THE OXFORD

Essential
Biographical
Dictionary

AMERICAN EDITION

Also Available

THE OXFORD

Essential
Biographical
Dictionary

AMERICAN EDITION

BERKLEY BOOKS, NEW YORK

THE OXFORD ESSENTIAL BIOGRAPHICAL DICTIONARY

A Berkley Book / published in mass market paperback
by arrangement with Oxford University Press, Inc.

PRINTING HISTORY
Berkley edition / August 1999

The Penguin Putnam Inc. World Wide Web site address is
http://www.penguinputnam.com

ISBN: 0-425-16993-6

BERKLEY®
Berkley Books are published by
The Berkley Publishing Group, a division of Penguin Putnam Inc.,
375 Hudson Street, New York, New York 10014.
BERKLEY and the "B" design are trademarks
belonging to Penguin Putnam Inc.

PRINTED IN THE UNITED STATES OF AMERICA

10 9 8 7 6 5 4 3 2 1

Contents

Staff

Editor in Chief:	Frank R. Abate
Managing Editor:	Elizabeth J. Jewell
Associate Editors:	Stephen P. Elliott
	Christine A. Lindberg
	Andrea R. Nagy
	Laurie H. Ongley
Pronunciation Editors:	John K. Bollard
	William A. Kretzschmar
	Katherine Sietsema
Assistant Editor, Research:	Patricia Baldwin
Editorial Assistant:	Karen A. Fisher
Proofreaders:	Deborah Argosy
	Linda Ciacchi
	Linda Costa
	Linda Legassie
	Sue Ellen Thompson
Data Entry:	Kimberly Roberts

Introduction

The *Oxford Essential Biographical Dictionary* provides concise biographical information for more than 7,500 prominent individuals, living and dead, selected from the annals of history, statecraft, science, business, entertainment, sports—indeed, any field of human activity that is of interest to people generally.

For each entry in this dictionary, the user will find the following information: the name of the individual, an indication of correct word division of the surname (if applicable), the pronunciation (unless an accurate pronunciation could not be determined); alternate names, nicknames, names at birth, and other names by which an individual may be known; and a concise definition identifying the individual's nationality/country of origin and principal occupation(s), as well as (in most cases) an indication of the particular significance of that individual in human affairs or in a certain field of activity.

The selection of individuals for inclusion in the *Oxford Essential Biographical Dictionary* was done with particular attention to American interests and history, such that the coverage in this dictionary is distinctly from an American point of view.

How to Use This Book

The "entry map" below explains the different parts of a typical entry in this dictionary: surname and given name(s), pronunciation, life date(s), any alternate names, the identifying information on that individual, and any information indicating significance.

> **Buck** |bək|, Pearl S. (1892–1973) U.S. writer; full name *Pearl Sydenstricker Buck*. Her upbringing and work in China inspired her earliest novels, including *The Good Earth* (Pulitzer Prize, 1931). Nobel Prize for Literature (1938).

Boldface entries: Surnames (family names) appear in **boldface**. Other names, including given names, nicknames, epithets, etc., appear in normal type.

Word division: Dots within the boldface main entries mark places where the name can be divided correctly, as at the end of a line of text. Many names will not have dots at each syllable, because the dots are intended to show optimum word division points. Thus, one-letter syllables at the beginning or end of a name are not marked with dots (•).

Pronunciation: Pronunciations are given for the great majority of surnames. For more details on pronunciation, including a complete pronunciation key, see the pages that follow this Introduction.

Cross-references appear in small capitals, for example:

> **Llo·sa** |'yōsə|, Mario Vargas see VARGAS
> LLOSA.

For individuals who are members of a single family, different family members who merit inclusion are covered under one main entry. Individuals in the single family entry are given in order chronologically by birth date, for example:

> **Ad·ams** |'ædəmz| U.S. political family, including: **John Adams** see box. **Abigail Smith Adams** (1744–1818), wife of John Adams and U.S. first lady (1797–1801). **John Quincy Adams** see box. **Louisa Catherine Johnson Adams** (1775–1852), wife of John Quincy Adams and U.S. first lady (1825–29). **Charles Francis Adams** (1807–86), U.S. diplomat and author. The son of John Quincy Adams, he was a member of the Massachusetts House of Representatives (1859–61) and U.S. ambassador to Great Britain (1861–68). **Charles Fran·cis Adams** (1835–1915), U.S. historian. The son of Charles Francis (1807–86), he was an expert on railroads.

But where a single surname and given name combination is spelled exactly the same for two *unrelated* individuals, two separate main entries are given, distinguished by a superscript number given after each surname. In the case of such "homographs" (names spelled exactly the same, although the two individuals have no familial relation to one another), entry order is chronological by birth date.

Abbreviations

Abbreviations (besides those that are quite standard and familiar) used in the text of the entries include the following:

AFL	American Football League
c.	circa
CIA	Central Intelligence Agency
Co.	Company
Corp.	Corporation
FBI	Federal Bureau of Investigation
fl.	floruit (date of prominence)
Inc.	Incorporated
LPGA	Ladies Professional Golfers Association
NAACP	National Association for the Advancement of Colored People
NASA	National Aeronautics and Space Administration
NATO	North Atlantic Treaty Organization
NBA	National Basketball Association
NCAA	National Collegiate Athletic Association
NFL	National Football League
NHL	National Hockey Association
PGA	Professional Golfers Association
U.S.	United States (of America)
UK	United Kingdom (Great Britain)
UN	United Nations
USSR	Union of Soviet Socialist Republics (Soviet Union)

Pronunciation Key

Main entries are followed by a pronunciation. The pronunciation appears within upright vertical lines immediately after the main entry, for example:

Chi·ca·go |shə'k gō; she'kawgō|

The pronunciations use a simple respelling system to represent English and some non-English sounds, as shown below. Pronunciations generally are an "Americanized" rendering that is acceptable in almost all contexts. In certain cases, especially with rarer, foreign names whose pronunciations are less well known, the pronunciations are approximations of the way the name is pronounced in the particular foreign language of origin. In a small number of cases, when reliable data could not be obtained, no pronunciation is given.

VOWELS:

Symbol:	as in:	Example:
æ	cat	**Adi·ron·dack Mountains** |,ædə'r n,dæk|
ā	mate	**Ma·con** |'mākən|
	father	**Ag·ra** |' grə|
e	let	**El·gin**[1] |'eljin|
ē	feet	**Eden** |'ēdn|
i	it	**It·aly** |'itl-ē|
ī	tide	**Eif·fel Tower** |'ifəl|
aw	fall	**Taun·ton**[2] |'tawntn|
ō	cove	**Ohio** |ō'hīō|
ŏŏ	hook	**Woos·ter** |'wŏŏstər|
ōō	loose	**Poole** |pōol|
ə	but, banana	**Aca·dia** |ə'kādēə|

DIPHTHONGS:

oi	foil	**Boyne River** |boin|
ow	couch	**Out·er Banks** |'owtər 'bænks|

CONSONANTS:

b	boot	**Bom·beck**	|'bäm,bek|
CH	church	**Charles**	|CHärlz|
d	dog	**Da·vis**	|'dāvəs|
f	fate	**Ford**	|fawrd|
g	go; bigger	**Gar·bo**	|'gärbō|
h	hot; behave	**Har·ri·son**	|'herəsən|
j	jack; magic	**John·son**	|'jänsən|
k	kettle; cut	**Col·lins**	|'kälənz|
l	lap; cellar; cradle	**La·Belle**	|lə'bel|
m	main	**Mc·Mil·lan**	|mək'milən|
n	honor; maiden	**No·lan**	|'nōlən|
NG	singer	**Lang** |'læNG|; **Planck**	|pläNGk|
p	put	**Pol Pot**	|,pōl 'pät; ,päl 'pät|
r	root; carry	**Rich·ards**	|'riCHərdz|
s	sit	**Scripps**	|'skrips|
SH	shape; wish	**Marsh**	|märSH|
t	top; butter	**Trot·sky**	|'trätskē|
TH	thing; path	**Lu·ther**	|'lōōTHər|
<u>TH</u>	this; mother	**Suth·er·land**	|'səTHərlənd|
v	never	**Vic·to·ria**	|vik'tawrēə|
w	wait; quick	**Wal·lace**	|'wawləs; 'wäləs|
y	yes; beyond	**Young**	|yəNG|
z	lazy; fuse	**Za·pa·ta** |zə'pätə|; **Lans·bury**	|'lænz,berē|
ZH	beige; leisure	**Pia·get**	|,pēä'ZHä|

FOREIGN SOUNDS:

KH	Bach	**Feu·er·bach**	|'foiər,bäKH|
N	vin	**Gau·guin**	|gō'gæN|
Œ	Goethe	**Gö·del**	|'gOEd(ə)l; 'gōd(ə)l|
Y	über	**Lul·ly**	|lY'lē; lōō'lē|

STRESS

Each stressed syllable is preceded by a small upright stroke, showing that the following syllable has a stressed vowel sound. Primary stress is shown by an upright stroke above the line, while secondary stress is shown by an upright stroke below the line:

West·ing·house \|'westiNG,hows\|

Aa

Aal·to |'ältaw|, Alvar (1898–1976) Finnish architect and designer. Full name *Hugo Alvar Henrik Aalto.* As a designer he is known as the inventor of bent plywood furniture.

Aar·on |'erən|, Hank (1934–) U.S. baseball player. Full name *Henry Louis Aaron.* He set the all-time career record for home runs (755) and runs batted in (2,297). Elected to the Baseball Hall of Fame (1982).

Ab·bas |'æbəs|, Ferhat (1899–1985) Algerian nationalist leader. He was president of the Algerian provisional government from 1958, and president of the constituent assembly of independent Algeria (1962–63).

Ab·be |'äbə|, Ernst (1840–1905) German physicist. He invented the apochromatic lens.

Ab·bey |'æbē|, Edwin Austin (1852–1911) U.S. painter and illustrator. He was a *Harper's Weekly* staff illustrator.

Ab·bot |'æbət|, Charles Greeley (1872–1973) U.S. astrophysicist. He was director of the astrophysical observatory of the Smithsonian Institution (1907–44).

Ab·bott |'æbət|, Berenice (1898–1991) U.S. photographer and author. She is known for her photographs of New York City and for preserving the photographs of Eugène Atget.

Ab·bott |'æbət|, Robert Sengstacke (1868–1940) U.S. publisher and editor. He founded and edited the *Chicago Defender* (1905–40).

Ab·duh |'äbdoō|, Muhammad (1849–1905) Egyptian Islamic scholar, jurist, and liberal reformer.

Ab·dul Ha·mid II |əb,doōl hä'mēd| (1842–1918) The last sultan of Turkey (1876–1909). An autocratic ruler, he was deposed after the revolt of the Young Turks (1908). He is remembered for the massacres of Christian Armenians (1894–96).

Abdul-Jabbar |æb,doōljə'bär|, Kareem (1947–) U.S. basketball player. Born *Ferdinand Lewis Alcindor;* known (until 1968) as **Lew Alcindor.** He set

more than 20 all-time records, including most games played (1,560) and most career points (38,387). Elected to the Basketball Hall of Fame (1995).

Ab·dul·lah ibn Hus·sein |äb'doōlə ib(ə)n hoō'sän| (1882–1951) king of Jordan (1946–51). He served as emir of Transjordan from 1921, becoming king of Jordan on its independence. He was assassinated in 1951.

Ab·dul Rah·man |əb'doōl rä'män|, Tunku (1903–90) Malayan statesman. He was the first prime minister of independent Malaya (1957–63) and of Malaysia (1963–70).

Abe |'äbä|, Kōbō (1924–93) Japanese author. Real name *Abe Kimifusa.*

Abel |'äbəl|, Niels Henrik (1802–29) Norwegian mathematician. He proved that equations of the fifth degree cannot be solved by conventional algebraic methods, and made advances in the fields of power series and elliptic functions.

Ab·e·lard |'æbə,lärd|, Peter (1079–1144) French scholar, theologian, and philosopher. He is famous for his tragic love affair with his pupil Héloïse (see HÉLOÏSE).

Ab·er·crom·bie |'æbər'krämbē|, Sir (Leslie) Patrick (1879–1957) English town planner and architect. He is known for his postwar "Greater London Plan," for which he was knighted in 1945.

Ab·er·deen |'æbər,dēn|, George Hamilton-Gordon, 4th Earl of (1784–1860) British Conservative statesman. He was prime minister (1852–55).

Ab·er·nathy |'æbər,næтнē|, Ralph David (1926–90) U.S. clergyman and civil rights activist. With Martin Luther King, Jr., he led the U.S. civil rights movement in the 1950s and 1960s and founded (1957) the Southern Christian Leadership Conference. He published his autobiography, *And the Walls Came Tumbling Down,* in 1989.

Abra·hams |'äbrə,hæmz|, Harold (Maurice) (1899–1978) English athlete. In 1924 he became the first Englishman to win the 100 meters in the

Olympic Games. His story was the subject of the movie *Chariots of Fire* (1981).

Abram·o·vitz |ə'brämə,vits|, Max (1908–) U.S. architect.

Abrams |'abrəmz|, Creighton William (1914–74) U.S. army officer. He became major general (1965) and vice-chief of the U.S. Army (1964–67) before commanding U.S. troops in Vietnam (1968–72) and overseeing U.S. withdrawal; he then served as army chief of staff (1972–74).

Ab·zug |'æbzoog|, Bella Savitsky (1920–98) U.S. antiwar, feminist and gay rights activist. She was a New York attorney and U.S. congresswoman (1971–77) and a founding member of the National Organization for Women.

Ache·be |ə'cHäbä|, Chinua (1930–) Nigerian novelist, poet, short-story writer, and essayist. Born *Albert Chinualumgu*. Notable works: *Things Fall Apart* (1958) and *Anthills of the Savanna* (1987). Nobel Prize for Literature (1989).

Ach·e·son |'æcHəsən|, Dean (Gooderham) (1893–1971) U.S. statesman and secretary of state (1949-53). He urged international control of nuclear power, was instrumental in the formation of NATO, and implemented the Marshall Plan and the Truman Doctrine.

Acuff |'a,kəf|, Roy (1903–92) U.S. country musician. Known as the "King of Country Music," he was a star of the Grand Ole Opry, and with Fred Rose he formed the Acuff-Rose Music Publishing Co. (1942).

Ad·am |'ædəm|, Robert (1728–92) Scottish architect. He was influenced by neoclassical theory and, assisted by his brother **James** (1730–94), he initiated a lighter, more decorative style than the Palladianism favored by the British architecture of the previous half-century.

Ad·ams |'ædəmz| U.S. political family, including: **John Adams** see box. **Abigail Smith Adams** (1744–1818), wife of John Adams and U.S. first lady (1797–1801). **John Quincy Adams** see box. **Louisa Catherine Johnson Adams** (1775–1852), wife of John Quincy Adams and U.S. first lady (1825–29). **Charles Francis Adams**

Adams, John
2nd U.S. president

Life dates: 1735–1826
Place of birth: Braintree (now Quincy), Massachusetts
Mother: Susanna Boylston Adams
Father: John Adams
Wife: Abigail Smith Adams
Children: Abigail, John Quincy (6th U.S. president), Susanna, Charles, Thomas
College/University: Harvard
Career: Lawyer; schoolmaster; writer
Political career: Massachusetts legislature; First Continental Congress; Second Continental Congress; minister to Great Britain and the Netherlands; vice president (under Washington); president
Party: Federalist
Home state: Massachusetts
Opponent in presidential race: Thomas Jefferson
Term of office: March 4, 1797–March 3, 1801
Vice president: Thomas Jefferson
Notable events of presidency: XYZ Affair; Judiciary Act; Alien and Sedition Acts
Other achievements: Admitted to the Massachusetts bar; president of the Massachusetts Society for Promoting Agriculture; wrote articles for the Boston *Patriot*
Place of burial: Quincy, Massachusetts

(1807–86), U.S. diplomat and author. The son of John Quincy Adams, he was a member of the Massachusetts House of Representatives (1859–61) and U.S. ambassador to Great Britain (1861–68). **Charles Francis Adams** (1835–1915), U.S. historian. The son of Charles Francis Adams (1807–86), he was an expert on railroads.

Ad·ams |'ædəmz|, Alice (1926–) U.S. author and editor.

Ad·ams |'ædəmz|, Ansel (Easton) (1902–84) U.S. photographer. He was noted for his black-and-white photographs of American landscapes. Many of Adams's collections, such as *My Camera in the National Parks* (1950) and *This is the American Earth* (1960), reflect his interest in conservation.

Ad·ams |'ædəmz|, Harriet Stratemeyer (c. 1893–1982) U.S. author. After the

---

Adams, John Quincy
6th U.S. president

Life dates: 1767–1848

Place of birth: Braintree (now Quincy), Massachusetts

Mother: Abigail Smith Adams

Father: John Adams (2nd U.S. president)

Wife: Louisa Catherine Johnson Adams

Children: George, John, Charles, Louisa

College/University: Harvard; also attended University of Leiden

Career: Lawyer

Political career: Massachusetts Senate; U.S. Senate; minister to Great Britain, Netherlands, Portugal, Prussia, and Russia; U.S. secretary of state; president; U.S. House of Representatives

Party: Whig; Federalist; Democratic-Republican

Home state: Massachusetts

Opponents in presidential race: Henry Clay; Andrew Jackson; William H. Crawford

Term of office: March 4, 1825–March 3, 1829

Vice president: John C. Calhoun

Notable events of presidency: Erie Canal opened; Pan-American Congress; Tariff of Abominations; construction of Baltimore and Ohio Railroad began; Treaty of Paris; Treaty of Ghent; South Carolina Exposition on nullification of federal tariffs

Other achievements: Admitted to the Massachusetts bar; only U.S. president elected to the House after presidency; secretary to his father, John Adams; wrote pamphlets and articles under the pseudonyms of "Publicola," "Marcellus," "Columbus," etc.; professor of rhetoric and belles lettres, Harvard College; nominated to U.S. Supreme Court, but declined

Place of burial: Quincy, Massachusetts

---

death of her father, Edward Stratemeyer (1862–1930), she continued to write the series of books he created, especially the Nancy Drew and Hardy Boys series.

Ad·ams |'ædəmz|, Henry Brooks (1838–1918) U.S. historian and scholar. Notable works: *Democracy* (1880) and *The Education of Henry Adams* (1907, Pulitzer Prize).

Ad·ams |'ædəmz|, Herbert Samuel (1858–1945) U.S. sculptor. He executed busts of John Marshall, William Ellery Channing, William Cullen Bryant, Will Rogers, and Joseph Story; he also created the bronze doors of St. Bartholomew's Church in New York City, and those of the Library of Congress.

Ad·ams |'ædəmz|, James Truslow (1878–1949) U.S. historian. He wrote *The Founding of New England* (1921, Pulitzer Prize) and edited the *Dictionary of American History* (1940) and *Atlas of American History* (1943).

Ad·ams |'ædəmz|, John Couch (1819–92) English astronomer. In 1843 he calculated the position of a supposed planet beyond Uranus; similar calculations performed by Le Verrier resulted in the discovery of Neptune three years later.

Ad·ams |'ædəmz|, Richard George (1920–   ) British novelist. Notable works: *Watership Down* (1972).

Ad·ams |'ædəmz|, Samuel (1722–1803) American Revolutionary politician. He was a leader of the Boston Tea Party (1773), a delegate to the First and Second Continental Congresses, and a signer of the Declaration of Independence.

Ad·ams |'ædəmz|, Scott (1957–   ) U.S. cartoonist. He created the comic strip "Dilbert."

Ad·ams |'ædəmz|, Thomas. U.S. inventor. He was the first person to make sticks of chewing gum from the plant sap chicle (1870).

Ad·dams |'ædəmz|, Charles (1912–88) U.S. cartoonist. He created macabre cartoons, many of which were published in *The New Yorker*.

Ad·dams |'ædəmz|, Jane (1860–1935) U.S. social reformer, feminist, and pacifist. In 1889 she founded Hull House, a center for the care and education of the poor of Chicago, and a national model for the combat of urban poverty and the treatment of young offenders. She was a leader of the women's suffrage movement and an active pacifist. Nobel Peace Prize (1931).

Ad·der·ly |'ædərlē|, Cannonball (1928–75) U.S. jazz alto saxophonist. Born *Julian Edwin Adderly*. He played in the Miles Davis Quintet (1957–59) and later formed a second quintet with his brother, Nat Adderly.

Ad·ding·ton |'ædiɴɢtən|, Henry, 1st Viscount Sidmouth (1757–1844) British Tory statesman, prime minister (1801–04), and home secretary (1812–21).

Ad·di·son |'ædəsən|, Joseph (1672–1719) English essayist, poet, dramatist, and Whig politician. In 1711 he founded the *Spectator* with Sir Richard Steele.

Ad·di·son |'ædəsən|, Thomas (1793–1860) English physician. A renowned clinical teacher, he described the disease now named for him, ascribing it correctly to defective functioning of the adrenal glands.

Ade·nau·er |'ædə,nowər|, Konrad (1876–1967) German statesman. He was first chancellor of the Federal Republic of Germany (1949–63).

Ad·ler |'ædlər|, Alfred (1870–1937) Austrian psychologist and psychiatrist. Adler disagreed with Freud's idea that mental illness was caused by sexual conflicts in infancy, arguing that society and culture were significant factors. He introduced the concept of the inferiority complex.

Ador·no |ä'dörnō|, Theodor Wiesengrund (1903–69) German philosopher, sociologist, and musicologist. Born *Theodor Wiesengrund*. A member of the Frankfurt School, Adorno argued that philosophical authoritarianism is inevitably oppressive.

Adri·an IV |'ädri,än| (c. 1100–59) Pope (1154–59). Born *Nicholas Breakspear*. He is the only Englishman to have held this office.

Ael·fric |'ælfrik| (c. 955–c. 1020) Anglo-Saxon monk, writer, and grammarian. Called **Grammaticus**. Notable works: *Lives of the Saints* (993–996).

Aes·chi·nes |'eskənēz| (c. 389–c. 314 BC) Athenian orator and statesman. He opposed Demosthenes' efforts to unite the Greek city states against Macedon, with which he attempted to make peace.

Aes·chy·lus |'eskələs| (c. 525–c. 456 BC) Greek dramatist. Aeschylus is best known for his trilogy the *Oresteia* (458 BC, consisting of the tragedies *Agamemnon*, *Choephoroe*, and *Eumenides*), which tells the story of Agamemnon's murder at the hands of his wife Clytemnestra and the vengeance of their son Orestes.

Ae·sop |'ē,säp| (c. 550 BC) Greek storyteller. The moral animal fables associated with him were probably collected from many sources and initially communicated orally.

Af·fleck |'æf,lek|, Ben (1972–) U.S. actor and screenwriter. Full name *Benjamin Geza Affleck*. His screenplay for the movie *GoodWill Hunting* (1997) won an Academy Award.

Agas·si |'ægəsē|, André (1970–) U.S. tennis player. He won at Wimbledon (1992), the U.S. Open (1994), and the Australian Open (1995).

Ag·as·siz |'ægəsē|, Jean Louis Rodolphe (1807–73) Swiss-born U.S. zoologist, geologist, and paleontologist. In 1837 Agassiz was the first to propose that much of Europe had once been in the grip of an ice age.

Agee |'ā,jē|, James Rufus (1909–55) U.S. author. He was widely recognized for *Let Us Now Praise Famous Men* (1941), his study of Alabama tenant farmers, co-authored with photographer Walker Evans. He also wrote poetry; movie scripts, including *The African Queen* (1952); and novels, including *A Death in the Family* (1957, Pulitzer Prize).

Ag·nes[1] |'ægnəs|, St. (died c. 304) Roman martyr. She is the patron saint of virgins and her emblem is a lamb (Latin *agnus*). Feast day, January 21.

Ag·nes[2] |'ægnəs|, St. (c. 1211–82) patron saint of Bohemia. She was canonized in 1989. Feast day, March 2.

Agne·si |än'yäzē|, Maria Gaetana (1718–99) Italian mathematician and philosopher. She is regarded as the first female mathematician of the Western world.

Ag·new |'ægnoo|, Spiro T. (1918–96) vice president of the U.S. (1969–73). He pleaded nolo contendere to charges of tax evasion on contractors' payments to him as governor of Maryland; as a result of this scandal, he resigned the vice presidency in 1973.

Agri·co·la |ə'grikələ|, Gnaeus Julius (AD 40–93) Roman general and governor of Britain (78–84). As governor he completed the subjugation of Wales and defeated the Scottish Highland tribes.

Agrip·pa |ə'gripə|, Marcus Vipsanius (63?–12 BC) Roman general. Augustus's adviser and son-in-law, he played an important part in the naval victories over Mark Antony.

Ai·dan |'adən|, St. (died AD 651) Irish missionary and evangelist of northern England.

Ai·ken |'aken|, Conrad Potter (1889–1973) U.S. poet, critic, and writer. Notable works: *Selected Poems*, which won the 1929 Pulitzer Prize.

Ai·ken |'aken|, Howard Hathaway (1900–73) U.S. mathematician and computer scientist.

Ai·ley |'alē|, Alvin (1931–89) U.S. dancer and choreographer. He founded the American Dance Theatre (1958), which helped to establish modern dance as an American art form; he incorporated ballet, jazz, and Afro-Carribbean idioms in his choreography.

Ait·ken |'atkən|, William Maxwell see BEAVERBROOK.

Ak·bar |'æk,bär|, Jala-lu-Din Muhammad (1542–1605) Mogul emperor of India (1556–1605). Called **Akbar the Great**. Akbar expanded the Mogul empire to incorporate northern India.

Akhe·na·ton |äk'nätən| (14th century BC) Egyptian pharaoh. Also **Amenhotep** or **Ikhnaton**. A pharaoh of the 18th dynasty, he came to the throne as *Amenhotep IV* and reigned 1379–1362 BC. The husband of Nefertiti, he introduced the monotheistic solar cult of Aten and moved the capital from Thebes to the newly built city of Akhetaten.

Akh·ma·to·va |æk'mätəvə|, Anna (1889–1966) Russian poet. Pseudonym of *Anna Andreevna Gorenko*. Akhmatova was a member of the Acmeist group of poets.

Aki·hi·to |äkē'hētō| (1933–) emperor of Japan (1989–). Full name *Tsugu Akihito*. The son of Emperor Hirohito.

Alain-Fournier |ä'län foŏr'nyä| (1886–1914) French novelist. Pseudonym of *Henri-Alban Fournier*.

al-Amin, Jamil Abdullah (1943–) U.S. political activist and author. Formerly known as **H. Rap Brown**, he was

chairman of the Student Nonviolent Coordinating Committee and, with Stokely Carmichael, an outspoken advocate of black power in the 1960s.

Alar·cón |älär'kawn|, Pedro Antonio de (1833–91) Spanish novelist and short-story writer. Notable works: *The Three-Cornered Hat* (1874).

Alarcón y Mendoza |,älär'kawn ē ,men 'dōsə| see RUIZ DE ALARCÓN Y MENDOZA.

Al·a·ric |'ælərik| (*c.* 370–410) king of the Visigoths (395–410). He captured Rome in 410.

Al·ban |'älbən|, St. (3rd century) the first British Christian martyr. He was a native of Verulamium (now St. Albans).

Al·bee |'älbē|, Edward Franklin (1928–) U.S. dramatist. He was initially associated with the Theater of the Absurd, but *Who's Afraid of Virginia Woolf* (1962) marked a more naturalistic departure. Another notable play is *A Delicate Balance* (1966).

Al·bers |'älbərz|, Josef (1888–1976) U.S. artist, designer, and teacher, born in Germany. His work is associated with the Bauhaus and constructivism.

Al·bert |'ælbərt|, Prince (1819–61) consort to Queen Victoria of Great Britain and prince of Saxe-Coburg-Gotha. Full name *Albert Francis Charles Augustus Emmanuel.*

Al·ber·ti |äl'bertē|, Leon Battista (1404–72) Italian architect, humanist, painter, and art critic. His book *On Painting* (1435) was the first account of the theory of perspective in the Renaissance.

Al·bert·son |'ælbərt,sən|, Jack (1907–81) U.S. actor. He was a character player in vaudeville, burlesque, Broadway, television, and movies. Notable movies: *The Subject Was Roses* (1968, Academy Award).

Al·ber·tus Mag·nus |æl'bərtəs 'mægnəs|, St. (*c.* 1200–80) Dominican theologian, philosopher, and scientist. Known as **Doctor Universalis**. A teacher of St. Thomas Aquinas, he was a pioneer in the study of Aristotle and contributed significantly to the comparison of Christian theology and pagan philosophy. Feast day, November 15.

Al·bi·no·ni |,ælbə'nōnē|, Tomaso

Giovanni (1671–1751) Italian composer of opera and instrumental works.

Al·bi·nus |æl'bēnəs| Another name for Alcuin.

Al·bright |'awlbrīt|, Madeleine Korbel (1937–) U.S. secretary of state (1997–), born in Czechoslovakia. She was the first woman to head the U.S. State Department.

Al·bu·quer·que |'ælbə,kerkē| Alfonso de (1453–1515) Portuguese colonial statesman. He conquered Goa (1510) and made it the capital of the Portuguese empire in the east.

Al·cae·us |'æl,sēəs| (c. 620–c. 580 BC) Greek lyric poet. He invented a new form of lyric meter, called the alcaic. His works were a model for the Roman poet Horace and the verse of the Renaissance.

Al·ci·bi·a·des |,ælsə'bīədēz| (c. 450–404 BC) Athenian general and statesman. He led the unsuccessful Athenian expeditions against Sparta and Sicily during the Peloponnesian War but fled to Sparta after being charged with sacrilege.

Al·cock |'awl,käk|, Sir John William (1892–1919) English aviator. Together with Sir Arthur Whitten Brown, he made the first nonstop transatlantic flight in June 1919.

Al·cott |'awl,kət| U.S. family name of: **Bronson Alcott** (1799–1888), an educator. Full name Amos Bronson Alcott. He advocated radical reforms in education, including racial integration in the classroom. Appointed superintendent of schools in Concord, Massachusetts, in 1859, he created the first parent-teacher association. His daughter, **Louisa May Alcott** (1832–88), was a novelist whose best known work was Little Women (1868–69).

Al·cuin |'ælkwən| (c. 735–804) English scholar, theologian, and adviser to Charlemagne. Also known as **Albinus**. He is credited with the transformation of Charlemagne's court into a cultural center in the period known as the Carolingian Renaissance.

Al·da |'awldə|, Alan (1936–) U.S. actor, director, and writer. He won five Emmys for his role as Hawkeye Pierce on the television series "M*A*S*H" (1972–83).

Al·diss |'awldəs|, Brian (Wilson) (1925–) English novelist and critic. He is best known for his science fiction. Notable works: Frankenstein Unbound (1973).

Al·drin |'awldrin|, Buzz (1930–) U.S. astronaut. Full name Edwin Eugene Aldrin, Jr. In 1969 he took part in the first moon landing, the Apollo 11 mission, becoming the second person to set foot on the moon, after Neil Armstrong.

Al·dus Ma·nu·ti·us |'awldəs mə-'nōōsh(ē)əs| (1450–1515) Italian scholar, printer, and publisher. Latinized name of Teobaldo Manucci; also known as **Aldo Manuzio**. He printed fine first editions of many Greek and Latin classics.

Ale·khine |,əl'yōкнyin|, Alexander (1892–1946) Russian-born French chess player. He was world champion from 1927 to 1935 and from 1937 until his death.

Al·ex·an·der[1] |,æləg'zændər| (356–323 BC) king of Macedon (336–323). Known as **Alexander the Great**. The son of Philip II, he conquered Persia, Egypt, Syria, Mesopotamia, Bactria, and the Punjab; in Egypt he founded the city of Alexandria.

Al·ex·an·der[2] |,æləg'zændər| (1777–1825) The name of three czars of Russia: **Alexander I** (1777–1825; reigned 1801–25); **Alexander II** (1818–81; reigned 1855–81), the son of Nicholas I. He was known as **Alexander the Liberator** after the emancipation of the serfs (1861). **Alexander III** (1845–94; reigned 1881–94), the son of Alexander II.

Al·ex·an·der[3] |,æləg'zændər| (c. 1080–1124) The name of three kings of Scotland: **Alexander I** (c. 1077–1124; reigned 1107–24), the son of Malcolm III; **Alexander II** (1198–1249; reigned 1214–49), the son of William I of Scotland; and **Alexander III** (1241–86; reigned 1249–86), the son of Alexander II.

Al·ex·an·der |,æləg'zændər|, Grover Cleveland (1887–1950) U.S. baseball player. Known as **Pete**. A 20-season pitcher (1911–30), he retired with 373 career wins and 90 shutouts. Elected to the Baseball Hall of Fame (1938).

Al·ex·an·der |ˌæləg'zændər|, Harold (Rupert Leofric George), 1st Earl Alexander of Tunis (1891–1969) British field marshal and Conservative statesman.

Al·ex·an·der |ˌæləg'zændər|, (Andrew) Lamar (1940–) U.S. politician and administrator. He was the governor of Tennessee (1979–87) and President Bush's secretary of education (1991–93).

Al·ex·an·der Nev·sky |ˌæləg'zændər 'nyefskē| (c. 1220–63) prince of Novgorod (1236–63). Also **Nevski**. He defeated the Swedes on the banks of the River Neva in 1240. Feast day, August 30 or November 23.

Al·ex·and·er·son |ˌæləg'zændərsən|, Ernst Frederik Werner (1878–1975) U.S. electrical engineer and inventor, born in Sweden. Having invented and perfected radio receiving and transmitting systems, he produced a complete television system (1927) and a color television receiver (1955).

Al·fon·so XIII |æl'fänsō| (1886–1941) king of Spain (1886–1931). He was forced into exile after elections indicating a preference for a republic.

Al·ford |'awlfərd|, Andrew (1904–92) U.S. inventor, born in Russia. He invented and developed antennas for radio-navigation and instrument-landing systems.

Al·fred |'ælfrəd| (849–99) king of Wessex (871–99). Known as **Alfred the Great**. Alfred's military resistance saved SW England from Viking occupation. A great reformer, he is credited with the foundation of the English navy and with a revival of learning.

Alf·vén |äl'vän|, Hannes Olof Gösta (1908–95) Swedish theoretical physicist. His work was important for controlled thermonuclear fusion. Nobel Prize for Physics (1970).

Al·ger |'æljər|, Horatio, Jr. (1832–99) U.S. author. His novels, most notably *Ragged Dick* (1867), were infused with the message that honest hard work can overcome poverty.

Al·gren |'awlgrən|, Nelson (Abraham) (1909–81) U.S. novelist. He drew on his childhood experiences in the slums of Chicago for his novels of social realism,

for example *The Man with the Golden Arm* (1949) and *Walk on the Wild Side* (1956).

Ali[1] |ä'lē|, Muhammad see MUHAMMAD ALI[1].

Ali[2] |ä'lē|, Muhammad see MUHAMMAD ALI[2].

Ali·ghie·ri |ä,lig'yerē|, Dante see DANTE.

Al·len |'ælən|, Ethan (1738–89) American Revolutionary soldier. He fought the British in the Revolutionary War and led an irregular force, the Green Mountain Boys, in their campaign to gain independence for Vermont, which became a state after his death.

Al·len |'ælən|, Frederick Lewis (1890–1954) U.S. historian and editor. He worked for *Harper's Magazine* on staff (1923–41) and as editor (1941–53). Notable books: *Only Yesterday* (1931) and *The Big Change* (1952).

Al·len |'ælən|, Gracie (c. 1905–64) U.S. comedian and television actress. She was the wife and comedy partner of George Burns.

Al·len |'ælən|, Sam Leeds U.S. businessman. He founded the Flexible Flyer sled company.

Al·len |'ælən|, Steve (1921–) U.S. television humorist and songwriter. Full name *Stephen Valentine Patrick William Allen*. He was host and creator of "The Tonight Show" (1953–57) and host of "The Steve Allen Show" (1956–60).

Al·len |'ælən|, Tim (1953–) U.S. actor. Born *Tim Allen Dick*. A comedian and writer, he starred in the television sitcom "Home Improvement" (1991–99).

Al·len |'ælən|, Woody (1935–) U.S. movie director, writer, and actor. Born *Allen Stewart Konigsberg*. Notable movies: *Play it Again, Sam* (1972), *Annie Hall* (1977, Academy Award), and *Hannah and Her Sisters* (1986, Academy Award).

Al·len·by |'ælənbē|, Edmund Henry Hynman, 1st Viscount (1861–1936) British soldier. Commander of the Egyptian Expeditionary Force against the Turks, he captured Jerusalem in 1917 and defeated the Turkish forces at Megiddo in 1918.

Al·len·de |ä'yen,dä| Family name of: **Salvador Allende** (1908–73), Chilean president (1970–73). The first avowed Marxist to win a presidency in a free election, Allende was overthrown and killed in a military coup led by General Pinochet. **Isabel Allende** (1942–　), Chilean author, born in Peru. Notable novels: *The House of the Spirits* (1985, Lillian Gish Prize) and *The Infinite Plan* (1993). She is the niece of Salvador Allende.

Al·li·son |'æləsən|, Dorothy (1949–　) U.S. author. She was a National Book Award finalist (1992) for her novel *Bastard Out of Carolina*.

All·man |'awlmən| U.S. musicians. **Duane Allman** (1946–71) was a guitarist for The Allman Brothers Band. His brother **Gregg** (1947–　) was keyboardist and guitarist for The Allman Brothers Band.

All·ston |'awlstən|, Washington (1779–1843) U.S. landscape painter. He was the first major artist of the American romantic movement.

Alma-Tadema |'ælmə 'tædəmə|, Sir Lawrence (1836–1912) British painter, born in the Netherlands. He is known for his lush genre scenes set in the ancient world.

Al·pert |'ælpərt|, Herb (1935–　) U.S. musician and producer. A jazz trumpeter, he cofounded A & M Records (1962) with Jerry Moss.

Alt·dor·fer |'ält,dawrfər|, Albrecht (c. 1480–1538) German painter and engraver. He was one of the first modern European landscape painters and was principal artist of the Danube School.

Alt·hus·ser |'ält,hoōsər|, Louis (1918–90) French philosopher. In giving a reinterpretation of traditional Marxism in the light of structuralist theories, his work had a significant influence on literary and cultural theory.

Alt·man |'awltmən|, Robert (1925–　) U.S. movie director. Notable movies: *M*A*S*H* (1970) and *The Player* (1992).

Al·va·rez |'ælvə,rez|, Luis Walter (1911–88) U.S. physicist. In 1980 Alvarez and his son identified iridium in sediment from the Cretaceous–Tertiary boundary and proposed that this resulted from a catastrophic meteorite impact.

Ama·do |ä'mäṭHō|, Jorge (1912–　) Brazilian author. Notable novels: *The Violent Land* (1944) and *Pen, Sword and Camisole: A Fable to Kindle Hope* (1985).

Ama·ti |ä'mäte| a family of Italian violin-makers from Cremona. In the 16th and 17th centuries, three generations of the Amatis developed the basic proportions of the violin, viola, and cello.

Ama·to |ə'mätō|, Pasquale (1878–1942) Italian operatic baritone. He sang 446 performances with the Metropolitan Opera, beginning in 1908.

Am·brose |'æm,brōz|, St. (c. 339–97) Doctor of the Church, a champion of orthodoxy, who introduced much Eastern theology and liturgical practice into the West. Feast day, December 7.

Ame·che |ə'mēcHē|, Don (1908–93) U.S. actor. Born *Dominic Felix Amici*. Notable movies: *Cocoon* (1985, Academy Award).

Amen·ho·tep |,æmən'hōtəp| see AKHENATON.

Am·herst |'æm(h)ərst|, Lord Jeffrey (1717–97) English soldier and military commander in North America. He was appointed Governor General of British North America (1760–63) and served as commander in chief of the British army (1772–95).

Am·i·don, Tom U.S. entrepreneur. He created Cream of Wheat cereal.

Amin |ä'mēn|, Idi (1925–　) Ugandan soldier and head of state (1971–79); full name *Idi Amin Dada*. He was deposed after a period of rule characterized by the murder of political opponents.

Amis |'ämis| English novelists. **Sir Kingsley Amis** (1922–95) achieved popular success with his first novel *Lucky Jim* (1954); his later novels include *The Old Devils* (1986, Booker Prize) and *The Folks that Live on the Hill* (1990). His son, **Martin (Louis) Amis** (1949–　), wrote *The Rachel Papers* (1973), *Money* (1984), and *Time's Arrow* (1991).

Am·mons, A. R. (1926–　) U.S. poet. Full name *Archie Randolph Ammons*. He is considered one of the leading transcendentalist American poets. He received the National Book Award for *Garbage* (1993).

Amos |'äməs|, Tori (1963–　) U.S. pop

singer. She was the youngest student ever to attend Peabody Conservatory in Baltimore.

Am·père |'æm,piər|, André-Marie (1775–1836) French physicist, mathematician, and philosopher, who analyzed the relationship between magnetic force and electric current.

Amund·sen |'æmənsən|, Roald (1872–1928) Norwegian explorer. Amundsen was the first to navigate the Northwest Passage (1903–6), during which expedition he located the site of the magnetic north pole. In 1911 he became the first to reach the South Pole.

Anac·re·on |ə'nækrēən| (c. 570–c. 478 BC) Greek lyric poet. He is best known for his celebrations of love and wine.

An·ax·ag·o·ras |,ænək'sægərəs| (c. 500–c. 428 BC) Greek philosopher. He taught in Athens and believed that all matter was infinitely divisible and motionless until animated by mind (nous).

An·ax·i·man·der |ə,næksə'mændər| (c. 610–c. 547 BC) Greek scientist who lived at Miletus. He believed the earth to be cylindrical and poised in space, and is reputed to have taught that life began in water and that humans originated from fish.

An·ax·im·e·nes |,ænək'simənēz| (c. 546 BC) Greek philosopher and scientist, who lived at Miletus. Anaximenes believed the earth to be flat and shallow, a view of astronomy that was a retrograde step from that of Anaximander.

An·der·sen |'ændərsən|, Hans Christian (1805–75) Danish author. He is famous for his fairy tales, published from 1835, such as "The Snow Queen," "The Ugly Duckling," and "The Little Match Girl."

An·der·son |'ændərsən|, Bradley Jay (1924–) U.S. cartoonist. He created the syndicated cartoons "Marmaduke" (1954) and "Grandpa's Boy" (1954).

An·der·son |'ændərsən|, Carl David (1905–91) U.S. physicist. In 1932 he discovered the positron—the first antiparticle known. Nobel Prize for Physics (1936, shared).

An·der·son |'ændərsən|, Elizabeth Garrett (1836–1917) English physician. She established a clinic for women and children in London and was the first

woman elected to the British Medical Association (1873).

An·der·son |'ændərsən|, Gillian (1968–) U.S. actress. She has won Emmy Awards for her role as FBI agent Dana Scully on the television show "The X-Files."

An·der·son |'ændərsən|, Ian (1947–) British flutist, born in Scotland. He performed with the rock group Jethro Tull.

An·der·son |'ændərsən|, John Bayard (1922–) U.S. lawyer and politician. He was an Independent Party presidential candidate in 1980.

An·der·son |'ændərsən|, Marian (c. 1902–93) U.S. operatic contralto. In 1955 she became the first black singer to perform at the New York Metropolitan Opera.

An·der·son |'ændərsən|, Maxwell (1888–1959) U.S. playwright. His plays, many of which are written in verse, deal with social and moral problems. He also wrote many historical dramas. Notable works: *Elizabeth the Queen* (1930), *Key Largo* (1939), *Anne of the Thousand Days* (1948), and *The Bad Seed* (1954).

An·der·son |'ændərsən|, Philip Warren (1923–) U.S. physicist. He made contributions to the study of solid-state physics, investigating magnetism and superconductivity. Research on molecular interactions has also been facilitated by his work on the spectroscopy of gases. Nobel Prize for Physics (1977).

An·der·son |'ændərsən|, Robert Woodruff (1917–) U.S. playwright and educator. Notable plays: *Tea and Sympathy* (1953), *You Know I Can't Hear You When the Water's Running* (1967), and *I Never Sang for My Father* (1968).

An·der·son |'ændərsən|, Sherwood (1876–1941) U.S. author. He is best known for *Winesburg, Ohio* (1919), a collection of interrelated short stories that explore the loneliness and frustration of small town life.

An·dré |'än,drā|, Carl (1935–) U.S. minimalist sculptor. His most famous works consist of ready-made units such as bricks, stacked according to a mathematical system and without adhesives or joints.

An·dré |'än,drā|, John (1750–80)

British soldier. He successfully negotiated with Benedict Arnold for the betrayal of West Point to the British (1779–80). Captured while on his return to New York, he was tried and hanged as a spy.

An·dret·ti |æn'dretē|, Mario (Gabriele) (1940–) Italian-born U.S. race-car driver.

An·drew |'æn,drōō|, Prince, Duke of York (1960–) British prince. Full name *Andrew Albert Christian Edward*. He is the second son of Elizabeth II. He married Sarah Ferguson in 1986 but the couple divorced in 1993; they have two children, Princess Beatrice (1988–) and Princess Eugenie (1990–).

An·drew |'æn,drōō|, St. died (c. 60 AD) an Apostle. He was the brother of St. Peter. The X-shaped cross is associated with him because he is said to have been crucified on such a cross. St. Andrew is the patron saint of Scotland and Russia. Feast day, November 30.

An·drews |'æn,drōōz|, Julie (1935–) English actress and singer. Born *Julia Elizabeth Wells*. She is best known for the movies *Mary Poppins* (1964) and *The Sound of Music* (1965).

An·drews |'æn,drōōz|, Roy Chapman (1884–1960) U.S. naturalist, explorer, and author. He discovered the first known clutch of fossil dinosaur eggs in Mongolia (1925).

An·drews |'æn,drōōz|, Thomas (1813–85) Irish physical chemist. He discovered the critical temperature of carbon dioxide and showed that ozone is an allotrope of oxygen.

An·drić |'ändrēt|, Ivo (1892–1975) Yugoslav novelist, essayist, and short-story writer. Nobel Prize for Literature (1961).

An·dro·pov |æn'drō,pawf|, Yuri (Vladimirovich) (1914–84) Soviet statesman, general secretary of the Communist Party of the USSR (1982–84) and president (1983–84). As president he initiated the reform process carried through by Mikhail Gorbachev, his chosen successor.

An·gel·ic Doctor the nickname of St. Thomas AQUINAS.

An·ge·li·co |'änje,likō|, Fra (c. 1400–55) Italian painter and Dominican friar.

Born *Guido di Pietro*; monastic name *Fra Giovanni da Fiesole*. Notable works: the frescoes in the convent of San Marco, Florence (c. 1438–47).

An·ge·lou |'ænjəlō|, Maya (1928–) U.S. novelist and poet. acclaimed for the first volume of her autobiography, *I Know Why the Caged Bird Sings* (1970).

Ång·ström |'æNGstrəm|, Anders Jonas (1814–1874) Swedish physicist. He proposed a relationship between the emission and absorption spectra of chemical elements, and measured optical wavelengths in the unit later named in his honor.

An·ka |'æNGkə|, Paul (1941–) Canadian musician. Among the hits that he composed and sang are "Lonely Boy" (1959) and "Put Your Head on My Shoulder" (1959).

An·nan |'ænən|, Kofi (Atta) (1938–) Ghanaian diplomat; secretary general of the United Nations (1997–).

Anne |æn| (1665–1714) queen of England and Scotland (known as Great Britain from 1707) and Ireland (1702–14). The last of the Stuart monarchs, daughter of the Catholic James II (but herself a Protestant), she succeeded her brother-in-law William III to the throne.

Anne |æn|, Princess (1950–) British princess. Full name *Anne Elizabeth Alice Louise*, the Princess Royal. Daughter of Elizabeth II.

Anne, St. traditionally the mother of the Virgin Mary. First mentioned by name in the apocryphal gospel of James (2nd century). Feast day, July 26.

Anne Boleyn |æn bŏŏ'lin| see BOLEYN.

An·nen·berg |'ænən,bərg|, Walter (Hubert) (1908–) U.S. publisher and philanthropist. He founded the magazines *Seventeen* (1944) and *TV Guide* (1953) and was US ambassador to Britain (1969–74).

Anne of Cleves |'æn| (1515–57) fourth wife of Henry VIII. Arranged for political purposes, the marriage was dissolved after only six months; Henry, initially deceived by a flattering portrait of Anne by Holbein, took an instant dislike to her.

An·ni·go·ni |,ænə'gawnē|, Pietro (1910–88) Italian painter. He is famous for his portraits of Queen Elizabeth II (1955, 1970) and President Kennedy (1961).

An·no |'änō|, Mitsumasu (1926–) Japanese author and illustrator of children's books.

Anouilh |ä'nōōē|, Jean (1910–87) French dramatist. He wrote many plays but is best known for his reworking of the Greek myth of Antigone in *Antigone* (1944).

An·selm |'ænsəlm|, St. (c. 1033–1109) Italian-born philosopher and theologian, Archbishop of Canterbury (1093–1109).

Antall |'æntæ|, Jozsef (1933–93) Hungarian statesman. He was prime minister (1990–93), elected premier in the country's first free elections for over forty years.

An·the·mi·us |æn'THēmē,əs| (6th century AD) Greek mathematician, engineer, and artist; known as **Anthemius of Tralles**.

An·tho·ny |'ænTHənē|, St. (c. 250–356) Also **Antony**. Egyptian hermit, the founder of monasticism. Feast day, January 17.

An·tho·ny |'ænTHənē|, Susan Brownell (1820–1906) U.S. social reformer and leader of the woman suffrage movement. She traveled, lectured, and campaigned throughout her life for women's rights. With Elizabeth Cady Stanton, she organized (1869) the National Woman Suffrage Association. With Stanton and Matilda Joslyn Gage, she compiled Volumes I to III of the *History of Woman Suffrage* (1881–86).

An·tho·ny of Pad·ua |'ænTHənē|, St. (1195–1231) Portuguese Franciscan friar. His devotion to the poor is commemorated by alms known as St. Anthony's bread; he is invoked to find lost articles. Feast day, June 13.

An·ti·o·chus |æn'tīəkəs| (c. 242–187 BC) the name of eight Seleucid kings, notably: **Antiochus III** (c. 242–187 BC; reigned 223–187 BC); known as **Antiochus the Great**. He restored and expanded the Seleucid empire. **Antiochus IV** (c. 215–163 BC; reigned 175–163 BC). Known as **Antiochus Epiphanes**. His firm control of Judaea and his attempt to Hellenize the Jews resulted in the revival of Jewish nationalism and the Maccabean revolt.

An·to·ni·nus Pi·us |æntə'ninəs 'pīəs| (86–161) Roman emperor 138–61. The adopted son and successor of Hadrian, he had a generally peaceful and harmonious reign.

An·to·nio·ni |æn'tōnē,ōnē|, Michelangelo (1912–) Italian movie director. Notable movies: *L'avventura* (1960), *Blow-Up* (1966), and *Zabriskie Point* (1970).

An·to·ny |'æntənē|, Mark (c. 82 or 81–30 BC) Roman general and triumvir; Latin name *Marcus Antonius*. A supporter of Julius Caesar, following Caesar's assassination in 44 he took charge of the Eastern Empire, where he established his association with Cleopatra. Quarrels with Octavian led finally to his defeat at the battle of Actium and to his suicide.

An·to·ny |'æntənē|, St. see ANTHONY, ST.

An·to·ny of Padua |'æntənē|, St. see ANTHONY OF PADUA, ST.

Apel·les |ə'pelēz| (4th century BC) Greek painter. He is now known only from written sources, but was highly acclaimed throughout the ancient world.

Apol·li·naire |ə,pälə'ner|, Guillaume (1880–1918) French poet. Pseudonym of *Wilhelm Apollinaris de Kostrowitzki*. He coined the term *surrealist* and was acknowledged by the surrealist poets as their precursor. Notable works: *Les Alcools* (1913) and *Calligrammes* (1918).

Ap·ol·lo·ni·us[1] |,æpə'lōnēəs| 3rd cent. BC. Greek poet called **Appollonius of Rhodes**. Notable work: *Argonautica*.

Ap·ol·lo·ni·us[2] |,æpə'lōnēəs| (c. 262–190 BC) Greek mathematician; **Apollonius of Perga**. He was the first to use the terms *ellipse, parabola*, and *hyperbola*.

Ap·pel |'æpəl|, Karel (1921–) Dutch painter, sculptor, and graphic artist.

Ap·ple |'æpəl|, Fiona (1977–) U.S. rock singer and songwriter. Born *Fiona Apple Maggart*. She won a 1998 Grammy Award for "Criminal."

Ap·ple·seed |'æpəl,sēd|, Johnny (1774–1845) U.S. folk hero. Born *John Chapman*. A missionary, he traveled throughout Ohio and Indiana planting and caring for apple orchards.

Ap·ple·ton |'æpəltən|, Sir Edward Victor (1892–1965) English physicist. He discovered a region of ionized gases (the Appleton layer) in the atmosphere above the Heaviside or E layer, and won the Nobel Prize for Physics in 1947.

Ap·u·le·ius |ˌapyə'lēəs| (*c.* 124–*c.* 170) Roman writer, born in Africa. Notable works: *Metamorphoses (The Golden Ass)*.

Aqui·nas |ə'kwinəs|, St. Thomas (1225–74) Italian philosopher, theologian, and Dominican friar. Known as *the Angelic Doctor*. He is regarded as the greatest figure of scholasticism; one of his most important achievements was the introduction of the work of Aristotle to Christian western Europe. Feast day, January 28.

Aqui·no |ə'kēnō|, (Maria) Corazon (1933–) Filipino stateswoman and president (1986–92).

Aq·ui·taine |'ækwiˌtān|, Eleanor of see ELEANOR OF AQUITAINE.

Ávila |'ävēlə|, Teresa of see TERESA OF ÁVILA, ST.

Ar·a·fat |'erəˌfæt|, Yasser (1929–) Palestinian statesman, chairman of the Palestine Liberation Organization from 1968 and Palestinian president since 1996.

Ar·a·gon |'erəˌgän|, Catherine of see CATHERINE OF ARAGON.

Ar·bus |'ärbəs|, Diane (1923–71) U.S. photographer. She is best known for her disturbing images of people on the streets of U.S. cities.

Ar·buth·not |är'bəтнnət|, John (1667–1735) Scottish physician and writer. His satirical *History of John Bull* (1712) was the origin of John Bull as the personification of the typical Englishman.

Ar·ca·ro |är'kærō; är'kerō|, Eddie (1916–) U.S. jockey. Full name *George Edward Arcaro*. He was the first two-time Triple Crown winner, riding Whirlaway (1941) and Citation (1948).

Ar·chil·o·chus |är'kiləkəs| (7th century BC) Greek poet. He is credited with the invention of iambic meter.

Ar·chi·me·des |ˌärkə'mēdēz| (*c.* 287–212 BC) Greek mathematician and inventor, of Syracuse. He is famous for his discovery of Archimedes' principle (legend has it that he made this discovery while taking a bath, and ran through the streets shouting "Eureka!"); among his mathematical discoveries are the ratio of the radius of a circle to its circumference, and formulas for the surface area and volume of a sphere and of a cylinder.

Ar·chi·pen·ko |ˌærki'peɴɢkō|, Alexander (Porfirevich) (1887–1964) Russianborn U.S. sculptor. He adapted cubist techniques to sculpture.

Ar·den |'ärdən|, Elizabeth (*c.* 1884–1966) Canadian-born U.S. executive in the cosmetics industry; born *Florence Nightingale Graham*.

Arendt |ə'rent|, Hannah (1906–75) German-born U.S. philosopher and political theorist.

Ari·as San·chez |'ärēäs 'sänchez|, Oscar (1941–) Costa Rican president (1986–94). Nobel Peace Prize (1987).

Ari·os·to |ˌärē'ästō|, Ludovico (1474–1533) Italian poet. He was noted for his romantic epic *Orlando Furioso* (final version 1532).

Ar·is·tar·chus[1] |ˌerə'stärkəs| (3rd century BC) Greek astronomer. Known as **Aristarchus of Samos**. Founder of an important school of Hellenic astronomy, he was aware of the rotation of the earth around the sun and so was able to account for the seasons.

Ar·is·tar·chus[2] |ˌerə'stärkəs| (*c.* 215–145 BC) Greek scholar. Known as **Aristarchus of Samothrace**. He was noted for his editions of the writings of Homer and other Greek authors.

Ari·stide |ˌærə'stēd|, Jean-Bertrand (1953–) Haitian president (1990–96). He led a movement against the dictatorship of Duvalier in the 1980s and was elected president of Haiti in 1990, but was forced into exile (1991–94) by a military coup. In 1994, the presence of U.S. troops facilitated his return.

Ar·is·ti·des |ˌerə'stīdēz| (*c.* 530–468 BC) Athenian statesman and general. Known as **Aristides the Just**.

Ar·is·tip·pus |ˌerə'stipəs| (*c.* 435–366 BC) Greek philosopher. Known as **Aristippus the Elder**. He is considered the founder of the Cyrenaic school.

Ar·is·toph·a·nes |ˌerə'stäfənēz| (*c.* 450–*c.* 388 BC) Greek comic dramatist Notable works: *Lysistrata*, the *Birds*, and the *Frogs*.

Ar·is·tot·le |'erəs'tädəl| (384–322 BC)

Greek philosopher and scientist. A pupil of Plato and tutor to Alexander the Great, he founded a school (the Lyceum) outside Athens. He is one of the most influential thinkers in the history of Western thought. His surviving works cover a vast range of subjects, including logic, ethics, metaphysics, politics, natural science, and physics.

Ark·wright |'ärk,rīt|, Sir Richard (1732–92) English inventor and industrialist. In 1767 he patented a water-powered spinning machine.

Ar·ledge |'ärlij|, Roone (1931–) U.S. television executive. He has won 36 Emmys for technical and editorial innovation in sports coverage, including 10 Olympic Games and "Monday Night Football."

Ar·ma·ni |är'mänē|, Giorgio (1935–) Italian fashion designer.

Ar·ma·tra·ding |'ärmə,trādiNG|, Joan (1950–) British musician, born in St. Kitts. Her music is a blend of folk, reggae, soul, and rock.

Ar·mour |'ärmər|, Philip Danforth (1832–1901) U.S. industrialist. He reorganized his brother Herman's grain commission house into the Armour & Co. meat-packing plant (1870).

Arm·strong |'ärm,strawNG|, Edwin Howard (1890–1954) U.S. electrical engineer, inventor of the superheterodyne radio receiver and the frequency modulation (FM) system.

Arm·strong |'ärm,strawNG|, Louis (Daniel) (1901–71) U.S. jazz musician. Known as **Satchmo**. A major influence on Dixieland jazz, he was a trumpet and cornet player as well as a bandleader and a distinctive singer.

Arm·strong |'ärm,strawNG|, Neil (Alden) (1930–) U.S. astronaut. He commanded the Apollo 11 mission, during which he became the first man to set foot on the moon (July 20, 1969).

Arne |ärn|, Thomas (1710–78) English composer of the tune for "Rule, Britannia," and of Shakespearean songs.

Ar·no |'är,nō|, Peter (1904–68) U.S. cartoonist. Born *Curtis Arnoux Peters*. He published satirical cartoons of New York society in *The New Yorker* and wrote musical revues.

Ar·nold |'ärnəld|, Benedict (1741–1801) Revolutionary War general and traitor to the American side. With Ethan Allan, he captured Fort Ticonderoga but later planned to betray West Point to the British. He was captured and hanged by the Americans, and his name became a synonym for "traitor."

Ar·nold |'ärnəld|, Hap (1886–1950) U.S. airman and author. Full name *Henry Harley Arnold*. He helped develop the U.S. Army Air Corps during the 1930s; later he served as general of the army (1944) and general of the air force (1949).

Ar·nold |'ärnəld|, Sir Malcolm (Henry) (1921–) English composer and trumpeter, noted especially for his orchestral works and movie scores.

Ar·nold |'ärnəld|, Matthew (1822–88) English poet, essayist, and social critic. In works such as *Culture and Anarchy* (1869) he criticized the Victorian age in terms of its materialism, philistinism, and complacency. Notable poems: "The Scholar Gipsy" (1853) and "Dover Beach" (1867.

Arp |ärp|, Jean (1887–1966) French painter, sculptor, and poet. Also known as **Hans Arp**. He was a co-founder of the Dada movement.

Ar·rhe·ni·us |ə'rānēəs|, Svante August (1859–1927) Swedish chemist, noted for his work on electrolytes. Nobel Prize for Chemistry (1903).

Ar·row |'erō|, Kenneth Joseph (1921–) U.S. economist. He is noted chiefly for his work on general economic equilibrium and social choice. Nobel Prize for Economics (1972).

Ar·taud |är'tō|, Antonin (1896–1948) French actor, director, and poet. He developed the concept of the nonverbal Theater of Cruelty, which concentrated on the use of sound, mime, and lighting.

Ar·ta·xer·xes |,ärtə'zərksēz| the name of three kings of ancient Persia: **Artaxerxes I** son of Xerxes I, reigned 464–424 BC. **Artaxerxes II** son of Darius II, reigned 404–358 BC. **Artaxerxes III** son of Artaxerxes II, reigned 358–338 BC.

Ar·thur |'ärTHər| (5th or 6th century) A legendary king of Britain, historically perhaps a 5th– or 6th–century Romano-British chieftain or general. Stories of his life, the exploits of his knights, and the

Round Table of the court at Camelot were developed by Malory, Chrétien de Troyes, and other medieval writers and became the subject of many legends.

Ar·thur |'ärᴛʜər|, Chester Alan see box.

Ellen Lewis Herndon Arthur (1837–80), wife of Chester Alan Arthur; she died before her husband became president.

Ar·ya·bha·ta I |'æryə'bətə| (476–c. 550) Indian astronomer and mathematician. His surviving work, the *Aryabhatiya* (499, has sections dealing with mathematics, the measurement of time, planetary models, the sphere, and eclipses.

Asch |äsн; æsн|, Sholem (1880–1957) U.S.author and playwright, born in Poland. Notable plays: *The God of Vengeance* (1910). Notable novels: *Mottke the Thief* (1935) and *The Prophet* (1955).

As·cham |'æskəm|, Roger (1515–68) English humanist scholar and writer. He was noted for his treatise on archery, *Toxophilus* (1545), and *The Scholemaster* (1570), a practical and influential tract on education.

Ash·bery |'æsнberē|, John Lawrence (1927–) U.S. poet. He is noted for his visionary poetry, as in *Self-Portrait in a Convex Mirror* (1975, National Book Award).

Ash·croft |'æsн,krawft|, Dame Peggy (1907–91) English actress; born *Edith Margaret Emily Ashcroft*. She made her name on the stage with a number of Shakespearean roles.

Ashe |æsн|, Arthur (Robert) (1943–93) U.S. tennis player. He won the U.S. Open championship in 1968 and Wimbledon in 1975, and was the first black male player to achieve world rankings.

Ash·ke·na·zy |,äsнkə'näzē|, Vladimir (Davidovich) (1937–) Russian-born pianist. A child prodigy, he left the Soviet Union in 1963, finally settling in Iceland in 1973.

Ash·ley |'æsнlē|, Laura (1925–85) Welsh fashion and textile designer, known for her use of floral patterns and romantic Victorian and Edwardian styles.

Ash·man |'æsн,mən|, Howard (1950–91) U.S. lyricist. His songs are featured

---

Arthur, Chester Alan
21st U.S. president

Life dates: 1829–1886
Place of birth: Fairfield, Vermont
Mother: Malvina Stone Arthur
Father: William Arthur
Wife: Ellen Lewis Herndon Arthur
Children: William, Chester, Ellen
College/University: Union College
Military service: during Civil War, brigadier-general, quartermaster-general in New York State Militia
Career: Lawyer; teacher
Political career: Collector, New York Custom House; vice president (under Garfield); president
Party: Republican
Home state: New York
Opponents in presidential race: none; succeeded to the presidency on the assassination of James Garfield
Term of office: Sept. 20, 1881 (following the death of Garfield)–March 3, 1885
Vice president: none
Notable events of presidency: Panic of 1883; Pendleton Act; Chinese Exclusion Act; Edmunds Anti-Polygamy Act; adoption of standard time; Korean Treaty of Peace, Amity, Commerce and Navigation; dedication of the Washington Monument; Civil Service Commission organized; establishment of territorial government in Alaska; Nicaragua Canal Treaty (later Panama Canal Treaty)
Other achievements: Admitted to the New York bar; delegate from New York to Republican National Convention, Chicago
Place of burial: Albany, New York

---

in *Little Shop of Horrors* and *The Little Mermaid.*

Ash·mole |'æsн,mōl|, Elias (1617–92) English antiquary. His collection of rarities, presented to Oxford University in 1677, formed the nucleus of the Ashmolean Museum.

Ash·ton |'æsнtən|, Sir Frederick (William Mallandaine) (1904–88) British ballet dancer, choreographer, and director. As a choreographer he created successful new works as well as popular adaptations of classical ballets.

Ashur·ba·ni·pal |ä,sнoͦr'bänipäl| (c. 668–627 BC) grandson of Sennacherib.

A patron of the arts, he established a library of more than 20,000 clay tablets at Nineveh.

As·i·mov |'æzə‚mawv|, Isaac (1920–92) Russian-born U.S. writer and scientist, particularly known for his works of science fiction and books on science for nonscientists. Notable science-fiction works: *I, Robot* (1950) and *Foundation* (trilogy, 1951–53).

As·ner |'æzner|, Edward (1929–) U.S. actor. He starred in *The Mary Tyler Moore Show* (1970–77) and *The Lou Grant Show* (1977–82), and has won 7 Emmys.

Aso·ka |ə'sōkə| (died *c.* 232 BC) emperor of India *c.* 269–232 BC. Also **Ashoka**. He converted to Buddhism and established it as the state religion.

As·quith |'æskwɔth|, Herbert Henry, 1st Earl of Oxford and Asquith (1852–1928) British Liberal statesman, prime minister (1908–16).

As·sad |ä'säd|, Hafiz al- (1928–) Syrian Baath statesman, president since 1971.

As·san·te |ä'sän‚te|, Armand (1949–) U.S. actor. His films include *Fatal Instinct* (1993); he has also won Emmy Awards for the television special "The Odyssey."

As·si·si[1] |ə'sēsē| see CLARE OF ASSISI, ST.

As·si·si[2] |ə'sēsē| see FRANCIS OF ASSISI, ST.

Astaire |ə'stær|, Fred (1899–1987) U.S. dancer, singer, and actor; born *Frederick Austerlitz*. He is famous for starring in a number of movie musicals, including *Top Hat* (1935), in a successful partnership with Ginger Rogers.

As·ton |'æstən|, Francis William (1877–1945) English physicist. He invented the mass spectrograph (with J. J. Thomson) and eventually discovered many of the 287 naturally occurring isotopes of nonradioactive elements. Nobel Prize for Chemistry (1922).

As·tor |'æstər|, John Jacob (1763–1848) U.S. merchant, born in Germany. He emigrated to the U.S. in 1784 and made a fortune in the fur trade.

As·tor |'æstər|, Nancy Witcher Langhorne, Viscountess (1879–1964) U.S.-born British Conservative politician.

She became the first woman to sit in the House of Commons when she succeeded her husband as a member of Parliament.

As·tu·ri·as |ä'stoor‚yäs|, Miguel Angel (1899–1974) Guatemalan novelist and poet, best known for his experimental novel *The President* (1946). Nobel Prize for Literature (1967).

Ata·türk |'ætətərk|, Kemal (1881–1938) Turkish general and statesman, president (1923–38); also called **Kemal Pasha**. He was elected the first president of the Turkish republic. He abolished the caliphate and introduced other policies designed to make Turkey a modern secular state.

At·get |ätzHe|, Eugène (1856–1927) French photographer. Full name *Jean-Eugène-Auguste Atget*. His is noted for his photographs of Paris, especially historic buildings, architectural decoration, and tradespeople.

Ath·a·na·sius |‚ætHə'näsHəs|, St. (*c.* 293–373) Greek theologian and upholder of Christian orthodoxy against the Arian heresy. Feast day, May 2.

Ath·el·stan |'ætHəl‚stæn| (895–939) king of England (925–39). Athelstan came to the thrones of Wessex and Mercia in 924 before effectively becoming the first king of all England.

At·kins |'ætkinz|, Chet (1924–) U.S. musician. A guitarist and country music producer, he established the "Nashville Sound" at RCA Records.

At·kin·son |'ætkinsən|, Sir Harry (Albert) (1831–92) British-born New Zealand statesman, prime minister (1876–77, 1883–84, and 1887–91).

At·ten·bor·ough |'ætn‚bərə| Family name of: **Richard (Samuel) Attenborough, Baron Attenborough of Richmond-upon-Thames** (1923–), English movie actor, producer, and director. His brother, **Sir David (Frederick) Attenborough** (1926–), English naturalist and broadcaster. He is known for movies of animals in their natural habitats, including *Life on Earth* (1979), *The Living Planet* (1983), and *The Trials of Life* (1990).

At·ti·la |ə'tilə| (*c.* 406–53) king of the Huns (434–53). Known as **Attila the Hun**. He ravaged vast areas between the

Rhine and the Caspian Sea, before being defeated by the joint forces of the Roman army and the Visigoths at Chèlons in 451.

Att·lee |'æt,lē|, Clement Richard, 1st Earl Attlee (1883–1967) British Labour statesman, prime minister (1945–51). His term saw the creation of the modern welfare state and nationalization of major industries.

At·tucks |'ætəks|, Crispus (1723?–1770) American revolutionary. Believed to be either an escaped or freed slave, he was one of five colonists killed by British soldiers in the Boston Massacre (March 5, 1770).

At·wood |'æt,wŏod|, Margaret (Eleanor) (1939–) Canadian novelist, poet, critic, and short-story writer. Notable novels: *The Edible Woman* (1969), *Cat's Eye* (1989).

Au·brey |'awbrē|, John (1626–97) English antiquarian and author. He is chiefly remembered for *Brief Lives*, a collection of biographies of eminent people.

Au·chin·closs |'awkən,kläs|, Louis Stanton (1917–) U.S. lawyer and author. Pseudonym (early novels) **Andrew Lee**.

Au·den |'awdən|, W. H. (1907–73) British-born poet, resident in America from 1939. Full name *Wystan Hugh Auden*. *Look, Stranger!* (1936) and *Spain* (1937, on the Civil War) secured his position as a leading left-wing poet. He was awarded the Pulitzer Prize for *The Age of Anxiety* (1947).

Au·du·bon |'awdə,bän|, John James (1785–1851) U.S. naturalist and artist. Notable works: *The Birds of America* (1827–38), in which he portrayed even the largest birds life-size, and painted them in action.

Au·er |'ow(ə)r|, Carl, Baron von Welsbach (1858–1929) Austrian chemist, who separated the supposed rare earth element didymium into neodymium and praseodymium.

Au·er·bach |'ow(ə)r,bäk|, Frank (1931–) German-born British painter.

Au·er·bach |'ow(ə)r,bäk|, Red (1917–) U.S. basketball coach. Full name *Arnold Jacob Auerach*. As coach of

the Boston Celtics (1950 –66), he led the team to nine NBA championships, eight of them consecutively (1959–66).

Au·gus·tine[1] |'awgə,stēn; ə'gəstin|, St. (354–430) Doctor of the Church; known as **St. Augustine of Hippo**. He became bishop of Hippo in North Africa in 396. His writings, such as the *City of God*, dominated subsequent Western theology. Feast day, August 28.

Au·gus·tine[2] |'awgə,stēn|, St. (died *c.* 604) Italian churchman. Known as **St. Augustine of Canterbury**. Sent from Rome by Pope Gregory the Great to refound the Church of England in 597, he founded a monastery at Canterbury and became its first archbishop. Feast day, May 26.

Au·gus·tus |ə'gəstəs| (63 BC–AD14) the first Roman emperor; born *Gaius Octavianus*; also called **Octavian**. He was adopted in the will of his great-uncle Julius Caesar and gained supreme power by his defeat of Antony in 31 BC. In 27 BC he was given the title Augustus ('venerable') and became in effect emperor.

Aung San |'owNG 'sän| (*c.* 1914–47) Burmese nationalist leader. As leader of the Council of Ministers he negotiated a promise of self-government from the British shortly before his assassination.

Aung San Suu Kyi |'owNG 'sän 'sŏo 'CHē|, Daw (1945–) Burmese political leader, daughter of Aung San and leader of the National League for Democracy (NLD) since 1988. She was kept under house arrest from 1989 to 1995, and the military government refused to recognize her party's victory in the 1990 elections. Nobel Peace Prize (1991).

Au·rang·zeb |aw,ræNG'zeb| (1618–1707) Mogul emperor of Hindustan (1658–1707), who increased the Mogul empire to its greatest extent.

Au·re·li·an |aw'rēlēən| (*c.* 215–75) Roman emperor (270–75); Latin name *Lucius Domitius Aurelianus*. Originally a common soldier, he rose through the ranks and was elected emperor by the army.

Au·re·li·us |aw'rēlēəs|, Marcus (121–80) Roman emperor (161–80); full name *Caesar Marcus Aurelius Antoninus Augustus*. He was occupied for much of his reign with wars against invading Germanic tribes. His *Meditations*, a collection of aphorisms and reflections, are evidence of his philosophical interests.

Au·ric |'awrik|, Georges (1899–1983) French composer. Auric was one of the anti-romantic group Les Six. He is probably best known for his scores for movies such as *The Lavender Hill Mob* (1951) and *Moulin Rouge* (1952).

Aus·ten |'awstən|, Jane (1775–1817) English novelist. Her major novels are *Sense and Sensibility* (1811), *Pride and Prejudice* (1813), *Mansfield Park* (1814), *Emma* (1815), *Northanger Abbey* (1818), and *Persuasion* (1818). They are notable for skillful characterization, dry wit, and penetrating social observation.

Aus·tin |'awstən|, Herbert, 1st Baron Austin of Longbridge (1866–1941) British automobile manufacturer. Among the cars produced by his factory the Austin Seven ("Baby Austin") was particularly popular. His company merged with Morris Motors in 1952 to form the British Motor Corp.

Aus·tin |'awstən|, J. L.(1911–60) English philosopher. Full name *John Langshaw Austin*. A careful exponent of linguistic philosophy, he pioneered the theory of speech acts, pointing out that utterances can be used to perform actions as well as to convey information. Notable works: *Sense and Sensibilia* and *How to Do Things with Words* (both 1962).

Aus·tin |'awstən|, John (1790–1859) English jurist. His work is significant for its strict delimitation of the sphere of law and its distinction from that of morality.

Aus·tin |'awstən|, Stephen Fuller (1793–1836) colonizer of Texas. He founded the first recognized Anglo-American settlement in Texas (1822) and served briefly as secretary of state of the Republic of Texas (1836).

Au·try |'awtrē|, (Orvon) Gene (1907–98) U.S. singer and actor. Known as the **Singing Cowboy**. His credits include the first cowboy song recording (1929) and 88 musical Westerns.

Av·a·lon |'ævə,län|, Frankie (1939–) U.S. musician. Full name *Francis Avalon*. He was a singer who made regular appearances on television's "American Bandstand" and costarred with Annette Funicello in several beach party movies.

Av·e·don |ævədän|, Richard (1923–) U.S. photographer and photojournalist. Among his noted works is *Observations* (1959), a book of celebrity portraits. His series of photos chronicling the civil rights and antiwar movements of the 1960s gained critical acclaim.

Aver·ro·ës |ə'verə,wēz; ,ævə'rōēz| (1126–98) Spanish-born Islamic philosopher, judge, and physician; Arabic name *ibn-Rushd*. His highly influential commentaries on Aristotle sought to reconcile Aristotle with Plato and the Greek philosophical tradition with the Arabic.

Avery |'āvərē|, Tex (1907–80) U.S. animator. Born *Frederick Bean Avery*. He created the cartoon characters Bugs Bunny and Porky Pig.

Av·i·cen·na |,ævə'senə| (980–1037) Persian-born Islamic philosopher and physician; Arabic name *ibn-Sina*. His philosophical system, drawing on Aristotle but in many ways closer to Neoplatonism, was the major influence on the development of scholasticism. His *Canon of Medicine* was a standard medieval medical text.

Avo·ga·dro |,āvə'gädrō|, Amedeo (1776–1856) Italian chemist and physicist. His law, formulated in 1811, was used to derive both molecular weights and a system of atomic weights.

Ax |æks|, Emanuel (1949–) U.S. pianist, born in Poland. A soloist with major international orchestras, he has won four Grammys and the Arthur Rubinstein International Competition (1974).

Ayatollah Kho·mei·ni |kō'mānē| see KHOMEINI.

Ayck·bourn |'ĭk,baw(ə)rn|, Sir Alan (1939–) English dramatist, known chiefly for comedies dealing with suburban and middle-class life. Notable plays: *Relatively Speaking* (1967), *Absurd Person Singular* (1973).

Ay·er |ær|, Sir A. J. (1910–89) English philosopher. Full name *Alfred Jules Ayer*. Involved with the Vienna Circle in 1932, he was an important proponent of logical positivism. Notable works: *Language, Truth, and Logic* (1936).

Ayl·ward |'alwawrd|, Gladys (May) (1902–70) English missionary. In 1932 she helped found an inn in Yangsheng (later portrayed in the 1959 movie *The Inn of the Sixth Happiness*). During the Sino-Japanese war she made a perilous journey to lead a hundred children to safety. She later settled in Taiwan as head of an orphanage.

Ayub Khan |ä'oob'kän|, Muhammad (1907–74) Pakistani soldier and statesman; he was president (1958–69).

Azi·ki·we, (Benjamin) Nnamdi (1904–96) Nigerian statesman, the first governor general of an independent Nigeria (1960–63) and its first president (1963–66).

Bb

Baa·de |'bädə|, (Wilhelm Heinrich) Walter (1893–1960) German-born U.S. astronomer. He proved that the Andromeda galaxy was much farther away than had been thought, which implied that the universe was much older and more extensive than had been supposed.

Bab·bage |'bæbij|, Charles (1792–1871) English mathematician, inventor, and pioneer of machine computing. He designed a mechanical computer with Ada Lovelace but was unable to complete it in his lifetime.

Bab·bitt |'bæbət|, Arthur (1907–92) U.S. cartoonist. He worked on several Disney projects, including "Snow White."

Bab·bitt |'bæbət|, Bruce Edward (1938–) U.S. politician. He has served as the governor of Arizona (1978–87) and the U.S. Secretary of the Interior (1993–).

Bab·bitt |'bæbət|, Milton (Byron) (1916–) U.S. composer and mathematician. His compositions developed from the twelve-note system of Schoenberg and Webern.

Ba·bel |'bæbəl|, Isaac Emmanuilovich (1894–1941) Russian author. He was exiled to Siberia c. 1937. Notable works: *Odessa Tales* (1916), *Konarmiya* (1926), and the plays *Zakat* (1928) and *Mariya* (1935).

Ba·bur |'bä,bŏŏr| (1483–1530) first Mogul emperor of India c. 1525–30, descendant of Tamerlane; born *Zahir ad-Din Muhammad*. He invaded India c. 1525 and conquered the territory from the Oxus to Patna.

Ba·call |bə'kawl|, Lauren (1924–) U.S. actress; born *Betty Jean Perske*. She co-starred with her husband, Humphrey Bogart, in a number of successful movies.

Bach |bäКH|, Johann Sebastian (1685–1750) German composer. An exceptional and prolific baroque composer, he produced works ranging from violin concertos, suites, and the six *Brandenburg Concertos* (1720–21) to clavier works and sacred cantatas. Large-scale choral works include *The Passion according to St. John* (1723), *The Passion according to St. Matthew* (1729), and the *Mass in B minor* (1733–38). He had twenty children: **Carl Philipp Emanuel Bach** (1714–88) wrote church music, keyboard sonatas, and a celebrated treatise on clavier playing, and **Johann Christian Bach** (1735–82) became music master to the British royal family and composed thirteen operas.

Bach·a·rach |'bækə,ræk|, Burt (1929–) U.S. writer of popular songs, many of which were written with lyricist Hal David (1921–).

Ba·con[1] |'bākən|, Francis, Baron Verulam and Viscount St. Albans (1561–1626) English statesman and philosopher. As a scientist he advocated the inductive method; his views were instrumental in the founding of the Royal Society in 1660. Notable works: *The Advancement of Learning* (1605) and *Novum Organum* (1620).

Ba·con[2] |'bākən|, Francis (1909–92) Irish painter. His work chiefly depicts human figures in grotesquely distorted postures, their features blurred or erased.

Ba·con |'bākən|, Henry (1866–1924) U.S. architect. He collaborated with sculptor Daniel Chester French in the creation of several American memorials, most notably the Lincoln Memorial (1911) in Washington, D.C., the design of which was Bacon's last major work.

Ba·con |'bākən|, Kevin (1958–) U.S. actor. In 1996 he made his directorial debut in the film *Losing Chase*.

Ba·con |'bākən|, Roger (1220–92) English philosopher, scientist, and Franciscan monk. Most notable for his work in the field of optics, he emphasized the need for an empirical approach to scientific study.

Baden-Powell |'bädn 'pōəl|, Robert (Stephenson Smyth), 1st Baron Baden-Powell of Gilwell (1857–1941) English soldier and founder of the Boy Scout movement.

Ba·der |'bädər|, Sir Douglas (Robert

Stuart) (1910–82) British airman. Despite having lost both legs in a flying accident in 1931, he saw action as a fighter pilot during the Battle of Britain (1940–41). After the war he was noted for his work on behalf of disabled people.

Ba·du |ˌbäˈdo͞o|, Erykah (1971–) U.S. rhythm and blues musician. Born *Erica Wright*. Grammy Award, 1998.

Baeck, Leo (1873–1956) German rabbi and theologian. As leader of the National Agency of Jews in Germany (1933–42), he was eventually sent (1942–45) to a German concentration camp. After the war, he became president of the World Union for Progressive Judaism in London and taught at the Hebrew Union College in Cincinnati, Ohio.

Bae·de·ker |ˈbā,dekər|, Karl (1801–59) German publisher. He is remembered chiefly for the series of travel guidebooks to which he gave his name and which are still published today.

Baeke·land |ˈbāk,lənd|, Leo Hendrik (1863–1944) U.S. chemist and inventor, born in Belgium. He invented and developed the synthetic resin Bakelite (1907).

Baer |bär|, Karl Ernst von (1792–1876) German biologist. He discovered that ova were particles within the ovarian follicles, and he formulated the principle that in the developing embryo general characteristics appear before special ones. His studies were used by Darwin in the theory of evolution.

Baer |bär|, Ralph U.S. engineer and inventor. He devised the first video game.

Baey·er |ˈbeyər|, (Johann FriedrichWilhelm) Adolf von (1835–1917) German organic chemist. He prepared the first barbiturates and investigated dyes, synthesizing indigo and determining its structural formula. Nobel Prize for Chemistry (1905).

Ba·ez |bīˈez|, Joan (1941–) U.S. folk singer and civil rights activist

Baf·fin |ˈbæfən|, William (*c.* 1584–1622) English navigator and explorer, the pilot of several expeditions in search of the Northwest Passage (1612–16).

Bage·hot |ˈbæjət|, Walter (1826–77)

English economist and journalist; editor of the *Economist* (1860–77).

Bai·ley |ˈbālē|, Donovan (1967–) Canadian sprinter, born in Jamaica. He set the world record for the 100 meters (9.84 seconds) at the 1996 Olympic Games.

Bai·ley |ˈbālē|, Mildred (1907–51) U.S. jazz and blues singer and pianist. She was the first white singer to successfully emulate jazz as performed by black contemporaries.

Baird |bærd|, John Logie (1888–1946) Scottish pioneer of television. He made the first transatlantic transmission and demonstration of color television in 1928 using a mechanical system which was soon superseded by an electronic system.

Bai·ul |bīˈyo͞ol|, Oksana (1977–) Ukranian figure skater. She was the 1993 world champion at age 15 and a 1994 Olympic gold medalist.

Ba·ker |ˈbākər|, Chet (1929–87) U.S. jazz trumpeter. Full name *Chesney Henry Baker*. He played with Gerry Mulligan in his "pianoless" quartet, as well as with others and on his own.

Ba·ker |ˈbākər|, George (1915–75) U.S. cartoonist. He created the syndicated comic strip "Sad Sack," depicting the beleaguered enlisted military man.

Ba·ker |ˈbākər|, Dame Janet (Abbott) (1933–) English operatic mezzo-soprano.

Ba·ker |ˈbākər|, Josephine (1906–75) U.S. dancer. She was a star of the Folies-Bergère in the 1930s, famed for her exotic dancing and risqué clothing.

Ba·ker |ˈbākər|, Russell (1925–) U.S. journalist. He won a Pulitzer Prize in 1983 for *Growing Up* and in 1979 for *Commentary*.

Bake·well |ˈbāk,wel|, Robert (1725–95) English pioneer in scientific methods of livestock breeding and husbandry. He produced pedigree herds of sheep and cattle and increased the meat production from his animals through selective breeding.

Bak·ker |ˈbākər|, Robert T. (1945–) U.S. paleontologist. He proposed the controversial idea that dinosaurs were both active and warm-blooded.

Bakst |bækst|, Léon (1866–1924) Russian painter and designer; born *Lev Samuilovich Rozenberg*. He was a member of the Diaghilev circle and the Ballets Russes, for which he designed exotic, richly colored sets and costumes.

Ba·ku·nin |bə'kōō,nyēn|, Mikhail (Aleksandrovich) (1814–76) Russian anarchist. He took part in the revolutions of 1848, and participated in the First International until his expulsion in 1872.

Bal·an·chine |bælən,SHēn|, George (1904–83) Russian-born U.S. ballet dancer and choreographer; born *Georgi Melitonovich Balanchivadze*. He was chief choreographer of Diaghilev's Ballets Russes during the 1920s, and in 1934 he co-founded the company which later became the New York City Ballet.

Bal·boa |bæl'bōə|, Vasco Núñez de (1475–1519) Spanish explorer. In 1513 he reached the western coast of the isthmus of Darien (Panama), thereby becoming the first European to see the eastern shores of Pacific Ocean.

Bald·win |'bawldwən|, Henry (1780–1844) U.S. Supreme Court Justice (1830–44). He was a member of the U.S. House of Representatives from Pennsylvania (1817–22).

Bald·win |'bawldwən|, James (Arthur) (1924–87) U.S. novelist and black civil rights activist. Notable works: *Go Tell It on the Mountain* (1953) and *Giovanni's Room* (1956).

Bald·win |'bawldwən|, Stanley, 1st Earl Baldwin of Bewdley (1867–1947) British Conservative statesman and prime minister (1923–24, 1924–29, and 1935–37). Despite the German occupation of the Rhineland and the outbreak of the Spanish Civil War (both 1936), Baldwin opposed demands for rearmament, believing that the public would not support it.

Ba·len·cia·ga |bə,lensē'ägə|, Cristóbal (1895–1972) Spanish couturier. In the 1950s he contributed to the move away from the tight-waisted New Look originated by Christian Dior to a looser, semifitted style.

Bal·four |'bæl,fər|, Arthur James, 1st Earl of Balfour (1848–1930) British Conservative statesman, prime minister (1902–05). In 1917, in his capacity as foreign secretary, Balfour issued the declaration in favor of a Jewish national home in Palestine that came to be known as the Balfour Declaration.

Ball |bawl|, John (died 1381) English rebel, a priest who preached an egalitarian social message. Following the Peasants' Revolt, he was hanged as a traitor.

Ball |bawl|, Lucille (1911–89) U.S. comedienne, known in particular for the popular television series "I Love Lucy" (1951–55).

Bal·la |'bälä|, Giacomo (1871–1958) Italian futurist painter. He created some of the earliest nonobjective paintings.

Bal·lan·tine |'bælən,tīn|, Ian (1916–95) U.S. publisher. He founded Penguin USA, Bantam Books, and Ballantine Books.

Bal·lan·tyne |'bælən,tīn|, R. M. (Robert Michael) (1825–94) Scottish author. He wrote acclaimed stories for boys, such as *The Coral Island* (1857).

Bal·lard |'bælərd|, J. G. (James Graham) (1930–) British novelist and short-story writer. He is known for dystopian science fiction such as his first novel, *The Drowned World* (1962), and *Crash* (1973).

Bal·lard |'bælərd|, Robert Duane (1942–) U.S. marine biologist and explorer. He found the wrecks of the *Bismarck* and the *Titanic* (1985).

Bal·le·ste·ros |bælə'ste,rōs|, Severiano (1957–) Spanish professional golfer. Known as **Sevvy**.

Bal·sam |'bawlsəm|, Martin (1919–96) U.S. actor. He won an Academy Award for *A Thousand Clowns* (1965).

Bal·zac |bawl'zäk|, Honoré de (1799–1850) French novelist. He is chiefly remembered for his series of ninety-one interconnected novels and stories known collectively as *La Comédie humaine*, which includes *Eugénie Grandet* (1833) and *Le Père Goriot* (1835).

Ban·croft |'bæn,krawft|, Anne (1931–) U.S. actress. Born *Anna Maria Luisa Italiano*. She won a 1959 Tony Award for her performance in the play *The Miracle Worker*, and an Academy Award for her performance in the movie version (1962) of the same work.

Ban·croft |'bæn,krawft|, George

(1800–91) U.S. historian and statesman. As U.S. secretary of the navy
(1845–46), he established the U.S.
Naval Academy at Annapolis (1845). He
was ambassador to Great Britain (1846–
49) and to Prussia and Germany (1867–
74). Notable works: *History of the United States* (ten volumes, 1834–74).

Ban·da |'bændə|, Hastings Kamuzu (*c.*
1906–) Malawian statesman, prime
minister (1964–94) and the first president of the Republic of Malawi (1966–
94).

Ban·da·ra·nai·ke |,bændərə'nīkə|, Sir-
imavo Ratwatte Dias (1916–) Sin-
halese stateswoman and prime minister
of Sri Lanka (1960–65, 1970–77, and
from 1994). The world's first woman
prime minister, she succeeded her husband, S. W. R. D. Bandaranaike, after his
assassination.

Ban·de·ras |,bæn'dārəs|, Antonio
(1960–) U.S. actor and director, born
in Spain.

Bank·head |'bæNGk,hed|, Tallulah
(1903–68) U.S. actress.

Banks |bæNGks|, Ernie (1931–) U.S.
baseball player. Full name *Ernest Banks*;
known as **Mr. Cub**. Elected to the Baseball Hall of Fame (1977).

Banks |bæNGks|, Sir Joseph (1743–
1820) English botanist. He accompanied Captain James Cook on his first
voyage to the Pacific, and helped to establish the Royal Botanic Gardens at
Kew.

Ban·ne·ker |'bænəkər|, Benjamin
(1731–1806) U.S. inventor, astronomer, and mathematician. Born to
a slave father and freed slave mother, he
published an almanac (1792–1802) that
featured his astronomical and tide cal-
culations. On the recommendation of
Thomas Jefferson, he was hired to assist
in the surveying of the District of Columbia (1791).

Ban·nis·ter |'bænəstər|, Sir Roger
(Gilbert) (1929–) British middle-dis-
tance runner and neurologist. In May
1954 he became the first man to run a
mile in under four minutes.

Ban·ting |'bæntiNG|, Sir Frederick
Grant (1891–1941) Canadian physiologist and surgeon. With the assistance
of C. H. Best, Banting discovered insulin

(1921–22), using it to treat the previ-
ously incurable and fatal disease dia-
betes. Nobel Prize for Physiology or
Medicine (1923, shared with J. J. R.
Macleod).

Ba·ra·ka |bə'räkə; 'bä'räkə|, Imamu
Amiri (1934–) U.S. author. Born
LeRoi Jones. An African-American Mus-
lim, he has written plays, short stories,
and nonfiction that reflect his black na-
tionalism.

Bar·ba·ros·sa[1] |,bärbə'rawsə| (died
1546) Barbary pirate; born *Khair ad-
Din*. He was notorious for his successes
against Christian vessels in the eastern
Mediterranean.

Bar·ba·ros·sa[2] |,bärbə'rawsə| see
FREDERICK I.

Bar·ber |'bärbər|, Samuel (1910–81)
U.S. composer. He developed a style
based on romanticism allied to classical
forms; his music includes operas and or-
chestral and chamber music.

Bar·be·ra |,bär'bärə|, Joseph (1911–)
U.S. animator. He was co-chairman and
cofounder of Hanna-Barbera Cartoons,
Inc., with partner William Hanna; together they created characters such as
the Flintstones, Tom and Jerry, The Jet-
sons, Yogi Bear, and Scooby Doo. He
won seven Academy Awards between
1943 and 1953 for MGM's animated
shorts.

Bar·bi·rol·li |,bärbə'rōlē|, Sir John
(Giovanni Battista) (1899–1970) English conductor, of Franco-Italian de-
scent.

Bar·bour |'bärbər|, John (*c.* 1325–95)
Scottish poet and prelate. The only
poem ascribed to him with certainty is
The Bruce, a verse chronicle relating the
deeds of Robert the Bruce.

Bar·bour |'bärbər|, Philip P. (1783–
1841) U.S. Supreme Court Justice
(1836–41).

Bar-Cochba |'bär 'kawKHbä| Jewish
rebel leader; known as **Simeon** in Jewish sources. He led the rebellion in AD
132 against the Romans, and was ac-
cepted by some of his Jewish contem-
poraries as the Messiah.

Bar·deen |,bär'dēn|, John (1908–91)
U.S. physicist. He won the Nobel Prize
in 1956 with William Shockley and Walter Brattain for developing a point-

contact transistor and again in 1972 with Leon N. Cooper and John R. Schreiffer for the theory of superconductivity.

Bar·dot |bär'dō|, Brigitte (1934–) French actress; born *Camille Javal*. The movie *And God Created Woman* (1956) established her reputation as an international sex symbol.

Bar·en·boim |'bærən,boim|, Daniel (1942–) Israeli pianist and conductor, musical director of the Orchestre de Paris 1975–88 and of the Chicago Symphony Orchestra from 1991.

Ba·rents |'berənts|, Willem (c. 1550–1597) Dutch explorer. The leader of several expeditions in search of the Northeast Passage to Asia, Barents discovered Spitsbergen and reached Novaya Zemlya, off the coast of which he died.

Bar·ker |'bärkər|, George (Granville) (1913–91) English poet, noted for his penchant for puns, distortion, and abrupt changes of tone.

Bark·ley |'bärklē|, Alben William (1877–1956) vice president of the U.S. (1949–53).

Bark·ley |'bärklē|, Charles (1963–) U.S. basketball player. He was a five-time All-NBA player, first with Philadelphia and then with Phoenix; he was also a member of the U.S.Olympic Dream Team (1992).

Bar·na·bas |'bärnəbəs|, St. (1st century AD) Cypriot Levite and Apostle. He accompanied St. Paul on the first missionary journey to Cyprus and Asia Minor. The traditional founder of the Cypriot Church, he is said to have been martyred in Cyprus. Feast day, June 11.

Bar·nard |'bär,närd|, Christiaan Neethling (1922–) South African surgeon. He pioneered human heart transplantation, performing the first operation of this kind in December 1967.

Bar·nard |'bär,närd|, Henry (1811–1900) U.S. educator. He was a public school system reformer and the first U.S. commissioner of education (1867–70).

Barnes |bärnz|, Djuna (1892–1982) U.S. poet, author, and artist. Also known by pseudonym **Linda Steptoe**. Notable works of verse: *Creatures in an Alphabet* (1982). Notable novels: *Ryder* (1928) and *Nightwood* (1936).

Bar·num |'bärnəm|, P. T. (Phineas Taylor) (1810–91) U.S. showman. He billed his circus, opened in 1871, as "The Greatest Show on Earth"; ten years later he founded the Barnum and Bailey Circus with his former rival Anthony Bailey (1847–1906).

Ba·ro·ja (y Nes·si) |,bä'rōKHə ē 'nesē|, Pío (1872–1956) Spanish novelist. He was a physician in Basque country who wrote nearly 100 novels, including the 22-volume *Memorias de un hombre de acción*.

Bar·rault |bä'rō|, Jean-Louis (1910–94) French actor and director. He directed a number of movies, including *Les Enfants du Paradis* (1945).

Bar·rett |'berət|, Elizabeth see BROWNING, ELIZABETH BARRETT.

Bar·rie |'berē|, Sir J. M. (James Matthew) (1860–1937) Scottish dramatist and novelist. Barrie's most famous play is *Peter Pan* (1904), a fantasy for children about a boy who would not grow up.

Bar·row |'berō|, Clyde (1909–34) U.S. bank robber and murderer. He and his partner, Bonnie Parker, shot and killed at least 13 persons during a notorious two-year crime spree across the Southwest. They were finally stopped and shot to death at a Louisiana roadblock.

Bar·ry |'berē|, Sir Charles (1795–1860) English architect, designer of the Houses of Parliament.

Bar·ry |'berē|, Dave (1947–) U.S. newspaper columnist and author. He writes a column for the *Miami Herald* (1983–), won the 1988 Pulitzer Prize for *Criticism or Commentary*, and has written humorous books.

Bar·ry[1] |'berē|, John (1745–1803) American naval officer, born in Ireland. After John Paul Jones, Barry ranks as the foremost naval hero of the American Revolution.

Bar·ry[2] |'berē|, John (1933–) English composer. A three-time Academy Award winner, he gained fame for the music of several James Bond movies.

Bar·ry |'berē|, Marion Shepilov, Jr. (1936–) U.S. politician. He was the mayor of Washington, D.C. (1979–91; 1995–98).

Bar·ry |'berē|, Philip James Quinn (1896–1949) U.S. playwright. Notable plays: *Holiday* (1928) and *The Philadelphia Story* (1939).

Bar·ry |'berē|, Rick (1944–) U.S. basketball player. Elected to the Basketball Hall of Fame (1986).

Bar·ry·more |'berē,mŏor| U.S. family of movie and stage actors, notably **Lionel** (1878–1954), his sister **Ethel** (1879–1959), their brother **John** (1882–1942), and John's granddaughter **Drew** (1975–).

Bart |bärt|, Lionel (1930–1999) English composer and lyricist. His musicals include *Oliver!* (1960).

Barth |bärt.|, John (Simmons) (1930–) U.S. novelist and short-story writer noted for complex experimental novels such as *The Sot-Weed Factor* (1960).

Barth |bärᴛн|, Karl (1886–1968) Swiss Protestant theologian. His seminal work *Epistle to the Romans* (1919) established a neo-orthodox or theocentric approach to contemporary religious thought that remains influential on Protestant theology.

Bar·thelme, Donald (1931–1989) U.S. author. Notable works: *Come Back, Dr. Caligari* (1964) and *Paradise* (1986).

Barthes |bärt|, Roland (1915–80) French writer and critic. Barthes was a leading exponent of structuralism and semiology in literary criticism, while later works were influential in the development of deconstruction and poststructuralism.

Bar·thol·di |bär'tôldē|, Frédéric-Auguste (1834–1904) French sculptor, known especially as the designer of the Statue of Liberty, which was presented to the U.S. in 1886.

Bar·thol·o·mew |bär'ᴛнälə,myŏo|, St. an Apostle, regarded as the patron saint of tanners. Feast day, August 24.

Bart·lett |'bärtlət|, John (1820–1905) U.S. publisher and lexicographer. His most famous work, Bartlett's *Familiar Quotations*, was first published in 1855.

Bart·lett |'bärtlət|, John Russell (1805–86) U.S. bibliographer and librarian. He served as Rhode Island's secretary of state (1855–72); his works include *Dictionary of Americanisms* (1848) and *Records of the Colony of Rhode Island, 1636–1792.*

Bart·lett |'bärtlət|, Josiah (1729–95) American Revolutionary leader and physician. He was a signer of the Declaration of Independence and the first governor of New Hampshire (1793–94).

Bart·lett |'bärtlət|, Paul Wayland (1865–1925) U.S. sculptor. He created the pediment on the House wing of the U.S. Capitol (1916).

Bart·lett |'bärtlət|, Robert Abram (1875–1946) U.S. explorer and author. Known as **Captain Bob Bartlett**. He commanded the ship *Roosevelt* on Robert Peary's Arctic voyages (1905–09) and made numerous other northern expeditions.

Bar·tók |'bär,tawk|, Béla (1881–1945) Hungarian composer. His work owes much to Hungarian folk music and includes six string quartets, three piano concertos, and the *Concerto for Orchestra* (1943).

Bar·to·lom·meo |,bärtōlō'meō|, Fra (*c.* 1472–1517) Italian painter; born *Baccio della Porta.* He was a Dominican friar and worked chiefly in Florence.

Bar·ton |'bärtən|, Clara (1821–1912) U.S. founder of the American Red Cross and its first president (1882–1904).

Bar·ton |'bärtən|, Sir Derek Harold Richard (1918–98) English chemist and educator. He added a third dimension to chemical analysis, which became central to research on new drugs. Nobel Prize, 1969.

Bar·ton |'bärtən|, Sir Edmund (1849–1920) Australian statesman and jurist, first prime minister of Australia (1901–03).

Ba·ruch |bə'rŏok|, Bernard Mannes (1870–1965) U.S. financier and economic adviser. As a sought-after presidential adviser, his many appointments included chairman of the War Industries Board (1918–19) and U.S. representative on the United Nations Atomic Energy Commision (1946).

Ba·rysh·ni·kov |bə'risнnə,kawv|, Mikhail (Nikolaevich) (1948–) U.S. ballet dancer, born in Latvia of Russian parents. In 1974 he defected to the West while touring with the Kirov Ballet.

Bar·zun |ˌbär'zən|, Jacques Martin (1907–) U.S. educator, author, and literary critic, born in France. He is known as a staunch and outspoken supporter of traditional standards of language and education. Notable books: *Teacher in America* (1945), *Music in American Life* (1956), and *Clio and the Doctors* (1974).

Ba·sie |'bāsē|, Count (William) (1904– 84) U.S. jazz pianist, organist, and bandleader. In 1935 he formed the Count Basie Orchestra, which became one of the most successful bands of the swing era.

Bas·il |'bæzəl|, St. (*c.* 329–79) Doctor of the Church, bishop of Caesarea; known as **St. Basil the Great**. Brother of St. Gregory of Nyssa, he staunchly opposed the Arian heresy and put forward a monastic rule that is still the basis of monasticism in the Eastern Church. Feast day, June 14.

Ba·sing·er |'bā,siNGgər|, Kim (1953–) U.S. actress. Academy Award, 1997.

Bas·ker·ville |'bæskər,vil|, John (1706– 75) British printer and typographer. His experiments in typefounding (1750s) led him to design the Baskerville type styles. He served as printer to Cambridge University (1758–68).

Bas·kin |'bæskən|, Burton (1913–67) U.S. businessman. He formed the Baskin-Robbins ice cream business in 1947 with brother-in-law Irvine Robbins (1917–).

Bas·qui·at, Jean-Michel (1960–1988) U.S. painter, sculptor, and draughtsman. He was a graffiti artist in New York City who eventually had exhibitions of his artwork.

Bate·man |'bātmən|, H. M. (Henry Mayo) (1887–1970) Australian-born British cartoonist.

Bates |bāts|, Daisy. U.S. civil rights activist. She was one of the students who integrated Central High School in Little Rock, Arkansas (1957); she reounted her experiences in *The Long Shadow of Little Rock*. She served as president of the Arkansas chapter of the NAACP. Spingarn Medal, 1958.

Bates |bāts|, H. E (1905–74) English novelist and short-story writer; full name *Herbert Ernest Bates*.

Bates |bāts|, Kathy (1948–) U.S. actress. Notable movies: *Misery* (1990, Academy Award), *Fried Green Tomatoes* (1991), and *Titanic* (1997).

Bate·son |'bātsən|, William (1861– 1926) English geneticist. He coined the term *genetics* in its current sense and publicized the work of Mendel.

Ba·tis·ta |bə'tēstə|, Fulgencio (1901– 73) Cuban soldier and statesman, president (1940–44 and 1952–59); full name *Fulgencio Batista y Zaldívar*. Despite support from the U.S. his second government was overthrown by Fidel Castro.

Bat·ten |'bætn|, Jean (1909–82) New Zealand aviator. She was the first woman to fly from England to Australia and back (1934–5), and in 1936 she made the first direct solo flight from England to New Zealand.

Bau·de·laire |ˌbōdə'ler|, Charles-Pierre (1821–67) French poet and critic. He is largely known for *Les Fleurs du mal* (1857), a series of 101 lyrics that explore his isolation and melancholy and the attraction of evil and the macabre.

Bau·dril·lard, Jean (1929–) French sociologist and cultural critic, associated with postmodernism.

Baugh |baw|, Sammy (1914–) U.S.football player. Full name *Samuel A. Baugh*; known as **Slingin' Sammy**. His trademark pinpoint passing revolutionized professional football by making the forward pass a routine play from scrimmage. He became the only player to lead the NFL in passing, punting, and interceptions in the same season (1943).

Baum |bawm|, L. Frank (1856–1919) U.S. journalist and author. Full name *Lyman Frank Baum*. Notable children's books: *Father Goose: His Book* (1899) and *The Wonderful Wizard of Oz* (1900). He also wrote under numerous pseudonyms, including Edith Van Dyne, Laura Bancroft, and Captain Hugh Fitzgerald.

Bausch |bowSH|, John Jacob (1830– 1926) U.S. businessman. He was a co-founder of the Bausch & Lomb Optical Co. (1853).

Bax |bæks|, Sir Arnold (Edward Trevor)

(1883–1953) English composer, noted for tone poems such as *Tintagel* (1917).

Bax·ter |'bækstər|, Anne (1923–85) U.S. actress. She won an Academy Award in 1946 for *The Razor's Edge*.

Bax·ter |'bækstər|, James Keir (1926–72) New Zealand poet, dramatist, and critic.

Ba·yard |bi'är; 'bāərd|, Pierre du Terrail, Chevalier de (*c.* 1473–1524) French soldier. He became known as the knight "sans peur et sans reproche" (fearless and above reproach).

Bay·lor |'bālər|, Elgin Gay (1934–) U.S. basketball player. Elected to the Basketball of Fame (1976).

Bea·dle |'bēdl|, Erastus Flavel (1821–94) U.S. publisher. He introduced the Dime Novel series (631 titles), Dime Library (1103 titles), and Half Dime Library (1168 titles).

Beale |bēl|, Dorothea (1831–1906) English educationist. She was principal of Cheltenham Ladies' College 1858–1906 and a campaigner for women's suffrage and higher education.

Bea·mon |'bēmən|, Bob (1946–) U.S. long jumper; full name *Robert Beamon*. At the 1968 Olympic Games he set a world record that stood until 1991.

Bean |bēn|, Leon Lenwood (1872–1967) U.S. outdoorsman and entrepreneur. He created the Maine Hunting Shoe and started the L.L. Bean Co.

Bean |bēn|, Roy (1825?–1903) U.S. frontiersman. Known as **Judge**. In 1882 he named himself justice of the peace in the Texas camp "Vinegaroon," which he renamed Langtry after his idol Lillie Langtry. He held court in his saloon, the Jersey Lily.

Beard |bird|, Charles Austin (1874–1948) U.S. historian and educator. He cowrote *The Development of Modern Europe* (1907), a pioneer text of economic, political and cultural history.

Beard |bird|, Daniel Carter (1850–1941) U.S. illustrator, author, and outsdoorsman. He founded the Sons of Daniel Boone (1905), a forerunner of the Boy Scouts of America, and authored the *American Boy's Handy Book* (1882).

Beard |bird|, James (1903–85) U.S. gastronome and author. He wrote many cookbooks, including *James Beard's American Cookery* (1980).

Beards·ley |'birdzlē|, Aubrey (Vincent) (1872–98) English artist and illustrator, associated with art nouveau and the Aesthetic movement. He is known for original and controversial illustrations, such as those for Oscar Wilde's *Salome* (1894).

Beas·ley |'bēzlē|, Delilah Leontium (1871–1934) U.S. journalist and historian. She wrote *The Negro Trail Blazers of California* (1919), which documented the role of blacks in the American westward expansion.

Bea·ton |'bētn|, Sir Cecil (Walter Hardy) (1904–80) English photographer, famous for his fashion features and portraits of celebrities, particularly the British royal family. He later diversified into costume and set design, winning two Oscars for the movie *My Fair Lady* (1964).

Be·a·trix |'bēətrics| (1938–) queen of the Netherlands (1980–).

Beat·tie |'bē‚tē|, Ann (1947–) U.S. author. Notable works of fiction: *Another You* (1995) and *Park City: New and Selected Stories* (1998).

Beat·ty |'bētē|, David, 1st Earl Beatty of the North Sea and of Brooksby (1871–1936) British admiral during World War I.

Beat·ty |'bātē|, Warren (1937–) U.S. movie actor, director, and screenwriter; born *Henry Warren Beaty*.

Beau·mar·chais |bō‚mär'sHä|, Pierre-Augustin Caron de (1732–99) French dramatist. He is chiefly remembered for his comedies *The Barber of Seville* (1775) and *The Marriage of Figaro* (1784), which inspired operas by Rossini and Mozart.

Beau·mont |'bō‚mänt|, Francis (1584–1616) English dramatist. He collaborated with John Fletcher on *Philaster* (1609), *The Maid's Tragedy* (1610–11), and many other plays.

Beau Nash |'bō 'næsH| see NASH, RICHARD.

Beau·re·gard |'bōrə‚gärd|, Pierre Gustave Toutant (1818–93) U.S. army officer. He served as superintendent of the U.S. Military Academy at West Point; on the eve of the Civil War, he resigned to join the Confederate army as a brigadier general.

Beck |bek|, C. C. (1910–89) U.S. cartoonist and artist. Full name *Charles Clarence Beck*. He was co-creator of the original "Captain Marvel."

Beck |bek|, Jeff (1944–) British musician. He played lead guitar in rock, blues rock, psychedelia and heavy metal bands.

Beck·en·bau·er |'bekən,bowər|, Franz (1945–) German professional soccer player and team manager.

Beck·er |'bekər|, Boris (1967–) German professional tennis player.

Beck·et |'bekət|, St. Thomas à (*c.* 1118–70) English prelate and statesman, Archbishop of Canterbury (1162–70). He came into open opposition with King Henry II, who uttered words in anger which led four knights to assassinate Becket in his cathedral. Becket's tomb became a major center of pilgrimage until its destruction under Henry VIII (1538). Feast Day, December 29.

Beck·ett |'bekət|, Samuel (Barclay) (1906–89)) Irish dramatist, novelist, and poet. He is best known for his plays, especially *Waiting for Godot* (1952), a seminal work in the Theater of the Absurd. Nobel Prize for Literature (1969).

Beck·ford |'bekfərd|, William (1760–1844) English writer and collector. As an author he is remembered for the oriental romance *Vathek* (1786, originally written in French).

Beck·man |'bekmən|, Arnold Orville (1900–) U.S. electrical engineer and inventor. He invented a quartz spectrophotometer, which made automatic chemical analysis possible.

Beck·mann |'bekmən|, Ernst Otto (1853–1923) German chemist. He devised a method of determining a compound's molecular weight by measuring the rise in boiling point of a solvent containing the compound.

Beck·mann |'bekmən|, Max (1884–1950) German painter and graphic artist. Beckmann's paintings reflect his first-hand experience of human evil during World War I.

Beck·wourth |'bek,wərTH|, James P. (1798–1867) U.S. western pioneer and fur trader. Born into slavery, but raised free in Missouri, he traveled west on fur-trading expeditions (1823–26) and lived among the Crow Indians (1826–37). The pass he discovered (1850) in the Sierra Nevada Mountains opened a route to California's Sacramento Valley. His *Life and Adventures of James P. Beckwourth* (1856) documents the life of the mountain men of the American West.

Bec·que·rel |bek'rel|, Antonie-Henri (1852–1908) French physicist. With Marie and Pierre Curie he discovered the natural radioactivity in uranium salts. Nobel Prize for Physics (1903, shared with the Curies).

Bede |bēd|, St. (*c.* 673–735) English monk, theologian, and historian; known as **the Venerable Bede**. Bede wrote *The Ecclesiastical History of the English People* (written in Latin, completed in 731), a primary source for early English history. Feast day, May 27.

Bee·cham |'bēCHəm|, Sir Thomas (1879–1961) English conductor and impresario, founder of the London Philharmonic (1932) and the Royal Philharmonic (1947). He did much to stimulate interest in new or neglected composers such as Sibelius, Delius, and Richard Strauss.

Bee·cher |'bēCHər|, Henry Ward (1813–87) U.S. Congregationalist clergyman, orator, and writer. He became famous as an orator attacking political corruption and slavery.

Beene |bēn|, Geoffrey (1927–) U.S. fashion designer. He won eight Coty Awards.

Beer·bohm |'bir,bōm|, Max (1872–1956) English caricaturist, essayist, and critic; full name *Sir Henry Maximilian Beerbohm*. A central figure of the Aesthetic Movement, he is remembered chiefly for his novel, *Zuleika Dobson* (1911).

Beers |bērz|, Clifford Whittingham (1876–1943) U.S. mental health reformer. After careful notations of his own mental breakdown and recovery, he founded the Connecticut Society for Mental Hygiene (1908) and the National Commission for Mental Hygiene (1909).

Bee·tho·ven |'bā,tōvən|, Ludwig van

(1770–1827) German composer. Despite increasing deafness Beethoven was responsible for a prodigious output; nine symphonies, thirty-two piano sonatas, sixteen string quartets, the opera *Fidelio* (1814), and the Mass in D (the *Missa Solemnis*, 1823). He is often seen as bridging the classical and romantic movements.

Bee·ton |'bētn|, Mrs. Isabella Mary (1836–65) English author on cookery, famous for her best-selling *Book of Cookery and Household Management* (1861).

Be·gin |bə'gin|, Menachem (1913–92) Israeli statesman and prime minister (1977–84). His hard line on Arab–Israeli relations softened in a series of meetings with President Sadat of Egypt, which led to a peace treaty between the countries. Nobel Peace Prize (1978, shared with Sadat).

Be·han |'bēən|, Brendan (Francis) (1923–64) Irish dramatist and poet who supported Irish nationalism and was convicted for terrorism. Notable works: *Borstal Boy* (novel, 1958) and *The Quare Fellow* (play, 1956).

Behn |bān|, Aphra (1640–89) English novelist and dramatist, regarded as the first professional woman writer in England. Notable works: *The Rover* (comic play, 1678) and *Oroonoko, or the History of the Royal Slave* (novel, 1688).

Beh·rens |'bārəns|, Peter (1868–1940) German architect and designer. He trained Walter Gropius and Le Corbusier.

Beh·ring |'beriNG|, Emil Adolf von (1854–1917) German bacteriologist and one of the founders of immunology. Nobel Prize for Physiology or Medicine (1901).

Bei·der·becke |'bīdər,bek|, Bix (1903–31) U.S. jazz musician and composer; born *Leon Bismarck Beiderbecke*. A self-taught cornettist and pianist, he was one of a handful of white musicians who profoundly influenced the development of jazz.

Bé·jart |bā'zHär|, Maurice (1927–) French ballet choreographer; born *Maurice Jean Berger*.

Bel·i·veau, Jean (1931–) Canadian hockey player. Known as **Le Gros Bill**.

Bell |bel|, Alexander Graham (1847–1922) Scottish-born U.S. scientist, the inventor of the telephone; he also made improvements to the telegraph and the phonograph.

Bell |bel|, Gertrude (Margaret Lowthian) (1868–1926) English archaeologist, traveler, and supporter of Arab independence.

Bell |bel|, Jocelyn (1943–) British radio astronomer. Full name *Susan Jocelyn Bell Burnell*. As a research student at Cambridge, working with Professor Antony Hewish, she discovered pulsars (1967).

Bell |bel|, Lawrence Dale (1894–1956) U.S. aircraft designer. The president of Bell Aircraft (1935–56), he designed and produced the first rocket-propelled airplane. Named the X-1, it was the first aircraft to break the sound barrier (1947).

Bell |bel|, Vanessa (1879–1961) English painter and designer; born *Vanessa Stephen*. Together with her sister Virginia Woolf she was a prominent member of the Bloomsbury Group.

Bel·la·my |'beləmē|, Edward (1850–1898) U.S. journalist and novelist. His utopian romance *Looking Backward: 2000–1887* (1888) led to the founding of the Nationalist party, which advocated socialist economic principles.

Bel·li·ni |bə'lēnē| Family of Italian painters in Venice: **Jacopo** (*c.*1400–70), **Gentile** (*c.*1429–1507), and **Gio·vanni** (*c.*1430–1516).

Bel·li·ni |bə'lēnē|, Vincenzo (1801–35) Italian opera composer. Notable operas: *La Sonnambula* (1831), *Norma* (1831), and *I Puritani* (1835).

Bel·loc |'belawk|, (Joseph) Hilaire (Pierre René) (1870–1953) French-born British writer, historian, and poet remembered chiefly for *Cautionary Tales* (1907).

Bel·low |'belō|, Saul (1915–) Canadian-born U.S. novelist, of Russian-Jewish descent. Notable works: *The Adventures of Augie March* (1953) and *Herzog* (1964). Nobel Prize for Literature (1976).

Bel·lows |'bel,ōz|, George Wesley (1882–1925) U.S. artist and lithographer. Known for his sporting scenes, portraits, and landscapes, he was also noted for a compelling series of antiwar paintings during World War I.

Bel·lus·chi, Pietro (1899–1994) U.S. architect, born in Italy. Noted for his use of "curtain wall" construction, he designed more than 1,000 buildings, including the Equitable Building (1945–48) in Portland, Oregon.

Bel·shaz·zar |bel'sнæ,zər| (died c. 539 BC) viceroy and son of the last king of Babylon. The Bible (Daniel 5) tells how his death in the sack of the city was foretold by a mysterious hand that wrote on the palace wall at a banquet.

Be·lu·shi |bə'lσσ,sнε|, John (1949–82) U.S. comedian and actor. He is best known for his comic characterizations on television's "Saturday Night Live" (1975–79) and as one of the title characters in the movie *The Blues Brothers* (1980).

Be·mel·mans |'bēməlmənz|, Ludwig (1898–1962) U.S. restaurant proprietor and author, born in the Austrian Tyrol. He wrote the *Madeleine* series of books for children, as well as nonfiction travel literature for adults.

Ben Bel·la |'ben 'belə|, (Mohammed) Ahmed (1918–) Algerian statesman, prime minister (1962–63) and president (1963–65). The first president of an independent Algeria, he was overthrown in a military coup.

Bench |benCH|, Johnny Lee (1947–) U.S. baseball player. Elected to the Baseball Hall of Fame (1989).

Bench·ley |'benCH,lē| Family of U.S. authors, including: **Robert Charles** (1889–1945), drama critic, actor, and humorist. He was a theater critic for *Life* magazine (1920–29) and *The New Yorker* (1929–40). His son, **Nathaniel Benchley** (1915–81), was the author of humorous novels, including *Lassiter's Folly* (1971). **Peter Benchley** (1940–), the son of Nathaniel, wrote *Jaws* (1974) and *The Deep* (1976).

Ben·e·dict |'benədikt|, St. (c. 480–c. 547) Italian hermit. He established a monastery at Monte Cassino and his *Regula Monachorum* (known as the Rule of St. Benedict) formed the basis of the Western monasticism. Feast day, July 11 (formerly March 21).

Be·neš |'ben,esн|, Edvard (1884–

1948) Czechoslovak statesman, prime minister (1921–22), and president (1935–38 and 1945–48). During World War II he served in London as head of the Czechoslovakian government in exile. In 1945 he regained the presidency but resigned after the 1948 communist coup.

Be·nét |bə'nā| . Family of U.S. authors, including: **William Rose Benét** (1886–1950), poet, novelist, and editor. Husband of Elinor Wylie, he won the Pulitzer Prize in 1941 for *The Dust Which Is God*. His brother, **Stephen Vincent Benét** (1898–1943), was the author of *John Brown's Body* (1928, Pulitzer Prize) and *Western Star* (1943, Pulitzer Prize).

Be·net·ton |'benə,tän| Italian entrepreneurs: **Luciano Benetton** (1938–) and his sister **Giuliana Benetton** (1938–) founded the multinational Benetton clothing company.

Ben-Gurion |ben'gəryən|, David (1886–1973) Israeli statesman, prime minister (1948–53 and 1955–63), Israel's first prime minister and minister of defense.

Ben·nett |'benət| U.S. journalists, including: Scottish-born **James Gordon Bennett** (1795–1872), who founded *The New York Herald*. His son **James Gordon Bennett** (1841–1918) sponsored Henry Stanley's expedition into Africa (1870–71) to find David Livingstone.

Ben·nett |'benət|, (Enoch) Arnold (1867–1931) English novelist, dramatist, and critic. His fame rests on the novels and stories set in the Potteries ("the Five Towns") of his youth, notably *Anna of the Five Towns* (1902), *The Old Wives' Tale* (1908), and the *Clayhanger* series (1902–08).

Ben·nett |'benət|, Michael (1943–87) U.S. choreographer and stage director. Notable productions *Promises, Promises* (1968) and *A Chorus Line* (1975).

Ben·nett |'benət|, Sir Richard Rodney (1936–) English composer, whose works include movie scores, operas, concertos, and chamber pieces.

Ben·nett |'benət|, Tony (1926–) U.S. musician. Born *Anthony Dominick Benedetto*. He was a popular jazz-inflected singer in the early 1950s. Grammy Award, 1998.

Ben·nett |'benət|, William John (1943–) U.S. statesman. He was chairman of the National Endowment for the Humanities (1981–85) and secretary of the U.S. Department of Education (1985–88).

Ben·nett |'benət|, Willard Harrison (1903–87) U.S. physicist. He invented the radio frequency mass spectrometer, which was first used in space by the Soviets aboard their satellite Sputnik (1957).

Ben·ny |'benē|, Jack (1894–1974) U.S. comedian and actor; born *Benjamin Kubelsky*. Working notably on radio and then television, he was renowned for his timing, delivery, and mordant, self-effacing humour.

Ben·tham |'benТНəm|, Jeremy (1748–1832) English philosopher and jurist, the first major proponent of utilitarianism. Bentham wanted to reform the law, arguing that the proper object of all legislation and conduct was to secure "the greatest happiness of the greatest number." Notable works: *Introduction to the Principles of Morals and Legislation* (1789).

Bent·ley |'bentlē|, Edmund Clerihew (1875–1956) English journalist and novelist, inventor of the comic verse form, the clerihew. Notable works: *Trent's Last Case* (detective novel, 1913) and *Clerihews Complete* (1951).

Ben·ton[1] |'bentən|, Thomas Hart (1782–1858) U.S. politician. He was a Democratic member of the U.S. Senate from Missouri (1820–50) and a supporter of frontier explorations.

Ben·ton[2] |'bentən|, Thomas Hart (1889–1975) U.S. painter. He was a leader of the American naturalist school and a great-nephew of Thomas Hart Benton.

Bent·sen |'bentsen|, Lloyd (1921–) U.S. politician. He was a member of the U.S. Senate from Texas (1971–93), a Democratic vice presidential candidate (1988), and secretary of the treasury (1993–94).

Benz |benz|, Carl Friedrich (1844–1929) German engineer and automotive manufacturer. In 1885 he built the first vehicle to be powered by an internal combustion engine.

Ber·e·nice |,berə'nēs| (3rd century BC) Egyptian queen, wife of Ptolemy III. She dedicated her hair as an offering for the safe return of her husband from an expedition; the hair was stolen and (according to legend) placed in the heavens. She is commemorated in the name of the constellation Coma Berenices (*Berenice's hair*).

Ber·en·son |'berənsən|, Bernard (1865–1959) U.S. art critic, born in Lithuania. He was an authority on Italian Renaissance art.

Berg |bərg|, Alban (Maria Johannes) (1885–1935) Austrian composer, a leading exponent of twelve-note composition. Notable works: the operas *Wozzeck* (1914–21) and *Lulu* (1928–35) and his violin concerto (1935).

Berg |bərg|, Patty (1918–) U.S. golfer. Full name *Patricia Jane Berg*.

Ber·gen |'bərgən|, Candice (1946–) U.S. actress and photojournalist. She won five Emmy Awards for her title role in television's "Murphy Brown" (1988–98). Notable movies: *Carnal Knowledge* (1971) and *Rich and Famous* (1981). She was the wife of director Louis Malle.

Ber·ger |'bərgər|, Hans (1873–1941) German psychiatrist who detected electric currents in the cerebral cortex and developed encephalography.

Ber·ger |'bərgər|, Thomas (1924–) U.S. author. Notable works: *Crazy in Berlin* (1958), *Little Big Man* (1964), and *The Feud* (1983).

Ber·ge·rac |'bərZHə,ræk| see CYRANO DE BERGERAC.

Ber·gi·us |'bər,gēyəs|, Friedrich Karl Rudolf (1884–1949) German industrial chemist. Nobel Prize for Chemistry (1931).

Berg·man |'bərgmən|, (Ernst) Ingmar (1918–) Swedish movie and theater director. He used haunting imagery and symbolism often derived from Jungian dream analysis. Notable movies: *Smiles of a Summer Night* (1955), *The Seventh Seal* (1956), and *Hour of the Wolf* (1968).

Berg·man |'bərgmən|, Ingrid (1915–82) Swedish actress. Notable roles: *Casablanca* (1942), *Anastasia* (1956), and *Murder on the Orient Express* (1974).

Berg·son |'bərgsən|, Henri (Louis) (1859–1941) French philosopher. Dividing the world into life (or consciousness) and matter, he rejected Darwinian evolution and argued that life possesses an inherent creative impulse (*elan vital*) that creates new forms as life seeks to impose itself on matter. Nobel Prize for Literature (1927).

Be·ria |'byer,yä|, Lavrenti (Pavlovich) (1899–1953) Soviet politician and head of the secret police 1938–53. He was involved in the elimination or deportation of Stalin's opponents, but after Stalin's death he was arrested and executed.

Ber·i·gan |'berə,gən|, Bunny (1908–42) U.S. jazz trumpeter and orchestra leader. Full name *Rowland Bernart Berigan*. He played with various bands, including Tommy Dorsey and Benny Goodman, until he started his own (1937).

Be·ring |'beriNG|, Vitus (Jonassen) (1681–1741) Danish navigator and explorer. He led several Russian expeditions aimed at discovering whether Asia and North America were connected by land. He sailed along the coast of Siberia and in 1741 reached Alaska from the east but died on the return journey; the Bering Sea and Bering Strait are named after him.

Ber·io |'berēō|, Luciano (1925–) Italian composer, an experimentalist who has adopted serial, aleatory, and electronic techniques. Notable works: *Circles* (1960), *Sequenza* series (1958–75), and *Un Re in Ascolto* (opera, 1984).

Berke·ley |'bərklē|, Busby (1895–1976) U.S. choreographer and movie director; born *William Berkeley Enos*. He is remembered for spectacular sequences in which dancers formed kaleidoscopic patterns on the screen. Notable movies: the *Gold Diggers* series (1922–37) and *Babes in Arms* (1939).

Berke·ley |'bərklē|, George (1685–1753) Irish philosopher and bishop. He argued that material objects exist solely by being perceived, so there are only minds and mental events. Since God perceives everything all the time, objects have a continuous existence in the mind of God. Notable works: *A Treatise Concerning the Principles of Human Knowledge* (1710).

Berke·ley |'bərklē|, Sir Lennox (Randall Francis) (1903–89) English composer of four operas, four symphonies, music for ballet and movie, and sacred choral music.

Ber·ko·witz |'bərkō,wits|, David (1953–) U.S. murderer. Known as **Son of Sam.**

Berle |bərl|, Milton (1908–) U.S. actor. Born *Milton Berlinger*. He began as a vaudeville entertainer and went on to star in radio, stage, movies, and television.

Ber·lin |bər'lin|, Irving (1888–1989) Russian-born U.S. composer of popular music; born *Israel Baline*. He wrote more than 800 songs many of which are regarded as popular "standards" or classics. Notable works: the songs "God Bless America" (1939) and "White Christmas" (1942) and the score for *Annie get Your Gun* (1946).

Ber·lin |bər'lin|, Sir Isaiah (1909–) Latvian-born British philosopher who concerned himself with the history of ideas. Notable works: *Karl Marx* (1939), *Four Essays on Liberty* (1959), and *Vico and Herder* (1976).

Ber·li·ner |'bərlənər|, Emile (1851–1929) U.S. inventor, born in Germany. He invented the Berliner loose-contact telephone transmitter (1877), devised a method of duplicating flat disk recordings (1888), and developed the first acoustic tiles (1915).

Ber·lioz |'berlē,ōz|, Hector (1803–69) French composer; full name *Louis-Hector Berlioz*. Notable works: *Les Troyens* (opera, 1856–9), *Symphonie fantastique* (1830), and *La Damnation de Faust* (cantata, 1846).

Ber·na·dette |'bərnədet|, St. (1844–79) French peasant girl; born *Marie Bernarde Soubirous*. Her visions of the Virgin Mary in Lourdes in 1858 led to the town's establishment as a center of pilgrimage. Feast day, February 18.

Ber·na·dotte |'bernədät|, Jean Baptiste Jules (1763–1844) French soldier, king of Sweden (as Charles XIV) (1818–44). One of Napoleon's marshals, he was adopted by Charles XIII of Sweden in

1810 and later became king, thus founding Sweden's present royal house.

Ber·na·dotte |'bernədät|, Folke, Count Bernadotte of Wisborg (1895–1948) Swedish statesman. As vice-president of the Swedish Red Cross he arranged the exchange of prisoners of war and in 1945 conveyed a German offer of capitulation to the Allies.

Ber·nard |bər'närd|, Claude (1813–78) French physiologist. Bernard showed the role of the pancreas in digestion, the method of regulation of body temperature, and the function of nerves supplying the internal organs.

Ber·nard |bər'närd|, St (died *c.* 1081) French monk who founded two hospices for travelers in the Alps. The St. Bernard passes, where the hospices were situated, and St. Bernard dogs, once kept by the monks and trained to aid travelers, are named after him. Feast day, May 28.

Ber·nard of Clair·vaux |,bər'närd əv kler'vō|, St. (1090–1153) French theologian and abbot. He was the first abbot of Clairvaux, and his monastery became one of the chief centers of the Cistercian order. Feast day, August 20.

Berners-Lee |'bərnərz 'lē|, Tim. U.S. computer scientist. He developed the World Wide Web (1989) and directs the W3 Consortium at MIT's Laboratory for Computer Science.

Bern·hard |'bərn,härt|, Sandra (1955–) U.S. actress and singer. Her movie and television credits include *The Apocalypse* (1997) and appearances on "Late Night with David Letterman" and "Roseanne."

Bern·hardt |'bərn,härt|, Sarah (1844–1923) French actress; born *Henriette Rosine Bernard*. She was best known for her portrayal of Marguerite in *La Dame aux Camélias* and Cordelia in *King Lear*.

Ber·ni·ni |bər'nēnē|, Gian Lorenzo (1598–1680) Italian baroque sculptor, painter, and architect. His work includes the great canopy over the altar and the colonnade round the piazza at St. Peter's in Rome.

Ber·noul·li |,bər'nōōlē| Family of Swiss mathematicians, including **Jakob Bernoulli** (1655–1705); also known as *Jacques* or *James*. He made discoveries

in calculus and contributed to geometry and the theory of probabilities. His brother, **Johann Bernoulli** (1667–1748), was also known as *Jean* or *John*. He contributed to differential and integral calculus. Johann's son, **Daniel Bernoulli** (1700–82), contributed to hydrodynamics and mathematical physics.

Bern·stein |'bərnstēn|, Carl (1944–) U.S. journalist and author. He was the *Washington Post* reporter who, with Bob Woodward, broke the story of the Watergate burglary and traced the financial payoffs to President Nixon.

Bern·stein |'bərnstīn|, Leonard (1918–90) U.S. composer, conductor, and pianist. He worked as a conductor with the New York Philharmonic Orchestra (1945–48 and 1957–69). As a composer he encompassed a wide range of forms and styles in his music. Notable works: *Candide* (operetta, 1954–6), *West Side Story* (musical, 1957), *Chichester Psalms* (1965), and movie music for *On the Waterfront* (1954).

Ber·ra |'berə|, Yogi (1925–) U.S. baseball player; born *Lawrence Peter Berra*. He was especially famous as a catcher with the New York Yankees, setting the record for the most home runs (313) by a catcher in the American League. He became known for his pithy saying such as (on baseball) "You can't think and hit at the same time".

Ber·ri·gan |'berə,gən| U.S. family that includes two brothers, priests and political activists: **Daniel** (1921–), a Jesuit priest, devoted his time to civil rights, antipoverty, and antiwar causes. He was convicted and sentenced to three years in prison for destroying selective service files in 1968. He later wrote his prison memoirs, *Lights On in the House of the Dead* (1974). His brother, **Philip** (1923–), a Roman Catholic priest, founded the Catholic Peace Fellowship. He, too, was convicted and sent to prison for destroying selective service files in 1967 and 1968. Notable works: *Prison Journals of a Revolutionary Priest* (1970) and *Widen the Prison Gates* (1973).

Ber·ry |'berē|, Chuck (1926–) U.S. rock-and-roll singer, guitarist, and songwriter; born *Charles Edward Berry*. Notable songs: "Johnny B Goode" (1958).

Ber·ry |'berē|, Jim (1932–) U.S. cartoonist and author. Full name *James Berry*. He created the comic "Berry's World."

Ber·ry |'berē|, Wendell (1934–) U.S. author and professor. His poems, novels, and essays reflect his native state of Kentucky.

Ber·ry·man |'berē,mən|, John (1914–1972) U.S. poet and educator. Notable works: *77 Dream Songs* (1964), which won the Pulitzer Prize.

Ber·til·lon |bertē'yōn|, Alphonse (1853–1914) French criminologist. He devised a system of body measurements for the identification of criminals, which was widely used until superseded by fingerprinting at the beginning of the 20th century.

Ber·to·luc·ci |,bərtə'lōōCHē|, Bernardo (1940–) Italian movie director. Notable works: *The Spider's Stratagem* (1970), *Last Tango in Paris* (1972), and *The Last Emperor* (1988).

Ber·ze·li·us |bər'zēlēəs|, Jöns Jakob (1779–1848) Swedish analytical chemist. He determined the atomic weights of many elements and discovered cerium, selenium, and thorium.

Bes·ant |'bezənt|, Annie (1847–1933) English theosophist, writer, and politician, president of the Theosophical Society. She settled in Madras, where she worked for Indian self-government.

Bes·sel |'besəl|, Friedrich Wilhelm (1784–1846) German astronomer and mathematician. He determined the positions of some 75,000 stars, obtained accurate measurements of stellar distances, and following a study of the orbit of Uranus, predicted the existence of an eighth planet.

Bes·se·mer |'besəmər|, Sir Henry (1813–98) English engineer and inventor. By 1860 he had developed the Bessemer process, the first successful method of making steel in quantity at low cost.

Best |best|, Charles Herbert (1899–1978) American-born Canadian physiologist who assisted F. G. Banting in research leading to the discovery of insulin in 1922.

Be·thune |bə'THyōōn|, Henry Norman (1899–1939) Canadian surgeon. He joined the Communist Party in 1935 and served in the Spanish Civil War against the Fascists, organizing the first mobile blood-transfusion service. Bethune then joined the Chinese army in their war against Japan as a surgeon, becoming a hero in the People's Republic; he died while in China.

Be·thune |bə'THyōōn|, Mary McLeod (1875–1955) U.S. educator. She was founder and first president (1935–49) of the National Council of Negro Women.

Bet·je·man |'beCHəmən|, Sir John (1906–84) British poet and author. He received the Queen's Medal for Poetry in 1960, was knighted in 1969, and became Poet Laureate in 1972.

Bet·tel·heim |'betl,hīm|, Bruno (1903–90) U.S. psychologist and author, born in Austria. His experiences in Nazi Germany helped him develop revolutionary theories and therapies for emotionally disturbed children

Bet·ter·ton |'betərtən|, Thomas (1635–1710) English actor. A leading actor of the Restoration period, he also adapted the plays of John Webster, Molière, and Beaumont and Fletcher for his own productions.

Bet·ti |'betē|, Ugo (1892–1953) Italian dramatist, poet, and short-story writer. Notable plays: *Corruption in the Palace of Justice* (1949), *Crime on Goat Island* (1950).

Bett·man |'betmən|, Otto Ludwig (1903–98) U.S. picture archivist and graphic historian, born in Germany. He founded the archive of photographs (1941) and was the author of many books of photographs, including *A Pictorial History of American Sports* (1952) and *A Pictorial History of Medicine* (1956).

Beuys |bois|, Joseph (1921–86) German artist. One of the most influential figures of the avant-garde movement in Europe in the 1970s and 1980s, his work consisted of "assemblages" of various articles of rubbish. In 1979 he co-founded the German Green Party.

Bew·ick |'byōōik|, Thomas (1753–1828) English artist and wood engraver, noted especially for the animal studies in such books as *A History of British Birds* (1797, 1804).

Be·zos, Jeff. U.S. businessman. He founded Amazon.com, the Internet bookstore (1995).

Bhut·to |'boŏtō| Family of Pakistani politicians, including: **Zulfikar Ali Bhutto** (1928–79), president (1971–73) and prime minister (1973–77). He was ousted by a military coup and executed for conspiring to murder a political rival. His daughter, **Benazir Bhutto** (1953–), was prime minister (1988–90 and 1993–96). She was the first woman prime minister of a Muslim country and took Pakistan back into the British Commonwealth.

Bich, Marcel (1914–) French manufacturer and inventor. He invented the Bic disposable ballpoint pen and cigarette lighter.

Bi·den |'bīdən|, Joseph Robinette, Jr. (1942–) U.S. politician. He is a member of the U.S. Senate from Delaware (1972–)

Bierce |birs|, Ambrose (Gwinnett) (1842–*c.* 1914) U.S. writer, best known for his sardonic short stories and *The Devil's Dictionary* (1911). In 1913 he traveled to Mexico and mysteriously disappeared.

Bier·stadt |'bir,stät|, Albert (1830–1902) U.S. painter, born in Germany. He was a member of the Hudson River school of landscape painters.

Bi·ko |'bēkō|, Steve (1946–77) South African radical leader; full name *Stephen Biko*. He was banned from political activity in 1973; after his death in police custody he became a symbol of heroic resistance to apartheid.

Bi·net |bə'nā|, Alfred (1857–1911) French psychologist. He devised a mental age scale that described performance in relation to the average performance of students of the same physical age, and with the psychiatrist **Théodore Simon**, (1873–1961) was responsible for a pioneering system of intelligence tests.

Bing |biNG|, Rudolf (1902–97) U.S. opera conductor and manager, born in Vienna. He was conductor and director of the Metropolitan Opera in New York

(1950–72); in 1955, he hired Marian Anderson, ending the Met's unwritten ban against African Americans.

Bing·ham |'biNGəm|, George Caleb (1811–79) U.S. artist. His paintings of the American frontier include *The Fur Traders Descending the Missouri* (1845) and *The Trappers Return* (1851). Several of his works, notably *The County Election* (1851–52), reflect a political theme.

Bing·ham |'biNGəm|, Hiram (1875–1956) U.S. explorer and politican. A Yale professor (1907–24), he discovered the Inca ruins of Machu Picchu (1911). He served as governor of Connecticut (1924–25) and in the U.S. Senate (1925–33).

Bin·ney |'bi,nē|, Edwin (1866–1934) U.S. entrepreneur. He was a cofounder of Crayola crayons.

Bin·nig |'bi,niKH|, Gerd Karl (1947–) German physicist and inventor. With Heinrich Rohrer, he developed the scanning tunneling microscope. Nobel Prize in Physics (1986).

Bi·on·di |bē'awndē|, Matt (1965–) U.S. swimmer. Full name *Matthew Biondi*. At the 1986 world championships, he won a record seven medals (three gold). He won eight Olympic gold medals (1984, 1988, 1992).

Bird |bərd|, Larry (1956–) U.S. basketball player and coach. Elected to the Basketball Hall of Fame (1998).

Birds·eye |'bərdz,ī|, Clarence (1886–1956) U.S. businessman and inventor. A former fur trader, he had observed food preservation techniques practiced by local people in Labrador. He developed a process of rapid freezing of foods in small packages suitable for retail, creating a revolution in eating habits.

Birk·hoff |'bər,kawf|, George David (1884–1944) U.S. mathematician. He proved Poincaré's last theorem, now known as the Poincaré-Birkhoff fixed-point theorem (1912).

Bish·op |'bishəp|, Elizabeth (1911–79) U.S. poet awarded the Pulitzer Prize for her first two collections, *North and South* (1946) and *A Cold Spring* (1955).

Bis·marck |'bizmärk|, Otto Eduard Leopold von, Prince of Bismarck, Duke of Lauenburg (1815–98) Prussian minister and German statesman, chancellor of the German Empire (1871–90); known as the **Iron Chancellor**. He was the driving force behind the unification of Germany, orchestrating wars with Denmark (1864), Austria (1866), and France (1870–71) in order to achieve this end.

Bi·zet |bi'zā|, Georges (1838–75) French composer; born *Alexandre César Léopold Bizet*. He is best known for the opera *Carmen* (1875).

Bjerk·nes |'byərk,näs|, Vilhelm Friman Koren (1862–1951) Norwegian geophysicist and meteorologist. He developed a theory of physical hydrodynamics for atmospheric and oceanic circulation, and mathematical models for weather prediction.

Björ·ling |'byœrling|, Jussi (1911–60) Swedish operatic tenor. He made his debut with the Metropolitan Opera in 1938 as Rudolfo in *La Bohème*, and he excelled in roles from Verdi and Puccini.

Black |blæk|, Harold Stephen (1898–1983) U.S. electrical engineer and inventor. In the late 1920s, he invented and developed a negative feedback amplifier, which countered the problem of distortion in telephone communications. He later applied this technology to systems useful to the blind and deaf.

Black |blæk|, Hugo Lafayette (1886–1971) U.S. Supreme Court Justice (1937–71). He was also a U.S. senator from Alabama (1927–37).

Black |blæk|, Joseph (1728–99) Scottish chemist. He was important in developing accurate techniques for following chemical reactions by weighing reactants and products, and formulated the concepts of latent heat and thermal capacity.

Black·beard |'blækbērd| (died 1718) pirate in the West Indies and Virginia–North Carolina coast. Born *Edward Teach* (also *Thatch* or *Thack*). He was originally a privateer during the War of the Spanish Succession (1701–14).

Black·ett |'blækət|, Patrick Maynard Stuart (Baron) (1897–1974) English physicist. Blackett was a member of the Maud Committee that dealt with the development of the atom bomb. He also modified the cloud chamber for the study of cosmic rays. Nobel Prize for Physics (1948).

Black Hawk |'blæk ,hawk| (1767–1838) chief of the Sauk and Fox Indians. He was a leader in the Black Hawk War (1832); in 1833 he published his *Autobiography*.

Black·more |'blæk,mŏŏr|, R. D. (Richard Doddridge) (1825–1900) English novelist and poet. He is known for his romantic novel *Lorna Doone* (1869).

Black·mun |'blækmən|, Harry Andrew (1908–1999) U.S. Supreme Court Justice (1970–94).

Black·mur |'blækmər|, R. P. (1904–65) U.S. poet and literary critic. Full name *Richard Palmer Blackmur*. With no formal education after high school, he served as a resident fellow (1940–48) and professor (1948–65) at Princeton. He was a prominent advocate of the New Criticism.

Black Prince |'blæk 'prins| (1330–76) eldest son of Edward III of England; name given to Edward, Prince of Wales and Duke of Cornwall. He was responsible for the English victory at Poitiers in 1356. He predeceased his father, but his son became king as King Richard II; the name Black Prince apparently derives from the black armor he wore when fighting.

Black·stone |'blæk,stōn|, Sir William (1723–80) English jurist. His major work was the *Commentaries on the Laws of England* (1765–9), an exposition of English law.

Blair |bler| U.S. political family, including: **Francis Preston Blair** (1791–1876), a journalist and politician. He was a member of President Andrew Jackson's "kitchen cabinet" and helped organize the Republican Party (1856), later becoming one of Abraham Lincoln's advisers. His son **Montgomery Blair** (1813–83), a jurist and politician, represented Dred Scott before the Supreme Court (1857). **Francis Preston Blair, Jr.**, (1821–75), the son of Francis Preston Blair and brother of Montgomery Blair, was a politician who helped establish the Free Soil Party (1848) and was an unsuccessful

Democratic vice presidential candidate (1868).

Blair |bler|, Bonnie (1964–) U.S. speed skater. She is the only U.S. woman to win five Olympic gold medals (500m, 1988; 500m and 1000m, 1992 and 1994).

Blair |bler|, Henry. U.S. inventor. He obtained patents for a corn planter (1834) and a cotton planter (1836).

Blair |bler|, John (1732–1800) U.S. Supreme Court Justice (1789–96). He was a member of the Consitutional Convention (1787).

Blair |bler|, Tony (1953–) British Labour statesman, prime minister from 1997; full name *Anthony Charles Lynton Blair*. His landslide victory in the election of 1997 gave his party its biggest-ever majority and made him the youngest prime minister since Lord Liverpool in 1812.

Blake |blak|, Eubie (1883–1983) U.S. jazz pianist and composer. One of the foremost ragtime pianists, he wrote over 300 songs, many in collaboration with Noble Sissle.

Blake |blak|, Peter (1932–) English painter, prominent in the pop art movement in the late 1950s and early 1960s. He is best known for the cover design for the Beatles album *Sergeant Pepper's Lonely Hearts Club Band* (1967).

Blake |blak|, William (1757–1827) English artist and poet. Blake's poems mark the beginning of romanticism and a rejection of the Age of Enlightenment. His watercolors and engravings, like his writings, were only fully appreciated after his death. Notable collections of poems: *Songs of Innocence* (1789) and *Songs of Experience* (1794).

Bla·key |'blakē|, Art (1919–90) U.S. jazz drummer, a pioneer of the bebop movement, known for his group the Jazz Messengers; full name *Arthur Blakey*.

Blan·chard |'blænCHərd|, Jean-Pierre-François (1753–1809) French balloonist. He made the first crossing of the English Channel by air, flying by balloon, on January 7, 1785.

Blan·da |'blændə|, George Frederick (1927–) U.S. football player. He is the all-time leading scorer (2,002 points) in professional football.

Blan·ding |'blæn,diNG|, Sarah G. (1899–1985) U.S. educator. She was president of Vassar College (1946–64).

Blan·ton |'blæntən|, Jimmy (1918–42) U.S. jazz bassist. He was hired by Duke Ellington in 1939.

Blass |'blæs|, Bill (1922–) U.S. fashion designer. Full name *William Ralph Blass*.

Blatch·ford |'blæCHfərd|, Samuel (1820–1893) U.S. Supreme Court Justice (1882–93).

Bla·vat·sky |blə'vætskē|, Helena (Petrovna) (1831–91) Russian spiritualist, born in Ukraine; born *Helena Petrovna Hahn*; known as **Madame Blavatsky**. In 1875 she co-founded the Theosophical Society in New York together with the American Henry Steel Olcott.

Blé·riot |'blāryō; 'blerē,ō|, Louis (1872–1936) French aviation pioneer. On July 25, 1909 he became the first to fly the English Channel (Calais to Dover), in a monoplane of his own design.

Blessed Virgin Mary Also **Blessed Virgin**. (abbrev.: **BVM**) a title given to Mary, the mother of Jesus. (see MARY 1).

Bligh |blī|, William (1754–1817) British naval officer, captain of HMS *Bounty*. In 1789 part of his crew, led by the first mate Fletcher Christian, mutinied and set Bligh adrift in an open boat, arriving safely at Timor, nearly 4,000 miles (6,400 km) away, a few weeks later.

Bliss |blis|, Sir Arthur (Edward Drummond) (1891–1975) English composer. He moved from the influence of Stravinsky, in works such as *A Colour Symphony* (1922), to a rich style closer to Elgar, as in his choral symphony *Morning Heroes* (1930).

Blixen, Karen (Christence), Baroness Blixen-Finecke (1885–1962) Danish novelist and short-story writer; born *Karen Dinesen*; also known by the pseudonym of **Isak Dinesen**. She is best known for *Seven Gothic Tales* (1934) and her autobiography *Out of Africa* (1937).

Bloch |bläk|, Ernest (1880–1959) Swiss-born U.S. composer, of Jewish descent. His work reflects the influence of the late 19th-century romanticism of Liszt and Richard Strauss and Jewish musical forms. Notable works: the *Israel Symphony* (1912–16) and *Solomon* (1916).

Bloch |bläk|, Felix (1905–83) U.S. physicist, born in Switzerland. With Edward Mills Purcell, he won the 1952 Nobel Prize for Physics for the discovery of nuclear magnetic resonance.

Bloch |bläk|, Henry Wollman (1922–) U.S. businessman. He founded the tax-preparation company H & R Block (1955).

Block |bläk|, Herbert L. (1909–) U.S. editorial cartoonist, author, and artist. Known as **Herblock**. He is a two-time winner of the Pulitzer Prize for cartooning (1942, 1954) and the recipient of several journalism awards.

Blon·din |'bländēn|, Charles (1824–97) French acrobat; born *Jean-François Gravelet*. He is famous for on several occasions walking across a tightrope suspended over Niagara Falls.

Bloody Mary the nickname of Mary I of England (see MARY 2).

Bloom |bloom|, Allan David (1936–92) U.S. political scientist and author. In his best-selling *The Closing of the American Mind: How Higher Education Has Failed Democracy and Impoverished the Souls of Today's Students* (1987), he denounced the decline of liberal education in the U.S.

Bloom |bloom|, Harold (1930–) U.S. literary critic, educator, and author. Notable works: *The Anxiety of Influence* (1973) and *Omens of Millennium* (1996).

Bloom·berg |'bloombərg|, Michael Rubens (1942–) U.S. businessman. He is founder, chairman, and CEO of the business news service, Bloomberg Financial Markets (begun 1981).

Bloom·er |'bloomər|, Amelia Jenks (1818–94) U.S. suffragette and social reformer. She founded and edited the feminist paper *Lily* (1849–55), and she wore full pants that came to be known as "bloomers."

Bloom·field |'bloom,fēld|, Leonard (1887–1949) U.S. linguist, one of the founders of American structural linguistics. His primary aim was to establish linguistics as an autonomous and

scientific discipline. Notable works: *Language* (1933).

Blü·cher |'blookər|, Gebhard Leberecht von, Prince of Wahlstatt (1742–1819) Prussian field marshal. Nickname **Marschall Vorwäts**. He served in the war against Napoléon (1813).

Blum |bloom|, Léon (1872–1950) French statesman, prime minister (1936–37, 1938, 1946–47). As France's first socialist and Jewish prime minister, Blum introduced significant labor reforms.

Blum·berg |'bloombərg; 'bləmbərg|, Baruch Samuel (1925–) U.S. research physician. He discovered a causative agent for hepatitis B (1963) and developed a hepatitis B vaccine (1982).

Blume |bloom|, Judy Sussman (1938–) U.S. author. She wrote best-selling children's fiction, including *Are You There, God? It's Me, Margaret* (1970), and adult fiction, including *Summer Sisters* (1998).

Blu·men·bach |'bloomən,bäk|, Johann Friedrich (1752–1840) German physiologist and anatomist. He is regarded as the founder of physical anthropology, though his approach has since been much modified. He classified modern humans into five broad categories (Caucasian, Mongoloid, Malayan, Ethiopian, and American) based mainly on cranial measurements.

Blun·den |'bləndən|, Edmund (Charles) (1896–1974) English poet and critic. His poetry reveals his love of the English countryside, while his prose work *Undertones of War* (1928) deals with his experiences in the First World War.

Blunt |blənt|, Anthony (Frederick) (1907–83) British art historian, Foreign Office official, and Soviet spy. He confessed in 1965 that he had been a Soviet agent since the 1930s and had facilitated the escape of Guy Burgess and Donald Maclean. When these facts were made public in 1979 he was stripped of his knighthood.

Bly |blī|, Robert Elwood (1926–) U.S. poet and author. Notable works: *The Light Around the Body* (1967, National Book Award) and *Iron John: A Book about Men* (1990).

Bly·ton |'blītn|, Enid (1897–1968) English writer of children's fiction. Her best-known creation for young children is the character Noddy, who first appeared in 1949; her books for older children include the series of *Famous Five* and *Secret Seven* adventure stories.

Bo·as |'bōæz|, Franz (1858–1942) German-born U.S. anthropologist. A pioneer of modern anthropology, he developed the linguistic and cultural components of ethnology. He did much to overturn the theory that Nordic peoples constitute an essentially superior race; his writings were burnt by the Nazis.

Boc·cac·cio |bō'käCHēō|, Giovanni (1313–75) Italian writer, poet, and humanist. He is most famous for the *Decameron* (1348–58), a collection of a hundred tales told by ten young people who have moved to the country to escape the Black Death.

Boc·che·ri·ni |,bōkə'rēnē|, Luigi (1743–1805) Italian composer and cellist, known chiefly for his cello concertos and sonatas.

Boch·co |'bäCH,kō|, Steven (1943–) U.S. television producer and screenwriter. He cocreated the Emmy Award-winning television series "Hill Street Blues" and was executive producer of the series "LA Law" and "NYPD Blue."

Bod·ley |'bädlē|, Sir Thomas (1545–1613) English scholar and diplomat. He refounded and greatly enlarged the Oxford University library, which was renamed the Bodleian in 1604.

Bo·do·ni |bō'dōnē|, Giambattista (1740–1813) Italian printer. He designed a typeface that is characterized by extreme contrast between uprights and diagonals.

Boe·ing |'bōiNG|, William Edward (1881–1956) U.S. industrialist. He founded the Boeing Aircraft Co.

Boe·sky |'bō,skē|, F. Ivan (1936–) U.S. stockbroker. Accused of insider trading on Wall Street, he pleaded guilty to an unspecified criminal count and paid a $100 million fine.

Bo·e·thi·us |bō'ēTHēəs|, Anicius Manlius Severinus (*c.* 480–524) Roman statesman and philosopher, best known for *The Consolation of Philosophy*, which he wrote while in prison on a charge of treason.

Bo·gan |,bō'gæn|, Louise (1897–1970) U.S. poet and critic. She was poetry editor of the *New Yorker* magazine for many years. Notable works: *Body of This Death* (1923), *The Blue Estuaries: Poems 1923–1968* (1968), and the literary history *Achievement in American Poetry, 1900–1950* (1951).

Bo·garde |'bō,gärd|, Sir Dirk (1921–) British actor and writer, of Dutch descent. Born *Derek Niven van den Bogaerde*. Notable movies: *The Servant* (1963) and *Death in Venice* (1971).

Bo·gart |'bōgärt|, Humphrey (DeForest) (1899–1957) U.S. actor. His many movies include *Casablanca* (1942), *The Big Sleep* (1946, in which he played opposite his fourth wife, Lauren Bacall), and *The African Queen* (1951, for which he won an Oscar).

Bohr |bôr|, Niels Henrik David (1885–1962) Danish physicist and pioneer in quantum physics. Bohr's theory of the structure of the atom incorporated quantum theory for the first time, and is the basis for present-day quantum-mechanical models. Bohr helped to develop the atom bomb in Britain and then in the US. Nobel Prize for Physics (1922).

Boi·leau |,bwä'lō|, Nicolas (1636–1711) French critic and poet; full name *Nicholas Boileau-Despréaux*. Boileau is considered particularly important as one of the founders of French literary criticism. His didactic poem *Art poétique* (1674) defined principles of composition and criticism.

Bo·kas·sa |bō'käsə|, Jean Bédel (1921–96) African statesman and military leader, president (1972–76) of the Central African Republic, and self-styled emperor (1976–79).

Bol·den |'bōl,dən|, Buddy (1877–1931) U.S. jazz musician. Born *Charles Joseph Bolden*. He was a cornetist and leader of several New Orleans bands in the 1890s.

Bol·dre·wood |'bōldər,wŏŏd|, Rolf (1826–1915) Australian novelist; pseudonym of *Thomas Alexander Browne*. His most enduring work was *Robbery Under Arms* (first published as a serial in 1882–

83), a narration of the life and crimes of a bushranger under sentence of death.

Bol·eyn |bŏŏ'lin|, Anne (1507?–36) second wife of Henry VIII and mother of Elizabeth I. Henry divorced Catherine of Aragon in order to marry Anne (1533), but she fell from favor when she failed to provide him with a male heir, and she was eventually executed because of alleged infidelities.

Bol·ger |'bŏljər|, James (Brendan) (1935–) New Zealand National Party statesman and prime minister (1990– 97).

Bo·ling·broke |'bawliNG,brŏŏk; 'bōliNG ,brŏk|, Henry the surname of Henry IV of England (see HENRY1).

Bo·lí·var |'bələ,vär|, Simón (1783– 1830) Venezuelan patriot and statesman; known as **the Liberator**. He succeeded in driving the Spanish from Venezuela, Colombia, Peru, and Ecuador although his dream of South American federation was never realized. Upper Peru was named Bolivia in his honor.

Böll |bäl|, Heinrich (Theodor) (1917– 85) German novelist and short-story writer. His later work, such as *The Lost Honour of Katharina Blum* (1974), is frequently critical of post-war German society. Nobel Prize for Literature (1972).

Bolt |bōlt|, Robert (Oxton) (1924–95) English writer best known for the play *A Man for All Seasons* (1960) and the screenplays for *Lawrence of Arabia* (1962) and *Dr Zhivago* (1965).

Boltz·mann |'bawltsmən|, Ludwig Eduard (1844–1906) Austrian physicist, who made contributions to the kinetic theory of gases, statistical mechanics, and thermodynamics.

Bom·beck |'bäm,bek|, Erma Louise (1927–96) U.S. journalist and author. Her syndicated column appeared in newspapers throughout the U.S. from 1965 until her death. Notable works: *Motherhood: The Second Oldest Profession* (1983); *Family: The Ties That Bind...and Gag!* (1987).

Bo·na·parte |'bōnə,pärt|, Napoleon a Corsican family including the three French rulers named Napoleon.

Bon·a·ven·tu·re |,bänəvən'cHŏŏr|, St. (c. 1217–74) Franciscan theologian;

born *Giovanni di Fidanza;* known as **the Seraphic Doctor**. He wrote the official biography of St. Francis and had a lasting influence as a spiritual writer. Feast day, July 15 (formerly 14).

Bond |bänd|, Edward (1934–) English dramatist. Many of his plays are marked by scenes of violence and cruelty. Notable works: *Saved* (1965) and *Lear* (1971).

Bon·hoef·fer |'bän,hawfər|, Dietrich (1906–45) German Lutheran theologian and pastor. He was an active opponent of Nazism and was involved in the German resistance movement. Arrested in 1943, he was sent to Buchenwald concentration camp and later executed.

Bon·i·face |'bänəfəs|, St. (c. 675–754) Anglo-Saxon missionary; born *Wynfrith;* known as **the Apostle of Germany**. He was sent to Frisia and Germany to spread the Christian faith and was appointed Primate of Germany in 732; he was martyred in Frisia. Feast day, June 5.

Bon·nard |baw'när|, Pierre (1867– 1947) French painter and graphic artist, member of the Nabi Group.

Bon·ney |'bänē|, William H. (1859–81) U.S. outlaw; born *Henry McCarty;* known as **Billy the Kid**. A notorious robber and murderer, he was captured by Sheriff Pat Garrett in 1880, and was shot by Garrett after he escaped.

Bonnie Prince Charlie see STUART 1.

Bon·nin |'bawnin|, Gertrude Simmons (1876–1938) Sioux-American author and Indian activist. Also known as **Zitkala-Sa** ("Red Bird."). One of the first Native Americans to translate and publish traditional Indian stories, she published her first book, *Old Indian Legends,* in 1901. She founded the National Council of American Indians (1926).

Bo·no |'bō,nō|, Sonny (1935–98) U.S. entertainer and politician. Born *Salvatore Bono.* Famed as half of the singing duo Sonny and Cher (1964–74), he became a Republican politician. He served as mayor of Palm Springs, California (1988–92) and in the U.S. House of Representatives (1994–98).

Bon·temps |,bän'täm|, Arna Wendell (1902–73) U.S. author and librarian. He was librarian of Fisk University and the author of novels about African American life; his nonfiction includes correspondence with Langston Hughes, published in 1979.

Boole |bōōl|, George (1815–64) English mathematician responsible for Boolean algebra. The study of mathematical or symbolic logic developed mainly from his ideas.

Boone |bōōn|, Daniel (c. 1734–1820) American pioneer. Boone made trips west from Pennsylvania into the unexplored area of Kentucky, organizing settlements and successfully defending them against hostile American Indians.

Boor·stin |'bawrstən; 'bərstən|, Daniel J. (1914–) U.S. educator and author. He was Librarian of Congress (1975–87). Notable works: *The Democratic Experience* (1973, Pulitzer Prize).

Booth |bōōTH|, George (1926–) U.S. cartoonist, artist, and author. He was on staff at *The New Yorker* magazine

Booth |bōōTH|, John Wilkes (1838–65) U.S. actor and assassin of Abraham Lincoln.

Booth |bōōTH|, Shirley (1898–1992) U.S. actress. She won an Academy Award in 1952 for *Come Back, Little Sheba*.

Booth |bōōTH|, William (1829–1912) English religious leader, founder and first general of the Salvation Army. A Methodist revivalist preacher, in 1865 he established a mission in the East End of London that later became the Salvation Army.

Bor·den |'bawrdən|, Gail (1801–74) U.S. businessman and inventor. He invented the process for making condensed milk and founded Borden's Milk & Ice Cream Co.

Bor·den |'bawrdən|, Lizzie Andrew (1860–1927) U.S. accused murderess. Accused of the murder of her father and stepmother in Fall River, Massachusetts, in 1892, she was acquitted in a trial that became a national sensation.

Bor·det |bawr'dā|, Jules-Jean-Baptiste-Vincent (1870–1961) Belgian bacteriologist and immunologist. He discovered the complement system of blood serum, and developed a vaccine for whooping cough. Nobel Prize for Physiology or Medicine (1919).

Borg |bawrg|, Björn (Rune) (1956–) Swedish tennis player. He won five consecutive men's singles titles at Wimbledon (1976–80), beating the record of three consecutive wins held by Fred Perry.

Bor·ges |'bawr,hās|, Jorge Luis (1899–1986) Argentinian poet, short-story writer, and essayist. The volume of short stories *A Universal History of Infamy* (1935, revised 1954) is regarded as a founding work of magic realism.

Bor·gia |'bawrzHə| Italian family, including: **Cesare Borgia** (c. 1476–1507), a statesman, cardinal, and general. The illegitimate son of Cardinal Rodrigo Borgia (later Pope Alexander VI) and brother of Lucrezia Borgia, he was captain general of the papal army from 1499, and became master of a large portion of central Italy. His sister, **Lucrezia Borgia** (1480–1519), married three times, according to the political alliances useful to her family; after her third marriage in 1501 she established herself as a patron of the arts.

Bor·glum |'bawrgləm|, Gutzon (1867–1941) U.S. sculptor. Full name *John Gutzon de la Mothe Borglum*. His most famous work is the Mount Rushmore National Memorial in South Dakota, which features the monumental heads of Presidents Washington, Jefferson, Lincoln, and T. Roosevelt. The work, begun in 1927, was completed in 1941 with the help of his son Lincoln Borglum (1912–86).

Borg·nine |'bawrg,nīn|, Ernest (1917–) U.S. actor. He won an Academy Award in 1955 for *Marty*.

Bo·ri |'bawrē|, Lucrezia (1887–1960) Italian operatic soprano, born in Spain. She made her debut with the Metropolitan Opera in 1912 as Manon in *Manon Lescaut* and sang there for 19 seasons; in 1935, she was first woman and first active artist to be elected a director of the Metropolitan Opera Association.

Boris Godunov |'bawris 'gōd(ə),nawf; 'gawd(ə),nawf| see GODUNOV.

Bork |bawrk|, Robert Heron (1927–) U.S. jurist and legal scholar. He was nominated to the Supreme Court by Ronald Reagan but rejected by the Senate in a controversial vote.

Bor·laug |'bawr,lawg|, Norman Ernest (1914–) U.S. agronomist. He developed high-yielding cereals for cultivation in the Third World. Nobel Peace Prize (1970).

Bor·mann |'bawrmən|, Martin Ludwig (1900–c. 1945) German Nazi politician. Considered to be Hitler's closest collaborator, he disappeared at the end of World War II; his skeleton, exhumed in Berlin, was identified in 1973.

Born |bawrn|, Max (1882–1970) German theoretical physicist, a founder of quantum mechanics. Nobel Prize for Physics (1954).

Bo·ro·din |bawrə'dēn|, Aleksandr (Porfiryevich) (1833–87) Russian composer. He is best known for the epic opera *Prince Igor* (completed after his death by Rimsky-Korsakov and Glazunov).

Bor·ro·mi·ni |,bawrə'mēnē|, Francesco (1599–1667) Italian architect, a leading figure of the Italian baroque.

Bor·row |'bärō|, George (Henry) (1803–81) English writer. His travels with gypsies provided material for the picaresque narrative *Lavengro* (1851) and its sequel *The Romany Rye* (1857).

Bosch |bawsH|, Carl (1874–1940) German industrial chemist. He was recognized for his invention and development of chemical high-pressure methods, specifically the Haber-Bosch process, by which hydrogen is obtained from water gas and superheated steam. Nobel Prize for Chemistry (1931).

Bosch |bawsH|, Hieronymus (1450–1516) Dutch painter. Bosch's highly detailed works are typically crowded with half-human, half-animal creatures and grotesque demons in settings symbolic of sin and folly. His individual style prefigures that of the surrealists.

Bose |bōz|, Sir Jagadis Chandra (1858–1937) Indian physicist and plant physiologist. He investigated the properties of very short radio waves, wireless telegraphy, and radiation-induced fatigue in inorganic materials. His physiological work involved comparative measurements of the responses of plants exposed to stress.

Bose |bōz|, Satyendra Nath (1894–1974) Indian physicist. With Einstein he described fundamental particles which later came to be known as *bosons*.

Boswell |'bäzwel|, James (1740–95) Scottish author, companion and biographer of Samuel Johnson. He is known for *Journal of a Tour to the Hebrides* (1785) and *The Life of Samuel Johnson* (1791).

Bo·tha |'bōtə|, Louis (1862–1919) South African soldier and statesman, first prime minister of the Union of South Africa (1910–19).

Bo·tha, P. W (1916–) South African statesman, prime minister (1978–84), state president (1984–89); full name *Pieter Willem Botha*. An authoritarian leader, he continued to enforce apartheid but in response to pressure introduced limited reforms; his resistance to more radical changes ultimately led to his fall from power.

Both·well |'bäTHwəl|, James Hepburn, 4th Earl of (c. 1535–78) Scottish nobleman and third husband of Mary, Queen of Scots. He was implicated in the murder of Mary's previous husband, Lord Darnley (1567), a crime for which he was tried but acquitted; he married Mary later the same year.

Bot·ti·cel·li |,bätə'cHelē|, Sandro (1445–1510) Italian painter; born *Alessandro di Mariano Filipepi*. He worked in Renaissance Florence under the patronage of the Medicis. Botticelli is best known for his mythological works such as *Primavera* (c.1478) and *The Birth of Venus* (c.1480).

Bou·cher |boo'sHa|, François (1703–70) French painter and decorative artist, one of the foremost artists of the rococo style in France. Notable paintings: *The Rising of the Sun* (1753) and *Summer Pastoral* (1749).

Bou·cher de Crèvecoeur de Perthes |boo'sHa də pert|, Jacques (1788–1868) French archaeologist. In 1837 he discovered some of the first evidence of man-made stone tools near the bones of extinct (Pleistocene) animals in the valley of the River Somme. He argued that these tools (and their makers) belonged to a pre-Celtic "antediluvian" age, but his findings were not accepted until the 1850s.

Bou·chet |bōō'sнä|, Edward Alexander (1852–1918) U.S. physicist. He became the first African American to earn a Ph.D. from an American university (Yale, 1876).

Bou·dic·ca |bōō'dikə| (died AD 60) a queen of the Britons, ruler of the Iceni tribe in eastern England; also known as **Boadicea**. Boudicca led her forces in revolt against the Romans and sacked Colchester, St. Albans, and London before being defeated by the Roman governor Suetonius Paulinus.

Bou·gain·ville |bōōgən'vēl|, Louis-Antoine de (1729–1811) French explorer. Bougainville led the first French circumnavigation of the globe 1766–69, visiting many of the islands of the South Pacific and compiling an invaluable scientific record of his findings.

Bou·lan·ger |bōōlän'zнä|, Nadia-Juliette (1887–1979) French music teacher, conductor, and composer. Her students included Aaron Copland, Roger Sessions, Virgil Thomson, and Leonard Bernstein.

Bou·lez |bōō'lez|, Pierre (1925–) French composer and conductor. His works explore and develop serialism and aleatory music, making use of both traditional and electronic instruments.

Boult |bōlt|, Sir Adrian (Cedric) (1899–1983) English conductor. Music director of the BBC 1930–49 and principal conductor of the London Philharmonic Orchestra 1950–57.

Boul·ton |'bōltən|, Matthew (1728–1809) English engineer and manufacturer. With his partner James Watt he pioneered the manufacture of steam engines, which they began to produce in 1774.

Bour·gui·ba |bōōr'gēbə|, Habib ibn Ali (1903–) Tunisian nationalist and statesman and the first president of independent Tunisia (1957–87).

Bourke-White |'bōōrk '(h)wīt|, Margaret (1906–71) U.S. photojournalist. During World War II she was the first female photographer with the U.S. armed forces, at the end of the war accompanying the Allied forces when they entered the Nazi concentration camps.

Boutros Ghali |,bōōtrōs'gälē|, Boutros (1922–) Egyptian diplomat and politician and Secretary General of the United Nations (1992–97).

Bow |bō|, Clara (1905–65) U.S. actress. One of the most popular stars and sex symbols of the 1920s, she was known as the "It Girl."

Bow·ditch |'baw,diсн|, Nathaniel (1773–1838) U.S. mathematician and astronomer. He expanded *The Practical Navigator* into *The New American Practical Navigator* (1802).

Bow·en |'bōən|, Elizabeth (Dorothea Cole) (1899–1973) British novelist and short-story writer, born in Ireland. Notable novels: *The Death of the Heart* (1938) and *The Heat of the Day* (1949).

Bow·er·man |'bowər,mən|, William J (1909–) U.S. businessman. While coaching track at the University of Oregon (1960–75), he founded the Nike company (1973–).

Bow·ie |'bōē|, David (1947–) English rock singer, songwriter, and actor; born *David Robert Jones*. He is known for his theatrical performances and unconventional stage personae.

Bow·ie |'bōē; 'bōōē|, Jim (1796–1836) American frontiersman Full name *James Bowie*. The Bowie knife was designed either by him or by his brother Rezin. He became a leader among the American settlers who opposed Mexican rule in Texas. He shared command of the garrison that resisted the Mexican attack on the Alamo, where he died.

Bow·ker |'bowkər|, Richard Rogers (1848–1933) U.S. editor and author. He was founder (with F. Leypoldt and Melvil Dewey) and editor of *The Library Journal*, publisher and editor of *Publishers 'Weekly*, and founder of the American Library Association (1876).

Bow·les |bōlz|, Paul (Frederick) (1910–) U.S. writer and composer. His novels, which include *The Sheltering Sky* (1949) and *The Spider's House* (1966), typically concern westerners in the Arab world.

Boyce |bois|, William (1711–79) English composer and organist. His compositions include songs, overtures, and eight symphonies; one of his most famous songs is "Hearts of Oak". He is also noted for his *Cathedral Music* (1760–73).

Boyd |boid|, Arthur (Merric Bloomfield) (1920–) Australian painter, potter, etcher, and ceramic artist. He is famous for his large ceramic sculptures and for his pictures inspired by his travels among the native people of Australia.

Boyd |boid|, John R (1927–97) U.S. military strategist. He was an expert on air-to-air combat and the architect of military reform in the U.S. Deptartment of Defense in the 1970s and 1980s.

Boyer |'boiər|, Charles (1899–1978) French-born U.S. actor. Before going to Hollywood in the 1930s he enjoyed a successful stage career in France. Notable movies: *Mayerling* (1936), *Gaslight* (1944), and *Barefoot in the Park* (1968).

Boyle |boil|, Robert (1627–91) Irish-born scientist. Boyle put forward a view of matter based on particles that was a precursor of the modern theory of chemical elements. He is best known for his experiments with the air pump, which led to the law named after him.

Boyle |boil|, T. Coraghessan (1948–) U.S. author. Notable works: *The Road to Wellville* (1993).

Boz |bäz| the pseudonym used by Charles Dickens in his *Pickwick Papers* and contributions to the *Morning Chronicle*.

Brad·bury |'bræd,berē|, Ray (1920–) U.S. writer of science fiction; full name *Raymond Douglas Bradbury*. Notable works: *The Martian Chronicles* (short story collection, 1950) and *Fahrenheit 451* (novel, 1951).

Brad·dock |'brædək|, Edward (1695–1755) British soldier. He was major general and commander in chief of the British forces in America in 1754.

Brad·ford |'brædfərd|, Barbara Taylor (1933–) U.S. author, born in England. Notable novels: *A Woman of Substance* (1974) and *A Sudden Change of Heart* (1999).

Brad·ford |'brædfərd|, William (1590–1657) U.S. religious and colonial leader. He was a signer of the Mayflower Compact (1620) and Governor of Plymouth Colony (1621–32; 1635; 1637; 1639–43; 1645–56).

Brad·ham |'brædəm|, Caleb D. U.S. inventor. He created the formula used in Pepsi-Cola.

Brad·lee |'brædlē|, Benjamin Crowninshield (1921–) U.S. journalist. He is the executive editor of the *Washington Post* (1968–).

Brad·ley |'brædlē|, Bill (1943–) U.S. basketball player and politician. He played for the New York Knicks in the NBA (1967–77) before entering politics. A New Jersey Democrat, he was elected to the U.S. Senate (1979–). Elected to the Basketball Hall of Fame (1983).

Brad·ley |'brædlē|, Edward R. (1941–) U.S. journalist. He is a news correspondent for the CBS television news show "60 Minutes" (1981–).

Brad·ley |'brædlē|, James (1693–1762) English astronomer. Bradley was appointed Astronomer Royal in 1742. He discovered the aberration of light and also observed the oscillation of the earth's axis, which he termed *nutation*. His star catalogue was published posthumously.

Brad·ley |'brædlē|, Joseph P. (1813–92) U.S. Supreme Court justice (1870–92).

Brad·ley |'brædlē|, Milton (1836–1911) U.S. publisher and manufacturer. His board game *The Checkered Game of Life* (1860) led to the formation of the Milton Bradley Co. (1864).

Brad·ley |'brædlē|, Omar Nelson (1893–1981) U.S. general. He was in charge of the land contingent during the Normandy campaign (1944–45) and served as chief of staff of the U.S. Army (1948–49), chairman of the U.S. Joint Chiefs of Staff (1949–53), and General of the Army (1950).

Brad·ley |'brædlē|, Thomas (1917–98) U.S. politician and lawyer. Elected mayor of Los Angeles (1973–93), he became the first African-American mayor of a largely white city. Awarded Spingarn Medal (1984).

Brad·shaw |'bræd,sHaw|, Terry Paxton (1948–) U.S. football player.

Brad·street |'bræd,strēt|, Anne Dudley (1612–72) U.S. poet. She came from England with her husband Simon Bradstreet to the Massachusetts Bay Colony in 1630. She was the first American poetess. Notable works: *The Tenth Muse Lately Sprung Up in America* (1650).

Bra·dy |'brādē|, James Buchanan (1856–1917) U.S. financier. He was a salesman for a railroad supply house and was known for his ostentatious display of jewelry, which gave him the nickname "Diamond Jim."

Bra·dy |'brādē|, Mathew B. (1823?–96) U.S. photographer. His photographs of Union armies taken during the Civil War became the basis for his National Photographic Collection, and the publication of his *Gallery of Illustrious Americans* (1850) established him as a leading American photographer.

Bragg |bræg|, Sir William Henry (1862–1942) English physicist, a founder of solid-state physics. He collaborated with his son, **Sir (William) Lawrence Bragg**, (1890–1971, in developing the technique of X-ray diffraction for determining the atomic structure of crystals; for this they shared the 1915 Nobel Prize for Physics.

Bra·he |'brä,hē|, Tycho (1546–1601) Danish astronomer. He built an observatory equipped with precision instruments, but despite demonstrating that comets follow sun-centered paths, he adhered to a geocentric view of the planets.

Brahms |brämz|, Johannes (1833–97) German composer and pianist. He eschewed program music and opera and concentrated on traditional forms. He wrote four symphonies, four concertos, chamber and piano music, choral works including the *German Requiem* (1857–68), and nearly 200 songs including *Wiegenlied*, (op. 49), for the melody for "Brahms Lullaby."

Braille |brāl|, Louis (1809–52) French educationist. Blind from the age of 3, by the age of 15 he had developed his own system of raised-point reading and writing, which was officially adopted two years after his death.

Braine |brān|, John (Gerard) (1922–86) English novelist, famous for his first novel, *Room at the Top* (1957), whose opportunistic hero was hailed as a representative example of an "angry young man."

Brai·thwaite |'brāTH,wāt|, William

Stanley Beaumont (1878–1962) U.S. poet and anthologist. He is noted for his poetry collection *The House of Falling Leaves* (1904) and for editing annual anthologies of magazine verse (1913–39). Spingarn Medal, 1918.

Bra·mah |'brämə|, Joseph (1748–1814) English inventor. One of the most influential engineers of the Industrial Revolution, Bramah is best known for his hydraulic press, used for heavy forging.

Bra·man·te |brä'mäntä|, Donato (d' Angelo) (1444–1514) Italian architect. As architect to Pope Julius II he drew up the first plan for the new St. Peter's (begun in 1506), instigating the concept of a huge central dome.

Bran·agh |'brænə|, Kenneth (Charles) (1960–   ) English actor, producer, and director. With the Royal Shakespeare Company he attracted critical acclaim for roles such as Henry V. He has also directed and starred in movies such as *Hamlet* (1996).

Bran·cu·și |'bränkʊʃ|, Constantin (1876–1957) Romanian sculptor, who spent much of his working life in France. His sculpture represents an attempt to move away from a representational art and to capture the essence of forms by reducing them to their ultimate, almost abstract, simplicity.

Bran·deis |'bræn,dīs|, Louis Dembitz (1856–1941) U.S. Supreme Court justice (1916–39). He gained an early reputation as the "people's attorney" by defending without a fee Boston residents seeking regulation of local public utilities. His "Brandeis brief" made use of social facts, rather than relying solely on precedent and general argument.

Bran·do |'brændō|, Marlon (1924–   ) U.S. actor. An exponent of method acting, he first attracted critical acclaim in the stage production of *A Streetcar Named Desire* (1947); he starred in the movie version four years later. Other notable movies: *On the Waterfront* (1954, for which he won an Oscar) and *The Godfather* (1972).

Brandt |brænt|, Bill (1904?–83) German-born British photographer; full name *Hermann Wilhelm Brandt*. He is best known for his almost abstract treatment of the nude, as in *Perspectives of Nudes* (1961).

Brandt |brænt|, Willy (1913–92) German statesman, chancellor of West Germany 1969–74; born *Karl Herbert Frahm*. He achieved international recognition for his policy of détente and the opening of relations with the countries of the Eastern bloc (Ostpolitik). Nobel Peace Prize (1971).

Bran·son |'brænsən|, Richard (1950–) English businessman and adventurer. He made his name with the company Virgin Records, which he set up in 1969. He later influenced the opening up of air routes with Virgin Atlantic Airways, established in 1984.

Braque |bräk|, Georges (1882–1963) French painter. His collages, which introduced commercial lettering and fragmented objects into pictures to contrast the real with the "illusory" painted image, were the first stage in the development of synthetic cubism.

Bras·sey |'bræsē|, Thomas (1805–70) English engineer and railway contractor. He built more than 10,000 km (6,500 miles) of railways in Europe, India, South America, and Australia.

Brat·tain |'brætn|, Walter Houser (1902–87) U.S. inventor. He co-invented the point-contact transistor (1947) with John Bardeen and William Shockley, with whom he share a Nobel Prize for Physics (1956).

Braun |brown|, Eva (1912–45) German mistress of Adolf Hitler. Braun and Hitler are thought to have married during the fall of Berlin, shortly before committing suicide together in the air-raid shelter of his Berlin headquarters.

Braun |brown|, Karl Ferdinand (1850–1918) German physicist. Braun invented the coupled system of radio transmission and the Braun tube (forerunner of the cathode ray tube), in which a beam of electrons could be deflected. Nobel Prize for Physics (1909).

Braun |brown|, Wernher Magnus Maximilian von (1912–77) German-born U.S. rocket engineer. Braun led development on the V-2 rockets used by Germany in World War II. After the war he moved to the U.S., where he pioneered

the work that resulted in the U.S. space program.

Brau·ti·gan |'brawtə,gən|, Richard (1935–84) U.S. author. His novels, particularly *Trout Fishing in America* (1967), reflect the ethos of the Beat generation.

Brax·ton |'brækstən|, Toni (1968–) U.S. pop singer. Grammy Award, 1997.

Braz·le·ton |'bræzl,tən; 'bräzl,tən|, T. Berry (1918–) U.S. pediatrician and educator. He was director of the child development unit at Children's Hopsital Medical Center in Boston (1972–) and the author of *Infants and Mothers: Individual Differences in Development* (1970).

Bream |brēm|, Julian (Alexander) (1933–) English guitarist and lute player. He formed the Julian Bream Consort for the performance of early consort music and revived and edited much early music. Britten, Walton, and others composed works for him.

Breath·ed |'breTH,əd|, Berke (1957–) U.S. cartoonist. Full name *Guy Berkeley Breathed*. He created the Pulitzer Prize-winning comic strip "Bloom County."

Brecht |brekt|, (Eugen) Bertolt (Friedrich) (1898–1956) German dramatist, producer, and poet. His interest in combining music and drama led to collaboration with Kurt Weill, for example in *The Threepenny Opera* (1928), an adaptation of John Gay's *The Beggar's Opera*. Brecht's later drama, written in exile after Hitler's rise to power, uses techniques of theatrical alienation and includes *Mother Courage* (1941) and *The Caucasian Chalk Circle* (1948).

Breck·in·ridge |'brekən,rij|, John Cabell (1821–75) U.S. politician and vice president of the U.S. (1857–61).

Brel |brel|, Jacques (1929–78) Belgian singer and composer. He gained a reputation in Paris as an original songwriter whose satirical wit was balanced by his idealism and hope.

Bren·dan |'brendən|, St (*c.* 486–*c.* 578) Irish abbot. The legend of the "Navigation of St. Brendan" (*c.*1050), describing his voyage with a band of monks to a promised land (possibly Orkney or the Hebrides), was widely popular in the Middle Ages. Feast day, May 16.

Bren·del |'brendəl|, Alfred (1931–) Austrian pianist.

Bren·nan |'brenən|, Walter (1894–1974) U.S. actor. He was the first actor to win three Academy Awards (1936, *Come and Get It*; 1938, *Kentucky*; 1940, *The Westerner*).

Bren·nan |'brenən|, William J., Jr (1906–97) U.S. Supreme Court Justice (1956–90).

Bres·lin |'brez,lin|, Jimmy (1930–) U.S. journalist and author. A syndicated columnist, he won a 1986 Pulitzer Prize in 1986. He wrote *The Gang That Couldn't Shoot Straight* (1969) and *He Got Hungry and Forgot His Manners* (1988).

Bre·ton |'bretn|, André (1896–1966) French poet, essayist, and critic. First involved with Dadaism, Breton later launched the surrealist movement, outlining the movement's philosophy in his manifesto of 1924. His creative writing is characterized by surrealist techniques such as "automatic" writing.

Brett |bret|, George (1953–) U.S. baseball player. He was the American League batting champion in three different decades (1976, 1980, 1990). Elected to the Baseball Hall of Fame (1999).

Brett |bret|, Jan (1949–) U.S. author and illustrator. Her lavishly illustrated children's books include *Trouble with Trolls* (1992).

Breu·er |'broiər|, Marcel Lajos (1902–81) U.S. architect, born in Hungary. Notable designs: UNESCO headquarters (1953–58) in Paris and the Whitney Museum of American Art (1965–66) in New York City.

Breuil |'broEy|, Henri-Édouard Prosper (1877–1961) French archaeologist. He is noted for his work on Paleolithic cave paintings, in particular those at Altamira in Spain, which he was able to authenticate.

Brew·er |'broöər|, David J. (1837–1910) U.S. Supreme Court Justice (1889–1910).

Brew·ster |'broöstər|, Sir David (1781–1868) Scottish physicist. He is best known for his work on the laws governing the polarization of light, and for his invention of the kaleidoscope.

Brey·er |'briər|, Stephen Gerald (1938–) U.S. Supeme Court justice (1994–)

Brezh·nev |'brezH,nev|, Leonid (Ilyich) (1906–82) Soviet statesman, general secretary of the Communist Party of the USSR (1966–82) and president (1977–82). His period in power was marked by intensified persecution of dissidents at home and by attempted détente followed by renewed Cold War in 1968; he was largely responsible for the invasion of Czechoslovakia (1968).

Brick·er |'brikər|, John W. (1893–1986) U.S. politician. He was a Republican vice presidential candidate (1944).

Bride, St. see BRIDGET, ST.

Bridge |brij|, Frank (1879–1941) English composer, conductor, and violist. His compositions include chamber music, songs, and orchestral works, among them *The Sea* (1910–11) and *Oration* (for cello and orchestra, 1930).

Bridg·es |'brijəz|, Lloyd Vernet, Jr. (1913–98) U.S. actor. Father of Jeff Bridges and Beau Bridges. His many movie credits include *High Noon* (1952) and *Airplane* (1980).

Bridg·es |'brijəz|, Robert (Seymour) (1844–1930) English poet and literary critic. His long philosophical poem *The Testament of Beauty* (1929), written in the Victorian tradition, was instantly popular. He was Poet Laureate 1913–30.

Bridg·et[1] |'brijət|, St. (*c.* 453–524) Irish abbess. Also **Bride** or **Brigid**; also known as **St. Bridget of Ireland**. She was venerated in Ireland as a virgin saint and noted in miracle stories for her compassion; her cult soon spread over most of western Europe. Feast day, July 23.

Bridg·et[2] |'brijət|, St. (*c.* 1303–73) Swedish nun and visionary. Also **Birgitta**; also known as **St. Bridget of Sweden**. She experienced her first vision of the Virgin Mary at the age of seven. Feast day, July 23.

Bridg·man |'brijmən|, Percy Williams (1882–1961) U.S. physicist. He worked with liquids and solids under very high pressures, and his techniques were later used in making artificial minerals (including diamonds). Nobel Prize for Physics (1946).

Briggs |brigz|, Clare A. (1875–1930) U.S. cartoonist. He created the comic strip "Mr. & Mrs."

Briggs |brigz|, Henry (1561–1630) English mathematician. He was renowned for his work on logarithms, in which he introduced the decimal base, made the thousands of calculations necessary for the tables, and popularized their use. Briggs also devised a standard method used for long division.

Bright |brīt|, John (1811–89) English Liberal politician and reformer. A noted orator, Bright was the leader, along with Richard Cobden, of the campaign to repeal the Corn Laws. He was also a vociferous opponent of the Crimean War (1854) and was closely identified with the 1867 Reform Act.

Brigid, St. see BRIDGET, ST.

Brind·ley |ˈbrindlē|, James (1716–72) pioneering English canal-builder. He designed some 600 km (375 miles) of waterway with a minimum of locks, cuttings, or tunnels, connecting most of the major rivers of England.

Brink |briNGk|, André (1935–) South African novelist, short-story writer, and dramatist. He gained international recognition with his novel *Looking on Darkness* (1973), which became the first novel in Afrikaans to be banned by the South African government. Other notable novels: *A Dry White Season* (1979) and *A Chain of Voices* (1982).

Brink·ley |ˈbriNGk,lē|, David (1920–) U.S. news commentator. He reported news for NBC (1951–81) and anchored ABC's *This Week* (1981–97).

Bris·bane |ˈbrizbən|, Sir Thomas Makdougall (1773–1860) Scottish soldier and astronomer. In 1790 he joined the army, becoming major general in 1813. He was governor of New South Wales (1821–25) and became an acclaimed astronomer.

Brit·ten |ˈbritn|, (Edward) Benjamin, Lord Britten of Aldeburgh (1913–76) English composer, pianist, and conductor. Notable operas: *Peter Grimes* (1945), *A Midsummer Night's Dream* (1960), and *Death in Venice* (1973) .

Brock |bräk|, Lou (1939–) U.S. baseball player. He was the National League stolen base leader eight times, and (until 1991) held the record for career stolen bases (938).

Bro·der |ˈbrōdər|, David Salzer (1929–) U.S. journalist and author. A syndicated columnist, he won a Pulitzer Prize in 1973 and became an associate editor of *The Washington Post* (1975–).

Brod·key |ˈbrawd,kē|, Harold (1930–1996) U.S. author. He wrote about Jewish family life in small-town midwestern America. Notable works: *First Love and Other Sorrows* (1958) and *Stories in an Almost Classical Mode* (1988).

Brod·sky |ˈbrädskē|, Joseph (1940–96) Russian-born U.S. poet; born *Iosif Aleksandrovich Brodsky*. Writing both in Russian and in English, he was most famous for his collection *The End of a Beautiful Era* (1977). Nobel Prize for Literature (1987); U.S. Poet Laureate (1991).

Bro·dy |ˈbrō,dē|, Jane (1941–) U.S. journalist and author. A science writer and personal health columnist for the *New York Times* (1965–), she also wrote *Jane Brody's Good Food Book* (1985).

Broglie, de see DE BROGLIE.

Bro·now·ski |,brəˈnowskē|, Jacob (1908–74) Polish-born British scientist, writer, and broadcaster. He popularized science with such books as *The Common Sense of Science* (1951) and the 1970s television documentary series "The Ascent of Man."

Bron·të |ˈbräntē| Family of English novelists, including: **Charlotte Brontë** (1816–55). Under the pseudonym *Currer Bell*, she published *Jane Eyre* (1847). Her sister **Emily Brontë** (1818–48), under the pseudonym *Ellis Bell*, published *Wuthering Heights* (1847). **Anne Brontë** (1820–49) was the sister of Charlotte and Emily. Under the pseudonym *Acton Bell*, she published *The Tenant of Wildfell Hall* (1847).

Bron·zi·no |,brawnˈzēnō|, Agnolo (1503–72) Italian mannerist painter; born *Agnolo di Cosimo*. He spent most of his career in Florence as court painter to Cosimo de' Medici. Notable works: *Venus, Cupid, Folly, and Time* (c.1546).

Brooke |bro͝ok|, Edward William (1919–) U.S. attorney and politician. He was a Republican member of the U.S. Senate from Massachusetts (1966–

79) and the first African American senator elected in 85 years. Spingarn Medal, 1967.

Brooke |brŏŏk|, Rupert (Chawner) (1887–1915) English poet. He is most famous for his wartime poetry *1914 and Other Poems* (1915). He died while on naval service in the Mediterranean.

Brook·ner |'brŏŏknər|, Anita (1928–) English novelist and art historian.

Brooks |brŏŏks|, Cleanth (1906–94) U.S. teacher and critic. A leading proponent of the New Criticism movement, he edited *The Southern Review* from 1935 to 1942 and taught at Yale University (1947–75). Notable works: *Modern Poetry and Tradition* (1939).

Brooks |brŏŏks|, Garth (1962–) U.S. country music singer and songwriter. Full name *Troyal Garth Brooks*. Notable albums: *No Fences* (1990) and *Ropin' the Wind* (1991).

Brooks |brŏŏks|, Gwendolyn (1917–) U.S. poet and author. She was the first African-American woman named as Poetry Consultant to the Library of Congress (1985–86). Notable works: *Annie Allen* (1949), which won the Pulitzer Prize.

Brooks |brŏŏks|, Henry Sands (1770?–1833) U.S. entrepreneur. A pioneer in men's ready-to-wear clothing, he was the founder of Brooks Brothers clothing stores.

Brooks |brŏŏks|, James L. (1940–) U.S. director. Notable movies: *Terms of Endearment* (1983, Academy Award).

Brooks |brŏŏks|, Mel (1926–) U.S. comedian, movie director and comic actor; born *Melvin Kaminsky*. He is known especially for his parodies and farces. His movie debut *The Producers* (1967) was followed by the spoof western *Blazing Saddles* (1974).

Brooks |brŏŏks|, Van Wyck (1886–1963) U.S. literary critic. Notable works: *The Wine of the Puritans* (1909), *America's Coming-of-Age* (1915), and *The Flowering of New England* (1936), which won the Pulitzer Prize.

Broon·zy |'brŏŏn,zē|, Big Bill (1893–1958) U.S. guitarist and blues singer. Full name *William Lee Conley Broonzy*.

Brou·wer |'brow,ər|, Adriaen (c. 1605–38) Flemish painter. Providing an important link between Dutch and Flemish genre painting, his most typical works represent peasant scenes in taverns.

Brown |brown|, Sir Arthur Whitten (1886–1948) Scottish aviator. He made the first transatlantic flight in 1919 with Sir John William Alcock.

Brown |brown|, Ford Madox (1821–93) English painter. His early work was inspired by the Pre-Raphaelites, and in 1861 he became a founding member of William Morris's company, designing stained glass and furniture.

Brown |brown|, Helen Gurley (1922–) U.S. editor and author. She was editor in chief of *Cosmopolitan* magazine (1972–) and author of *Sex and the Single Girl* (1962).

Brown |brown|, Henry Billings (1836–1913) U.S. Supreme Court Justice (1890–1906).

Brown |brown|, H. Rap (1943–) see AL-AMIN, Jamil Abdullah.

Brown[1] |brown|, James (1800–55) U.S. publisher. In partnership with Charles C. Little, he founded Little, Brown & Co. (1847).

Brown[2] |brown|, James (1928–) U.S. soul and funk singer and songwriter. In the 1960s he played a leading role in the development of funk with songs such as "Papa's Got a Brand New Bag" (1965).

Brown |brown|, Jerry, Jr. (1938–) U.S. politician. Full name *Edmund Gerald Brown*. He was governor of California (1975–83) and a Democratic presidential candidate (1990).

Brown |brown|, Jim (1936–) U.S. football player and actor. He was the NFL's premier running back, leading the league in rushing in eight of his nine seasons (1957–66). He was later featured in several action-adventure movies, including *Ice Station Zebra* (1968).

Brown |brown|, John (1800–59) U.S. radical abolitionist. In 1859 he was executed after raiding a government arsenal at Harpers Ferry, Virginia, intending to arm black slaves and start a revolt. He became a hero of the abolitionists in the Civil War; he is commemorated in the song "John Brown's Body."

Brown |brown|, John Carter (1797–

1874) U.S. bibliophile. He assembled over 7,500 volumes of early Americana, which became the John Carter Brown Library at Brown University.

Brown |brown|, Lancelot (1715–83) English landscape gardener; known as **Capability Brown**. He evolved an English style of natural-looking landscape parks. Notable examples of his work are at Blenheim Palace, Chatsworth House in Derbyshire, and Kew Gardens.

Brown |brown|, Marc Tolon (1946–) U.S. author and artist. He wrote the "Arthur" series of books for children.

Brown |brown|, Margaret Wise (1910–52) U.S. author. She was a prolific writer of books for young children, including "Good Night, Moon" (1947).

Brown |brown|, Paul (1908–91) U.S. football coach. He led the Cleveland Browns to three NFL titles (1950, 1954, 1955). He founded the Cincinnati Bengals (1968).

Brown |brown|, Rachel Fuller (1898–1980) U.S. inventor. With Elizabeth Lee Hazen, she developed Nystatin, the first nontoxic antifungal antibiotic.

Brown |brown|, Sterling Allen (1901–89) U.S. poet, literary critic, and educator. Considered a founder of black literary criticism, he wrote *Negro Poetry and Drama* (1937).

Brown |brown|, Tina (1953–) U.S. editor, born in England. She edited *Vanity Fair* (1984–92) and *The New Yorker* (1992–98).

Brown |brown|, William Wells (1816?–84) U.S. author. After securing freedom from slavery, Brown aided other fugitive slaves. Notable works: *Clotelle: or, The President's Daughter* (1852), said to be the first novel published by an African American.

Browne |brown|, Dik (1917–89) U.S. cartoonist, advertising artist, and author. Full name *Richard Arthur Allen*. He was creator of the comic strip "Hagar the Horrible" and co-creator of the comic strip "Hi and Lois."

Browne |brown|, Jackson (1948–) U.S. rock singer and songwriter.

Browne |brown|, Sir Thomas (1605–82) English author and physician. He achieved prominence with *Religio Medici* (1642), a collection of opinions on a vast number of subjects connected with religion.

Brow·ning |'browniNG| English poets: **Elizabeth Barrett Browning** (1806–61); born *Elizabeth Barrett*. She established her reputation with *Poems* (1844). In 1846 she eloped to Italy with **Robert Browning** (1812–89). In 1842 he established his name with *Dramatic Lyrics*, containing "The Pied Piper of Hamelin" and "My Last Duchess."

Bru·beck |'brōōbek|, Dave (1920–) U.S. jazz pianist, composer, and bandleader; full name *David Warren Brubeck*. He formed the Dave Brubeck Quartet in 1951 and won international recognition with the album *Time Out*, which included "Take Five" (1959).

Bruce |brōōs|, Lenny (1925–66) U.S. comedian; born *Leonard Alfred Schneider*. He gained notoriety for flouting the bounds of respectability with his humor, and was imprisoned for obscenity in 1961. He died following an accidental drug overdose.

Bruce |brōōs|, James (1730–94) Scottish explorer. In 1770 he was the first European to discover the source of the Blue Nile, although his *Travels to Discover the Sources of the Nile* (1790), recounting his expedition, was dismissed by his contemporaries as fabrication.

Bruce |brōōs|, Robert the see ROBERT I.

Bruck·ner |'brōōknər|, Anton (1824–1896) Austrian composer and organist. He wrote ten symphonies, four masses, and a *Te Deum* (1884).

Brue·gel |'broigəl|, Pieter (*c.* 1525–69) Flemish artist Family of Flemish artists, including: **Pieter Bruegel** (*c.* 1525–69); known as **Pieter Bruegel the Elder**. He produced landscapes, religious allegories, and satires of peasant life. Notable works: *The Procession to Calvary* (1564), *The Blind Leading the Blind* (1568), and *The Peasant Dance* (1568). His son, **Pieter Bruegel** (1564–1638), known as **Pieter Bruegel the Younger** or as **Hell Bruegel**, was a very able copyist of his father's work; he is also noted for his paintings of devils. **Jan Bruegel** (1568–1625), son of Pieter Bruegel the Elder, was known as **Velvet**. He was a celebrated painter of flower, landscape, and mythological pictures.

Brum·mell |'brəməl|, George Bryan (1778–1840) English dandy; known as **Beau Brummell**. He was the arbiter of British fashion for the first decade and a half of the 19th century, owing his social position to his friendship with the Prince Regent.

Brundt·land |'brənt,lənd|, Gro Harlem (1939–) Norwegian Labor stateswoman and prime minister (1981, 1986–89, and 1990–96). As Norway's first woman prime minister, she chaired the World Commission on Environment and Development (known as the Brundtland Commission), which produced the report *Our Common Future* in 1987.

Bru·nel |brə'nel| Family of English engineers, including French-born **Sir Marc Isambard Brunel** (1769–1849). He introduced mass-production machinery to the Portsmouth dockyard and designed other machines for woodworking, bootmaking, knitting, and printing. He also worked to construct the first tunnel under the Thames (1825–43). His son, **Isambard Kingdom Brunel** (1806–59), was chief engineer of the Great Western Railway. His achievements include designing the Clifton suspension bridge (1829–30) and the first transatlantic steamship, the *Great Western* (1838).

Bru·nel·les·chi |,broōnl-'eskē|, Filippo (1377–1446) Italian architect; born *Filippo di Ser Brunellesco*. He is especially noted for the dome of Florence cathedral (1420–61), which he raised without the use of temporary supports. He is often credited with the Renaissance "discovery" of perspective.

Bru·no |'broōnō|, Frank (1961–) English heavyweight boxing champion. Full name *Franklin Ray Bruno*.

Bru·no |'broōnō|, Giordano (1548–1600) Italian philosopher. He was a follower of Hermes Trismegistus and a supporter of the heliocentric Copernican view of the solar system. Bruno was tried by the Inquisition for heresy and burned at the stake.

Bru·no |'broōnō|, St. (*c.* 1030–1101) German-born French churchman. In 1084 he withdrew to the mountains of Chartreuse and founded the Carthusian order at La Grande Chartreuse. Feast day, October 6.

Bru·ton |'broōtən|, John (Gerard) (1947–) Irish Fine Gael statesman and Taoiseach (prime minister) (1994–97).

Bru·tus |'broōtəs|, Lucius Junius (6th century BC) legendary founder of the Roman Republic. Traditionally he led a popular uprising, after the rape of Lucretia, against the king (his uncle) and drove him from Rome. He and the father of Lucretia were elected as the first consols of the Republic (509 BC).

Bru·tus |'boōtəs|, Marcus Junius (85–42 BC) Roman senator. With Cassius he led the conspirators who assassinated Julius Caesar in 44 BC. They were defeated by Caesar's supporters, Antony and Octavian, at the battle of Philippi in 42 BC, after which Brutus committed suicide.

Bry·an |'brīən| U.S. political family, including **William Jennings Bryan** (1860–1925); known as **The Great Commoner**. His "Cross of Gold" speech (1896) won him the Democratic nomination for the U.S. presidency, and he was nominated and defeated two other times (1900 and 1908). He was the prosecutor of evolutionist John T. Scopes and had notable debates with Clarence Darrow (1925). His brother, **Charles Wayland Bryan** (1867–1945), served as governor of Nebraska (1923–25) and was a Democratic vice presidential candidate in 1924.

Bry·ant |'brīənt|, Lane (1879–1951) U.S. businesswoman, born in Lithuania. Born *Lena Himmelstein Bryant*. She founded Lane Bryant Apparel, which specializes in women's garments in larger sizes.

Bry·ant |'brīənt|, Paul William (1913–83) U.S. college football coach. Known as **Bear**. He set a record for most career wins (323) for a collegiate football coach.

Bry·ant |'brīənt|, William Cullen (1794–1878) U.S. poet and editor. He was co-owner and editor of the *New York Evening Post* (1829–78); his poems "Thanatopsis" and "An Indian at the Burial Place of His Fathers" established him as the leading poet of his time.

Bryn·ner |'brinər|, Yul (1920–85) U.S. actor, born in Russia. Born *Taidje Khan*. He is best known as the king of Siam in the musical *The King and I*, a role he performed on stage more than 4,500 times (1951–85). Notable movies: *The King and I* (1956, Academy Award) and *The Magnificent Seven* (1960).

Buat·ta, Mario (1935–   ) U.S. interior designer. Known as the "prince of chintz," with Mark Hampton, he redecorated Blair House in Washington, D.C. (1985).

Buber, Martin (1878–1965) Israeli religious philosopher, born in Austria. In his existentialist work *I and Thou* (1923), he argues that religious experience involves reciprocal relationships with a personal subject, rather than knowledge of some "thing."

Bub·ka |'bəbkə|, Sergei (1963–   ) Ukrainian pole vaulter. A six-time world champion and Olympic gold medalist (1991), he became the first man to clear 20 feet both indoors and out (1991).

Buch·an |'bəkən|, Alexander (1829–1907) Scottish meteorologist. He wrote a textbook on meteorology and produced maps and tables of atmospheric circulation, and of ocean currents and temperatures, based largely on information gathered on the voyage of HMS *Challenger* in 1872–6.

Buch·an |'bəkən|, John, 1st Baron Tweedsmuir (1875–1940) Scottish novelist. His adventure stories feature recurring heroes such as Richard Hannay. Notable works: *The Thirty-Nine Steps* (1915).

Bu·chan·an |byoo'kænən|, James see box.

Bu·chan·an |byoo'kænən|, Pat (1938–   ) U.S. journalist. Full name *Patrick Joseph Buchanan*. Noted for his political conservatism, he has been a syndicated newspaper columnist, radio commentator, and cohost of a television forum of political discussion.

Buch·ner |'booкHnər|, Eduard (1860–1917) German organic chemist. He studied the chemistry of alcoholic fermentation and identified several enzymes, notably zymase. Nobel Prize for Chemistry (1907).

Buch·wald |'bək,wawld|, Art (1925–   )

Buchanan, James
15th U.S. president

Life dates: 1791–1868
Place of birth: Stony Batter, Pennsylvania
Mother: Elizabeth Speer Buchanan
Father: James Buchanan
Wife: none
Children: none
College/University: Dickinson College
Military service: Company of Dragoons, War of 1812
Career: Lawyer; writer
Political career: Pennsylvania legislature; U.S. House of Representatives; minister to Russia; U.S. Senate; minister to Great Britain; U.S. secretary of state; president
Party: Federalist (till 1824); Democratic
Home state: Pennsylvania
Opponents in presidential race: John Charles Frémont; Millard Fillmore
Term of office: March 4, 1857–March 3, 1861
Vice president: John C. Breckinridge
Notable events of presidency: Panic of 1857; Pony Express; raid by John Brown on Harper's Ferry; Dred Scott decision; Minnesota admitted as the 32nd state, Oregon admitted as the 33rd state; Kansas admitted as the 34th state; secession of South Carolina, Mississippi, Florida, Alabama, Georgia, Louisiana, and Texas from the Union; Confederate States of America organized
Other achievements: Admitted to the Pennsylvania bar; co-author of proslavery Ostend Manifesto calling for immediate acquisition of Cuba
Place of burial: Lancaster, Pennsylvania

U.S. journalist and author. A syndicated columnist and 1982 Pulitzer Prize winner, he wrote *I Am Not A Crook* (1974) and *I Think I Don't Remember* (1987).

Buck |bək|, Pearl S. (1892–1973) U.S. writer; full name *Pearl Sydenstricker Buck*. Her upbringing and work in China inspired her earliest novels, including *The Good Earth* (Pulitzer Prize, 1931). Nobel Prize for Literature (1938).

Buck·land |'bəklənd|, William (1784–1856) English geologist. He helped to redefine geology, correlating deposits and associated fossils with former conditions, and developed the idea of an ice age. He was the first to describe and name a dinosaur (*Megalosaurus*), in 1824.

Buck·ley |'bəklē|, William F., Jr. (1925–) U.S. journalist and author. Full name *William Frank Buckley, Jr.*. Founder of the politically conservative *National Review* magazine (1955), he has hosted the television discussion program "Firing Line" since 1966.

Bud·dha |'bōōdə| Often **the Buddha**, a title given to the founder of Buddhism, Siddartha Gautama (*c.* 563–*c.* 460 BC). Born an Indian prince, he renounced wealth and family to become an ascetic, and after achieving enlightenment while meditating, taught all who came to learn from him.

Budge |bəj|, Don (1915–) U.S. tennis champion; born *John Donald Budge*. He was the first to win the four major singles championships, the "Grand Slam"—Australia, France, Wimbledon, and the U.S.—in one year (1938).

Bu·ell |'byōōl|, Marjorie (1904–93) U.S. cartoonist. She created "Little Lulu," originally a panel in the *Saturday Evening Post*.

Buf·fa·lo Bill |'bəfə,lō'bil| (1846–1917) U.S. showman; born *William Frederick Cody*. He gained his nickname for killing 4,280 buffalo in eight months to feed the Union Pacific Railroad workers, and subsequently devoted his career to his traveling Wild West Show.

Buf·fett |'bəfət|, Jimmy (1946–) U.S. musician and author. He is known for the hit song "Margaritaville."

Buf·fett |'bəfət|, Warren Edward (1930–) U.S. businessman. He is the CEO of Berkshire Hathaway and an influential board member of Salomon Brothers.

Buf·fon |,byōō'fōn|, Georges-Louis Leclerc, Comte de (1707–88) French naturalist. A founder of paleontology, he emphasized the unity of all living species, minimizing the apparent differences between animals and plants. He produced a compilation of the animal kingdom, the *Histoire Naturelle*, which had reached thirty-six volumes by the time of his death.

Bu·ick |'byōōik|, David Dunbar (1854–1929) U.S. inventor and manufacturer. He formed the Buick Manufacturing Co. (1902) to build automobiles.

Bu·kha·rin |bōō'kär,yēn|, Nikolay (Ivanovich) (1888–1938) Russian revolutionary activist and theorist. Editor of *Pravda* (1918–29) and *Izvestia* (1934–37), a member of the Politburo (1924–29), and chairman of Comintern from 1926, he was executed in one of Stalin's purges.

Bul·finch |'bōōl,finCH| U.S. family, including: **Charles Bulfinch** (1763–1844), an architect. He was the first professional architect in the U.S. and designed many buildings in his native Boston, including the Boston State House (1795–98). He succeeded Benjamin Henry Latrobe as architect of the National Capitol (1817–30). His son, **Thomas Bulfinch** (1796–1867), was an author. Notable works: *The Age of Fable* (1855) and *The Age of Chivalry* (1958).

Bul·ga·kov |,bōōl'gäkəf|, Mikhail Afanasyevich (1891–1940) Russian author. Notable novels: *The White Guard* (1925) and *The Master and Margarita* (1938). Such satirical works were banned and did not reemerge until the 1960s.

Bul·ga·nin |,bōōl'gänyēn|, Nikolay (Aleksandrovich) (1895–1975) Soviet statesman and chairman of the Council of Ministers (premier) (1955–58). He was vice-premier in the government of Georgi Malenkov in 1953, and in 1955 shared the premiership with Khrushchev.

Bult·mann |'bōōlt,män|, Rudolf (Karl) (1884–1976) German Lutheran theologian. He emphasized the "existential" rather than the historical significance of the Gospel story. Notable works: *The History of the Synoptic Tradition* (1921).

Bulwer-Lytton |,bōōlwər 'lit(ə)n| see LYTTON.

Bunche |'bənCH|, Ralph Johnson (1904–71) U.S. diplomat. Nobel Peace Prize, 1950.

Bu·nin |'bōōn,yin|, Ivan (Alekseyevich) (1870–1953) Russian poet and prose writer. An opponent of modernism, he concentrated on the themes of peasant life and love. Nobel Prize for Literature (1933, the first Russian prizewinner).

Bun·sen |'bənsən|, Robert Wilhelm Eberhard (1811–99) German chemist. With Gustav Kirchhoff he pioneered spectroscopy, detecting new elements (caesium and rubidium) and determining the composition of many substances and of the sun and stars. He designed numerous items of chemical apparatus, notably the Bunsen burner (1855).

Bun·shaft |'bən,ʃæft|, Gordon (1909–90) U.S. architect. He is best known for his use of the International style in corporate architecture. Notable designs: Pepsi-Cola Building (1960) in New York City, and the Hirshhorn Museum and Sculpture Garden (1974) in Washington, D.C.

Bu·ñu·el |,bōōnyə'wel|, Luis (1900–83) Spanish movie director. Influenced by surrealism, he wrote and directed his first movie, *Un Chien andalou* (1928), jointly with Salvador Dali. Other notable movies: *Belle de jour* (1967) and *The Discreet Charm of the Bourgeoisie* (1972).

Bun·yan |'bənyən|, John (1628–88) English writer. A Nonconformist, he was imprisoned twice for unlicensed preaching, during which time he wrote his spiritual autobiography, *Grace Abounding* (1666), and began his major work, *The Pilgrim's Progress* (1678–84).

Buon·a·parte |,bwōnä'pärte| see BONAPARTE.

Buo·nar·ro·ti |,bwōnä'rōtē|, Michelangelo see MICHELANGELO.

Bur·bage |'bərbij|, Richard (*c.* 1567–1619) English actor. He was the creator of most of Shakespeare's great tragic roles: Hamlet, Othello, Lear, and Richard III, and was also associated with the building of the Globe Theatre.

Bur·bank |'bər,bæNGk|, Luther (1849–1926) U.S. horticulturist. His experiments in cross-breeding led to new types and improved varieties of plants, especially the Shasta daisy and the potato.

Burck·hal·ter |'bərk,hawltər|, Joseph H. (1912–   ) U.S. inventor. With Robert J. Seiwald, he developed dyes that could be utilized in the diagnosis of infectious diseases.

Bur·don |'bərdən|, Eric (1941–   ) British rock singer and guitarist.

Bur·ger |'bərgər|, Warren Earl (1907–95) U.S. Supreme Court justice (1969–86). Appointed as chief justice to the Supreme Court by President Richard Nixon, he was a conservative and an advocate of judicial restraint.

Bur·gess |'bərjəs|, Anthony (1917–93) English novelist and critic; pseudonym of *John Anthony Burgess Wilson*. One of his best-known novels is *A Clockwork Orange* (1962), a disturbing, futuristic vision of juvenile delinquency, violence, and high technology. Other notable works: *The Malayan Trilogy* (1956–59) and *Earthly Powers* (1980).

Bur·gess |'bərjəs|, Edward (1848–91) U.S. naval architect. He designed the America's Cup winners *Puritan* (1850), *Mayflower* (1886), and *Volunteer* (1887).

Bur·gess |'bərjəs|, Thornton Waldo (1874–1965) U.S. author of children's books. He wrote the *Old Mother West Wind* series (1910–18), as well as hundreds of stories about Peter Rabbit.

Burgh·ley |'bərlē|, William Cecil, 1st Baron (1520–98) English statesman. Secretary of State to Queen Elizabeth I 1558–72 and Lord High Treasurer 1572–98, he was the queen's most trusted councilor and minister.

Bur·goyne |'bər,goin|, John (1722–92) English general and dramatist; known as **Gentleman Johnny**. He surrendered to the Americans at Saratoga (1777) in the Revolutionary War.

Burke |bərk|, Edmund (1729–97) British man of letters and Whig politician. Burke wrote on the issues of political emancipation and moderation, notably with respect to Roman Catholics and the American colonies.

Burke |bərk|, John (1787–1848) Irish genealogical and heraldic writer. He compiled the first edition of *Burke's Peerage* (1826), still regarded as the authoritative guide to the British aristocracy.

Burke |bərk|, Robert O'Hara (1820–61) Irish explorer. He led a successful expedition from south to north across Australia in the company of William Wills and two others—the first white men to make this journey. On the return journey, however, Burke, Wills, and a third companion died of starvation.

Burke |bərk|, William (1792–1829)

Irish murderer. He was a bodysnatcher operating in Edinburgh with his accomplice **William Hare**. Burke was hanged for his crimes.

Bur·leigh |'bərlē|, Harry Thacker (1866–1949) U.S. singer and composer. He is known especially for his arrangements of negro spirituals.

Burne-Jones |'bərn'jōnz|, Sir Edward (Coley) (1833–98) English painter and designer. His work, which included tapestry and stained-glass window designs, reflected his interest in medieval and literary themes and is typical of the later Pre-Raphaelite style. Notable paintings: *The Golden Stairs* (1880) and *The Mirror of Venus* (1867–77).

Bur·nett |bər'net|, Carol (1936–) U.S. actress. A five-time Emmy Award winner, she is best known for the television program "The Carol Burnett Show" (1966–77).

Bur·nett |bər'net|, Frances (Eliza) Hodgson (1849–1924) British-born U.S. novelist. She is remembered chiefly for her novels for children, including *Little Lord Fauntleroy* (1886), *A Little Princess* (1905), and *The Secret Garden* (1911).

Bur·ney |'bərnē|, Fanny (1752–1840) English novelist; born *Frances Burney*. Notable works: *Evelina* (1778), *Cecilia* (1782), and *Letters and Diaries* (1846).

Burn·ham |'bərnəm|, Daniel H. (1846–1912) U.S. architect. Notable designs: Flatiron Building (1901) in New York City, and Union Railroad Station (1909) in Washington, D.C.

Burns |bərnz|, George (1896–1996) U.S. comedian. Born *Nathan Birnbaum*. Known for his comedy partnership with his wife Gracie Allen (*c.* 1905–64), he won an Academy Award for the movie *The Sunshine Boys* (1975).

Burns |bərnz|, Ken (1953–) U.S. filmmaker. He has created American historical documentary epics, including *The Civil War* (1990) and *Baseball* (1994).

Burns |bərnz|, Robert (1759–96) Scottish poet, best known for poems such as "The Jolly Beggars" (1786) and "Tam o' Shanter" (1791), and for old Scottish songs that he collected, including "Auld Lang Syne". Burns Night celebrations

are held in Scotland and elsewhere on his birthday, January 25.

Burn·side |'bərn,sīd|, Ambrose Everett (1824–81) U.S. army officer. He was appointed General of the Army of the Potomac (1862), but his incompetence at the Battle of Fredericksburg (1862) led to his transfer to Ohio.

Bur·pee |'bər,pē|, Washington Atlee (1858–1915) U.S. businessman. He began a mail-order poultry business at age 17, and incorporated the W. Atlee Burpee & Co. (1878), which sold livestock and farm seed.

Burr |bər|, Aaron (1756–1836) U.S. statesman. In 1804, while vice-president, he killed his rival Alexander Hamilton in a duel. He then plotted to form an independent administration in Mexico and was tried for treason but acquitted.

Bur·ra |'bərə|, Edward (1905–76) English painter, noted for his low-life subjects, as in *Harlem* (1934), and the bizarre and fantastic, as in *Dancing Skeletons* (1934).

Bur·roughs |'bərōz|, Edgar Rice (1875–1950) U.S. novelist and writer of science fiction. He is chiefly remembered for his adventure stories about Tarzan, who first appeared in *Tarzan of the Apes* (1914).

Bur·roughs |'bərōz|, William (Seward) (1914–97) U.S. novelist. In the 1940s he became addicted to heroin, and his best-known writing, for example *Junkie* (1953) and *The Naked Lunch* (1959), deals with life as a drug addict in a unique, surreal style.

Burt |bərt|, Cyril (Lodowic) (1883–1971) English psychologist. Using studies of identical twins, he claimed that intelligence is inherited, but he was later accused of fabricating data.

Bur·ton |'bərtən|, Harold Hitz (1888–1964) U.S. Supreme Court Justice (1945–58).

Bur·ton |'bərtən|, Richard (1925–84) Welsh actor; born *Richard Jenkins*. He often co-starred with Elizabeth Taylor (to whom he was twice married). Notable movies: *The Spy Who Came in from the Cold* (1966) and *Who's Afraid of Virginia Woolf* (1966).

Bur·ton |'bərtən|, Sir Richard (Francis)

(1821–90) English explorer, anthropologist, and translator. He and John Hanning Speke were the first Europeans to see Lake Tanganyika (1858). Notable translations: the *Arabian Nights* (1885–8), the *Kama Sutra* (1883), and *The Perfumed Garden* (1886).

Bur·ton |'bərtən|, William Meriam (1865–1954) U.S. chemist. He developed a thermal process of manufacturing gasoline (1912). He was president of the Standard Oil Co. (1918–27).

Bu·sca·glia |ˌbəs'kæliə|, Leo (1924–98) U.S. educator and author. Full name *Felice Leonardo Buscaglia*. His works include *The Fall of Freddie the Leaf* (1982) and *Loving Each Other: The Challenge of Human Relationships* (1984).

Busch |bʊsH|, Adolphus (1839–1913) U.S. businessman, born in Germany. As president of the Anheuser-Busch Brewing Association (1879–1913), he was a pioneer in the pasteurization of beer and introduced the Budweiser brand.

Bush |bʊsH|, George (Herbert Walker) see box. **Barbara Pierce Bush** (1925–), wife of George Bush and U.S. first lady (1989–93).

Bush·mil·ler |'bʊsH,milər|, Ernie (1905–82) U.S. cartoonist, comedy writer, and animator. Full name *Ernest Paul Bushmiller*. He created the comic strips "Fritzi Ritz" and the internationally syndicated "Nancy."

Bush·nell |'bʊsH,nel|, David (1742?–1824) U.S. inventor. He invented a submarine that was first used in warfare (1775) called "Bushnell's Turtle."

Bu·so·ni |,bʊ'zōnē|, Ferruccio (Benvenuto) (1866–1924) Italian composer, conductor, and pianist. As a composer he is best known for his piano works and his unfinished opera *Doktor Faust* (1925).

Buss |bəs|, Frances Mary (1827–94) English educationist. She was in charge of the North London Collegiate School for Ladies (1850–94) and campaigned for higher education for women with her friend Dorothea Beale.

Bute |byōōt|, John Stuart, 3rd Earl of (1713–92) Scottish courtier and Tory statesman, prime minister (1762–63).

Bu·the·le·zi |'bʊōdə,lāzē|, Chief Mangosuthu (Gatsha) (1928–) South

---

Bush, George Herbert Walker
41st U.S. president

Life dates: 1924–
Place of birth: Milton, Massachusetts
Mother: Dorothy Walker Bush
Father: Prescott Sheldon Bush
Wife: Barbara Pierce Bush
Children: George, Robin, John, Neil, Marvin, Dorothy
College/University: Yale
Military service: U.S. Navy pilot
Career: Businessman
Political career: U.S. House of Representatives; ambassador to the United Nations; director of the Central Intelligence Agency; vice president (under Reagan); president
Party: Republican
Home state: Texas
Opponent in presidential races: Michael Dukakis; Bill Clinton
Term of office: Jan. 20, 1989–Jan. 20, 1993
Vice president: Dan (James Danforth) Quayle
Notable events of presidency: Americans with Disabilities Act; Iraq's invasion of Kuwait and Persian Gulf War; Iran-Contra Affair
Other achievements: Distinguished Flying Cross and three air medals for combat in the Pacific in World War II

African politician. He became leader of the Inkatha movement in 1975 and minister of home affairs in 1994.

But·kus |'bətkəs|, Dick (1942–) U.S. football player. Elected to the Football Hall of Fame (1979).

But·ler |'bətlər|, Nicholas Murray (1862–1947) U.S. educator. He was organizer and first president of the New York College for Training of Teachers, now Teachers College, Columbia University. Nobel Peace Prize, 1931.

But·ler |'bətlər|, Pierce (1866–1939) U.S. Supreme Court Justice (1922–39).

But·ler[1] |'bətlər|, Samuel (1612–80) English poet, most notable for his three-part satirical poem *Hudibras* (1663–78).

But·ler[2] |'bətlər|, Samuel (1835–1902) English novelist. Notable works: *Erewhon* (1872), *Erewhon Revisited* (1901), and *The Way of All Flesh* (1903).

But·ter·field |'bətər,fēld|, William (1814–1900) English architect, an exponent of the Gothic revival. Notable designs: All Saints', Margaret Street, London (1850–59) and Keble College, Oxford (1867–83).

But·ter·ick |'bətər,ik|, Ebenezer (1826–1903) U.S. tailor and inventor. He invented the dress pattern made of tissue paper (1859).

But·ton |'bətn|, Dick (1929–) U.S. figure skater. Full name *Richard Button*. He was five-time world champion (1948–52) and won two Olympic gold medals (1948, 1952).

But·tons |'bətnz|, Red (1919–) U.S. actor. Born *Aaron Chwatt*. Notable movies: *Sayonara* (1957, Academy Award).

Bux·te·hu·de |bəkstə'hoōdə|, Dietrich (1637–1707) Danish organist and composer. Working in Lübeck, Germany, he wrote mainly for the organ.

By·as |'biəs|, Don (1912–72) U.S. jazz tenor saxophonist. Born *Carlos Wesley*. He played with various bands, including those led by Lionel Hampton, Coleman Hawkins, Dizzy Gillespie, Cout Basie, and Duke Ellington, as well as his own.

By·att |'biət|, A. S. (1936–) English novelist and literary critic; born *Antonia Susan Byatt*. She is the elder sister of Margaret Drabble. Notable novels: *The Virgin in the Garden* (1978) and *Possession* (1990).

Byrd |bərd|, Richard (Evelyn) (1888–1957) American explorer, naval officer, and aviator. He claimed to have made the first aircraft flight over the North Pole (1926, although his actual course has been disputed. He was the first to fly over the South Pole (1929).

Byrd |bərd|, Robert (1917–) U.S. senator from West Virginia (1950–52; 1959–).

Byrd |bərd|, William (1543–1623) English composer. He was joint organist of the Chapel Royal with Tallis and is famous for his Latin masses and his Anglican Great Service.

Byrnes |bərnz|, James F. (1879–1972) U.S. Supreme Court Justice (1941–42), politician, and author. He served as director of the Office of Economic Stabilization (1942–43), as director of war mobilization (1943–45); and as secretary of state (1945–47).

By·ron |'birən|, George Gordon, 6th Baron (1788–1824) English poet. Byron's poetry exerted considerable influence on the romantic movement, particularly on the Continent. Having joined the fight for Greek independence, he died of malaria before seeing serious action. Notable works: *Childe Harold's Pilgrimage* (1812–18) and *Don Juan* (1819–24)

Cc

Ca·bal·lé |kə'bälyä; kəbäl'yä|, Montserrat (1933–) Spanish operatic soprano.

Cab·ell |'kæbəl|, James Branch (1879–1958) U.S. author. He wrote novels, poetry, criticism, and nonfiction, including the 18-volume *Biography of Manuel* (1917–29).

Ca·be·za de Va·ca |kä,besə de 'väkə|, Á Núñez (c. 1490–c. 1560) Spanish explorer. He began an expedition to Florida in 1528 that eventually led him across the Southwest to the Gulf of California.

Cab·ot |'kæbət|, George (1752–1823) U.S. businessman and senator from Massachusetts (1791–96).

Cab·ot |'kæbət|, Italian explorers, including: **John Cabot** (c. 1450–c. 1499). While in the service of England, he sailed from Bristol in 1497 in search of Asia, but in fact discovered the mainland of North America. His son, **Sebastian Cabot** (c. 1476–1557), accompanied his father on his voyage in 1497 and made further voyages after the latter's death, most notably to Brazil and the River Plate (1526).

Ca·bri·ni |kə'brēnē|, St. Frances Xavier (1850–1917) U.S. religious leader, born in Italy. Born *Maria Francesca Cabrini*; known as **Mother Cabrini**. She became the first American saint in 1946.

Cad·bury |'kædbərē| George (1839–1922) and **Richard** (1835–99) English cocoa and chocolate manufacturers and social reformers.

Cade |kād|, Jack (died 1450) Irish rebel. Full name *John Cade*. In 1450 he assumed the name of Mortimer and led the Kentish rebels against Henry VI. They occupied London for three days and executed the treasurer of England and the sheriff of Kent.

Ca·dil·lac |'kædə,læk|, Antoine Laumet de La Mothe (1658–1730) French soldier and colonialist. He founded military posts at Mackinac (1694) and Detroit; from 1713 to 1716 he was governor of Louisiana.

Caed·mon |'kædmən| (7th century) Anglo-Saxon monk and poet, said to have been an illiterate herdsman inspired in a vision to compose poetry on biblical themes. The only authentic fragment of his work is a song in praise of the Creation, quoted by Bede.

Caen |kän|, Herb (1916–97) U.S. journalist and author. He wrote for San Francisco newspapers (1936–58) and authored numerous books. He received a special Pulitzer citation for journalism in 1996.

Caesar, Gaius Julius (100–44 BC) Roman general and statesman. He established the First Triumvirate with Pompey and Crassus (60), and became consul in 59. Between 58 and 51 he fought the Gallic Wars, invaded Britain (55–54), and acquired immense power. After civil war with Pompey, which ended in Pompey's defeat at Pharsalus (48), Caesar became dictator of the Roman Empire; he was murdered on the Ides (15th) of March in a conspiracy led by Brutus and Cassius.

Cae·sar |'sēzər|, Sid (1922–) U.S. actor. He was one of the comedy stars featured on television's "Your Show of Shows" (1950–54).

Cage |kāj|, John (Milton) (1912–92) U.S. composer, pianist, and writer. He was notable for his experimental approach, which included the use of aleatory music and periods of silence.

Cag·ney |'kægnē|, James (1899–1986) U.S. actor. He is chiefly remembered for playing gangster roles in movies such as *The Public Enemy* (1931).

Cahn |kän|, Sammy (1913–93) U.S. lyricist. Notable songs: "High Hopes," "Love and Marriage," and "The Second Time Around."

Cain |kän|, James Mallahan (1892–1977) U.S. novelist and journalist. Notable works: *The Postman Always Rings Twice* (1934) and *Double Indemnity* (1936).

Caine |kän|, Sir Michael (1933–) English actor. Born *Maurice Micklewhite*. Notable movies: *The Ipcress File* (1965) and *Hannah and Her Sisters* (1986, Academy Award).

Ca·lam·i·ty Jane |ˌkəˈlæmitē ˈjān| (c. 1852–1903) U.S. frontierswoman. Born *Martha Jane Cannary*. She was noted for her skill at shooting and riding.

Cal·de·cott |ˈkäldəˌkät|, Randolph (1846–86) English graphic artist and watercolor painter. He is best known for his illustrations for children's books.

Cal·der |ˈkäldər|, Alexander (1898–1976) U.S. sculptor and painter. He introduced movement into sculpture, making the first pieces to be called "mobiles." His static sculptures are known by contrast as "stabiles."

Cal·de·rón de la Bar·ca |ˌkäldəˈrōn de lä ˈbärkə|, Pedro (1600–81) Spanish dramatist and poet. He wrote some 120 plays and more than 70 of them religious dramas.

Cal·de·rone |ˌkäldəˈrōn|, Mary Steichen (1904–98) U.S. physician. The daughter of Edward Steichen, she was an advocate of family planning and sexual education in schools and communities. She cofounded the Sex Information and Education Council of the U.S. (SIECUS, 1964) and wrote *Talking With Your Child About Sex* (1982).

Cald·well |ˈkawldwel|, Erskine Preston (1903–87) U.S. novelist and short-story writer. He reproduced the dialect of poor whites in his realistic, earthy, and popular novels, such as *Tobacco Road* (1932).

Cal·houn |kælˈho͞on|, John Caldwell (1782–1850) U.S. politician. A South Carolina Democrat, he served as U.S. vice president (1825–32) and in the U.S. Senate (1832–1844).

Ca·lig·u·la |kəˈligyələ| (AD 12–41) Roman emperor (37–41). Born *Gaius Julius Caesar Germanicus*. His reign was notorious for its tyrannical excesses.

Cal·i·sher |ˈkælisHər|, Hortense (1911–) U.S. author.

Cal·la·ghan |ˈkælə,hæn|, (Leonard) James, Baron Callaghan of Cardiff (1912–) British Labour statesman; prime minister (1976–79).

Cal·las |ˈkæləs|, Maria (1923–77) U.S.-born operatic soprano, of Greek parentage. Born *Maria Cecilia Anna Kalageropoulos*. She was a coloratura soprano whose bel canto style of singing was especially suited to early Italian opera.

Ca·lles |ˈkīyäs|, Plutarco Elías (1877–1945) Mexican president (1924–28). Opposed to the the the policies of President Cardenas, he was forced into exile in the U.S. (1936–41).

Cal·ley |ˈkælē|, William Laws, Jr. (1943–) U.S. army officer. He was convicted in 1971 of the premeditated murder of 22 South Vietnamese at My Lai (1968).

Cal·lic·ra·tes |ˌkəˈlikrətēz| (5th century BC) Greek architect. He was the leading architect in Periclean Athens, and with Ictinus designed the Parthenon (447–438 BC).

Cal·lil |kəˈlil|, Carmen (Thérèse) (1938–) Australian publisher. She founded the feminist publishing house Virago in 1972.

Cal·lim·a·chus |kəˈliməkəs| (c. 305–c. 240 BC) Greek poet and scholar. He is famed for his hymns and epigrams, and was head of the library at Alexandria.

Cal·lo·way |ˈkæləwä|, Cab (1907–94) U.S. jazz singer and bandleader. Full name *Cabell Calloway*. He was famous for his style of scat singing and for songs such as "Minnie the Moocher" (1931).

Cal·vert |ˈkælvərt| British and colonial American family, including **George Calvert, 1st Baron Baltimore** (c. 1580–1632), who was granted the territory of what is now Maryland but died before the charter was issued. The charter was instead issued to his son, **Cecilius Calvert, 2nd Baron Baltimore** (1605–75), who established the colony of Maryland. His brother **Leonard Calvert** (1606–47) was the first governor (1634–47) of the province of Maryland. **Charles Calvert, 3rd Baron Baltimore** (1637–1715) was the son of Cecilius Calvert. He served as governor of Maryland (1661–75) and as proprietor (1675–89).

Cal·vin |ˈkælvən|, John (1509–64) French Protestant theologian and reformer. He established the first Presbyterian government in Geneva (1536–38). His *Institutes of the Christian Religion* (1536) was the first systematic account of reformed Christian doctrine.

Cal·vin |ˈkælvən|, Melvin (1911–97)

U.S. biochemist. He investigated photosynthesis and discovered the cycle of reactions (the *Calvin cycle*) that constitute the dark reaction. Nobel Prize for Chemistry (1961).

Cal·vi·no |kälˈvēnō|, Italo (1923–85) Italian novelist and short-story writer, born in Cuba. His later works, such as *If on a Winter's Night a Traveler* (1979), are associated with magic realism.

Cam·by·ses II |kæmˈbisēz| (died 522 BC) King of Persia (529–522 BC), son of Cyrus. He is chiefly remembered for his conquest of Egypt in 525 BC.

Cam·er·on |ˈkæmrən| U.S. political family, including: **Simon Cameron** (1799–1889), a financier and U.S. senator (1845–49, 1857–61, 1867–77). He established and maintained control of the Republican party machine in Pennsylvania. **James Donald Cameron** (1833–1918), the son of Simon Cameron, was U.S. secretary of war (1876–77) and a U.S. senator from Pennsylvania (1877–97).

Cam·er·on |ˈkæmrən|, James (1954–) U.S. director, born in Canada. Notable movies: *The Terminator* (1984) and *Titanic* (1997, Academy Award).

Cam·er·on |ˈkæmrən|, Julia Margaret (1815–79) English photographer, credited with being the first to use soft-focus techniques. Her work often reflects the influence of contemporary painting, especially that of the Pre-Raphaelites.

Ca·mõ·es |kəˈmoisH|, Luis (Vaz) de (*c.* 1524–80) Portuguese poet. Also **Camoëns**. His most famous work, *The Lusiads* (1572), describes Vasco da Gama's discovery of the sea route to India.

Camp |kæmp|, Walter Chauncey (1859–1925) U.S. football coach. One of the first to play American football, he coached at Yale and was influential in shaping the rules of the sport.

Cam·pa·nel·la |ˌkæmpəˈnelə|, Roy (1921–93) U.S. baseball player. Known as **Campy**. Elected to Baseball Hall of Fame (1969).

Camp·bell |ˈkæmbəl|, Earl (1955–) U.S. football player. Awarded the Heisman Trophy (1977).

Camp·bell |ˈkæmbəl|, John A. (1811–89) U.S. Supreme Court justice (1853–61). He served as assistant secretary of war in the Confederate cabinet (1862–65).

Camp·bell |ˈkæmbəl|, Joseph (1817–1900) U.S. businessman. He entered the canning business in 1869 and introduced the Campbell Soup Co. in 1898.

Camp·bell |ˈkæmbəl|, Mrs. Patrick (1865–1940) English actress. Born *Beatrice Stella Tanner*. George Bernard Shaw wrote the part of Eliza Doolittle in *Pygmalion* (1914) for her.

Camp·bell |ˈkæmbəl|, Roy (1901–57) South African poet. Full name *Ignatius Royston Dunnachie Campbell*. His long poem *Flowering Rifle* (1939) shows strong right-wing sympathies. He fought for Franco's side in the Spanish Civil War.

Camp·bell |ˈkæmbəl|, Thomas (1777–1844) Scottish poet. He published *Gertrude of Wyoming* (1809) among other volumes of verse, and is known for his patriotic lyrics such as "The Battle of Hohenlinden" and "Ye Mariners of England."

Campbell-Bannerman |ˈkæmbəl ˈbænərmən|, Sir Henry (1836–1908) British Liberal statesman and prime minister (1905–08).

Cam·pi·on |ˈkæmpēən|, St. Edmund (1540–81) English Jesuit priest and martyr. Feast day, December 1.

Cam·pi·on |ˈkæmpēən|, Jane (1954–) New Zealand movie director and screenwriter. Notable works: *An Angel at My Table* (1990) and *The Piano* (1993).

Cam·ras |ˈkæmrəs|, Marvin (1916–95) U.S. inventor. In the 1930s, he developed a wire recorder. His inventions revolutionized the field of electronic communications.

Ca·mus |käˈmoo|, Albert (1913–60) French novelist, dramatist, and essayist, closely aligned with existentialism. Notable works: *The Outsider* (novel, 1942), *The Plague* (novel, 1947), and *The Rebel* (essay, 1951). Nobel Prize for Literature (1957).

Ca·na·let·to |ˌkänəˈletō| (1697–1768) Italian painter. Born *Giovanni Antonio Canale*. He is well known for his paintings of Venetian festivals and scenery.

Can·dler |'kæn(də)lər|, Asa Griggs (1851–1929) U.S. manufacturer and politician. He bought the formula for Coca-Cola (1887) and was president and organizer of the Coca-Cola Co. (until 1916); after selling the company he became mayor of Atlanta (1917–18).

Can·dolle |kæn'dawl|, Augustin-Pyrame de (1778–1841) Swiss botanist. He introduced a new scheme of plant classification based on morphological characteristics, which prevailed for many years.

Can·dy |'kændē|, John (1950–94) U.S. comedian, born in Canada. He acted in television and movies, including *The Blues Brothers* (1980) and *Planes, Trains, and Automobiles* (1987).

Ca·net·ti |kə'netē|, Elias (1905–94) Bulgarian-born British writer. Notable works: *Auto-da-Fé* (1936) and *Crowds and Power* (1960). Nobel Prize for Literature (1981).

Ca·niff |kə'nif|, Milton Arthur (1907–88) U.S. cartoonist. He created two of the longest-running comic strips in daily newspaper syndication history, "Terry and the Pirates" and "Steve Canyon."

Can·ion |'kænyən|, Joseph Rod (1945–) U.S. businessman. He founded Compaq Computers (1982).

Can·more |'kaenmawr| the nickname of Malcolm III of Scotland (see MALCOLM).

Can·ning |'kæniNG|, George (1770–1827) British Tory statesman; prime minister (1827).

Can·niz·za·ro |,kænəd'zärō|, Stanislao (1826–1910) Italian chemist. He revived Avogadro's hypothesis and used it to distinguish clearly between atoms and molecules, and to introduce the unified system of atomic and molecular weights.

Can·non |'kænən|, James W. (1852–1921) U.S. manufacturer. He began producing towels in 1894.

Ca·no·va |kə'nōvə|, Antonio (1757–1822) Italian sculptor, a leading exponent of neoclassicism. Notable works: *Cupid and Psyche* (1792) and *The Three Graces* (1813–16).

Can·tor |'kæntər|, Georg (1845–1918) Russian-born German mathematician. His work on numbers laid the foundations for the theory of sets and stimu-lated 20th-century exploration of number theory.

Ca·nute |kə'nyo͞ot| (died 1035) Danish king of England (1017–35), Denmark (1018–35), and Norway (1028–35), son of Sweyn I. Also **Cnut** or **Knut**.

Capability Brown see BROWN.

Ca·pek, Karel (1890–1938) Czech novelist and dramatist He is known for *R.U.R. (Rossum's Universal Robots)* (1920), which introduced the word *robot* to the English language, and *The Insect Play* (1921), written with his brother **Josef** (1887–1945).

Ca·pet |'kāpət; kä'pā|, Hugh (938–96) king of France 987–96, founder of the Capetian dynasty.

Ca·pone |kə'pōn|,Al (1899–1947) U.S. gangster. Full name *Alphonse Capone*; known as **Scarface**. He dominated organized crime in Chicago in the 1920s and was believed responsible for many murders, including the St. Valentine's Day Massacre. However, it was for federal income tax evasion that he was eventually imprisoned in 1931.

Ca·po·te |kə'pō,tē|, Truman (1924–84) U.S. writer. Born *Truman Streckfus Persons*. Notable works: *Breakfast at Tiffany's* (1958) and *In Cold Blood* (1966), a meticulous re-creation of a brutal multiple murder.

Capp |kæp|, Al (1909–79) U.S. cartoonist. Born *Alfred Gerald Caplin*. He is best known for his comic strip "Li'l Abner" (1934–1977).

Cap·ra |'kæprə|, Frank (1897–1991) Italian-born U.S. movie director. Notable movies: *It Happened One Night* (1934), *Arsenic and Old Lace* (1944), and *It's a Wonderful Life* (1946). He won six Academy Awards.

Ca·ra·cal·la |,kerə'kälə| (188–217) Roman emperor 211–17. Born *Septimius Bassanius*; later called *Marcus Aurelius Severus Antoninus Augustus*. In 212 he granted Roman citizenship to all free inhabitants of the Roman Empire.

Ca·rac·ta·cus |kə'ræktəkəs| variant spelling of CARATACUS.

Ca·rat·a·cus |kə'rätəkəs| (1st century AD) British chieftain, son of Cymbeline. Also **Caractacus**. He took part in the resistance to the Roman invasion of AD 43.

Ca·ra·vag·gio |ˌkerə'väjēō|, Michelangelo Merisi da (c. 1573–1610) Italian painter. An influential figure in the transition from late mannerism to baroque, he made use of naturalistic realism and dramatic light and shade.

Cár·de·nas |'kärdənəs|, Lázaro (1895–1970) Mexican revolutionary leader and president (1934–40).

Car·din |kär'dæn|, Pierre (1922–) French couturier, the first designer in the field of haute couture to show a collection of clothes for men as well as women.

Car·do·zo |kär'dōzō|, Benjamin Nathan (1870–1938) U.S. Supreme Court justice (1932–38).

Ca·rew |kə'rōō|, Rod (1945–) U.S. baseball player. Born *Rodney Cline Carew*. He was a seven-time American League batting champion.

Car·ey |'kerē|, George (Leonard) (1935–) English Anglican churchman, Archbishop of Canterbury from 1991. The controversial introduction of women priests into the Church of England was approved under his leadership.

Car·ey |'kerē|, Mariah (1970–) U.S. singer and songwriter. Grammy Awards (1991).

Carle |kärl|, Eric (1929–) U.S. author and illustrator of children's books. Notable works: The Very Busy Spider (1984).

Carl·son |'kärlsən|, Chester Floyd (1906–68) U.S. inventor. He invented the electrostatic "xerography" process (1938), the development of which gave rise to the Xerox Corp.

Carl·ton |'kärltn|, Effie (1857–1940) U.S. actress. Under the pen name **Effie Canning** she wrote the lullaby *Rock-a-Bye-Baby* (1887).

Carl·ton |'kärltn|, Steve (1944–) U.S. baseball player. Born *Steven Norman Carlton*. He was the first pitcher to win four Cy Young Awards (1972, 1977, 1980, 1982). Elected to Baseball Hall of Fame (1994).

Car·lyle |'kär,līl|, Thomas (1795–1881) Scottish historian and political philosopher. He established his reputation as a historian with his *History of the French Revolution* (1837). Influenced by German Romanticism, many of his works,

including *Sartor Resartus* (1833–34), celebrate the force of the "strong, just man" as against the degraded masses.

Car·mi·chael |'kär,mīkl|, Hoagy (1899–1981) U.S. jazz pianist, composer, and singer. Born *Howard Hoagland Carmichael*. His best-known songs include "Stardust" (1929), "Georgia on My Mind" (1930), and "In the Cool, Cool, Cool of the Evening" (1951).

Car·nap |'kärnəp|, Rudolf (1891–1970) German-born U.S. philosopher, a founding member of the logical positivist Vienna Circle. Notable works: *The Logical Structure of the World* (1928) and *The Logical Foundations of Probability* (1950).

Car·né |kär'nā|, Marcel (1906?–96) French movie director. He gained his reputation for the movies he made with the poet and scriptwriter **Jacques Prévert** (1900–77), notably *Le Jour se lève* (1939) and *Les Enfants du paradis* (1945).

Car·ne·gie |'kärnəgē; kär'negē|, Andrew (1835–1919) Scottish-born U.S. industrialist and philanthropist. He built up a fortune in the steel industry in the U.S., then retired from business in 1901 and devoted his wealth to charitable purposes, in particular libraries, education, and the arts.

Car·ne·gie |'kärnəgē; kär'negē|, Dale (1888–1955) U.S. lecturer and author. Born *Dale Carnagey*. He wrote *How to Win Friends and Influence People* (1936).

Car·ne·gie |'kärnəgē; kär'negē|, Hattie (1889–1956) U.S. fashion designer, born in Austria. Born *Henriette Kanengesier*. She popularized the "little Carnegie suit" and the simple black cocktail dress

Car·ney |'kärnē|, Art (1918–) U.S. actor. He played Ed Norton, upstairs neighbor to Ralph Cramden, on television's "The Honeymooners." Notable movies: *Harry and Tonto* (1974, Academy Award).

Car·ney |'kärnē|, Harry (Howell) (1910–74) U.S. jazz baritone saxophonist. He was the first and for many years the only soloist on his instrument.

Car·not |kär'nō|, Nicolas-Léonard-Sadi (1796–1832) French scientist. His work in analyzing the efficiency of steam engines was posthumously recognized as being of crucial importance to the theory of thermodynamics.

Ca·roth·ers |kə'rəTHərz|, Wallace Hume (1896–1937) U.S. industrial chemist. He developed the first successful synthetic rubber, neoprene, and the synthetic fiber nylon 6.6.

Car·pac·cio |kär'pätcHō|, Vittore (c. 1460–c. 1525) Italian painter noted especially for his paintings of Venice.

Car·pen·ter |'kärpəntər|, John Alden (1876–1951) U.S. composer. Works include the ballets *Krazy Kat* (1921) and *Skyscraper* (1923–24) and the suite *Jazz Orchestra Pieces* (1925–26).

Carr |kär|, Emily (1871–1945) Canadian painter and writer. Her paintings, inspired by the wilderness of British Columbia, often drew on motifs of American Indian folk art. From 1927 she came into contact with the Group of Seven and produced such expressionist works as *Forest Landscape II* and *Sky* (both 1934–35).

Car·rac·ci |kä'rätcHē| Italian painters. **Lidovico Carracci** (1555–1619) is remembered chiefly as a distinguished teacher. With his cousins **Annibale Carracci** (1560–1609) and **Agostino Carracci** (1557–1602) he established an academy at Bologna which was responsible for training many important painters. Annibale is is famed for the ceiling of the Farnese Gallery (1597–1600) in Rome; he developed a style that was the foundation of the Italian baroque and is also remembered for his invention of the caricature. Agostino was chiefly an engraver but he also worked with his brother in the Farnese Gallery.

Car·rel |'kerəl|, Alexis (1873–1944) French surgeon and biologist. He developed improved techniques for suturing arteries and veins, and carried out some of the first organ transplants. Nobel Prize for Physiology or Medicine (1912).

Car·re·ras |kə'rerəs|, José (1946–   ) Spanish operatic tenor.

Car·rère |kə'rer|, John Merven (1858–1911) U.S. architect, born in Brazil. He designed the Hotel Ponce de Leon (St. Augustine, Florida, 1887), the Carnegie Institution (Washington, D.C., 1906) and the New York Public Library (completed 1911).

Car·rey |'kerē|, Jim (1962–   ) U.S. actor, born in Canada. Notable movies: *Liar, Liar* (1996), *The Cable Guy* (1996), and *The Truman Show* (1997).

Car·ri·er |'kerēər|, Willis Haviland (1876–1950) U.S. engineer and inventor. He invented and developed air-conditioning technology and was the first to create an air-conditioning system for skyscrapers (1939).

Car·ring·ton |'keriNGtən|, Dora (1893–1932) English painter. She was a member of the Bloomsbury Group.

Car·roll |'kerəl|, Earl (1893–1948) U.S. theatrical producer and composer. He produced Broadway shows and lavish revues, including *The Earl Carroll Vanities* (1923–35).

Car·roll |'kerəl|, Lewis (1832–98) English writer; pseudonym of *Charles Lutwidge Dodgson*. He wrote the children's classics *Alice's Adventures in Wonderland* (1865) and *Through the Looking Glass* (1871), which were inspired by Alice Liddell, the young daughter of the dean at the Oxford college where Carroll was a mathematics lecturer.

Car·ruth |kə'rōōTH|, Hayden (1921–   ) U.S. poet. National Book Award (1996).

Car·sey |'kärsē|, Marcia Lee Peterson (1944–   ) U.S. television producer. Co-owner of the Carsey-Werner Co. (1982–), she was executive producer of "The Cosby Show" and "A Different World."

Car·son |'kärsən|, Kit (1809–68) U.S. frontiersman and scout. Full name *Christopher Carson*. He was a U.S. Indian agent in the Southwest (1853–60, 1865–68) and organized Union scouts in the West during the Civil War.

Car·son |'kärsən|, Johnny (1925–   ) U.S. television personality. Full name *John William Carson*, host of "The Tonight Show" (1962–92).

Car·son |'kärsən|, Rachel Louise (1907–64) U.S. biologist and author. Works include *The Sea Around Us* (1941) and *Silent Spring* (1962).

Car·ter |'kärtər|, Angela (1940–92) English novelist and short-story writer, whose fiction is characterized by fantasy, black humor, and eroticism. Notable works: *The Magic Toyshop* (1967) and *Nights at the Circus* (1984).

Car·ter |'kärtər|, U.S. musicians, including: **A. P. Carter** (1891–1960). Full name *Alvin Pleasant Carter*. He was the founder of the Carter Family Singers (1927–43), who popularized Appalachian folk music. His sister-in-law, **Maybelle Addington Carter** (1909–78), was the featured singer of the Carter Family.

Car·ter |'kärtər|, Elliott (Cook) (1908–) U.S. composer. He is noted for his innovative approach to meter and his choice of sources as diverse as modern jazz and Renaissance madrigals.

Car·ter |'kärtər|, Howard (1873–1939) English archeologist. In 1922, while excavating in the Valley of the Kings at Thebes, he discovered the tomb of Tutankhamen.

Car·ter |'kärtər|, Jimmy see box.

(Eleanor) Rosalynn Smith Carter (1927–), wife of Jimmy Carter and U.S. first lady (1977–81).

Car·tier |kärtē'a|, Jacques (1491–1557) French explorer. The first to establish France's claim to North America, he made three voyages to Canada between 1534 and 1541.

Cartier-Bresson |ˌkärtē'a bres'ōN|, Henri (1908–) French photographer and film director. He is famed for his collection of photographs *The Decisive Moment* (1952) and his documentary film about the Spanish Civil War, *Return to Life* (1937).

Cart·land |'kärtlənd|, Dame Barbara (1901–) English author. Full name *Mary Barbara Hamilton Cartland*. She is best known for her light romantic fiction.

Cart·wright |'kärt,rīt|, Alexander Joy (1820–92) U.S. sportsman. He founded the Knickerbocker Baseball Club and was influential in developing the rules of baseball. Elected to Baseball Hall of Fame (1938).

Cart·wright |'kärt,rīt|, Edmund (1743–1823) English engineer, inventor of the power loom.

Ca·ru·so |kə'rōōsō|, Enrico (1873–1921) Italian operatic tenor. He was the

---

Carter, Jimmy (James Earl, Jr.)
39th U.S. president

Life dates: 1924–
Place of birth: Plains, Georgia
Mother: Lillian Gordy Carter
Father: James Earl Carter, Sr.
Wife: Rosalynn Smith Carter
Children: John (Jack), James (Chip), Donnel Jeffrey (Jeff), Amy
College/University: Georgia Southwestern College; Georgia Institute of Technology; U.S. Naval Academy
Military service: Lieutenant senior grade, U.S. Navy
Career: Peanut farmer; lecturer; writer
Political career: Georgia Senate; governor of Georgia; president
Party: Democratic
Home state: Georgia
Opponents in presidential races: Gerald R. Ford, Eugene McCarthy; Ronald Reagan
Term of office: Jan. 20, 1977–Jan. 20, 1981
Vice president: Walter Mondale
Notable events of presidency: SALT II Treaty; fall of the shah of Iran and seizure of U.S. embassy and American hostages in Teheran; Camp David accords; Panama Canal treaty; Department of Education created; U.S. boycott of Moscow Olympics
Other achievements: Led several international election observer teams

---

first major tenor to be recorded on phonograph records.

Car·ver |'kärvər|, George Washington (1864?–1943) U.S. botanist. He was born into slavery; later, he became the director of agricultural research at Tuskegee Institute (1896) and developed many products from soybeans, sweet potatoes, and peanuts.

Car·ville |'kärvil|, James (1944–) U.S. political strategist and author. He managed Bill Clinton's presidential campaign in 1992 and wrote *We're Right, They're Wrong* (1996).

Cary |'kerē|, Joyce (1888–1957) English novelist. Full name *Arthur Joyce Lunel Cary*. Notable works: *The Horse's Mouth* (1944) and *Not Honour More* (1955).

Ca·sals |kə'säls|, Pablo (1876–1973) Spanish cellist, conductor, and composer.

Cas·a·no·va |ˌkæsəˈnōvə|, Giovanni (1725–98) Full name *Giovanni Jacopo Casanova de Seingalt*. Italian adventurer.

Case·ment |ˈkāsmənt|, Sir Roger (David) (1864–1916) Irish diplomat and nationalist. In 1914 he sought German support for an Irish uprising, and was subsequently hanged by the British for treason.

Ca·sey |ˈkāsē|, William Joseph (1913–87) U.S. intelligence official. He was the director of the CIA (1981–87). Under his leadership, the CIA assisted Nicaraguan contras and was alleged to have been involved in the arms-for-hostages deal known as the "Iran-contra affair."

Cash |kæsH|, Johnny (1932–) U.S. country music singer and songwriter. Notable songs: "I Walk the Line" (1956) and "A Boy Named Sue" (1969).

Cas·per |ˈkæspər|, Billy (1931–) U.S. golfer.

Cas·satt |kəˈsæt|, Mary Stevenson (1844–1926) U.S. painter, who worked mostly in Paris. Her paintings display a close interest in everyday subject matter.

Cas·si·ni |kəˈsēnē|, Giovanni Domenico (1625–1712) Italian-born French astronomer. He discovered the gap in the rings of Saturn known as Cassini's division.

Cas·sius |ˈkæsHəs|, Gaius (died 42 BC) Roman general; full name *Gaius Cassius Longinus*. He was one of the leaders of the conspiracy in 44 BC to assassinate Julius Caesar.

Cas·ta·ne·da |ˌkæstəˈnädə|, Carlos (1931–98) Brazilian author. His works include *The Teachings of Don Juan* (1968).

Cas·te·lla·nos |ˌkæstəˈyänōs|, Rosario (1925–74) Mexican author and literary critic.

Cas·tle |ˈkæsəl|, Vernon Blythe (1887–1918) British dancer and aviator. Born *Vernon Blythe*. With his wife Irene (1893–1969), he originated the one-step, the turkey trot, the Castle walk, and the hesitation waltz.

Cas·tle·reagh |ˈkæsəlrā|, Robert Stewart, Viscount (1769–1822) British Tory statesman. He became foreign secretary

in 1812 and represented Britain at the Congress of Vienna (1814–15).

Cas·tro |ˈkæstrō|, Fidel (1927–) Cuban statesman, prime minister (1959–76), and president from 1976. After overthrowing President Batista, he set up a communist regime that survived the abortive Bay of Pigs invasion, the Cuban Missile Crisis, and the collapse of the Soviet bloc.

Cas·tro |ˈkæstrō|, José María (1818–93) Costa Rican politician. He was president (1847–49) at the time of the Costa Rican Declaration of Independence (1848), and again for a later term (1866–68).

Cath·er |ˈkæTHər|, Willa (Sibert) (1873–1947) U.S. novelist and short-story writer. Her home state of Nebraska provides the setting for some of her best writing. Notable novels: *O Pioneers!* (1913) and *Death Comes for the Archbishop* (1927).

Cath·e·rine |ˈkæTHrən|, St. (died *c.* 307) early Christian martyr; known as **St. Catherine of Alexandria**. According to tradition she opposed the persecution of Christians under the emperor Maxentius and refused to recant or to marry the emperor. She is said to have been tortured on a spiked wheel and then beheaded. Feast day, November 25.

Ca·the·rine de' Me·di·ci |kə,trän də me ˈdēcHē| (1519–89) queen of France, wife of Henry II. She ruled as regent (1560–74) during the minority reigns of her three sons, Francis II, Charles IX, and Henry III, and it was at her instigation that Huguenots were killed in the Massacre of St. Bartholomew (1572).

Cath·e·rine II |ˈkæTHrən| (1729–96) empress of Russia, reigned 1762–96; known as **Catherine the Great**. She became empress after her husband, Peter III, was deposed; her attempted social and political reforms were impeded by the aristocracy. She formed alliances with Prussia and Austria, and made territorial advances at the expense of the Turks and Tartars.

Cath·e·rine of Ar·a·gon |ˌkæTHrən əv ˈerə,gän| (1485–1536) first wife of Henry VIII, youngest daughter of Ferdinand and Isabella of Castile, mother of Mary I. Henry's wish to annul his marriage to Catherine (due to her failure to produce a male heir) led eventually to England's break with the Roman Catholic Church.

Cat·i·line |'kætə,līn| (c. 108–162 BC) Roman nobleman and conspirator; Latin name *Lucius Sergius Catilina*. In 63 BC he planned an uprising which was suppressed; his fellow conspirators were executed and he died in battle in Etruria.

Cat·lin |'kætlən|, George (1796–1872) U.S. artist and author. He contributed 300 engravings to *The Manners, Customs and Condition of North American Indians* (1841), *Last Rambles Amongst the Indians of the Rocky Mountains and the Andes* (1867), and *Life Among the Indians* (1867).

Ca·to |'kātō|, Marcus Porcius (234–149 BC) Roman statesman, orator, and writer; known as **Cato the Elder** or **Cato the Censor**. As censor he initiated a vigorous program of reform, and attempted to stem the growing influence of Greek culture.

Ca·tron |'kātrən|, John (1786?–1865) U.S. Supreme Court justice (1837–65).

Catt |kæt|, Carrie Clinton Chapman Lane (1859–1947) U.S. suffragist. As president of the National American Woman Suffrage Association (1900–04; 1915–47) and of the International Woman Suffrage Alliance (1904–23), she was instrumental in the adoption of the 19th amendment to U.S. Constitution (1920).

Cat·tell |kə'tel|, James McKeen (1860–1944) U.S. psychologist. He was a pioneer in developing psychological tests and experimental methods.

Ca·tul·lus |kə'tələs|, Gaius Valerius (c. 84–c. 54 BC) Roman poet. He is best known for his love poems.

Cau·chy |kō'sHē|, Augustin-Louis, Baron (1789–1857) French mathematician. He transformed the theory of complex functions by developing his integral theorems. He founded the modern theory of elasticity, and contributed substantially to the founding of group theory and analysis.

Ca·va·fy |kä'väfē|, Constantine (Peter) (1863–1933) Greek poet; born *Konstantinos Petrou Kavafis*. His poems refer mainly to the Hellenistic and Graeco-Roman period of his native Alexandria.

Cav·ell |'kævəl|, Edith (Louisa) (1865–1915) English nurse. During World War I, she helped Allied soldiers to escape from occupied Belgium. She was subsequently executed by the Germans and became a heroine of the Allied cause.

Cav·en·dish |'kævəndisH|, Henry (1731–1810) English chemist and physicist. He identified hydrogen, studied carbon dioxide, and determined their densities relative to atmospheric air. He also established that water is a compound, and determined the density of the earth.

Ca·vour |kə'vŏŏr|, Camillo Benso, Conte di (1810–61) Italian statesman. A supporter of Italian unification under Victor Emmanuel II, he was premier of Piedmont (1852–59; 1860–61), and in 1861 became the first premier of a unified Italy.

Caw·ley |'kawlē|, Yvonne (Fay) (1951–) Australian professional tennis player; born *Evonne Fay Goolagong*.

Cax·ton |'kækstən|, William (c. 1422–91) English printer. He printed the first book in English in 1474 and went on to produce about eighty other texts, including editions of *Le Morte d'Arthur* and *Canterbury Tales*.

Cay·ley |'kālē|, Arthur (1821–95) English mathematician and barrister. He wrote almost a thousand mathematical papers, including articles on determinants, group theory, and the algebra of matrices. The *Cayley numbers*, a generalization of complex numbers, are named after him.

Cay·ley |'kālē|, Sir George (1773–1857) British engineer, the father of British aeronautics. He is best known for his understanding of the principles of flight and for building the first manned glider, which was flown in 1853. He was also a founder of the original Polytechnic Institution.

Ceauşescu |cHow'cHeskŏŏ|, Nicolae (1918–89) Romanian Communist statesman, first president of the Socialist Republic of Romania (1974–89). His regime became increasingly totalitarian and corrupt; a popular uprising in December 1989 resulted in its downfall and in his execution.

Ce·cil |'sesəl|, William see BURGHLEY.

Ce·cil·ia |sə'sēlyə|, St. (2nd or 3rd century) Roman martyr. According to legend, she took a vow of celibacy but when forced to marry converted her husband to Christianity and both were martyred. She is the patron saint of church music. Feast day, November 22.

Cé·line |sə'lēn|, Louis-Ferdinand (1894–1961) French novelist; pseudonym of *Louis-Ferdinand Destouches*. He is best known for his autobiographical novel, the satirical *Voyage au bout de la nuit* (1932).

Cel·li·ni |CHə'lēnē|, Benvenuto (1500–71) Italian goldsmith and sculptor, the most renowned goldsmith of his day.

Cel·si·us |'selsēəs|, Anders (1701–44) Swedish astronomer, best known for his temperature scale.

Cerf |sərf|, Bennett Alfred (1898–1971) U.S. publisher, editor, and author. He was a cofounder of Random House publishers (1927).

Cer·van·tes |sər'väntäs|, Miguel de (1547–1616) Spanish novelist and dramatist; full name *Miguel de Cervantes Saavedra*. His most famous work is *Don Quixote* (1605–15), a satire on chivalric romances that greatly influenced the development of the novel.

Cet·shwayo |keCH'wīō| (*c.* 1826–84) Zulu king. Also **Cetewayo**. He became ruler of Zululand in 1873 and was involved in a series of battles with the Afrikaners and British; he was deposed as leader after the capture of his capital by the British in 1879.

Cé·zanne |sā'zän|, Paul (1839–1906) French painter. He is closely identified with post-Impressionism and his later work had an important influence on cubism. Notable works: *Bathers* (sequence of paintings 1890–1905).

Cha·brol |sHä'brôl|, Claude (1930–) French movie director, a member of the *nouvelle vague*. His movies typically combine suspense with studies of personal relationships, and include *Les Biches* (1968).

Chad·wick |'CHæd,wik|, George Whitefield (1854–1931) U.S. conductor and composer. He was director of the New England Conservatory of Music (from 1897).

Chad·wick |'CHæd,wik|, Henry (1824–1908) U.S. sportswriter. Compiled a baseball handbook that later became *Spalding's Official Baseball Guide*. Elected to Baseball Hall of Fame (1938).

Chad·wick |'CHæd,wik|, Sir James (1891–1974) English physicist. He discovered the neutron, for which he received the 1935 Nobel Prize for Physics.

Chaf·fee |'CHæfē|, Roger Bruce (1935–67) U.S. astronaut. He died in a flash fire in the Apollo 1 space capsule.

Cha·gall |sHə'gäl|, Marc (1887–1985) Russian-born French painter and graphic artist. His work was characterized by the use of rich emotive color and dream imagery, and had a significant influence on surrealism.

Chain |CHān|, Sir Ernst Boris (1906–79) German-born British biochemist. With Howard Florey he isolated and purified penicillin and in 1945 they shared a Nobel Prize with Alexander Fleming.

Cha·lia·pin |sHäl'yä,pyin|, Fyodor (Ivanovich) (1873–1938) Russian operatic bass.

Cham·ber·lain |'CHämbərlən|, Neville (1869–1940) British Conservative statesman, prime minister (1937–40). Full name *Arthur Neville Chamberlain*. He pursued a policy of appeasement with Nazi Germany, signing the Munich Agreement (1938), but was forced to abandon this policy following Hitler's invasion of Czechoslovakia in 1939.

Cham·ber·lain |'CHämbərlən|, Owen (1920–) American physicist. He investigated subatomic particles and in 1955 discovered the antiproton with E. G. Segrè, 1905–89, for which they shared the 1959 Nobel Prize for Physics.

Cham·ber·lain |'CHämbərlən|, Wilt (1936–) U.S. basketball player. Full name *Wilton Norman Chamberlain*; known as **Wilt the Stilt**. Elected to the Basketball Hall of Fame (1978).

Cham·ber·lin |'CHämbərlən|, Thomas Chrowder (1843–1928) U.S. geologist. He founded the *Journal of Geology*.

Cham·bers |'CHämbərz|, Whittaker (1901–61) U.S. journalist. Full name *Jay David Whittaker Chamberlain*. He accused Alger Hiss of Communist party membership and of passing State Department documents to Soviet agents.

Cham·pion |'CHæmpēən|, Gower (1921–80) U.S. choreographer, dancer, and director.

Cham·plain |ˌsHæm'plān|, Samuel de (1567–1635) French explorer and colonial statesman. He established a settlement at Quebec (Canada) in 1608, developing alliances with the native peoples, and was appointed lieutenant governor in 1612.

Cham·pol·lion |ˌsHämpawl'yawn|, Jean-François (1790–1832) French Egyptologist. A pioneer in the study of ancient Egypt, he is best known for his success in deciphering some of the hieroglyphic inscriptions on the Rosetta Stone in 1822.

Chan |CHæn|, Jackie (1954–) U.S. actor, director, and screenwriter, born in China. He is known for his stunts, which he choreographs and performs himself.

Chan·cel·lor |'CHænsələr|, John William (1927–) U.S. journalist. He has provided news coverage for NBC since 1967 as a correspondent, television anchorman, and commentator.

Chan·dler |'CHændlər|, Raymond (Thornton) (1888–1959) U.S. novelist. He is remembered as the creator of the private detective Philip Marlowe. Notable novels: *The Big Sleep* (1939).

Chan·dra·gup·ta Maurya |ˌCHəndrə 'gŏŏptə| (c. 325–297 BC) Indian emperor. He founded the Mauryan empire and annexed provinces deep into Afghanistan from Alexander's Greek successors.

Chan·dra·se·khar |ˌCHändrə'sākər|, Subrahmanyan (1910–95) Indian-born American astronomer. He suggested how some stars could eventually collapse to form a dense white dwarf, provided that their mass does not exceed an upper limit (the *Chandrasekhar limit*).

Cha·nel |sHə'nel|, Coco (1883–1971) French couturière; born *Gabrielle Bonheur Chanel.* Her simple but sophisticated garments were a radical departure from the stiff corseted styles of the day. She also diversified into perfumes, costume jewelry, and textiles.

Cha·ney |'CHānē|, Lon (1883–1930)

U.S. movie actor; born *Alonso Chaney.* He played a wide variety of deformed villains and macabre characters in more than 150 movies, including *The Hunchback of Notre Dame* (1923).

Chan·ning |'CHāniNG|, Carol (1923–) U.S. actress. She starred on Broadway in *Hello, Dolly!* (1964–67; Tony Award 1964) and has received a Tony Lifetime Achievement Award (1995).

Chan·ning |'CHæniNG|, Walter (1786–1876) U.S. obstetrician. Professor and dean at Harvard Medical School (1819–47), he introduced the use of ether in childbirth delivery (1847).

Chan·ning |'CHæniNG|, William Ellery (1818–1901) U.S. poet. He was a transcendentalist colleague of Thoreau and Emerson.

Cha·nute |sHə'nŏŏt|, Octave (1832–1910) French-born American aviation pioneer. From 1898 he produced a number of gliders, including a biplane that made over 700 flights. He assisted the Wright brothers in making the world's first controlled powered flight.

Cha·pin |'CHāpən|, Roy Dikeman (1880–1936) U.S. industrialist. He was the organizer of the Hudson Motor Car Co. (with Howard E. Coffin, 1909) and the U.S. secretary of commerce (1932–33).

Chap·lin |'CHæplən|, Charlie (1889–1977) British movie actor and director. Full name *Sir Charles Spencer Chaplin.* He directed and starred in many short silent comedies, mostly playing a bowler-hatted tramp, a character that was his trademark for more than 25 years. A master who combined pathos with slapstick clowning, he was best suited to the silent medium. Notable movies: *The Kid* (1921).

Chap·man |'CHæpmən|, Frank Michler (1864–1945) U.S. ornithologist and author. Author of *Handbook of Birds of Eastern North America* (1895), he became curator of the American Museum of Natural History (1908–42).

Chap·man |'CHæpmən|, George (c. 1559–1634) English poet and dramatist. He is chiefly known for his translations of Homer; the complete *Iliad* and *Odyssey* were published in 1616. They are commemorated in Keats's sonnet *"On First Looking into Chapman's Homer"* (1817).

Chap·man, John see APPLESEED, JOHNNY.

Chap·man |ˈCHæpmən|, Mark David (1955–) U.S. convicted murderer of John Lennon.

Chap·man |ˈCHæpmən|, Tracy (1964–) U.S. folk-rock singer and songwriter. Grammy Awards, 1988 and 1997.

Char·cot |sHärˈkō|, Jean-Martin (1825–93) French neurologist, regarded as one of the founders of modern neurology. He established links between neurological conditions and particular lesions in the central nervous system. His work on hysteria was taken up by his pupil Sigmund Freud.

Char·don·net |sHärdəˈnā|, Louis-Marie-Hilaire, Comte de Bernigaud (1839–1924) French chemist. He patented rayon (1884) and established factories for its manufacture.

Char·le·magne |ˈsHärlə,män| (742–814) king of the Franks (768–814) and Holy Roman emperor (as Charles I) (800–814). Latin name *Carolus Magnus*; known as **Charles the Great**. As the first Holy Roman emperor, Charlemagne promoted the arts and education, and his court became the cultural center of the Carolingian Renaissance, the influence of which outlasted his empire.

Charles[1] |CHärlz| the name of two kings of England, Scotland, and Ireland: **Charles I** (1600–49; reigned 1625–49), the son of James I. His reign was dominated by the deepening religious and constitutional crisis that resulted in the English Civil War (1642–49). After the battle of Naseby, Charles tried to regain power in alliance with the Scots, but his forces were defeated in 1648 and he was tried by a special Parliamentary court and beheaded. **Charles II** (1630–85; reigned 1660–85), the son of Charles I. Charles was restored to the throne after the collapse of Cromwell's regime and displayed considerable adroitness in handling the difficult constitutional situation, although continuing religious and political strife dogged his reign.

Charles[2] |CHärlz| the name of four kings of Spain: **Charles I** (1500–58; reigned 1516–56), the son of Philip I. He was Holy Roman emperor (as Charles V) (1519–56). His reign was characterized by the struggle against Protestantism in Germany, rebellion in Castile, and war with France (1521–44). Exhausted by these struggles, Charles handed Naples, the Netherlands, and Spain over to his son Philip II and the imperial crown to his brother Ferdinand, and retired to a monastery. **Charles II** (1661–1700; reigned 1665–1700). He inherited a kingdom already in a decline which he was unable to halt. His choice of Philip of Anjou, grandson of Louis XIV of France, as his successor gave rise to the War of the Spanish Succession. **Charles III** (1716–88; reigned 1759–88). He improved Spain's position as an international power through an increase in foreign trade, and brought Spain a brief cultural and economic revival. **Charles IV** (1748–1819; reigned 1788–1808). During the Napoleonic Wars he suffered the loss of the Spanish fleet, destroyed along with that of France at Trafalgar in 1805. Following the French invasion of Spain in 1807, Charles was forced to abdicate.

Charles[3] |CHärlz| the name of seven Holy Roman Emperors. **Charles I** see CHARLEMAGNE. **Charles II** (823–87; reigned 875–877). **Charles III** (839–888; reigned 881–887). **Charles IV** (1316–1378; reigned 1355–1378). **Charles V** Charles I of Spain (see CHARLES[2]). **Charles VI** (1685–1740; reigned 1711–40). His claim to the Spanish throne instigated the War of the Spanish Succession, but he was ultimately unsuccessful. He drafted the Pragmatic Sanction in an attempt to ensure that his daughter succeeded to the Habsburg dominions; this triggered the War of the Austrian Succession after his death. **Charles VII** (1697–1745; reigned 1742–45).

Charles VII |CHärlz| (1403–61) king of France; reigned 1422–61. At the time of his accession, much of northern France was under English occupation. After the intervention of Joan of Arc, however, the French experienced a dramatic military revival, and the defeat of the English ended the Hundred Years War.

Charles XII |ᴄʜärlz| (1682–1718) king of Sweden. Also **Karl XII.** In 1700 he embarked on the Great Northern War against Denmark, Poland-Saxony, and Russia. Initially successful, in 1709 he embarked on an expedition into Russia that ended in the destruction of his army and his internment.

Charles |ᴄʜärlz|, Prince (1948–) British prince. Full name **Charles Philip Arthur George,** Prince of Wales (1948–), heir apparent to Elizabeth II. He married Lady Diana Spencer in 1981; the couple had two children, Prince William Arthur Philip Louis (1982–) and Prince Henry Charles Albert David (known as Prince Harry; 1984–), and were divorced in 1996.

Charles |ᴄʜärlz|, Ray (1930–) U.S. pianist and singer; born *Ray Charles Robinson.* Totally blind from the age of 6, he drew on blues, jazz, and country music for songs such as "What'd I Say" (1959), "Georgia On My Mind" (1960), and "Busted" (1963).

Charles Mar·tel |ˌᴄʜärlz mär'tel| (*c.* 688–741) Frankish ruler. He ruled the eastern part of the Frankish kingdom from 715 and the whole kingdom from 719 and was the grandfather of Charlemagne. His rule marked the beginning of Carolingian power.

Chase |ᴄʜās|, Salmon Portland (1808–73) Chief Justice of the U.S. (1864–73). He defended fugitive slaves; as U.S. secretary of the treasury (1861–64), he issued the first "greenbacks" (1863).

Chase |ᴄʜās|, Samuel (1741–1811) U.S. Supreme Court justice (1796–1811). He was a delegate to the Continental Congress (1774–78, 1784, 1785) and a signer of the Declaration of Independence. In 1804 he was impeached but was reinstated to the bench in 1805.

Chast |ᴄʜæst|, Roz (1954–) U.S. cartoonist and illustrator. She was on staff with the *New Yorker* magazine and has illustrated several children's books.

Chat·eau·bri·and |sʜæˌtōbrē'awn|, François-Auguste-René, Vicomte de (1768–1848) French writer and diplomat. He was an important figure in early French romanticism. Notable works: *Le Génie du Christianisme* (1802) and *Mémoires d'outre-tombe* (autobiography, 1849–50).

Chat·ham |'ᴄʜætəm|, 1st Earl of see Pɪᴛᴛ.

Chat·ter·ton |'ᴄʜætərtən|, Thomas (1752–70) English poet. He is chiefly remembered for his fabricated poems professing to be those of a 15th-century monk. He committed suicide at the age of 17.

Chau·cer |'ᴄʜawsər|, Geoffrey (*c.* 1342–1400) English poet. His most famous work, *The Canterbury Tales* (*c.* 1387–1400), is a cycle of linked tales told by a group of pilgrims. His skills of characterization, humor, and versatility established him as the first great English poet. Other notable works: *Troilus and Criseyde* (1385).

Chau·liac |sʜōl'yäk|, Guy de (*c.* 1300–68) French physician. His *Chirurgia Magna* (1363) was the first work to describe many surgical techniques.

Cha·vez |'sʜävez|, Cesar Estrada (1927–93) U.S. labor leader. He founded the organization that became the United Farm Workers (1962), and he used nonviolent tactics to gain union contracts with California vineyard owners.

Cha·vis |'ᴄʜāvəs; 'ᴄʜævəs|, Benjamin U.S. minister and black activist. He was executive director of the NAACP (1993–94) until fired for misuse of funds.

Cha·yef·sky |ˌᴄʜī'efskē; ˌᴄʜī'evskē|, Paddy (Sidney) (1923–81) U.S. writer. He wrote television dramas, films, plays, and a science fiction novel, *Altered States* (1978).

Chea·tam |'ᴄʜētəm|, Adolphus (1905–97) U.S. jazz trumpeter.

Cheat·ham |'ᴄʜētəm|, Doc (1906–97) U.S. musician. He was a jazz and big band trumpeter whose career spanned eight decades.

Check·er |'ᴄʜekər|, Chubby (1941–) U.S. singer. Born *Ernest Evans.* He popularized dance crazes such as "The Twist" (1960).

Chee·ver |'ᴄʜēvər|, John (1912–82) U.S. short-story writer and novelist. His stories frequently satirize affluent suburban New Englanders. Notable novels: *The Wapshot Chronicle* (1957).

Che·khov |'CHekawv|, Anton (Pavlovich) (1860–1904) Russian dramatist and short-story writer. Chekhov's work, portraying upper-class life in pre-revolutionary Russia with a blend of naturalism and symbolism, had a considerable influence on 20th-century drama. Notable plays: *The Seagull* (1895), *Uncle Vanya* (1900), *The Three Sisters* (1901), and *The Cherry Orchard* (1904).

Cheng Ho |'jeNG 'hō| (c. 1371–c. 1433) Chinese admiral and explorer.

Chen·nault |SHə'nält|, Claire Lee (1890–1958) U.S. aviator. In 1941 she formed the American volunteer group the "Flying Tigers" to aid China.

Che·ops |'kē,äps| (26th century BC) Egyptian pharaoh of the 4th dynasty. Egyptian name **Khufu**. He commissioned the building of the Great Pyramid at Giza.

Cher |SHer| (1946–   ) U.S. actress and singer. Born *Cherilyn LaPiere Sarkisian*. She was married to Sonny Bono, with whom she cohosted a television show, and to musician Gregg Allman. Notable movies: *Moonstruck* (1987, Academy Award) and *Tea With Mussolini* (1999).

Che·ren·kov |CHə'reNG,kawv|, Pavel (Alekseyevich) (1904–90) Soviet physicist. Also **Cerenkov**. He investigated the effects of high-energy particles and shared the 1958 Nobel Prize for Physics for discovering the cause of blue light (now called *Cerenkov Radiation*) emitted by radioactive substances underwater.

Cher·nen·ko |CHer'nyeNGkō|, Konstantin (Ustinovich) (1911–85) Soviet statesman. He was General Secretary of the Communist Party of the USSR and president (1984–85). He died after only thirteen months in office and was succeeded by Mikhail Gorbachev.

Cher·ry |'CHerē|, Don (1936–95) U.S. jazz trumpeter. Full name *Donald Eugene Cherry*. He was a leading figure in free jazz.

Che·ru·bi·ni |,kərə'bēnē|, (Maria) Luigi (Carlo Zenobio Salvadore) (1760–1842) Italian composer. He spent most of his composing career in

Paris and is principally known for his church music and operas.

Cher·well |'CHer,wel|, Frederick Alexander Lindemann, 1st Viscount (1886–1957) German-born British physicist. He was Winston Churchill's scientific adviser during World War II.

Chese·brough |'CHēzbrə|, Robert (1837–1933) U.S. inventor. He discovered and patented Vaseline (1870).

Ches·ter·ton |'CHestərtən|, G. K. (1874–1936) English essayist, novelist, and critic. Full name *Gilbert Keith Chesterton*. His novels include *The Napoleon of Notting Hill* (1904) and a series of detective stories featuring Father Brown, a priest with a talent for crime detection.

Chest·nutt |'CHestnət|, Charles Waddell (1858–1932) U.S. author. He wrote *Life of Frederick Douglass* (1899), as well as novels and short stories with a subtle treatment of racial themes.

Che·va·lier |SHəvȧl'yā|, Maurice-Auguste (1888–1972) French singer and actor. Notable movies: *Innocents of Paris* (1929), *Love Me Tonight* (1932), and *Gigi* (1958).

Chev·ro·let |,SHevrə'lā|, Louis (1879–1941) U.S. automobile racer, designer, and manufacturer. He founded the Chevrolet Motor Co. (1911) and designed its first car.

Chiang Kai-shek |'CHæNG 'kī 'SHek| (1887–1975) Chinese statesman and general. Also **Jiang Jie Shi**. He was president of China (1928–31, 1943–49) and of Taiwan (1950–75). He tried to unite China by military means in the 1930s but was defeated by the Communists. Forced to abandon mainland China in 1949, he set up a separate Nationalist Chinese State in Taiwan.

Chi·ches·ter |'CHiCHəstər|, Sir Francis (Charles) (1901–72) English yachtsman. In his yacht *Gipsy Moth IV* he was the first person to sail alone around the world with only one stop (1966–67).

Chif·ley |'CHiflē|, Joseph Benedict (1885–1951) Australian Labour statesman. He was prime minister (1945–49).

Child |CHīld|, Julia (McWilliams) (1912–   ) U.S. chef and author. Known as **the French Chef**. She has hosted several televsion cooking programs since

1963. She co-authored the two-volume *Mastering the Art of French Cooking* (1961–70).

Child |CHīld|, Lydia Marie (1802–80) U.S. abolitionist and author. She was editor of the *National Anti-Slavery Standard* (1841–43) and the author of novels, children's books, and the poem "Thanksgiving Day," which begins, "Over the river and through the woods."

Chil·ders |ˈCHildərz|, (Robert) Erskine (1870–1922) English-born Irish writer and political activist. He was court-martialed and shot for his involvement in the Irish civil war. Notable works: *The Riddle of the Sands* (novel, 1903). His son **Erskine Hamilton Childers** (1905–74) was president of Ireland (1973–74).

Chip·pen·dale |ˈCHipən,dāl|, Thomas (1718–79) English furniture-maker and designer. He produced furniture in a neoclassical vein, with elements of the French rococo, chinoiserie, and Gothic revival styles, and his book of furniture designs *The Gentleman and Cabinetmaker's Director* (1754) was immensely influential.

Chi·rac |SHiˈräk|, Jacques (René) (1932–) French statesman. He was prime minister (1974–76 and 1986–88) and president from 1995.

Chi·ri·co |ˈkēri,kō|, Giorgio de (1888–1978) Greek-born Italian painter. His disconnected and unsettling dream images exerted a significant influence on surrealism.

Chis·holm |ˈCHizəm|, Shirley Anita St. Hill (1924–) U.S. politician and educator. The first African-American woman elected to Congress, she was a member of the U.S. House of Representatives from New York (1968–83).

Chis·um |ˈCHizəm|, John Simpson (1824–84) U.S. rancher frontiersman. He developed the largest cattle herd in the U.S. during the 1870s.

Choate |CHōt|, Joseph Hodges (1832–1917) U.S. lawyer and diplomat. He was U.S. ambassador to Britain (1899–1905) and head of the U.S. delegation to the second International Peace Conference at The Hague (1907).

Choate |CHōt|, Rufus (1799–1859) U.S. lawyer. He was a Massachusetts member of the U.S. House of Repre-

sentatives (1831–34) and the U.S. Senate (1841–45).

Chom·sky |ˈCHämskē|, (Avram) Noam (1928–) U.S. theoretical linguist. He is noted for expounding the theory of generative grammar. He also theorized that linguistic behavior is innate, not learned, and that all languages share the same underlying grammatical base. Chomsky is known also for his opposition to U.S. involvement in the Vietnam War and the Gulf War. Notable works: *Syntactic Structures* (1957) and *Aspects of the Theory of Syntax* (1965).

Cho·pin |SHōˈpæn|, Frédéric (François) (1810–49) Polish-born French composer and pianist. Polish name *Fryderyk Franciszek Szopen*. Writing almost exclusively for the piano, he composed numerous mazurkas and polonaises inspired by Polish folk music, as well as nocturnes, preludes, and two piano concertos (1829; 1830).

Cho·pin |ˈSHōˈpən|, Kate (O'Flaherty) (1851–1904) U.S. novelist and short-story writer. Notable works: *Bayou Folk* (1894), *A Night in Acadie* (1897), and *The Awakening* (1899).

Chré·tien |krāˈtyen|, Jean (1934–) Canadian Liberal statesman. Full name *Joseph-Jacques Jean* He became prime minister in 1993.

Chré·tien de Troyes |krā,tyen də ˈtrwä| (1130–1183) French poet. His courtly romances on Arthurian themes include *Lancelot* (*c.*1177–88) and *Perceval* (1181–90, unfinished).

Chris·tian |ˈkrisCHən|, Charles (1919–42) U.S. jazz guitarist. He was a pioneer of electrically amplified guitar and played with Benny Goodman's band (1939–42).

Chris·tian |ˈkrisCHən|, Fletcher (*c.* 1764–*c.* 1793) English seaman and mutineer. As first mate under Captain Bligh on the HMS *Bounty*, in April 1789 Christian seized the ship and cast Bligh and others adrift. In 1790 the mutineers settled on Pitcairn Island, where Christian was probably killed by Tahitians.

Chris·tie |ˈkristē|, Dame Agatha (1890–1976) English writer of detective fiction. Notable works: *Murder on the Orient Express* (1934), *Death on the Nile* (1937), and *The Mousetrap* (play, 1952). She created the detectives Miss Marple and Hercule Poirot.

Chris·tie |'kristē|, Julie (1940–) British actress, born in India. Notable movies: *Darling* (1965, Academy Award), *Dr. Zhivago* (1965), and *Shampoo* (1975).

Chris·to·pher |'kristəfər|, Warren (1925–) U.S. statesman and lawyer. He served as Bill Clinton's secretary of state (1993–97).

Chris·ty |'kristē|, Edwin Pearce (1815–62) U.S. actor and singer. He founded the Christy Minstrels singing group.

Chris·ty |'kristē|, Howard Chandler (1873–1952) U.S. illustrator and painter. An illustrator for periodicals, he popularized the image of the "Christy girl."

Chrys·ler |'krīslər|, Walter Percy (1875–1940) U.S. automobile manufacturer. He was president and general manager of Buick Motor Co. (1916–19). He introduced the Chrysler automobile (1924) and became chairman of Chrysler Corp. (1935–40).

Chrys·os·tom |'krisəstəm|, St. John (*c.* 347–407) Doctor of the Church, bishop of Constantinople. He attempted to reform the corrupt state of the court, clergy, and people; this offended many, including the Empress Eudoxia, who banished him in 403. His name means "golden-mouthed" in Greek, referring to his preaching ability. Feast day, January 27.

Chung |CHəNG|, Connie (1946–) U.S. broadcast journalist. Full name *Constance Yu-Hwa Chung.*Since 1987 she has been a news correspondent and anchor for NBC.

Church |CHərCH|, Frank Forrester (1924–84) U.S. politician. A U.S. senator from Idaho, he was a leading liberal voice and civil rights champion who opposed the Vietnam War.

Church |CHərCH|, Frederick Edwin (1826–1900) U.S. painter. He was a student of Thomas Cole and was known for his landscapes.

Chur·chill |'CHərCHəl|, Sir Winston (Leonard Spencer) (1874–1965) British Conservative statesman. He served as prime minister (1940–45, 1951–55). A consistent opponent of ap-

peasement during the 1930s, he replaced Neville Chamberlain as British prime minister in 1940 and led Britain throughout World War II, forging and maintaining the alliance that defeated the Axis Powers. His writings include *The Second World War* (1948–53) and *A History of the English-Speaking Peoples* (1956–58); he won the Nobel Prize for Literature in 1953.

Church·ward |'CHərCHwərd|, George Jackson (1857–1933) English railway engineer. The standard 4-6-0 locomotives that he built at the Swindon works of the Great Western Railway were the basis of many later designs.

Cic·e·ro |'sisərō|, Marcus Tullius (106–43 BC) Roman statesman, orator, and writer. As an orator and writer Cicero established a model for Latin prose; his surviving works include speeches, treatises on rhetoric, philosophical works, and letters. A supporter of Pompey against Julius Caesar, in the *Philippics* (43 BC) he attacked Mark Antony, who had him put to death.

Cid, El |sid|, Count of Bivar (*c.* 1043–99) Spanish soldier. Born *Rodrigo Díaz de Vivar.* He was a champion of Christianity against the Moors. In 1094 he captured Valencia, which he went on to rule. He is immortalized in the Spanish *Poema de Cid* (12th century) and in Corneille's play *Le Cid* (1637).

Ciof·fi |'CHōfē|, Lou (1926–98) U.S. journalist. He covered the Korean and Vietnam wars.

Cis·ne·ros |,sis'nerəs|, Sandra (1954–) U.S. poet and author. Works include *The House on Mango Street* (1983), which received an American Book Award.

Clai·borne |'klā,bawrn|, Craig (1920–) U.S. editor and cookbook author. He is the food editor for the New York Times and author of *Classic French Cuisine* (1970).

Clai·borne |'klā,bawrn|, Liz (1929–) U.S. fashion designer and manufacturer. Full name *Elisabeth Claiborne Ortenberg.*

Clan·cy |'klænsē|, Tom (1947–) U.S. author. Notable novels: *Hunt for Red October* (1985), *Patriot Games* (1987), and *Rainbow Six* (1998).

Clap·ton |'klæptən|, Eric (1945–) English blues and rock guitarist, singer, and composer. He is noted as a virtuoso guitarist and interpreter of the blues.

Clare |kler|, John (1793–1864) English poet. He wrote in celebration of the natural world. In 1837 he was certified insane and spent the rest of his life in an asylum. Notable works: *Poems Descriptive of Rural Life and Scenery* (1820) and *The Rural Muse* (1835).

Clar·en·don |'klerəndən|, Edward Hyde, Earl of (1609–74) English statesman and historian. He was chief adviser to Charles II and chancellor of Oxford University (1660–67). Notable works: *History of the Rebellion and Civil Wars in England* (published posthumously 1702–04).

Clare of As·si·si |,kler əv ə'sēsē|, St. (1194–1253) Italian saint and abbess. With St. Francis she founded the order of Poor Ladies of San Damiano ("Poor Clares"), of which she was abbess. Feast day, August 11 (formerly 12).

Clark |klärk|, Dick (1929–) U.S. performer and producer. He hosted television's "American Bandstand" (1952–87) and formed Dick Clark Productions in 1956.

Clark |klärk|, George Rogers (1752–1818) American Revolutionary War leader and frontiersman. He defended the Illinois frontier against the British.

Clark |klärk|, Joe (1939–) Canadian statesman. Full name *Charles Joseph Clark*. A leader of the Progressive Conservative Party (1976–83), he became Canada's youngest prime minister (1979–80).

Clark |klärk|, Kenneth Bancroft (1914–) U.S. educator, author, and psychologist. Notable works: *Desegregation: An Appraisal of the Evidence* (1953) and *The War Against Poverty* (1968). Spingarn Medal, 1961.

Clark |klärk|, MarkWayne (1896–1984) U.S. army officer. He served as chief of staff of the U.S. Army ground forces (1942), as UN commander and commander in chief of the U.S. Far East command (1952–53). He signed the Korean armistice.

Clark |klärk|, Mary Higgins (1931–) U.S. author. Notable novels: *A Stranger is Watching* (1978) and *All Through the Night* (1998).

Clark |klärk|, Tom Campbell (1899–1977) U.S. Supreme Court justice (1949–67).

Clark |klärk|, William (1770–1838) U.S. explorer. With Meriwether Lewis, he commanded the Lewis and Clark expedition (1804–06) across the North American continent.

Clarke |klärk|, Sir Arthur Charles (1917–) English writer of science fiction. He wrote the book *2001: A Space Odyssey* in 1968 and cowrote (with Stanley Kubrick) the screenplay for the movie in the same year.

Clarke |klärk|, Bobby (1949–) U.S. hockey player.

Clarke |klärk|, John H. (1857–1945) U.S. Supreme Court justice (1916–22). He was president of the League of Nations Non-Partisan Committee (1922–28).

Clarke |klärk|, Kenny (1914–85) U.S. jazz drummer and bandleader. Full name *Kenneth Spearman Clarke*. A pioneer of modern drums, he composed "Salt Peanuts" with Dizzy Gillespie and "Epistrophy" with Thelonius Monk.

Claude Lor·rain |,klawd law'rän| (1600–82) Also **Lorrain**. French painter; born *Claude Gellée*. He is noted for the use of light in his landscapes. Notable works: *Ascanius and the Stag* (1682).

Claudius (10 BC–AD 54) Roman emperor (41–54); full name *Tiberius Claudius Drusus Nero Germanicus*. His reign was noted for its restoration of order after Caligula's decadence and for its expansion of the Empire, in particular the invasion of Britain in AD 43. His fourth wife, Agrippina, is said to have poisoned him.

Clau·se·witz |'klowzə,vits|, Carl von (1780–1831) Prussian general and military theorist. His study *On War* (1833) had a marked influence on strategic studies in the 19th and 20th centuries.

Clau·si·us |'kläzēəs|, Rudolf (1822–88) German physicist, one of the founders of modern thermodynamics. He was the first, in 1850, to formulate the second law of thermodynamics, developing the concept of a system's available thermal energy and coining the term *entropy* for it.

Cla·vell |klə'vel|, James (1924–94) Australian author and filmmaker. Born *Charles Edmund DuMaresq de Clavell*. Notable novels: *King Rat* (1962) and *Shogun* (1975). Notable movies (as writer and producer): *The Great Escape* (1963) and *To Sir with Love* (also directed; 1967).

Clay, Cassius see MUHAMMAD ALI.

Clay |klā|, Henry (1777–1852) U.S. politician and statesman. He was a leader of the "War Hawks" (1811); for his role as a champion of the Missouri Compromise (1820), he was nicknamed "the Great Pacificator." He served as U.S. secretary of state (1825–29) and as a U.S. senator from Kentucky (1831– 42); his oratory favoring the Compromise of 1850 earned him a second nickname, "the Great Compromiser."

Clay |klā|, Lucius DuBignon (1897– 1978) U.S. army officer. He served as commander in chief of U.S. forces in Europe (1947–49) and was in charge of the Berlin airlift (1948).

Clay·ton |'klātn|, Buck (1911–91) U.S. jazz trumpeter and arranger. Full name *Wilbur Dorsey Clayton*. He was a leading soloist with Count Basie's band and a central figure of mainstream jazz.

Cleary |'klirē|, Beverly (Bunn) (1916–) U.S. author. Notable children's books: *Henry Huggins* (1950) and *Ramona the Pest* (1968).

Clea·ver |'klēvər|, Eldridge (1935–98) U.S. civil rights activist.

Cleese |klēz|, John (Marwood) (1939–) English comic actor and writer. He became famous for television's "Monty Python's Flying Circus" (1969–74) and the situation comedy "Fawlty Towers" (1975–79).

Cleis·the·nes |'klīsTHə,nēz| (*c.* 570 BC–*c.* 508 BC) Athenian statesman. His reforms consolidated the Athenian democratic process begun by Solon and influenced the policies of Pericles.

Cle·men·ceau |,klemən'sō|, Georges (Eugène Benjamin) (1841–1929) French statesman, prime minister (1906–09, 1917–20). At the Versailles peace talks he pushed hard for a punitive settlement with Germany, but failed

to obtain all that he demanded (notably the Rhine River as a frontier).

Clem·ens |'klemənz|, Roger (1962–) U.S. baseball player. Full name *William Roger Clemens*, known as **the Rocket**. He set a major league record by twice striking out 20 batters during a nine-inning game. Received four Cy Young Awards (1986, 1987, 1991, 1997).

Clemens, Samuel Langhorne see TWAIN, MARK.

Clem·ent |'klemənt|, St. (1st century AD) Pope (bishop of Rome) *c.* 88–*c.* 97. He was probably the third pope after St. Peter; known as **St. Clement of Rome**. Feast day, November 23.

Cle·men·te |klə'mentē|, Roberto Walker (1934–72) U.S. baseball player, born in Puerto Rico. He was a four-time National League batting champion. Elected to the Baseball Hall of Fame (1973).

Clem·ent of Al·ex·an·dria |'klemənt əv ,æleg'zændrēə|, St. (*c.* 150–*c.* 215) Greek theologian. Latin name *Titus Flavius Clemens*. His main contribution to theological scholarship was to relate the ideas of Greek philosophy to the Christian faith. Feast day, December 5.

Cle·o·pat·ra |,klēə'pætrə| (69–30 BC) queen of Egypt (47–30). Also called **Cleopatra VII**. She was the last Ptolemaic (Macedonian dynasty) ruler. After a brief liaison with Julius Caesar she formed a political and romantic alliance with Mark Antony. Their ambitions ultimately brought them into conflict with Rome, and she and Antony were defeated at the battle of Actium in 31. She is reputed to have committed suicide by allowing herself to be bitten by an asp.

Cleve·land |'klēvlənd|, (Stephen) Grover (1837–1908) see box. **Frances Folsom Cleveland** (1864–1947), wife of Grover Cleveland and U.S. first lady (1886–89, 1893–97).

Cleve·land |'klēvlənd|, James (1931– 91) U.S. gospel singer and composer.

Clif·ford |'klifərd|, Clark M. (1906–98) U.S. attorney and public official. A key adviser to four Democratic presidents, he helped draft legislation establishing the CIA.

Clif·ford |'klifərd|, Nathan (1803–81) U.S. Supreme Court justice (1858–81).

Cleveland, Grover
22nd and 24th U.S. president
(two separate terms)

Life dates: 1837–1908
Place of birth: Caldwell, New Jersey
Mother: Anne Neal Cleveland
Father: Richard Falley Cleveland
Wife: Frances Folsom Cleveland
Children: Ruth, Esther, Marion, Richard, Francis
College/University: none
Career: Lawyer; sheriff
Political career: Mayor of Buffalo, New York; governor of New York; president
Party: Democratic
Home state: New York
Opponents in presidential races: James G. Blaine (in 1884); Benjamin Harrison, James B. Weaver (in 1888 and 1892)
Terms of office: March 4, 1885–March 3, 1889 (first term); March 4, 1893–March 3, 1897 (second term)
Vice presidents: Thomas A. Hendricks (first term); Adlai E. Stevenson (second term)
Notable events of presidency: (first term) Interstate Commerce Act; Presidential Succession Act; (second term) financial panic of 1893; labor unrest, including Pullman strike of 1894; gold crisis of 1895; Statue of Liberty dedication; Department of Agriculture established; Utah admitted as 45th state
Place of burial: Princeton, New Jersey

He helped negotiate the Treaty of Guadeloupe Hidalgo with Mexico (1848).

Clift |klift|, Montgomery (1920–66) U.S. actor. Full name *Edward Montgomery Clift*. He received four Oscar nominations for movies that included *From Here to Eternity* (1953) and *Judgment at Nuremberg* (1961).

Cline |klīn|, Patsy (1932–63) U.S. country singer. Born *Virginia Petterson Hensley*. She was discovered in 1957 when she sang "Walkin' After Midnight" on a television show. She had hits with "Crazy" (1961) and "Sweet Dreams of You" (1963).

Clin·ton |ˈklintən|, DeWitt (1769–1828) U.S. politician. Among his political positions, he was a member of the New York legislature (1798–1802), a U.S. senator (1802–03), and mayor of New York City (1803–07, 1808–10, 1811–15). As governor of New York (1817–23, 1825–28), he was a champion of the Erie Canal.

Clin·ton |ˈklintən|, George (1739–1812) U.S. politician. He was governor of New York (1777–95) and vice president of the U.S. (1805–12).

Clin·ton |ˈklintən|, Sir Henry (1738–95) English soldier. He fought at the battles of Bunker Hill (1775) and Long Island (1776) and became commander in chief of British troops in America (1778).

Clin·ton |ˈklintən|, William Jefferson (1946–) see box. **Hillary Rodham**

Clinton, Bill (William Jefferson)
42nd U.S. president

Life dates: 1946–
Place of birth: Hope, Arkansas
Name at birth: William Jefferson Blythe IV
Mother: Virginia Cassidy Blythe (later married Roger Clinton, Sr.)
Father: William Jefferson Blythe II (died before son's birth)
Stepfather: (from the age of 4) Roger Clinton, Sr.
Wife: Hillary Rodham Clinton (married 1975; adopted her husband's last name in 1982)
Child: Chelsea
College/University: Georgetown; Oxford (as Rhodes scholar); Yale Law School
Career: Lawyer
Political career: Governor of Arkansas (two separate terms); president
Party: Democratic
Home state: Arkansas
Opponents in presidential races: George Bush; Robert Dole
Term of office: Jan. 20, 1993–
Vice president: Albert Gore, Jr.
Notable events of presidency: North American Free Trade Agreement (NAFTA); Anti-Crime Bill; Israeli-PLO Peace Accord; Bosnian Civil War treaty (Dayton accords); Good Friday Peace Agreement in Northern Ireland; Paula Jones sexual-harassment lawsuit; Monica Lewinsky scandal; impeachment in the U.S. House of Representatives and acquittal in U.S. Senate trial

Clinton (1947–), wife of Bill Clinton and U.S. first lady (1993–).

Clive |kliv|, Robert (1725–74) (1st Baron Clive of Plassey) British general and colonial administrator; known as **Clive of India**. In 1757 he recaptured Calcutta, following the Black Hole incident, and gained control of Bengal. He served as governor of Bengal 1765–67, but was implicated in the East India company's corruption scandals and committed suicide.

Close |klōz|, Glenn (1947–) U.S. actress. Her movies include *Fatal Attraction* (1987), and her stage appearances include *The Real Thing* (1984–85) and *Sunset Boulevard* (1995).

Clou·et |kloō'a| French court portrait painters. **Jean Clouet** (*c.* 1485–1541) worked as court painter to Francis I; the monarch's portrait in the Louvre is attributed to him. His son **François Clouet** (*c.* 1516–72) succeeded his father as court painter, and is chiefly known for his undated portraits of Elizabeth of Austria (now in the Louvre) and Mary, Queen of Scots (now in the Wallace Collection in London).

Clough |klʌf|, Arthur Hugh (1819–61) English poet. Notable poems: "Amours de Voyage" (1858).

Clo·vis |'klōvəs| (*c.* 466–511) king of the Franks (481–511). He extended Merovingian rule to Gaul and Germany, making Paris his capital. After his conversion to Christianity he championed orthodoxy against the Arian Visigoths, finally defeating them in the battle of Poitiers (507).

Clu·ett |'kloō,ət|, Sanford Lockwood (1874–1968) U.S. engineer. He invented the Sanforizing process of mechanically preshrinking fabrics.

Co·bain |'kō'bān|, Kurt (Donald) (1967–94) U.S. rock singer, guitarist, and songwriter. As leader of the Seattle band Nirvana, his style helped characterize the alternative music scene. His notoriety reached cult proportions, undiminished by his suicide in April 1994.

Cobb |käb|, Ty (1886–1961) U.S. baseball player. Full name *Tyrus Raymond Cobb*; also known as **Georgia Peach**. He holds the highest lifetime batting average (.367) in baseball history.

Cob·bett |'käbət|, William (1763–1835) English writer and political reformer. He started his political life as a Tory, but later became a radical and in 1802 founded the periodical *Cobbett's Political Register*. Notable works: *Rural Rides* (1830).

Cob·den |'käbdn|, Richard (1804–65) English political reformer. He was one of the leading spokesmen of the free-trade movement in Britain. From 1838, together with John Bright, he led the Anti-Corn Law League in its successful campaign for the repeal of the Corn Laws (1846).

Co·burn |'kōbərn|, Charles (1877–1961) U.S. actor. Notable movies: *The Devil and Miss Jones* (1941) and *The More the Merrier* (1943, Academy Award).

Co·chise |kō'CHēs| (1812?–74) Apache Indian chief.

Coch·ran |'käkrən|, Sir Charles Blake (1872–1951) English theatrical producer. He was noted for musical revues including Noël Coward's *Bitter Sweet* (1929) and *Cavalcade* (1931). He was also agent for Houdini.

Coch·ran |'käkrən|, Eddie (1938–60) U.S. rock-and-roll singer and songwriter. Full name *Edward Cochrane*. He was killed in a car crash during a British tour. Notable songs: "Summertime Blues" (1958) and "Three Steps to Heaven" (1960).

Coch·ran |'käkrən|, Jacqueline (1910?–80) U.S. aviator. The first woman to break the sound barrier, she set many speed and altitude records

Coch·ran |'käkrən|, Johnnie L., Jr. (1937–) U.S. attorney. He was the lead defense attorney for O. J. Simpson in his murder trial (1995)

Cock·croft |'kä,krawft|, Sir John Douglas (1897–1967) English physicist. In 1932 he succeeded (with E. T. S. Walton) in splitting the atom, ushering in the whole field of nuclear and particle physics. Nobel Prize for Physics (1951, shared with Walton).

Cock·er |'käkər|, Joe (1944–) British musician. Full name *Robert John Cocker*. Known for his gritty, powerful white-soul and rock voice, his performance at Woodstock of "A Little Help from My

Friends" became an archetypal rock performance.

Cock·er·ell |'käkrəl|, Sir Christopher Sydney (1910–) English engineer, the inventor of the hovercraft.

Coc·teau |käk'tō|, Jean (1889–1963) French dramatist, novelist, and movie director. His plays are noted for their striking blend of poetry, irony, and fantasy. Notable works: *La Machine infernale* (play, 1934), *La Belle et la bête* (movie, 1946), and *Les Enfants terribles* (novel, 1929).

Co·dy |'kōdē|, William Frederick see BUFFALO BILL.

Coe |kō|, Sebastian (1956–) British middle-distance runner and Conservative politician. He was an Olympic gold medal winner in the 1,500 meters in 1980 and 1984.

Coen |kōn| U.S. filmmakers. **Joel Coen** (1954–), a director, and his brother **Ethan Coen** (1957–), a producer, together created such movies as *Barton Fink* (1991) and *Fargo* (1996, Academy Award).

Coet·zee |'kootsir|, J. M. (1940–) South African novelist; full name *John Maxwell Coetzee*. Notable novels: *In the Heart of the Country* (1977) and *Life and Times of Michael K* (1983).

Cof·fin |'kawfən|, Howard Earle (1873–1937) U.S. engineer. He designed the Hudson automobile and helped found National Air Transport (1925), which was the forerunner of United Airlines.

Cof·fin |'kawfən|, Levi (1798–1877) U.S. abolitionist. He was active in the Underground Railroad and opened a Quaker school for slaves.

Cof·fin |'kawfən|, William Sloan (1924–) U. S. minister. As a Presbyterian clergyman and Yale University chaplain during the 1960s, he was a leader of antiwar protests.

Co·han |'kō,hæn|, George Michael (1878–1942) U.S. actor, playwright, composer, and producer. Among his most famous tunes are "Yankee Doodle Dandy" and "Give My Regards to Broadway."

Cohn |kōn|, Al (1925–88) U.S. jazz tenor saxophonist and composer. Full name *Alvin Gilbert Cohn*. He was the principal arranger for the musicals

Raisin (1973), *Music, Music, Music* (1974), and *Sophisticated Ladies* (1981).

Cohn |kōn|, Ferdinand Julius (1828–98) German botanist, a founder of bacteriology and the first to devise a systematic classification of bacteria into genera and species.

Cohn |kōn|, Harry (1891–1958) U.S. founder of Columbia Pictures.

Col·bert |kōl'bert|, Jean Baptiste (1619–83) French statesman, chief minister to Louis XIV 1665–83. He was responsible for reforming the country's finances and the navy, and for boosting industry and commerce.

Cole |kōl| U.S. musicians: **Nat King Cole** (1919–65), a singer and pianist, was born *Nathaniel Adams Coles*. His mellow vocal tones won him international recognition as a singer. He became the first black man to have his own radio (1948–49) and television (1956–57) series. Notable songs: "Mona Lisa" (1950) and "Ramblin' Rose" (1962). His daughter **Natalie Cole** (1950–), a singer, won three Grammy Awards for her album *Unforgettable* (1991).

Cole |kōl|, Cozy (1909–81) U.S. jazz drummer. Born *William Randolph Cole*. He performed with Cab Calloway's orchestra (1938–42) and with Louis Armstrong's All Stars (1949–53). He opened a drum school in New York with Gene Krupa.

Cole |kōl|, Thomas (1801–48) U.S. artist. He was founder of the Hudson River School.

Cole·man |'kōlmən|, Ornette (1930–) U.S. jazz saxophonist, trumpeter, violinist, and composer, whose music is noted for its lack of harmony and chordal structure.

Cole·man |'kōlmən|, William (1870–1957) U.S. businessman. He founded Coleman Camping Equipment and marketed the "Coleman Arc Lamp" gas lamp to homes without electricity in 1903.

Cole·ridge |'kōl(ə)rij|, Samuel Taylor (1772–1834) English poet, critic, and philosopher. His *Lyrical Ballads* (1798), written with William Wordsworth, marked the start of English romanticism and included "The Rime of the Ancient Mariner." Other notable poems:

"Christabel" and "Kubla Khan" (both 1816).

Coles |kōl|, Joanna (1944–) U.S. author. Her nonfiction books for children include the *Magic School Bus* series.

Coles |kōlz|, Robert Martin (1929–) U.S. psychiatrist, educator, and author. A specialist in child psychology, he wrote the Pulitzer Prize–winning series *Children of Crisis* (1967–78).

Co·lette |kō'let| (1873–1954) French novelist. Born *Sidonie Gabrielle Claudine*. Notable novels: *Chéri* (1920) and *La Fin de Chéri* (1926). Her novel *Gigi* (1945) was filmed in 1948 and again as a musical in 1958.

Col·fax |'kawlfæks|, Schuyler (1823–85) U.S. vice president (1869–73).

Col·gate |'kōl,gāt|, William (1783–1857) U.S. manufacturer and philanthropist, born in England. He started out making candles and then (1806) set up a tallow factory in New York to make soap. His firm later became the Colgate-Palmolive-Peet Co. Colgate University was named in his honor.

Col·lier |'kälyər|, Peter Fenelon (1849–1909) U.S. publisher. He founded *Collier's Weekly* (1896).

Col·lins |'kälənz|, Edward Knight (1802–78) U.S. shipowner. He founded the Collins Line (1847), with steamships that were then the fastest in transatlantic service.

Col·lins |'kälənz|, Joan (Henrietta) (1933–) English actress. She was a sex symbol in movies such as *Our Girl Friday* (1953) and was later known for the television series "Dynasty" (1981–89). She is the sister of the novelist Jackie Collins.

Col·lins |'kälənz|, Judy (1939–) U.S. singer, songwriter, author, and actress. Her lyrical voice helped to define folk rock in the 1960s.

Col·lins |'kälənz|, Michael (1890–1922) Irish nationalist leader and politician. A member of Parliament for Sinn Fein, he was one of the negotiators of the Anglo-Irish Treaty of 1921. He commanded the Irish Free State forces in the civil war and became head of state but was assassinated ten days later.

Col·lins |'kälənz|, Phil (1951–) U.S. rock musician. Full name *Phillip David*

Charles Collins. He was a singer with many top hits and a drummer for Genesis, Eric Clapton, and Led Zeppelin.

Col·lins |'kälənz|, (William) Wilkie (1824–89) English novelist. He is noted for his detective stories *The Woman in White* (1860) and *The Moonstone* (1868).

Col·man |'kōlmən|, Ronald (1891–1958) English actor. Notable movies: *A Tale of Two Cities* (1935), *The Prisoner of Zenda* (1937), and *Random Harvest* (1942).

Col·son |'kōlsən|, Charles Wendell (1931–) U.S. lay minister. As special counsel to President Nixon (1969–72), he became a principal in the Watergate scandal.

Colt |kōlt|, Samuel (1814–62) U.S. inventor. He is remembered chiefly for the revolver named after him, which he patented originally in 1836; it was adopted by the U.S. Army in 1846. His armory at Hartford, Connecticut, advanced the manufacturing techniques of interchangeable parts and the production line.

Col·ton |'kawltn|, Frank Benjamin (1923–) U.S. chemist, born in Poland. He developed Enovid, the first oral contraceptive (1960).

Col·trane |'kōl,trān|, John William (1926–67) U.S. jazz saxophonist. He was a leading figure in avant-garde jazz, bridging the gap between the harmonically dense jazz of the 1950s and the free jazz that evolved in the 1960s. Notable recordings: *My Favorite Things* (1960).

Co·lum·ba |kə'ləmbə|, St. (*c.* 521–97) Irish abbot and missionary. He established the monastery at Iona *c.*563 and converted the Picts to Christianity. Feast day, June 9.

Co·lum·bus |kə'ləmbəs|, Christopher (1451–1506) Italian-born Spanish explorer. Spanish name *Cristóbal Colón*. His four pioneering voyages to the Americas (1492–1504) led to Spanish colonization of the New World.

Co·ma·ne·ci |kōmə'nēCH|, Nadia (1961–) Romanian gymnast; emigrated to the U.S. in 1989. In 1976 she became the first Olympic gymnast to earn seven perfect scores and won three gold medals at the 1976 Olympics.

Co·mis·key |kə'miskē|, Charles Albert (1859–1931) U.S. baseball executive. A professional baseball player and the founder, owner, and president of the Chicago White Sox (1900), he built Comiskey Park and was inducted into the Baseball Hall of Fame (1939).

Com·ma·ger |'kəmə,jər|, Henry Steele (1902–98) U.S. educator and author. Notable works: *The American Mind* (1951) and *Freedom, Loyalty, Dissent* (1954).

Co·mo |'kō,mō|, Perry (1912–) U.S. singer. A nightclub entertainer with movie and television credits, he starred in the television program "The Perry Como Show."

Comp·ton |'kämptn|, Arthur Holly (1892–1962) American physicist. He observed the Compton effect and thus demonstrated the dual particle and wave properties of electromagnetic radiation and matter, as predicted by quantum theory. Nobel Prize for Physics (1927).

Compton-Burnett |'kämptn bər'net|, Dame Ivy (1884–1969) English novelist. Notable novels: *Brothers and Sisters* (1929), *A Family and a Fortune* (1939), and *Manservant and Maidservant* (1947).

Com·stock |'käm,stäk|, John Henry (1849–1931) U.S. entomologist and author. He wrote pioneering work in the classification of scale insects, moths, and butterflies.

Com·stock |'käm,stäk|, Anthony (1844–1915) U.S. reformer. He campaigned against pornographic literature and helped pass the federal Comstock Law (1873) banning such literature from the mails. As founder and secretary for the Society for the Suppression of Vice in New York, he carried out raids on publishers and vendors of "obscene" materials.

Comte |kawnt|, Auguste (1798–1857) French philosopher, one of the founders of sociology. Comte's positivist philosophy attempted to define the laws of social evolution and to found a genuine social science that could be used for social reconstruction.

Co·nan Doyle |'kōnən 'doil| see DOYLE.

Co·ne·glia·no |kawnel'yänō|, Emmanuele see DA PONTE.

Con·fu·cius |kən'fyōōSHəs| (551–479 BC) Chinese philosopher. Latinized name of *Kongfuze* (*K'ung Fu-tzu*). Known as **Kong the master**. His ideas about the importance of practical moral values, collected by his disciples in the *Analects*, formed the basis of the philosophy known as Confucianism.

Con·greve |'käNG,grēv|, William (1670–1729) English dramatist. A close associate of Swift, Pope, and Steele, he wrote plays such as *Love for Love* (1695) and *The Way of the World* (1700), which epitomize the wit and satire of Restoration comedy.

Con·nell |'känəl|, Evan Shelby, Jr. (1924–) U.S. author. His works of nonfiction include the historical *Son of the Morning Star* (1984). Notable novels: *Mrs. Bridge* (1959) and *Mr. Bridge* (1969).

Con·nery |'känərē|, Sean (1930–) Scottish actor. Born *Thomas Connery*. He is best known for his portrayal of British secret agent James Bond in a number of movies. Other notable work: *The Untouchables* (1987, Academy Award).

Con·nol·ly |'känəlē|, Cyril (Vernon) (1903–74) English writer and journalist. His works include one novel, *The Rock Pool* (1936), and collections of essays, aphorisms, and reflections, among which are *Enemies of Promise* (1938) and *The Unquiet Grave* (1944). He worked for the *Sunday Times* from 1951 until 1974.

Con·nol·ly |'känəlē|, Maureen Catherine (1934–69) U.S. tennis player. Known as **Little Mo**. She was 16 when she first won the U.S. singles title and 17 when she took the Wimbledon title. In 1953 she became the first woman to win the tennis Grand Slam. She retired in 1954 after a riding accident.

Con·nor |'känər|, Dennis (1942–) U.S. yachtsman. Three-time winner of the America's Cup (1980, 1987, 1988), he is also the first American skipper to lose the Cup (1983).

Con·nors |'känərz|, Jimmy (1952–) U.S. professional tennis player. Full name *James Scott Connors*. He won Wimbledon in 1974 and 1982, and the U.S. Open championship five times.

Con·over |'känəvər|, Lloyd H. (1923–) U.S. inventor. He created the broad-spectrum antibiotic tetracycline (patented 1955).

Con·rad |'kän,ræd|, Paul Francis (1924–) U.S. political cartoonist. Pulitzer Prizes, 1964 and 1971.

Con·rad |'kän,ræd|, Joseph (1857–1924) Polish-born British novelist. Born *Józef Teodor Konrad Korzeniowski*. Although French was his first foreign language, Conrad wrote in English and became a British citizen in 1886. Much of his work, including his story *Heart of Darkness* (1902) and the novel *Nostromo* (1904), explores the darkness within human nature.

Con·roy |'kän,roi|, Pat (1945–) U.S. author. Full name *Donald Patrick Conroy*. Notable novels: *The Great Santini* (1976) and *The Prince of Tides* (1986).

Con·sta·ble |'känstəbəl|, John (1776–1837) English painter. Among his best-known works are early paintings like *Flatford Mill* (1817) and *The Hay Wain* (1821), inspired by the landscape of his native Suffolk.

Con·stan·tine |'känstən,tēn| (*c.* 274–337) Roman emperor. Known as **Constantine the Great**. He was the first Roman emperor to be converted to Christianity and in 324 made Christianity the Empire's state religion. In 330 he moved his capital from Rome to Byzantium, renaming it Constantinopolis (Constantinople). In the Orthodox Church he is venerated as a saint.

Cook |kook|, George Cram (1873–1924) U.S. playwright, novelist, and poet.

Cook |kook|, Captain James (1728–79) English explorer. On his first expedition to the Pacific (1768–71), he charted the coasts of New Zealand and New Guinea as well as exploring the east coast of Australia and claiming it for Britain. He made two more voyages to the Pacific before being killed in a skirmish with native people in Hawaii.

Cook |kook|, Peter (Edward) (1937–95) English comedian and actor.

Cook |kook|, Robin (1940–) U.S. author. He is known as the master of the medical thriller. Notable novels: *Fatal Cure* (1994) and *Chromosome 6* (1997).

Cook |kook|, Thomas (1808–92) English founder of the travel firm Thomas Cook. In 1841 he organized the first publicly advertised excursion train in England; the success of this venture led him to organize further excursions both in Britain and abroad, laying the foundations for the British tourist and travel-agent industry.

Cooke |kook|, Jay (1821–1905) U.S. financier. He was the founder of Jay Cooke and Co., a leading Philadelphia bank (1861); his financing of western railroads precipitated the Panic of 1873.

Cooke |kook|, Sam (1935–64) U.S. musician. He was a singer, songwriter, and producer who mixed gospel and rock to provide the foundation of soul music.

Cooke |kook|, Sir William Fothergill (1806–79) English inventor. With Sir Charles Wheatstone he invented the electric telegraph alarm.

Cook·son |'kooksən|, Dame Catherine (Ann) (1906–1998) English writer. She is a prolific author of romantic fiction.

Coo·lidge |'koolij|, (John) Calvin (1872–1933) see box. **Grace Anna Goodhue Coolidge** (1879–1957), wife of Calvin Coolidge and U.S. first lady (1923–29).

Coo·lidge |'koolij|, William David (1873–1975) U.S. physical chemist and inventor. His invention of ductile tungsten (1908) revolutionized the production of light bulbs and enabled him to make significant strides in x-ray technology.

Coo·ney |'koonē|, Joan Ganz (1929–) U.S. broadcasting executive. A pioneer of educational children's television, she founded the Children's Television Workshop (1968) and created "Sesame Street" (1968–) for the Public Broadcasting System.

Coo·per |'koopər|, Alice (Vincent Damon Furnier) (1948–) U.S. rock singer and songwriter.

Coo·per |'koopər|, Gary (1901–61) U.S. movie actor. Born *Frank James Cooper*. He is noted for his performances in such westerns as *The Virginian* (1929) and *High Noon* (1952).

Coo·per |'koopər|, James Fenimore

Coolidge, Calvin (born John Calvin)
30th U.S. president

Life dates: 1872–1933
Place of birth: Plymouth Notch, Vermont
Mother: Victoria Josephine Moor Coolidge
Stepmother: Caroline Athelia Brown Coolidge
Father: John Calvin Coolidge
Wife: Grace Anna Goodhue Coolidge
Children: John; Calvin, Jr.
Nickname: "Silent Cal"
College/University: Amherst College
Career: Lawyer; bank vice president; newspaper columnist
Political career: Massachusetts House of Representatives; mayor, Northampton, Mass.; Massachusetts Senate; lieutenant governor and governor of Massachusetts; vice president (under Harding); president
Party: Republican
Home state: Massachusetts
Opponents in presidential race: John W. Davis, Robert M. La Follette
Term of office: Aug. 3, 1923–March 3, 1929 (succeeded to the presidency on the death of Warren G. Harding; won 1924 election)
Vice president: none (1st term); Charles G. Dawes (2nd term)
Notable events of presidency: Teapot Dome scandal; Immigration Act of 1924; Scopes monkey trials; Japanese Exclusion Act; Charles Lindbergh's transatlantic solo flight; Kellogg-Briand Peace Pact; U.S. Foreign Service created
Other achievements: Admitted to the Pennsylvania bar; settled Boston police strike; chairman, Nonpartisan Railroad Commission; president, American Antiquarian Society; wrote syndicated newspaper column
Place of burial: Plymouth Notch, Vermont

(1789–1851) U.S. novelist. He is renowned for his tales of American Indians and frontier life, in particular *The Last of the Mohicans* (1826).

Coo·per |'kōōpər|, Peter (1791–1883) U.S. manufacturer and philanthropist. He designed and built the first steam locomotive, *Tom Thumb* (1830), and founded Cooper Union in New York City (1859).

Coo·per |'kōōpər|, Susie (1902–95) English ceramic designer and manufacturer. Full name *Susan Vera Cooper*. Her work was noted for its functional shapes and simple, vivid designs.

Coors |koorz|, Adolph (1847–1929) U.S. businessman, born in Germany. He founded the Coors brewery.

Co·per·ni·cus |kə'pərnəkəs|, Nicolaus (1473–1543) Polish astronomer. Latinized name of *Mikołaj Kopernik*. He proposed a model of the solar system in which the planets orbited in perfect circles around the sun, and his work ultimately led to the overthrow of the established geocentric cosmology. He published his astronomical theories in *De Revolutionibus Orbium Coelestium* (1543).

Cop·land |'kōplənd|, Aaron (1900–90) U.S. composer, pianist, and conductor, of Lithuanian descent. He established a distinctive American style in his compositions, borrowing from jazz, folk, and other traditional music. Notable works: *Appalachian Spring* (1944), *Fanfare for the Common Man* (1942), and *Music for the Theater* (1925).

Cop·ley |'käplē|, John Singleton (1738–1815) U.S. painter. He is noted for his portraits and for paintings such as *The Death of Chatham* (1779–80), one of the first large-scale paintings of contemporary events.

Cop·per·field |'käpər,fēld|, David (1956–) U.S. magician. Born *David Seth Kotkin*. He has appeared extensively on television and Broadway, performing illusions such as walking through the Great Wall of China.

Cop·po·la |'käpələ|, Francis Ford (1939–) U.S. movie director, writer, and producer. Notable movies: *The Godfather* (1972) and *Apocalypse Now* (1979).

Cor·bett |'kawrbət|, James John (1866–1933) U.S. boxer. Known as **Gentleman Jim**. He won two world heavyweight championships (1892, 1897).

Cor·bin |'kawrbin|, Margaret (1751–1800) American Revolutionary heroine. After her husband's death in the attack on Fort Washington (1776), she took his place at his cannon until becoming severly wounded. She was the first woman to be pensioned by the American government.

Cor·day |kawr'dā|, Charlotte (1768–93) French political assassin. Full name *Marie Anne Charlotte Corday d'Armont.* She became involved with the Girondists and in 1793 assassinated the revolutionary leader Jean Paul Marat in his bath; she was found guilty of treason and guillotined.

Cor·dero |kawrderō|, Angel (1942–) U.S. jockey, born in Puerto Rico.

Co·rel·li |kə'relē|, Arcangelo (1653–1713) Italian violinist and composer. His best-known works are his trio and solo sonatas for the violin and his concerti grossi (published posthumously in 1714), especially the "Christmas" concerto.

Co·rel·li |kə'relē|, Marie (1855–1924) English writer of romantic fiction; pseudonym of *Mary Mackay.* The sales of her novels *Thelma* (1887), *Barabbas* (1893), and *The Sorrows of Satan* (1895) broke records for book sales in the UK, although her popularity was not matched by critical acclaim.

Cor·i·o·la·nus |,kawrēə'lānəs|, Gnaeus Marcius (6th–5th century BC) Roman general, who got his name from the capture of the Volscian town of Corioli. According to legend, after his banishment from Rome he led a Volscian army against the city and was turned back only by the pleas of his mother and wife.

Cor·mack |'kawrmək|, Allan MacLeod (1924–98) U.S. physicist and educator, born in South Africa. He helped to invent the CAT scan. Nobel Prize, 1979.

Cor·neille |kawr'nā|, Pierre (1606–84) French dramatist, generally regarded as the founder of classical French tragedy. Notable plays: *Le Cid* (1637), *Cinna* (1641), and *Polyeucte* (1643).

Cor·nell |kawr'nel|, Ezra (1807–74) U.S. financier and philanthropist. He was an organizer of the Magnetic Telegraph Co., which connected New York and Washington. He later helped found the Western Union Telegraph Co.

Cor·nish |'kawrnisн|, Samuel E (1793–1858) U.S. journalist. He cofounded the first newspaper for African Americans, *Freedom's Journal* (1827).

Corn·wal·lis |,kawrn'wäləs|, Charles, 1st Marquis (1738–1805) English soldier. He surrendered the British forces at Yorktown (1781), ending the fighting in the American Revolution.

Co·ro·na·do |,kawrə'nädō|, Francisco Vásquez de (1510?–54) Spanish explorer. His explorations into Arizona and New Mexico from Mexico opened the Southwest to Spanish colonization.

Co·rot |kə'rō|, Jean-Baptiste-Camille (1796–1875) French landscape painter, who worked in an essentially classical style despite his contact with the Barbizon School. Corot had a significant influence on the Impressionists.

Cor·reg·gio |kə'rejēō|, Antonio Allegri da (1494–1534) Italian painter. The soft, sensual style of his devotional and mythological paintings influenced the rococo of the 18th century. He is best known for his frescoes in Parma Cathedral.

Cort |kawrt|, Henry (1740–1800) English ironmaster. He patented a process for producing iron bars by passing iron through grooved rollers, thus avoiding a hammering stage.

Côrte-Real |'kawr,tə rē'äl|, Gaspar (1450?–?1501) Portuguese navigator and explorer. He explored the coasts of Labrador and Newfoundland (1500).

Cor·tés |kawr'tez|, Hernando (1485–1547) First of the Spanish conquistadors. Also **Cortez.** Cortés overthrew the Aztec empire, conquering its capital, Tenochtitlán, in 1519 and deposing its emperor, Montezuma. In 1521 he destroyed Tenochtitlán completely and established Mexico City as the new capital of Mexico (then called New Spain).

Cos·by |'käzbē|, Bill (1937–) U.S. comedian, actor, and author. Full name *William Henry Cosby, Jr.* He was the first African American to star in a weekly television drama ("I Spy"; 1965–68). His comedy series "The Cosby Show" (1984–92) was one of the most successful programs in television history. Notable books: *Fatherhood* (1987) and *Congratulations! Now What?: A Book for Graduates* (1999).

Co·sell |kō'sel|, Howard (1918–95)

U.S. sports journalist. He was a television and radio commentator whose abrasive "tell it like it is" style found many followers.

Cos·i·mo de' Me·di·ci |'käzə,mō de me 'dēCHē| (1389–1464) Italian statesman and banker. Known as **Cosimo the Elder.** He laid the foundations for the Medici family's power in Florence, becoming the city's ruler in 1434 and using his considerable wealth to promote the arts and learning.

Cos·ta |'kawstə|, Lúcio (1902–63) French-born Brazilian architect, town planner, and architectural historian. He achieved a worldwide reputation with his design for Brazil's new capital, Brasilia, which was chosen by an international jury in 1956.

Cost·ner |'kawstnər|, Kevin (1955–) U.S. actor, director, and producer. Notable movies: *Dances with Wolves* (1990, Academy Award).

Cot·man |'kätmən|, John Sell (1782–1842) English watercolorist and landscape painter. He is regarded as one of the leading figures of the Norwich School.

Cot·sa·kos |kət'säkōs|, Christos Michael (1948–) U.S. businessman. He is the president and CEO of E*Trade Group, Inc. (1996–).

Cot·ten |'kätn|, Joseph (1905–94) U.S. actor. A star of Broadway (*The Philadelphia Story*, 1939), Hollywood (*Citizen Kane*, 1941), and television, his credits include over 60 movies.

Cot·ton |'kätn|, John (1585–1652) English Puritan clergyman. He was a 1633 emigrant to the Massachusetts Bay Colony and a leading exponent of Congregationalism.

Cot·trell |'kätrəl|, Frederick Gardner (1877–1948) U.S. physical chemist and inventor. He invented electrostatic precipitators (1911) and developed practical methods for producing synthetic ammonia.

Cou·ber·tin |koō'bərtän|, Pierre de, Baron (1863–1937) French educator and sportsman. As president of the International Olympic Committee (1894–1925), he revived the Olympic Games.

Cou·lomb |'koō,läm|, Charles-Augustin de (1736–1806) French military engineer. He is best known for Coulomb's Law (1785), which describes the inverse square law of electrostatic force. From this a quantity of electric charge may be defined.

Coul·ter |'kōltər|, Ernest Kent (1871?–1952) U.S. lawyer and humanitarian. A children's rights advocate in the legal system, he founded the Big Brother movement (1904) and was president of the Society for the Prevention of Cruelty to Children (1914–36).

Cou·pe·rin |,koōp'rän|, François (1668–1733) French composer, organist, and harpsichordist. A composer at the court of Louis XIV, he is principally known for his harpsichord works.

Cour·bet |koōr'bā|, Gustave (1819–77) French painter. A leader of the 19th-century realist school of painting, he favored an unidealized choice of subject matter that did not exclude the ugly or vulgar. Notable works: *Burial at Ornans* (1850) and *Painter in his Studio* (1855).

Cour·ic |'koōrik|, Katie (1957–) U.S. TV journalist. She coanchors NBC's *The Today Show* (1991–).

Cour·règes |kaw'reZH|, André (1923–) French fashion designer. He is famous for his futuristic and youth-oriented styles, in particular the use of plastic and metal and unisex fashion such as trouser suits for women.

Court |kawrt|, Margaret Smith (1942–) Australian tennis player. She won more Grand Slam events (66) than any other player.

Cour·tauld |kawr'tōld|, Samuel (1876–1947) English industrialist. He was a director of his family's silk firm and a collector of French Impressionist and post-Impressionist paintings. He presented his collection to the University of London, endowed the Courtauld Institute of Art, and bequeathed to it his house in Portman Square, London.

Cous·teau |koō'stō|, Jacques-Yves (1910–97) French oceanographer and movie director. He devised the scuba apparatus, but is known primarily for several feature films and a popular television series on marine life.

Cou·sy |'koōzē|, Bob (1928–) U.S. basketball player. Full name *Robert*

Joseph Cousy. Elected to the Basketball Hall of Fame (1970).

Cov·er·dale |'kəvər,dāl|, Miles (1488?–1569) English biblical scholar. He translated the first complete printed English Bible (1535), published in Zurich while he was in exile for preaching against confession and images. He also edited the Great Bible of 1539.

Cow·ard |'kowərd|, Sir Noël (Pierce) (1899–1973) English dramatist, actor, and composer. He is remembered for witty, satirical plays, such as *Hay Fever* (1925) and *Private Lives* (1930), as well as revues and musicals featuring songs such as "Mad Dogs and Englishmen" (1932).

Cow·en |'kowən|, Joshua Lionel (1877–1965) U.S. inventor. He invented batteries, electric fuses, and Lionel trains.

Cow·per |'kōōpər|, William (1731–1800) English poet. He is best known for his long poem *The Task* (1785) and the comic ballad *John Gilpin* (1782).

Cox |käks|, James Middleton (1870–1957) U.S. newspaper publisher and politician. He was owner of the Dayton (Ohio) *Daily News*, the Springfield (Ohio) *Press-Republican*, and the Springfield *Sun*, and was a Democratic nominee for president of the U.S. in 1920.

Coxe |käks|, Tench (1755–1824) U.S. political economist. He was assistant U.S. secretary of the treasury (1790–92), commissioner of the revenue (1792–98), and purveyor of public supplies (1803–12).

Coz·zens |'kəzənz|, James Gould (1903–78) U.S. author. Notable works: *Guard of Honor* (1948, Pulitzer Prize) and *By Love Possessed* (1957).

Crabbe |kræb|, George (1754–1832) English poet. He is best known for grimly realistic narrative poems, such as "The Village" (1783) and "The Borough" (1810); the latter included tales of Peter Grimes and Ellen Orford and later provided the subject matter for Benjamin Britten's opera *Peter Grimes* (1945).

Cram |kræm|, Ralph Adams (1863–1942) U.S. architect. Notable designs: Cathedral of St. John the Divine (1912) in New York City, and Princeton University (1909–31).

Cra·nach |'kränək| German painters. **Lucas Cranach** (1472–1553); known as **Cranach the Elder**. He was a member of the Danube School who was noted for his early religious pictures, such as *The Rest of the Flight into Egypt* (1504). He also painted portraits, including several of Martin Luther. His son, **Lucas Cranach** (1515–86), was known as **Cranach the Younger**. He continued to work in the same tradition as his father.

Crane |krān|, Hart (1899–1932) U.S. poet. Full name *Harold Hart Crane*. He published only two books before committing suicide: the collection *White Buildings* (1926) and *The Bridge* (1930), a mystical epic poem concerned with American life and consciousness.

Crane |krān|, Roy (1901–77) U.S. cartoonist. Full name *Royston C. Crane*. One of the earliest cartoonists to produce an adventure strip, he was the creator of the characters Wash Tubbs, Captain Easy, and Buz Sawyer.

Crane |krān|, Stephen (1871–1900) U.S. writer. His reputation rests on his novel *The Red Badge of Courage* (1895), a study of an inexperienced soldier in the Civil War. It was hailed as a masterpiece of psychological realism, even though Crane himself had no personal experience of war.

Cran·mer |'krænmər|, Thomas (1489–1556) English Protestant cleric and martyr. After helping to negotiate Henry VIII's divorce from Catherine of Aragon, he was appointed the first Protestant Archbishop of Canterbury in 1532. He was responsible for liturgical reform and the compilation of the Book of Common Prayer (1549). In the reign of Mary Tudor, Cranmer was tried for treason and heresy and burned at the stake.

Cras·sus |'kræsəs|, Marcus Licinius (*c.* 115–53 BC) Roman politician. After defeating the slave rebellion led by Spartacus in 71 BC, Crassus joined Caesar and Pompey in the First Triumvirate in 60. In 55 he was made consul and given a special command in Syria, where, after some successes, he was defeated and killed.

Cra·ter |'krātər|, Joseph Force (1889–?1937) U.S. jurist. He disappeared on August 6, 1930, while hearing a case on the New York Supreme Court; his disappearance was linked to possible political corruption. He was never found but was declared dead in July 1937.

Craw·ford |'krawfərd| Family name of **Thomas Crawford** (1814–57), a U.S. sculptor. His "Armed Freedom" crowns the dome of the National Capitol; he also sculpted the pediments in the Senate wing of the Capitol. His son, **Francis Marion Crawford** (1854–1909), was a U.S. novelist, born in Italy.

Craw·ford |'krawfərd|, Cindy (1966–) U.S. model.

Craw·ford |'krawfərd|, Joan (1908–73) U.S. movie actress. Born *Lucille LeSueur*. Her movie career lasted for over forty years, during which she played the female lead in movies such as *Rain* (1932), *The Women* (1939), and *Mildred Pierce* (1945). She later appeared in mature roles, such as in the horror movie *Whatever Happened to Baby Jane?* (1962).

Craw·ford |'krawfərd|, Osbert Guy Stanhope (1886–1957) British archaeologist. He pioneered the use of aerial photography in the detection of previously unlocated or buried archeological sites and monuments.

Cray |krā|, Seymour Robert (1925–96) U.S. computer designer. He designed the first computer made with transistors, the Cray-1 and Cray-2.

Cra·zy Horse |'krāzē ˌhawrs| (*c.* 1842–77) Sioux chief. Sioux name *Ta-Sunko-Witko*. In 1876 he led a successful rearguard action of Sioux and Cheyenne warriors against U.S. army forces in Montana. A leading figure in the resistance to white settlement on American Indian land, he was at the center of the confederation that defeated General Custer at Little Bighorn (1876). He surrendered in 1877 and was killed in custody.

Creel |krēl|, George Edward (1876–1953) U.S. journalist and author. He founded and edited the *Kansas City Independent* (1899–1909).

Cree·ley |'krēlē|, Robert White (1926–) U.S. poet. He was editor of *Black Mountain Review* (1954–57).

Cret |krā|, Paul Philippe (1876–1945) U.S. architect, born in France. He designed the Folger Shakespeare Library and the Federal Reserve Board building in Washington, D.C.

Crews |krōōz|, Harry (1935–) U.S. author and educator.

Crich·ton |'krītn|, James (1560–1582) Scottish adventurer. Known as **the Admirable Crichton**. Crichton was an accomplished swordsman, poet, and scholar. He served in the French army and made a considerable impression on French and Italian universities with his skills as a polyglot orator.

Crich·ton |'krītn|, Michael (1942–) U.S. author. Notable novels: *Jurassic Park* (1990) and *The Lost World* (1995).

Crick |krik|, Francis Harry Compton (1916–) English biophysicist. Together with J. D. Watson he proposed the double helix structure of the DNA molecule, thus broadly explaining how genetic information is carried in living organisms and how genes replicate. Shared the Nobel Prize for Physiology or Medicine (1962).

Crip·pen |'kripən|, Hawley Harvey (1862–1910) U.S.-born British murderer. Known as **Doctor Crippen**. Crippen poisoned his wife at their London home and sailed to Canada with his former secretary. His arrest in Canada was achieved through the intervention of radiotelegraphy, the first case of its use in apprehending a criminal; Crippen was later hanged.

Cro·ce |'krōchā|, Benedetto (1866–1952) Italian philosopher and politician. In his *Philosophy of Spirit*, he denied the physical reality of a work of art and identified philosophical endeavor with a methodological approach to history. A former minister of education, he helped to rebuild democracy in Italy after the fall of Mussolini.

Crock·er |'krākər|, Charles (1822–88) U.S. financier. He merged the Southern Pacific and Central Pacific railroads (1884).

Crock·er |'krākər|, Francis Bacon (1861–1921) U.S. electrical engineer. Along with others, he developed the standard electrical motor (1886).

Crock·ett |'krākət|, Davy (1786–1836)

U.S. frontiersman, soldier, and politician. Full name *David Crockett*. He was a member of the U.S. House of Representatives (1827–35) and cultivated the image of a rough backwoods legislator. On leaving politics he returned to the frontier, where he took up the cause of independence for Texas and was killed at the siege of the Alamo.

Croe·sus |'krēsəs| (died *c.* 546 BC) The last king of Lydia (*c.* 560–546 BC). Renowned for his great wealth, he subjugated the Greek cities on the coast of Asia Minor before being overthrown by Cyrus the Great of Persia.

Cro·ker |'krōkər|, Richard (1841–1922) U.S. politician, born in Ireland. Known as **Boss Croker**. He was recognized as the leader of Tammany Hall (1884–1901).

Cro·ly |'krōlē| U.S. family of editors. Irish-born **David Goodman Croly** (1829–89), a journalist, was the managing editor of *New York World* (1862–72) and editor of the *Daily Graphic* (1873–78). His wife, **Jane Cunningham Croly** (1829–1901), born in England, was an editor. Pseudonym **Jennie June**. She founded the women's club Sorosis and the Woman's Press Club in New York. Their son, **Herbert David Croly** (1869–1930), an editor and author, founded *The New Republic*.

Crome |krōm|, John (1768–1821) English painter. Founder and leading member of the Norwich School, he later developed a distinctive romantic style of his own, exemplified in such landscapes as *Slate Quarries*.

Cromp·ton |'krämtn|, Richmal (1890–1969) English writer. Pseudonym of *Richmal Crompton Lamburn*. She made her name with *Just William* (1922), a collection of stories for children about a mischievous schoolboy, William Brown. She published a further thirty-seven collections based on the same character, as well as some fifty books for adults.

Cromp·ton |'krämtn|, Samuel (1753–1827) English inventor. Famed for his invention of the spinning mule, he lacked the means to obtain a patent and sold his rights to an industrialist for £67. The House of Commons subsequently gave him £5,000 in compensation.

Crom·well |'krämwel|, Oliver (1599–1658) English general and statesman. He was Lord Protector of the Commonwealth (1653–58). Cromwell was the leader of the victorious Parliamentary forces (or Roundheads) in the English Civil War. As head of state he styled himself Lord Protector, and refused Parliament's offer of the Crown in 1657. His rule was notable for its Puritan reforms in the Church of England. He was briefly succeeded by his son **Richard** (1626–1712), who was forced into exile in 1659.

Crom·well |'krämwel|, Thomas (1485?–1540) English statesman. He was chief minister to Henry VIII (1531–40). He presided over the king's divorce from Catherine of Aragon (1533) and his break with the Roman Catholic Church as well as the dissolution of the monasteries and the 1534 Act of Supremacy. He fell from favor over Henry's marriage to Anne of Cleves and was executed on a charge of treason.

Cro·nin |'krōnən|, A. J. (1896–1981) Scottish novelist. Full name *Archibald Joseph Cronin*. His novels, including *The Citadel* (1937), often reflect his early experiences as a doctor.

Cron·kite |'kräNGkīt|, Walter Leland, Jr. (1916–) U.S. television journalist. He anchored the "CBS Evening News" from its debut (1962) until his retirement (1981).

Crook |krŏŏk|, George (1829–90) U.S. army officer. He fought against American Indians and was defeated by Crazy Horse (1876); he also fought against the Apaches and Geronimo (1882–85).

Crookes |krŏŏks|, Sir William (1832–1919) English physicist and chemist. In 1861 he discovered the element thallium. This led him indirectly to the invention of the radiometer in 1875. He later developed a vacuum tube (the precursor of the X-ray tube) and in 1903 invented the spinthariscope.

Cros·by |'krawzbē|, Bing (1904–77) U.S. singer and actor; born *Harry Lillis Crosby*. His songs include "White Christmas" (from the movie *Holiday*

Inn, 1942) one of the best selling songs of all time. He also starred in the series of *Road* movies (1940–62) with Bob Hope and Dorothy Lamour.

Cros·by |'krawzbē|, David (1941–) U.S. rock guitarist and singer. Born *David Van Cartland.* He was a member of the Byrds and of Crosby, Stills, Nash (and Young).

Cross |kraws|, (Charles) Whitman (1854–1949) U.S. geologist. With Iddings, Pirsson, and Washington, he wrote *Quantitative Classification of Igneous Rocks* (1903).

Crow |krō|, Sheryl (1963–) U.S. rock singer, songwriter, and guitarist. Grammy Awards, 1997.

Crown·in·shield |'krownən,SHēld|, Francis Welch (1872–1947) U.S. editor, born in France. He was the publisher of *The Bookman* (1895–1900) and editor of *Vanity Fair* (1914–36).

Cruik·shank |'krŏŏk,SHæNGk|, George (1792–1878) English painter, illustrator, and caricaturist, the most eminent political cartoonist of his day. His later work includes illustrations for Charles Dickens's *Sketches by Boz* (1836), and a series of etchings supporting the temperance movement.

Cruise |krŏŏz|, Tom (1962–) U.S. actor. Born *Thomas Cruise Mapother, IV.*

Crumb |krəm|, Robert (1943–) U.S. cartoonist and author. He was the leading member of a group of "underground" cartoonists producing controversial work satirizing American society.

Crys·tal |'kristl|, Billy (1947–) U.S. actor, comedian, writer, and director.

Cu·kor |'kŏŏkər|, George Dewey (1899–1983) U.S. movie director. Notable movies: *My Fair Lady* (1964, Academy Award).

Cul·bert·son |'kəlbərtsən|, Ely (1891–1955) U.S. bridge player. An authority on contract bridge, he revolutionized the game by formalizing a system of bidding. This helped to establish this form of the game in preference to auction bridge.

Cul·ha·ne |kəl'hānē|, Shamus (1908–96) U.S. producer and animator. He was an animator with Walt Disney Studios and others before opening his own studio (1946). Notable movies: *Snow White* (1937, Academy Award).

Cul·len |'kələn|, Countee (1903–46) U.S. poet and leader of the Harlem Renaissance.

Cul·pep·er |'kəl,pepər|, Nicholas (1616–54) English herbalist. His *Complete Herbal* (1653) popularized herbalism and, despite embracing ideas of astrology and the doctrine of signatures, was important in the development of botany and pharmacology.

Cum·ber·land |'kəmbərlənd|, William Augustus, Duke of (1721–65) English military commander, third son of King George II. He gained great notoriety (and his nickname "the Butcher") for the severity of his suppression of the Jacobite clans in the aftermath of his victory at the Battle of Culloden in Scotland (1746).

cum·mings |'kəmiNGz|, e. e. (1894–1962) U.S. poet and novelist; full name *Edward Estlin Cummings.* His poems are characterized by their experimental typography (most notably in the avoidance of capital letters), technical skill, frank vocabulary, and the sharpness of his satire.

Cum·mings |'kəmiNGz|, Homer Stillé (1870–1956) U.S. lawyer and politician. As U.S. attorney general (1933–39), he drafted Pres. Franklin D. Roosevelt's plan to "pack" the U.S. Supreme Court (1937).

Cu·nard |kyŏŏ'närd|, Sir Samuel (1787–1865) Canadian-born British shipowner. One of the pioneers of the regular transatlantic passenger service, he founded the steamship company that still bears his name with the aid of a contract to carry the mail between Britain and Canada. The first such voyage for the company was made in 1840.

Cun·ning·ham |'kəniNG,hæm|, Imogen (1883–1976) U.S. photographer. She is best known for her black-and-white portraits and nature studies.

Cun·ning·ham |'kəniNG,hæm|, Merce (1919–) U.S. dancer and choreographer. A dancer with the Martha Graham Dance Company (1939–45), he began to experiment with choreography, collaborating with the composer John Cage in solo performances in 1944. He formed his own company in 1953 and explored new abstract directions for modern dance.

Cu·rie |'kyŏōrē| French physicists. **Pierre Curie** (1859–1906) and his wife, Polish-born **Marie Curie** 1867–1934), were pioneers in studying radioactivity. Working together on the mineral pitchblende, they discovered the elements polonium and radium, for which they shared the 1903 Nobel Prize for Physics with A. H. Becquerel. After her husband's accidental death Marie received another Nobel Prize (for chemistry) in 1911 for her isolation of radium. She died of leukemia, caused by prolonged exposure to radioactive materials.

Cur·ley |'kôrlē|, James Michael (1874–1958) U.S. politician. An urban political boss, he was a member of the U.S. House of Representatives (1911–14, 1943–47), mayor of Boston (four terms between 1914 and 1950), and governor of Massachusetts (1935–37).

Cur·ri·er |'kərēər|, Nathaniel (1813–88) U.S. lithographer. He partnered with James Ives in 1857 to establish the company of Currier & Ives, which produced hand-colored prints of American scenes.

Cur·ry |'kərē|, John (Anthony) (1949–94) English figure skater.

Cur·ry |'kərē|, John Steuart (1897–1946) U.S. artist. Much of his work portrayed legendary American folk heroes, such as his depiction of abolitionist John Brown in *Tragic Prelude*, part of a mural series (1938–40) in the Kansas State Capitol.

Cur·tin |'kərtn|, Jane (1947–) U.S. actress. She was an original cast member of television's "Saturday Night Live" (1975–80) and later starred in the television sitcom "Third Rock from the Sun."

Cur·tin |'kərtn|, John (Joseph Ambrose) (1885–1945) Australian Labour statesman, prime minister (1941–45).

Cur·tis |'kərtəs| U.S. family, including: **Benjamin Robbins Curtis** (1809–74), a U.S. Supreme Court justice (1851–57). He resigned in protest over the Supreme Court's handling of the Dred Scott case. He served as chief counsel to Andrew Johnson during Johnson's impeachment. His brother, **George Tick-**

nor Curtis (1812–94), a lawyer and author, argued for the plaintiff before the U.S. Supreme Court in the Dred Scott case.

Cur·tis |'kərtəs|, Charles (1860–1936) U.S. politician. A member from Kansas of the U.S. House of Representatives (1893–1907) and the U.S. Senate (1907–13, 1915–29), he was vice president of the U.S. (1929–33) under Herbert Hoover.

Cur·tis |'kərtəs|, Cyrus Hermann Kotzschmar (1850–1933) U.S. publisher. He was head of the Curtis Publishing Co. (1890–1933), which published the *Ladies' Home Journal*, the *Saturday Evening Post*, and the *Philadelphia Inquirer*.

Cur·tis |'kərtəs|, Edward Sheriff (1868–1952) U.S. photographer. He photographed the Harriman Alaskan expedition (1899) and was known for his photographs of American Indians.

Cur·tis |'kərtəs|, George William (1824–92) U.S. author. He was a member of the Brook Farm community, a leader in civil service reform, and the editor of *Harper's Weekly* from 1863.

Cur·tiss |'kərtəs|, Glenn (Hammond) (1878–1930) U.S. air pioneer and aircraft designer. In 1908 Curtiss made the first public U.S. flight, of more than a kilometer. He built his first airplane in 1909, invented the aileron, and demonstrated the first practical seaplane two years later.

Cur·tiz |'kərtəs|, Michael (1888–1962) U.S. director, born in Hungary. Notable movies: *Casablanca* (1943, Academy Award)

Cush·ing |'kŏōSHiNG|, Harvey Williams (1869–1939) American surgeon. He introduced techniques that greatly increased the likelihood of success in neurosurgical operations, and described the hormonal disorder that was later named after him.

Cush·ing |'kŏōSHiNG|, Peter (1913–94) English actor, known particularly for his roles in horror movies.

Cush·ing |'kŏōSHiNG|, William (1732–1810) U.S. Supreme Court justice (1789–1810). He also served as Chief Justice of the Massachusetts Supreme Court (1777–89).

Cus·ter |'kəstər|, George Armstrong (1839–76) U.S. cavalry officer He served with distinction in the Civil War, but led his 266 men to their deaths in a clash (popularly known as Custer's Last Stand) with the Sioux at Little Bighorn in Montana (1876). Controversy over his conduct in the final battle still continues.

Cuth·bert |'kəтнbərt|, St. (635–687) English monk, bishop, and missionary to Northumbria. Feast day, March 20.

Cut·ter |'kətər|, Charles Ammi (1837–1903) U.S. librarian. He developed a system of labeling books using initial letters and numbers for the authors' names.

Cu·vier |kōōvē'ā|, Georges Léopold Chrétien Frédéric Dagobert, Baron (1769–1832) French naturalist. Cuvier founded the science of paleontology and made pioneering studies in comparative anatomy and classification.

Cym·be·line |'simbəlēn| (died c. 42 AD) British chieftain. Also **Cunobelinus**. A powerful ruler, he made Camulodunum (Colchester) his capital, and established a mint there. He was the subject of a medieval fable used by Shakespeare for his play *Cymbeline*.

Cyn·e·wulf |'kinə,wŏŏlf| (9th century) Anglo-Saxon poet. Modern scholarship attributes four poems to him: *Juliana*, *Elene*, *The Fates of the Apostles*, and *Christ II*.

Cyp·ri·an |'siprēən|, St. (died 258) Carthaginian bishop and martyr. The author of a work on the nature of true unity in the Church in its relation to the episcopate, he was martyred in the reign of the Roman emperor Valerian. Feast day, September 16 or 26.

Cyr·a·no de Ber·ge·rac |,sirənō də 'bərzнəræk|, Savinien (1619–55) French soldier, duelist, and writer. He is chiefly remembered for the large number of duels that he fought (many on ac-

count of his proverbially large nose), as immortalized in a play by Edmond Rostand (*Cyrano de Bergerac*, 1897).

Cyr·il |'sirəl|, St. (c. 827–69) Greek missionary. The invention of the Cyrillic alphabet is ascribed to him. He and his brother, St. Methodius, were sent to Moravia where they taught in the vernacular, which they adopted also for the liturgy, and circulated a Slavic version of the scriptures. Feast day (in the Eastern Church) May 11; (in the Western Church) February 14.

Cyr·il of Al·ex·an·dria |,sirəl əv æleg-'zændrēə|, St. (c. 375–444) Doctor of the Church and patriarch of Alexandria. A champion of orthodoxy, he is best known for his vehement opposition to the views of the patriarch of Constantinople, Nestorius, whose condemnation he secured at the Council of Ephesus in 431. Feast day, February 9.

Cy·rus[1] |'sirəs| (died c. 530 BC) king of Persia 559–530 BC and founder of the Achaemenid dynasty, father of Cambyses; known as **Cyrus the Great**. He defeated the Median empire in 550 BC and went on to conquer Asia Minor, Babylonia, Syria, Palestine, and most of the Iranian plateau. He is said to have ruled with wisdom and moderation, maintaining good relations with the Jews (whom he freed from the Babylonian Captivity) and the Phoenicians.

Cy·rus[2] |'sirəs| (424–401 BC) Persian prince; known as **Cyrus the Younger**. On the death of his father, Darius II, in 405 BC, Cyrus led an army of mercenaries against his elder brother, who had succeeded to the throne as Artaxerxes II. His campaign is recounted by the historian Xenophon.

Czer·ny |'cHərnē|, Karl (1791–1857) Austrian pianist, teacher, and composer. The bulk of his output is made up of more than 1,000 exercises and studies for the piano.

Dd

Dadd |dæd|, Richard (1819–87) English painter. After killing his father while suffering a mental breakdown, he was confined in asylums, where he produced a series of visionary paintings.

da Ga·ma |dəˈgämə|, Vasco (c. 1469–1524) Portuguese explorer. He led the first European expedition around the Cape of Good Hope in 1497, sighting and naming Natal on Christmas Day before crossing the Indian Ocean and arriving in Calicut (Kozhikode, in India) in 1498. He also established colonies in Mozambique.

Da·guerre |dəˈger|, Louis-Jacques-Mandé (1789–1851) French physicist, painter, and inventor of the first practical photographic process. He went into partnership with **Joseph-Nicéphore Niépce**, (1765–1833) to improve the latter's heliography process, and in 1839 he presented his daguerreotype process to the French Academy of Sciences.

Dahl |däl|, Roald (1916–90) British writer, of Norwegian descent. His fiction and drama, such as the short-story collection *Tales of the Unexpected* (1979), typically include macabre plots and unexpected outcomes. Notable works for children: *Charlie and the Chocolate Factory* (1964), and *The BFG* (1982).

Dahl·berg |ˈdälber|, Edward (1900–77) U.S. author. He wrote novels, including *Kentucky Blue Grass* (1932); essays, including *Can These Bones Live?* (1941); and an autobiography, *Because I Was Flesh* (1964).

Dai·ley |ˈdälē|, Janet (1944–) U.S. author. She wrote many historical and romantic novels.

Daim·ler |ˈdämlər|, Gottlieb Wilhelm (1834–1900) German engineer and automobile manufacturer. An employee of Nikolaus Otto, he produced a small engine using the Otto cycle in 1884 and made it propel a bicycle using gasoline. He founded the Daimler automobile company in 1890.

Da·la·dier |dälä'dyä|, Édouard (1884–1970) French prime minister (1933, 1934, 1938–40).

Da·lai La·ma |ˈdälē ˈlämə| (1935–) Tibetan Buddhist leader. Born *Tenzin Gyatso*. He won a Nobel Peace Prize (1989) for his nonviolent movement to end Chinese domination of Tibet.

Dale |dāl|, Sir Henry Hallett (1875–1968) English physiologist and pharmacologist. He investigated the role of histamine in anaphylactic shock and allergy, and the role of acetylcholine as a natural neurotransmitter. Nobel Prize for Physiology or Medicine (1936).

Dale |dāl|, Sir Thomas (died 1619) English naval commander and colonial administrator. As colonial governor of Virginia, he enforced "Dale's Code," a legislative code that caused 1611–16 to be known as "5 years of slavery."

d'Alem·bert |dälän'ber|, Jean Le Rond (1717–83) French mathematician, physicist, and philosopher. His most famous work was the *Traité de dynamique* (1743), in which he developed his own laws of motion. From 1746 to 1758 he was Diderot's chief collaborator on the *Encyclopédie*.

Da·ley |ˈdälē|, Richard Joseph (1902–76) U.S. politician. As mayor of Chicago (1955–76) he was known as a big-city boss; he also led the National Democratic Party.

Dal·hou·sie |dæl'hōōzē|, James Andrew Broun Ramsay, 1st Marquess of (1812–60) A British colonial administrator, he was a progressive governor general of India (1847–56).

Da·li |ˈdälē; dä'lē|, Salvador Felipe Jacinto (1904–89) Spanish painter. A surrealist, he portrayed dream images with almost photographic realism against backgrounds of arid Catalan landscapes. Dali also collaborated with Buñuel in the production of the movie *Un Chien andalou* (1928). Notable works: *The Persistence of Memory* (1931).

Dal·la·pic·co·la |ˌdäləpi'kōlə|, Luigi (1904–75) Italian composer. He combined serialism with lyrical polyphonic writing. Notable works: *Songs of Prison* (1938–41).

Dal·las |ˈdæləs|, U.S. political family.

Jamaican-born **Alexander James Dallas** (1759–1817) was a lawyer and secretary of the treasury (1814–16). He restored public faith in U.S. credit after the War of 1812; he also established the second bank of the U.S. His son **George Mifflin Dallas** (1792–1864) was U.S. vice president (1845–49). The city of Dallas, Texas, is named for him.

Dal·ton |'dawltən|, John (1766–1844) English chemist, father of modern atomic theory. He defined an atom as the smallest part of a substance that could participate in a chemical reaction and argued that elements are composed of atoms. He stated that elements combine in definite proportion and produced the first table of comparative atomic weights.

Dal·trey |'dältrē; 'dawltrē|, Roger Harry (1944–) British rock singer. He was a member of the rock band The Who.

Da·ly |'dālē|, (John) Augustin (1838–99) U.S. playwright and theatrical manager. He managed theaters in New York and London while also writing drama criticism for New York daily newspapers.

Da·ly |'dālē|, Marcus (1841–1900) U.S. businessman. In partnership with others, he organized the Anaconda Mining Company (1891) and the Amalgamated Copper Company (1891).

Da·ly |'dālē|, Tyne (1947–) U.S. actress. She won four Emmys as costar of the television series "Cagney and Lacey."

Dam |dæm|, (Carl Peter) Henrik (1895–1976) Danish biochemist. He discovered vitamin K and shared the 1943 Nobel Prize for Medicine or Physiology with E. A. Doisy.

Da·ma·di·an, Raymond Vahan (1936–) U.S. biophysicist. He invented the magnetic resonance imaging (MRI) scanner (1989).

Da·mien |'dāmēən|, Father Joseph (1840–89) Belgian priest. Born *Joseph Damien de Veuster*. He ministered to a Hawaiian leper colony from 1873 until his death from leprosy.

Da·mon |'dāmən|, Matt (1970–) U.S. actor. Notable movies: *Good Will Hunting* (1997, Academy Award).

Dam·pi·er |'dæmpēər|, William (1652–1715) English explorer, buccaneer, and adventurer. He is notable for having sailed around the world twice. In 1683 he set out from Panama, crossing the Pacific and reaching England again in 1691; in 1699 the government commissioned him to explore the northwest coast of Australia.

Dam·rosch |'däm,rawsH|, Leopold (1832–85) U.S. symphony conductor, born in Prussia. As founder and conductor of the New York Symphony, he introduced U.S. audiences to operas by Wagner and symphonic music by Brahms and other Europeans. When he died, his son Walter (1862–1950) assumed his post at the New York Symphony and also conducted at the Metropolitan Opera.

Da·na |'dānə|, Charles Anderson (1819–97) U.S. newspaper editor. He was a resident of the Brook Farm commune (1841–46) and the owner and editor of the *New York Sun* (1868–97).

Da·na |'dānə|, James Dwight (1813–95) U.S. naturalist, geologist, and mineralogist. He founded an important classification of minerals based on chemistry and physics. His view of the earth as a unit was an evolutionary one, but he was slow to accept Darwin's theory of evolution.

Da·na |'dānə|, Richard Henry (1815–82) U.S. adventurer, lawyer, and writer, known for his classic account of his voyage on a brig from Boston around Cape Horn to California, *Two Years Before the Mast* (1840).

Dan·dridge |'dændrij|, Dorothy (1923–65) U.S. actress. She was the first African-American woman nominated for an Oscar in the Best Actress category (*Carmen Jones*, 1954).

Dane |dān|, Nathan (1752–1835) U.S. jurist. He was a delegate to the Continental Congress (1785–87), and as a Massachusetts state senator (1790–98) revised many Massachusetts laws.

Dan·iel |'dænyəl|, Jack Newton (1846–1911) U.S. entrepreneur. He founded the Jack Daniels distillery.

Dan·iel |'dænyəl|, Peter Vivian (1784–1860) U.S. Supreme Court justice (1841–60).

Da•ni•lo•va |də'nēləvə|, Alexandra (1904–97) U.S. ballet dancer and teacher, born in Russia. She taught at the School of American Ballet (1964–89).

Dan•nay |də'nā|, Frederic (1905–82) U.S. author. With Manfred Bennington Lee (1905–71), he wrote over 40 detective novels under the pseudonym **Ellery Queen** and a series of novels under the pseudonym **Barnaby Ross.**

d'An•nun•zio |dän'no͞ontsyō|, Gabriele (1863–1938) Italian novelist, dramatist, and poet. He is best known for his "Romances of the Rose" trilogy, including *The Triumph of Death* (1894), which shows the influence of Nietzsche.

Dan•te |'däntā| (1265–1321) Italian poet; full name *Dante Alighieri*. His reputation rests chiefly on *The Divine Comedy* (*c.*1309–20), an epic poem describing his spiritual journey through Hell and Purgatory and finally to Paradise. His love for Beatrice Portinari is described in *Vita nuova* (*c.*1290).

Dan•ton |'dæntən|, Georges-Jacques (1759–94) French revolutionary. A noted orator, he won great popularity in the early days of the French Revolution. He was initially an ally of Robespierre but later revolted against the severity of the Revolutionary Tribunal and was executed on Robespierre's orders.

Da Pon•te |dä'pōntā|, Lorenzo (1749–1838) Italian poet and librettist; born *Emmanuele Conegliano*. He became poet to the Court Opera in Vienna in 1784 and wrote the libretti for Mozart's *Marriage of Figaro* (1786), *Don Giovanni* (1787), and *Così fan tutte* (1790).

Dare |der|, Virginia (1587–?) First English child born in North America. Born on Roanoke Island, Virginia, to Ananias Dare and Elinor White, she disappeared with the other 117 Roanoke colonists, as was discovered in 1591.

Dar•in |'derən|, Bobby (1936–73) U.S. pop singer and songwriter. Born *Walden Robert Cassotto*. He was a film star and teen idol of the 1950s. Notable songs: "Splish Splash" and "Mack the Knife."

Da•ri•us I |də'rīəs; 'derdə'rīəs; 'derēəs| (550–486 BC) king of Persia 521–486 BC. Known as **Darius the Great**. He divided the empire into provinces, governed by satraps, developed commerce, built a network of roads, and connected the Nile with the Red Sea by canal. After a revolt by the Greek cities in Ionia (499–494 BC) he invaded Greece but was defeated at Marathon (490 BC).

Dar•ley |'därlē|, Felix Octavius Carr (1822–88) U.S. illustrator and author. He illustrated the works of Irving, Cooper, Longfellow, Dickens, and others.

Dar•ling |'därliNG|, Jay Norwood (1876–1962) U.S. political cartoonist. Pseudonym **Ding**. He worked for the *Des Moines Register* (1906–11; 1913–49) and was nationally syndicated from 1917. Pulitzer Prizes, 1923 and 1943.

Darn•ley |'därnlē|, Henry Stewart, Lord (1545–65) Scottish nobleman, second husband of Mary, Queen of Scots, and father of James I of England. Also **Henry Stuart**. He was implicated in the murder of his wife's secretary Rizzio in 1566, and was later killed in a mysterious gunpowder explosion in Edinburgh.

Dar•row |'derō|, Clarence Seward (1857–1938) U.S. lawyer. He served as defense counsel in several well-publicized trials, including that of John T. Scopes of Dayton, Tennessee, who was charged with violating state law for teaching evolution in a public school (1925).

Dart |därt|, Raymond Arthur (1893–1988) Australian-born South African anthropologist and anatomist. In 1925 he found the first specimen of a hominid for which he coined the genus name *Australopithecus*.

Dar•win |'därwən| English scientists. **Erasmus Darwin** (1731–1802) was a physician, scientist, inventor, and poet. He is chiefly remembered for his scientific and technical writing, much of which appeared in the form of long poems. These include *Zoonomia* (1794–96), which proposed a Lamarckian view of evolution. He was the grandfather of Francis Galton (see GALTON, FRANCIS) and **Charles (Robert) Darwin** (1809–82), a natural historian and geologist, proponent of the theory of evolution by natural selection. Darwin was the naturalist on HMS *Beagle* for its voyage around the southern hemisphere (1831–36), during which he collected the material that became the basis for his ideas on natural selection. His works *On the Origin of Species* (1859) and *The Descent of Man* (1871) had a fundamental effect on the concepts of nature and humanity's place within it.

Dau·bi·gny |ˌdōbēˈnyä|, Charles-François (1817–78) French landscape painter. He was a member of the Barbizon School and is often regarded as a linking figure between this group and the Impressionists.

Dau·det |dōˈdä|, Alphonse (1840–97) French novelist and dramatist. He is best known for his sketches of life in his native Provence, particularly the *Lettres de mon moulin* (1869).

Daugh·er·ty |ˈdōərtē|, Harry Micajah (1860–1941) U.S. politician. A U.S. attorney general (1921–24), he managed the political career of Warren Harding. In 1927, he was tried and acquitted of charges of conspiracy to defraud the U.S. government.

Daum·ier |dōmˈyä|, Honoré (1840–97) French painter and lithographer. From the 1830s he worked as a cartoonist for periodicals such as *Charivari*, where he produced lithographs satirizing French society and politics.

Dav·en·port |ˈdævən,pawrt|, Charles Benedict (1866–1944) U.S. zoologist, eugenicist, and author.

Dav·en·port |ˈdævən,pawrt|, John (1597–1670) U.S. clergyman, born in England. He was the Puritan founder of the New Haven Colony and of the Third (Old South) Church, Boston.

Da·vid |ˈdāvəd| (died *c.* 962 BC) king of Judah and Israel *c.* 1000–*c.* 962 BC. In the biblical account, he was the youngest son of Jesse. He killed the Philistine Goliath and, on Saul's death, became king, making Jerusalem his capital. He is traditionally regarded as the author of the Psalms, although this has been disputed.

Da·vid |ˈdāvəd| the name of two kings of Scotland: **David I** (*c.* 1084–1153; reigned 1124–53). He was the sixth son of Malcolm III. In 1136 he invaded England in support of his niece Matilda's claim to the throne, but was defeated at the Battle of the Standard in 1138. **David II** (1324–71; reigned 1329–71)

was the son of Robert the Bruce. His reign witnessed a renewal of fighting in England, with Edward III supporting the pretender Edward de Baliol. His death without issue left the throne to the Stuarts.

Da·vid |ˈdāvəd|, Jacques-Louis (1748–1825) French painter, famous for neoclassical paintings such as *The Oath of the Horatii* (1784). He became actively involved in the French Revolution, voting for the death of Louis XVI and supporting Robespierre.

Da·vid |ˈdāvəd|, St. (*c.* 520–600) Welsh monk; Welsh name **Dewi**. Since the 12th century he has been regarded as the patron saint of Wales. Little is known of his life, but it is generally accepted that he transferred the center of Welsh ecclesiastical administration from Caerleon to Mynyw (now St. David's). Feast day, March 1.

Da·vies |ˈdāvēz|, W. H. (1871–1940) English poet; full name *William Henry Davies*. He emigrated to the U.S. and lived as a vagrant and laborer, writing *The Autobiography of a Super-Tramp* (1908) about his experiences.

Da·vies |ˈdāvēz|, Arthur Bowen (1862–1928) U.S. artist. He painted romantic landscapes and experimented with Cubism.

Da·vies |ˈdāvēz|, Ray (1944–) British musician. He was a rock guitarist and vocalist with The Kinks.

Da·vies |ˈdāvēz|, (William) Robertson (1913–95) Canadian novelist, dramatist, and journalist. He won international recognition with his Deptford trilogy of novels, comprising *Fifth Business* (1970), *The Manticore* (1972), and *World of Wonders* (1975).

da Vin·ci |dəˈvinCHē|, Leonardo (1452–1519) see LEONARDO DA VINCI.

Da·vis |ˈdāvəs|, Alexander Jackson (1803–92) U.S. architect. He is known for his Gothic and Italianate country houses.

Da·vis |ˈdāvəs|, Angela Yvonne (1944–) U.S. civil rights leader and author.

Da·vis |ˈdāvəs|, Benjamin Oliver (1877–1970) U.S. military leader. He was the first African-American general in the U.S. Army (1940).

Da·vis |'dāvəs|, Bette (1908–89) U.S. actress; born *Ruth Elizabeth Davis*. She established her Hollywood career playing a number of strong, independent female characters in such movies as *Dangerous* (1935). Her flair for suggesting the macabre and menacing emerged in later movies, such as *Whatever Happened to Baby Jane?* (1962).

Da·vis |'dāvəs|, Charles Henry (1807–77) U.S. naval officer. He commanded a Union gunboat flotilla on the Mississippi (1862).

Da·vis |'dāvəs|, David (1815–86) U.S. Supreme Court justice (1862–77).

Da·vis |'dāvəs|, Dwight Filley (1879–1945) U.S. public official. An independently wealthy amateur tennis player, he donated the Davis Cup (1900); he later became U.S. secretary of war (1925–29) and governor general of the Philippines (1929–32). A founding trustee of the Brookings Institution, he was also its chairman (1937–45).

Da·vis |'dāvəs|, Geena (1957–) U.S. actress. Notable movies: *The Accidental Tourist* (1988, Academy Award)

Da·vis |'dāvəs|, Henry Winter (1817–65) U.S. politician. As a member of the U.S. House of Representatives from Maryland (1855–61, 1863–65), he was a leader of the Radical Republicans.

Da·vis |'dāvəs|, Jefferson (1808–89) U.S. politician and president of the Confederate States of America. As a U.S. senator from Mississippi (1847–51) and a defender of slavery, he withdrew from the Senate when Mississippi seceded from the union and was later elected president of the Confederate States of America (1862). He wrote *The Rise and Fall of the Confederate Government* (1881).

Da·vis |'dāvəs|, Jim (1945–) U.S. cartoonist. Full name *James Robert Davis*. He created the "Garfield" comic strip (1978), as well as books and television scripts based on the Garfield character.

Da·vis |'dāvəs|, John (c.1550–1605) English navigator. On searches for the Northwest Passage to Asia, he discovered Cumberland Sound off Baffin Island (1585) and sailed through Davis Strait (1587) into Baffin Bay.

Da·vis |'dāvəs|, John William (1873–1955) U.S. politician. He was a Democratic presidential candidate in 1924.

Da·vis |'dāvəs|, Miles (Dewey) (1926–91) U.S. jazz trumpeter, composer, and bandleader. In the 1950s he played and recorded arrangements in a new style that became known as "cool" jazz, heard on albums such as *Kind of Blue* (1959). In the 1960s he pioneered the fusion of jazz and rock.

Da·vis |'dāvəs|, Sammy, Jr (1925–90) U.S. actor, singer and dancer. Spingarn Medal, 1968.

Da·vis |'dāvəs|, Stuart (1894–1964) U.S. artist. He experimented with Cubism and abstract paintings.

Da·vis |'dāvəs|, William Augustine (1809–75) U.S. postal authority. He devised a system of sorting mail on trains, originating railroad post-office service.

Da·vi·son |'dāvəsən|, Wild Bill (1906–89) U.S. Chicago jazz cornetist. Full name *William Edward Davison*.

Da·vis·son |'dāvəsən|, Clinton Joseph (1881–1958) U.S. physicist. With **L. H. Germer** (1896–1971), he discovered electron diffraction, thus confirming de Broglie's theory of the wave nature of electrons. Nobel Prize for Physics (1937).

Da·vy |'dāvē|, Sir Humphry (1778–1829) English chemist, a pioneer of electrochemistry. He discovered nitrous oxide (laughing gas) and the elements sodium, potassium, magnesium, calcium, strontium, and barium. He also identified and named the element chlorine, determined the properties of iodine, and demonstrated that diamond was a form of carbon. In 1815 he invented the miner's safety lamp.

Dawes |dawz|, Charles Gates (1865–1951) U.S. politican, lawyer, and financier. He was vice president of the U.S. (1925–29). Nobel peace prize, 1925, with Sir Austen Chamberlain.

Dawes |dawz|, Henry Laurens (1816–1903) U.S. politician. As a U.S. senator from Massachusetts (1875–93), he was chairman of the Senate Committee on Indian Affairs. The Dawes Act (1887) ended the status of Indian tribal lands as "domestic nations."

Dawes |dawz|, William (1745–99) U.S. patriot. With Paul Revere, he rode from

Lexington to Concord, Massachusetts, to warn of approaching British soldiers (April 18, 1775).

Daw·kins |'dawkənz|, Richard (1941–) English biologist. Dawkins's book *The Selfish Gene* (1976) did much to popularize the theory of sociobiology. In *The Blind Watchmaker* (1986) Dawkins discussed evolution by natural selection and suggested that the theory could answer the fundamental question of why life exists.

Daw·son |'dawsən|, William Levi (1886–1970) U.S. politician. A member of the U.S. House of Representatives from Illinois (1943–70), he was the first African-American chairman of a major House committee.

Day |da| U.S. family, including: **Benjamin Henry Day** (1810–89), a newspaperman. He founded the first one-cent daily paper, the *New York Sun* (1833). His son, **Benjamin Day** (1838–1916), a printer, invented the Ben Day process for shading and color in printing illustrations. Benjamin Henry Day's grandson, **Clarence Shepard Day, Jr.** (1874–1935), was a writer. Notable works:*Life with Father* (1935).

Day |da|, Doris (1924–) U.S. actress and singer. Born *Doris Kappelhoff*. She became a movie star in the 1950s with roles in light-hearted musicals, comedies, and romances such as *Calamity Jane* (1953) and *Pillow Talk* (1959).

Day |da|, Dorothy (1897–1980) U.S. journalist and reformer. She founded the Catholic Worker newspaper with Peter Maurin (1933).

Day |da|, William Rufus (1849–1923) U.S. Supreme Court justice (1903–22).

Da·yan |dī'yän|, Moshe (1915–81) Israeli statesman and general. As Minister of Defense he oversaw Israel's victory in the Six Day War and as Foreign Minister he played a prominent role in negotiations towards the Camp David agreements of 1979.

Day-Lewis |'da 'loowəs|, C(ecil) (1904–72) English poet and critic. His early verse, such as *Transitional Poems* (1929), reflects the influence of revolutionary thinking. After 1940, he increasingly became an Establishment figure and was Poet Laureate 1968–72.

Dea·kin |'dēkən|, Alfred (1856–1919) Australian Liberal statesman, prime minister (1903–04, 1905–08, and 1909–10).

Dean |dēn|, Dizzy (1911–74) U.S. baseball player. Born *Jay Hanna Dean*. He led National League pitchers in strikeouts (1932–36).

Dean |dēn|, James (1931–55) U.S. actor. Although he starred in only three movies before dying in a car accident, he became a cult figure closely identified with the title role of *Rebel Without a Cause* (1955), symbolizing for many the disaffected youth of the postwar era.

Dean |dēn|, John, III (1938–) U.S. political adviser. After serving as presidential counsel to Richard Nixon, he became the chief witness in the Watergate hearings. He was convicted of conspiracy and served four months in prison.

de Beau·voir |dəbōv'wär|, Simone (1908–86) French existentialist philosopher, novelist, and feminist. Her best-known work is *The Second Sex* (1949), a central book of the "second wave" of feminism. She is strongly associated with Jean-Paul Sartre, with whom she had a lifelong association.

De·Beck, Billy (1890–1942) U.S. cartoonist. Full name *William Morgan De-Beck*. He created Barney Google, Spark Plug, and other popular cartoon characters.

De·brett |də'bret|, John (c.1750–1822) English publisher. He compiled *The Peerage of England, Scotland, and Ireland* (first issued in 1803), which, with its periodic updatings, is regarded as the authority on the British nobility.

de Bro·glie |də 'brawglē|, Louis-Victor-Pierre-Raymond (1892–1987) French physicist. His experiments initiated the study of wave mechanics. Nobel Prize for Physics (1929).

Debs |debz|, Eugene Victor (1855–1926) U.S. labor leader. The chief organizer of the Social Democratic Party (1897), he ran as a Socialist candidate for U.S. president five times from 1900 to 1920. He was a founder of the Industrial Workers of the World (1905).

De·Buss·chere |də'boosHər|, Dave (1940–) U.S. professional athlete. After playing at the major league level in both baseball and basketball, he became the youngest coach in NBA history.

De·bus·sy |ˌdebyōōˈsē|, (Achille) Claude (1862–1918) French composer and critic. Debussy carried the ideas of Impressionist art and symbolist poetry into music, using melodies based on the whole-tone scale and delicate harmonies exploiting overtones. Notable works: *Prélude à l'après-midi d'un faune* (1894).

De·bye |dəˈbī|, Peter Joseph William (1884–1966) Dutch-born U.S. chemical physicist. Debye is best known for establishing the existence of permanent electric dipole moments in many molecules, demonstrating the use of these to determine molecular size and shape, and modifying Einstein's theory of specific heats as applied to solids. Nobel Prize for Chemistry (1936).

De·ca·tur |dəˈkātər|, Stephen (1779–1820) U.S. naval officer. He was a daring commander in the Tripolitan War and gave the famous toast, "Our Country! In her intercourse with foreign nations may she always be in the right; but our country, right or wrong!"

De·cius |ˈdēsHēəs|, Gaius Messius Quintus Trajanus (*c.*201–251) Roman emperor (249–51). He was the first Roman emperor to promote systematic persecution of the Christians in the empire.

De·de·kind |ˈdādəkint|, (Julius Wilhem) Richard (1831–1916) Full name *Julius Wilhelm Richard Didekind.* German mathematician, one of the founders of abstract algebra and modern mathematics.

de Du·ve |ˌdəˈdōōvə|, Christian René (1917–) British-born Belgian biochemist. A pioneer in the study of cell biology, he won the Nobel Prize for Physiology or Medicine in 1974.

Dee |dē|, John (1527–1608) English alchemist, mathematician, and geographer. He was Elizabeth I's astrologer, and in later life he absorbed himself in alchemy and acquired notoriety as a sorcerer.

Deere |dir|, John (1804—86) U.S. manufacturer. He founded John Deere & Co. (1868), originally manufacturing plows.

Deer·ing |ˈdēriNG|, William (1826–

1913) U.S. industrialist. He established a harvester manufacturing business and merged with International Harvester Co. (1902).

de Falla |də ˈfäyə|, Manuel see FALLA.

De·foe |dəˈfō|, Daniel (1660–1731) English novelist and journalist. His best-known novel, *Robinson Crusoe* (1719), is loosely based on the true story of the shipwrecked sailor Alexander Selkirk; it has a claim to being the first English novel. Other notable works: *Moll Flanders* (novel, 1722) and *A Journal of the Plague Year* (historical fiction, 1722).

De For·est |dēˈfawrəst|, John William (1826–1906) U.S. author. He wrote the first American realistic novel, *Miss Ravenel's Conversion* (1867).

De For·est |dēˈfawrəst|, Lee (1873–1961) U.S. physicist and electrical engineer. He designed a triode valve that was crucial to the development of radio communication, television, and computers.

De For·est |dēˈfawrəst|, Robert Weeks (1848–1931) U.S. lawyer. He helped found the New York Charity Organization Society (1882), where he served as president (1888–1931).

De·Frantz, Anita Lucette (1952–) U.S. sports executive and attorney. After winning an Olympic bronze medal in rowing (1976), she became one of two U.S. delegates to the International Olympic Committee and a member of the USOC Executive Committee.

De·gas |dāˈgä|, (Hilaire-Germain) Edgar (1834–1917) French painter and sculptor. An Impressionist painter, Degas is best known for his paintings of ballet dancers.

de Gaulle |də ˈgawl|, Charles (André Joseph Marie) (1890–1970) French general and statesman, head of government (1944–46), president (1959–69). A wartime organizer of the Free French movement, de Gaulle became President after having been asked to form a government, going on to establish the French presidency as a democratically elected office (1962). He is remembered particularly for his assertive foreign policy and for quelling the student uprisings and strikes of May 1968.

De·gen·er·es |dəˈgenərəs|, Ellen

(1958–   ) U.S. actress and comedian. She was star of the sitcom "Ellen," a television show whose main character is revealed to be a homosexual.

de Hav·il·land |dəˈhævələnd|, Sir Geoffrey (1882–1965) English aircraft designer and manufacturer. He designed and built many aircraft, including the Mosquito of World War II.

de Hav·il·land |dəˈhævələnd|, Olivia (1916–   ) U.S. actress, born in Japan. Notable movies: *To Each His Own* (1946, Academy Award) and *The Heiress* (1949, Academy Award).

de Hooch |dəˈhōk|, Pieter (c.1629–c.1684) Also **de Hoogh**. Dutch genre painter. He is noted for his depictions of domestic interior and courtyard scenes.

Deigh·ton |ˈdātn|, Len (1929–   ) English writer; full name *Leonard Cyril Deighton*. His reputation is based on his spy thrillers, several of which have been adapted as movies and for television.

Dek·ker |ˈdekər|, Thomas (c.1572–c.1632) English dramatist, author of the revenge tragedy *The Witch of Edmonton* (1623), in which he collaborated with John Ford and William Rowley, and *The Honest Whore* (1604) with Thomas Middleton.

de Klerk |dəˈklerk|, F. W. (1936–   ) South African statesman, president (1989–94); full name *Frederik Willem de Klerk*. As state president, he freed Nelson Mandela in 1990, lifted the ban on membership in the African National Congress (ANC), and opened the negotiations that led to the first democratic elections in 1994. Nobel Peace Prize with Nelson Mandela (1993).

de Koon·ing |dəˈkŏŏniNG|, Willem (1904–97) Dutch-born U.S. painter, a leading exponent of abstract expressionism. The female form became a central theme in his later work, notably in the *Women* series (1950–53).

De Ko·ven |dəˈkōvən|, (Henry Louis) Reginald (1859–1920) U.S. composer. He composed operas and songs.

de la Beche |ˈdelə,besH|, Sir Henry Thomas (1796–1855) English geologist. He traveled extensively and produced the first geological description and map of Jamaica. He was involved in the establishment of the Geological Survey of Great Britain in 1835, directing it from then until his death.

De·la·croix |,delə'krwä|, (Ferdinand Victor) Eugène (1798–1863) French painter, the chief painter of the French romantic school. He is known for his use of vivid color, free drawing, and exotic, violent, or macabre subject matter. Notable works: *The Massacre at Chios* (1824).

de la Hoya |,dələ'hoiyə|, Oscar (1973–   ) U.S. boxer. A 1992 Olympic gold medalist, he has been the world lightweight (1995), super lightweight (1996), and welterweight (1997) champion.

de la Mare |,delə'mær|, Walter (John) (1873–1956) English poet. He is known particularly for his verse for children. Notable work: *The Listeners* (1912).

De·la·ney |də'lānē|, Kim (1961–   ) U.S. television actress. She won Emmy Awards (1996, 1997) for her role in "NYPD Blue."

de la Ren·ta |dälə'rentə|, Oscar (1932–   ) U.S. fashion designer, born in the Dominican Republic. He is known especially for lavish evening gowns.

de la Roche |dələ'rawsH|, Mazo (1885–1961) Canadian novelist. She won acclaim for *Jalna* (1927), the first of a series of novels about the Whiteoak family. The "Jalna" cycle was noted for its characterization and its evocation of rural Ontario.

De·lau·nay |dəlaw'nä|, Robert (1885–1941) French painter. For most of his career he experimented with the abstract qualities of color, and he painted some of the first purely abstract pictures. He was one of the founding members of Orphism together with Sonia Delaunay-Terk.

Delaunay-Terk |dəlaw'nä 'tərk|, Sonia (Terk) (1885–1979) Russian-born French painter and textile designer, wife of Robert Delaunay. She created abstract paintings based on harmonies of form and color.

Del·brück |ˈdel,brŏŏk|, Max (1906–81) U.S. biologist, born in Germany. With Salvador Luria and Alfred Hershey, he discovered the recombination of viral DNA (1946) and won a Nobel Prize in Physiology or Medicine (1969).

de Len·clos, Ninon see LENCLOS.

Del·font |del'fänt|, Bernard, Baron Delfont of Stepney (1909–94) Russianborn British impresario; born *Boris Winogradsky*. From the early 1940s onward he presented more than 200 shows in London's West End theatrical district.

De·libes |də'leb|, (Clément Philibert) Léo (1836–91) French composer and organist. His best-known works are the ballets *Coppélia* (1870) and *Sylvia* (1876).

De Lil·lo, Don (1936–) U.S. author. Notable works: *White Noise* (1985).

De·li·us |'dēlēəs|, Frederick Theodore Albert (1862–1934) English composer, of German and Scandinavian descent. He is best known for pastoral works such as *Brigg Fair* (1907), but he also wrote songs, concertos, and choral and theater music.

Dell |del|, Michael (1965–) U.S. manufacturing executive. He founded the Dell Computer Corp. (1984).

del·la Fran·ces·ca |,delə ,fræn-'CHeskə| see PIERO DELLA FRANCESCA.

della Quer·cia |,dälä 'kwerCHä|, Jacopo (c.1374–1438) Italian sculptor. He is noted for his tomb of Ilaria del Carretto in Lucca cathedral (c.1406) and for the biblical reliefs on the portal of San Petronio in Bologna (1425–35).

Della Rob·bia |,dälä'rawbyä|, Luca (c.1400–82) Italian sculptor and ceramicist. He is best known for his relief panels in Florence cathedral and his color-glazed terracotta figures.

De·Lor·e·an |də 'lawrēən|, John Z. (1925–) U.S. automobile designer and manufacturer.

De·lors |də'lawr|, Jacques (Lucien Jean) (1925–) French socialist politician, president of the European Commission (1985–94). During his presidency he pressed for closer European union and oversaw the introduction of a single market within the European Community, which came into effect on January 1, 1993.

del Sar·to |del 'särtō|, Andrea see SARTO

de Main·te·non |də ,mæNt(ə)nawN| see MAINTENON.

de Mau·pas·sant |də ,mōpə'sän|, Guy see MAUPASSANT.

de' Medici, Catherine see CATHERINE DE' MEDICI.

de' Medici, Cosimo see COSIMO DE' MEDICI.

de Medici, Giovanni the name of Pope Leo X (see LEO).

de' Medici, Lorenzo see LORENZO DE' MEDICI.

de' Medici see MEDICI.

de Mé·di·cis |də ,medə'sēs|, Marie see MARIE DE MÉDICIS.

De·Mille |də'mil|, Cecil B. (1881–1959) U.S. movie producer and director, famous for his spectacular epics; full name *Cecil Blount DeMille*. Notable movies: *The Ten Commandments* (1923; remade 1956) and *Samson and Delilah* (1949).

de Mille |də'mil|, Agnes (George) (c. 1905–93) U.S. dancer and choreographer. She is known for her choreography of the ballet *Rodeo* (1942) and the Broadway musical *Oklahoma* (1943). She is a niece of Cecil B. DeMille.

De·moc·ri·tus |də'mäkrətəs| (c. 460–c. 370 BC) Greek philosopher. He developed the atomic theory originated by his teacher, Leucippus, which explained natural phenomena in terms of the arrangement and rearrangement of atoms moving in a void.

de Mon·tes·pan |də ,mawntəs'pän|, Marquise de see MONTESPAN.

de Mont·fort |də 'män(t)fərt|, Simon see MONTFORT.

De·mos·the·nes |də'mäsTHənēz| (384–322 BC) Athenian orator and statesman. He is best known for his political speeches on the need to resist the aggressive tendencies of Philip II of Macedon (the *Philippics*).

Demp·sey |'dempsē|, Jack (1895–1983) U.S. profesional boxer; full name *William Harrison Dempsey*. He was world heavyweight champion 1919–26.

Den·by |'denbē|, Edwin (1870–1929) U.S. politician. He resigned as U.S. secretary of the navy (1921–24) after being implicated in the Teapot Dome Scandal.

Dench |'denCH|, Dame Judi (1934–) English actress; full name *Judith Olivia Dench*. She has performed in numerous theatrical, movie, and television productions. She won an Oscar as best supporting actress for *Shakespeare in Love* (1998).

De·neuve |də'nōōv|, Catherine (1943–) French actress; born *Catherine Dorléac*. Notable movies: *Repulsion* (1965) and *Belle de jour* (1967).

Deng Xiao·ping |'dəNG'SHOW'piNG| (1904–97) Also **Teng Hsiao-p'ing**. Chinese communist statesman, vice premier (1973–76, 1977–80); vice chairman of the Central Committee of the Chinese Communist Party (1977–80). Discredited during the Cultural Revolution, he was reinstated in 1977, becoming the de facto leader of China. He worked to modernize the economy and improve relations with the West, although in 1989 his orders led to the massacre of some 2,000 prodemocracy demonstrators in Beijing's Tiananmen Square.

De·ni·kin |dyin'yĕkyin|, Anton Ivanovich (1872–1947) Russian soldier. He established the South Russian government but was defeated by the Bolsheviks (1919).

De·Niro |də'nērō|, Robert (1943–) U.S. actor and director. He has starred in many movies, often playing tough characters, and has worked frequently with director Martin Scorsese. He won Oscars for *The Godfather, Part II* (1974) and *Raging Bull* (1980). Other movies include *Taxi Driver* (1976), *The Deer Hunter* (1978), *the Untouchables* (1987), *Goodfellas* (1990), and *Casino* (1995).

Den·is |'denəs|, St. (died *c*.250) Also **Denys**. Italian-born French bishop, patron saint of France; Roman name *Dionysius*. According to tradition he was one of a group of seven missionaries sent from Rome to convert Gaul; he became bishop of Paris and was martyred in the reign of the emperor Valerian. Feast day, October 9.

Den·is |'denəs|, Maurice (1870–1943) French painter, designer, and art theorist. A member of the Nabi Group, he wrote many works on art, including *Théories* (1913) and *Nouvelles Théories* (1921).

Den·ver |'denvər|, John (1943–97) U.S. country and pop singer and songwriter. Born *John Henry Deutschendorf*. He celebrated the state of Colorado in his music.

Denys, St. see DENIS, ST.

de Pao·la, Tomie (1934–) U.S. author and illustrator. Full name *Thomas Anthony de Paola*. His children's books, including the "Strega Nona" stories, have received several awards for typography and illustration.

Dé·par·dieu |dāpär'dyōō|, Gérard (1948–) French actor.

de Pi·san, Christine (*c*.1364–*c*.1430) Also **de Pizan**. Italian writer, resident in France from 1369. The first professional woman writer in France, she is best known for her works in defense of women's virtues and achievements, such as *Le Livre des trois vertus* (1406).

De Quin·cey |di'kwinsē|, Thomas (1785–1859) English essayist and critic. He achieved fame with his *Confessions of an English Opium Eater* (1822), a study of his addiction to opium and its psychological effects.

De·rain |də'ræn|, André (1880–1954) French painter, one of the exponents of fauvism. He also designed theater sets and costumes, notably for the Ballets Russes.

Der·by |'dərbē|, Edward George Geoffrey Smith Stanley, 14th Earl of (1799–1869) British Conservative statesman, prime minister (1852, 1858–59, 1866–68).

Der·in·ger |'derənjər|, Henry (1786–1869) U.S. gun manufacturer. He invented the pistol that became known as the Derringer.

Dern |dern|, George Henry (1872–1936) U.S. mining executive and politician. He was governor of Utah (1925–32) and author of the workmen's compensation law.

Der·r·da |dəri'dä|, Jacques (1930–) French philosopher and literary critic, the most important figure in the theory of deconstructionism. Notable works: *Of Grammatology* (1967) and *Writing and Difference* (1967).

de Sade |də'säd|, Marquis see SADE.

De·sai |də'sī|, (Shri) Morarji (Ranchhodji) (1896–1995) Indian prime minister (1977–79).

Des·cartes |dā'kärt|, René (1596–1650) French philosopher, mathematician, and man of science. Aiming to reach totally secure foundations for knowledge, he concluded that everything was open to doubt except his own conscious experience, and his existence as a necessary condition of this: *"Cogito, ergo sum"* (I think, therefore I am). From this certainty he developed a dualistic theory regarding mind and matter as separate though interacting. In mathematics, Descartes developed the use of coordinates to locate a point in two or three dimensions.

De Si·ca |də'sēkə|, Vittorio (1901–74) Italian movie director and actor, a key figure in Italian neorealist cinema. Notable movies: *The Bicycle Thief* (1948) and *Two Women* (1960), both of which won Oscars.

de So·to |də'sōtō|, Hernando (*c.* 1496–1542) Spanish soldier and explorer. Landing in Florida in 1539, he explored much of what is now the southeastern U.S., as far west as Oklahoma. He died of a fever on the banks of the Mississippi River.

de Spinoza, Baruch see SPINOZA.

des Prez |da'prā|, Josquin (*c.* 1440–1521) Also **des Prés** or **Desprez**. Flemish musician, he was a leading Renaissance composer.

de Staël |də 'stäl|, Madame (1766–1817) French novelist and critic, a precursor of the French romantics, born *Anne Louise Germaine Necker*. Her best-known critical work, *De l'Allemagne* (1810), introduced late 18th-century German writers and thinkers to France.

de Troyes, Chrétien see CHRÉTIEN DE TROYES.

Dett |det|, Robert Nathaniel (1882–1943) U.S. conductor and composer. He authored *The Dett Collection of Negro Spirituals* (1937).

de Va·le·ra |,davə'lerə|, Eamon (1882–1975) U.S.-born Irish statesman, prime minister (1937–48, 1951–54, and 1957–59), and president of the Republic of Ireland (1959–73). He was the leader of Sinn Fein (1917–26) and the founder of the Fianna Fáil Party in 1926. As president of the Irish Free State from 1932, de Valera was largely responsible for the new constitution of 1937 that created the state of Eire.

de Val·ois |də väl'wä|, Dame Ninette (1898–) Irish choreographer, ballet dancer, and teacher; born *Edris Stannus*.

A former soloist with Diaghilev's Ballets Russes, she formed the Vic-Wells Ballet (which eventually became the Royal Ballet) and the Sadler's Wells ballet school.

de Va·ro·na |,davə'rōnə|, Donna (1947–) U.S. swimmer. Winner of 2 gold medals in the 1964 Olympic Games, she set 18 world records during her career; she was a cofounder of the Women's Sports Foundation (1974).

De·vers |'dēvərz|, Gail (1966–) U.S. track and field athlete. She won Olympic gold medals in the 100 meters (1992, 1996) and was a 3-time world champion in the 100 meters and 100-meter hurdles.

De Vinne |də'vinē|, Theodore Low (1828–1914) U.S. printer and author. He founded and served as the first president of the Grolier Club (1884).

De Vo·to |di'vōtō|, Bernard Augustine (1897–1955) U.S. author, editor, and educator. He edited "The Easy Chair" in *Harper's Magazine* (1935–55). Notable works: *Across the Wide Missouri* (1947, Pulitzer Prize).

de Vries |dəv'rēs|, Hugo Marie (1848–1935) Dutch plant physiologist and geneticist. De Vries did much work on osmosis and water relations in plants, coining the term *plasmolysis*. His subsequent work on heredity and variation contributed substantially to the chromosome theory of heredity.

De Vries |di'vrēs|, Peter (1910–93) U.S. author. Although known for his comic touch, he also wrote a harrowing autobiographical novel, *The Blood of the Lamb* (1961), after his young daughter died of leukemia. Notable works: *No, But I Saw the Movie(s)* (1952), *Reuben, Reuben* (1964), and *Slouching Towards Kalamazoo* (1983).

Dew·ar |'dōōwər|, Sir James (1842–1923) Scottish chemist and physicist. He is chiefly remembered for his work in cryogenics, in which he devised the vacuum flask, achieved temperatures close to absolute zero, and was the first to produce liquid oxygen and hydrogen in quantity.

Dew·ey |'dōōē|, George (1837–1917) U.S. naval officer. Appointed commodore of the navy in 1896, he was the hero of the battle of Manila (May 1, 1898) during the Spanish-American War.

Dew·ey |'dōōē|, John (1859–1952) U.S. philosopher and educational theorist. Working in the pragmatic tradition of William James and C. S. Pierce, he defined knowledge as successful practice, and evolved the educational theory that children would learn best by doing. Notable work: *The School and Society* (1899).

Dew·ey |'dōōē|, Melvil (1851–1931) U.S. librarian. He devised a decimal system of classifying books, using ten main subject categories.

Dew·ey |'dōōē|, Thomas Edmund (1902–71) U.S. attorney. He served as governor of New York (1943–55) and was a Republican presidential candidate (1944,1948).

Dew·hurst |'dōō,hərst|, Colleen (1926–1991) U.S. actress. A star of film and stage, she has won two Tony Awards (1960, 1973).

Dia·ghi·lev |'dyägyəlyəf|, Sergey (Pavlovich) (1872–1929) Russian ballet impresario. In 1909 he formed the Ballets Russes, which he directed until his death. With Nijinsky, and later Massine, as his star performer, he transformed the European ballet scene, pooling the talents of leading choreographers, painters, and composers of his day.

Dia·mond |'dīmənd|, Neil (1941–) U.S. pop singer and songwriter.

Di·ana, Prin·cess of Wales |di'ænə| (1961–1997) Former wife of Prince Charles; her title before marriage was *Lady Diana Frances Spencer*. The daughter of the 8th Earl Spencer, she married Prince Charles in 1981; the couple were divorced in 1996. They had two children, *Prince William Arthur* (1982–) and *Prince Henry Charles Albert David* (known as Prince Harry, 1984–). She became a popular figure through her charity work and media appearances, and her death in a car crash in Paris gave rise to intense international mourning.

Di·as |'dēäsh|, Bartolomeu (c.1450–1500) Also **Diaz**. Portuguese navigator and explorer. He was the first European to round the Cape of Good Hope

(1488), thereby establishing a sea route from the Atlantic to Asia.

Dí·az |'dēæz|, Porfirio (1830–1915) Mexican general and statesman, president (1877–80, 1884–1911).

Diaz variant spelling of DIAS.

Dick·ens |'dikənz|, Charles (John Huffam) (1812–70) English novelist. His novels and stories are notable for their satirical humor and treatment of contemporary social problems, including the plight of the urban poor and the corruption and inefficiency of the legal system. Memorable characters such as Scrooge and Mr. Micawber contributed to his work's popular appeal. Some of his most famous works are *Oliver Twist* (1837–38), *Nicholas Nickleby* (1838–39), *A Christmas Carol* (1843), *David Copperfield* (1850), *Bleak House* (1852–53), and *Great Expectations* (1860–61).

Dick·en·son |'dikənsən|, Vic (1906–84) U.S. jazz trombonist and composer. He played with many groups and was known as one of the most consistent mainstream jazz musicians.

Dick·er·son |'dikərsən|, Eric (1960–) U.S. football player. He set the NFL's single-season rushing record of 2,105 yards in 1984.

Dick·ey |'dikē|, James (Lafayette) (1923–97) U.S. poet and author. Notable works: *Buckdancer's Choice* (1965, National Book Award) and *Deliverance* (1970).

Dick·in·son |'dikənsən|, Emily (Elizabeth) (1830–86) U.S. poet. From the age of 24, she led the life of a recluse; her poems use an elliptical language, emphasizing assonance and alliteration rather than rhyme, reflecting the struggles of her reclusive life. Although she wrote nearly 2,000 poems, only seven were published in her lifetime; the first notable collection appeared in 1890.

Did·dley |'didlē|, Bo (1928–) U.S. rock singer and songwriter. Born *Ellas Bates*.

Di·de·rot |'dēdə,rō|, Denis (1713–84) French philosopher, writer, and critic. A leading figure of the Enlightenment in France, he was principal editor of the *Encyclopédie* (1751–76), through which he disseminated and popularized philosophy and scientific knowledge. Other notable works: *Le Rêve de D'Alembert* (1782) and *Le Neveu de Rameau* (1805).

Did·i·on |'didiən|, Joan (1934–) U.S. author. Winner of the National Book Award for *Play It As It Lays* (1970), she is best known for writing about the extremes of life in her native California. Notable works: *Run, River* (1963), *Slouching Towards Bethlehem* (1968), and *After Henry* (1992).

Die·fen·ba·ker |'dēfən,bäkər|, John George (1895–1979) Canadian politician. He was prime minister (1957-63) and a member of the House of Commons (1940-79).

Die·sel |'dēzəl|, Rudolf (Christian Karl) (1858–1913) French-born German engineer, inventor of the diesel engine. In 1892 he patented a design for his new type of internal combustion engine, and developed it, exhibiting the prototype in 1897.

Die·trich |'dē,trik|, Marlene (c.1901–92) German-born U.S. actress and singer; born *Maria Magdelene von Losch*. She became famous for her part as Lola in *The Blue Angel* (1930), one of many movies she made with Josef von Sternberg. From the 1950s she was also successful as an international cabaret star.

Dietz |dēts|, Howard (1896–1983) U.S. lyricist. In collaboration with George Gershwin, Jerome Kern, and Arthur Schwartz, he wrote over 500 songs, including *You and the Night and the Music, Dancing in the Dark,* and *That's Entertainment.*

Di·fran·co |də'frænkō|, Ani (1970–) U.S. musician and punk-folk feminist.

Dil·lard |'dilərd|, Annie (1945–) U.S. author. She is the writer of essays on ecological subjects, including *Pilgrim at Tinker Creek* (1974, Pulitzer Prize).

Dil·ler |'dilər|, Barry (1942–) U.S. corporate executive. He has been chairman of the board of Paramount Pictures Corp. (1974–84) and CEO of 20th Century Fox (1984–) and Fox Television (1985–).

Dil·lin·ger |'dilənjər|, John (1903–34) U.S. outlaw. He was a bank robber who made daring escapes from jail and was named "Public Enemy Number 1" by the FBI; he was eventually betrayed by the "Lady in Red."

Di·Mag·gio |di'mæjēō|, Joe (1914–99) U.S. baseball player; Full name *Joseph Paul DiMaggio*; called *Joltin' Joe* and *the Yankee Clipper.* Star of the New York Yankees teams of 1936–51, he was renowned for his outstanding batting ability and for his outfield play. In 1941 he hit safely in 56 consecutive games, a record that has not been challenged. He was briefly married to Marilyn Monroe in 1954.

Ding·ley |'diNGlē|, Nelson (1832–99) U.S. politician. As a member of the U.S. House of Representatives from Maine (1881–99), he authored the Dingley Tariff Act (1897).

Di·o·cle·tian |,dīə'klēsHən| (c.245–c.313) Roman emperor (284–305); full name *Gaius Aurelius Valerius Diocletianus.* Faced with mounting military problems, in 286 he divided the empire between himself in the east and Maximian in the west. Diocletian launched the final persecution of the Christians (303).

Di·og·e·nes |dī'äjənēz| (c.412–c.323 BC) Greek philosopher. The most famous of the Cynics, he lived ascetically in Athens (according to legend, he lived in a tub) and was accordingly nicknamed *Kuōn* ("the dog"), from which the Cynics derived their name. He emphasized self-sufficiency and the need for natural, uninhibited behaviour, regardless of social conventions.

Di·on |'dē,än|, Celine (1968–) Canadian rock singer. She won a Grammy Award for the song "My Heart Will Go On," from the movie *Titanic* (1997).

Di·o·ny·sius |,dīə'nisēəs; ,dīə'nisHəs| name of two rulers of Syracuse: **Dionysius I** (c.430–367 BC; reigned 405–367); known as **Dionysius the Elder**. A tyrannical ruler, he waged three wars against the Carthaginians for control of Sicily, later becoming the principal power of Greek Italy after the capture of Rhegium (386) and other Greek cities in southern Italy. His son, **Dionysius II** (c. 397–344 BC; reigned 367–357 and 346–344), was known as **Dionysius the Younger**. He lacked his father's military ambitions and signed a peace treaty with Carthage in 367. Despite his patronage of philosophers, he resisted the attempt by Plato to turn him into a philosopher king.

Di·o·ny·sius Ex·i·gu·us |eg'zigyŏŏəs| (c.500–c.560) Scythian-born monk and scholar. He is notable for having developed in 525, at the behest of Pope John I, the system of dates BC and AD that is still in use today, calculating 753 years from the founding of Rome as the year of Jesus Christ's Incarnation; this has since been shown to be mistaken by several years. He is said to have taken the nickname *Exiguus* ('little') as a sign of humility.

Di·o·ny·sius of Hal·i·car·nas·sus |ˌhælicär'næsəs| (1st century BC) Greek historian, literary critic, and rhetorician. He lived in Rome from 30 BC and is best known for his detailed history of the city, written in Greek; this covers the period from the earliest times until the outbreak of the first Punic War (264 BC).

Di·o·ny·sius the Are·op·a·gite |ˌærē-'äpəˌgīt| (1st century AD) Greek churchman. His conversion by St. Paul is recorded in Acts 17:34, and according to tradition he went on to become the first bishop of Athens. He was later confused with St. Denis and with a mystical theologian, Pseudo-Dionysius the Areopagite, who exercised a profound influence on medieval theology.

Di·o·phan·tus |ˌdīə'fæntəs| (*fl.* c.250) Greek mathematician. Diophantus was the first to attempt an algebraical notation, showing in *Arithmetica* how to solve simple and quadratic equations. His work led to Pierre de Fermat's discoveries in the theory of numbers.

Di·or |dē'awr|, Christian (1905–57) French fashion designer. His first collection (1947) featured narrow-waisted tightly fitted bodices and full pleated skirts; this became known as the New Look. He later created the first A-line garments and built up a range of quality accessories.

Di·rac |də'räk|, Paul Adrien Maurice (1902–84) English theoretical physicist. He described the properties of the electron, including its spin, and postulated the existence of the positron by applying Einstein's theory of relativity to quantum mechanics. Nobel Prize for Physics (1933).

Dirks |dərks|, Rudolph (1877–1968) U.S. cartoonist, born in Germany. He was creator of "The Katzenjammer Kids."

Dirk·sen |'dərksən|, Everett McKinley (1896–1969) U.S. politician. An Illinois Republican, he was a member of the U.S. House of Representatives (1933–48), a U.S. Senator (1950–69), and a Senate Republican leader (1959–69).

Dis·ney |'diznē|, Walt (1901–1966) U.S. animator and movie and television producer. Founder of Disney entertainment company; full name *Walter Elias Disney*. He made his name with the creation of cartoon characters such as Mickey Mouse (who first appeared in 1928), Donald Duck, Goofy, and Pluto. *Snow White and the Seven Dwarfs* (1937) was the first full-length cartoon feature film with sound and color. Other notable films: *Pinocchio* (1940), *Dumbo* (1941), and *Bambi* (1942). He also founded the Disneyland amusement park in California.

Dis·rae·li |diz'rālē|, Benjamin, 1st Earl of Beaconsfield (1804–81) British Tory statesman, of Italian-Jewish descent; prime minister (1868, 1874–80). He was largely responsible for the introduction of the second Reform Act (1867), which doubled the electorate, and introduced measures to improve public health and working conditions in factories. He also ensured that Britain bought a controlling interest in the Suez Canal (1875) and made Queen Victoria Empress of India.

Dit·ko |'ditkō|, Steven (1927–) U.S. cartoonist. He created the character Spider-Man.

Dix |diks|, Dorothea Lynde (1802–87) U.S. reformer. She was a pioneer of American prison reform, a creator of almshouses and insane asylums, and superintendent of women nurses in the Civil War.

Dix·on |'diksən|, George (c. 1755–c. 1800) English navigator. He sailed with Cook on his third expedition (1776–69), and in 1787 discovered Queen Charlotte Islands, Norfolk Sound, Port Mulgrave, Dixon Entrance, and Alexander Archipelago.

Dix·on |'diksən|, George (1870–1909)

U.S. boxer, born in Canada. He was the first African-American boxer to win a world bantamweight title (1980), and he later became the world featherweight champion (1891–97 and 1898–1900).

Dix·on |'diksən|, Jeremiah (died 1777) English surveyor. With Charles Mason, he determined the boundary between Maryland and Pennsylvania that became known as the Mason-Dixon line.

Dix·on |'diksən|, Thomas (1864–1946) U.S. clergyman and writer. He was an extremist Southerner, strongly supportive of the Ku Klux Klan; his 20 novels include the trilogy *The Leopard's Spots* (1902), *The Clansman* (1905), and *The Traitor* (1907).

Dix·on |'diksən|, Willie (1915–92) U.S. songwriter. His classics, such as "You Shook Me," "Little Red Rooster," and "Bring It On Home, " linked rock and roll with the blues.

Dje·ras·si, Carl (1923–) U.S. physician, born in Bulgaria. He invented a machine for white blood cell transfusions (1970); his contributions to cancer therapy include chemotherapy and platelet transfusions.

Do·bell |dō'bel|, Sir William (1899–1970) Australian painter.

Dö·be·rei·ner |'dœɛbə,rīnər|, Johann Wolfgang (1780–1849) German chemist. His work contributed to the formation of the periodic table of elements.

Do·by |'dōbē|, Larry (1924–) U.S. baseball player and manager.

Dob·zhan·sky |dəb'zHänskē|, Theodosius Grigorievich (1900–75) U.S. geneticist, author, and educator, born in Ukraine. He studied genetic variation and the philosophical implications of evolution.

Doc·tor·ow |'däktə,rō|, E. L. (1931–) U.S. author. Born *Edgar Lawrence Doctorow*. He won a National Book Critics Circle Award for *Ragtime* (1975).

Dodge |däj| U.S. family, including **David Low Dodge** (1774–1852), a businessman and pacifist. He founded the New York Peace Society (1815), the first group of its kind. His son, **William Earl Dodge** (1805–83), a businessman and philanthropist, founded Phelps, Dodge & Co. (1883), and was an orga-

nizer of the YMCA in the U.S. David Low Dodge's great-granddaughter, **Grace Hoadley Dodge** (1856–1914), was a social worker. She organized a club for young working women (1885).

Dodge |däj|, Grenville Mellen (1831–1916) U.S. Army officer and civil engineer. He supervised the building of the Union Pacific Railroad (1866–70).

Dodge |däj|, Mary Elizabeth Mapes (1831–1905) U.S. author. Notable works: *Hans Brinker, or The Silver Skates* (1865).

Dodgson, Charles Lutwidge see CARROLL.

Doe·nitz |'dənits|, Karl (1891–1980) German admiral. He was commander in chief of the German navy (1943) and delivered the German surrender (1945).

Doi, Takako (1935–) Japanese author. Works include *Chinese Painting* (1983).

Dois·neau, Robert (1912–94) French photographer, best known for his photos of the city and inhabitants of Paris. Notable works: "The Kiss at the Hôtel de Ville" (1950).

Doi·sy |'doizē|, Edward Adelbert (1893–1986) U.S. biochemist. He isolated sex homones and discovered Vitamin K, and with Henrik Dam won the Nobel Prize (1943) for Physiology or Medicine.

Dole |dōl| U.S. political family, including: **Bob Dole** (1923–); full name *Robert Joseph Dole*. A senator from 1968, he became leader of the Republican Party in 1992, and was defeated by Bill Clinton in the presidential election of 1996. His wife, **Elizabeth Hanford Dole** (1936–), was U.S. secretary of transportation (1983–89) and U.S. secretary of labor (1989–91) before becoming president of the American Red Cross (1991–99).

Do·lin |'dōlən|, Sir Anton (1904–83) English ballet dancer and choreographer; born *Sydney Francis Patrick Chippendall Healey-Kay*. He was the first artistic director of the London Festival Ballet (1950–61), as well as first soloist.

Doll |däl|, Sir Richard (1912–) English physician. Full name *William Richard Shaboe Doll*. With **Sir A. Bradford Hill** (1897–1991), he was the first to show a statistical link between smoking and lung cancer.

Dol·lar |'dälər|, Robert (1844–1932) U.S. businessman, born in Scotland. He founded Dollar Steamship Co. (1901) for trade with Asia and expanded to around-the-world passenger service (1924).

Doll·fuss |'dälfəs|, Engelbert (1892–1934) Austrian statesman, chancellor of Austria 1932–34. From 1933 Dollfuss attempted to block Austrian Nazi plans to force the *Anschluss* (German annexation of Austria) by governing without Parliament. He was assassinated by Austrian Nazis.

Do·magk |'dō,mäk|, Gerhard (1895–1964) German bacteriologist and pathologist. Nobel Prize for Physiology or Medicine, 1939.

Do·men·i·ci |də'menəCHē|, Pete (1932–) U.S. politician and lawyer. He was a member of the U.S. Senate from New Mexico (1972–).

Do·min·go |də'miNGgō|, Placido (1941–) Spanish-born operatic tenor; emigrated to Mexico in 1950.

Dom·i·nic |'dämənik|, St. (c.1170–1221) Spanish priest and friar; Spanish name *Domingo de Guzmán*. In 1216 he founded the Order of Friars Preachers at Toulouse in France; its members became known as Dominicans or Black Friars. Feast day, August 8.

Do·mi·nio |'dämə,nō|, Fats (1928–) U.S. pianist, singer, and songwriter; born *Antoine Domino*. His music represents part of the transition from rhythm and blues to rock and roll, and shows the influence of jazz, boogie-woogie, and gospel music. Notable songs: "Ain't That a Shame" (1955) and "Blueberry Hill" (1956).

Do·mi·tian |də'misHən| (AD 51–96) Son of Vespasian, Roman emperor (81–96); full name *Titus Flavius Domitianus*. An energetic but autocratic ruler, he embarked on a major building program, but was assassinated following a lengthy period of terror.

Don·a·hue |'dänə,hyōō|, Phil (1935–) U.S. talk show host. He began the award-winning *Phil Donahue Show* in 1967 and retired in 1996.

Don·ald |'dawnəld|, David Herbert (1920–) U.S. historian and biographer. Notable works: *Charles Sumner and the Coming of the Civil War* (1960, Pulitzer prize) and *Look Homeward: A Life of Thomas Wolfe* (1987, Pulitzer prize).

Don·a·tel·lo |,dänə'telō| (c.1386–1466) Italian sculptor; born *Donato di Betto Bardi*. He was one of the pioneers of scientific perspective, and is especially famous for his lifelike sculptures, including the bronze *David* (c.1430–60).

Do·na·tus |,dō'nätəs|, Aelius (4th century) Roman grammarian. The *Ars Grammatica*, containing his treatises on Latin grammar, was the sole textbook used in schools in the Middle Ages.

Don·i·zet·ti |,dänə'zetē|, Gaetano (1797–1848) Italian composer. His operas include tragedies such as *Lucia di Lammermoor* (1835) and comedies such as *Don Pasquale* (1843).

Don·kin |'dänkən|, Bryan (1768–1855) English engineer. He developed a method of food preservation by heat sterilization, sealing the food inside a container made of sheet steel and so producing the first tin can.

Donne |'dən|, John (1572–1631) English poet and preacher. A metaphysical poet, he is most famous for his *Satires* (c.1590–99), *Elegies* (c.1590–99), and love poems, which appeared in the collection *Songs and Sonnets*. He also wrote religious poems and, as dean of St. Paul's in London from 1621, was one of the most celebrated preachers of his age.

Don·o·van |'dänəvən| (1946–) British folk-rock singer. Born *Donovan Leitch*. Notable songs: "Mellow Yellow" (1966).

Doo·ley |'dōōlē|, Thomas Anthony (1927–61) U.S. physician and author. He established a medical mission in Northern Laos (1956) and hospitals in Cambodia, Laos, and Vietnam; in 1957 he established Medico, an international medical aid mission.

Doo·lit·tle |'dōō,litəl|, Hilda (1886–1961) U.S. poet; Pseudonym **H. D.** Her work shows the influence of Ezra Pound and other imagist poets. Notable works: *Sea Garden* (1916).

Dop·pler |'däplər|, Christian Johann (1803–53) Austrian physicist, famous for his discovery, in 1842, of what is now known as the Doppler effect.

Do·ran |'dōrən|, George Henry (1869–1956) U.S. publisher, born in Canada. He joined with F. N. Doubleday to form Doubleday, Doran & Co. (1927).

Do·ra·ti |də'rätē|, Antal (1906–88) U.S. composer and conductor, born in Budapest. As musical director of symphonies in Dallas; Minneapolis; Stockholm; Washington, D.C.; and Detroit, he made over 500 recordings.

Do·ré |daw'rā|, Gustave (1832–83) French book illustrator, known for his woodcut illustrations of books such as Dante's *Inferno* (1861), Cervantes' *Don Quixote* (1863), and the Bible (1865–66).

Dorr |'dawr|, Thomas Wilson (1805–54) U.S. lawyer and political reformer. He formed the "People's Party" in Rhode Island and was elected governor (1842). As a result of his attempts to reform established government, civil war broke out in the state (Dorr's Rebellion). He was sentenced to prison in 1844.

Dor·sey |'dawrsē| U.S. musicians. **Jimmy Dorsey** (1904–57), a jazz clarinetist and alto saxophonist, and his brother **Tommy Dorsey** (1905–56), a jazz trombonist, led popular dance and jazz bands both individually and jointly.

Dos Pas·sos |də'spæsəs|, John (Roderigo) (1896–1970) U.S. novelist, chiefly remembered for his portrayal of American life in such novels as *Manhattan Transfer* (1925) and *USA* (1938).

Do·sto·ev·sky |,dästə'yefskē|, Fyodor (Mikhailovich) (1821–81) Russian novelist. Also **Dostoyevsky**. Dostoevsky's novels reveal his psychological insight, savage humor, and concern with the religious, political, and moral problems posed by human suffering. Notable novels: *Crime and Punishment* (1866), *The Idiot* (1868), and *The Brothers Karamazov* (1880).

Dou·ble·day |'dəbl,dā|, Abner (1819–93) U.S. army officer. A Union general in the Civil War, he is credited with creating the modern game of baseball, although this claim has been largely disputed.

Dou·ble·day |'dəbl,dā|, Frank Nelson (1862–1934) U.S. publisher. With S. S.

McClure he founded Doubleday & McClure (1897–1900) and with Walter Hines Page he formed Doubleday, Page & Co. (1900–27); he served as chairman of Doubleday, Doran & Co. (1927–34).

Doug·las |'dəgləs| U.S. actors. **Kirk Douglas** (1916–); born *Issur Danielovitch Demsky*. Notable movies: *Lust for Life* (1956) and *Spartacus* (1960). His son, **Michael Douglas** (1944–), is also a director, and producer. Notable movies: *Romancing the Stone* (1984), *Wall Street* (1987, Academy Award), and *The American President* (1995).

Doug·las |'dəgləs|, Aaron (1899–1979) U.S. painter.

Doug·las |'dəgləs|, Lord Alfred (Bruce) (1870–1945) English poet. Enraged by his long intimacy with Oscar Wilde, Douglas's father, the 8th Marquess of Queensberry, cut off Douglas's allowance and had Wilde imprisoned.

Doug·las |'dəgləs|, Donald Wills (1892–1981) U.S. businessman and aircraft engineer. He was an early engineer of passenger and military airplanes and president of the Douglas Aircraft Co. (1928–57), which merged to become the McDonnell Douglas Corp. (1967).

Doug·las |'dəgləs|, Melvyn (1901–81) U.S. actor. Born *Melvyn Hesselberg*. Notable movies: *Being There* (1979, Academy Award).

Doug·las |'dəgləs|, Stephen Arnold (1813–61) U.S. attorney and politician. Known as **the Little Giant**. An Illinois Democrat who served as a U.S. congressman (1843–47) and senator (1847–61), he is best remembered for a series of seven senatorial-campaign debates (1858) with Republican candidate Abraham Lincoln, in which Douglas advocated states' rights. He won the Senate seat in 1858, but lost his 1860 bid for the presidency to Lincoln, after which he was an outspoken supporter of the Lincoln administration.

Doug·las |'dəgləs|, William Orville (1898–1980) U.S. Supreme Court justice (1939–75). He was noted as a consistent liberal, especially concerning freedom of speech.

Douglas-Home |'dəgləs hōm|, Sir Alex, Baron Home of the Hirsel of Coldstream (1903–95) British Conservative statesman, prime minister (1963–64). Full name *Alexander Frederick Douglas-Home*.

Doug·lass |'dɒgləs|, Frederick (1817–95) U.S. abolitionist and author. Born *Frederick Augustus Washington Bailey*. He escaped from slavery in 1838 and became an antislavery lecturer. He established an antislavery newspaper, *North Star* (1847–64), and published his autobiography, *Narrative of the Life of Frederick Douglass* (1845, revised 1892).

Dove |dʌv|, Rita (1952–) U.S. author. She was the youngest poet and the first African-American woman to hold the post of Poet Laureate of the U.S. (1993–94). Notable works: *Thomas and Beulah* (1986, Pulitzer prize).

Dow |dow|, Charles Henry (1851–1902) U.S. journalist. With Edward D. Jones (1856–1920), he founded Dow Jones & Co.(1882) and *The Wall Street Journal* (1889).

Dow |dow|, Herbert Henry (1866–1930) U.S. chemist and businessman, born in Canada. He founded Dow Chemical Co. (1897) and developed and patented over 100 chemical processes.

Dowd |dowd|, Maureen (1952–) U.S. journalist. She writes an opinion/editorial column for the *New York Times* (1995–).

Dow·ding |'dowdiNG|, Hugh (Caswall Tremenheere), Baron (1882–1970) British Marshal of the Royal Air Force. He was commander in chief of the British air defense forces that defeated the Luftwaffe during the Battle of Britain in 1940.

Dow·son |'dowsən|, Ernest (Christopher) (1867–1900) English poet, associated with the "decadent" school of Oscar Wilde and Aubrey Beardsley. His two books of poems, *Verses* (1896) and *Decorations* (1899), deal with themes of ennui and world-weariness.

Doyle |doil|, Sir Arthur Conan (1859–1930) Scottish novelist and short-story writer, chiefly remembered for his creation of the private detective Sherlock Holmes. Holmes first appeared in *A Study in Scarlet* (1887), and was featured in more than fifty stories and in novels such as *The Hound of the Baskervilles* (1902).

D'Oy·ly Carte |'doilē 'kärt|, Richard (1844–1901) English impresario and producer. He brought together the librettist Sir W. S. Gilbert and the composer Sir Arthur Sullivan, producing many of their operettas in London's Savoy Theatre, which he had established in 1881.

Drab·ble |'dræbəl|, Margaret (1939–) English novelist, the younger sister of A. S. Byatt. Notable works: *The Millstone* (1966), *The Ice Age* (1977), and *The Radiant Way* (1987).

Dra·co |'drākō| (7th century BC) Athenian legislator. His codification of Athenian law was notorious for its severity in that the death penalty was imposed even for trivial crimes; this gave rise to the adjective draconian in English.

Drake |drāk|, Sir Francis (*c.* 1540–96) English sailor and explorer. He was the first Englishman to circumnavigate the globe (1577–80), in his ship the *Golden Hind*. He played an important part in the defeat of the Spanish Armada.

Dra·per |'drāpər| U.S. scientists. English-born **John William Draper** (1811–82) was an organizer and president (1850–73) of New York University Medical School and the author of *Human Physiology, Statical and Dynamical* (1856), for many years the field's standard text. His son, **Henry Draper** (1837–82), was an astronomer. In his self-built observatory, he obtained the first photograph of a stellar spectrum (Vega, 1872) and the first photograph of a nebula (Orion, 1880).

Dra·per |'drāpər|, Charles Stark (1901–87) U.S. aeronautical engineer. He invented the gyroscope-stabilized gunsight used by the U.S. armed forces and directed the development of guidance technology for fighter planes, submarines, missiles, and Apollo spacecraft.

Drei·ser |'drīzər|, Theodore (Herman Albert) (1871–1945) U.S. novelist. His first novel, *Sister Carrie* (1900), caused controversy for its frank treatment of the heroine's sexuality and ambition. Other notable works: *America Is Worth Saving* (1941).

Drew |drōō|, Charles Richard (1904–50) U.S. physician. He was a pioneer in the development of blood banks (1940). Spingarn medal, 1944.

Drew |drōō|, Daniel (1797–1879) U.S. financier. In 1844 he joined the Wall Street banking firm, Drew, Robinson and Co.; later, he manipulated the stock of the Erie Railroad to prevent Cornelius Vanderbilt from gaining a majority interest. Drew Theological Seminary (now Drew University) benefitted from his contributions.

Drew |drōō|, Elizabeth (1935–) U.S. journalist. She wrote for *New Yorker* magazine as a Washington correspondent (1973–92) is a commentator on Monitor Radio.

Drex·el |'dreksəl|, Anthony Joseph (1826–93) U.S. banker and philanthropist. He joined his father's brokerage firm (1847) and merged with J. P. Morgan (1871), making Drexel, Morgan and Co. the most powerful investment banking house in the U.S. He was the founder and benefactor (1892) of Drexel Institute of Technology.

Drey·fus |'drāfəs|, Alfred (1859–1935) French army officer, of Jewish descent. In 1894 he was falsely accused of providing military secrets to the Germans; his trial and imprisonment caused a major political crisis in France. He was eventually fully exonerated in 1906.

Drey·fuss |'drifəs|, Richard (1947–) U.S. actor. Notable movies: *Close Encounters of the Third Kind* (1977) and *The Goodbye Girl* (1977, Academy Award).

Druck·er |'drəkər|, Mort (1929–) U.S. cartoonist and artist. He was on staff at *Mad* magazine.

Dry·den |'drīdən|, John (1631–1700) English poet, critic, and dramatist of the English Augustan Age. He is best known for *Marriage à La mode* (comedy, 1673), *All for Love* (tragedy based on Shakespeare's *Antony and Cleopatra*, 1678), and *Absalom and Achitophel* (verse satire in heroic couplets, 1681).

Drys·dale |'drīz,dāl|, Sir Russell (1912–81) British-born Australian painter. He dealt with life in the Australian bush, for example in *The Rabbiter and Family* (1938), and with the plight of Aboriginals in contact with white settlement, as in *Mullaloonah Tank* (1953).

Duane |dwān| U.S. family, including:

William Duane (1760–1835), a journalist. He was co-editor of the *Philadelphia Aurora*, which strongly supported Jeffersonian policies. His great-grandson, **William Duane** (1872–1935), was a physicist. He developed methods and equipment for using radium and X rays in medicine.

Duar·te |'dwärtē; 'dwärtā|, José Napoleón (1925–90) Salvadoran politician. After a corrupt military deprived him of his elected presidency (1972), he hid in exile in Venezuela for 7 years and returned in 1980 as a figurehead for the ruling junta; he was elected president (1984–89).

Du Bar·ry |dōō 'berē|, Marie Jeanne Bécu, Comtesse (1743–93) French courtier and mistress of Louis XV. During the French Revolution she was arrested by the Revolutionary Tribunal and guillotined.

Dub·ček |'dōōb,CHek|, Alexander (1921–92) Czechoslovak statesman, first secretary of the Czechoslovak Communist Party (1968–69). Dubček was the driving force behind the Czechoslovakian political reforms of 1968 (the Prague Spring), which prompted the Soviet invasion of Czechoslovakia in 1968 and his removal from office. After the collapse of communism in 1989, he was elected speaker of the Federal Assembly in the new Czechoslovak parliament.

Du·bin·sky |də'binskē|, David (1892–1982) U.S. labor leader and social reformer, born in Russia. He served as president of the International Ladies' Garment Workers Union (1932–66).

Du Bois |dōō'bois|, W. E. B. (1868–1963) U.S. writer, sociologist, and political activist; full name *William Edward Burghardt Du Bois*. He was an important figure in campaigning for equality for black Americans arguing in *The Souls of Black Folk* (1903) that racial equality could be achieved only by political organization and struggle. He co-founded the National Association for the Advancement of Colored People (NAACP) in 1909.

Du·buf·fet |dOEboE'fä|, Jean (1901–85) French painter. He rejected traditional techniques, incorporating materials such as sand and plaster in his paintings and producing sculptures made from rubbish.

Duc·cio |'dōōtCHŌ|, di Buoninsegna (*c.*1255–1318) Italian painter, founder of the Sienese school of painting; full name *Duccio di Buoninsegna*. The only fully documented surviving work by him is the *Maestà* for the high altar of Siena Cathedral (completed 1311).

Du·ce |'dōōCHĀ|, Il the title assumed by Benito Mussolini in 1922.

Du·champ |dōō'sHäm|, Marcel (1887–1968) French-born artist, a U.S. citizen from 1955. A leading figure of the Dada movement and originator of conceptual art, he invented "ready-mades," mass-produced articles selected at random and displayed as works of art—most famously a bicycle wheel and a urinal.

Du·chov·ny |dōō'kəvnē|, David (1960–) U.S. actor. He won awards for his role as FBI agent Fox Mulder on "The X-Files."

Dud·ley |'dədlē|, Robert, Earl of Leicester (*c.*1532–88) English nobleman, military commander, and court favorite of Elizabeth I.

Due·sen·berg |'dōōzən,bərg|, Frederick Samuel (1877–1932) U.S. manufacturer, born in Germany. He founded the Duesenberg Motor Co. (1917) and designed racing and luxury cars.

Du·fay |dōō'fā|, Guillaume (*c.*1400–74) French composer. He made a significant contribution to the development of Renaissance polyphony.

Dufy, Raoul (1877–1953) French painter and textile designer His characteristic style involved calligraphic outlines sketched on brilliant background washes.

Du·ka·kis |də'käkəs|, Michael Stanley (1933–) U.S. politician. He was governor of Massachusetts (1975–79, 1983–91) and a Democratic presidential candidate (1988). Olympia Dukakis is his cousin.

Du·ka·kis |də'käkəs|, Olympia (1931–) U.S. actress. Notable movies: *Steel Magnolias* (1989) and *Moonstruck* (1987, Academy Award). Michael Dukakis is her cousin.

Duke |dōōk|, U.S. industrialists. **Benjamin Newton Duke** (1855–1929) and

his brother **James Buchanan Duke** (1856–1925) established a tobacco factory (1874) and joined with rival companies in the American Tobacco Co. Benjamin served as the company's president. James founded Duke University. James's daughter, **Doris Duke** (1912–93), was a philanthopist and heiress to the Duke tobacco fortune.

Dul·les |'dələs|, John Foster (1888–1959) U.S. statesman and international lawyer. He was the U.S. adviser at the founding of the United Nations in 1945 and negotiated the peace treaty with Japan in 1951. As U.S. secretary of state at the height of the Cold War (1953–59) he urged the stockpiling of nuclear arms to deter Soviet aggression.

Du·luth |də'lōōTH|, Daniel Greysolon (1636–1710) French explorer. He was sent by Comte de Frontenac to establish forts and trading posts in the western part of the Great Lakes region (1678). Duluth, Minnesota, is named after him.

Du·mas |dōō'mä| French authors, including **Alexandre Dumas** (1802–70); known as **Dumas pére** (father). Although he was a pioneer of the romantic theater in France, his reputation now rests on his historical adventure novels *The Three Musketeers* (1844–45) and *The Count of Monte Cristo* (1844–45). His son, **Alexandre Dumas** (1824–95), was known as **Dumas fils** (son). He wrote the novel (and play) *La Dame aux camélias* (1848 and 1852), which formed the basis of Verdi's opera *La Traviata* (1853).

Du Mau·ri·er |də'mawrē,ā| English authors, including French-born **George (Louis Palmella Busson) du Maurier** (1834–96), a novelist, cartoonist, and illustrator. He is chiefly remembered for his novel *Trilby* (1894), which included the character Svengali and gave rise to the word *Svengali*, for a person who has a hypnotic influence over someone else. His granddaughter **Dame Daphne du Maurier** (1907–89) was a novelist. Many of her popular novels and period romances are set in the West Country of England, where she spent most of her life. Notable works: *Jamaica Inn* (1936) and *Rebecca* (1938).

Du Mont |'dōō,mänt; ,dōō'mänt|, Allen Balcom (1901–65) U.S. engineer, inventor, and manufacturer. He established Du Mont Laboratories (1931) and developed and manufactured commercial television receivers.

Du·mont d'Ur·ville |dōō'mōndōōr-'vēl|, Jules-Sébastien-César (1790–1842) French naval commander and explorer. He explored Polynesia and the South Seas (1826–29).

Dun |dən|, Robert Graham (1826–1900) U.S. businessman. He established R. G. Dun & Co., which merged into Dun & Bradstreet, Inc. (1933), and published *Dun's Review* business report (from 1893).

Dun·bar |'dən,bär|, Paul Laurence (1872–1906) U.S. poet. The son of escaped slaves, he published a volume of poetry (1893) whose reputation was established by favorable notice from William Dean Howells.

Dun·bar |'dən,bär|, William (*c*.1460–*c*.1520) Scottish poet. He was the author of satires such as the political allegory "The Thrissill and the Rois" ("The Thistle and the Rose", 1503) and of elegies such as "Lament for the Makaris."

Dun·bar |'dən,bär|, William (1749–1810) U.S. scientist. He explored the old Southwest for President Thomas Jefferson, noting the existence of Hot Springs in Arkansas and exploring the Mississippi Delta.

Dun·can |'dəNGkən|, Isadora (1877–1927) U.S. dancer and teacher. She was a pioneer of modern dance, famous for her "free" barefoot dancing. She died in a freak accident, strangled when her long scarf became entangled in the wheels of a car.

Dun·can I |'dəNGkən| (*c*.1010–40) king of Scotland (1034–40). He was killed in battle by Macbeth.

Dun·lap |'dənlawp|, William (1766–1839) U.S. playwright, painter, and historian. He was the first American to make a serious business of writing for the stage and is honored as the father of the American theater.

Dun·lop |'dənläp|, John Boyd (1840–1921) Scottish inventor. He developed the first successful pneumatic bicycle tire (1888), manufactured by the company he founded.

Dunne |dən|, Finley Peter (1867–1936) U.S. columnist and editor of the *Chicago Journal*. He is best known for creating the character of Mr. Dooley, Irish saloonkeeper and humorous commentator on current events.

Dunne |dən|, John Gregory (1932–) U.S. writer. He is the author of fiction such as *True Confessions* (1977) and nonfiction such as *Vegas* (1974).

Dunne |dən|, John William (1875–1949) English philosopher. His work is especially concerned with time and includes *An Experiment with Time* (1927) and *The Serial Universe* (1934), both of which influenced the plays of J. B. Priestley.

Duns Sco·tus |dən'skōtəs|, John (*c*.1266–1308) Scottish theologian and scholar. A profoundly influential figure in the Middle Ages, he was the first major theologian to defend the theory of the Immaculate Conception, and opposed St. Thomas Aquinas in arguing that faith was a matter of will rather than something dependent on logical proofs.

Dun·sta·ble |'dənstəbəl|, John (*c*.1390–1453) English composer. He was a significant early exponent of counterpoint.

Dun·stan |'dənstən|, St. (*c*.924–88) Anglo-Saxon prelate. As Archbishop of Canterbury he introduced the strict Benedictine rule into England and succeeded in restoring monastic life. Feast day, May 19.

du Pont |dōō'pän|, E. I. (1771–1834) U.S. industrialist, born in France. Full name *Eleuthère Irenee du Pont*. The gunpowder manufacturing plant that he established near Wilmington, Delaware, in 1802 became an American corporate giant, due largely to the government contracts that ensured its early success, especially during the War of 1812.

Du Pré |dōō'prā|, Jacqueline (1945–87) English cellist. She made her solo debut at the age of 16 and became famous for her interpretations of cello concertos. Her performing career was halted in 1972 by multiple sclerosis.

Du·rand |də'rænd|, Asher Brown (1796–1886) U.S. artist. He was one of the earliest landscape painters of the Hudson River School.

Du·rand |də'rænd|, William Frederick (1859–1958) U.S. mechanical engineer and educator. He was a consultant for the Hoover, Grand Coulee, and other dams.

Du·rant |də'rænd| U.S. historians. **Will** (1885–1981; full name *William James Durant*) and his wife **Ariel** (1898–1981; born *Chaya "Ida" Kaufman* in Ukraine) wrote the 11-volume "Story of Civilization" series, works that were published over a 40-year period (1935–75). Volume 10, *Rousseau and Revolution* (1967) won a Pulitzer Prize. The Durants were awarded the Presidential Medal of Freedom (1977).

Du·rant |də'rænd|, Graham J. (1934–) English inventor. With John Colin Emmett (1939-) and C. Robin Ganellin (1934-) he discovered antiulcer compounds (trade name Tagamet).

Du·rant |də'rænd|, Thomas Clark (1820–85) U.S. businessman. He was an organizer (1863–69) and president (1863–67) of the Union Pacific Railroad Co.

Du·rant |də'rænd|, William Crapo (1861–1947) U.S. industrialist. He created or took over several automobile companies, including Buick (1904), General Motors (1908), and Chevrolet (1911). He invested poorly and ended his life bankrupt.

Du·ran·te |də'ræntē|, Jimmy (1893–1980) U.S. entertainer. Born *James Francis Durante*. The gravelly-voiced star of Broadway, movies, radio, and television, his career began in vaudeville.

Du·ras |dōō'räs|, Marguerite (1914–96) French novelist, movie director, and dramatist; pseudonym of *Marguerite Donnadieu*. She is best known for the screenplay to Alain Resnais' movie *Hiroshima mon amour* (1959) and for her semiautobiographical novel *L'Amant* (1984).

Dü·rer |'dərər|, Albrecht (1471–1528) German engraver and painter. He was the leading German artist of the Renaissance, important for his technically advanced woodcuts and copper engravings and also noted for his watercolors and drawings.

Du·rey |dōō'rā|, Louis-Edmond (1888–1979) French composer. A member until 1921 of the group Les Six, he later wrote music of a deliberate mass appeal, in accordance with communist doctrines on art. Notable works: *La Longue marche* (cantata, 1949).

Durk·heim |'dərk,hīm|, Émile (1858–1917) French sociologist, one of the founders of modern sociology. He became the first professor of sociology at the Sorbonne (1913). Notable works: *The Division of Labor in Society* (1893) and *Suicide* (1897).

Du·ro·cher |də'rōSHər|, Leo Ernest (1905–91) U.S. baseball player and manager. He is noted for coining the remark, "nice guys finish last."

Dur·rell |dŏŏ'rel| English family, including: **Lawrence (George) Durrell** (1912–90), a novelist, poet, and travel writer. He spent much of his life abroad, particularly in the Mediterranean. Notable works: *Alexandria Quartet* (four novels, 1957–60) and *Prospero's Cell* (travel, 1945). His brother, **Gerald (Malcolm) Durrell** (1925–95), was a zoologist and writer. In 1958 he founded a zoo (later the Jersey Wildlife Preservation Trust) devoted to the conservation and captive breeding of endangered species. Notable works: *My Family and Other Animals* (1956).

Dürrenmatt, Friedrich (1921–90) Swiss playwright, novelist, and critic. Notable works: *The Visit* (1958).

Dur·yea |'dŏŏr,yä| U.S. inventors and manufacturers. **Charles Edgar Duryea** (1861–1938) and his brother **James Frank Duryea** (1869–1967) built a gasoline automobile (1893) and organized Duryea Motor Wagon Co. (1895).

Du·se |'dōōzä|, Eleonora (1858–1924) Italian actress, best known for her tragic roles, particularly in plays by Ibsen and Gabriele d'Annunzio.

Dus·ton |'dəstən|, Hannah (1657– *c.* 1736) American heroine. After being captured by Indians (1697), she escaped and returned home after killing and scalping her captors.

Du Toit |də'toi|, Stephanus Jacobus (1847–1911) South African clergyman and politician. He founded the Society of True South Africans (1875) and helped establish the language (Afrikaans) and political identity of Boers.

Dut·ton |'dətn|, Clarence Edward (1841–1912) U.S. geologist. He worked for the U.S. Geological Survey (1875–90), studying the plateau regions of Utah, Arizona, and New Mexico, and developing the concept of isotasy.

Dut·ton |'dətn|, Edward Payson (1831–1923) U.S. publisher. He founded E. P. Dutton & Co.(1858).

Du·val |doo'väl|, Gabriel (1752–1844) U.S. Supreme Court justice (1811–35). He served as comptroller of the U.S. Treasury (1802–11).

Du·val·ier |doo,väl'yä|, François (1907–71) Haitian statesman, president (1957–71); known as **Papa Doc**. His regime was noted for its oppressive nature, opponents being assassinated or forced into exile by his security force, the Tontons Macoutes. He was succeeded by his son **Jean-Claude Duvalier** (1951–) known as **Baby Doc**, who was overthrown by a mass uprising in 1986.

Du·vall |doo'väl; də'väl|, Robert (1931–) U.S. actor, director, producer, and screenwriter. Notable movies: *Tender Mercies* (1983, Academy Award).

Du·Vig·neaud |doo'vinyō|, Vincent (1901–78) U.S. biochemist. He studied vitamins and hormones, especially insulin, methionine, and biotin, and isolated and synthesized oxytocin and vasopressin, for which he received the Nobel Prize for Chemistry (1955).

Duy·ckinck |'dī,kiNGk|, Evert Augustus (1816–78) U.S. editor. With his brother George Long (1823–63), he edited the influential *New York Literary World* (1848–53) and compiled the two-volume *Cyclopaedia of American Literature* (1855).

Dvoř·ák |də'vawr,ZHäk|, Antonín (1841–1904) Czech composer Czech composer. Combining ethnic folk elements with the Viennese musical tradition, he wrote chamber music, operas, and songs, but is probably best known for his ninth symphony (*From the New World,* 1892–95).

Dwig·gins |'dwigənz|, William Addison (1880–1956) U.S. book designer. He designed the typefaces Metro (1929), Electra (1935), Caledonia (1939), and Eldorado (1953).

Dwight |dwīt|, John Sullivan (1813–93) U.S. music critic. He founded and edited *Dwight's Journal of Music* (1852–81) and was an organizer of the Boston Philharmonic society (1865).

Dwight |dwīt|, Timothy (1752–1817) U.S. clergyman and educator. He was grandson of Jonathan Edwards and a leading Calvinist and Federalist. From 1795 to 1817, he served as president of Yale University.

Dy·lan |'dilən|, Bob (1941–) U.S. singer and songwriter; born *Robert Allen Zimmerman.* The leader of an urban folk-music revival in the 1960s, he became known for political and protest songs such as "The Times They Are A-Changin'" (1964). When on tour in 1966 he caused controversy for using an amplified backing group. His lyrics are noted for their poetic imagery. Notable albums: *Highway 61 Revisited* (1965) and *Blood on the Tracks* (1975).

Dzer·zhin·sky |jər'zHinskē|, Feliks (Edmundovich) (1877–1926) Russian Bolshevik leader, of Polish descent. He was the organizer and first head of the postrevolutionary Soviet security police (the Cheka, later the OGPU).

Ee

Eads |ēdz|, James Buchanan (1820–87) U.S. engineer and inventor. He invented the diving bell and built the first bridge across the Mississippi at St. Louis (Eads Bridge, 1867–74).

Ead·wig variant spelling of EDWY.

Ea·ker |'ākər|, Ira Clarence (1896–1987) U.S. general. An air force commander during World War II, he was a leader in creating a separate branch of the armed services for the U.S. Air Force (1947).

Ea·kins |'ākinz|, Thomas (1844–1916) U.S. painter and photographer noted for his portraits and genre pictures of life in Philadelphia. His picture *The Gross Clinic* (1875) aroused controversy because of its explicit depiction of surgery.

Eames |ēmz|, Wilberforce (1855–1937) U.S. bibliographer. He was bibliographer of the New York Public Library and the editor of *Sabin's Dictionary*.

Ear·hart |'er,härt|, Amelia (1898–1937) U.S. aviator. In 1932 she became the first woman to fly across the Atlantic solo. Her aircraft disappeared over the Pacific Ocean during a subsequent round-the-world flight.

Ear·ly |'ərlē|, Jubal Anderson (1816–94) U.S. Confederate army officer. He nearly reached the capital in his 1864 raid on Washington, but was defeated several months later by Sheridan in the Shenandoah Valley and was relieved of his command.

Earn·hardt |'ərnhhärt|, Dale (1952–) U.S. racecar driver. He was a seven-time NASCAR national champion.

Earp |ərp|, Wyatt (Berry Stapp) (1848–1929) U.S. marshal and frontiersman. He is famous for the gunfight at the OK Corral (1881), in which Wyatt with his brothers and his friend Doc Holliday fought the Clanton brothers at Tombstone, Arizona.

East·man |'ēs(t)mən|, George (1854–1932) U.S. inventor and manufacturer of photographic equipment. He invented flexible roll film coated with light-sensitive emulsion and, in 1888, the Kodak camera for use with it.

East·wood |'ēs(t),wŏŏd|, Clint (1930–) U.S. movie actor and director. He became famous with his role in *A Fistful of Dollars* (1964), the first cult "spaghetti western" (movie about the Old West filmed in Italy); other successful movies include *Dirty Harry* (1971). Movies directed include *Bird* (1988) and the western *Unforgiven* (1992).

E·ber·hart, Richard (Ghormley) (1904–) U.S. poet. He won the 1962 Bollingen Prize, the 1966 Pulitzer Prize for his *Selected Poems*, and the National Book Award.

E·bert |'ēbərt|, Roger (1942–) U.S. movie critic. With critic Gene Siskel, he was co-host of a syndicated television program in which they reviewed current films.

Ec·cles |'ekəlz|, Sir John Carew (1903–97) Australian physiologist, who demonstrated the way in which nerve impulses are conducted by means of chemical neurotransmitters. Nobel Prize for Physiology or Medicine (1963).

Eck·ardt |'ekərt|, (Arthur) Roy (1918–98) U.S. clergyman and educator. He was a pioneer in Christian-Jewish relations.

Eck·ert |'ekərt|, John Presper, Jr. (1919–) U.S. electrical engineer. A pioneer in the development of the modern computer working for the Sperry Rand Corp., he designed BINAC, a step towards the UNIVAC 1.

Eco |'e,kō|, Umberto (1932–) Italian novelist and semiotician. Notable works: *The Name of the Rose* (novel, 1981), *Travels in Hyperreality* (writings on semiotics, 1986).

Ed·berg |'edbərg|, Stefan (1966–) Swedish tennis player.

Ed·ding·ton |'ediNGtən|, Sir Arthur Stanley (1882–1944) English astronomer, considered the founder of astrophysics. He used Einstein's theory of relativity to explain the bending of light by gravity that he observed in the 1919 solar eclipse.

Ed·dy |'edē|, Mary Baker (1821–1910) U.S. religious leader and founder of the

Christian Science movement. Long a victim of various ailments, she believed herself cured by a faith healer, Phineas Quimby, and later evolved her own system of spiritual healing.

Edel, (Joseph) Leon (1907–97) U.S. literary critic. His five-volume *Life of Henry James* (1953–72) won a Pulitzer Prize and a National Book Award for two of its volumes.

Edel·man, Marian Wright (1939–) U.S. human rights activist. She was founder and president of the Children's Defense Fund.

Eden |'ēdən|, (Robert) Anthony, 1st Earl of Avon (1897–1977) British Conservative statesman, prime minister (1955–57). His premiership was dominated by the Suez crisis of 1956; widespread opposition to Britain's role in this led to his resignation.

Eder·le, Gertrude Caroline (1906–) U.S. swimmer. The winner of three Olympic medals (1924), she became the first woman to swim the English Channel (1926), breaking the existing men's record by two hours.

Ed·gar |'edgər| king of England (959–75), younger brother of Edwy. He became king of Northumbria and Mercia in 957 when these regions renounced their allegiance to Edwy, succeeding to the throne of England on Edwy's death.

Ed·ger·ton |'ejərtən|, Harold Eugene (1903–90) U.S. electrical engineer. He invented stroboscopic photography.

Edge·worth |'ej,wərTH|, Maria (1767–1849) Irish novelist, born in England. Notable works: *Castle Rackrent* (1800) and *Belinda* (1801).

Ed·in·burgh, Duke of |'ed(ə)n,bərə; 'ed(ə)n,bərō| see PHILIP, PRINCE.

Ed·i·son |'edəsən|, Thomas (Alva) (1847–1931) U.S. inventor. He took out the first of more than a thousand patents at the age of 21. His inventions include automatic telegraph systems, the carbon microphone for telephones, the phonograph, and the carbon filament lamp.

Ed·mund I |'edmənd| (921–46) king of England, reigned 939–46. After succeeding Athelstan, Edmund spent much of his reign trying to win his northern lands back from the Norse control.

Ed·mund II |'edmənd| (*c.*980–1016)

king of England, son of Ethelred the Unready, reigned 1016; known as **Edmund Ironside.** Edmund led the resistance to Canute's forces in 1015, but was eventually defeated and forced to divide the kingdom with Canute. On Edmund's death Canute became king of all England.

Ed·mund |'edmənd|, St. (*c.*1175–1240) English churchman and teacher, archbishop of Canterbury (1234–40); born *Edmund Rich.* He was the last primate of all England. Feast day, November 16.

Ed·mund Cam·pi·on, St. |'edmənd 'kæmpēən| see CAMPION.

Ed·mund Iron·side |'edmənd 'īərn,sīd| Edmund II of England (see EDMUND).

Ed·munds |'edmən(d)z|, George Franklin (1828–1919) U.S. lawyer and politician. As a member of the U.S. Senate from Vermont (1866–91), he helped draft the Sherman Antitrust Act (1890) and the Edmunds Act (1882), which outlawed polygamy in the territories.

Ed·mund the Martyr |'edmənd|, St. (*c.*841–70) king of East Anglia (855–70). After the defeat of his army by the invading Danes in 870, tradition holds that he was captured and shot with arrows for refusing to reject the Christian faith or to share power with his pagan conqueror. Feast day, November 20.

Ed·ward |'edwərd| the name of six kings of England and also one of Great Britain and Ireland and one of the United Kingdom: **Edward I** (1239–1307; reigned 1272–1307), the son of Henry III. He was known as **the Hammer of the Scots.** His campaign against Prince Llewelyn ended with the annexation of Wales in 1284, but he failed to conquer Scotland, where resistance was led by Sir William Wallace and later Robert the Bruce. **Edward II** (1284–1327; reigned 1307–27), the son of Edward I. In 1314 he was defeated by Robert the Bruce at Bannockburn. In 1326 Edward's wife, Isabella of France, and her lover, Roger de Mortimer, invaded England; Edward was deposed in favor of his son and murdered. **Edward III** (1312–77; reigned 1327–77), the son of Edward II. In 1330 he took control of his kingdom, banishing Isabella and executing Mortimer.

He supported Edward de Baliol, the pretender to the Scottish throne, and started the Hundred Years War. **Edward IV** (1442–83; reigned 1461–83), the son of Richard, Duke of York. He became king after defeating the Lancastrian Henry VI. Edward was briefly forced into exile (1470–71) by the Earl of Warwick but regained his position with victory at Tewkesbury in 1471. **Edward V** (1470–c. 1483; reigned 1483 but not crowned), the son of Edward IV. Edward and his brother Richard (known as the Princes of the Tower) were probably murdered and the throne was taken by their uncle, Richard III. **Edward VI** (1537–53; reigned 1547–53), the son of Henry VIII. His reign saw the establishment of Protestantism as the state religion. **Edward VII** (1841–1910; reigned 1901–10), the son of Queen Victoria. Although he played little part in government on coming to the throne, his popularity helped revitalize the monarchy. **Edward VIII** (1894–1972; reigned 1936 but not crowned), the son of George V. Edward abdicated eleven months after coming to the throne in order to marry the American divorcee Mrs. Wallis Simpson. Upon the accession by his brother George VI, Edward became Duke of Windsor.

Ed·ward |'edwərd|, Prince (1964–) British prince. Full name *Edward Antony Richard Louis*; he is the third son of Elizabeth II.

Edward, Prince of Wales see BLACK PRINCE.

Ed·wards |'edwərdz|, Jonathan (1703–58) American clergyman and theologian. Widely known as a powerful preacher, he served as a missionary to the Indians at Stockbridge, Massachusetts, and is considered the greatest theologian of American Puritanism.

Ed·ward the Confessor |'edwərd|, St. (c. 1003–66) son of Ethelred the Unready, king of England (1042–66). Famed for his piety, Edward founded Westminster Abbey, where he was eventually buried. Feast day, October 13.

Ed·ward the Elder |'edwərd| (c. 870–924) son of Alfred the Great, king of Wessex (899–924). His military successes against the Danes made it possible for his son Athelstan to become the first king of all England in 925.

Ed·ward the Martyr |'edwərd|, St. (c. 963–78) son of Edgar, king of England (975–78). Edward was faced by a challenge for the throne from supporters of his half-brother, Ethelred, who eventually had him murdered at Corfe Castle in Dorset. Feast day, March 18.

Edwy |'edwē| (died 959) king of England (955–57). Also **Eadwig**. He was probably only 15 years old when he became king; after Mercia and Northumbria renounced him in favor of his brother Edgar, he ruled over only the lands south of the Thames.

Egas Moniz, Antonio Caetano de Abreu Freire (1874–1955) Portuguese neurologist. He developed cerebral angiography as a diagnostic technique, and pioneered the treatment of certain psychotic disorders by the use of prefrontal lobotomy. Nobel Prize for Physiology or Medicine (1949).

Eg·bert |'egbərt| (died 839) king of Wessex (802–39). In 825 he won a decisive victory that temporarily brought Mercian supremacy to an end and foreshadowed the supremacy that Wessex later secured over all England.

Eh·ren·burg |'ärinbərg|, Ilya (Grigorevich) (1891–1967) Russian novelist and journalist. He became famous during World War II for his anti-German propaganda in *Pravda* and *Red Star*. His novels include *The Thaw* (1954), a work criticizing Stalinism.

Eh·ricke |'arik|, Krafft A. (1917–84) U.S. aeronautical engineer and physicist. The chief scientific adviser to Rockwell International Corp.'s space division, he designed and developed the Atlas and Centaur rockets.

Ehr·lich |'erlik|, Paul (1854–1915) German medical scientist. One of the founders of modern immunology and chemotherapy, he developed techniques for staining specific tissues, believing that a disease organism could be destroyed by an appropriate "magic bullet." The effective treatment of syphilis in 1911 proved his theories.

Ehr·lich·man |'erlikmän|, John Daniel (1925–) U.S. government official. A domestic policy adviser to President Nixon, he resigned (1973) and was convicted (1975) of perjury, conspiracy, and obstruction of justice in the Watergate scandal.

Eich·mann |'ĭkmən|, (Karl) Adolf (1906–62) German Nazi administrator who was responsible for administering the concentration camps. In 1960 he was traced by Israeli agents and executed after trial in Israel.

Eif·fel |'ĭfəl|, Alexandre Gustave (1832–1923) French engineer, best known as the designer and builder of the Eiffel Tower and architect of the inner structure of the Statue of Liberty.

Eijk·man |'ĭkmän|, Christiaan (1858–1930) Dutch physician. Eijkman's work resulted in a simple cure for the disease beriberi and led to the discovery of the vitamin thiamine. Nobel Prize for Physiology or Medicine (1929).

Ein·stein |'ĭn,stĭn|, Albert (1879–1955) German-born U.S. theoretical physicist, founder of the theory of relativity. Einstein is often regarded as the greatest scientist of the 20th century. In 1905 he published his special theory of relativity and in 1915 he succeeded in incorporating gravitation in his general theory of relativity, which was vindicated when one of its predictions was observed during the solar eclipse of 1919. However, Einstein searched without success for a unified field theory embracing electromagnetism, gravitation, relativity, and quantum mechanics. He influenced the decision to build an atom bomb, but after World War II he spoke out passionately against nuclear weapons.

Eint·ho·ven |'ĭnt,hōvən|, Willem (1860–1927) Dutch physiologist. He devised the first electrocardiograph, through which he was able to identify specific muscular contractions in the heart.

Eise·ley |'āzlē|, Loren Corey (1907–77) U.S. anthropologist, educator, and author. Notable works: *The Immense Journey* (1957) and *The Man Who Saw Through Mirrors* (1973).

Ei·sen·how·er |'īzən,howər|, Dwight David (1890–1969) see box. **Mamie Geneva Doud Eisenhower** (1896–

Eisenhower, Dwight David
34th U.S. president

Life dates: 1890–1969
Place of birth: Denison, Texas
Mother: Ida Elizabeth Stover Eisenhower
Father: David Jacob Eisenhower
Wife: Mamie (Marie) Geneva Doud Eisenhower
Children: Dwight, John
Nickname: Ike
College/University: U.S. Military Academy, West Point
Military service: directed tank training during World War I; general staff positions between the wars; commanding general of U.S. forces in the European theater during World War II; directed amphibious invasions of North Africa, Sicily, and Italy; as supreme commander of the Allied Expeditionary Force in Europe, directed Normandy invasion; U.S. Army chief of staff; supreme commander of NATO
Political career: none prior to presidency
Party: Republican
Home state: Kansas (family moved to Abilene in his infancy)
Opponent in presidential races: Adlai E. Stevenson
Term of office: Jan. 20, 1953–Jan. 20, 1961
Vice president: Richard M. Nixon
Notable events of presidency: McCarthy hearings; Supreme Court rules racial segregation of schools unconstitutional; Salk polio vaccine introduced; Suez Canal crisis; National Guard ordered to integrate schools in Little Rock, Ark.; interstate highway system begun; St. Lawrence Seaway completed; Soviet Sputnik launched; first U.S. satellite, Explorer I, launched; Alaska admitted as 49th state; Hawaii admitted as 50th state
Other achievements: Graduated first in his class at Command and General Staff School, Fort Leavenworth, Kansas; president, Columbia University
Place of burial: Abilene, Kansas

1979), wife of Dwight D. Eisenhower and U.S. first lady (1953–61).

Ei·sen·staedt |'īzən,stæt|, Alfred (1898–1995) U.S. photojournalist, born in Dirschau, Germany (now

Tczew, Poland). He was one of the original photographers for *Life* magazine (1932–72).

Ei·sen·stein |'īzən,sнtīn|, Sergei (Mikhailovich) (1898–1948) Soviet movie director, born in Latvia. He is chiefly known for *The Battleship Potemkin* (1925), a commemoration of the Russian Revolution of 1905 celebrated for its pioneering use of montage.

Eis·ner |'iznər|, Michael Dammann (1942–) U.S. corporate executive. He is the CEO of Walt Disney Corp. (1984–).

Eis·ner |'äznər|, Will (1917–) U.S. cartoonist, publisher, and educator. Full name *William E. Eisner*. He created "The Spirit," a weekly adventure series that appeared as an insert in Sunday newspapers (1940–51).

Ek·man |äkmin|, Vagn Walfrid (1874–1954) Swedish oceanographer. He recognized the importance of the Coriolis effect on ocean currents, showing that it can be responsible for surface water moving at an angle to the prevailing wind direction.

El·ton |'eltən|, Charles Sutherland (1900–91) English zoologist. Elton pioneered the study of animal ecology, and his research into rodent populations found practical application in vermin control.

Ed Cid |el 'sid| see CID, EL.

El·dridge |'eldrij|, (David) Roy (1911–89) U.S. jazz trumpeter. He was one of the first African Americans to play in formerly all-white swing bands, including those of Gene Krupa (1941) and Artie Shaw (1944).

El·ea·nor of Aquitaine |'elənər əv 'ækwi,tän; 'elənawr| (*c.*1122–1204) daughter of the Duke of Aquitaine, queen of France (1137–52) and of England (1154–89). She was married to Louis VII of France in 1137; in 1152, with the annulment of their marriage, she married the future Henry II of England.

El·gar |'elgär|, Sir Edward (William) (1857–1934) British composer He is known particularly for the *Enigma Variations* (1899), the oratorio *The Dream of Gerontius* (1900), and for patriotic

pieces such as the five *Pomp and Circumstance* marches.

El·gin |'el,gən|, James Bruce, 8th Earl of (1811–63) British colonial statesman. As Governor General of Canada (1847–54) he commissioned Louis Hippolyte Lafontaine to form Canada's first cabinet government in 1848. He maintained good relationships with subsequent administrations and successfully negotiated a reciprocity treaty between Canada and the U.S. in 1854.

El·gin |'el,gən|, Thomas Bruce, 7th Earl of (1766–1841) British diplomat and art connoisseur. Between 1803 and 1812 he controversially transported a number of classical sculptures (the "Elgin Marbles") to England from the Parthenon and elsewhere in Greece, which was then under Turkish control.

El Gre·co |el 'grekō| (1541–1614) Cretan-born Spanish painter; born *Domenikos Theotokopoulos*, he is better known by the Spanish name meaning 'the Greek'. El Greco's portraits and religious works are characterized by distorted perspective, elongated figures, and strident use of color.

Elia |'ɛlyə| the pseudonym adopted by Charles Lamb in his *Essays of Elia* (1823) and *Last Essays of Elia* (1833).

Eli·jah |ə'lī(d)zнə| (9th century BC) a Hebrew prophet in the time of Jezebel who maintained the worship of Jehovah against that of Baal and other pagan gods.

El·iot |'elēət|, Charles William (1834–1926) U.S. educator. He was president of Harvard University (1869–1909) and editor of the *Harvard Classics* (1910).

El·iot |'elēət|, George (1819–80) English novelist. Pseudonym of *Mary Ann Evans*. Her novels of provincial life are characterized by their exploration of moral problems and their development of the psychological analysis that marks the modern novel. Notable works: *Adam Bede* (1859), *The Mill on the Floss* (1860), and *Middlemarch* (1871–72).

El·iot |'elēət|, T. S. (1888–1965) U.S.-born British poet, critic, and dramatist; full name *Thomas Stearns Eliot*. Associated with the rise of literary modernism, he was established as the voice of a disillusioned generation by *The Waste Land*

(1922). *Four Quartets* (1943) revealed his increasing involvement with Christianity. Nobel Prize for Literature (1948).

Eli·sha |əˈlīshə| (9th century) Hebrew prophet, disciple and successor of Elijah.

Eliz·a·beth |əˈlizəbəTH| the name of two English monarchs, including: **Elizabeth I** (1533–1603; reigned 1558–1603), the daughter of Henry VIII; queen of England and Ireland. Succeeding her Catholic sister Mary I, Elizabeth re-established a moderate form of Protestantism as the state religion. Her reign was dominated by the threat of a Catholic restoration and by war with Spain, culminating in the defeat of the Armada in 1588. Shakespeare, Marlowe, and Spenser were all active during her reign, which saw a flowering of national culture. Although frequently courted, she never married. **Elizabeth II** (1926–; reigned 1952–), the daughter of George VI. Born *Princess Elizabeth Alexandra Mary.* She married Prince Philip in 1947. They have four children: Prince Charles, Princess Anne, Prince Andrew, and Prince Edward.

Eliz·a·beth |iˈlizəbəTH|, the Queen Mother (1903–) wife of George VI; born *Lady Elizabeth Angela Marguerite Bowes-Lyon.* She married George VI in 1923, when he was Duke of York; they had two daughters, Elizabeth (later Queen Elizabeth II) and Margaret.

Eli·zon·do, Hector (1936–) U.S. actor. He won Emmy Awards in 1996 and 1997 for the television series "Chicago Hope".

El·lery |ˈelərē|, William (1727–1820) U.S. politician. He was a member of the Continental Congress (1776–81 and 1783–85) and a signer of the Declaration of Independence.

El·let |ˈelət|, Charles (1810–62) U.S. engineer. He built the first wire suspension bridge in America, over the Schuylkill River in Philadelphia (1841–42).

El·li·cott |ˈeləcət|, Andrew (1754–1820) U.S. surveyor. He surveyed many state boundaries, including those of New York, Pennsylvania, the District of Columbia, Georgia, South Carolina, and Florida.

El·ling·ton |ˈeliNGtən|, Duke (1899–1974) U.S. jazz pianist, composer, and bandleader; born *Edward Kennedy Ellington.* Coming to fame in the early 1930s, Ellington wrote over 900 compositions and was one of the first popular musicians to write extended pieces. Notable works: *Mood Indigo* (1930).

El·lis |ˈeləs|, (Henry) Havelock (1859–1939) English psychologist and writer, remembered as the pioneer of the scientific study of sex. His major work was the six-volume *Studies in the Psychology of Sex* (1897–1910), with a seventh volume added in 1928).

El·lis |ˈeləs|, Perry (1940–86) U.S. fashion designer.

El·li·son |ˈeləsən|, Ralph (Waldo) (1914–94) U.S. author. Notable works: *Invisible Man* (1952, National Book Award).

El·mann |ˈelmən|, Richard David (1918–87) U.S. literary critic and professor. He won a Pulitzer Prize for the biography *Oscar Wilde* (1988).

Ells·berg |ˈelzbərg|, Daniel (1931–) U.S. political analyst and activist. A former adviser to President Nixon on policy in Southeast Asia, he became an avid opponent of the Vietnam War. Indicted for leaking classified Vietnam-related papers (the "Pentagon Papers") to the press in 1971, he was freed of charges when it was disclosed that Nixon had authorized the theft of Ellsberg's psychiatric records as a means of discrediting him.

Ells·worth |ˈelz,wərTH|, Lincoln (1880–1951) U.S. explorer. He participated in a number of polar expeditions and was the first person to fly over both the North (1926) and South (1935) Poles.

Ells·worth |ˈelz,wərTH|, Oliver (1745–1807) U.S. Supreme Court justice (1796–1800). He was a member of the Continental Congress (1777–84), author of the "Connecticut Compromise," and drafter of the Judiciary Act of 1789.

Éluard |ˈelwär|, Paul (1895–1952) French poet; pseudonym of *Eugène Grindel.* He was a leading figure in the surrealist movement.

El·ze·vir |ˈelzə,vir| a family of Dutch printers. Fifteen members were active between 1581 and 1712, including **Louis** (c. 1542–1617), who founded the business c. 1580. **Bonaventure** (1583–1652) and **Abraham** (1592–1652) managed the firm in its prime.

Em·er·son |'emərsən|, Ralph Waldo (1803–82) U.S. philosopher and poet. While visiting England in 1832, he met Coleridge, Wordsworth, and Carlyle, through whom he became associated with German idealism. On his return to the U.S. he evolved the concept of Transcendentalism, which found expression in his essay *Nature* (1836).

Em·mett |'emət|, Daniel Decatur (1815–1904) U.S. songwriter and minstrel-show performer. A member of early blackface minstrel troupes, he composed the song "Dixie."

Em·ped·o·cles |em'pedə,klēz| (c. 490–430 BC) Greek philosopher, born in Sicily. He taught that the universe is composed of fire, air, water, and earth, which mingle and separate under the influence of the opposing principles of Love and Strife. According to legend he lept into the crater of Mount Etna in order that he might be thought a god.

Emp·son |'em(p)sən|, Sir William (1906–84) English poet and literary critic. His influential literary criticism includes *Seven Types of Ambiguity* (1930).

En·ders |'endərz|, John Franklin (1897–1985) U.S. virologist. With **Frederick C. Robbins** (1916–92) and **Thomas H. Weller** (1915–92), he devised a method of growing viruses in tissue cultures which led to the development of vaccines against mumps, polio, and measles. The three scientists shared a Nobel Prize for Physiology or Medicine in 1954.

Ene·scu |e'neskoo|, George (1881–1955) Romanian violinist, composer, conductor, and teacher. He taught the concert violinist Yehudi Menuhin.

Eng·els |'eNGgəlz|, Friedrich (1820–95) German socialist and political philosopher. He collaborated with Marx in the writing of the *Communist Manifesto* (1848) and translated and edited Marx's later work. Engels's own writings include *The Condition of the Working Classes in England in 1844* (1845).

En·ni·us |'enēəs|, Quintus (239–169 BC) Roman epic poet and dramatist. He was largely responsible for the creation of a native Roman literature based on Greek models, but only fragments of his many works survive.

En·right |'enrīt|, Elizabeth (1909–68) U.S. author. Notable children's books: *Thimble Summer* (1938, Newbery Medal) and *Then There Were Five* (1944).

En·sor |'ensawr|, James (Sydney), Baron (1860–1949) Belgian painter and engraver, noted for his macabre subjects. His work is significant both for symbolism and for the development of 20th-century expressionism.

En·ver Pa·sha |en'vər pä'sHä| (1881–1922) Turkish political and military leader. A leader of the Young Turks in 1908, he came to power as part of a ruling triumvirate following a coup d'état in 1913.

En·ya |'enyə| (1961–) Irish singer and musician. Born *Eithne Ni Bhronain*. Notable songs: "The Memory of Trees" (1997, Grammy Award).

Eph·ron |'efrən|, Nora (1941–) U.S. journalist. A contributing editor for *New York Magazine* and *Esquire*, she also wrote the novel *Heartburn* (1983).

Ep·ic·te·tus |,epək'tētəs| (c. 55–135) Greek philosopher who preached the common brotherhood of man and advocated a Stoic philosophy.

Ep·i·cu·rus |'epə,kyŏŏrəs| (341–270 BC) Greek philosopher, founder of Epicureanism. His physics is based on Democritus' theory of a materialist universe composed of indestructible atoms moving in a void, unregulated by divine providence.

Ep·stein |'ep,stīn|, Brian (1935–67) English manager of the Beatles.

Ep·stein |'ep,stīn|, Sir Jacob (1880–1959) U.S.-born British sculptor. A founding member of the vorticist group, he later had great success in his modeled portraits of the famous, in particular his *Einstein* (1933).

Equi·a·no |,ekwē'änō|, Olaudah (c. 1750–97) African slave and writer. Known as **Gustavus Vassa**. He became an active abolitionist in England and published his autobiographical narrative in 1789.

Eras·mus |ə'ræzməs|, Desiderius (*c.*1466–1536) Dutch humanist and scholar. Dutch name *Gerhard Gerhards.* He was the foremost Renaissance scholar of northern Europe, paving the way for the Reformation with his satires on the Church, including the *Colloquia Familiaria* (1518). However, he opposed the violence of the Reformation and condemned Luther in *De Libero Arbitrio* (1523).

Eras·tus |ə'ræstəs| (1524–83) Swiss theologian and physician. Swiss name *Thomas Lieber,* also *Liebler* or *Lüber.* Professor of medicine at Heidleberg from 1558, he opposed the imposition of a Calvinistic system of Church government in the city. The doctrine of Erastianism was later wrongly attributed to him.

Er·a·tos·the·nes |ˌerə'tästHəˌnēz| (*c.*276–194 BC) Greek scholar, geographer, and astronomer. The first systematic geographer of antiquity, he accurately calculated the circumference of the earth and attempted (less successfully) to determine the size and distance of the sun and of the moon.

Er·drich |'ərdrik|, Louise (1954–) U.S. author. Notable works: *Love Medicine* (1984, National Book Critics Circle Award).

Er·ics·son |'eriksən|, John (1803–89) Swedish engineer whose inventions included a steam railway locomotive to rival Stephenson's *Rocket,* and the marine screw propeller (1836).

Er·ics·son |'eriksən|, Leif (970–1020) Norse explorer, son of Erik the Red. Also **Ericson** or **Eriksson.** He sailed westward from Greenland (*c.* 1000) and reputedly discovered land (variously identified as Labrador, Newfoundland, or New England), which he namedVinland because of the vines he claimed to have found growing there.

Er·ik·son |'eriksən|, Erik Homburger (1902–94) U.S. psychoanalyst, born in Germany. His writings include *Childhood and Society* (1950), *Ghandhi's Truth* (1969, Pulitzer Prize), and *Identity and the Life Cycle* (1980).

Er·ik the Red |'erik| (*c.*940–*c.*1010) Norse explorer. He left Iceland in 982 in search of land to the west, exploring Greenland and establishing a Norse settlement there in 986.

Er·lang·er |'ər,læNGgər|, Abraham Lincoln (1860–1930) U.S. theatrical manager and producer. With others, he formed the Theatrical Syndicate (1896), which virtually monopolized American theatrical business.

Er·lang·er |'ər,læNGgər|, Joseph (1874–1965) U.S. physiologist. Collaborating with Herbert Gasser, he showed that the velocity of a nerve impulse is proportional to the diameter of the fiber. Nobel Prize for Physiology or Medicine (1944, shared with Gasser).

Ernst |ərnst|, Max (1891–1976) German artist. He was a leader of the Dada movement and developed the techniques of collage, photomontage, and frottage. He is probably best known for his surrealist paintings, such as *L'Eléphant de Célèbes* (1921).

Erté |'ertā| (1892–1990) Russian fashion illustrator and set designer. Born *Romain de Tirtoff.*

Ertegun, Ahmet Munir (1923–) U.S. record company executive, born in Turkey. He was cofounder of Atlantic Records (1947) and has been elected to the Rock and Roll Hall of Fame.

Er·ving |'ərviNG|, Julius Winfield (1950–) U.S. basketball player. Known as **Dr. J.** He was elected to the Basketball Hall of Fame (1993).

Esaki |i'säkē|, Leo (1925–) Japanese physicist. He investigated and pioneered the development of quantum-mechanical tunneling of electrons in semiconductor devices, and designed the tunnel diode (also called the Esaki diode). Nobel Prize for Physics (1973).

Esch·er |'esHər|, M.C. (1898–1972) Dutch graphic artist. Full name *Maurits Corneille Escher.* His prints are characterized by their sophisticated use of visual illusion.

Es·cof·fier |ˌeskawf'yā|, Georges-Auguste (1846–1935) French chef. He gained an international reputation while working in London at the Savoy Hotel (1890–9) and later at the Carlton (1899–1919).

Es·po·si·to |espə'zētō|, Phil (1942–) U.S. hockey player. He was elected to Hockey Hall of Fame (1984).

Es·py |es'pī|, James Pollard (1785–1860) U.S. meteorologist. As an adviser to the War Department (from 1842) and the Navy Department (from 1848), he pioneered scientific weather forecasting.

Es·qui·vel, Laura (1950–) Mexican author. Notable works: *Like Water for Chocolate* (1992) and *The Law of Love* (1996).

Es·te·fan |'estə,fän|, Gloria (1957–) U.S. musician, born in Cuba. Born *Gloria Fajardo*. A singer and songwriter of the disco-pop and salsa band Miami Sound Machine, she released her first solo album in 1989.

Es·tes |'estēz|, Eleanor (1906–) U.S. author and librarian. Notable children's books: *Rufus M.* (1941) and *Ginger Pye* (1951, Newbery Medal).

Eth·el·red I |'eTHəl,red| (died 871) king of Wessex and Kent (865–71), elder brother of Alfred. His reign was marked by the continuing struggle against the invading Danes. Alfred joined Ethelred's campaigns and succeeded him on his death.

Eth·el·red II |'eTHəl,red| (c.968–1016) king of England (978–1016); known as **Ethelred the Unready**. Ethelred's inability to confront the Danes after he succeeded his murdered half-brother St. Edward the Martyr led to his payment of tribute to prevent their attacks. In 1013 he briefly lost his throne to the Danish king Sweyn I.

Eth·er·idge |,eTH(ə)rəj|, Melissa (1961–) U.S. singer, songwriter and guitarist. She won Grammy Awards in 1992 and 1994.

Eu·clid |'yo͞o,klid| (c.300 BC) Greek mathematician. His great work, *Elements of Geometry*, which covered plane geometry, the theory of numbers, irrationals, and solid geometry, was the standard text until other kinds of geometry were discovered in the 19th century.

Eugénie |ō'zHänə| (1826–1920) Spanish-born empress of France (1853–70) and wife of Napoleon III; born *Eugénia María de Montijo de Guzmán*. She contributed much to her husband's court and was an important influence on his foreign policy.

Eu·ler |'oilər|, Leonhard (1707–83) Swiss mathematician. He attempted to elucidate the nature of functions, and his study of infinite series led his successors, notably Abel and Cauchy, to introduce ideas of convergence and rigorous argument into mathematics.

Euler-Chelpin |'oilər 'kelpən| Swedish scientists, including: German-born **Hans Karl August Simon von Euler-Chelpin** (1873–1964), a biochemist. He worked mainly on enzymes and vitamins, and explained the role of enzymes in the alcoholic fermentation of sugar. Nobel Prize for Chemistry (1929). His son **Ulf Svante von Euler-Chelpin** (1905–83), a physiologist, was the first to discover a prostaglandin, which he isolated from semen. Euler also identified noradrenaline as the principal chemical neurotransmitter of the sympathetic nervous system. Nobel Prize for Physiology or Medicine (1970).

Eu·rip·i·des |yə'ripə,dēz| (c.484–406 BC) Greek dramatist. His nineteen surviving plays show important innovations in the handling of traditional myths, such as the introduction of realism, an interest in feminine psychology, and the portrayal of abnormal and irrational states of mind. Notable works: *Medea*, *Hippolytus*, *Electra*, *Trojan Women*, and *Bacchae*.

Eusebius (c.264–340 AD) bishop and Church historian; known as **Eusebius of Caesaria**. His *Ecclesiastical History* is the principal source for the history of Christianity (especially in the Eastern Church) from the age of the Apostles until 324.

Ev·ans |'evənz|, Sir Arthur (John) (1851–1941) English archaeologist. His excavations at Knossos (1899–1935) resulted in the discovery of the Bronze Age civilization of Crete, which he named Minoan after the legendary Cretan king Minos.

Ev·ans |'evənz|, Bill (1929–80) U.S. jazz pianist. Full name *William John Evans*. He developed a bop language based on the style of Bud Powell.

Ev·ans |'evənz|, Dame Edith (Mary) (1888–1976) English actress. She appeared in a wide range of Shakespearean and contemporary roles but is particularly remembered as Lady Bracknell in Oscar Wilde's *The Importance of Being Earnest.*

Ev·ans |'evənz|, Gil (1912–87) Canadian jazz pianist, composer, and arranger; born *Ian Ernest Gilmore Green.* In 1947 he began a long association with Miles Davis, producing albums such as *Porgy and Bess* (1958) and *Sketches of Spain* (1959).

Ev·ans |'evənz|, Herbert McLean (1882–1971) U.S. anatomist and educator. He discovered the 48 human chromosomes (1918) and vitamin E (1922).

Ev·ans |'evənz|, Janet (1971–) U.S. swimmer. She won four Olympic gold medals (three in 1988, one in 1992).

Evans-Pritchard |'evənz 'priCHərd|, Sir Edward (Evan) (1902–73) English anthropologist. He is noted for his studies of the Azande and Nuer peoples of the Sudan, with whom he lived in the 1920s and 1930s.

Ev·arts |'evərtz|, William Maxwell (1818–1901) U.S. lawyer and statesman. He was the U.S. secretary of state (1877–81) and a member of the U.S. Senate from New York (1885–91).

Eve·lyn |'ev(ə)lən|, John (1620–1706) English diarist and writer. He is remembered chiefly for his *Diary* (published posthumously in 1818), which describes such important historical events as the Great Plague and the Great Fire of London.

Ev·er·ly |'evərlē| U.S. singers and songwriters. **Don Everly** (1937–) and his brother **Phil Everly** (1939–) formed the rock-folk-country duo known as the Everly Brothers.

Ev·ers |'evərz|, Medgar Wiley (1925–63) U.S. civil rights leader. He was Mississippi field secretary of the NAACP (1952); his assassination was a factor in President Kennedy's call for new, comprehensive civil rights legislation.

Ev·ert |'evərt|, Chris (1954–) U.S. professional tennis player; full name *Christine Marie Evert.*

Ew·ell |'yo͞oəl|, Richard Stoddert (1817–72) U.S. soldier. He resigned from the U.S. Army to join Confederate forces in charge of Richmond defenses (1861).

Ew·ing |'yo͞oiNG|, Patrick (1962–) U.S. basketball player. A center for the New York Knicks, he led the U.S. Olympic team to gold medals in 1984 and 1992.

Ew·ry |'yo͞o(ə)rē|, Ray C. (1873–1937) U.S. track and field athlete. He won eight Olympic gold medals (two in each year:1900, 1904, 1906, 1908).

Eyre |e(ə)r|, Edward John (1815–1901) British-born Australian explorer and colonial statesman. He undertook explorations in the interior deserts of Australia (1840–1) and later served as lieutenant governor of New Zealand and governor of Jamaica.

Ey·senck |'īzəNGk|, Hans (Jürgen) (1916–97) German-born British psychologist. He is best known for his development of behavior therapy.

Ff

Fa·ber |'fābər|, John Eberhard (1822–79) U.S. businessman, born in Germany. He established the Eberhard Faber Pencil Co. in the U.S. (1861) from his family's German pencil-making business.

Fa·ber |'fābər|, Sir Geoffrey Cust (1889–1961) English publisher and author. He was the founding president (1924–61) of Faber and Faber, Ltd.

Fa·ber·gé |'fæbər,ZHā|, Peter Carl (1846–1920) Russian goldsmith and jeweler, of French descent. He is famous for the intricate Easter eggs that he made for Czar Alexander III and other royal households.

Fa·bi·us |'fābēəs| (died 203 BC) Roman general and statesman; full name *Quintus Fabius Maximus Verrucosus*; known as **Fabius Cunctator** ("Fabius the Delayer"). After Hannibal's defeat of the Roman army at Cannae in 216 BC, Fabius successfully pursued a strategy of caution and delay in order to wear down the Carthaginian invaders.

Fa·bre |fäb(ə)r|, Jean-Henri (1823–1915) French entomologist. Fabre became well known for his meticulous observations of insect behavior, notably the life cycles of dung beetles, oil beetles, and solitary bees and wasps.

Fa·bri·a·no, Gentile da see GENTILE DA FABRIANO.

Fa·bri·ci·us |fä'brētsēoos|, Johann Christian (1745–1808) Danish entomologist. Fabricius studied for two years under Linnaeus, and named and described some 10,000 new species of insect.

Fac·tor |'fæktər|, Max (1877–1938) U.S. businessman, born in Russia. A Russian immigrant who founded the Max Factor makeup company, he developed the first greasepaint cream makeup for use on Hollywood movie actors.

Fag·gin, Federico (1941–) U.S. electronics executive and inventor, born in Italy. In the 1960s, he invented the silicon gate technology that enabled him to codesign and build the first microprocessor (1971).

Fahd |fäd| (1923–) king of Saudi Arabia (1982–). Full name *Fahd ibn Abd al-Aziz al Saud*.

Fah·ren·heit |'ferən,hīt|, Daniel Gabriel (1686–1736) German physicist. Fahrenheit is best known for his thermometer scale, but also set up his own business to manufacture scientific instruments. He also improved the performance of thermometers, developed an instrument to determine atmospheric pressure from the boiling point of water, and designed a hydrometer.

Fair·banks |'ferbæNGks| U.S. actors. **Douglas (Elton) Fairbanks** (1883–1939), was born *Julius Ullman*. He co-founded United Artists in 1919 and became famous for his swashbuckling movie roles. His son, **Douglas Fairbanks, Jr.**, (1909–) played similar roles.

Fair·banks |'ferbæNGks|, Charles Warren (1852–1918) Vice president of the U.S. (1905–09) and member of the U.S. Senate from Indiana (1897–1905).

Fair·fax |'ferfæks|, Thomas, 3rd Baron Fairfax of Cameron (1612–71). English Parliamentary general. Fairfax helped to secure the restoration of Charles II.

Fai·sal |'fīsəl| name of two kings of Iraq: **Faisal I** (1885–1933; reigned 1921–33). A British-sponsored ruler, he was also supported by fervent Arab nationalists. Under his rule Iraq achieved full independence in 1932. His grandson, **Faisal II** (1935–58; reigned 1939–58), was assassinated in a military coup, after which a republic was established.

Fal·do |'fawldō|, Nick (1959–) English professional golfer; full name *Nicholas Alexander Faldo*.

Falk |fawk|, Peter (1927–) U.S. actor. A stage, movie, and television actor, he was the star of the television series "Columbo."

Fal·la |'fälyə; 'fīə|, Manuel de (1876–1946) Spanish composer and pianist. He composed the ballets *Love, the Magician* (1915) and *The Three-Cornered Hat* (1919); the latter was produced by Diaghilev, with designs by Picasso.

Fal·lop·pio |fäl'lōpyō|, Gabriele (1523–62) Italian anatomist. He discovered the function of oviducts (Fallopian tubes).

Fal·well |'fawl,wel|, Jerry L. (1933–) U.S. Baptist clergyman. He was the founder and president of the Moral Majority conservative political action group (1979), which later became the Liberty Foundation.

Fan·euil |'fænyəl|, Peter (1700–43) U.S. merchant. He offered the building known as Faneuil Hall to the city of Boston (1742).

Fan·gio |'fänj(ē)ō|, Juan Manuel (1911–95) Argentinian racecar driver. He first won the world championship in 1951 and then held the title from 1954 until 1957.

Far·a·day |'ferə,dā|, Michael (1791–1867) English physicist and chemist. He contributed significantly to the field of electromagnetism, discovering electromagnetic induction and demonstrating electromagnetic rotation (the key to the electric dynamo and motor). Faraday also discovered the laws of electrolysis and set the foundations for the classical field theory of electromagnetic behavior.

Fard |färd|, Wallace D. (1877– c.1934) U.S. religious leader. He founded the Black Muslim movement (1930).

Far·go |'färgō|, William George (1818–81) U.S. businessman. He was an organizer of Wells, Fargo & Co. (1852).

Far·ley |'färlē|, Harriet (1817–1907) U.S. factory worker and writer. She edited *Lowell Offering* (1842–45), which became *New England Offering* (1847–50), a periodical collecting the writings of women mill hands.

Far·mer |'färmər|, Fannie Merritt (1857–1915) U.S. educator and author. She opened Miss Farmer's School of Cookery in 1902; her *Boston Cooking School Cook Book* (1896) was known as "the mother of level measurements."

Far·mer |'färmər|, Moses Gerrish (1820–93) U.S. inventor. He was a co-inventor of the electric fire alarm system and helped develop torpedo warfare.

Far·ne·se |fär'neze|, Alessandro, Duke of Parma (1545–92) Italian general and statesman. While in the service of Philip II of Spain he acted as Governor General of the Netherlands (1578–92). He captured Antwerp in 1585, securing the southern Netherlands for Spain.

Farn·ham |'färnəm|, Eliza Wood (1815–64) U.S. reformer and author. As matron of the Ossining, New York, prison women's department (1844–48) she instituted many reforms.

Farns·worth |'färns,wərTH|, Philo Taylor (1906–71) U.S. engineer and inventor. A pioneer in television technology, he created the first all-electronic television image (1926). His other inventions include cold cathode ray tubes and an electron microscope.

Fa·rouk |fə'rook| (1920–65) king of Egypt, reigned 1936–52. Farouk's defeat in the Arab–Israeli conflict of 1948, together with the general corruption of his reign, led to a military coup in 1952, masterminded by Nasser. Farouk was forced to abdicate in favor of his infant son, Fuad.

Far·quhar |'färkwär|, George (1678–1707) Irish dramatist. He was a principal figure in Restoration comedy. Notable works: *The Recruiting Officer* (1706) and *The Beaux' Stratagem* (1707).

Far·ra·gut |'ferəgət|, David Glasgow (1801–70) U.S. admiral. Tthe outstanding naval commander of the Civil War, he captured the city of New Orleans (April 1862) and extended Union control of the Mississippi north to Vicksburg.

Far·ra·khan |'ferə,kæn|, Louis (1933–) U.S. Muslim minister and African-American nationalist.

Far·rand |'färənd|, Livingston (1867–1939) U.S. psychologist, anthropologist, and educator. A scholar specializing in American Indian studies, he served as president of Columbia University (1901–14), the University of Colorado (1914–19), and Cornell University (1921–37).

Far·rar |'färər|, John Chipman (1896–1974) U.S. publisher and author. He was chairman of Farrar, Straus & Giroux (1929–44).

Far·rell |'ferəl|, J. G. (1935–79) English novelist; full name *James Gordon Farrell*. Notable works: *The Siege of Krishnapur* (1973) and *The Singapore Grip* (1978).

Far·rell |'ferəl|, J.T. (1904–79) U.S. novelist. Full name *James Thomas Farrell*. He achieved fame with his trilogy about Studs Lonigan, a young Chicago Catholic of Irish descent, which began with *Young Lonigan* (1932).

Far·rell |'ferəl|, Suzanne (1945–) U.S. dancer. Born *Roberta Sue Ficker*. She performed with the New York City Ballet (1961–69), where she was principal dancer (1965–69). She is noted for her performance in the movie version of *A Midsummer Night's Dream* (1966).

Far·well |'färwel|, Arthur (1877–1952) U.S. composer and critic. He is known for his American Indian songs.

Far·well |'färwel|, John Villiers (1825–1908) U.S. businessman. He donated the land for the first YMCA building in the U.S. (Chicago).

Fass·bin·der |'fæs,bindər|, Rainer Werner (1946–82) German movie director. His movies dealt largely with Germany during World War II and postwar West German society. Notable movies: *The Bitter Tears of Petra von Kant* (1972).

Fast |fæst|, Howard Melvin (1914–) U.S. author. He is best known as a writer of historical novels and as a member of the Communist party (1943–56) who was imprisoned (1950) for refusing to cooperate with the House Committee on Un-American Activities. He was awarded the Stalin Peace Prize in 1953. Notable works: *Spartacus* (1951), *The Naked God* (1957), and *The Immigrant's Daughter* (1985).

Fa·ti·ma |fə'tēmə; 'fætimə| (c.616–633 AD) youngest daughter of the prophet Muhammad and wife of the fourth caliph, Ali. The descendants of Muhammad trace their lineage through her; she is revered especially by Shiite Muslims as the mother of the imams Hasan and Husayn.

Faulk·ner |'fawknər|, William (1897–1962) U.S. novelist. His works deal with the history and legends of the American South and have a strong sense of a society in decline. Notable works: *The Sound and the Fury* (1929), *As I Lay Dying* (1930), and *Absalom! Absalom!* (1936). Nobel Prize for Literature (1949).

Fau·ré |faw'rā; fô'rā|, Gabriel-Urbain (1845–1924) French composer and organist. His best-known work is the *Requiem* (1887) for solo voices, choir, and orchestra; he also wrote songs, piano pieces, chamber music, and incidental music for the theater.

Fau·set, Jessie Redmon (1882–1961) U.S. author and editor. She edited DuBois's *The Crisis*; her four novels feature African-American heroines.

Faust |fowst|, Frederick Schiller (1892–1944) U.S. writer. Pseudonym **Max Brand**. He wrote over 100 western novels, including *Destry Rides Again* (1930); he also wrote scripts for the *Dr. Kildare* movie series.

Faust |fowst|, Johann (c.1480–1540) German astronomer and necromancer. Also **Faustus**. Reputed to have sold his soul to the Devil, he became the subject of dramas by Marlowe and Goethe, an opera by Gounod, and a novel by Thomas Mann.

Favre |färv|, Brett (1969–) U.S. football player.

Faw·cett |'fawsət|, Farrah (1947–) U.S. actress. She was a star in the "Charlie's Angels" television program, as well as a number of television movies, including *The Burning Bed* (1984).

Fawkes |fawks|, Guy (1570–1606) English conspirator. He was hanged for his part in the Gunpowder Plot of November 5, 1605. The occasion is commemorated annually in England on Bonfire Night with fireworks, bonfires, and the burning of an effigy called *guy*.

FDR the nickname of President Franklin Delano Roosevelt (see ROOSEVELT, FRANKLIN DELANO).

Fech·ner |'feknər|, Gustav Theodor (1801–87) German physicist and psychologist. Fechner hoped to make psychology a truly objective science and coined the termed *psychophysics* to define his study of the quantitative relationship between degrees of physical stimulation and the resulting sensations.

Feif·fer |'fīfər|, Jules (1929–) U.S. cartoonist and author. He is best known for his satirical cartoons, which first appeared in *The Village Voice* and later were internationally syndicated.

Fein·stein |'fīnstīn|, Dianne (1933–) U.S. politician. She was mayor of San

Francisco, California (1978–88), and U.S. senator (1992–).

Fel·ler |ˈfelər|, Bob (1918–) U.S. baseball player. Full name *RobertWilliam Andrew Feller*; known as **Rapid Robert**. He led American League pitchers in strikeouts seven times. Elected to Baseball Hall of Fame (1962).

Fel·li·ni |fəˈlēnē|, Federico (1920–93) Italian movie director. He rose to international fame with *La Strada* (1954), which won an Oscar for best foreign movie. Other major movies include *La dolce vita* (1960), a satire on Rome's high society and winner of the Grand Prix at Cannes.

Fen·der |ˈfendər|, Leo (1907–91) U.S. guitar maker. He pioneered the production of electric guitars, designing the first solid-body electric guitar to be widely available and founding the Fender company.

Fe·nol·lo·sa |ˌfenəlˈōsə|, Ernest Francisco (1853–1908) U.S. educator and author. He led a revival of the Japanese school of painting and a movement to preserve Japanese temples and works of art.

Fer·ber |ˈfərbər|, Edna (1887–1968) U.S. author. Notable novels: *So Big* (1924, Pulitzer Prize) and *Giant* (1952).

Fer·di·nand II |ˈfərd(ə),nænd|, of Aragon (1452–1516) king of Castile (1474–1516) and of Aragon (1479–1516); known as **Ferdinand the Catholic**. His marriage to Isabella of Castile in 1469 ensured his accession (as Ferdinand V) to the throne of Castile with her. Ferdinand subsequently succeeded to the throne of Aragon (as Ferdinand II) and was joined as monarch by Isabella. They instituted the Spanish Inquisition in 1478 and supported Columbus's expedition in 1492. Their capture of Granada from the Moors in the same year effectively united Spain as one country.

Fer·en·czi |fəˈren(t)sē|, Sándor (1873–1933) Hungarian psychoanalyst. He was a friend and collaborator of Freud.

Fer·gu·son |ˈfərgəsən| U.S. politicians. **James Edward Ferguson** (1871–1944) was the governor of Texas until impeached (1915–17). His wife **Miriam Amanda Ferguson** (1875–1961);

known as **Ma** Ferguson. She became governor of Texas (1925–27 and 1933–35) after her husband James was impeached.

Fer·lin·ghet·ti |ˌfərlinˈgetē|, Lawrence (Monsanto) (1919–) U.S. poet and publisher; born *Lawrence Ferling*. Identified with San Francisco's Beat movement, he founded the publishing house City Lights, which produced works such as Allen Ginsberg's *Howl* (1957). Notable works: *A Coney Island of the Mind* (1958).

Fer·mat |fərˈmä(t)|, Pierre de (1601–65) French mathematician. His work on curves led directly to the general methods of calculus introduced by Newton and Leibniz. He is also recognized as the founder of the theory of numbers.

Fer·mi |ˈfer,mē|, Enrico (1901–54) Italian-born U.S. atomic physicist, who directed the first controlled nuclear chain reaction in 1942. Nobel Prize for Physics (1938).

Fer·ra·ga·mo |ˌferəˈgämō|, Salvatore (1898–1960) Italian shoe designer and manufacturer.

Fer·ran·ti |fəˈräntē|, Sebastian Ziani de (1864–1930) English electrical engineer. He was one of the pioneers of electricity generation and distribution in Britain, his chief contribution being the use of high voltages for economical transmission over a distance.

Fer·ra·ri |fəˈrärē|, Enzo (1898–1988) Italian car designer and manufacturer. In 1929 he founded the company named after him, producing a range of high-quality sports and racing cars. Since the early 1950s Ferraris have won the greatest number of world championship Grands Prix of any car.

Fer·ra·ro |fəˈrärō|, Geraldine Anne (1935–) U.S. politician. She ran unsuccessfully for vice president of the U.S., with Walter Mondale (1984).

Fer·rel |ˈferəl|, William (1817–91) U.S. meteorologist and author. His research led to Ferrel's Law (1856) on the deflection of air currents on the rotating earth.

Fer·rer |fəˈrär; fəˈrer|, José (1912–92) U.S. actor and director, born in Puerto

Rico. Notable movies: *Cyrano de Bergerac* (1950, Academy Award).

Fer·ri·er |'ferēər|, Kathleen (1912–53) English contralto. She is particularly famous for her performance in 1947 of Mahler's song cycle *Das Lied von der Erde.*

Fer·ris |'ferəs|, George Washington Gale, Jr. (1859–96) U.S. engineer and inventor. He invented the Ferris wheel (1893).

Fes·sen·den |'fesəndən|, Reginald Aubrey (1866–1932) Canadian-born U.S. pioneer of radio-telephony, who invented the heterodyne receiver.

Fet·ter·man |'fetərmən|, William Judd (c. 1833–66) U.S. army officer. A Civil War Union officer, he was killed by the Sioux and Cheyenne in the "Fetterman massacre" (Dec. 21, 1866).

Feu·er·bach |'fȯiər,bäкн|, Ludwig (Andreas) (1804–72) German materialist philosopher. In his best-known work, *The Essence of Christianity* (1841), he argued that the dogmas and beliefs of Christianity are figments of human imagination, fulfilling a need inherent in human nature.

Fey·deau |fā'dō|, Georges (1862–1921) French dramatist. His name has become a byword for French bedroom farce. He wrote some forty plays, including *Hotel Paradiso* (1894) and *Le Dindon* (1896).

Feyn·man |'finmən|, Richard Phillips (1918–88) U.S. theoretical physicist, noted for his work on quantum electrodynamics. Nobel Prize for Physics (1965).

Fi·bo·nac·ci |,fibə'näcнē|, Leonardo (c. 1170–c. 1250) Italian mathematician; known as **Fibonacci of Pisa**. Fibonacci popularized the use of the "new" Arabic numerals in Europe. He made many original contributions in complex calculations, algebra, and geometry, and pioneered number theory and indeterminate analysis, discovering the Fibonacci series.

Fich·te |'fiкнtə|, Johann Gottlieb (1762–1814) German philosopher. A pupil of Kant, he postulated that the ego is the basic reality; the world is posited by the ego in defining and delimiting itself. His political addresses had some influence on the development of German nationalism and the overthrow of Napoleon.

Fied·ler |'fēdlər|, Arthur (1894–1979) U.S. conductor. An accomplished violist, he became renowned as conductor of the Boston Pops Orchestra (1930–74).

Fied·ler |'fēdlər|, Leslie A. (1917–) U.S. educator and author. His writings include literary criticism, such as *Love and Death in the American Novel* (1960), and works of fiction.

Field |fēld| U.S. family, including: **David Dudley Field** (1805–94), a lawyer. He wrote the code of civil procedure that was adopted by many U.S. states, Great Britain, and several British colonies. His brother **Stephen Johnson Field** (1816–99) was a U.S. Supreme Court justice (1863–97). David and Stephen's brother, **Cyrus West Field** (1819–92), was an engineer and financier. He promoted the laying of the transatlantic cable (1857–66).

Field |fēld|, Eugene (1850–95) U.S. poet and journalist. He wrote children's verses, including "Little Boy Blue."

Field |fēld|, John (1782–1837) Irish composer and pianist. He is noted for the invention of the nocturne and for his twenty compositions in this form.

Field |fēld|, Marshall (1834–1906) U.S. merchant. He organized the Marshall Field & Co. (1881) and expanded it into the largest wholesale and retail drygoods establishment in the world. He made major donations to the University of Chicago, the Art Institute of Chicago, and the Field Museum of Natural History.

Field |fēld|, Sally (1946–) U.S. actress. Born *Sally Mahoney*. Notable movies: *Norma Rae* (1979, Academy Award).

Field·ing |'fēldiNG|, Henry (1707–54) English novelist. He provoked the introduction of censorship in theaters with his political satire *The Historical Register for 1736.* He then turned to writing picaresque novels, notably *Joseph Andrews* (1742) and *Tom Jones* (1749).

Fields |fēldz|, James Thomas (1817–81) U.S. editor, author, and publisher. He was a partner in the firm Ticknor &

Fields (1854) and editor of *Atlantic Monthly* (1861–70).

Fields |fēldz|, Dorothy (1905–74) U.S. songwriter. She wrote lyrics for Broadway musicals such as *Annie Get Your Gun* (1946) and *Sweet Charity* (1965).

Fields |feldz|, Dame Gracie (1898–1979) English singer and comedienne; born *Grace Stansfield*.

Fields |fēldz|, W. C. (1880–1946) U.S. comedian; born *William Claude Dukenfield*. Having made his name as a comedy juggler he became a vaudeville star, appearing in the *Ziegfeld Follies* revues between 1915 and 1921. Notable movies: *The Bank Dick* (1940).

Fier·stein, Harvey (1954–) U.S. playwright, actor, and AIDS activist. Born *Harvey Forbes*. Notable works: *Torch Song Trilogy* (1981).

Fi·lene |fi'lēn|, Edward Albert (1860–1937) U.S. merchant. The president of Wm. Filene & Sons, he helped establish the Credit Union National Extension Bureau and the International Chamber of Commerce.

Fill·more |'fil,mawr|, Millard see box.

Abigail Powers Fillmore (1798–1853), wife of Millard Fillmore and U.S. first lady (1850–53).

Fil·son |'filsən|, John (*c.* 1747–88) American frontiersman. He published the earliest account of Daniel Boone's adventures and helped found Cincinnati, Ohio (1788).

Fink |fiNGk|, Albert (1827–97) U.S. engineer. He invented the Fink truss used in railroad bridges, and founded the science of railroad economics.

Fink |fiNGk|, Mike (*c.* 1770–1823) U.S. frontiersman. He was a famed marksman and Indian scout.

Fin·ley |'finlē|, Martha Farquharson (1828–1909) U.S. author. As Martha Farquharson, she wrote over 100 novels for children, including 28 *Elsie* books.

Fin·sen |'finsən|, Niels Ryberg (1860–1904) Danish physician. He developed the light treatment method for skin diseases. Nobel Prize for Physiology or Medicine (1903).

Fio·ruc·ci |,fēə'rōōcHē|, Elio (1935–) Italian designer and retailer.

Fire·stone |'firstōn|, Harvey Samuel (1868–1938) U.S. industrialist. He or-

---

Fillmore, Millard
13th U.S. president

Life dates: 1800–1874
Place of birth: Locke, New York
Mother: Phoebe Millard Fillmore
Father: Nathaniel Fillmore
Wives: Abigail Powers Fillmore (died 1853); Caroline Carmichael McIntosh (married 1858)
Children: Millard, Mary (by first wife)
College/University: none
Military service: Commander, Home Guard corps, Mexican War
Career: Lawyer (New York Supreme Court); teacher; wool carder; clothdresser
Political career: New York State Assembly; U.S. House of Representatives; vice president (under Taylor); president
Party: Whig
Home state: New York
Term of office: Jul. 10, 1850–March 3, 1853 (succeeded to the presidency on the death of Zachary Taylor)
Vice president: none
Notable events of presidency: Compromise of 1850; California admitted as 31st state; territorial governments established in Utah and New Mexico; Fugitive Slave Law; Capitol partially destroyed by fire; Washington Territory created
Other achievements: admitted to the New York bar; first chancellor, University of Buffalo; president, Buffalo Historical Society
Place of burial: Buffalo, New York

---

ganized the Firestone Tire & Rubber Co. (1900), which he served as president (1903–32) and chairman (1932–38).

Firth |fərTH|, J. R. (1890–1960) English linguist. Full name *John Rupert Firth*. Noted for his contributions to linguistic semantics and prosodic phonology and for his insistence on studying both speech sounds and words in context. He was a major influence on the development of systemic grammar.

Fisch·er |'fisHər|, Bobby (1943–) U.S. chess player; full name *Robert James Fischer*. He defeated Boris Spassky in 1972 to take the world championship, which he held until 1975. He emerged from seclusion to defeat Gary Kasparov in 1992, although the match was not held under the auspices of the international chess federation.

Fisch·er |'fɪsHər|, Emil Hermann (1852–1919) German organic chemist. He studied the structure of sugars, other carbohydrates, and purines, and synthesized many of them. He also confirmed that peptides and proteins consist of chains of amino acids. Nobel Prize for Chemistry (1902).

Fisch·er |'fɪsHər|, Hans (1881–1945) German organic chemist. He determined the structure of the porphyrin group of many natural pigments, including the red oxygen-carrying part of hemoglobin, the green chlorophyll pigments found in plants, and the orange bile pigment bilirubin. Nobel Prize for Chemistry (1930).

Fischer-Dieskau |,fɪsHər'dē,skow|, Dietrich (1925–) German baritone. He is noted for his interpretations of German lieder, in particular Schubert's song cycles.

Fish |fɪsH|, Hamilton (1808–1893) U.S. politician. He held many political offices, including U.S. secretary of state (1869–77).

Fish·er |'fɪsHər|, Bud (1884–1954) U.S. cartoonist. Full name *Harry Conway Fisher*. He created in 1907 the world-famous comic strip "Mutt & Jeff," which he drew until his death.

Fish·er |'fɪsHər|, Ham (1900–55) U.S. cartoonist. Full name *Hammond Edward Fisher*. He was creator of the comic strip "Joe Palooka"

Fish·er |'fɪsHər|, M. F. K. (1908–92) U.S. author. Full name *Mary Frances Kennedy Fisher*. Her writings, including *How to Cook a Wolf* (1942) and *Long Ago in France* (1991), describe fictional and nonfictional culinary experiences.

Fish·er |'fɪsHər|, Sir Ronald Aylmer (1890–1962) English statistician and geneticist. Fisher made major contributions to the development of statistics, publishing influential books on statistical theory, the design of experiments, statistical methods for research workers, and the relationship between Mendelian genetics and evolutionary theory.

Fish·er |'fɪsHər|, St. John (1469–1535) English churchman. In 1504 he became bishop of Rochester and earned the dis-

favor of Henry VIII by opposing his divorce from Catherine of Aragon. When he refused to accept the king as supreme head of the Church, he was condemned to death. Feast day, June 22.

Fisk |fɪsk|, James (1834–72) U.S. financier. He made his fortune in the stock manipulation that ruined the Erie Railroad, and with Jay Gould he engineered events that involved the U.S. Treasury in the Black Friday scandal (1869).

Fiske |fɪsk|, Bradley Allen (1854–1942) U.S. naval officer and inventor. He invented electrical military devices, including the electric range finder.

Fiske |fɪsk|, John (1842–1901) U.S. philosopher, writer, professor, and historian. Born *Edmund Fisk Green*. He was a leading exponent and popularizer of Darwinism.

Fitch |fɪcH|, John (1743–98) U.S. inventor. Although he received the U.S. patent and built the first steamboat (1787), he was never commercially successful.

Fit·ti·pal·di |,fɪti'pawldē|, Emerson (1946–) Brazilian racecar driver. He was the Formula One world champion in 1972 and 1974, and won the Indianapolis 500 in 1989.

Fitts |fɪts|, Dudley (1903–68) U.S. teacher and translator. He wrote a colloquial metrical translation of Aristophanes' play *Lysistrata* (1954) and edited the Yale Series of Younger Poets (1960–68).

Fitz·ger·ald |,fits'jerəld| U.S. authors: **F. Scott Fitzgerald** (1896–1940); full name *Francis Scott Key Fitzgerald*. His novels, in particular *The Great Gatsby* (1925), provide a vivid portrait of the U.S. during the jazz era of the 1920s. His wife, **Zelda Sayre Fitzgerald** (1899–1948), wrote *Save Me the Waltz* (1932), an account of her life with her husband.

Fitz·ger·ald |,fits'jerəld|, Barry (1888–1961) U.S. actor, born in Ireland. Born *William Shields*. Notable movies: *Going My Way* (1944, Academy Award).

Fitz·ger·ald |,fits'jerəld|, Edward (1809–83) English scholar and poet. Notable works: *The Rubáiyát of Omar Khayyám* (translation, 1859).

Fitz·ger·ald |ˌfits'jerəld|, Ella (1918–96) U.S. jazz singer, known for her distinctive style of scat singing.

Fitz·ger·ald |ˌfits'jerəld|, Frances (1940–) U.S. author and foreign correspondent. Notable works: *Fire in the Lake: The Vietnamese and the Americans in Vietnam* (1972, Pulitzer Prize and National Book Award).

Fitz·Ger·ald |ˌfits'jerəld|, George Francis (1851–1901) Irish physicist. He suggested that length, time, and mass depend on the relative motion of the observer, while the speed of light is constant. This hypothesis, postulated independently by Lorentz, prepared the way for Einstein's special theory of relativity.

Fitz·ger·ald |ˌfits'jerəld|, Robert Stuart (1910–85) U.S. educator and writer. He has written poetry and a well-known translation of Homer's *Odyssey* (1961). Bollingen Prize, 1961.

Fitz·patrick |fits'pætrək|, Thomas (c. 1799–1854) U.S. frontiersman, born in Ireland. A fur trapper, trader, and scout, he was the guide for Frémont's second expedition (1843–44) in the American West and Kearny's expeditions (1845 and 1846).

Fixx |fiks|, Jim (1932–84) U.S. runner. He popularized the sport of running with his bestseller *The Complete Book of Running* (1977).

Flack |flæk|, Roberta (1939–) U.S. pop vocalist.

Flagg |flæg|, James Montgomery (1877–1960) U.S. artist. He created the World War I recruiting poster featuring Uncle Sam's pointing finger and the caption "I Want You."

Flag·ler |'flæglər|, Henry Morrison (1830–1913) U.S. financier. With John D. Rockefeller, he developed the Standard Oil Co.

Flah·er·ty |'flertē|, Robert Joseph (1884–1951) U.S. movie director, author, and explorer. He is known as the father of documentary film. Notable movies: *Nanook of the North* (1922).

Flam·steed |'flæm,stēd|, John (1646–1719) English astronomer. He was the first Astronomer Royal at the Royal Greenwich Observatory and produced the first star catalog (for use in navigation).

Flan·a·gan |'flænəgən|, John Bernard (1895–1942) U.S. sculptor. He is known for his small, primitive sculptures of animals, birds, and fish.

Flat·ley |'flætlē|, Michael (1958–) U.S. dancer. He performed Irish step dancing with "Riverdance" before forming his own show, "Lord of the Dance."

Flatt |flæt|, Lester (1914–79) U.S. country singer and guitarist. Notable songs: "Foggy Mountain Breakdown."

Flau·bert |flō'ber|, Gustave (1821–80) French novelist and short-story writer. A dominant figure in the French realist school, he achieved fame with his first published novel, *Madame Bovary* (1857). Its portrayal of the adulteries and suicide of a provincial doctor's wife caused Flaubert to be tried for immorality (and acquitted).

Flax·man |'flæksmən|, John (1755–1826) English sculptor and draftsman, noted for his church monuments and his engraved illustrations to Homer (1793).

Fleck·er |'flekər|, James (Herman) Elroy (1884–1915) English poet. Notable works: *The Golden Journey to Samarkand* (collection, 1913) and *Hassan* (play, 1922).

Fle·gen·hei·mer |'flägən,hīmər|, Arthur (1902–35) U.S. gangster. Known as **Dutch Schultz**. As head of the New York crime syndicate, he was notorious for bootlegging, extortion, and the numbers racket.

Fleisch·er |'flīsHər|, Max (1883–1972) U.S. cartoonist and animator, born in Austria. He created the character Betty Boop and animated the comic strip character Popeye.

Flem·ing |'fleming|, Sir Alexander 1881–1955. Scottish bacteriologist. In 1928, Fleming discovered the effect of penicillin on bacteria.

Flem·ing |'fleming|, Ian (Lancaster) (1908–64) English novelist. He is known for his spy novels that feature the secret agent James Bond.

Flem·ing |'fleming|, Sir John Ambrose (1849–1945) English electrical engineer, chiefly remembered for his invention of the thermionic valve (1900).

Flem·ing |'fleming|, Victor (1883–1949) U.S. movie director. Notable movies: *Gone With the Wind* (1939, Academy Award).

Fletch·er |'fleCHər|, John (1579–1625) English dramatist. A writer of Jacobean tragicomedies, he wrote some fifteen plays with Francis Beaumont, including *The Maid's Tragedy* (1610–11). He is also believed to have collaborated with Shakespeare on such plays as *The Two Noble Kinsmen* and *Henry VIII* (both *c.*1613).

Fletch·er |'fleCHər|, Horace (1849–1919) U.S. nutritionist. He wrote and lectured on the value of thoroughly masticating food.

Flick·in·ger |'flikən,gər|, Donald D. (1907–97) U.S. physician. He helped develop life support systems for high-altitude flight and space travel.

Flin·ders |'flindərz|, Matthew (1774–1814) English explorer. He explored the coast of New South Wales (1795–1800) and circumnavigated Australia (1801–03) for the Royal Navy, charting much of the west coast of the continent for the first time.

Flint |flint|, Austin (1812–86) U.S. physician and educator. He founded Bellevue Hospital Medical College (New York, 1861) and wrote *Treatise on the Principles and Practice of Medicine* (1866).

Flip·per |'flipər|, Henry Ossian (1856–1940) U.S. soldier and engineer. The first black graduate of West Point (1877), he was court-martialed on false charges (1882), to which the army formally admitted in 1976.

Flood |fləd|, Curt (1938–97) U.S. baseball player. He challenged baseball's reserve clause in 1972, which led to new rules for free agency.

Flo·rey |'flawrē|, Howard Walter, Baron (1898–1968) Australian pathologist. With Ernst Chain he isolated and purified penicillin; in 1945 they shared a Nobel Prize for Physiology or Medicine with Alexander Fleming.

Flo·rio |'flawrēō|, John (*c.*1553–1625) English lexicographer, of Italian descent. He produced an Italian–English dictionary entitled *A Worlde of Wordes* (1598) and translated Montaigne's essays into English (1603).

Flynn |flin|, Errol (1909–59) Aus-

tralian-born U.S. actor; born *Leslie Thomas Flynn*. His usual role was the swashbuckling hero of romantic costume dramas in movies such as *Captain Blood* (1935) and *The Adventures of Robin Hood* (1938).

Fo |fō|, Dario (1926–) Italian dramatist. Notable works: *Accidental Death of an Anarchist* (political satire, 1970) and *Open Couple* (farce, 1983). Nobel Prize for Literature (1997).

Foch |'fawSH|, Ferdinand (1851–1929) French general. He supported the use of offensive warfare, which resulted in many of his 20th Corps being killed in August 1914. He was later the senior French representative at the Armistice negotiations.

Fo·gar·ty |'fōgərtē|, Anne (1919–1981) U.S. fashion designer.

Fo·ger·ty |'fōgərtē|, John (1945–) U.S. musician. He performed with Creedence Clearwater Revival. Grammy Award, 1998.

Fo·kine |'fawkyin; faw'kēn|, Michel (1880–1942) Russian-born U.S. dancer and choreographer; born *Mikhail Mikhailovich Fokin*. He was a reformer of modern ballet; as Diaghilev's chief choreographer he staged the premières of Stravinsky's *The Firebird* (1910) and Ravel's *Daphnis and Chloë* (1912).

Fok·ker |'fäkər|, Anthony Herman Gerard (1890–1939) Dutch-born U.S. aircraft designer and pilot. Having built his first aircraft in 1908, he designed fighters used by the Germans in World War I and founded the Fokker Co.

Fo·ley |'fōlē|, Red (1910–68) U.S. country singer. Notable songs: "Blues in My Heart."

Fol·ger |'fōljər|, Henry Clay (1857–1930) U.S. businessman. An executive with Standard Oil (1879–1928), he amassed a large library collection and endowed the Folger Shakespeare Library, Washington, D.C. (1928).

Fol·mer |'fōlmər|, William Frederic (1861–1936) U.S. inventor. He patented over 300 inventions, including gas burners, lamps, and photographic equipment; his photographic manufacturing firm, Folmer & Schwing, was acquired by Eastman Kodak (1905).

Fon·da |'fändə| U.S. actors, including:

Henry Fonda (1905–82). He was noted for his roles in such films as *The Grapes of Wrath* (1939) and *Twelve Angry Men* (1957). He won his only Oscar for his role in his final film, *On Golden Pond* (1981). His daughter, **Jane Fonda** (1937–), is known for films including *Klute* (1971), for which she won an Oscar, and *The China Syndrome* (1979); she also acted alongside her father in *On Golden Pond*. Jane's brother **Peter Fonda** (1939–) and his daughter Bridget Fonda (1964–) are also actors.

Fon·taine |fän′tän|, Joan (1917–) U.S. actress, born in Tokyo. Born *Joan de Havilland*. Notable movies: *Suspicion* (1941, Academy Award).

Fon·tanne |fän′tän|, Lynn (1887–1983) British actress. She worked with her husband, U.S. actor Alfred Lunt.

Fon·teyn |ˌfän′tän|, Dame Margot (1919–91) English ballet dancer; born *Margaret Hookham*. In 1962 she began a celebrated partnership with Rudolf Nureyev, dancing with him in *Giselle* and *Romeo and Juliet*. In 1979 she was named *prima ballerina assoluta*, a title given only three times in the history of ballet.

Foote |foŏt|, Andrew Hull (1806–63) U.S. naval officer. As a commander off the African coast, he worked at breaking up slave trade (1849–51); he also served as the Union commander of naval operations on the upper Mississippi (1861–62).

Foote |foŏt|, Horton (1916–) U.S. author. He wrote numerous screenplays, including *To Kill a Mockingbird* (1962) and *Tender Mercies* (1983, Academy Award).

Forbes |fawrbz| family of U.S. magazine publishers, including: **Bertie Charles** (1880–1954). Born in Scotland, his full name was *Robert Charles Forbes*. He was the founder, editor, and publisher of *Forbes* magazine (1916). His son **Malcolm Stevenson** (1919–90) published *Forbes* magazine after the death of his father and was a member of the U.S. Senate from New Jersey (1952–58). He was the first person to fly coast-to-coast across the U.S. in a hot air balloon. His son, **Malcolm Stevenson, Jr.** (1947–) worked for *Forbes* from 1970

and served as editor in chief from 1982. He was a U.S. presidential candidate in the Republican primary in 1996.

Forbes |fawrbz|, Esther (1891–1967) U.S. writer. Notable works: *Johnny Tremaine* (1943), *The Running of the Tide* (1948), and *Paul Revere and the World He Lived In* (1942, Pulitzer Prize).

Ford |fawrd|, Gerald (Rudolph) see box.

Betty Ford (1918–); born *Elizabeth Bloomer Warren*; the wife of Gerald Ford and U.S. first lady (1974–77).

Ford |fawrd|, Ford Madox (1873–1939) English novelist and editor; born *Ford Hermann Hueffer*. He is chiefly remembered as the author of the novel *The Good Soldier* (1915). As founder of both the *English Review* (1908) and the *Transatlantic Review* (1924), he published works by such writers as Ernest

---

Ford, Gerald Rudolph
38th U.S. president

Life dates: 1913–
Place of birth: Omaha, Nebraska
Name at birth: Leslie Lynch King, Jr.
Mother: Dorothy Ayer Gardner King
Father: Leslie Lynch King (natural); Gerald R. Ford (adoptive)
Wife: Elizabeth (Betty) Bloomer Ford
Children: Michael, John (Jack), Steven, Susan
College/University: University of Michigan; Yale Law School
Military service: officer in U.S. Navy during World War II
Career: Lawyer
Political career: U.S. House of Representatives; House minority leader; vice president (under Nixon; appointed to replace Spiro Agnew, 1973); president
Party: Republican
Home state: Michigan
Opponent in presidential race: Jimmy Carter
Term of office: Aug. 9, 1974 (succeeded to the presidency on the resignation of Richard M. Nixon)–Jan. 20, 1977
Vice president: Nelson A. Rockefeller
Notable events of presidency: granted unconditional pardon to former President Nixon; clemency for Vietnam draft evaders; end of Vietnam War and evacuation of Americans in Saigon
Other achievements: Eagle Scout; admitted to the Michigan bar

Hemingway, James Joyce, and Ezra Pound. He was the grandson of the Pre-Raphaelite painter Ford Madox Brown.

Ford |fawrd|, Harrison (1942–) U.S. actor. He became internationally famous with the science-fiction movie *Star Wars* (1977) and its two sequels. Other notable movies include *American Graffiti* (1973), *Raiders of the Lost Ark* (1981), *Witness* (1985), and *Air Force One* (1997).

Ford |fawrd|, Henry (1863–1947) U.S. automobile manufacturer. A pioneer of large-scale mass production, he founded the Ford Motor Co., which in 1909 produced his famous Model T. Control of the company passed to his grandson, **Henry Ford II** (1917–1987) in 1945.

Ford[1] |fawrd|, John (1586–*c.* 1639) English dramatist. His plays, which include *'Tis Pity She's a Whore* (1633) and *The Broken Heart* (1633), explore human delusion, melancholy, and horror.

Ford[2] |fawrd|, John (1895–1973) U.S. movie director; born *Sean Aloysius O'Feeney*. He is chiefly known for his westerns, including *Stagecoach* (1939) and *She Wore a Yellow Ribbon* (1949).

Ford |fawrd|, Richard (1944–) U.S. writer. Notable works: *The Sportswriter* (1986).

Ford |fawrd|, Tennessee Ernie (1919–91) U.S. country singer and songwriter. Notable song: "Sixteen Tons."

Ford |fawrd|, Whitey (1928–) U.S. baseball player. Born *Edward Charles Ford*. His career win percentage (.690) is the highest among 20th-century pitchers. Elected to Baseball Hall of Fame (1974).

Fore·man |'fawrmən|, Carl (1914–84) U.S. screenwriter. He was blacklisted for being an "uncooperative witness" before the House Committee on Un-American Activities. His movie credits include *High Noon* (1952), *The Bridge on the River Kwai (1957)*, and *The Guns of Navarone* (1961).

Fore·man |'fawrmən|, George (1949–) U.S. boxer. Having held the world heavyweight championship (1973–74), he regained the title in 1994, becoming the oldest man to do so.

For·es·ter |'fawrəstər|, C. S. (1899–1966) English novelist. Full name *Cecil*

Scott Forester, pseudonym of *Cecil Lewis Troughton Smith.* He is remembered for his seafaring novels set during the Napoleonic Wars, featuring Captain Horatio Hornblower. His other works include *The African Queen* (1935), later made into a celebrated film by John Huston.

Fork·beard |'fawrk,bērd|, Sweyn see SWEYN I.

For·man |'fawrmən|, Milos (1932–) Czech-born U.S. movie director. He made *One Flew Over the Cuckoo's Nest* (1975), which won five Oscars, and *Amadeus* (1983), which won eight Oscars, including that for best director.

Form·by |'fawrmbē|, George (1904–61) English comedian; born *George Booth.* He became famous for his numerous musical movies in the 1930s in which he projected the image of a Lancashire working lad and accompanied his songs on the ukulele.

For·rest |'fawrəst|, John, 1st Baron (1847–1918) Australian explorer and statesman, first premier of Western Australia (1890–1901).

For·rest |'fawrəst|, Nathan Bedford (1821–77) Confederate cavalry officer. He led a massacre of 300 black Union soldiers at the surrender of Fort Pillow, Tennessee (April 12, 1864). He became Grand Wizard of the Ku Klux Klan (1867–69).

For·res·ter |'fawrəstər|, Jay Wright (1918–) U.S. computer engineer. He invented the first random-access magnetic core memory storage for electronic digital computers (1949).

Forss·mann |'fawrs,män|, Werner Theodor Otto (1904–79) German physician. A pioneer in heart research, he shared the 1956 Nobel Prize for Physiology or Medicine with A. Cournand and D. Richards.

For·ster |'fawrstər|, E. M. (1879–1970) English novelist and literary critic. Full name *Edward Morgan Forster.* His novels, several of which have been made into successful movies, include *A Room with a View* (1908) and *A Passage to India* (1924).

For·syth |'fawr,sïTH|, Frederick (1938–) English novelist, known for political thrillers such as *The Day of the*

Jackal (1971), *The Odessa File* (1972), and *The Fourth Protocol* (1984).

For·tas |'fawrtəs|, Abe (1910–82) U.S. Supreme Court justice (1965–69). Criticized for his financial dealings, he was the first justice ever forced to resign due to public scorn.

For·ten |'fawrt(ə)n|, James (1766–1842) U.S. businessman and reformer. An abolitionist born to free black parents, he made his fortune in the sailmaking business.

Fos·bury |'fäs‚berē|, Richard (1947–) U.S. high jumper. He originated the now standard style of jumping known as the "Fosbury flop," in which the jumper clears the bar headfirst and with back to the bar. In 1968 he won the Olympic gold medal using this technique.

Fos·se |'fawsē|, Bob (1927–87) U.S. jazz dancer, choreographer, and director. Full name *Robert Louis Fosse*. He directed and choreographed Broadway musicals such as *The Pajama Game* (1954) and movies such as *Cabaret* (1972, Academy Award)

Fos·ter |'fästər|, Hal (1892–1982) U.S. cartoonist, born in Canada. Full name *Harold Rudolf Foster*. He drew the comic-strip versions of adventure heroes Tarzan and Prince Valiant.

Fos·ter |'fästər|, Jodie (1962–) U.S. movie actress and director; born *Alicia Christian Foster*. She won Oscars for her performances in *The Accused* (1988) and *Silence of the Lambs* (1991). She directed *Little Man Tate* (1991).

Fos·ter |'fästər|, Sir Norman (Robert) (1935–) English architect. His work is notable for its sophisticated engineering approach and technological style.

Fos·ter |'fästər|, Stephen (Collins) (1826–64) U.S. composer. He wrote more than 200 songs and, though a Northerner, was best known for songs that captured the Southern plantation spirit, such as "Oh! Susannah" (1848) and "Camptown Races" (1850).

Fos·ter |'fästər|, Vincent, Jr. (1945–93) U.S. attorney. He was deputy White House counsel to President Clinton (1993).

Fos·ter |'fästər|, William Zebulon

(1881–1961) U.S. labor leader and politician. He was the Communist Party candidate for president of the U.S.(1924, 1928, and 1932).

Fou·cault |fōō'kō|, Jean-Bernard-Léon (1819–68) French physicist. He is chiefly remembered for the huge pendulum which he hung from the roof of the Panthéon in Paris in 1851 to demonstrate the rotation of the earth. He also invented the gyroscope and was the first to determine the velocity of light reasonably accurately.

Fou·cault |fōō'kō|, Michel (Paul) (1926–84) French philosopher. A student of Louis Althusser, he was mainly concerned with exploring how society defines categories of abnormality such as insanity, sexuality, and criminality, and the manipulation of social attitudes towards such things by those in power.

Fou·rier |‚fōōrē'ā|, Jean-Baptiste-Joseph, Baron (1768–1830) French mathematician. His studies involved him in the solution of partial differential equations by the method of separation of variables and superposition; this led him to analyze the series and integrals that are now known by his name.

Four·nier |‚fōōrn'yā|, Pierre-Simon (1712–68) French type designer and engraver. He designed many new characters, and was noted for his decorative ornaments in the Rococo style.

Fow·ler |'fowlər|, H. W. (1858–1933) English lexicographer and grammarian. Full name *Henry Watson Fowler*. He compiled the first edition of the *Concise Oxford Dictionary* (1911) with his brother F. G. Fowler, and wrote the moderately prescriptive guide to style and idiom, *Modern English Usage*, first published in 1926.

Fowles |fowls|, John (Robert) (1926–) English novelist. His works include the psychological thriller *The Collector* (1963), the magic realist novel *The Magus* (1966), and the semihistorical novel *The French Lieutenant's Woman* (1969).

Fox |fäks|, Charles James (1749–1806) British statesman. He became a Whig member of Parliament in 1768, supporting American independence and the French Revolution, and collaborated with Lord North to form a coalition government (1783–84).

Fox |fäks|, Fontaine (1884–1964) U.S. cartoonist. He created the suburban-rural town of Toonerville and the panel "Toonerville Folks."

Fox |fäks|, George (1624–91) English preacher and founder of the Society of Friends (Quakers). He taught that truth in the inner voice of God speaking to the soul and rejected priesthood and ritual. Despite repeated imprisonment, he established a society called the "Friends of the Truth" (*c*.1650), which later became the Society of Friends.

Fox |fäks|, Paula (1923–) U.S. author of children's fiction. Notable works: *One-Eyed Cat* (1984, Newbery Honor Book).

Fox |fäks|, William (1879–1952) U.S. corporate executive. He founded the Fox Film Corp. (1915), which later became Twentieth Century Fox.

Foxe |fäks|, John (1516–87) English religious writer. He is famous for his *Actes and Monuments* popularly known as *The Book of Martyrs*, which appeared in England in 1563. This passionate account of the persecution of English Protestants fueled hostility to Catholicism for generations.

Fox Tal·bot |'fäks 'tawlbət|, William Henry see TALBOT.

Foxx |fäks|, Jimmie (1907–67) U.S. baseball player. Full name *James Emory Foxx*; known as **Double X** and **the Beast**. Elected to Baseball Hall of Fame (1951).

Foyt |foit|, A. J. (1935–) U.S. racecar driver. Full name *Anthony Joseph Foyt*. He was a four-time winner of the Indianapolis 500 (1961, 1964, 1967, 1977).

Fra·go·nard |ˌfrægə'när|, Jean-Honoré (1732–1806) French painter in the rococo style. He is famous for landscapes and for erotic canvases such as *The Progress of Love* (1771).

Frame |främ|, Janet (Paterson) (1924–) New Zealand novelist. Her novels draw on her experiences of psychiatric hospitals after she suffered a severe mental breakdown. Her three-volume autobiography (1982–85) was made into the movie *An Angel at My Table* (1990).

France |fræns|, Anatole (1844–1924) French writer; pseudonym of *Jacques-Anatole-François Thibault*. Works include the novel *Le Crime de Sylvestre Bonnard* (1881) and his ironic version of the Dreyfus case, *L'Ile des pingouins* (1908). Nobel Prize for Literature (1921).

Fran·cis I |'frænsəs| (1494–1547) king of France (1515–47). Much of his reign (1521–44) was spent at war with Charles V of Spain. He supported the arts and commissioned new buildings, including the Louvre.

Fran·cis of Assisi |'frænsəs|, St. (1181–1226) Italian monk, founder of the Franciscan order; born *Giovanni di Bernardone*. He founded the Franciscan order in 1209 and drew up its original rule (based on complete poverty). He is revered for his generosity, simple faith, humility, and love of nature. Feast day, October 4.

Fran·cis of Sales |'frænsəs|, St. (1567–1622) French bishop. One of the leaders of the Counter Reformation, he was bishop of Geneva (1602–22). The Salesian order (founded in 1859) is named after him. Feast day, January 24.

Fran·cis Xa·vier |'frænsis 'zävyər|, St. see XAVIER, ST. FRANCIS.

Franck |fräNgk|, César (Auguste) (1822–90) Belgian-born French composer and organist. His reputation as a composer rests on the *Symphonic Variations* for piano and orchestra (1885), the D minor Symphony (1886–8), and the *String Quartet* (1889).

Franck |fräNgk|, James (1882–1964) German-born U.S. physicist. He worked on the bombardment of atoms by electrons and became involved in the U.S. atom bomb project; he advocated the explosion of the bomb in an uninhabited area to demonstrate its power to Japan.

Fran·co |'fræNgkō|, Francisco (1892–1975) Spanish general and statesman, head of state (1939–75). Leader of the Nationalists in the Civil War, in 1937 Franco became head of the Falange Party and proclaimed himself *Caudillo* ("leader") of Spain. With the defeat of the republic in 1939, he took control of the government and established a dictatorship that ruled Spain until his death.

Frank |fræNGk|, Anne (1929–1945) German Jewish girl known for her diary, which records the experiences of her family living for two years in hiding from the Nazis in occupied Amsterdam. They were eventually betrayed and sent to concentration camps; Anne died in Belsen.

Frank·fur·ter |'fræNGk,fərtər|, Felix (1882–1965) U.S. Supreme Court justice (1939–62), born in Austria. He helped found the American Civil Liberties Union (1920) and was awarded the Presidential Medal of Freedom (1963).

Frank·lin |'fræNGklən|, Aretha (1942–) U.S. soul and gospel singer. Her best-known songs include Respect and I Never Loved a Man the Way I Love You (1967).

Frank·lin |'fræNGklən|, Benjamin (1706–90) American statesman, inventor, and scientist. He was one of the signatories to the peace treaty between the U.S. and Great Britain after the American Revolution. His main scientific achievements were the formulation of a theory of electricity, which introduced positive and negative electricity, and a demonstration of the electrical nature of lightning, which led to the invention of the lightning conductor.

Frank·lin |'fræNGklən|, Sir John (1786–1847) British explorer. He and all his crew died during his Arctic expedition (1845–47), but their found remains and records proved the existence of the Northwest Passage.

Frank·lin |'fræNGklən|, John Hope (1915–) U.S. educator, historian, and author. He was the first African American to become president of the American Historical Association (1978–79). Notable works: *From Slavery to Freedom: A History of American Negroes* (1947) and *Racial Equality in America* (1976). Awarded Spingarn Medal (1995).

Frank·lin |'fræNGklən|, (Stella Maria Sarah) Miles (1879–1954) Australian novelist. She wrote the first true Australian novel, *My Brilliant Career* (1901). She also produced a series of chronicle novels under her pseudonym "Brent of Bin Bin" (1928–56).

Frank·lin |'fræNGklən|, Rosalind Elsie (1920–58) English physical chemist and molecular biologist. Together with Maurice Wilkins she investigated the structure of DNA by means of X-ray crystallography, and contributed to the discovery of its helical structure.

Franz |frænz; fränz|, Dennis (1944–) U.S. actor and playwright. He won an Emmy Award (1996–97) for his role in the television show "NYPD Blue."

Franz Josef |'frænz 'yōsef; fränz| (1830–1916) emperor of Austria (1848–1916) and king of Hungary (1867–1916). He gave Hungary equal status with Austria in 1867. His annexation of Bosnia–Herzegovina (1908) contributed to European political tensions, and the assassination in Sarajevo of his heir apparent, Archduke Franz Ferdinand, precipitated World War I.

Fra·ser |'frāzər|, Dawn (1937–) Australian swimmer. She won the Olympic gold medal for the 100-meters freestyle in 1956, 1960, and 1964, the first competitor to win the same title at three successive Olympics.

Fra·ser |'frāzər|, (John) Malcolm (1930–) Australian Liberal statesman, prime minister (1975–83). He was the youngest-ever Australian member of Parliament when elected in 1955.

Fra·ser |'frāzər|, Peter (1884–1950) New Zealand politician, born in Scotland. He was a founder of the Labour Party (1916) and prime minister of New Zealand (1940–49), as well as one of the architects of the United Nations (1945).

Fraun·ho·fer |'frown,hōfər|, Joseph von (1787–1826) German optician and pioneer in spectroscopy. He observed and mapped the dark lines in the solar spectrum (Fraunhofer lines) that result from the absorption of particular frequencies of light by elements present in the outer layers; these are now used to determine the chemical composition of the sun and stars.

Fra·zer |'frāzər|, Sir James George (1854–1941) Scottish anthropologist. In *The Golden Bough* (1809–1915) he proposed an evolutionary theory of the development of human thought, from the magical and religious to the scientific.

Fra·zier |'frāzHər; 'frāzər|, Joe

(1944–) U.S. heavyweight boxing champion; full name *Joseph Frazier*.

Fred·er·ick I |'fred(ə)rik| (*c.*1123–90) king of Germany and Holy Roman emperor (1152–90); known as **Frederick Barbarossa** ("Redbeard"). He made a sustained attempt to subdue Italy and the papacy, but was eventually defeated at the battle of Legnano in 1176.

Fred·er·ick II |'fred(ə)rik| (1712–86) king of Prussia (1740–86); known as **Frederick the Great**. His campaigns in the War of the Austrian Succession (1740–48) and the Seven Years War (1756–63) succeeded in considerably strengthening Prussia's position; by the end of his reign he had doubled the area of his country.

Fred·er·ick Wil·liam |'fred(ə)rik 'wilyəm| (1620–88) elector of Brandenburg (1640–88); known as **the Great Elector**. His program of reconstruction and reorganization following the Thirty Years War brought stability to his country and laid the basis for the expansion of Prussian power in the 18th century.

Freed |frēd|, Alan (1922–65) U.S. radio disc jockey. He helped break barriers in the music industry of the 1950s by broadcasting the rhythm and blues music of black performers to white audiences and by promoting integrated concerts. He is credited with coining the term "rock and roll."

Free·man |'frēmən|, Douglas Southall (1886–1953) U.S. editor, educator, and author. He was editor of the *Richmond News Leader* (1915–33). Notable works: *R. E. Lee* (4 vols., 1934–35, Pulitzer Prize); and *George Washington* (6 vols., 1948–54, Pulitzer Prize).

Fre·ge |'frāgə|, Gottlob (1848–1925) German philosopher and mathematician, founder of modern logic. He developed a logical system for the expression of mathematics. He also worked on general questions of philosophical logic and semantics and devised his influential theory of meaning, based on his use of a distinction between what a linguistic term refers to and what it expresses.

Fre·leng |Friz (1906–95) U.S. animator. Born *Isadore Freleng*. His animation of the cartoon characters Yosemite Sam,

Porky Pig, Sylvester, and Tweety Bird won him three Oscars.

Fré·mont |'frē,mänt|, John Charles (1813–90) U.S. explorer and politician. He was responsible for exploring several viable routes to the Pacific across the Rockies in the 1840s. He made an unsuccessful bid for the presidency in 1856, losing to James Buchanan.

French |frenCH|, Daniel Chester (1850–1931) U.S. sculptor. Among his works is the seated figure of Abraham Lincoln in the Lincoln Memorial, Washington, D.C. (1922).

French |frenCH|, Marilyn (1929–) U.S. author. Notable works: *The Women's Room* (1977).

Fre·neau |fri'nō|, Philip Morin (1752–1832) U.S. poet. He was known as "the poet of the American Revolution" and was publisher of the Jeffersonian newspaper, *The National Gazette*.

Fres·nel |frə'nel|, Augustin Jean (1788–1827) French physicist and civil engineer. He correctly postulated that light has a wavelike motion transverse to the direction of propagation, contrary to the longitudinal direction suggested by Christiaan Huygens and Thomas Young.

Freud |froid| Family name of: **Sigmund Freud** (1856–1939), an Austrian neurologist and psychotherapist. He was the first to emphasize the significance of unconscious processes in normal and neurotic behavior, and was the founder of psychoanalysis as both a theory of personality and a therapeutic practice. He proposed the existence of an unconscious element in the mind that influences consciousness, and of conflicts in it between various sets of forces. Freud also stated the importance of a child's semi-consciousness of sex as a factor in mental development; his theory of the sexual origin of neuroses aroused great controversy. His youngest child, **Anna Freud** (1895–1982), was an Austrian-born British psychoanalyst. She introduced important innovations in method and theory to her father's work, notably with regard to disturbed children, and set up a child therapy course and clinic in London.

Freud |froid|, Lucian (1922–)

German-born British painter, grandson of Sigmund Freud. His subjects, typically portraits and nudes, are painted in a powerful naturalistic style.

Frick |frik|, Henry Clay (1849–1919) U.S. industrialist. He was chairman of the Carnegie Steel Co. (1889–1900); the Frick collection of art is housed in his former house in New York City.

Frie·dan |frĕ'dæn|, Betty (1921–) U.S. feminist and writer, known for *The Feminine Mystique* (1963), which presented femininity as an artificial construct and traced the ways in which American women are socialized to become mothers and housewives. In 1966 she founded the National Organization for Women, serving as its president until 1970.

Fried·man |'frēdmən|, Bruce Jay (1930–) U.S. author. Notable works: *A Mother's Kisses* (1964), *The Dick* (1970), and *The Lonely Guy's Book of Life* (1978).

Fried·man |'frēdmən|, Milton (1912–) U.S. economist. A principal exponent of monetarism, he acted as a policy adviser to President Reagan from 1981 to 1989. Nobel Prize for Economics (1976).

Frie·drich |'frēdriĸH|, Caspar David (1774–1840) German painter, noted for his romantic landscapes. He caused controversy with his altarpiece *The Cross in the Mountains* (1808), which lacked a specifically religious subject.

Friend·ly |'fren(d)lē|, Fred (1915–1998) U.S. journalist. He collaborated with Edward R. Murrow and Walter Cronkite in radio and television to produce various historical series, such as *Hear It Now* and *See It Now.*

Frisch |frisĦ|, Karl von (1886–1982) Austrian zoologist. He worked mainly on honeybees, studying particularly their vision, navigation, and communication. He showed that they perform an elaborate dance in the hive to indicate the direction and distance of food.

Frisch |frisĦ|, Otto Robert (1904–79) Austrian-born British physicist. With his aunt, Lise Meitner, he recognized that Otto Hahn's experiments with uranium had produced a new type of nuclear reaction. Frisch named it nuclear fission, and indicated the explosive potential of its chain reaction.

Frisch |frisĦ|, Ragnar (Anton Kittil) (1895–1973) Norwegian economist. A pioneer of econometrics, he shared the first Nobel Prize for Economics with Jan Tinbergen (1969).

Frith |friTĦ|, William Powell (1819–1909) English painter. He is remembered for his panoramic paintings of Victorian life, including *Derby Day* (1858) and *The Railway Station* (1862).

Friz·zell |fri'zel|, Lefty (1928–75) U.S. country singer and guitarist. Full name *William Orville Frizzell*. His honky-tonk, literate country music hits included "If You've Got the Money, I've Got the Time," "Always Late with Your Kisses," and "Long Black Veil."

Fro·bi·sher |'frōbisĦər|, Sir Martin (c.1535–94) English explorer. In 1576 he led an unsuccessful expedition in search of the Northwest Passage. Frobisher served in Sir Francis Drake's Caribbean expedition of 1585–86 and played a prominent part in the defeat of the Spanish Armada.

Froe·bel |'frōEbəl|, Friedrich (Wilhelm August) (1782–1852) German educationist and founder of the kindergarten system. Believing that play materials, practical occupations, and songs are needed to develop a child's real nature, he opened a school for young children in 1837, later naming it the Kindergarten ("children's garden"). He also established a teacher-training school.

Fromm |frōm; främ|, Erich (1900–80) German-born U.S. psychoanalyst and social philosopher. His works, which include *Escape from Freedom* (1941), *Man for Himself* (1947), and *The Sane Society* (1955), emphasize the role of culture in neurosis and strongly criticize materialist values.

Fromm-Reichmann |,främ'rīkmän|, Frieda (1889–1957) U.S. psychiatrist and psychoanalyst, born in Germany.

Fron·te·nac |frawtənäk|, Louis de Buade, Comte de (1622–98) French politician. He served as governor of New France (1672–82, 1689–98).

Frost |frawst|, A. B. (1851–1928) U.S. illustrator and cartoonist. Full name

Arthur Burdett Frost. He illustrated works by Lewis Carroll, Charles Dickens, Mark Twain, and others.

Frost |frawst|, Robert (Lee) (1874–1963) U.S. poet, noted for his ironic tone and simple language. Much of his poetry reflects his affinity with New England, including the collections *North of Boston* (1914) and *New Hampshire* (1923). He won the Pulitzer Prize on three occasions (1924; 1931; 1937).

Frueh |frōō|, Al (1880–1968) U.S. caricaturist and cartoonist. Full name *Alfred Frueh.* He was on staff at the *New Yorker* magazine.

Fry |frī|, Christopher (Harris) (1907–) English dramatist. He is known chiefly for his comic verse dramas, especially *The Lady's not for Burning* (1948) and *Venus Observed* (1950).

Fry |frī|, Elizabeth (1780–1845) English Quaker. She was a leading figure in the early 19th-century campaign for penal reform.

Fry |frī|, Roger (Eliot) (1866–1934) English art critic and painter. He argued for an esthetics of pure form, regarding content as incidental.

Frye |frī|, (Herman) Northrop (1912–91) Canadian literary critic. His work explores the use of myth and symbolism. Notable works: *Fearful Symmetry* (1947) and *The Great Code:The Bible and Literature* (1982).

Fu·ad |fōō'äd| the name of two kings of Egypt: **Fuad I** (1868–1936; reigned 1922–36). Formerly sultan of Egypt (1917–1922), he became Egypt's first king after independence. **Fuad II** (1952–; reigned 1952–53), the grandson of Fuad I. Named king as an infant on the forced abdication of his father, Farouk, he was deposed when Egypt became a republic.

Fuchs |f(y)ōōks|, Klaus (Emil Julius) (1911–88) German-born British physicist. He was a communist who fled Nazi persecution. During the 1940s he passed to the USSR secret information acquired while working on the development of the atom bomb in the U.S., and while engaged in research in Britain.

Fuchs |f(y)ōōks|, Sir Vivian (Ernest) (1908–) English geologist and explorer. He led the Commonwealth Trans-Antarctic Expedition (1955–58), making the first overland crossing of the Antarctic.

Fuen·tes |'fwentās|, Carlos (1928–) Mexican novelist and writer. Notable works: *Where the Air is Clear* (1958), *Terra nostra* (1975), and *The Old Gringo* (1984).

Fu·gard |'f(y)ōō,gärd|,Athol (1932–) South African dramatist. His plays, including *Blood Knot* (1963) and *The Road to Mecca* (1985), are mostly set in contemporary South Africa and deal with social deprivation and other aspects of life under apartheid.

Ful·bright |'fōol,brīt|, (James) William (1905–95) U.S. senator. He sponsored the Fulbright Act of 1946, which authorized funds from the sale of surplus war materials overseas to be used to finance exchange programs of students and teachers between the U.S. and other countries. The program has continued, supported by federal grants.

Ful·ler |'fōolər|, Albert Carl (1885–1973) U.S. businessman, born in Canada. He created the Capital Brush Co. (1906), which was later known as the Fuller Brush Co. (1910).

Ful·ler |'fōolər|, Charles (1939–) U.S. author. Notable works: *A Soldier's Play* (1981, Pulitzer Prize).

Ful·ler |'fōolər|, (Sarah) Margaret (1810–50) U.S. literary critic and social reformer. An advocate of cultural education for women, she conducted "Conversations," a popular series of discussion groups in the Boston area before becoming literary critic of the *New York Tribune* (1844–46). Among her books is the feminist classic *Woman in the Nineteenth Century* (1845).

Ful·ler |'fōolər|, Melville Weston (1833–1910) U.S. Supreme Court justice (1888–1910). He was also a member of the Court of International Arbitration, The Hague (1900–10).

Ful·ler |'fōolər|, R. Buckminster (1895–1983) U.S. designer and architect; full name *Richard Buckminster Fuller.* He is best known for his invention of the geodesic dome and for his ideals of using the world's resources with maximum purpose and least waste.

Ful·ler |'fōolər|, Thomas (1608–61)

English cleric and historian. He is chiefly remembered for *The History of the Worthies of England* (1662), a description of counties with short biographies of local personages.

Ful·ton |'fŏoltən|, Robert (1765–1815) U.S. pioneer of the steamship. He constructed a steam-propelled "diving-boat" in 1800, which submerged to a depth of 25 ft., and in 1806 he built the first successful paddle steamer, the *Clermont*.

Funk |fəNGk|, Casimir (1884–1967) Polish-born U.S. biochemist. He showed that a number of diseases, including scurvy, rickets, beriberi, and pellagra, were each caused by the deficiency of a particular dietary component, and coined the term *vitamins* for the chemicals concerned.

Furt·wäng·ler |'fŏort,veNG(g)lər|, Wilhelm ((1886–1954)) German conductor, chief conductor of the Berlin Philharmonic Orchestra from 1922. He is noted particularly for his interpretations of Beethoven and Wagner.

Fu·seli |fyŏo'zelē|, Henry (1741–1825) Swiss-born British painter and art critic; born *Johann Heinrich Füssli*. A prominent figure of the romantic movement, he tended toward the horrifying and the fantastic, as in *The Nightmare* (1781).

Fus·sell |'fəsəl|, Paul (1924–) U.S. educator and author. Notable works: *The Great War and Modern Memory* (1975, National Book Award).

Gg

Gable |'gābəl|, (William) Clark (1901–60) U.S. actor, famous for leading man roles in movies such as *It Happened One Night* (1934), for which he won an Oscar, *Mutiny on the Bounty* (1935), *Gone with the Wind* (1939), and *The Misfits* (1961).

Ga·bo |'gäbō|, Naum (1890–1977) Russian-born U.S. sculptor, brother of Antoine Pevsner; born *Naum Neemia Pevsner*. A founder of Russian constructivism, Gabo experimented with kinetic art and transparent materials. Nobel Prize for Physics (1971).

Ga·bor |gə'bawr| Hungarian-born U.S. actresses. **Zsa Zsa Gabor** (*c.* 1919–) and her sister **Eva Gabor** (*c.* 1921–95). Eva played the comedic leading role in television's "Green Acres" (1965–71).

Ga·bor |gə'bawr|, Dennis (1900–79) Hungarian-born British electrical engineer, who conceived the idea of holography. Nobel Prize for Physics (1971).

Ga·bri·eli |,gäbrē'elē|, Giovanni (*c.* 1556–1612) Italian composer and organist. He was a leading Venetian musician who wrote a large number of motets with instrumental accompaniments for St. Mark's Cathedral.

Gad·dafi |gə'däfē|, Mu'ammar Muhammad al (1942–) Libyan colonel, head of state since 1970. Also **Qaddafi**. After leading the coup that overthrew King Idris in 1969, he established the Libyan Arab Republic and has since pursued an anti-colonial policy at home; he has also been accused of supporting international terrorism.

Gad·dis |'gædis|, William (1922–) U.S. author. Notable works: *J R* (National Book Award, 1975) and *A Frolic of His Own* (National Book Award, 1994).

Ga·ga·rin |gə'gärən|, Yury Alekseyevich (1934–68) Russian cosmonaut. In 1961 he made the first manned space flight, completing a single orbit of the earth in 108 minutes.

Gage |gäj|, Thomas (1596–1656) English priest. He was a Christian missionary to Central America and the West Indies.

Gains·bor·ough |'gänz,bərō|, Thomas (1727–88) English painter. He was famous for his society portraits, including *Mr. And Mrs. Andrews* (1748) and *The Blue Boy* (*c.* 1770), and for landscapes such as *The Watering Place* (1777).

Gait·skell |'gätskəl|, Hugh (Todd Naylor) (1906–63) British Labour statesman, chancellor of the exchequer (1950–51) and leader of the Labour Party (1955–63).

Gal·a·had |'gælə,hæd|, Sir the noblest of King Arthur's legendary knights, renowned for immaculate purity and destined to find the Holy Grail.

Gal·ba |'gawlbə|, Servius Sulpicius (*c.* 3BC–69 AD) Roman emperor (AD 68–69). The successor to Nero, he aroused hostility by his severity and parsimony and was murdered in a conspiracy organized by his successor, Otho.

Gal·braith |'gawl,brāTH|, John Kenneth (1908–) Canadian-born U.S. economist. He is well known for his criticism of consumerism and of the power of large multinational corporations. Notable works: *The Affluent Society* (1958) and *The New Industrial State* (1967).

Ga·len |'gālən| (129–*c.* 199) Greek physician; full name *Claudios Galenos*; Latin name *Claudius Galenus*. He attempted to systematize the whole of medicine, making important discoveries in anatomy and physiology. His works became influential in Europe when retranslated from Arabic in the 12th century.

Ga·li·leo Ga·li·lei |,gælə'lāō ,gæli'lā(ē) | (1564–1642) Italian astronomer and physicist. He discovered the constancy of a pendulum's swing, formulated the law of uniform acceleration of falling bodies, and described the parabolic trajectory of projectiles. He applied the telescope to astronomy and observed craters on the moon, sunspots, Jupiter's moons, and the phases of Venus.

Gal·la·tin |'gælətən|, (Abraham Alfonse) Albert (1761–1849) U.S. politician, born in Switzerland. As a member of the U.S. House of Representatives from Virginia (1795–1801), he helped establish the House Committee on Finance, now the Ways and Means Committee; he served as U.S. secretary of the treasury (1801–14).

Gal·lau·det |ˌgælɔ'det|, Thomas Hopkins (1787–1851) U.S. educator. In 1817 he founded the first free American school for the deaf, the Connecticut (later, American) Asylum, in Hartford, Connecticut.

Gal·lo |'gælō| U.S. winemakers. **Ernest Gallo** (1910–) and his brother **Julio Gallo** (1911–93) started a winery to manufacture California wines.

Gal·lo·way |'gælɔ,wā|, Joseph (1731–1803) U.S. lawyer and politician. He was a loyalist writer and statesman and an adviser to the British crown.

Gal·lup |'gæləp|, George Horace (1901–84) U.S. statistician. He pioneered public opinion polls.

Ga·lois |gäl'wä|, Évariste (1811–32) French mathematician. His memoir on the conditions for solubility of polynomial equations was highly innovative but was not published until 1846, after his death.

Gals·wor·thy |'gawlz,wərTHē|, John (1867–1933) English novelist and dramatist. He is remembered chiefly for *The Forsyte Saga* (1906–28), a series of novels that was adapted for television in 1967. Nobel Prize for Literature (1932).

Gal·ti·eri |ˌgältē'erē|, Leopoldo Fortunato (1926–) Argentinian general and statesman, president (1981–82). Galtieri's military junta ordered the invasion of the Falkland Islands in 1982, precipitating the Falklands War.

Gal·ton |'gawltən|, Sir Francis (1822–1911) English scientist. He founded eugenics and introduced methods of measuring human mental and physical abilities. He also pioneered the use of fingerprints as a means of identification.

Gal·va·ni |gäl'vänē|, Luigi (1737–98) Italian anatomist. He studied the structure of organs and the physiology of tissues, but he is best known for his discovery of the twitching of frogs' legs in an electric field.

Gal·way |'gawl,wä|, James (1939–) British flutist.

Ga·ma |'gämə|, Vasco da see DA GAMA.

Gam·ow |'gæmawf|, George (1904–68) Russian-born U.S. physicist. He was a proponent of the "big bang" theory and also suggested the triplet code of bases in DNA, which governs the synthesis of amino acids.

Gance |gäns|, Abel (1889–1981) French movie director. He was an early pioneer of technical experimentation in movies. Notable movies: *La Roue* (1921) and *Napoléon* (1926).

Gan·dhi |'gändē| Indian political family. **Indira Gandi** (1917–84) was prime minister (1966–77 and 1980–84). The daughter of Jawaharlal Nehru, she sought to establish a secular state and to lead India out of poverty. She was assassinated by her own Sikh bodyguards following prolonged religious disturbances. Her son, **Rajiv Gandi** (1944–91), was prime minister (1984–89) after her assassination. His premiership was marked by continuing unrest, and he was assassinated during an election campaign.

Gan·dhi |'gändē|, Mahatma (1869–1948) Indian nationalist and spiritual leader; full name *Mohandas Karamchand Gandhi*. He became prominent in the opposition to British rule in India, pursuing a policy of non-violent civil disobedience. He never held government office, but was regarded as the country's supreme political and spiritual leader; he was assassinated by a Hindu following his agreement to the creation of the state of Pakistan.

Gar·bo |'gärbō|, Greta (1905–90) Swedish-born U.S. actress. Born *Greta Gustafsson*. She traveled to Hollywood and gained international recognition. Notable movies: *Anna Christie* (1930), *Mata Hari* (1931), and *Anna Karenina* (1935). After her retirement in 1941, she lived as a recluse.

Gar·cia |gär'sēə|, Jerry (1942–95) U.S. rock singer and guitarist; full name *Jerome John Garcia*. Garcia was the central figure of the Grateful Dead, a group formed *c*. 1966. Mixing psychedelic rock with country and blues influences in lengthy improvisations, the band toured extensively until Garcia's death.

Gar·cía Lor·ca |gär'sēə 'lawrkə|, Federico (1899–1936) Spanish poet and dramatist. Notable works: *Romancero gitano* (1953).

Gar·cía Már·quez |gär'sēə 'mär,kes|, Gabriel (1928–) Colombian novelist. His works include *One Hundred Years of Solitude* (1967), a classic example of magic realism, and *Chronicle of a Death Foretold* (1981). Nobel Prize for Literature (1982).

Gard·ner |'gärdnər|, Alexander (1821–82) U.S. photographer, born in Scotland. His early Civil War photos were credited to Mathew Brady, his employer (1856–63). He published *Gardner's Photographic Sketch Book of the Civil War* (1866) and was hired as the official photographer of the Union Pacific Railroad (1867).

Gard·ner |'gärdnər|, Ava (Lavinnia) (1922–90) U.S. actress. Notable movies: *The Killers* (1946), *Bhowani Junction* (1956), and *The Night of the Iguana* (1964).

Gard·ner |'gärdnər|, Erle Stanley (1889–1970) U.S. novelist and short-story writer. He practiced as a defense lawyer before writing his novels featuring the lawyer-detective Perry Mason.

Gard·ner |'gärdnər|, Isabella Stewart (1840–1924) U.S. socialite and art collector. Her house in Boston was a gathering-place for artists, writers, musicians, and other celebrities. With the help of art connoisseur Bernard Berenson, she assembled an outstanding collection of classical and contemporary art. The palazzo she built in Boston (1903) to house her collection was bequeathed to the city as the Isabella Stewart Gardner Museum.

Gard·ner |'gärdnər|, John Champlin, Jr. (1933–82) U.S. educator and author. Notable works: *October Light* (National Book Critics Circle Award, 1976) and *Mickelsson's Ghosts* (1982).

Gar·field |'gär,fēld|, James Abram see box. **Lucretia Randolph Garfield** (1832–1918), wife of James Garfield and U.S. first lady (1881).

Gar·fun·kel |'gär,fəNGkəl|, Art (1942–) U.S. singer and songwriter. He was part of the pop-folk duo Simon and Garfunkel (1958–70), which won four Grammy Awards (1968 and 1970).

Gar·i·bal·di |,geri'bawldē|, Giuseppe

Garfield, James Abram
20th U.S. president

Life dates: 1831–1881
Place of birth: Orange, Ohio
Mother: Eliza Ballou Garfield
Father: Abram Garfield
Wife: Lucretia Rudolph Garfield
Children: Eliza, Harry, James, Mary (Molly), Irvin, Abram, Edward
College/University: Western Reserve Eclectic Institute; Williams College
Military service: during Civil War, rose to rank of major general in the Ohio volunteers
Career: Lawyer; college professor and college president; lay preacher
Political career: Ohio Senate; U.S. House of Representatives; president
Party: Republican
Home state: Ohio
Opponents in presidential race: Neal Dow; James Baird Weaver, John Wolcott Phelps; Winfield Scott Hancock
Term of office: March 4, 1881–Sept. 19, 1881 (died in office after being shot by Charles J. Guiteau on July 2, 1881)
Vice president: Chester Alan Arthur
Other achievements: President, Western Reserve Eclectic Institute; member, Electoral Commission that settled the disputed Tilden-Hayes election of 1876
Place of burial: Cleveland, Ohio

(1807–82) Italian patriot and military leader of the Risorgimento (unification of Italy). With his volunteer force of "Red Shirts" he captured Sicily and southern Italy from the Austrians in 1860–61, thereby playing a key role in the establishment of a united kingdom of Italy.

Gar·land |'gärlənd|, Judy (1922–69) U.S. singer and actress; born *Frances Gumm*. Her most famous early movie role was in *The Wizard of Oz* (1939), in which she played Dorothy and sang "Over the Rainbow". Other notable movies: *Meet Me in St. Louis* (1944) and *A Star is Born* (1954).

Gar·ner |'gärnər|, Errol (Louis) (1923–77) U.S. jazz pianist and composer. He formed his own trio and also recorded with Charlie Parker. Notable songs: "Misty."

Gar·ner |'gärnər|, James (1928–   ) U.S. actor. Born *James Scott Bumgarner.* He starred in the television series "The Rockford Files" (1974–80). Notable movies: *Victor/Victoria* (1982) and *Murphy's Romance* (1985)

Gar·ner |'gärnər|, John Nance (1868–1967) Vice president of the U.S. (1933–41). Known as **Cactus Jack**. He was a member of the U.S. House of Representatives from Texas (1903–33) and speaker of the House (1931–33).

Gar·ret·son |'gerətsən|, James Edmund (1828–95) U.S. physician. He was a pioneer in oral surgery and published the first textbook on dental surgery.

Gar·rick |'gerik|, David (1717–79) English actor and dramatist. He was a notably versatile actor and the manager of the Drury Lane Theatre.

Gar·ri·son |'gerəsən|, William Lloyd (1805–79) U.S. social liberal and spearhead for New England abolitionism.

Gar·son |'gärsən|, Greer (1908–96) U.S. actress. Notable movies: *Mrs. Miniver* (1942, Academy Award).

Gar·vey |'gärvē|, Marcus (Moziah) (1887–1940) Jamaican political activist and black nationalist leader. He was the leader of the "Back to Africa" movement, which advocated the establishment of an African homeland for black Americans. He attracted a large following in the U.S., and his thinking was later an important influence on Rastafarianism.

Gary |'gerē|, Elbert Henry (1846–1927) U.S. lawyer and businessman. He organized the United States Steel Corp. (1901); Gary, Indiana, is named for him.

Gas·kell |'gæskəl|, Mrs. Elizabeth (Cleghorn) (1810–65) English novelist. Notable works: *Mary Barton* (1848), *Cranford* (1853), and *North and South* (1855). She also wrote a biography (1857) of her friend Charlotte Brontë.

Gass |gæs|, William H(oward) (1924–   ) U.S. educator and author. Notable works: *Omensetter's Luck* (1966) and *On Being Blue* (1976).

Gas·sen·di |gə'sendē; gä'sändē|, Pierre (1592–1655) French astronomer and philosopher. He is best known for his atomic theory of matter, which was based on his interpretation of the works of Epicurus.

Gas·ser |'gæsər|, Herbert Spencer (1888–1963) U.S. physiologist. Collaborating with Joseph Erlanger, he used an oscilloscope to show that the velocity of a nerve impulse is proportional to the diameter of the fibre. Nobel Prize for Physiology or Medicine (1944, shared with Erlanger).

Gates |gāts|, Bill (1955–   ) U.S. computer entrepreneur; full name *William Henry Gates*. He co-founded the computer software company Microsoft. Overseas expansion and the successful marketing of the MS-DOS and Windows operating systems for personal computers made the firm a leading multinational computer company by 1990. He became the youngest multibillionaire in U.S. history.

Gates |gāts|, Henry Louis, Jr. (1950–   ) U.S. educator and author. He wrote *The Future of the Race* (1996) and edited *Bearing Witness* (1991).

Gates |gāts|, Horatio (1728–1806) American Revolutionary War army officer, born in England. He was commanding general in the Saratoga Campaign (1777); his friends formed the Conway Cabal in an attempt to replace George Washington with Gates as commander in chief.

Gat·ling |'gætliNG|, Richard Jordan (1818–1903) U.S. inventor. He is best known for the Gatling gun, invented in 1862.

Gau·dí |gow'dē|, Antonio (1852–1926) Spanish architect; full name *Antonio Gaudi y Cornet.* He was a leading but idiosyncratic exponent of art nouveau, known mainly for his ornate and extravagant church of the Sagrada Familia in Barcelona (begun 1884).

Gaudier-Brzeska |,gōdyä'bzHeskä|, Henri (1891–1915) French sculptor, a leading member of the vorticist movement. Notable works: the faceted bust of Horace Brodzky (1912) and *Bird Swallowing a Fish* (1913).

Gau·guin |gō'gæN|, (Eugène Henri) Paul (1848–1903) French painter. From 1891 on he lived mainly in Tahiti, painting in a post-Impressionist style that was influenced by primitive art. Notable works: *The Vision after the Sermon* (1888) and *Faa Iheihe* (1898).

Gaulle, Charles de see DE GAULLE.

Gaul·tier |'gōtyä|, Jean Paul (1952–   ) French fashion designer.

Gaunt, John of see JOHN OF GAUNT.

Gauss |gows|, Carl Friedrich (1777–1855) German mathematician, astronomer, and physicist. Gauss laid the foundations of number theory, and applied rigorous mathematical analysis to geometry, geodesy, electrostatics, and electromagnetism.

Gau·ta·ma |'gowtəmə|, Siddhartha see BUDDHA.

Gau·tier |'gōtyä|, Théophile (1811–72) French author. His works, written in the Romantic tradition, include the novel *Mademoiselle de Maupin* (1835).

Gay |gā|, John (1685–1732) English poet and dramatist. He is chiefly known for *The Beggar's Opera* (1728), a low-life ballad opera combining burlesque and political satire.

Gaye |gā|, Marvin (1939–84) U.S. singer, composer, and musician. Known for hits including "I Heard It Through the Grapevine" (1968), he later recorded the albums *What's Goin' On* (1971), *Let's Get It On* (1973), and *Midnight Love* (1982). He was shot dead by his father in a quarrel.

Gay-Lussac |ˌgälə'sæk|, Joseph-Louis (1778–1850) French chemist and physicist. He is best known for his work on gases, and in 1808 he formulated the law usually known by his name. He also developed techniques of quantitative chemical analysis, confirmed that iodine was an element, discovered cyanogen, and made two balloon ascents to study the atmosphere and terrestrial magnetism.

Ge·ber |'jēbər| (*c.* 721–*c.* 815) Arab chemist; Latinized name of *Jabir ibn Hayyan*. Many works are attributed to him, but his name was used by later writers. He was familiar with many chemicals and laboratory techniques, including distillation and sublimation.

Gef·fen |'gefən|, David (1943–   ) U.S. recording company executive. He founded Asylum Records (1970), Geffen Records (1980), and the Geffen Film Co.

Geh·rig |'gerig|, Lou (Henry Louis) (1903–41) U.S. baseball player. Known as **the Iron Horse**. He played a then-record 2,130 consecutive major league games for the New York Yankees from 1925 to 1939. His consecutive-game streak was ended by the disease that he ultimately died from, amyotrophic lateral sclerosis, often called Lou Gehrig's disease.

Gei·ger |'gīgər|, Johannes Hans Wilhelm (1882–1945) German nuclear physicist. In 1908 he developed his prototype radiation counter for detecting alpha particles, later improved in collaboration with Walther Müller.

Gei·kie |'gikē|, Sir Archibald (1835–1924) Scottish geologist. He specialized in Pleistocene geology, especially the geomorphological effects of glaciations and the resulting deposits.

Gei·sel |'gīzəl|, Theodor Seuss (1904–91) U.S. author and illustrator. His numerous children's books include *And to Think That I Saw It on Mulberry Street* (1937), *The Cat in the Hat* (1957), and *Green Eggs and Ham* (1960).

Gel·bart |'gelbärt|, Larry (1925–   ) U.S. movie and television writer. He won an Emmy Award (1972) for his episodes of "M*A*S*H," as well as Tony Awards (1962 and 1989).

Gell·horn |'gelhörn|, Martha (1908–   ) U.S. journalist and author. She was a foreign correspondent for *Collier's* Magazine (1937–45) and was married to Ernest Hemingway (1940–43).

Gell-Mann |'gel 'mæn|, Murray (1929–   ) U.S. theoretical physicist. He coined the word *quark* and proposed the concept of strangeness in quarks. Nobel Prize for Physics (1969).

Ge·may·el |jə'mīəl|, Pierre (1905–84) Lebanese political leader. A Maronite Christian, he founded the right-wing Phalange Party in 1936 and served as a member of Parliament (1960–84). His youngest son, **Bashir** (1947–82), was assassinated while president-elect; his eldest son, **Amin** (1942–   ), served as president (1982–88).

Ge·net |zʜə'nā|, Jean (1910–86) French novelist, poet, and dramatist. Much of his work portrayed life in the criminal and homosexual underworlds, of which he was a part. Notable works: *Our Lady of the Flowers* (novel, 1944), *The Thief's Journal* (autobiography, 1949), and *The Maids* (play, 1947).

Gen·ghis Khan |'geNGgəs 'kän| (1162–1227) founder of the Mongol empire; born *Temujin*. He took the name Genghis Khan ('ruler of all') in 1206 after uniting the nomadic Mongol tribes, and by the time of his death his empire extended from China to the Black Sea. His grandson Kublai Khan completed the conquest of China.

Gen·ti·le |jen'tēlā|, Giovanni (1875–1944) Italian philosopher and educator. He was a proponent of the fascist philosophy of "actualism" and a Mussolini supporter.

Gen·ti·le da Fa·bri·a·no |jen'tēlā dä ,fäbrē'änō| (*c.* 1370–1427) Italian painter. His major surviving work is the altarpiece *The Adoration of the Magi* (1423), most others having been destroyed.

Geof·frey of Mon·mouth |'jefrē| (*c.* 1110–*c.* 1154) Welsh chronicler. His *Histroia Regum Britanniae* (*c.* 1139; first printed in 1508), an account of the kings of Britain, was a major source for English literature but is now thought to contain little historical fact.

George |jawrj| the name of four kings of Great Britain and Ireland, one of Great Britain and Ireland (from 1920 of the United Kingdom), and one of the United Kingdom: **George I** (1660–1727; reigned 1714–27), king of Great Britain and Ireland, great-grandson of James I, Elector of Hanover (1698–1727). He succeeded to the British throne as a result of an Act of Settlement (1701). Unpopular in England as a foreigner who never learned English, he left administration to his ministers. **George II** (1683–1760; reigned 1727–60), son of George I. King of Great Britain and Ireland as well as Elector of Hanover (1727–60). He depended heavily on his ministers, although he took an active part in the War of the Austrian Succession (1740–48). His later withdrawal from active politics allowed the development of constitutional monarchy. **George III** (1738–1820; reigned 1760–1820), grandson of George II. He was

king of Great Britain and Ireland, as well as Elector of Hanover (1760–1815) and King of Hanover (1815–20). He reigned during the time of the Revolutionary War and the War of 1812. He exercised considerable political influence, but it declined from 1788 after bouts of mental illness, as a result of which his son was made regent in 1811. **George IV** (1762–1830; reigned 1820–30), son of George III. King of Great Britain and Ireland. Known as a patron of the arts and *bon vivant*, he gained a bad reputation, which further damaged his attempt to divorce his estranged wife Caroline of Brunswick. **George V** (1865–1936; reigned 1910–36), son of Edward VII. King of Great Britain and Ireland (of the United Kingdom from 1920). He exercised restrained but important influence over British politics, playing an especially significant role in the formation of the government in 1931. **George VI** (1895–1952; reigned 1936–52), son of George V. King of the United Kingdom. He came to the throne on the abdication of his elder brother Edward VIII. Despite a retiring disposition, he became a popular monarch, gaining respect for the staunch example he and his family set during the London Blitz.

George |jawrj|, Henry (1839–97) U.S. economist. He theorized the formula of the single tax, generating taxes from land ownership.

George |jawrj|, St. (*c.* 3rd century) patron saint of England. He is reputed in legend to have slain a dragon, and may have been martyred near Lydda in Palestine some time before the reign of Constantine. His cult did not become popular until the 6th century, and he probably became patron saint of England in the 14th century. Feast day, April 23.

Gep·hardt |'gep,härt|, Richard Andrew (1941–) U.S. politician. He is a member of the U.S. House of Representatives from Missouri (1979–) and was a 1988 U.S. presidential nominee.

Ge·rard |jə'rärd|, John (1545–1612) English herbalist. He was curator of the physic garden of the College of Surgeons and published his *Herball*, containing over 1,800 woodcuts, in 1597.

Ger·ber |'gərbər|, Daniel Frank (1873–1952) U.S. businessman. He owned a small cannery with his father, and in 1928 he and his wife Dorothy began making and marketing strained baby food.

Gé·ri·cault |ˌzHārē'kō|, (Jean Louis André) Théodore (1791–1824) French painter, criticized for his rejection of classicism in favor of a more realistic style. His most famous work, *The Raft of the Medusa* (1819), depicts the survivors of a famous shipwreck of 1816.

Ger·mer |'germər|, Edmund (1901–87) U.S. scientist, born in Germany. He developed the flourescent lamp and high-pressure mercury-vapor lamp.

Gern·reich, Rudi (1922–85) U.S. fashion designer, born in Austria.

Gerns·back |'gernz,bäk|, Hugo (1884–1967) U.S. inventor and publisher, born in Luxembourg. He patented over 80 electronic inventions and founded *Amazing Stories* magazine (1926), establishing science fiction as literary form. The Hugo Award is named for him.

Ge·ro·ni·mo |jə'ränə,mō| (c. 1829–1909) Apache chief. He led his people in resisting white encroachment on tribal reservations in Arizona before surrendering in 1886.

Ger·ry |'jerē|, Elbridge (1744–1814) vice president of the U.S. (1813–14). His political maneuvering in Massachusetts gave rise to the term "gerrymander."

Gersh·win |'gərsHwin| U.S. musicians of Russian-Jewish descent. **Ira Gershwin** (1896–1983), a lyricist, collaborated with his brother **George Gershwin** (1898–1937). Ira won the first Pulitzer Prize awarded to a lyricist for *Of Thee I Sing* (1931). George, who was born *Jacob Gershovitz*, was a composer and pianist. He made his name in 1919 with the song "Swanee." He went on to compose many successful songs and musicals, the orchestral work *Rhapsody in Blue* (1924), and the opera *Porgy and Bess* (1935).

Ger·vin, George (1952–) U.S. basketball player. Known as **the Iceman**.

Get·ty |'getē|, Jean Paul (1892–1976) U.S. industrialist. He made a large for-

tune in the oil industry and was also a noted art collector. He founded the J. Paul Getty Museum in Los Angeles.

Getz |gets|, Stan (1927–91) U.S. jazz saxophonist; born *Stanley Gayetsky*. He was a leader of the "cool" school of jazz; his recordings include "Early Autumn" (1948) and "The Girl from Ipanema" (1963).

Ghi·ber·ti |gē'bertē|, Lorenzo (1378–1455) Italian sculptor and goldsmith. His career was dominated by his work on two successive pairs of bronze doors for the baptistery in Florence.

Ghir·lan·daio |ˌgirlən'däyō| (c. 1449–94) Italian painter; born *Domenico di Tommaso Bigordi*. He is noted for his religious frescoes, particularly *Christ Calling Peter and Andrew* (1482–4) in the Sistine Chapel, Rome.

Gia·co·met·ti |ˌjäkə'metē|, Alberto (1901–66) Swiss sculptor and painter. His most typical works feature emaciated and extremely elongated human forms, such as *Pointing Man* (1947).

Gia·mat·ti |j(ē)ə'mäti|, A. Bartlett (1938–89) U.S. educator and sports administrator. He was president of Yale University (1978–86), president of the National Baseball League (1986–89), and the 7th commissioner of baseball (1989).

Giap, Vo Nguyen (1912–) Vietnamese military and political leader. As North Vietnamese vice-premier and defense minister, he was responsible for the strategy leading to the withdrawal of U.S. forces from South Vietnam in 1973 and the subsequent reunification of the country in 1976. His book *People's War, People's Army* (1961) was an influential text for revolutionaries.

Gib·bon |'gibən|, Edward (1737–94) English historian. He is best known for his multi-volume work *The History of the Decline and Fall of the Roman Empire* (1776–88), chapters of which aroused controversy for their critical account of the spread of Christianity.

Gib·bon |'gibən|, Lewis Grassic (1901–35) Scottish writer; pseudonym of *James Leslie Mitchell*.

Gib·bons |'gibənz|, Grinling (1648–1721) Dutch-born English sculptor. He is famous for his decorative carvings, chiefly in wood, as in the choir stalls of St. Paul's Cathedral, London.

Gib·bons |'gibənz|, Orlando (1583–1625) English composer and musician. He was the organist of Westminster Abbey from 1623 and composed mainly sacred music, although he is also known for madrigals such as *The Silver Swan* (1612).

Gibbs |gibz|, Sir Philip Hamilton (1877–1962) British journalist and author. He was knighted for his behind-the-lines work as a correspondent during World War I.

Gibbs |gibz|, James (1682–1754) Scottish architect. He developed Christopher Wren's ideas for London's city churches, especially in his masterpiece, *St. Martin's-in-the-Fields* (1722–26).

Gibbs |gibz|, Josiah Willard (1839–1903) U.S. physical chemist. He pioneered chemical thermodynamics and statistical mechanics, although his theoretical work was not generally appreciated until after his death.

Gibran |jə'brän|, Khalil (1883–1931) Lebanese-born U.S. writer and artist. Also **Jubran**. His writings in both Arabic and English are deeply romantic, displaying his religious and mystical nature.

Gib·son |'gibsən|, Althea (1927–) U.S. tennis player. She was the first black player to succeed at the highest level of tennis, winning all the major world women's singles titles in the late 1950s.

Gib·son |'gibsən|, Bob (1935–) U.S. baseball player. Full name *Robert Gibson*. Elected to Baseball Hall of Fame (1981).

Gib·son |'gibsən|, Charles Dana (1867–1944) U.S. artist. He was a magazine illustrator and creator of the "Gibson Girl."

Gib·son |'gibsən|, Mel (Columcille Gerard) (1956–) U.S.-born Australian actor and director. Notable movies: *Mad Max* (1979), the *Lethal Weapon* series (1987, 1989, 1992, and 1998) and *Braveheart* (1995), which he also directed and which won five Oscars.

Gib·son |'gibsən|, William (1914–) U.S. playwright. Notable works: *The Miracle Worker* (1960) and *Golda* (1977).

Gid·dings |'gidiNGz|, Joshua Reed (1795–1864) U.S. politician and abolitionist. He was a member of the U.S. House of Representatives from the Western Reserve district of Ohio (1838–59) and was censured for his militant abolitionist tactics (1842).

Gide |zHēd|, André-Paul-Guillaume (1869–1951) French novelist, essayist, and critic, regarded as the father of modern French literature. Notable works: *The Immoralist* (1902), *La Porte Étroite* (1909, *Strait is the Gate*), *The Counterfeiters* (1927), and his *Journal* (1939–50). Nobel Prize for Literature (1947).

Giel·gud |'gēl,good|, Sir (Arthur) John (1904–) English actor and director. A notable Shakespearean actor, particularly remembered for his interpretation of the role of Hamlet, he has also appeared in contemporary plays and films and won an Oscar for his role as a butler in *Arthur* (1980).

Gi·gli |'jēlyē|, Beniamino (1890–1597) Italian operatic tenor. He made his Milan debut with the conductor Toscanini in 1918, and retained his singing talents to a considerable age.

Gil·bert |'gilbərt|, Cass (1859–1934) U.S. architect. He designed the Woolworth building in New York City (1913) and the U.S. Supreme Court building (1935).

Gil·bert |'gilbərt|, Sir Humphrey (*c.* 1539–83) English explorer. He claimed Newfoundland for Elizabeth I in 1583, but was lost when his ship foundered in a storm on the way home.

Gil·bert |'gilbərt|, William (1544–1603) English physician and physicist. He discovered how to make magnets, and coined the term *magnetic pole*. His book *De Magnete* (1600) is an important early work on physics.

Gil·bert |'gilbərt|, Sir W. S. (1836–1911) English dramatist; full name *William Schwenck Gilbert*. He is best known as a librettist who collaborated on light operas with the composer Sir Arthur Sullivan. Notable works: *HMS Pinafore* (1878), *The Pirates of Penzance* (1879), and *The Mikado* (1885).

Gill |gil|, (Arthur) Eric (Rowton) (1882–1940) English sculptor, engraver, and typographer. He designed the first sans serif typeface, Gill Sans.

Gil·les·pie |gi'lespē|, Dizzy (1917–93) U.S. jazz trumpet player and bandleader; born *John Birks Gillespie*. He was a virtuoso trumpet player and a leading exponent of the bebop style.

Gil·lette |jə'let|, King Camp (1855–1932) U.S. inventor and manufacturer. He invented the disposable safety razor.

Gil·man |'gilmən|, Charlotte Anna (Perkins) (1860–1935) U.S. author and feminist lecturer. Notable works: *The Yellow Wallpaper* (1892).

Gil·man |'gilmən|, Daniel Coit (1831–1908) U.S. educator and professor. He founded the Sheffield Scientific School at Yale (1856) and served as the first president of Johns Hopkins University (1875–1901).

Gil·pin |'gilpən|, Charles Sidney (1878–1930) U.S. actor. He was one of the first black actors to gain success on the American stage.

Gil·roy |'gilroi|, Frank D. (1925–) U.S. author. Notable works: *The Subject Was Roses* (1964, Pulitzer Prize).

Gim·bel |'gimbəl|, Isaac (1856–1931) U.S. businessman, born in Germany. With his brothers Charles (1861–1932) and Ellis A. (1865–1950) Gimbel, he founded the department store chain Gimbel Brothers, Inc. (1922).

Ging·rich |'giNG(g)riCH|, Newt (1943–) U.S. politician and speaker of the U.S. House of Representatives. Full name *Newton Leroy Gingrich*. He served as a representative from Georgia (1979–98).

Gins·berg |'ginzbərg|, Allen (1926–97) U.S. poet. A leading poet of the beat generation, and later influential in the hippy movement of the 1960s, he is notable for *Howl and Other Poems* (1956), in which he attacked American society for its materialism and complacency. He later campaigned for civil rights, gay liberation, and the peace movement.

Gins·burg |'ginzbərg|, Charles P. (1920–92) U.S. scientist. He invented a videotape recorder, which was first used by a television network in 1956.

Gins·burg |'ginzbərg|, Ruth Bader (1933–) U.S. Supreme Court justice (1993–).

Gio·lit·ti |jō'lētē|, Giovanni (1842–1928) Italian statesman, prime minister five times between 1892 and 1921. He was responsible for the introduction of a wide range of social reforms, including national insurance (1911) and universal male suffrage (1912).

Gior·gio·ne |jawr'j(ē)awnā| (*c.* 1477–1511) Italian painter; also called **Giorgio Barbarelli** or **Giorgio da Castelfranco**. An influential figure in Renaissance art, he introduced the small easel picture in oils intended for private collectors. Notable works: *The Tempest* (*c.*1505) and *Sleeping Venus* (*c.*1510).

Giot·to |'jawtō| (*c.* 1266–1337) Italian painter; full name *Giotto di Bondone*. He introduced a naturalistic style showing human expression. His name is associated with the legend of "Giotto's O", in which he is said to have proven his mastery to the pope by drawing a perfect circle freehand. Notable works include the frescoes in the Arena Chapel, Padua (1305–08) and the church of Santa Croce in Florence (*c.*1320).

Gio·van·ni de' Me·di·ci the name of the Pope Leo X (see LEO).

Gis·card d'Es·taing |ZHis'kär des 'tæN|, Valéry (1926–) French statesman, president (1974–81).

Gish |'giSH| U.S. actresses. **Lillian Gish** (1893–1993) and her sister **Dorothy Gish** (1898–1968) appeared in a number of D. W. Griffith's silent movies, including *Hearts of the World* (1918) and *Orphans of the Storm* (1922).

Gis·sing |'gisiNG|, George (Robert) (1857–1903) English novelist. Notable works: *New Grub Street* (1891), *Born in Exile* (1892), and *The Private Papers of Henry Ryecroft* (1903).

Gi·ven·chy |,ZHēväN'SHē|, Hubert (1927–) French fashion designer.

Glad·stone |'glæd,stōn|, William Ewart (1809–98) British Liberal statesman, prime minister (1868–74, 1880–85, 1886, and 1892–94).

Glas·gow |'glæz,gō|, Ellen (Anderson Gholson) (1873–1945) U.S. author. Notable works: *In This Our Life* (1941, Pulitzer Prize).

Glash·ow |'glæSHō|, Sheldon Lee (1932–) U.S. theoretical physicist. He independently developed a unified theory to explain electromagnetic interactions and the weak nuclear force, and extended the quark theory of Murray Gell-Mann. Nobel Prize for Physics (1979).

Glas·pell |'glæs,pel|, Susan (1882–1948) U.S. novelist and playwright. She won a Pulitzer Prize for her play *Alison's House* (1930), based on the life of Emily Dickinson.

Glass |glæs|, Philip (1937–) U.S. composer, a leading minimalist. Notable works: *Einstein on the Beach* (opera 1976), *Glass Pieces* (ballet 1982), and *Low Symphony* (1993).

Gla·zu·nov |'gläzə,nawf|, Aleksandr (Konstantinovich) (1865–1936) Russian composer, a pupil of Rimsky-Korsakov. Notable work: *The Seasons* (ballet, 1901).

Glea·son |'glēsən|, Jackie (1916–87) U.S. entertainer. Born *Herbert John Gleason*; known as **the Great One**. He is best known for his comedic work in television, especially his role as bus driver Ralph Kramden in "The Honeymooners" (1955–56), one of the most frequently rebroadcast programs in television history.

Glen·dow·er |'glendowər|, Owen (*c.* 1359–*c.* 1416) Also **Glyndwr**. Welsh chief. He proclaimed himself Prince of Wales and led a national uprising against Henry IV.

Glenn |glen|, John Herschel, Jr. (1921–) U.S. astronaut and senator. In 1962, he became the first American to orbit the earth. An Ohio Democrat, he served several terms in the U.S. Senate (1975–99). In 1998, he joined the crew of the Space Shuttle in order to help study the effects of space travel on older people.

Glid·den |'glidən|, Joseph Farwell (1813–1906) U.S. farmer and inventor. He invented the first commercially sucessful barbed wire (1874).

Glin·ka |'gliNGkə|, Mikhail (Ivanovich) (1804–57) Russian composer. Regarded as the father of the Russian national school of music, he is best known for his operas *A Life for the Tsar* (1836) and *Russlan and Ludmilla* (1842).

Glo·ri·a·na |,glawrē'änə| the nickname of Queen Elizabeth I.

Gluck |glŏŏk|, Christoph Willibald (1714–87) German composer, notable for operas in which he sought a balance of music and drama and reduced the emphasis on the star singer. Notable operas: *Orfeo ed Euridice* (1762) and *Iphigénie en Aulide* (1774).

Gob·bi |'gäbē|, Tito (1915–84) Italian operatic baritone, famous for his interpretations of Verdi's baritone roles.

Go·bin·eau |'gäbə,nō|, Joseph-Arthur, Comte de (1816–82) French writer and anthropologist. His stated view that the races are innately unequal and that the white Aryan race is superior to all others later influenced the ideology and policies of the Nazis.

Go·dard |,gō'därd|, Jean-Luc (1930–) French movie director. He was one of the leading figures of the *nouvelle vague*. His movies include *Breathless* (1960), *Alphaville* (1965), and the more overtly political *Wind from the East* (1969).

God·dard |'gädərd|, Robert Hutchings (1882–1945) U.S. physicist. He carried out pioneering work in rocketry, and designed and built the first successful liquid-fueled rocket. NASA's Goddard Space Flight Center is named after him.

Gö·del |'gœd(ə)l; 'gōd(ə)l|, Kurt (1906–78) Austrian-born U.S. mathematician. He made several important contributions to mathematical logic, especially the incompleteness theorem.

God·frey |'gädfrē|, Arthur (1903–83) U.S. actor. He starred in radio and television variety shows.

Go·di·va |gə'dīvə|, Lady (*c.* 1140–1180) English noblewoman, wife of Leofric, Earl of Mercia. According to 13th century legend, she agreed to her husband's proposition that he would reduce unpopular taxes only if she rode naked on horseback through the marketplace of Coventry. According to later versions of the story, all the townspeople refrained from watching, except for peeping Tom, who was struck blind in punishment.

Go·du·nov |'gōd(ə),nawf; 'gawd(ə),nawf|, Boris Fyodorovich (1551–1605) czar of Russia (1598–1605). A counselor of Ivan the Terrible, he succeeded Ivan's son as czar. His reign was marked by famine, doubts over his involvement in the earlier death of Ivan's eldest son, and the appearance of a pretender, the so-called False Dmitri.

God·win |'gädwən|, Gail (1937–) U.S. author. Notable works: *A Mother and Two Daughters* (1982).

God·win |'gädwən|, William (1756–1836) English social philosopher and novelist. He advocated a system of anarchism based on a belief in the goodness of human reason and on his doctrine of extreme individualism. His wife was Mary Wollstonecraft, and their daughter, Mary, was the wife of Shelley.

Goeb·bels |'gOEbəlz; 'gəbəlz|, (Paul) Joseph (1897–1945) Also **Göbbels**. German Nazi leader and politician. From 1933 Goebbels was Hitler's Minister of Propaganda, with control of the press, radio, and all aspects of culture, which he manipulated in order to further Nazi aims. He committed suicide rather than surrender to the Allies.

Goe·ring |'gOEriNG; 'gəriNG|, Hermann Wilhelm (1893–1946) German Nazi leader and politician. Goering was responsible for the German rearmament program, founded the Gestapo, and from 1936 until 1943 directed the German economy. He was also the de facto head of the Luftwaffe, the German air force, until he lost face when it failed to win the Battle of Britain or prevent Allied bombing of Germany. Sentenced to death at the Nuremberg war trials, he committed suicide in his cell.

Goes |gOOs|, Hugo van der (c. 1440–82) Flemish painter, born in Ghent. His best-known work is the large-scale *Portinari Altarpiece* (1475), commissioned for a church in Florence.

Goe·thals |'gOTHəlz|, George Washington (1858–1928) U.S. army officer and engineer. As chief engineer and chairman of the Panama Canal Commission (1907), he oversaw construction of the Panama Canal.

Goe·the |'gOEtə|, Johann Wolfgang von (1749–1832) German Romanticist poet, dramatist, and scholar. Involved at first with the *Sturm und Drang* movement, Goethe changed to a more measured and classical style, as in the "Wilhelm Meister" novels (1796–1829). Notable dramas: *Göltz von Berlichingen*

(1773), *Tasso* (1790), and *Faust* (1808–32).

Goetz |gets|, Bernhard Hugo (1948–) U.S. murderer. When four teenagers on the New York subway asked him for money, he shot them and killed one, claiming that he was acting in self defense.

Gof·fin |'gawfən|, Gerry (1939–) U.S. lyricist. Notable songs: "Will You Still Love Me Tomorrow" and "Up on the Roof."

Go·gol |'gOgawl|, Nikolay Vasilyevich (1809–52) Russian novelist, dramatist, and short-story writer, born in Ukraine. His writings are satirical, often exploring themes of fantasy and the supernatural. Notable works: *The Government Inspector* (play, 1836), *Notes of a Madman* (short fiction, 1835), and *Dead Souls* (novel, 1842).

Goi·zue·ta, Roberto Crispulo (1931–) U.S. businessman, born in Cuba. With the Coca-Cola Co. since 1954, he became chairman of the board and CEO (1980–).

Go·kha·le |'gOkə,lä|, Gopal Krishna (1866–1915) Indian political leader and social reformer, president of the Indian National Congress from 1905. He was a leading advocate of Indian self-government through constitutional or moderate means.

Gold·berg |'gOl(d),bərg|, Arthur Joseph (1908–90) U.S. Supreme Court justice (1962–65). He served as U.S. ambassador to the U. N. (1965–68) but resigned, protesting the escalation of the Vietnam War.

Gold·berg |'gOl(d),bərg|, Rube (1883–1970) U.S. cartoonist. Full name *Reuben Lucius Goldberg*. As creator of the comic strip characters Professor Lucifer Gorgonzola Butts, Boob McNutt, and Lala Palooza, he satirized American folkways and modern technology. Pulitzer Prize, 1948.

Gold·berg |'gOl(d),bərg|, Whoopi (1955–) U.S. actress. Born *Caryn Johnson*. She has appeared in the movies *The Color Purple* (1985) and *Sister Act* (1992) and in the television series "Star Trek: The Next Generation."

Gold·ber·ger |'gOl(d),bərgər|, Joseph (1874–1929) U.S. physician, born in

Austria. He discovered and developed a cure for pellagra (1913–25).

Gold·ing |'gōldiNG|, Sir William (Gerald) (1911–93) English novelist. He achieved literary success with his first novel *Lord of the Flies* (1954), about boys stranded on a desert island who revert to savagery. Nobel Prize for Literature (1983).

Gold·man |'gōl(d)mən|, Emma (1869–1940) Lithuanian-born U.S. political activist. Involved in New York's anarchist movement, she was imprisoned in 1917 with lifelong associate Alexander Berkman; in 1919 they were released and deported to Russia. Notable works: *Anarchism and Other Essays* (1910) and *My Disillusionment in Russia* (1923).

Gold·man |'gōl(d)mən|, William (1931–) U.S. author of adult and children's fiction. Pseudonym **Harry Longbaugh**. Notable works: *Boys and Girls Together* (1964).

Gold·mark |'gōl(d),märk|, Peter Carl (1906–77) Hungarian-born U.S. inventor and engineer. He made the first color television broadcast in 1940, invented the long-playing record in 1948, and pioneered video cassette recording.

Gold·schmidt |'gōl(d),sHmit|, Victor Moritz (1888–1947) Swiss-born Norwegian chemist. Considered the founder of modern geochemistry, he carried out fundamental work on crystal structure, suggesting a law relating it to chemical composition.

Gold·smith |'gōl(d),smiTH|, Oliver (1730–74) Irish novelist, poet, essayist, and dramatist. Notable works: *The Vicar of Wakefield* (novel, 1766), *The Deserted Village* (poem, 1770), and *She Stoops to Conquer* (play, 1773).

Gold·wa·ter |'gōl(d),wawtər|, Barry Morris (1909–98) U.S. politician. He was a member of the U.S. Senate from Arizona (1953–65, 1969–87) and a Republican presidential candidate (1964).

Gold·wyn |'gōldwən|, Samuel (1882–1974) Polish-born U.S. movie producer; born *Schmuel Gelbfisz*; changed to *Samuel Goldfish* then *Goldwyn*. He produced his first film in 1913; with Louis B. Mayer, he founded the movie company Metro-Goldwyn-Mayer (MGM) in 1924.

Gol·gi |'gawljē|, Camillo (1843–1926) Italian histologist and anatomist. He devised a staining technique to study nerve tissue, classified types of nerve cells, and described the structure of dendritic nerve cells, now called "Golgi cells." Received the Nobel Prize for Physiology or Medicine (1906).

Gol·lancz |gə'länts|, Sir Victor (1893–1967) British publisher and philanthropist. A committed socialist, Gollancz compaigned against the rise of Fascism in the 1930s and founded the Left Book Club (1936). He also organized aid for World War I refugees.

Gom·pers |'gämpərz|, Samuel (1850–1924) U.S. labor leader, born in England. He helped to found (1881) the Federation of Organized Trades and Labor Unions, which was later reorganized as The American Federation of Labor (1886). He served as president of the A.F. of L. until his death and did much to win respect for organized labor.

Gon·cha·rov |'gänCHə,rawf|, Ivan (Aleksandrovich) (1812–91) Russian novelist. His novel *Oblomov* (1857) is regarded as one of the greatest works of Russian realism.

Gon·court |gawn'koŏr| French novelists and critics. **Edmond de Goncourt** (1822–96) and his brother **Jules de Goncourt** (1830–70) wrote art criticism, realist novels, and social history. In his will Edmond provided for the establishment of the Académie Goncourt, which awards the annual Prix Goncourt to a work of French literature.

Good·all |'goŏdawl|, Jane (1934–) English zoologist. After working with Louis Leakey in Tanzania from 1957, she made prolonged and intimate studies of chimpanzees at the Gombe Stream Reserve by Lake Tanganyika from 1970.

Good·hue |'goŏd(h)yoŏ|, Bertram Grosvenor (1869–1924) U.S. architect. Notable designs: additions to West Point (1903–10) and the Nebraska State Capitol (1920–32).

Good·ing |'goŏdiNG|, Cuba, Jr. (1968–) U.S. actor. Notable movies: *Jerry Maguire* (Academy Award, Best Supporting Actor, 1997); *As Good As It Gets* (1997); and *What Dreams May Come* (1998).

Good·man |'go͝odmən|, Benny (1909–86) U.S. jazz and classical clarinetist and bandleader. Full name *Benjamin David Goodman*; known as **the King of Swing**. He was the first major white bandleader to integrate black and white musicians and the first musician to give a jazz concert at Carnegie Hall (1938).

Good·man |'go͝odmən|, Ellen Holtz (1941–) U.S. journalist and author. An associate editor of the *Boston Globe* (1986–), she writes a syndicated colum of the Washington Post Writers Group (1976–); she won a 1980 Pulitzer Prize in commentary.

Good·man |'go͝odmən|, John (1952–) U.S. actor. He had a leading role in the television series "Roseanne" (1988–96). Notable movies: *Sea of Love* (1989) and *King Ralph* (1991).

Good·man |'go͝odmən|, Paul (1911–72) U.S. psychoanalyst and author. He wrote *Growing Up Absurd* (1960) and *Compulsory Mis-Education* (1964), as well as fiction and poetry.

Good·rich |'go͝odriCH|, Samuel Griswold (1793–1860) U.S. publisher and writer. He published an annual gift book, *The Token* (1827–42); under the pseudonym **Peter Parley**, he wrote 116 children's tales.

Good·son |'go͝odsən|, Mark (1915–) U.S. television producer. He formed Goodson-Todman Productions (1946), which created the television game shows "What's My Line," " Password," "I've Got a Secret," "The Price is Right," and "To Tell the Truth."

Good·win |'go͝odwin|, Doris Kearns (1943–) U.S. journalist, historian, and author. She received the 1995 Pulitzer Prize for *No Ordinary Time*.

Good·year |'go͝od,yir|, Charles (1800–60) U.S. inventor. He developed the vulcanization process for rubber, after accidentally dropping some rubber mixed with sulfur and white lead on a hot stove.

Goos·sens |'go͝osəns|, Sir (Aynsley) Eugene (1893–1962) English conductor, violinist, and composer, of Belgian descent. After conducting in the U.S. (1923–45), he was appointed the director (1947) of the New South Wales Conservatorium and conductor of the Syd-ney Symphony Orchestra. His compositions include opera, ballet, and symphonies.

Gor·ba·chev |'gawrbə,CHawf|, Mikhail (Sergeyevich) (1931–) Soviet statesman, general secretary of the Communist Party of the USSR (1985–91), and president (1988–91). His foreign policy helped bring about an end to the Cold War, while within the USSR he introduced major reforms, both in the economy and in freedom of information. He resigned following an attempted coup. Nobel Peace Prize (1990).

Gor·di·mer |'gawrdəmər|, Nadine (1923–) South African novelist and short-story writer. Her experience of the effects of apartheid underlies much of her work. Notable novels: *The Conservationist* (1974). Nobel Prize for Literature (1991).

Gor·don |'gawrdən|, Charles George (1833–85) British general and colonial administrator. He made his name by crushing the Taiping Rebellion (1863–64) in China. In 1884 he fought Mahdist forces in Sudan led by Muhammad Ahmad (see MAHDI) but was trapped at Khartoum and killed.

Gor·don |'gawrdən|, Dexter Keith (1923–90) U.S. jazz tenor saxophonist. He defined the bebop style.

Gor·don |'gawrdən|, Jeff (1971–) U.S. racecar driver. He became the youngest winner of the Daytona 500 (1997).

Gor·don |'gawrdən|, Mary Catherine (1949–) U.S. author. Notable works: *The Company of Women* (1981).

Gor·don |'gawrdən|, Ruth (1896–1985) U.S. actress and writer. Born *Ruth Gordon Jones*. Notable movies: *Pat and Mike* (1952), *Rosemary's Baby* (1968, Academy Award), and *Harold and Maude* (1971).

Gor·dy |'gawrdē|, Berry, Jr. (1929–) U.S. recording-company executive and popular music producer. He founded the Motown record company in 1959, which had huge success in the 1960s and 1970s, popularizing black rhythm-and-blues and soul music.

Gore |gawr|, Al (1948–) U.S. vice president (1993–). Full name *Albert Arnold Gore, Jr.* A Tennessee Democrat, he served in the U.S. House of Representatives (1977–85) and U.S. Senate (1985–93). Noted for his commitment to environmental issues, he wrote *Earth in the Balance: Healing the Global Environment* (1992).

Górecki, Henryk Mikolaj (1933–   ) Polish composer. His works, influenced by religious music, include the *Third Symphony* (1976), known as the *Symphony of Sorrowful Songs*.

Gor·ey |'gawrē|, Edward (St. John) (1925–   ) U.S. author and illustrator. He published numerous hand-lettered books with brief, cryptic narratives and morbidly comic pen and ink illustrations.

Gor·ges |'gōrjəz|, Sir Ferdinando (*c.* 1566–1647) English soldier and colonizer. He was an organizer of the Plymouth Company (1606) and the Council for New England (1620), which gave rise to the Plymouth Colony and the Massachusetts Bay Company.

Gor·ky |'gawrkē|, Arshile (1905–48) Turkish-born U.S. painter. An exponent of abstract expressionism, he is best known for his work of the early 1940s, for example *Waterfall* (1943).

Gor·ky |'gawrkē|, Maksim (1868–1936) Russian writer and revolutionary; pseudonym of **Aleksei Maksimovich Peshkov**. After the Revolution he was honored as the founder of the new, officially sanctioned socialist realism. His best-known works include the play *The Lower Depths* (1901) and his autobiographical trilogy (1915–23).

Gor·ton |'gawrtən|, Samuel (1592–1677) U.S. religious leader, born in England. He was an Antinomian who was banished to England for heresy (1637–38) but returned and founded a settlement at Warwick, Rhode Island.

Gos·nold |'gäs,nōld|, Bartholomew (*c.* 1572–1607) English navigator. He explored the Maine coast and Narragansett Bay (1602); he was second in command on the Jamestown expedition (1606–07).

Gos·sett |'gäsət|, Louis, Jr. (1936–   ) U.S. actor. Notable movies: *An Officer and a Gentleman* (1982, Academy Award).

Got·ti |'gätē|, John, Jr. (1940–   ) U.S.

mobster. He was head of the Gambino underworld crime organization.

Gott·schalk |'gät,SHawk|, Louis Moreau (1829–69) U.S. pianist and composer. He was the first U.S. pianist to tour Europe with critical success.

Gou·dy |'gowdē|, Frederic William (1865–1947) U.S. printer and type designer.

Gould |gŏŏld|, Chester (1900–85) U.S. cartoonist and author. He was the creator of "Dick Tracy" (1931), the first dramatic comic strip with crime and violence.

Gould |gŏŏld|, Glenn (Herbert) (1932–82) Canadian pianist and composer. Best known for his performances of works by Bach, he retired from the concert stage in 1964 to concentrate on recording and broadcasting.

Gould |gŏŏld|, Gordon (1920–   ) U.S. physicist. A member of the Manhattan Project (1943–45), he worked on the development of the atomic bomb. He devised several laser devices, including a laser amplifier (patented 1978).

Gould |gŏŏld|, Jay (1836–92) U.S. financier. With James Fisk and Daniel Drew, he gained control of the Erie Railroad (1868) through stock manipulation; with Fisk, he attempted to corner the gold market, which created the Black Friday panic on September 24, 1869.

Gould |gŏŏld|, John (1804–81) English bird artist. He produced many large illustrated volumes, though it is believed that many of the finest plates were actually drawn by Gould's wife and other employed artists.

Gould |gŏŏld|, Stephen Jay (1941–   ) U.S. paleontologist. A noted popularizer of science, he has studied modifications of Darwinian evolutionary theory, proposed the concept of punctuated equilibrium, and written on the social context of scientific theory.

Gou·nod |gŏŏ'nō|, Charles-François (1818–93) French composer, conductor, and organist. He is best known for his opera *Faust* (1859).

Go·won, Yakubu Francisco José de (1934–   ) Nigerian general and statesman, head of state (1966–75).

Go·ya y Lucientes |'goiə| (1746–1828) Spanish painter and etcher; full name *Francisco José de Goya y Lucientes*. He is famous for his works treating the French occupation of Spain (1808–14), including *The Shootings of May 3rd 1808* (painting, 1814) and *The Disasters of War* (etchings, 1810–14), depicting the cruelty and horror of war.

Gra·ble |'grāb(ə)l|, Betty (1916–73) U.S. actress. Born **Ruth Elizabeth Grable**. A leading movie star, she was most famous for her 1942 pinup poster. Notable movies: *Moon Over Miami* (1941) and *How to Marry a Millionaire* (1953).

Grac·chus |'grækəs| Roman tribunes. **Tiberius Sempronius Gracchus** (*c.* 163–133 BC) and his brother **Gaius Sempronius Gracchus** (*c.* 153–121 BC) were also known as **the Gracchi**. They were responsible for radical social and economic legislation, especially concerning the redistribution of land to the poor.

Graf |gräf|, Steffi (1969–) German professional tennis player; full name *Stephanie Graf*.

Graf·ton |'græftən|, Augustus Henry Fitzroy, 3rd Duke of (1735–1811) British Whig statesman, prime minister (1768–70).

Graf·ton |'græftən|, Sue (1940–) U.S. author. Her alphabet series of mysteries includes *I is for Innocent* (1992), *J is for Judgment* (1994), and *K is for Killer* (1994).

Graham |græm|, Billy (1918–) U.S. evangelical preacher and author; full name *William Franklin Graham*. A minister of the Southern Baptist Church. He is world-famous for preaching to mass religious meetings.

Graham |græm|, Katherine Meyer (1917–) U.S. publisher. Wife of Philip Graham, head of a communications empire that included *Newsweek* magazine and the *Washington Post*, she became the company's president upon her husband's death (1963), and most notably publisher of the *Post* (1969–79).

Graham |græm|, Martha (1894–1991) U.S. dancer, teacher, and choreographer. She evolved a new dance language using more flexible movements intended to express psychological complexities and emotional power. Notable works: *Appalachian Spring* (1931) and *Care of the Heart* (1946).

Graham |græm|, Otto (1921–) U.S. football player.

Graham |græm|, Sylvester (1794–1851) U.S. reformer. A promotor of temperance and vegetarianism, he invented the graham cracker and established the breakfast cereal industry.

Graham |græm|, Thomas (1805–69) Scottish physical chemist. He studied diffusion and osmosis, coining the word *osmose* (now *osmosis*) and *colloid* in its modern chemical sense.

Grahame |'grāəm|, Kenneth (1859–1932) Scottish-born writer of children's stories, resident in England from 1864. He is remembered for the children's classic *The Wind in the Willows* (1908).

Grain·ger |'grānjər|, (George) Percy (Aldridge) (1882–1961) Australian-born U.S. composer and pianist. From 1901 he lived in London, where he collected, edited, and arranged English folk songs. Notable works: *Shepherd's Hey* (1911).

Gramm |græm|, Phil (1942–) U.S. politician. Full name *William Philip Gramm*. He is a member of the U.S. Senate from Texas (1985–).

Gram·sci |'græmshē|, Antonio (1891–1937) Italian political theorist and activist, co-founder and leader of the Italian Communist Party. Imprisoned in 1926 when the Fascists banned the Communist Party, he died shortly after his release. *Letters from Prison* (1947) remains an important work.

Grange |grānj|, Red (1903–91) U.S. football player. Born *Harold Edward Grange*; also called **the Galloping Ghost**. Elected to the NFL Hall of Fame (1963).

Grant |grænt|, Cary (1904–86) British-born U.S. actor; born *Alexander Archibald Leach*. He made his Hollywood screen debut in *This is the Night* (1932) after appearing in Broadway musicals. He acted in more than seventy movies, usually as the debonair male lead, including *Holiday* (1938), *The Philadelphia Story* (1940), *To Catch a Thief* (1955), and *North by Northwest* (1959).

Grant |grænt|, Duncan (James Corrow)

(1885–1978) Scottish painter and designer, a pioneer of abstract art in Britain. He was a cousin of English writer Lytton Strachey and a member of the Bloomsbury Group.

Grant |grænt|, Ulysses S. see box. **Julia Boggs Dent Grant** (1826–1902), wife of Ulysses S. Grant and U.S. first lady (1869–77).

Granville-Barker |'grænvil 'bärkər|, Harley (1877–1946) English dramatist, critic, theater director, and actor. His *Prefaces to Shakespeare* (1927–46) influenced subsequent interpretation of Shakespeare's work. Notable plays: *The Voysey Inheritance* (1905).

Grap·pel·li |grə'pelē|, Stephane (1908–97) French jazz violinist. With Django Reinhardt, he founded the group known as the Quintette du Hot Club de France in 1934.

Grass |gräs|, Günter (Wilhelm)

Grant, Ulysses Simpson
18th U.S. president

Life dates: 1822–1885
Place of birth: Point Pleasant, Ohio
Name at birth: Hiram Ulysses Grant
Mother: Hannah Simpson Grant
Father: Jesse Root Grant
Wife: Julia Boggs Dent Grant
Children: Frederick, Ulysses, Ellen ("Nellie"), Jesse
College/University: U.S. Military Academy, West Point
Military service: U.S. Army, Mexican War; during Civil War, officer in and ultimately commander of all Union armies
Career: Farming; real estate
Political career: Secretary of war (interim appointment)
Party: Republican
Home state: Ohio
Opponents in presidential races: Horatio Seymour; Horace Greeley
Term of office: March 4, 1869–March 3, 1877
Vice presidents: Henry Wilson (died in office in 1875); Schuyler Colfax
Notable events of presidency: Black Friday gold panic of 1869; Financial Panic of 1873; Credit Mobilier stock scandal; Whiskey Ring Conspiracy; Colorado admitted as the 38th state
Place of burial: New York, New York

(1927–   ) German novelist, poet, and dramatist. Notable novels: *The Tin Drum* (1959) and *The Flounder* (1977).

Grau |grow|, Shirley Ann (1929–   ) U.S. author. Notable works: *The Keepers of the House* (Pulitzer Prize, 1964).

Graup·ner |'grownpər|, (Johann Christian) Gottlieb (1767–1836) U.S. musician, born in Prussia. He organized the Philharmonic Society in Boston (1810–24), the first symphony orchestra in the U.S.

Graves |grävz|, Robert (Ranke) (1895–1985) English poet, novelist, and critic, known for his interest in classics and mythology. Notable prose works: *Goodbye to All That* (autobiography, 1929), *I, Claudius* (historical fiction, 1934), and *The White Goddess* (non-fiction, 1948).

Gray |grā|, Asa (1810–88) U.S. botanist and author. He wrote many textbooks that greatly popularized botany. He also supported Darwin's theories at a time when they were anathema to many.

Gray |grā|, Elisha (1835–1901) U.S. inventor. He was a rival of Alexander Graham Bell for the telephone patent; his Gray and Barton Co. became Western Electric.

Gray |grā|, Hanna Holborn (1930–   ) U.S. historian and educator, born in Germany. A history professor, she was president of the University of Chicago (1978–93).

Gray |grā|, Harold Lincoln (1894–1968) U.S. cartoonist. He created the comic strip "Little Orphan Annie" and was the first strip cartoonist to use the medium as a vehicle for expressing political opinions.

Gray |grā|, Horace (1828–1902) U.S. Supreme Court justice (1881–1902).

Gray |grā|, Thomas (1716–71) English poet, best known for "Elegy Written in a Country Church-Yard" (1751).

Gre·co |'grekō|, El see EL GRECO.

Gree·ley |'grēlē|, Horace (1811–72) U.S. journalist and political leader of abolitionism.

Gree·ly |'grēlē|, Adolphus Washington (1844–1935) U.S. army officer and explorer. He conducted an expedition to map unknown segments of Greenland

and Ellesmere Island (1881), and he established telegraph communication in outlying U.S. possessions.

Green |grēn|, Hetty (1834–1916) U.S. financier. Full name *Henrietta Howland Green*; known as the **Witch of Wall Street**. Through shrewd investing, she turned her inherited wealth into the largest fortune held by a woman, but she obscured her identity by living in tenement houses.

Green·a·way |'grēn(ə),wā|, Kate (1846–1901) English artist; full name *Catherine Greenaway*. She is known especially for her illustrations of children's books such as *Mother Goose* (1881).

Green·a·way |'grēn(ə),wā|, Peter (1942–) English movie director. Notable movies: *The Cook, the Thief, His Wife, and Her Lover* (1989) and *The Pillow Book* (1996).

Greene |grēn|, (Henry) Graham (1904–91) English novelist. The moral paradoxes he saw in his Roman Catholic faith underlie much of his work. Notable works: *Brighton Rock* (1938), *The Power and the Glory* (1940), and *The Third Man* (written as a screenplay, and filmed in 1949; novel 1950).

Greene |grēn|, Joe (1946–) U.S. football player. He was chosen All-Pro five times and led Pittsburgh to four Super Bowl titles in the 1970s.

Greene |grēn|, Leonard Michael (1918–) U.S. aerospace inventor and manufacturer. He invented numerous flight safety instruments, most notably the airplane stall warning device, developed during World War II.

Greene |grēn|, Nathanael (1742–86) American revolutionary general. He forced the British out of Georgia and the Carolinas in a series of battles (1781) during the American Revolution and was much admired as a military strategist.

Green·field |'grēn,fēld|, Meg (1930–99) U.S. journalist. An editorial page writer for the *Washington Post* (1979–) and *Newsweek* columnist (1974–), she won a 1978 Pulitzer Prize in editorial writing.

Green·ough |'grēnō|, Horatio (1805–52) U.S. sculptor. His seated *Washington* was intended for the national Capitol rotunda but now resides in the Smithsonian.

Green·span |'grēnspæn|, Alan (1926–) U.S. economist. As chairman of the National Commission on Social Security Reform (1981–83), he helped prevent the bankruptcy of the Social Security system. Appointed chairman of the Federal Reserve Board (1987).

Greer |grir|, Germaine (1939–) Australian feminist and writer. She first achieved recognition with her influential book *The Female Eunuch* (1970), an analysis of women's subordination in a male-dominated society.

Greg·o·ry XIII |'greg(ə)rē| (1502–85) pope (1572–85), born in Italy. He was a major sponsor of numerous educational programs and institutes. The Gregorian calendar, still in use, was introduced in 1582 as a result of his efforts to correct the errors in the Julian calendar.

Greg·o·ry |'greg(ə)rē|, St. (*c*. 540–604) pope (as Gregory I) (590–604) and Doctor of the Church; known as **St. Gregory the Great**. An important reformer, he did much to establish the temporal power of the papacy. He sent St. Augustine to England to lead the country's conversion to Christianity, and is also credited with the introduction of Gregorian chant. Feast day, March 12.

Greg·o·ry of Na·zi·an·zus |'greg(ə)rē əv ,nāzē'änzəs|, St. (329–89) Doctor of the Church, bishop of Constantinople. With St. Basil and St. Gregory of Nyssa he upheld orthodoxy against the Arian and Apollinarian heresies, and was influential in restoring adherence to the Nicene Creed. Feast day, (in the Eastern Church) January 25 and 30; (in the Western Church) January 2 (formerly May 9).

Greg·o·ry of Nys·sa |'greg(ə)rē əv 'nisə|, St. (*c*. 330–*c*. 395) Doctor of the Eastern Church, bishop of Nyssa in Cappadocia. The brother of St. Basil, he was an orthodox follower of Origen and joined with St. Basil and St. Gregory of Nazianzus in opposing Arianism. Feast day, March 9.

Greg·o·ry of Tours |'greg(ə)rē əv 'toŏrz|, St. (*c*. 540–94) Frankish bishop and historian. He was elected bishop of Tours in 573; his writings provide the chief authority for the early Merovingian period of French history. Feast day, November 17.

Greg·o·ry the Great |'greg(ə)rē| see GREGORY, ST.

Gren·fell |'gren‚fel|, Joyce (Irene Phipps) (1910–79) English entertainer and writer.

Gren·ville |'grenvəl|, George (1712–70) British Whig statesman, prime minister (1763–65). The American Stamp Act (1765), which aroused great opposition in the North American colonies, was passed during his term of office.

Gre·sham |'greSHəm|, Sir Thomas (c. 1519–79) English financier. He founded the Royal Exchange in 1566 and served as the chief financial adviser to the Elizabethan government.

Gres·ley |'grezlē|, Sir (Herbert) Nigel (1876–1941) British railway engineer. He is most famous for designing express steam locomotives, such as the A4 class exemplified by the *Mallard*.

Gretz·ky |'gretskē|, Wayne (1961–) Canadian hockey player. He is the all-time leading point-scorer in the National Hockey League, and was voted Most Valuable Player nine times.

Greuze |grœz|, Jean-Baptiste (1725–1805) French painter, noted for his genre paintings and portraits.

Grey |grā|, Charles, 2nd Earl (1764–1845) British statesman, prime minister (1830–34). His government passed the first Reform Act (1832) as well as important factory legislation and the Act abolishing slavery throughout the British Empire.

Grey |grā|, Sir George (1812–98) British statesman, colonial administrator, and a scholar of Maori culture.

Grey |grā|, Lady Jane (1537–54) queen of England (July 9–19, 1553) and niece of Henry VIII. In 1553, to ensure a Protestant succession, John Dudley, the Duke of Northumberland, forced Jane to marry his son and persuaded the dying Edward VI to name Jane as his successor. She was quickly deposed by forces loyal to Edward's (Catholic) sister Mary, who had popular support, and was executed the following year.

Grey |grā|, Joel (1932–) U.S. actor. Born *Joe Katz*. Notable movies: *Cabaret* (1972, Academy Award).

Grey |grā|, Zane (1872–1939) U.S. writer; born *Pearl Grey*. He wrote 54 westerns in a somewhat romanticized and formulaic style, which sold over 13 million copies during his lifetime.

Grieg |grēg|, Edvard (1843–1907) Norwegian composer, conductor, and violinist. Famous works include the Piano Concerto in A minor (1869) and the incidental music to Ibsen's play *Peer Gynt* (1876).

Grier |grir|, Robert Cooper (1794–1870) U.S. Supreme Court justice (1846–70).

Grif·fey |'grifē|, Ken, Jr. (1969–) U.S. baseball player. Full name *George Kenneth Griffey, Jr.*; known as **Junior**.

Grif·fith |'grifiTH|, Arthur (1872–1922) Irish nationalist leader and statesman, president of the Irish Free State (1922). In 1905 he founded and became president of Sinn Fein. He became vice-president of the newly declared Irish Republic in 1919 and negotiated the Anglo-Irish Treaty (1921).

Grif·fith |'grifiTH|, D. W. (1875–1948) U.S. movie director; full name *David Lewelyn Wark Griffith*. A pioneer in movies, he is responsible for introducing many cinematic techniques, including flashback and fade-out. Notable movies: *The Birth of a Nation* (1915), *Intolerance* (1916), and *Broken Blossoms* (1919).

Gri·mal·di |gri'mäldē|, Francesco Maria (1618–63) Italian physicist and astronomer who discovered the diffraction of light and verified Galileo's law of the uniform acceleration of falling bodies.

Gri·mal·di |gri'mäldē|, Joseph (1779–1837) English circus entertainer who created the role of the circus clown and performed at Covent Garden, where he became famous for his acrobatic skills.

Grim·ké |'grimkē|, Archibald Henry (1849–1930) U.S. lawyer, editor, author, and civil rights leader. He was a member of the original Committee of Forty (1909) who helped found the National Association for the Advancement of Colored People (NAACP). Spingarn Medal, 1919.

Grim·ké |'grimkē| U.S. reformers, abolitionists, and feminists. **Sarah Moore Grimké** (1792–1872) and her sister, **Angelina Emily Grimké** (1805–79), wrote for the American Anti-Slavery Society. Sarah later wrote pamphlets for women's rights, and, with her husband, Theodore Dwight Weld, *American Slavery as It Is: Testimony of a Thousand Witnesses* (1839).

Grimm |grim| German philologists and folklorists. **Jacob (Ludwig Carl) Grimm** (1785–1863) and his brother **Wilhelm (Carl) Grimm** (1786–1859) jointly inaugurated a dictionary of German on historical principles (1852), which was eventually completed by other scholars in 1860. They also compiled an anthology of German fairy tales, which appeared in three volumes between 1812 and 1822.

Gri·mond |'grimənd|, Jo, Baron (1913–93) British Liberal politician, leader of the Liberal Party (1956–67); full name *Joseph Grimond*.

Gris |grēs|, Juan (1887–1927) Spanish painter; born *José Victoriano Gonzales*. His main contribution was to the development of the later phase of synthetic cubism. His work features the use of collage and paint in simple fragmented shapes.

Grish·am |'grisHəm|, John (1955–) U.S. author and lawyer. Notable novels: *The Firm* (1991).

Gris·som |'grisəm|, Gus (1926–67) U.S. astronaut. Full name *Virgil Ivan Grissom*. Part of the original Project Mercury astronaut team (1959), he was killed in a flash fire in the Apollo 1 capsule along with Edward H. White and Roger B. Chaffee.

Gri·vas |'grēvās|, George (Theodorou) (1898–1974) Greek Cypriot patriot and soldier. A supporter of the union of Cyprus with Greece, he led the guerrilla campaign against British rule, which culminated in the country's independence in 1959.

Groen·ing |'grāniNG|, Matt (1954–) U.S. cartoonist and author. He created "The Simpsons" television comedy and the weekly comic strip "Life in Hell."

Gro·my·ko |grə'mēkō|, Andrei (Andreevich) (1909–89) Soviet statesman, foreign minister (1957–85), president of the USSR (1985–88). He represented the Soviet Union abroad throughout most of the Cold War.

Gro·pi·us |'grōpēəs|, Walter (1883–1969) German-born U.S. architect. He was the first director of the Bauhaus School of Design (1919–28) and a pioneer of the international style. He settled in the U.S. in 1938, where he was professor of architecture at Harvard University until 1952.

Gross |grōs|, Samuel David (1805–84) U.S. surgeon, educator, and author. He was a founder of the American Surgical Association (1880) and author of *A System of Surgery* (1859), which he constantly revised as a result of his teaching

Grosse·teste |'grōs,test|, Robert (c. 1175–1253) English churchman, philosopher, and scholar. His experimental approach to science, especially in optics and mathematics, inspired his pupil, Roger Bacon.

Grosz |grōs|, George (1893–1959) German painter and draughtsman. His satirical drawings and paintings characteristically depict a decadent society in which gluttony and depraved sensuality are juxtaposed with poverty and disease.

Gro·tius |'grōsH(ē)əs|, Hugo (1583–1645) Dutch jurist and diplomat; Latinized name of *Huig de Groot*. His legal treatise *De Jure Belli et Pacis* (1625) established the basis of modern international law.

Grove |grōv|, Sir George (1820–1900) English musicologist. He was the founder and first editor of the multi-volume *Dictionary of Music and Musicians* (1879–89), now named for him in its later editions, and served as the first director of the Royal College of Music (1883–94).

Grove |grōv|, Lefty (1900–75) U.S. baseball player. Full name *Robert Moses Grove*. A pitcher, he led the American League in strikeouts seven times. Elected to Baseball Hall of Fame (1947).

Grü·ne·wald |'grŏonə,vält; grYnə,vält|, Mathias (c. 1460–1528) German painter; born *Mathis Nithardt*; also called **Mathis Gothardt**. His most famous work is the nine-panel *Isenheim Altar* (completed 1516).

Guar·di |'gärdē|, Francesco (1712–93) Italian painter. A pupil of Canaletto, he produced paintings of Venice notable for their free handling of light and atmosphere.

Guare, John (1938–) U.S. playwright. Notable works: *The House of Blue Leaves* (1971) and *Six Degrees of Separation* (1990).

Guar·ne·ri |gwär'nerē|, Giuseppe (1687–1744) Italian violin-maker; known as **del Gesù**. He is the most famous of a family of three generations of violin-makers based in Cremona.

Gue·ricke |'gärikə|, Otto von (1602–86) German engineer and physicist. He was the first to investigate the properties of a vacuum, and he devised the Magdeburg hemispheres to demonstrate atmospheric pressure.

Guest |gest|, Edgar A. (1881–1959) U.S. journalist and poet, born in England. Full name *Edgar Albert Guest.* He was on the staff of the Detroit *Free Press.* Notable works: *A Heap o' Livin'* (1916), *Just Folks* (1917), and *Life's Highway* (1933).

Gue·va·ra |gwə'värə|, Che (1928–67) Argentinian revolutionary and guerrilla leader; full name *Ernesto Guevara de la Serna.* He played a significant part in the Cuban revoluation (1956–59) and became a government minister under Castro. He was captured and executed by the Bolivian army while training guerrillas for a planned uprising in Bolivia.

Gug·gen·heim |'gŏŏgən,hīm|, U.S. family, including: Swiss-born industrialist **Meyer Guggenheim** (1828–1905). With his seven sons he established large mining and metal-processing companies. His son **Solomon Guggenheim** (1861–1949), a philanthropist, set up several foundations providing support for the arts, including the Guggenheim Museum in New York. Meyer's son **Daniel Guggenheim** (1856–1930), an industrialist and philanthropist, expanded the family copper industry to include gold, rubber, and tin; with his wealth he established the Daniel and Florence Guggenheim Foundation (1924) and the Guggenheim Foundation for the Promotion of Aeronautics (1926). Meyer's son

Simon Guggenheim (1867–1941), a politician and philanthropist, was a member of the U.S. Senate from Colorado (1907–13). He established the John Simon Guggenheim Memorial Foundation (1925). Meyer's granddaughter **Peggy Guggenheim** (1898–1979) was a patron of the arts and an author. Full name *Marguerite Guggenheim.* She was a collector of modern art (especially Pollock and Motherwell) and financed galleries in London, New York, and Venice.

Gui·do of Arezzo |'gwēdō əv ə'retsō| (*c.* 991–1050) Italian monk and music theorist. A member of the Benedictine Order, he is credited with devising the four-line musical staff and naming the notes of the scale with syllables.

Giu·li·a·ni |'jŏŏlē'änē|, Rudolph (1944–) U.S. politician. He is the mayor of New York City (1993–).

Guinier, Ewart (1911–90) U.S. educator and union official.

Guin·ness |'ginis|, Sir Alec (1914–) English actor. He gave memorable performances in the movies *Bridge on the River Kwai* (1957) and *Star Wars* (1977) and as espionage chief George Smiley in television versions of John Le Carré's books.

Güi·ral·des |gē'räldäs|, Ricardo (1886–1927) Argentinian author. His novels include *Don Segundo Sombra* (1926).

Guise·wite |'gīz,wīt|, Cathy (1950–) U.S. cartoonist and author. She created the syndicated comic strip "Cathy."

Gu·lick |'g(y)ŏŏlik|, Luther Halsey (1865–1918) U.S. educator. She was a cofounder of the Campfire Girls (1910).

Gunn |gən|, Thom (1929–) English poet, resident in California from 1954; full name *Thomson William Gunn.* His works, written in a predominantly lowkey, laconic, and colloquial style, include *Fighting Terms* (1954), *My Sad Captains* (1961), and *The Passages of Joy* (1982).

Gur·djieff |'gərdyef|, George (Ivanovich) (1877–1949) Russian spiritual leader and occultist. He founded the Institute for the Harmonious Development of Man in Paris (1922).

Gur·ney |'gərnē|, A. R., Jr. (1930–) U.S. educator and playwright. Full name *Albert Ramsdell Gurney*. Notable works: *The Dining Room* (1981) and *The Cocktail Hour* (1987).

Gur·ney |'gərnē|, Ivor (Bertie) (1890–1937) English poet and composer He fought on the Western Front during World War I, and wrote the verse collections *Severn and Somme* (1917) and *War's Embers* (1919).

Gus·ta·vus Adol·phus |gə'stävəs ə'dawlfəs| (1594–1632) king of Sweden (1611–32). His repeated victories in battle made Sweden a European power, and in 1630 he intervened on the Protestant side in the Thirty Years War. His domestic reforms laid the foundation of the modern Swedish state.

Gu·ten·berg |'gōōtn,bərg|, Johannes (*c.* 1400–68) German printer. He was the first in the West to print using movable type; he introduced typecasting using a matrix, an alloy for type metal, and an oil-based ink for printing, and was the first to use a press. By *c.* 1455 he had produced what later became known as the Gutenberg Bible.

Guth·rie |'gəTHrē| U.S. folksingers and songwriters. **Woody Guthrie** (1912–67); full name *Woodrow Wilson Guthrie*. His radical politics and the rural hardships of the Depression inspired many of his songs. His son **Arlo Guthrie** (1947–) was the founder of Rising Son Records. Notable songs: "Alice's Restaurant" (1967) and "City of New Orleans."

Gu·tiér·rez |gōō'tyerez|, Gustavo (1928–) Peruvian theologian. He was an important figure in the emergence of liberation theology in Latin America, outlining its principles in *A Theology of Liberation* (1971).

Gwynn |gwin|, Nell (1650–87) English actress; full name *Eleanor Gwynn*. She became famous as a comedienne at the Theatre Royal, Drury Lane, London. She was a mistress of Charles II.

Gwynn |gwin|, Tony (1960–) U.S. baseball player. Full name *Anthony Keith Gwynn*.

Hh

Ha·ber·mas, Jürgen (1929–) German philosopher. Notable books: *Theory of Communicative Action* (1982).

Ha·bi·bie |haˈbēbē|, B. J. (1936–) president of Indonesia (1998–). Full name *Bacharuddin Jusuf Habibie*.

Ha·chette |äˈSHet|, Louis-Christophe-François (1800–64) French editor and publisher. He founded the publishing house Hachette et Cie (1826).

Hack·ett |ˈhækət|, Bobby (1915–76) U.S. jazz cornetist and bandleader. Full name *Robert Leo Hackett*. A melodic improviser, he played in clubs with many different small bands.

Hack·man |ˈhækmən|, Gene (1930–) U.S. actor. Notable movies: *The French Connection* (1971, Academy Award).

Ha·dri·an |ˈhādrēən|, (AD 76–138) Roman emperor 117–138; full name *Publius Aelius Hadrianus*. The adopted successor of Trajan, he toured the provinces of the Empire and secured the frontiers.

Haeck·el |ˈhekəl|, Ernst Heinrich (1834–1919) German biologist and philosopher. He popularized Darwin's theories and saw evolution as providing a framework for describing the world, with the German Empire representing the highest evolved form of a civilized nation.

Ha·gen |ˈhāgən|, Walter Charles (1892–1969) U.S. golfer.

Hag·gard |ˈhægərd|, Sir (Henry) Rider (1856–1925) English novelist. He is famous for adventure novels such as *King Solomon's Mines* (1885) and *She* (1889).

Hahn |hän|, Otto (1879–1968) German chemist, codiscoverer of nuclear fission. Together with Lise Meitner he discovered the new element protactinium in 1917. The pair discovered nuclear fission in 1938 with **Fritz Strassmann**, (1902–80). Nobel Prize for Chemistry (1944).

Haig |hāg|, Douglas, 1st Earl Haig of Bemersyde (1861–1928) British field marshal during World War I.

Hai·le Se·las·sie |ˈhīlē səˈlæsē| (1892–1975) emperor of Ethiopia 1930–74; born *Tafari Makonnen*. In exile in Britain during the Italian occupation of Ethiopia (1936–41), he was restored to the throne by the Allies and ruled until deposed by a military coup. He is revered by the Rastafarian religious sect.

Hai·ley |ˈhālē|, Arthur (1920–) Canadian author. Notable works: *Hotel* (1965) and *Airport* (1968).

Hai·tink |ˈhītiNGk|, Bernard (Johann Herman) (1929–) Dutch musical director and conductor.

Hak·luyt |ˈhæklət|, Richard (c. 1552–1616) English geographer and historian. He compiled *Principal Navigations, Voyages, and Discoveries of the English Nation* (1598), a collection of accounts of great voyages of discovery.

Hal·as |ˈhæləs|, George (1895–1983) U.S. football player, coach, and owner. Full name *George Stanley Halas*; known as **Papa Bear**. He founded the Chicago Bears (originally the Decatur Staleys) in 1920. As a coach, he set an NFL record with 325 wins. Elected to NFL Hall of Fame (1963).

Hal·ber·stam |ˈhælbər,stæm|, David (1934–) U.S. journalist and author. Notable books: *The Making of a Quagmire* (1965, Pulitzer Prize) and *The Children* (1998).

Hal·dane |ˈhawl,dān|, J. B. S. (John Burdon Sanderson) (1892–1964) Scottish mathematical biologist. As well as contributing to the development of population genetics, Haldane became well known as a popularizer of science and as an outspoken Marxist.

Hal·de·man |ˈhawldəmən|, H. R. (1926–93) U.S. government official. Full name *Harry Robbins Haldeman*. White House chief of staff under President Nixon (1969–73), he resigned and was convicted of perjury, conspiracy, and obstruction of justice in the Watergate scandal.

Hale |hāl|, Edward Everett (1822–1909) U.S. clergyman, author, and philanthropist. A Unitarian minister, he wrote *The Man Without a Country* (1863).

Hale |hāl|, George Ellery (1868–1938)

U.S. astronomer. He discovered that sunspots are associated with strong magnetic fields and invented the spectroheliograph. He also initiated the construction of several large telescopes.

Hale |hāl|, Nathan (1755–76) American revolutionary hero. He volunteered (1776) to spy behind British lines on Long Island, disguised as a schoolmaster, but he was captured by the British and hanged without trial. His last words are said to have been, "I only regret that I have but one life to lose for my country."

Hale |hāl|, Sarah Josepha (Buell) (1788–1879) U.S. author. She is best known for the nursery rhyme "Mary Had a Little Lamb," from her *Poems for Our Children* (1830).

Ha·ley |'hālē|, Alex (1921–92) U.S. author. Full name *Alexander Murray Palmer Haley*. His best-selling work *Roots: The Saga of an American Family* chronicled the ancestors of his African-American family from its entry into America as slaves. The book and subsequent television miniseries (1977) each won a Pulitzer Prize.

Ha·ley |'hālē|, Bill (William John Clifton) (1925–81) U.S. rock-and-roll singer; full name *William John Clifton Haley*. His song "Rock Around the Clock" (1954) helped pioneer the popularity of rock and roll.

Hall |hawl|, Arsenio (1955–) U.S. actor and comedian. He was the first African American to host a late night television program (1989–94).

Hall |hawl|, Charles Francis (1821–71) U.S. explorer. He made three expeditions to explore the Arctic (1860–62, 1864–69, and 1871); on his first, he discovered the remains of Martin Frobisher's expedition of 1578.

Hall |hawl|, Charles Martin (1863–1914) U.S. chemist and manufacturer. He devised the commercial method for producing aluminium from bauxite, which involves the electrolysis of alumina dissolved in molten cryolite.

Hall |hawl|, Donald Andrew (1928–) U.S. poet, author, and educator. Notable works: *The Happy Man* (1986), *Seasons at Eagle Pond* (1987), and *Lucy's Summer* (1995).

Hall |hawl|, Granville Stanley (1844–1924) U.S. psychologist and educator. The founder of child psychology in the U.S., he was a leader in the development of educational psychology. He founded the *American Journal of Psychology* (1887) and the American Psychological Association (1891).

Hall |hawl|, James (1793–1868) U.S. lawyer and historian. His books on the early American frontier include *The Romance of Western History* (1857).

Hall |hawl|, J. C. (1891–1982) U.S. businessman. Full name *Joyce Clyde Hall*. He founded Hallmark Greeting Cards.

Hall |hawl|, James, Jr. (1811–98) U.S. geologist and paleontologist. The leading stratigraphic geologist and invertebrate paleontologist of his day, he wrote the 13-volume *Paleontology of New York* (1847–94).

Hall |hawl|, Lyman (1724–90) American revolutionary leader. He was a member of the Continental Congress (1775–78, 1780) and a signer of the Declaration of Independence.

Hall |hawl|, (Marguerite) Radclyffe (1886–1943) English novelist and poet. She is chiefly remembered for her novel *The Well of Loneliness* (1928), an exploration of a lesbian relationship, which caused outrage and was banned in Britain for many years.

Hal·lé |'hälə|, Sir Charles (1819–95) German-born pianist and conductor; born *Karl Halle*. He left Paris in 1848 and settled in Manchester, where he founded the Hallé Orchestra (1858).

Hal·ler |'hälər|, Albrecht von (1708–77) Swiss anatomist and physiologist. He pioneered the study of neurology and experimental physiology and wrote the first textbook of physiology.

Hal·ley |'hælē; 'hālē|, Edmond (1656–1742) English astronomer and mathematician. He is best known for identifying a bright comet (later named after him), and for successfully predicting its return.

Hal·li·day |'hælə,dā|, Michael (Alexander Kirkwood) (1925–) English linguist. He built on the work of J. R. Firth in pursuit of a psychologically and sociologically realistic overall theory of language and its functions.

Hal·lowes |'hælōz|, Odette (1912–95) French heroine of World War II; born *Marie Céline*. She worked as a British secret agent in occupied France.

Hal·prin |'hælprin|, Lawrence (1916–) U.S. architect. Notable designs: Freeway Park (1972–76) in Seattle, Washington, and Lovejoy Fountain Plaza (1966) in Portland, Oregon.

Hals |häls|, Frans (c. 1581–1666) Dutch portrait and genre painter. He endowed his portraits with vitality and humor, departing from conventional portraiture with works such as *The Banquet of the Officers of the St. George Militia Company* (1616) and *The Laughing Cavalier* (1624).

Hal·sey |'hawlzē|, William Frederick (1882–1959) U.S. naval officer. Known as **Bull**. He was commander of Allied naval forces in the South Pacific (1942–44) and of the U.S. Third Fleet (1944–45), and became a fleet admiral in 1945.

Hal·ston |'hawlstən| (1932–90) U.S. fashion designer. Born *Roy Halston Frowick*.

Ha·ma·da |hə'mädə|, Shoji (1894–1978) Japanese potter. He collaborated with Bernard Leach, working mainly in stoneware to produce utilitarian items of unpretentious simplicity.

Ha·mil·car Bar·ca |hə'mil,kär 'bärkə| (c. 270–229 BC) Carthaginian general, father of Hannibal. He fought Rome in the first Punic War and negotiated the terms of peace after Carthaginian defeat.

Ham·il·ton |'hæməltən|, Sir William Rowan (1806–65) Irish mathematician and theoretical physicist. Hamilton made influential contributions to optics and to the foundations of algebra and quantum mechanics.

Ham·il·ton |'hæməltən|, Alexander (1757–1804) U.S. politician. He established the U.S. central banking system as the first secretary of the treasury under Washington (1789–95), and advocated strong central government. He was killed in a duel with Aaron Burr.

Ham·il·ton |'hæməltən|, Sir Charles (1900–78) New Zealand inventor and automobile-racing driver, best known for his development of the jet boat.

Ham·il·ton |'hæməltən|, Lady Emma (c. 1765–1815) English beauty and mistress of Lord Nelson; born *Amy Lyon* or **Emily Lyon**.

Ham·il·ton |'hæməltən|, Scott (1958–) U.S. figure skater. He won four world championships (1981–84) and an Olympic gold medal (1984).

Ham·il·ton |'hæməltən|, Virginia Esther (1936–) U.S. author. A biographical and children's fiction author, her works include *M. C. Higgins, the Great* (1974), the first book in history to receive the National Book Award and the Newbery Medal.

Ham·lin |'hæmlən|, Hannibal (1809–91) U.S. politician. He was vice president of the U.S. (1861–65), a member of the U.S. Senate (1869–81), and minister to Spain (1881–82).

Ham·lisch |'hæmlisн|, Marvin (1944–) U.S. composer. His compositions include *A Chorus Line* (1975) and *They're Playing Our Song* (1979).

Hammarskjöld |'hämərsнəld|, Dag (Hjalmar Agne Carl) (1905–61) Swedish diplomat and politician. As secretary general of the United Nations (1953–61) he was influential in the establishment of the UN emergency force in Sinai and Gaza (1956), and also initiated peace moves in the Middle East (1957–58). Killed in a plane crash while on a peace mission in Congo, he was posthumously awarded the 1961 Nobel Peace Prize.

Ham·mer |'hæmər|, Armand (1898–1990) U.S. industrialist and philanthropist. He had many business interests in the U.S. and the U.S.S.R. and served as chairman and chief executive officer of Occidental Petroleum Corp. (1957–90).

Ham·mer·stein |'hæmər,stīn|, Oscar II (1895–1960) U.S. lyricist. He collaborated with various composers, most notably Richard Rodgers, with whom he wrote *Oklahoma!* (1943), *South Pacific* (1949), and *The Sound of Music* (1959).

Ham·mett |'hæmət|, (Samuel) Dashiell (1894–1961) U.S. novelist. He developed the hard-boiled style of detective fiction in works such as *The Maltese Falcon* (1930) and *The Thin Man* (1932) (both made into successful movies). He lived for many years with Lillian Hellman; they were both persecuted for their left-wing views during the McCarthy era.

Ham·mon |'hæmən|, Jupiter (c. 1720– c. 1800) U.S. poet. His "An Evening Thought" (1761) was the first published poem by an African American.

Ham·mond |'hæmənd| U.S. engineers. **John Hays Hammond** (1855–1936) was a mining engineer, an associate of Cecil Rhodes in the development of South African mining resources, and a leader in the Transvaal reform movement (1895–96). His son, **John Hays Hammond, Jr.** (1888–1965), was an electrical and radio engineer and inventor. He established the Hammond Radio Research Laboratory (1911).

Ham·mond |'hæmənd|, Dame Joan (1912–96) Australian operatic soprano, born in New Zealand.

Ham·mond |'hæmənd|, Laurens (1895–1973) U.S. inventor. He developed the Hammond electric organ (1933).

Ham·mu·ra·bi |ˌhæməˈräbē| (died 1750 BC) the sixth king of the first dynasty of Babylonia, reigned 1792–1750 BC. He extended the Babylonian empire and instituted one of the earliest known collections of laws.

Hamp·ton |'hæm(p)tən|, Lionel (1909–) U.S. jazz vibraphonist, drummer, pianist, singer, and bandleader. He played with Benny Goodman in small ensembles before forming his own big band (1940).

Ham·sun |'hämsən|, Knut (1859–1952) Norwegian novelist; pseudonym of *Knut Pedersen.* Notable works: *Hunger* (1890) and *Growth of the Soil* (1917). Nobel Prize for Literature (1920).

Han·cock |'hæn,käk|, John (1737–93) American revolutionary and politician. Noted as the first signer of the Declaration of Independence (1776), he was a member of the Continental Congress (1775–80; 1785; 1786) and its first president (1775–77). He was later governor of Massachusetts (1780–85; 1787–93).

Han·cock |'hæn,käk|, Winfield Scott (1824–86) U.S. army officer. A Union general, he was famed for his defense of Cemetery Ridge in the Battle of Gettysburg (1863). He was the 1880 De-

mocratic presidential candidate, narrowly losing to Garfield.

Hand |hænd|, (Billings) Learned (1872–1961) U.S. jurist and author. He wrote over 2000 opinions as judge of the U.S. Court of Appeals, 2nd Circuit (1924–51). Notable works: *The Spirit of Liberty* (1952).

Han·del |'hændəl|, George Frideric (1685–1759) German-born composer and organist, resident in England from 1712; born *Georg Friedrich Händel.* A prolific composer, he is chiefly remembered for his choral works, especially the oratorio *Messiah* (1742), and for orchestra, his *Water Music* suite (c.1717) and *Music for the Royal Fireworks* (1749).

Handley Page, Frederick see PAGE.

Han·dy |'hændē|, W. C. (William Christopher) (1873–1958) U.S. blues musician. He set up a music-publishing house in 1914, and his transcriptions of traditional blues helped establish the pattern of the modern twelve-bar blues.

Hanks |hæNGks|, Tom (1956–) U.S. actor, director and producer; full name *Thomas J. Hanks.* Light-hearted films such as *Splash!* (1984) and *Big* (1988) brought him international success. He won Oscars for his performances in *Philadelphia* (1993) and *Forrest Gump* (1994).

Han·na |'hænə|, Bill (1910–) U.S. cartoonist and motion picture and televison producer. Full name *William Denby Hanna.* With longtime partner Joseph Barbera, he created cartoon characters such as the Flintstones, Top Cat, Huckleberry Hound, Yogi Bear, and Tom and Jerry.

Han·ni·bal |'hænəbəl| (247–183 BC) Carthaginian general. In the second Punic War he attacked Italy via the Alps, repeatedly defeating the Romans, although he failed to take Rome itself.

Hans·ber·ry |'hænz,berē|, Lorraine (1930–65) U.S. playwright. Her *A Raisin in the Sun* (1959) was the first play by an African-American woman to be produced on Broadway.

Han·sen |'hænsən|, Austin (1910–96) U.S. photographer.

Hap·good |'hæpgo͝od|, Norman (1868–1937) U.S. editor and author. He was editor of the magazines *Collier's* (1903–

12), *Harper's Weekly* (1913–16), and *Hearst's International* (1923–25).

Har·court |'härkawrt|, Alfred (1881–1954) U.S. publisher. He cofounded the firm that eventually became Harcourt Brace Jovanovich (1919).

Har·die |'härdē|, (James) Keir (1856–1915) Scottish Labour politician. A miner before becoming a member of Parliament in 1892, he became the first leader of both the Independent Labour Party (1893) and the Labour Party (1906).

Har·ding |'härdiNG|, Tonya (1970–) U.S. figure skater. She was a world champion figure skater (1991) involved in a plot to injure competitor Nancy Kerrigan and prevent her from competing on the Olympic team.

Har·ding |'härdiNG|, Warren (Gamaliel) see box. **Florence Kling De Wolfe Harding** (1860–1924), wife of Warren Harding and U.S. first lady (1921–23).

Hard·wick |'härdwik|, Elizabeth (1916–) U.S. author and editor.

Harding, Warren Gamaliel
29th U.S. president

Life dates: 1865–1923
Place of birth: Corsica, Ohio (now Blooming Grove)
Mother: Phoebe Elizabeth Dickerson Harding
Father: George Tryon Harding
Wife: Florence Kling De Wolfe Harding
College/University: Ohio Central College
Career: Publisher; schoolteacher; newspaper editor; insurance salesman
Political career: Ohio Senate; lieutenant governor of Ohio; U.S. Senate; president
Party: Republican
Home state: Ohio
Opponents in presidential race: James M. Cox, Eugene Debs
Term of office: March 4, 1921–Aug. 2, 1923 (died while in office)
Vice president: Calvin Coolidge
Notable events of presidency: peace treaties with Austria, Germany, and Hungary; Teapot Dome Oil Scandal (revealed during Coolidge administration); dedication of the Tomb of the Unknown Soldier at Arlington, Va.
Place of burial: Marion, Ohio

Har·dy |'härdē|, Oliver (1892–1957) see LAUREL, STAN.

Har·dy |'härdē|, Thomas (1840–1928) English novelist and poet. Much of his work deals with the struggle against the indifferent force that inflicts the sufferings and ironies of life. Notable novels: *The Mayor of Casterbridge* (1886), *Tess of the D'Urbervilles* (1891), and *Jude the Obscure* (1896).

Hare, William see BURKE.

Harefoot, Harold see HAROLD.

Har·greaves |'här,grēvz|, James (*c.* 1720–78) English inventor; invented the spinning jenny (*c.* 1764).

Har·i·ot |'herēət|, Thomas (1560–1621) English mathematician and geographer. Also **Thomas Harriot** or **Thomas Harriott**. His *Briefe and True Report of the New-Found Land of Virginia* (1588) was the first English book written about the first English colony in America.

Hark·ness |'härknəs|, Anna M. (1837–1926) U.S. philanthropist. She endowed the Harkness Quadrangle at Yale University (1921) and established the Commonwealth Fund (1920).

Har·lan |'härlən| U.S. jurists. **John Marshall Harlan** (1833–1911) was a U.S. Supreme Court justice (1877–1911). In *Plessy v. Ferguson* (1896), he declared in a dissenting opinion that the Constitution is "color-blind." His grandson, **John Marshall Harlan** (1899–1971), was also a U.S. Supreme Court justice (1955–71).

Har·low |'härlō|, Harry Frederick (1905–81) U.S. ethologist and primate researcher.

Har·low |'härlō|, Jean (1911–37) U.S. movie actress; born *Harlean Carpenter*. Howard Hughes's *Hell's Angels* (1930) launched her career, her platinum blonde hair and sex appeal bringing immediate success. Her movies include *Platinum Blonde* (1931) and six movies with Clark Gable, including *Red Dust* (1932) and *Saratoga* (1937).

Harms·worth |'härmzwərTH|, Alfred Charles William see NORTHCLIFFE.

Har·old I |'herəld| (died 1040) king of England, reigned 1035–40; known as **Harold Harefoot**. An illegitimate son of Canute, he came to the throne when his half-brother Hardecanute (Canute's legitimate heir) was king of Denmark and thus absent when Canute died.

Har·old II |'herəld| (c. 1022–66) king of England, reigned 1066, the last Anglo-Saxon king of England. Succeeding Edward the Confessor, he was faced with two invasions within months of his accession. He resisted his half-brother Tostig and the Norse king Harald Hardrada at Stamford Bridge, but was killed and his army defeated by William of Normandy at the Battle of Hastings.

Har·per |'härpər|, Frances Ellen Watkins (1825–1911) U.S. author and social reformer. She was a founding member of the National Association for the Advancement of Colored Women (1896). Notable works: *Poems on Miscellaneous Subjects* (1854) and "The Two Offers" (1859).

Har·per |'härpər|, James (1795–1869) U.S. publisher. With his brothers John (1797–1875), Joseph Wesley (1801–70), and Fletcher (1806–77), he founded Harper & Brothers (1833), which published books and the magazines *Harper's New Monthly* (1850), *Harper's Weekly* (1957), and *Harper's Bazaar* (1867).

Har·per |'härpər|, Valerie (1940–) U.S. actress. Her television credits include the programs "The Mary Tyler Moore Show" (1970–74), "Rhoda" (1974–78), and "Valerie" (1986–87).

Har·ri·man |'herəmən| U.S. family, including: **Edward Henry Harriman** (1848–1909), a financier and railroad executive. His son, **(William) Averell Harriman** (1891–1986), was a U.S. diplomat. He served as U.S. representative to the Paris talks about peace in Vietnam.

Har·ring·ton |'heriNGtən|, Michael (1928–89) U.S. author and educator. He was a democratic socialist whose book *The Other America: Poverty in the United States* (1962) led to President Johnson's War on Poverty programs.

Har·ris |'herəs|, Sir Arthur Travers (1892–1984) British Marshal of the Royal Air Force; known as **Bomber Harris**. As commander in chief of Bomber Command (1942–45) in World War II, he organized mass bombing raids against German towns that resulted in large-scale civilian casualties.

Har·ris |'herəs|, Chapin Aaron (1806–60) U.S. dentist. He founded the first dental periodical, the *American Journal of Dental Science* (1939) and cofounded the first dental college, Baltimore College of Dental Surgery (1840).

Har·ris |'herəs|, Emmylou (1947–) U.S. country musician. Her hits include "If I Could Only Win Your Love" (1975) and "We Believe in Happy Endings" (1988).

Har·ris |'herəs|, Frank (1856–1931) Irish writer; born *James Thomas Harris*.

Har·ris |'herəs|, Joel Chandler (1848–1908) U.S. author. He is best known for his Brer Rabbit and Brer Fox stories as told by the fictional Uncle Remus.

Har·ris |'herəs|, William Torrey (1835–1909) U.S. educator and philosopher. He served as U.S. commissioner of education (1889–1906) and was the leading American interpreter of German philosophical thought.

Har·ri·son |'herəsən|, Benjamin see box. **Caroline Lavinia Scott Harrison** (1832–92), wife of Benjamin Harrison and U.S. first lady (1889–92).

Har·ri·son |'herəsən|, George (1943–) English rock and pop guitarist and songwriter, the lead guitarist of the Beatles.

Har·ri·son |'herəsən|, John (1693–1776) English horologist and inventor. He developed a marine chronometer for determining longitude at sea (1730–63).

Har·ri·son |'herəsən|, Peter (1716–75) U.S. architect.

Har·ri·son |'herəsən|, Sir Rex (1908–90) English actor; full name *Reginald Carey Harrison*. Notable movies: *Blithe Spirit* (1944), *My Fair Lady* (1964), and *Dr. Dolittle* (1967).

Har·ri·son |'herəsən|, Richard Berry (1864–1935) U.S. actor, born in Canada. He won national reputation in the African-American community as a Shakespearean actor and starred in *Green Pastures* (1930, Pulitzer Prize). Spingarn Medal, 1931.

Har·ri·son |'herəsən|, Wallace Kirkman (1895–1981) U.S. architect. His designs in New York City include the Metropolitan Opera House, Lincoln Center, and the United Nations complex.

Harrison, Benjamin
23rd U.S. president

Life dates: 1833–1901
Place of birth: North Bend, Ohio
Mother: Elizabeth Ramsey Irwin Harrison
Father: John Scott Harrison
Wives: Caroline Lavinia Scott Harrison (died 1892); Mary Scott Lord Dimmick Harrison (married 1896)
Children: (by first wife) Russell, Mary; (by second wife) Elizabeth
College/University: Miami University of Ohio
Military service: during Civil War, rose to the rank of brigadier general with Indiana volunteers
Career: Lawyer; law professor
Political career: Indianapolis city attorney; U.S. Senate; president
Party: Republican
Home state: Indiana
Opponents in presidential races: Grover Cleveland
Term of office: March 4, 1889–March 3, 1893
Vice president: Levi P. Morton
Notable events of presidency: Sherman Anti-Trust Act; Sherman Silver Purchase Act; McKinley Tariff Act; Dependent Pension Act; Pan American Union created; Oklahoma opened to settlers; North and South Dakota admitted as the 39th and 40th states; Montana admitted as the 41st state; Wyoming admitted as the 42nd state
Place of burial: Indianapolis, Indiana

Harrison, William Henry
9th U.S. president

Life dates: 1773–1841
Place of birth: Berkeley plantation, Charles City County, Virginia
Mother: Elizabeth Bassett Harrison
Father: Benjamin Harrison
Wife: Anna Tuthill Symmes Harrison
Children: Elizabeth, John (died in infancy), Lucy, William, John, Benjamin, Mary, Carter, Anna, James
College/University: Hampden-Sydney College
Military service: Battle of Tippecanoe (1811); U.S. Army major general in War of 1812
Career: Farmer; soldier
Political career: governor of the Indiana Territory; U.S. House of Representatives; Ohio Senate; U.S. Senate; minister to Colombia; president
Party: Whig
Home state: Ohio
Opponent in presidential races: Martin Van Buren
Term of office: March 4, 1841–Apr. 4, 1841 (died after 31 days in office)
Vice president: John Tyler
Place of burial: North Bend, Ohio

Har·ri·son |ˈherəsən|, William Henry see box. **Anna Tuthill Symmes Harrison** (1775–1864), wife of William Henry Harrison and U.S. first lady (1841). She had not yet moved to Washington, D.C., when word arrived of her husband's death one month after taking office.

Har·rod |ˈherəd|, Charles Henry (1800–85) English grocer and tea merchant. In 1853 he took over a shop in Knightsbridge, London, which, after expansion by his son **Charles Digby Harrod** (1841–1905), became the prestigious Harrod's department store.

Har·ry |ˈherē|, Deborah (1945–) U.S. punk rock vocalist. She was known as "Blondie" and performed with the group by the same name.

Hart |härt|, Johnny (1931–) U.S. cartoonist and author. Full name *John Lewis Hart*. He created the comic strips "B.C." and "The Wizard of Id."

Hart |härt|, Lorenz Milton (1895–1943) U.S. lyricist. His collaborations with composer Richard Rodgers include the scores for the Broadway shows *Babes in Arms* (1937) and *Pal Joey* (1940). Notable songs: "The Lady Is a Tramp," "My Funny Valentine," and "Blue Moon."

Hart |härt|, Moss (1904–61) U.S. playwright. His collaborations with George S. Kaufman include *You Can't Take It With You* (1936, Pulitzer Prize) and *The Man Who Came to Dinner* (1939).

Har·tack |ˈhärtæk|, Bill (1932–) U.S. jockey. Full name *William John Hartack, Jr.*. He won the Kentucky Derby five times.

Harte |härt|, (Francis) Brett (1836–1902) U.S. short-story writer and poet. He is chiefly remembered for his stories about life in a Californian gold-mining settlement.

Hart·ley |'härtlĕ|, L. P. (Leslie Pôles) (1895–1972) English novelist and short-story writer.

Hart·nell |'härtnəl|, Sir Norman (1901–78) English couturier; dressmaker to Queen Elizabeth II (whose coronation gown he designed) and the Queen Mother.

Harun ar-Rashid |hä'rōͦon är rä'sHĕd| (763–809) Also **Haroun-al-Raschid** (763–809), fifth Abbasid caliph of Baghdad (786–809). The most powerful of the Abbasid caliphs, he was made famous by his portrayal in the *Arabian Nights*.

Har·vard |'härvərd|, John (1607–38) American clergyman. He left his library and half of his estate to the newly founded college in Massachusetts which became Harvard University.

Har·vey |'härvĕ|, Alfred (1913–94) U.S. cartoonist. The founder of Harvey Comics, he created the cartoon character Casper the Friendly Ghost.

Har·vey |'härvĕ|, Paul (1918–) U.S. radio journalist and commentator. He is a syndicated columnist for the *Los Angeles Times* (1954–).

Har·vey |'härvĕ|, William (1578–1657) English physician, discoverer of the circulation of the blood. In *De Motu Cordis* (1628), Harvey described the motion of the heart and concluded that the blood leaves the heart through the arteries and returns to the heart through the veins after it had passed through the flesh.

Has·dru·bal |hæz'drōͦobəl| (died 221 BC) Carthaginian general. He accompanied his father-in-law, Hamilcar, to Spain in 237 and advanced the Carthaginian boundary to the Ebro.

Ha·šek |'häsHek|, Jaroslav (1883–1923) Czech novelist and short-story writer.

Hass |häs|, Robert (1947–) U.S. author. He was Poet Laureate of the U.S. (1995–97).

Has·sam |'hæsəm|, Childe (1859–1935) U.S. artist. Full name *Frederick Childe Hassam*.

Has·sel·blad |'häsel,bläd|, Victor (1906–78) Swedish inventor. He served as president of Hasselblad Photography, Inc. (1944–66).

Hass·ler |'häslər|, Ferdinand Rudolph (1770–1843) U.S. geodesist, born in Switzerland. He was superintendent of the U.S. Coast Survey (1816–18, 1832–43).

Has·tie |'hästĕ|, William H. (1904–76) U.S. jurist. He served as the first black federal judge (appointed 1937) and as governor of the U.S. Virgin Islands (1946–49).

Has·tings |'hästiNGz|, Thomas (1860–1929) U.S. architect. With John Merven Carrère (1858–1911), he designed the New York Public Library (1902 –11) and the Manhattan Bridge (1904–11).

Has·tings |'hästiNGz|, Warren (1732–1818) British colonial administrator. India's first governor general (1774–84), he introduced vital administrative reforms.

Hath·a·way |'hæTHə,wā|, Anne (*c.* 1556–1623) the wife of Shakespeare, whom she married in 1582.

Hat·shep·sut |hæt'sHep,sōͦot| (died 1482 BC) Egyptian queen of the 18th dynasty, reigned *c.* 1503–1482 BC. On the death of her husband Tuthmosis II, she became regent for her nephew Tuthmosis III. She then named herself Pharaoh and was often portrayed as male.

Haupt·mann |'howp(t),mæn|, Gerhart (1862–1946) German dramatist. An early pioneer of naturalism, he is known for *Before Sunrise* (1889) and *The Ascension of Joan* (1893). Nobel Prize for Literature (1912).

Ha·vel |'hävəl|, Václav (1936–) Czech dramatist and statesman, president of Czechoslovakia (1989–92) and of the Czech Republic since 1993. His plays, such as *The Garden Party* (1963), were critical of totalitarianism, and he was twice imprisoned as a dissident. He was elected president following the fall of the Communist leadership.

Hav·ell |'hævəl|, Robert, Jr. (1793–1878) U.S. engraver and painter. He made most of the plates for Audubon's *Birds of America*.

Hav·li·cek |'hæv,ləcHek|, John (1940–) U.S. basketball player.

Hawke |hawk|, Bob (1929–) Australian Labour statesman, prime minister (1983–91); full name *Robert James Lee Hawke*.

Haw·king |'hawkiNG|, Stephen (William) (1942–) English theoretical physicist. His main work has been on space–time, quantum mechanics, and black holes. His book *A Brief History of Time* (1988) proved a popular best-seller.

Haw·kins |'hawkinz|, Alma (1904–94) U.S. pioneer of modern dance.

Haw·kins |'hawkinz|, Coleman (Randolph) (1904–69) U.S. jazz saxophonist. During the 1920s and 1930s he was influential in making the tenor saxophone popular as a jazz instrument.

Haw·kins |'hawkinz|, Sir John (1532–95) English sailor. Also **Hawkyns**. Involved in the slave trade and privateering, he later helped build up the fleet that defeated the Spanish Armada in 1588.

Hawks |hawks|, Howard (Winchester) (1896–1977) U.S. movie director, producer, and screenwriter. He directed such movies as *The Big Sleep* (1946), *Gentlemen Prefer Blondes* (1953), and *Rio Bravo* (1959).

Hawks·moor |'hawks,mawr|, Nicholas (1661–1736) English architect. He worked with Vanbrugh at Castle Howard and Blenheim Palace and designed six London churches.

Hawn |hawn|, Goldie (1945–   ) U.S. actress. Notable movies: *Cactus Flower* (1969, Academy Award).

Ha·worth |'haw,wərTH|, Sir Walter Norman (1883–1950) English organic chemist. He was a pioneer in carbohydrate chemistry and was the first person to make a vitamin artificially when he synthesized vitamin C. Nobel Prize for Chemistry (1937).

Haw·thorne |'hawTHawrn| U.S. authors. **Nathaniel Hawthorne** (1804–64) was a novelist and short-story writer. Much of his fiction explores guilt, sin, and morality. Notable works: *Twice-Told Tales* (short stories, 1837) and *The House of Seven Gables* (novel, 1851). His son, **Julian Hawthorne** (1846–1934), wrote *Garth* (1877) and *Nathaniel Hawthorne and His Wife* (1884).

Hay |hā|, John Milton (1838–1905) U.S. diplomat and author. He was President Lincoln's private secretary (1861–65) and U.S. ambassador to Great Britain (1897–98). As U.S. secretary of state (1898–1905), he negotiated the Hay-Pauncefote Treaty (1901), making possible the construction of the Panama Canal.

Hay·den |'hād(ə)n|, Charles (1870–1937) U.S. banker and philanthropist. He donated the projector in the planetarium in New York City named in his honor.

Hay·den |'hād(ə)n|, Robert (1913–80) U.S. poet. Notable works: *Words in the Mourning Time* (1970) and *American Journal* (1978).

Hay·dn |'hīdn|, (Franz) Joseph (1732–1809) Austrian composer. A major exponent of the classical style, he taught both Mozart and Beethoven. His work includes 108 symphonies, 67 string quartets, 12 masses, and the oratorio *The Creation* (1796–98).

Hay·ek |'hīyek|, Friedrich August von (1899–1992) Austrian-born British economist. Strongly opposed to Keynesian economics, he was a leading advocate of the free market. Nobel Prize for Economics (1974).

Hayes |hāz|, Helen (1900–93) U.S. actress. Born *Helen Hayes Brown*; known as **the first lady of the American theater**. Her Broadway career spanned seven decades and included Tony-winning roles in *Happy Birthday* (1946) and *Time Remembered* (1957). Notable movies: *The Sin of Madelon Claudet* (1932, Academy Award) and *Airport* (1970, Academy Award).

Hayes |hāz|, Isaac (1942–   ) U.S. songwriter, pianist, and singer. His scoring for the film *Shaft* made him the first African-American composer to win an Academy Award (1971); his hits include "Walk On By" and "By the Time I Get to Phoenix."

Hayes |hāz|, Isaac Israel (1832–81) U.S. explorer and author. He made three expeditions to the Arctic and recounted his experiences in *An Arctic Boat Journey* (1860).

Hayes |hāz|, Roland (1887–1976) U.S. musician, a singer of classical music and spirituals. Spingarn Medal, 1925.

Hayes, Rutherford (Birchard) see box. **Lucy Ware Webb Hayes** (1831–89), wife of Rutherford Hayes and U.S. first lady (1877–81). She was known as **Lemonade Lucy** for her prohibition of alcoholic beverages in the White House.

Hayes, Rutherford Birchard
19th U.S. president

Life dates: 1822–1893
Place of birth: Delaware, Ohio
Mother: Sophia Birchard Hayes
Father: Rutherford Hayes, Jr.
Wife: Lucy Ware Webb Hayes
Children: Birchard, James, Rutherford, Joseph, George, Fanny, Scott, Manning
College/University: Kenyon College; Harvard Law School
Military service: officer in Ohio volunteers during Civil War; rose to the rank of brevet major general
Career: Farmer; lawyer
Political career: U.S. House of Representatives; governor of Ohio; president
Party: Republican
Home state: Ohio
Opponent in presidential race: Samuel J. Tilden
Term of office: March 4, 1877–March 3, 1881
Vice president: William Almon Wheeler
Notable events of presidency: railroad strikes of 1877; civil service reform, specie payments resumption; Bland-Allison Silver Purchase Act; Permanent Exhibition, Philadelphia; end of War with Idaho Indians
Other achievements: Admitted to the Ohio bar
Place of burial: Fremont, Ohio

Hayes |hāz|, Woody (1913–87) U.S. football coach. Full name *Wayne Woodrow Hayes*. He coached at Ohio State University (1951–78), where he won 13 Big Ten Championships and four Rose Bowl victories.

Hay·ward |'hāwərd|, Susan (1919–75) U.S. actress. Born *Edythe Marrener*. Notable movies: *I Want to Live* (1958, Academy Award).

Hay·worth |'hāwərTH|, Rita (1918–87) U.S. actress and dancer; born *Margarita Carmen Cansino*. She achieved stardom in movie musicals such as *Cover Girl* (1944) before going on to play roles in *film noir*, notably in *Gilda* (1946) and *The Lady from Shanghai* (1948).

Ha·zel·tine |'hāzəl,tin|, Louis Alan (1886–1964) U.S. electrical engineer. He invented the neutrodyne circuit, which suppressed the noise inherent in radio receivers and made commercial broadcasting possible.

Ha·zen |'hāzən|, Elizabeth Lee (1885–1975) U.S. microbiologist. With Rachel Brown, she developed Nystatin, the first nontoxic antifungal antibiotic.

Haz·litt |'hæzlət|, William (1778–1830) English essayist and critic. His diverse essays, collected in *Table Talk* (1821), were marked by a clarity and conviction that brought new vigor to English prose writing.

Haz·zard |'hæzərd|, Shirley (1931–) Australian author and diplomat. Notable works: *The Bay of Noon* (1970) and *Countenance of Truth* (1990).

H. D. see DOOLITTLE.

Head |hed|, Edith (1907–81) U.S. costume designer. She worked on a wide range of movies, winning Oscars for costume design in *All About Eve* (1950) and *The Sting* (1973).

Hea·ney |'hēnē|, Seamus (Justin) (1939–) Irish poet. Born in Northern Ireland, in 1972 he took Irish citizenship. Notable works: *North* (1975) and *The Haw Lantern* (1987). Nobel Prize for Literature (1995).

Hearst |hərst| U.S. family, including: **George Hearst** (1820–91), a mining magnate. He had holdings in Nevada, Utah, Montana, South Dakota, and Mexico. He served as a member of the U.S. Senate from California (1886–91). His son, **William Randolph Hearst** (1863–1951), was a newspaper publisher and tycoon. His introduction of features such as large headlines and sensational crime reporting revolutionized American journalism. He was the model for the central character of Orson Welles's movie *Citizen Kane* (1941). William Randolph Hearst's granddaughter, heiress **Patricia Campbell Hearst** (1954–), was kidnapped by the Symbionese Liberation Army (1974), found by FBI agents (1975), and convicted of bank robbery (1976). She was known as **Patty**.

Heath |hēTH|, Sir Edward (Richard George) (1919–) British Conservative statesman, prime minister (1970–74). He negotiated Britain's entry into the European Economic Community and faced problems caused by a marked increase in oil prices. Attempts to restrain wage rises led to widespread strikes, and he lost a general election after a second national coal strike.

Heat-Moon |'hētmōon|, William Least (1939–) U.S. author. Also known as **William Trogdon**. His books include *Blue Highways* (1982).

Heav·i·side |'hevē,sīd|, Oliver (1850–1925) English physicist and electrical engineer, important in the development of telephone communication and telegraphy. In 1902 he suggested (independently of A. E. Kennelly) the existence of a layer in the atmosphere responsible for reflecting radio waves back to earth.

Hecht |hekt|, Anthony Evan (1923–) U.S. poet. His books of verse include *The Hard Hours* (1967, Pulitzer Prize).

Hecht |hekt|, Ben (1894–1964) U.S. author and dramatist. With Charles MacArthur, he wrote *The Front Page* (1928).

Heck·er |'hekər|, Isaac Thomas (1819–88) U.S. clergyman. He founded the Congregation of the Missionary Priests of St. Paul the Apostle ("Paulists") and served as its first superior (1858–88).

Heck·e·wel·der |'hekə,weldər|, John Gottlieb Ernestus (1743–1823) U.S. missionary and author, born in England. A Moravian missionary to Indians of the Susquehanna Valley, he wrote *Account of the History, Manners, and Customs of the Indian Nationals Who Once Inhabited Pennsylvania* (1819).

Hedge |hej|, Frederic Henry (1805–90) U.S. clergyman and author. Notable works: *Prose Writers of Germany* (1848) and *Martin Luther and Other Essays* (1888).

He·din |he'dēn|, Sven Anders (1865–1952) Swedish explorer and geographer. Notable books: *Mount Everest* (1922) and *The Silk Road* (1938).

Hef·lin |'heflən|, Van (1910–71) U.S. actor. Notable movies: *Johnny Eager* (1942, Academy Award).

Hef·ner |'hefnər|, Hugh (1926–) U.S. publisher. He was the founder of *Playboy Magazine* (1953) and Playboy Clubs International, Inc. (1959).

He·gel |'hāgəl|, Georg Wilhelm Friedrich (1770–1831) German

philosopher. In his *Science of Logic* (1812–16) Hegel described the three-stage process of dialectical reasoning, on which Marx based his theory of dialectical materialism. He believed that history, the evolution of ideas, and human consciousness all develop through idealist dialectical processes as part of the Absolute or God coming to know itself.

Hei·deg·ger |'hīdəgər|, Martin (1889–1976) German philosopher. In *Being and Time* (1927) he examined the ontology of being, in particular human existence as involvement with a world of objects (*Dasein*). His writings on *Angst* (dread) as a fundamental part of human consciousness due to radical freedom of choice and awareness of death had a strong influence on existentialist philosophers such as Sartre.

Hei·fetz |'hīfəts|, Jascha (1901–87) U.S. violinist, born in Lithuania. Recognized as a musical prodigy at age three, he made his U.S. debut at Carnegie Hall in 1917 and went on to become the most celebrated violinist of the century.

Hei·ne |'hīnə|, (Christian Johann) Heinrich (1797–1856) German poet; born *Harry Heine*. Much of his early lyric poetry was set to music by Schumann and Schubert. In 1830 Heine emigrated to Paris, where his works became more political.

Hein·lein |'hīn,līn|, Robert Anson (1907–88) U.S. author. Notable works of science fiction: *Stranger in a Strange Land* (1961) and *I Will Fear No Evil* (1970). His pseudonyms include Anson MacDonald, Lyle Monroe, John Riverside, Caleb Saunders, and Simon York.

Heinz |hīn(t)s|, Henry John (1844–1919) U.S. food manufacturer. In 1869 he established a family firm for the manufacture and sale of processed foods. Heinz devised the marketing slogan "57 Varieties" in 1896 and erected New York's first electric sign to promote his company's pickles in 1900.

Hei·sen·berg |'hīzən,bərg|, Werner Karl (1901–76) German mathematical physicist and philosopher. He developed a system of quantum mechanics based on matrix algebra in which he stated his famous uncertainty principle

(1927). For this and his discovery of the allotropic forms of hydrogen he was awarded the 1932 Nobel Prize for Physics.

Held |held|, John, Jr. (1889–1958) U.S. cartoonist, illustrator and artist. He visually defined Jazz Age with the images of flappers and flaming youths.

Hel·e·na |'helənə|, St. (c. 248–c. 328 AD) Roman empress and mother of Constantine the Great. In 326 she visited the Holy Land and founded basilicas on the Mount of Olives and at Bethlehem. She is credited with the finding of the cross on which Christ was crucified. Feast day (in Eastern Church) May 21; (in Western Church) August 18.

He·lio·gab·a·lus |ˌhēlēə'gæbələs| (AD 204–22) Roman emperor (218–22). Also **Elagabalus**. Born *Varius Avitus Bassianus*. He took his name from the Syro-Phoenician sun god Elah-Gabal, of whom he was a hereditary priest. He became notorious for his dissipated lifestyle and neglect of state affairs; he and his mother were both murdered.

Hel·ler |'helər|, Joseph (1923–) U.S. novelist. His experiences in the U.S. Army Air Forces during World War II inspired his best-known novel *Catch-22* (1961), an absurdist black comedy satirizing war, the source of the expression "catch-22."

Hell·man |'helmən|, Lillian (Florence) (1905–84) U.S. dramatist. Her plays, such as *The Children's Hour* (1934) and *The Little Foxes* (1939), often reflected her socialist and feminist concerns. She lived with the detective-story writer Dashiell Hammett, and both were blacklisted during the McCarthy era.

Helm·holtz |'helm,hōlts|, Hermann Ludwig Ferdinand von (1821–94) German physiologist and physicist. He formulated the principle of the conservation of energy in 1847. Other achievements include his studies in sense perception, hydrodynamics, and non-Euclidean geometry.

Hel·mont |'helmänt|, Jan Baptista van (1579–1644) Belgian chemist and physician. He made early studies on the conservation of matter, was the first to distinguish gases, and coined the word *gas*.

Helms |helmz|, Jesse (1921–) U.S. senator from North Carolina (1973–).

Helms·ley |'helmzlē| U.S. business family, including **Harry B. Helmsley** (1909–97) and his wife **Leona Helmsley**. They built a real estate empire, Helmsley-Spear, Inc., but he was eventually convicted of tax evasion. She was president of Helmsley Hotels, Inc. (1980–) and also served time in prison for tax evasion.

Hé·lo·ïse |'elə,wēz| (c. 1098–1164) French abbess. She is known for her tragic love affair with the theologian Abelard, which began after she became his pupil. When the affair came to light, Abelard persuaded her to enter a convent; she later became abbess of the community of Paraclete. See also ABELARD.

Help·mann |'helpmən|, Sir Robert (Murray) (1909–86) Australian ballet dancer, choreographer, director, and actor. He joined the Vic-Wells Ballet shortly after coming to England in 1933, and in 1935 began a long partnership with Margot Fonteyn.

Hel·prin |'helprən|, Mark (1947–) U.S. author. Notable works: *Winter's Tale* (1983).

Hem·ings |'heminGz|, Sally (1773–1835) U.S. slave. A slave at Thomas Jefferson's estate, Monticello, she was reported to be his mistress in the *Richmond Recorder* (1802).

Hem·ing·way |'heminGgwā|, Ernest (Miller) (1899–1961) U.S. novelist, short-story writer, and journalist. He achieved success with *The Sun Also Rises* (1926), which reflected the disillusionment of the postwar "lost generation." Other notable works: *A Farewell to Arms* (1929), *For Whom the Bell Tolls* (1940), and *The Old Man and the Sea* (1952, Pulitzer Prize 1953). Nobel Prize for Literature (1954).

Hen·der·son |'hendərsən|, (James) Fletcher (1898–1952) U.S. jazz pianist, bandleader, and arranger. He was a big band leader during the swing era.

Hen·der·son |'hendərsən|, Richard (1735–85) U.S. colonizer. He sent Daniel Boone to explore beyond the Cumberland Gap (1769), and he helped to settle colonies in Kentucky and in Nashville, Tennessee.

Hen·der·son |'hendərsən|, Rickey (1958–) U.S. baseball player. He set a major league record by stealing 130 bases in one season (1982).

Hen·drick |'hendrik|, Burton Jesse (1870–1949) U.S. journalist and historian. Pulitzer Prize–winning works: *The Victory at Sea* (1920, written with Admiral William S. Sims), *The Life and Letters of Walter Hines Page* (1922), and *The Training of an American: The Earlier Life and Letters of Walter Hines Page* (1928).

Hen·dricks |'hendriks|, Thomas Andrews (1819–85) U.S. vice president (1885).

Hen·drix |'hendriks|, Jimi (1942–70) U.S. rock musician; full name *James Marshall Hendrix*. Remembered for the flamboyance and originality of his improvisations, he greatly widened the scope of the electric guitar. Notable songs: "Purple Haze" (1967), and "All Along the Watchtower" (1968).

Hen·gist and Horsa |'heNGgəst ænd 'hawrsə| (died 488) semimythological Jutish leaders. According to Bede, the brothers were invited to Britain by the British king Vortigern in 449 to assist in defeating the Picts and later established an independent Anglo-Saxon kingdom in Kent.

Hen·ie |'henē|, Sonja (1912–69) Norwegian figure skater. She won ten consecutive world championships (1927–36) and three Olympic gold medals (1928, 1932, 1936).

Hen·ley |'henlē|, Beth (1952–) U.S. playwright. She won a Pulitzer Prize for *Crimes of the Heart* (1979).

Hen·ne·pin |'henəpən|, Louis (1640–c. 1701) French missionary, explorer, and author. He accompanied La Salle through the Great Lakes.

Hen·ri |'henrē|, Robert (1865–1929) U.S. painter. An advocate of realism, he believed that the artist must be a social force. The Ashcan School was formed largely as a result of his influence.

Hen·ri·et·ta |ˌhenrē'etə|, Maria (1609–69) daughter of Henry IV of France, queen consort of Charles I of England (1625–49). Her Roman Catholicism heightened public anxieties about the court's religious sympathies and was a contributory cause of the English Civil War.

Hen·ry[1] |'henrē| (1068–1135) the name of eight kings of England: **Henry I** (1068–1135; reigned 1100–35). King of England, youngest son of William I. His only son drowned in 1120, and although Henry extracted an oath of loyalty to his daughter Matilda from the barons in 1127, his death was followed almost immediately by the outbreak of civil war. **Henry II** (1133–89; reigned 1154–89); the son of Matilda. The first Plantagenet king, he restored order after the reigns of Stephen and Matilda. Opposition to his policies on reducing the power of the Church was led by Thomas à Becket, who was eventually murdered by four of Henry's knights. **Henry III** (1207–72; reigned 1216–72), the son of John. King of England. His ineffectual government caused widespread discontent, ending in Simon de Montfort's defeat and capture of Henry in 1264. Although he was restored a year later, real power resided with his son, who eventually succeeded him as Edward I. **Henry IV** (1366–1413; reigned 1399–1413), son of John of Gaunt. King of England; known as **Henry Bolingbroke**. He overthrew Richard II, establishing the Lancastrian dynasty. His reign was marked by rebellion in Wales and the north, where the Percy family raised several uprisings. **Henry V** (1387–1422; reigned 1413–22). King of England, son of Henry IV. He renewed the Hundred Years War soon after coming to the throne and defeated the French at Agincourt in 1415. **Henry VI** (1421–71; reigned 1422–61 and 1470–71), son of Henry V. King of England. He was unfit to rule effectively on his own due to a recurrent mental illness. Government by the monarchy became increasingly unpopular and after intermittent civil war with the House of York (the Wars of the Roses), Henry was deposed in 1461 by Edward IV. He briefly regained his throne following a Lancastrian uprising. **Henry VI** (1457–1509; reigned 1485–1509), the son of Ednund Tudor, Earl of Richmond. The first Tudor king; known as **Henry Tudor**. Although the grandson of

Owen Tudor, he inherited the Lancastrian claim to the throne through his mother, a great-granddaughter of John of Gaunt. He defeated Richard III at Bosworth Field and eventually established an unchallenged Tudor dynasty. **Henry VIII** (1491–1547; reigned 1509–47), son of Henry VII. King of England. Henry had six wives (Catherine of Aragon, Anne Boleyn, Jane Seymour, Anne of Cleves, Catherine Howard, Katherine Parr); he executed two and divorced two. His first divorce, from Catherine of Aragon, was opposed by the Pope, leading to England's break with the Roman Catholic Church.
Hen·ry[2] |'henrē| (1394–1460) Portuguese prince; known as **Henry the Navigator**. The third son of John I of Portugal, he organized many voyages of discovery, most notably south along the African coast, thus laying the foundation for Portuguese imperial expansion around Africa to the Far East.
Hen·ry[3] |'henrē| the name of seven kings of the Germans, six of whom were also Holy Roman emperors: **Henry I** (c. 876–936; reigned 919–936). King of the Germans; known as **Henry the Fowler**. He waged war successfully against the Slavs in Brandenburg, the Magyars, and the Danes. **Henry II** (973–1024; reigned 1002–24). King of the Germans. Holy Roman emperor (1014–24); also known as **Saint Henry. Henry III** (1017–56; reigned 1039–56). King of the Germans. Holy Roman emperor (1046–56). He brought stability and prosperity to the empire, defeating the Czechs and fixing the frontier between Austria and Hungary. **Henry IV** (1050–1106; reigned 1056–1105), son of Henry III. King of the Germans. Holy Roman emperor (1084–1105). Increasing conflict with Pope Gregory VII led Henry to call a council in 1076 to depose the Pope, who excommunicated Henry. Henry obtained absolution by doing penance before Gregory in 1077 but managed to depose him in 1084. **Henry V** (1081–1125; reigned 1099–1125). King of the Germans. Holy Roman emperor (1111–25). **Henry VI** (1165–97; reigned 1069–97). King of the Germans. Holy Roman emperor (1191–97). **Henry VII** (c.

1275–1313; reigned 1308–13). King of the Germans. Holy Roman emperor (1312–13).
Hen·ry IV |'henrē| (1553–1610) king of France 1589–1610; known as **Henry of Navarre**. Although leader of Huguenot forces in the latter stages of the French Wars of Religion, on succeeding the Catholic Henry III he became Catholic himself in order to guarantee peace. He established religious freedom with the Edict of Nantes (1598) and restored order after the prolonged civil war.
Hen·ry |'henrē|, Joseph (1797–1878) U.S. physicist and educator. His electrical inventions include the first electromagnetic motor (1829). He was the first secretary and director of the Smithsonian Institution (1846–77). The "henry" unit of inductance is named after him.
Hen·ry |'henrē|, Marguerite (1902–   ) U.S. author of children's books. Notable works: *Misty of Chincoteague* (1947, Newbery Award).
Hen·ry |'henrē|, O (1862–1910) U.S. short-story writer; pseudonym of *William Sydney Porter*. Jailed for embezzlement in 1898, he started writing short stories in prison. Collections include *Cabbages and Kings* (1904) and *The Voice of the City* (1908).
Hen·ry |'henrē|, Patrick (1736–99) American revolutionary. As a member of the Continental Congress (1774–76), he was a noted orator. He is best remembered for an impassioned speech in which he stated, "Give me liberty, or give me death."
Henry Bolingbroke |'bawliNG,brŏŏk| Henry IV of England (see HENRY[1]).
Henry the Fowler Henry I, king of the Germans (see HENRY[3]).
Henry Tudor Henry VII of England (see HENRY[1]).
Hen·son |'hensən|, Jim (1936&en90) U.S. puppeteer. Full name *James Maury Henson*. He created the Muppets, the most commercially successful puppets in history. Since gaining fame as principal characters on television's "Sesame Street" (1969–   ), the Muppets have been featured in numerous television shows and movies.
Hen·son |'hensən|, Josiah (1789–1883) U.S. slave and clergyman. A Methodist

preacher, he escaped from Maryland to Canada (1830). His autobiography, *The Life of Josiah Henson* (1849) includes an introduction by Harriet Beecher Stowe.

Hen·son |'hensən|, Matthew Alexander (1866–1955) U.S. explorer. He accompanied Peary on his 1908 expedition to the North Pole.

Hep·burn |'hepbərn|, Audrey (1929–93) British actress, born in Belgium. After pursuing a career as a stage and movie actress in England, she moved to Hollywood, where she starred in such movies as *Roman Holiday* (1953), for which she won an Oscar, and *My Fair Lady* (1964).

Hep·burn |'hepbərn|, Katharine (1907–) U.S. actress. She starred in a wide range of movies, often opposite Spencer Tracy; movies include *Woman of the Year* (1942), *The African Queen* (1951), and *On Golden Pond* (1981), for which she won her fourth Oscar.

Hep·ple·white |'hepəl,(h)wīt|, George (died1786) English cabinetmaker and furniture designer. The posthumously published book of his designs, *The Cabinetmaker and Upholsterer's Guide* (1788), contains almost 300 designs, characterized by light and elegant lines, which sum up neoclassical taste.

Hep·worth |'hep,wərTH|, Dame (Jocelyn) Barbara (1903–75) English sculptor. A pioneer of abstraction in British sculpture, she worked in wood, stone, and bronze and is noted for her simple monumental works in landscape and architectural settings, including *The Family of Man* (nine-piece group, 1972).

Her·a·cli·tus |,herə'klītəs| (*c.* 540–480 BC) Greek philosopher. He believed that fire is the origin of all things and that permanence is an illusion, everything being in a (harmonious) process of constant change.

Her·bert |'hərbərt|, Sir A. P. (1890–1970) English writer and politician Full name *Alan Patrick Herbert*. He wrote novels, items for the magazine *Punch*, and libretti for comic operas.

Her·bert |'hərbərt|, George (1593–1633) English metaphysical poet. He was vicar of Bemerton, near Salisbury; his poems are pervaded by simple piety and reflect the spiritual conflicts he ex-

perienced before submitting his will to God.

Her·bert |'hərbərt|, Victor (1859–1924) U.S. cellist, conductor, and composer, born in Ireland. Notable operettas: *Babes in Toyland* (1903) and *Naughty Marietta* (1910).

Herbst |hərbst|, Josephine Frey (1892–1969) U.S. author and journalist. Her novel *Pity Is Not Enough* (1933) was the first in a popular trilogy based on her family's history from the Civil War to the Depression.

Her·e·ward the Wake |'herəwərd THə 'wāk| (11th cent) semilegendary Anglo-Saxon rebel leader. A leader of Anglo-Saxon resistance to William I's new Norman regime, he is thought to have been responsible for an uprising centered on the Isle of Ely in 1070.

Her·man |'hərmən|, Woody (1913–87) U.S. jazz clarinetist, saxophonist, and bandleader. Full name *Woodrow Charles Herman*; known as "the Boy Wonder of the Clarinet." The *Ebony Concerto*, written for him by Stravinsky, was performed at Carnegie Hall (1946).

He·ro |'hērō| (1st century) Greek mathematician and inventor; known as **Hero of Alexandria**. His surviving works are important as a source for ancient practical mathematics and mechanics. He described a number of hydraulic, pneumatic, and other mechanical devices, including elementary applications of the power of steam.

Her·od |'herəd| (*c.* 73–4 BC) ruler of ancient Palestine (37–34 BC). Known as **Herod the Great**. He built the palace of Masada and rebuilt the Temple in Jerusalem. According to the New Testament, the birth of Jesus during his reign led Herod to order the massacre of the innocents (Matt. 2:16).

Her·od Agrip·pa |'herəd ə'gripə| the name of two rulers of ancient Palestine: **Herod Agrippa I** (10 BC–AD 44; reigned AD 41–44), grandson of Herod the Great. King of Judaea. He imprisoned St. Peter and put St. James the Great to death. His son, **Herod Agrippa II** (*c.* AD 27–*c.* 93; reigned 50–*c.*93). He was king of various territories in northern Palestine. He presided over the trial of St. Paul (Acts 25:13).

Her·od An·ti·pas |'herəd 'äntəpəs| (21 BC–39 AD) ruler of ancient Palestine, son of Herod the Great, tetrarch of Galilee and Peraea 4 BC–AD 40. He married Herodias and was responsible for the beheading of John the Baptist. According to the New Testament (Luke 23:7), Pilate sent Jesus to be questioned by him before the Crucifixion.

He·rod·o·tus |he'rädətəs| (5th century BC) Greek historian. His *History* tells of the Persian Wars of the early 5th century BC. He was the first historian to collect his materials systematically, test their accuracy to a certain extent, and arrange them in a well-constructed and vivid narrative.

He·roph·i·lus |hə'räfələs| (*c.* 335–*c.* 280 BC) Greek anatomist. He is regarded as the father of human anatomy for his fundamental discoveries concerning the anatomy of the brain, eye, and reproductive organs. Herophilus also studied the physiology of nerves, arteries, and veins.

Herr |her|, Herbert Thacker (1876–1933) U.S. engineer. He invented locomotive air-brake equipment and made improvements to turbine, oil, and gas engines.

Her·res·hoff |'herəs,hawf| U.S. family, including **James Brown Herreshoff** (1834–1930), an inventor. He invented a sliding seat for rowboats and improved marine steam boilers. His brother, **Nathanel Greene Herreshoff** (1848–1938), was a yacht manufacturer. He designed many America's Cup defenders, including *Vigilant* (1892) and *Defender* (1895); he also built the first seagoing torpedo boat for the U.S. Navy.

Her·rick |'herik|, Robert (1591–1674) English cavalier poet. He is best known for his collection *Hesperides* (1648), containing both secular and religious poems.

Her·rick |'herik|, Robert Welch (1868–1938) U.S. author and educator. Notable novels: *The Gospel of Freedom* (1898), *The Common Lot* (1904), and *Sometime* (1933).

Her·ri·man |'herəmən|, George Joseph (1880–1944) U.S. cartoonist and illustrator. He created the "Krazy Kat" comic strip and illustrated the "Archy and Mehitabel" books.

Her·ri·ot |'hereət|, James (1916–95) English short-story writer and veterinary surgeon; pseudonym of *James Alfred Wight*. His experiences as a veterinarian in North Yorkshire inspired a series of stories (the basis for a television series), including *All Creatures Great and Small* (1972).

Her·schel |'hərSHəl|, Sir (Frederick) William (1738–1822) German-born British astronomer. His cataloging of the skies resulted in the discovery of the planet Uranus. He was the first to appreciate the great remoteness of stars and developed the idea that the sun belongs to the star system of the Milky Way.

Her·schel |'hərSHəl|, Sir John (Frederick William) (1792–1871) English astronomer and physicist, son of William. He extended the sky survey to the southern hemisphere, carried out pioneering work in photography, and made contributions to meteorology and geophysics.

Her·sey |'hərsē|, John Richard (1914–93) U.S. author. Notable works: *A Bell for Adano* (1944, Pulitzer Prize) and *Hiroshima* (1946).

Her·shey |'hərsHē|, Alfred D. (1908–97) U.S. biologist. He conducted genetic research with Max Delbrück and Salvador Luria and discovered the recombination of viral DNA (1946). Nobel Prize for Physiology or Medicine, 1969.

Her·shey |'hərsHē|, Milton Snavely (1857–1945) U.S. industrialist. He established the Hershey chocolate company (1903).

Hertz |hərts|, Heinrich Rudolf (1857–94) German physicist and pioneer of radio communication. He continued the work of Maxwell on electromagnetic waves and was the first to broadcast and receive radio waves. Hertz also showed that light and radiant heat were electromagnetic in nature.

Herzl |'hərtsəl|, Theodor (1860–1904) Hungarian-born journalist, dramatist, and Zionist leader. The founder of the Zionist movement (1897), he worked for most of his life as a writer and journalist in Vienna.

Her·zog |'hərtsawg|, Werner (1942–) German movie director; born *Werner Stipetic*. Themes of remoteness in time and space are dominant elements throughout his movies, which include *Aguirre, Wrath of God* (1972) and *Fitzcarraldo* (1982).

He·si·od |'hesēəd| (*c.* 800 BC) Greek poet. One of the earliest known Greek poets, he wrote the *Theogony*, an epic poem on the genealogies of the gods, and *Works and Days*, which gave moral and practical advice and was the chief model for later ancient didactic poetry.

Hess |hes|, Harry Hammond (1906–69) U.S. geophysicist and educator. He made numerous discoveries regarding Pacific seamounts, island arcs, and sea-floor spreading. He was chosen by NASA to be one of the first scientists to examine lunar rocks.

Hess |hes|, Dame Myra (1890–1965) English pianist. She was noted for her performances of the music of Schumann, Beethoven, Mozart, and Bach.

Hess |hes|, Rudolf (1894–1987) German Nazi politician, deputy leader of the Nazi Party (1934–41). Full name *Walther Richard Rudolf Hess*. In 1941, secretly and on his own initiative, he parachuted into Scotland to negotiate peace with Britain. He was imprisoned for the duration of the war and, at the Nuremberg war trials, sentenced to life imprisonment in Spandau prison, Berlin, where he died.

Hess |hes|, Victor Franz (1883–1964) Austrian-born U.S. physicist; born *Victor Franz Hess*. He showed that some ionizing radiation (later termed cosmic rays) was extraterrestrial in origin but did not come from the sun. Nobel Prize for Physics (1936), shared with C. D. Anderson.

Hes·se |'hesə|, Hermann (1877–1962) German-born Swiss novelist and poet. His work reflects his interest in spiritual values as expressed in Eastern religion and his involvement in Jungian analysis. Notable works: *Siddhartha* (1922), *Der Steppenwolf* (1927), and *The Glass Bead Game* (1943). Nobel Prize for Literature (1946).

Hes·ton |'hestən|, Charlton (1924–) U.S. actor. Notable movies: *Ben-Hur* (1959, Academy Award).

He·ve·sy |'hevəsĥē|, George Charles de (1885–1966) Hungarian-born radio-

chemist. He studied radioisotopes and invented the technique of labeling with isotopic tracers. Hevesy was also co-discoverer of the element hafnium (1923). Nobel Prize for Chemistry (1943).

Hew·itt |'hyo͞oət|, Abram Stevens (1822–1903) U.S. industrialist and politican. His iron manufacturing business featured the first open-hearth furnace (1862) in the U.S. and made the nation's first steel (1870). He served in the U.S. House of Representatives (1875–79, 1881–86) and as mayor of New York (1887–88).

Hew·itt |'hyo͞oət|, Don (1922–) U.S. television producer. He created and produced news programs and special events, including "60 minutes," the Kennedy-Nixon debates, and rocket launchings at Cape Canaveral.

Hew·lett |'hyo͞olət|, William R. (1913–) U.S. electrical engineer, inventor, and businessman. He invented an audio oscillator and cofounded the Hewlett-Packard Co. (1939).

Hey·er |'hīər|, Georgette (1902–74) English novelist. She is noted especially for her historical novels, which include numerous Regency romances such as *Regency Buck* (1935).

Hey·er·dahl |'hīər,däl|, Thor (1914–) Norwegian anthropologist. He is noted for his ocean voyages in primitive craft to demonstrate his theories of cultural diffusion, the best known of which was that of the balsa raft *Kon-Tiki* from Peru to the islands east of Tahiti in 1947.

Hey·ward |'hāwərd|, (Edwin) DuBose (1885–1940) U.S. author and poet. Full name *Edwin DuBose Heyward*. His first novel, *Porgy* (1925), dramatized with wife Dorothy, won a Pulitzer Prize and was made into the Gershwin opera *Porgy and Bess* (1935).

Hi·a·wa·tha |,hīə'wäTHə| (*fl. c.* 1570) Mohawk Indian chief. Possibly a leader of mere legend, he is credited with establishing an Iroquois confederacy comprised of Onondaga, Mohawk, Oneida, Cayuga, and Seneca tribes. His name is said to mean "He Makes Rivers."

Hick·ok |'hikäk|, James Butler (1837–76) U.S. frontiersman and marshal; known as **Wild Bill Hickok**. The legend of his invincibility in his encounters with frontier desperadoes became something of a challenge to gunmen, and he was eventually murdered at Deadwood, South Dakota.

Hicks |'hiks|, Edward (1780–1849) U.S. artist. A primitive folk painter, he is noted for his *The Peaceable Kingdom* series of paintings.

Hicks |'hiks|, Sir John Richard (1904–89) English economist. He did pioneering work on general economic equilibrium (the theory that economic forces tend to balance one another rather than simply reflect cyclical trends), for which he shared a Nobel Prize with K. J. Arrow in 1972.

Hig·gin·both·am |'higən,bäTHəm|, A. Leon, Jr. (1928–   ) U.S. jurist. He became head of the U.S. Commission on Civil Rights in 1995. Awarded Spingarn Medal (1996).

Hig·gins |'higənz|, George Vincent (1939–   ) U.S. author. Notable novels *Friends of Eddie Coyle* (1971) and *Wonderful Years, Wonderful Years* (1988).

Hig·gin·son |'hēgənsən|, Thomas Wentworth Storrow (1823–1911) U.S. clergyman, journalist, and author. He was an activist for abolition and woman suffrage. He was also known for the correspondence he maintained with Emily Dickinson until her death (1886).

High·smith |'hīsmiTH|, Patricia (1921–95) U.S. writer of detective fiction; born *Patricia Plangman*. Her novels are noted for their black humor, particularly those featuring Tom Ripley, an amoral antihero resident in France. Her *Strangers on a Train* (1949) was filmed by Alfred Hitchcock in 1951.

Hi·jue·los |ē'hwelōs|, Oscar (1951–   ) U.S. author. His novels include *The Mambo Kings Play Songs of Love* (1989, Pulitzer Prize).

Hil·a·ry |'hilərē|, St. (*c.* 315–*c.* 367) French bishop. In *c.*350 he was appointed bishop of Poitiers, in which position he became a leading opponent of Arianism. Feast day, January 13.

Hil·da |'hildə|, St. (614–80) English abbess. Related to the Anglo-Saxon kings of Northumbria, she founded a monastery for both men and women at Whitby around 658, and was one of the

leaders of the Celtic Church delegation at the Synod of Whitby. Feast day, November 17.

Hil·de·gard von Bing·en |'hildəgärd vawn 'biNGən|, St. (1098–1179) German abbess, scholar, composer, and mystic. A nun of the Benedictine order, she wrote scientific works, poetry, and music, and described her mystical experiences in *Scivias*.

Hil·dreth |'hildreTH|, Richard (1807–65) U.S. historian, author, and jurist. His works include the six-volume *A History of the United States* (1849–52).

Hil·fi·ger |'hil,figər|, Tommy (1952–   ) U.S. fashion designer

Hill |hil|, Anita (1956–   ) U.S. educator and author. Her book *Speaking Truth to Power* (1977), is based on her testimony of sexual harassment against Clarence Thomas during his Supreme Court nomination hearings (1991).

Hill |hil|, Benny (1925–92) English comedian; born *Alfred Hawthorne*. His risqué humor, as seen in the television series "The Benny Hill Show," had an international appeal.

Hill |hil|, George Roy (1922–   ) U.S. movie director. Notable movies: *The Sting* (1973, Academy Award).

Hill |hil|, (Norman) Graham (1929–75) English racecar driver. He became Formula One world champion in 1962 and 1975.

Hill |hil|, James Jerome (1838–1916) U.S. railroad executive, born in Canada.

Hill |hil|, Octavia (1838–1912) English housing reformer and cofounder of Britain's National Trust (1895).

Hill |hil|, Patty Smith (1868–1946) U.S. educator. She was an advocate in the nursery school movement.

Hill |hil|, Sir Rowland (1795–1879) English educationist, administrator, and inventor. He is chiefly remembered for his introduction of the penny postagestamp system in 1840.

Hil·la·ry |'hilərē|, Sir Edmund (Percival) (1919–   ) New Zealand mountaineer and explorer. In 1953 Hillary and Tenzing Norgay were the first people to reach the summit of Mount Everest, as members of a British expedition.

Hil·lier |'hilyər|, James (1915–   ) U.S.

researcher and technology management executive. He co-invented and developed the first electron microscope in North America (1937).

Hill·man |'hilmən|, Sidney (1887–1946) U.S. labor leader, born in Lithuania. He helped to organize the Congress of Industrial Organizations (1935).

Hill·yer |'hilyər|, Robert Silliman (1895–1961) U.S. poet and educator. His *Collected Verse* (1933) won a Pulitzer Prize.

Hil·ton |'hiltən|, Conrad Nicholson (1887–1979) U.S. businessman. He formed the Hilton Hotels Corp. (1946).

Hil·ton |'hiltən|, James (1900–54) English author. Notable novels: *Lost Horizon* (1933), *Goodbye, Mr. Chips* (1934), and *Random Harvest* (1941).

Himes |hīmz|, Chester Bomar (1909–84) U.S. author. His books include a series of crime novels (1957–80) that feature the detective "Grave Digger" Johnson.

Himm·ler |'himlər|, Heinrich (1900–45) German Nazi leader, chief of the SS (1929–45) and of the Gestapo (1936–45). He established and oversaw the systematic genocide of over 6 million Jews and other disfavored groups between 1941 and 1945. Captured by British forces in 1945, he committed suicide.

Hi·nault |ē'nō|, Bernard (1954–) French racing cyclist. He won the Tour de France five times between 1978 and 1985 and won the Tour of Italy three times between 1980 and 1985.

Hin·de·mith |'hində,miTH|, Paul (1895–1963) German composer. A leading figure in the neoclassical trend which began in the 1920s and an exponent of *Gebrauchsmusik* ("utility music"), he believed that music should have a social purpose. Notable works: *Mathis der Maler* (opera, 1938).

Hin·den·burg |'hindən,bərg|, Paul Ludwig von Beneckendorff und von (1847–1934) German field marshal and statesman, president of the Weimar Republic (1925–34). Elected president in 1925 and reelected in 1932, he reluctantly appointed Hitler as chancellor in 1933.

Hine |hīn|, Lewis Wickes (1874–1940) U.S. photographer.

Hines |hīnz|, Earl (Kenneth) (1905–83) U.S. jazz pianist and band leader. Known as **Fatha Hines**. He originated the "trumpet style" of piano playing.

Hines |hīnz|, Gregory (1946–) U.S. dancer and choreographer.

Hin·gis |'hiNGgəs|, Martina (1981–) U.S. tennis player.

Hin·shel·wood |'hinsHəl,wood|, Sir Cyril Norman (1897–1967) English physical chemist. He made fundamental contributions to reaction kinetics in gases and liquids. He later applied the laws of kinetics to bacterial growth, and suggested the role of nucleic acids in protein synthesis. Nobel Prize for Chemistry (1956).

Hin·ton |'hin(t)ən|, S. E. (Susan Eloise) (1948–) U.S. author. She is the author of young adult novels, including *That Was Then, This Is Now* (1971).

Hin·ton |'hin(t)ən|, William Augustus (1883–1959) U.S. physician. Noted for his development of tests for syphillis, he became the first black professor at Harvard Medical School (1949).

Hip·par·chus |hi'pärkəs| (c. 146–127 BC) Greek astronomer and geographer. He is best known for his discovery of the precession of the equinoxes and is credited with the invention of trigonometry.

Hip·poc·ra·tes |hi'päkrətēz| (c. 460–377 BC) Greek physician, traditionally regarded as the father of medicine. His name is associated with the medical profession's Hippocratic oath from his attachment to a body of ancient Greek medical writings, probably none of which was written by him.

Hi·ro·hi·to |'hirō'hitō| (1901–89) emperor of Japan (1926–89); full name *Michinomiya Hirohito*. Regarded as the 124th direct descendant of Jimmu, he refrained from involvement in politics, though he was instrumental in obtaining Japan's agreement to the unconditional surrender that ended World War II. In 1946 the new constitution imposed by the U.S. obliged him to renounce his divinity and become a constitutional monarch.

Hirsch·feld |'hərsHfeld|, Al (1903–) U.S. artist. He was a *New York Times* theater caricaturist (1925–); his murals and sculpture are represented in musuems nationally.

Hirsh·horn |'hərsHawrn|, Joseph Herman (1899–1981) U.S. financier and art collector, born in Latvia. He began as an office boy on Wall Street (1913) and built a fortune in mining and petroleum stocks; he built the Hirshhorn Museum in Washington, D.C. (1974) to house his art collection.

Hiss |his|, Alger (1904–96) U.S. public official. In 1948 he was accused of passing State Department documents to a Soviet agent. He pleaded innocent to these charges, but was later convicted of perjury in connection with the case, which became a political cause célèbre.

Hitch·cock |'hiCH,käk|, Sir Alfred (Joseph) (1899–1980) English movie director. Acclaimed in Britain for movies such as *The Thirty-Nine Steps* (1935), he moved to Hollywood in 1939. Among his later works, notable for their suspense and their technical ingenuity, are the thrillers *Strangers on a Train* (1951), *Psycho* (1960), and *The Birds* (1963).

Hitch·cock |'hiCH,käk|, Edward (1793–1864) U.S. geologist and educator. He performed a geological survey of Massachusetts (1830–33, 1837–41) and discovered dinosaur tracks in the Connecticut Valley; he also served as president of Amherst College (1845–54).

Hitch·ens |'hiCHənz|, Ivon (1893–1979) English painter. He is known chiefly for landscapes represented in an almost abstract style using areas of vibrant color.

Hit·ler |'hitlər|, Adolf (1889–1945) Austrian-born Nazi leader, chancellor of Germany (1933–45). He cofounded the National Socialist German Workers' (Nazi) Party in 1919, and came to prominence through his powers of oratory. While imprisoned for an unsuccessful putsch in Munich (1923–24) he wrote *Mein Kampf* (1925), an exposition of his political ideas. Becoming chancellor in 1933, he established the totalitarian Third Reich. His expansionist foreign policy precipitated World War II, while his fanatical anti-Semitism led to the Holocaust.

Hoag·land |'hōglənd|, Edward (1932–) U.S. author. His novels include *Seven Rivers West* (1986).

Ho·ban |'hōbən|, James (1762–1831) U.S. architect, born in Ireland. He designed the White House in Washington, D.C. (1793–1801) and its restoration and redesign after the War of 1812 (1815–29).

Ho·ban |'hōbən|, Russell Conwell (1925–) U.S. author and illustrator. His works include more than 50 children's books.

Ho·bart |'hōbərt; 'hōbärt|, Garret Augustus (1844–99) Vice president of the U.S. (1897–99).

Hob·be·ma |'häbəmə|, Meindert (*c.* 1638–1709) Dutch landscape painter. A pupil of Jacob van Ruisdael, he was one of the last 17th-century Dutch landscape painters.

Hobbes |häbz|, Thomas (1588–1679) English philosopher. Hobbes was a materialist, claiming that there was no more to the mind than the physical motions discovered by science, and he believed that human action was motivated entirely by selfish concerns, notably fear of death. In *Leviathan* (1651) he argued that absolute monarchy was the most rational, hence desirable, form of government.

Ho Chi Minh |'hō CHē ,min| (1890–1969) Vietnamese communist statesman, president of North Vietnam (1954–69); born *Nguyen That Thanh*. He led the Viet Minh against the Japanese during World War II, fought the French until they were defeated in 1954 and Vietnam was divided into North and South Vietnam, and deployed his forces in the guerrilla struggle that became the Vietnam War.

Hock·ing |'häkiNG|, William Ernest (1873–1966) U.S. educator and author. Notable books: *The Meaning of God in Human Experience* (1912) and *Science and the Idea of God* (1944).

Hock·ney |'häknē|, David (1937–) English painter and draftsman. He is best known for his association with pop art and for his Californian work of the mid-1960s, which depicts flat, almost shadowless architecture, lawns, and swimming pools.

Hodge |häj|, Frederick Webb (1864–1956) U.S. anthropologist and author. His books include the two-volume *Handbook of American Indians North of Mexico* (1907–10).

Hodg·es |'häjəz|, Johnny (1906–70) U.S. jazz alto saxophonist. Known as **Rabbit**. He was the mainstay of Duke Ellington's orchestra (1928–68), known for his earthy blues playing and ballad interpretation.

Hodg·kin |'häjkən|, Sir Alan Lloyd (1914–) English physiologist. With Andrew Huxley he demonstrated the role of sodium and potassium ions in the transmission of nerve impulses between cells. Nobel Prize for Physiology or Medicine (1963).

Hodg·kin |'häjkən|, Dorothy (Crowfoot) (1910–94) British chemist. She developed Sir Lawrence Bragg's X-ray diffraction technique for investigating the structure of crystals and applied it to complex organic compounds. Using this method she determined the structures of penicillin, vitamin B_{12}, and insulin. Nobel Prize for Chemistry (1964).

Hoe |hō|, Richard March (1812–86) U.S. inventor and industrialist. In 1846 he became the first printer to develop a successful rotary press, which greatly increased the speed of printing.

Hoff |hawf|, Marcian Edward, Jr. (1937–) U.S electronics engineer. His developments in computer technology include integrated circuits and the single-chip, general-purpose computer central processor.

Hof·fa |'hawfə|, Jimmy (1913–*c.* 75) U.S. labor union leader; full name *James Riddle Hoffa*. President of the Teamsters Union from 1957, he was imprisoned (1967–71) for attempted bribery of a federal court judge, fraud, and looting pension funds. His sentence was commuted by President Nixon and he was given parole in 1971 on condition that he resign as president of the union. He disappeared in 1975 and is thought to have been murdered.

Hoff·man |'hawfmən|, Dustin (Lee) (1937–) U.S. actor. A versatile method actor, he won Oscars for *Kramer vs Kramer* (1979) and *Rain Man* (1989).

Other notable movies: *The Graduate* (1967) and *Tootsie* (1983).

Hoff·man |'hawfmən|, Malvina (1887–1966) U.S. sculptor. He created bronzes of 110 racial types for the Field Museum in Chicago (1930–33).

Hoff·mann |'hawfmän|, E. T. A. (Ernst Theodor Amadeus) (1776–1822) German novelist, short-story writer, and music critic. His extravagantly fantastic stories provided the inspiration for Offenbach's opera *Tales of Hoffmann* (1881).

Hof·mann |'hawfmän|, Hans (1880–1966) U.S. artist, born in Germany. He was a leader in the style of abstract expressionism.

Hof·manns·thal |'hawfmän,stäl|, Hugo von (1874–1929) Austrian poet and dramatist. He wrote the libretti for many of the operas of Richard Strauss, including *Elektra* (1909). With Strauss and Max Reinhardt he helped found the Salzburg Festival.

Hof·stadt·er |'höf,stætər|, Richard (1916–70) U.S. historian and author. Pulitzer Prize–winning works: *The Age of Reform: From Bryan to F.D.R.* (1955) and *Anti-Intellectualism in American Life* (1963).

Ho·gan |'hōgən|, Ben (1912–97) U.S. golfer.

Ho·garth |'hōgärTH|, Burne (1911–96) U.S. cartoonist. He created and illustrated the comic strip "Tarzan."

Ho·garth |'hōgärTH|, William (1697–1764) English painter and engraver. Notable works include his series of engravings on "modern moral subjects," such as *A Rake's Progress* (1735), which satirized the vices of both high and low life in 18th-century England.

Hogg |hawg|, James (1770–1835) Scottish poet.

Ho·kin·son |'hōkənsən|, Helen (1893–1949) U.S. cartoonist and author. She was best known for satirizing clubwomen; her cartoon characters, the "Hokinson Girls," frequently appeared in the *New Yorker* magazine.

Ho·ku·sai |'hōkoo,sī|, Katsushika (1760–1849) Japanese painter and wood engraver. A leading artist of the *ukiyo-e* school, he represented aspects of Japanese everyday life in his woodcuts and strongly influenced European Impressionist artists.

Hol·a·bird |'häləbərd|, William (1854–1923) U.S. architect. With Martin Roche (1881), he began a firm that helped to develop the Chicago School of commercial architecture.

Hol·bein |'hōlbīn| German artists. **Hans Holbein** (c. 1465–1524); known as **Holbein the Elder**. His chiefly religious works include numerous cathedral altarpieces and such paintings as *Presentation of Christ* (1502) and *Fountain of Life* (1519). His son, **Hans Holbein** (c. 1497–1543), a painter and engraver, was known as **Holbein the Younger**. He became a well-known court portraitist in England and was commissioned by Henry VIII to supply portraits of the king's prospective brides. Notable works: *Dance of Death* (series of woodcuts, c. 1523–36); *Anne of Cleves* (miniature, 1539).

Hol·brook |'hōlbrŏŏk|, Hal (1925–) U.S. actor. A five-time Emmy winner, he is known for his stage portrayals of Mark Twain.

Hol·brook |'hōlbrŏŏk|, Josiah (1788–1854) U.S. educator.

Hol·den |'hōldən|, William (1918–81) U.S. actor. Born *William Beadle*. Notable movies: *Stalag 17* (1953, Academy Award).

Höl·der·lin |'hawldər,lēn; 'hœldər,lēn|, (Johann Christian) Friedrich (1770–1843) German poet. Most of his poems express a romantic yearning for harmony with nature and beauty. While working as a tutor he fell in love with his employer's wife, who is portrayed in his novel *Hyperion* (1797–99).

Hol·i·day |'hälədā|, Billie (1915–59) U.S. jazz singer; born *Eleanora Fagan*. She began her recording career with Benny Goodman's band in 1933, going on to perform with many small jazz groups. Her autobiography *Lady Sings the Blues* (1956) was made into a film in 1972.

Hol·in·shed |'hälənz,hed|, Raphael (died 1580) English chronicler. Although the named compiler of *The Chronicles of England, Scotland, and Ireland* (1577), Holinshed wrote only the *Historie of England* and had help with the

remainder. The revised (1587) edition was used by Shakespeare.

Hol·land |'hälənd|, Clifford Milburn (1883–1924) U.S. civil engineer. He oversaw the construction of double subway tunnels under the East River in Manhattan and the Holland Tunnel under the Hudson River (1919–24).

Hol·land |'hälənd|, John Philip (1840–1914) U.S. inventor, born in Ireland. He designed the first submarine with an internal combustion engine for surface power and an electric motor for submerged cruising; his company became the Electric Boat Co.

Hol·lan·der |'häləndər|, John (1929–) U.S. poet and educator. Since 1986, he has been the A. Bartlett Giamatti Professor of English at Yale University. Winner of the Bollingen Prize (1983), he has published more than 20 volumes of poetry as well as nonfiction, plays, anthologies, and children's books. Notable works: *The Night Mirror* (1971), *Reflections on Espionage* (1976), and *Powers of Thirteen* (1983).

Hol·lan·der |'häləndər|, Nicole (1939–) U.S. cartoonist. She created the comic strip "Sylvia."

Hol·le·rith |'hälə,riTH|, Herman (1860–1929) U.S. engineer. He invented a tabulating machine using punched cards for computation, an important precursor of the electronic computer, and founded a company that later expanded to become the IBM Corp..

Hol·ley |'hälē|, Alexander Lyman (1832–82) U.S. engineer. He purchased the American rights to the Bessemer process (1863) and established the first steel plant in the U.S. (1865). He became known as "the father of modern American steel manufacture."

Hol·ly |'hälē|, Buddy (1936–59) U.S. rock-and-roll singer, guitarist, and songwriter; born *Charles Hardin Holley*. He recorded such hits as "That'll be the Day" with his band, The Crickets, before going solo in 1958. He was killed in an airplane crash.

Holm |hōm|, Celeste (1919–) U.S. actress. Notable movies: *Gentleman's Agreement* (1947, Academy Award).

Holmes |hōmz|, Arthur (1890–1965) English geologist, geophysicist and educator. He pioneered the isotopic dating of rocks and was one of the first supporters of the theory of continental drift. His *Principles of Physical Geology* (1944) became a standard text.

Holmes |hōmz|, Oliver Wendell (1809–94) U.S. physician, poet, and essayist. His best-known literary works are the humorous essays known as "table talks," which began with *The Autocrat of the Breakfast Table* (1857–58).

Holmes |hōmz|, Oliver Wendell (1841–1935) U.S. Supreme Court justice (1902–32). He became well known for his strong, articulate, and often dissenting opinions.

Holst |hōlst|, Gustav (Theodore) (1874–1934) English composer, of Swedish and Russian descent. He made his reputation with the orchestral suite *The Planets* (1914–16). Other notable works: *Choral Hymns from the Rig Veda* (1908–12).

Holt |hōlt| U.S. family, including: **Henry Holt** (1840–1926), a publisher and author. He organized Henry Holt and Co. (1873). His daughter **Winifred Holt** (1870–1945), a welfare worker, founded the New York Association for the Blind (1905).

Holt |hōlt|, John (1923–85) U.S. educational reformer and author. He was a leader in the home schooling movement in the 1970s. Notable works: *How Children Fail* (1964) and *How Children Learn.*

Ho·ly·field |'hōlē,fēld|, Evander (1962–) U.S. boxer. He was a three-time world heavyweight champion.

Ho·ly·oake |'hōlē,ōk|, Sir Keith (Jacka) (1904–83) New Zealand statesman, prime minister (1957 and 1960–72), governor general (1977–80).

Home of the Hirsel of Coldstream, Baron see DOUGLAS-HOME.

Ho·mer |'hōmər| (*c.* 7th–8th century BC) Greek epic poet. He is traditionally held to be the author of the *Iliad* and the *Odyssey*, though modern scholarship has revealed the place of the Homeric poems in a preliterate oral tradition. In later antiquity Homer was regarded as the greatest poet, and his poems were constantly used as a model and source by others.

Ho·mer |'hōmər|, Winslow (1836–1910) U.S. painter. He is best known for his seascapes, such as *Cannon Rock* (1895), painted in a vigorous naturalistic style considered to express the American pioneering spirit.

Hon·da |'händə|, Soichiro (1906–92) Japanese manufacturer. Opening his first factory in 1934, he began motorcycle manufacture in 1948 and expanded into car production during the 1960s.

Hon·eck·er |'hänəkər|, Erich (1912–94) East German communist statesman, head of state 1976–89. His repressive regime was marked by a close allegiance to the Soviet Union. He was ousted in 1989 as communism collapsed throughout eastern Europe.

Ho·neg·ger |'hänəgər|, Arthur (1892–1955) French composer, of Swiss descent. He lived and worked chiefly in Paris, where he became a member of the antiromantic group Les Six. His first major success was the orchestral work *Pacific 231* (1924).

Hooch |hōk|, Pieter de see DE HOOCH.

Hood |hŏŏd|, Raymond Mathewson (1881–1934) U.S. architect. Notable designs: the Tribune Tower (1922) in Chicago, and Rockefeller Center (1929–40) in New York City.

Hood |hŏŏd|, Thomas (1799–1845) English poet and humorist. He wrote much humorous verse but is chiefly remembered for serious poems such as "The Song of the Shirt".

Hooke |hŏŏk|, Robert (1635–1703) English scientist. He formulated the law of elasticity (Hooke's law), proposed an undulating theory of light, introduced the term *cell* to biology, postulated elliptical orbits for the earth and moon, and proposed the inverse square law of gravitational attraction. He also invented or improved many scientific instruments and mechanical devices, and designed a number of buildings in London after the Great Fire.

Hook·er |'hŏŏkər|, John Lee (1917–) U.S. blues singer and guitarist. He helped define the electric blues, which linked the blues with rock and roll.

Hook·er |'hŏŏkər|, Sir Joseph Dalton (1817–1911) English botanist and pioneer in plant geography. Hooker applied

Darwin's theories to plants and, with **George Bentham,** (1800–84), he produced a work on classification, *Genera Plantarum* (1862–83).

Hook·er |'hŏŏkər|, Thomas (*c.* 1586–1647) American clergyman, born in England. A founding settler of Hartford, Connecticut (1636), he wrote *Fundamental Orders* (1639), which was Connecticut's original constitution.

hooks |hŏŏks|, bell (*c.* 1955–) U.S. educator and author. Born *Gloria Watkins.* A champion of African-American and women's rights, she wrote *Teaching to Transgress: Education as Practice of Freedom* (1994).

Hooks |hŏŏks|, Benjamin Lawson (1925–) U.S. lawyer, clergyman, and civil rights leader. He was executive director of the NAACP (1977–93). Awarded Spingarn Medal (1986).

Hoo·ver |'hŏŏvər|, Herbert (Clark) see box. **Lou Henry Hoover** (1875–1944), wife of Herbert Clark Hoover and U.S. first lady (1929–33).

Hoo·ver |'hŏŏvər|, J. Edgar (1895–1972) U.S. government official, director of the FBI (1924–72); full name *John Edgar Hoover.* He reorganized the FBI into an efficient, scientific law-enforcement agency, but came under criticism for the organization's role during the McCarthy era and for its reactionary political stance in the 1960s.

Hoo·ver |'hŏŏvər|, William (Henry) (1849–1932) U.S. industrialist; manufacturer of Hoover vacuum cleaners.

Hope |hōp|, Bob (1903–) British-born U.S. comedian; born *Leslie Townes Hope.* He often adopted the character of a cowardly incompetent, cheerfully failing to become a romantic hero, as in the series of *Road* movies (1940–62).

Hope |hōp|, John (1868–1936) U.S. educator and civil rights leader. He was president of Morehouse College (1906–31) and of Atlanta University (1929–36).

Hope-Jones |hōp jōnz|, Robert (1859–1914) U.S. organ builder, born in England. He made numerous improvements in electrified organs. His Hope-Jones Organ Co. was sold to the Wurlitzer Co. (1910).

Hop·kins |'häpkənz|, Sir Anthony

Hoover, Herbert Clark
31st U.S. president

Life dates: 1874–1964
Place of birth: West Branch, Iowa (first president born west of the Mississippi River)
Mother: Hulda Randall Minthorn Hoover
Father: Jesse Clark Hoover
Wife: Lou Henry Hoover
Children: Herbert, Allan
College/University: Stanford University
Career: Mining engineer; entrepreneur
Political career: headed U.S. Food Administration in Europe during World War I; secretary of commerce; president; chairman of Commission on Organization of the Executive Branch of Government ("Hoover Commission")
Party: Republican
Home state: California
Opponents in presidential race: Alfred E. Smith
Term of office: March 4, 1929–March 3, 1933
Vice president: Charles Curtis
Notable events of presidency: Stock Market crash of October 1929; Great Depression; Reconstruction Finance Corporation created; London Naval Treaty; independence for the Philippines; "Star Spangled Banner" adopted as national anthem
Other achievements: Mining engineer/consultant in North America, Europe, Asia, Africa and Australia; after presidency, chairman of Famine Emergency Commission
Place of burial: West Branch, Iowa

(Philip) (1937–) Welsh actor. He won an Oscar for his performance in *The Silence of the Lambs* (1991). Other notable movies: *The Elephant Man* (1980) and *The Remains of the Day* (1993).

Hop·kins |'häpkənz|, Donald (1941–) U.S. public health physician. As a member of the U.S. delegation to the World Health Assembly in Geneva (1977–78, 1980–86) and deputy director of the Centers for Disease Control (1984–87), he worked to eradicate smallpox throughout the world.

Hop·kins |'häpkənz|, Sir Frederick Gowland (1861–1947) English biochemist. He carried out pioneering work on "accessory food factors" essential to the diet, later called vitamins. Nobel Prize for Physiology or Medicine (1929).

Hop·kins |'häpkənz|, Gerard Manley (1844–89) English poet. A shipwreck in 1876 inspired him to write "The Wreck of the Deutschland". Like his poems "Windhover" and "Pied Beauty" (both 1877), it makes use of Hopkins's "sprung rhythm" technique.

Hop·kins |'häpkənz|, Harry Lloyd (1890–1946) U.S. social worker and government official. He headed the Works Progress Administration (1935–38) and served as adviser to President Franklin D. Roosevelt.

Hop·kins |'häpkənz|, Mark (1802–87) U.S. philosopher and educator.

Hop·kins |'häpkənz|, Pauline (1859–1930) U.S. author. Her works include *Contending Forces: A Romance Illustrative of Negro Life North and South* (1900).

Hop·kins |'häpkənz|, Sam (1912–82) U.S. blues singer and guitarist. Known as **Lightnin'**.

Hop·kin·son |'häpkənsən|, Francis (1737–91) U.S. public official, musician, and author. He was a signer of the Declaration of Independence (1776) and helped design the first U.S. flag (1777). A gifted harpsichordist, he is considered the first native-born American composer of classical music.

Hop·per |'häpər|, Edward (1882–1967) U.S. realist painter. He is best known for his mature works, such as *Early Sunday Morning* (1930), often depicting isolated figures in bleak scenes from everyday urban life.

Hop·per |'häpər|, Grace Murray (1906–92) U.S. admiral, mathematician, and computer scientist.

Hop·per |'häpər|, Hedda (1890–1966) U.S. newspaper columnist. Born *Elda Furry*. She wrote a syndicated gossip column (1938–66).

Hor·ace |'hawrəs| (65–8 BC) Roman poet of the Augustan period; full name *Quintus Horatius Flaccus*. A notable satirist and literary critic, he is best known for his *Odes*, much imitated by later ages, especially by the poets of 17th-century England. His other works include *Satires* and *Ars Poetica*.

Hor·dern |'hawrdərn|, Sir Michael (Murray) (1911–95) English actor.

Hor·gan |'hawrgən|, Paul (1903–95) U.S. author. His books include *Great River* (1954, Pulitzer Prize).

Hork·heim·er |'hawrk,hīmər|, Max (1895–1973) German philosopher and sociologist. A leading figure of the Frankfurt School, he wrote *Dialectic of the Enlightenment* (1947), with his colleague Theodor Adorno, and *Critical Theory* (1968).

Hor·mel |hawr'mel|, George A. (1860–1946) U.S. businessman. The founder of Hormel Foods, he spoke out on economic issues and wrote a booklet called "The Golden Way to Unemployment Relief" (1935).

Horne |hawrn|, Lena Calhoun (1917–) U.S. singer and actress. In the early 1940s, she became the first African American to have a long-term contract with a Hollywood studio. Notable movies: *Stormy Weather* (1943) and *Till the Clouds Roll By* (1946). Awarded Spingarn Medal (1983).

Hor·ney |'hawrnī|, Karen (1885–1952) U.S. psychoanalyst, born in Germany. Born *Karen Danielsen*. Expelled from the New York Psychoanalytic Institute for her critique of Freudian practices (1941), she was the founder of the Association for Advancement of Psychoanalysis and the American Institute for Psychoanalysis.

Horns·by |'hawrnzbē|, Rogers (1896–1963) U.S. baseball player. Known as **Rajah**. Elected to Baseball Hall of Fame (1942).

Hor·nung |'hawrnəNG|, Paul (1935–) U.S. football player.

Ho·ro·witz |'hawrə,wits|, Vladimir (1903–89) Russian-born U.S. pianist. He first toured the U.S. in 1928, and settled there soon afterward. A leading international virtuoso, he was best known for his performances of Scarlatti, Liszt, Scriabin, and Prokofiev.

Hor·sa |'hawrsə| (died 455) see HENGIST AND HORSA.

Hor·ta |'hawrtə|, Victor (1861–1947) Belgian architect. He was a leading figure in art nouveau architecture and his work was notable for its innovative use of iron and glass.

Hotspur |'hätspər| The nickname of Sir Henry Percy (see PERCY).

Hou·di·ni |hoo'dēnē|, Harry (1874–1926) Hungarian-born U.S. magician and escape artist; born *Erik Weisz*. In the early 1900s he became famous for his ability to escape from all kinds of bonds and containers, from prison cells to aerially suspended straitjackets.

Hou·dry |'hoodrē; 'ŏdrē|, Eugene Joules (1892–1962) French chemical engineer and inventor. In the 1920s, he discovered and developed a catalytic method for producing gasoline from crude oil. During World War II, he developed a method for producing synthetic rubber.

Hough·ton |'hōtn|, Henry Oscar (1823–95) U.S. publisher. His printing company, known as The Riverside Press, eventually became the Houghton Mifflin Co. (1864).

House·man |'howsmən|, John (1902–88) U.S. actor, born in Romania. Born *Jacques Haussmann*. Notable movies: *The Paper Chase* (1973, Academy Award).

Hous·man |'howsmən|, A. E. (Alfred Edward) (1859–1936) English poet and classical scholar. He is now chiefly remembered for the poems collected in *A Shropshire Lad* (1896), a series of nostalgic verses largely based on ballad forms.

Hous·ton |'hyoōstən|, Charles Hamilton (1895–1950) U.S. attorney and educator.

Hous·ton |'hyoōstən|, Samuel (1793–1863) U.S. soldier and politician. He was the first president of the Republic of Texas (1836–38; 1841–44) and the first U.S. senator from the state of Texas (1846–59). He was governor of Texas (1859–61) until ousted for refusing to swear allegiance to the Confederacy.

Hous·ton |'hyoōstən|, Whitney (1963–) U.S. singer. Her songs, a blend of gospel, ballad, pop, rock and rhythm and blues, include "I Will Always Love You" (1992).

How·ard |'howərd|, Catherine (*c.* 1520–42) fifth wife of Henry VIII. She married Henry soon after his divorce from Anne of Cleves in 1540. Accused of infidelity, she confessed and was beheaded.

How·ard |'howərd|, John (Winston) (1939–) Australian Liberal statesman, prime minister from 1996 with a Liberal–National Party coalition.

How·ard |'howərd|, Leslie (1893–1943) English actor; born *Leslie Howard Stainer*. He was best known for his roles as the archetypal English gentleman in movies such as *The Scarlet Pimpernel* (1935) and *Pygmalion* (1938). Other notable movies: *Gone with the Wind* (1939).

How·ard |'howərd|, Ron (1954–) U.S. actor and director. He was the child television star of "The Andy Griffith Show" (1960–68) and a star of "Happy Days" (1974–80). His film appearances include *The Music Man* (1962) and *American Graffiti* (1974). He directed *Backdraft* (1991) and *Apollo 13* (1995).

How·ard |'howərd|, Trevor (Wallace) (1916–88) English actor. He starred in *Brief Encounter* (1945) and *The Third Man* (1949) and later played character roles in movies such as *Gandhi* (1982).

Howe |how| . English officers. **Sir Richard Howe** (1726–99) was a naval officer. During the American Revolution, he was commander of the British fleet. His brother, **Sir William Howe** (1729–1814), was an army officer. He commanded the British troops at the Battle of Bunker Hill (1775) and succeeded Gage as commander in chief in North America (1775–78).

Howe |how| U.S. social reformers. **Samuel Gridley Howe** (1801–76). His success in educating a blind deaf-mute girl gained international attention. He was devoutly involved in such causes as public education, abolition, prison reform, and humane treatment of the mentally ill. His wife, **Julia Ward Howe** (1819–1910), was an author, poet, and social reformer. An activist in the causes of abolition, pacifism, and suffrage, she is best known as the author of "The Battle Hymn of the Republic" (1862). She was the first woman elected to the American Academy of Arts and Letters (1908).

Howe |how|, Elias (1819–67) U.S. mechanic and inventor. In 1846 he patented the first sewing machine. Its principles were adapted by Isaac Merritt Singer and others in violation of Howe's patent rights, and it took a seven-year litigation battle to secure the royalties.

Howe |how|, Gordie (1928–) U.S. hockey player.

Howe |how|, Irving (1920–93) U.S. educator, literary, and social critic. His books include *World of Our Fathers* (1976, National Book Award).

How·ells |'howəlz|, William Dean (1837–1920) U.S. novelist and critic. He was editor in chief of *Atlantic Monthly* (1971–81). His novels include *A Traveler from Altruria* (1894).

Howl·in' Wolf |'howlin ,woolf| (1910–76) U.S. blues singer, harmonica player, and guitarist. Born *Chester Arthur Burnett*. His hits include "Smokestack Lightnin'," "Little Red Rooster," and "I Ain't Superstitious."

Ho·xha |'hä,jə|, Enver (1908–85) Albanian statesman, founder of the Albanian Communist Party (1941), prime minister (1944–54), and first secretary of the Albanian Communist Party (1954–85). He rigorously isolated Albania from Western influences and implemented a Stalinist program of nationalization and collectivization.

Hoyle |hoil|, Sir Fred (1915–) English astrophysicist and writer. He was one of the proponents of the steady state theory of cosmology

Hua Guo Feng |,hwä ,gwō 'fəNG| (1920–) Chinese prime minister (1976-80) and chairman of the Communist Party (1976-81).

Hub·bard |'həbərd|, Cal (1900–77) U.S. sportsman. Full name *Robert Calvin Hubbard*. He was a football player and a baseball umpire, and was the only person to be a member of the halls of fame in both sports.

Hub·bard |'həbərd|, Elbert (1856–1915) U.S. author. His books include *A Message to Garcia* (1899).

Hub·bard |'həbərd|, Gardiner Greene (1822–97) U.S. lawyer. He was a financial backer of his son-in-law Alexander Graham Bell (from 1876) and the founder and first president of the National Geographic Society (1888–97).

Hub·bell |'həbəl|, Carl Owen (1903–88) U.S. baseball player. Known as **King Carl**. Elected to Baseball Hall of fame (1947).

Hub·ble |'həbəl|, Edwin Powell (1889–1953) U.S. astronomer. He studied galaxies and devised a classification scheme for them. In 1929 he proposed what is now known as Hubble's law with its constant of proportionality (Hubble's constant).

Hud·son |'hədsən|, Henry (*c.* 1575–1611) English explorer. He discovered the North American bay, river, and strait that bear his name. In 1610 he attempted to winter in Hudson Bay, but his crew mutinied and set Hudson and a few companions adrift, never to be seen again.

Hud·son |'hədsən|, Manley Ottmer (1886–1960) U.S. jurist. He was a judge at the Permanent Court of International Justice (1936–45) and author of *Progress in International Organization* (1932).

Hud·son |'hədsən|, William Henry (1841–1922) British naturalist and author, born in Argentina. An astute observer and lover of nature, he wrote *The Naturalist in La Plata* (1892) and *Nature in Downland* (1900).

Hug·gins |'həgənz|, Sir William (1824–1910) British astronomer. He pioneered spectroscopic analysis in astronomy, showing that nebulae are composed of luminous gas. He discovered the red shift in stellar spectra, attributing it to the Doppler effect and using it to measure recessional velocities.

Hughes |hyōōz|, Charles Evans (1862–1948) U.S. jurist and politcian. He was a U.S. Supreme Court justice (1910–16), a U.S. presidential candidate (1916), and Chief Justice of the U.S. (1930–41).

Hughes |hyōōz|, Howard (Robard) (1905–76) U.S. industrialist, movie producer, and aviator. He made his fortune through the Hughes Tool Co., made his debut as a movie director in 1926, and from 1935 to 1938 broke many world aviation records. Notable movies: *Hell's Angels* (1930) and *The Outlaw* (1941). For the last twenty-five years of his life he lived as a recluse.

Hughes |hyōōz|, (James Mercer) Langston (1902–67) U.S. writer. A leading voice of the Harlem Renaissance. He began a prolific literary career with *The Weary Blues* (1926), a series of poems on black themes using blues and jazz rhythms. Other poetry collections include *The Negro Mother* (1931).

Hughes |hyo͞oz|,Ted (1930–98) English poet; full name *Edward James Hughes*. His vision of the natural world as a place of violence, terror, and beauty pervades his work. He served as Britain's Poet Laureate (1984–98). Hughes was married to Sylvia Plath, a marriage he recounted in *Birthday Letters* (1998).

Hu·go |'hyo͞ogō|, Richard Franklin (1923–82) U.S. poet, author, and educator. Notable works: *A Run of Jacks* (1961) and *Selected Poems* (1979).

Hu·go |Y'gō; 'hyo͞ogō|,Victor (1802–85) French poet, novelist, and dramatist; full name *Victor-Marie Hugo*. A leading figure of French romanticism, he brought a new freedom to French poetry, and his belief that theater should express both the grotesque and the sublime of human existence overturned existing conventions. His political and social concern is shown in his novels. Notable works: *Hernani* (drama, 1830) and *Les Misérables* (novel, 1862).

Hui·zen·ga |hī'zeNGä|, (Harry) Wayne (1939–) U.S. businessman and corporate executive. The founder, chairman, and CEO of Blockbuster Entertainment Corp. (1987–94), he is an owner of the Florida Marlins, Miami Dolphins, and Florida Panthers.

Hull |həl|, Bobby (1939–) Canadian hockey player. Elected to the Hockey Hall of Fame, 1983.

Hull |həl|, Cordell (1871–1955) U.S. statesman. He served as a member of the U.S. House of Representatives (1907–21, 1923–31) and as U.S. secretary of state (1933–44). Received Nobel Peace Prize (1945).

Hull |həl|, Isaac (1773–1843) U.S. naval officer. As commander of the USS *Constitution* during the War of 1812, he won a stunning victory over the British *Guerrière*.

Hum·boldt |'həmbōlt|, Friedrich Heinrich Alexander Baron von (1769–1859) German explorer and scientist. He traveled in Central and South America (1799–1804) and wrote on natural history, meteorology, and physical geography.

Hume |'hyo͞om|, David (1711–76) Scottish philosopher, economist, and historian. He rejected the possibility of certainty in knowledge and claimed that all the data of reason stem from experience. Notable works: *A Treatise of Human Nature* (1739–40) and *History of England* (1754–62).

Humes |hyo͞omz|, H. L. (1926–) U.S. author. Full name *Harold Louis Humes*.

Hum·mel |'həməl|, Berta (1909–46) German artist. Also known as **Sister Maria Innocentia**. She created the sketches upon which M. I. Hummel figurines, made by the Franz Goebel Co., are based.

Hum·per·dinck |'həmpər,diNGk|, Engelbert (1854–1921) German composer. Influenced by Wagner, he is remembered as the composer of the opera *Hänsel und Gretel* (1893).

Hum·phrey |'həmfrē|, Doris (1895–1958) U.S. dancer and choreographer. She is known especially for her exploration of imbalance, fall, and recovery.

Hum·phrey |'həmfrē|, Hubert Horatio (1911–78) U.S. politican. He was vice president of the U.S. (1965–68) and a U.S. Democratic presidential candidate in 1968.

Hum·phreys |'həmfrēz|, David (1752–1818) U.S. author. During the American Revolution, he served as aide-de-camp to George Washington.

Hum·phreys |'həmfrēz|, Joshua (1751–1838) U.S. naval builder. Designed and supervised the construction of frigates (including the *Constitution* and *Constellation*) that formed the nucleus of the U.S. Navy in the War of 1812.

Hunt |hənt| U.S. family, including **William Morris Hunt** (1824&79), an artist. His paintings include *The Bathers* (1877). His brother, **Richard Morris Hunt** (1827–95), was an architect. Notable designs: Presbyterian Hospital (1872) in New York City, and Biltmore House (1895), a 225-room mansion in North Carolina.

Hunt |hənt|, Helen (1963–) U.S. actress. She won a 1997 Academy Award for *As Good as It Gets* and a 1997 Emmy Award for her role in the television series "Mad About You."

Hunt |hənt|, Henry Alexander (1866–1938) U.S. educator and social reformer. He was president of Fort Valley State College (1904–38). Spingarn Medal, 1930.

Hunt |hənt|, Ward (1810–86) U.S. Supreme Court justice (1873–82).

Hunt |hənt|, (William) Holman (1827–1910) English painter, one of the founders of the Pre-Raphaelite Brotherhood. He painted biblical scenes with extensive use of didactic and moral symbolism. Notable works: *The Light of the World* (1854) and *The Scapegoat* (1855).

Hun·ter |'hən(t)ər|, Holly (1958–) U.S. actress. Notable movies: *The Piano* (1993, Academy Award).

Hun·ter |'hən(t)ər|, Jim (1946–) U.S. baseball player. Full name *James Augustus Hunter;* known as **Catfish**. Elected to Baseball Hall of Fame (1987).

Hun·ter |'hən(t)ər|, John (1728–93) Scottish anatomist, regarded as a founder of scientific surgery. He also made valuable investigations in pathology, physiology, dentistry, and biology.

Hun·ting·ton |'hən(t)iNGtən|, Collis Potter (1821–1900) U.S. industrialist. He organized the Southern Pacific Railroad (1884).

Hunt·ley |'həntlē|, Chet (1911–74) U.S. television journalist. Born *Chester Robert Huntley.* With David Brinkley he coanchored *The Huntley-Brinkley Report* (1956–70).

Hurd |hərd|, Peter (1904–84) U.S. artist. He created sun-drenched landscapes of the American Southwest.

Hurs·ton |'hərstən|, Zora Neale (1903–60) U.S. novelist. Her novels reflect her interest in folklore, especially that of the Deep South. Notable works: *Jonah's Gourd Vine* (1934) and *Seraph on the Suwanee* (1948).

Hurt |hərt|, William (1950–) U.S. actor. Notable movies: *Kiss of the Spider Woman* (1985, Academy Award).

Husain variant spelling of HUSSEIN.

Hu·sák |'hōōsäk; 'hyōōsæk|, Gustáv (1913–91) Czechoslovak statesman, leader of the Communist Party of Czechoslovakia (1969–87) and president (1975–89). He succeeded Alexander Dubček following the Prague Spring of 1968 and purged the party of its reformist elements.

Huss |həs|, John (*c.* 1372–1415) Bohemian religious reformer; Czech name *Jan Hus.* A rector of Prague University, he supported the views of Wyclif, attacked ecclesiastical abuses, and was excommunicated in 1411. He was later tried and burnt at the stake. See also HUSSITE.

Hus·sein |hōō'sän|, ibnTalal (1935–99) Also **Husain**. King of Jordan (1953–99). Throughout his reign Hussein sought to maintain good relations both with the West and with other Arab nations, but his moderate policies created problems with the Palestinian refugees from Israel within Jordan. During the Gulf War he supported Iraq, but in 1994 he signed a treaty normalizing relations with Israel. He was succeeded by his son **Abdullah** (see ABDULLAH IBN HUSSEIN).

Hus·sein |hōō'sän|, Saddam (1937–) Also **Husain**. Iraqi president, prime minister, and head of the armed forces since 1979; full name *Saddam bin Hussein at-Takriti.* During his presidency Iraq fought a war with Iran (1980–88) and invaded Kuwait (1990), from which Iraqi forces were expelled in the Gulf War of 1991. He also ordered punitive attacks on Kurdish rebels in the north of Iraq and on the Marsh Arabs in the south.

Hus·serl |'hōōsərl|, Edmund (Gustav Albrecht) (1859–1938) German philosopher. His work forms the basis of the school of phenomenology; he rejected metaphysical assumptions about what actually exists, and explanations of why it exists, in favor of pure subjective consciousness as the condition for all experience, with the world as the object of this consciousness.

Hus·ton |'hyōōstən| U.S. acting family, including: Canadian-born **Walter Huston** (1884–1950). Born *Walter Houghston.* Notable movies: *Treasure of the Sierra Madre* (1948, Academy Award). His son, **John Huston** (1906–87), a director, was born in the U.S. but became an Irish citizen in 1964. He made his debut as a movie director in 1941 with *The Maltese Falcon.* Other notable movies: *The Treasure of the Sierra Madre* (1948; Academy Award), *The African Queen*

(1951), and *Prizzi's Honor* (1985). John's daughter, **Anjelica Huston** (1951–), is an actress. Notable movies: *Prizzi's Honor* (1985, Academy Award) and *The Addams Family* (1991).

Hutch·ins |'həCHənz|, Robert Maynard (1899–1977) U.S. educator and author.

Hutch·ins |'həCHənz|, Thomas (1730–89) U.S. cartographer. Appointed by Congress as "geographer to the U.S." (1781), he created maps that were the basis for all subsequent surveying in the West.

Hutch·in·son |'həCHənsən|, Anne Marbury (1591–1643) American religious leader, born in England. She was banished from Massachusetts Bay Colony in 1637 for her liberal views of grace and salvation. Having settled in New York in 1642, she and most of her family were killed by Indians.

Hut·son |'hətsən|, Don (1913–97) U.S. football player.

Hut·ton |'hətn|, James (1726–97) Scottish geologist. Although controversial at the time, his uniformitarian description of the processes that have shaped the surface of the earth is now accepted as showing that it is very much older than had previously been believed.

Hux·ley |'həkslē| English family, including: **Thomas Henry Huxley** (1825–95), a biologist. A surgeon and leading supporter of Darwinism, he coined the word *agnostic* to describe his own beliefs. Notable works: *Man's Place in Nature* (1863). His grandson, **Sir Julian Sorell Huxley** (1887–1975), was a biologist. He studied animal behavior

and was a notable interpreter of science to the public. His brother, **Aldous (Leonard) Huxley** (1894–1963), was a novelist and essayist. After writing *Antic Hay* (1923) and *Brave New World* (1932), in 1937 he moved to California, where in 1953 he experimented with psychedelic drugs, writing of his experiences in *The Doors of Perception* (1954).

Huy·gens |'hoigənz|, Christiaan (1629–95) Dutch physicist, mathematician, and astronomer. His wave theory of light enabled him to explain reflection and refraction. He also patented a pendulum clock, improved the lenses of his telescope, discovered a satellite of Saturn, and recognized the nature of Saturn's rings, which had eluded Galileo.

Hy·att |'hīət|, Alpheus (1838–1902) U.S. zoologist and paleontologist. He helped to established the Marine Biological Labratory at Woods Hole, Massachusetts.

Hy·att |'hīət|, John Wesley (1837–1920) U.S. inventor. Creator of many inventions, including celluloid (1870).

Hyde, Edward see CLARENDON.

Hyde |hīd|, Henry Baldwin (1834–99) U.S. businessman. He founded the Equitable Life Assurance Society of the U.S. (1859).

Hy·pa·tia |ˌhī'pashə| (c. 370–415) Greek philosopher, astronomer, and mathematician. Head of the Neoplatonist school at Alexandria, she wrote several learned treatises as well as devising inventions such as an astrolabe.

Ii

Ia·coc·ca |ˌīə'kōkə|, Lee (1924–) U.S. industrialist. Full name *Lido Anthony Iacocca*. He is chairman of the board and chief executive officer of Chrysler Corp. (1979–).

Ibár·ruri Gó·mez |i'bärōōrē 'gōmez|, Dolores (1895–1989) Spanish communist politician and leader of the Republicans during the Spanish Civil War; known as **La Pasionaria**.

Ibn Ba·tu·ta |ˌibən bæ'tōōtä| (*c.* 1304–68) Arab explorer. From 1325 to 1354 he journeyed through North and West Africa, India, and China, and wrote a vivid account of his travels in the *Rihlah*.

ibn Hus·sein, Abdullah see ABDULLAH IBN HUSSEIN.

Ibn Sa·ud |ˌibən sä'ōōd| (*c.* 1880–1953) king of Saudi Arabia (1932–53). Full name *Abd al-Aziz ibn Abd ar-Rahman ibn Faysal ibn Turki Abd Allah ibn Muhammad Al Saud*. A powerful Muslim leader, he founded Saudi Arabia (1932), having unified the various domains over which he had assumed sovereignty.

Ib·sen |'ibsən|, Henrik (1828–1906) Norwegian dramatist. He is credited with being the first major dramatist to write tragedy about ordinary people in prose. Ibsen's later works, such as *The Master Builder* (1892), deal increasingly with the forces of the unconscious and were admired by Sigmund Freud. Other notable works: *Peer Gynt* (1867), *A Doll's House* (1879), *Ghosts* (1881).

Ick·es |'ikəs|, Harold LeClair (1874–1952) U.S. lawyer and public official. He served as head of the federal Public Works Administration (1933–39) and as U.S. secretary of the interior (1933–46).

Ic·ti·nus |ik'tīnəs| (5th century BC) Greek architect. He is said to have designed the Parthenon in Athens with the architect Callicrates and the sculptor Phidias between 448 and 437 BC.

Igle·sias |ē'glásyäs; i'gläzēəs|, Julio (1943–) Spanish singer. He has recorded more than sixty albums and is famous for love songs and ballads.

Ig·na·tius of Loy·o·la |ig'näsHəs əv loi 'ōlə|, St. (1491–1556) Spanish theologian and founder of the Society of Jesus (the Jesuit order). His *Spiritual Exercises* (1548), an ordered scheme of meditations, is still used in the training of Jesuits. Feast day, July 31.

Ig·na·tow, David (1914–97) U.S. poet. His works include *New and Collected Poems: 1970–1985* (1987).

Ikh·na·ton |ik'nät(ə)n| see AKHENATON.

Il·lich |'iliCH|, Ivan (1926–) Austrianborn U.S. educationist and writer. He advocated the deinstitutionalization of education, religion, and medicine. Notable works: *Deschooling Society* (1971) and *Limits to Medicine* (1978).

Iman |'ēmän| (1955–) U.S. model and entrepreneur, born in Somalia. The wife of David Bowie, she developed a line of cosmetics for women of color.

Im·ho·tep |im'hō,tep| (27th century BC) Egyptian architect and scholar, later deified. He probably designed the step pyramid built at Saqqara for the 3rd dynasty pharaoh Djoser.

Imus |'īməs|, Don (1940–) U.S. radio host and author. Host of the radio talk show "Imus in the Morning" (1988–) on WFAN, New York, as well as a television host for MS/NBC (1996–).

In·du·rain |'indyōō,rin|, Miguel (1964–) Spanish cyclist. He was the first person to win the Tour de France five consecutive times, (1991–95).

Ine |'inə| (688–726) king of Wessex (688–726). He extended the prestige and power of the throne, developing an extensive legal code.

Inge |'iNG|, William Motter (1913–73) U.S. playwright. Notable plays: *Come Back, Little Sheba* (1950), *Picnic* (1953), and *Bus Stop* (1955).

In·ger·soll |'iNGgər,sawl|, Robert Green (1833–99) U.S. lawyer and orator. During his lecture circuit (1870s), he promoted a secular religion that was labeled "agnosticism."

In·ger·soll |'iNGgər,sawl|, Robert Hawley (1859–1928) U.S. industrialist. He developed the mail-order business and chain-store system, and introduced the Ingersoll one-dollar watch (1892).

In·gra·ham |'iNGgrəhəm; 'iNGgrəm|, Prentiss (1843–1904) U.S. author. Using his own name as well as numerous pseudonyms, he wrote hundreds of dime novels, including *The Masked Spy* (1872).

In·gres |'æNGgrəs|, Jean Auguste Dominique (1780–1867) French painter. A pupil of Jacques-Louis David, he vigorously upheld neoclassicism in opposition to Delacroix's romanticism. Notable works: *Ambassadors of Agamemnon* (1801) and *The Bather* (1808).

In·man |'inmən|, Henry (1801–46) U.S. artist. A leading portraitist of his day, he helped found the National Academy of Design (1826).

In·ness |'inəs|, George (1825–94) U.S. artist. Notable paintings: *Peace and Plenty* (1865) and *The Home of the Heron* (1893).

In·sull |'insəl|, Samuel (1859–1938) U.S. financier, born in England. Private secretary to Thomas A. Edison, he built his financial empire based on holdings of electric companies. He fled the country when his businesses failed (1932).

Io·nes·co |yaw'neskō|, Eugène (1912–94) Romanian-born French dramatist, a leading exponent of the Theatre of the Absurd. Notable plays: *The Bald Soprano* (1950), *Rhinoceros* (1960).

Ipa·tieff |i'pät,yef|, Vladimir Nikolaievich (1867–1952) Russian-born U.S. chemist. He worked mainly on the catalysis of hydrocarbons, developing high octane fuels and techniques important to the petrochemical industry.

Iq·bal |,ik'bäl|, Sir Muhammad (1875–1938) Indian poet and philosopher, generally regarded as the father of Pakistan. As president of the Muslim League in 1930, he advocated the creation of a separate Muslim state in NW India; the demands of the League led ultimately to the establishment of Pakistan in 1947.

Ire·dell |'ī(ə)r,del|, James (1751–1799) U.S. Supreme Court justice (1790–99), born in England.

Ire·land |'īrlənd|, John (1838–1918) U.S. prelate, born in Ireland. He became Archbishop of St.Paul in 1884 and was a founder of Catholic University (1889) in Washington, D.C.

Ire·land |'īrlənd|, Patricia (1945–) U.S. lawyer and social reformer. She is president of the National Organization for Women (1991–).

Ire·nae·us |ī'rēnēəs|, St. (*c.* 130–*c.* 200 AD) Greek theologian, the author of *Against Heresies* (*c.*180), a detailed attack on Gnosticism. Feast day (in the Eastern Church) August 23; (in the Western Church) June 28.

Iron Chancellor see BISMARCK.

Iron Duke see WELLINGTON.

Iron Lady the nickname of Margaret Thatcher while she was British prime minister.

Irons |ī(ə)rnz|, Jeremy John (1948–) English stage, film, and television actor. Notable movies: *Reversal of Fortune* (1990, Academy Award).

Ir·ving |'ərviNG|, Sir Henry (1838–1905) English actor-manager; born *John Henry Brodribb*. He managed the Lyceum Theatre from 1878 to 1902, during which period he entered into a celebrated acting partnership with Ellen Terry.

Ir·ving |'ərviNG|, John (1942–) U.S. author. Notable works: *The Hotel New Hampshire* (1981) and *The World According to Garp* (1978).

Ir·ving |'ərviNG|, Washington (1738–1859) U.S. writer. He is best known for *The Sketch Book of Geoffrey Crayon, Gent* (1819–20), which contains such tales as "Rip Van Winkle" and "The Legend of Sleepy Hollow."

Is·a·bel·la I |,izə'belə| (1451–1504) queen of Castile (1474–1504) and of Aragon (1479–1504). Her marriage in 1469 to Ferdinand of Aragon helped to join together the Christian kingdoms of Castile and Aragon, marking the beginning of the unification of Spain. They instituted the Spanish Inquisition (1478) and supported Columbus's famous expedition of 1492.

Isa·bel·la of France |,izə'belə əv 'fræns| (1292–1358) daughter of Philip IV of France and wife of Edward II of England (1308–27). After returning to France in 1325, she organized an invasion of England in 1326 with her lover

Roger de Mortimer, murdering Edward and replacing him with her son, Edward III. Edward took control in 1330, executing Mortimer and sending Isabella into retirement.

Ish·er·wood |'iSHər,wŏŏd|, Christopher (William Bradshaw) (1904–86) British-born U.S. novelist. Notable novels: *Mr. Norris Changes Trains* (1935), *Goodbye to Berlin* (1939; filmed as *Cabaret*, 1972).

Ishi·gu·ro |'iSHi'gŏŏ,rō|, Kazuo (1954–) Japanese-born British novelist. Notable novels: *The Remains of the Day* (1989).

Is·i·dore of Se·ville |'izə,dawr əv sə'vil|, St. (c. 560–636) Spanish archbishop and Doctor of the Church; also called **Isidorus Hispalensis**. He is noted for his *Etymologies*, an encyclopedic work used by many medieval authors. Feast day, April 4.

Isoc·ra·tes |ī'säkrə,tēz| (436–338 BC) Athenian orator whose written speeches are among the earliest political pamphlets.

Ito |'ē,tō|, Prince Hirobumi (1841–1909) Japanese statesman, premier four times between 1884 and 1901. He was prominent in drafting the Japanese constitution (1889) and helped to establish a bicameral national diet (1890). He was assassinated by a member of the Korean independence movement.

Ivan |'ivən; ē'vän| the name of six rulers of Russia: **Ivan I** (c. 1304–41). He was the grand duke of Muscovy (1328–40). He strengthened and enlarged the duchy, making Moscow the ecclesiastical capital in 1326. **Ivan II** (1326–59) was the grand duke of Muscovy (1353–59); known as **Ivan the Red**. **Ivan III** (1440–1505) was the grand duke of Muscovy (1462–1505); known as **Ivan the Great**. He consolidated and enlarged his territory, defending it against a Tartar invasion in 1480 and adopting the title "Ruler of all Russia" in 1472. **Ivan IV** (1530–84), grand duke of Muscovy (1533–47) and first czar of Russia (1547–84); known as **Ivan the Terrible**. He captured Kazan, Astrakhan, and Siberia, but the Tartar siege of Moscow and the Polish victory in the Livonian War (1558–82) left Russia weak and divided. In 1581 Ivan killed his eldest son Ivan in a fit of rage, the succession passing to his mentally handicapped second son Fyodor. **Ivan V** (1666–96), nominal czar of Russia (1682–96). **Ivan VI** (1740–64), infant czar of Russia (1740–01).

Ivan the Great Ivan III of Russia (see IVAN).

Ivan the Terrible Ivan IV of Russia (see IVAN).

Ives |'īvz|, Burl (1909–95) U.S. actor and folk singer. Born *Icle Ivanhoe*. Notable movies: *The Big Country* (1958, Academy Award).

Ives |'īvz|, Charles (Edward) (1874–1954) U.S. composer, noted for his use of polyrhythms, polytonality, quartertones, and aleatoric techniques. Notable works: *The Unanswered Question* (chamber work, 1906) and *Three Places in New England* (for orchestra, 1903–14).

Ives |'īvz|, Frederic Eugene (1856–1937) U.S. inventor. He was responsible for many improvements in photographic printing, including the halftone photogravure process.

Ivo·ry |'īv(ə)rē|, James (1928–) U.S. movie director. He has made a number of movies in partnership with producer Ismail Merchant, including *Heat and Dust* (1983), *Howard's End* (1992), *A Room with a View* (1986), and *The Remains of the Day* (1993).

Jj

Jack·son |'jæksən|. U.S. pop singers: **Michael Jackson** (1958–) was the top-selling pop artist of the 1980s; his hit albums include *Dangerous* and *Thriller*. **Janet Damita Jackson** (1966–), his sister and the youngest of the Jackson family, sang hits including "That's the Way Love Goes" (1993).

Jack·son |'jæksən|, Glenda (1936–) British actress. Notable movies: *Women in Love* (1970, Academy Award).

Jack·son |'jæksən|, Howell Edmunds (1832–95) U.S. Supreme Court justice (1893–95).

Jack·son |'jæksən|, Jesse (Louis) (1941–) U.S. political and social activist; civil rights leader, U.S. civil rights activist, politician and clergyman. After working with Martin Luther King in the civil rights struggle, he competed for but failed to win the Democratic Party's 1984 and 1988 presidential nominations.

Jack·son |'jæksən|, Mahalia (1911–72) U.S. gospel singer and musician. Her 1947 recording of "Move Up a Little Higher" sold over a million copies.

Jack·son |'jæksən|, Reggie (1946–) U.S. baseball player. Full name *Reginald Martinez Jackson*; known as **Mr. October**. Elected to Baseball Hall of Fame (1993).

Jack·son |'jæksən|, Robert Houghwout (1892–1954) U.S. Supreme Court justice (1941–54). He was chief prosecutor for the U.S. at the Nuremberg war crimes tribunal (1945–46).

Jack·son |'jæksən|, Scoop (1912–83) U.S. politician. Full name *Henry Martin Jackson*. As a member of the U.S. Senate from Washington (1953–83), he led the Democratic neo-conservatives and twice campaigned unsuccessfully for the Democratic presidential nomination (1972 and 1976).

Jack·son |'jæksən|, Shirley (1919–65) U.S. author. She is best known for her tales of the macabre or supernatural. Notable novels: *The Bird's Nest* (1954) and *The Haunting of Hill House* (1959).

Jack·son |'jæksən|, Stonewall (1824–

Jackson, Andrew
7th U.S. president

Life dates: 1767–1845
Place of birth: in Carolinas, perhaps in Waxhaw, South Carolina
Mother: Elizabeth Hutchinson Jackson
Father: Andrew Jackson
Wife: Rachel Donelson Robards Jackson
Children: none (adopted his wife's nephew, renamed Andrew Jackson, Jr.)
Nickname: "Old Hickory"
College/University: none
Military service: served at the age of 13 in the S. Car. militia in the Revolutionary War; defeated Creek Indians, Battle of Horseshoe Bend, 1813; victorious over British at Battle of New Orleans, 1815; defeated Seminole Indians in Florida, 1817
Career: Lawyer; businessman
Political career: U.S. House of Representatives; U.S. Senate; justice, Tennessee Supreme Court; provisional governor of Florida; U.S. Senate; president
Home state: Tennessee
Party: Democratic
Opponents in presidential races: John Quincy Adams; Henry Clay
Term of office: March 4, 1825–March 3, 1837
Vice presidents: John Caldwell Calhoun; Martin Van Buren
Notable events of presidency: vetoed renewal of charter of the Bank of the United States; Indian Removal Act of 1830; proclamation opposing nullification issued; Specie Circular issued; Texas declaration of independence; Arkansas admitted as 25th state; Wisconsin Territory organized; Michigan admitted as 26th state; independence of Texas recognized
Other achievements: admitted to the North Carolina and Tennessee bars; successful real estate speculator; delegate to Tennessee State Constitutional Convention
Place of burial: The Hermitage, near Nashville, Tennessee

63) Confederate general. Full name *Thomas Jonathan Jackson.* The brilliant commander of the Shenandoah campaign (1861–62), he was mortally wounded by one of his own sharpshooters at Chancellorsville.

Jack·son |'jæksən|, William Henry (1843–1942) U.S. photographer. His photographs chronicled the expansion of the American West and particularly the construction of the Union Pacific Railroad.

Jack the Rip·per |jæk| (19th century) An unidentified English murderer. In 1888 at least six prostitutes were brutally killed in the East End of London, the bodies being mutilated in a way that indicated a knowledge of anatomy. The authorities received taunting notes from a person calling himself Jack the Ripper and claiming to be the murderer, but the cases remain unsolved.

Ja·co·bi |jə'kōbē; yä'kōbē|, Karl Gustav Jacob (1804–51) German mathematician. He worked on the theory of elliptic functions, in competition with Niels Abel.

Ja·cobs |'jäkəbz|, Bernard B. (1916–) U.S. Broadway producer. With Gerald Schoenfeld (1924–), he took over the Shubert Organization.

Jacopo della Quercia see DELLA QUERCIA.

Jac·quard |zHä'kär(d)|, Joseph-Marie (1752–1834) French inventor. He invented the Jacquard loom (1801).

Ja·cuz·zi |jə'kōozē|, Candido (1903–) U.S. businessman. Developed the "jacuzzi," a portable aerating jet pump designed for home hydrotherapy.

Jag·ger |'jægər|, Mick (1943–) English rock singer and songwriter; full name *Michael Philip Jagger.* He formed the Rolling Stones *c.* 1962 with guitarist Keith Richards (1943–), a childhood friend.

Jakes |jäks|, John (1932–) U.S. author. Pseudonyms **Alan Payne** and **Jay Scotland.** He was a prolific author of such works as the *Kent Family Chronicles.*

Ja·kob·son |'yäkəbsən|, Roman (Osipovich) (1896–1982) Russian-born U.S. linguist. His most influential work described universals in phonology.

Jalal ad-Din ar-Rumi |jə'läl ood'dēn ər 'rōomē| (1207–73) Persian poet and Sufi mystic, founder of the order of whirling dervishes; also called **Mawlana.**

James[1] the name of seven Stuart kings of Scotland: **James I** (1394–1437), son of Robert III, reigned 1406–37. A captive of the English until 1424, he returned to a country divided by baronial feuds, but managed to restore some measure of royal authority. **James II** (1430–60), son of James I, reigned 1437–60. He considerably strengthened the position of the Crown by crushing the powerful Douglas family (1452–55). **James III** (1451–88), son of James II, reigned 1460–88. His nobles raised an army against him in 1488, using his son, the future James IV, as a figurehead. The king was defeated and killed in battle. **James IV** (1473–1513), son of James III, reigned 1488–1513. He forged a dynastic link with England through his marriage to Margaret Tudor, the daughter of Henry VII, and revitalized the traditional pact with France. When England and France went to war in 1513 he invaded England, but died in defeat at Flodden. **James V** (1512–42), son of James IV, reigned 1513–42. During his reign Scotland was dominated by French interests. Relations with England deteriorated in the later years, culminating in an invasion by Henry VIII's army. **James VI** (1566–1625), James I of England (see JAMES[2]). **James VII** (1633–1701), James II of England (see JAMES[2]).

James[2] the name of two kings of England, Ireland, and Scotland: **James I** (1566–1625), son of Mary, Queen of Scots, king of Scotland (as James VI) 1567–1625, and of England and Ireland 1603–25. He inherited the throne of England from Elizabeth I, as great-grandson of Margaret Tudor, daughter of Henry VII. His declaration of the divine right of kings and his intended alliance with Spain made him unpopular with Parliament. **James II** (1633–1701), son of Charles I, king of England, Ireland, and (as James VII) Scotland 1685–88. His Catholic beliefs led to the rebellion of the Duke of Monmouth in

1685 and to James's later deposition in favor of William of Orange and Mary II. Attempts to regain the throne resulted in James's defeat at the Battle of the Boyne in 1690.

James³ |jāmz| U.S. family of intellectuals: **Henry James** (1811–82), father of Henry and William, a philosopher who wrote on theology and social philosophy and was a friend of many literary figures. His more prominent son, **Henry James** (1843–1916), an author and critic. His early novels, notably *The Portrait of a Lady* (1881), deal with the relationship between European civilization and American life, while later works, such as *What Maisie Knew* (1897), depict English life. **William James** (1842–1910), brother of Henry James the novelist. He was a psychologist, philosopher, and educator. A leading exponent of pragmatism, he sought a functional definition of truth, and in psychology he is credited with introducing the concept of the stream of consciousness.

James |jāmz|, Daniel, Jr. (1920–78) U.S. air force officer. Known as **Chappie**. He headed the North American Air Defense Command (1975–78), and became the first African American in U.S. military history to attain the rank of four-star general (1976).

James |jāmz|, Edmund Janes (1855–1925) U.S. political scientist and educator. He founded the American Economic Association (1885) and the American Academy of Political and Social Science (1889).

James |jāmz|, Etta (1938–   ) U.S. soul singer. Born *Jamesetta Hawkins*. Grammy Award, 1994.

James |jāmz|, Jesse Woodson (1847–82) U.S. outlaw. With brother Frank (1843–1915), he was a member of a notorious gang of train and bank robbers.

James |jāmz|, St. (died *c.* 44 AD) an Apostle, son of Zebedee and brother of John; known as **St. James the Great**. He was put to death by Herod Agrippa I; afterward, according to a Spanish tradition, his body was taken to Santiago de Compostela. Feast day, July 25.

James |jāmz|, St. (1st century) an Apostle; known as **St. James the Less**. Feast day (in the Eastern Church) October 9; (in the Western Church) May 1.

James |jāmz|, St. (died *c.* 62 AD) leader of the early Christian Church at Jerusalem; known as **St. James the Just** or **the Lord's Brother**. He was put to death by the Sanhedrin. Feast Day, March 1.

James |jāmz|, Thomas (*c.* 1593–1635) English navigator. During his search for the Northwest Passage (1631, 1633), he explored the southern extension of Hudson Bay (James Bay).

Jame·son |'jāmsən|, John Franklin (1859–1937) U.S. historian and educator. He was a founder of the American Historical Association (1884) and headed the division of manuscripts at the Library of Congress (1928–37).

Ja·mi·son |'jāməsən|, Judith (1944–   ) U.S. dancer and choreographer. She performed with the Alvin Ailey American Dance Theater in New York City from 1965 and was star of the Broadway show *Sophisticated Ladies* (1980).

Ja·ná·ček |'yänə,cHek|, Leoš (1854–1928) Czech composer. His works, much influenced by Moravian folk songs, include the opera *The Cunning Little Vixen* (1924) and the *Glagolitic Mass* (1927).

Jan·sen |'jænsən|, Cornelius Otto (1585–1638) Flemish Roman Catholic theologian and founder of Jansenism. A strong opponent of the Jesuits, he proposed a reform of Christianity through a return to St. Augustine.

Jansens (also **Janssen van Ceulen**) variant spelling of JOHNSON, CORNELIUS.

Jan·sky |'jænskē|, Karl Guthe (1905–50) U.S. electrical engineer. He founded the science of radio astronomy when he discovered radio waves that originated in distant space (1931).

Jan·son |'yänsawn|, Anton (1620–87) Dutch type designer. He designed the Janson typeface.

Jaques-Dal·croze |'zHäk däl'krōz|, Émile (1865–1950) Austrian-born Swiss music teacher and composer. He evolved the eurhythmics method of teaching music and dance, establishing a school for eurhythmics instruction in 1910.

Jar·man |'järmən|, Derek (1942–94) English movie director and painter.

Jar·rell |jə'rel|, Randall (1914–65) U.S. author, poet, and educator. His works include *The Woman at the Washington Zoo* (1960, National Book Award).

Jar·ry |'zHäri|, Alfred (1873–1907) French dramatist. His satirical farce *Ubu Roi* (1896) anticipated surrealism and the Theatre of the Absurd.

Ja·ru·zel·ski |,yärə'zelski|, Wojciech (1923–) Polish general and statesman, prime minister (1981–85), head of state (1985–89), and president (1989–90). He responded to the rise of Solidarity by imposing martial law and banning labor union activities, but following the victory of Solidarity in the 1989 elections he supervised Poland's transition to a democracy.

Jar·vik |'järvik|, Robert K. (1946–) U.S. biomedical research scientist. He patented an artificial heart driven by compressed air.

Ja·wor·ski |jə'wawrski|, Leon (1905–1982) U.S. lawyer and politician. He became the Watergate special prosecutor after Archibald Cox was fired (1973).

Jay |jā|, John (1745–1829) U.S. jurist and statesman. With James Madison and Alexander Hamilton, he was author of *The Federalist* (1787–88). He served as Chief Justice of the U.S. (1789–95).

Jean Paul |,zHän 'pawl| (1763–1825) German novelist; pseudonym of **Johann Paul Friedrich Richter**. He is noted for his romantic novels, including *Hesperus* (1795), and for comic works such as *Titan* (1800–03).

Jeans |'jēnz|, Sir James Hopwood (1877–1946) English physicist and astronomer. Jeans proposed a theory for the formation of the solar system and was the first to propose that matter is continuously created throughout the universe, one of the tenets of the steady state theory.

Jef·fers |'jefərz|, Robinson (1887–1962) U.S. poet. Full name *John Robinson Jeffers*. Notable books of verse: *Tamar and Other Poems* (1924) and *The Women at Point Sur* (1927).

Jef·fer·son |'jefərsən|, Thomas see box.

Martha Wayles Skelton Jefferson (1748–82), wife of Thomas Jefferson.

Jefferson, Thomas
3rd U.S. president

Life dates: 1743–1826
Place of birth: Shadwell, Goochland (now Albemarle) County, Va.
Mother: Jane Randolph Jefferson
Father: Peter Jefferson
Wife: Martha Wayles Skelton
Children: Martha, Jane, Mary ("Marie," "Polly"), Lucy, Lucy Elizabeth
Nickname: Sage of Monticello
College/University: College of William and Mary
Career: Lawyer; writer
Political career: member of Virginia House of Burgesses; delegate, Second Continental Congress; member, Virginia House of Delegates; governor of Virginia; U.S. House of Representatives; U.S. secretary of state; vice president (under John Adams); president
Party: Democratic-Republican
Home state: Virginia
Opponents in presidential races: John Adams, Thomas Pinckney; Aaron Burr, John Adams, Charles C. Pinckney; Charles C. Pinckney
Term of office: March 4, 1801–March 3, 1809
Vice presidents: Aaron Burr; George Clinton
Notable events of presidency: war with Barbary States; *Marbury vs. Madison* Supreme Court decision; Louisiana Territory purchased from France; Lewis and Clark expedition; Embargo Act; prohibition of the importation of slaves; Ohio admitted as 17th state; Michigan Territory established; Illinois Territory established; Non-Intercourse Act prohibiting trade with Grade Britain and France
Other achievements: Admitted to the Virginia bar; published influential pamphlet "A Summary View of the Rights of British America" (1774); chairman of the committee to prepare the Declaration of Independence; minister plenipotentiary to France; championed the founding of the University of Virginia
Place of burial: at Monticello, in Charlottesville, Va.

Jef·fer·son |'jefərsən|, Blind Lemon (1897–1930) U.S. blues singer and guitarist. His hit song "Booger Rooger

Blue" coined the term that became "boogie-woogie."

Jehu |'jē,h(y)ōō| (842–815 BC) king of Israel. He was famous for driving his chariot furiously (2 Kings 9).

Jel·li·coe |'jeləkō|, John Rushworth, 1st Earl (1859–1935) British admiral, commander of the Grand Fleet at the Battle of Jutland (1916).

Jen·kins |'jeNGkənz|, Roy (Harris), Baron Jenkins of Hillhead (1920–) English politician and scholar.

Jen·ney |'jenē|, William Le Baron (1832–1907) U.S. architect. His designs include the Home Insurance Co. Building (1884–85) in Chicago.

Jen·nings |'jeniNGz|, Peter Charles (1938–) U.S. television news anchorman, born in Canada. He anchors ABC's *World News Tonight* (1983–).

Jen·nings |'jeniNGz|, Waylon (1937–) U.S. country musician. Notable songs: "Momas Don't Let Your Babies Grow Up to be Cowboys" and "The Eagle."

Jen·son |'jensən|, Nicolas (c. 1420–80) French engraver and printer. An apprentice to Gutenberg, he established his own business in Venice and perfected roman type (1470).

Jer·e·miah |,jerə'mīə| (c. 650–c. 585 BC) Hebrew prophet. He foresaw the fall of Assyria, the conquest of his country by Egypt and Babylon, and the destruction of Jerusalem. The biblical Lamentations are traditionally ascribed to him.

Je·rit·za |'yeritsə|, Maria (1887–1982) Czech operatic soprano. Born *Mizzi Jedička*. She sang with the Metropolitan Opera (1921–32).

Je·rome |jə'rōm|, St. (c. 342–420) Doctor of the Church. He is chiefly known for his compilation of the Vulgate Bible. Feast day, September 30.

Jer·vis |'jərvəs|, John, Earl St. Vincent (1735–1823) British admiral. In 1797, as commander of the British fleet, he defeated a Spanish fleet off Cape St. Vincent, for which he was created Earl St. Vincent.

Jes·per·sen |'yespərsən|, (Jens) Otto (Harry) (1860–1943) Danish philologist, grammarian, and educationist. He promoted the use of the "direct method" In language teaching with the publica-

tion of his theoretical work *How to Teach a Foreign Language* (1904). Other notable works: *Modern English Grammar* (1909–49).

Jes·sel |'jesəl|, George Albert (1898–1981) U.S. entertainer. He is best known as a master of ceremonies.

Je·sus |'jēzəs| (c. 6 BC–c. 30 AD) the central figure of the Christian religion. Also **Jesus Christ** or **Jesus of Nazareth**. Jesus conducted a mission of preaching and healing (with reported miracles) in Palestine in about AD 28–30, which is described in the Gospels. His followers considered him to be the Christ or Messiah and the Son of God, and belief in his resurrection from the dead is the central tenet of Christianity.

Jett |jet|, Joan (1960–) U.S. rock guitarist and singer. Notable albums: *Up Your Alley* (1988).

Jew·ett |'jōōət|, Charles Coffin (1816–68) U.S. librarian. He was the first librarian of the Smithsonian Institution (1848–54) and later became superintendent of the Boston Public Library (1855–68).

Jew·ett |'jōōət|, Sarah Orne (1849–1909) U.S. author and poet. Her works include *The Country of the Pointed Firs* (1896).

Jew·i·son |'jōōəsən|, Norman (1929–) Canadian movie director and producer. He is known particularly for the drama *The Cincinnati Kid* (1965) and *In the Heat of the Night* (1971), which won five Oscars, the musical *Fiddler on the Roof* (1971), and the romantic comedy *Moonstruck* (1987).

Je·ze·bel |'jezəbel| (9th century BC) a Phoenician princess, traditionally the great-aunt of Dido and in the Bible the wife of Ahab king of Israel. She was denounced by Elijah for introducing the worship of Baal into Israel (1 Kings 16:31, 21:5–15, 2 Kings 9:30–37). Her use of make-up shocked Puritan England.

Jiang Jie Shi variant form of CHIANG KAI-SHEK.

Ji·mé·nez de Cis·ne·ros |hi'menəs də sis'nerōs|, Francisco (1436–1517) Spanish cardinal and statesman, regent of Spain (1516–17). Also **Ximenes de Cisneros**. He was Grand Inquisitor for

Castile and Léon from 1507 to 1517, during which time he undertook a massive campaign against heresy, having some 2,500 alleged heretics put to death.

Jin·nah |'jinə|, Muhammad Ali (1876–1948) statesman and founder of Pakistan. He headed the Muslim League in its struggle with the Hindu-oriented Indian National Congress over Indian independence, and in 1947 he became the first governor general and president of Pakistan.

Joan of Arc |jön əv 'ärk|, St. (c. 1412–31) French national heroine; known as **the Maid of Orleans**. She led the French armies against the English in the Hundred Years War, relieving besieged Orleans (1429) and ensuring that Charles VII could be crowned in previously occupied Reims. Captured by the Burgundians in 1430, she was handed over to the English, convicted of heresy, and burnt at the stake. She was canonized in 1920. Feast day, May 30.

Jobs |jäbz|, Steven (Paul) (1955–) U.S. computer entrepreneur. He set up the Apple computer company in 1976 with *Steve Wozniak* (1950–), remaining chairman of the company until 1985.

Joel |jöl|, Billy (1949–) U.S. pop singer and songwriter. His many top 10 hits include "Just the Way You Are" (1977), "Tell Her About It" (1983), and "River of Dreams" (1993).

Jof·fre |'zHawfrə|, Joseph Jacques Césaire (1852–1931) French marshal, commander in chief of the French army on the Western Front during World War I.

Jof·frey |'jawfrē|, Robert (1930–88) U.S. ballet dancer and choreographer. Born *Abdullah Jaffa Anver Bey Khan*. He founded the Joffrey Ballet (1966).

John[1] |jän| (1165–1216) son of Henry II, king of England (1199–1216); known as **John Lackland**. He lost most of his French possessions, including Normandy, to Phillip II of France. In 1209 he was excommunicated for refusing to accept Stephen Langton as Archbishop of Canterbury. Forced to sign the Magna Carta by his barons (1215), he ignored its provisions and civil war broke out.

John[2] |jän| the name of six kings of Por-

tugal: **John I** (1357–1433), reigned 1385–1433; known as **John the Great**. Reinforced by an English army, he defeated the Castilians at Aljubarrota (1385), winning independence for Portugal. **John II** (1455–95), reigned 1481–95. **John III** (1502–57), reigned 1521–57. **John IV** (1604–56), reigned 1640–56; known as **John the Fortunate**. The founder of the Braganza dynasty, he expelled a Spanish usurper and proclaimed himself king. **John V** (1689–1750), reigned 1706–50. **John VI** (1767–1826), reigned 1816–26.

John |jän|, Augustus (Edwin) (1878–1961) Welsh painter. Frequent subjects of his work are the gypsies of Wales; he was also noted for his portraits of the wealthy and famous, particularly prominent writers. He was the brother of Gwen John.

John |jän|, Sir Elton (Hercules) (1947–) English pop and rock singer, pianist, and songwriter; born *Reginald Kenneth Dwight*. Notable songs: "Goodbye, Yellow Brick Road" (1973) and "Can You Feel the Love Tonight?" (1994).

John |jän|, Gwen (1876–1939) Welsh painter. The sister of Augustus John, she settled in France. In 1913 she converted to Catholicism; her paintings, noted for their grey tonality, often depict nuns or girls in interior settings.

John |jän|, St. (1st century) an Apostle, son of Zebedee and brother of James; known as **St. John the Evangelist** or **St. John the Divine**. He has traditionally been credited with the authorship of the fourth Gospel, Revelation, and three epistles of the New Testament. Feast day, December 27.

John III |jän| (1624–96) king of Poland (1674–96); known as **John Sobieski**. In 1683 he relieved Vienna when it was besieged by the Turks, thereby becoming the hero of the Christian world.

John V |jän| (1689–1750) king of Portugal, reigned 1706–50.

John VI |jän| (1767–1826) king of Portugal, reigned 1816–26.

John of Da·mas·cus |,jän əv də 'mæskəs|, St. (c. 675–c. 749) Syrian theologian and Doctor of the Church. A champion of image worship against the iconoclasts, he wrote the influential encyclopedic work on Christian theology *The Fount of Wisdom*. Feast day, December 4.

John of Gaunt |ˌjän əv 'gawnt| (1340–99) son of England's Edward III. John of Gaunt was the effective ruler of England during the final years of his father's reign and the minority of Richard II. His son Henry Bolingbroke later became King Henry IV.

John of the Cross |ˌjän|, St. (1542–91) Spanish mystic and poet; born *Juan de Yepis y Alvarez*. A Carmelite monk and priest, he joined with St. Teresa of Ávila in founding the "discalced" Carmelite order in 1568. Feast day, December 14.

John the Baptist |ˌjän|, St. (1st century) Jewish preacher and prophet, a comtemporary of Jesus. In *c.*27 AD he preached and baptized on the banks of the Jordan River. Among those whom he baptized was Christ. He was beheaded by Herod Antipas after denouncing that latter's marriage to Herodias, the wife of Herod's brother Philip (Matt. 14:1–12). Feast day, June 24.

John the Evangelist, St (also **John the Divine**) see JOHN, ST.

John the Fortunate John IV of Portugal (see JOHN²).

John the Great John I of Portugal (see JOHN²).

John Paul II |ˌjän 'pawl| (1920–) Polish cleric, pope since 1978; born *Karol Jozef Wojtyla*. The first non-Italian pope since 1522, he traveled abroad extensively during his papacy and upheld the Roman Catholic Church's traditional opposition to artificial means of contraception and abortion, homosexuality, the ordination of women, and the relaxation of the rule of celibacy for priests.

Johns |'jänz|, Jasper (1930–) U.S. painter, sculptor, and printmaker. A key figure in the development of pop art, he depicted commonplace and universally recognized images. His notable series of works include *Flags*, *Targets*, and *Numbers* (all produced in the mid-1950s).

John·son |'jänsən| Andrew, see box.

Eliza McCardle Johnson (1810–76), wife of Andrew Johnson and U.S. first lady (1865–69).

Johnson, Andrew
17th U.S. president

Life dates: 1808–1875
Place of birth: Raleigh, N. Carolina
Mother: Mary McDonough Johnson
Father: Jacob Johnson
Stepfather: Turner Dougherty
Wife: Eliza McCardle Johnson
Children: Martha, Charles, Mary, Robert, Andrew
College/University: none
Military service: during Civil War, appointed by Lincoln as military governor of Tennessee
Career: Tailor
Political career: alderman and mayor; Greenville, Tenn.; Tennessee House of Representatives; U.S. House of Representatives; governor of Tennessee; U.S. Senate; vice president (under Lincoln); president; U.S. Senate
Party: Democratic; National Union Party
Home state: Tennessee
Opponents in presidential race: none (succeeded to the presidency after the assassination of Abraham Lincoln)
Term of office: Apr. 15, 1865–March 3, 1869
Vice president: none
Notable events of presidency: Reconstruction Act; Alaska Purchase; Thirteenth Amendment to the Constitution ratified, abolishing slavery; Nebraska admitted as 37th state; Tenure of Office Act; Fourteenth Amendment to the Constitution ratified; impeachment by U.S. House of Representatives and acquittal in U.S. Senate trial
Place of burial: Greenville, Tenn.

John·son |'jänsən|, Betsey (1942–) U.S. fashion designer.

John·son |'jänsən|, Byron Bancroft (1864–1931) U.S. baseball organizer. Known as **Ban**. He organized the American League (1900) and inaugurated the World Series.

John·son |'jänsən|, Cornelius (1593–*c.* 1661) English-born Dutch portrait painter. Also **Jansens** or **Janssen van Ceulen**. He painted for the court of Charles I; after the outbreak of the English Civil War, he emigrated to Holland (1643).

John·son |'jänsən|, Earvin (1959–) U.S. basketball player; known as **Magic Johnson**. He played for the Los

Johnson, Lyndon Baines
36th U.S. president

Life dates: 1908–1973
Place of birth: near Stonewall, Texas
Mother: Rebekah Baines Johnson
Father: Sam Ealy Johnson, Jr.
Wife: Lady Bird Johnson (born Claudia Alta Taylor)
Children: Lynda Bird, Luci
Nickname: LBJ
College/University: Southwest Texas State Teachers College
Military service: during World War II, served as a special duty officer, U.S. Naval Intelligence
Career: Teacher
Political career: U.S. House of Representatives; U.S. Senate (minority and majority leader); vice president (under Kennedy); president
Party: Democratic
Home state: Texas
Opponent in presidential race: Barry M. Goldwater
Term of office: Nov. 22, 1963–Jan. 20, 1969 (succeeded to the presidency after the assassination of John F. Kennedy)
Vice president: None (1st term); Hubert H. Humphrey (2nd term)
Notable events of presidency: Civil Rights Act; Voting Rights Act; Economic Opportunity Act; Nuclear Non-Proliferation Treaty; Vietnam War; Arab-Israeli War; Department of Transportation established
Other achievements: awarded Silver Star for gallantry, World War II
Place of burial: (near) Johnson City, Texas

Angeles Lakers from 1979 to 1991. After being diagnosed HIV-positive, he won an Olympic gold medal in 1992 and then briefly returned to the Lakers.

John·son |'jänsən|, Hiram Warren (1866–1945) U.S. politician. He served as governor of California (1911–17) and in the U.S. Senate (1917–45). A founder of the U.S. Progressive Party, he was the vice-presidential candidate on Theodore Roosevelt's "Bull Moose" ticket (1912).

John·son |'jänsən|, Howard Deering (c. 1896–1972) U.S. businessman. His Howard Johnson's restaurants were America's first franchise chain.

John·son |'jänsən|, Jack (1878–1946) U.S. boxer. He was the first black world heavyweight champion (1908–15).

John·son |'jänsən|, James P. (1894–1955) U.S. jazz pianist and composer. He wrote large-scale orchestral works such as *Harlem Symphony* (1932) and *Symphony in Brown* (1935), as well as songs.

John·son |'jänsən|, James Weldon (1871–1938) U.S. poet, novelist, and diplomat He was a leader in the civil rights movement and the Harlem Renaissance, and he edited *The Book of American Negro Poetry* (1922, enlarged 1931).

John·son |'jänsən|, John H. (1918–) U.S. publisher. He was chairman and chief executive officer of the Johnson Publishing Co., Inc. (1942–), the publisher of *Ebony* and *Jet* magazines. Spingarn Medal, 1966.

John·son |'jänsən| Lyndon Baines, see box. **Lady Bird Johnson**, born *Claudia Alta Taylor* (1912–), wife of Lyndon Johnson and U.S. first lady (1963–69).

John·son |'jänsən|, Martin Elmer (1884–1937) U.S. explorer and naturalist. He produced motion pecures such as *Simba, the King of the Beasts* (1928); with his wife Osa Helen (1894-1953), who was also his pilot and a hunter, he coauthored several books.

John·son |'jänsən|, Mordecai W. (1890–1976) U.S. educator. Spingarn Medal, 1929.

John·son |'jänsən|, Philip Courtelyou (1906–) U.S. architect and author. He designed many buildings in New York City, including Lincoln Center, the AT&T headquarters building, and Bobst Library at New York University. He is the author of *Architecture Since 1922.*

John·son |'jänsən|, Reverdy (1796–1876) U.S. politician. He represented the defense in the Dred Scott Supreme Court case.

John·son |'jänsən|, Richard Mentor (1780–1850) vice president of the U.S. (1837–41).

John·son |'jänsən|, Robert (1911–38) U.S. blues singer and guitarist. Despite his mysterious early death, he was very influential on the 1960s blues movement. Notable songs: "I Was Standing at the Crossroads."

John·son |'jänsən|, Samuel (1709–84) English lexicographer, writer, critic, and conversationalist. Known as **Dr. Johnson**. A leading figure in the literary London of his day, he is noted particularly for his *Dictionary of the English Language* (1755), edition of Shakespeare (1765), and *The Lives of the English Poets* (1777). James Boswell's biography of Johnson records details of his life and conversation.

John·son |'jänsən|, Thomas (1732–1819) U.S. Supreme Court justice (1791–93).

John·son |'jänsən|, Walter Perry (1887–1946) U.S. baseball player. Known as **Big Train**. He pitched a record 113 career shutouts and led the American League in strikeouts for 12 seasons. Elected to Baseball Hall of Fame (1936).

John·son |'jänsən|, William (1771–1834) U.S. Supreme Court justice (1804–34).

John·ston |'jänstən|, Annie (1863–1931) U.S. author. She wrote a series of children's stories, beginning with "The Little Colonel" (1895).

John·ston |'jänstən|, Joseph Eggleston (1807–91) U.S. army officer and politician. He was defeated by Grant at Vicksburg and surrendered to Sherman. He was a member of the U.S. House of Representatives from Virginia (1879–81).

John·ston |'jänstən|, Lynn (1947–) Canadian cartoonist, author, and illustrator. She created the comic strip "For Better or For Worse."

Jo·liot |ZHŌ'lyŌ|, Jean-Frédéric (1900–58) French nuclear physicist. Marie Curie's assistant at the Radium Institute; he worked with her daughter Irène (1897–1956) and they later married. Together they discovered artificial radioactivity. Nobel Prize for Chemistry (1935, shared with his wife).

Jo·liot-Cu·rie |ZHŌ,lyŌkyŌŌ'rē|, Irène (1897–1956) French physicist. Nobel Prize for Chemistry, 1935.

Jol·liet |ZHAwl'ye; ZHŌlē'(y)et|, Louis (1645–1700) French-Canadian explorer. With Jacques Marquette, he explored the upper Mississippi River.

Jol·son |'jōlsən|, Al (1886–1950) Russian-born U.S. singer, movie actor, and comedian; born *Asa Yoelson*. He made the Gershwin song "Swanee" his trademark, and appeared in blackface in the first full-length talking movie, *The Jazz Singer* (1927).

Jones |jōnz|, Bobby (1902–71) U.S. golfer; full name *Robert Tyre Jones*. In a short competitive career (1923–30), and as an amateur, he won thirteen major competitions, including four American and three British open championships.

Jones |jōnz|, Chuck (1912–) U.S. writer, producer, and director. Full name *Charles Martin Jones*. He was the creator of the cartoon characters Pepe le Pew, the Road Runner, Coyote, and others, and director of "How the Grinch Stole Christmas."

Jones |jōnz|, Daniel (1881–1967) British phonetician. He developed the International Phonetic Alphabet from 1907 and went on to invent the system of cardinal vowels. Notable works: *English Pronouncing Dictionary* (1917).

Jones |jōnz|, Edward D. (1856–1920) U.S. business journalist. With Charles Henry Dow, he founded Dow Jones & Co. (1882) and *The Wall Street Journal* (1889).

Jones |jōnz|, Howard Mumford (1892–1980) U.S. educator and author. Notable works: *O Strange New World* (1964, Pulitzer Prize).

Jones |jōnz|, Inigo (1573–1652) English architect and stage designer. He introduced the Palladian style to England; notable buildings include the Queen's House at Greenwich (1616) and the Banqueting Hall at Whitehall (1619).

Jones |jōnz|, James (1921–77) U.S. author. Notable works: *From Here to Eternity* (1951).

Jones |jōnz|, James Earl (1931–) U.S. actor. A star of stage, film, and television, he performed in the *Star Wars* movies and the play *Fences*.

Jones |jōnz|, Jennifer (1919–) U.S. actress. Born *Phyllis Isley*. Notable movies: *The Song of Bernadette* (1943, Academy Award).

Jones |jōnz|, Jo (1911–85) U.S. jazz drummer. Full name *Jonathan Jones*. He performed with Count Basie's

Orchestra (1934–48); his innovations revolutionized the timbre of the jazz rhythm section.

Jones |jōnz|, John Paul (1747–92) Scottish-born U.S. admiral; born *John Paul*. He became famous for his raids off the northern coasts of Britain during the American Revolution and in his ship *Bonhomme Richard* defeated the *Serapis* in 1779. He served in the Russian Navy in 1788–89.

Jones |jōnz|, Paula Corbin (1966–) U.S. plaintiff. Her 1994 suit charging President Bill Clinton with sexual harassment while he was governor of Arkansas in 1991 led to the exposure of Clinton's affair with Monica Lewinsky.

Jones |jōnz|, Quincy Delight, Jr. (1933–) U.S. composer, conductor, and jazz trumpeter. He founded his own recording label, Qwest Records, and wrote television and movie scores and the theme for "The Bill Cosby Show."

Jones |jōnz|, Shirley (1934–) U.S. stage, film, and television actress. Notable movies: *Elmer Gantry* (1960 Academy Award).

Jones |jōnz|, Tom (1940–) Welsh pop singer; born *Thomas Jones Woodward*. Hits include "It's Not Unusual" (1965), "The Green, Green Grass of Home" (1966), and "Delilah" (1968).

Jong |'jawNG|, Erica (Mann) (1942–) U.S. poet and novelist. She is best known for her picaresque novels *Fear of Flying* (1973), recounting the sexual exploits of its heroine Isadora Wing, and *Fanny* (1980), written in a pseudo-18th-century style.

Jon·son |'jänsən|, Ben (1572–1637) English dramatist and poet; full name *Benjamin Jonson*. With his play *Every Man in his Humour* (1598) he established his "comedy of humours," whereby each character is dominated by a particular obsession. He became the first Poet Laureate in the modern sense. Other notable works: *Volpone* (1606) and *Bartholomew Fair* (1614).

Jop·lin |'jäplin|, Janis (1943–70) U.S. singer. She died from a heroin overdose just before her most successful album, *Pearl*, and her number-one single "Me and Bobby McGee" were released.

Jop·lin |'jäplin|, Scott (1868–1917)

U.S. pianist and composer. He was the first of the creators of ragtime to write down his compositions. Notable compositions: "Maple Leaf Rag" (1899), "The Entertainer" (1902), and "Gladiolus Rag" (1907).

Jor·daens |'yawrdäns|, Jacob (1593–1678) Flemish painter. Influenced by Rubens, he is noted for his boisterous peasant scenes painted in warm colors. Notable works: *The King Drinks* (1638).

Jor·dan |'jawrdən|, Barbara (1936–96) U.S. lawyer, educator, and politician. She was a member of the U.S. House of Representatives from Texas (1972–78) and a member of the Texas Senate (1966–72).

Jor·dan |'jawrdən|, Michael (Jeffrey) (1963–) U.S. basketball player. Playing for the Chicago Bulls (1984–93, 1995–98), he led them to six titles and was the NBA's (National Basketball Association) Most Valuable Player five times. He retired in 1993 to play professional baseball, but returned in 1995. He has endorsed products and appeared in movies.

Jo·seph |'jōzəf; 'jōsəf|, St. (1st cent. BC–1st cent. AD) husband of the Virgin Mary. A carpenter of Nazareth, he was betrothed to Mary at the time of the Annunciation. Feast day, March 19.

Jo·seph |'jōzəf; 'jōsəf|, Chief (1840–1904) American Indian chief. Indian name *Inmuttooyahlatlat*. As chief of the Nez Percé tribe, he defied the efforts of the U.S. government to move his people from Oregon until he was captured in 1877.

Jo·se·phine |'jōzəfēn; 'jōsəfēn| (1763–1814) Empress of France (1804–09); full name *Marie Joséphine Rose Tascher de la Pagerie*. She married to the Viscount de Beauharnais before marrying Napoleon in 1796. Their marriage proved childless, and she was divorced by Napoleon in 1809.

Jo·seph·son |'jōzəfsən; 'jōsəfsən|, Matthew (1899–1978) U.S. author. Notable works: *Zola and His Time* (1928) and *Infidel in the Temple* (1967).

Jo·se·phus |jō'sēfəs|, Flavius (c. 37–c. 100) Jewish historian, general, and Pharisee; born *Joseph ben Matthias*. His *Jewish War* gives an eyewitness account of the events leading up to the Jewish re-volt against the Romans in 66, in which he was a leader.

Josh·ua |'jäsH(ə)wə| (*c.* 13th century BC) the Israelite leader who succeeded Moses and led his people into the Promised Land.

Josquin des Prez see DES PREZ.

Joule |jōol|, James Prescott (1818–89) English physicist. Joule established that all forms of energy were interchange-able—the first law of thermodynamics. The Joule–Thomson effect, discovered with William Thomson, later Lord Kelvin, in 1852, led to the development of the refrigerator and to the science of cryogenics. Joule also measured and de-scribed the heating effects of an electric current passing through a resistance.

Joyce |jois|, James (Augustine Aloysius) (1882–1941) Irish author. One of the most important writers of the modernist movement, he made his name with *Dubliners* (short stories, 1914). His novel *Ulysses* (1922) revolutionized the struc-ture of the modern novel and developed the stream-of-consciousness technique. Other notable novels: *A Portrait of the Artist as a Young Man* (1914–15) and *Finnegan's Wake* (1939).

Joy·ner |'joinər|, Florence Griffith (1959–98) U.S. track and field athlete. She established world records in the 100- and 200-meter races in 1988, win-ning three gold medals in the 1988 Olympic Games.

Joy·ner-Ker·see |'joinər 'kərsē|, Jack-ie (1962–) U.S. track and field ath-lete. She won gold medals in the hep-tathalon in the 1988 and 1992 Olympic Games.

Juan Car·los |,(h)wän 'kärlōs| (1938–) grandson of Alfonso XIII, king of Spain since 1975; full name *Juan Carlos Victor María de Borbón y Borbón*. Franco's chosen successor, he became king after Franco's death. His reign has seen Spain's increasing liberalization and its entry into NATO and the Euro-pean Community.

Juá·rez |'hwärez|, Benito Pablo (1806–72) Mexican statesman, president (1858–72). Between 1864 and 1867 he was replaced by Emperor Maximilian, who was supported by the French.

Judas |jōodəs| see JUDE, ST.

Ju·das Is·car·iot |'jōodəs is'kerēət| (1st century AD) an Apostle. He betrayed Jesus to the Jewish authorities in return for thirty pieces of silver; the Gospels leave his motives uncertain. Overcome with remorse, he later committed sui-cide.

Ju·das Mac·ca·bae·us |'jōodəs ,mækə 'bēyəs| (died *c.* 161 BC) Jewish leader. Leading a Jewish revolt in Judaea against Antiochus IV Epiphanes from around 167, he recovered Jerusalem and dedi-cated the Temple anew. He is the hero of the two books of the Maccabees in the Apocrypha.

Jude |jōod|, St. an Apostle, supposed brother of James; also known as **Judas**. Thaddaeus is traditionally identified with him. According to tradition, he was martyred in Persia with St. Simon. Feast day (with St. Simon), October 28.

Judge |jəj|, Mike (1962–) U.S. ani-mator, producer, and movie director. He created the television comedies "Beavis and Butt-head" and "King of the Hill."

Jud·son |'jədsən|, Arthur Leon (1881–1975) U.S. musician and businessman. He organized a network of stations to air radio broadcasts of concerts (1927), which later became the Columbia Broadcasting System; he also formed Columbia Records.

Ju·gur·tha |jōo'gərTHə| (died 104 BC) joint king of Numidia (*c.* 118–104). His attacks on his royal partners prompted intervention by Rome and led to the outbreak of the Jugurthine War (112–105). He was eventually captured by the Roman general Marius and executed in Rome.

Juil·li·ard |'jōolēärd|, Augustus D. (1840–1919) U.S. merchant and patron of music. He founded the Juilliard Mu-sical Foundation (1920), which later be-came the Juilliard School of Music (1926).

Jul·ian |'jōolyən| (*c.* 331–363 AD) Roman emperor (360–363), nephew of Constantine; full name *Flavius Claudius Julianus*; known as **the Apostate**. He re-stored paganism as the state cult in place of Christianity, but this move was re-versed after his death during a campaign against the Persians.

Jul·ian |'jo͞olyən|, Percy Lavon (1899–1975) U.S. chemist. He synthesized cortisone and developed numerous soya protein derivatives. He was founder and president of Julian Laboratories (1953).

Jul·i·an of Nor·wich |'jo͞olyən əv 'nawriCH| (c. 1342–c. 1413) English mystic. She is said to have lived as a recluse outside St. Julian's Church, Norwich. She is chiefly associated with the *Revelations of Divine Love* (c. 1393), a description of a series of visions she had in which she depicts the Holy Trinity as Father, Mother, and Lord.

Jul·i·us Cae·sar |'jo͞olyəs 'sēzər|, Gaius (100–44 BC) Roman general and statesman. He established the First Triumvirate (60) with Pompey and Crassus, and became consul in 59. Between 58 and 51 he fought the Gallic Wars, invaded Britain (55–54), and acquired immense power. After civil war with Pompey, which ended in Pompey's defeat at Pharsalus (48), Caesar became dictator at Rome and began to introduce reforms. He was murdered on the Ides (15th) of March in a conspiracy led by Brutus and Cassius.

Jung |yo͝oNG|, Carl (Gustav) (1875–1961) Swiss psychologist. He originated the concept of introvert and extrovert personality, and of the four psychological functions of sensation, intuition, thinking, and feeling. He collaborated with Sigmund Freud in developing the psychoanalytic theory of personality, but later disassociated himself from Freud's preoccupation with sexuality as the determinant of personality, preferring to emphasize a mystical or religious factor in the unconscious.

Jus·sieu |zHo͞os'yoE|, Antoine Laurent de (1748–1836) French botanist. Jussieu grouped plants into families on the basis of common essential properties and, in *Genera Plantarum* (1789), developed the system on which modern plant classification is based.

Jus·tin |'jəstən|, St. (c. 100–165) Christian philosopher; known as **St. Justin the Martyr.** According to tradition he was martyred in Rome together with some of his followers. He is remembered for his *Apologia* (c. 150). Feast day, June 1.

Jus·tin·i·an |jəs'tinēən| (483–565) Byzantine emperor (527–65); Latin name *Flavius Petrus Sabbatius Justinianus.* Through his general, Belisarius, he regained North Africa and Spain. He codified Roman law (529) and carried out a building program throughout the Empire, of which St. Sophia at Constantinople (532) was a part.

Ju·ve·nal |'jo͞ovənəl| (c. 60–c. 140) Roman satirist; Latin name *Decimus Junius Juvenalis.* His sixteen verse satires present a savage attack on the vice and folly of Roman society, chiefly in the reign of the emperor Domitian.

Kk

Ka·bi·la |kä'bēlə|, Laurent (1937–)
African statesman, president of the
Democratic Republic of Congo (formerly Zaire). Kabila's forces overthrew
President Mobutu in 1997. On taking
power Kabila changed the name of the
country from Zaire to Democratic Republic of Congo.

Ká·dár |'kä,där|, János (1912–89) Hun-
garian statesman, First Secretary of the
Hungarian Socialist Workers' Party
(1956–88) and prime minister (1956–
58 and 1961–65). After crushing the
Hungarian uprising of 1956, Kádár con-
sistently supported the Soviet Union.
His policy of "consumer socialism"
made Hungary the most affluent state
in eastern Europe.

Kael |käl|, Pauline (1919–) U.S.
movie critic. She was a reviewer for *The
New Yorker*; her collections of reviews include *Deeper into Movies* (1973, National Book Award).

Kaf·ka |'käfkə|, Franz (1883–1924)
Czech novelist who wrote in German.
His work is characterized by its portrayal
of an enigmatic and nightmarish reality
where the individual is perceived as
lonely, perplexed, and threatened. Notable works: *The Metamorphosis* (1917)
and *The Trial* (1925).

Ka·ha·na·mo·ku |kə,hänə'mōkōō|,
Duke Paoa (1890–1968) U.S. swimmer
and surfer. The developer of the flutter
kick, he won the 100-yard freestyle gold
medals in the 1912 and 1920 Olympic
Games, as well as the 800-meter relay
gold medal in the 1920 Olympics.

Kah·lo |'kälō|, Frieda (1907–54) Mex-
ican artist. Her many self-portraits deal
with her battle to survive after a crip-
pling bus accident.

Kahn |kän|, Albert (1869–1942) U.S.
architect. He designed the General Mo-
tors Building in Detroit, Michigan.

Kahn |kän|, Louis Isadore (1901–74)
U.S. architect, born in Estonia. He designed the Salk Lab in La Jolla, California, and the Yale Art Gallery in New
Haven, Connecticut.

Kahn |kän|, Otto Hermann (1867–

1934) U.S. banker and philanthropist,
born in Germany. He worked for the
banking firm Kuhn, Loeb & Co. in New
York from 1897. He is also noted as one
of the greatest patrons of arts and served
as president of the Metropolitan Opera
Co. (1918–31).

Kai·ser |'kīzər|, Henry John (1882–
1967) U.S. industrialist. He was an executive with companies involved in dam
construction, shipbuilding, steel production, and automobile manufacture,
and he founded the Kaiser Foundation
for health services.

Kai·ser |'kīzər|, Georg (1878–1945)
German dramatist. He is best known for
his expressionist plays *The Burghers of
Calais* (1914), and *Gas I* (1918) and *Gas
II* (1920); the last two provide a grue-
some vision of futuristic science, ending
with the extinction of all life by poiso-
nous gas.

Kai·ser Wil·helm Wilhelm II of Germany (see WILHELM II).

Kaler, James Otis (1848–1912) U.S. author. Pseudonym **James Otis**. He wrote
stories for boys, including *Toby Tyler: or,
Ten Weeks with a Circus* (1881).

Ka·li·da·sa |'kälē'däsə| (5th century
AD) Indian poet and dramatist. He is
best known for his drama *Sakuntala*, the
love story of King Dushyanta and the
maiden Sakuntala.

Ka·li·nin |kə'lēnin; kə'lyenyin|, Mikhail
(Ivanovich) (1875–1946) Soviet statesman, head of state of the USSR 1919–
46. He founded the newspaper *Pravda*
(1912).

Ka·ma·li |kə'mälē|, Norma (1945–)
U.S. fashion designer.

Ka·me·ha·me·ha |kä'mähä'mähä| five
kings of Hawaii: **Kamehameha I**
(c.1758–1819; reigned 1795–1819).
Born *Paiea*; known as **Kamehameha
the Great**. **Kamehameha II** (1797–
1824; reigned 1819–24). Born *Liholiho*;
son of Kamehameha I. **Kamehameha
III** (1813–54; reigned 1825–54).
Born *Kauikeaouli*; brother of Kamehameha II. **Kamehameha IV** (1834–
63; reigned 1854–63). Also known as

Alexander Liholiho; nephew of Kamehameha III. **Kamehameha V** (1830–72; reigned 1863–72). Born *Lot*; brother of Kamehameha IV.

Ka·mer·lingh On·nes |'kämərliNG 'awnəs|, Heike (1853–1926) Dutch physicist. During his studies of cryogenic phenomena he achieved a temperature of less than one degree above absolute zero and succeeded in liquefying helium. Onnes discovered the phenomenon of superconductivity in 1911, and was awarded the Nobel Prize for Physics in 1913.

Kan·din·sky |kæn'dinskē|, Wassily (1866–1944) Russian painter. He pioneered abstract painting.

Kane |kān|, Bob (1916–   ) U.S. cartoonist. With neighbor Bill Finger, he was cocreator of the character Batman.

Kan·in |'kænən|, Garson (1912–   ) U.S. actor, director, and producer. Notable works: *Born Yesterday* (1946) and *Moviola* (1979).

Kant |känt|, Immanuel (1724–1804) German philosopher. In the *Critique of Pure Reason* (1781) he countered Hume's skeptical empiricism by arguing that any affirmation or denial regarding the ultimate nature of reality ("noumenon") makes no sense. He maintained that all we can know are the objects of experience ("phenomena"), interpreted by space and time and ordered according to twelve key concepts. Kant's *Critique of Practical Reason* (1788) affirms the existence of an absolute moral law—the categorical imperative.

Kap·lin |'kæplən|, Justin (1925–   ) U.S. author. Notable works: *Mr. Clemens and Mark Twain* (1966, Pulitzer Prize and National Book Award).

Ka·ra·džić |kä'räjiCH|, Vuk Stefanović (1787–1864) Serbian writer, grammarian, lexicographer, and folklorist. He modified the Cyrillic alphabet for Serbian written usage and compiled a Serbian dictionary in 1818. Widely claimed to be the father of modern Serbian literature, he collected and published national folk stories and poems.

Ka·ra·jan |'kärä,yän|, Herbert von (1908–89) Austrian conductor, chiefly remembered as the principal conductor

of the Berlin Philharmonic Orchestra (1955–89).

Ka·ra·man·lis |,kerə'mænləs|, Constantine (1907–1998) Greek politician. He served as president of Greece (1980–85 and 1990–94), rebuilding democracy after a 1967–74 junta.

Ka·ran |'kerən; kə'ræn|, Donna (1948–   ) U.S. fashion designer.

Kar·loff |'kärlawf|, Boris (1887–1969) British-born U.S. actor; born *William Henry Pratt*. His name is chiefly linked with horror movies, such as *Frankenstein* (1931) and *The Body Snatcher* (1945).

Kar·pov |'kärpawf|, Anatoli (Yevgenevich) (1951–   ) Russian chess player. He was world champion from 1975 until defeated by Gary Kasparov in 1985.

Ka·sem |'käsəm|, Casey (1933–   ) U.S. radio disk jockey.

Kas·pa·rov |'kæspə,rawf|, Gary (1963–   ) Russian chess player. He has been world chess champion since 1985.

Kas·se·baum |'kæsə,bawm; 'kæsə-,bowm|, Nancy Landon (1932–   ) U.S. senator from Kansas (1979–96).

Kauff·mann |'kowfmən|, (Maria Anna Catherina) Angelica (1740–1807) Swiss painter. Also **Kauffman**. In London from 1766, she became well known for her neoclassical and allegorical paintings. She was a founding member of the Royal Academy of Arts (1768).

Kauf·man |'kawfmən|, George Simon (1889–1961) U.S. journalist, playwright, and director. He collaborated with George Gershwin to write *Of Thee I Sing* (1931, Pulitzer Prize), and with Moss Hart to write *You Can't Take It With You* (1936, Pulitzer Prize).

Kaunda, Kenneth (David) (1924–   ) Zambian statesman, president (1964–91). He led the United National Independence Party to electoral victory in 1964, becoming prime minister and the first president of independent Zambia.

Ka·wa·ba·ta |käwä'bätä|, Yasunari (1899–1972) Japanese novelist. Known as an experimental writer in the 1920s, he reverted to traditional Japanese novel forms in the mid 1930s. He was the first Japanese writer to win the Nobel Prize for Literature (1968).

Kaye |kā|, Danny (1913–87) U.S. actor

and comedian; born *David Daniel Kominski*. He was known for his mimicry, comic songs, and slapstick humor. Notable movies: *The Secret Life of Walter Mitty* (1947), *Hans Christian Andersen* (1952).

Ka·zan |kə'zæn|, Elia (1909–) Turkish-born U.S. movie and theater director; born *Elia Kazanjoglous*. In 1947 he co-founded the Actors' Studio, one of the leading centers of method acting. Kazan directed *A Streetcar Named Desire* on stage (1947) and then on screen (1953). Other notable movies: *On the Waterfront* (1954) and *East of Eden* (1955). He received an Academy Award for lifetime achievement 1999.

Kazin, Alfred (1915–98) U.S. literary critic. Notable works: *On Native Ground* (1942).

Kean |kēn|, Edmund (1787–1833) English actor, renowned for his interpretations of Shakespearean tragic roles, notably those of Macbeth and Iago.

Keane |kēn|, Bill (1922–) U.S. cartoonist. Full name *William Keane*. He created the comic strips "The Family Circus" and "Channel Chuckles."

Kea·ting |'kētiNG|, Paul (John) (1944–) Australian Labour statesman, prime minister (1991–96).

Kea·ton |'kētn|, Buster (1895–1966) U.S. actor and director; born *Joseph Francis Keaton*. His deadpan face and acrobatic skills made him one of the biggest comedy stars of the silent-movie era. He starred in and directed movies including *The Navigator* (1924) and *The General* (1926).

Kea·ton |'kētn|, Diane (1946–) U.S. actress. Born *Diane Hall*. Notable moves: *Annie Hall* (1977, Academy Award).

Keats |kēts|, Ezra Jack (1916–) U.S. children's author and illustrator.

Keats |kēts|, John (1795–1821) English poet. A principal figure of the romantic movement, he wrote all of his most famous poems, including "La Belle Dame sans Merci", "Ode to a Nightingale", and "Ode on a Grecian Urn", in 1818 (published in 1820).

Ke·ble |'kēbəl|, John (1792–1866) English churchman. His sermon on national apostasy (1833) is generally held to

mark the beginning of the Oxford Movement, which he founded with John Henry Newman and Edward Pusey.

Keck·ley |'keklē|, Elizabeth (1827– 1907) U.S. former slave. She earned her emancipation as a dressmaker and served Mrs. Abraham Lincoln. Notable works: *Behind the Scenes; or Thirty Years a Slave and Four Years in the White House* (1868), used by all Lincoln biographers.

Kee·ler |'kēlər|, Christine (1942–) English model and showgirl. She achieved notoriety in 1963 in a scandal arising from her affair with the Conservative cabinet minister John Profumo when she was also mistress of a Soviet attaché. Profumo resigned and Keeler was imprisoned on related charges.

Keene |kēn|, Charles Samuel (1823– 91) English illustrator and caricaturist. He is remembered for his work in the weekly journal *Punch* from 1851.

Kee·shan |'kēsHən|, Robert James (1927–) U.S. actor and producer. He played Clarabell on the "Howdy Doody Show" (1947–52), and he produced and starred in "Captain Kangaroo" (1955– 85).

Ke·fau·ver |'kē,fawvər|, (Carey) Estes (1903–63) U.S. politician. He was a member of the U.S. House of Representatives from Tennessee (1939–49), a member of the U.S. Senate (1949–63), and a Democratic vice presidential candidate (1956). As a senator, he conducted hearings to investigate organized crime in interstate commerce (1950– 51).

Keil·lor |'kēlər|, Garrison (Edward) (1942–) U.S. writer and radio entertainer. He is creator of the radio program "A Prairie Home Companion" and the author of fiction such as *Wobegon Boy* (1996) and *The Sandy Bottom Orchestra* (1996, with J. Nilsson).

Keith |kēTH|, Damon Jerome (1922–) U.S. jurist. He served as a judge on the U.S. 6th Circuit Court of Appeals for Detroit (1977–). Spingarn Medal, 1974.

Ke·kulé |'kakŏŏla|, Friedrich August (1829–96) German chemist; full name *Friedrich August Kekulé von Stradonitz*. One of the founders of structural organic chemistry, he is best known for discovering the ring structure of benzene.

Kel·ler |'kelər|, Helen (Adams) (1880–1968) U.S. writer, social reformer, and academic. Blind and deaf from the age of nineteen months, she learned how to read, type, and speak with the help of tutor Anne Sullivan. She went on to champion the cause of blind and deaf people throughout the world.

Kel·logg |'kelawg| U.S. nutritionists: **Will Keith Kellogg** (1860–1951), food manufacturer, collaborated with his brother, **John Harvey Kellogg** (1852–1943), a physician, to develop a breakfast cereal for sanatorium patients, of crisp flakes of rolled and toasted wheat and corn. He established the W. K. Kellogg company in 1906, whose successful breakfast cereals brought about a revolution in Western eating habits.

Kel·logg |'kelawg|, Frank Billings (1856–1937) U.S. statesman. As secretary of state (1925–29), he negotiated the Kellogg-Briand Pact of 1928 to outlaw war. Nobel Peace Prize, 1929.

Kel·logg |'kelawg|, Steven (1941–) U.S. children's author and illustrator.

Kel·ly |'kelē|, Emmett Lee (1898–1979) U.S. clown. He played the mournful tramp with the Ringling Brothers and Barnum and Bailey Circus (1942–57).

Kel·ly |'kelē|, Gene (1912–96) U.S. dancer and choreographer; full name *Eugene Curran Kelly*. He began his career on Broadway in 1938, making a successful transition to movies with *For Me and My Girl* (1942). He performed in and choreographed many movie musicals, including *An American in Paris* (1951) and *Singin' in the Rain* (1952).

Kel·ly |'kelē|, George (1887–1974) U.S. actor and playwright. Notable works: *Craig's Wife* (1925, Pulitzer Prize).

Kel·ly |'kelē|, Grace (Patricia) (1928–82) U.S. movie actress; also called (from 1956) **Princess Grace of Monaco**. She starred in *High Noon* (1952) and also made three Hitchcock movies, including *Rear Window* (1954), before retiring from movies in 1956 on her marriage to Prince Rainier III of Monaco. She died in an automobile accident.

Kel·ly |'kelē|, Ned (1855–80) Australian outlaw; full name *Edward Kelly*. Leader of a band of horse and cattle thieves and bank robbers, he was eventually hanged.

Kel·ly |'kelē|, Walt (1913–73) U.S. cartoonist, book illustrator, and author. Full name *Walter Crawford Kelly*. He created the popular comic strip "Pogo."

Kel·vin |'kelvən|, William Thomson 1st Baron (1824–1907) British physicist and natural philosopher. Best known for introducing the absolute scale of temperature. He also reinstated the second law of thermodynamics and was involved in the laying of the first Atlantic cable, for which he invented several instruments.

Ke·mal Pa·sha |ke'mäl päshə| see ATATÜRK.

Kem·ble |'kembəl|, Fanny (1809–93) English actress; full name *Frances Anne Kemble*. The daughter of Charles Kemble and the niece of Sarah Siddons, she was a success in Shakespearean comedy and tragedy.

Kem·ble |'kembəl|, Gouverneur (1786–1875) U.S. manufacturer and politician. The producer of the finest cannon of his day, he was also a member of the U.S. House of Representatives from New York (1837–41).

Kem·ble |'kembəl|, John Philip (1757–1823) English actor-manager, brother of Sarah Siddons. Noted for his performances in Shakespearean tragedy, he was manager of Drury Lane (1788–1803) and Covent Garden (1803–17) theaters. His younger brother **Charles Kemble** (1775–1854) was also a successful actor-manager.

Kem·e·ny |'kemənē|, John George (1926–92) U.S. mathematician. At one time an assistant to Albert Einstein, he also contributed to the Manhattan Project and (with Thomas Kurtz) invented BASIC computer language (1964). He later became president of Dartmouth College (1970–91).

Kemp |kemp|, Jack F. (1935–) U.S. politician. He was a professional football player for 13 years and a member of the U.S. House of Representatives from New York (1971–); he was a Republican vice presidential candidate (1996).

Kempe |kemp|, Margery (*c.* 1373–*c.*

1440) English mystic. From about 1432 to 1436 she dictated one of the first autobiographies in English, *The Book of Margery Kempe*. It gives an account of her series of pilgrimages, as well as details of her mystic self-transcendent visions.

Kem·pis |'kempis|, Thomas à see THOMAS À KEMPIS.

Ken·dall |'kendl|, Edward Calvin (1886–1972) U.S. biochemist. He isolated crystalline thyroxine from the thyroid gland, and from the adrenal cortex he obtained a number of steroid hormones, one of which was later named cortisone. Nobel Prize for Physiology or Medicine (1950).

Ke·neal·ly |kə'næle|, Thomas (Michael) (1935–) Australian novelist. He first gained recognition for *The Chart of Jimmy Blacksmith* (1972), but is probably best known for his prize-winning novel *Schindler's List* (1982), filmed by Steven Spielberg in 1993.

Ken·nan |'kenən|, George Frost (1904–) U.S. author and diplomat. He held ambassadorships to the Soviet Union and Yugoslavia. Notable works: *Russia Leave the Ward* (1956, Pulitzer Prize) and *Memoirs* (1967, Pulitzer Prize and National Book Award).

Ken·ne·dy |'kenəde| U.S. political family, including: **John Fitzgerald Kennedy** see box. His wife, **Jacqueline Kennedy** see ONASSIS. **Robert Francis Kennedy** (1925–68), U.S. attorney general (1961–64); known as **Bobby**. He closely assisted his brother John in domestic policy and was also a champion of the civil rights movement. He was assassinated during his campaign for the Democratic presidential nomination. **Edward Moore Kennedy** (1932–), brother of John and Robert, U.S. senator since 1962; known as **Ted** or **Teddy**. His political career has been overshadowed by his involvement in an automobile accident at Chappaquiddick Island (1969), in which his assistant Mary Jo Kopechne drowned. **John Fitzgerald Kennedy, Jr.,** (1960–), son of John Kennedy. U.S. lawyer and editor. He was cofounder and editor in chief of the magazine *George* (1995–98).

Ken·ne·dy |'kenəde|, Anthony McLeod

Kennedy, John Fitzgerald
35th U.S. president

Life dates: 1917–1963
Place of birth: Brookline, Mass.
Mother: Rose Elizabeth Fitzgerald Kennedy
Father: Joseph Patrick Kennedy
Wife: Jacqueline (Jackie) Lee Bouvier Kennedy
Children: Caroline; John, Jr.; Patrick (died 2 days after birth)
Nicknames: JFK; Jack
College/University: Harvard; Princeton; London School of Economics
Military service: U.S. Navy lieutenant and PT boat commander, World War II
Political career: U.S. House of Representatives; U.S. Senate; president
Party: Democratic
Home state: Massachusetts
Opponent in presidential race: Richard M. Nixon
Term of office: Jan. 20, 1961–Nov. 22, 1963 (assassinated)
Vice president: Lyndon Baines Johnson
Notable events of presidency: Peace Corps created; established Committee on Equal Employment Opportunity; Berlin Wall built; Cuban Missile Crisis; Nuclear Test-Ban Treaty; Alan Shepard first U.S. astronaut in space; President Diem and brother Ngo Dinh Nhu assassinated in Vietnam coup
Other achievements: Awarded Navy and Marine Corps Medal and Purple Heart; Pulitzer Prize for biography *Profiles in Courage*
Place of burial: Arlington National Cemetery, Va.

(1935–) U.S. Supreme Court justice (1988–).

Ken·ne·dy |'kenəde|, George (1925–) U.S. actor. Notable movies: *Cool Hand Luke* (1967, Academy Award).

Ken·ne·dy |'kenəde|, Joseph Patrick (1888–1969) U.S. businessman and diplomat. Father of John Fitzgerald, Robert Francis, and Edward T. Kennedy, he made his fortune in banking, the stock market, shipbuilding, and motion pictures.

Ken·ne·dy |'kenəde|, William (1928–) U.S. author. Notable works: *Ironweed* (1983, National Book Award and Pulitzer Prize).

Ken·nel·ly |'kenəlē|, Arthur Edwin (1861–1939) U.S. electrical engineer. His principal work was on the theory of alternating currents. Independently of O. Heaviside, he also discovered the layer in the atmosphere responsible for reflecting radio waves back to the earth.

Ken·neth I |'kenəTH| (died 858) king of Scotland (c.844–58); known as **Kenneth MacAlpin**. He is traditionally viewed as the founder of the kingdom of Scotland, which was established following his defeat of the Picts in about 844.

Kent |kent|, Rockwell (1882–1971.) U.S. author and artist. His books recount sea voyages and residences in the Arctic and South America.

Ken·ton |'ken(t)ən|, Stan (1912–79) U.S. bandleader, composer, and arranger; born *Stanley Newcomb.* He formed his own orchestra in 1940 and is particularly associated with the big-band jazz style of the 1950s.

Ken·yat·ta |ken'yätə|, Jomo (c. 1891–1978) Kenyan statesman, prime minister of Kenya (1963) and president (1964–78). Imprisoned for alleged complicity in the Mau Mau uprising (1952–61), on his release he was elected president of the Kenya African National Union and led Kenya to independence in 1963, subsequently serving as its first president.

Ken·zo |'kenzō| (1940–) Japanese fashion designer. Full name *Kenzo Takada.* His store, Jungle Jap, is known for trendsetting knitwear.

Kep·ler |'keplər|, Johannes (1571–1630) German astronomer. His analysis of Tycho Brahe's planetary observations led him to discover the three laws governing orbital motion.

Kern |kərn|, Jerome (David) (1885–1945) U.S. composer. A major influence in the development of the musical, he wrote several musical comedies, including *Showboat* (1927).

Kern |kərn|, John W. (1849–1917) U.S. politician. He was a member of the U.S. Senate from Indiana (1911–17) and a vice presidential Democratic candidate (1908).

Ker·ou·ac |'kerəwæk|, Jack (1922–69) U.S. novelist and poet, of French-Canadian descent; born *Jean-Louis Lebris de Kérouac.* A leading figure of the Beat Generation, he is best known for his semi-autobiographical novel *On the Road* (1957).

Kerr |kər; kär| U.S. authors: **Walter Francis Kerr** (1913–), a drama critic and playwright, wrote for the *New York Herald Tribune* (1951–66) and *The New York Times* (1966–83). Pulitzer Prize, 1978. **Jean Collins Kerr** (1923–) wrote *Please Don't Eat the Daisies* (1957) and collaborated with her husband Walter in writing plays.

Ker·ri·gan |'kerəgən|, Nancy (1969–) U.S. figure skater. The 1993 U.S. women's champion and an Olympic medalist (1992, bronze; 1994, silver), she was the victim of an assault planned by rival Tonya Harding.

Ker·tész |kər'teSH|, André (1894–1985) U.S. photographer, born in Hungary. He pioneered and refined the use of the handheld 35mm camera, and his photographs of Paris in the 1920s had a profound influence on modern photojournalism.

Ke·sey |'kēzē|, Ken (Elton) (1935–) U.S. novelist. His best-known novel, *One Flew over the Cuckoo's Nest* (1962), is based on his experiences as a ward attendant in a mental hospital.

Ketch·am |'keCHəm|, Hank (1920–) U.S. cartoonist and author. Full name *Henry King Ketcham.* He created the "Dennis the Menace" comic strip.

Ket·ter·ing |'ketəriNG|, Charles Franklin (1876–1958) U.S. automobile engineer. His first significant development was the electric starter (1912). As head of research at General Motors he discovered tetraethyl lead as an anti-knock agent and defined the octane rating of fuels; he also did important work on diesel engines, synchromesh gearboxes, automatic transmissions, and power steering.

Ke·vor·kian |kə'vawrkēən|, Jack (1928–) U.S. physician. He was an advocate and practicioner of assisted suicide but was convicted of murder in the death of one of his patients.

Key |kē|, Francis Scott (1779–1843) U.S. lawyer and poet. A witness to the successful U.S. defense against the British bombardment of Fort McHenry in Baltimore (Sept. 13–14, 1814), he wrote the poem "Defence of Fort M'Henry." The poem was later set to music, renamed "The Star-Spangled Banner," and adopted as the U.S. national anthem (1931).

Key |kē|, Ted (1912–) U.S. cartoonist and writer. Full name *Theodore Key*. He is best known as the creator of "Hazel," which appeared in the *Saturday Evening Post*; he was also a cartoonist and writer for the *New Yorker* and other magazines.

Keynes |kānz|, John Maynard, 1st Baron (1883–1946) English economist. He laid the foundations of modern macroeconomics with *The General Theory of Employment, Interest and Money* (1936), in which he argued that full employment is determined by effective demand and requires government spending on public works to stimulate this. His theories influenced Roosevelt's decision to introduce the New Deal.

Kha·cha·tu·ri·an |ˌkäCHəˈtŏŏrēən|, Aram (Ilich) (1903–78) Soviet composer, born in Georgia. His music is richly romantic and reflects his lifelong interest in the folk music of Armenia, Georgia, and Russia. Notable works include *Gayane* (ballet, 1942), his Second Symphony (1943), and *Spartacus* (ballet, 1954).

Kha·ma |ˈkämə|, Sir Seretse (1921–80) Botswanan statesman, prime minister of Bechuanaland (1965) and first president of Botswana (1966–80).

Khan |kän|, Ayub see AYUB KHAN.

Kho·mei·ni |kōˈmānē|, Ruhollah (1900–89) Iranian Shiite Muslim leader; known as **Ayatollah Khomeini**. He returned from exile in 1979 to lead an Islamic revolution that overthrew the shah. He established Iran as a fundamentalist Islamic republic and relentlessly pursued the Iran–Iraq War (1980–89).

Khru·schev |krŏŏSHˈCHawf|, Nikita (Sergeevich) (1894–1971) Soviet statesman, premier of the USSR (1958–64). He was First Secretary of the Communist Party of the USSR (1953–64) after the death of Stalin, whom he denounced in 1956. He came close to war with the U.S. over the Cuban Missile Crisis in 1962 and also clashed with China, which led to his being ousted by Brezhnev and Kosygin.

Khu·fu |ˈkŏŏfŏŏ| see CHEOPS.

Kidd |kid|, William (1645–1701) Scottish pirate; known as **Captain Kidd**. Sent to the Indian Ocean in 1695 in command of an anti-pirate expedition, Kidd became a pirate himself. In 1699 he went to Boston in the hope of obtaining a pardon, but was arrested and later hanged in London.

Kid·der |ˈkiddər|, (John) Tracy (1945–) U.S. author. Works include *The Soul of a New Machine* (1982, Pulitzer Prize, American Book Award).

Kid·man |ˈkidmən|, Nicole (1967–) U.S. actress. Notable movies: *To Die For* (1995), *Portrait of a Lady* (1996), and *Eyes Wide Shut* (1999). She is married to actor Tom Cruise.

Kier·ke·gaard |ˈkirkegärd|, Søren (Aabye) (1813–55) Danish philosopher. A founder of existentialism, he affirmed the importance of individual experience and choice and believed one could know God only through a "leap of faith," and not through doctrine. Notable works: *Either-Or* (1843) and *The Sickness unto Death* (1849).

Kie·slow·ski |kēˈslawfskē|, Krzysztof (1941–96) Polish movie director. Noted for their mannered style and their artistic, philosophical nature, his movies include *Dekalog* (1988), a series of visual interpretations of the Ten Commandments, and the trilogy *The Double Life of Véronique* (1991).

Kil·le·brew |ˈkilə,brŏŏ|, Harmon (1936–) U.S. baseball player. He led the American League in home runs six times.

Kil·ly |ˈkēyē|, Jean-Claude (1943–) French alpine skier. He won three gold medals at the 1968 Olympic Games and was a two-time World Cup champion.

Kil·mer |ˈkilmər|, Joyce (1888–1918) U.S. poet. Full name *Alfred Joyce Kilmer*. He was killed in action during World War I. Notable books: *Summer of Love* and *Trees and Other Poems* (1914).

Kim Il Sung |kim il sŏŏNG| (1912–94) Korean communist statesman, first premier of North Korea (1948–72) and president (1972–94); born *Kim Song Ju*.

He precipitated the Korean War (1950–53), and remained committed to the reunification of the country. He maintained a one-party state and created a personality cult around himself and his family; on his death he was quickly replaced in power by his son **Kim Jong Il**.

King |kiNG| U.S. civil rights leaders. **Martin Luther King, Jr.** (1929–68), a Baptist minister, opposed discrimination against blacks by organizing nonviolent resistance and peaceful mass demonstrations, and was a notable orator. He was assassinated in Memphis. Nobel Peace Prize (1964). His birthday, January 15, is a legal holiday. **Coretta Scott King** (1927–), his wife, founded the Martin Luther King, Jr. Center for Nonviolent Social Change in Atlanta.

King |kiNG|, Albert (1923–92) U.S. blues guitarist. Born *Albert Nelson*. Notable songs: "Laundromat Blues" (1966).

King |kiNG|, B. B. (1925–) U.S. blues singer and guitarist; born *Riley B. King*. An established blues performer, he came to the notice of a wider audience in the late 1960s, when his style of guitar playing was imitated by rock musicians.

King |kiNG|, Billie Jean (1943–) U.S. tennis player and promoter of professional women's tennis. She won a record twenty Wimbledon titles, including six singles titles (1966–68; 1972–73; 1975), ten doubles titles, and four mixed doubles titles.

King |kiNG|, Carole (1942–) U.S. singer and songwriter. Born *Carole Klein*. With Gerry Goffin, she cowrote hits such as "Will You Still Love Me Tomorrow" (1961) and "Up on the Roof."

King |kiNG|, Ernest J. (1878–1956) U.S. naval officer. He served as commander in chief of the U.S. Atlantic fleet (1940) and combined fleet (Dec. 1941), as chief of naval operations (1942–45), and as admiral of the fleet (1945).

King |kiNG|, Larry (1933–) U.S. television and radio broadcaster. Born *Larry Zeiler*. He hosts the call-in television program "Larry King, Live."

King |kiNG|, Rufus (1755–1827) U.S. politician. A member of the Continental Congress (1784–87), he ran unsuccessfully for U.S. vice president (1804 and 1808) and president (1816).

King |kiNG|, Stephen Edwin (1947–) U.S. author. He is best known for his writings of horror and suspense. Notable novels: *Carrie* (1974), *The Shining* (1977), and *Bag of Bones* (1998).

King |kiNG|, William Lyon Mackenzie (1874–1950) Canadian Liberal statesman, prime minister (1921–26, 1926–30, and 1935–48). The grandson of William Lyon Mackenzie, he played an important role in establishing the status of the self-governing nations of the Commonwealth.

King |kiNG|, William Rufus de Vane (1786–1853) vice president of the U.S. (1853).

Kings·ley |'kiNGzlē|, Charles (1819–75) English novelist and clergyman. He is remembered for his historical novel *Westward Ho!* (1855) and for his classic children's story *TheWater-Babies* (1863).

King·sol·ver, Barbara (1955–) U.S. author. Notable works: *The Bean Trees* (1992) and *High Tide in Tucson: Essays Now or Never* (1995).

Kin·nell |kĭ'nel|, Galway (1927–) U.S. author of fiction and poetry. Notable works: *Mortal Words, Mortal Acts* (1980).

Kin·sey |'kinzē|, Alfred Charles (1894–1956) American zoologist and sex researcher. He carried out pioneering studies into sexual behavior by interviewing large numbers of people. His best-known work, *Sexual Behavior in the Human Male* (1948, also known as the *Kinsey Report*), was controversial but highly influential.

Kip·ling |'kipliNG|, (Joseph) Rudyard (1865–1936) British novelist, short-story writer, and poet. Born in India, he is known for his poems, such as "If" and "Gunga Din," and his children's tales, notably *The Jungle Book* (1894) and the *Just So Stories* (1902). Nobel Prize for Literature (1907).

Kir·by |'kɔrbē|, Jack (1917–94) U.S. cartoonist. He made important contributions to the history of the comic book with the creation of the characters Captain America, Spider-Man, the Incredible Hulk, and the Fantastic Four.

Kir·by |'kərbē|, Rollin (1875–1952) U.S. cartoonist and author. He was a newspaper cartoonist and the writer of verse, short stories, and editorials for magazines. Pulitzer Prize for cartooning (1921, 1924, and 1928).

Kirch·hoff |'kerKHhawf|, Gustav Robert (1824–87) German physicist, a pioneer in spectroscopy. Working with Bunsen, he developed a spectroscope and discovered that solar absorption lines are specific to certain elements. He also developed the concept of black-body radiation and discovered the elements cesium and rubidium.

Kirch·ner |'kerKHnər|, Ernst Ludwig (1880–1938) German expressionist painter. In 1905 he was a founder of the first group of German expressionists. His paintings are characterized by the use of bright, contrasting colors and angular outlines and often depict claustrophobic street scenes.

Kirk·pat·rick |ˌkərk'pætrik|, Jeane Duane Jordan (1926–) U.S. political scientist and public official. U.S. representative to the U.N. (1981–85).

Kir·stein |'kərstīn|, Lincoln (1907–96) U.S. ballet promoter and author. With George Balanchine, he founded and then directed the School of American Ballet and the New York City Ballet.

Kis·sin·ger |'kisənjər|, Henry (Alfred) (1923–) German-born U.S. statesman and diplomat, Secretary of State 1973–77. In 1973 he helped negotiate the withdrawal of U.S. troops from South Vietnam, for which he shared the Nobel Peace Prize. He later restored U.S. diplomatic relations with Egypt in the wake of the Yom Kippur War and subsequently mediated between Israel and Syria. His numerous trips to foster Middle East negotiations led to the term "shuttle diplomacy."

Kitch·e·ner |'kiCH(ə)nər|, (Horatio) Herbert, 1st Earl Kitchener of Khartoum (1850–1916) British soldier and statesman. At the outbreak of World War I, he was made secretary of state for war. He had previously defeated the Mahdist forces at Omdurman in 1898, served as chief of staff in the Second Boer War, and been commander in chief (1902–09) in India.

Kit·tredge |'kitrij|, George Lyman (1860–1941) U.S. literary critic. Notable works: *Shakespeare* (1916).

Klap·roth |'kläp,rōt|, Martin Heinrich (1743–1817) German chemist, one of the founders of analytical chemistry. He discovered three new elements (zirconium, uranium, and titanium) in certain minerals, and contributed to the identification of others. A follower of Lavoisier, he helped to introduce the latter's new system of chemistry into Germany.

Klee |klā|, Paul (1879–1940) Swiss painter, resident in Germany from 1906. He joined Kandinsky's *Blaue Reiter* group in 1912 and later taught at the Bauhaus (1920–33). His work is characterized by his sense of color, and moves freely between abstraction and figuration. Although some of his paintings have a childlike quality, his later work became increasingly somber.

Klein |klīn|, Calvin (Richard) (1942–) U.S. fashion designer, known for his understated fashions for both men and women.

Klein |klīn|, Melanie (1882–1960) Austrian-born psychoanalyst. Klein was the first psychologist to specialize in the psychoanalysis of small children. Her discoveries led to an understanding of some of the more severe mental disorders found in children.

Klem·per·er |'klempərər|, Otto (1885–1973) German-born U.S. conductor and composer. While conductor at the Kroll Theatre in Berlin (1927–31), he was noted as a champion of new work. He became a U.S. citizen in 1937 and subsequently became known for his interpretations of Beethoven, Brahms, and Mahler.

Klerk |klerk|, F. W. de see DE KLERK.

Kliegl |'klēg(ə)l|, U.S. businessman, born in Germany. **Anton T. Kliegl** (1872–1927) and his brother **John H. Kliegl** (1869–1959) were pioneers in the development of electric stage lighting equipment.

Klimt |klimt|, Gustav (1862–1918) Austrian painter and designer. Co-founder of the Vienna Secession (1897), he is known for his decorative and allegorical paintings and his portraits of women. Notable works: *The Kiss* (1908).

Kline |klīn|, Kevin (1947–) U.S. actor. Notable movies: *A Fish Called Wanda* (1988, Academy Award).

Klugman |'kləgmən|, Jack (1922–) U.S. actor. Film credits include *Days of Wine and Roses* (1962). He starred in the television series "The Odd Couple" (1970–75) and "Quincy" (1976–83).

Knight |nīt|, Bob (1940–) U.S. basketball coach. He coached the 1984 gold medal Olympic team.

Knight |nīt|, Gladys (1944–) U.S. musician. She formed Gladys Knight and the Pips. Notable songs: "That's What Friends are For."

Knight |nīt|, John Shively (1894–1981) U.S. newspaper publisher. He merged his newspapers in Detroit, Chicago, New York, etc. with the Ridder Publications chain (1974) to form Knight-Ridder Newspapers, Inc., which includes 34 daily papers and 4 television stations.

Knight |nīt|, Philip H. (1938–) U.S. businessman. He was cofounder of the Blue Ribbon Sports athletic shoe company, which became Nike, Inc.

Knopf |(kə)'näpf|, Alfred A. (1892–1984) U.S. publisher. He was founder of Alfred A. Knopf (1915).

Knotts |näts|, Don (1924–) U.S. actor. Performer in movies and on television, and five-time Emmy Award winner for his supporting role as Barney Fife in the television series "The Andy Griffith Show."

Knowles |nōlz|, John (1926–) U.S. author. Notable works: *Selected Poems* (1982, Pulitzer Prize).

Knox |näks|, Frank (1874–1944) U.S. newspaper publisher and politician. Full name *William Franklin Knox*. He was a Republican vice presidential candidate (1936) and served as secretary of the U.S. Navy (1940–44).

Knox |näks|, Henry (1750–1806) American Revolutionary War general and first U.S. secretary of war (1785–94).

Knox |näks|, John (*c.* 1505–72) Scottish Protestant reformer. Knox played a central part in the establishment of the Church of Scotland within a Scottish Protestant state and led opposition to the Catholic Mary, Queen of Scots, when she returned to rule in her own right in 1561.

Koch |käCH|, Edward I. (1924–) U.S. politician. Mayor of New York City (1978–89).

Koch |käCH|, Kenneth (1925–) U.S. author and educator. Notable works: *Selected Poems* (1985). Bollingen Prize, 1995.

Kö·chel |'kOEKHəl; 'kərSHəl|, Ludwig Alois Ferdinand Ritter von (1800–77) Austrian music bibliographer. In his *Chronologisch-thematisches Verzeichnis* (1862), he numbered all of Mozart's works; hence the prefatory "K" or "KV" number on Mozart program listings.

Ko·dály |'kōdī; 'kōdäē|, Zoltán (1882–1967) Hungarian composer. His main source of inspiration was his native land; he was also involved in the collection and publication of Hungarian folk songs. Notable works: *Psalmus Hungaricus* (choral, 1923) and *Háry János* (operetta, 1925–27).

Koest·ler |'kest(l)ər|, Arthur (1905–83) Hungarian-born British novelist and essayist. His best-known novel *Darkness at Noon* (1940) exposed the Stalinist purges of the 1930s. He left money in his will to found a university chair in parapsychology.

Koff·ka |'kawfkə|, Kurt (1886–1941) German psychologist, educator, and author. Chief developer of Gestalt psychology and its application to child development.

Ko·foid |'kō,foid|, Charles Atwood (1865–1947) U.S. zoologist. Played a major role in the establishment of the Scripps Institution of Oceanography and invented the Kofoid horizontal net and Kofoid self-closing bucket for the collection of plankton.

Kohl |kōl|, Helmut (1930–) German statesman, chancellor of the Federal Republic of Germany (1982–90), and of Germany (1990–98). As chancellor he showed strong commitment to NATO and to closer European unity within the European Union.

Kolff |kawlf|, Willem Johan (1911–) U.S. surgeon and educator, born in Holland. He developed an artificial kidney for clinical use (1943) and an oxygenator (1956).

Kooning |kooninG|, Willem de see DE KOONING.

Koontz |kōonts|, Dean Ray (1945–) U.S. author. Pseudonyms **Richard Paige** and **Owen West**. He is the author of over 70 best-sellers including *Sole Survivor* (1996).

Koop |kōop|, C. Everett (1916–) U.S. physician and government official. Full name *Charles Everett Koop*. U.S. surgeon general (1981–89).

Kop·lik |'käplik|, Henry (1858–1927) U.S. pediatrician. He described Koplik's spots to diagnose measles and established the first milk distribution center for infants of the poor.

Kor·but |'kawrbət|, Olga (1955–) Soviet gymnast, born in Belarus. She won two individual gold medals at the 1972 Olympic Games.

Kor·da |'kawrdə|, Sir Alexander (1893–1956) Hungarian-born British movie producer and director; born *Sándor Kellner*. He produced *The Thief of Baghdad* (1940) and *The Third Man* (1949) and produced and directed *The Private Life of Henry VIII* (1933).

Koren, Edward B. (1935–) U.S. cartoonist, author, and illustrator. He is best known for his creation of a cast of woolly characters appearing in the *New Yorker* magazine.

Kor·man |'kawrmən|, Harvey Herschel (1927–) U.S. actor. He starred in the television series "The Carol Burnett Show" (1967–70) and movies such as *Blazing Saddles* (1974) and *High Anxiety* (1978).

Kor·ni·lov |kawr'n(y)iləf|, Lavr Georgyevich (1870–1918) Russian general. He commanded the troops in Petrograd after the Bolshevik Revolution (1917) but was checked by the Bolsheviks in an attempt to make himself dictator.

Kos·cius·ko |,käsē'əs,kō|, Thaddeus (1746–1817) Polish soldier and patriot; full Polish name *Tadeusz Andrzej Bonawentura Kościuszko*. After fighting for the Americans during the Revolutionary War, he led a nationalist uprising against Russia in Poland in 1794.

Ko·sin·ski |kə'zinskē|, Jerzy (Nikodem) (1933–91) U.S. author, born in Poland. Notable works: *Being There* (1971).

Kos·suth |'kä,sōoTH|, Lajos (1802–94) Hungarian statesman and patriot. He led the 1848 insurrection against the Hapsburgs, but after a brief success the uprising was crushed and he began a lifelong period of exile.

Ko·sy·gin |kə'sēgən|, Aleksei (Nikolaevich) (1904–80) Soviet statesman, premier of the USSR (1964–80). He devoted most of his attention to internal economic affairs, being gradually eased out of the leadership by Brezhnev.

Kot·ze·bue |'kawtsə,bōo|, August von (1761–1819) German dramatist. His many plays were popular in both Germany and England. He was a political informant to Tsar Alexander I and was assassinated by the Germans.

Kou·fax |'kōfæks|, Sandy (1935–) U.S. baseball player. Elected to the Baseball Hall of Fame (1972).

Kous·se·vitz·ky |,kōosə'vitskē|, Serge (1874–1951) U.S. conductor, born in Russia. He was director of the Boston Symphony Orchestra (1924–49) and organizer of the Berkshire Music Center at Tanglewood.

Ko·vacs |'kōvæks|, Ernie (1919–62) U.S. television comedian.

Krafft-Ebing |'kräf't ēbiNG|, Richard von (1840–1902) German physician and psychologist. He established the relationship between syphilis and general paralysis and pioneered the systematic study of aberrant sexual behaviour.

Kraft |kræft|, James Lewis (1874–1953) U.S. businessman, born in Canada. The founder of the Kraft Cheese Co., he patented a method of blending, pasteurizing, and packaging cheddar cheese (1916).

Krantz |kræn(t)s|, Judith (1928–) U.S. author. Notable works: *Princess Daisy* (1980).

Krebs |krebz|, Sir Hans Adolf (1900–81) German-born British biochemist. He discovered the cycle of reactions (Krebs cycle) by which urea is synthesized in the liver as a nitrogenous waste product. Nobel Prize for Physiology or Medicine (1953).

Krebs |krebz|, Johann Ludwig (1713–80) German organist and composer. He was a student of J. S. Bach.

Kreis·ler |'krīslər|, Fritz (1875–1962) Austrian-born U.S. violinist and composer. A noted virtuoso, in 1910 he gave the first performance of Elgar's violin concerto, which was dedicated to him.

Kress |kres|, Samuel Henry (1863–1955) U.S. merchant. He was the founder of S. H. Kress & Co., a chain of 5-, 10-, and 25-cent stores.

Krish·na·mur·ti |ˌkrisHnəˈmərtē|, Jiddu (1895–1986) Indian spiritual leader. His spiritual philosophy is based on a rejection of organized religion and the attainment of self-realization by introspection.

Kris·tof·fer·son |kriˈstawfərsən|, Kris (1936–) U.S. singer, songwriter, and actor.

Kroc |kräk|, Ray (1902–84) U.S. entrepreneur. Full name *Raymond Albert Kroc*. In 1955, he founded the franchise empire of McDonald's fast-food restaurants.

Kro·ne |ˈkrōnə|, Julie (1963–) U.S. jockey. She was the first woman to capture a Triple Crown horse-racing title (1993).

Kro·pot·kin |krəˈpätkən|, Prince Peter (1842–1921) Russian anarchist. Imprisoned in 1874, he escaped abroad in 1876 and did not return to Russia until after the Revolution. His works include *Modern Science and Anarchism* (1903).

Kru·ger |ˈkrōōgər|, Stephanus Johannes Paulus (1825–1904) South African soldier and statesman, president of Transvaal (1883–99). He led the Afrikaners to victory in the First Boer War in 1881. His refusal to allow equal rights to non-Boer immigrants was one of the causes of the Second Boer War.

Kru·pa |ˈkrōōpə|, Gene (1909–73) U.S. jazz drummer and bandleader. He was the first major popular drum soloist.

Krupp |krōōp; krəp|, Alfred (1812–87) German arms manufacturer. His company played a preeminent role in German arms production from the 1840s through the end of World War II.

Krutch |krōōCH|, Joseph Wood (1893–1970) U.S. educator and author. Notable works: *The Modern Temper* (1929).

Ku·be·lík |ˈkōōbəlik|, (Jeronym) Rafael (1914–) Czech conductor and composer. He served as director of the Chicago Symphony (1950–53), Covent Garden (1955–58), and the Bavarian Radio Orchestra (1961–80), and music

director of the Metropolitan Opera (1973–74).

Ku·blai Khan |ˌkōōbləˈkän| (1216–94) Mongol emperor of China, grandson of Genghis Khan. With his brother Mangu (then Mongol Khan) he conquered southern China (1252–59). After Mangu's death in 1259 he completed the conquest of China, founded the Yuan dynasty, and established his capital on the site of modern Beijing.

Ku·brick |ˈkōōbrik|, Stanley (1928–99) U.S. film director, producer, and writer. Notable films: *Dr. Strangelove* (1964), *2001: A Space Odyssey* (1968), and *A Clockwork Orange* (1971).

Kuhn |k(y)ōōn|, Maggie (1905–95) U.S. organization executive. Full name *Margaret Kuhn*. An advocate for women and the elderly, she was a founder of the Gray Panthers (1971) and author of *Maggie Kuhn on Aging* (1977).

Ku·min |ˈkōōmin|, Maxine (Winokur) (1925–) U.S. author. Notable works: *Up Country* and *Poems of New England* (1972, Pulitzer Prize).

Kun·de·ra |ˈkōōndərə|, Milan (1929–) Czech novelist. He emigrated to France in 1975 after his books were banned in Czechoslovakia following the Soviet military invasion of 1968. Notable works: *The Book of Laughter and Forgetting* (1979) and *The Unbearable Lightness of Being* (1984).

Ku·nitz |ˈkōōnits|, Stanley Jasspon (1905–) U.S. poet and editor. He is the author of *Selected Poems* (1958, Pulitzer Prize) and of reference works including *American Authors, 1600–1900* (1938, with Howard Haycraft).

Kunst·ler |ˈkəns(t)lər|, William (1919–95) U.S. attorney and civil rights activist. His clients included the Southern Christian Leadership Conference, the Black Panthers, and the Chicago Seven.

Ku·ralt |kəˈrawlt|, Charles (1934–97) U.S. television and radio journalist. He chronicled life in America with his "On the Road" reports.

Ku·ro·sa·wa |ˌkŏŏrəˈsäwə|, Akira (1910–98) Japanese movie director. Notable movies: *Rashomon* (1950) and *Ran* (1985), a Japanese version of Shakespeare's *King Lear*.

Kurtz·man |ˈkərtsmən|, Harvey (1921–

93) U.S. illustrator and cartoonist. He helped to create *Mad* magazine.

Kurz·weil |ˈkərts,wīl|, Raymond C. (1948–) U.S. computer scientist and entrepreneur. He is the chairman of Kurzweil Applied Intelligence, Inc. (1982–).

Ku·tu·zov |kōōˈtōōzəf; kōōˈtōō,zawf|, Mikhail Illarionovich, Prince (1745–1813) Russian field marshal. He was an army commander in the wars against Napoleon (1805–12), the Turks (1811–12), and the French (1812).

Kwo·lek, Stephanie Louise (1923–) U.S. chemist. She invented processes that resulted in new polymers, the best known of which is Kevlar.

Kyd |kid|, Thomas (1558–64) English dramatist. His anonymously published *The Spanish Tragedy* (1592), an early example of revenge tragedy, was very popular on the Elizabethan stage.

Ll

La·ban |'läbən|, Rudolf von (1879–1958) Hungarian choreographer and dancer. A pioneer of the central European school of modern dance, in 1920 he published the first of several volumes outlining his system of dance notation.

la Bar·ca |lä 'bärkə|, Pedro Calderón de see CALDERÓN DE LA BARCA.

La·Belle |lə'bel|, Patti (1944–) U.S. singer and actress. Born *Patricia Louise Holt*. Grammy Award, 1991.

La Bru·yére |'lä brōō'yer|, Jean de (1645–96) French writer and moralist. He is known for his *Caractères* (1688), consisting of a translation of the *Characters* based on Theophrastus and exposing the vanity and corruption of human behavior by satirizing Parisian society.

La·can |lä'käN|, Jacques (1901–81) French psychoanalyst and writer. A notable post-structuralist, he reinterpreted Freudian psychoanalysis, especially the theory of the unconscious, in the light of structural linguistics and anthropology.

La·chaise |lä'sHez|, Gaston (1882–1935) U.S. figurative sculptor, born in France. He is known for his massively proportioned female nudes, including *Standing Woman* (1912–27).

La·clos |lä'klō|, Pierre Choderlos de (1741–1803) French novelist; full name *Pierre-Ambroise-François Choderlos de Laclos*. He is chiefly remembered for his epistolary novel *Les Liaisons dangereuses* (1782).

Lad·is·laus I |'lädĕs,läs| (c. 1040–95) king of Hungary (1077–95); canonized as **St. Ladislaus**. He extended Hungarian power and advanced the spread of Christianity. Feast day, June 27.

Lad·is·laus II |'lädĕs,läs| (c. 1351–1434) king of Poland (1386–1434); Polish name *Władysław*. As grand duke of Lithuania, he acceded to the Polish throne on his marriage to the Polish monarch, **Queen Jadwiga**, thus uniting Lithuania and Poland.

La Farge |lə 'färzH; lə 'färj| U.S. family, including: **John La Farge** (1835–1910), an artist known for his panels in St. Thomas' Church (New York City) and for the stained glass at Second Presbyterian Church (Chicago). His son **Christopher Grant La Farge** (1862–1938), an architect. He designed the Roman Catholic chapel at West Point, New York. **Oliver (Hazard Perry) La Farge** (1901–63), son of Christopher Grant La Farge. He was an ethnologist and author who wrote *Laughing Boy* (1929, Pulitzer Prize).

La·fa·yette |,läfä'yet; ,läfē'yet; ,læfē 'yet|, Marie-Joseph-Paul-Yves-Roch-Gilbert du Motier, Marquis de (1757–1834) French soldier and statesman. He fought alongside the American colonists in the Revolutionary War and commanded the National Guard (1789–91) in the French Revolution.

La Fol·lette |lə'fälət|, Robert Marion (1855–1925) U.S. politician. He was a member of the U.S. House of Representatives from Wisconsin and a member of the U.S. Senate; he served as governor of Wisconsin and was a Progressive Party presidential candidate (1924).

La Fon·taine |'läfawn,tän|, Jean de (1621–95) French poet. He is chiefly remembered for his *Fables* (1668–94), drawn from oriental, classical, and contemporary sources.

La·ger·feld |'lägər,felt|, Karl (1938–) French fashion designer, born in Germany.

La·ger·löf |'lägər,lœv|, Selma (Ottiliana Lovisa) (1858–1940) Swedish novelist. She made her name with *Gösta Berlings Saga* (1891) and was the first woman to be the sole winner of a Nobel Prize (Literature, 1909).

La·grange |lä'gränzH; lə'gränj|, Joseph-Louis Comte de (1736–1813) Italian-born French mathematician. He is remembered for his proof that every positive integer can be expressed as a sum of at most four squares, and for his work on mechanics and its application to the description of planetary and lunar motion.

La Guar·dia |lə'gwär,dēə|, Fiorello Henry (1882–1947) U.S. politician. He was mayor of New York City (1933–45).

Lahr |lär|, Bert (1895–1967) U.S. comedian. Born *Irving Lahrheim*. He starred in *The Wizard of Oz* as the Cowardly Lion.

Laing |læNG|, R. D. (1927–89) Scottish psychiatrist; full name *Ronald David Laing*. He became famous for his controversial views on insanity and in particular on schizophrenia, linking what society calls insanity with politics and family structure.

Lake |lāk|, Simon (1866–1945) U.S. naval architect. He invented the even-keel submarine torpoedo boat.

La·lique |lä'lēk|, René (1860–1945) French jeweler, famous for his art nouveau brooches and combs and his decorative glassware.

La·mar |lə'mär|, Joseph Rucker (1857–1916) U.S. Supreme Court justice (1910–16).

La·mar |lə'mär|, Lucius Quintus Cincinnatus (1825–1893) U.S. Supreme Court justice (1888–93).

La·marck |lə'märk|, Jean-Baptiste de Monet de (1744–1829) French naturalist. French naturalist. He was an early proponent of organic evolution, although his theory is not widely accepted today. He suggested that species could have evolved from each other by small changes in their structure, and that the mechanism of such change (not now generally considered possible) was that characteristics acquired in order to survive could be passed on to offspring.

La·mar·tine |lämär'tēn|, Alphonse-Marie-Louis de Prat de (1790–1869) French poet, statesman, and historian. He was Minister of Foreign Affairs in the provisional government following the Revolution of 1848. Notable works: *Méditations poétiques* (1820).

Lamb |lăm|, Charles (1775–1834) English essayist and critic. Together with his sister Mary he wrote *Tales from Shakespeare* (1807). Other notable works: *Essays of Elia* (1823).

Lamb |lăm|, Wally (1950–) U.S. author. Notable works: *She's Come Undone* (1992) and *I Know This Much Is True* (1998).

Lamb |lăm|, Willis Eugene, Jr. (1913–) U.S. physicist. He discovered the Lamb shift. Nobel Prize for Physics (1955).

Lam·bert |'lămbərt|, (Leonard) Constant (1905–51) English composer, conductor, and critic. He wrote the music for the ballet *Romeo and Juliet* (1926) and the jazz work *The Rio Grande* (1929), later becoming musical director of Sadler's Wells (1930–47).

L'Amour |lə'mawr; lə 'mŏŏr|, Louis (Dearborn) (1908–88) U.S. author. Born *Louis LaMoore*. He wrote over 200 novels about the American West. Presidential Medal of Freedom, 1984.

Lam·pe·du·sa |,lămpə'dōŏsə|, Giuseppe Tomasi di (1896–1957) Italian novelist. His only novel *Il Gattopardo* (*The Leopard*) was originally rejected by publishers but won worldwide acclaim on its posthumous publication in 1958.

Lan·cas·ter |'læNG,kæstər|, Burt (1913–94) U.S. movie actor; full name *Burton Stephen Lancaster*. He starred in movies such as *From Here to Eternity* (1953), *Elmer Gantry* (1960), for which he won an Oscar, and *Field of Dreams* (1989).

Land |lănd|, Edwin (1909–91) U.S. inventor. He invented a new polarizing filter with wide use in optical instruments; in 1937, he founded the Polaroid Corp. and introduced the first Polaroid Land Camera (1947).

Lan·dau |'læn,dow|, Lev (Davidovich) (1908–68) Soviet theoretical physicist, born in Russia. Active in many fields, Landau was awarded the Nobel Prize for Physics in 1962 for his work on the superfluidity and thermal conductivity of liquid helium.

Lan·ders |'lændərz|, Ann (1918–) U.S. journalist. Born *Esther Pauline Friedman*. Author of the "Ann Landers" advice column, she competed with her twin sister, Abigail Van Buren ("Dear Abby").

Lan·don |'lændən|, Alfred Mossman (1887–1987) U.S. politician. He was a Republican presidential candidate (1936).

Lan·don |'lændən|, Michael (1936–91) U.S. actor. Born *Eugene Maurice*

Orowitz. He starred in the television series "Bonanza" (1959–73) and "Little House on the Prairie" (1974–82).

Lan·dor |'lændər|, Walter Savage (1775–1864) English poet and essayist. His works include the oriental epic poem *Gebir* (1798), and *Imaginary Conversations of Literary Men and Statesmen* (prose, 1824–8).

Lan·dry |'lændrē|, Tom (1924–) U.S. football coach and player. He was the Dallas Cowboys coach for 29 years.

Land·seer |'læn(d)sir|, Sir Edwin Henry (1802–73) English painter and sculptor. He is best known for his animal subjects such as *The Monarch of the Glen* (1851). As a sculptor he is chiefly remembered for the bronze lions in London's Trafalgar Square (1867).

Land·stei·ner |'län(d),SHtīnər|, Karl (1868–1943) Austrian-born U.S. physician. In 1930 Landsteiner was awarded a Nobel Prize for devising the ABO system of classifying blood. He was also the first to describe the rhesus factor in blood.

Lane |lān|, John (19th c) U.S. blacksmith. He constructed the first steel plow (1833) and manufactured plows in Chicago (1824–97) with his son **John**.

Lang |'læNG|, Fritz (1890–1976) Austrian-born movie director, resident in the U.S. from 1933. He directed the silent dystopian movie *Metropolis* (1927), making the transition to sound in 1931 with the thriller *M*. His later work included *The Big Heat* (1953).

Lange |'læNG|, Dorothea (1895–1965) U.S. photographer. She is known for her documentary photographs of the Great Depression, including "White Angel Breadline"; her later photo-essays were published in *Life* magazine.

Lange |'læNG|, Jessica (1949–) U.S. actress. Notable movies: *Tootsie* (1982, Academy Award).

Lang·er |'læNGər|, Susanne K. (1895–1985) U.S. philosopher and educator. Notable works: *An Introduction to Symbolic Logic* (1937).

Lang·ford |'læNGfərd|, Nathaniel Pitt (1832–1911) U.S. explorer and conservationist. He was instrumental in the creation of Yellowstone National Park (1872).

Lang·land |'læNGlənd|, William (*c.* 1330–*c.*1400) English poet. He is best known for *Piers Plowman* (*c.*1367–70), a long allegorical poem which takes the form of a spiritual pilgrimage.

Lang·ley |'læNGlē|, Samuel Pierpont (1834–1906) U.S. astronomer and aviation pioneer. He invented the bolometer (1879–81) and contributed to the design of early aircraft.

Lang·muir |'læNG,myŏŏər|, Irving (1881–1957) U.S. chemist and physicist. His principal work was in surface chemistry, especially applied to catalysis. He also worked on high-temperature electrical discharges in gases and studied atomic structure. Nobel Prize for Chemistry, 1932.

Lang·ton |'læNGtən|, Stephen (*c.* 1150–1228) English prelate, Archbishop of Canterbury 1207–15; 1218–28. A champion of the English Church, he was involved in the negotiations leading to the signing of Magna Carta.

Lang·try |'læNGtrē|, Lillie (1853–1929) British actress; born *Emilie Charlotte le Breton*. She made her stage debut in 1881 and later became the mistress of the Prince of Wales, later Edward VII.

Lans·bury |'lænz,berē|, Angela Brigid (1925–) English actress. She starred in the television series "Murder, She Wrote" (1984–96) and the Broadway shows *Mame* (1966) and *Gypsy* (1974).

Lan·sing |'lænsiNG|, Robert (1864–1928) U.S. lawyer and public official. He was an authority on international law and served as U.S. secretary of state (1915-20).

Lan·ston |'lænstən|, Tolbert (1844–1913) U.S. inventor. He patented the typesetting machine (1887) and introduced Monotype (1897).

Lantz |'læn(t)s|, Walter (1900–94) U.S. cartoonist, producer, painter, and animator. He was the creator of the cartoon character Woody Woodpecker. Academy Award, 1979.

Lan·vin, Jeanne (1867–1946) French couturier.

Lan·za |'länzə|, Mario (1921–59) U.S. tenor. Born *Alfredo Arnold Cocozza*. He became an international star as the portrayer of Enrico Caruso in the movies

The Great Caruso (1951) and The Seven Hills of Rome (1958).

Lao-tzu |ˌlowˈtsoō| (6th century BC) Chinese philosopher traditionally regarded as the founder of Taoism and author of the Tao-te-Ching, its most sacred scripture.

La·place |läˈpläs|, Pierre Simon de (1749–1827) French applied mathematician and theoretical physicist. His treatise Méchanique céleste (1799–1825) is an extensive mathematical analysis of geophysical matters and of planetary and lunar motion.

Lard·ner |ˈlärdnər|, Ring (1885–1933) U.S. author and journalist. Full name Ringgold Wilmer Lardner. Notable works: How to Write Short Stories (1924).

Lar·kin |ˈlärkən|, Philip (Arthur) (1922–85) English poet. His poetry is characterized by an air of melancholy and bitterness and by stoic wit. Notable works: The Whitsun Weddings (1964) and High Windows (1974).

La Roche·fou·cauld |lä ˌrōsHfoōˈkō|, François de Marsillac, Duc de (1613–80) French writer and moralist. Notable works: Réflexions, ou sentences et maximes morales (1665).

La·rousse |ləˈroōs|, Pierre-Athanase (1817–75) French lexicographer and encyclopedist. He edited the fifteen-volume Grand dictionnaire universel du XIXᵉ siècle (1866–76), which aimed to treat every area of human knowledge. In 1852 he cofounded the publishing house of Larousse.

Lar·ro·quette |ˌlærəˈket|, John Bernard (1947–) U.S. actor. He starred in the television series "Night Court."

Lar·son |ˈlärsən|, Gary (1950–) U.S. cartoonist and author. His one-panel comic, "The Far Side," was syndicated in over 900 newspapers.

La Salle |ləˈsæl|, René-Robert Cavelier de (1643–87) French explorer. He sailed from Canada down the Ohio and Mississippi Rivers to the Gulf of Mexico in 1682, naming the Mississippi basin Louisiana in honor of Louis XIV. In 1684 he led an expedition to establish a French colony on the Gulf of Mexico, but was murdered when his followers mutinied.

Lasch |læsH|, Christopher (1932–94)

U.S. historian and social critic. Notable works: The Culture of Narcissism (1979).

Las·ker |ˈlæskər|, Albert Davis (1880–1952) U.S. advertising executive and philanthropist, born in Germany. He owned the Chicago advertising firm Lord and Thomas (1912–42)

Las·ker |ˈlæskər|, Emanuel (1868–1941) German chess player. He was the world champion from 1894 to 1921.

Las·ki |ˈlæskē|, Harold Joseph (1893–1950) British political scientist, author, and educator. He was a prominent Labour party member who embraced Marxism in the 1930s. His Authority in the Modern State (1919) influenced socialist thinking.

Las·ky |ˈlæsˌkē|, Jesse Louis (1880–1958) U.S. movie producer. He made over 1,000 movies, including The Great Caruso (1951).

Las·sus |ˈläsoōs|, Orlandus de (1532–94) Flemish composer; Italian name Orlando di Lasso. A notable composer of polyphonic music, he wrote over 2,000 secular and sacred works.

Lath·rop |ˈläTHrəp|, George Parsons (1851–98) U.S. author and editor. He married Rose Hawthorne and edited her father Nathaniel Hawthorne's works. Notable works: A Study of Hawthorne (1876).

Lat·i·mer |ˈlætəmər|, Hugh (c. 1485–1555) English Protestant prelate and martyr. One of Henry VIII's chief advisers when the king broke with the papacy, under Mary I he was condemned for heresy and burnt at the stake at Oxford with Nicholas Ridley.

Lat·i·mer |ˈlætəmər|, Lewis H. (1848–1928) U.S. inventor. An associate of Thomas Edison, he supervised the installation of the first electric street lighting in New York City.

La Tour |lä ˈtoŌr|, Georges de (1593–1652) French painter. He is best known for his nocturnal religious scenes and his subtle portrayal of candlelight. Notable works: St. Joseph the Carpenter (1645) and The Denial of St. Peter (1650).

La·trobe |ləˈtrōb|, Benjamin H. (1764–1820) U.S. architect, born in England. He designed the south wing of the U.S. Capitol in Washington, D.C. and rebuilt the Capitol after its destruction by the British (1815–17).

Lat·ti·more |'lætə,mawr|, Owen (1900–89) U.S. author and educator. Brother of Richmond Lattimore. He is noted for his writings on his travels, on geography and history, and on current events.

Lat·ti·more |'lætə,mawr|, Richmond Alexander (1906–84) U.S. author. Brother of Owen Lattimore. His translations include Homer's *Illiad* (1951) and Aristophanes' *The Frogs* (1962).

Laud |lawd|, William (1573–1645) English prelate, Archbishop of Canterbury 1633–45. His attempts to restore some pre-Reformation practices in England and Scotland aroused great hostility and were a contributory cause of the English Civil War. He was executed for treason.

Lau·da |'lowdə|, Niki (1949–) Austrian racing-car driver; full name *Nikolaus Andreas Lauda*.

Lau·der |'lawdər|, Estee (1908–) U.S. businesswoman. She is chairman of the board of the Estee Lauder Co. (1946–).

Laugh·lin, James Laurence (1850–1933) U.S. educator and economist. He edited the *Journal of Political Economy* for 40 years.

Laugh·ton |'lawtn|, Charles (1899–1962) British-born U.S. actor. He is remembered for character roles such as Henry VIII (*The Private Life of Henry VIII*, 1933) and Captain Bligh (*Mutiny on the Bounty*, 1935); he also played Quasimodo in *The Hunchback of Notre Dame* (1939).

Lau·rel |'lawrəl|, Stan (1890–1965) British-born U.S. comedian. Full name *Arthur Stanley Jefferson Laurel*. He played the scatterbrained and tearful innocent alongside Oliver Hardy, his pompous, overbearing, and frequently exasperated friend. They brought their distinctive slapstick comedy to many movies from 1927 onwards.

Lau·ren |lə'ren|, Ralph (1939–) U.S. fashion and textile designer. Born *Ralph Lifshitz*. He began his Polo clothing line for men in 1968 and expanded to include a women's collection in 1971.

Lau·rence |'lawrəns|, (Jean) Margaret (1926–87) Canadian novelist. Her life in Somalia and Ghana (1950–57) influ-enced her early work, including *This Side Jordan* (1960). Other notable works: *The Stone Angel* (1964).

Lau·rens |'lawrəns|, Henry (1724–92) U.S. merchant and colonial leader. He was president of the Second Continental Congress (1777–78).

Lau·rents |'lawrən(t)s|, Arthur (1918–) U.S. playwright and author. Notable works: *The Way We Were* (1972) and *The Turning Point* (1977).

Lau·ri·er |'lawrē,ā|, Sir Wilfrid (1841–1919) Canadian Liberal statesman, prime minister (1896–1911). He was Canada's first French-Canadian and Roman Catholic prime minister. He worked to achieve national unity and oversaw the creation of the provinces of Alberta and Saskatchewan.

La·ver |'lāvər|, Rod (1938–) Australian tennis player; full name *Rodney George Laver*. In 1962 he became the second man (after Don Budge in 1938) to win the four major singles championships (British, American, French, and Australian) in one year, called the "Grand Slam"; in 1969 he was the first to repeat this.

La·voi·sier |lə,vwä'zyā|, Antoine-Laurent (1743–94) French scientist, regarded as the father of modern chemistry. He caused a revolution in chemistry by his description of combustion as the combination of substances with air, or more specifically the gas oxygen.

Law |law|, (Andrew) Bonar (1858–1923) Canadian-born British Conservative statesman and prime minister (1922–23). He was leader of the Conservative Party (1911–21). He retired in 1921, but returned in 1922, following Lloyd George's resignation, to become prime minister for six months.

Law·less |'lawləs|, Theodore K. (1892–1971) U.S. physician. He was one of the first physicians to treat cancer with radium. Spingarn Medal, 1954.

Law·rence |'lawrəns|, St. (died 258) Roman martyr and deacon of Rome; Latin name *Laurentius*. According to tradition, Lawrence was ordered by the prefect of Rome to deliver up the treasure of the Church; when in response to this order he presented the poor people of Rome to the prefect, he was roasted to death on a gridiron. Feast day, August 10.

Law·rence |'lawrəns|, D. H. (1885–1930) English novelist, poet, and essayist; full name *David Herbert Lawrence*. His work is characterized by its condemnation of industrial society and by its frank exploration of sexual relationships, as in *The Rainbow* (1915) and *Lady Chatterley's Lover*, originally published in Italy in 1928, but not available in unexpurgated form until 1960. Other notable works: *Sons and Lovers* (1913).

Law·rence |'lawrəns|, Ernest Orlando (1901–58) U.S. physicist. 1939 Nobel Prize for Physics U.S. physicist. He developed the first circular particle accelerator, later called a cyclotron, and opened the way for high-energy physics. He also worked on providing fissionable material for the atom bomb. Nobel Prize for Physics (1939).

Law·rence |'lawrəns|, Jacob (1917–   ) U.S. artist and educator. His murals grace space at the Kingdome Stadium in Seattle and at Howard University; Spingarn Medal, 1970.

Law·rence |'lawrəns|, T. E. (1888–1935) British soldier and writer; full name *Thomas Edward Lawrence*; known as **Lawrence of Arabia**. From 1916 he helped to organize the Arab revolt against the Turks in the Middle East, contributing to General Allenby's eventual victory in Palestine in 1918. Lawrence described this period in *The Seven Pillars of Wisdom* (1926).

Law·rence |'lawrəns|, Sir Thomas (1769–1830) English painter. He achieved success with his full-length portrait (1789) of Queen Charlotte, the wife of King George III, and by 1810 he was recognized as the leading portrait painter of his time.

Law·son |'lawsən|, Thomas William (1857–1925) U.S. stockbroker. His sensational attacks on abusive money practices instigated an insurance investigation in 1905.

Lay·a·mon |'laə,män| (late 12th cent) English poet and priest. He wrote the verse chronicle known as the *Brut*, a history of England which introduces for the first time in English the story of King Arthur.

Laz·a·rus |'læzərəs|, Emma (1849–87) U.S. poet. She is known for her sonnet to the Statue of Liberty, which is carved on the pedestal of the statue.

Laz·a·rus |'læzərəs|, Mell (1929–   ) U.S. cartoonist. Full name *Melvin Lazarus*. He was creator of the comic strips "Miss Peach" and "Momma."

Leach·man |'lēcHmən|, Cloris (1930–   ) U.S. actress. She performed in the "Mary Tyler Moore Show" and starred in her own television program, "Phyllis" (1975–77). She won an Academy Award in 1971 for *The Last Picture Show*.

Lea·cock |'lē,käk|, Stephen (Butler) (1869–1944) Canadian humorist and economist. He is chiefly remembered for his many humorous short stories, parodies, and essays. Notable works: *Sunshine Sketches of a Little Town* (1912) and *Arcadian Adventures with Idle Rich* (1914).

Lea·key |'lēkē| British family of anthropologists and archaeologists, including: **Louis Seymour Bazett Leakey** (1903–72), a Kenyan-born anthropologist and author who discovered fossil hominids at the Olduvai Gorge in Tanzania. His wife **Mary (Douglas) Leakey** (1913–96), an archaeologist and anthropologist. She discovered fossilized footprints in Tanzania. Their son **Richard (Erskine Frere) Leakey** (1944–   ), a Kenyan-born archaeologist and anthropologist. He proved theories regarding the origins of *Homo sapiens*.

Lean |lēn|, Sir David (1908–91) English movie director. He made many notable movies, including *Lawrence of Arabia* (1962), *Doctor Zhivago* (1965), and *A Passage to India* (1984).

Lear |lir|, Edward (1812–88) English humorist and illustrator. He wrote *A Book of Nonsense* (1845) and *Laughable Lyrics* (1877).

Lear |lir|, Norman Milton (1922–   ) U.S. television writer, producer, and director. His award-winning shows include *All in the Family* and *Sanford and Son*.

Lear |lir|, William P. (1902–78) U.S.

inventor. He obtained over 150 patents for such inventions as the automobile radio, the eight-track stereo cartridge, and the Lear jet (1963).

Learn·ed |'lərnəd|, Michael (1939–) U.S. actress. She starred in the television series "The Waltons."

Leary |'lirē|, Timothy (Francis) (1920–96) U.S. psychologist. After experimenting with consciousness-altering drugs including LSD, he was dismissed from his teaching post at Harvard University in 1963 and became a symbol of the hippy drug culture.

Lea·vis |'lēvis|, F. R. (1895–1978) English literary critic; full name *Frank Raymond Leavis*. Founder and editor of the quarterly *Scrutiny* (1932–53), he emphasized the value of critical study of English literature to preserving cultural continuity. Notable works: *The Great Tradition* (1948).

Leav·itt |'levit|, Henrietta Swan (1868–1921) U.S. astronomer. She discovered four novae and some 2,400 variable stars.

Le Brun |lə'brəN|, Charles (1619–90) French painter, designer, and decorator. He was prominent in the development and institutionalization of French art and was a leading exponent of French classicism. In 1648 he helped to found the Royal Academy of Painting and Sculpture.

Le Car·ré |lə,kär'ā|, John (1931–) English novelist; pseudonym of *David John Moore Cornwell*. He is known for his unromanticized and thoughtful spy novels, which often feature the British agent George Smiley and include *The Spy Who Came in from the Cold* (1963) and *Tinker, Tailor, Soldier, Spy* (1974).

Le·conte de Lisle |lə'cöNt də ,lēl; lə 'cawnt də ,lēl|, Charles-Marie-René (1818–94) French poet and leader of the Parnassians. His poetry often draws inspiration from mythology, biblical history, and exotic Eastern landscape. Notable works: *Poèmes antiques* (1852).

Le Cor·bu·sier |ləkawrbYzyə| (1887–1965) French architect and city planner, born in Switzerland; born *Charles Édouard Jeanneret*. A pioneer of the international style, he developed theories on functionalism, the use of new mate-

rials and industrial techniques, and the Modulor, a modular system of standard-sized units.

Led·bet·ter |'led,betər|, Huddie (1885–1949) U.S. blues singer. Known as **Leadbelly**. His many recordings include "Good Morning, Blues" (1940).

Le·der·berg |'lādər,bərg|, Joshua (1925–) U.S. geneticist. He won the 1958 Nobel Prize for Physiology or Medicine for his discovery of genetic recombination in bacteria.

Led·yard |'led,yərd|, John (1751–89) U.S. explorer. He joined Captain James Cook's last voyage to the Sandwich Islands.

Lee |lē| Family of early American statesmen. **Richard Henry Lee** (1732–94) was a delegate to the Continental Congress (1774–79) and authored a resolution that led to the writing of the Declaration of Independence; he was later elected to the U.S. Senate from Virginia (1789–92). His brother **Francis Lightfoot Lee** (1734–97) was a delegate to the Continental Congress (1775–79) and a signer of the Declaration of Independence. Their brother **Arthur Lee** (1740–92) was a member of the Continental Congress (1781–85) and the U.S. Treasury Board (1784–89).

Lee |lē| U.S. family, including: **Henry** (1756–1818), soldier and politician. Known as **Light-Horse Harry**. Noted as a brilliant Revolutionary War cavalry commander, he later became governor of Virginia (1792–95) and a member of the U.S. House of Representatives (1799–1801). His brother **Charles** (1758–1815) was attorney general of the U.S. (1795–1801). **Robert E. Lee** (1807–70), Confederate general and the son of Henry Lee. Full name *Robert Edward Lee*. He was the commander of the Confederate Army of Northern Virginia for most of the Civil War. A noted tactician and strategist, his invasion of the North was repulsed at the Battle of Gettysburg (1863), and he surrendered in 1865. **Fitzhugh Lee** (1835–1905), army officer and politician, nephew of Robert E. Lee and grandson of Henry Lee. He was the governor of Virginia (1886–90).

Lee |lē|, Ann (1736–84) U.S. religious

leader, born in England. Known as **Mother Ann**. A Shaker leader, she founded the first Shaker colony in the U.S. at Watervliet, NY (1776).

Lee |lē|, Bruce (1940–73) U.S. actor; born *Lee Yuen Kam*. An expert in kung fu, he starred in a number of martial arts movies, such as *Enter the Dragon* (1973). He also played Kato in the television series "The Green Hornet" (1966).

Lee |lē|, Gypsy Rose (1914–70) U.S. striptease artist; born *Rose Louise Hovick*. In the 1930s she became famous on Broadway for her sophisticated striptease act. He autobiography, *Gypsy* (1957) was filmed in 1962.

Lee |lē|, (Nelle) Harper (1926–   ) U.S. novelist. She won a Pulitzer Prize with her only novel, *To Kill a Mockingbird* (1960), about the sensational trial of a black man falsely charged with raping a white woman.

Lee |lē|, Henry D. (1849–1928) U.S. merchant and manufacturer. He invented Lee blue jeans.

Lee |lē|, Spike (1957–   ) U.S. movie director; born *Shelton Jackson Lee*. Lee's declared intention is to express the richness of black American culture; movies such as *Do the Right Thing* (1989) and *Malcolm X* (1992) sparked controversy with their treatment of racism.

Lee |lē|, Stan (1922–   ) U.S. publisher and author. He was the publisher of Marvel Comics and creator, former writer, and editor of "The Fantastic Four," "The Incredible Hulk," and "Spiderman."

Leeu·wen·hoek |'lāvən,hŏŏk|, Antoni van (1632–1723) Dutch naturalist. He developed a lens for scientific purposes and was the first to observe bacteria, protozoa, and yeast. He accurately described red blood cells, capillaries, striated muscle fibers, spermatozoa, and the crystalline lens of the eye.

Lé·ger |la'zнɑ|, Fernand (1881–1955) French painter. From about 1909 he was associated with the cubist movement, but then developed a style inspired by machinery and modern technology; works include the *Contrast of Forms* series (1913).

Le·Guin |lə'gwin|, Ursula (1929–   ) U.S. author. She has written science fic-

tion for children and adults, as well as novels and poetry, including *The Dispossessed* (1975).

Le·hár |'lȧ,här|, Franz (Ferencz) (1870–1948) Hungarian composer. He is chiefly known for his operattas, of which the most famous is *The Merry Widow* (1905).

Leh·man |'lēmən; 'lȧmən|, Herbert Henry (1878–1963) U.S. banker and politician. He was a partner with Lehman Brothers bankers and served as governor of New York (1932–42) and as a member of the U.S. Senate from New York (1949–57).

Leh·mann |'lāmən; 'lāmän|, Lilli (1848–1929) German soprano. She was known especially as an interpreter of Wagner and Mozart and of lieder.

Leh·mann |'lāmən; lāmän|, Lotte (1888–1976) U.S. lyric soprano, born in Germany. She was known especially for her interpretations of Mozart, Beethoven, Wagner, Strauss, and Schumann.

Leh·rer |'lerər|, Jim (1934–   ) U.S. television journalist. Born *James Charles Lehrer*. With Robert MacNeil he co-anchored the *MacNeil/Lehrer News Hour* (1983–95) and now anchors the *NewsHour* (1995–   ).

Leib·niz |'līb,nits|, Gottfried Wilhelm (1646–1716) German rationalist philosopher, mathematician, and logician. He argued that the world is composed of single units (monads), each of which is self-contained but acts in harmony with every other, as ordained by God, and so this world is the best of all possible worlds. Leibniz also made the important distinction between necessary and contingent truths and devised a method of calculus independently of Newton.

Lei·bo·vitz |'lēbə,vits|, Annie (1949–   ) U.S. photographer. She was chief photographer of *Rolling Stone* magazine (1973–83) before moving to *Vanity Fair*.

Leicester, Earl of see DUDLEY.

Lei·dy |'līdē|, Joseph (1823–91) U.S. educator and anatomist. He was the first to identify extinct species of horse and tiger.

Leif Er·ics·son |'eriksən| see ERICS-SON.

Leigh |lē|, Vivien (1913–67) British actress, born in India. Born *Vivian Hartley*. She won 1939 Academy Awards for her role as Scarlett O'Hara in *Gone With the Wind*.

Leigh·ton |'lātn|, Frederick, 1st Baron Leighton of Stretton (1830–96) English painter and sculptor. He was a leading exponent of Victorian neoclassicism and chiefly painted large-scale mythological and genre scenes.

Le·land |'lēlənd|, Henry Martyn (1843–1932) U.S. automobile manufacturer. He founded the Cadillac Motor Car Co. (1904) and the Lincoln Motor Co. (1917).

Le·land |'lēlənd|, Mickey (1944–89) U.S. politician. He was a member of the U.S. House of Representatives from Texas (1979–89) and a chairman of the Congressional Black Caucus.

Le·ly |'lēlē|, Sir Peter (1618–80) Dutch portrait painter, resident in England from 1641; Dutch name *Pieter van der Faes*. He became principal court painter to Charles II. Notable works include *Windsor Beauties*, a series painted during the 1660s.

Le·May |lə'mā|, Curtis Emerson (1906–90) U.S. air force officer. Known as **Old Iron Pants**. He was the commanding general of the U.S. Strategic Air Command (1948–57) and Air Force chief of staff (1961–65).

Lem·el·son |'leməlsən|, Jerome H. (1923–97) U.S. inventor. His more than 500 patents include the bar-code scanner, the fax machine, and the cassette drive mechanism.

Le·mieux |lə'myōō; lə'myOE|, Mario (1965–) U.S. hockey player, born in Canada.

Lem·mon |'lemən|, Jack (1925–) U.S. actor; born *John Uhler*. He made his name in comedy movies, such as *Some Like It Hot* (1959), later playing serious dramatic parts and winning an Oscar for *Save the Tiger* (1973).

Lem·nitz·er |'lem,nitsər|, Lyman Louis (1899–1988) U.S. army officer. He played a key role in the Allied invasions of Africa in World War II and in the negotiated surrender of Italy; later he served as commander of U.N. forces in Korea (1955–57) and as chairman

of the U.S. joint chiefs of staff (1960–62).

Len·clos |länklō|, Ninon de (1620–1705) French courtesan; born *Anne de Lenclos*. She was a famous wit and beauty who advocated a form of Epicureanism in her book *La Coquette vengée* (1659) and later presided over one of the most distinguished literary salons of the age.

Len·dl |'lendl|, Ivan (1960–) Czech-born U.S. tennis player. He won many singles titles in the 1980s and early 1990s, including the U.S., Australian, and French Open championships.

L'En·fant |länfän|, Pierre Charles (1754–1825) U.S. architect and soldier, born in France. He submitted plans for the design of Washington, D.C.

L'Eng·le |'leNGgəl|, Madeleine (1918–) U.S. author. She has written numerous works of adult and children's fiction and nonfiction, including *A Wrinkle in Time* (1962, Newbery Award).

Le·nin |'lenən| (1870–1924) the principal figure in the Russian Revolution and first premier of the Soviet Union (1918–24); born *Vladimir Ilich Ulyanov*. Lenin was the first political leader to attempt to put Marxist principles into practice. In 1917 he established Bolshevik control after the overthrow of the czar, and in 1918 became head of state (Chairman of the Council of People's Commissars). With Trotsky he defeated counter-revolutionary forces in the Russian Civil War but was forced to moderate his policies to allow the country to recover from the effects of war and revolution.

Len·non |'lenən|, John (1940–80) English pop and rock singer, guitarist, and songwriter. A founding member of the Beatles, he wrote most of their songs in collaboration with Paul McCartney. After the group broke up in 1970, he continued recording material, such as *Imagine* (1971), some with his second wife Yoko Ono. He was assassinated outside his home in New York.

Len·nox |'lenəks|, Annie (1954–) U.S. singer, born in Scotland. She was the lead singer of the Eurythmics before launching a solo career.

Leno |'lenō|, Jay (1950–) U.S. actor

and comedian. Full name *James Douglas Muir Leno*. He replaced Johnny Carson as host of "The Tonight Show" (1992). Emmy Award, 1995.

Le Nô·tre |lənōtrə|, André (1613–1700) French landscape gardener. He designed many formal gardens, including the parks of Vaux-le-Vicomte and Versailles, which incorporated his ideas on geometric formality and equilibrium.

Len·ox |'lenəks|, James (1800–80) U.S. philanthropist. His personal library became part of the New York Public Library.

Leo |'lē(y)ō| The name of thirteen popes, notably: **Leo I** (*c.* 400–461), pope from 440 and Doctor of the Church; known as **Leo the Great**; canonized as **St. Leo I**. He defined the doctrine of the Incarnation at the Council of Chalcedon (451) and extended the power of the Roman See to Africa, Spain, and Gaul. Feast day (in the Eastern Church), February 18; (in the Western Church), April 11. **Leo X** (1475–1521), pope from 1513; born *Giovanni de' Medici*. He excommunicated Martin Luther and bestowed on Henry VIII of England the title of Defender of the Faith. He was a noted patron of learning and the arts.

Leo III |'lē(y)ō| (*c.* 680–741) Byzantine emperor (717–41). He repulsed several Muslim invasions and carried out an extensive series of reforms. In 726 he banned icons and other religious images; the resulting iconoclastic controversy led to over a century of political and religious turmoil.

Leon·ard |'lenərd|, Elmore (John) (1925–) U.S. novelist and screenwriter Notable works: *Freaky Deaky* (1988), *Get Shorty* (1990), and *Be Cool* (1999).

Leon·ard |'lenərd|, Sugar Ray (1956–) U.S. boxer. Full name *Ray Charles Leonard*. He won world championship titles in three different weight divisions.

Le·o·nar·do da Vin·ci |,lē(y)ə'närdō də 'vin,CHē| (1452–1519) Italian painter, scientist, and engineer. His paintings are notable for their use of the technique of *sfumato* and include *The Virgin of the Rocks* (1483–85), *The Last Supper*

(1498), and the enigmatic *Mona Lisa* (1504–05). He devoted himself to a wide range of other subjects, from anatomy and biology to mechanics and hydraulics: his nineteen notebooks include studies of the human circulatory system and plans for a type of aircraft and a submarine.

Le·on·ti·ef |lē'(y)awn,tyef|, Wassily (1906–) U.S. economist, educator, and author, born in Russia. Notable works: The Structure of the American Economy, 1919–29 (2nd ed. 1976). Nobel Prize for Economics, 1973.

Le·o·pold I |'lē(y)ə,pōld| (1790–1865) first king of Belgium (1831–65). The fourth son of the Duke of Saxe-Coburg-Saalfield, Leopold was an uncle of Britain's Queen Victoria. In 1830 he refused the throne of Greece, but a year later he accepted that of the newly independent Belgium.

Leo the Great Pope Leo I (see LEO).

Le·pi·dus |'lepədəs|, Marcus Aemilius (died *c.* 13 BC) Roman statesman and triumvir. A supporter of Julius Caesar in the civil war against Pompey, he was elected consul in 46 and was appointed one of the Second Triumvirate with Octavian and Antony in 43.

Ler·ner |'lərnər|, Alan J. (1918–1986) U.S. lyricist and dramatist; full name *Alan Jay Lerner*. He wrote a series of musicals with composer Frederick Loewe (1904–88) that were also filmed, including *Paint Your Wagon* (1951; filmed 1969) and *My Fair Lady* (1956; filmed 1964). He won Oscars for the movies *An American in Paris* (1951) and *Gigi* (1958).

Le·sage |lə'säZH|, Alain-René (1668–1747) French novelist and dramatist. He is best known for the picaresque novel *Gil Blas* (1715–35).

Les·caze |,les'käz|, William (1896–1969) U.S. architect, born in Switzerland. He designed the Philadelphia Savings Fund Society building and the Church Peace Center building in New York City.

Les·seps |lä'seps; 'lesəps|, Ferdinand-Marie, Vicomte de (1805–94) French diplomat. From 1854 onwards, while in the consular service in Egypt, he devoted himself to the project of the Suez

Canal. In 1881 he embarked on the building of the Panama Canal, but the project was abandoned in 1889.

Les·sing |'lesɪNG|, Doris (May) (1919–) British novelist and short-story writer, brought up in Rhodesia. An active communist in her youth, she frequently deals with social and political conflicts in her fiction, especially as they affect women. Notable novels: *The Grass is Singing* (1950), *Canopus in Argus* (1979–83), and *The Good Child* (1988).

Les·sing |'lesɪNG|, Gotthold Ephraim (1729–81) German dramatist and critic. In his critical works, such as *Laokoon* (1766), he suggested that German writers look to English literature rather than the French classical school. He also wrote both tragedy and comedy.

Let·ter·man |'letərmən|, David (1947–) U.S. writer and comedian. He hosted "The David Letterman Show" and "Late Night with David Letterman"

Leu·tze |'loitsə|, Emanuel Gottlieb (1816–68) U.S. artist. He is noted for his historical paintings, especially *Washington Crossing the Deleware* (1851).

Le·ver·hulme |'levər,hyo͞om|, 1st Viscount (1851–1925) English industrialist and philanthropist; born *William Hesketh Lever*. He and his brother manufactured soap; their company, Lever Bros., came to form the basis of the international corporation Unilever.

Lever·rier |ləvāryā|, Urbain-Jean-Joseph (1811–77) French mathematician. His analysis of the motions of the planets suggested that an unknown body was disrupting the orbit of Uranus. Le Verrier prompted the German astronomer **Johann Galle**, (1812–1910) to investigate, and the planet Neptune was discovered in 1846.

Lev·er·tov |'levər,tawf|, Denise (1923–97) U.S. poet, born in England. Notable works: *The Poet in the World* (1973).

Le·vi |'lāvē|, Primo (1919–87) Italian novelist and poet, of Jewish descent. His experiences as a survivor of Auschwitz are recounted in his first book *If This is a Man* (1947).

Lev·in |'levən|, Ira (1929–) U.S. author. Notable works: *Rosemary's Baby* (1967) and *Deathtrap* (1978).

Lev·in |'levən|, Meyer (1905–81) U.S. author. Notable works: *Compulsion* (1956).

Le·vine |lə'vēn|, David (1926–) U.S. caricaturist and painter. He was reknowned for his political, social, and literary caricatures appearing in *Esquire* and the *New York Review of Books*.

Le·vine |lə'vēn|, Philip (1928–) U.S. poet and educator. Notable works: *Simple Truth* (1995, Pulitzer Prize).

Le·vin·son |'levən,sən|, Barry (1942–) U.S. director. Notable movies: *Rain Man* (1988, Academy Award).

Lé·vi-Strauss |,levē'strows|, Claude (1908–) French social anthropologist A pioneer in the use of a structuralist analysis to study cultural systems, he regarded language as an essential common denominator underlying cultural phenomena.

Le·win·sky |lə'winskē|, Monica (1973–) U.S. White House intern. She gained notoriety for her "inappropriate relationship" with President Bill Clinton.

Lew·is |'loōəs|, Carl (1961–) U.S. track and field athlete; full name *Frederick Carleton Lewis*. He won Olympic gold medals in 1984, 1988, 1992, and 1996 (his ninth) for sprinting and the long jump and broke the world record for the 100 meters on several occasions.

Lew·is |'loōəs|, Cecil Day see DAY LEWIS.

Lew·is |'loōəs|, C. S. (1898–1963) British novelist, religious writer, and literary scholar; full name *Clive Staples Lewis*. He broadcast and wrote on religious and moral issues, and created the imaginary land of Narnia for a series of children's books. Notable works: *The Lion, the Witch, and the Wardrobe* (1950).

Lew·is |'loōəs|, Henry (1932–1996) U.S. conductor. He was founder of the Los Angeles Chamber Orchestra (1958) and music director of the Los Angeles Opera (1965–68). He made his Metropolitan Opera conducting debut in 1972 in *La Bohème*.

Lew·is |'loōəs|, Jerry Lee (1935–) U.S. rock-and-roll singer and pianist. In 1957 he had hits with "Whole Lotta Shakin' Going On" and "Great Balls of

Fire". His career was interrupted when his marriage to his fourteen-year-old cousin caused a public outcry.

Lew·is |'lŏŏəs|, John Llewellyn (1880–1969) U.S. labor leader. He headed the United Mine Workers (1920–60) and organized the Committee for Industrial Organization (1935), which became the Congress of Industrial Organizations.

Lew·is |'lŏŏəs|, Mel (1929–90) U.S. jazz drummer and orchestra leader. Born *Melvin Sokoloff*. He formed the Thad Jones-Mel Lewis Orchestra in 1965 and became the sole leader after 1979.

Lew·is |'lŏŏəs|, Meriwether (1774–1809) U.S. explorer. Together with William Clark he led an expedition to explore the newly acquired Louisiana Purchase (1804–06). They travelled from St. Louis to the Pacific Northwest and back. He then served as governor of Louisiana Territory (1807–09).

Lew·is |'lŏŏəs|, R.W. B. (1917–) U.S. literary critic and educator. Full name *Richard Warrington Baldwin Lewis*. Notable works: *The American Adam* (1955) and *Edith Warton* (1975, Pulitzer Prize).

Lew·is |'lŏŏəs|, Shari (1934–98) U.S. television puppeteer and ventriloquist. Born *Shari Hurwitz*. She was known for her children's television programs featuring the puppets Lamb Chop, Charlie Horse, and Hush Puppy.

Lew·is |'lŏŏəs|, (Harry) Sinclair (1885–1951) U.S. novelist, known for satirical works such as *Main Street* (1920), *Babbitt* (1922), and *Elmer Gantry* (1927). He was the first American writer to receive the Nobel Prize for Literature (1930).

Lew·is |'lŏŏəs|, (Percy) Wyndham (1884–1957) British novelist, critic, and painter, born in Canada. He was a leader of the vorticist movement, and with Ezra Pound edited the magazine *Blast* (1914–15). Notable novels: *The Apes of God* (1930).

Lib·by |'libē|, Willard Frank (1908–80) U.S. chemist. He was a member of the Atomic Energy Commission (1954–59) and won the Nobel Prize in Chemistry in 1960 for his discovery of radioactive carbon dating.

Lib·e·ra·ce |ˌlibə'räCHē| (1919–87) U.S. pianist and entertainer; full name

Wladziu Valentino Liberace. He was known for his romantic arrangements of popular piano classics and for his flamboyant costumes.

Lich·ten·stein |'liktən,stīn|, Roy (1923–97) U.S. painter and sculptor. A leading exponent of pop art, he became known for paintings inspired by comic strips. Notable works: *Whaam!* (1963).

Lid·dell |'lidəl|, Eric (Henry) (1902–45) British runner and missionary, born in China. In the 1924 Olympic Games he won the 400 meters in a world record time. His exploits were celebrated in the movie *Chariots of Fire* (1981).

Lid·dell Hart |ˌlidəl 'härt|, Sir Basil Henry (1895–1970) British military historian and theorist. He developed principles of mobile warfare, which were adopted by both sides in World War II.

Lie |lē|, Trygve Halvdan (1896–1968) Norwegian Labor politician, first secretary general of the United Nations (1946–53).

Lie·ber |'lēbər|, Francis (1800–1872) U.S. political philosopher, born in Germany. His work, *A Code for the Government of Armies* (1863), was reissued by the War Department as General Orders No. 100 and became a standard international work on military law and conduct of war.

Lie·big |'lēbig|, Justus von (Baron) (1803–73) German chemist and teacher. With Friedrich Wöhler he discovered the benzoyl radical, and demonstrated that such radicals were groups of atoms that remained unchanged in many chemical reactions.

Li·ge·ti |'ligətē|, György Sándor (1923–) Hungarian composer. His orchestral works *Apparitions* (1958–59) and *Atmosphères* (1961) dispense with the formal elements of melody, harmony, and rhythm.

Light·foot |'lit,fŏŏt|, Gordon (1938–) Canadian singer and songwriter. His hits include "If You Could Read My Mind" and "The Wreck of the Edmund Fitzgerald."

Li·li·u·o·ka·la·ni |li,lēəwōkə'länē| (1838–1917) Hawaiian queen. Also known as **Lydia Paki Liliuokalani** and **Liliu Kamakaeha**. The last reigning queen of the Hawaiian Islands (1891–

93), she ascended the throne in 1891; she was deposed by U.S. marines in 1893 and formally renounced her royal claim in 1895.

Lim·baugh |limbaw|, Rush (1951–) U.S. talk show host and political commentator. His daily three-hour radio show, combining conservative political commentary with satire, has the largest audience of any radio talk show.

Li·món |lĕ'mōn|, José Arcadio (1908–72) U.S. modern dancer and choreographer, born in Mexico. He founded his own dance company (1947).

Lin |'lin|, Leslie Charles Bowyer (1907–93) U.S. author, born in Singapore. Pseudonym **Leslie Charteris**. He wrote popular thrillers featuring the character Simon Templar, the Saint. Notable works: *The Saint Steps In* (1943) and *Vendetta for Saint* (1964).

Lin |'lin|, Maya (1960–) U.S. architect. She designed the Vietnam Veterans' Memorial in Washington, D.C.

Lin·a·cre |linəkər|, Thomas (c. 1460–1524) English physician and classical scholar. In 1518 he founded the College of Physicians in London, and became its first president. He translated Galen's Greek works on medicine and philosophy into Latin, reviving studies in anatomy, botany, and clinical medicine in Britain.

Lin Biao |,lin 'byow| (c. 1907–71) Also **Lin Piao**. Chinese communist statesman and general. He was nominated to become Mao's successor in 1969. Having staged an unsuccessful coup in 1971, he was reported to have been killed in a plane crash while fleeing to the Soviet Union.

Lin·coln |'liNGkən|, Abraham see box.
Mary Todd Lincoln (1818–82), wife of Abraham Lincoln and U.S. first lady (1861–65). Their son **Robert Todd Lincoln** (1843–1926), U.S. lawyer. The only one of four sons of Abraham Lincoln to live to adulthood, he served as secretary of war (1881–85) and as president of the Pullman Co. (1897–1911).

Lind |'lind|, Jenny (1820–87) Swedish soprano; born *Johanna Maria Lind Goldschmidt*. She was known as "the Swedish nightingale" for the purity and agility of her voice.

Lincoln, Abraham
16th U.S. president

Life dates: 1809–1865
Place of birth: Hodgenville, Hardin (now Larue) County, Ky.
Mother: Nancy Hanks Lincoln
Stepmother: Sarah Bush Johnston Lincoln
Father: Thomas Lincoln
Wife: Mary Todd Lincoln
Children: Robert, Edward, William, Thomas ("Tad")
Nickname: Honest Abe
College/University: None
Military service: captain, Company of Volunteers; private, U.S. Army, Black Hawk War
Career: Lawyer; surveyor; postmaster
Political career: Illinois General Assembly; U.S. House of Representatives; president
Party: Whig; Republican
Home state: Illinois
Opponents in presidential races: Stephen A. Douglas, John C. Breckinridge, John Bell; George B. McClellan
Term of office: Mar. 4, 1861–Apr. 15, 1865 (assassinated)
Vice presidents: Hannibal Hamlin; Andrew Johnson
Notable events of presidency: Civil War; Emancipation Proclamation; Homestead Act; Gettysburg Address; Morrill Land-Grant College Act; West Virginia and Nevada admitted as 35th and 36th states; Gen. Robert E. Lee surrendered to Gen. Ulysses S. Grant at Appomattox Courthouse, Va.
Other achievements: Admitted to the Illinois bar; Lincoln-Douglas debates in Illinois (senatorial campaign); first Republican president
Place of burial: Springfield, Ill.

Lind·bergh |'lin(d)bərg| U.S. family, including: **Charles (Augustus) Lindbergh** (1902–74), aviator. In 1927 he made the first solo transatlantic flight in a single-engined monoplane, *Spirit of St. Louis*, and was known thereafter as "Lucky Lindy." He recounted his adventures in the Pulitzer Prize-winning *The Spirit of St. Louis* (1953). His wife **Anne Morrow Lindbergh** (1906–), U.S. author and poet. Notable works: *North to the Orient* (1935) and *Listen! The Wind* (1938). With her husband Charles, she moved to Europe to escape the publicity surrounding the kidnap and murder of their two-year-old son in 1932.

Lind·gren |'lin(d),grən|, Astrid (1907–) Swedish author of children's books. Notable works: *Pippi Longstocking*.

Lind·say |'linzē| Family of Australian artists. **Sir Lionel Lindsay** (1874–1961) was an art critic, watercolor painter, and graphic artist. His brother **Norman Lindsay** (1879–1969) was a graphic artist, painter, critic, and novelist.

Lind·say |'linzē|, Howard (1889–1968) U.S. playwright, producer, and actor. With Russel Crouse (1893–1966) he coauthored Broadway shows, including *Anything Goes* (1934), *State of the Union* (1946, Pulitzer Prize) and *Sound of Music* (1959).

Lind·say |'linzē|, Vachel (1879–1931) U.S. poet. Full name *Nicholas Vachel Lindsay*. Notable books: *General William Booth Enters into Heaven and Other Poems* (1913), *The Congo and Other Poems* (1914), and *The Candle in the Cabin* (1926).

Link |liNGk|, Edwin Albert (1904–81) U.S. inventor and businessman. With brother George, he made a flight simulator for pilot classroom training (1929) and was the founder and president of Link Aviation, Inc. (1935–53).

Lin·nae·us |lə'nā(y)əs|, Carolus (1707–78) Swedish botanist, founder of modern systematic botany and zoology. Latinized name of *Carl von Linné*. He devised an authoritative classification system for flowering plants involving binomial Latin names (later superseded by that of Antoine Jussieu), and also a classification method for animals.

Lip·chitz |'lip,SHits|, Jacques (1891–1973) Lithuanian-born French sculptor; born *Chaim Jacob Lipchitz*. After producing cubist works such as *Sailor with a Guitar* (1914), he explored the interpenetration of solids and voids in his series of "transparent" sculptures of the 1920s.

Li·pin·ski |lə'pinskē|, Tara (1982–) U.S. figure skater. She became the youngest woman to win the U.S. and

world figure skating championship (1997).

Li Po |'lē pō; 'lē 'bō| (AD 701–62) Also **Li Bo** or **Li T'ai Po**. Chinese poet. Typical themes in his poetry are wine, women, and the beauties of nature.

Lip·pi |'lipē|, Filippino (c. 1457–1504) Italian painter, son of Fra Filippo Lippi. Having trained with his father and Botticelli he completed a fresco cycle begun by Masaccio in the Brancacci Chapel, Florence; other works include the series of frescoes in the Carafa Chapel in Rome and the painting *The Vision of St. Bernard* (c. 1486).

Lip·pin·cott |'lipən,kät|, Joshua Ballinger (1813–86) U.S. publisher. He founded J. B. Lippincott & Co. (1936).

Lipp·mann |'lipmən|, Gabriel-Jonas (1845–1921) French physicist. He is best known today for his production of the first fully orthochromatic color photograph in 1893.

Lipp·mann |'lipmən|, Walter (1889–1974) U.S. journalist. He was a founder and associate editor of *The New Republic* and a columnist for *The New York Herald Tribune* (1931–67). Pulitzer Prizes, 1958 and 1962.

Lip·ton |'liptən|, Sir Thomas Johnstone (1850–1931) Scottish merchant and yachtsman. He developed a chain of food stores in Scotland before investing in tea. He entered five yachts in the America's Cup races.

Li·sa |'lēsə|, Manuel (1772–1820) U.S. fur trader. He built Fort Manuel, the first trading post in Montana, and he formed the Missouri Fur Co. with members of the Chouteau family.

Lis·ter |'listər|, Joseph (1st Baron) (1827–1912) English surgeon, inventor of antiseptic techniques in surgery. He realized the significance of Louis Pasteur's germ theory in connection with sepsis, and in 1865 he used carbolic acid dressings on patients who had undergone surgery.

Lis·ton |'listən|, Sonny (1932?–70) U.S. heavyweight boxing champion; born *Charles Liston*.

Liszt |list|, Franz (1811–86) Hungarian composer and pianist. He was a key figure in the romantic movement; many of his piano compositions combine lyricism with great technical complexity, while his twelve symphonic poems (1848–58) created a new musical form.

Lith·gow |'liTHgow|, John (1945–) U.S. actor. He won 1996–97 Emmy Awards for his role in the television show "Third Rock from the Sun."

Lit·tle |'litəl|, Arthur Dehon (1863–1935) U.S. chemical engineer. He organized a chemical consulting firm that was later reorganized as Arthur D. Little, Inc. (1909).

Lit·tle |'litəl|, Charles Coffin (1799–1869) U.S. publisher. With James Brown, he founded Little, Brown and Co. (1847), publishers of legal and general works.

Little Corporal a nickname for Napoleon.

Lit· Rich·ard |'litl 'riCHərd| (1932–) U.S. rock and roll musician. Born *Richard Wayne Penniman*. His hits include "Tutti Frutti," "Long Tall Sally," and "Good Golly, Miss Molly."

Lit·tle Tur·tle |'litl 'tərtl| (1752?–1812) chief of the Miami Indians. He led raids on settlers in the Northwest Territory and was forced to sign the Treaty of Greenville (1795).

Lit·tle·wood |'litl,wŏŏd|, (Maudie) Joan (1914–) English theater director. She cofounded the Theatre Workshop (1945), and is particularly remembered for her production of the musical *Oh, What a Lovely War* (1963).

Lit·tré |lētrā|, Maximilien-Paul-Émile (1801–81) French lexicographer and philosopher. He was the author of the major *Dictionnaire de la langue française* (1863–77). A follower of Auguste Comte, he became the leading exponent of positivism after Comte's death.

Liv·er·pool |'livər,pŏŏl|, Robert Banks Jenkinson, 2nd Earl of (1770–1828) British Tory statesman, prime minister (1812–27).

Liv·ing·ston |'liviNGstən| Family of early American jurists and statesmen. **Robert R. Livingston** (1746–1813) was a member of the Continental Congress (1775–55, 1779–81) and one of the five drafters of the Declaration of Independence. His brother **Edward Livingston** (1764–1836) authored the penal code for Louisiana, which became

the model for state penal codes throughout the U.S. and internationally. They were great-grandsons of Robert Livingston.

Liv·ing·ston |'liviNGstən|, Robert (1654–1728) U.S. fur trader, born in Scotland. He married Alida Van Rensselaer and established an estate of 160,000 acres in upstate New York; he became a prominent influence in New York state politics.

Liv·ing·ston |'liviNGstən|, Henry Brockholst (1757–1823) U.S. Supreme Court justice (1806–23).

Liv·ing·stone |'liviNGstən|, David (1813–73) Scottish missionary and African explorer. He went to Bechuanaland as a missionary in 1841. On extensive travels, he discovered Lake Ngami (1849), the Zambezi River (1851), and the Victoria Falls (1855). In 1866 he went in search of the source of the Nile, and was found in poor health by Sir Henry Morton Stanley in 1871.

Livy |'livē| (59 BC–AD 17) Roman historian; Latin name *Titus Livius*. His history of Rome from its foundation to his own time contained 142 books, of which thirty-five survive (including the earliest history of the war with Hannibal).

Llo·sa |'yōsə|, Mario Vargas see VARGAS LLOSA.

Lloyd |loid|, Harold (Clayton) (1894–1971) U.S. movie comedian. Performing his own hair-raising stunts, he used physical danger as a source of comedy in silent movies such as *High and Dizzy* (1920), *Safety Last* (1923), and *The Freshman* (1925).

Lloyd George |'loid 'jawrj|, David, 1st Earl Lloyd George of Dwyfor (1863–1945) British Liberal statesman, prime minister (1916–22). His coalition government was threatened by economic problems and trouble in Ireland, and he resigned when the Conservatives withdrew their support in 1922.

Lloyd Web·ber |'loid 'webər|, Sir Andrew, Baron Lloyd-Webber of Sydmonton (1948–) English composer. His many successful musicals, several of them written in collaboration with the lyricist Sir Tim Rice, include *Jesus Christ Superstar* (1970), *Cats* (1981), and *The Phantom of the Opera* (1986).

Lly·wel·yn |lŏō'(w)elən| (died 1282) prince of Gwynedd in North Wales; also known as **Llywelyn ap Gruffydd**. Proclaiming himself prince of all Wales in 1258, he was recognized by Henry III in 1265. His refusal to pay homage to Edward I led the latter to invade and subjugate Wales (1277–84); Llewelyn died in an unsuccessful rebellion.

Lo·ba·chev·sky |ˌlŏbə'CHefskē|, Nikolay Ivanovich (1792–1856) Russian mathematician. At about the same time as Gauss and **János Bolyai,** (1802–60), he independently discovered non-Euclidean geometry. His work was not widely recognized until the non-Euclidean nature of space–time was revealed by the general theory of relativity.

Lo·bo |'lŏbō|, Rebecca (1973–) U.S. basketball player. She was the women's college basketball Player of the Year in 1995, when she led the University of Connecticut to an undefeated season and a national title. She was also on the 1996 U.S. Olympic women's basketball team and a premier player for the New York Liberty in the Women's National Basketball League.

Locke |läk|, Alain (LeRoy) (1886–1954) U.S. author and educator. His anthology *The New Negro: An Interpretation* (1925) started the Harlem Renaissance.

Locke |läk|, John (1632–1704) English philosopher, a founder of empiricism and political liberalism. His *Two Treatises of Government* (1690) argues that the authority of rulers has a human origin and is limited. In *An Essay concerning Human Understanding* (1690) he argued that all knowledge is derived from sense-experience.

Lock·yer |'läkyər|, Sir (Joseph) Norman (1836–1920) English astronomer. His spectroscopic analysis of the sun led to his discovery of a new element, which he named *helium.* He founded both the Science Museum in London and the scientific journal *Nature,* which he edited for fifty years.

Lodge |läj|, David (John) (1935–) English novelist and academic Honorary professor of Modern English Literature at the University of Birmingham since 1976, he often satirizes academia and literary criticism in his novels, which include *Changing Places* (1975) and *Small World* (1984).

Lodge[1] |läj|, Henry Cabot (1850–1924) U.S. politician and author. He was a member of the U.S. House of Representatives and the U.S. Senate from Massachusetts; the great-grandson of George Cabot and grandfather of Henry Cabot Lodge.

Lodge[2] |läj|, Henry Cabot (1902–85) U.S. politician and diplomat. He was a Republican vice presidential candidate (1960), ambassador to South Vietnam (1963–63, 1965–67), and chief negotiator at the Vietnam peace talks in Paris. He was grandson of Henry Cabot Lodge (1850–1924).

Lodge |läj|, Sir Oliver (Joseph) (1851–1940) English physicist. He made important contributions to the study of electromagnetic radiation, and was a pioneer of radio-telegraphy.

Loeb |lōb|, James Morris (1867–1933) U.S. banker and philanthropist. With the banking firm Kuhn, Loeb and Co. (1888–1901), he subsidized the publication of the *Loeb Classical Library* (1910).

Loes·ser |'lesər|, Frank Henry (1910–69) U.S. composer and lyricist. He composed movie scores and songs, including *Baby, It's Cold Outside* (1948, Academy Award) and *Guys and Dolls* (1950).

Loew |lō|, Marcus (1870–1927) U.S. theater owner and movie producer. He owned a chain of movie theaters and then formed Loew's Inc., which purchased Metro Pictures and Goldwyn Pictures to become Metro-Goldwyn-Mayer.

Loewe |lō|, Frederick (1901–88) U.S. composer. The collaboration he began with lyricist Alan Jay Lerner in 1942 became one of the most successful in the history of musical theater. Notable scores: *Brigadoon* (1947), *My Fair Lady* (1956), *Gigi* (1958), and *Camelot (1960).*

Lof·ting |'lawf,tiNG|, Hugh (1886–1947) British author and U.S. resident. He wrote numerous children's books, including *The Story of Dr. Doolittle* (1922) and its many sequels.

Lo·gan |'lōgən|, Joshua Lockwood

(1908–88) U.S. director and playwright. He directed Broadway shows, including *South Pacific* (1949), which he also cowrote, and *Annie Get Your Gun* (1946).

Lo·gan |'lōgən|, Rayford W. (1897–1982) U.S. historian and educator. Spingarn Medal, 1980

Lomb |läm|, Henry (1828–1908) U.S. optician. He was a cofounder of Bausch & Lomb Optical Co.

Lom·bar·di |läm'bärdē|, Vincent Thomas (1913–70) U.S. football coach. He coached the Green Bay Packers (1959–67) to five National Football League championships and two Super Bowl titles.

Lom·bar·do |ləm'bär,dō|, Guy Albert (1902–77) U.S. band leader, born in Canada. His dance band, the Royal Canadians (from 1927), played the "sweetest music this side of heaven," and his New Year's Eve broadcasts became a national tradition.

Lon·don |'ləndən|, Jack (1876–1916) U.S. novelist; pseudonym of *John Griffith Chaney*. The Klondike gold rush of 1897 provided the material for his famous works depicting struggle for survival. Notable works: *The Call of the Wild* (1903) and *White Fang* (1906).

Long |lawNG|, Huey Pierce (1893–1935) U.S. politician. Known as **the Kingfish**. He was governor of Louisiana (1928–31) and a U.S. senator (1932–35), known as a dictatorial demagogue with politically radical ideas, most notably his "Share the Wealth" program. Not long after he announced his plans to run for the U.S. presidency, he was assassinated.

Long |lawNG|, John Luther (1861–1927) U.S. author. He wrote the short story *Madame Butterfly* (1898), which was adapted for the stage and used as a source for Puccini's opera.

Long |lawNG|, Stephen Harriman (1784–1864) U.S. Army officer and explorer. His expeditions included the upper Mississippi and the Rocky Mountain region; he discovered Longs Peak in Colorado.

Long·a·cre |'lawNG,äkər|, James Barton (1794–1869) U.S. engraver. He created *The National Portrait Gallery of Distinguished Americans* (4 vols., 1834–39)

and was chief engraver of the U.S. Mint (1844–69).

Long·fel·low |'lawNG,felō|, Henry Wadsworth (1807–82) U.S. poet. He is known for "The Wreck of the Hesperus" and "The Village Blacksmith" (both 1841) and narrative poems such as *Evangeline* (1847), *The Song of Hiawatha* (1855), and *Paul Revere's Ride* (1861).

Lon·gi·nus |län'jīnəs| (1st century AD) Greek scholar. He is the supposed author of a Greek literary treatise *On the Sublime*, concerned with the moral function of literature, which influenced Augustan writers such as Dryden and Pope.

Long·street |'lawNG,strēt|, James (1821–1904) Confederate army officer. He surrendered with Robert E. Lee at Appomattox and recounted his experiences in *From Manassas to Appomattox* (1896).

Loos |'lōōs|, Anita (1893–1981) U.S. author. She wrote books and movie scripts, including *Gentlemen Prefer Blondes* (1925).

Lor·ca |lawrkə|, Federico García (1898–1936) Spanish poet and dramatist. His works include *Gypsy Ballads* (verse, 1928) and intense, poetic tragedies evoking the passionate emotions of Spanish life, notably *Blood Wedding* (1933) and *The House of Bernada Alba* (1945).

Lorde |lawrd|, Audre (1934–92) U.S. poet. Notable works: *The Marvelous Arithmetics of Distance: Poems 1987–1992*.

Lo·ren |lə'ren|, Sophia (1934–) Italian actress; born *Sofia Scicolone*. She has starred in both Italian and American movies, including the slapstick comedy *The Millionairess* (1960) and the wartime drama *La Ciociara* (1961), for which she won an Oscar.

Lo·rentz |'lawrənts|, Hendrik Antoon (1853–1928) Dutch theoretical physicist. He worked on the forces affecting electrons and realized that electrons and cathode rays were the same thing. For their work on electromagnetic theory he and his pupil **Pieter Zeeman**, (1865–1943) shared the 1902 Nobel Prize for Physics.

Lo·renz |'lawrənz; 'lawrənts|, Konrad

(Zacharias) (1903–89) Austrian zoologist. He pioneered the science of ethology, emphasizing innate rather than learned behaviour or conditioned reflexes. Lorenz extrapolated his studies in ornithology to human behaviour patterns, and compared the ill effects of the domestication of animals to human civilizing processes. He shared a Nobel Prize in 1973 with Karl von Frisch and Nikolaas Tinbergen.

Lo·ren·zo de' Me·di·ci |lə'renzō dä 'medə,CHē; mə'dēCHē| (1449–92) Italian statesman and scholar. A patron of the arts and humanist learning, he supported Botticelli, Leonardo da Vinci, and Michelangelo, among others. He was also a noted poet and scholar in his own right.

Lor·i·mer |'lawrəmər|, George Horace (1867–1937) U.S. editor. He was editor in chief of the *Saturday Evening Post* (1889–1936).

Lor·rain, Claude |law'rän| see CLAUDE LORRAIN.

Lor·raine, Claude |law'rän| see CLAUDE LORRAINE.

Lor·re |'lawrē; 'lärē|, Peter (1904–64) Hungarian-born U.S. actor; born *Laszlo Lowenstein*. He was known for the sinister roles he played, as in the German movie *M* (1931), *The Maltese Falcon* (1941), and *The Raven* (1963).

Lo·throp |'lōTHrəp|, Harriet Mulford Stone (1844–1924) U.S. author. Pseudonym **Margaret Sidney**. Notable works: *Five Little Peppers and How They Grew* (1881).

Lo·ti |lō'tē|, Pierre (1850–1923) French novelist; pseudonym of *Louis Marie Julien Viaud*. His voyages as a naval officer provided the background for works such as *Pêcheur d'Islande* (1886) and *Matelot* (1893).

Lott |lät; 'lawt|, Trent (1941–) U.S. politician. Member of the U.S. House of Representatives from Michigan (1989–).

Lot·to |'lätō|, Lorenzo (c. 1480–1556) Italian painter. He chiefly painted religious subjects, though he also produced a number of notable portraits, such as *A Lady as Lucretia* (c. 1533).

Lou·ga·nis |,lōō'gänəs|, Greg (1960–) U.S. diver. He won two gold medals at the 1984 Olympic Games and two at the 1988 Olympics.

Lou·is II |'lōō(w)ē| (846–79) king of France, reigned 877–79.

Lou·is |'lōō(w)ē| The name of 18 kings of France: **Louis I** (778–840), son of Charlemagne. He was king of the West Franks and Holy Roman Emperor (814–40). **Louis II** (846–879; reigned 877–879). **Louis III** (863–882; reigned 879–882), son of Louis II. **Louis IV** (921–954; reigned 936–954). **Louis V** (967–987; reigned 979–987). **Louis VI** (1081–1137; reigned 1108–37). **Louis VII** (c. 1120–80; reigned 1137–80). **Louis VIII** (1187–1226; reigned 1223–26). **Louis IX** (1214–70; reigned 1226–70), son of Louis VIII, canonized as **St. Louis**. He conducted two unsuccessful crusades, dying of plague in Tunis during the second. Feast day, August 25. **Louis X** (1289–1316; reigned 1314–16). **Louis XI** (1423–83; reigned 1461–83), son of Charles VII. He continued his father's work in laying the foundations of a united France ruled by an absolute monarchy. **Louis XII** (1462–1515; reigned 1498–1515). **Louis XIII** (1601–43; reigned 1610–43), son of Henry IV of France. During his minority the country was ruled by his mother Marie de Médicis. From 1624 he was heavily influenced in policy-making by his chief minister Cardinal Richelieu. **Louis XIV** (1638–1715; reigned 1643–1715), son of Louis XIII; known as **the Sun King**. His reign represented the high point of the Bourbon dynasty and of French power in Europe, and in this period French art and literature flourished. His almost constant wars of expansion united Europe against him, however, and gravely weakened France's financial position. **Louis XV** (1710–74; reigned 1715–74), great-grandson and successor of Louis XIV. He led France into the Seven Years' War (1756–63). **Louis XVI** (1754–93; reigned 1774–92), grandson and successor of Louis XV. His minor concessions and reforms in the face of the emerging French Revolution proved disastrous. As the Revolution became more extreme, he was executed with his wife, Marie Antoinette, and the monarchy was abolished. **Louis XVII** (1785–95), son of Louis XVI. He was the titular king who died in prison during the Revolution. **Louis XVIII** (1755–1824; reigned 1814–24), brother of Louis XVI. After his nephew Louis XVII's death he became titular king in exile until the fall of Napoleon in 1814, when he returned to Paris on the summons of Talleyrand and was officially restored to the throne.

Lou·is I |'lōō(w)ē| (1326–82) king of Hungary (1342–82) and of Poland (1370–82); known as **Louis the Great**. Under his rule Hungary became a powerful state; he fought two successful wars against Venice (1357–58; 1378–81), and the rulers of Serbia, Wallachia, Moldavia, and Bulgaria became his vassals.

Lou·is |'lōōis|, Joe (1914–81) U.S. heavyweight boxing champion; born *Joseph Louis Barrow*; known as the **Brown Bomber**. He was heavyweight champion of the world 1937–49, defending his title twenty-five times during that period. He retired undefeated and then lost a comeback fight.

Lou·is |'lōōwis|, Morris (1912–62) U.S. artist. Born *Morris Bernstein*. He was an abstract Expressionist painter influenced by Jackson Pollack.

Lou·is-Phi·lippe |'lōō(w)ē fə'lēp| (1773–1850) king of France (1830–48). After the restoration of the Bourbons he became the focus for liberal discontent and was made king, replacing Charles X. His regime was gradually undermined by radical discontent and eventually overthrown.

Louis the Great Louis I of Hungary (see LOUIS I).

Love·lace |'ləvləs|, Augusta Ada King, Countess of (1815–52) English mathematician. The daughter of Lord Byron, she became assistant to Charles Babbage and worked with him on his mechanical computer.

Love·lace |'ləvləs|, Maud Hart (1892–1980) U.S. author. She wrote children's fiction, including the "Betsy-Tacy" series.

Love·lace |'ləvləs|, Richard (1618–57) English poet. A supporter of Charles I, he was imprisoned during the English Civil War in 1642, when he probably wrote his famous poem "To Althea, from Prison."

Lov·ell |'ləvəl|, Sir (Alfred Charles) Bernard (1913–) English astronomer and physicist, and pioneer of radio astronomy. He founded Manchester University's radio observatory at Jodrell Bank, where he directed the construction of the large radio telescope that is now named after him.

Lov·ell |'ləvəl|, James A., Jr. (1928–) U.S. astronaut. He was aboard the Apollo 8 first journey to the moon (1968) and the Apollo 13 aborted mission to the moon (1970).

Love·lock |'ləvläk|, James (Ephraim) (1919–) English scientist. He is best known for the *Gaia hypothesis*, first presented by him in 1972 and discussed in several popular books, including *Gaia* (1979).

Lov·ett |'ləvət|, Lyle (1957–) U.S. country singer and actor. Grammy Award, 1997. Notable movies: *The Player* and *Short Cuts*.

Low |lō|, Sir David (Alexander Cecil) (1891–1963) British cartoonist, born in New Zealand, famous for his political cartoons and for inventing the character Colonel Blimp.

Low |lō|, Juliette Gordon (1860–1927) U.S. youth leader. She founded the Girl Scouts of America (1912).

Lowe |lō|, Edwin S. (1910–86) U.S. manufacturer. He manufactured games such as bingo, Yahtzee, chess, and checkers.

Low·ell |'lōəl|, Amy (Lawrence) (1874–1925) U.S. poet. A leading imagist poet, she is known for her polyphonic prose and sensuous imagery. Notable works: *A Critical Fable* (1922) and *What's O'-Clock* (Pulitzer Prize, 1925).

Low·ell |'lōəl|, James Russell (1819–91) U.S. poet, essayist, and diplomat. He was the first editor of the *Atlantic Monthly* (1857–61).

Low·ell |'lōəl|, Percival (1855–1916) U.S. astronomer. Lowell inferred the existence of a ninth planet beyond Neptune, and when it was eventually discovered in 1930 it was given the name Pluto, with a symbol that also included his initials. He was the brother of Amy Lowell.

Low·ell |'lōəl|, Robert (Traill Spence) (1917–77) U.S. poet. His poetry, often describing his manic depression, is notable for its intense confessional nature and for its complex imagery.

Low·ry |'low(ə)rē|, Lois (1937–) U.S. author of novels for adolescents.

Low·ry |'low(ə)rē|, L. S. (1887–1976) English painter; full name *Laurence Stephen Lowry*. He painted small matchstick figures set against the iron and brick expanse of urban and industrial landscapes.

Low·ry |'low(ə)rē|, (Clarence) Malcolm (1909–57) English novelist. His experiences living in Mexico in the 1930s provided the background for his symbolic semi-autobiographical novel *Under the Volcano* (1947).

Loy |loi|, Myrna (1905–93) U.S. actress. Born *Myrna Williams*. She played Nora Charles in *The Thin Man* (1934).

Loyd |loid|, Samuel (1841–1911) U.S. puzzlemaker. He devised chess problems and invented the Parcheesi board game.

Lu·bitsch |'lōōbicH|, Ernst (1892–1947) U.S. movie director, born in Germany. Notable works: *Heaven Can Wait* (1943).

Lu·can |'lōōkən| (AD 39–65) Roman poet, born in Spain; Latin name *Marcus Annaeus Lucanus*. His major work is *Pharsalia*, a hexametric epic in ten books dealing with the civil war between Julius Caesar and Pompey.

Lu·cas |'lōōkəs|, George (1944–) hollywood U.S. movie director, producer, and screenwriter. He wrote and directed the science-fiction movie *Star Wars* (1977), Steven Spielberg's *Raiders of the Lost Ark* (1981), and the two sequels of each movie.

Lu·cas van Ley·den |'lōōkəs væn 'lidən| (c. 1494–1533) Dutch painter and engraver. He produced his most significant work as an engraver, including *Ecce Homo* (1510). His paintings include portraits, genre scenes, and religious subjects.

Luce |lōōs| U.S. family, including: **Henry Robinson Luce** (1898–1967), editor and publisher. He was a co-founder of *Time, Fortune, Life*, and *Sports Illustrated* magazines. His wife **Clare**

Boothe Luce (1903–87), playwright and public official. She served as a war correspondent for *Life* magazine during World War II and as ambassador to Italy (1953–57).

Luck·man |'ləkmən|, Sid (1916–) U.S. football player. Elected to the NFL Hall of Fame (1965).

Lu·cre·tius |lōō'krēsHəs| (c. 94–c. 55 BC) Roman poet and philosopher; full name *Titus Lucretius Carus*. His didactic hexametric poem *On the Nature of Things* is an exposition of the materialist atomist physics of Epicurus, which aims to give peace of mind by showing that fear of the gods and of death is without foundation.

Lu·den·dorff |'lōōdn,dawrf|, Erich (1865–1937) German general, Chief of Staff to General von Hindenburg during the First World War and later a Nazi Party support.

Lud·lum |'lədləm|, Robert (1927–) U.S. author. Pseudonyms **Jonathan Ryder, Michael Shepherd**. He has written suspense novels, including *The Bourne Identity* (1980).

Lud·wig |'lōōdwig; 'lədwig; 'lōōdvig| Name of three kings of Bavaria: **Ludwig I** (1786–1868; reigned 1825–48). He became unpopular due to his reactionary policies, lavish expenditure, and his domination by the dancer Lola Montez, and he was forced to abdicate in favor of his son **Maximilian II. Ludwig II** (1845–86; reigned 1864–86). A patron of the arts, he became a recluse and built a series of elaborate castles. He was declared insane and deposed in 1886. **Ludwig III** (1845–1921; reigned 1913–18).

Lu·gar |'lōōgər|, Richard Green (1932–) U.S. senator from Indiana (1977–).

Lu·go·si |lə'gōsē|, Bela (born Béla Ferenc Blasko) (1884–1956) Hungarian-born U.S. actor famous for his roles in horror movies such as *Dracula* (1931), *Mark of the Vampire* (1935), and *The Wolf Man* (1940).

Lu·han |,lōō'hän|, Mabel Dodge (Ganson) (1879–1962) U.S. author and patron of artists. Notable works: *Lorenzo in Taos* (1932) and *Intimate Memories* (4 vols., 1933–37).

Lu·kács |'lōō,käcH|, György (1885–

1971) Hungarian philosopher, literary critic, and politician. His best-known work is *History and Class Consciousness* (1923), in which he stresses the central role of alienation in Marxist thought.

Lu·kas |ˈlo͝okəs|, J. Anthony (1933–97) U.S. journalist and author. Notable works: *Common Ground* (1986, Pulitzer Prize).

Lu·kas |ˈlo͝okəs|, Paul (1895–1971) U.S. actor, born in Hungary. Notable movies: *Watch on the Rhine* (1943, Academy Award).

Luke |lo͝ok|, St. (1st century AD) an evangelist, closely associated with St. Paul and traditionally the author of the third Gospel and the Acts of the Apostles. Feast day, October 18.

Lul·ly |lyˈlē; lo͞oˈlē|, Jean-Baptiste (1632–87) French composer, born in Italy; Italian name *Giovanni Battista Lulli*. His operas, which include *Alceste* (1674) and *Armide* (1686), mark the beginning of the French operatic tradition.

Lu·miére |ˌlo͞omēˈer|, Auguste-Marie-Louis-Nicolas (1862–1954) French inventors and movie pioneers. In 1895 the brothers patented their "Cinématographe," which combined a movie camera and projector. They also invented the improved "autochrome" process of color photography.

Lunce·ford |ˈlənsfərd|, Jimmie (1902–47) U.S. jazz band leader and saxophonist. Full name *James Melvin Lunceford*. Jimmie Lunceford's Orchestra (1929) had a national reputation as an outstanding black swing band.

Lun·den |ˈləndən|, Joan (1950–) U.S. television journalist. She was co-host of ABC's "Good Morning, America" (1980–97).

Lu·pi·no |ləˈpēˌnō; lo͞oˈpēnō|, Ida (1918–95) U.S. actress and director, born in England. She starred in *Anything Goes* (1936), *Artists and Models* (1937), and *the Sea Wolf* (1941).

Lu·ria |ˈlo͝orē(y)ə|, Salvador Edward (1912–91) U.S. microbiologist, born in Italy. He won a National Book Award for *Life: The Unfinished Experiment* (1974) and shared the 1969 Nobel Prize for Physiology or Medicine.

Lu·rie |ˈlo͝orē|, Alison (1926–) U.S. author and educator. She has written

adult and children's fiction and nonfiction, including *The War Between the Tates* (1974).

Lur·ton |ˈlərt(ə)n|, Horace Harmon (1844–1914) U.S. Supreme Court justice (1910–14). He served in the Confederate army for three years.

Lu·ther |ˈlo͞oTHər|, Martin (1483–1546) German Protestant theologian, the principal figure of the German Reformation. He preached the doctrine of justification by faith rather than by works and attacked the sale of indulgences (1517) and papal authority. In 1521 he was excommunicated at the Diet of Worms. His translation of the Bible into High German (1522–34) contributed significantly to the development of German literature in the vernacular.

Lu·thu·li |ləˈto͝olē|, Albert John Mvumbi (1898–1967) Also **Lutuli**. South African political leader. His presidency of the African National Congress (1952–60) was marked by a program of civil disobedience for which he was awarded the Nobel Peace Prize (1960).

Lu·to·slaw·ski |ˌlo͞otəˈslawvskē|, Witold (1913–94) Polish composer noted for his orchestral music. From the early 1960s his works were characterized by a blend of notational composition and aleatroic sections.

Lut·yens |ˈlətyenz| English family, including: **Sir Edwin (Landseer) Lutyens** (1869–1944), architect. He established his reputation designing country houses, but is particularly known for his plans for New Delhi (1912), where he introduced an open garden-city layout, and for the Cenotaph in London (1919–21). His daughter **(Agnes) Elizabeth** (1906–83), composer. She was one of the first English composers to use the twelve-tone system, as in her *Chamber Concerto No. 1* (1939).

Lux·em·burg |ˈləksəmˌbərg|, Rosa (1870–1919) Polish-born German revolutionary leader. Together with the German socialist **Karl Liebknecht** (1871–1919) she founded the revolutionary group known as the Spartacus League in 1916 and the German Communist Party in 1918.

Ly·cur·gus |lī'kərgəs| (9th century BC) Spartan lawgiver. He is traditionally held to have been the founder of the constitution and military regime of ancient Sparta.

Lyd·gate |'lid,gāt|, John (c. 1370–c. 1450) English poet and monk. His copious output of verse, often in Chaucerian style, includes the poetical translations the *Troy Book* (1412–20) and *The Fall of Princes* (1431–38).

Ly·ell |'lī(ə)l|, Sir Charles (1797–1875) Scottish geologist. His textbook *Principles of Geology* (1830–33) influenced a generation of geologists and held that the earth's features were shaped over a long period of time by natural processes, thus clearing the way for Darwin's theory of evolution.

Ly·ly |'lilē|, John (c. 1554–1606) English prose writer and dramatist. His prose romance in two parts, *Euphues, The Anatomy of Wit* (1578) and *Euphues and his England* (1580) was written in an elaborate style that became known as *euphuism*.

Lynn |lin|, Loretta (1935–) U.S. country singer and songwriter. Born *Loretta Webb*. Notable songs: "Don't Come Home a Drinkin' (With Lovin' on Your Mind)" and "Coal Miner's Daughter."

Lynn |lin|, Dame Vera (1917–) English singer; born *Vera Margaret Lewis*. She is known chiefly for her rendering of such songs as "We'll Meet Again" and "White Cliffs of Dover", which she sang to the troops in World War II.

Ly·on |'liən|, Mary Mason (1797–1849) U.S. educator. She founded Mount Holyoke Seminary (later Mount Holyoke College) in South Hadley, Massachusetts (1837), and served as its first president (1837–49).

Lyo·tard |,lēə'tär|, Jean-François (1924–) French philosopher and literary critic. He outlined his "philosophy of desire," based on the politics of Nietzsche, in *L'Économie libidinale* (1974). In later books he adopted a postmodern quasi-Wittgensteinian linguistic philosophy.

Ly·san·der |lī'sændər| (died 395 BC) Spartan general. He defeated the Athenian navy in 405 and captured Athens in 404, so bringing the Peloponnesian War to an end.

Ly·sen·ko |li'seNGkō|, Trofim Denisovich (1898–1976) Soviet biologist and geneticist. He was an adherent of Lamarck's theory of evolution by the inheritance of acquired characteristics. Since his ideas harmonized with Marxist ideology he was favoured by Stalin and dominated Soviet genetics for many years.

Ly·sip·pus |'lī'sipəs| (4th century BC) Greek sculptor. He is said to have introduced a naturalistic scheme of proportions for the human body into Greek sculpture.

Lyt·ton |'litn|, 1st Baron (1803–73) British novelist, dramatist, and statesman; born *Edward George Earle Bulwer-Lytton*. He achieved literary success with *Pelham* (1828), a novel of fashionable society, and also wrote historical romances (such as *The Last Days of Pompeii*, 1834) and plays. As a diplomat, he served as Viceroy of India (1876–80).

Mm

Ma |mä|, Yo-Yo (1955–) U.S. cellist, born in Paris. Made his debut in New York's Carnegie Hall at age 9, and currently performs throughout the world with major orchestras.

Ma·bu·se |mə'byzə|, Jan (c. 1478–c. 1532) Flemish painter; Flemish name *Jan Gossaert*. He was one of the first artists to disseminate the Italian style in the Netherlands.

MacAlpin |mək'ælpən|, Kenneth see KENNETH I.

Mac·Ar·thur |mə'kärTHər|, Douglas (1880–1964) U.S. general. Commander of U.S. (later Allied) forces in the SW Pacific during World War II, he accepted Japan's surrender in 1945 and administered the ensuing Allied occupation. He was in charge of UN forces in Korea 1950–51, before being forced to relinquish command by President Truman.

Ma·cau·lay |mə'kawlē|, Dame (Emilie) Rose (1881–1958) English novelist and essayist. Notable novels: *Potterism* (1920), *The World My Wilderness* (1950), and *The Towers of Trebizond* (1956).

Ma·cau·lay |mə'kawlē|, Thomas Babington, 1st Baron (1800–59) English historian, essayist, and philanthropist. He was a civil servant in India, where he established a system of education and a new criminal code, before returning to Britain and devoting himself to literature and politics. Notable works: *The Lays of Ancient Rome* (1842) and *History of England* (1849–61).

Mac·beth |mək'beTH| (c. 1005–57) king of Scotland 1040–57. He came to the throne after killing his cousin Duncan I in battle, and was himself defeated and killed by Malcolm III. Shakespeare's tragedy *Macbeth* considerably embroiders the historical events.

Mac·ca·bae·us |,mækə'bēyəs|, Judas see JUDAS MACCABAEUS.

Mac·Diar·mid |mək'derməd|, Hugh (1892–1978) Scottish poet and nationalist; pseudonym of *Christopher Murray Grieve*. The language of his poems drew on the language of various regions of Scotland and historical periods. He was a founding member (1928) of the National Party of Scotland (later the Scottish National Party).

Mac·Don·ald |mək'dänəld|, Dwight (1906–82) U.S. journalist and author. Notable works: *Against the American Grain* (1963).

Mac·Don·ald |mək'dänəld|, Flora (1722–90) Scottish Jacobite heroine. She aided Charles Edward Stuart's escape from English pursuit after his defeat at Culloden in 1746, by smuggling him to the island of Skye, disguised as her maid.

Mac·don·ald |mək'dänəld|, Sir John Alexander (1815–91) Scottish-born Canadian statesman, prime minister (1867–73 and 1878–91). He played a leading role in the confederation of the Canadian provinces and was appointed first prime minister of the Dominion of Canada.

Mac·Don·ald |mək'dänəld|, (James) Ramsay (1866–1937) British Labour statesman, prime minister (1924, 1929–31, and 1931–35). He served as Britain's first Labour prime minister.

Mac·Dow·ell |mək'dowəl|, Edward Alexander (1860–1908) U.S. composer. He is known for his symphonic poems, including *Hamlet and Ophelia* (1885). His widow established the MacDowell Colony for artists and musicians in 1910.

Ma·chia·vel·li |,mækēə'velē|, Niccolò di Bernardo dei (1469–1527) Italian statesman and political philosopher. His best-known work is *The Prince* (1532), which advises rulers that the acquisition and effective use of power may necessitate unethical methods.

Mack |mæk|, Connie (1862–1956) U.S. baseball player and manager. Born *Cornelius Alexander McGillicuddy*. A manager of the Philadelphia Athletics for 50 years, he led the team to 9 American League pennants and 5 World Series championships. He was elected to the Hall of Fame in 1937.

Mac·ken·zie |mə'kenzē|, Sir Alexander

(1764–1820) Scottish explorer of Canada. He discovered the Mackenzie River in 1789 and in 1793 became the first European to reach the Pacific Ocean by land along a northern route.

Mac·ken·zie |məˈkenzē|, Sir Compton (1883–1972) English novelist, essayist, and poet; full name *Edward Montague Compton Mackenzie.* He is best known for his novels, which include *Sinister Street* (1913–14) and *Whisky Galore* (1947).

Mac·ken·zie |məˈkenzē|, William Lyon (1795–1861) Scottish-born Canadian politician and journalist, involved with the movement for political reform in Canada. In 1837 he led an unsuccessful rebellion in Toronto and fled to New York.

Mack·in·tosh |ˈmakən,täSH|, Charles Rennie (1868–1928) Scottish architect, designer, and painter. A leading exponent of art nouveau, he pioneered the new concept of functionalism in architecture and interior design. Notable among his designs is the Glasgow School of Art (1898–1909).

Mac·Lach·lan |məˈklaklən|, Patricia (1938–) U.S. children's author.

Mac·Laine |məˈklān|, Shirley (1934–) U.S. actress. Born *Shirley Beaty.* Notable movies: *Terms of Endearment* (1983, Academy Award).

Mac·lean |məˈklän|, Alistair (1922–87) Scottish novelist, writer of thrillers including *The Guns of Navarone* (1957) and *Where Eagles Dare* (1967).

Mac·lean |məˈklän|, Donald (Duart) (1913–83) British Foreign Office official and Soviet spy. After acting as a Soviet agent from the late 1930s he fled to the USSR with Guy Burgess in 1951.

Mac·Leish |məˈklēSH|, Archibald (1892–1982) U.S. poet. Pulitzer Prize-winning works: *Conquistador* (1932), *Collected Poems* (1952), and *J.B.* (1958).

Mac·leod |məˈklowd|, John James Rickard (1876–1935) Scottish physiologist. He directed the research on pancreatic extracts by F. G. Banting and C. H. Best that led to the discovery and isolation of insulin. Macleod shared a Nobel Prize for Physiology or Medicine with Banting in 1923.

Mac·Mil·lan |məkˈmilən|, Donald Bax-

ter (1874–1970) U.S. explorer and author. He accompanied Robert Peary on his expeditions to the North Pole (1908–09) and to Greenland, Baffin Island, and Labrador (before 1950).

Mac·mil·lan |məkˈmilən|, (Maurice) Harold, 1st Earl of Stockton (1894–1986) British Conservative statesman, prime minister (1957–63). His term of office saw the signing of the Test Ban Treaty (1963) with the U.S. and the USSR. Macmillan resigned on grounds of ill health shortly after the scandal surrounding a member of his government, John Profumo.

Mac·Neice |məkˈnēs|, (Frederick) Louis (1907–63) Northern Irish poet. His work, such as *Collected Poems* (1966), is characterized by the use of assonance, internal rhymes, and balladlike repetitions.

Mac·Neil |məkˈnēl|, Robert Breckenridge Ware (1931–) U.S. broadcast journalist, born in Canada. With Jim Lehrer he co-anchored the *MacNeil/Lehrer News Hour* (1983–95).

Mac·Nel·ly |məkˈnelē|, Jeff (1947–) U.S. political cartoonist. Full name *Jeffrey Kenneth MacNelly.* Pulitzer Prizes for Political Cartooning, 1972, 1978, and 1985.

Ma·con |ˈmākən|, Uncle Dave (1870–1952) U.S. country singer, banjo player, and comedian.

Mac·quar·ie |məˈkwärē|, Lachlan (1761–1824) Scottish-born Australian colonial administrator, governor of New South Wales (1809–21).

Ma·da·ri·a·ga y Ro·jo |,mädərē'ägə ē 'rōhō|, Salvador de (1886–1978) Spanish writer and diplomat. He was a delegate to the League of Nations (1931–36). Notable works: *The Rise and Fall of the Spanish Empire* (1947).

Mad·dux |ˈmadəks|, Greg (1966–) U.S. baseball pitcher. He won an unprecendented four straight National League Cy Young Awards.

Mad·i·son |ˈmadəsən|, James see box.

Dolley Madison (1768–1849), born *Dorothea Payne Todd,* wife of James Madison and U.S. first lady (1809–17). She is remembered for saving the portrait of George Washington from the burning White House.

Madison, James
4th U.S. president

Life dates: 1751–1836
Place of birth: Port Conway, Va.
Mother: Eleanor ("Nelly") Rose Conway Madison
Father: James Madison
Wife: Dolley Payne Todd Madison
Children: none
Nickname: Father of the Constitution
College/University: College of New Jersey (now Princeton)
Military service: colonel, Orange County militia
Political career: Virginia State Council; Second Continental Congress; U.S. House of Representatives; U.S. secretary of state; president
Party: Democratic-Republican
Home state: Virginia
Opponents in presidential races: Charles Cotesworth Pinckney; DeWitt Clinton
Term of office: March 4, 1809–March 3, 1817
Vice president: George Clinton; Elbridge Gerry
Notable events of presidency: War of 1812; Washington D.C. burned by the British; "Star Spangled Banner" written by Francis Scott Key; Missouri Territory organized; Louisiana and Indiana admitted as the 18th and 19th states
Other achievements: Admitted to the Virginia bar; drafted Virginia guarantee of religious liberty and helped write state constitution; wrote essays on constitutional government for *The Federalist*; member, Virginia Ratification Convention; rector, University of Virginia; delegate to Virginia Constitutional Convention; chief author of the Bill of Rights
Place of burial: Montpelier, Va.

Ma·don·na |mə'dänə| (1958–) U.S. pop singer and actress; born *Madonna Louise Ciccone*. Albums such as *Like a Virgin* (1984) and her image as a sex symbol brought her international stardom from the mid-1980s. She starred in the movie *Desperately Seeking Susan* (1985).

Mae·ce·nas |,mī'sēnəs|, Gaius (*c.* 70–8 BC) Roman statesman. He was a trusted adviser of Augustus and a notable patron of poets such as Virgil and Horace.

Mae·ter·linck |'metər,liNGk|, Count Maurice (1862–1949) Belgian poet, dramatist, and essayist. His prose dramas *La Princesse Maleine* (1889) and *Pelléas et Mélisande* (1892) established him as a leading figure in the symbolist movement. Nobel Prize for Literature (1911).

Ma·gel·lan |mə'jelən|, Ferdinand (*c.* 1480–1521) Portuguese explorer; Portuguese name *Fernão Magalhães*. In 1519 he sailed from Spain, rounding South America through the strait that now bears his name, and reached the Philippines in 1521. He was killed in a skirmish on Cebu; the survivors sailed back to Spain around Africa, completing the first circumnavigation of the globe (1522).

Ma·gritte |mə'grēt|, René (François Ghislain) (1898–1967) Belgian surrealist painter. His paintings display startling or amusing juxtapositions of the ordinary, the strange, and the erotic, depicted in a realist manner.

Mah·fouz |mä'fōōz|, Naguib (1911–) Egyptian novelist and short-story writer. He was the first writer in Arabic to be awarded the Nobel Prize for Literature (1988). Notable works: *Miramar* (1967).

Mah·ler |'mälər|, Gustav (1860–1911) Austrian composer, conductor, and pianist. Forming a link between romanticism and the experimentalism of Schoenberg, his works include nine complete symphonies (1888–1910) and the symphonic song cycle *Das Lied von der Erde* (1908).

Mai·ler |'mālər|, Norman (1923–) U.S. novelist and essayist. His novels, in which he frequently deals with the effect of war and violence on human relationships, include *The Naked and the Dead* (1948) and *Ancient Evenings* (1983). His nonfiction works combine a wide range of styles from autobiography to political commentary and include the prize-winning *The Armies of the Night* (1968) and *The Executioner's Song* (1979).

Mai·mo·ni·des |mī'mänədēz| (1135–1204) Jewish philosopher and Rabbinic scholar, born in Spain; born *Moses ben*

Maimon. His *Guide for the Perplexed* (1190) attempts to reconcile Talmudic scripture with the philosophy of Aristotle.

Main·te·non |ˌmæNt(ə)'nawN|, Françoise d'Aubigné, Marquise de (1635–1719) Mistress and later second wife of the French king Louis XIV.

Ma·jor |'mājər|, John (1943–) British Conservative statesman, prime minister (1990–97). His premiership saw the negotiations leading to the Maastricht Treaty and progress toward peace in Northern Ireland.

Ma·ka·ri·os III |mə'kärē,ōs| (1913–77) Greek Cypriot archbishop and statesman, first president of the republic of Cyprus (1960–77); born *Mikhail Christodolou Mouskos.* He was primate and archbishop of the Greek Orthodox Church in Cyprus from 1950.

Ma·la·mud |'mæləməd|, Bernard (1914–86) U.S. novelist and short-story writer. Notable works: *The Fixer* (1967), *Dubin's Lives* (1979), and *Stories of Bernard Malamud* (1983).

Mal·colm |'mælcəm| Name of four kings of Scotland: **Malcolm I** (died 954; reigned 943–54). **Malcolm II** (*c.* 953–1034; reigned 1005–34). **Malcolm III** (*c.* 1031–93; reigned 1058–93), son of Duncan I; known as **Malcolm Canmore** (from Gaelic *Ceann-mor,* "great head"). He came to the throne after killing Macbeth in battle (1057), and was responsible for helping to form Scotland into an organized kingdom. **Malcolm IV** (1141–65; reigned 1153–65), grandson of David I; known as **Malcolm the Maiden**. His reign witnessed a progressive loss of power to Henry II of England; he died young and without an heir.

Mal·colm X |'mælcəm 'eks| (1925–65) U.S. political activist; born *Malcolm Little.* He joined the Nation of Islam in 1946 and became a vigorous campaigner for black rights, initially advocating the use of violence. In 1964 he converted to orthodox Islam and moderated his views on black separatism; he was assassinated the following year.

Mal·den |'mawldən|, Karl (1914–) U.S. actor. Born Miaden Sekulovich. He starred in the television series "The Streets of San Francisco" (1972–77) and won an Academy Award for his role in *A Streetcar Named Desire* (1951).

Ma·len·kov |mə'len,kawf|, Georgi (Maksimilianovich) (1902–88) Soviet statesman, born in Russia. He became prime minister and first secretary of the Soviet Communist Party in 1953, but was forced to resign in 1955 following internal party struggles.

Ma·le·vich |mə'lävicH|, Kazimir (Severinovich) (1878–1935) Russian painter and designer, founder of the suprematist movement. In his abstract works he used only basic geometrical shapes and a severely restricted range of color.

Malf·man, Theodore Harold (1927–) U.S. inventor of Ruby Laser Systems.

Mal·herbe |ˌmä'lərb|, François de (1555–1628) French poet. An architect of classicism in poetic form and grammar, he criticized excess of emotion and ornamentation and the use of Latin and dialectal forms.

Ma·li·now·ski |ˌmælə'nawfskē|, Bronisław Kaspar (1884–1942) Polish anthropologist. He initiated the technique of "participant observation" and developed the functionalist approach to anthropology.

Mal·lar·mé |ˌmälär'mä|, Stéphane (1842–98) French poet. A symbolist, he experimented with rhythm and syntax by transposing words and omitting grammatical elements. Notable poems: "Hérodiade" (*c.*1871) and "L'Après-midi d'un faune" (1876).

Malle |mäl|, Louis (1932–95) French movie director. His movies *Ascenseur pour l'échafaud* (1958) and *Les Amants* (1959) are seminal examples of the French *nouvelle vague.* Other notable movies: *Pretty Baby* (1978) and *Au revoir les enfants* (1987).

Mal·lon |'mælən|, Mary (1870?–1938) U.S. cook. Known as **Typhoid Mary**. Immune to typhoid herself, she spread the disease while working in New York City; she was institutionalized for life from 1914 to protect others

Ma·lone |mə'lōn|, Dorothy (1925–) U.S. actress. Notable movies: *Written on the Wind* (1956, Academy Award).

Ma·lone |mə'lōn|, John C. (1941–)

U.S. telecommunications executive. He is the CEO of Tele-Communications, Inc. (1996–).

Ma·lone |məˈlōn|, Karl (1963–) U.S. basketball player.

Ma·lone |məˈlōn|, Moses (1955–) U.S. basketball player.

Mal·o·ry |ˈmælərē|, Sir Thomas (died 1471) English writer. His major work, *Le Morte d'Arthur* (printed 1483), is a prose translation of a collection of the legends of King Arthur, selected from French and other sources.

Mal·raux |ˌmälˈrō|, André (1901–76) French novelist, politician, and art critic. Involved in the Chinese communist uprising of 1927 and the Spanish Civil War, he was later appointed France's first minister of cultural affairs (1959–69). Notable novels: *La Condition humaine* (1933).

Mal·thus |ˈmawlᴛнəs|, Thomas Robert (1766–1834) English economist and clergyman. In *Essay on Population* (1798) he argued that without the practice of "moral restraint" the population tends to increase at a greater rate than its means of subsistence, resulting in the population checks of war, famine, and epidemic.

Mam·et |ˈmæmət|, David (1947–) U.S. dramatist, director, and screenwriter. Notable plays: *Glengarry Glen Ross* (Pulitzer Prize, 1984) and *Oleanna* (1992).

Man·ches·ter |ˈmæn,cнəstər|, William (1922–) U.S. historian and biographer. Notable works: *The Death of a President* (1967).

Man·ci·ni |ˌmænˈsēnē|, Henry (1924–94) U.S. composer and conductor. He wrote many movie themes, including "The Pink Panther."

Man·de·la |ˌmænˈdelə| Family of South African political figures, including: **Nelson (Rolihlahla) Mandela** (1918–), president of South Africa since 1994. He was sentenced to life imprisonment in 1964 as an activist for the African National Congress (ANC). Released in 1990, as leader of the ANC he engaged in talks on the introduction of majority rule with President F. W. de Klerk, with whom he shared the Nobel Peace Prize in 1993. He became the country's first democratically elected president in 1994. His former wife **Winnie Mandela** (1934–). Despite her conviction on kidnapping and assault charges (1990), she continues to be a prominent figure in the African National Congress.

Man·del·brot |ˈmændl,brō|, Benoit (1924–) Polish-born French mathematician. Mandelbrot is known as the pioneer of fractal geometry.

Man·del·stam |ˈmändl,stäm|, Osip (Emilevich) (1891–1938) Also **Mandelshtam**. Russian poet, a member of the Acmeist group. Sent into internal exile in 1934, he died in a prison camp. Notable works: *Stone* (1913) and *Tristia* (1922).

Man·de·ville |ˈmændə,vil|, John (14th cent) English nobleman. He is remembered as the reputed author of a book of travels and travelers' tales that was actually compiled by an unknown hand from the works of several writers.

Ma·net |ˌmäˈnā|, Édouard (1832–83) French painter. He adopted a realist approach that greatly influenced the Impressionists, using pure color to give a direct unsentimental effect. Notable works: *Déjeuner sur l'herbe* (1863), *Olympia* (1865), and *A Bar at the Folies-Bergère* (1882).

Man·e·tho |ˈmænə,ᴛнō| (3rd century BC) Egyptian priest. He wrote a history of Egypt from mythical times to 323, in which he arbitrarily divided the succession of rulers known to him into thirty dynasties, an arrangement that is still followed.

Man·kie·wicz |ˈmænkə,wits|, Joseph Leo (1909–93) U.S. director, producer, and screenwriter. Notable movies: *All About Eve* (1950, Academy Award).

Man·kil·ler |ˈmæn,kilər|, Wilma Pearl (1945–) U.S. Cherokee Nation tribal leader and historian. She is a women's rights leader and author of *Mankiller: A Chief and Her People* (1993).

Man·ley |ˈmænlē|, Michael (Norman) (1923–97) Jamaican statesman, prime minister (1972–80 and 1989–92). A socialist, he introduced policies to strengthen Jamaica's economy through the expansion of public works and the encouragement of local industry.

Mann |ˈmæn|, Horace (1796–1859)

U.S. educator and politician. Known as **the father of American public education.** While serving in the Massachusetts state legislature (1927–37), he helped establish the first state board of education, over which he presided (1937–48).

Mann |'män|, Thomas (1875–1955) German novelist and essayist. The role and character of the artist in relation to society is a constant theme in his works. Notable works: *Buddenbrooks* (1901), *Death in Venice* (1912), and *Dr. Faustus* (1947). Nobel Prize for Literature (1929).

Man·ner·heim |'mänər,hām|, Baron Carl Gustaf Emil von (1867–1951) Finnish soldier and politician. He planned and supervised the construction of the Mannerheim line of defense against Russia (1939–40), and he was president of Finland (1944–46).

Man·nes |'mænəs|, Leopold (1899–1964) U.S. scientist, musician, and inventor. He was a co-inventor of Kodachrome color film and a faculty member of the Mannes School of Music, which was founded by his father David (1866–1959).

Man Ray |'mæn 'rā| see RAY, MAN.

Man·sart |,män'sär(t)|, François (1598–1666) French architect. He rebuilt part of the château of Blois, which incorporated the type of roof now named after him.

Mans·field |'mæns,fēld|, Katherine (1888–1923) New Zealand short-story writer; pseudonym of *Kathleen Mansfield Beauchamp*. Her stories range from extended impressionistic evocations of family life to short sketches.

Man·son |'mænsən|, Charles (1934–) U.S. cult leader. He founded a commune based on free love and complete subordination to him. In 1969 its members carried out a series of murders, including that of the U.S. actress Sharon Tate, for which he and some followers received the death sentence (later commuted to life imprisonment).

Man·son |'mænsən|, Sir Patrick (1844–1922) Scottish physician, pioneer of tropical medicine. He discovered the organism responsible for elephantiasis and established that it was spread by the bite

of a mosquito; he then suggested a similar role for the mosquito in spreading malaria.

Man·stein |'män,stīn|, Fritz Erich von (1887–1973) German army officer. Born *Fritz Erich von Lewinski*. He planned an assault against France in World War II and was imprisoned for war crimes.

Man·te·gna |,män'tenyə|, Andrea (1431–1506) Italian painter and engraver, noted especially for his frescoes.

Man·tell |,mæn'tel|, Gideon Algernon (1790–1852) English geologist. Mantell is best known as the first person to recognize dinosaur remains as reptilian. In 1825 he published a description of the teeth of a "giant fossil lizard" which he named *Iguanodon*.

Man·tle |'mæn(t)əl|, Mickey Charles (1931–95) U.S. baseball player. Elected to the Baseball Hall of Fame, 1974.

Ma·nu·tius |mə'nōōSH(ē)əs|, Aldus see ALDUS MANUTIUS.

Man·zo·ni |,män'zōnē|, Alessandro (1785–1873) Italian novelist, dramatist, and poet. He is remembered chiefly as the author of the novel *I Promessi sposi* (1825–42), a historical reconstruction of 17th-century Lombardy.

Mao Ze·dong |'mow ,zə'dawNG| (1893–1976) Also **Mao Tse-tung**. Chinese statesman, chairman of the Communist Party of the Chinese People's Republic (1949–76) and head of state (1949–59). A cofounder of the Chinese Communist Party in 1921 and its effective leader from the time of the Long March (1934–35), he eventually defeated both the occupying Japanese and rival Kuomintang nationalist forces to create the People's Republic of China in 1949, becoming its first head of state. At first Mao followed the Soviet Communist model, but from 1956 he introduced his own measures, such as the economically disastrous Great Leap Forward (1958–60). Despite having resigned as head of state Mao instigated the Cultural Revolution (1966–68), during which he became the focus of a personality cult.

Ma·ra·do·na |,merə'dawnə|, Diego (Armando) (1960–) Argentinian soccer player. He captained the Argentina team that won the World Cup in 1986, arousing controversy when his apparent handball scored a goal in the quarterfinal match against England.

Ma·rat |mə'rä(t)|, Jean Paul (1743–93) French revolutionary and journalist. A virulent critic of the moderate Girondists, he was instrumental (with Danton and Robespierre) in their fall from power in 1793.

Mar·a·vich |'merə,viCH|, Pete (1948–88) U.S. basketball player. Known as **Pistol Pete**. Elected to the Basketball Hall of Fame (1986).

Mar·ceau |,mär'sō|, Marcel (1923–) French mime artist. He is known for appearing as the white-faced Bip, a character he developed from the French Pierrot character.

March |märCH|, Fredric (1897–1975) U.S. stage and movie actor. Born *Frederick Bickel*. Notable moveis: *Dr. Jekyll and Mr. Hyde* (Academy Award, 1932) and *The Best Years of Our Lives* (Academy Award, 1946).

Mar·ci·a·no |märsē'änō|, Rocky (1923–69) U.S. boxer; born *Rocco Francis Marchegiano*. He became world heavyweight champion in 1952 and successfully defended his title six times before he retired, undefeated, in 1956.

Mar·co·ni |mär'kōnē|, Guglielmo (1874–1937) Italian physicist, electrical engineer, and inventor. He produced the continuously oscillating wave (1912), which is essential for the transmission of sound. Known as the father of radio, he went on to develop short-wave transmissions over long distances and received the Nobel Prize for Physics (1909).

Mar·co Po·lo |'märkō 'pōlō| (c. 1254–1324) Italian explorer. With his father and uncle he traveled to China and the court of Kublai Khan via central Asia (1271–75). He eventually returned home (1291–95) via Sumatra, India, and Persia. His book recounting his travels spurred the European quest for Eastern riches.

Mar·cos |'mär,kōs|, Ferdinand Edralin (1917–89) President of the Philippines (1965–86). Amid charges of corruption and political intrigue, he was unable to secure his 1986 reelection and was forced into exile.

Mar·cus Au·re·lius |'märkəs aw'rēlēəs| see AURELIUS.

Mar·cu·se |mär'ko͞ozə|, Herbert (1898–1979) German-born U.S. philosopher. A member of the Frankfurt School, in *Soviet Marxism* (1958) he argued that revolutionary change can come only from alienated elites such as students.

Mare, Walter de la see DE LA MARE.

Mar·garet |'märgrət|, St. (c. 1046–93) Scottish queen, wife of Malcolm III. She exerted a strong influence over royal policy during her husband's reign, and was instrumental in the reform of the Scottish Church. Feast day, November 16.

Mar·garet, Prin·cess |'märgrət|, Margaret Rose (1930–) member of the British royal family, only sister of Elizabeth II.

Mar·gre·the II |mär'grätə| (1940–) queen of Denmark (1972–).

Ma·ria de' Med·i·ci |mə'rēə dä 'medəCHē; me'dēCHē| see MARIE DE MÉDICIS.

Ma·ria The·re·sa |mə'rēə tə'rāsə| (1717–80) Archduchess of Austria, queen of Hungary and Bohemia (1740–80). The daughter of the Emperor Charles VI, she succeeded to the Habsburg dominions in 1740 by virtue of the Pragmatic Sanction. Her accession triggered the War of the Austrian Succession, which in turn led to the Seven Years War (1756–63).

Ma·rie An·toi·nette |mə'rē ,æntwə'net| (1755–93) French queen, wife of Louis XVI. A daughter of Maria Theresa, she married the future Louis XVI of France in 1770. Her extravagant lifestyle led to widespread unpopularity and, like her husband, she was executed during the French Revolution.

Ma·rie de Mé·di·cis |mə'rē də 'medə,sēs| (1573–1642) queen of France; Italian name *Maria de' Medici*. The second wife of Henry IV of France, she ruled as regent during the minority of her son Louis XIII (1610–17) and retained her influence after her son came to power.

Ma·rin |mə'rin|, John Cheri (1870–1953) U.S. artist. He is known especially for his expressionistic watercolor seascapes and views of Manhattan.

Ma·ri·net·ti |ˌmerə'nedē |, Filippo Tommaso (1876–1944) Italian poet and dramatist. He launched the futurist movement with a manifesto (1909) that exalted technology, glorified war, and demanded revolution in the arts.

Ma·ri·ni |məˈrēnē |, Marino (1901–80) Italian sculptor, painter, and graphic artist. He is known especially for his expressionistic horse-and-rider series (from 1935).

Ma·ri·no |məˈrēnō |, Dan (1961–) U.S. football player.

Mar·i·on |'merēən |, Francis (c. 1732–c. 1795) American Revolutionary commander. Known as **The Swamp Fox**. He commanded militia troops in South Carolina and evaded the British by hiding in swamps.

Mar·is |'merəs |, Roger Eugene (1934–85) U.S. baseball player. A New York Yankees right fielder, he broke Babe Ruth's record (60 home runs, 1927) for most home runs in a season by hitting 61 in 1961.

Mar·i·us |'merēəs |, Gaius (c. 157–86 BC) Roman general and politician. Elected consul in 107 BC, he defeated Jugurtha and invading Germanic tribes. After a power struggle with Sulla he was expelled from Italy, but returned to take Rome by force in 87 BC.

Mark |märk |, St. an Apostle, companion of St. Peter and St. Paul, traditional author of the second Gospel. Feast day, April 25.

Mar·ko·va |märˈkōvə |, Dame Alicia (1910–) English ballet dancer; born Lilian Alicia Marks. She founded the Markova–Dolin Ballet with Anton Dolin in 1935 and was prima ballerina with the London Festival Ballet 1950–52.

Marks |'märks |, Simon, 1st Baron Marks of Broughton (1888–1964) English businessman; established the retail chain Marks & Spencer.

Marl·bor·ough |'mär(l),bərə |, John Churchill, 1st Duke of (1650–1722) British general. He was commander of British and Dutch troops in the War of the Spanish Succession and won a series of victories (notably at Blenheim in 1704) over the French armies of Louis XIV.

Mar·lette |märˈlet |, Doug (1949–) U.S. editorial cartoonist. Full name Douglas Nigel Marlette. He was creator and author of the comic strip "Kudzu." Pulitzer Prize for Editorial Cartooning, 1988.

Mar·ley |'märlē |, Bob (1945–81) Jamaican reggae singer, guitarist, and songwriter; full name Robert Nesta Marley. Having formed the trio the Wailers in 1965, in the 1970s he was instrumental in popularizing reggae. His lyrics often reflected his commitment to Rastafarianism.

Mar·lowe |'mär,lō |, Christopher (1564–93) English dramatist and poet. As a dramatist he brought a new strength and vitality to blank verse; his work influenced Shakespeare's early historical plays. Notable plays: Doctor Faustus (c.1590) and The Jew of Malta (1592).

Mar·quand |ˌmärˈkwänd |, J. P. (1893–1960) U.S. author. Full name John Phillips Marquand. He created the character Mr. Moto, a Japanese detective featured in several of his stories. Notable novels: The Late George Apley (1937, Pulitzer Prize), Point of No Return (1949), and Women and Thomas Harrow (1958).

Mar·quette |ˌmärˈket |, Jacques (1637–75) French Jesuit missionary and explorer. Arriving in Canada in 1666, he played a prominent part in the attempt to Christianize the American Indians, and explored the Wisconsin and Mississippi Rivers.

Már·quez |'mär,kes |, Gabriel García see García Márquez.

Mar·quis |'märkwəs |, Don (1878–1937) U.S. journalist and author. Full name Donald Robert Perry Marquis. Notable works: archy and mehitabel (1927) and sequels.

Mar·quis de Sade |säd | see Sade.

Mar·ri·ott |'meri,ät |, John Willard, Jr. (1932–) U.S. businessman. Founder of the Marriott hotel chain (1964), he is president and CEO (1972–) of Marriott Corp..

Mar·ry·at |'meriət |, Frederick (1792–1848) English novelist and naval officer; known as **Captain Marryat**. Notable works: Peter Simple (1833), Mr.

Midshipman Easy (1836), and *The Children of the New Forest* (1847).

Mar·sal·is |ˌmärˈsæləs|, Wynton (1961–) U.S. jazz trumpeter. He formed his own group in 1981 and was the first musician to win Grammy awards for both a jazz and a classical recording (1984). He is the brother of saxophonist Branford Marsalis.

Marsh |märsʜ|, James (1794–1842) U.S. clergyman and educator. He was influential in the American Transcendental movement and served as president of the University of Vermont (1826–33).

Marsh |märsʜ|, Dame Ngaio (Edith) (1889–1982) New Zealand writer of detective fiction. Her works include *Vintage Murder* (1937) and *Final Curtain* (1947).

Marsh |märsʜ|, Othniel Charles (1831–99) U.S. paleontologist. He was a nephew of George Peabody and the originator of "authentic skeletal restorations" of dinosaurs.

Marsh |märsʜ|, Reginald (1898–1954) U.S. artist. He is known especially for his paintings of New York City, including *The Bowery* (1930).

Mar·shall |ˈmärsʜəl|, George C. (1880–1959) U.S. general and statesman; full name *George Catlett Marshall*. A career army officer, he served as U.S. Army chief of staff (1939–45) in World War II. As U.S. secretary of state (1947–49) he initiated the program of economic aid to European countries known as the Marshall Plan. Nobel Peace Prize (1953).

Mar·shall |ˈmärsʜəl|, John (1755–1835) Chief Justice of the U.S. (1801–35). He is considered the father of the American system of constitutional law.

Mar·shall |ˈmärsʜəl|, Thomas Riley (1854–1925) vice president of the U.S. (1913–21). He opposed woman's suffrage and prohibition, and he is noted for the remark "What this country needs is a really good five-cent cigar."

Mar·shall |ˈmärsʜəl|, Thurgood (1908–93) U.S. Supreme Court justice (1967–93). The first black justice appointed to the U.S. Supreme Court, he had previously won 29 of the 32 cases he argued before the Court, including the land-

mark civil rights case *Brown* v. *Board of Education* (1954).

Mar·tel |märˈtel|, Charles see CHARLES MARTEL.

Mar·tial |ˈmärsʜəl| (*c.* 40–*c.* 104 AD) Roman epigrammatist, born in Spain; Latin name *Marcus Valerius Martialis*. His fifteen books of epigrams, in a variety of meters, reflect all facets of Roman life.

Mar·tin |ˈmärtn|, Dean (1917–95) U.S. singer and actor; born *Dino Paul Crocetti*. He joined with Frank Sinatra and Sammy Davis, Jr. in a number of movies, including *Bells are Ringing* (1960), and had his own television show.

Mar·tin |ˈmärtn|, Glenn Luther (1886–1955) U.S. airplane manufacturer. He founded the Glenn L. Martin Co. (1917), which manufactured bombers, transoceanic flying boats, and clipper airplanes.

Mar·tin |ˈmärtn|, Mary (1913–90) U.S. actress. She starred in the Broadway musicals *South Pacific* (1949), *The Sound of Music* (1959), and *Peter Pan* (1954).

Mar·tin |ˈmärtn|, St. (*c.* 316–397) French bishop (Bishop of Tours from 371), a patron saint of France. When giving half his cloak to a beggar he received a vision of Christ, after which he was baptized. Feast day, November 11.

Mar·tin |ˈmärtn|, Steve (1945?–) U.S. actor and comedian. He made his name with farcical movie comedies such as *The Jerk* (1979) and went on to write, produce, and star in *Roxanne* (1987) and *LA Story* (1991).

Mar·ti·neau |ˈmärtə,nō|, Harriet (1802–76) English writer. She wrote mainly on social, economic, and historical subjects, and is known for her twenty-five-volume series *Illustrations of Political Economy* (1832–4) and her translation of Auguste Comte's *Philosophie positive* (1853).

Mar·ti·ni |ˌmärˈtēnē|, Simone (*c.* 1284–1344) Italian painter. His work is characterized by strong outlines and the use of rich color, as in *The Annunciation* (1333).

Mar·vell |ˈmärvəl|, Andrew (1621–78) English metaphysical poet. He was best known during his lifetime for his verse satires and pamphlets attacking the corruption of Charles II and his ministers; most of his poetry was published posthumously and was not recognized until the 20th century. Notable poems: "To his Coy Mistress" and "An Horatian Ode on Cromwell's Return from Ireland."

Mar·vin |'märvən|, Lee (1924–87) U.S. actor. Notable movies: *Cat Ballou* (1965, Academy Award).

Marx Brothers |märks| A family of U.S. comedians, consisting of the brothers **Chico** (Leonard, 1886–1961), **Harpo** (Adolph Arthur, 1893–1964), **Groucho** (Julius Henry, 1890–1977), and **Zeppo** (Herbert, 1901–79). Their movies, which are characterized by their anarchic humor, include *Duck Soup* (1933) and *A Night at the Opera* (1935).

Marx |märks|, Karl (Heinrich) (1818–83) German political philosopher and economist, resident in England from 1849. The founder of modern communism with Friedrich Engels, he collaborated with him in the writing of the *Communist Manifesto* (1848) and enlarged it into a series of books, most notably the three-volume *Das Kapital*.

Mary[1] |'merē| mother of Jesus; known as **the (Blessed) Virgin Mary**, or **St. Mary**, or **Our Lady**. According to the Gospels she was a virgin betrothed to Joseph and conceived Jesus by the power of the Holy Spirit. She has been venerated by Catholic and Orthodox Churches from the earliest Christian times. Feast days, January 1 (Roman Catholic Church), March 25 (Annunciation), August 15 (Assumption), September 8 (Immaculate Conception).

Mary[2] |'merē| Name of two queens of England: **Mary I** (1516–58, reigned 1553–58), daughter of Henry VIII; known as **Mary Tudor** or **Bloody Mary**. In an attempt to reverse the country's turn toward Protestantism she instigated the series of religious persecutions by which she earned her nickname. **Mary II** (1662–94; reigned 1689–94), daughter of James II. Having been invited to replace her Catholic father on the throne after his deposition in 1689, she insisted that her husband, William of Orange, be crowned along with her.

Mary, Queen of Scots |'merē| (1542–87) daughter of James V and queen of

Scotland (1542–67); known as **Mary Stuart**. A devout Catholic, she was unable to control her Protestant lords and fled to England in 1567. She became the focus of several Catholic plots against Elizabeth I and was eventually beheaded.

Mary, St. see MARY[1].

Mary Mag·da·lene |'merē 'mægdələn; 'mægdə,lēn |, St. Also **Magdalen**. (in the New Testament) a woman of Magdala in Galilee. She was a follower of Jesus, who cured her of evil spirits (Luke 8:2); she is also traditionally identified with the "sinner" of Luke 7:37. Feast day, July 22.

Mary Stu·art |'merē 'stŏŏərt| see MARY, QUEEN OF SCOTS.

Ma·sac·cio |mə'zächō| (1401–28) Italian painter; born *Tommaso Giovanni di Simone Guidi*. The first artist to apply the laws of perspective to painting, he is remembered particularly for his frescoes in the Brancacci Chapel in Florence (1424–27).

Ma·sa·ryk |'mäsə,rik|, Tomáš (Garrigue) (1850–1937) Czechoslovak statesman, president (1918–35). He became Czechoslovakia's first president when the country achieved independence in 1918.

Mas·ca·gni |mä'skänyē|, Pietro (1863–1945) Italian composer and conductor. He is especially remembered for the opera *Cavalleria Rusticana* (1890).

Mase·field |'mās,fēld|, John (Edward) (1878–1967) English poet and novelist. He was appointed Poet Laureate in 1930. Notable works: *Salt-Water Ballads* (1902).

Mas·low |'mæzlō |, Abraham (1908–70) U.S. psychologist. He was a leader of the humanistic school of psychology, and he postulated a " hierarchy of needs" to explain human motivation.

Ma·son |'māsən|, Bobby Ann (1940–) U.S. author. Notable works: *Midnight Magic* (1998) and *In Country* (1985).

Ma·son |'māsən|, Charles (1728–86) English astronomer. With Jeremiah Dixon he surveyed the boundary line between Maryland and Pennsylvania (1763–68) that became known as the Mason-Dixon Line.

Ma·son |'māsən|, George (1725–92) U.S. political philosopher and politician. A Virginia statesman and Revolutionary leader, he refused to sign the Constitution because it lacked a Bill of Rights, which he wrote.

Ma·son |'māsən|, James (1909–84) English actor He acted in more than a hundred films, notably *A Star is Born* (1954), *Lolita* (1962), *Georgy Girl* (1966), and *The Verdict* (1982).

Ma·son |'māsən|, Lowell (1792–1872) U.S. musician. He founded the Boston Academy of Music (1833) and established the first public school music program in the U.S.

Mas·sa·soit |ˌmæsə'soit| (1580?–1661) chief of the Wampanoag Indians. He signed the treaty at Plymouth in 1621 and remained a friend to white settlers. His son was named King Philip.

Mas·sey |'mæsē|, Raymond (1896–1983) U.S. actor and producer, born in Canada.

Mas·sine |mə'sēn|, Léonide Fédorovitch (1896–1979) Russian-born choreographer and ballet dancer, a French citizen from 1944; born *Leonid Fyodorovich Myasin*. He was the originator of the symphonic ballet, and danced in and choreographed the movie *The Red Shoes* (1948).

Mas·sin·ger |'mæsənjər|, Philip (1583–1640) English dramatist. Notable works: *The Duke of Milan* (1621–22), *A New Way to Pay Old Debts* (1625–26), and *The City Madam* (1632).

Mas·son |mə'sän|, André (1896–1987) French painter and graphic artist. He joined the surrealists in the mid-1920s and pioneered "automatic" drawing, a form of fluid, spontaneous composition intended to express images emerging from the unconscious.

Mas·ters |'mæstərz|, Edgar Lee (1869–1950) U.S. writer. Notable books of verse: *Spoon River Anthology* (1915) and *Domesday Book* (1920). Notable biographies: *Lincoln—The Man* (1931) and *Mark Twain* (1938).

Mas·tro·ian·ni |ˌmästroi'änē|, Marcello (1924–96) Italian actor. He appeared in over 140 films, including *La Dolce Vita* (1960) and *Divorce, Italian Style* (1962).

Ma·ta Ha·ri |'mätə 'härē| (1876–1917) Dutch dancer and secret agent; born *Margaretha Geertruida Zelle*. She probably worked for both French and German intelligence services before being executed by the French in 1917.

Math·er |'mæTHər| Family of early New England clergymen, including: **Richard** (1596–1669), born in England. He helped define New England Congregationalism and broadened the power and membership of the Congregational Church. His son **Increase Mather** (1639–1723), clergyman and educator. He was a Congregational leader credited with ending executions for witchcraft. **Cotton Mather** (1663–1728), son of Increase Mather, Congregational clergyman and author. His ecclesiastical history of New England, *Magnalia Christi Americana* (1702), is considered a masterpiece of 17th-century scholarship.

Math·er |'mæTHər|, Stephen Tyng (1867–1930) U.S. conservationist. A descendant of Richard Mather, he organized and served as the first director of the National Parks Service (1917–29).

Math·ews |'mæTHyōōz|, Eddie (1931–) U.S. baseball player. Elected to the Baseball Hall of Fame (1978).

Math·ew·son |'mæTHyōōsən|, Christy (1880–1925) U.S. baseball player. He won 22 or more games for 12 straight years, for a total of 373 career wins. He pitched three shutouts in 1905 World Series. Elected to the Baseball Hall of Fame (1936).

Ma·thi·as |mə'THīəs|, Bob (1930–) U.S. track and field athlete and politician. He was the youngest winner of the decathlon with a gold medal in the 1948 Olympic Games and another in the 1952 Olympics; later he served as a member of the U.S. House of Representatives from California (1967–74).

Math·is |'mæTHəs|, Johnny (1935–) U.S. pop singer. His popular ballads include "Wonderful, Wonderful," "It's Not for Me to Say," and "Chances Are."

Ma·til·da |mə'tildə| (1102–67) English princess, daughter of Henry I and mother of Henry II; known as **the Empress Maud**. Henry's only legitimate child, she was named his heir, but her cousin

Stephen seized the throne on Henry's death in 1135. She waged an unsuccessful civil war against Stephen until 1148.

Ma·tisse |mə'tēs|, Henri (Emile Benoît) (1869–1954) French painter and sculptor. His use of nonnaturalistic color led him to be regarded as a leader of the Fauvists. His later painting and sculpture displays a trend toward formal simplification and abstraction and includes large figure compositions and abstracts made from cut-out colored paper.

Mat·lin |'mætlən|, Marlee (1965–) U.S. actress. Notable movies: *Children of a Lesser God* (1986, Academy Award).

Mat·thau |'mæTHow|, Walter (1920–) U.S. actor. Born *Walter Matuschanskayasky*. Notable stage performances: *The Odd Couple* (1964); notable movies: *The Fortune Cookie* (1966, Academy Award) and *The Odd Couple* (1966)

Mat·thew |'mæTHyōō|, St. an Apostle, a tax collector from Capernaum in Galilee, traditionally the author of the first Gospel. Feast day, September 21.

Mat·thew Pa·ris |'mæTHyōō 'perəs| (*c.* 1199–1259) English chronicler and Benedictine monk, noted for his *Chronica Majora*, a history of the world from the Creation to the mid-13th century.

Mat·thi·as |mə,THīəs|, St. an Apostle, chosen by lot after the Ascension to replace Judas. Feast day (in the Western Church) May 14; (in the Eastern Church) August 9.

Mat·thies·sen |'mæTH(y)əsən|, F. O. (1902–50) U.S. educator and author. Full name *Francis Otto Matthiessen*. Notable works: *American Renaissance* (1941).

Mat·thies·sen |'mæTH(y)əsən|, Peter (1927–) U.S. author. Notable works: *The Snow Leopard* (1978, National Book Award).

Mat·zel·i·ger |mət'seləgər|, Jan Ernst (1852–89) U.S. inventor, born in Suriname. His lasting machine, which revolutionized the shoe industry, was patented in 1883.

Mauch·ly |'mäklē|, John William (1907–80) U.S. physicist and engineer. With John P. Eckert he invented the first electronic computer, ENIAC (1946), and later models Binac and Univac I.

Maud·lin |'mawdlən|, William H. (1921–) U.S. cartoonist and author. He depicted the squalid life of the G.I. in World War II. Notable works: *Bill Maudlin's Army* (1951) and *The Brass Ring* (1971).

Maugham |'mawm|, (William) Somerset (1874–1965) British novelist, short-story writer and dramatist, born in France. Notable works: *Of Human Bondage* (1915), *The Moon and Sixpence* (1919), *East of Suez* (1922), and *Cakes and Ale* (1930).

Mau·pas·sant |,mōpə'sän|, (Henri René Albert) Guy de (1850–93) French novelist and short-story writer. He wrote about 300 short stories and six novels in a simple, direct narrative style. Notable novels: *Une Vie* (1883) and *Bel-Ami* (1885).

Mau·riac |,mawrē'äk|, François (1885–1970) French novelist, dramatist, and critic. His stories show the conflicts of convention, religion, and human passions suffered by prosperous bourgeoisie. Notable works: *Thérèse Desqueyroux* (1927). Nobel Prize for Literature (1952).

Mau·ry |'mawrē|, Matthew Fontaine (1806–73) U.S. oceanographer. He conducted the first systematic survey of oceanic winds and currents, and published charts of his findings.

Maw·la·na another name for JALAL AD-DIN AR-RUMI.

Max |mæks|, Peter (1937–) U.S. artist, born in Germany. His works include art for U.S. postage stamps, murals for border stations between the U.S. and Canada and the U.S. and Mexico, and an annual series of Statue of Liberty paintings.

Max·im U.S. family of inventors, including: **Sir Hiram Stevens Maxim** (1840–1916). He invented incandescent lamps and the Maxim machine gun. His brother **Hudson** (1853–1927), born *Isaac Maxim*. He was an inventor and explosives expert. **Hiram Percy Maxim** (1896–1936), son of Sir Hiram. He invented the Maxim firearms silencer and adapted the same idea to mufflers and air compressors.

Max·i·mil·ian |,mæksə'milyən| (1832–67) Austrian emperor of Mexico 1864–

7; full name *Ferdinand Maximilian Joseph*. Brother of Franz Josef, Maximilian was established as emperor of Mexico under French auspices in 1864. American pressure forced Napoleon III to withdraw his support in 1867. He was executed by a popular uprising led by President Benito Juárez.

Max·well |'mækswəl|, Elsa (1883–1963) U.S. columnist and socialite. She was a syndicated gossip columnist and legendary hostess for high society and royalty in Europe and U.S.

Max·well |'mækswəl|, James Clerk (1831–79) Scottish physicist. He extended the ideas of Faraday and Kelvin in his equations of electromagnetism and succeeded in unifying electricity and magnetism, identifying the electromagnetic nature of light, and postulating the existence of other electromagnetic radiation.

Max·well |'mækswəl|, (Ian) Robert (1923–91) Czech-born British publisher and media entrepreneur; born *Jan Ludvik Hoch*. He died in mysterious circumstances while yachting off Tenerife; it subsequently emerged that he had misappropriated company pension funds.

Max·well |'mækswəl|, William (1908–) U.S. author. Notable works: *So Long, See You Tomorrow* (1979).

Ma·ya·kov·sky |ˌmäyə'kawfskē|, Vladimir (Vladimirovich) (1893–1930) Soviet poet and dramatist, born in Georgia. A fervent futurist, he wrote in a declamatory, aggressive avant-garde style, which he altered to have a comic mass appeal after the Bolshevik revolution.

May·all |'mä,awl|, John Brumwell (1933–) English blues singer and musician. He formed the group John Mayall's Bluesbreakers in 1963.

May·beck |'mä,bek|, Bernard Ralph (1862–1957) U.S. architect. He designed Hearst Hall and other buildings at the University of California, Berkeley.

May·er |'mäər|, Jean (1920–93) U.S. nutritionist and educator, born in France. His work on nutrition led to the expansion of the federal school lunch program and the food stamp program.

May·er |'mäər|, Louis B. (1885–1957) Russian-born U.S. movie executive; full name *Louis Burt Mayer*; born *Eliezer Mayer*. In 1924 he formed Metro-Goldwyn-Mayer (MGM) with Samuel Goldwyn; he headed the company until 1951.

May·er |'mīər|, Oscar F. (1859–1955) U.S. businessman, born in Germany. He founded the Oscar Mayer Co., best known for the Oscar Mayer weiner.

May·field |'mä,fēld|, Curtis (1942–) U.S. musician. He performed with the Impressions (1958–70); his solo hits include the soundtrack to the film *Superfly* (1972).

Mayle |māl|, Peter (1939–) U.S. author. Notable works: *A Year in Provence* (1990) and *Under the Tuscan Sun* (1997).

Mayo |'māō|, William Worrall (1819–1911) U.S. physician, born in England. With his sons **William James Mayo** (1861–1939) and **Charles Horace Mayo** (1865–1939), both surgeons, he helped the Sisters of St. Francis found St. Mary's Hospital in Rochester, Minnesota, with the Mayos as its sole staff (1889).

Mayo |'māō|, George Elton (1880–1949) U.S. psychologist, born in Australia. He practiced social and industrial psychology.

Mayr |'mäər|, Ernst Walter (1904–) German-born U.S. zoologist. He argued for a neo-Darwinian approach to evolution in his classic *Animal Species and Evolution* (1963).

Mays |māz|, Benjamin E. (1895–1984) U.S. educator and civil rights leader.

Mays |māz|, Willie (1931–) U.S. baseball player. Known as **Say Hey Kid**. Elected to the Baseball Hall of Fame, 1979.

Ma·za·rin |'mäzərən|, Jules (1602–61) Italian-born French statesman; Italian name *Giulio Mazzarino*. Sent to Paris as the Italian papal legate (1634), he became a naturalized Frenchman, and was made a cardinal in 1641 and then chief minister of France (1642).

Maz·zi·ni |mə'zēnē|, Giuseppe (1805–72) Italian nationalist leader. He founded the patriotic movement Young Italy (1831) and was a leader of the Risorgimento. Following the country's unification as a monarchy in 1861, he continued to campaign for a republican Italy.

Mbo·ya |əm'boiyə|, Tom (1930–69) Kenyan statesman. Full name *Thomas Joseph Mboya*. As secretary of the Kenya Federation of Labour (1953–63), he successfully campaigned for Kenyan independence and more representation for blacks in the legislature. He served as minister of justice (1963) and minister of economic affairs (1964–69). Regarded as the likely successor to President Kenyatta, he was assassinated in Nairobi.

Mc·Al·lis·ter |mə'kæləstər|, (Samuel) Ward (1827–95) U.S. lawyer and social leader. He coined the term "The Four Hundred" to refer to the socialites left after he cut a guest list to 400 to accommodate Mrs. William Astor's Newport ballroom.

Mc·Car·thy |mə'kärTHē|, Cormac (1933–) U.S. author. Notable works: *The Orchard Keeper* (1965).

Mc·Car·thy |mə'kärTHē|, Joseph Raymond (1908–57) U.S. politician. A Wisconsin Republican, he was a U.S. senator (1947–57). Having charged the U.S. State Department with an infiltration of Communists, he headed a Senate subcommittee that investigated suspected government subversives. Marked by unsubstantiated accusations and highly questionable invasions of privacy, these investigations were finally halted and McCarthy was censured by the Senate (1954).

Mc·Car·thy |mə'kärTHē|, Mary (Therese) (1912–89) U.S. novelist and critic. Notable novels: *The Groves of Academe* (1952) and *The Group* (1963).

Mc·Cart·ney |mə'kärtnē|, Sir (James) Paul (1942–) English pop and rock singer, songwriter, and bass guitarist. A founding member of the Beatles, he wrote most of their songs in collaboration with John Lennon. After the group broke up in 1970 he formed the band Wings.

Mc·Cart·ney |mə'kärtnē|, Linda (1941–98) U.S. photographer and musician. Wife of former Beatle Paul McCartney.

Mc·Caw |mə'kaw|, Craig O. (1949–) U.S. communications executive. He founded McCaw Cellular Communications, Inc. (1968) and NextLink.

Mc·Cay |mə'kā|, Winsor Zenic (1869–1934) U.S. cartoonist. He is best known for the comic strip "Little Nemo in Slumberland."

Mc·Clel·lan |mə'klelən|, George Brinton (1826–85) U.S. army officer. Known as **Little Mac**. He became general in chief of the U.S. Army (1861) during the Civil War. Although the victor at Antietam (1862), he was removed from command due to a lack of military aggressiveness. The Democratic presidential candidate in 1864, he was defeated by incumbent Abraham Lincoln.

Mc·Clin·tock |mə'klin,(t)äk|, Barbara (1902–92) U.S. geneticist. The discovery of DNA vindicated her earlier findings of transposable genetic elements (1951), earning her the 1983 Nobel Prize for Physiology or Medicine.

Mc·Clos·ky |mə'klawskē|, Robert (1914–) U.S. children's author and illustrator. Notable works: *Make Way for Ducklings* (Caldecott Medal, 1958).

Mc·Cor·mack |mə'kawrmək|, John (1884–1945) U.S. tenor, born in Ireland. He sang with the Chicago, Boston, Metropolitan, and Monte Carlo opera companies.

Mc·Cor·mick |mə'kawrmək|, Cyrus Hall (1809–84) U.S. inventor and industrialist. His patented reaper (1834) was the cornerstone of his harvesting machinery company, and the innovative deferred-payment plans he offered customers became a model in American consumerism.

Mc·Cor·mick |mə'kawrmək|, Katharine Dexter (1875–1967) U.S. women's rights activist. She cofounded the League of Women Voters.

Mc·Court |mə'kawrt|, Frank (1930–) U.S. author. Notable works: *Angela's Ashes* (1996, Pulitzer Prize).

Mc·Cov·ey |mə'kəvē|, Willie (1938–) U.S. baseball player. Elected to the Baseball Hall of Fame (1986).

Mc·Cul·lers |mə'kələrz|, (Lula) Carson (1917–67) U.S. writer. Her work deals sensitively with loneliness and the plight of the eccentric. Notable works: *The Heart is a Lonely Hunter* (1940), *The Member of the Wedding* (1946), and *The Ballad of The Sad Cafe* (1951).

Mc·Cul·lough |mə'kələ(k)|, Colleen

(1937–) Australian author. Notable works: *The Thorn Birds* (1977) and *The Song of Troy* (1998).

Mc·Cutch·eon |məˈkəCHən|, John Tinney (1870–1949) U.S. cartoonist and author. He is best known for his cartoons depicting midwestern rural life.

Mc·Don·ald |məkˈdänəld|, Maurice (1902–71) U.S. entrepeneur. With brother **Richard** he founded McDonald's hamburger restaurant, beginning the concept of fast-food drive-ins.

Mc·Dou·gall |məkˈdo͞ogl|, Alexander (1732–86) American Revolutionary patriot, born in Scotland. He was a member of the Contintental Congress (1781–82, 1784–85).

Mc·En·roe |ˈmækən,rō|, John (Patrick) (1959–) U.S. tennis player. A temperamental player, he dominated the game in the early 1980s. He won seven Wimbledon titles (three for singles: 1981, 1983, 1984) and four U.S. Open singles championships (1979–84).

Mc·En·tire |ˈmækən,tī(ə)r|, Reba (1954–) U.S. country singer. Her song credits include "You Lie," "The Greatest Man I Never Knew," and "Take It Back."

Mc·Gov·ern |mə(k)ˈgəvərn|, George S. (1922–) U.S. politician. He was a Democratic presidential candidate (1972).

Mc·Graw |mə(k)ˈgraw|, John (1873–1934) U.S. baseball manager. He was manager of the New York Giants 1905–24. Elected to Baseball Hall of Fame (1936).

Mc·Guane, Thomas (1939–) U.S. author. Notable works: *Ninety-Two in the Shade* (1974).

Mc·Guf·fey |məˈgəfē|, William Holmes (1800–73) U.S. public education reformer. He is best known for his series of *Eclectic Readers.*

Mc·Gwire |mə(k)ˈgwī(ə)r|, Mark David (1963–) U.S. athlete. In 1998, he hit 70 home runs, breaking Roger Maris's record (61) for the most home runs in a season.

Mc·Iner·ney |ˈmækə,nərnē|, Jay (1955–) U.S. author. Notable works: *Bright Lights, Big City* (1984).

Mc·Kay |məˈkā|, Donald (1810–80) U.S. shipbuilder. He designed famous clipper ships, including *Flying Cloud,* as well as ships for the U.S. Navy.

Mc·Kay |məˈkā|, Jim (1921–) U.S. television sports commentator. He was commentator for the Winter and Summer Olympic Games (1960–84) and host of ABC's *Wide World of Sports* (1986–).

Mc·Ken·na |məˈkenə|, Joseph (1843–1926) U.S. Supreme Court justice (1898–1925).

Mc·Kim |məˈkim|, Charles F. (1847–1909) U.S. architect. He designed the Public Library in Boston, the Columbia University Library, and Penn Station in New York City.

Mc·Kim |məˈkim|, Charles M. (1920–) U.S. architect. He designed the KUHT-TV transmitter building in Houston, Texas.

Mc·Kin·ley |məˈkinlē|, John (1780–1852) U.S. Supreme Court justice (1837–52).

Mc·Kin·ley |məˈkinlē|, William see box.

Ida Saxton McKinley (1847–1907), wife of William McKinley and U.S. first lady (1897–1901).

Mc·Ku·en |məˈkyo͞o(w)ən|, Rod (1933–) U.S. poet, composer, and singer.

Mc·Lach·lan |məˈkläklən|, Sarah (1968–) U.S. pop musician, born in Canada. Grammy Award, 1998.

Mc·Lean |məˈklēn|, John (1785–1861) U.S. Supreme Court justice (1829–61). He dissented in the Dred Scott case and was an unsuccessful candidate for the Republican nomination for the presidency (1856, 1860).

Mc·Lu·han |məˈklo͞oən|, (Herbert) Marshall (1911–80) Canadian writer and thinker. He became famous in the 1960s for his phrase "the medium is the message" and his argument that it is the characteristics of a particular medium rather than the information it disseminates that influence and control society.

Mc·Man·us |məkˈmænəs|, George (1884–1954) U.S. cartoonist. He created the comic strip "Bringing Up Father."

Mc·Mas·ter |məkˈmæstər|, John Bach (1852–1932) U.S. historian. Notable works: *History of the People of the U.S.* (8 vols., 1883–1912).

McKinley, William
25th U.S. president

Life dates: 1843–1901
Place of birth: Niles, Ohio
Mother: Nancy Campbell Allison McKinley
Father: William McKinley
Wife: Ida Saxton Mc Kinley
Children: Katherine, Ida
College/University: Allegheny College; Albany Law School
Military service: brevet major, Civil War
Career: Lawyer; teacher
Political career: U.S. House of Representatives; governor of Ohio; president
Party: Republican
Home state: Ohio
Opponent in presidential races: William Jennings Bryan
Term of office: Mar. 4, 1897–Sept. 14, 1901 (assassinated by Leon Czolgosz)
Vice presidents: Garret A. Hobart; Theodore Roosevelt
Notable events of presidency: Gold Rush in Klondike; Dingley Tariff Act; Hague Peace Conference; Treaty of Paris; Spanish-American War; Hawaii annexed to U.S.; Philippines, Puerto Rico, and Guam acquired from Cuba; American Samoa acquired by Treaty of 1900; Gold Standard Act
Other achievements: Admitted to the Ohio bar; prosecuting attorney, Stark County, Ohio
Place of burial: Canton, Ohio

Mc·Mil·lan |mək'milən|, Edwin Mattison (1907–91) U.S. physicist. He discovered neptunium. Nobel Prize for Chemistry, 1951.

Mc·Mur·try |mək'mərtrē|, Larry (1936–) U.S. author. Notable works: *Lonesome Dove* (1985).

Mc·Na·ma·ra |'mæknə,merə|, Robert Strange (1916–) U.S. businessman and public official. He was secretary of the U.S. Department of Defense (1961–68) and president of the World Bank (1968–81).

Mc·Part·land |mək'pärtlənd|, Jimmy (1907–91) U.S. jazz trumpeter. Full name *James Dougald McPartland*. He defined the style that was later termed "Chicago jazz."

Mc·Phee |mək'fē|, John (Angus) (1931–) U.S. journalist and author.

Notable works: *Coming into the Country* (1977).

Mc·Rae |mə'krā|, Carmen (1922–94) U.S. jazz singer. She began as a club singer in New York City; she became an inventive scat singer directly influenced by the emergence of bop.

Mc·Rey·nolds |mək'renəl(d)z|, James C. (1862–1946) U.S. Supreme Court justice (1914–41).

Mc·Veigh |mək'vā|, Timothy (1968–) U.S. terrorist. He was convicted in 1997 of federal conspiracy, murder, and other charges for his role in the bombing of the Alfred P. Murrah Federal Building in Oklahoma City in 1995.

Mc·Wil·liams |mək'wilyəmz|, Carey (1905–80) U.S. journalist and author. He was editor of *The Nation* (1955–79). Notable works: *Factories in the Field* (1939).

Mead |mēd|, Margaret (1901–78) U.S. anthropologist and social psychologist. She worked in Samoa and the New Guinea area and wrote a number of studies of primitive cultures, including *Coming of Age in Samoa* (1928). Her writings made anthropology accessible to a wide readership and demonstrated its relevance to Western society.

Meade |mēd|, George Gordon (1815–72) U.S. army officer. He was the commander of the Army of the Potomac (1863–65) during the Civil War, and is most noted for his victory at Gettysburg (1863).

Mea·ny |'mēnē|, George (1894–1980) U.S. labor leader. He was president of the AFL-CIO (1955–79).

Meara |'mirə|, Anne (1929–) U.S. actress. She and her husband Jerry Stiller form the comedy duo Stiller & Meara.

Meat Loaf |'mēt ,lōf| (1947–) U.S. rock musician and actor. Born *Marvin Lee Aday*. Notable songs: "I'd Do Anything for Love (But I Won't Do That)"; notable movies: *The Rocky Horror Picture Show*.

Med·a·war |'medəwər|, Sir Peter (Brian) (1915–87) English immunologist. He studied the biology of tissue transplantation, and showed that the rejection of grafts was the result of an immune mechanism. Nobel Prize for Physiology or Medicine (1960).

Me·di·ci Also **de' Medici.** A powerful Italian family of bankers and merchants whose members effectively ruled Florence for much of the 15th century and from 1569 were grand dukes of Tuscany. **Cosimo** and **Lorenzo de' Medici** were notable rulers and patrons of the arts in Florence; the family also provided four popes (including **Leo X**) and two queens of France (**Catherine de' Medici** and **Marie de Médicis**).

Mé·di·cis |'medə,sēs|, Marie de see MARIE DE MÉDICIS.

Meh·ta |'mätä|, Zubin (1936–) U.S. symphony conductor, born in India. He has been music director of the Los Angeles Philharmonic (1962–78), the New York Philharmonic (1978–91), and the Israel Philharmonic (1991–).

Mei·er |'mīər|, Richard (1934–) U.S. architect. He designed the Getty Center Museum in Los Angeles and the High Museum of Art in Georgia.

Mei·ji Ten·no |,mājē 'tenō| (1852–1912) emperor of Japan (1868–1912); born *Mutsuhito*. He took the name Meiji Tenno when he became emperor. He encouraged Japan's rapid modernization and political reform.

Mei·kle·john |'mĭkl,jän|, Alexander (1872–1964) U.S. educator and social reformer, born in England. Notable works: *The Liberal College* (1920).

Me·ir |mä'ir|, Golda (1898–1978) Israeli stateswoman, prime minister (1969–74); born *Golda Mabovich*. Born in Ukraine, she emigrated to the U.S. in 1907 and then to Palestine in 1921. Following Israel's independence she served in cabinet posts from 1949 to 1966 before being elected prime minister. She resigned (1974) in the wake of criticism for Israel's losses in the Arab-Israeli War (1973).

Meit·ner |'mītnər|, Lise (1878–1968) Austrian-born Swedish physicist. She worked in the field of radiochemistry with Otto Hahn, discovering the element protactinium with him in 1917. She formulated the concept of nuclear fission with her nephew Otto Frisch.

Me·lanch·thon |mə'læNGkTHän|, Philipp (1497–1560) German Protestant reformer; born *Philipp Schwarzerd*. He succeeded Martin Luther as leader of the Reformation movement in Germany in 1521 and drew up the Augsburg Confession (1530).

Mel·ba |'melbə|, Dame Nellie (1861–1931) Australian operatic soprano; born *Helen Porter Mitchell*. She was born near Melbourne, from which city she took her professional name. Melba gained worldwide fame with her coloratura singing.

Mel·bourne |'melbərn|, William Lamb, 2nd Viscount (1779–1848) British Whig statesman, prime minister (1834 and 1835–41). He became chief political adviser to Queen Victoria after her accession in 1837.

Mel·chi·or |'melkē,awr|, Lauritz Lebrecht Hommel (1890–1973) U.S. tenor, born in Denmark. He was considered the outstanding heldentenor of his day.

Mel·e·a·ger |,melē'āgər| (1st century BC) Greek poet, best known as the compiler of *Stephanos*, one of the first large anthologies of epigrams.

Mel·len·camp |'melən,kæmp|, John (Cougar) (1951–) U.S. rock musician. Notable albums: *American Fool* (1982).

Mel·lon |'melən|, Andrew (William) (1855–1937) U.S. financier and philanthropist. He served as secretary of the treasury (1921–32). He donated his art collection and made gifts to establish the National Gallery of Art in Washington D.C. in 1941.

Mel·ville |'melvil|, Herman (1819–91) U.S. novelist and short-story writer. His experiences on a whaling ship formed the basis of several novels, notably *Moby Dick* (1851). Other notable works: *White-Jacket* (1850), *The Confidence Man* (1857), and *Billy Budd* (first published in 1924).

Me·nan·der |mə'nændər| (c. 342–292 BC) Greek dramatist. His comic plays deal with domestic situations and capture colloquial speech patterns. The sole complete extant play is *Dyskolos*.

Men·ci·us |'men,SHēəs| (c. 371–c. 289 BC) Chinese philosopher; Latinized name of *Meng-tzu* or *Mengzi* ("Meng the Master"). Noted for developing Confucianism, he believed that rulers should provide for the welfare of the people and that human nature is intrinsically good.

Menck·en |'meNGkən|, H. L. (1880–1956) U.S. journalist and literary and social critic; full name *Henry Louis Mencken*. From 1908 he attacked the political and literary establishment. In his book *The American Language* (1919) he opposed the dominance of European culture in America, arguing for and establishing the study of American English in its own right.

Men·del |'mendəl|, Gregor Johann (1822–84) Moravian monk, the father of genetics. From systematically breeding peas he demonstrated the transmission of characteristics in a predictable way by factors (genes) that remain intact and independent between generations and do not blend, though they may mask one another's effects.

Men·de·le·ev |ˌmendə'lāəf|, Dmitri (Ivanovich) (1834–1907) Russian chemist. He developed the periodic table and successfully predicted the discovery of several new elements.

Men·dels·sohn |'mendlsən|, Felix (1809–47) German composer and pianist; full name *Jakob Ludwig Felix Mendelssohn-Bartholdy*. His romantic music is elegant, light, and melodically inventive. Notable works include the oratorio *Elijah* (1846) and eight volumes of *Songs without Words* for piano.

Men·do·za |ˌmen'dōzə|, Antonio de (*c.* 1490–1552) Spanish colonial administrator, the first viceroy of New Spain (1535–50).

Me·nes |'mē,nēz| (*c.* 3100 BC) Egyptian pharaoh. He founded the first dynasty that ruled Egypt.

Meng-tzu |meNG 'tso͞o| Also **Mengzi**. Chinese name for MENCIUS.

Men·nen |'menən|, Gerhard H. (1856–1902) U.S. manufacturer. He founded the Mennen Chemical Co. (1892), maker of talcum powder, creams, and beauty products.

Men·nin·ger |'menənjər|, Karl Augustus (1893–1990) U.S. psychiatrist. He founded the Menninger Clinic, where he began training psychiatrists in psychoanalysis.

Me·not·ti |mə'nätē|, Gian Carlo (1911–) U.S. composer, born in Italy.

Notable operas: *The Old Maid and the Thief* (1939; Pulitzer Prize) and *Amahl and the Night Visitors* (1951).

Men·u·hin |'menyo͞oin|, Sir Yehudi (1916–99) U.S.-born British violinist. He founded a school of music, named after him, in 1962.

Men·zies |'menzēz|, Sir Robert Gordon (1894–1978) Australian Liberal statesman, prime minister (1939–41 and 1949–66). He is Australia's longest-serving prime minister.

Mer·ca·tor |mər'kātər|, Gerardus (1512–94) Flemish geographer and cartographer, resident in Germany from 1552; Latinized name of *Gerhard Kremer*. He invented the system of map projection that is named after him.

Mer·cer |'mərsər|, Johnny (1909–76) U.S. songwriter. Full name *John Herndon Mercer*. He wrote lyrics for hundreds of popular songs, including "Moon River" (1961) and "Days of Wine and Roses" (1962).

Mer·chant |'mərCHənt|, Ismail (1936–) Indian movie producer. In 1961 he became a partner with James Ivory in Merchant Ivory Productions. Together they have made a number of movies, such as *Shakespeare Wallah* (1965), *The Bostonians* (1984), and *Howard's End* (1992).

Merckx |mərks|, Eddy (1945–) Belgian racing cyclist. During his professional career he won the Tour de France five times (1969–72 and 1974).

Mer·cou·ri |mərk(y)o͞orē|, Melina (1923–94) Greek actress and politician; born *Anna Amalia Mercouri*. Her movies include *Never on Sunday* (1960). Exiled for opposing the military junta in 1967, she was elected to Parliament in the socialist government of 1978, becoming minister of culture in 1985.

Mer·cu·ry |'mər,kyərē|, Freddie (1946–91) British pop star. He was the founder (1971) and lead singer of the heavy metal rock band Queen.

Mer·e·dith |'merə,diTH|, George (1828–1909) English novelist and poet. His semiautobiographical verse collection *Modern Love* (1862) describes the disillusionment of married love. Other notable works: *The Egoist* (1871).

Mer·e·dith |'merə,diTH|, James Howard

(1933–) U.S. business executive. He was the first African American to attend Jackson (Mississippi) State College (1960–62) after 3,000 troops quelled riots.

Mer·e·dith |'merə,diTH|, William (Morris) (1919–) U.S. poet. Notable works: *Partial Accounts* (1987, Pulitzer Prize).

Mer·gen·tha·ler |'mərgən,tälər|, Ottmar (1854–99) U.S. inventor, born in Germany. He developed the first Linotype typesetting machine (1884).

Mer·man |'mərmən|, Ethel (1908?–84) U.S. singer and actress. Born *Ethel Zimmerman*. The "queen of Broadway" for 3 decades, she performed in many Broadway plays and musicals, including *Gypsy* (1959) and *Hello, Dolly!* (1970).

Mer·ri·am |'merēəm| Brothers **George** (1803–80) and **Charles** (1806–87), U.S. publishers, formed the G. & C. Merriam Co., which published the first version of the Merriam-Webster dictionary.

Mer·rill |'merəl|, Frank Dow (1903–55) U.S. army officer. He organized the volunteer regiment known as "Merrill's Marauders," who trained for jungle warfare (1943).

Mer·rill |'merəl|, James (1926–95) U.S. poet. Notable works: *Nights and Days* (National Book Award, 1966) and *Divine Comedies* (1976, Pulitzer Prize). Bollingen Prize, 1973.

Mer·ton |'mərtən|, Thomas (1915–68) U.S. monk and author, born in France. He was ordained as Father M. Louis. Notable works: *The Seven Storey Mountain* (1948).

Mer·win |'mərwən|, W. S. (1927–) U.S. poet and author. Full name *William Stanley Merwin*. Notable works: *The Carrier of Ladders* (1970, Pulitzer Prize). Bollingen Prize, 1979.

Mes·mer |'mezmər|, Franz Anton (1734–1815) Austrian physician. Mesmer is chiefly remembered for introducing a therapeutic technique involving hypnotism; it was bound up with his ideas about "animal magnetism," however, and steeped in sensationalism.

Mes·sa·li·na |,mesə'lēnə|, Valeria (c. 22–48 AD) Also **Messallina**. Roman empress, third wife of Claudius. She be-

came notorious in Rome for the murders she instigated in court and for her extramarital affairs, and was executed on Claudius's orders.

Mes·ser·schmitt |'mesər,SHmit|, Willy (1898–1978) German aircraft designer and manufacturer of German warplanes.

Mes·sia·en |'mesä,ən|, Olivier (Eugène Prosper Charles) (1908–92) French composer. His music was influenced by Greek and Hindu rhythms, birdsong, Stravinsky and Debussy, and the composer's Roman Catholic faith. Notable works: *Quartet for the End of Time* (1941).

Mes·sick |'mesək|, Dalia (1906–) U.S. cartoonist. Pseudonym **Dale Messick**. She created the comic strip "Brenda Starr, Reporter."

Me·tes·ky |mə'teskē|, George ·(1903–) U.S. terrorist. Known as **The Mad Bomber**. He confessed to planting 32 bombs and causing 15 injuries between 1947 and 1957 in New York City.

Me·tho·di·us |mə'THōdēəs|, St. the brother of St. Cyril (see CYRIL, ST.).

Met·ter·nich |'metər,nik|, Klemens Wenzel Nepomuk Lothar, Prince of Metternich-Winnebург-Beilstein (1773–1859) Austrian statesman. As foreign minister (1809–48), he was one of the organizers of the Congress of Vienna (1814–15), which devised the settlement of Europe after the Napoleonic Wars.

Mey·er |'mīər|, Adolf (1866–1950) U.S. psychiatrist and educator, born in Switzerland. He was a leading exponent of psychobiology.

Mey·er·beer |'mīərbir|, Giacomo (1791–1864) German composer; born *Jakob Liebmann Beer*. He settled in Paris, establishing himself as a leading exponent of French grand opera with a series of works including *Les Huguenots* (1836).

Mey·er·hof |'mīərhawf|, Otto Fritz (1884–1951) German-born U.S. biochemist. He worked on the biochemical processes involved in muscle action and provided the basis for understanding the process by which glucose is broken down to provide energy. Nobel Prize for Physiology or Medicine (1922).

Mi·chel·an·ge·lo |,mikəl'ænjəlō; ,mīkəl'ænjəlō| (1475–1564) Italian sculptor, painter, architect, and poet; full name *Michelangelo Buonarroti*. A leading figure of the High Renaissance, Michelangelo established his reputation with sculptures such as the *Pietà* (*c.* 1497–1500) and *David* (1501–04). Under papal patronage he decorated the ceiling of the Sistine Chapel in Rome (1508–12) and painted the fresco *The Last Judgment* (1536–41), both important mannerist works. His architectural achievements include the completion of St. Peter's in Rome (1546–64).

Mi·che·lin |'misHəlɜn|, André (1853–1931) French industrialist. He and his brother Édouard founded the Michelin Tire Co. in 1888 and pioneered the use of tires on automobiles.

Mi·che·loz·zo |,mēkə'lätsō| (1396–1472) Italian architect and sculptor; full name *Michelozzo di Bartolommeo*. In partnership with Ghiberti and Donatello he led a revival of interest in Roman architecture.

Mi·chel·son |'mīkəlsən|, Albert Abraham (1852–1931) U.S. physicist. He specialized in precision measurement in experimental physics, and in 1907 became the first American to be awarded a Nobel Prize.

Miche·ner |miCH(ə)nər|, James Albert (1907–97) U.S. author. Notable novels: *Tales of the South Pacific* (1947, Pulitzer Prize), *The Bridges at Toko-ri* (1953), and *Caribbean* (1989).

Mid·dle·ton ·|'midl-tən|, Thomas (*c.* 1570–1627) English dramatist. He is best known for the tragedies *The Changeling* (1622), written with the dramatist William Rowley, and *Women Beware Women* (1620–27).

Mid·ler |'midlər|, Bette (1945–) U.S. actress and musician. Known as **The Divine Miss M**. She is noted for her 1989 hit "Wind Beneath My Wings," taken from the movie in which she starred, *Beaches*.

Mies van der Rohe |,mēs ,væn dər 'rō|, Ludwig (1886–1969) German-born architect and designer. He designed the German pavilion at the 1929 International Exhibition at Barcelona and the Seagram Building in New York (1954–58), and was noted for his tubular steel furniture. He was director of the

Bauhaus 1930–33 before emigrating to the U.S. in 1937.

Miff·lin |'miflin|, George Harrison (1845–1921) U.S. publisher. He was president of Houghton Mifflin Co. (1908–21).

Mi·hai·lo·vić |mə'hīlə,viCH|, Draža (1893–1946) Yugoslav soldier; full name *Dragoljub Mihailović*. Leader of the Chetniks during World War II, in 1941 he became minister of war for the Yugoslav government in exile. After the war he was executed on the charge of collaboration with the Germans.

Mi·kan |'mīkən|, George (1924–) U.S. basketball player, born in Czechoslovakia. Elected to the Basketball Hall of Fame (1959).

Mi·ki·ta |mə'kētə|, Stanley (1940–) U.S. hockey player, born in Czechoslovakia. He led the NHL in scoring four times.

Mil·haud |mē'(y)ō|, Darius (1892–1974) French composer. A member of the group Les Six, he composed the music to Cocteau's ballet *Le Boeuf sur le toit* (1919). Much of his music was polytonal and influenced by jazz.

Mil·ken |'milkən|, Michael (1946–) U.S. junk bond trader. He was convicted of fraud and racketeering in 1989.

Mill |mil|, John Stuart (1806–73) English philosopher and economist. Mill is best known for his political and moral works, especially *On Liberty* (1859), which argued for the importance of individuality, and *Utilitarianism* (1861), which extensively developed Bentham's theory.

Mil·lais |mə'lā|, Sir John Everett (1829–96) English painter. A founding member of the Pre-Raphaelite Brotherhood, he went on to produce lavishly painted portraits and landscapes. Notable works: *Christ in the House of his Parents* (1850) and *Bubbles* (1886).

Mil·land |mə'lænd|, Ray (1905–86) U.S. actor. Notable movies: *The Lost Weekend* (1945, Academy Award).

Mil·lay |mə'lā|, Edna St. Vincent (1892–1950) U.S. poet and author. Notable works: *The Ballad of the Harp-Weaver* (1923, Pulitzer Prize).

Mille |mil|, Cecil B. de see DeMille.

Mil·ler |'milər|, Alfred Jacob (1810–

74) U.S. artist. His Rocky Mountain sketches of Indians and mountain men were first published to illustrate *DeVoto's Across the Wide Missouri* (1947).

Mil·ler |'milər|, Arthur (1915–) U.S. dramatist. He established his reputation with *Death of a Salesman* (1949; Pulitzer Prize). *The Crucible* (1953) used the Salem witch trials of 1692 as an allegory for McCarthyism in America in the 1950s. Miller was married to Marilyn Monroe (1955–61). Notable works: *All My Sons* (1947), *A View From the Bridge* (1955), and *After the Fall* (1964).

Mil·ler |'milər|, Glenn (1904–44) U.S. jazz trombonist and bandleader. Full name *Alton Glenn Miller*. He led a celebrated swing big band, with whom he recorded his signature tune "Moonlight Serenade." He died when his aircraft disappeared over the English Channel.

Mil·ler |'milər|, Henry (Valentine) (1891–1980) U.S. novelist. His autobiographical novels *Tropic of Cancer* (1934) and *Tropic of Capricorn* (1939) were banned in the U.S. until the 1960s due to their frank depiction of sex and use of obscenities.

Mil·ler |'milər|, J. D. (1923–96) U.S. country songwriter. Notable songs: "Honky-Tonk Angels."

Mil·ler |'milər|, Joaquin (1837–1913) U.S. author and poet. Born *Cincinnatus Hiner Miller*.

Mil·ler |'milər|, Roger Dean (1936–92) U.S. country singer and songwriter. Notable songs: "King of the Road" and "Dang Me," as well as music for the Broadway show, *Big River*.

Mil·ler |'milər|, Samuel Freeman (1816–90) U.S. Supreme Court justice (1862–90).

Mil·ler |'milər|, Shannon (1977–) U.S. gymnast. She won 5 medals in 1992 Olympics and 2 gold medals in the 1996 Olympics, and was the All-Around Women's World Champion in 1993 and 1994.

Mil·ler |'milər|, Steve (1943–) U.S. musician. He started his Steve Miller Blues Band in 1966.

Mil·let |mə'la|, Jean (François) (1814–75) French painter. He was famous for the dignity he brought to the treatment of peasant subjects, which he concentrated on from 1850. Notable works: *The Gleaners* (1857).

Mil·lett |'milit|, Kate (1934–) U.S. feminist; full name *Katherine Millett*. She became involved in the civil rights movement of the 1960s, and advocated a radical feminism in *Sexual Politics* (1970).

Mil·li·kan |'miləkən|, Robert Andrews (1868–1953) U.S. physicist. He was the first to give an accurate figure for the electric charge on an electron. Nobel Prize for Physics, 1923.

Mills |milz|, Clark (1815–83) U.S. sculptor. He executed a bronze equestrian statue of Andrew Jackson in Washington, D.C.

Mills |milz|, John (1908–) U.S. actor. Notable movies: *Ryan's Daughter* (1970, Academy Award).

Mills |milz|, Sir John (Lewis Ernest Watts) (1908–) English actor. He is best known for his roles in war and adventure movies, such as *Scott of the Antarctic* (1948). He won an Oscar for his portrayal of a village idiot in *Ryan's Daughter* (1971). His daughters Juliet Mills (b.1941) and Hayley Mills (b.1946) have also had acting careers.

Mills |milz|, Robert (1781–1855) U.S. architect. He designed the Washington Monument in Washington, D.C.

Milne |'mil(n)|, A. A. (1882–1956) English writer of stories and poems for children; full name *Alan Alexander Milne*. He created the character Winnie the Pooh for his son Christopher Robin. Notable works: *Winnie-the-Pooh* (1926) and *When We Were Very Young* (verse collection, 1924).

Mi·losz |'mēlawsH|, Czeslaw (1911–) U.S. poet and author, born in Lithuania. Notable works: *Collected Poems* (1988). Nobel Prize, 1980.

Mil·sap |'mil,sæp|, Ronnie (1944–) U.S. country singer.

Mil·ton |'miltən|, John (1608–74) English poet. His three major works, completed after he had gone blind (1652), show his mastery of blank verse: they are the epic poems *Paradise Lost* (1667, revised 1674) and *Paradise Regained* (1671), and the verse drama *Samson Agonistes* (1671).

Min·ghel·la, Anthony (1954–) U.S.

director. Notable movies: *The English Patient* (Academy Award, 1996).

Min·gus |'miNGgəs|, Charles (1922–79) U.S. jazz bassist and composer. A leading figure of the 1940s jazz scene, he experimented with atonality and was influenced by gospel and blues. His compositions include "Goodbye Porkpie Hat."

Min·nel·li |mə'nelē| U.S. family, including: **Vincente Minnelli** (1910–86), movie director. He directed classic Hollywood musicals, including *Gigi* (1958, Academy Award). He was married to actress Judy Garland. His daughter **Liza Minnelli** (1946–), actress and entertainer. Notable movies: *Cabaret* (1972, Academy Award).

Min·ton |'min(t)ən|, Sherman (1890–1965) U.S. Supreme Court justice (1949–56).

Min·ton |'min(t)ən|, Thomas (1765–1836) English pottery manufacturer. He made majolica, bone china, and reproductions of works of della Robbia and Palissy.

Min·u·it |'minyəwət|, Peter (1580–1638) Dutch colonial administrator. He was the first director general of the North American Dutch colony of New Netherland (1626–31). He purchased Manhattan Island from the Algonquin Indians (1626) for 60 guilders ($24).

Mi·ra·beau |'mirə,bō|, Honoré Gabriel Riqueti, Comte de (1749–91) French revolutionary politician. Pressing for a form of constitutional monarchy, Mirabeau was prominent in the early days of the French Revolution.

Mi·ró |,mi'rō|, Joan (1893–1983) Spanish painter. One of the most prominent figures of surrealism, he painted a brightly colored fantasy world of variously spiky and amebic calligraphic forms against plain backgrounds.

Mi·shi·ma |'misHē,mä|, Yukio (1925–70) Japanese writer; pseudonym of *Hiraoka Kimitake*. His books include the four-volume *The Sea of Fertility* (1965–70), which looks at reincarnation and the sterility of modern life. An avowed imperialist, he committed hara-kiri after failing to incite soldiers against the postwar regime.

Mis·so·ni, Tai Otavio (1921–) Italian

fashion designer, born in Yugoslavia. With his wife Rosita, he founded the Missoni Co. in Milan (1953)

Mitch·ell |'miCHəl|, Billy (1879–1936) U.S. army officer, born in France. An outspoken advocate of air power, he was court-martialed for his criticism of the War and Navy Departments (1925).

Mitch·ell |'miCHəl|, John (1870–1919) U.S. labor leader. He was United Mine Workers president (1898–1908).

Mitch·ell |'miCHəl|, John (1913–88) U.S. statesman. He was U.S. attorney general under President Nixon (1969–72).

Mitch·ell |'miCHəl|, John Ames (1845–1918) U.S. artist, editor, and novelist. He founded and edited *Life* magazine (1883–1918).

Mitch·ell |'miCHəl|, Joni (1943–) Canadian singer and songwriter; born *Roberta Joan Anderson*. Starting to record in 1968, she moved from folk to a fusion of folk, jazz, and rock. Notable albums: *Blue* (1971) and *Hejira* (1976).

Mitch·ell |'miCHəl|, Margaret (1900–49) U.S. novelist, famous as the author of the Pulitzer Prize–winning novel *Gone with the Wind* (1936), set during the Civil War.

Mitch·ell |'miCHəl|, Maria (1818–89) U.S. astronomer. She established the orbit of a newly discovered comet (1847) and became the first woman elected to the American Academy of Arts and Sciences.

Mitch·ell |'miCHəl|, S. Weir (1829–1914) U.S. author. Full name *Silas Weir Mitchell*. Notable works: *Hugh Wynne, Free Quaker* (1897).

Mitch·um |'miCHəm|, Robert (1917–97) U.S. actor. He was a professional boxer before rising to stardom in movies such as *Out of the Past* (1947), and *Night of the Hunter* (1955).

Mit·ford |'mitfərd|, Nancy (Freeman) (1904–73) She and her sister **Jessica (Lucy)** (1917–96) were English writers. Nancy achieved fame with comic novels including *Love in a Cold Climate* (1949). Jessica became a U.S. citizen in 1944 and is best known for her works on American culture, notably *The American Way of Death* (1963). Among their four sisters were **Unity** (1914–48), who was an admirer of Hitler, and **Diana** (1910–), who married Sir Oswald Mosley in 1936.

Mith·ri·da·tes VI |ˌmĭTHrə'dāˌtēz| (*c.* 132–63 BC) Also **Mithradates VI.** king of Pontus (120–63 BC); known as **Mithridates the Great**. His expansionist policies led to three wars with Rome (88–85, 83–82, and 74–66 BC). He was finally defeated by Pompey.

Mit·ter·rand |'mitə,rän(d)|, François (Maurice Marie) (1916–96) French statesman, president (1981–95). As president he initially moved to raise basic wages, increase social benefits, nationalize key industries, and decentralize government. The Socialist Party lost its majority vote in the 1986 general election and Mitterrand made the conservative Jacques Chirac prime minister, resulting in a reversal of some policies.

Mi·ya·ke, Issey (1938–) Japanese fashion designer. Worked with Guy Laroche, Hubert de Givenchy, and Geoffrey Beene before opening a design studio (1970).

Mö·bi·us |'mOEbēəs; 'mōbēəs|, August Ferdinand (1790–1868) German mathematician and astronomer. He discovered the one-sided figure the Möbius strip (1958).

Mö·bi·us |'mOEbēəs; 'mōbēəs|, Karl August (1825–1908) German zoologist. He introduced the concept of the ecosystem.

Mo·bu·tu Se·se Se·ko |mə'bōōtōō 'sāzē 'sākō| (1930–97) president of Zaire, now the Democratic Republic of Congo (1965–97); born *Joseph-Désiré Mobutu*. Seizing power in a military coup in 1965, he retained control despite opposition until 1997, when he was finally forced to resign.

Mo·di·glia·ni |ˌmōdēl'yänē|, Amedeo (1884–1920) Italian painter and sculptor, resident in France from 1906. His portraits and nudes are noted for their elongated forms, linear qualities, and earthy colors.

Moholy-Nagy |'mawhəlē 'näj|, László (1895–1946) Hungarian-born U.S. painter, sculptor, and photographer. He pioneered the experimental use of plastic materials, light, photography, and movie.

Mois·san |ˌmwä'sän|, Ferdinand Frédéric Henri (1852–1907) French chemist. In 1886 he succeeded in isolating the very reactive element fluorine. In 1892 he invented the electric-arc furnace that bears his name. Nobel Prize for Chemistry (1906).

Mo·lière |ˌmōl'yer| (1622–73) French dramatist; pseudonym of *Jean-Baptiste Poquelin*. He wrote more than twenty comic plays about contemporary France, developing stock characters from Italian *commedia dell'arte*. Notable works: *Don Juan* (1665), *Le Misanthrope* (1666), and *Le Bourgeois gentilhomme* (1670).

Mol·nar |'mawlnär|, Ferenc (1878–1952) Hungarian playwright and novelist. Notable plays: *Liliom* (1909) and *The Good Fairy* (1930). Notable novels: *The Paul Street Boys* (1907) and *Andor* (1918).

Mo·lo·tov |'mälə,tawf|, Vyacheslav (Mikhailovich) (1890–1986) Soviet statesman; born *Vyacheslav Mikhailovich Skryabin*. As commissar (later minister) for foreign affairs (1939–49; 1953–56), he negotiated the nonaggression pact with Nazi Germany (1939) and after 1945 represented the Soviet Union at meetings of the United Nations.

Molt·ke |'mawltkə|, Helmuth Karl Bernhard Graf von (1800–91) Prussian soldier. He devised strategic and tactical command methods for modern mass armies engaged on broad fronts.

Momm·sen |'mämsən|, Theodor (1817–1903) German historian. He is noted for his three-volume *History of Rome* (1854–56; 1885) and his treatises on Roman constitutional law (1871–88). Nobel Prize for Literature (1902).

Monck |məNGk|, George, 1st Duke of Albemarle (1608–70) English general. Initially a Royalist, he became a supporter of Oliver Cromwell and later suppressed the Royalists in Scotland (1651). Concerned at the growing unrest following Cromwell's death (1658), Monck negotiated the return of Charles II in 1660.

Mon·dale |'män,dāl|, Walter Frederick (1928–) U.S. vice president (1977–81). A Minnesota Democrat, he served in the U.S. Senate (1964–76). He ran for the U.S. presidency in 1984, losing to incumbent Ronald Reagan. He was U.S. ambassador to Japan (1993–96).

Mon·dri·an |'mawndrēən|, Piet (1872–1944) Dutch painter; born *Pieter Cornelis Mondriaan*. He was a cofounder of the De Stijl movement and the originator of neoplasticism, one of the earliest and strictest forms of geometrical abstract painting.

Mo·net |ˌmō'nā|, Claude (1840–1926) French painter. A founding member of the Impressionists, his fascination with the play of light on objects led him to produce a series of paintings of single subjects painted at different times of day and under different weather conditions, such as the *Haystacks* series (1890–91), *Rouen Cathedral* (1892–95), and the *Water lilies* sequence (1899–1906; 1916 onward).

Mon·i·ca |'mänikə|, St. (332–*c.* 387) mother of St. Augustine of Hippo. She is often regarded as the model of Christian mothers for her patience with her son's spiritual crises, which ended with his conversion in 386. Feast day, August 27 (formerly May 4).

Mo·nier |'mawn,yā|, Joseph (1823–1906) French gardener and inventor. He was the first to reinforce concrete with wire netting (1867).

Monk |məNGk|, Thelonious (Sphere) (1920–82) U.S. jazz pianist and composer, one of the founders of the bebop style in the early 1940s, he became popular in the late 1950s, as the new style of "cool" jazz reached a wider audience. Notable compositions: "Round Midnight," "Straight, No Chaser," and "Well, You Needn't."

Mon·mouth |'mänməTH|, James Scott, Duke of (1649–85) English claimant to the throne of England. The illegitimate son of Charles II, he became the focus for Whig supporters of a Protestant succession. In 1685 he led a rebellion against the Catholic James II, but was defeated at the Battle of Sedgemoor and executed.

Mo·nod |mə'nō(d)|, Jacques Lucien (1910–76) French biochemist; 1965 Nobel Prize for Physiology or Medicine French biochemist. Together with fellow

French biochemist François Jacob (1920–   ), with whom he was awarded a Nobel Prize in 1965, he formulated a theory to explain how genes are activated and in 1961 proposed the existence of messenger RNA.

Mon·roe |mən'rō|, James see box. **Elizabeth Kortright Monroe** (1768–1830), wife of James Monroe and U.S. first lady (1817–25).

Mon·roe |mən'rō|, Bill (1911–96) U.S. country singer, songwriter, and man-

---

Monroe, James
5th U.S. president

Life dates: 1758–1831
Place of birth: Westmoreland County, Va.
Mother: Elizabeth Jones Monroe
Father: Spence Monroe
Wife: Elizabeth ("Eliza") Kortright Monroe
Children: Eliza, Maria
College/University: College of William and Mary
Military service: lieutenant colonel, Continental Army, Revolutionary War
Career: lawyer
Political career: Virginia Assembly; Congress of the Confederation; U.S. Senate; minister to Spain, France, and Great Britain; governor of Virginia; U.S. secretary of state; U.S. secretary of war; president
Party: Democratic-Republican
Home state: Virginia
Opponents in presidential races: Rufus King; John Quincy Adams
Term of office: March 4, 1817–March 3, 1825
Vice president: Daniel D. Tompkins
Notable events of presidency: construction of Erie Canal; Seminole Wars; Financial Panic of 1819; Missouri Compromise; Monroe Doctrine; legislation established flag of the United States; Rush-Bagot Agreement; Mississippi, Illinois, Alabama, Maine, and Missouri admitted as 20th–24th states
Other achievements: Delegate to Virginia state convention to ratify Federal Constitution; chairman, Virginia Constitutional Convention; headed diplomatic mission to Spain; commissioned to negotiate treaty with England
Place of burial: Richmond, Va.

dolin player. Known as **the father of bluegrass**. With his group the Blue Grass Boys, he joined the Grand Ole Opry (1939) and toured; his 1988 song "Southern Flavor" won the first Grammy for bluegrass music.

Mon·roe |mən'rō|, Marilyn (1926–62) U.S. actress; born *Norma Jean Mortenson*; later *Norma Jean Baker*. Her movie roles, largely in comedies, made her the definitive Hollywood sex symbol. Her husbands included playwright Arthur Miller and baseball player Joe DiMaggio. She is thought to have died of an overdose of sleeping pills. Notable movies: *Gentlemen Prefer Blondes* (1953), *Some Like it Hot* (1959), and *The Misfits* (1961).

Mon·ta·gna |mawn'tänyə|, Bartolommeo Cincani (c. 1450–1523) Italian painter. He is noted for his altarpiece *Sacra Conversazione* (1499).

Mon·taigne |män'tän|, Michel (Eyquem) de (1533–92) French essayist. Widely regarded as the originator of the modern essay, he wrote about prominent personalities and ideas of his age in his skeptical *Essays* (1580; 1588).

Mon·ta·le |,mōn'tälä|, Eugenio (1896–1981) Italian poet, critic, and translator. Nobel Prize for Literature, 1975

Mon·tana |män'tænə|, Bob (1920–75) U.S. cartoonist. He created the comic strip "Archie."

Mon·tana |män'tænə|, Joe (1956–) U.S. football player.

Mont·calm |,män(t)'käm|, Louis Joseph de Montcalm-Gozon, Marquis de (1712–59) French general. He defended Quebec against British troops under General Wolfe, but was defeated and fatally wounded in the battle on the Plains of Abraham during the French and Indian War.

Mon·tes·pan |,mawntəs'pän|, Françoise-Athénaïs de Rochechouart, Marquise de (1641–1707) French noblewoman. She was mistress of Louis XIV from 1667 to 1679, and had seven children by him. She subsequently fell from favor when the king became attracted to the children's governess, Madame de Maintenon.

Mon·tes·quieu |,män(t)əs'kyōō|, Charles Louis de Secondat, Baron de La Brède et de (1689–1755) French political philosopher. His reputation rests chiefly on *L'Esprit des lois* (1748), a comparative study of political systems in which he championed the separation of judicial, legislative, and executive powers as being most conducive to individual liberty.

Mon·tes·so·ri |,män(t)ə'sawrē|, Maria (1870–1952) Italian educationist. In her book *The Montessori Method* (1909) she advocated a child-centered approach to education, developed from her success with mentally handicapped children.

Mon·teux |,mawn'tœ|, Pierre (1875–1964) U.S. conductor, born in France. He was a noted interpreter of 20th-century music.

Mon·te·ver·di |,mäntə'verdē|, Claudio (1567–1643) Italian composer. His madrigals are noted their use of harmonic dissonance; other important works include his opera *Ofeo* (1607) and his sacred *Vespers* (1610).

Mon·tez |män'tez|, Lola (1818–61) Irish dancer; born *Marie Dolores Eliza Rosanna Gilbert*. She became the mistress of Ludwig I of Bavaria in 1846 and exercised great influence over him until banished the following year.

Mon·te·zu·ma II |,män(t)ə'zōōmə| (1466–1520) Aztec emperor (1502–20). The last ruler of the Aztec empire in Mexico, he was defeated and imprisoned by the Spanish under Cortés in 1519. He was killed while trying to pacify some of his former subjects during an uprising against his captors.

Mont·fort |'män(t)fərt| Family of soldiers, including: **Simon de Montfort** (c. 1165–1218), French soldier. From 1209 he led the Albigensian Crusade against the Cathars in southern France. His son **Simon de Montfort, Earl of Leicester** (c. 1208–65), English soldier, born in Normandy. He led the baronial opposition to Henry III, defeating the king at Lewes in 1264 and summoning a Parliament (1265). He was defeated and killed by reorganized royal forces under Henry's son (later Edward I).

Mont·gol·fier |,män(t)'gawlfēər|, **Joseph Michel** (1740–1810) and **Jacques Étienne** (1745–99), French brothers; inventors and pioneers in hot-air ballooning. They built a large balloon from linen and paper and successfully lifted a number of animals; the first human ascents followed in 1783.

Mont·gom·er·y |ˌmän(t)ˈgəm(ə)rē|, Bernard Law, 1st Viscount Montgomery of Alamein (1887–1976) British Field Marshal; known as **Monty**. His victory at El Alamein in 1942 proved the first significant Allied success in World War II. He commanded the Allied ground forces in the invasion of Normandy in 1944 and accepted the German surrender on May 7, 1945.

Mont·go·me·ry |ˌmän(t)ˈgəm(ə)rē|, L. M. (1874–1942) Canadian novelist; full name *Lucy Maud Montgomery*. She is noted for her best-selling first novel *Anne of Green Gables* (1908).

Mont·rose |ˈmäntrōz|, James Graham, 1st Marquis of (1612–50) Scottish general. Montrose supported Charles I in the English Civil War and inflicted a dramatic series of defeats on the stronger Covenanter forces in the north before being defeated. In 1650 he attempted to restore Charles II, but was betrayed to the Covenanters and hanged.

Moo·dy |ˈmoōdē|, John (1868–1958) U.S. financial analyst. He published various investment magazines; in 1941 he merged with Henry V. Poor, and their firm became Standard and Poor.

Moo·dy |ˈmoōdē|, William Henry (1853–1917) U.S. Supreme Court justice (1906–10).

Moon |moōn|, Sun Myung (1920–) Korean industrialist and religious leader. In 1954 he founded the Holy Spirit Association for the Unification of World Christianity, which became known as the Unification Church. Disciples are popularly called "Moonies."

Moore |moŏr|, Alfred (1755–1810) U.S. Supreme Court justice (1799–1804).

Moore |moŏr|, Archie (1913?–) U.S. boxer.

Moore |moŏr|, Charles (1925–93) U.S. architect. He designed Sea Ranch near San Francisco and the Piazza d'Italia in Los Angeles.

Moore |moŏr|, Clement Clarke (1779–1863) U.S. author. His poetry includes "A Visit from St. Nicholas," published anonymously (1923).

Moore |moŏr|, Dudley (Stuart John) (1935–) English actor, comedian, and musician. He appeared with Peter Cook in the television shows "Beyond the Fringe" (1959–64) and "Not Only … But Also" (1964–70). His movies include *Arthur* (1981).

Moore |moŏr|, G. E. (1873–1958) English moral philosopher and member of the Bloomsbury Group; full name *George Edward Moore*. Notable works: *Principia Ethica* (1903).

Moore |moŏr|, George (Augustus) (1852–1933) Irish novelist. Notable works: *A Mummer's Wife* (1885) and *Esther Waters* (1894).

Moore |moŏr|, Gordon E. (1929–) U.S. businessman. He was cofounder of Intel Corp (1968) with Robert Norton Noyce.

Moore |moŏr|, Henry (Spencer) (1898–1986) English sculptor and draftsman. His work is characterized by semi-abstract reclining forms, large upright figures, and family groups, which Moore intended to be viewed in the open air.

Moore |moŏr|, Marianne Craig (1887–1972) U.S. poet. Notable works: *Collected Poems* (1951, Pulitzer Prize) and *Tell Me, Tell Me* (1966).

Moore |moŏr|, Mary Tyler (1936–) U.S. actress. She starred in the television series "The Dick Van Dyke Show" (1961–66) and "The Mary Tyler Moore Show" (1970–77).

Moore |moŏr|, Thomas (1779–1852) Irish poet and musician. He wrote patriotic and nostalgic songs set to Irish tunes, notably "The Harp that once through Tara's Halls" and "The Minstrel Boy," and is also known for the oriental romance *Lalla Rookh* (1817).

Moores |moŏrs|, Dick (1909–86) U.S. cartoonist. Full name *Richard Moores*. He created the comic strip "Gasoline Alley."

Mo·ra·via |məˈrävēə|, Alberto (1907–90) Italian author. Born *Alberto Pincherle*. His novels and short stories were censored by Fascists and condemned by the Vatican.

More |mawr|, Sir Thomas (1478–1535) English scholar and statesman, Lord Chancellor (1529–32); canonized as **St. Thomas More**. His *Utopia* (1516), describing an ideal city state, established him as a leading humanist of the Renaissance.

Mo·reau |mə'rō|, Jeanne (1928–) French actress. Notable movies: *Les Liaisons dangereuses* (1959), *Jules et Jim* (1961), and *Nikita* (1990).

Mo·renz, Howie (1902–37) Canadian hockey player. He was voted Outstanding Player of the Half-Century, 1950.

Mor·gan |'mawrgən|, Daniel (1736–1802) American Revolutionary soldier and politican. He served as a member of the U.S. House of Representatives (1797–99).

Mor·gan |'mawrgən|, J. P. (1837–1913) U.S. financier, philanthropist, and art collector; full name *John Pierpont Morgan.* He created General Electric (1891) and the U.S. Steel Corp. (1901). He bequeathed his large art collection to the Museum of Modern Art in New York.

Mor·gan |'mawrgən|, Thomas Hunt (1866–1945) U.S. geneticist. His studies on inheritance using the fruit fly *Drosophila* showed that the genetic information was carried by genes arranged along the length of the chromosomes. Nobel Prize for Physiology or Medicine (1933).

Mo·ri |,maw'rē|, Hanae (1926–) Japanese fashion designer.

Mor·i·son |'mawrəsən|, Samuel Eliot (1887–1976) U.S. historian. Notable works: *Oxford History of the United States* (1927), *Admiral of the Ocean Sea* (1942, Pulitzer Prize), and *John Paul Jones* (1959, Pulitzer Prize).

Mor·i·son |'mawrəsən|, Stanley (1889–1967) English typographer. He was on the staff of the London *Times* (1929–60); he designed Times New Roman typeface (1932).

Mo·ri·sot |,mawri'sō|, Berthe (Marie Pauline) (1841–95) French painter, the first woman to join the Impressionists. Her works typically depicted women and children and waterside scenes.

Mor·land |'mawrlənd|, George (1763–1804) English painter. Although indebted to Dutch and Flemish genre painters such as David Teniers the Younger, he drew his inspiration for his pictures of taverns, cottages, and farm-

yards from local scenes, as with *Inside a Stable* (1791).

Mor·ley |'mawrlē|, Edward Williams (1838–1923) U.S. chemist. In 1887 he collaborated with Albert Michelson in an experiment to determine the speed of light, the result of which disproved the existence of the ether.

Mo·ro |'maw,rō|, Aldo (1916–78) Italian statesman and Christian Democrat prime minister (1963–68, 1974–76). He was assassinated by the Red Brigades.

Mor·ris |'mawrəs|, Desmond John (1928–) British zoologist. He studied animal behavior and the implications for the human condition. Notable works: *The Naked Ape* (1967).

Mor·ris |'mawrəs|, Gouverneur (1752–1816) American politician. An active proponent of American independence, he represented New York as a member of the Continental Congress (1777–79), the Constitutional Convention (1787), and the U.S. Senate (1800–03). It was while serving as Robert Morris's assistant superintendent of finance (1781–85) that he proposed the adoption of a decimal monetary system based on dollars and cents.

Mor·ris |'mawrəs|, Robert (1734–1806) American politician and financier. He represented Pennsylvania as a member of the Continental Congress (1775–78) and was a reluctant signer of the Declaration of Independence. He provided extensive financial support for the colonial war effort and was later appointed superintendent of finance (1781–84) by the Continental Congress. After serving in the U.S. Senate (1789–95), he lost all his money in western land speculations and spent his final years in poverty.

Mor·ris[1] |'mawrəs|, William (1834–96) English designer, craftsman, poet, and writer. A leading figure in the Arts and Crafts Movement, in 1861 he established Morris & Co., an association of craftsmen whose members included Edward Burne-Jones and Dante Gabriel Rossetti, to produce hand-crafted goods for the home. His many writings include *News from Nowhere*, which portrays a socialist Utopia.

Mor·ris[2] |'mawrəs|, William (1873–

1932) U.S. theatrical agent. He organized the William Morris Agency.

Mor·ris |'mawrəs|, William Richard, 1st Viscount Nuffield (1877–1963) English automobile manufacturer and philanthropist.

Mor·ris |'mawrəs|, Wright (Marion) (1910–) U.S. author, educator and photographer. Notable works: *Earthly Delights, Unearthly Adornments* (1978).

Mor·ri·son |'mawrəsən|, Jim (1943–71) U.S. rock singer; full name *James Douglas Morrison.* Morrison was the lead singer of the Doors.

Mor·ri·son |'mawrəsən|, Toni (1931–) U.S. novelist; full name *Chloe Anthony Morrison.* Her novels depict the black American experience and heritage, often focusing on rural life in the South, as in *The Bluest Eye* (1970). *Beloved* (1987) won the Pulitzer Prize, and Morrison became the first black woman to receive the Nobel Prize for Literature in 1993. Notable works: *Sula* (1973), *Song of Solomon* (1977), *Tar Baby* (1981), and *Jazz* (1992).

Mor·ri·son |'mawrəsən|, Van (1945–) Northern Irish singer, instrumentalist, and songwriter; full name *George Ivan Morrison.* He developed a distinctive personal style from a background of blues, soul, folk music, and rock. Notable albums: *Astral Weeks* (1968) and *Moondance* (1970).

Mor·ris·sey |'mawrəsē|, Stephen Patrick (1959–) British rock musician.

Mor·ti·mer |'mawrtəmər|, Roger de, 8th Baron of Wigmore and 1st Earl of March (c. 1287–1330) English noble. In 1326 he invaded England with his lover Isabella of France, replacing her husband, England's Edward II, with her son, the future Edward III. When Edward III assumed royal power in 1330 he had Mortimer executed.

Mor·ton |'mawrtən|, Jelly Roll (1885–1941) U.S. jazz pianist, composer, and bandleader; born *Ferdinand Joseph La Menthe Morton.* He was one of the principal links between ragtime and New Orleans jazz.

Mor·ton[1] |'mawrtən|, John (c. 1420–1500) English prelate and statesman. He was appointed Archbishop of Can-

terbury in 1486 and Chancellor under Henry VII a year later. The Crown's stringent taxation policies made the regime in general and Morton in particular widely unpopular.

Mor·ton[2] |'mawrtən|, John (1724?–77) American Revolutionary patriot. He was a member of the Continental Congress (1774–77) and a signer of the Declaration of Independence.

Mor·ton |'mawrtən|, Julius Sterling (1832–1902) U.S. agriculturist. The U.S. secretary of agriculture (1893–97), he originated Arbor Day.

Mor·ton |'mawrtən|, Levi Parsons (1824–1920) vice president of the U.S. (1889–93) and governor of New York (1895–97).

Mor·ton |'mawrtən|, Oliver Hazard Perry Throck (1823–77) U.S. politician. A founder of the Indiana Republican Party, he served in the U.S. Senate (1867–77).

Mor·ton |'mawrtən|, Thomas (1590?–1647) U.S. colonist, born in England. He was arrested twice for anti-Puritan polemics and activites; his *New English Canaan* (1637) satirizes Myles Standish as "Captain Shrimp."

Mor·ton |'mawrtən|, William Thomas Green (1819–68) U.S. dentist and pioneer in surgical anesthesia.

Mo·san·der |mə'sændər|, Carl Gustaf (1797–1858) Swedish chemist. Mosander continued Berzelius's work on the rare earth elements and discovered the new elements lanthanum, erbium, and terbium, and the supposed element didymium.

Mose·ley |'mōzlē|, Henry Gwyn Jeffreys (1887–1915) English physicist. He determined the atomic numbers of elements from their X-ray spectra, demonstrated that an element's chemical properties are determined by this number, and showed that there are only 92 naturally occurring elements.

Mo·ses |'mōzəs| (c. 14th–13th century BC) Hebrew prophet and lawgiver, brother of Aaron. According to the biblical account, he was born in Egypt and led the Israelites away from servitude there, across the desert toward the Promised Land. During the journey he was inspired by God on Mount Sinai to write down the Ten Commandments on tablets of stone (Exod. 20).

Mo·ses |'mōzəs|, Edwin (1955–) U.S. track athlete; full name *Edwin Corley Moses*. He won Olympic gold medals for the 400-meters hurdles in 1976 and 1984, and set successive world records in the event throughout those years.

Mo·ses |'mōzəs|, Grandma (1860–1961) U.S. painter; full name *Anna Mary Robertson Moses*. She took up painting as a hobby when widowed in 1927, producing more than a thousand paintings in primitive style, mostly of American rural life.

Mo·ses |'mōzəs|, Robert (1889–1981) U.S. public official. As New York City parks commissioner (1934–60), he built 416 miles of parkways.

Moss |maws|, Jeffrey A. (1942–98) U.S. children's author and songwriter. He created the "Sesame Street" characters Cookie Monster and Oscar the Grouch and wrote *The Butterfly Jar*.

Moss |maws|, Stirling (1929–) English racecar driver.

Möss·bau·er |'maws,bowər|, Rudolf Ludwig (1929–) German physicist. He discovered the Mössmauer effect, for which he shared the 1961 Nobel Prize for Physics.

Mo·ten |'mōtn|, Bennie (1894–1935) U.S. jazz pianist. Full name *Benjamin Moten*. He was a principal developer of the "Southwestern" style of orchestral jazz.

Mother Te·re·sa |tə'rēsə; tə'rāsə| see TERESA, MOTHER.

Moth·er·well |'məTHər,wel|, Robert (1915–91) U.S. artist. He was a founder and leading exponent of the New York school of abstract expressionism.

Mot·ley |'mätlē|, Willard (1912–65) U.S. author. Notable works: *Let No Man Write My Epitaph* (1958).

Mo·ton |'mōtn|, Robert Russa (1867–1940) U.S. educator. He was principal of the Tuskegee Normal and Industrial Institute (1915–35). Spingarn Medal, 1932.

Mott |mät|, Lucretia (Coffin) (1793–1880) U.S. social reformer. A progressive Quaker minister, she was a highly motivated activist in the causes of abolition, women's rights, and freedom of religion.

Mou·hot |,mōō'ō|, Henri (1826–61) French naturalist and photographer. Full name *Alexandre-Henri Mouhot*. He discovered ancient Cambodian temples at Angkor (1860).

Mount·bat·ten |,mown(t)'bætn|, Louis (Francis Albert Victor Nicholas), 1st Earl Mountbatten of Burma (1900–79) British admiral and administrator. He was supreme Allied commander in Southeast Asia (1943–45) and the last viceroy (1947) and first governor general of India (1947–48). He was killed by an IRA bomb while on his yacht.

Moy·er |'moiər|, Andrew J. (1899–1959) U.S. inventor. He developed a method for the production of penicillin, which became a model for the development of all other antibiotic fermentations.

Moy·ers |'moiərz|, Bill (1934–) U.S. journalist. He worked for public and commercial television as a news analyst.

Moy·ni·han |'moinə,hæn|, Daniel Patrick (1927–) U.S. senator from New York (1977–).

Moy·roud, Louis Marius (1914–) French inventor. With Rene Higonnet, he built the first practical phototypsesetting machine, the Lumitype, later known as the Photon (1946).

Mo·zart |'mō,tsärt|, (Johann Chrysostom) Wolfgang Amadeus (1756–91) Austrian composer. A child prodigy as a harpsichordist, pianist, and composer, he came to epitomize classical music in its purity of form and melody. A prolific composer, he wrote more than forty symphonies, nearly thirty piano concertos, over twenty string quartets, and sixteen operas, including *The Marriage of Figaro* (1786), *Don Giovanni* (1787), *Così fan tutte* (1790), and *The Magic Flute* (1791).

Mu·ba·rak |mōō'bärək|, (Muhammad) Hosni (Said) (1928–) Egyptian statesman, president since 1981. He did much to establish closer links between Egypt and other Arab nations, while opposing militant Islamic fundamentalism in Egypt.

Mu·cha |'mōōkə|, Alphonse (1860–1939) Czech painter and designer; born

Alfons Maria. He was a leading figure in the art nouveau movement, noted for his flowing poster designs, typically featuring the actress Sarah Bernhardt.

Mudd |məd|, Roger Harrison (1928–) U.S. journalist. He was the CBS News chief Washington correspondent (1961–87).

Mu·ga·be |mŏŏ'gäbē|, Robert (Gabriel) (1924–) Zimbabwean statesman, prime minister (1980–87) and president since 1987. He became prime minister in Zimbabwe's first post-independence elections. In 1987 his party ZANU merged with ZAPU and Mugabe became executive president of a one-party state.

Mug·ler, Thierry (1948–) French fashion designer.

Mu·ham·mad |mə'häməd| (c. 570–632) Also **Mohammed.** Arab prophet and founder of Islam. In c. 610 in Mecca he received the first of a series of revelations that, as the Koran, became the doctrinal and legislative basis of Islam. In the face of opposition to his preaching he and his small group of supporters were forced to flee to Medina in 622 (the Hegira). Muhammad led his followers into a series of battles against the Meccans. In 630 Mecca capitulated, and by his death Muhammad had united most of Arabia.

Mu·ham·mad |mə'häməd|, Elijah (1897–1975) U.S. activist. He directed the growth of the Black Muslim movement.

Mu·ham·mad |mə'häməd|, Mahathir (1925–) Malaysian statesman, prime minister since 1981.

Mu·ham·mad Ah·mad see MAHDI.

Mu·ham·mad A·li[1] |mə'häməd ,älē| (1769–1849) Ottoman viceroy and pasha of Egypt (1805–49), possibly of Albanian descent. He modernized Egypt's infrastructure, making it the leading power in the eastern Mediterranean, and established a dynasty that survived until 1952.

Mu·ham·mad A·li[2] |mə'häməd ,ä'lē| (1942–) U.S. boxer; born *Cassius Marcellus Clay.* He was an Olympic gold medalist as a light heavyweight in 1960. He won the world heavyweight title in 1964, 1974, and 1978, becoming the only boxer to be world heavyweight champion three times. After converting to Islam and changing his name, he was stripped of his title for refusing army service on conscientious objector grounds, a decision that was overthrown by the U.S. Supreme Court in 1971.

Mu·ji·bur Rah·man |mŏŏ'jēbŏŏr rə 'män| (1920–75) Bangladeshi statesman, first prime minister of independent Bangladesh (1972–75) and president (1975); known as **Sheikh Mujib.** After failing to establish parliamentary democracy as prime minister, he assumed dictatorial powers in 1975. He and his family were assassinated in a military coup.

Mul·doon |məl'dōōn|, Sir Robert (David) (1921–92) New Zealand statesman, prime minister (1975–84). His premiership was marked by domestic measures to tackle low economic growth and high inflation.

Mul·ler |'mələr|, Hermann Joseph (1890–1967) U.S. geneticist. He discovered that X-rays induce mutations in the genetic material of the fruit fly *Drosophila* and thus recognized the danger of X-radiation to living things. Nobel Prize for Physiology or Medicine (1946).

Mül·ler |'mələr|, Johannes Peter (1801–58) German anatomist and zoologist. He was a pioneer of comparative and microscopical methods in biology.

Mül·ler |'mələr|, (Friedrich) Max (1823–1900) German-born British philologist. He is remembered for his edition of the Sanskrit *Rig-veda* (1849–75).

Mül·ler |'mələr|, Paul Hermann (1899–1965) Swiss chemist. He synthesized DDT in 1939 and soon patented it as an insecticide. Nobel Prize for Physiology or Medicine (1948).

Mul·li·gen |'mələgən|, Gerry (1927–96) U.S. jazz baritone saxophonist and songwriter. Full name *Gerald Joseph Mulligen.* He helped create the "Cool Jazz" idiom.

Mul·li·ken |'mələkən|, Robert Sanderson (1896–1986) U.S. chemist, physicist and educator. Nobel Prize for Chemistry, 1966.

Mul·lin |'mələn|, Willard (1902–78) U.S. cartoonist and artist. He created the characters of the baseball-playing "Bum" and "Kid."

Mul·ro·ney |məl'rōnē|, (Martin) Brian (1939–) Canadian Progressive Conservative statesman, prime minister (1984–93).

Mum·ford |'məmfərd|, Lewis (1895–1990) U.S. social philosopher. He was an expert on regional and city planning. Notable works: *The Myth of the Machine* (1967, 1971).

Munch |mYNSH|, Charles (1891–1968) French violinist and conductor. He was conductor of the Paris Philharmonic and the Boston Symphony and director of the Berkshire Music Center at Tanglewood.

Munch |mo͞oNGk|, Edvard (1863–1944) Norwegian painter and engraver. He infused his subjects with an intense emotionalism, exploring the use of vivid color and linear distortion to express feelings about life and death. Notable works: his *Frieze of Life* sequence, incorporating *The Scream* (1893).

Mun·ro |mən'rō|, Alice (1931–) Canadian author. Notable works: *The Moons of Jupiter* (1983) and *Selected Stories* (1996).

Mun·ro |mən'rō|, H. H. see SAKI.

Mu·ra·sa·ki Shi·ki·bu |,mo͞orə'säkē 'SHēkē,bo͞o| (c. 978–c. 1031) Japanese author. Notable works: the *Tale of Genji*.

Mu·rat |,myo͞o'rä|, Joachim (c. 1767–1815) French general, king of Naples 1808–15. Murat made his name as a cavalry commander in Napoleon's Italian campaign (1800) and was made king of Naples. He attempted to become king of all Italy in 1815, but was captured in Calabria and executed.

Mur·doch |'mərdäk|, Dame (Jean) Iris (1919–99) British novelist and philosopher, born in Ireland. She is primarily known for her novels, many of which explore complex sexual relationships and spiritual life. Notable novels: *The Sandcastle* (1957) and *The Sea, The Sea* (Booker Prize, 1978), and *The Philosopher's Pupil* (1983).

Mur·doch |'mərdäk|, (Keith) Rupert (1931–) Australian-born U.S. publisher and media entrepreneur. As the founder and head of the News International Communications empire he owns

major newspapers in Australia, Britain, and the U.S., together with movie and television companies and the publishing firm HarperCollins.

Mu·ril·lo |m(y)o͞o'rēyō|, Bartolomé Esteban (c. 1618–82) Spanish painter. He is noted for his genre scenes of urchins and peasants and for his devotional pictures.

Mur·nau |'mo͞or,now|, F. W. (1888–1931) German movie director; born *Frederick Wilhelm Plumpe*. His revolutionary use of cinematic techniques to record and interpret human emotion paralleled the expressionist movement in art and drama. Notable movies: *Nosferatu* (1922), *Der letzte Mann* (1924), and *Sunrise* (1927), which won three Oscars.

Mur·phy |'mərfē|, Audie (1924–71) U.S. soldier and actor. The most decorated soldier of World War II, he appeared in war adventure movies such as *Beyond Glory* (1948) and *To Hell and Back* (1955).

Mur·phy |'mərfē|, Carl (1889–1967) U.S. journalist, publisher, and civil rights leader, and educator. He was editor of the *Baltimore Afro-American* (1922–61) and was on the board of directors of the NAACP. Spingarn Medal, 1955.

Mur·phy |'mərfē|, Eddie (1961–) U.S. actor. Notable movies: *Beverly Hills Cop* (1984) and *Coming to America* (1988).

Mur·phy |'mərfē|, Frank (1890–1949) U.S. Supreme Court justice (1940–49). Full name *Willian Francis Murphy*.

Mur·phy |'mərfē|, Turk (1915–87) U.S. jazz trombonist and band leader. Born *Melvin Edward Alton Murphy*. He formed his own band in 1947 and led it into the 1980s; he opened the Traditional Jazz Museum in San Francisco (1986).

Mur·ray |'mərē|, (George) Gilbert (Aimé) (1866–1957) Australian-born British classical scholar. His translations of Greek dramatists helped to revive interest in Greek drama. He was also a founder of the League of Nations and later a joint president of the United Nations.

Mur·ray |'mərē|, Sir James (Augustus

Henry) (1837–1915) Scottish lexicographer. He was chief editor of the *Oxford English Dictionary*, but did not live to see the work completed.

Mur·ray |'mərē|, Phillip (1886–1952) U.S. labor leader, born in Scotland. He served as president of the Congress of Industrial Organizations (1940–52) and as president of the United Steel Workers of America (1942–52).

Mur·row |'mərō |, Edward R. (1908–65) U.S. journalist. Born *Egbert Roscoe Murrow*. He produced and narrated the radio series "Hear It Now" and the television series "See It Now."

Mu·se·ve·ni, Yoweri (Kaguta) (1945–) Ugandan statesman, president since 1986. He came to power after ousting Milton Obote and brought some stability to a country that had suffered under the dictatorial Obote and Idi Amin.

Mu·si·al |'myōŏzēəl |, Stan (1920–) U.S. baseball player. Known as **Stan the Man**. He led the National League in batting seven times. Elected to the Baseball Hall of Fame (1969).

Mus·kie |'məskē |, Edmund Sixtus (1914–96) U.S. lawyer and politician. He was a member of the U.S. Senate from Maine (1959–80) and a Democratic vice presidential candidate (1968); he also served as U.S. secretary of state (1980–81).

Mus·so·li·ni |,mōŏsə'lēnē |, Benito (Amilcaro Andrea) (1883–1945) Italian Fascist statesman, prime minister (1922–43); known as **Il Duce** ("the leader"). He founded the Italian Fascist

Party in 1919. He annexed Abyssinia in 1936 and entered World War II on Germany's side in 1940. Forced to resign after the Allied invasion of Sicily, he was rescued from imprisonment by German paratroopers, but was captured and executed by Italian communist partisans.

Mus·sorg·sky |mə'zawr(g)skē |, Modest (Petrovich) (1839–81) Also **Moussorgsky**. Russian composer. His best-known works include the opera *Boris Godunov* (1874), *Songs and Dances of Death* (1875–77) and the piano suite *Pictures at an Exhibition* (1874).

Mutsuhito see MEIJI TENNO.

My·ers |'mīərz |, Russell (1938–) U.S. cartoonist. He created the comic strip, "Broom Hilda."

Myr·dal |'m(i)ər,däl| Swedish family, including: **(Karl) Gunnar Myrdal** (1898–1987), economist. He was a leading analyst of Third World development policies. Nobel Prize for Economics, 1974. His wife **Alva Myrdal** (1902–86), sociologist, government official, and peace activist. With her husband she implemented a national program for children's welfare; she shared the 1982 Nobel Peace Prize with Alfonso Garcia Robles.

My·ron |'mīrən| (*c.* 480–440 BC) Greek sculptor. None of his original work is known to survive, but there are two certain copies, one being the *Discobolus* (*c.*450 BC), a figure of a man throwing the discus, which demonstrates a remarkable interest in symmetry and movement.

Nn

Na·bo·kov |'näbə,kawf|, Vladimir (Vladimorovich) (1899–1977) Russian-born U.S. novelist and poet. He is best known for *Lolita* (1958), his novel about a middle-aged man's obsession with a twelve-year-old girl.

Na·der |'nädər|, Ralph (1934–) U.S. consumer-rights advocate. His campaign on behalf of public safety gave impetus to the consumer-rights movement from the 1960s onward and prompted legislation concerning car design, radiation hazards, food packaging, and insecticides.

Na·ga·no |nä'gänō|, Osami (1880–1947) Japanese admiral. He planned and executed the attack on Pearl Harbor.

Na·gur·ski |nə'gərskē|, Bronko (1908–90) U.S. football player. He was a charter member of the college and professional football halls of fame.

Nagy |näj|, Imre (1896–1958) Hungarian communist statesman and prime minister (1953–55 and 1956). In 1956 he withdrew Hungary from the Warsaw Pact, seeking neutral status. He was executed after the Soviet Army crushed the uprising of 1956 later that year.

Nai·paul |'nī,pawl|, V. S. (1932–) Trinidadian writer of Indian descent, resident in Britain since 1950; full name *Sir Vidiadhar Surajprasad Naipaul*. He is best known for his satirical novels, such as *A House for Mr. Biswas* (1961); *In a Free State* (1971) won the Booker Prize.

Nai·smith |'nā,smiTH|, James A. (1861–1939) U.S. physical educator. He invented the game of basketball (1891).

Na·math |'nämƏTH|, Joe (1943–) U.S. football player. Nicknamed "Broadway Joe," he was a professional quarterback (1965–78) who led the New York Jets to a 1969 Super Bowl title. Elected to the NFL Hall of Fame, 1985.

Na·nak |'nänək| (1469–1539) Indian religious leader and founder of Sikhism; known as **Guru Nanak**. Not seeking to create a new religion, he preached that spiritual liberation could be achieved through meditating on the name of God.

His teachings are contained in a number of hymns that form part of the Adi-granth.

Nan·sen |'nænsən|, Fridtjof (1861–1930) Norwegian Arctic explorer. In 1888 he led the first expedition to cross the Greenland ice fields, and five years later he sailed from Siberia for the North Pole, which he failed to reach, on board the *Fram*. He received the Nobel Peace Prize in 1922.

Na·po·le·on |nə'pōlyən; nə'pōlē(y)ən| three rulers of France: **Napoleon I** (1769–1821), emperor 1804–14 and 1815; full name *Napoleon Bonaparte*; known as **Napoleon**. In 1799 Napoleon joined a conspiracy which overthrew the Directory, becoming the supreme ruler of France. He declared himself emperor in 1804, establishing an empire stretching from Spain to Poland. After defeats at Trafalgar (1805) and in Russia (1812), he abdicated and was exiled to the island of Elba (1814). He returned to power in 1815, but was defeated at Waterloo and exiled to the island of St. Helena. **Napoleon II** (1811–1832), son of Napoleon I and Empress Marie-Louise; full name *Napoleon François Charles Joseph Bonaparte*. In 1814 Napoleon I abdicated on behalf of himself and Napoleon II, who had no active political role. **Napoleon III** (1808–73), emperor 1852–70; full name *Charles Louis Napoleon Bonaparte*; known as **Louis-Napoleon**. A nephew of Napoleon I, Napoleon III was elected President of the Second Republic in 1848 and staged a coup in 1851. He abdicated in 1870 after defeat in the Franco-Prussian War.

Na·ra·yan |nə'rīən|, R. K. (1906–) Indian novelist and short-story writer; full name *Rasipuram Krishnaswamy Narayan*. His best-known novels are set in an imaginary small Indian town, and portray its inhabitants in an affectionate yet ironic manner; they include *Swami and Friends* (1935) and *The Man-Eater of Malgudi* (1961)

Na·ra·ya·nan |nə'rīənən|, K. R.

(1920–　) Indian statesman, president since 1997; full name *Kocheril Raman Narayanan.*

Nar·vá·ez |ˌnärväˈyez|, Pánfilo de (1470?–1528) Spanish conquistador. He landed near Tampa Bay (1528) and went as far as Tallahassee in search of gold.

Nash |næSH|, Graham (1942–　) British rock musician. He was a guitarist, keyboardist, and singer with the group Crosby, Stills, Nash (and Young).

Nash |næSH|, John (1752–1835) English town planner and architect. He planned the layout of Regent's Park (1811–25), Trafalgar Square (1826–*c.*1835), and many other parts of London, and designed the Marble Arch.

Nash |næSH|, (Frederic) Ogden (1902–71) U.S. poet. His sophisticated light verse comprises puns, epigrams, and other verbal eccentricities.

Nash |næSH|, Paul (1889–1946) English painter and designer. He was a war artist in both world wars. Notable works: *Totes Meer* (1940–1).

Nash |næSH|, Richard (1674–1762) Welsh dandy; known as **Beau Nash**. He was an arbiter of fashion and etiquette in the early Georgian age.

Nashe |næSH|, Thomas (1567–1601) English pamphleteer, prose writer, and dramatist. Notable works: *The Unfortunate Traveller* (1594).

Nas·ser |ˈnæsər|, Gamal Abdel (1918–70) Egyptian colonel and statesman, prime minister (1954–56) and president (1956–70). He deposed King Farouk in 1952 and President Muhammad Neguib in 1954. His nationalization of the Suez Canal brought war with Britain, France, and Israel in 1956; he also waged two unsuccessful wars against Israel (1956 and 1967).

Nast |næst|, Thomas (1840–1902) U.S. cartoonist. He was staff artist of *Harper's Weekly* (1862–86) and creator of the Republican elephant and the Democratic donkey symbols as well as the U.S. image of Santa Claus.

Na·than |ˈnātHən|, George Jean (1882–1958) U.S. journalist. He cofounded the magazine *American Mercury* (1924) and wrote the *Encyclopaedia of the Theatre* (1940).

Na·than |ˈnātHən|, Robert (Gruntal) (1894–1985) U.S. author. Notable works: *Sleeping Beauty* (1950).

Na·tion |ˈnāSHən|, Carry Amelia (Moore) (1846–1911) U.S. temperance reformer. Her prohibitionist activism was characterized by scenes of hatchet-wielding saloon smashing, primarily in Kansas.

Na·var·ro |nəˈvärō; ˌnäˈvärō|, Fats (1923–50) U.S. jazz trumpeter. Full name *Theodore Navarro.* He was among the foremost players in the bop idiom.

Nav·ra·ti·lo·va |ˌnævrətəˈlōvə|, Martina (1956–　) Czech-born U.S. tennis player. She dominated women's tennis throughout the 1980s and won nine Wimbledon singles titles (1978–79; 1982–87; 1990).

Nde·ti |n-ˈdetē; en'detē|, Cosmas (1971–　) Kenyan runner. He won the Boston Marathon three times (1993, 1994, 1995) and set the course record of 2:07:15 (1994).

Neal |nēl|, John (1793–1876) U.S. author. Notable works: *The Down-Easters* (1833).

Neal |nēl|, Joseph Clay (1807–47) U.S. author. Notable works: *Charcoal Sketches; or, Scenes in a Metropolis* (1838).

Neal |nēl|, Patricia (1926–　) U.S. stage and movie actress. Notable movies: *Hud* (1963, Academy Award).

Near·ing |ˈnēriNG|, Scott (1883–1983) U.S. environmentalist and economist. His book *Living the Good Life* (1954) became one of the foundations of the 1960s counterculture.

Neb·u·chad·nez·zar II |ˌnebəkəd'nezər| (*c.* 630–562 BC) king of Babylon (605–562 BC). He rebuilt the city with massive walls, a huge temple, and a ziggurat and extended his rule over neighboring countries. In 586 BC he captured and destroyed Jerusalem and deported many Israelites in what is known as the Babylonian Captivity.

Nec·ker |ˈnekər|, Jacques (1732–1804) Swiss-born banker and director general of French finances (1777–81; 1788–89). In 1789 he recommended summoning the States General and was dismissed, this being one of the factors that triggered the French Revolution.

Need·ham |ˈnēdəm|, Joseph (1900–95)

English scientist and historian. Notable works: *History of Embryology* (1934) and *Science and Civilization in China* (1954).

Nee·son |'nēsən|, Liam (1952–   ) U.S. actor, born in Ireland. Notable movies: *Schindler's List* (1994).

Nef·er·ti·ti |,nefər'tētē| (14th century BC) Also **Nofretete**. Egyptian queen, wife of Akhenaten and half-sister of Tutankhamen. She is best known from the painted limestone bust of her, now in Berlin (*c.* 1350).

Ne·he·mi·ah |,nēə'mīə| (5th century BC) Hebrew leader who supervised the rebuilding of the walls of Jerusalem (*c.*444) and introduced moral and religious reforms (*c.* 432).

Neh·ru |'näro͞o|, Jawaharlal (1889–1964) Indian statesman, prime minister (1947–64); known as **Pandit Nehru**. An early associate of Mahatma Gandhi, Nehru was elected leader of the Indian National Congress in 1929. He was imprisoned nine times by the British for his nationalist campaigns, but went on to become the first prime minister of independent India.

Neill |nēl|, A. S. (1883–1973) Scottish teacher and educationist; full name *Alexander Sutherland Neill*. He founded the progressive school Summerhill, which has attracted both admiration and hostility for its anti-authoritarian ethos.

Neill |nēl|, Sam (1948–   ) New Zealand actor; born *Nigel John Dermot*. He starred in the British television series "Reilly: The Ace of Spies" (1983) and achieved international recognition with *Jurassic Park* and *The Piano* (both 1993).

Nel·son |'nelsən| U.S. family of entertainers, including: **Ozzie Nelson** (1906–75), bandleader and actor. Full name *Oswald George Nelson*. He is best remembered as the father in "The Adventures of Ozzie and Harriet," a comedy series on radio (1944–54) and television (1952–66) starring Ozzie, his wife, Harriet Hilliard Nelson, and (from 1949) their sons, David and Ricky. His son **Ricky Nelson** (1940–85), musician and actor. Full name *Eric Hilliard Nelson*. He became a teen idol with many song hits including "Hello, Mary Lou."

Nel·son |'nelsən|, Byron (1912–   )

U.S. golfer. He set the all-time PGA stroke average with 68.33 strokes per round over 120 rounds in 1945.

Nel·son |'nelsən|, Horatio, Viscount Nelson, Duke of Bronte (1758–1805) British admiral. Nelson became a national hero as a result of his victories at sea in the Napoleonic Wars, especially the Battle of Trafalgar, in which he was mortally wounded.

Nel·son |'nelsən|, Samuel (1792–1873) U.S. Supreme Court justice (1845–72).

Nel·son |'nelsən|, Willie (1933–   ) U.S. country singer and songwriter. He is noted for hits such as "A Good Hearted Woman" (1976) and the album *Red Haired Stranger* (1975).

Nem·e·rov |'nemə,rawv|, Howard (1920–91) U.S. poet and professor. U.S. poet laureate, 1988.

Nen·ni·us |'nenēəs| (*c.* 800) Welsh chronicler. He is traditionally credited with the compilation or revision of the *Historia Britonum*, which includes one of the earliest known accounts of King Arthur.

Nernst |nərnst|, Walther Hermann (1864–1941) German physical chemist. He is best known for his discovery of the third law of thermodynamics (also known as *Nernst's heat theorem*). Nobel Prize for Chemistry (1920).

Ne·ro |'nirō| (AD 37–68) Roman emperor 54–68; full name *Nero Claudius Caesar Augustus Germanicus*. Infamous for his cruelty, he wantonly executed leading Romans. His reign witnessed a fire that destroyed half of Rome in 64.

Ne·ru·da |nə'ro͞odə|, Pablo (1904–73) Chilean poet and diplomat; born *Ricardo Eliezer Neftalí Reyes*. He took his pseudonym from the Czech poet Jan Neruda. His *Canto General* (completed 1950), is an epic covering the history of the Americas. Nobel Prize for Literature (1971).

Ner·va |'nərvə|, Marcus Cocceius (*c.* 30–98 AD) Roman emperor 96–8. He returned to a liberal and constitutional form of rule after the autocracy of his predecessor, Domitian.

Ner·vi |'nervē|, Pier Luigi (1891–1979) Italian engineer and architect. A pioneer of reinforced concrete, he codesigned the UNESCO building in Paris (1953) and designed the Pirelli skyscraper in Milan (1958) and San Francisco cathedral (1970).

Nes·bit |'nesbət|, E. (1858–1924) English novelist; full name *Edith Nesbit*. She is best known for her children's books, including *Five Children and It* (1902) and *The Railway Children* (1906).

Net·an·ya·hu |ˌnet(ə)n'yähoo|, Benjamin (1949–) Israeli Likud statesman, prime minister since 1996. Leader of the right-wing Likud coalition since 1993, he narrowly defeated Shimon Peres in the elections of 1996.

Neu·mann |'noimän|, John von (1903–57) Hungarian-born U.S. mathematician and computer pioneer. He pioneered game theory and the design and operation of electronic computers.

Neu·tra |'noitrə; 'n(y)ootrə|, Richard Josef (1892–1970) U.S. architect, born in Austria. Notable designs: Mathematics Park (New Jersey) and Orange County courthouse (California).

Neu·wirth |'n(y)oo'(w)ərth|, Bebe (1958–) U.S. actress. Tony Award, 1997.

Nev·ers |'nevərz|, Ernest Alonzo (1903–76) U.S. athlete. A professional player of both baseball and football, he set an NFL single-game scoring record of 40 points (1929).

Nev·ille |'nevəl|, Richard see WARWICK, RICHARD NEVILLE.

Nev·ins |'nevənz|, Allan (1890–1971) U.S. historian and author. Notable works: *Grover Cleveland* (1932, Pulitzer Prize) and *Hamilton Fish* (1936, Pulitzer Prize).

Nev·sky |'nevskē|, Alexander see ALEXANDER NEVSKY.

New·cas·tle |'n(y)oo,kæsəl|, Thomas Pelham-Holles, 1st Duke of (1693–1768) British Whig statesman, prime minister (1754–56 and 1757–62). During his second term in office he headed a coalition with William Pitt the Elder.

New·comb |'n(y)ookəm|, Simon (1835–1909) U.S. astronomer, born in Canada. His tables of the planetary system were used throughout the world.

New·combe |'n(y)ookəm|, John (1944–) Australian tennis player. He won Wimbledon three times and the

U.S. and Australian championships twice each.

New·ell |'n(y)ooəl|, Robert Henry (1836–1901) U.S. journalist and humorist. Pseudonym **Orpheus C. Kerr** (a play on the words "office seeker&cqq). Notable works: *The Orpheus C. Kerr Papers* (1862–71).

New·hart |'n(y)oohärt|, Bob (1929–) U.S. entertainer He starred in the television series "The Bob Newhart Show" (1971–78) and "Newhart" (1982–90).

New·house |'n(y)oohows|, Samuel I., Jr. (1895–1979) U.S. publisher and philanthropist. He served as the chairman of Conde Nast Publications, Inc.

Ne Win |'ne 'win|, U (1911–) Burmese general and socialist statesman, prime minister (1958–60), head of state (1962–74), and president (1974–81). After the military coup in 1962 he established a military dictatorship and formed a one-party state.

New·lands |'n(y)oolən(d)z|, John Alexander Reina (1837–98) English industrial chemist. He proposed a form of periodic table shortly before Dmitri Mendeleev, based on a supposed *law of octaves* according to which similar chemical properties recurred in every eighth element.

New·man |'n(y)oomən|, Barnett (1905–70) U.S. painter A seminal figure in color-field painting, he juxtaposed large blocks of uniform color with narrow marginal strips of contrasting colors.

New·man |'n(y)oomən|, John Henry (1801–90) English prelate and theologian. A founder of the Oxford Movement, in 1845 he turned to Roman Catholicism, becoming a cardinal in 1879.

New·man |'n(y)oomən|, Paul (1925–) U.S. actor and movie director. Among his many movies are *Butch Cassidy and the Sundance Kid* (1969), *The Sting* (1973), *The Color of Money* (1987), for which he won an Oscar, and *The Glass Menagerie* (1987), which he also directed. He was also known for his philanthropic activities.

New·port |'n(y)oo,pawrt|, Christopher (1565?–1617) English sailor. The founder of Jamestown, Virginia (1606–

7), he was shipwrecked on Bermuda (1609), procuring it as a colony for England.

New·ton |'n(y)ōōtn|, A. Edward (1863–1940) U.S. book collector and author. Full name *Alfred Edward Newton*.

New·ton |'n(y)ōōtn|, Sir Isaac (1642–1727) English mathematician and physicist, considered the greatest single influence on theoretical physics until Einstein. In his *Principia Mathematica* (1687), Newton gave a mathematical description of the laws of mechanics and gravitation, and applied these to planetary motion. *Opticks* (1704) records his optical experiments and theories, including the discovery that white light is made up of a mixture of colors. His work in mathematics included the binomial theorem and differential calculus.

Ney |nā|, Michel (1769–1815) French marshal. He was one of Napoleon's leading generals, and commanded the French cavalry at Waterloo (1815).

Nga·ta |'NGätä;en'gätə|, Sir Apirana Turupa (1874–1950) New Zealand Maori leader and politician. As Minister for Native Affairs he devoted much time to Maori resettlement, seeking to preserve the characteristic elements of their life and culture.

Ngo Dinh Diem |(ə)'NGō 'din di'(y)em| (1901–63) President of the Republic of South Vietnam (1956–63) He was assassinated in a military coup d'état.

Nich·o·las |'nik(ə)ləs|, St. (4th century) Christian prelate. Said to have been bishop of Myra in Lycia, he is the patron saint of children, sailors, Greece, and Russia. The persona of Santa Claus (a corruption of his name) originated from the Dutch custom of giving gifts to children on his feast day (December 6).

Nich·o·las I |'nikələs| two czars of Russia: **Nicholas I** (1796–1855; reigned 1825–55), brother of Alexander I. At home he pursued rigidly conservative policies, while his expansionism in the Near East led to the Crimean War. **Nicholas II** (1868–1918; reigned 1894–1917), son of Alexander III. Forced to abdicate after the Russian Revolution in 1917, he was shot along with his family a year later.

Nich·ols |'nikəlz|, Mike (1931–) U.S.

director. Born *Michael Igor Peschowsky*. Notable movies: *The Graduate* (1967, Academy Award).

Nich·ols |'nikəlz|, Red (1905–65) U.S. jazz cornetist and band leader. Full name *Ernest Loring Nichols*. He was the most prolifically recorded white jazz bandleader of the 1920s.

Nich·ols |'nikəlz|, Terry (1955–) U.S. terrorist. A coconspirator with Timothy McVeigh, he was sentenced to life imprisonment for his role in the bombing of Oklahoma City's Alfred P. Murrah Federal Building in 1995.

Nich·ols |'nikəlz|, Thomas Low (1815–1901) U.S. journalist and author. Notable works: *Forty Years of American Life: 1821–61* (1864).

Nich·ol·son |'nikəlsən|, Ben (1894–1981) English painter; full name *Benjamin Lauder Nicholson*. He was a pioneer of British abstract art, noted for his painted reliefs with circular and rectangular motifs.

Nich·ol·son |'nikəlsən|, Jack (1937–) U.S. actor. He won Oscars for *One Flew Over the Cuckoo's Nest* (1975), *Terms of Endearment* (1983), and *As Good As It Gets* (1997). Other movies include *Easy Rider* (1969), *Chinatown* (1974), *The Shining* (1980), *Prizzi's Honor* (1985), and *Batman* (1989).

Nick·laus |'nikləs|, Jack William (1940–) U.S. golfer. He has won more than eighty tournaments during his professional career, including six wins in the PGA championship, five in the Masters, four in the U.S. Open, and three in the British Open.

Nicks |niks|, Stevie (1948–) U.S. rock musician. Full name *Stephanie Nicks*. She performed with the group Fleetwood Mac.

Nic·o·lay |'nikə,lā|, John George (1832–1901) U.S. journalist, born in Germany. He was Abraham Lincoln's private secretary and biographer.

Ni·col·let |,nikə'let|, Joseph Nicolas (1786–1843) U.S. explorer, born in France. With John Fremont, he mapped the region between the upper Mississippi and Missouri rivers.

Nie·buhr |'nēbər|, Reinhold (1892–1971) U.S. theologian and political activist. Notable works: *Moral Man and*

Immoral Society (1932) and *The Irony of American History* (1952).

Niel·son |'nilsən|, Carl August (1865–1931) Danish composer. He is best known for his six symphonies (1890–1925).

Nie·mey·er |'nē,mīər|, Oscar (1907–) Brazilian architect. An early exponent of modernist architecture in Latin America, he designed the main public buildings of Brasilia (1950–60).

Nie·möl·ler |'nē,mOElər; 'nē,mələr|, Martin (1892–1984) German Lutheran pastor. An outspoken opponent of Nazism, he was imprisoned in Sachsenhausen and Dachau concentration camps (1937–45).

Nietz·sche |'nēCHə; 'nēCHē|, Friedrich Wilhelm (1844–1900) German philosopher. He is known for repudiating Christianity's compassion for the weak, exalting the "will to power," and formulating the idea of the *Übermensch* (superman), who can rise above the restrictions of ordinary morality.

Nieuw·land |'n(y)o͞o,lənd|, Julius Arthur (1878–1936) U.S. chemist and botanist, born in Belgium. He synthesized organic compounds, including rubber.

Night·in·gale |'nītn,gāl|, Florence (1820–1910) English nurse and medical reformer. In 1854, during the Crimean War, she improved sanitation and medical procedures at the army hospital at Scutari, achieving a dramatic reduction in the mortality rate. She became known as the "Lady of the Lamp" for her nightly rounds.

Ni·jin·sky |ni'zHinskē; ni'jinskē|, Vaslav (Fomich) (1890–1950) Russian ballet dancer and choreographer. The leading dancer with Diaghilev's Ballets Russes from 1909, he went on to choreograph Debussy's *L'Après-midi d'un faune* (1912) and Stravinsky's *The Rite of Spring* (1913).

Nils·son |'nilsən|, (Märta) Birgit (1922–) Swedish operatic soprano. She gained international success in the 1950s, being particularly noted for her interpretation of Wagnerian roles.

Nim·itz |'nimits|, Chester William (1885–1966) U.S. naval officer. He was chief of the Bureau of Navigation

(1939–41) and became commander in chief of the Pacific Fleet after Pearl Harbor (1941). Aboard his flagship, the USS *Missouri*, he was the U.S. signatory on the occasion of Japanese surrender (1945). He then served as chief of naval operations (1945–47).

Nin |nēn|, Anaïs (1903–77) U.S. writer. She published her first novel, *House of Incest*, in 1936 and went on to produce collections of short stories, essays, diaries, and erotica.

Ni·ño |'nēn,yō|, Pedro Alonzo (1468?–1505) Spanish navigator. He navigated the ship *Niña* on Columbus's first voyage to the New World.

Ni·ro |'nērō|, Robert De see DE NIRO.

Niv·en |'nivən|, David (1909–83) U.S. actor. Notable movies: *Separate Tables* (1958, Academy Award).

Nix·on |'niksən| Richard Milhous, see box. **Pat Nixon** (1912–93), wife of Richard Nixon and U.S. first lady (1969–74); born *Thelma Catherine Ryan*.

Nko·mo |(ə)NG'kawmō|, Joshua (Mqabuko Nyongolo) (1917–) Zimbabwean statesman, leader of the Zimbabwe African People's Union (ZAPU). He returned to the cabinet in 1988, when the Zimbabwe African National Union and ZAPU agreed to merge, and became vice president in 1990.

Nkru·mah |(ə)NG'kro͞omə|, Kwame (1909–72) Ghanaian statesman, prime minister (1957–60), president (1960–66). The first prime minister after independence, he became increasingly dictatorial and was finally overthrown in a military coup.

No·bel |nō'bel|, Alfred Bernhard (1833–96) Swedish chemist and engineer. He invented dynamite (1866), gelignite, and other high explosives, making a large fortune which enabled him to endow the prizes that bear his name.

No·gu·chi |nō'go͞oCHē|, Isamu (1904–88) U.S. sculptor and designer. Notable designs: two bridges for Peace Park (Hiroshima, 1952); the Billy Rose Sculpture Garden (the Israeli Museum, Jerusalem, 1960–65).

No·lan |'nōlən|, Sir Sidney Robert (1917–92) Australian painter, known

Nixon, Richard Milhous
37th U.S. president

Life dates: 1913–1994
Place of birth: Yorba Linda, California
Mother: Hannah Milhous Nixon
Father: Francis Anthony Nixon
Wife: Pat (Thelma Catharine Ryan) Nixon
Children: Patricia (Tricia), Julie
College/University: Whittier College; Duke University Law School
Military service: U.S. Navy lieutenant, World War II
Career: lawyer
Political career: U.S. House of Representatives; U.S. Senate; vice president (under Eisenhower); president
Party: Republican
Home state: New York
Opponents in presidential races: defeated by John F. Kennedy in 1960; Hubert H. Humphrey, George C. Wallace (1968); George McGovern (1972)
Term of office: Jan. 20, 1969–Aug. 9, 1974 (resigned)
Vice presidents: Spiro T. Agnew (resigned); Gerald R. Ford
Notable events of presidency: U.S. troops sent to Cambodia and Laos; Kent State University incident; Environmental Protection Agency created; Daniel Ellsberg disclosed "Pentagon Papers"; Twenty-Sixth Amendment to the Constitution (lowering voting age to 18) ratified; U.S. combat ground troops departed from Vietnam; burglary of Democratic National Convention headquarters at Watergate Hotel; Watergate scandal; Wounded Knee incident; Arab-Israeli War; Federal Energy Administration created; impeachment hearings in the House Judiciary Committee
Other achievements: first president to visit Communist China; published *Six Crises; RN: The Memoirs of Richard Nixon;* and *The Real War*
Place of burial: New York, New York

for his paintings of famous characters and events from Australian history.

Noll |nŏl|, Chuck (1932–) U.S. football coach. Full name *Charles Henry Noll.* He coached the Pittsburgh Steelers to four Super Bowl titles.

Nor·di·ca |'nawrdəkə|, Lillian (1857–1914) U.S. soprano. Born Lillian Norton. She was the first American opera singer to gain international fame.

Nord·strom |'nawrdstrəm|, Ursula (1910–88) U.S. editor. She worked for Harper & Row from 1936 and became its first female vice president in 1960; she launched the careers of many authors, including Charlotte Zolotow and Maurice Sendak.

No·ri·e·ga |ˌnawrē'ägə|, Manuel (Antonio Morena) (1939–) Panamanian statesman and general, head of state 1983–9. Charged with drug trafficking by a U.S. grand jury in 1988, he eventually surrendered to U.S. troops sent into Panama and was brought to trial, convicted, and imprisoned in 1992.

Nor·man |'nawrmən|, Greg (1955–) Australian golfer; full name *Gregory John Norman.* He has won the world match-play championship three times (1980; 1983; 1986) and the British Open twice (1986; 1993).

Nor·man |'nawrmən|, Jessye (1945–) U.S. operatic soprano. She is noted for her interpretations of the works of Wagner, Schubert, and Mahler.

Nor·ris |'nawrəs|, Frank (1870–1902) U.S. author. Born *Benjamin Franklin Norris.* His unfinished trilogy *Epic of Wheat* documents the history of muckraking.

Nor·ris |'nawrəs|, George William (1861–1944) U.S. politician. As a member of the U.S. Senate from Nebraska (1913–43), he founded the Tennessee Valley Authority.

North |nawrᴛн|, Frederick, Lord (1732–92) British Tory statesman and prime minister 1770–82. He sought to avoid the Revolutionary War, but was regarded as responsible for the loss of the American colonies.

North |nawrᴛн|, Oliver (1943–) U.S. soldier. He provided testimony to Congress on the Iran-contra affair, saying he believed that all of his activities were authorized by his superiors (1986).

North·cliffe |'nawrᴛнklif|, Alfred Charles William Harmsworth, 1st Viscount (1865–1922) British newspaper publisher. He built up a large newspaper empire, including *The Times,* the *Daily Mail,* and the *Daily Mirror.*

Nor·ton |'nawrtən|, Charles Eliot (1827–1908) U.S. educator and author. He was the editor of *North American Review* (1864–68) and the first American professor of fine arts (Harvard, 1874–98).

Nor·ton |'nawrtən|, Eleanor Holms (1937–) U.S. lawyer and educator. She has been assistant director of the ACLU (1965–70) and professor of law at Georgetown University (1982–).

Nor·ton |'nawrtən|, Mary (1903–92) English author and actress. She wrote *The Borrowers* series of books for children.

Nos·tra·da·mus |,nawstrə'däməs| (1503–66) French astrologer and physician; Latinized name of *Michel de Nostredame*. His cryptic and apocalyptic predictions in rhyming quatrains appeared in two collections (1555 and 1558), and their interpretation continues to be the subject of controversy.

No·vel·lo |nō'velō|, Ivor (1893–1951) Welsh composer, songwriter, actor, and dramatist; born *David Ivor Davies*. In 1914 he wrote "Keep the Home Fires Burning," which became one of the most popular songs of World War I.

No·verre |naw'ver|, Jean-Georges (1727–1810) French choreographer and dance theorist, who stressed the importance of dramatic motivation in ballet as opposed to technical virtuosity.

No·vot·ný |'nawvawt,nē|, Antonín (1904–75) Czechoslovak communist statesman, president 1957–68. A founding member of the Czechoslovak Communist Party (1921), he played a major part in the communist seizure of power in 1948. He was ousted by the reform movement in 1968.

Noyce |nois|, Robert Norton (1927–90) U.S. engineer. He was a co-inventor of the integrated circuit, and with Gordon Moore he founded Intel Corp. (1968).

Noyes |noiz|, Alfred (1880–1958) English poet. Notable works: *The Flower of Old Japan* (1903) and *Drake* (1908).

Noyes |noiz|, John Humphrey (1811–86) U.S. social reformer. A propounder of the doctrine of Perfectionism, which held that human moral and spiritual perfection is attainable, he formed societies at Putney, Vermont (1839) and Oneida, New York (1848–79).

Nuf·field |'nəfēld|, William Richard Morris, 1st Viscount (1877–1963) British automotive manufacturer and philanthropist, who opened the first Morris automobile factory in Oxford in 1912. He endowed Nuffield College, Oxford (1937) and created the Nuffield Foundation (1943) for medical, social, and scientific research.

Nu·re·yev |noo'räef; 'noorä,(y)ev|, Rudolf (1938–93) Russian-born ballet dancer and choreographer. He defected to the West in 1961, joining the Royal Ballet in London, where he began his noted partnership with Margot Fonteyn. He became a naturalized Austrian citizen in 1982.

Nur·mi |'nərmē|, Paavo Johannes (1897–1973) Finnish distance runner. He won seven Olympic gold medals (1920–28) and held a world record for the mile (1923–31).

Nye·re·re |ni'rerē|, Julius Kambarage (1922–) Tanzanian statesman, president of Tanganyika (1962–64) and of Tanzania (1964–85). He led Tanganyika to independence in 1961 and in 1964 successfully negotiated a union with Zanzibar, creating the new state of Tanzania.

Ny·ro |'nērō|, Laura (1947–97) U.S. songwriter and singer. Born *Laura Nigro*. Notable songs: "Wedding Bell Blues," "Blowin' Away," and "And When I Die."

Oo

Oak·ley |'ōklē|, Annie (1860–1926) U.S. markswomen; full name *Phoebe Anne Oakley Mozee.* In 1885 she joined Buffalo Bill's Wild West Show, of which she became a star attraction for the next 17 years.

Oates |'ōts|, Joyce Carol (1938–) U.S. author and educator. Notable works: *A Sentimental Education* (1981).

Oates |'ōts|, Titus (1649–1705) English clergyman and conspirator, remembered as the fabricator of the Popish Plot (1678). Convicted of perjury in 1685, Oates was imprisoned in the same year, but subsequently was released and granted a pension.

Oba·ta |ˌō'bätə|, Gyo (1923–) U.S. architect. Notable designs: the National Air and Space Museum of the Smithsonian Institution (Washington, D.C.).

Obo·te |aw'baw,tā|, (Apollo) Milton (1924–) Ugandan statesman, prime minister (1962–66), president (1966–71 and 1980–85). Overthrown by Idi Amin in 1971, he was re-elected president in 1980. He was removed in a second military coup in 1985.

O'Bri·an |ˌō'brīən|, Patrick (1932–) English author. He wrote the Aubrey-Maturin novels and works of British naval history.

O'Bri·en |ō'brīən|, Conan (1963–) U.S. television actor, producer, and writer. He wrote for "Saturday Night Live" and hosted the "Late Night" program.

O'Bri·en |ō'brīən|, Edna (1932–) Irish novelist and short-story writer, noted especially for her novel *The Country Girls* (1960).

O'Bri·en |ō'brīən|, Flann (1911–66) Irish novelist and journalist; pseudonym of *Brian O'Nolan.* Writing under the name of Myles na Gopaleen, he contributed a satirical column to the *Irish Times* for nearly twenty years. Notable novels: *At Swim-Two-Birds* (1939); *The Third Policeman* (1967).

O'Bri·en |ō'brīən|, Tim (1946–) U.S. author. Notable works: *Tomcat in Love*

(1998), *In the Lake of the Woods* (1994), and *Going After Cacciato* (1978).

O'Ca·sey |ō'kāsē|, Sean (1880–1964) Irish dramatist. His plays, such as *The Shadow of a Gunman* (1923) and *Juno and the Paycock* (1924), deal with the Irish poor before and during the civil war that followed the establishment of the Irish Free State (1922). He also wrote an autobiography in several volumes.

Oc·cam, William of |'äkəm| see WILLIAM OF OCCAM.

Ochs |ōks|, Adolph Simon (1858–1935) U.S. publisher. He acquired *The New York Times* (1896) and made it one of the nation's preeminent newspapers.

Ochs |ōks|, Phil (1940–76) U.S. folksinger and songwriter. He was popular in 1960s protest circles for his songs "I Ain't a Marchin'" and "Draft Dodger Rag."

Ock·ham, William of see WILLIAM OF OCCAM.

O'Con·nell |ō'känəl|, Daniel (1775–1847) Irish nationalist leader and social reformer; known as **the Liberator**. His election to Parliament in 1828 forced the British government to grant Catholic Emancipation in order to enable him to take his seat in the House of Commons. In 1839 he established the Repeal Association to abolish the union with Britain.

O'Con·nor |ō'känər|, Carroll (1924–) U.S. actor, writer, and producer. He starred in the television series "All in the Family" (1971–79).

O'Con·nor |ō'känər|, Flannery (1925–64) U.S. novelist and short-story writer. Full name *Mary Flannery O'Connor.* Notable novels: *Wise Blood* (1952) and *The Violent Bear It Away* (1960).

O'Con·nor |ō'känər|, Sandra Day (1930–) U.S. Supreme Court justice (1981–). She was the first woman appointed to the U.S. Supreme Court.

O'Con·nor |ō'känər|, Sinéad (1966–) Irish pop singer.

Oc·ta·vi·an |äk'tāvēən| see AUGUSTUS.

Odets |ō'dets|, Clifford (1906–63) U.S.

dramatist. He was a founding member in 1931 of the avant garde Group Theater, which staged his best-known play, *Waiting for Lefty* (1935). His plays of the 1930s reflect the experiences of the Depression.

O'Don·nell |ō'dänəl|, Rosie (1962–) U.S. actress and talk show host. She has hosted television's "Rosie O'Donnell Show" since 1995; her acting credits include the movies *A League of Their Own* (1992) and *Harriet the Spy* (1996) and the stage musical *Grease* (1994).

Oer·ter |'awrtər|, Al (1936–) U.S. track and field athlete. He holds an Olympic record for consecutive medals, winning the discus 1956–68.

Of·fa |'awfə| (died 796) king of Mercia 757–96. He organized the construction of Offa's Dyke.

Of·fen·bach |'awfən,bäk|, Jacques (1819–80) German composer, resident in France fromx 1833; born *Jacob Offenbach*. He is associated with the rise of the operetta, whose style is typified by his *Orpheus in the Underworld* (1858). Other notable works: *The Tales of Hoffmann* (1881).

Og·den |'ägdən|, Peter Skene (1794–1854) Canadian explorer. He discovered the Humboldt River (1828); Ogden, Utah, is named for him.

Ogle·thorpe |'ōgəl,THawrp|, James Edward (1696–1785) British soldier, philanthropist, and member of Parliament (1722–54). He received the charter for the colony of Georgia (1732) and founded Savannah.

O'Ha·ra |ō'herə|, Frank (1926–66) U.S. poet and art critic. He won a National Book Award for *Selected Poems* (1973).

O'Ha·ra |ō'herə|, John (Henry) (1905–70) U.S. author. Notable works: *Butterfield 8* (1935); *A Rage to Live* (1949); and *From the Terrace* (1958).

O'Hig·gins |ō'higinz|, Bernardo (*c.* 1778–1842) Chilean revolutionary leader and statesman, head of state 1817–23. With the help of José de San Martín, he led the army that defeated Spanish forces in 1817 and paved the way for Chilean independence the following year.

Ohm |ōm|, Georg Simon (1789–1854) German physicist. The units ohm and

mho are named after him, as is Ohm's Law on electricity.

O'Keeffe |ō'kēf|, Georgia (1887–1986) U.S. painter. Her best-known paintings depict enlarged flowers and are often regarded as sexually symbolic (for example, *Black Iris*, 1926). She married photographer Alfred Stieglitz in 1924.

Olaf |'ō,läf; 'ōləf| five kings of Norway: **Olaf I Tryggvason** (969–1000; reigned 995–1000). **Olaf II Haraldsson** (*c.* 995–1030; reigned 1016–30). Canonized as **St. Olaf** for his attempts to spread Christianity in his kingdom, he is the patron saint of Norway. Feast day, July 29. **Olaf III Haraldsson** (died 1093; reigned 1066–93). **Olaf IV Haakonsson** (1370–87; reigned 1380–87). **Olaf V** (1903–91; reigned 1957–91). Full name *Olaf Alexander Edmund Christian Frederik*.

Ola·ju· |ə'läzHə,wän|, Hakeem (1963–) U.S. basketball player, born in Nigeria.

Ol·den·burg |'ōldən,bərg|, Claes Thure (1929–) U.S. pop artist and sculptor, born in Sweden.

Old Pretender see STUART, JAMES.

Olds |ōldz|, Ransom Eli (1864–1950) U.S. inventor and manufacturer. He created the Oldsmobile, the first commercially successful American car (1901).

Olds |ōldz|, Sharon (1942–) U.S. poet. Notable works: *The Father*(1993).

Oli·phant |'äləfənt|, Pat (1935–) U.S. political cartoonist and artist, born in Australia. He is syndicated internationally.

Ol·i·ver |'äləvər|, King (1885–1938) U.S. jazz cornetist and band leader. Full name *Joe Oliver*. In Chicago and New Orleans he played with newcomer Louis Armstrong in King Oliver's Creole Jazz Band.

Ol·i·ver |'äləvər|, Mary (1935–) U.S. poet. Notable works: *American Primitive* (1983, Pulitzer Prize) and *New and Selected Poems* (1992, National Book Award).

Ol·i·ver |'äləvər|, Sy (Melvin James) (1910–88) U.S. jazz trumpeter, composer, and conductor. He played with Tommy Dorsey's orchestra.

Oliv·ier |ə'livē,ā|, Laurence (Kerr), Baron Olivier of Brighton (1907–89)

English actor and director. Following his professional debut in 1924, he performed all the major Shakespearean roles; he was also director of the National Theatre (1963–73). His movies include *Rebecca* (1940), *HenryV* (1944), and *Hamlet* (1948).

Olm·sted |'ŏm͵sted|, Frederick Law (1822–1903) U.S. architect. He designed Central Park in New York and Fairmount Park in Philadelphia.

Ol·sen |'ōlsən|, Kenneth H. (1926–) U.S. engineer and inventor. The inventor of magnetic core memory, he helped develop the modern computer.

Ol·sen |'ōlsən|, Tillie (1913–) U.S. author. Notable works: *Silences* (1978).

Omar I |'ō͵mär| (*c.* 581–644) Muslim caliph (634–44). He conquered Syria, Palestine, and Egypt.

Omar Khay·yám |'ō͵mär ͵kī'(y)äm; ͵kī(y)æm| (*c.* 1048–1131) Persian poet, mathematician, and astronomer. His *rubáiyát* (quatrains), found in *The Rubáiyát of Omar Khayyám* (translation published 1859), are meditations on the mysteries of existence and celebrations of worldly pleasures.

Onas·sis |ō'næsəs|, Aristotle (Socrates) (1900?–75) Greek shipping magnate and international businessman. He owned a substantial shipping empire and founded the Greek national airline, Olympic Airways (1957).

Onas·sis |ō'næsəs|, Jacqueline Lee Bouvier Kennedy (1929–94) U.S. first lady; known as **Jackie O**. She married John F. Kennedy in 1953, serving as first lady during his presidency (1961–63). Widowed in 1963, she married Aristotle Onassis (1968). After his death (1975), she pursued a career in publishing.

On·daat·je |än'dätyə|, (Philip) Michael (1943–) Sri Lankan-born Canadian writer. Notable works: *Running in the Family* (autobiography, 1982); *The English Patient* (novel; Booker Prize, 1992).

O'Neal |ō'nēl|, Shaquille (1972–) U.S. basketball player.

O'Neill |ō'nēl|, Eugene (Gladstone) (1888–1953) U.S. dramatist. He was awarded the Pulitzer Prize for his first full-length play, *Beyond the Horizon* (1920). Other notable works: *The Em-*

peror Joves (1920), *Anna Christie* (1921), *Desire Under the Elms* (1924), *Mourning Becomes Electra* (1931), and *The Iceman Cometh* (1946). *Long Day's Journey into Night* appeared posthumously in 1956. Nobel Prize for Literature (1936).

Ono |'ōnō|, Yoko (1933–) U.S. musician and artist, born in Japan. She married John Lennon in 1969 and collaborated with him on various experimental recordings. Ono also recorded her own albums.

Oort |awrt|, Jan Hendrik (1900–92) Dutch astronomer. He proved that the Galaxy is rotating, and determined the position and orbital period of the sun within it.

Opel |'ōpel|, Wilhelm von (1871–1948) German automotive manufacturer. His company was the first in Germany to introduce assembly-line production, selling over one million cars.

Opie |'ōpē|, John (1761–1807) English painter. His work includes portraits and history paintings such as *The Murder of Rizzio* (1787).

Op·pen·hei·mer |'äp(ə)n͵hīmər|, Julius Robert (1904–67) U.S. theoretical physicist. He was director of the laboratory at Los Alamos during the development of the first atom bomb, but opposed the development of the hydrogen bomb after the Second World War.

Op·per |'äpər|, Frederick Burr (1857–1937) U.S. cartoonist. He is best known for the comic strips "Happy Hooligan," "And Her Name Was Maud!" and "Alphonse and Gaston."

Orange, William of William III of Great Britain and Ireland (see WILLIAM).

Or·bi·son |'awrbə͵sən|, Roy (1936–88) U.S. rock-and-roll singer and songwriter. Notable songs: "Only the Lonely" (1960) and "Oh, Pretty Woman" (1964).

Or·ca·gna |awr'känyä| (*c.* 1308–68) Italian painter, sculptor, and architect; born *Andrea di Cione*. His paintings include frescoes and an altarpiece in the church of Santa Maria Novella, Florence (1357).

Or·czy |'awrtsē|, Baroness Emmusca (1865–1947) Hungarian-born British novelist. Her best-known novel is *The Scarlet Pimpernel* (1905).

Orff |awrf|, Carl (1895–1982) German composer. He is best known for his secular cantata *Carmina Burana* (1937), based on a collection of characteristically bawdy medieval Latin poems.

Or·i·gen |'awri,jen| (*c.* 185–*c.* 254) Christian scholar and theologian, probably born in Alexandria, Egypt. His most famous work was the *Hexapla*, an edition of the Old Testament with six or more parallel versions. His Neoplatonist theology was ultimately rejected by Church orthodoxy.

Or·man·dy |'awrməndē|, Eugene (1899–1985) U.S. conductor, born in Hungary. Born *Jeno Blau*. He was conductor of the Philadelphia Orchestra from 1938 to 1980, the longest directorship in U.S. history.

Oroz·co |ō'rōskō; ō'rawskō|, José Clemente (1883–1949) Mexican artist. He was the most important 20th-century muralist to work in fresco.

Orr |awr|, Bobby (1948–   ) U.S. hockey player (1966–77), born in Canada. Full name **Robert Gordon Orr**. Led the National Hockey League in scoring twice and assists five times.

Or·te·ga |awr'tāgə|, Daniel (1945–   ) Nicaraguan statesman, president (1985–90); full name *Daniel Ortega Saavedra*. He became the leader of the Sandinista National Liberation Front (FSLN) in 1966 and became president after the Sandinista election victory in 1984.

Or·te·ga y Gas·set |,awr'tāgə ē 'gäsət|, José (1883–1955) Spanish philosopher. His works include *The Revolt of the Masses* (1930), in which he proposed leadership by an intellectual elite.

Or·ton |'awrtən|, Joe (1933–67) English dramatist; born *John Kingsley Orton*. He wrote a number of unconventional black comedies, examining corruption, sexuality, and violence; they include *Entertaining Mr. Sloane* (1964) and *Loot* (1965).

Or·well |'awr,wel|, George (1903–50) British novelist and essayist, born in India; pseudonym of *Eric Arthur Blair*. His work is characterized by his concern about social injustice. His most famous works are *Animal Farm* (1945), a satire on Communism as it developed under

Stalin, and *Nineteen Eighty-four* (1949), a dystopian account of a future state in which every aspect of life is controlled by Big Brother.

Ory |'awrē|, Kid (1886–1973) U.S. jazz trombonist and bandleader. Full name *Edward Ory*. He composed "Muskrat Ramble" and was the leader of the Spikes' Seven Pods of Pepper, the first New Orleans style jazz band to record.

Os·borne |'äz,bawrn|, Thomas Mott (1859–1926) U.S. prison reformer. He resigned as warden of Sing Sing prison (1914–15) because of public hostility toward his system of self-government for inmates.

Os·bourne |'äz,bawrn; 'äzbərn|, John (James) (1929–94) English dramatist His first play, *Look Back in Anger* (1956), ushered in a new era of kitchen-sink drama; its hero Jimmy Porter personified contemporary disillusioned youth, the so-called "angry young man." Later plays include *The Entertainer* (1957) and *Luther* (1961).

Os·ce·o·la |,äsē'ōlə; ,ōsē'ōlə| (*c.* 1804–38) Native American leader of the Seminole Indians. A successful leader during the Seminole Wars (1835–42), he was captured while bearing a flag of truce.

Os·ler |'äslər|, Sir William (1849–1919) Canadian-born physician and classical scholar. His *Principles and Practice of Medicine* (1892) became the chosen clinical textbook for medical students.

Os·man I |'äs,män; 'äsmən| (1258–1326) Also **Othman**. Turkish conqueror, founder of the Ottoman (Osmanli) dynasty and empire. Osman reigned as sultan of the Seljuk Turks from 1288, conquering NW Asia Minor. He assumed the title of emir in 1299.

Os·ta·de |'äs,tädə|, Adriaen van (1610–85) Dutch painter and engraver. His work chiefly depicts lively genre scenes of peasants carousing or brawling in crowded taverns or barns.

O'Sul·li·van |ō'sələvən|, Maureen (1911–98) U.S. actress, born in Ireland. She starred as Jane in the *Tarzan* series and appeared in Woody Allen's *Hannah and Her Sisters*(1986).

O'Sul·li·van |ō'sələvən|, Timothy H. (1840–82) U.S. photographer. He took photographs of Civil War battles, the southwestern U.S., and Panama.

Os·wald |'äz,wawld|, Lee Harvey (1939–63) U.S. alleged assassin of President John F. Kennedy. He denied the charge of assassinating the president, but was murdered before he could be brought to trial. Oswald's role in the assassination remains the focus for a number of conspiracy theories.

Os·wald of York |'äs,wawld|, St. (c. 925–992) English prelate and Benedictine monk. As Archbishop of York, he founded several monasteries and, with St. Dunstan, revived the Church and learning in 10th-century England. Feast day, February 28.

Oth·man Variant form of OSMAN I.

Otho |'ōTHō|, Marcus Salvius (AD 32–69) Roman emperor (January–April 69). He was proclaimed emperor after he had procured the death of Galba in a conspiracy of the praetorian guard, but the German legions, led by their imperial candidate, Vitellius, defeated his troops, and Otho committed suicide.

Otis |'ōtəs|, Elisha Graves (1811–61) U.S. inventor and manufacturer. He produced the first efficient elevator with a safety device to prevent it from falling (1852).

Otis |'ōtəs|, James (1725–83) American revolutionary statesman. He led the majority in the Massachusetts legislature (1766–69) and opposed various revenue acts.

O'Toole |ō'tōōl|, Peter (Seamus) (1932–) Irish-born British actor. Notable movies include *Lawrence of Arabia* (1962) and *Goodbye Mr. Chips* (1969); he is especially noted for his portrayals of eccentric characters.

Ott |ät|, Mel (1909–58) U.S. baseball player. Full name *Melvin Thomas Ott*. He was the first to hit 500 home runs in the National League.

Ot·to |'ätō|, Nikolaus August (1832–91) German engineer whose name is given to the four-stroke cycle on which most internal-combustion engines work.

Ot·to I |'ätō| (912–73) king of the Germans 936–73, Holy Roman emperor 962–73; known as **Otto the Great**. As king of the Germans he carried out a policy of eastward expansion, and as

Holy Roman emperor he established a presence in Italy to rival that of the papacy.

Ot·way |'ätwā|, Thomas (1652–85) English dramatist. He is chiefly remembered for his two blank verse tragedies, *The Orphan* (1680) and *Venice Preserved* (1682).

Oui·da |'wēdə| (1839–1908) English novelist; pseudonym of *Marie Louise de la Ramée*. Her novels, such as *Under Two Flags* (1867), are romances that are typically set in a fashionable world far removed from reality.

Out·cault |'owt,kawlt|, Richard Felton (1863–1928) U.S. cartoonist. He created the characters Yellow Kid (1895) and Buster Brown (1902).

Ovid |'ävid| (43 BC–c. 17AD) Roman poet; full name *Publius Ovidius Naso*. He is particularly known for his elegiac love poems (such as the *Amores* and the *Ars Amatoria*) and for the *Metamorphoses*, a hexametric epic which retells Greek and Roman myths.

Ow·en |'ō(w)ən|, Sir Richard (1804–92) English anatomist and paleontologist. Owen made important contributions to evolution, taxonomy, and palaeontology and coined the word *dinosaur* in 1841. He was a strong opponent of Darwinism.

Ow·en |'ō(w)ən|, Robert Dale (1801–77) U.S. politician and social reformer, born in England. As a member of the U.S. House of Representatives from Indiana (1843–47), he drafted legislation to create the Smithsonian Institution; his letter to Abraham Lincoln, published as *Policy of Emancipation* (1863), influenced Lincoln's views.

Ow·ens |'ō(w)ənz|, Jesse (1913–80) U.S. track and field athlete; born *James Cleveland Owens*. In 1935 he equalled or broke six world records in 45 minutes, and in 1936 won four gold medals at the Olympic Games in Berlin. The success in Berlin of Owens, as a black man, outraged Hitler.

Oz |äz|, Frank Richard (1944–) U.S. puppeteer, born in England. He created many of the Muppet characters, including Miss Piggy, Grover, and Bert.

Oza·wa |ō'zäwə|, Seiji (1935–) Japanese conductor. He was conductor of the Toronto Symphony Orchestra from 1965 to 1970, and in 1973 he became music director and conductor of the Boston Symphony Orchestra. He conducts frequently with major symphony and opera companies.

Ozick |'ō,zik|, Cynthia (1928–   ) U.S. author and critic. Notable works: *The Puttermesser Papers* (1997).

Ozu |'ōzo͞o|, Yasujirō (1903–63) Japanese movie director. He was the originator of films about lower middle class families, such as *Tokyo Monogatari* (1953).

Pp

Pabst |ˈpæbst|, Captain Frederick (1836–1904) U.S. steamship captain and businessman. He entered his father-in-law's brewery business and turned it into the Pabst brewing company.

Pa·chel·bel |ˈpäkHəl,bel|, Johann (1653–1706) German composer and organist. His compositions include seventy-eight chorale preludes, thirteen settings of the Magnificat, and the Canon and Gigue in D for three violins and continuo.

Pa·ci·no |pəˈcHēnō|, Al (1940–) U.S. movie actor; full name *Alfredo James Pacino*. Nominated for an Oscar eight times, winning once for *Scent of a Woman* (1992), he first achieved recognition with *The Godfather* (1972). Other notable movies: *Scarface* (1983), *Dick Tracy* (1990), and *Carlito's Way* (1993).

Pack·wood |ˈpæk,wʊd|, Robert (1932–) U.S. politician. A member of the U.S. Senate from Oregon (1969–95), he resigned following charges of sexual harassment.

Pa·de·rew·ski |ˌpædəˈrefskē|, Ignacy Jan (1860–1941) Polish pianist, composer, and statesman, prime minister (1919). He was the first prime minister of independent Poland, but resigned after only ten months in office and resumed his musical career.

Pa·ga·ni·ni |ˌpägəˈnēnē|, Niccolò (1782–1840) Italian violinist and composer. His virtuoso violin recitals, including widespread use of pizzicato and harmonics, established him as a major figure of the romantic movement.

Page |pāj|, Geraldine (Sue) (1924–87) U.S. actress. Her Broadway credits include *Sweet Bird of Youth* (1959), *Strange Interlude* (1963), and *Agnes of God* (1982). Notable movies: *The Trip to Bountiful* (1985, Academy Award).

Page |pāj|, Jimmy (1944–) British rock guitarist, composer, and producer.

Page |pāj|, Thomas Nelson (1853–1922) U.S. author. Notable works: *In Ole Virginia* (1887).

Page |pāj|, Walter Hines (1855–1918) U.S. diplomat, journalist, and philanthropist. A partner in Doubleday, Page & Co., he advocated mass education and welfare.

Pag·lia |ˈpæglēə|, Camille (Anna) (1947–) U.S. cultural critic. Her first book, *Sexual Personae* (1990), brought her to public attention. Other notable works: *Sex, Art, and American Culture* (1992) and *Vamps and Tramps* (1994).

Pa·gnol |pənˈyōl|, Marcel (1895–1974) French dramatist, movie director, and writer. His novels include *La Gloire de mon père* (1957) and *Le Chateau de ma mère* (1958); the movies *Jean de Florette* and *Manon des Sources* (both 1986) were based on Pagnol's *L'Eau des collines* (1963).

Pah·la·vi |ˈpäləvē| two shahs of Iran: **Reza Pahlavi** (1878–1944; ruled 1925–41). Born *Reza Khan*. An army officer, he took control of the Persian government after a coup in 1921. He was elected Shah in 1925 but abdicated following the occupation of Iran by British and Soviet forces. His son, **Muhammad Reza Pahlavi** (1919–80; ruled 1941–79). Also known as **Reza Shah**. Opposition to his regime culminated in the Islamic revolution of 1979 under Ayatollah Khomeini; he was forced into exile and died in Egypt.

Paige |pāj|, Satchel (1906–82) U.S. baseball player. Born *Leroy Robert Paige*. A pitcher for the Negro leagues (1924–47) and the major leagues, he pitched 55 career no-hitters. Elected to the Baseball Hall of Fame (1971).

Paine |pān|, Albert Bigelow (1861–1937) U.S. editor, dramatist, and biographer. He edited Mark Twain's letters and authored *The Great White Way* (1901).

Paine |pān|, John Knowles (1839–1906) U.S. organist and composer. He held the first chair of music in an American university (Harvard).

Paine |pān|, Thomas (1737–1809) English political writer. His pamphlet *Common Sense* (1776) called for American independence and *The Rights of Man* (1791) defended the French Revolution. His radical views prompted the British government to indict him for treason, and he fled to France. Other notable works: *The Age of Reason* (1794).

Pais·ley |'pāzlē|, Ian (Richard Kyle) (1929–) Northern Irish clergyman and politician. cofounder of the Ulster Democratic Unionist Party (1972), he has been a vociferous and outspoken defender of the Protestant Unionist position in Northern Ireland.

Pa·les·tri·na |ˌpælə'strēnə|, Giovanni Pierluigi da (*c.* 1525–94) Italian composer. Palestrina is chiefly known for his sacred music, including 105 masses, over 250 motets, and the *Missa Papae Marcelli* (1567).

Pa·ley |'pālē|, Grace (1922–) U.S. novelist and short story writer. Notable works: *Collected Stories* (1994).

Pa·ley |'pālē|, William Samuel (1901–90) U.S. television and radio executive. He built the CBS communications empire and served as its president (1928–46) and chairman of the board (1946–90).

Pal·grave |'pawl,grāv|, Francis Turner (1824–97) English critic and poet, known for his anthology *The Golden Treasury of Songs and Lyrical Poems in the English Language* (1861).

Pa·lis·sy |'pælisē|, Bernard (*c.* 1510–89) French potter, known for his richly colored earthenware decorated with reliefs of plants and animals.

Pal·la·dio |pə'lädēō|, Andrea (1508–80) Italian architect; born *Andrea di Pietro della Gondola*. He led a revival of classical architecture, in particular promoting the Roman ideals of harmonic proportions and symmetrical planning. A notable example of his many villas, palaces, and churches is the church of San Giorgio Maggiore in Venice.

Pal·me |'pälmə|, (Sven) Olof (Joachim) (1927–86) Swedish statesman, prime minister (1969–76 and 1982–86). He was killed by an unknown assassin.

Pal·mer |'pä(l)mər|, Arnold (Daniel) (1929–) U.S. golfer. His many championship victories include the Masters (1958; 1960; 1962; 1964), the U.S. Open (1960), and the British Open (1961–2). The huge galleries that were attracted by the ever-popular Palmer whenever he played came to be called "Arnie's Army."

Pal·mer |'pä(l)mər|, Erastus Dow (1817–1904) U.S. sculptor. Notable works: *The White Captive* (1859).

Pal·mer |'pä(l)mər|, Jim (1945–) U.S. baseball player. He won the Cy Young Award three times.

Pal·mer |'pä(l)mər|, Samuel (1805–81) English painter and etcher. His friendship with William Blake resulted in the mystical, visionary landscape paintings, such as *Repose of the Holy Family* (1824), for which he is best known. He was leader of a group of artists called The Ancients.

Pal·mer·ston |'pä(l)mərstən|, Henry John Temple, 3rd Viscount (1784–1865) British Whig statesman, prime minister (1855–58 and 1859–65). Palmerston declared the second Opium War against China in 1856 and oversaw the successful conclusion of the Crimean War in 1856 and the suppression of the Indian Mutiny in 1858. He also maintained British neutrality during the U.S. Civil War.

Pan·dit |'pændət|, Vijaya (Lakshmi) (1900–90) Indian politician and diplomat, sister of Jawaharlal Nehru. Imprisoned three times by the British for nationalist activities, after independence she became the first woman to serve as president of the United Nations General Assembly (1953–54).

Pa·net·ta |pə'netə|, Leon Edward (1938–) U.S. politician. He was White House chief of staff to President Clinton (1994–97).

Pa·ni·ni |'pāninē| (*fl. c.* 400 BC) Indian grammarian. Sources vary as to when he lived, with dates ranging from the 4th to the 7th century BC. He is noted as the author of the *Eight Lectures*, a grammar of Sanskrit.

Pank·hurst |'pæNGk,hərst|, Emmeline (1858–1928) English suffragette. In 1903 Emmeline and her daughters Christabel (1880–1958) and (Estelle) Sylvia (1882–1960) founded the Women's Social and Political Union, with the motto "Votes for Women." Following the imprisonment of Christabel in 1905, Emmeline initiated the militant suffragette campaign that continued until the outbreak of World War I.

Pao·loz·zi |ˌpow'lätsē|, Eduardo (Luigi) (1924–) Scottish artist and sculptor, of Italian descent. He was a key figure in the development of pop art in Britain in the 1950s.

Pa·pa·dop·ou·los |ˌpäpə'däpələs|, Georgios (1919–) Greek military and political leader. He headed the military junta that ruled Greece from 1967 to 1973, after which he became prime minister (1967–73) and then president (1973).

Pa·pan·dre·ou |ˌpäpən'drăōō|, George (1888–1968) Greek political leader. He was exiled in 1936, headed the government-in-exile (1944–45), and was elected premier in 1963. He was arrested after a military coup in April 1967.

Pa·pi·neau |päpē'nō|, Louis Joseph (1786–1871) French-Canadian politician. The leader of the French-Canadian party in Lower Canada (later Quebec province), he campaigned against the union of Lower and Upper Canada (later Ontario) and pressed for greater French-Canadian autonomy. He was forced to flee the country after leading an abortive French rebellion against British rule in 1837.

Papp |pæp|, Joseph (1921–91) U.S. producer and director. Born *Joseph Papirofsky*. He was managing director of the Hollywood's Actors Laboratory (1948–50) and founded the Shakespearean Theatre Workshop (1954), which became the New York Shakespeare Festival.

Pap·pus |'pæpəs| (*fl. c.* 300–350) Greek mathematician; known as **Pappus of Alexandria**. Little is known of his life, but his *Collection* of six books (another two are missing) is the principal source of knowledge of the mathematics of his predecessors.

Pa·quin |'pækwin|, Anna (1982–) U.S. actress. Notable movies: *The Piano* (1993, Academy Award).

Pa·ra·cel·sus |ˌperə'selsəs| (*c.* 1493–1541) Swiss physician; born *Theophrastus Phillipus Aureolus Bombastus von Hohenheim*. He developed a new approach to medicine and philosophy based on observation and experience. He saw illness as having a specific external cause (rather than resulting from an imbalance of the bodily humors), and introduced chemical remedies to replace traditional ones.

Par·is |'peris|, Matthew see MATTHEW PARIS.

Park |pärk|, Mungo (1771–1806) Scottish explorer. He undertook a series of explorations in West Africa (1795–7), among them the navigation of the Niger. He drowned on a second expedition to the Niger (1805–6).

Park Chung Hee |ˌpärk CHəNG 'hē| (1917–79) South Korean statesman, president (1963–79). After staging a coup in 1961 he was elected president, assuming dictatorial powers in 1971. Under Park's presidency South Korea emerged as a leading industrial nation.

Par·ker |'pärkər|, Alton Brooks (1852–1926) U.S. jurist and politician. He served as chief justice of the New York court of appeals (1898–1904) and was a Democratic presidential candidate in 1904.

Par·ker |'pärkər|, Bonnie (1911–34) U.S. bank robber. The romantic partner of Clyde Barrow, who was known for a criminal spree, she wrote a poem that inspired the movie *The Ballad of Bonnie and Clyde*.

Par·ker |'pärkər|, Charlie (1920–55) U.S. saxophonist; full name *Charles Christopher Parker*; known as **Bird** or **Yardbird**. From 1944 he played with Thelonious Monk and Dizzy Gillespie, and became one of the key figures of the bebop movement. He is noted especially for his recordings with Miles Davis in 1945.

Par·ker |'pärkər|, Dorothy (Rothschild) (1893–1967) U.S. humorist, literary critic, and writer. From 1927 Parker wrote book reviews and short stories for the *New Yorker* magazine, becoming one of its legendary wits.

Par·ker |'pärkər|, Francis Wayland (1837–1902) U.S. educator. A school principal and superintendent, he was a pioneer of progressive education in the U.S.

Par·ker |'pärkər|, Horatio William (1863–1919) U.S. composer. The dean of the Yale School of Music (1904–19), he wrote oratorios, operas, and choral works.

Par·ker |'pärkər|, Louis W. (1906–93) U.S. inventor, born in Hungary. He invented the first color television.

Par·ker |'pärkər|, Theodore (1810–60) U.S. clergyman and social reformer. A liberal and radical Unitarian and later Congregational minister, he was a leading Transcendentalist of his day.

Park·man |'pärkmən|, Francis (1823–93) U.S. historian. He traveled the Oregon Trail in 1846 to improve his health and later wrote an account of his journey, *The California and Oregon Trail* (1849).

Parks |pärks|, Gordon Roger Alexander Buchanan (1912–   ) U.S. movie director, composer, author, and photographer. He directed the movie *Shaft* (1972) and was the author of *Flash Photography* (1947); Spingarn Medal, 1972.

Parks |pärks|, Rosa L. (1913–   ) On December 1, 1955, she refused to give up her bus seat to a white man in Montgomery, Alabama; after the ensuing boycott and NAACP protest, bus segregation was ruled unconstitutional. Spingarn Medal, 1979.

Par·men·i·des |pär'menə,dēz| (5th century BC) Greek philosopher. Born in Elea in SW Italy, he founded the Eleatic school of philosophers. In his work *On Nature*, written in hexameter verse, he maintained that the apparent motion and changing forms of the universe are in fact manifestations of an unchanging and indivisible reality.

Par·mi·gia·ni·no |,pärməjə'nē,nō| (1503–40) Also **Parmigiano**. Italian painter; born *Girolano Francesco Maria Mazzola*. He made an important contribution to early mannerism with the graceful figure style of his frescoes and portraits. Notable works: *Madonna with the Long Neck* (1534).

Par·nell |pär'nel|, Charles Stewart (1846–91) Irish nationalist leader. Parnell became leader of the Irish Home Rule faction in 1880 and raised the profile of Irish affairs through obstructive parliamentary tactics. He was forced to retire from public life in 1890 after the exposure of his adultery with Mrs. Kitty O'Shea.

Parr |pär|, Katherine (1512–48) English queen, sixth and last wife of Henry VIII. Having married the king in 1543, she influenced his decision to restore the succession to his daughters Mary and Elizabeth (later Mary I and Elizabeth I, respectively).

Par·ry |'perē|, Sir (Charles) Hubert (Hastings) (1848–1918) English composer. Parry's best-known work is his setting of William Blake's poem "Jerusalem" (1916), which has acquired the status of a national song.

Par·sons |'pärsənz|, Sir Charles (Algernon) (1854–1931) British engineer, scientist, and manufacturer. He patented and built the first practical steam turbine in 1884, designed to drive electricity generators. He also developed steam turbines for marine propulsion, and his experimental vessel *Turbinia* caused a sensation in 1897.

Par·sons |'pärsənz|, Estelle (1927–   ) U.S. stage and movie actress. Notable movies: *Bonnie and Clyde* (1967, Academy Award).

Par·sons |'pärsənz|, John T. (1913–   ) U.S inventor. He built a machine that cut airplane wings automatically on a contour; the machine now has many applications in manufacturing.

Par·ton |'pärtn|, Dolly (Rebecca) (1946–   ) U.S. country music singer and songwriter. Her hits include "Jolene" (1974). She has also made a number of movies, including *Nine to Five* (1980) and *Steel Magnolias* (1989), and founded a theme park, Dollywood.

Pas·cal |pæ'skæl|, Blaise (1623–62) French mathematician, physicist, and religious philosopher. He founded the theory of probabilities and developed a forerunner of integral calculus, but is best known for deriving the principle that the pressure of a fluid at rest is transmitted equally in all directions. His *Lettres Provinciales* (1656–7) and *Pensées* (1670) argue for his Jansenist Christianity.

Pa·šić |'päsHicH|, Nikola (1845–1926) Serbian statesman, prime minister of Serbia five times between 1891 and 1918, and of the Kingdom of Serbs, Croats, and Slovenes (1921–24 and 1924–26). He was a party to the formation of the Kingdom of Serbs, Croats, and Slovenes (called Yugoslavia from 1929) in 1918.

Pa·so·li·ni |ˌpäsə'lēnē|, Pier Paolo (1922–75) Italian film director and novelist. A Marxist, he drew on his experiences in the slums of Rome for his work, but became recognized for his controversial, bawdy literary adaptation, such as *The Gospel According to St. Matthew* (1964) and *The Canterbury Tales* (1973).

Pass |pæs|, Joe (1929–94) U.S. jazz guitarist. Born *Joseph Anthony Jacobi Passalaqua*. He achieved recognition with his 1973 solo album, *Virtuoso*.

Pas·sos, John Dos see DOS PASSOS.

Pas·ter·nak |'pæstər,næk|, Boris (Leonidovich) (1890–1960) Russian poet, novelist, and translator. His best-known novel, *Doctor Zhivago* (1957), describes the experience of the Russian intelligentsia during the Revolution; it was banned in the Soviet Union. Pasternak was awarded the Nobel Prize for Literature in 1958, but turned it down under pressure from Soviet authorities.

Pas·teur |päs'tœr|, Louis (1822–95) French chemist and bacteriologist. He introduced pasteurization and made pioneering studies in vaccination techniques.

Pa·ter |'pātər|, Walter (Horatio) (1839–94) English essayist and critic. His *Studies in the History of the Renaissance* (1873) had a major impact on the development of the Aesthetic Movement.

Pa·ter·no |pə'tərnō|, Joe (1926–) U.S. college football coach.

Pat·er·son |'pætərsən|, William (1745–1806) U.S. Supreme Court justice (1793–1806), born in Ireland. He was a member of the Constitutional Convention (1787), a member of the U.S. Senate from New Jersey (1789–90), and governor of New Jersey (1790–93).

Pa·thé |pä'tā; pə'THä|, Charles (1863–1957) French movie pioneer. In 1896 he and his brothers founded a company that came to dominate the production and distribution of movies. It became internationally known for its newsreels, first introduced in France in 1909.

Pa·ton |'pātn|, Alan (Stewart) (1903–88) South African writer and politician. He is best known for his novel *Cry, the Beloved Country* (1948), a passionate indictment of the apartheid system.

Pa·tou |pə'tōō|, Jean (1887–1936) French couturier and perfume-maker.

Pat·rick |'pætrik|, St. (5th cent) Apostle and patron saint of Ireland. Of Romano-British parentage, he was taken as a slave to Ireland, where he experienced a religious conversion. He founded the archiepiscopal see of Armagh in about 454. Feast day, March 17.

Pat·ter·son |'pætərsən|, Floyd (1935–) U.S. boxer. An Olympic middleweight champion (1952), he was also world heavyweight champion (1956–59, 1960–62).

Pat·ter·son |'pætərsən| U.S. family of journalists, including: **Robert Wilson Patterson** (1850–1910), editor of the *Chicago Tribune* (1873–1910.). **Joseph Medill Patterson** (1879–1946), the son of Robert Patterson. With his cousin Robert McCormick he founded the *New York Daily News* (1925). **Eleanor Medill Patterson** (1884–1948), the daughter of Robert Patterson; known as **Cissy**. She was the editor and later the owner (1939) of the *Washington Herald*, which she merged with the *Washington Times*.

Pat·ti |'pætē|, Adelina (1843–1919) U.S. operatic soprano, born in Spain of Italian parentage. Born *Adela Juana Maria*. One of the greatest coloratura singers of the 19th century, she made her New York debut in 1859.

Pat·ton |'pætn|, George Smith (1885–1945) U.S. army general. During World War II, he commanded the ground forces in the Allied invasion of northwest Africa (1942–43) and the U.S. Third Army in the drive through France (1944). He wrote his autobiography, *War as I Knew It* (1947).

Paul III |pawl| (1468–49) Italian pope (1534–49); born *Alessandro Farnese*. He excommunicated Henry VIII of England in 1538, instituted the order of the Jesuits in 1540, and initiated the Council of Trent in 1545. Paul III was also a patron of Michelangelo.

Paul |pawl|, Les (1915–) U.S. jazz guitarist and guitar designer; born *Lester Polfus*. In 1946 he invented the solid-body electric guitar, which was promoted from 1952 as the Gibson Les Paul guitar. Paul was also among the first to use such recording techniques as over-dubbing. His style of play influenced many rock guitarists.

Paul |pawl|, St. (died *c.* 64) Christian missionary of Jewish descent; known as **Paul the Apostle,** or **Saul of Tarsus,** or **the Apostle of the Gentiles.** He first opposed the followers of Jesus, assisting at the martyrdom of St. Stephen. On a journey to Damascus he was converted to Christianity after a vision and became one of the first major Christian missionaries and theologians. His epistles form part of the New Testament. Feast day, June 29.

Paul·ding |'pawldiNG|, Hiram (1797–1878) U.S. naval officer. He was acting lieutenant on the *Ticonderoga* at the Battle of Lake Champlain (1814).

Paul·ding |'pawldiNG|, James Kirke (1778–1860) U.S. author. He authored *Westward Ho!* (1832) and served as secretary of the navy under Martin Van Buren (1838–41).

Paul·ey |'pawlē|, Jane (1950–) U.S. journalist. She cohosted NBC's *The Today Show* (1976–90) and is coanchor of *Dateline NBC* (1992–).

Paul·i |'powlē|, Wolfgang (1900–58) Austrian-born U.S. physicist. He made a major contribution to quantum theory with his exclusion principle, according to which only two electrons in an atom could occupy the same quantum level, provided they had opposite spins. In 1931 he postulated the existence of the neutrino, later discovered by Enrico Fermi. Nobel Prize for Physics (1945).

Paul·ing |'pawliNG|, Linus Carl (1901–94) U.S. chemist. He is renowned for his study of molecular structure and chemical bonding, for which he received the 1954 Nobel Prize for Chemistry. His suggestion of a helical structure for proteins formed the foundation for the elucidation of the structure of DNA.

Pau·sa·ni·as |paw'sānēəs| (2nd cent) Greek geographer and historian. His *Description of Greece* (also called the *Itinerary of Greece*) is a guide to the topography and remains of ancient Greece and is still considered an invaluable source of information.

Pa·va·rot·ti |ˌpävä'rawtē; ˌpævə'rätē|,

Luciano (1935–) Italian operatic tenor. He made his debut as Rodolfo in Puccini's *La Bohème* in 1961 and has since gained international acclaim and popularity for his bel canto singing.

Pa·ve·se |pə'vā,zā|, Cesare (1908–50) Italian novelist, poet, and translator. He is best known for his last novel *La Luna e i falò* (1950), in which he portrays isolation and the failure of communication as a general human predicament.

Pav·lov |'päv,lawv|, Ivan (Petrovich) (1849–1936) Russian physiologist. He was awarded a Nobel Prize in 1904 for his work on digestion, but is best known for his studies on the conditioned reflex. He showed by experiment with dogs how the secretion of saliva can be stimulated not only by food but also by the sound of a bell associated with the presentation of food.

Pav·lo·va |päv'lōvə|, Anna (Pavlovna) (1881–1931) Russian dancer, resident in Britain from 1912. Her highly acclaimed solo dance *The Dying Swan* was created for her by Michel Fokine in 1905. On settling in Britain she formed her own company.

Pay·ton |'pātn|, Walter (1954–) U.S. football player. He set an NFL career rushing record with 16,726 yards.

Paz |päz|, Octavio (1914–98) Mexican poet and essayist. His poems reflect a preoccupation with Aztec mythology. He also wrote essays in response to the brutal suppression of student demonstrations in 1968. Nobel Prize for Literature (1990).

Pea·body |'pē,bädē|, Elizabeth Palmer (1804–94) U.S. education pioneer. Her Boston bookshop became a focus for Transcendentalist activities, including the publication of the *Dial.* She also published elementary textbooks and founded the first American kindergarten (1860).

Pea·body |'pē,bädē|, George (1795–1869) U.S. banker and philanthropist. He founded the U.S. Peabody Education Fund and a number of scientific museums (Yale, Harvard, Baltimore).

Peake |pēk|, Mervyn (Laurence) (1911–68) British novelist, poet, and artist, born in China. He is principally remembered for the trilogy comprising

Titus Groan (1946), *Gormenghast* (1950), and *Titus Alone* (1959).

Peale |pēl| American family of artists, including: **Charles Willson Peale** (1741–1827). He painted more than 1,000 portraits of prominent Americans, including the first known portrait of George Washington (1772). **Rembrandt Peale** (1778–1860), his son. He painted historical scenes and portraits of George Washington, Thomas Jefferson, and Napoleon Bonaparte.

Peale |pēl|, Norman Vincent (1898–1993) U.S. clergyman. He preached "applied Christianity," encouraging people to think positively. Notable books: *The Art of Living* (1937) and *The Power of Positive Thinking* (1952).

Pearl |pərl|, Minnie (1912–96) U.S.comedian and country music singer. Born *Sarah Ophelia Colley Cannon*. She was a Grand Ole Opry star who made recordings and television appearances.

Pears |perz|, Sir Peter (1910–86) English operatic tenor. In his lifelong partnership with Benjamin Britten he performed the title roles in all of Britten's operas and with Britten cofounded the Aldeburgh Festival in 1948.

Pear·son |'pirsən|, Lester Bowles (1897–1972) Canadian diplomat and Liberal statesman, prime minister (1963–68). As secretary of state for External Affairs (1948–57) he acted as a mediator in the resolution of the Suez crisis (1956). Nobel Peace Prize (1957).

Pea·ry |'pirē|, Robert Edwin (1856–1920) U.S. explorer. He made eight Arctic voyages before becoming the first person to reach the North Pole, on April 6, 1909.

Peck |pek|, (Eldred) Gregory (1916–) U.S. actor. Peck won an Oscar for his role as the lawyer Atticus in the movie of the novel *To Kill a Mockingbird* (1962).

Peck·ham |'pekəm|, Rufus Wheeler (1838–1909) U.S. Supreme Court justice (1896–1909).

Peel |pēl|, Sir Robert (1788–1850) British Conservative statesman, prime minister (1834–35 and 1841–46). As home secretary (1828–30) he established (in the UK) the Metropolitan Police (hence the nicknames *bobby* and *peeler*). His repeal of the Corn Laws in 1846 split the Conservatives and forced his resignation.

Peerce |pirs|, Jan (1904–84) U.S. operatic tenor. Born *Jacob Pincus Perelmuth*. He was a regular soloist with Toscanini at Radio City Music Hall, and he sang with the Metropolitan Opera for 26 seasons beginning in 1941, as well as in films and on Broadway.

Peg·ler |'peglər|, (James) Westbrook (1894–1969) U.S. journalist. He wrote a syndicated column (Pulitzer Prize, 1941).

Pei |pā|, I. M. (1917–) U.S. architect, born in China. Full name *Iwoh Ming Pei*. He designed monumental public buildings, including the East Wing of the National Gallery of Art in Washington, D.C., and the Pyramid at the Louvre in Paris.

Pei·erls, Sir Rudolph Ernst (1907–95) British physicist, born in Germany. On staff at the Los Alamos National Laboratory, with Otto Frisch he was the first physicist to calculate that an atomic bomb could be made.

Peirce |pirs|, Charles Sanders (1839–1914) U.S. philosopher and logician. A founder of American pragmatism, he argued that the meaning of a belief is to be understood by the actions and uses to which it gives rise.

Pei·sis·tra·tus variant spelling of PISISTRATUS.

Pe·la·gius |pə'lāj(ē)əs| (*c.* 360–*c.* 420) British monk. He denied the doctrines of original sin and predestination, defending innate human goodness and free will. His beliefs were opposed by St. Augustine of Hippo and condemned as heretical by the Synod of Carthage in about 418.

Pe·lé |'pā,lā| (1940–) Brazilian soccer player; born *Edson Arantes do Nascimento*. Regarded as one of the greatest goalscorers of all time, he ended his career with the New York Cosmos (1975–77), and is credited with over 1,200 goals in first-class soccer.

Pel·ham |'peləm|, Henry (1696–1754) British Whig statesman, prime minister (1743–54).

Pelle·tier |,pel'tyā; ,pelə'tir|, Pierre-Joseph (1788–1842) French chemist.

With his friend **Joseph-Bienaimé Caventou** (1795–1877), he isolated a number of alkaloids for the first time. Pelletier and Caventou also isolated the green pigment of leaves and gave it the name *chlorophyll*.

Pel·li |'pelē|, Cesar (1926–) U.S. architect. Notable designs: the World Financial Center and Carnegie Hall Tower (New York).

Pem·ber·ton |'pembərtən|, John Stith (1831–1888) U.S. inventor. He invented the soft drink Coca-Cola.

Pen·de·rec·ki |ˌpendə'retskē|, Krzysztof (1933–) Polish composer. His music frequently features sounds drawn from extramusical sources and note clusters, as in his *Threnody for the Victims of Hiroshima* (1960) for fifty-two strings. Notable religious works: *Stabat Mater* (1962) and *Polish Requiem* (1980–4).

Pen·der·gast |'pendər,gæst|, Thomas Joseph (1872–1945) U.S. politician. A supporter of Harry Truman, he was the acknowledged Democratic boss of Kansas City and Missouri.

Pen·field |'pen,fēld|, Wilder Graves (1891–1976) Canadian neurologist. He devised a surgical method for treating epilepsy.

Penn |pen|, William (1644–1718) English Quaker, founder of Pennsylvania. Having been imprisoned in 1668 for his Quaker writings, he successfully petitioned King Charles II for a grant of land in North America to repay a debt. He founded the colony of Pennsylvania as a sanctuary for Quakers and other Nonconformists in 1682.

Pen·ney |'penē|, James Cash (1875–1971) U.S. businessman. He developed the J. C. Penney department store chain and served as the company's president (1913–17) and chairman (1917–46).

Pe·pin III |'pepin| (c. 714–768) King of the Franks (751–768). Called **Pepin the Short**. He founded the Carolingian dynasty (751) and was the father of Charlemagne.

Pep·per |'pepər|, Art, Jr. (1925–82) U.S. jazz alto saxophonist. Born *Arthur Edward Pepper, Jr.* He toured with Stan Kenton (1946–51) and was associated with "West Coast jazz."

Pep·per·rell |'pepərəl|, Sir William (1696–1759) American jurist and naval hero. A Maine fish and lumber merchant, he was a hero in King George's War (1744).

Pepys |pēps|, Samuel (1633–1703) English diarist and naval administrator. He is particularly remembered for his *Diary* (1660–9), which describes events such as the Great Plague and the Fire of London.

Per·ce·val |'pərsəvəl|, Spencer (1762–1812) British Tory statesman, prime minister (1809–12). He was shot dead in the lobby of the House of Commons by a bankrupt merchant who blamed the government for his insolvency.

Per·cy |'pərsē|, Sir Henry (1364–1403) English soldier; known as **Hotspur** or **Harry Hotspur**. Son of the 1st Earl of Northumberland, he was killed at the battle of Shrewsbury during his father's revolt against Henry IV.

Per·cy |'pərsē|, Walker (1916–90) U.S. author. Notable works: *The Moviegoer* (1961, National Book Award).

Per·due |ˌpər'do͞o|, Frank (1920–) U.S. entrepreneur. He founded Perdue Farms, a company that raises and markets chickens.

Pe·rei·ra |pə'rerə|, William (1909–85) U.S. architect. Notable designs: Los Angeles International Airport and the Transamerica Building (San Francisco).

Pe·rel·man |'pər(ə)lmən|, S. J. (1904–79) U.S. humorist and writer; full name *Sidney Joseph Perelman*. In the early 1930s he worked in Hollywood as a scriptwriter, and from 1934 his name is linked with the *New Yorker* magazine, for which he wrote most of his short stories and sketches.

Pe·res |pə'rez|, Shimon (1923–) Polish-born Israeli statesman, prime minister (1984–86 and 1995–96); Polish name *Szymon Perski*. As foreign minister under Yitzhak Rabin he played a major role in negotiating the PLO–Israeli peace accord (1993). Nobel Peace Prize (1994), shared with Rabin and PLO leader Yasser Arafat.

Pé·rez de Cué·llar |'perez də 'kweyär|, Javier (1920–) Peruvian diplomat and secretary general of the United Nations 1982–91.

Per·i·cles |'perə‚klēz| (*c.* 495–429 BC) Athenian statesman and general. A champion of Athenian democracy, he pursued an imperialist policy and masterminded Athenian strategy in the Peloponnesian War. He commissioned the building of the Parthenon in 447 and promoted the culture of Athens in a golden age that produced such figures as Aeschylus, Socrates, and Phidias.

Per·kin |'pərkən|, Sir William Henry (1838–1907) English chemist and pioneer of the synthetic organic chemical industry. He prepared and manufactured the first synthetic dyestuff, mauve, from aniline.

Per·kins |'pərkənz|, Carl (1932–98) U.S. singer and songwriter. A rockabilly artist, he wrote "Blue Suede Shoes."

Per·kins |'pərkənz|, Frances (1882–1965) U.S. public official. As U.S. secretary of labor (1933–45) and the first woman to hold a federal cabinet post, she promoted the adoption of the Social Security Act.

Per·kins |'pərkənz|, Max (1884–1947) U.S. editor. Full name *William Maxwell Evarts Perkins*. He was the intellectual champion and publisher of daring new writers, including F. Scott Fitzgerald and Ernest Hemingway.

Perl·man |'pərlmən|, Itzhak (1945–) Israeli violinist. He has appeared with most of the world's major orchestras and has won 6 Grammy awards.

Perl·man |'pərlmən|, Rhea (1948–) U.S. actress. She starred in the television series "Taxi" (1978–82) and "Cheers" (1982–93).

Perls |pərlz|, Fritz (1893–1970) U.S. psychiatrist, born in Germany. Born *Frederick Salomon Perls*. He was a founder and practitioner of Gestalt psychotherapy.

Pe·rón |pə'rōn| Argentinian political family, including: **Juan Domingo Perón** (1895–1974), soldier and statesman . He participated in the 1943 military coup and was later elected president (1946–55, 1973–74), winning popular support with his social reforms. The faltering economy and conflict with the Church led to his removal and exile. Perón returned to power in 1973, but died in office. **María Eva Duarte Ibar-**

guren de Perón (1919–52), his second wife; known as **Evita**. A former actress, after her marriage in 1945 she became de facto minister of health and of labor until her death from cancer; her social reforms earned her great popularity with the poor.

Pe·rot |pə'rō|, H. Ross (1930–) U.S. businessman and politician. Full name *Henry Ross Perot*. He mounted a third-party candidacy for president of the U.S. in 1992.

Per·rault |pə'rō|, Charles (1628–1703) French writer. He is remembered for his *Mother Goose Tales* (1697), containing such fairy tales as "Sleeping Beauty," "Little Red Riding Hood," "Puss in Boots," and "Cinderella."

Per·rin |pə'ræn; 'perən|, Jean Baptiste (1870–1942) French physical chemist. He provided the definitive proof of the existence of atoms, proved that cathode rays are negatively charged, and investigated Brownian motion. Nobel Prize for Physics (1926).

Per·ry |'perē| Family of U.S naval officers, including: **Oliver Hazard Perry** (1785–1819) He built up and commanded the American fleet that fought the British on Lake Erie during the War of 1812. Upon defeating the British fleet (Sept. 10, 1813), he sent the dispatch to General William Henry Harrison, "We have met the enemy and they are ours." **Matthew Calbraith Perry** (1794–1858), his brother. He commanded (1837) the *Fulton*, the first steam vessel in the U.S. navy. He negotiated a treaty with Japan (signed 1854) that opened diplomatic relations and trade with the U.S.

Per·ry |'perē|, Bliss (1860–1954) U.S. educator, editor, and author. He edited *Atlantic Monthly* (1899–1909) and *The American Mind* (1912).

Per·ry |'perē|, Fred (1909–95) British-born U.S. tennis player; full name *Frederick John Perry*. His record of winning three consecutive singles titles at Wimbledon (1934–36) was unequaled until 1978.

Per·ry |'perē|, Harold R. (1916–91) U.S. religious leader. He became the first black American Roman Catholic bishop in the 20th century (1966).

Per·shing |'pərsHiNG; 'pərZHiNG|, John Joseph (1860–1948) U.S. army officer. Known as **Black Jack**. His early military years included active duty in Cuba (1898) and the Philippines (1899–1903). He led the force that pursued Pancho Villa into Mexico (1916–17) before becoming commander in chief of the American Expeditionary Forces (1917–19) in World War I. His Meuse-Argonne offensive (1918) led to the final collapse of the Germans. In 1919, he was named General of the Army and served as U.S. Army chief of staff (1921–24). His memoir, *My Experiences in the World War* (1931), won the Pulitzer Prize.

Perthes |pert|, Jacques Boucher de see BOUCHER DE PERTHES.

Pe·rutz |pə'rōōtz|, Max Ferdinand (1914–) British biochemist, born in Austria. He discovered the molecular structure of blood pigment; with John C. Kendrew, he won the 1962 Nobel Prize for Chemistry.

Pes·ci |'pesHē|, Joe (1943–) U.S. actor. Notable movies: *Good Fellas* (1990, Academy Award).

Pes·ta·loz·zi |,pestə'lawtsē|, Johann Heinrich (1746–1827) Swiss educational reformer. He pioneered education for poor children and had a major impact on the development of primary education.

Pé·tain |,pa'tæN|, (Henri) Philippe (1856–1951) French soldier and politician. He was the premier of the Fascist-dominated Vichy government in France (1940–44).

Pe·ter |'pētər|, St. (died c. 67) an Apostle. Born *Simon*. Peter ("stone") is the name given him by Jesus, signifying the rock on which he would establish his church. He is regarded by Roman Catholics as the first bishop of the church at Rome, where he is said to have been martyred in about AD 67. He is often represented as the keeper of the door of heaven. Feast day, June 29.

Pe·ter I |'pētər| (1672–1725) czar of Russia (1682–1725); known as **Peter the Great**. Peter modernized his armed forces before waging the Great Northern War (1700–21) and expanding his territory in the Baltic. His extensive administrative reforms were instrumental

in transforming Russia into a significant European power. In 1703 he made the new city of St. Petersburg his capital.

Pe·ter the Hermit |,pētər| (c. 1050–1115) French monk. His preaching on the First Crusade was a rallying cry for thousands of peasants throughout Europe to journey to the Holy Land; most were massacred by the Turks in Asia Minor. Peter later became prior of an Augustinian monastery in Flanders.

Pe·ter·kin |'pētərkən|, Julia (Mood) (1880–1961) U.S. author. Notable works: *Scarlet Sister Mary* (1928, Pulitzer Prize).

Pe·ters |'pētərz|, Mike (1943–) U.S. editorial and political cartoonist. He created the comic "Mother Goose & Grimm."

Pe·ter·son |'pētərsən|, Charles Jacobs (1819–87) U.S. author and publisher. He founded *Ladies' National Magazine* (1842).

Pe·ter·son |'pētərsən|, Oscar (Emmanuel) (1925–) Canadian jazz pianist and composer. He became internationally famous in the 1960s, often appearing with Ella Fitzgerald.

Pe·ter·son |'pētərsən|, Roger Tory (1908–96) U.S. ornithologist and artist. Peterson produced his first book for identifying birds in the field in 1934, introducing the concept of illustrating similar birds in similar postures with their differences highlighted. The format of his field guides has become standard in field guides for all groups of animals and plants.

Pe·ti·pa |,pa'tēpə|, Marius (Ivanovich) (1818–1910) French ballet dancer and choreographer, resident in Russia from 1847. Petipa choreographed more than fifty ballets, working with Tchaikovsky on *Sleeping Beauty* (1890) and *The Nutcracker* (1892).

Pe·trarch |'pe,trärk| (1304–74) Italian poet; Italian name *Francesco Petrarca*. His reputation is chiefly based on the *Canzoniere* (c. 1351–53), a sonnet sequence in praise of a woman he calls Laura.

Pe·trie |'pētrē|, Sir (William Matthew) Flinders (1853–1942) English archaeologist and Egyptologist. He began excavating the Great Pyramid in 1880.

Petrie was the first to establish the system of sequence dating, now standard archaeological practice, by which sites are excavated layer by layer and historical chronology determined by the dating of artefacts found *in situ*.

Pe·tro·ni·us |pə'trōnēəs|, Gaius (died AD 66) Roman writer; known as **Petronius Arbiter**. Petronius is generally accepted as the author of the *Satyricon*, a work in prose and verse satirizing the excesses of Roman society.

Pe·try |'pētrē|, Ann (1908–   ) U. S. author. She was the first African-American woman author to receive broad critical acclaim. Notable works: *The Street* (1946).

Pet·ti·ford |'petəfərd|, Oscar (1922–60) U.S. jazz double bassist, cellist, and bandleader. He played with Dizzy Gillespie, Duke Ellington, and Woody Herman and is remembered for his lasting influence on bop style.

Pet·tit |'petət|, Bob (1932–   ) U.S. basketball player. Elected to the Basketball Hall of Fame (1970).

Pet·ty |'petē|, Richard (1937–   ) U.S. racecar driver. He was the first stock car driver to win $1 million in his career.

Pet·ty |'petē|, Tom (1952–   ) U.S. rock vocalist, composer, and guitarist. He formed his own band The Heartbreakers (1976); his solo releases include the album *Wildflowers* (1994).

Pevs·ner |'pevznər|, Antoine (1886–1962) Russian-born French sculptor and painter, brother of Naum Gabo. With his brother he was a founder of Russian constructivism; the theoretical basis of the movement was put forward in their *Realistic Manifesto* (1920).

Phei·dip·pi·des |fi'dipə,dēz| (5th century BC) Athenian messenger. He was sent to Sparta to ask for help after the Persian landing at Marathon in 490 and is said to have covered the 250 km (150 miles) in two days on foot.

Phid·i·as |'fidēəs| (5th century BC) Athenian sculptor. He is noted for the sculptures on the Parthenon (the Elgin marbles) and his vast statue of Zeus at Olympia (*c.*430), which was one of the Seven Wonders of the Ancient World.

Phil·by |'filbē|, Kim (1912–88) British Foreign Office official and spy; born

Harold Adrian Russell Philby. While working at the British Embassy in Washington, DC (1949–51), Philby was asked to resign on suspicion of being a Soviet agent. He defected to the USSR in 1963 and was officially revealed to have spied for the Soviets from 1933.

Phil·ip[1] |'filəp|, St. an Apostle. He is commemorated with St. James the Less on May 1.

Phil·ip[2] |'filəp|, St. deacon of the early Christian Church; known as **St. Philip the Evangelist**. He was one of seven deacons appointed to superintend the secular business of the Church at Jerusalem (Acts 6:5–6). Feast day, June 6.

Phil·ip[3] |'filəp| the name of five kings of ancient Macedonia, notably: **Philip II** (382–336 BC; reigned 359–336 BC), father of Alexander the Great; he reigned and was known as **Philip II of Macedon**. He unified and expanded ancient Macedonia as well as carrying out a number of army reforms. His victory over Athens and Thebes at the battle of Chaeronea in 338 established his hegemony over Greece. **Philip V** (238–179 BC; reigned 221–179 BC). His expansionist policies led to a series of confrontations with Rome, culminating in his defeat and resultant loss of control over Greece.

Phil·ip[4] |'filəp| the name of six kings of France: **Philip I** (1052–1108; reigned 1059–1108). **Philip II** (1165–1223; reigned 1180–1223), son of Louis VII; known as **Philip Augustus**. After mounting a series of campaigns against the English kings Henry II, Richard I, and John, Philip succeeded in regaining Normandy (1204), Anjou (1204), and most of Poitou (1204–05). **Philip III** (1245–1285; reigned 1270–85), known as **Philip the Bold**. **Philip IV** (1268–1314; reigned 1285–1314), son of Philip III; known as **Philip the Fair**. He continued to extend French dominions, waging wars with England (1294–1303) and Flanders (1302–05). **Philip V** (1294–1322; reigned 1316–1322), known as **Philip the Tall**. **Philip VI** (1293–1350; reigned 1328–50); known as **Philip of Valois**. The founder of the Valois dynasty, Philip came to the throne on the death of Charles IV, whose only child, a girl, was barred from ruling. His claim was challenged by Edward III of England; the dispute developed into the Hundred Years War.

Phil·ip[5] |'filəp| the name of five kings of Spain: **Philip I** (1478–1506; reigned 1504–06); known as **Philip the Handsome**. Son of the Holy Roman Emperor Maximilian I, in 1496 Philip married the infanta Joanna, daughter of Ferdinand of Aragon and Isabella of Castile. After Isabella's death he ruled Castile jointly with Joanna, establishing the Hapsburgs as the ruling dynasty in Spain. **Philip II** (1527–98; reigned 1556–98), son of Charles I (Holy Roman Emperor Charles V). Philip came to the throne following his father's abdication. His reign was dominated by an anti-Protestant crusade that exhausted the Spanish economy. **Philip III** (1578–1621; reigned 1598–1621). **Philip IV** (1605–1665; reigned 1621–1665). **Philip V** (1683–1746; reigned 1700–24 and 1724–46), grandson of Louis XIV. The selection of Philip as successor to Charles II, and Louis XIV's insistence that Philip remain an heir to the French throne, gave rise to War of the Spanish Succession (1701–14). In 1724 Philip abdicated in favor of his son Louis I, but returned to the throne following Louis's death.

Phil·ip[6] |'filəp|, Prince (1921–   ) Duke of Edinburgh and husband of Elizabeth II. The son of Prince Andrew of Greece and Denmark, he married Princess Elizabeth in 1947; on the eve of his marriage he was created Duke of Edinburgh.

Phil·ip Au·gus·tus |'filəp ə'gəstəs| Philip II of France (see PHILIP[4]).

Phil·ip the Bold Philip III of France (see PHILIP[4]).

Phil·ip the Fair Philip IV of France (see PHILIP[4]).

Phil·ip the Handsome Philip I of Spain (see PHILIP[5]).

Phil·ip the Tall Philip V of France (see PHILIP[4]).

Phil·ip of Valois |väl'wä| Philip VI of France (see PHILIP[4]).

Phil·lips |'filəps| U.S. entrepreneurs: Brothers **Frank Phillips** (1873–1950) and **Lee Eldas Phillips** (1876–1944) founded Phillips Petroleum Co.

Phil·lips |'filəps|, David Graham (1867–1911) U.S. journalist and novelist. His novels were written to expose corruption and other evils. Notable works: *Susan Lenox* (1917).

Phil·lips |'filəps|, Samuel (1752–1802) U.S. industrialist and political leader. He manufactured gunpowder for the Continental army and founded Phillips Academy at Andover (1778), the first endowed academy in America.

Phi·lo Ju·dae·us |'filō jōō'dāəs| (c. 15 BC–c. 50 AD) Jewish philosopher of Alexandria. He is particularly known for his commentaries on the Pentateuch (written in Greek), which he interpreted allegorically in the light of Platonic and Aristotelian philosophy.

Phiz |fiz| (1815–82) English illustrator; pseudonym of *Hablot Knight Browne*. He illustrated many of Dickens's works, including *Martin Chuzzlewit*, *Pickwick Papers*, and *Bleak House*. He took his pseudonym to complement Dickens's "Boz."

Phoe·nix |'fēniks|, River (1970–93) U.S. actor.

Pho·ti·us |'fōtēəs| (c. 820–c. 891) Byzantine scholar and patriarch of Constantinople. His most important work is the *Bibliotheca*, a critical account of 280 earlier prose works and an invaluable source of information about many works now lost.

Phyfe |fif|, Duncan (1768–1854) U.S. cabinetmaker, born in Scotland. He made chairs, sofas, and tables noted for their graceful proportions with simple ornaments precisely carved.

Piaf |'pēäf|, Edith (1915–63) French singer, cabaret artiste, and songwriter. Born *Edith Giovanna Gassion*; known as **The Kid**. She gained international fame with her songs of tragic love affairs.

Pia·get |,pēä'zHā|, Jean (1896–1980) Swiss psychologist. Piaget's work on the intellectual and logical abilities of children provided the single biggest impact on the study of the development of human thought processes. He described the mind as proceeding through a series of fixed stages of cognitive development, each being a prerequisite for the next.

Pi·cas·so |pə'käsō|, Pablo (1881–1973) Spanish painter, sculptor, and graphic artist, resident in France from 1904. His prolific inventiveness and technical versatility made him the dominant figure in avant-garde art in the first half of the 20th century. Following his Blue Period (1901–04) and Rose Period (1905–06), *Les Demoiselles d'Avignon* (1907) signaled his development of cubism (1908–14). In the 1920s and 1930s he adopted a neoclassical figurative style and produced semisurrealist paintings using increasingly violent imagery, notably *The Three Dancers* (1935) and *Guernica* (1937).

Pi·cas·so |pə'käsō|, Paloma (1949–) French jewelry designer. She is the daughter of Pablo Picasso.

Pick·er·ing |'pik(ə)riNG|, John (1777–1846) U.S. linguist and lexicographer. The son of Timothy Pickering, he wrote the first dictionary of Americanisms.

Pick·er·ing |'pik(ə)riNG|, Timothy (1745–1829) U.S. government official. He was the U.S. secretary of war (1795) and secretary of state (1795–1800) as well as a member of the U.S. Senate (1803–11) and House of Representatives (1813–17).

Pick·er·ing |'pik(ə)riNG|, William Hayward (1910–) New Zealand-born U.S. engineer, director of the Jet Propulsion Laboratory (JPL) at the California Institute of Technology (1954–76). During his directorate the JPL launched America's first satellite, Explorer I (1958), and several unmanned probes to the moon and planets.

Pick·ett |'pikət|, George Edward (1825–75) U.S. army officer. Last in his class at West Point (1846), he became distinguished as a Confederate general during the Civil War. His military reputation was marred at Gettysburg (1863) when, under orders, he led a disastrous charge ("Pickett's Charge") across an open field.

Pick·ett |'pikət|, Wilson (1941–) U.S. soul-rock singer and songwriter. Notable songs: "In the Midnight Hour."

Pick·ford |'pikfərd|, Mary (1893–1979) Canadian-born U.S. actress; born *Gladys Mary Smith*. She was a star of silent movies, usually playing the innocent young heroine, as *Rebecca of Sunnybrook Farm* (1917), *Pollyanna* (1920).

She won an Academy Award for *Coquette* (1929). She also cofounded United Artists (1919).

Pierce |pirs|, Franklin (1804–69) see box. **Jane Means Appleton Pierce** (1806–63), wife of Franklin Pierce and U.S. first lady (1853–57).

Pier·cy |'pirsē|, Marge (1936–) U.S. author. Notable works: *City of Darkness, City of Light* (1996).

Pie·ro del·la Fran·ces·ca |'pyerō ˌdelə frän'CHeskə| (c. 1420–92) Italian painter. He used perspective, proportion, and geometrical relationships to create ordered and harmonious pictures in which the figures appear to inhabit real space. He is best known for his fres-

---

Pierce, Franklin
14th U.S. president

Life dates: 1804–1869
Place of birth: Hillsborough (now Hillsboro), New Hampshire
Mother: Anna Kendrick Pierce
Father: General Benjamin Pierce
Wife: Jane Means Appleton Pierce
Children: Franklin (died 3 days after birth), Frank, Benjamin
College/University: Bowdoin College
Military service: U.S. Army brigadier general, Mexican War
Career: lawyer
Political career: New Hampshire state legislature; U.S. House of Representatives; U.S. Senate; president
Party: Democratic
Home state: New Hampshire
Opponents in presidential race: Winfield Scott
Term of office: March 4, 1853–March 3, 1857
Vice president: William R. D. King
Notable events of presidency: Tariff Act of 1857; civil war in Kansas; first U.S. World's Fair; Ostend Manifesto; Gadsden Purchase; Treaty of Kanagawa; Republican Party formed; Japanese ports opened to American trade; Kansas-Nebraska Act
Other achievements: Admitted to the New Hampshire bar; declined appointment as U.S. attorney general under President Polk; member and president, New Hampshire Fifth State Constitutional Convention
Place of burial: Concord, N.H.

coes, notably a cycle in Arezzo depicting the story of the True Cross (begun 1452).

Pike |pīk|, Zebulon Montgomery (1779–1813) U.S. explorer. He led expeditions to the Louisiana Purchase region; Pike's Peak, Colorado, is named for him although he never climbed it.

Pi·late |'pīlət|, Pontius (died *c.* 36 AD) Roman procurator of Judaea *c.*26–*c.*36. He is remembered for presiding at the trial of Jesus Christ and authorizing his crucifixion.

Pills·bury |'pilz,berē|, Charles Alfred (1842–99) U.S. businessman. He began as a small flour miller in Minneapolis (1869) and became the largest flour producer in the world (1889).

Pin·cay |pin'kī|, Laffit, Jr. (1946–) U.S. jockey.

Pin·chot |'pinSHō|, Gifford (1865–1946) U.S. forester. He was the first professional American forester and a leader in the land conservation movement; he was also governor of Pennsylvania (1923–27, 1931–35).

Pinck·ney |'piNGknē| U.S. political family, including: **Charles Cotesworth Pinckney** (1746–1825). A Federalist, he ran unsuccessfully for U.S. vice president (1800) and president (1804, 1808). **Thomas Pinckney** (1750–1828), brother of Charles Cotesworth Pinckney. As Washington's minister to England (1792–96) he negotiated Pinckney's Treaty with Spain. **Charles Pinckney** (1757–1824), cousin of Thomas and Charles Cotesworth Pinckney. He was governor of South Carolina (1789–92, 1796–98, 1806–08) and a U.S. Senator (1819–21).

Pin·dar |'pin,där| (*c.* 518–*c.* 438 BC) Greek lyric poet. He is famous for his odes (the *Epinikia*), which celebrate victories in athletic contests at Olympia and elsewhere and relate them to religious and moral themes.

Pi·ne·ro |pi'nerō|, Sir Arthur Wing (1855–1934) English dramatist and actor. Notable works: *The Second Mrs. Tanqueray* (1893).

Pin·ker·ton |'piNGkərtən|, Allan (1819–84) Scottish-born U.S. detective. In 1850 he established the first American private detective agency, be-

coming famous after solving a series of train robberies. He served as *Dandy Dick* (1887). From 1889 he embarked on a number of serious plays dealing with social issues, especially the double standards of morality for men and women.

Pink·ham |'piNGkəm|, Lydia (1819–83) U.S. inventor and saleswoman. She concocted and marketed Mrs. Lydia E. Pinkham's Vegetable Compound, a patented herbal medicine for female complaints (1865).

Pi·no·chet |,pēnō'sHā|, Augusto (1915–) Chilean general and statesman, president (1974–90); full name *Augusto Pinochet Ugarte*. Having masterminded the military coup that overthrew President Allende in 1973, he imposed a military dictatorship until forced to call elections, giving way to a democratically elected president in 1990.

Pin·sky |'pinskē|, Robert (1940–) U.S. author, educator and poet. Notable works: *Sadness and Happiness* (1975) and *The Sounds of Poetry* (1997).

Pin·ter |'pintər|, Harold (1930–) English dramatist, actor, and director. His plays are associated with the Theatre of the Absurd and are typically marked by a sense of menace. Notable plays: *The Birthday Party* (1958), *The Caretaker* (1960), and *Party Time* (1991).

Pin·za |'pinzə|, Ezio (1892–1957) Italian operatic bass. He performed with the Metropolitan Opera for 22 years beginning in 1926 and was responsible for the return of Mozart's operas to the Met repertory by mid-century.

Pi·per |'pīpər|, John (1903–92) English painter and decorative designer. He is best known for his watercolors and aquatints of buildings and for his stained glass in Coventry and Llandaff cathedrals.

Pip·pen |'pipən|, Scottie (1965–) U.S. basketball player.

Pi·ran·del·lo |,pirən'delō|, Luigi (1867–1936) Italian dramatist and novelist. His plays, including *Six Characters in Search of an Author* (1921) and *Henry IV* (1922), challenged the conventions of naturalism. Notable novels: *The Outcast* (1901) and *The Late Mattia Pascal*

(1904). Nobel Prize for Literature (1934).

Pi·ra·ne·si |ˌpirəˈnäzi|, Giovanni Battista (1720–78) Italian engraver. Notable works: *Prisons* (1745–61).

Pir·sig |ˈpərsig|, Robert Maynard (1928–) U.S. author. Notable works: *Zen and the Art of Motorcycle Maintenance* (1974).

Pi·san |ˈpēzän|, Christine de see DE PISAN.

Pi·sa·no[1] |piˈzänō| Italian sculptors: **Andrea** (*c.*1290–*c.*1348) and **Nino**, his son (died *c.*1368). Andrea created the earliest pair of bronze doors for the baptistery at Florence (completed 1336). Nino was one of the earliest to specialize in free-standing life-size figures.

Pi·sa·no[2] |piˈzänō| two Italian sculptors: **Nicola** (*c.*1220–*c.*1278) and his son **Giovanni** (*c.*1250–*c.*1314). Nicola's work departed from medieval conventions and signaled a revival of interest in classical sculpture. His most famous works are the pulpits in the baptistery at Pisa and in Siena cathedral. Giovanni's works include the richly decorated facade of Siena cathedral.

Pi·sis·tra·tus |pəˈsistrətəs| (*c.* 600–*c.* 527 BC) Also **Peisistratus**. Tyrant of Athens. He seized power in 561 and after twice being expelled ruled continuously from 546 until his death. He reduced aristocratic power in rural Attica and promoted the financial prosperity and cultural pre-eminence of Athens.

Pis·sar·ro |piˈsärō|, Camille (1830–1903) French painter and graphic artist. He was a leading figure of the Impressionist movement, typically painting landscapes and cityscapes. He also experimented with pointillism in the 1880s.

Pit·man |ˈpitmən|, Sir Isaac (1813–97) English inventor of a shorthand system, published as *Stenographic Sound Hand* (1837). Pitman shorthand is still widely used.

Pit·ney |ˈpitnē|, Mahlon (1858–1924) U.S. Supreme Court justice (1912–22).

Pitt |pit| the name of two British statesmen: **William**, 1st Earl of Chatham (1708–78); known as **Pitt the Elder**. As Secretary of State (effectively Prime Minister), he headed coalition govern-

ments 1756–61 and 1766–68. He brought the Seven Years War to an end in 1763 and also masterminded the conquest of French possessions overseas, particularly in Canada and India. **William** (1759–1806), Prime Minister 1783–1801 and 1804–06, the son of Pitt the Elder; known as **Pitt the Younger**. The youngest-ever Prime Minister, he introduced financial reforms to reduce the national debt.

Pitt |pit|, Brad (1963–) U.S. actor. He starred in the movie *Seven Years in Tibet* (1997).

Pitt-Rivers |ˌpit ˈrivərz|, Augustus Henry Lane Fox (1827–1900) English archaeologist and anthropologist. He developed a new scientific approach to archaeology. His collection of weapons and artifacts from different cultures formed the basis of the ethnological museum in Oxford that bears his name.

Pi·us XII |ˈpīəs| (1876–1958) pope 1939–58; born *Eugenio Pacelli*. He upheld the neutrality of the Roman Catholic Church during World War II, and was criticized after the war for failing to condemn Nazi atrocities.

Pi·zan, Christine de see DE PISAN.

Pi·zar·ro |piˈzärō|, Francisco (*c.* 1475–1541) Spanish conquistador. He defeated the Inca empire of Peru and in 1533 set up a puppet monarchy at Cuzco, building his own capital at Lima (1535), where he was assassinated.

Planck |plänGk|, Max (Karl Ernst Ludwig) (1858–1947) German theoretical physicist who founded quantum theory, announcing the radiation law named after him in 1900. Nobel Prize for Physics (1918).

Plank |plænGk|, Charles J. (1915–89) U.S. inventor, born in India. With Edward Rosinski he developed the first commercially useful zeolite catalyst in the petroleum industry.

Plante |plænt|, Jacques (1929–86) Canadian hockey player. He was the first goalie to wear a mask during games. Elected to the Hockey Hall of Fame (1978).

Plath |plæTH|, Sylvia (1932–63) U.S. poet, wife of Ted Hughes. Her work is notable for its treatment of extreme and painful states of mind. In 1963 she committed suicide. Notable works: *Ariel* (poems, 1965) and *The Bell Jar* (novel, 1963).

Pla·to |'plātō| (*c.* 429–*c.* 347 BC) Greek philosopher. A disciple of Socrates and the teacher of Aristotle, he founded the Academy in Athens. An integral part of his thought is the theory of "ideas" or "forms," in which abstract entities or *universals* are contrasted with their objects or *particulars* in the material world. His philosophical writings are presented in the form of dialogues, with Socrates as the principal speaker; they include the *Symposium* and the *Timaeus*. Plato's political theories appear in the *Republic*, in which he explored the nature and structure of a just society.

Plau·tus |'plawtəs|, Titus Maccius (*c.* 250–184 BC) Roman comic dramatist. His plays, such as *Rudens*, are modeled on Greek New Comedy.

Play·er |'plāər|, Gary (1935–) South African golfer. He has won numerous championships including the British Open (1959; 1968; 1974), the Masters (1961; 1974; 1978), the PGA (1962; 1972), and the U.S. Open (1965).

Play·fair |'plā,fer|, John (1748–1819) Scottish mathematician and geologist. A friend of James Hutton, he summarized the latter's views for a wider readership in his *Illustrations of the Huttonian Theory of the Earth* (1802).

Plimp·ton |'plimptən|, George Ames (1927–) U.S. author, editor, and television host. He was editor in chief of *Paris Review* (1953–), a contributor to *Sports Illustrated* (1968–), and editor of *Writers at Work*.

Pliny[1] |'plinē| (23–79) Roman statesman and scholar; Latin name *Gaius Plinius Secundus*; known as **Pliny the Elder**. His *Natural History* (77) is a vast encyclopedia of the natural and human worlds. He died while observing the eruption of Vesuvius.

Pliny[2] |'plinē| (*c.* 61–*c.* 112) Roman senator and writer, nephew of Pliny the Elder; Latin name *Gaius Plinius Caecilius Secundus*; known as **Pliny the Younger**. He is noted for his books of letters, which deal with both public and private affairs and which include a de-

scription of the eruption of Vesuvius in 79.

Plo·ti·nus |plə'tīnəs| (*c.* 205–70) philosopher, probably of Roman descent. He was the founder and leading exponent of Neoplatonism; his writings were published after his death by his pupil Porphyry.

Plum·mer |'pləmər|, (Arthur) Christopher (Orme) (1929–) U.S. actor, born in Canada. His award-winning stage, television, and film credits include the movie *The Sound of Music* (1965, Academy Award).

Plu·tarch |'ploo,tärk| (*c.* 46–*c.* 120) Greek biographer and philosopher; Latin name *Lucius Mestrius Plutarchus*. He is chiefly known for *Parallel Lives*, a collection of biographies of prominent Greeks and Romans.

Po·ca·hon·tas |'pōkə'häntəs| (*c.* 1595–1617) American Indian, daughter of Powhatan, an Algonquian chief in Virginia. According to John Smith, Pocahontas rescued him from death at the hands of her father. In 1612 she was seized as a hostage by the English, and she later married colonist John Rolfe.

Pod·ho·retz |päd'hawrəts|, Norman (1930–) U.S. literary critic. The editor of *Commentary* (1960–), he authored *The Bloody Crossroads: Where Literature and Politics Meet* (1986).

Poe |pō|, Edgar Allan (1809–49) U.S. short-story writer, poet, and critic. His fiction and poetry are Gothic in style and characterized by their exploration of the macabre and the grotesque. Notable works: "The Fall of the House of Usher" (short story, 1840), "The Murders in the Rue Morgue" (detective story, 1841), and "The Raven" (poem, 1845).

Poin·ca·ré |,pwænkä'rä|, Jules-Henri (1854–1912) French mathematician and philosopher of science, who transformed celestial mechanics and was one of the pioneers of algebraic topology. He proposed a relativistic philosophy which implied the absolute velocity of light, which nothing could exceed.

Pois·son |,pwä'sōN|, Siméon-Denis (1781–1840) French mathematical physicist. His major contributions were in probability theory, in which he greatly improved Laplace's work and developed several concepts that are now named after him.

Poi·tier |'pwäte͞,a|, Sidney (1924–) U.S. actor and movie director, the first black American actor to achieve superstar status. Notable movies: *Lilies of the Field* (1963) and *In the Heat of the Night* (1967).

Po·lan·ski |pə'lænske͞|, Roman (1933–) French movie director, of Polish descent. His second wife, the actress **Sharon Tate** (1943–69), was one of the victims of a multiple murder by followers of the cult leader Charles Manson. Notable movies: *Rosemary's Baby* (1968) and *Chinatown* (1974).

Polk |po͞k|, James Knox (1795–1849) see box. **Sarah Childress Polk** (1803–91), wife of James Knox Polk and U.S. first lady (1845–49).

Pol·lack |'pälək|, Sydney (1934–) U.S. television and movie director. Notable movies: *The Way We Were* (1973), *Three Days of the Condor* (1975), and *Out of Africa* (1985, Academy Award).

Pol·lai·uo·lo |ˌpo͞li'wo͞lo͞|, Italian sculptors, painters, and engravers: **Antonio** (*c.*1432–98) and **Piero** (1443–96). Both brothers worked on the monuments to Popes Sixtus IV and Innocent VIII in St. Peter's, and Antonio is particularly known for his realistic depiction of the human form.

Pol·lock |'pälək|, (Paul) Jackson (1912–56) U.S. painter. He was a leading figure in the abstract expressionist movement and from 1947 became the chief exponent of the style known as action painting. Fixing the canvas to the floor or wall, he poured, splashed, or dripped paint on it, covering the whole canvas and avoiding any point of emphasis in the picture.

Po·lo |'po͞lo͞|, Marco see MARCO POLO.

Pol Pot |ˌpo͞l 'pät; ˌpäl 'pät| (1925–98) Cambodian communist leader of the Khmer Rouge, prime minister (1976–79); born *Saloth Sar*. During his regime the Khmer Rouge embarked on a brutal reconstruction program in which millions of Cambodians were killed. Overthrown in 1979, Pol Pot led the Khmer Rouge in a guerrilla war against the new Vietnamese-backed government. In 1997 he was denounced by the Khmer Rouge and put under house arrest.

Po·lyb·i·us |pə'libēəs| (*c.* 200–*c.* 118 BC) Greek historian His forty books of *Histories* (only partially extant) chronicled the rise of the Roman Empire from 220 to 146 BC.

Pol·y·carp |'pälē͞,kärp|, St. (*c.* 69–*c.* 155) Greek bishop of Smyrna in Asia Minor. The leading Christian figure in Smyrna, he was arrested during a pagan festival, refused to recant his faith, and was burned to death. Feast day, February 23.

Pol·y·cli·tus |ˌpälē'klītəs| (5th century BC) Greek sculptor, known for his statues of idealized male athletes. Two Roman copies of his works survive, the *Doryphoros* (spear-bearer) and the *Diad-*

Polk, James Knox
11th U.S. president

Life dates: 1795–1849
Place of birth: near Pineville, Mecklenburg County, North Carolina
Mother: Jane Knox Polk
Father: Samuel Polk
Wife: Sarah Childress Polk
Children: none
College/University: University of North Carolina
Career: lawyer
Political career: Tennessee state legislature; U.S. House of Representatives; Speaker of the House; governor of Tennessee; president
Party: Democratic
Home state: Tennessee
Opponent in presidential race: Henry Clay
Term of office: March 4, 1845–March 3, 1849
Vice president: George M. Dallas
Notable events of presidency: U.S. Naval Academy opened; Elias Howe patented sewing machine; Mexican War; California Gold Rush; Women's Rights Convention, Seneca Falls, New York; Oregon admitted as a territory; Department of Interior created; Texas, Iowa, and Wisconsin admitted as 28th, 29th, and 30th states
Other achievements: Admitted to the Tennessee bar
Place of burial: Polk Place, Nashville, Tennessee

umenos (youth fastening a band around his head).

Pom·pa·dour |ˌpämpə'dawr|, Jeanne Antoinette Poisson, Marquise de (1721–64) French noblewoman; known as **Madame de Pompadour**. In 1744 she became the mistress of Louis XV, gaining considerable influence at court, but she later became unpopular as a result of her interference in political affairs.

Pom·pey |'pämpē| (106–48 BC) Roman general and statesman; Latin name *Gnaeus Pompeius Magnus*; known as **Pompey the Great**. He founded the First Triumvirate, but later quarreled with Julius Caesar, who defeated him at the battle of Pharsalus. He then fled to Egypt, where he was murdered.

Pom·pi·dou |'pämpə,dōō|, Georges (Jean Raymond) (1911–74) French statesman, prime minister (1962–68) and president (1969–74). He was instrumental in ending the conflict in Algeria between French forces and nationalist guerrillas.

Ponce de Le·ón |ˌpän(t)s də 'lēän; ˌpän(t)sə ˌdā lē'ōn|, Juan (c. 1460–1521) Spanish explorer. He accompanied Columbus on his second voyage to the New World in 1493, became governor of Puerto Rico (1510–12), and landed on the coast of Florida near what became St. Augustine in 1513, claiming the area for Spain.

Pons |pänz|, Lily (1898–1976) U.S. operatic soprano, born in France. Born *Alice-Joséphine Pons*. She made her debut at the Metropolitan Opera in 1931 as Lucia in *Lucia de Lammermoor* and was the reigning diva at the Met for 25 years.

Pon·selle |pän'sel|, Rosa (1897–1981) U.S. operatic soprano. Born *Rosa Ponzillo*. She sang with the Metropolitan Opera for 19 seasons, beginning in 1918 with her debut as Leonora in *Fidelio*.

Pon·te |'pōntā|, Lorenzo Da see Da Ponte.

Pon·ti·ac |'pän(t)ē,æk| (c. 1720–69) Ottawa Indian chief. He is credited with organizing and leading a rebellion against the British, during which he led a year-long siege of Fort Detroit (1763–64). He agreed to terms of peace in 1766.

Pon·tor·mo |pawn'tawr,mō|, Jacopo da (1494–1557) Italian painter, whose use of dynamic composition, anatomical exaggeration, and bright colors placed him at the forefront of early mannerism.

Pope |pōp|, Alexander (1688–1744) English poet. A major figure of the Augustan age, he is famous for his caustic wit and metrical skill, in particular his use of the heroic couplet. Notable works: *The Rape of the Lock* (1712; enlarged 1714) and *An Essay on Man* (1733–34).

Pope |pōp|, John Russell (1874–1937) U.S. architect. Notable designs: the National Gallery (Washington D.C.).

Pop·per |'päpər|, Sir Karl Raimund (1902–94) Austrian-born British philosopher. In *The Logic of Scientific Discovery* (1934) he argued that scientific hypotheses can never be finally confirmed as true, but are tested by attempts to falsify them. In *The Open Society and its Enemies* (1945) he criticized the historicist social theories of Plato, Hegel, and Marx.

Por·phy·ry |'pawrfərē| (c. 232–303) Neoplatonist philosopher; born *Malchus*. He was a pupil of Plotinus, whose works he edited after the latter's death.

Porsche |'pawrSH(ə)|, Ferdinand (1875–1952) Austrian car designer. In 1934 he designed the Volkswagen ("people's car"), while his name has since become famous for the high-performance sports and racing cars produced by his company, originally to his designs.

Por·sen·na |pawr'senə|, Lars (6th century BC) Also **Porsena** . A legendary Etruscan chieftain, king of the town of Clusium. Summoned by Tarquinius Superbus after the latter's overthrow and exile from Rome, Porsenna subsequently laid siege to the city but did not succeed in capturing it.

Por·ter |'pawrtər|, Cole (1891–1964) U.S. songwriter. He made his name with a series of Broadway musicals and also wrote songs for films, including *High Society* (1956). Notable songs: "Let's Do It," "Night and Day," and "Begin the Beguine." Notable musicals *Anything Goes* (1934) and *Kiss Me, Kate* (1948).

Por·ter |'pawrtər|, David (1780–1843)

U.S. military leader. He served in the wars against France (1799) and Tripoli (1801–05) and in the War of 1812; David Glasgow Farragut was his adopted son.

Por·ter |'pawrtər|, Katherine Anne (1890–1980) U.S. short-story writer and novelist. Notable works: *Pale Horse, Pale Rider* (short stories, 1939), *Ship of Fools* (novel, 1962), and *Collected Short Stories* (1965), for which she won a Pulitzer Prize.

Por·ter |'pawrtər|, Peter (Neville Frederick) (1929–) Australian poet, resident chiefly in England since 1951.

Por·tis |'pawrtəs|, Charles (McColl) (1933–) U.S. author. Notable works: *True Grit* (1968).

Post |pōst|, Charles W. (1854–1914) U.S. inventor. He invented a coffee substitute called Postum, Grape Nuts cereal, and other food products.

Post |pōst|, Emily (Price) (1873–1960) U.S. author. Notable works: *Etiquette* (1922).

Post |pōst|, George Brown (1837–1913) U.S. architect. Notable designs: the New York Stock Exchange and the Wisconsin State Capitol (Madison).

Post |pōst|, Wiley (1899–1935) U.S. aviator. He was the first man to fly solo around the world (1933).

Po·tok, Chaim (1929–) U.S. author and artist. Notable works: *The Chosen* (1967) and *The Gift of Asher Lev* (1991).

Pot·ter |'pätər|, (Helen) Beatrix (1866–1943) English writer for children. She is known for her series of animal stories, illustrated with her own delicate watercolors, which began with *The Tale of Peter Rabbit* (first published privately in 1900).

Pou·lenc |'pōōläNGk|, Francis (Jean Marcel) (1899–1963) French composer. He was a member of Les Six. His work is characterized by lyricism as well as the use of idioms of popular music such as jazz. His work includes songs and the ballet *Les Biches* (1923).

Pound |pownd|, Ezra (Weston Loomis) (1885–1972) U.S. poet and critic, resident in Europe 1908–45. Initially associated with imagism, he later developed a highly eclectic poetic voice, drawing on a vast range of classical and other references and establishing a reputation as a modernist poet. In 1945 he was charged with treason following his pro-Fascist radio broadcasts from Italy during World War II; adjudged insane, he was committed to a mental institution until 1958. Notable works: *Hugh Selwyn Mauberley* (1920) and *Cantos* (series, 1917–70).

Pound |pownd|, Roscoe (1870–1964) U.S. educator. A scholar of modern jurisprudence, he wrote hundreds of books.

Pous·sin |pōō'seN|, Nicolas (1594–1665) French painter. He is regarded as the chief representative of French classicism and a master of the grand manner. His subject matter included biblical scenes (*The Adoration of the Golden Calf*, c.1635), classical mythology (*Et in Arcadia Ego*, c.1655), and historical landscapes.

Pow·der·ly |'powdərlē|, Terence Vincent (1849–1924) U.S. labor leader. He was largely responsible for the first Chinese Exclusion Act (1882) and the Contract Labor Act (1885).

Pow·ell |'powəl|, Adam Clayton, Jr. (1908–72) U.S. clergyman and politician. He was a long-time member of the U.S. House of Representatives from New York (1945–67; 1969–71) and authored over 50 pieces of social legislation.

Pow·ell |'powəl|, Anthony (Dymoke) (1905–) English novelist. He is best known for his sequence of twelve novels *A Dance to the Music of Time* (1951–75), a satirical portrayal of the English upper middle classes between the two world wars.

Pow·ell |'powəl|, Bud (1924–66) U.S. jazz pianist. Full name *Earl Powell*. He was the most important pianist in the early bop style.

Pow·ell |'powəl|, Colin Luther (1937–) U.S. army officer. Decorated for heroism in Vietnam, he later held a series of commands posts and became a White House assistant for national security affairs (1987–89). The first black American to become chairman of the Joint Chiefs of Staff (1989), he was commander in chief of the 1990–91 U.S. military operations (Desert Shield and Desert Storm) against Iraq.

Pow·ell |'powəl|, John Wesley (1834–1902) U.S. geologist and author. He directed the U.S. Geological Survey (1880–94).

Pow·ell |'powəl|, Lewis F., Jr. (1907–98) U.S. Supreme Court justice (1972–87).

Pow·ell |'powəl|, Mel (1923–98) U.S. composer. Born *Melvin Epstein*. He began as a jazz musician before studying with Paul Hindemith (1952).

Pow·ell |'powəl|, Michael (Latham) (1905–90) English movie director, producer, and scriptwriter. He founded The Archers Co. with the Hungarian scriptwriter **Emeric Pressburger** (1902–88); their movies included *The Red Shoes* (1948), *The Tales of Hoffman* (1951), and *A Matter of Life and Death* (1945).

Pow·ha·tan |pow'hætn| (*c.* 1550–1618) Algonquian Indian chief. Indian name *Wa-hun-sen-a-cawh* or *Wahunsonacock*. He was the leader of an alliance ("Powhatan's Confederacy") of some 30 tribes, primarily in eastern Virginia. He is thought to be the first Native American leader to have contact with English settlers in North America. Often noted for his ruthlessness, he made peace with the colonists after his daughter Pocahontas married Englishman John Rolfe (1614).

Prandtl |'präntl|, Ludwig (1875–1953) German physicist. He established the existence of the boundary layer and made important studies on streamlining.

Prax·it·e·les |,præk'sitl,ēz| (mid 4th century BC) Athenian sculptor. Only one of his works, *Hermes Carrying the Infant Dionysus*, survives. He is also noted for a statue of Aphrodite, of which there are only Roman copies.

Prem·in·ger |'preminjər|, Otto (Ludwig) (1906–86) Austrian-born U.S. movie director. Notable productions: *The Moon is Blue* (1953), *The Man with the Golden Arm* (1955), and *Bonjour Tristesse* (1959).

Pren·der·gast |'prendər,gæst|, Maurice Brazil (1859–1924) U.S. artist, born in Canada. A post-Impressionist watercolorist, he painted *Central Park* (1901) and *Promenade* (1914–15).

Pres·cott |'preskät|, William Hickling (1796–1859) U.S. historian. An expert in Spanish history, he authored *The History of the Reign of Ferdinand and Isabella the Catholic* (1838).

Pres·ley |'preslē; 'prezlē|, Elvis (Aron) (1935–77) U.S. singer and actor known as **King of Rock and Roll**. He was the dominant personality of early rock and roll with songs such as "Heartbreak Hotel," "Don't Be Cruel," and "Hound Dog" and was noted for the frank sexuality of his performances. He also made numerous movies, including *King Creole* (1958). He became a cult figure after his death.

Prev·in |'prevən|, André (George) (1929–   ) German-born U.S. conductor, pianist, and composer. He is most famous as a conductor, notably with the London Symphony Orchestra (1968–79), the Pittsburgh Symphony Orchestra (1976–86), and the Royal Philharmonic Orchestra (1987–91).

Pré·vost d'Ex·iles |,prä'vō deg'zēl|, Antoine-François (1697–1763) French novelist; known as **Abbé Prévost**. A Benedictine monk and priest, he is remembered for his novel *Manon Lescaut* (1731), which inspired operas by Jules Massenet and Puccini.

Prez |prä|, Josquin des see DES PREZ.

Price |prīs|, Edison Avery (1918–97) U.S. inventor of track lighting.

Price |prīs|, George (1901–95) U.S. cartoonist. He was a regular contributor to the *New Yorker* magazine.

Price |prīs|, Leontyne (1927–   ) Full name *Mary Violet Leontyne Price*. U.S. singer. Her 1952 Broadway success in *Four Saints in Three Acts* and *Porgy and Bess* led to an international career as an operatic and concert soprano. She made her Metropolitan Opera debut in 1961.

Price |prīs|, Vincent (1911–93) U.S. actor, best known for his performances in a series of movies based on stories by Edgar Allan Poe.

Priest·ley |'prēs(t)lē|, J. B. (1894–1984) English novelist, dramatist, and critic; full name *John Boynton Priestley*. Notable works: *The Good Companions* (1929), a picaresque novel, and the mystery drama *An Inspector Calls* (1947).

Priest·ley |'prēs(t)lē|, Joseph (1733–

1804) English scientist and theologian. Priestley was the author of about 150 books, mostly theological or educational. His chief work was on the chemistry of gases, in which his most significant discovery was of "dephlogisticated air" (oxygen) in 1774; he demonstrated that it was important to animal life, and that plants give off this gas in sunlight.

Pri·mo de Ri·ve·ra |'prēmō ˌdä rē-'verä|, Miguel (1870–1930) Spanish general and statesman, head of state 1923–30. He assumed dictatorial powers after leading a military coup. His son, **José Antonio Primo de Rivera** (1903–36), founded the Falange in 1933 and was executed by Republicans in the Spanish Civil War.

Prince |prins| (1958–) U.S. rock, pop, and funk singer, songwriter, and musician; full name *Prince Rogers Nelson*. An eccentric, prolific performer with an enormously varied output, Prince is perhaps best known for the album and movie *Purple Rain* (1984).

Prince |prins|, Harold S. (1928–) U.S. theatrical producer. He produced *Fiorello* (Pulitzer Prize), *Cabaret*, *Evita*, and *Phantom of the Opera*.

Prince Albert, Prince Charles, etc. see ALBERT, PRINCE; CHARLES, PRINCE, etc.

Princes in the Tower, see EDWARD V.

Princess Anne, Princess Margaret, etc. see ANNE, PRINCESS; MARGARET, PRINCESS, etc.

Pri·scian |'prisH(ē)ən| (6th century AD) Byzantine grammarian; full name *Priscianus Caesariensis*. His *Grammatical Institutions* became one of the standard Latin grammatical works in the Middle Ages.

Pritch·ett |'priCHət|, Sir V. S. (1900–97) English writer and critic; full name *Victor Sawdon Pritchett*. He is chiefly remembered for his short stories.

Pro·co·pi·us |prō'kōpēəs| (c. 500–c. 532) Byzantine historian, born in Caesarea in Palestine. He accompanied Justinian's general Belisarius on his campaigns between 527 and 540. His principal works are the *History of the Wars of Justinian* and *On Justinian's Buildings*.

Proc·tor |'präktər|, William C. (1862–1934) U.S. businessman. Beginning in 1890, he headed the company that invented and marketed Ivory soap. He instituted labor reforms such as profit-sharing and pensions.

Pro·fu·mo |prə'f(y)o͞omō|, John (Dennis) (1915–) British Conservative politician. In 1960 he was appointed secretary of state for war under Harold Macmillan. Three years later news broke of his relationship with Christine Keeler, the mistress of a Soviet diplomat, precipitating a government crisis and his resignation.

Pro·ko·fi·ev |prō'kawfē,ef|, Sergei (Sergeevich) (1891–1953) Russian composer. Notable works include seven symphonies, the opera *The Love for Three Oranges* (1919), the *Lieutenant Kijé* suite (1934), the ballet music for *Romeo and Juliet* (1935–36), and *Peter and the Wolf* (1936), a young person's guide to the orchestra.

Pro·per·tius |prō'pərsH(ē)əs|, Sextus (c. 50–c. 16 BC) Roman poet. His four books of elegies are largely concerned with his love affair with a woman whom he called Cynthia.

Prost |prawst|, Alain (1955–) French racecar driver, four-time winner of the Formula One championship (1985–86, 1989, 1993).

Prou·dhon |prō'dōN|, Pierre-Joseph (1809–65) French social philosopher and journalist. His pamphlet *What Is Property?* (1840) argues that property, in the sense of the exploitation of one person's labor by another, is theft.

Proulx |pro͞o|, E. Annie (1935–) U.S. author. Notable works: *The Shipping News* (1994, Pulitzer Prize).

Proust |pro͞ost|, Joseph-Louis (1754–1826) French analytical chemist. He proposed the law of constant proportions, demonstrating that any pure sample of a chemical compound (such as an oxide of a metal) always contains the same elements in fixed proportions.

Proust |pro͞ost|, Marcel (1871–1922) French novelist, essayist, and critic. He devoted much of his life to writing his novel *À la recherche du temps perdu* (published in seven sections between 1913 and 1927). Its central theme is the recovery of the lost past and the releasing of its creative energies through the stimulation of unconscious memory.

Prout |prowt|, William (1785–1850) English chemist and biochemist. He developed the hypothesis that hydrogen is the primary substance from which all other elements are formed, which, although incorrect, stimulated research in atomic theory.

Prou·ty |'prowtē|, Olive Higgins (1882–1974) U.S. author. Notable works: *Stella Dallas* (1922).

Prud·homme |ˌprōō'dəm|, Paul (1940–) U.S. chef. Established as an expert in traditional cajun and creole cooking, he became renowned for his innovative blackened fish and meats. Notable cookbooks: *Paul Prudhomme's Louisiana Kitchen* (1984).

Ptol·e·my |'täləmē| (2nd century) Greek astronomer and geographer. His teachings had enormous influence on medieval thought, the geocentric view of the cosmos being adopted as Christian doctrine until the late Renaissance. Ptolemy's *Geography*, giving lists of places with their longitudes and latitudes, was also a standard work for centuries, despite its inaccuracies.

Puc·ci |'pōōCHē|, Emilio (1914–) Italian skiwear designer.

Puc·ci·ni |pōō'CHēnē|, Giacomo (1858–1924) Italian composer. Puccini's sense of the dramatic, gift for melody, and skillful use of the orchestra have contributed to his enduring popularity. Notable operas: *La Bohème* (1896), *Tosca* (1900), and *Madama Butterfly* (1904).

Puck·ett |'pəkət|, Kirby (1961–) U.S. baseball player. He led the Minnesota Twins to World Series titles in 1987 and 1991.

Pu·las·ki |pə'læskē|, Casimir (1747–79) Polish count and commissioned American cavalry officer. Having fled from his involvement in a Polish rebellion (1768–72), he arrived in America (1777) on the recommendation of Benjamin Franklin. He joined the cause of American independence and soon became a general (1778). He was invaluable in the defense of Charleston (1779) and was mortally wounded at the siege of Savannah.

Pul·it·zer |'pŏŏlətsər; 'pyŏŏlətsər|, Joseph (1847–1911) Hungarian-born U.S. newspaper proprietor and editor. A pioneer of popular journalism, he owned a number of newspapers, including the *New York World*, and competed for readers with William Randolph Hearst. He made provisions in his will for the establishment of the annual Pulitzer Prizes.

Pul·len |'pŏŏlən|, Don (Gabriel) (1941–95) U.S. jazz pianist. His style mixed bop, soul, and free jazz.

Pull·man |'pŏŏlmən|, George Mortimer (1831–97) U.S. industrialist. The founder of the Pullman Palace Car Co. (1867), he converted railroad coaches into sleeping cars.

Pur·cell |'pərsəl; pər'sel|, Henry (1659–95) English composer. Organist for Westminster Abbey (1679–95), he composed choral odes and songs for royal occasions. His main interest was music for the theater; he composed the first English opera *Dido and Aeneas* (1689) and the incidental music for many plays.

Pu·sey |'pyōōzē|, Edward Bouverie (1800–82) English theologian. In 1833, while professor of Hebrew at Oxford, he founded the Oxford Movement and became its leader after the withdrawal of John Henry Newman (1841). His many writings include a series of *Tracts for the Times*.

Push·kin |'pŏŏSH,kin|, Aleksandr (Sergeevich) (1799–1837) Russian poet, novelist, and dramatist. He wrote prolifically in many genres; his first success was the romantic narrative poem *Ruslan and Ludmilla* (1820). Other notable works include the verse novel *Eugene Onegin* (1833) and the blank-verse historical drama *Boris Godunov* (1831).

Putt·nam |'pətnəm|, Sir David (Terence) (1941–) English movie director. He directed *Chariots of Fire* (1981), which won four Oscars, *The Killing Fields* (1984), and *The Mission* (1986).

Pu·zo |'pōōzō|, Mario (1920–) U.S. author. Notable works: *The Godfather* (1969) and *The Last Don* (1996).

Pyle |pīl|, Ernest Taylor (1900–45) U.S. journalist. A syndicated war correspondent, he won a Pulitzer Prize (1944).

Pym |pim|, Barbara (Mary Crampton)

(1913–80) English novelist. She wrote a number of novels dealing satirically with English middle-class village life, including *Excellent Women* (1952), *Less than Angels* (1955), and *Quartet in Autumn* (1977).

Pyn·chon |'pinCHən|, Thomas (Ruggles) (1937–) U.S. novelist. He is an elusive author who shuns public attention, while his works abandon the normal conventions of the novel. Notable works: *V* (1963), *The Crying of Lot 49* (1966), *Gravity's Rainbow* (1973, National Book Award), *Vineland* (1990), and *Mason and Dixon* (1997).

Pyr·rho |'pirō| (*c.* 365–*c.* 270 BC) Greek philosopher, regarded as the founder of skepticism. He is credited with arguing that happiness comes from suspending judgment because certainty of knowledge is impossible.

Pyr·rhus |'pirəs| (*c.* 318–272 BC) king of Epirus *c.*307–272. After invading Italy in 280, he defeated the Romans at Asculum in 279, but sustained heavy losses; the term *pyrrhic victory* is named in allusion to this.

Py·thag·o·ras |pə'THægərəs| (*c.* 580–500 BC) Greek philosopher; known as **Pythagoras of Samos**. Pythagoras sought to interpret the entire physical world in terms of numbers, and founded their systematic and mystical study; he is best known for the theorem of the right-angled triangle. His analysis of the courses of the sun, moon, and stars into circular motions was not set aside until the 17th century.

Qq

Quant |kwänt|, Mary (1934–   ) English fashion designer. She was a principal creator of the "1960s look," launching the miniskirt in 1966 and promoting bold colors and geometric designs. She was also one of the first to design for the ready-to-wear market.

Qua·si·mo·do |ˌkwäzēˈmō,dō|, Salvatore (1901–68) Italian poet, whose early work was influenced by French symbolism. His later work is more concerned with political and social issues. Nobel Prize for Literature (1959).

Quayle |kwāl|, James Danforth (1947–   ) vice president of the U.S. (1989–93). He served as a member of the U.S. Senate from Indiana (1981–89).

Queen |kwēn|, Ellery. U.S. writer of detective novels; pseudonym of *Frederic Dannay* (1905–82) and *Manfred Bennington Lee* (1905–71), who wrote as a team. Their novels feature a detective also called Ellery Queen.

Quer·cia |ˈkwerCHä|, Jacopo della see DELLA QUERCIA.

Que·zon y Mo·li·na |ˈkäzän ē mōˈlēnə|, Manuel Luis (1878–1944) Filipino politician. He was the first president of the Commonwealth of the Philippines (1935–44).

Quin·cey |ˈkwinsē|, Thomas De see DE QUINCEY.

Quind·len |ˈkwindlən|, Anna (1953–   ) U.S. author and journalist. She wrote *One True Thing* and won a Pulitzer Prize for commentary in *The New York Times* (1992).

Quine |kwīn|, Willard Van Orman (1908–   ) U.S. philosopher and logician. A radical critic of modern empiricism, Quine took issue with the philosophy of language proposed by Rudolf Carnap, arguing that "no statement is immune from revision" and that even the principles of logic themselves can be questioned and replaced. In *Word and Object* (1961) he held that there is no such thing as satisfactory translation.

Quinn |kwin|, Anthony Rudolph Oaxaca (1915–   ) U.S. actor. Notable movies: *Viva Zapata!* (1952, Academy Award).

Quinn |kwin|, Jane Bryant (1939–   ) U.S. journalist. She writes a syndicated financial column (1974–   ) and authored *Everyone's Money Book* (1979).

Quin·te·ro |kwin'terō; kēn'terō|, Jose Benjamin (1924–   ) U.S. theatrical director, born in Panama. He directed *A Moon for the Misbegotten, Long Days Journey into Night,* and *Strange Interlude.*

Quin·til·ian |kwin'tilyən| (*c.* 35–*c.* 96 AD) Roman rhetorician; Latin name *Marcus Fabius Quintilianus.* He is best known for his *Education of an Orator,* a comprehensive treatment of the art of rhetoric and the training of an orator.

Rr

Ra |rä|, Sun (c. 1915–93) U.S. jazz bandleader, pianist, and composer.

Ra·banne, Paco (1934–) Spanish fashion designer.

Rab·bitt |'ræbət|, Eddie (1944–98) U.S. singer and songwriter. Born *Edward Thomas Rabbitt*. He wrote pop and country music, including "Kentucky Rain" and "Suspicious."

Rabe, David (1940–) U.S. author and playwright. Notable works: *Streamers* (1977).

Rab·e·lais |'ræbə,lā|, François (c. 1483–1553) French satirist. His writings are noted for their earthy humor, their parody of medieval learning and literature, and their affirmation of humanist values. Notable works: *Pantagruel* (c. 1532) and *Gargantua* (1534).

Ra·bi |'räbē|, Isidor Isaac (1898–1988) U.S. physicist, born in Austria. He invented the resonance method to measure the magnetic properties of atomic nuclei and won the Nobel Prize in Physics (1944).

Ra·bin |rä'bēn|, Yitzhak (1922–95) Israeli statesman and military leader, prime minister (1974–77 and 1992–95). In 1993 he negotiated a PLO–Israeli peace accord with Yasser Arafat, for which he shared the 1994 Nobel Peace Prize with Arafat and Shimon Peres. He was assassinated by a Jewish extremist.

Rach·ma·ni·nov |räk'mänənawf|, Sergei (Vasilevich) (1873–1943) Russian composer and pianist, resident in the U.S. from 1917. Part of the Russian romantic tradition, he is primarily known for his compositions for piano, including concertos and the Prelude in C sharp minor (1892).

Ra·cine |rə'sēn|, Jean (1639–99) French dramatist, the principal tragedian of the French classical period. Central to most of his tragedies is a perception of the blind folly of human passion, continually enslaved and unsatisfied. Notable works: *Andromaque* (1667) and *Phèdre* (1677).

Rack·ham |'rækəm|, Arthur (1867–1939) English illustrator, noted for his illustrations of books such as the Grimm brothers' *Fairy Tales* (1900) and Washington Irving's *Rip Van Winkle* (1905).

Ra·dis·son |,rädə'sōn|, Pierre Espirit (1636–1710) French explorer. A fur trader in the Lake Superior region, he inspired the organization of the Hudson's Bay Co. (1670).

Rad·ner |'rædnər|, Gilda (1946–82) U.S. comedian and actress. She was an original cast member of "Saturday Night Live."

Rae·burn |'rā,bərn|, Sir Henry (1756–1823) Scottish artist. The leading Scottish portraitist of his day, he depicted the local intelligentsia and Highland chieftains in a bold and distinctive style.

Raf·fi |'ræfē| (1948–) Canadian songwriter and children's entertainer. Full name *Raffi Cavoukian*.

Raf·fles |'ræfəlz|, Sir (Thomas) Stamford (1781–1826) British colonial administrator. As lieutenant general of Sumatra (1818–23), he persuaded the East India Company to purchase the undeveloped island of Singapore (1819), undertaking much of the preliminary work for transforming it into an international port and center of commerce.

Ra·fi·nesque |,räfē'nesk|, Constantine Samuel (1783–1840) U.S. educator and naturalist, born in Turkey.

Raf·san·ja·ni |,räfsən'jänē|, Ali Akbar Hashemi (1934–) Iranian statesman and religious leader, president (1989–97). In 1978 he helped organize the mass demonstrations that led to the shah's overthrow. As leader of Iran he sought to improve the country's relations with the West.

Ra·ha·krish·nam |,rähä'krēsHnäm|, Sir Sarvepalli (1888–1975) Indian philosopher and statesman, president (1962–67). He introduced classiscal Indian philosophy to the West through works such as *Indian Philosophy* (1923–27).

Rah·man |'rämän| see ABDUL RAHMAN, MUJIBUR RAHMAN.

Rahv |räv|, Philip (1908–73) U.S. editor and educator, born in Ukraine. He cofounded and edited the *Partisan Review* (1933).

Rain·ey |'rānē|, Joseph Hayne (1832–87) U.S. politician. He was the first African American elected to the U.S. House of Representatives, from South Carolina (1870–79).

Rain·ey |'rānē|, Ma (1886–1939) U.S. blues singer. Full name *Gertrude Rainey*. She made over 100 recordings with Louis Armstrong and her Georgia Jazz Band.

Rain-in-the-Face (d. 1905) Teton Sioux commander. With Sitting Bull and others, he annihilated the forces under Custer at Little Bighorn (1876).

Raitt |rāt|, Bonnie (1949–) U.S. singer, songwriter, and guitarist. Her style incorporates blues, pop, folk, and rhythm and blues; her album *Nick of Time* won a 1990 Grammy Award.

Raj·neesh |,räj'nēsн|, Bhagwan Shree (1931–90) Indian guru; born *Chandra Mohan Jain*; known as **the Bhagwan** (Sanskrit, "lord"). He founded an ashram in Poona, India, and a commune in Oregon, becoming notorious for his doctrine of communal therapy and salvation through free love. He was deported from the U.S. in 1985 for immigration violations.

Rá·ko·si |'räkəsнē|, Mátyás (1892–1971) Hungarian Communist statesman, first secretary of the Hungarian Socialist Workers' Party 1945–56 and prime minister (1952–53 and 1955–56). After the Communist seizure of power in 1945 he did much to establish a firmly Stalinist regime. He was ousted as premier by the more liberal Imre Nagy in 1953.

Ra·leigh |'rälē|, Sir Walter (*c.* 1552–1618) Also **Ralegh**. English explorer, courtier, and writer. A favorite of Elizabeth I, he organized several voyages of exploration and colonization to the Americas and introduced potato and tobacco plants to England. Imprisoned in 1603 by James I on a charge of conspiracy, he was released in 1616 to lead an expedition in search of El Dorado, but was executed on the original charge when he returned empty-handed.

Ra·ma·krish·na |,rämə'krisнnə| (1836–86) Indian yogi and mystic; born *Gadadhar Chatterjee*. He condemned lust, money, and the caste system, preaching that all religions leading to the attainment of mystical experience are equally good and true.

Ra·man |'rämən|, Sir Chandrasekhara Venkata (1888–1970) Indian physicist. He discovered the Raman effect, one of the most important proofs of the quantum theory of light. Nobel Prize for Physics (1930).

Ra·ma·nu·jan |rə'mänəjən|, Srinivasa Aaiyangar (1887–1920) Indian mathematician. He made a number of original discoveries in number theory, especially, in collaboration with **G. H. Hardy**, 1877–1947, a theorem concerning the partition of numbers into a sum of smaller integers.

Ram·bert |,räm'ber|, Dame Marie (1888–1982) British ballet dancer, teacher, and director, born in Poland; born *Cyvia Rambam*. After moving to London in 1917 she formed and directed the Ballet Club, which became known as the Ballet Rambert in 1935.

Ra·meau |,rä'mō|, Jean-Philippe (1683–1764) French composer, musical theorist, and organist. He is best known for his four volumes of harpsichord pieces (1706–41), which are noted for their bold harmonies and textural diversity.

Ra·món y Ca·jal |rə'mōn ē kə'häl|, Santiago (1852–1934) Spanish physician and histologist. He was a founder of the science of neurology, identifying the neuron as the fundamental unit of the nervous system. Nobel Prize for Physiology or Medicine (1906), shared with Camillo Golgi.

Ram·say |'ræmzē|, Allan (1713–84) Scottish portrait painter. His style is noted for its French rococo grace and sensitivity, particularly in his portraits of women.

Ram·say |'ræmzē|, Sir William (1852–1916) Scottish chemist, discoverer of the noble gases. He first discovered argon, helium, and (with the help of **M. W. Travers**, 1872–1961) neon, krypton, and xenon, determining their atomic weights and places in the periodic table. In 1910, with Frederick Soddy and **Sir Robert Whytlaw-Gray**, 1877–1958, he identified the last noble gas, radon. Nobel Prize for Chemistry (1904).

Ram·ses |'ræmzēz; 'ræmsēz| also **Rameses**. the name of eleven Egyptian pharaohs, notably: **Ramses II** (died *c*.1225 BC), reigned *c*.1292–*c*.1225 BC; known as **Ramses the Great**.The third pharaoh of the 19th dynasty, he built vast monuments and statues, including the two rock temples at Abu Simbel. **Ramses III** (died *c*.1167 BC), reigned *c*.1198–*c*.1167 BC. The second pharaoh of the 20th dynasty, he fought decisive battles against the Libyans and the Sea Peoples. After his death the power of Egypt declined.

Rand |rænd|, Ayn (1905–82) Russian-born U.S. writer and philosopher; born *Alissa Rozenbaum*. She developed a philosophy of "objectivism," arguing for "rational self-interest," individualism, and laissez-faire capitalism, which she presented in both non-fiction works and novels. Notable novels: *The Fountainhead* (1943) and *Atlas Shrugged* (1957).

Ran·dall |'rændəl|, Tony (1920–) U.S. actor. Born *Leonard Rosenberg*. He starred in the television series "The Odd Couple" (1970–74).

Ran·dolph |'ræn,dawlf| American colonial political family, including: **Peyton Randolph** (*c*. 1721–75), the president of the First Continental Congress. **Edmund Jennings Randolph** (1753–1813). The nephew of Peyton Randolph, he was a member of the Continental Congress (1779–82), governor of Virginia (1786–88), U.S. attorney general (1789–94), and U.S. secretary of state (1794–95).

Ran·dolph |'ræn,dawlf|, Asa Philip (1889–1979) U.S. labor and civil rights leader.

Ran·dolph |'ræn,dawlf|, Jennings (1902–98) U.S. politician. He was a Democratic member of the U.S. Senate from West Virginia (1958–85).

Ran·dolph |'ræn,dawlf|, John (1773–1833) U.S. politician. Known as **John Randolph of Roanoke**. A member of the U.S. House of Representatives from Virginia (1799–1813, 1815–17, 1819–25, 1827–29), he was a vigorous proponent of states' rights.

Ran·jit Singh |'rənjət 'siNG| (1780–1839) Indian maharaja, founder of the Sikh state of Punjab; known as the **Lion of the Punjab**. He proclaimed himself maharaja of Punjab in 1801 and went on to make it the most powerful state in India. Most of his territory was annexed by Britain after the Sikh Wars that followed his death.

Rank |ræNGk|, J. Arthur, 1st Baron (1888–1972) English industrialist and film executive; full name *Joseph Arthur Rank*. In 1941 he founded the Rank Organization, a movie production and distribution company that acquired control of the leading British studios and movie theaters in the 1940s and 1950s.

Ran·som |'rænsəm|, John Crowe (1888–1974) U.S. poet and critic. With *The New Criticism* (1941) he started a school of criticism that rejected the Victorian emphasis on literature as a moral force and advocated a close analysis of textual structure in isolation from the social background of the text.

Rao |row|, P. V. Narasimha (1921–) Indian statesman and prime minister (1991–96); full name *Pamulaparti Venkata Narasimha Rao*.

Raph·a·el |'ræfeəl; ,räfi'el| (1483–1520) Italian painter and architect; Italian name *Raffaello Sanzio*. Regarded as one of the greatest artists of the Renaissance, he is particularly noted for his madonnas, including his altarpiece the *Sistine Madonna* (*c*.1513).

Ras·mus·sen |'ræs,mo͞osən|, Knud Johan Victor (1879–1933) Danish explorer and ethnologist of Greenland.

Ra·spu·tin |ræs'pyo͞otn|, Grigori (Efimovich) (1872–1916) Russian monk. He came to exert great influence over Tsar Nicholas II and his family during World War I; this influence, combined with his reputation for debauchery, steadily discredited the imperial family, and he was assassinated by a group loyal to the tsar.

Ra·ta·na |rə'tänə|, Tahupotiki Wiremu (1870–1939) Maori political and religious leader in New Zealand. He founded the Ratana Church (1920), a religious revival movement that aimed to unite all Maori people.

Rath·er |'ræTHər|, Dan (1931–) U.S. journalist. He is managing editor and anchorman for *CBS Evening News* (1981–).

Rat·ti·gan |'rætəgən|, Sir Terence (Mervyn) (1911–77) English dramatist. Notable plays: *The Winslow Boy* (1946), *The Browning Version* (1948), and *Ross* (1960), based on the life of T. E. Lawrence.

Rat·tle |'rætəl|, Sir Simon (Denis) (1955–) English conductor. He was principal conductor with the City of Birmingham Symphony Orchestra 1980–91 and is noted particularly for his interpretation of works by early 20th-century composers such as Mahler.

Rau·schen·berg |'rowSHən,bərg|, Robert (1925–) U.S. artist. His series of "combine" paintings, such as *Charlene* (1954) and *Rebus* (1955), incorporate three-dimensional objects such as nails, rags, and bottles.

Ra·vel |rə'vel|, Maurice (Joseph) (1875–1937) French composer. Noted for their colorful orchestration, his works have a distinctive tone and make use of unresolved dissonances. Notable works: *Daphnis and Chloë* (ballet) (1912); *Boléro* (orchestral work) (1928).

Raw·lings |'rawliNGz|, Marjorie Kinnan (1896–1953) U.S. journalist and author. Notable works: *The Yearling* (1938, Pulitzer Prize).

Rawls |rawlz|, John (1921–) U.S. philosopher. His books *A Theory of Justice* (1971) and *Political Liberalism* (1993) consider the basic institutions of a just society as those chosen by rational people under conditions that ensure impartiality.

Ray |rā|, Man (1890–1976) U.S. photographer, painter, and filmmaker; born *Emmanuel Rudnitsky*. A leading figure in the New York and European Dada movements, he is perhaps best known for his photograph the *Violin d'Ingres* (1924), which achieved the effect of making the back of a female nude resemble a violin.

Ray |rā|, Satyajit (1921–92) Indian movie director, the first to bring Indian movies to the attention of Western audiences. Notable movies: *Pather Panchali* (1955).

Ray·burn |'rā,bərn|, Samuel Taliaferro (1882–1961) U.S. politician. He was a member of the House of Representatives from Texas (1913–61) and speaker of the House (1940–46; 1949–61).

Ray·leigh |'rālē|, John William Strutt (3rd Baron) (1842–1919) English physicist. He established the electrical units of resistance, current, and electromotive force. With William Ramsay he discovered argon and other inert gases. Nobel Prize for Physics (1904).

Ray·mond |'rāmənd|, Alex (1909–56) U.S. cartoonist. Full name *Alexander Gillespie Raymond*. He created the comic strips "Secret Agent X-9," "Flash Gordon," "Jungle Jim," and "Rip Kirby."

Ray·mond |'rāmənd|, Henry Jarvis (1820–69) U.S. journalist. He founded *The New York Times* (1851), which helped launch the Republican Party (1854).

Reade |rēd|, Charles (1814–84) English novelist and dramatist, remembered for his historical romance *The Cloister and the Hearth* (1861).

Rea·gan |'rāgən|, Ronald (Wilson) (1911–) see box. **Nancy Reagan** (1923–), wife of Ronald Reagan and U.S. first lady (1981–89). Born *Anne Frances Robbins Davis*. She campaigned for young people to "Just Say No" to drugs.

Ré·au·mur |'rāə,myōōr|, René Antoine Ferchault de (1683–1757) French naturalist. He is chiefly remembered for his thermometer scale, now obsolete, which set the melting point of ice at 0° and the boiling point of water at 80°. Réaumur also carried out pioneering work on insects and other invertebrates.

Red Cloud |'red 'klowd| (1822–1909) Native American leader of the Oglala Indians. Indian name *Mahpiua Luta*. He opposed the U.S. government's attempts to build forts along the Bozeman Trail in Wyoming and Montana.

Red·ding |'rediNG|, Otis (1941–67) U.S. soul singer. One of the most influential soul singers of the late 1960s, it was not until the Monterey pop festival in 1967 that he gained widespread recognition. "Dock of the Bay," released after Redding's death in an airplane crash, became a number-one hit in 1968.

Red·en·bach·er |'redn,bäkər|, Orville (1907–95) U.S. agricultural scientist.

<table>
<tr><td>

Reagan, Ronald Wilson
40th U.S. president

Life dates: 1911–

Place of birth: Tampico, Illinois

Mother: Nelle Clyde Wilson Reagan

Father: John Edward Reagan

Wives: Jane Wyman (born Sarah Jane Fulks); divorced 1948; married Nancy Davis (born Anne Frances Robbins) in 1952

Children: (with first wife) Maureen, Michael (adopted); (with second wife) Patricia, Ronald (Skip)

Nickname: Dutch

College/University: Eureka College

Military service: U.S. Army Air Forces during World War II

Career: Radio announcer; motion picture and television actor

Political career: Governor of California

Party: Republican (Democrat until 1962)

Home state: California

Opponents in presidential races: Jimmy Carter, John Anderson; Walter F. Mondale

Term of office: Jan. 20, 1981–Jan. 20, 1989

Vice president: George Bush

Notable events of presidency: Economic Recovery Tax Act of 1981; assassination attempt by John Hinckley Jr.; dismissal of 13,000 striking air traffic controllers; Sandra Day O'Connor appointed first woman Supreme Court justice; 241 die in bombing of U.S. Marine Corps building in Lebanon; U.S. invasion of Caribbean island of Grenada; space shuttle *Challenger* disaster; Chernobyl nuclear power plant disaster; Intermediate-Range Nuclear Forces Treaty; Iran-contra affair

Other achievements: president, Screen Actors Guild (six terms, five consecutively); television series host

</td></tr>
</table>

He founded the Orville Redenbacher popcorn company.

Red·field |ˈredfēld|, William C. (1789–1857) U.S. scientist. He discovered that hurricanes are revolving storms (1840) and served as the first president of the American Association for the Advancement of Science.

Red·ford |ˈredfərd|, (Charles) Robert (1937–   ) U.S. movie actor and director. He made his name playing opposite Paul Newman in *Butch Cassidy and the Sundance Kid* (1969), costarring again with him in *The Sting* (1973). Other notable movies include *The Way We Were* (1973), *The Great Gatsby* (1974), *All the President's Men* (1976), and *Ordinary People* (1980), for which he won an Oscar as director. He sponsors the annual Sundance Film Festival for independent filmakers

Red·grave |ˈred,grāv| the name of a family of English actors, notably: **Sir Michael (Scudamore)** (1908–85). A well-known stage actor, he played numerous Shakespearean roles and also starred in films such as *The Browning Version* (1951) and *The Importance of Being Earnest* (1952). **Vanessa** (1937–   ), Sir Michael's eldest daughter. Her successful career in the theater and movies includes the films *Mary Queen of Scots* (1972), *Julia* (1976), for which she won an Oscar, and *Howard's End* (1992) Her sister **Lynn** (1943–   ) has appeared in many films, including *Georgy Girl* (1966, Academy Award) and *Gods and Monsters* (1998)..

Red Jack·et |ˈred ˈjækət| (c. 1758–1830) Native American leader of the Seneca Indians. He received a symbolic medal from President Washington (1792).

Red·man |ˈredmən|, Don (1900–64) U.S. composer, bandleader, and saxophonist. Full name *Donald Matthew Redman.* He formed his own band (1931) and is noted for such songs as "Flight of the Jitterbugs" (1939) and "Deep Purple."

Red·mond |ˈredmənd|, John (Edward) (1856–1918) Irish politician, leader of the Irish Nationalist Party in the House of Commons 1891–1918. The Home Rule Bill of 1912 was introduced with his support, although it was never implemented because of World War I.

Re·don |rəˈdawn; rəˈdōN|, Odilon (1840–1916) French painter and graphic artist. He was a leading exponent of symbolism and forerunner of surrealism, especially in his early charcoal drawings of fantastic or nightmarish subjects.

Red·stone |ˈred,stōn|, Sumner Murray (1923–   ) U.S. businessman and lawyer. He is president and CEO of National Amusements, Inc. (1967–) and chairman of the board of Viacom, Inc. (1987–).

Reed |rēd|, Donna (1921–86) U.S. actress. Born *Donna Belle Mullenger*. Notable movies: *From Here to Eternity* (1953, Academy Award).

Reed |rēd|, Ishmael (1938–) U.S. author. Full name *Ishmael Scott Emmett Coleman Reed*. Notable works: *Japanese by Spring* (1993).

Reed |rēd|, John (1887–1920) U.S. journalist and poet. He organized the first communist party in the U.S. (1919) and edited its journal *The Voice of Labor*.

Reed |rēd|, Lou (1942–) U.S. rock singer, guitarist, and songwriter; full name *Lewis Allan Reed*. Reed led the Velvet Underground, his literate songs dealing with hitherto taboo subjects such as heroin addiction and sado-masochism. His best-known solo recordings are the song "Walk on the Wild Side" and album *Transformer* (both 1972).

Reed |rēd|, Stanley Forman (1884–1980) U.S. Supreme Court justice (1938–57).

Reed |rēd|, Willis (1942–) U.S. basketball player.

Reeve |rēv|, Christopher (1952–) U.S. actor and director. Notable movies: *Superman* (1978).

Reeve |rēv|, Tapping (1744–1823) U.S. lawyer and educator. He founded the Litchfield Law School (1784), the first law school in the U.S.

Reeves |rēvz|, Jim (1924–64) U.S. country singer and songwriter. Notable songs: "Four Walls."

Reeves |rēvz|, Martha (1941–) U.S. pop and soul singer. She was the lead singer of Martha and the Vandellas. Notable songs: "Dancing in the Streets," "Heat Wave," and Jimmy Mack."

Rehn·quist |'ren,kwist|, William Hubbs (1924–) Chief Justice of the U.S. (1986–). As President Nixon's assistant attorney general (1969–71), he held to a conservative stance that opposed civil rights legislation. He was appointed U.S. Supreme Court justice in 1972 and chief justice in 1986.

Re·ho·bo·am |,rē(h)ə'bōəm| (c. 930–c.

915) son of Soloman, king of anicent Israel (*c.*930–*c.*915 BC). His reign witnessed the secession of the northern tribes and their establishment of a new kingdom under Jeroboam, leaving Rehoboam as the first king of Judah (1 Kings 11–14).

Reich |rīk|, Steve (1936–) U.S. composer; full name *Stephen Michael Reich*. A leading minimalist, he uses the repetition of short phrases within a simple harmonic field. Influences include Balinese and West African music.

Reid |rēd|, Whitelaw (1837–1912) U.S. journalist and diplomat. He was the managing editor of *The New York Tribune* (1872–1905) and the U.S. minister to France and ambassador to England.

Rei·ner |'rīnər| U.S. family of actors. **Carl Reiner** (1922–) produced and wrote for the television series "The Dick Van Dyke Show." **Rob Reiner** (1947–), his son, acted in the television series "All in the Family" and directed the movies *Stand By Me* (1986) and *The Princess Bride* (1987).

Rein·hardt |'rīn,härt|, Django (1910–53) Belgian jazz guitarist; born *Jean Baptiste Reinhardt*. He became famous in Paris in the 1930s for his improvisational style, blending swing with influences from his gypsy background.

Rein·hardt |'rīn,härt|, Max (1873–1943) Austrian director and impresario; born *Max Goldmann*. He produced large-scale versions of such works as Sophocles' *Oedipus Rex* (1910), and helped establish the Salzburg Festival, with Richard Strauss and Hugo von Hofmannsthal.

Rein·king |'rinkiNG|, Ann (1950–) U.S. actress and dancer. Her stage, film, and television appearances include *A Chorus Line*, *All That Jazz*, and *Chicago* (1997, Tony Award).

Reith |rēTH|, John (Charles Walsham), 1st Baron (1889–1971) Scottish administrator and politician, first general manager (1922–27) and first director general (1927–38) of the BBC.

Re·marque |rə'märk|, Erich Maria (1898–1970) German-born U.S. novelist. His first novel, *All Quiet on the Western Front* (1929, movie 1930), was a huge international success. All of his ten novels deal with the horror of war and its aftermath.

Rem·brandt |'rem,brænt| (1606–69) Dutch painter; full name *Rembrandt Harmensz van Rijn*. He made his name as a portrait painter with the *Anatomy Lesson of Dr Tulp* (1632). With his most celebrated painting, the *Night Watch* (1642), he used chiaroscuro to give his subjects a more spiritual and introspective quality, a departure that was to transform the Dutch portrait tradition. Rembrandt is especially identified with the series of more than sixty self-portraits painted from 1629 to 1669.

Re·ming·ton |'remiNGtən| , Frederic (1861–1909) U.S. painter and sculptor. He painted scenes of the American West. Notable sculptures: *Bronco Buster*.

Re·nan |rə'nän| , (Joseph) Ernest (1823–92) French historian, theologian, and philosopher. He provoked a controversy with the publication of his *Life of Jesus* (1863), which rejected the supernatural element in Jesus' life.

Re·nault |rə'nō| , Louis (1877–1944) French engineer and automotive manufacturer. He and his brothers established the Renault company in 1898, manufacturing racing cars, and later industrial and agricultural machinery and military technology.

Re·nault |rə'nō| , Mary (1905–83) British novelist, resident in South Africa from 1948; pseudonym of *Mary Challans*. She wrote historical novels set in the ancient world, notably a trilogy dealing with Alexander the Great (1970–81).

Ren·dell |'rendəl| , Ruth (Barbara) (1930–) English writer of detective fiction and thrillers. She is noted for her psychological crime novels and her character Chief Inspector Wexford; she also writes under the pseudonym of Barbara Vine.

Re·no |'rēnō| , Janet (1938–) U.S. attorney general (1993–). She was the first woman to be appointed to this office.

Re·noir |,ren'wär| French family, including: **(Pierre) Auguste Renoir** (1841–1919), French painter. An early Impressionist, he developed a style characterized by light, fresh colors and indistinct, subtle outlines. Notable works: *Les Grandes baigneuses* (1884–87). **Jean Renoir** (1894–1979), French movie director, his son. He is famous for movies including *La Grande illusion* (1937) and *La Règle du jeu* (1939).

Ren·wick |'renwik| , James, Jr. (1818–95) U.S. architect. Notable designs: St. Patrick's Cathedral (New York, 1853); the Smithsonian Institution (1848); and Vassar College (1865).

Res·nais |rə'nā| , Alain (1922–) French movie director. One of the foremost directors of the *nouvelle vague*, he used experimental techniques to explore memory and time. Notable movies: *Hiroshima mon amour* (1959) and *L'Année dernière à Marienbad* (1961).

Re·spig·hi |rə'spēgē| , Ottorino (1879–1936) Italian composer. He is best known for his suites the *Fountains of Rome* (1917) and the *Pines of Rome* (1924), based on the poems of Gabriele d'Annunzio.

Reu·ter |'roitər| , Paul Julius, Baron von (1816–99) German pioneer of telegraphy and news reporting; born *Israel Beer Josaphat*. After establishing a service for sending commercial telegrams in Aachen (1849), he moved his headquarters to London, where he founded the news agency Reuters.

Reu·ther |'rōōTHər| , Walter (1907–70) U.S. labor leader. He was president of the United Automobile Workers (1946–70) and of the Congress of Industrial Organizations (1952–55).

Rev·els |'revəlz| , Hiram Rhoades (1822–1901) U.S. politician, educator, and clergyman. He was the first African American elected to the U.S. Senate, from Mississippi (1870–71).

Re·vere |rə'vir| , Paul (1735–1818) American patriot and silversmith. In 1775 he rode from Boston to Lexington to warn fellow American revolutionaries of the approach of British troops, immortalized in Longfellow's poem "Paul Revere's Ride" (1863).

Rex·roth |'reks,rawTH| , Kenneth (1905–82) U.S. poet and critic. Notable works: *New Poems* (1974); *Classics Revisited* (1969).

Rey·nolds |'renəldz| , Albert (1933–) Irish Fianna Fáil statesman, prime minister (1992–94). He was involved with British prime minister John Major in drafting the Downing Street Declaration (1993), intended as the basis of a peace initiative in Northern Ireland.

Rey·nolds |'renəldz|, Sir Joshua (1723–92) English painter. The first president of the Royal Academy (1768), he sought to raise portraiture to the status of historical painting by adapting poses and settings from classical statues and Renaissance paintings.

Re·za Shah |'räzə 'sHä| see PAHLAVI.

Rhead, Louis John (1857–1926) U.S. artist. His work was often featured on the covers of magazines such as *Harper's*.

Rhee |rē|, Syngman (1875–1965) president of the Republic of Korea (1948–60). Having been the principal leader in the movement for Korean independence, he became president of the exiled Korean provisional government (1919–41). Following World War II, he returned from exile and became the first elected president of the Republic of Korea (South Korea). Amid social and political unrest, he resigned one month into his fourth term (1960) and went into exile in Hawaii.

Rhine |rīn|, Joseph Banks (1895–1980) U.S. parapsychologist. He was founder and director of the Institute of Parapsychology in North Carolina (1964–68), which investigated extra-sensory perception.

Rhodes |rōdz|, Cecil (John) (1853–1902) British-born South African statesman, prime minister of Cape Colony (1890–96). He expanded British territory in southern Africa, annexing Bechuanaland (now Botswana) in 1884 and developing Rhodesia from 1889. By 1890 he had acquired 90 percent of the world's production of diamonds.

Rhodes |rōdz|, Richard Lee (1937–) U.S. author. Notable works include *The Making of the Atomic Bomb* (1988, Pulitzer Prize).

Rhys |rēs|, Jean (1894–1979) British novelist and short-story writer, born in Dominica; pseudonym of *Ella Gwendolen Rees Williams*. Her novels include *Good Morning, Midnight* (1939) and *Wide Sargasso Sea* (1966).

Rib·ben·trop |'rib(ə)n,träp|, Joachim von (1893–1946) German Nazi politician. As foreign minister (1938–45) he signed the nonaggression pact with the Soviet Union (1939). He was convicted as a war criminal in the Nuremberg trials and hanged.

Ri·be·ra |rə'berə|, José (or Jusepe) de (*c.* 1591–1652) Spanish painter and etcher, resident in Italy from 1616; known as **Lo Spagnoletto** ("the little Spaniard"). He is best known for his religious and genre paintings, for example the *Martyrdom of St. Bartholomew* (*c.*1630).

Rice |rīs|, Anne (1941–) U.S. author. Notable works: *Pandora: New Tales of the Vampire* (1998).

Rice |rīs|, Jerry (1962–) U.S. football player. He set NFL records in pass receptions and passing touchdowns.

Rice |rīs|, Thomas Dartmouth (1808–60) U.S. minstrel singer and playwright. He introduced the song and dance "Jim Crow" (1828).

Rice |rīs|, Sir Tim (1944–) English lyricist and entertainer; full name *Timothy Miles Bindon Rice*. Together with Andrew Lloyd Webber he cowrote a number of hit musicals, including *Joseph and the Amazing Technicolor Dreamcoat* (1968), *Jesus Christ Superstar* (1971), and *Evita* (1978). He has also won two Oscars for best original movie song (1992 and 1994).

Rich |riCH|, Adrienne (Cecile) (1929–) U.S. author and poet. Notable works: *Dark Fields of the Republic: Poems, 1991–1995* (1995).

Rich |riCH|, Buddy (1917–87) U.S. jazz drummer and bandleader; born *Bernard Rich*. He played for bandleaders such as Artie Shaw and Tommy Dorsey and formed his own band in 1946.

Rich |riCH|, Charlie (1932–95) U.S. country singer and songwriter. Known as **Silver Fox**. Notable songs: "Behind Closed Doors" and "The Most Beautiful Girl."

Rich |riCH|, Frank (1949–) U.S. journalist. He wrote for *The New York Times* as a drama critic (1980–93) and an op-ed columnist (1994–).

Rich·ard I |'riCHərd| (1157–99) king of England son of Henry II, reigned

1189–99; known as **Richard Coeur de Lion** or **Richard the Lionheart**. He led the Third Crusade, defeating Saladin at Arsuf (1191), but failing to capture Jerusalem. Returning home, he was held hostage by the Holy Roman Emperor Henry VI until being released in 1194 on payment of a huge ransom.

Rich·ard II |'riCHərd| (1367–1400) king of England son of the Black Prince, reigned 1377–99. Following his minority, he executed or banished most of his former opponents. His confiscation of John of Gaunt's estate on the latter's death provoked Henry Bolingbroke's return from exile to overthrow him.

Rich·ard III |'riCHərd| (1452–85) king of England brother of Edward IV, reigned 1483–85. He served as Protector to his nephew Edward V, who, after two months, was declared illegitimate and subsequently disappeared. Richard's brief rule ended at Bosworth's Field, where he was defeated by Henry Tudor and killed.

Rich·ard |'riCHərd|, Cliff (1940–) British pop singer, born in India; born *Harry Roger Webb*.

Rich·ard |'riCHərd|, Maurice (1921–) Canadian hockey player. He was the first player to score 50 goals in one season.

Richard Coeur de Lion Richard I of England (see RICHARD).

Rich·ards |'riCHərdz|, I. A. (1893–1979) English literary critic and poet; full name *Ivor Armstrong Richards*. He emphasized the importance of close textual study, and praised irony, ambiguity, and allusiveness. Notable works: *Practical Criticism* (1929).

Rich·ards |'riCHərdz|, Keith (1943–) British rock guitarist and vocalist. He performed with the Rolling Stones; his solo albums include *Main Offender* (1992).

Rich·ards |'riCHərdz|, Laura Elizabeth (1850–1943) U.S. author. She wrote over 80 children's books and, with her sister Maud Howe Elliott, a biography of their mother, *Julia Ward Howe* (1915, Pulitzer Prize).

Rich·ards |'riCHərdz|, Michael (1949–) U.S. actor. He is noted for

his role in the television show "Seinfeld" (1990–98).

Rich·ard·son |'riCHərdsən|, Elliot Lee (1920–) U.S. lawyer. The U.S. attorney general under President Nixon, he resigned in protest when Nixon fired Watergate special prosecutor Archibald Cox (1973).

Rich·ard·son |'riCHərdsən|, Henry Hobson (1838–86) U.S. architect. A pioneer in designing an indigenous American style of architecture, he created Trinity Church (Boston, 1872–77) and the Marshall Field Building (Chicago, 1885–87).

Rich·ard·son |'riCHərdsən|, Natasha (1963–) U.S. actress. Notable movies: *The Parent Trap* (1998).

Rich·ard·son |'riCHərdsən|, Sir Ralph (David) (1902–83) English actor. He played many Shakespearean roles as well as leading parts in plays including Harold Pinter's *No Man's Land* (1975) and movies including *Oh! What a Lovely War* (1969).

Rich·ard·son |'riCHərdsən|, Samuel (1689–1761) English novelist. His first novel *Pamela* (1740–41), entirely in the form of letters and journals, popularized the epistolary novel. He experimented further with the genre in *Clarissa Harlowe* (1747–48).

Richard the Lionheart Richard I of England (see RICHARD).

Rich·e·lieu |'risHəl,(y)o͞o|, Armand Jean du Plessis, duc de (1585–1642) French cardinal and statesman. As chief minister of Louis XIII (1624–42) he dominated French government. In 1635 he established the Académie Française.

Rich·ie |'riCHē|, Lionel B., Jr. (1949–) U.S. singer, songwriter, and producer. His hits include "We Are the World" (1985), "Truly" (1982), and "Say You, Say Me" (1987).

Rich·ler |'riCHlər|, Mordecai (1931–) Canadian writer. His best-known novel is probably *The Apprenticeship of Duddy Kravitz* (1959). Notable works: *St. Urbain's Horseman* (1971), and *Simon Gursky Was Here* (1989).

Rich·ter |'riktər|, Conrad (Michael) (1890–1968) U.S. author. Notable works: *The Town* (1950, Pulitzer Prize).

Richt·ho·fen |'rikt,hawfən|, Manfred,

Freiherr von (1882–1918) German fighter pilot; known as **the Red Baron**. He joined a fighter squadron in 1915, flying a distinctive bright red aircraft. He was eventually shot down after destroying eighty enemy planes.

Rick·ey |'rikē|, Branch (1881–1965) U.S. baseball manager. He revolutionized the game with the creation of the modern farm system, and he integrated the major leagues when he brought Jackie Robinson to the Brooklyn Dodgers (1947).

Rick·o·ver |'rik,ōvər|, Hyman George (1900–86) U.S. naval officer, born in Poland (then part of Russia). A rear admiral in 1953 and a vice admiral in 1959, he was the individual most responsible for creating the U.S. nuclear-powered navy. The world's first nuclear-powered submarine, the USS *Nautilus*, was launched under his direction (1954). He received the Presidential Medal of Freedom (1980).

Ride |rīd|, Sally (1951–) U.S.astronaut. She was the first U.S. woman to travel in space, on the shuttle *Challenger* (1983).

Rid·ley |'ridlē|, Nicholas (*c.* 1500–55) English Protestant bishop and martyr. He was appointed bishop of Rochester (1547) and then of London (1550). He opposed the Catholic policies of Mary I, for which he was burnt at the stake.

Rie |rē|, Lucie (1902–95) Austrian-born British potter. Her pottery and stoneware were admired for their precise simple shapes and varied subtle glazes.

Rie·fen·stahl |'rēfən,stawl|, Leni (1902–) German filmmaker and photographer; full name *Bertha Helene Amalie Riefenstahl.* She is chiefly known for *Triumph of the Will* (1934), a depiction of the 1934 Nuremberg Nazi Party rallies. Though she was not working for the Nazi Party, outside Germany her work was regarded as Nazi propaganda.

Riel |rē'el|, Louis (1844–85) Canadian political leader. He led the rebellion of the Metis at Red River Settlement in 1869, later forming a provisional government and negotiating terms for the union of Manitoba with Canada. He was

executed for treason after leading a further rebellion.

Rie·mann |'rēmän|, (Georg Friedrich) Bernhard (1826–66) German mathematician. He founded Riemannian geometry, which is of fundamental importance to both mathematics and physics. The *Riemann hypothesis,* about the complex numbers which are roots of a certain transcendental equation, remains an unsolved problem.

Riis |rēs|, Jacob August (1849–1914) U.S. journalist and reformer, born in Denmark. He was police reporter for *The New York Tribune* (1877–88) and *The New York Evening Sun* (1888–99) and a crusader for parks, playgrounds, and improved schools and housing in urban areas.

Riles |rīlz|, Wilson Camanza (1917–) U.S. educational consultant. Spingarn Medal, 1973.

Ri·ley |'rīlē|, Bridget (Louise) (1931–) English painter. A leading exponent of op art, she worked with flat patterns to create optical illusions of light and movement. Notable paintings: *Fall* (1963).

Ri·ley |'rīlē|, James Whitcomb (1849–1916) U.S. poet. Notable works: *The Old Swimmin'-Hole and 'Leven More Poems* (1883).

Ri·ley |'rīlē|, Pat (1945–) U.S. professional basketball player and coach. He coached the Los Angeles Lakers to four of their five NBA titles.

Ril·ke |'rilkə|, Rainer Maria (1875–1926) Austrian poet, born in Bohemia; pseudonym of *René Karl Wilhelm Josef Maria Rilke.* His conception of art as a quasi-religious vocation culminated in his best-known works, the *Duino Elegies* and *Sonnets to Orpheus* (both 1923).

Ril·lieux, Norbert (1806–94) U.S. inventor. He revolutionized the sugar-refining industry (1846) .

Rim·baud |ræm'bō|, (Jean Nicholas) Arthur (1854–91) French poet. Known for poems such as "Le Bateau ivre" (1871) and the collection of symbolist prose poems *Une Saison en enfer* (1873), and for his stormy relationship with Paul Verlaine, he stopped writing at about the age of 20 and spent the rest of his life traveling.

Rimes |rīmz|, LeAnn (1982–) U.S. country singer and songwriter. Grammy Award, 1997.

Rimsky-Korsakov |ˌrimskē ˈkawrsə kawf|, Nikolai (Andreevich) (1844–1908) Russian composer. He achieved fame with his orchestral suite *Scheherazade* (1888) and his many operas drawing on Russian and Slavic folk tales.

Rines |rinz|, Robert Harvey (1922–) U.S. inventor and lawyer. He invented high-resonance image-scanning radar and sonar.

Rip·ken |ˈripkin|, Cal, Jr. (1960–) U.S. baseball player. He holds the major league record of 2,632 consecutive games.

Rip·ley |ˈriplē|, George (1802–80) U.S. critic and reformer. A Unitarian minister who withdrew from the profession, he became associated with the New England Transcendentalists and founded the Brook Farm commune (1841–47). He created the first daily book review in U.S., at the *New York Tribune* (1849–80).

Rit·ten·house |ˈrit(ə)n‚hows|, David (1732–96) U.S. astronomer, surveyor, and clockmaker. He settled the dispute over the boundaries of the Mason-Dixon line.

Rit·ter |ˈritər|, Tex (1907–74) U.S. country singer, songwriter. Notable songs: "Jingle, Jangle, Jingle."

Ri·ve·ra |rəˈverə|, Diego (1886–1957) Mexican painter. He inspired a revival of fresco painting in Latin America and the U.S. His largest mural is a history of Mexico for the National Palace in Mexico City (unfinished, 1929–57).

Riv·ers |ˈrivərz|, Joan (1937–) U.S. entertainer. She has appeared on many television shows with her trademark line, "Can we talk?"

Ro·bards |ˈrōˌbärds|, Jason Nelson, Jr. (1922–) U.S. actor. Notable movies: *Long Day's Journey into Night* (1962) and *All The President's Men* (1976, Academy Award).

Robbe-Grillet |ˌräbgrēˈye|, Alain (1922–) French novelist. His first novel, *The Erasers* (1953), was an early example of the *nouveau roman*. He also wrote essays and screenplays.

Rob·bia |ˈrawbyä| see DELLA ROBBIA.

Rob·bins |ˈräbənz|, Harold (1916–97) U.S. novelist He wrote best-sellers such as *The Carpetbaggers* (1961) and *The Betsy* (1971).

Rob·bins |ˈräbənz|, Jerome (1918–98) U.S. ballet dancer and choreographer. He choreographed a number of successful musicals, including *The King and I* (1951), *West Side Story* (1957), and *Fiddler on the Roof* (1964).

Rob·bins |ˈräbənz|, Marty (1925–82) U.S. country singer and songwriter. Notable songs: "A White Sport Coat and a Pink Carnation."

Rob·bins |ˈräbənz|, Tom (1936–) U.S. author. Notable works: *Even Cowgirls Get the Blues* (1976) and *Half Asleep in Frog Pajamas* (1994).

Rob·ert |ˈräbərt| the name of three kings of Scotland: **Robert I** (1274–1329), reigned 1306–29; known as **Robert the Bruce**. He campaigned against Edward I and defeated Edward II at Bannockburn (1314). He re-established Scotland as a separate kingdom, negotiating the Treaty of Northampton (1328). **Robert II** (1316–90), grandson of Robert the Bruce, reigned 1371–90. He was steward of Scotland from 1326 to 1371 and the first of the Stuart line. **Robert III** (*c.* 1337–1406), son of Robert II, reigned 1390–1406; born *John*. An accident made him physically disabled, resulting in a power struggle among members of his family.

Rob·erts |ˈräbərts|, Cokie (1943–) U.S. journalist. Full name *Corinne Boggs Roberts*. She is a correspondent for National Public Radio. (1977–), a co-anchor on the television program "This Week" (1996–), and the author of *We Are Our Mother's Daughters* (1998).

Rob·erts |ˈräbərts|, Frederick Sleigh, 1st Earl Roberts of Kandahar (1832–1914) British field marshal.

Rob·erts |ˈräbərts|, Owen Josephus (1875–1955) U.S. Supreme Court justice (1930–45). He also served as dean of the University of Pennsylvania Law School (1948–51).

Rob·ert·son |ˈräbərtsən|, Cliff (1925–) U.S. actor. Notable movies: *Charly* (1968, Academy Award).

Rob·ert·son |ˈräbərtsən|, Oscar (1938–) U.S. basketball player. He led the 1960 U.S. Olympic team to a gold medal.

Rob·ert the Bruce see ROBERT.

Robe·son |'rōb(ə)sən|, Paul (Bustill) (1898–1976) U.S. singer and actor. His singing of "Ol' Man River" in the musical *Showboat* (1927) established his international reputation. As an actor Robeson was particularly identified with the title role of *Othello*. His black activism and Communist sympathies led to ostracism in the 1950s.

Robes·pierre |ˌrōbz'pyer|, Maximilien François Marie Isidore de (1758–94) French revolutionary. As leader of the radical Jacobins in the National Assembly he backed the execution of Louis XVI, implemented a purge of the Girondists, and initiated the Terror, but the following year he fell from favor and was guillotined.

Rob·in·son |'räbənsən|, Brooks (1937–) U.S. baseball player. He led the American League in fielding 12 times (1960–72).

Rob·in·son |'räbənsən|, Edward G. (1893–1972) Romanian-born U.S. actor; born *Emanuel Goldenberg*. He appeared in a number of gangster movies in the 1930s, starting with *Little Caesar* (1930).

Rob·in·son |'räbənsən|, Edwin Arlington (1869–1935) U.S. poet. His verse was largely unnoticed until 1905, when President T. Roosevelt praised his dramatic, often ironic work, setting into motion much recognition. Pulitzer Prize–winning works: *Collected Poems* (1921), *The Man Who Died Twice* (1924), and *Tristram* (1927).

Rob·in·son |'räbənsən|, Frank (1935–) U.S. baseball player and manager. He won MVP honors in both the National League and the American League, and became the first African-American manager in the major leagues (1975).

Rob·in·son |'räbənsən|, Jackie (1919–72) U.S. baseball player (1947–56). Born *Jack Roosevelt Robinson*. Joining the Brooklyn Dodgers in 1947, he became the first black player in the major leagues. In 1949, he led the National League with a .342 batting average and was named the league's Most Valuable

Player. Elected to the Baseball Hall of Fame (1962).

Rob·in·son |'räbənsən|, Joseph Taylor (1872–1937) U.S. politician. He was a member of the U.S. House of Representatives (1903–13) and of the U.S. Senate from Arkansas (1913–37) and a Democratic vice presidential candidate (1928).

Rob·in·son |'räbənsən|, Mary (Terese Winifred) (1944–) Irish Labour stateswoman, president (1990–97). She became Ireland's first woman president, noted for her platform of religious toleration and her liberal attitude. She became United Nations High Commissioner for Human Rights in 1997.

Rob·in·son |'räbənsən|, Max (1939–88) U.S. television journalist. He became the first African American to anchor a network news show (1978).

Rob·in·son |'räbənsən|, Smokey (1940–) U.S. soul singer and songwriter; born *William Robinson*. He is known for a series of successes with his group the Miracles, such as "Tracks of my Tears" (1965).

Rob·in·son |'räbənsən|, Sugar Ray (1920–89) U.S. boxer; born *Walker Smith*. He was world welterweight champion and seven times middleweight champion.

Rob Roy |'räb 'roi| (1671–1734) Scottish outlaw; born *Robert Macgregor*. His reputation as a Scottish Robin Hood was exaggerated in Sir Walter Scott's novel of the same name (1817).

Rob·son |'räbsən|, Dame Flora (1902–84) English actress. She was noted for her performance as the Empress Elizabeth in *Catherine the Great* (1934), and later for her many character roles.

Ro·cham·beau |ˌrawsHəm'bō|, Jean Baptiste Donatien de Vimeur, Comte de (1725–1807) French soldier. He commanded a French force that came to George Washington's aid at White Plains, New York, during the Revolutionary War (1781).

Roche |rōsH|, (Eamonn) Kevin (1922–) U.S. architect, born in Ireland. Notable designs: the Oakland Museum (Oakland, California, 1961–68) and the UN Plaza (New York, 1969–75).

Roch·es·ter |'räCHəstər|, John Wilmot,

2nd Earl of (1647–80) English poet and courtier. Infamous for his dissolute life at the court of Charles II, he wrote sexually explicit love poems and verse satires.

Rock |räk|, John (1890–1984) U.S. obstretrician-gynecologist. With Gregory Pincus and M.C. Chang he pioneered oral contraceptive pills (1960).

Rock·e·fel·ler |'räkə,felər| U.S. business and political family, including: **John D. Rockefeller,** (1839–1937), U.S. industrialist and philanthropist; full name *John Davison Rockefeller.* He founded the Standard Oil company in 1870, and by 1880 he exercised a virtual monopoly over oil refining in the U.S. Both he and his son, **John D. Rockefeller, Jr.** (1874–1960), established many philanthropic institutions. **Nelson Rockefeller** (1908–1979), son of John D. Rockefeller, Jr., and U.S. vice president (1974–77), known as **Rocky**. He held several government posts under Presidents F. D. Roosevelt, Truman, and Eisenhower before becoming governor of New York (1958–73). Nominated by Gerald Ford, he was named vice president when Ford acceded to the presidency following President Nixon's resignation (1974).

Rock·ne |'räknē|, Knute (1888–1931) U.S. college football coach. He coached Notre Dame to three consecutive national titles.

Rock·well |'räk,wel|, Norman (Percevel) (1894–1978) U.S. illustrator. Known for his typically sentimental portraits of small-town American life, he was an illustrator for *The Saturday Evening Post,* for which he created 317 covers (1916–63).

Rod·den·ber·ry |'rädn,berē|, Gene (1921–91) U.S. television producer and scriptwriter; full name *Eugene Wesley Roddenberry.* He created and wrote many scripts for the television science-fiction drama series "Star Trek," first broadcast 1966–69.

Rod·dick |'rädək|, Anita (Lucia) (1943–) English businesswoman. In 1976 she opened a shop selling cosmetics with an emphasis on environmentally conscious products. This developed into the Body Shop chain.

Rod·gers |'räjərz|, Jimmie (1897–1933) U.S. country singer and songwriter. Full name *James Charles Rodgers*; known as **The Singing Brakeman**. After retiring from his work on the railroad, he recorded over 100 songs, including "Waiting for a Train" and "T for Texas."

Rod·gers |'räjərz|, Richard (Charles) (1902–79) U.S. composer. He worked with lyricist **Lorenz Hart** (1895–1942) before collaborating with Oscar Hammerstein II on a succession of popular musicals, including *Oklahoma!* (1943), *South Pacific* (1949), *The King and I* (1951), and *The Sound of Music* (1959).

Ro·din |,rō'dæN|, Auguste (1840–1917) French sculptor. He was chiefly concerned with the human form. Notable works: *The Thinker* (1880) and *The Kiss* (1886).

Rod·man |'rädmən|, Dennis (1961–) U.S. basketball player. He led the National Basketball Association in rebounding six years in a row (1991–97).

Rod·ney |'rädnē|, Red (1927–94) U.S. jazz trumpeter. Born *Robert Chudnick*. Originally a swing player, he modernized his style after hearing Dizzy Gillespie and Charlie Parker; he played bop style in Charlie Parker's quintet (1949–51).

Ro·dri·go |raw'drēgō|, Joaquín (1901–) Spanish composer. He is best known for his guitar concerto (1939) and for his *Concerto Pastorale* (1978) for flute and orchestra, commissioned by James Galway.

Roe |rō|, Sir (Edwin) Alliott Verdon (1877–1958) English engineer and aircraft designer. With his brother H. V. Roe he founded the Avro Co. and built a number of planes, including the Avro 504 biplane of World War I; in 1928 he formed the Saunders-Roe Co. to design and manufacture flying boats.

Roeb·ling |'rōbliNG|, John Augustus (1806–69) U.S. engineer and bridge builder, born in Germany. He designed the railroad span at Niagara Falls (1851–55) and made plans for the Brooklyn Bridge, which his son Washington Augustus Roebling (1837–1926) completed as chief engineer of construction.

Roeg |rōg|, Nicholas (Jack) (1928–)

English movie director. His work is often impressionistic, and uses cutting techniques to create disjointed narratives. Notable works: *Performance* (1970) and *The Man Who Fell to Earth* (1975).

Roeth·ke |'retkĕ; 'reTHkĕ|, Theodore (1908–63) U.S. educator and poet. Notable works: *The Waking* (1953, Pulitzer Prize) and *Words for the Wind* (1958, Bollingen Prize).

Rog·ers |'räjərz|, Edith (1881–1960) U.S. politician. Born *Edith Nourse*. As a member of the U.S. House of Representatives from Massachusetts (1925–60), she introduced legislation that created the Women's Army Corps and the GI Bill of Rights.

Rog·ers |'räjərz|, Fred McFeely (1928–) U.S. television producer, actor, and author. He created and stars in the television program "Mister Rogers' Neighborhood" (1965–).

Rog·ers |'räjərz|, Ginger (1911–95) U.S. actress and dancer; born *Virginia Katherine McMath*. She is known for her dancing partnership with Fred Astaire, during which she appeared in movie musicals, including *Top Hat* (1935). Her solo acting career included the movie *Kitty Foyle* (1940), for which she won an Oscar.

Rog·ers |'räjərz|, Henry Huttleston (1840–1909) U.S. financier. While an executive with Standard Oil, he patented machinery for separating naphtha from crude oil and originated the idea of pipeline transportation.

Rog·ers |'räjərz|, James Gamble (1897–1947) U.S. architect. Notable designs: the Columbia-Presbyterian Medical Center (New York) and much of Yale University.

Rog·ers |'räjərz|, Kenny (1938–) U.S. country singer. Full name *Kenneth Ray Rogers*. His hits include "Lucille," "The Gambler," and "We've Got Tonight."

Rog·ers |'räjərz|, Sir Richard (George) (1933–) British architect, born in Italy. A leading exponent of high-tech architecture, his major works include the Pompidou Centre in Paris (1971–77), designed with the Italian architect Renzo Piano, and the Lloyd's Building in London (1986).

Rog·ers |'räjərz|, Roy (1912–98) U.S. actor and singer. Born *Leonard Slye*. He was one of the "Original Sons of the Pioneers" country singers.

Rog·ers |'räjərz|, Will (1879–1935) U.S. humorist and actor. Full name *William Penn Adair Rogers*. A vaudeville headliner with his rope twirling and homespun humor (from 1902), he wrote a syndicated column for *The New York Times* (1922–35). He died in a plane crash with aviator Wiley Post.

Ro·get |rō'zнā|, Peter Mark (1779–1869) English scholar. He worked as a physician but is remembered as the compiler of *Roget's Thesaurus of English Words and Phrases*, first published in 1852.

Roh·mer |'rōmər|, Sax (1883–1959) British author. Born *Arthur Sarsfield Ward*. Under the pseudonym Sax Rohmer he wrote novels featuring the fictional Chinese criminal Fu Manchu.

Rohr·er |'rawrər|, Heinrich (1933–) U.S. physicist, born in Switzerland. He invented the scanning tunneling microscope (Nobel Prize, 1986).

Rolfe |rawlf|, John (1585–1622) Virginia colonist, born in England. He perfected the process of curing tobacco, and he was married to the American Indian Pocahontas.

Rol·land |raw'läN|, Romain (1866–1944) French novelist, dramatist, and essayist. His interest in genius led to a number of biographies, and ultimately to *Jean-Christophe* (1904–12), a cycle of ten novels about a German composer. Nobel Prize for Literature (1915).

Rolls |rōlz|, Charles Stewart (1877–1910) English automotive and aviation pioneer. He and Henry Royce formed the company Rolls-Royce Ltd in 1906. Rolls, the first Englishman to fly across the English Channel, was killed in an airplane crash. The Rolls-Royce company established its reputation with luxury cars such as the Silver Ghost and the Silver Shadow, and produced aircraft engines used in both world wars, and later for commercial airliners.

Röl·vaag |'rōl,väg|, Öle Edvart (1876–1931) U.S. author and educator, born in Norway. Notable novels: *Giants in the Earth* (1927) and *Their Fathers' God* (1931).

Rom·berg |'räm,bərg|, Sigmund (1887–1951) Hungarian-born U.S. composer. He wrote a succession of popular operettas, including *The Student Prince* (1924), *The Desert Song* (1926), and *New Moon* (1928).

Rom·mel |'räməl|, Erwin (1891–1944) German field marshal; known as **the Desert Fox**. As commander of the Afrika Korps he deployed a series of surprise maneuvers and succeeded in capturing Tobruk (1942), but was defeated by Montgomery at El Alamein later that year. He was forced to commit suicide after being implicated in the officers' conspiracy against Hitler in 1944.

Rom·ney[1] |'rämnē|, George (1734–1802) English portrait painter. From the early 1780s he produced over fifty portraits of Lady Hamilton in historical costumes and poses.

Rom·ney[2] |'rämnē|, George (1907–95) U.S. businessman and politician, born in Mexico. He was president of American Motors, governor of Michigan (1963–69), and U.S. secretary of Housing and Urban Development (1969–72).

Ron·stadt |'rän,stæt|, Linda (1946–) U.S. pop and folk musician. Notable songs: "You're No Good" and "I Can't Help It If I'm Still in Love with You" (Grammy Award, 1975).

Rönt·gen |'rentgən; 'rɒentgən|, Wilhelm Conrad (1845–1923) German physicist, the discoverer of X-rays. He was a skillful experimenter and worked in a variety of areas as well as radiation. He was awarded the first Nobel Prize for Physics (1901).

Roo·ney |'rōōnē|, Andy (1919–) U.S. journalist and author. Full name *Andrew Aitkin Rooney.* He is a writer and producer for CBS News (1959–), a syndicated columnist (1979–), and a commentator on television's "60 Minutes" (1978–).

Roo·ney |'rōōnē|, Mickey (1920–) U.S. actor; born *Joseph Yule, Jr.* He played Andy Hardy in sixteen comedy-drama films about the Hardy family. He received Oscar nominations for his roles in *Babes in Arms* (1939) and *The Human Comedy* (1943).

Roo·se·velt |'rōzə,velt| **Theodore Roosevelt** see box. **Alice Hathaway**

Lee Roosevelt (1861–84), first wife of Theodore Roosevelt, whom she married in 1880. **Edith Kermit Carow Roosevelt** (1861–1948), wife of Theodore Roosevelt and U.S. first lady (1901–09).

Roo·se·velt |'rōzə,velt| **Franklin D. Roosevelt** see box. **(Anna) Eleanor Roosevelt** (1884–1962), wife of Franklin D. Roosevelt and U.S. first lady (1933–45). She was the niece of

---

Roosevelt, Theodore
26th U.S. president

Life dates: 1858–1919

Place of birth: New York, New York

Mother: Martha Bulloch Roosevelt

Father: Theodore Roosevelt

Wife: Alice Hathaway Lee (died 1884); Edith Kermit Carow (married 1886)

Children: (by first wife) Alice Lee; (by second wife) Theodore, Jr., Kermit, Ethel, Archibald, Quentin

Nicknames: Teddy; TR

College/University: Harvard

Military service: during Spanish-American War, organized and commanded a volunteer cavalry known as the "Rough Riders"

Career: Rancher; soldier; writer

Political career: New York State Assembly; U.S. Civil Service Commissioner; governor of New York; vice president (under McKinley); president; organized Progressive (Bull Moose) Party

Party: Republican

Home state: New York

Opponents in presidential races: Alton B. Parker (1904); William Howard Taft, Woodrow Wilson (1912)

Term of office: Sept. 14, 1901 (succeeded to the presidency after the assassination of William McKinley)–March 3, 1909

Vice president: none (first term); Charles W. Fairbanks (second term)

Notable events of presidency: breaking up of trusts; Sherman Anti-Trust Act; Department of Commerce and Labor created; U.S. Forest Service established; Panama Canal Zone acquired by U.S.; Federal Food and Drugs Act; Oklahoma admitted as 46th state

Other achievements: Awarded Nobel Prize in 1906 for mediation leading to the Russo-Japanese Peace Treaty

Place of burial: Oyster Bay, New York

Theodore Roosevelt and married Franklin Roosevelt in 1905. She was involved in a wide range of liberal causes; as chair of the U.N. Commission on Human Rights she helped draft the Declaration of Human Rights (1948).

Root |rŏŏt|, Elihu (1845–1937) U.S. lawyer and diplomat. He served as secretary of war (1898–1904) and as secretary of state (1905–09). He won the Nobel Peace Prize for the Root-Takahira Agreement with the Japanese (1912).

Root |rŏŏt|, John Wellborn (1887–1963) U.S. architect. He designed the Palmo-

---

Roosevelt, Franklin Delano
32nd U.S. president

Life dates: 1882–1945
Place of birth: Hyde Park, New York
Mother: Sara Roosevelt
Father: James Roosevelt
Wife: (Anna) Eleanor Roosevelt
Children: Anna Eleanor, James, Franklin Delano, Jr. (died in infancy, 1909), Elliott, Franklin Delano Jr. (born 1914), John
Nickname: FDR
College/University: Harvard; Columbia University Law School
Career: lawyer; bank officer
Political career: New York Senate; assistant secretary of the Navy; governor of New York; president
Party: Democratic
Home state: New York
Opponents in presidential races: Herbert C. Hoover (1932); Alfred M. Landon (1936); Wendell Lewis Willkie (1940); Thomas E. Dewey (1944)
Term of office: March 4, 1933–Apr. 12, 1945 (died during fourth term)
Vice presidents: John Nance Garner; Henry A. Wallace (third term); Harry S. Truman (fourth term)
Notable events of presidency: banking crisis ended with bank holiday declaration; New Deal programs enacted; Federal Housing Administration authorized; Federal Communications Commission created; Social Security Act; Fair Labor Standards Act; World War II; "Four Freedoms" enunciated; Lend-Lease Act; Yalta Conference
Other achievements: vice president, Fidelity and Deposit Company
Place of burial: Hyde Park, New York

---

live Building (Chicago) and the Hotel Statler (Washington, D.C.).

Ro·sa |'rōzə|, Salvator (1615–73) Italian painter and etcher. The picturesque and "sublime" qualities of his landscapes, often peopled with bandits and containing scenes of violence in wild natural settings, were an important influence on the romantic art of the 18th and 19th centuries.

Ros·ci·us |'räsH(ē)əs| (died 62 BC) Roman actor; full name *Quintus Roscius Gallus*. Many notable English actors from the 16th century onward were nicknamed in reference to his great skill.

Rose |rōz|, Axl (1962–) U.S. hard rock vocalist. Born *William Bailey*. He formed the Guns 'n' Roses band with Izzy Stradlin (1985).

Rose |rōz|, Fred (1898–1954) U.S. country singer, songwriter and musician. Notable songs: "Honest and Truly" and "Deed I Do."

Rose |rōz|, Pete (1941–) U.S. baseball player and manager. He holds the major league record for hits with 4,256.

Rose·anne |rō'zæn| (1952–) U.S. actress. Born *Roseanne Barr*. She was the award-winning star of the television program "Roseanne" (1988–97).

Rose·bery |'rōz,berē|, Archibald Philip Primrose, 5th Earl of (1847–1929) British Liberal statesman, prime minister (1894–95).

Ro·sen·berg |'rōzən,bərg| U.S. spies. **Ethel Greenglass Rosenberg** (1915–53) and her husband **Julius Rosenberg** (1918–53) were Communist Party members executed for espionage.

Ro·sen·berg |'rōzən,bərg|, Howard (1942–) U.S. journalist. A writer for the *Los Angeles Times*, he won a Pulitzer Prize for criticism (1985).

Ro·so·li·no |,räsə'lēnō|, Frank (1926–78) U.S. jazz trombonist. He performed with Howard Rumsey's Lighthouse All Stars (1954–60) and with Donn Trenner's band on television's "Steve Allen Show" (1962–64).

Ross |raws| British explorers. **Sir John Ross** (1777–1856) led an expedition to Baffin Bay in 1818 and another in search of the Northwest Passage between 1829 and 1833. His nephew, **Sir James Clark Ross** (1800–62), discovered the north magnetic pole in 1831 and headed an expedition to the Antarctic from 1839 to 1843, in the course of which he discovered Ross Island, Ross Dependency, and the Ross Sea.

Ross |raws|, Betsy (1752–1836) American patriot and seamstress. Full name *Elizabeth Griscom Ross*. She is credited with having made the first flag of the U.S. (June 1776).

Ross |raws|, Diana (1944–) U.S. pop and soul singer. Originally the lead singer of the Supremes, she went on to become a successful solo artist. She received an Oscar for her role as Billie Holiday in the movie *Lady Sings the Blues* (1973).

Ross |raws|, Harold Wallace (1892–1951) U.S. editor. He was founder and editor of *The New Yorker* magazine (1925–51).

Ross |raws|, Sir Ronald (1857–1932) British physician. Ross confirmed that the *Anopheles* mosquito transmitted malaria, and went on to elucidate the stages in the malarial parasite's life cycle. Nobel Prize for Physiology or Medicine (1902).

Ros·sel·li·ni |ˌrawsəˈlēnē|, Roberto (1906–77) Italian movie director. He is known for his neorealist movies, particularly his quasidocumentary trilogy about World War II, *Open City* (1945).

Ros·set·ti |rəˈzetē| English family, including: **Dante Gabriel Rossetti** (1828–82), poet and painter; full name *Gabriel Charles Dante Rossetti*. A founding member of the Pre-Raphaelite brotherhood (1848), he is best known for his idealized images of women, including *Beata Beatrix* (*c.*1863) and *The Blessed Damozel* (1871–79). **Christina (Georgina) Rossetti** (1830–94), his sister and a poet. She wrote much religious poetry (reflecting her High Anglican faith), love poetry, and children's verse. Notable works: *Goblin Market and Other Poems* (1862).

Ros·si·ni |rəˈsēnē|, Gioacchino Antonio (1792–1868) Italian composer, one of the creators of Italian bel canto. He wrote over thirty operas, including *The Barber of Seville* (1816) and *William Tell* (1829).

Ros·tand |ˈrästənd|, Edmond (1868–1918) French dramatist and poet. He romanticized the life of the 17th-century soldier, duelist, and writer Cyrano de Bergerac in his poetic drama of that name (1897).

Ros·ten |ˈrawstən|, Leo (Calvin) (1908–97) U.S. political scientist and humorist, born in Poland. Pseudonym **Leonard Q. Ross**. Notable works: *The Joys of Yinglish* (1989).

Ros·tro·po·vich |ˌrawstrəˈpōvicH|, Mstislav Leopoldovich (1927–) Russian cellist, pianist, and conductor. He was music director and conductor of the National Symphony Orchestra in Washington, D.C. (1977–94).

Roth |rawTH|, Ann (1931–) U.S. costume designer. She was a leading costumer for Broadway plays from the late 1950s and for Hollywood films from the mid 1960s.

Roth |rawTH|, Henry (*c.* 1906–) U.S. author, born in Austria. Notable works: *Call It Sleep* (1934).

Roth |rawTH|, Philip (Milton) (1933–) U.S. novelist and short-story writer. He often writes with irony and humor about the complexity and diversity of contemporary American Jewish life. Notable works: *Portnoy's Complaint* (1969), which records the intimate confessions of an adolescent boy to his psychiatrist; *Zuckerman Bound* (1985); and *American Pastoral* (1997).

Roth·ko |ˈrawTHkō|, Mark (1903–70) U.S. painter, born in Latvia; born *Marcus Rothkovich*. A leading figure in color-field painting, he painted hazy and apparently floating rectangles of color.

Roth·schild |ˈrawTH,cHīld|, Meyer Amschel (1743–1812) German financier. He founded the Rothschild banking house in Frankfurt at the end of the 19th century and was financial adviser to the landgrave of Hesse. His five sons all entered banking.

Rou·ault |rōōˈō|, Georges (Henri) (1871–1958) French painter and engraver. Associated with expressionism, he used vivid colors and simplified forms enclosed in thick black outlines.

Rous |rows|, (Francis) Peyton (1879–1970) U.S. pathologist. He was a pioneering cancer researcher; in 1966 he won the Nobel Prize for Physiology or Medicine with C. B. Huggins for the discovery of tumor-inducing viruses (1910).

Rous·seau |rŏŏ'sō|, Henri (Julien) (1844–1910) French painter; known as **le Douanier** ("customs officer"). After retiring as a customs official in 1893, he created bold and colorful paintings of fantastic dreams and exotic jungle landscapes, such as *Sleeping Gypsy* (1897) and *Tropical Storm with Tiger* (1891).

Rous·seau |rŏŏ'sō|, Jean-Jacques (1712–78) French philosopher and writer, born in Switzerland. He believed that civilization warps the fundamental goodness of human nature, but that the ill effects can be moderated by active participation in democratic consensual politics. Notable works: *Émile* (1762) and *The Social Contract* (1762).

Rous·seau |rŏŏ'sō|, (Pierre Étienne) Théodore (1812–67) French painter. A leading landscapist of the Barbizon School, his works typically depict the scenery and changing light effects of the forest of Fontainebleau, for example *Under the Birches, Evening* (1842–44).

Ro·vere, Richard (Halworth) (1915–79) U.S. journalist. A writer for *The New Yorker* (1944–79), he also wrote *Arrivals and Departures* (1976).

Row·an |'rōən|, Carl Thomas (1925–) U.S. journalist. He has written a nationally syndicated column since 1965; he was U.S. ambassador to Finland (1963–64) and director of the U.S. Information Agency (1964–65).

Rowe |rō|, Nicholas (1647–1718) English dramatist. Notable works: *Tamerlane* (1701) and *The Fair Penitent* (1703).

Row·land·son |'rōlən(d)sən|, Mary White (c. 1635–c. 1678) American writer. She and her three children were abducted (1676) by hostile Indians during King Philip's War; she published her narrative in 1682.

Row·land·son |'rōlən(d)sən|, Thomas (1756–1827) English painter, draftsman, and caricaturist. Some of his watercolors and drawings are featured in the series *Tours of Dr. Syntax* (1812–21).

Rowles, Jimmy (1918–96) U.S. jazz composer and pianist. Born *James George Hunter*. He was an accompanist to singers such as Billie Holiday and Peggy Lee.

Royce |rois|, Sir (Frederick) Henry (1863–1933) English engine designer. He founded the company of Rolls-Royce Ltd. with Charles Stewart Rolls in 1906, becoming famous as the designer of the Rolls-Royce Silver Ghost automobile and later also becoming known for his aircraft engines.

Roy·ko |'roikō|, Mike (1932–) U.S. journalist. A reporter and columnist for the *Chicago Daily News* (1959–78) and *Chicago Tribune* (1984–97), he won a Pulitzer Prize for commentary (1972).

Roy·ster |'roistər|, Vermont Connecticut (1914–96) U.S. journalist. On the staff of *The Wall Street Journal* for 60 years (1936–96), he won a Pulitzer Prize for commentary (1984).

Rub·bra |'rəbrə|, (Charles) Edmund (1901–86) English composer and pianist. He wrote many songs and eleven symphonies.

Ru·bens |'rŏŏbenz|, Sir Peter Paul (1577–1640) Flemish painter. The foremost exponent of northern Baroque, he is best known for his portraits and mythological paintings featuring voluptuous female nudes, as in *Venus and Adonis* (c. 1635).

Ru·bik |'rŏŏbik|, Ernö (1944–) Hungarian professor and inventor. He devised the Rubik's Cube puzzle (1974).

Ru·bin |'rŏŏbən|, Benjamin A. (1917–) U.S. inventor. He invented the bifurcated vaccination needle, which can be used in primitive conditions.

Ru·bin |'rŏŏbən|, Jerry (1938–94) U.S. radical. A 1960s standard-bearer of counterculture, he led student opposition to Vietnam War.

Ru·bin·stein |'rŏŏbən,stīn|, Anton (Grigorevich) (1829–94) Russian composer and pianist. In 1862 he founded the St. Petersburg Conservatory and was its director 1862–67 and 1887–91. He composed symphonies, operas, songs, and piano music.

Ru·bin·stein |'rŏŏbən,stīn|, Artur (1888–1982) Polish-born U.S. pianist. He toured extensively in Europe and the U.S. and among his many recordings are the complete works of Chopin.

Ru·bin·stein |'rŏŏbən,stīn|, Helena

(1882–1695) U.S. beautician and businesswoman. Her organization became an international cosmetics manufacturer and distributor.

Ru·by |'roobē|, Jack (1911–67) U.S. assassin. He shot and killed Lee Harvey Osward, the man accused of murdering President Kennedy.

Ruck·ey·ser, Muriel (1913–80) U.S. poet and author. Her poetry reflects her liberal political activism.

Rud·kin |'rədkin|, Margaret Fogarty (1897–1967) U.S. entrepreneur. She began the Pepperidge Farms company by baking bread at home.

Ru·dolph |'roodawlf|, Paul (1918–) U.S. architect. Notable designs: the Jewitt Art Center (Wellesley College) and the Art and Architecture building at Yale University.

Ru·dolph |'roodawlf|, Wilma (1940–94) U.S. runner. She was the first woman to win three gold medals in track and field in one Olympics (1960).

Ruis·dael |'roisdäl|, Jacob van (c. 1628–82) Dutch landscape painter. Also **Ruysdael**. Born in Haarlem, he painted the surrounding landscape from the mid-1640s until his move to Amsterdam in 1657.

Ru·iz de Alar·cón y Men·do·za |roo 'ēs dä ,älär'kawn ē ,men'dōsə|, Juan (1580–1639) Spanish dramatist, born in Mexico City. His most famous play, the moral comedy *La Verdad sospechosa*, was the basis of Corneille's *Le Menteur* (1642).

Ru·key·ser |'roo,kīzər|, Louis (1933–) U.S. economic commentator. He hosts the television program "Wall Street Week."

Rund·stedt |'roond,stet|, Karl Rudolf Gerd von (1875–1953) German field marshal. He was the German commander in chief on the Western Front during World War II (1942–45).

Run·yon |'rənyən|, (Alfred) Damon (1884–1946) U.S. author and journalist. His short stories about New York's Broadway underworld characters are written in a highly individual style with much use of colorful slang. His collection *Guys and Dolls* (1932) formed the basis for the musical of the same name (1950).

Ru·pert, Prince |'roopərt| (1619–82) English Royalist general, son of Frederick V (elector of the Palatinate) and nephew of Charles I. The Royalist leader of cavalry, he initially won a series of victories, but was defeated by Parliamentarian forces at Marston Moor (1644) and Naseby (1645).

Rupp |rəp|, Adolph (1901–77) U.S. college basketball coach. He coached the University of Kentucky to four NCAA championships.

Rush |rəsH|, Benjamin (1745–1813) American physician, educator, and patriot. He was a member of the Continental Congress (1776–77) and a signer of the Declaration of Independence. As surgeon general of the Continental Army, he established the first free dispensary in the U.S. (1786).

Rush·die |'rəsHdē|, (Ahmed) Salman (1947–) Indian-born British novelist. His work, chiefly associated with magic realism, includes the prize-winning *Midnight's Children* and *The Satanic Verses* (1988). The latter, regarded by Muslims as blasphemous, caused Iran's Ayatollah Khomeini to issue a fatwa (death penalty) in 1989 condemning Rushdie to death. Other works: *Haroun and the Sea of Stories* (1990, for children) and *The Moor's Last Sigh* (1995).

Rush·ing |'rəsHiNG|, Jimmy (1903–72) U.S. blues singer. Full name *James Andrew Rushing*; known as **Mr. Five by Five**. He performed with Count Basie's Band (1935–50).

Rusk |rəsk|, (David) Dean (1909–94) U.S. educator and statesman. He was secretary of state under Presidents Kennedy and Johnson (1961–69).

Rus·kin |'rəskən|, John (1819–1900) English art and social critic. His prolific writings include attacks on Renaissance art in *The Stone of Venice* (1851–53), capitalism in "The Political Economy of Art" (1857), and utilitarianism in *Unto This Last* (1860).

Rus·sell |'rəsəl|, Bertrand (Arthur William), 3rd Earl Russell (1872–1970) British philosopher, mathematician, and social reformer. In *Principia Mathematica* (1910–13) he and A. N. Whitehead attempted to express all of mathematics in formal logic terms. He expounded logical atomism in *Our Knowledge of the External World* (1914) and neutral monism in *The Analysis of Mind* (1921). A conscientious objector during World War I, he also campaigned for women's suffrage and against nuclear arms. Nobel Prize for Literature (1950).

Rus·sell |'rəsəl|, Bill (1934–) U.S. basketball player and coach. He became the first African-American head coach in the NBA (1966).

Rus·sell |'rəsəl|, Charles Marion (1865–1926) U.S. artist. He was noted for his paintings of cowboy and Indian life and Western landscapes.

Rus·sell |'rəsəl|, George William (1867–1935) Irish poet and journalist. After the performance of his poetic drama *Deirdre* (1902) Russell became a leading figure in the Irish literary revival.

Rus·sell |'rəsəl|, Henry Norris (1877–1959) U.S. astronomer. He worked mainly in astrophysics and spectroscopy, and is best known for his independent discovery of the relationship between stellar magnitude and spectral type, which he represented diagrammatically.

Rus·sell |'rəsəl|, John, 1st Earl Russell (1792–1878) British Whig statesman, prime minister (1846–52 and 1865–66). He was responsible for introducing the Reform Bill of 1832 into Parliament and resigned his second premiership when his attempt to extend the franchise further was unsuccessful.

Rus·sell |'rəsəl|, Ken (1927–) English movie director. Full name *Henry Kenneth Alfred Russell*. Characterized by extravagant and extreme imagery, his movies, for example *Women in Love* (1969), have often attracted controversy for their depiction of sex and violence.

Rus·sell |'rəsəl|, Pee Wee (1906–69) U.S. jazz clarinetist. Full name *Charles Ellsworth Russell*. He played dixieland music mainly in New York and intermittently with Eddie Condon for 30 years.

Russ·wurm |'rəs,wərm|, John Brown (1799–1851) U.S. publisher. With Samuel E. Cornish he founded the nation's first black newspaper, *Freedom's Journal* (1827, New York).

Rus·tin |'rəstən|, Bayard (1910–87) U.S. civil rights leader. He helped organized the March on Washington (1963).

Ruth |rōŏTH|, Babe (1895–1948) U.S. baseball player; born *George Herman Ruth*; also known as the **Bambino**. He played for the Boston Red Sox (1914–19), New York Yankees (1919–34), and Boston Braves (1935). Originally a pitcher, he later became noted for his hitting, setting a record of 714 career home runs that remained unbroken until 1974 and a single-season record in 1927 of 60 home runs that was not broken until 1961. In 1936 he became one of the original inductees into the Baseball Hall of Fame.

Ruth·er·ford |'rəTHərfərd|, Johnny (1938–) U.S. racecar driver. He won the Indy 500 championship three times.

Ruth·er·ford |'rəTHərfərd|, Dame Margaret (1892–1972) English actress. Chiefly remembered for her roles as a formidable but jovial eccentric, she won an Oscar for *The VIPs* (1963).

Rut·ledge |'rətləj|, John (1739–1800) U.S. Supreme Court justice (1789–91). He was appointed Chief Justice of the U.S. in 1795 and served one term but was not confirmed by the U.S. Senate.

Rut·ledge |'rətləj|, Wiley Blount, Jr. (1894–1949) U.S. Supreme Court justice (1943–49).

Ruys·dael variant spelling of RUISDAEL.

Ry·an |'rīən|, Nolan (1947–) U.S. baseball player. He holds the pitching records for no-hitters (7) and strikeouts (5,714).

Ry·an |'rīən|, Thomas Fortune (1851–1926) U.S. financier. Among many investments, he was a founder of the American Tobacco Co. in the early 1890s.

Ry·der |'rīdər|, Albert Pinkham (1847–1917) U.S. artist. He is known for seascapes and pastoral landscapes.

Ry·der |'rīdər|, Winona (1971–) U.S. actress. Born *Winona Laura Horowitz*. Notable movies: *Age of Innocence* (1993) and *Little Women* (1994).

Ry·kiel, Sonia (1930–) French fashion designer.

Ryle |rīl|, Gilbert (1900–76) English philosopher. In *The Concept of Mind* (1949) he attacks the mind–body dualism of Descartes. He was a cousin of the astronomer Sir Martin Ryle.

Ryle |rīl|, Sir Martin (1918–84) English astronomer. His demonstration that remote objects appeared to be different from closer ones helped to establish the big bang theory of the universe. Nobel Prize for Physics (1974). He was a cousin of the philosopher Gilbert Ryle.

Ry·sa·nek |'rēzä,nek|, Leonie (1926–98) Austrian operatic soprano. She made her debut at Innsbruck in 1949 as Agathe in *Der Freischütz*, and with the New York Metropolitan Opera in 1959 as Lady Macbeth; for the next 37 years she sang 299 performances of 24 roles.

Ss

Saa·di variant spelling of SADI.

Saa·ri·nen |'särənən|, Eero (1910–61) U.S. architect, born in Finland. Notable designs: Memorial Arch in St. Louis (1948) and the U.S. Embassy in London (1955–60).

Sa·bin |'sābən|, Albert Bruce (1906–93) U.S. physician, born in Russia. He developed an oral vaccine against poliomyelitis (adopted by World Health Organization 1957).

Sa·ble |'sābəl|, Jean Baptiste Point (c. 1750–1818) U.S. fur trader and pioneer, born in Haiti. Also known as *Point du Sable*. He founded a trading settlement at the present site of Chicago (1779).

Sac·a·ja·wea |ˌsækəjə'wēə; ˌsækəjə 'wäə| (c. 1786–1812) Shoshone guide and interpreter. Also **Sacagawea** ("Bird Woman"). She joined the Lewis and Clark expedition in what is now North Dakota and guided their expedition through the wilderness and across the Rockies (1804–05).

Sac·co |'sækō|, Nicola (1891–1927) U.S. political radical. Along with Bartolomeo Vanzetti, she was accused of murder in a sensational trial.

Sachs |zäks; säks|, Hans (1494–1576) German poet and dramatist. Some of his poetry celebrated Luther and furthered the Protestant cause, while other pieces were comic verse dramas.

Sack·ler |'sæklər|, Howard (1929–82) U.S. playwright and director. Notable works: *The Great White Hope* (1967; Pulitzer Prize).

Sackville-West |'sæk,vil 'west|, Vita (1892–1962) English novelist and poet. Full name *Victoria Mary Sackville-West*.

Sa·dat |sə'dät|, (Muhammad) Anwar al- (1918–81) Egyptian statesman, president 1970–81.

Saddam Hussein See HUSSEIN, Saddam.

Sade |säd|, Donatien-Alphonse-François, Comte de (1740–1814) French writer and soldier; known as **the Marquis de Sade**. His career as a cavalry officer was interrupted by periods of imprisonment for cruelty and debauchery. While in prison he wrote a number of sexually explicit works, including *Les 120 Journées de Sodome* (1784) and *Justine* (1791).

Sa·di |sä'dē| (c. 1213–c. 1291) Persian poet; born *Sheikh Muslih Addin*. His principal works were the collections known as the *Bustan* (1257) and the *Gulistan* (1258).

Sa·fer |'säfər|, Morley (1931–) U.S. journalist, born in Canada. He cohosts the television program "60 Minutes" (1971–).

Saf·ire |'sæf,ir|, William (1929–) U.S. journalist and author. He is a conservative political commentator and writer of the "On Language" column for *The New York Times*.

Sa·gan |'sāgən|, Carl (Edward) (1934–96) U.S. astronomer. Sagan showed that amino acids can be synthesized in an artificial primordial soup irradiated by ultraviolet light—a possible origin of life on the earth. He wrote several popular science books, and was coproducer of the television series *Cosmos* (1980).

Sa·gan |'sāgən|, Françoise (1935–) French novelist, dramatist, and short-story writer; pseudonym of *Françoise Quoirez*. She rose to fame with her first novel, *Bonjour Tristesse* (1954); in this and subsequent novels she examined the transitory nature of love as experienced in brief liaisons. Notable works: *Un Certain sourire* (1956) and *Aimez-vous Brahms?* (1959).

Sa·gen·dorf |'sægən,dawrf|, Bud (1915–94) U.S. cartoonist. Full name *Forrest Cowles Sagendorf*. He was assistant to the creator of Popeye and continued Popeye after the death of the creator (Elzie Segar).

Sa·ha |'sähä|, Meghnad (1894–1956) Indian theoretical physicist. Saha worked on thermal ionization in stars and laid the foundations for modern astrophysics. He devised an equation expressing the relationship between ionization and temperature.

Sa·id |sä'ēd|, Edward W. (1935–) U.S. critic, born in Palestine; full name

Edward Wadi Said. He came to public notice with *Orientalism* (1978), a study of Western attitudes towards Eastern culture. Other notable works: *Culture and Imperialism* (1993).

Saint |sānt|, Eva Marie (1924–) U.S. actress. Her television, stage, and film credits include *On the Waterfront* (1954, Academy Award).

Sainte-Beuve |seNt'bOEv|, Charles Augustin (1804–69) French critic and writer. In his criticism he concentrated on the influence of social and other factors in the development of character.

Saint-Exupéry |ˌseNtăgzYpä'rē|, Antoine-Marie-Roger de (1900–44) French writer and aviator, best known for the fable *The Little Prince* (1943). Other works: *Night Flight* (1931).

Saint-Gaudens |sānt'gawdnz|, Augustus (1848–1907) U.S. sculptor, born in Ireland. Notable works: *Farragut* (in Madison Square, New York City) and *Shaw Memorial* on Boston Common.

Saint Lau·rent |ˌseNlaw'räN|, Yves (Mathieu) (1936–) French couturier. After working with Christian Dior, he opened his own fashion house in 1962, later launching Rive Gauche boutiques to sell ready-to-wear garments and expanding the business to include perfumes.

Saint-Saëns |seN'säN|, (Charles) Camille (1835–1921) French composer, pianist, and organist. He is best known for his Third Symphony (1886), the symphonic poem *Danse macabre* (1874), and the *Carnaval des animaux* (1886).

Saint-Simon |ˌseNsē'mawN|, Claude-Henri de Rouvroy, Comte de (1760–1825) French social reformer and philosopher. Later claimed as the founder of French socialism, he argued that society should be organized by leaders of industry and given spiritual direction by scientists.

Saint-Simon |ˌseNsē'mawN|, Louis de Rouvroy, Duc de (1675–1755) French writer. He is best known for his *Mémoires*, a detailed record of court life between 1694 and 1723, in the reigns of Louis XIV and XV.

Sa·jak |'sā,jæk|, Pat (1947–) U.S. game show host. He is host of the tele-

vision game show "Wheel of Fortune" (1981–).

Sa·kha·rov |'säKHə,rawf; 'säkə,rawv|, Andrei (Dmitrievich) (1921–89) Russian nuclear physicist and civil rights campaigner. Having helped to develop the Soviet hydrogen bomb, he campaigned against nuclear proliferation. He fought for reform and human rights in the USSR, for which he was awarded the Nobel Peace Prize in 1975 but was also sentenced to internal exile 1980–86.

Sa·ki |'säkē| (1870–1916) British short-story writer, born in Burma; pseudonym of *Hector Hugh Munro*. His stories encompass the satiric, comic, macabre, and supernatural and frequently depict animals as agents seeking revenge on humankind.

Sal·a·din |'sæləd(ə)n| (1137–93) sultan of Egypt and Syria 1174–93; Arabic name *Salah-ad-Din Yusuf ibn-Ayyub*. Saladin reconquered Jerusalem from the Christians in 1187, but he was defeated by Richard the Lionheart at Arsuf (1191). He earned a reputation not only for military skill but also for honesty and chivalry.

Sa·lam |sä'läm|, Abdus (1926–96) Pakistani theoretical physicist. He independently developed a unified theory to explain electromagnetic interactions and the weak nuclear force. In 1979 he shared the Nobel Prize for Physics.

Sa·la·zar |'sælə,zär|, Antonio de Oliveira (1889–1970) Portuguese statesman and prime minister (1932–68). During his long premiership he ruled the country as a virtual dictator, enacting a new authoritarian constitution along Fascist lines. Salazar maintained Portugal's neutrality throughout the Spanish Civil War and World War II.

Sa·lie·ri |säl'yerē|, Antonio (1750–1825) Italian composer. Salieri was hostile to Mozart and a rumor arose that he poisoned him, though the story is now thought to be without foundation.

Sal·in·ger |'sælənjər|, J. D. (1919–) U.S. novelist and short-story writer; full name *Jerome David Salinger*. He is best known for his influential colloquial novel of adolescence *The Catcher in the Rye* (1951). He lived reclusively and did not publish after 1965. Other notable works: *Franny and Zooey* (1961), *Raise High the Roof Beam, Carpenter* (1963), and *Seymour: An Introduction* (1963), all short-story collections.

Salis·bury |'sawlz,berē; 'sawlzb(ə)rē|, Robert Arthur Talbot Gascoyne-Cecil, 3rd Marquess of (1830–1903) British Conservative statesman and prime minister (1885–86, 1886–92, and 1895–1902). He supported the policies that resulted in the Second Boer War (1899–1902).

Salk |'saw(l)k|, Jonas Edward (1914–95) American microbiologist. He developed the standard *Salk vaccine* against polio, using virus inactivated by formalin, in the early 1950s, and later became the director of the institute in San Diego that now bears his name.

Sal·lust |'sæləst| (*c.* 86–35 BC) Roman historian and politician; Latin name *Gaius Sallustius Crispus*. As a historian he was concerned with the political and moral decline of Rome after the fall of Carthage in 146 BC. His chief surviving works deal with the Catiline conspiracy and the Jugurthine War.

Sam·pras |'sæmprəs|, Peter (1971–) U.S. tennis player. He was the youngest man ever to win the U.S. Open, in 1990, and repeated as champion in 1993 and 1995–96. He won the Wimbledon title in 1993–95 and 1997–98, as well as the Australian Open in 1994 and 1997.

Sam·so·nov |,səm'sawnəf|, Aleksandr Vasiliyevich (1859–1914) Russian military leader. He commanded the army that invaded East Prussia (August 1914).

Sam·u·el·son |'sæmyə(wə)lsən|, Paul Anthony (1915–) U.S. economist. He has held many international advisory positions, including a seat on the Federal Reserve Board (1965–). Nobel Prize, 1970.

Sand |säN(d); sænd |, George (1804–76) French novelist; pseudonym of *Amandine-Aurore Lucile Dupin, Baronne Dudevant*. Her earlier novels, including *Lélia* (1833), portray women's struggles against conventional morals; she later wrote a number of pastoral novels, such as *La Mare au diable* (1846). Sand had a ten-year affair with Chopin.

Sand·burg |'sæn(d),bərg|, Carl (1878–1967) U.S. poet and biographer. Notable books of verse: *Chicago Poems* (1915), *Smoke and Steel* (1920), and *Complete Poems* (1950, Pulitzer Prize). Notable biographies: *Abraham Lincoln—The Prairie Years* (1926) and *Abraham Lincoln—The War Years* (1939, Pulitzer Prize).

San·de·man |'sændəmən|, Robert (1718–71) U.S. clergyman, born in Scotland. He was the leader of the religious sect known as the Sandemanians.

San·ders |'sændərz|, Barry (1968–) U.S. football player. He was twice named NFL Player of the Year.

San·ders |'sændərz|, Colonel Harland David (1890–1980) U.S. entrepreneur. He founded Kentucky Fried Chicken.

San·ders |'sændərz|, Lawrence (1920–) U.S. author. Notable works: *Guilty Pleasures* (1998) and *McNally's Puzzle* (1996).

San·ford |'sænfərd|, Edward Terry (1865–1930) U.S. Supreme Court justice (1923–30).

Sang·er |'sæNGər|, Margaret Louise (Higgins) (*c.* 1879–1966) U.S. birth-control campaigner. Her experiences as a nurse prompted her to distribute the pamphlet *Family Limitation* in 1914 and to found the first American birth-control clinic in 1916. She was the first president of the International Planned Parenthood Federation (1953).

San Mar·tín |,sän mär'tēn|, José Francisco de (1778–1850) Argentinian soldier and statesman. Having assisted in the liberation of his country from Spanish rule (1812–13), he went on to aid Bernardo O'Higgins in the liberation of Chile (1817–18) and Peru (1820–4). He was also involved in gaining Peruvian independence and was Protector of Peru (1821–22).

San·som |'sænsəm|, Art (1920–91) U.S. cartoonist and author. Full name *Arthur Baldwin Sansom*. He originated the character Brutus Applethorp for the syndicated comic strip "The Born Loser."

San·so·vi·no |,sänsə'vēnō |, Jacopo Tatti (1486–1570) Italian sculptor and architect. He was city architect of Venice, where his buildings, including the Palazzo Corner (1533) and St. Mark's Library (begun 1536), show the development of classical architectural style for contemporary use.

San·ta An·na |ˌsæntə ˈænə; ˌsäntə ˈänə|, Antonio López de (1794–1876) Mexican general and political leader. A militant revolutionary, he controlled Mexico as its president (1833–36), its dictator (1844–45), and again its president (1853–55). In most of the interim years, he was essentially still in control and engaged in several military actions against the U.S., including his defeat at San Jacinto (1836) and Buena Vista (1847).

San·ta·na |ˌsænˈtænə|, Carlos (1947–) U.S. rock musician, born in Mexico. He formed the Afro-Latin rock group Santana (1968); his eighth solo album hit, "Blues for Salvador," won a 1987 Grammy Award.

San·ta·ya·na |ˌsäntəˈyänə|, George (1863–1952) Spanish philosopher and writer; born *Jorge Augustin Nicolás Ruiz de Santayana*. His works include *The Realms of Being* (1924), poetry, and the novel *The Last Puritan* (1935).

Sa·pir |səˈpir|, Edward (1884–1939) German-born U.S. linguistics scholar and anthropologist. One of the founders of American structural linguistics, he carried out important research on American Indian languages and linguistic theory.

Sap·pho |ˈsæfō| (*c.* 610 BC–*c.* 580 BC) Greek lyric poet who lived on Lesbos. Many of her poems express her affection and love for women and have given rise to her association with female homosexuality.

Sa·ran·don |səˈrændən|, Susan (1946–) U.S. actress. Born *Susan Tomalin*. Notable movies: *Thelma and Louise* (1991), *The Client* (1994), and *Dead Man Walking* (1995).

Sar·a·zen |ˈsærəzən|, Gene (1902–99) U.S. golfer. He was one of only four players to win all four Grand Slam titles.

Sa·rett |səˈret|, Lewis Hastings (1917–) U.S. inventor. He prepared the first synthetic cortisone.

Sar·gent |ˈsärjənt|, Sir (Harold) Malcolm (Watts) (1895–1967) English conductor and composer. In 1921 he made

an acclaimed debut conducting his own *Impressions of a Windy Day*.

Sar·gent |ˈsärjənt|, John Singer (1856–1925) U.S. painter. He is best known for his portraiture in a style noted for its bold brushwork. He was much in demand in Parisian circles, but following a scandal over the supposed eroticism of *Madame Gautreau* (1884) he moved to London.

Sar·gon |ˈsärˌgän| (2334–2279 BC) the semi-legendary founder of the ancient kingdom of Akkad.

Sar·gon II |ˈsärˌgän| (died 705 BC) king of Assyria 721–705. He was probably a son of Tiglath-pileser III and is famous for his conquest of cities in Syria and Palestine.

Sar·noff |ˈsärˌnawf|, David (1891–1971) U.S. broadcaster and businessman. He pioneered the development of radio and televison broadcasting in the U.S.; later he became chairman of RCA and founder of NBC.

Sa·roy·an |səˈroiən|, William (1908–81) U.S. author. Notable books of short stories: *The Daring Young Man on the Flying Trapeze* (1934) and *My Name Is Aram* (1940). Notable plays: *The Time of Your Life* (1939) and *Razzle Dazzle* (1942). Notable novels: *The Human Comedy* (1943) and *The Laughing Matter* (1953).

Sar·raute |säˈrōt|, Nathalie (1902–) French author, born in Russia.

Sar·to |ˈsärtō|, Andrea del (1486–1531) Italian painter; born *Andrea d'Agnolo*. He worked chiefly in Florence, where his works include fresco cycles in the church of Santa Annunziata and the series of grisailles in the cloister of the Scalzi (1511–26).

Sar·ton |ˈsärtn|, (Eleanor) May (1912–95) U.S. author and poet, born in Belgium.

Sar·tre |särt; ˈsärtrə|, Jean-Paul (1905–80) French philosopher, novelist, dramatist, and critic. A leading existentialist, he dealt in his work with the nature of human life and the structures of consciousness. In 1945 he founded the review *Les Temps modernes* with his lifelong associate, Simone de Beauvoir. He refused the Nobel Prize for Literature in 1964. Notable works: *Nausée* (novel, 1938), *Being and Nothingness* (treatise,

1943), and *Huis clos* (play, 1944).

Sas·soon |sə'sōōn|, Vidal (1928–) English hairstylist. Opening a London salon in 1953, he introduced the cut and blow-dry styles that became popular for both men and women.

Sas·soon |sæ'sōōn|, Siegfried (Lorraine) (1886–1967) English poet and novelist. He is known for his starkly realistic poems written while serving in World War I, expressing his contempt for war leaders as well as compassion for his comrades.

Sa·tie |sä'tē|, Erik (Alfred Leslie) (1866–1925) French avant-garde composer. He formed an irreverent avant-garde artistic set associated with Les Six, Dadaism, and surrealism. Notable works: *Gymnopédies* (1888).

Sa·to |'sätō|, Eisaku (1901–75) Japanese prime minister (1964–72). He shaped post-war economic growth and improved relations with Asian neighbors; in 1974 he shared the Nobel Peace Prize for his opposition to nuclear weapons.

Saul |sawl| (11th century BC) (in the Bible) the first king of Israel (11th century BC).

Saul of Tarsus see PAUL, ST.

Saus·sure |sō'sYr|, Ferdinand de (1857–1913) Swiss linguistics scholar. He was one of the founders of modern linguistics, and his work is fundamental to the development of structuralism. Saussure made a distinction between *langue* (the total system of language) and *parole* (individual speech acts), and stressed that linguistic study should focus on the former.

Sav·age |'sævij|, Michael Joseph (1872–1940) New Zealand Labor statesman and prime minister (1935–40).

Sa·vo·na·ro·la |,sævənə'rōlə|, Girolamo (1452–98) Italian preacher and religious reformer. A Dominican monk and strict ascetic, he became popular for his passionate preaching against immorality and corruption. Savonarola became virtual ruler of Florence (1494–95) but in 1497 he was excommunicated and later executed as a heretic.

Saw·yer |'soiər; 'sawyər|, (L.) Diane (1945–) U.S. journalist. She is co-an-

chor of the television program "60 Minutes" (1981–).

Say·ers |'säərz|, Dorothy Leigh (1893–1957) English novelist and dramatist; full name *Dorothy Leigh Sayers*. She is chiefly known for her detective fiction featuring the amateur detective Lord Peter Wimsey; titles include *The Nine Tailors* (1934).

Say·ers |'saərz|, Gale (Eugene) (1943–) U.S. football player. He set an NFL record of 22 touchdowns in his rookie year (1965).

Sca·lia |skə'lē(y)ə|, Antonin (1936–) U.S. Supreme Court justice (1986–)

Scal·i·ger |'skæləjər|, Joseph Justus French family, including: **Julius Caesar Scaliger** (1484–1558), Italian-born French classical scholar and physician. **Joseph Justus Scaliger** (1540–1609), French scholar, his son. His *De Emendatione Temporum* (1583) gave a more scientific foundation to the understanding of ancient chronology by comparing and revising the computations of time made by different civilizations, including those of the Babylonians and Egyptians.

Scar·lat·ti |skär'lätē| two Italian composers. **(Pietro) Alessandro (Gaspare)** (1660–1725) was an important and prolific composer of operas which carried Italian opera through the baroque period and into the classical. His son **(Giuseppe) Domenico** (1685–1757) wrote over 550 sonatas for the harpsichord, and his work made an important contribution to the development of the sonata form.

Scar·ry |'skærē; 'skerē|, Richard (McClure) (1919–94) U.S. author and illustrator. As a writer of books for children, he has penned and illustrated more than 250 titles.

Schaw·low |'SHawlō|, Arthur Leonard (1921–) U.S. inventor. With Charles H. Townes he invented the laser. Nobel Prize (1981).

Schee·le |'SHälə|, Carl Wilhelm (1742–86) Swedish chemist. He discovered a number of substances including glycerol, chlorine, and oxygen.

Schell |SHel|, Maximilian (1930–) U.S. actor. Notable movies: *Judgment at Nuremberg* (1961, Academy Award).

Schenck |SHeNGk|, Joseph M. (1878–1961) U.S. corporate executive, born in Russia. He founded Twentieth Century Pictures.

Schia·pa·rel·li |ˌsk(y)äpə'relē; ˌSHäpə'relē|, Elsa (1896–1973) Italian-born French fashion designer.

Schia·pa·rel·li |ˌsk(y)äpə'relē; ˌSHäpə'relē|, Giovanni Virginio (1835–1910) Italian astronomer. He studied the nature of cometary tails, and observed Mars in detail.

Schick |SHik|, Lieutenant Colonel Jacob (1877–1937) U.S. inventor. He invented the dry shaver.

Schie·le |'SHēlə|, Egon (1890–1918) Austrian painter and draughtsman. His style is characterized by an aggressive linear energy and a neurotic intensity. Notable works: *The Cardinal and the Nun* (1912) and *Embrace* (1917).

Schil·ler |'SHilər|, (Johann Christoph) Friedrich von (1759–1805) German dramatist, poet, historian, and critic. Initially influenced by the *Sturm und Drang* movement, he was later an important figure of the Enlightenment. His historical plays include the trilogy *Wallenstein* (1800), *Mary Stuart* (1800), and *William Tell* (1804). Among his best-known poems is "Ode to Joy," which Beethoven set to music in his Ninth Symphony.

Schin·dler |'SHindlər|, Oskar (1908–74) German industrialist. He saved more than 1,200 Jews from concentration camps by employing them first in his enamelware factory in Cracow and then in an armaments factory that he set up in Czechoslovakia in 1944. This was celebrated in the film *Schindler's List* (1993).

Schle·gel |'SHlägəl|, August Wilhelm von (1767–1845) German romantic poet and critic, who was among the founders of art history and comparative philology.

Schles·in·ger |'SHläziNGər|, Arthur Meier (1888–1965) U.S. historian. Notable works: *The Colonial Merchants and the American Revolution, 1763–1776* (1918) and *The American Reformer* (1950).

Schles·in·ger |'slesənjər; 'slesiNGər|, John Richard (1926–) British movie, telvision, and theater director. Notable movies: *Midnight Cowboy* (1969, Academy Award).

Schles·sin·ger |'slesənjər; 'slesiNGər|, Laura U.S. radio psychologist and author. Known as **Dr. Laura**. She offers advice to callers on her syndicated radio show.

Schlick |SHlik|, Friedrich Albert Moritz (1882–1936) German philosopher and physicist, founder of the Vienna Circle. Notable works: *General Theory of Knowledge* (1918).

Schlie·mann |'SHlē,män|, Heinrich (1822–90) German archaeologist. In 1871 he began excavating the mound of Hissarlik on the NE Aegean coast of Turkey, where he discovered the remains of nine superimposed cities, identifying the second oldest as Homer's Troy, although it was later found to be pre-Homeric. He subsequently undertook excavations at Mycenae (1876).

Schmidt |SHmit|, Helmut (Heinrich Waldemar) (1918–) German politician. He was chancellor of the Federal Republic of Germany (1974–82).

Schmidt |SHmit|, Mike (1949–) U.S. baseball player. Full name *Michael Jack Schmidt.*

Schna·bel |'SHnäbəl|, Artur (1882–1951) U.S. pianist, born in Austria. He is known for his performances of Beethoven, Brahms, and Schubert; he also composed works for piano, orchestra, and voice, and he edited and recorded Beethoven's piano sonatas.

Schnei·der |'SHnīdər|, Ralph Edward (1909–64) U.S. businessman and inventor. He launched the Diners Club, which offered the world's first credit card.

Schoen·berg |'SHOEn,berg; 'SHərn,bərg|, Arnold (Franz Walter) (1874–1951) Austrian-born U.S. composer and music theorist. His major contribution to modernism was the development of atonality and serialism. He introduced atonality into his second string quartet (1907–08), while *Serenade* (1923) is the first example of the technique of serialism.

Scholl |SHōl|, William (1882–1968) U.S. doctor, inventor, and manufacturer. Known as **Dr. Scholl**. He developed and patented arch-support and other foot products and wrote *The Human Foot: Anatomy, Deformities & Treatment* (1915).

Schon·berg |'sHōn,bərg|, Harold C. (1915–) U.S. journalist and author. A writer on music and culture for *The New York Times* (1950–85), he won a Pulitzer Prize for criticism (1971).

School·craft |'skōol,kræft|, Henry Rowe (1793–1864) U.S. ethnologist and explorer. He discovered the source of the Mississippi River at Lake Itasca, Minnesota (1832), and he married an Ojibwa woman and wrote pioneering works on American Indian ethnology.

Scho·pen·hau·er |'sHōpən,(h)owər|, Arthur (1788–1860) German philosopher. According to his philosophy, as expressed in *The World as Will and Idea*, the will is identified with ultimate reality and happiness is only achieved by abnegating the will (as desire).

Schrei·ner |'sHrīnər|, Olive (Emilie Albertina) (1855–1920) South African novelist and feminist. Notable works: *The Story of an African Farm* (novel, 1883) and *Woman and Labour* (1911).

Schrö·ding·er |'sHrōdiNGər|, Erwin (1887–1961) Austrian physicist. He founded the study of wave mechanics, deriving the equation whose roots define the energy levels of atoms. Nobel Prize for Physics (1933).

Schroe·der |'sHrOEdər; 'sHrōdər|, Gerhard (Fritz Kurt) (1944–) German politician. The chancellor of Germany (1998–), he is a Social Democrat allied with the Green Party.

Schroe·der |'sHrōdər|, Patricia (Scott) (1940–) U.S. politician. She was a member of the U.S. House of Representatives from Colorado (1973–).

Schu·bert |'sHōōbərt|, Franz (Peter) (1797–1828) Austrian composer. His music is associated with the romantic movement for its lyricism and emotional intensity, but belongs in formal terms to the classical age. His works include more than 600 songs, the "Trout" piano quintet (1819), and nine symphonies.

Schul·berg |'skōōl,bərg|, Budd (Wilson) (1914–) U.S. author and screenwriter. He won an Academy Award for his screenplay *On the Waterfront* (1954).

Schul·yer |'sHōōlyer|, James (Marcus) (1923–91) U.S. author. Notable works: *The Morning of the Poet* (1980, Pulitzer Prize).

Schulz |sHōōlts|, Charles (Monroe) (1922–) U.S. cartoonist. He is the creator of the widely syndicated "Peanuts" comic strip., featuring a range of characters including the boy Charlie Brown and the dog Snoopy.

Schu·ma·cher |'sHōō,mäkər|, E. F. (1911–77) German economist and conservationist; full name *Ernst Friedrich Schumacher*. His most famous work is *Small is Beautiful: Economics as if People Mattered* (1973), which argues that mass production needs to be replaced by smaller, more energy-efficient enterprises.

Schu·mann |'sHōō,män|, Robert (Alexander) (1810–56) German composer. He was a leading romantic composer, particularly noted for his songs (including settings of poems by Heinrich Heine and Robert Burns) and piano music. His other works include four symphonies and much chamber music. His wife **Clara** (1819–96) was a noted pianist and composer.

Schurz |sHōōrts; 'sHərts|, Carl (1829–1906) U.S. political reformer, journalist, and army officer, born in Germany. He served as a Union army general at Bull Run and Gettysburg and as a member of the U.S. Senate from Missouri (1869–75); later he was an editorial writer for *Harper's* (1892–98) and president of the National Civil Service Reform League (1892–1901).

Schu·ster |'sHōōstər|, Max Lincoln (1897–1970) U.S. publisher. He was co-founder and partner of Simon and Schuster book publishers (1924).

Schütz |sHōōts|, Heinrich (1585–1672) German composer and organist. He is regarded as the first German baroque composer, and composed what is thought to have been the first German opera (*Dafne*, 1627; now lost).

Schwab |sHwäb|, Charles Michael (1862–1939) U.S. steel industrialist. He was the first President of the U.S. Steel Corp. (1901–03) and the founder of the Bethlehem Steel Co. (1903).

Schwann |sHwän; sHwän|, Theodor

Ambrose Hubert (1810–82) German physiologist. He showed that animals (as well as plants) are made up of individual cells and that the egg begins life as a single cell. He is best known for discovering the cells forming the myelin sheaths of nerve fibres (Schwann cells).

Schwann |ˈsHwän|, William Joseph (1913–98) U.S. organist, musicologist, and publisher. He founded the Schwann catalog of recordings.

Schwartz |ˈsHwawrts|, Delmore (1913–66) U.S. author. He was editor of *The Partisan Review* (1943–55) and author of *Summer Knowledge* (1959, Bollingen Prize).

Schwar·ze·neg·ger |ˈsHwawrtzə-ˌnegər|, Arnold (Alois) (1947–) Austrian-born U.S. actor. He won the bodybuilding title Mr. Olympia seven times (1970–75; 1980) before retiring to concentrate on acting. Noted for his action roles, for instance in *The Terminator* (1984), he diversified in films such as the comedy *Kindergarten Cop* (1990) and the spy thriller *True Lies* (1994).

Schwarz·kopf |ˈsHwawrts,kaw(p)f; sHwarts,kä(p)f|, Dame (Olga Maria) Elisabeth (Friederike) (1915–) German operatic soprano. She is especially famous for her roles in works by Richard Strauss, such as *Der Rosenkavalier*.

Schwarz·kopf |ˈsHwawrts,kaw(p)f; sHwarts,kä(p)f|, H. Norman (1934–) U.S. army officer. He was deputy commander of U.S. forces during the invasion of Grenada (1983). Promoted to full general in 1988 and appointed commander in chief of the U.S. Central Command (1988–91), he led the Allied forces against Iraq in the Persian Gulf War (1991). He retired in 1991.

Schweit·zer |ˈsHwītsər|, Albert (1875–1965) German theologian, musician, and medical missionary born in Alsace. *The quest for the Historical Jesus* (1906) emphasized the importance of understanding Jesus within the context of the Jewish apocalyptic thought of his day. In 1913 he qualified as a doctor and went as a missionary to Gabon, where he established a hospital. Nobel Peace Prize (1952).

Scip·io Ae·mil·i·an·us |ˈsipē,ō ə,milē-

'änəs| (*c.* 185–129 BC) Roman general and politician; full name *Publius Cornelius Scipio Aemilianus Africanus Numantinus Minor*, adoptive grandson of Scipio Africanus. He achieved distinction in the siege of Carthage (146 BC) during the third Punic War and in his campaign in Spain (133BC).

Scip·io Af·ri·can·us |ˈsipē,ō ˌæfri-'känəs| (236–*c.* 184 BC) Roman general and politician; full name *Publius Cornelius Scipio Africanus Major*. He was successful in concluding the second Punic War, firstly by the defeat of the Carthaginians in Spain in 206 BC and then by the defeat of Hannibal in Africa At Zama in 202 BC.

Scor·se·se |ˌskawr'säzē|, Martin (1942–) U.S. movie director. Notable works: *Mean Streets* (1973), *Taxi Driver* (1976), and *The Last Temptation of Christ* (1988).

Scott |skät|, Dred (*c.* 1795–1858) U.S. slave. He brought suit for his freedom based on his five-year residence in free territories, but the U.S. Supreme Court ruled against him (1857) in a case that became the focus of much heated political controversy. Scott was emancipated later that year and became a hotel porter in St. Louis.

Scott |skät|, George C. (1927–) U.S. actor. Full name: *George Campbell Scott*. Notable movies: *Patton* (1970 Academy Award).

Scott |skät|, Paul Mark (1920–78) British novelist. Notable works: *Raj Quartet*.

Scott |skät|, Sir Peter (Markham) (1909–89) English naturalist and artist, son of Sir Robert Scott. In 1946 he founded the Wildfowl Trust at Slimbridge in Gloucestershire.

Scott |skät|, Ridley (1939–) English movie director. Notable works: *Alien* (1979), *Blade Runner* (1982), and *Thelma and Louise* (1991).

Scott |skät|, Sir Robert (Falcon) (1868–1912) English explorer and naval officer. In 1910–12 Scott and four companions made a journey to the South Pole by sled, arriving there in January 1912 to discover that Roald Amundsen had beaten them by a month. Scott and his companions died on the journey back to base; their bodies and diaries were discovered eight months later.

Scott |skät|, Sir Walter (1771–1832) Scottish novelist and poet. He established the form of the historical novel in Britain and was influential in his treatment of rural themes and use of regional speech. Notable novels: *Waverley* (1814), *Ivanhoe* (1819), *Kenilworth* (1821), and *Quentin Durward* (1823).

Scott |skät|, Winfield (1786–1866) U.S. army officer. Known as **Old Fuss and Feathers**. A hero of the War of 1812, he became supreme commander of the U.S. Army (1841–61). During the Mexican War, he waged a victorious campaign from Veracruz to Mexico City (1847). He ran for the office of U.S. president as the Whig candidate (1852) but was defeated by Democrat Franklin Pierce.

Scria·bin |skrē'äbən|, Aleksandr (Nikolayevich) (1872–1915) Russian composer and pianist. Also **Skryabin**. Notable works: *The Divine Poem* (symphony, 1903) and *Prometheus: The Poem of Fire* (symphonic poem, 1909–10).

Scrib·ner |'skribnər|, Charles (1821–71) U.S. publisher. With Isaac D. Baker he founded the publishing company Baker & Scribner (1846), later Scribner's Sons.

Scripps |'skrips| U.S. newspaper publishers. **Edward Wyllis Scripps** (1854–1926) founded the Scripps-McRae League newspaper chain (1894) with his brother George Scripps and Milton A. McRae, and in 1907 he organized the United Press Association. His son, **Robert Paine Scripps** (1895–1938), founded the Scripps-Howard newspapers (1922) with Roy W. Howard.

Sea·borg |'sē,bawrg|, Glenn (Theodore) (1912–) American nuclear chemist. During 1940–58 Seaborg and his colleagues produced nine of the transuranic elements (plutonium to nobelium) in a cyclotron. Seaborg and his early collaborator **Edwin McMillan** (1907–91) shared the Nobel Prize for Chemistry in 1951.

Seale |sēl|, John Clement (1942–) U.S. cinematographer, born in Australia. Notable movies: *Rainman* (1988).

Sea·man |'sēmən|, Elizabeth Cochrane (1867–1922) U.S. journalist. Pseudonym **Nelly Bly**. Her employer Joseph Pulitzer dispatched her to make reality out of Jules Verne's fictional *Around the World in 80 Days*. She returned in 72 days, 6 hours, and 11 minutes (1889–90).

Searle |sərl|, Ronald (William Fordham) (1920–) English artist and cartoonist.

Sears |sirz|, Richard Warren (1863–1914) U.S. businessman. He founded his first mail-order business in Minneapolis (1886), moved to Chicago and sold it, then began a partnership with A. C. Roebuck in a new business, which became Sears, Roebuck & Co. (1893).

Se·at·tle |sē'ætl|, Chief (1786–1866) Native American leader of the Suquamish and Dewamish tribes. He signed the Treaty of Port Elliott (1855), guaranteeing a reservation for his people in what became the state of Washington.

Sea·ver |'sēvər|, Tom (1944–) U.S. baseball player. Full name *George Thomas Seaver*. He won three Cy Young Awards.

Se·bas·tian |sə'bæsCHən|, St. (late 3rd cent) Roman martyr. According to legend he was a soldier who was shot by archers on the order of Diocletian, but who recovered, confronted the emperor, and was then clubbed to death. Feast day, January 20.

Se·da·ka |sə'dækə|, Neil (1939–) U.S. singer and songwriter. Notable songs: "Love Will Keep Us Together" and "Laughter in the Rain"

See·ger |'sēgər|, Pete (1919–) U.S. folk musician and songwriter. Seeger was a prominent figure in the American folk revival. He was also concerned with environmental issues, especially on the Hudson River. Notable songs: "If I Had a Hammer" (c. 1949) and "Where Have All the Flowers Gone?" (1956).

Se·gar |'sē,gär|, Elzie Crisler (1894–1938) U.S. cartoonist. He was the creator of "Popeye."

Se·go·via |sə'gōvēə|, Andrés (1893–1987) Spanish guitarist and composer. He was largely responsible for the revival of the classical guitar, elevating it to use as a concert instrument and making a large number of transcriptions of classical music to increase the repertoire of the instrument.

Sein·feld |'sīn,feld|, Jerry (1955–) U.S. comedian and actor. He was star of the television sitcom "Seinfeld."

Sel·craig see SELKIRK.

Sel·den |'seldən|, George Baldwin (1846–1922) U.S. lawyer and inventor. He received the first American patent for a gasoline-driven car (1895), and he sold rights to the patent on a royalty basis.

Sel·es |'seləs|, Monica (1973–) U.S. tennis player, born in Yugoslavia. She became the youngest woman to win a grand slam singles title with her victory in the French Open in 1990. She was stabbed on court by a fan of Steffi Graf in 1993, but she returned to play in 1995 and won the Australian Open in 1996.

Se·leu·cus I |sə'lōōkəs| (died 281 BC) King of the Seleucid Empire (306–281 BC). Also known as **Seleucus Nicator**. A Macedonian general under Alexander the Great, he founded the Seleucid Empire.

Sel·kirk |'sel,kərk|, Alexander (1676–1721) Scottish sailor; also called *Alexander Selcraig*. While on a privateering expedition in 1704, Selkirk quarreled with his captain and was put ashore, at his own request, on one of the uninhabited Juan Fernandez Islands, where he remained until 1709. His experiences formed the basis of Daniel Defoe's novel *Robinson Crusoe* (1719).

Sel·lers |'selərz|, Peter (1925–80) English comic actor. Full name *Peter Richard Henry Sellers*. He is best known for the "Pink Panther" series of movies of the 1960s and 1970s, in which he played the French detective Inspector Clouseau. Other notable films: *The Lady Killers* (1955) and *Dr. Strangelove* (1964).

Se·lous |sə'lōōs|, Frederick Courteney (1851–1917) English explorer, naturalist, and soldier. From 1890 he was involved in the British South Africa Company, negotiating mineral and land rights. The Selous Game Reserve in Tanzania is named after him.

Sel·ye |'selyā|, Hans Hugo Bruno (1907–82) Austrian-born Canadian physician. He showed that environmental stress and anxiety could result in the release of hormones that, over a long period, could produce biochemical and physiological disorders.

Selz·nick |'selznik|, David O. (1902–65) U.S. movie producer; full name *David Oliver Selznick*. He produced such movies as *King Kong* (1933) for RKO and *Anna Karenina* (1935) for MGM before establishing his own production company in 1936 and producing such screen classics as *Gone with the Wind* (1939) and *Rebecca* (1940).

Sem·mel·weis |'zeməl,vīs|, Ignaz Philipp (1818–65) Hungarian obstetrician; Hungarian name *Ignác Fülöp Semmelweis*. He discovered the infectious character of puerperal fever and advocated rigorous cleanliness and the use of antiseptics by doctors examining patients.

Se·na·na·yake |,sänänä'yäkä|, Don Stephen (1884–1952) Sinhalese statesman, prime minister of Ceylon (now Sri Lanka) (1947–52). As prime minister he presided over Ceylon's achievement of full dominion status within the Commonwealth.

Sen·dak |'sen,dæk|, Maurice Bernard (1928–) U.S. author and illustrator of children's books. He received a Caldecott Award for *Where the Wild Things Are* (1963).

Sen·e·ca |'senikə|, Roman writers. **Marcus (or Lucius) Annaeus Seneca** (*c.* 55 BC–*c.* 39 AD), was a Roman rhetorician born in Spain and known as **Seneca the Elder**. He is best known for his works on rhetoric, only parts of which survive. **Lucius Annaeus Seneca** (*c.* 4 BC–AD 65), his son, was a Roman statesman, philosopher, and dramatist known as **Seneca the Younger**. He became tutor to Nero in 49 and was appointed consul in 57. His *Epistulae Morales* is a notable Stoic work.

Sen·ghor |sän'gawr|, Léopold Sédar (1906–) president of Senegal (1960–80). His *Poèmes* were published in 1984.

Sen·nach·er·ib |sə'nækə,rib| (died 681 BC) king of Assyria (705–681), son of Sargon II. In 701 he put down a Jewish rebellion, laying siege to Jerusalem but sparing it from destruction (according to 2 Kings 19:35). He also rebuilt the city of Nineveh and made it his capital.

Sen·nett |'senət|, Mack (1880–1960) U.S. movie director, producer, and actor, born in Canada. Born *Michael Sinnott*. He produced over 1,000 slapstick comedy shorts and created the Keystone Kops; his films include *The Shriek of Araby* (1923).

Se·quoya |sə'kwoiə| (*c.* 1770–1843) Cherokee scholar. Also **Sequoia**; also known (in later years) as **George Guess**. He invented a writing system for the Cherokee language (1809–21) and with it taught thousands of Cherokee Indians to read and write. The giant sequoia trees of California are named for him.

Se·raph·ic Doc·tor the nickname of St. Bonaventura.

Ser·gi·us |'sərjēəs|, St. (1314–92) Russian monastic reformer and mystic; Russian name *Svyatoi Sergi Radonezhsky*. He founded forty monasteries, reestablishing the monasticism that had been lost through the Tartar invasion, and inspired the resistance that saved Russia from the Tartars in 1380. Feast day, September 25.

Ser·ling |'sərliNG|, Rod (1924–75) U.S. writer and television producer. He hosted the television series "The Twilight Zone" (1959–65).

Ses·sions |'seSHənz|, Roger Huntington (1896–1985) U.S. composer. He composed eight symphonies, as well as operas and the cantata *When Lilacs Last in the Dooryard Bloom'd* (1970). Pulitzer Prizes, 1974 and 1981.

Se·ton |'sētn|, St. Elizabeth Ann (Bayley) (1774–1821) U.S. religious leader, educator, and social reformer. She became the first native-born American to be canonized as a saint (1975).

Seu·rat |sə'rä|, Georges-Pierre (1859–91) French painter. The founder of neo-Impressionism, he is chiefly associated with pointillism, which he developed during the 1880s. Among his major paintings using this technique is *Sunday Afternoon on the Island of La Grande Jatte* (1884–6).

Seuss |sōōs|, Dr. see GEISEL, THEODOR SEUSS.

Sev·a·reid |'sevə,rīd|, Eric (Arnold) (1912–92) U.S. broadcast journalist and author.

Se·ve·rus |sə'virəs|, Septimius (146–211) Roman emperor 193–211; full name *Lucius Septimius Severus*. He reformed the imperial administration and the army. In 208 he led an army to Britain to suppress a rebellion in the north of the country and later died at York.

Sew·all |'sōōəl|, Samuel (1652–1730) American colonial merchant and jurist. He presided over the Salem witchcraft trials (1692); his *Diary* (published 1878–82) covers the years 1674–77 and 1685–1729.

Sew·ard |'sōō(w)ərd|, William Henry (1801–72) U.S. statesman and politician. An outspoken antislavery politician, he was governor of New York (1839–43), U.S. senator (1849–61), and U.S. secretary of state (1861–69). He negotiated the purchase of Alaska from Russia (1867), which was widely mocked as "Seward's Icebox" and "Seward's Folly."

Sex·ton |'sekstən|, Anne (1928–74) U.S. poet. Notable works: *Live or Die* (1966, Pulitzer Prize).

Sey·mour |'sē,mawr|, Jane (*c.* 1509–37) third wife of Henry VIII and mother of Edward VI. She married Henry in 1536 and finally provided the king with the male heir he wanted, although she died twelve days later.

Sey·mour |'sē,mawr|, Lynn (1939–) Canadian ballet dancer; born *Lynn Springbett*. From 1957 she danced for the Royal Ballet. Her most acclaimed roles came in Frederick Ashton's *Five Brahms Waltzes in the Manner of Isadora Duncan* and *A Month in the Country* (both 1976).

Sha·ba·ka |'sHæbəkə| (died 695 BC) Egyptian pharaoh, founder of the 25th dynasty, reigned 712–698 BC; known as **Sabacon**. He promoted the cult of Amun and revived the custom of pyramid burial in his own death arrangements.

Shack·le·ton |'sHækəltən|, Sir Ernest Henry (1874–1922) British explorer. During one of his Antarctic expeditions (1914–16), Shackleton's ship *Endurance* was crushed in the ice. Shackleton and his crew eventually reached an island, from where he and five others made a 800-mile (1,300-km) open-boat voyage to South Georgia Island to get help.

Shaftes·bury |'sнæf(t)s,berē|, Anthony Ashley Cooper, 7th Earl of (1801–85) English philanthropist and social reformer. A dominant figure of the 19th-century social reform movement, he inspired much of the legislation designed to improve conditions for the large working class created as a result of the Industrial Revolution. His reforms included the introduction of the ten-hour work day (1847).

Shah |sнā|, Karim Al-Hussain see AGA KHAN.

Shah |sнā|, Reza see PAHLAVI.

Shahn |sнän|, Ben (1898–1969) U.S. artist, born in Lithuania. His paintings are devoted to political and social themes.

Sha·ka |'sнäkə| (c. 1787–1828) Also **Chaka**. Zulu chief (1816–28). He reorganized his forces and waged war against the Nguni clans, subjugating them and forming a Zulu empire in SE Africa.

Shake·speare |'sнāk,spir|, William (1564–1616) English dramatist. His plays are written mostly in blank verse and include comedies, such as *A Midsummer Night's Dream* and *As You Like It*; historical plays, including *Richard III* and *Henry V*; the Greek and Roman plays, which include *Julius Caesar* and *Antony and Cleopatra*; enigmatic comedies such as *All's Well that Ends Well* and *Measure for Measure*; the great tragedies, *Hamlet*, *Othello*, *King Lear*, and *Macbeth*; and the group of tragicomedies with which he ended his career, such as *The Winter's Tale* and *The Tempest*. He also wrote more than 150 sonnets, published in 1609.

Sha·li·kash·vi·li |,sнälē,käsн'vēlē|, John Malchase (1936–) U.S. army officer, born in Poland. He was chairman of the Joint Chiefs of Staff (1993–97).

Shal·ma·ne·ser III |,sнælmə'nēzər| (died 824 BC) king of Assyria (859–824 BC). Most of his reign was devoted to the expansion of his kingdom and the conquest of neighboring lands. According to Assyrian records he defeated an alliance of Syrian kings and the king of Israel in a battle at Qarqar on the Orontes in 853 BC.

Sha·mir |sнə'mir|, Yitzhak (1915–) Polish-born Israeli statesman, prime minister (1983–84 and 1986–92); Polish name *Yitzhak Jazernicki*. Under his leadership Israel did not retaliate when attacked by Iraqi missiles during the Gulf War, thereby possibly averting an escalation of the conflict.

Shan·kar |'sнäNG,kär|, Ravi (1920–) Indian sitar player and composer. From the mid-1950s he toured Europe and the U.S. giving sitar recitals, doing much to stimulate contemporary Western interest in Indian music.

Shan·kar |'sнäNG,kär|, Uday (1900–77) Indian dancer, brother of Ravi Shankar. He introduced Anna Pavlova to Indian dance and performed with her in his ballet *Krishna and Radha* (1923). He later toured the world with his own company, introducing Indian dance to European audiences.

Shank·er |'sнæNGkər|, Albert (1928–97) U.S. labor organizer. As head of the American Federation of Teachers, he was responsible for doubling its size.

Shan·non |'sнænən|, Claude Elwood (1916–) American engineer. He was the pioneer of mathematical communication theory, which has become vital to the design of both communication and electronic equipment. He also investigated digital circuits, and was the first to use the term *bit* to denote a unit of information.

Sha·pi·ro |sнə'pirō|, Karl (Jay) (1913–) U.S. author and educator. Notable works: *V-Letter and Other Poems* (1944, Pulitzer Prize).

Shap·ley |'sнæplē|, Harlow (1885–1972) American astronomer. He carried out an extensive survey of galaxies and used his studies on the distribution of globular star clusters to locate the likely centre of the Galaxy and to infer its structure and dimensions. He found that the solar system is located on the Galaxy's edge and not at its center.

Shar·ma |'sнärmə|, Shankar Dayal (1918–) Indian statesman, president (1992–97). A member of the Congress

Party, Sharma served as vice president (1987–92).

Sharp |sʜärp|, Cecil (James) (1859–1924) English collector of folk songs and folk dances.

Sharp |sʜärp|, William (1856–1905) Scottish author. Also called **Fiona Macleod**.

Sharp·ton |ˈsʜärptən|, Al (1954–) U.S. civil rights activist and Baptist minister. Full name *Alfred Charles Sharpton, Jr.*

Shat·ner |ˈsʜætnər|, William (1931–) U.S. actor, director, and producer, born in Canada. He starred in the "Star Trek" movies and television series.

Shaw |sʜaw|, Artie (1910–) U.S. jazz clarinetist and bandleader. Born *Arthur Jacob Arshawsky*. He was a leading musician of the swing period and formed several small groups, including the Gramercy Five.

Shaw |sʜaw|, George Bernard (1856–1950) Irish dramatist and writer. His best-known plays combine comedy with a questioning of conventional morality and thought; they include *Man and Superman* (1903), *Pygmalion* (1913), and *St. Joan* (1923). A socialist, he became an active member of the Fabian Society. Nobel Prize for Literature (1925). Other noted works: *Candida* (1897) and *Major Barbara* (1905).

Shaw |sʜaw|, Henry Wheeler (1818–85) U.S. author. Pseudonym **Josh Billings**. Notable works: *Josh Billings, His Sayings* (1865).

Shaw |sʜaw|, Irwin (1913–84) U.S. author. Notable works: *Bury the Dead* (1936) and *Rich Man, Poor Man* (1970).

Shear·er |ˈsʜirər|, Moira (1926–) Scottish ballet dancer and actress; full name *Moira Shearer King*. A ballerina with Sadler's Wells from 1942, she is perhaps best known for her portrayal of a dedicated ballerina in the film *The Red Shoes* (1948).

Shear·er |ˈsʜirər|, Norma (1902–83) U.S. actress, born in Canada. Born *Edith Norma Shearer*. She made a successful transition from silent to talking movies. Notable movies: *The Divorcee* (1929–30 Academy Award).

Sheed |sʜēd|, Wilfrid (John Joseph) (1930–) U.S. author, born in England. Notable works: *A Middle Class Education* (1961).

Shee·han |ˈsʜēən|, John Clark (1915–92) U.S. research chemist. He invented semisynthetic penicillin.

Shee·ler |ˈsʜēlər|, Charles (1883–1965) U.S. artist. He photographed and painted industrial-commercial subjects.

Shel·don |ˈsʜeldən|, Charles Monroe (1857–1946) U.S. clergyman and author. A Congregational minister, he edited the *Christian Herald* and wrote *In His Steps* (1896).

Shel·don |ˈsʜeldən|, Edward (Brewster) (1886–1946) U.S. author. Notable works: *The Nigger* (1909).

Shel·don |ˈsʜeldən|, Sidney (1917–) U.S. novelist. Notable works: *Tell Me Your Dreams* (1998).

Shel·ley |ˈsʜelē| English writers. **Percy Bysshe Shelley** (1792–1822) was a leading poet of the romantic movement with radical politcal views. Notable works include *Queen Mab* (political poems, 1813), *Prometheus Unbound* (lyrical drama, 1820), *The Defence of Poetry* (essay, 1821), and *Adonais* (1821), an elegy on the death of Keats. His wife, **Mary (Wollstonecraft) Shelley** (1797–1851), daughter of William Godwin and Mary Wollstonecraft, eloped with him in 1814 and married him in 1816. She is chiefly remembered as the author of the Gothic novel *Frankenstein, or the Modern Prometheus* (1818).

Shep·ard |ˈsʜepərd|, Sam (1943–) U.S. playwright and actor. Born *Samuel Shepard Rogers*. He wrote the plays *Buried Child* (1979, Pulitzer Prize) and *Fool for Love* (1984); he acted in the movies *Fool for Love* (1985) and *Baby Boom* (1987).

Shep·hard |ˈsʜepərd|, Thomas (1605–49) U.S. clergyman, born in England. He helped found Harvard and wrote *The Sincere Convert* (1641).

Shep·herd |ˈsʜepərd|, Cybill (1950–) U.S. actress. She appeared in the movie *The Last Picture Show* (1971) and had a starring role in the television series "Moonlighting."

Sher·er |ˈsʜirər|, Moshe (1921–98) U.S. rabbi. He contributed to the rise of Jewish Orthodoxy in the U.S.

Sher·i·dan |ˈsʜerəd(ə)n|, Philip Henry

(1831–88) U.S. army officer. A severe and effective Union cavalry commander in the Civil War, he was noted for his decisive victories and plundering raids. In April 1865, he cut off the Confederate retreat at Appomattox, forcing the surrender of General Lee.

Sher·i·dan |'sHerəd(ə)n|, Richard Brinsley (1751–1816) Irish dramatist and Whig politician. His plays are comedies of manners; they include *The Rivals* (1775) and *The School for Scandal* (1777). In 1780 he entered Parliament, becoming a celebrated orator and holding senior government posts.

Sher·man |'sHərmən|, James Schoolcraft (1855–1912) vice president of the U.S. (1909–12).

Sher·man |'sHərmən|, Roger (1721–93) American politician. A Connecticut legislator and jurist, he was an avid proponent of American independence. He was the only person to sign all of the following: the Articles of Association (1774), the Declaration of Independence (1776), the Articles of Confederation (1777), and the Constitution (1787).

Sher·man |'sHərmən|, William Tecumseh (1820–91) U.S. general. In 1864 in the Civil War he was appointed commander of Union forces in the West. He set out with 60,000 men on a "March to the Sea" through Georgia from Atlanta to Savannah, then north through the Carolinas, during which he crushed Confederate forces and broke civilian morale by his policy of deliberate destruction of the territory he passed through. He served as commander of the army (1869–84).

Sher·ring·ton |'sHeriNGtən|, Sir Charles Scott (1857–1952) English physiologist. He contributed greatly to the understanding of the nervous system and introduced the concept of reflex actions and the reflex arc. Nobel Prize for Physiology or Medicine (1932).

Shev·ard·na·dze |ˌsHevərd'nädzə|, Eduard (Amvrosiyevich) (1928–) Soviet statesman. He was Minister of Foreign Affairs 1985–90 under President Gorbachev before becoming head of state of his native Georgia in 1992.

Shields |sHēldz|, (Christa) Brooke

(Camille) (1965–) U.S. actress. She began her career as a model, before acting in movies and in the starring role of the television program "Suddenly Susan."

Shields |sHēldz|, Carol Ann (1935–) U.S. author. Notable works: *Larry's Party* (1997).

Shil·la·ber |'sHil,äbər|, Benjamin Penhallow (1814–90) U.S. editor and humorist. He edited a weekly humor magazine called *The Carpet-Bag* (1851–53) and wrote *The Life and Sayings of Mrs. Partington* (1854).

Shi·ma |'sHēmə|, Hideo (1901–98) Japanese engineer. He designed the Shinkansen bullet train.

Ship·ley |'sHiplē|, Jenny (1952–) New Zealand stateswoman. Full name *Jennifer Mary Shipley*. She is the prime minister of New Zealand (1997–).

Shi·ras |'sHīrəs|, George, Jr. (1832–1924) U.S. Supreme Court justice (1892–1903).

Shi·va·ji |'sHiväjē| (1627–80) Indian raja of the Marathas (1674–80). Also **Sivaji**. He raised a successful Hindu revolt against Muslim rule in 1659 and expanded Maratha territory. After being crowned raja, he blocked Mogul expansionism by forming an alliance with the sultans in the south.

Shock·ley |'sHäklē|, William (Bradford) (1910–89) U.S. physicist. Shockley and his researchers at Bell Laboratories developed the transistor in 1948, and in 1958 he shared with them the Nobel Prize for Physics. He later became a controversial figure because of his views on a supposed connection between race and intelligence.

Shoe·maker |'sHoo,mäkər|, Willie (1931–) U.S. jockey. Full name *William Lee Shoemaker*. He holds the record for all-time career wins (8,833).

Sholes |sHōlz|, Christopher Latham (1819–90) U.S. journalist and inventor. With his two collaborators, Samuel W. Soulé and Carols Glidden, he received a patent for the first practical typewriter.

Sho·lo·khov |'sHawlə,KHawf|, Mikhail Aleksandrovich (1905–84) Soviet novelist. Notable works: *Quiet Flows the Don*. Nobel Prize for Literature, 1965.

Sho·lom Alei·chem |'sHōləm ə'läkəm|

(1859–1916) U.S. author, born in Ukraine. Born *Solomon Rabinowitz*. *Fiddler on the Roof* is based on his writings.

Shore |ˈSHawr|, Dinah (Frances Rose) (1921–93) U.S. singer. She was a radio, television, and film star, as well as host of the television programs "Dinah's Place" (1970–74) "Dinah!" (1974–79), and "Dinah! And Friends." She won 10 Academy Awards.

Sho·sta·ko·vich |ˌSHästəˈkōviCH|, Dmitri (Dmitriyevich) (1906–75) Russian composer. He developed a highly personal style, and, although he experimented with atonality and twelve-note techniques, his music always returned to a basic tonality. He is best known for his fifteen symphonies.

Shri·ver |ˈSHrīvər|, (Robert) Sargent, Jr. (1915–) U.S. lawyer and politician. He was a Democratic vice presidential candidate (1972)

Shu·la |ˈSHo͞olə|, Don (Francis) (1930–) U.S. football coach. He retired with the NFL record of 347 career wins. Elected to the NFL Hall of Fame (1997).

Shu·ster |ˈSHo͞ostər|, Joe (1914–92) U.S. cartoonist. He was the co-creator of Superman with childhood friend Jerry Siegel.

Shute |SHo͞ot|, Nevil (1899–1960) English novelist; pseudonym of *Nevil Shute Norway*. After World War II he settled in Australia, which provides the setting for his later novels. Notable works: *A Town Like Alice* (1950) and *On the Beach* (1957), which depicts a community facing gradual destruction in the aftermath of a nuclear war.

Si·be·li·us |səˈbālēəs|, Jean (1865–1957) Finnish composer; born *Johan Julius Christian Sibelius*. His affinity for his country's landscape and legends, especially the epic *Kalevala*, is expressed in a series of symphonic poems including *The Swan of Tuonela* (1893), *Finlandia* (1899), and *Tapiola* (1925).

Sick·ert |ˈsikərt|, Walter Richard (1860–1942) British painter, of Danish and Anglo-Irish descent. His subjects are mainly urban scenes and figure compositions, particularly pictures of the theater and music hall, and drab domestic interiors.

Sid·dons |ˈsidnz|, Sarah (1755–1831) English actress, sister of John Kemble; born *Sarah Kemble*. She was an acclaimed tragic actress, noted particularly for her role as Lady Macbeth.

Sid·ney |ˈsidnē|, Sir Philip (1554–86) English poet, courtier, and soldier. His best-known work is *Arcadia* (published posthumously in 1590), a pastoral prose romance including poems in a wide variety of verse forms.

Sie·gel |ˈsēgəl|, Jerry (1914–96) U.S. cartoonist. Full name *Jerome Siegel*. He was the co-creator of Superman with childhood friend Joe Shuster

Sie·mens |ˈzēmənz| German family of scientific entrepreneurs and engineers. **Ernst Werner von Siemens** (1816–92) was an electrical engineer who developed the process of electroplating, devised an electric generator which used an electromagnet, and pioneered electrical traction. His brother **Karl Wilhelm** (1823–83) (also known as *Sir Charles William Siemens*) moved to England, where he developed the open-hearth steel furnace and designed the cable-laying steamship *Faraday*. Their brother **Friedrich** (1826–1904) applied the principles of the open-hearth furnace to glass-making.

Si·gnac |sēnˈyäk|, Paul (1863–1935) French neo-Impressionist painter. A pointillist painter, he had a technique that was freer than Seurat's and was characterized by the use of small dashes and patches of pure color rather than dots.

Si·ha·nouk |ˈsēə,no͞ok|, Norodom (1922–) Cambodian king (1941–55 and since 1993), prime minister (1955–60), and head of state (1960–70 and 1975–76). After Cambodian independence in 1953, Sihanouk abdicated in favor of his father in order to become prime minister. On his father's death Sihanouk proclaimed himself head of state. He was ousted in a U.S.-backed coup and was briefly reinstated by the Khmer Rouge. Sihanouk was crowned for the second time in 1993.

Si·kor·ski |SHēˈkawrskē|, Wladyslaw Eugeniusz (1881–1943) Polish general and statesman. He was prime minister of Poland (Dec. 1922–May 1923), as well as minister of war (1924–25) and prime minister in exile (1939–43).

Si·kor·sky |sə'kawrskē|, Igor (Ivanovich) (1889–1972) Russian-born American aircraft designer. He built the first large four-engined aircraft, the Grand (1913), in his native country and went on to establish the Sikorsky company in the US. In 1939 he developed the first mass-produced helicopter.

Sil·li·toe |'silə,tō|, Alan (1928–) English writer, noted for his novels about working-class provincial life. Notable works: *The Loneliness of the Long-Distance Runner* (1959) and *Saturday Night and Sunday Morning* (1958).

Sills |silz|, Beverly (1929–) U.S. singer. Born *Belle Miriam Silverman*; known as **Bubbles**. Her association with the New York City Opera included a brilliant career as a soprano (1955–80) and the positions of general director (1979–88) and president (1989–90). She became the first woman chairperson of the Lincoln Center for the Performing Arts (1993–).

Sil·ver·stein |'silvər,stīn; 'silvər,stēn|, Shel (1932–99) U.S. author. Full name *Shelby Silverstein*. Notable works: *A Light in the Attic* (1981), *The Giving Tree* (1964), and *Where the Sidewalk Ends* (1974).

Si·me·non |,sēme'nawN|, Georges-Joseph-Christian (1903–89) Belgian-born French novelist. He is best known for his series of detective novels featuring Commissaire Maigret.

Sim·n Sty·li·tes |'simēən stī'lītēz|, St. (*c.* 390–459) Syrian monk. After living in a monastic community he became the first to practise an extreme form of asceticism which involved living on top of a pillar.

Sim·ic |'simik|, Charles (1938–) U.S. author, born in Yugoslavia. Notable works: *The World Doesn't End* (1989, Pulitzer Prize).

Sim·jian |'simyən|, Luther (1905–97) U.S. inventor, born in Turkey. He holds more than 200 patents for mechanisms including a 1960 bank-deposit machine that was the basis for the modern automatic teller machine, the teleprompter, and the automatic postal meter machine.

Sim·mons |'simənz|, Al (1902–56) U.S. baseball player. Full name *Aloysius Harry Simmons*; born *Aloys Szymanski*. He twice led the American League in batting.

Sim·mons |'simənz|, Gene (1949–) U.S. rock musician, born in Israel. He was founder and member of the group Kiss (1973).

Simms |simz|, William Gilmore (1806–70) U.S. author. He wrote frontier romances and historical novels about the history of South Carolina.

Si·mon |'sīmən|, Carly (1945–) U.S. singer and songwriter. Notable songs: "You're So Vain," "Let the River Run," and "Anticipation."

Si·mon |'sīmən|, (Marvin) Neil (1927–) U.S. dramatist. Most of his plays are wry comedies portraying aspects of middle-class life; they include *Barefoot in the Park* (1963) and *The Odd Couple* (1965). Many of his plays were made into movies.

Si·mon |'sīmən|, Paul (1942–) U.S. singer and songwriter. He achieved fame with **Art Garfunkel** (1941–) for the albums *Sounds of Silence* (1966) and *Bridge Over Troubled Water* (1970). The duo split up in 1970 and Simon went on to pursue a successful solo career, recording albums such as *Graceland* (1986).

Si·mon |'sīmən|, Richard Leo (1899–1960) U.S. publisher. He was cofounder of Simon and Schuster book publishers (1924).

Si·mon |'sīmən|, St. an Apostle; known as **Simon the Zealot**. According to one tradition he preached and was martyred in Persia along with St. Jude. Feast day (with St. Jude), October 28.

Si·mon·i·des |sī'mänə,dēz| (*c.* 556–*c.* 468 BC) Greek lyric poet. Much of his poetry, which includes elegies, odes, and epigrams, celebrates the heroes of the Persian Wars.

Simp·son |'sim(p)sən|, Sir James Young (1811–70) Scottish surgeon and obstetrician. He discovered the usefulness of chloroform as an anesthetic shortly after the first use of ether.

Simp·son |'sim(p)sən|, George Gaylord (1902–84) U.S. paleontologist. He excavated and researched North American vertebrae fossils.

Simp·son |'sim(p)sən|, O. J. (1947–) U.S. football player, actor, and celebrity; full name *Orenthal James Simpson*. Following a successful career as a running back, Simpson became a sports commentator on television. He was arrested in 1994, accused of murdering his ex-wife and her male companion, but was acquitted after a lengthy, high-profile trial.

Simp·son |'sim(p)sən|, Wallis (1896–1986) U.S.-born wife of Edward, Duke of Windsor (Edward VIII); born *Wallis Warfield*. Her relationship with the king caused a scandal in view of her impending second divorce and forced the king's abdication in 1936. The couple were married shortly afterward, and she became the Duchess of Windsor.

Sims |simz|, Zoot (1925–85) U.S. jazz tenor saxophonist and bandleader. Full name *John Haley Sims*. He performed with Woody Herman's big band (1947–49) as one of the Four Brothers.

Si·na·tra |sə'nätrə|, Frank (1915–98) U.S. singer and actor; full name *Francis Albert Sinatra*. He became a star in the 1940s with a large teenage following; his many hits include "Night and Day" and "My Way". Notable movies: *From Here to Eternity* (1953), for which he won an Oscar.

Sin·clair |'sin,kler; sin'kler|, Sir Clive (Marles) (1940–) English electronics engineer and entrepreneur.

Sin·clair |sin'kler|, Upton (Beall) (1878–1968) U.S. novelist and social reformer. He agitated for social justice in seventy-nine books, including *The Jungle* (1906) and the eleven-volume "Lanny Budd" series (1940–53).

Sing·er |'siNGər|, Isaac Bashevis (1904–91) Polish-born U.S. novelist and short-story writer. His work blends realistic detail and elements of fantasy, mysticism, and magic to portray the lives of Polish Jews from many periods. Notable works: *The Magician of Lublin* (novel, 1955), *The Slave* (novel, 1962), *The Spinoza of Market Street* (short stories, 1961), and *Collected Stories* (1982). Nobel Prize for Literature (1978).

Sing·er |'siNGər|, Isaac Merritt (1811–75) U.S. inventor. In 1851 he designed and built the first commercially successful sewing machine, which included features already developed by Elias Howe. Singer's company became the world's largest sewing machine manufacturer.

Sin·gle·ton |'siNGgəltən|, Zutty (1898–1975) U.S. jazz drummer. Full name *Arthur James Singleton*. He was among the first drummers to use sock cymbals and wire brushes.

Sis·kel |'siskəl|, Gene (1946–99) U.S. movie critic. Full name *Eugene Kal Siskel*. He wrote for the *Chicago Tribune* (1969–98) and was co-host of the syndicated television program "Siskel & Ebert & the Movies" (1986–98).

Sis·ler |'sislər|, George Harold (1893–1973) U.S. baseball player. He set a record of 257 hits (1920).

Sis·ley |sislē; sē'slä|, Alfred (1839–99) French Impressionist painter, of English descent. He is chiefly remembered for his paintings of the countryside around Paris in the 1870s, with their concentration on reflecting surfaces and fluid brushwork.

Sit·ting Bull |,sitiNG 'bŏŏl| (*c.* 1831–90) Sioux chief; Sioux name *Tatanka Iyotake*. As the main chief of the Sioux peoples from about 1867, Sitting Bull led the Sioux in the fight to retain their lands; this resulted in the massacre of Lt. Col. George Custer and his men at Little Bighorn. He was killed by reservation police during the Ghost Dance turmoil.

Sit·well |'sit,wel; 'sitwəl|, Dame Edith (Louisa) (1887–1964) English poet and critic. Her early verse, with that of her brothers **Osbert** (1892–1969) and **Sacheverell** (1897–1988) marked a revolt against the prevailing Georgian style of the day.

Si·va·ji variant spelling of SHIVAJI.

Skel·ton |'skeltn|, John (*c.* 1460–1529) English poet. Court poet to Henry VIII, he wrote verse consisting of short irregular rhyming lines with rhythms based on colloquial speech.

Skel·ton |'skeltn|, Red (1913–97) U.S. comedian. Born *Richard Skelton*. A stage, circus, and movie performer, he starred in the television series "The Red Skelton Show" (1951–71).

Skid·more |'skid,mawr|, Louis (1897–1962) U.S. architect. Notable designs: U.S. Air Force Academy.

Skin·ner |'skinər|, B. F. (1904–90) U.S. behavioral psychologist. Full name *Burrhus Frederic Skinner*. He promoted the view that the proper aim of psychology should be to predict behavior, and hence be able to control it.

Skrya·bin variant spelling of SCRIABIN.

Sla·ter |'slātər|, Samuel (1768–1835) U.S. industrialist, born in England. He established textile mills at Pawtucket, Rhode Island, (1793) and elsewhere in New England.

Slick |slik|, Grace (1943–) U.S. rock vocalist. Born *Grace Barnett Wing*. She was a member of the Haight-Ashbury rock group Jefferson Airplane, which later became Jefferson Starship. Notable songs: "Somebody to Love" and "White Rabbit."

Sloan |slōn|, Alfred Pritchard, Jr. (1875–1966) U.S. industrialist. He was an executive with General Motors (1923–66).

Sloan |slōn|, John French (1871–1951) U.S. artist. He depicted scenes of New York City and gained fame as part of the "Ashcan School."

Sloane |slōn|, Sir Hans (1660–1753) Irish physician and naturalist. He endowed the Chelsea Physic Garden, and his books and specimens formed the basis of the British Museum Library and the Natural History Museum in London.

Slo·cum |'slōkəm|, Joshua (1844–c. 1910) U.S. mariner and author, born in Canada. He was the first man to sail alone around the world (1900).

Smalls |smawlz|, Robert (1839–1915) U.S. naval officer and politician. Born a slave, after he was impressed into the Confederate navy he commandeered a frigate, delivered it into Union hands, and became a pilot in the Union navy (1862). He later became a member of the U.S. House of Representatives from South Carolina (1875–79, 1881–87).

Smea·ton |'smētn|, John (1724–92) English engineer. He produced the first diving bell fed by compressed air, and

founded the Society of Engineers (1771).

Sme·ta·na |'smetn-ə|, Bedřich (1824–84) Czech composer. Regarded as the founder of Czech music, he was dedicated to the cause of Czech nationalism, as is apparent in his operas, such as *The Bartered Bride* (1866) and in the cycle of symphonic poems *MaVlast ("My Country"* 1874–9).

Smi·ley |'smilē|, Jane Graves (1949–) U.S. author. Notable works: *A Thousand Acres* (1991) and *Moo* (1995).

Smith |smiTH|, Adam (1723–90) Scottish economist and philosopher. Often regarded as the founder of modern economics, he advocated minimal state interference in economic matters and discredited mercantilism. Notable works: *Inquiry into the Nature and Causes of the Wealth of Nations* (1776).

Smith |smiTH|, Alfred Emanuel (1873–1944) U.S. politician. He served as governor of NewYork (1919–20 and 1923–28) and was a Democratic presidential candidate (1928).

Smith |smiTH|, Andrew (c. 1836–94) U.S. manufacturer. His cough drops were among the first "factory-filled" boxes of any confection.

Smith |smiTH|, Ashbel (1805–86) U.S. politician and physician. He negotiated a treaty by which Mexico acknowledged the independence of Texas (1845).

Smith |smiTH|, Bessie (1894–1937) Full name *Elizabeth Smith*. U.S. blues singer. She made over 150 recordings, including some with Benny Goodman and Louis Armstrong.

Smith |smiTH|, Betty (Wehner) (1904–72) U.S. author. Notable works: *A Tree Grows in Brooklyn* (1943).

Smith |smiTH|, Clarence (1904–29) U.S. jazz pianist and singer. Known as **Pinetop**. His recording "Pinetop's Boogie Woogie" (1928–29) was a pioneer of boogie-woogie.

Smith |smiTH|, David (Roland) (1906–65) U.S. sculptor. His early work is marked by recurring motifs of human violence and greed. These later give way to a calmer, more monumental style, as in the *Cubi* series.

Smith |smiTH|, Dean (Edwards) (1931–) U.S. college basketball coach. He coached the U.S. Olympic team to a gold medal in 1976 and remains number one on the all-time Division I victory list.

Smith |smiTH|, Emmitt J., III (1969–) U.S. football player. He was a three-time NFL rushing leader.

Smith |smiTH|, Horace (1808–93) U.S. inventor and manufacturer. With Daniel Baird Wesson he patented and manufactured revolvers (1854, 1857).

Smith |smiTH|, Ian (Douglas) (1919–) Rhodesian statesman and prime minister (1964–79). In 1965 he issued a unilateral declaration of independence from Britain because he would not agree to black majority rule. He eventually resigned in 1979 but remained active in politics in the independent state of Zimbabwe.

Smith |smiTH|, Jedediah Strong (1799–1831) U.S. explorer. He made expeditions in the Rocky Mountains (1822–26), California, and the Oregon coast (1826–69).

Smith |smiTH|, John (c. 1580–1631) American colonist, born in England. One of the leading promoters of English colonization in America, he helped found the colony of Jamestown (1607) and served as its president (1608–09).

Smith |smiTH|, Joseph (1805–44) U.S. religious leader and founder of the Church of Jesus Christ of Latter-Day Saints (the Mormons). In 1827, according to his own account, he was led by divine revelation to find the sacred texts written by the prophet Mormon, which he published as *The Book of Mormon* in 1830. He founded the Mormon Church in the same year and later established a large community in Illinois, where he was arrested and murdered by a mob.

Smith |smiTH|, Kate (1909–86) U.S. singer. Full name *Kathryn Elizabeth Smith*. She began a radio show in 1931 and started singing her trademark song "God Bless America" in 1938.

Smith |smiTH|, Lee (Arthur) (1957–) U.S. baseball pitcher. He retired in 1997 as the all-time saves leader with 478.

Smith |smiTH|, Lillian (Eugenia) (1897–1966) U.S. author and civil rights activist. Her *Strange Fruit* (1944),

an interracial love story, became a best-seller.

Smith |smiTH|, (Lloyd) Logan Pearsall (1865–1946) U.S. author. Notable works: *Reperusals and Re-collections* (1936).

Smith |smiTH|, Maggie (1934–) U.S. actress. Notable movies: *The Prime of Miss Jean Brodie* (1969, Academy Award).

Smith |smiTH|, Margaret Chase (1897–1995) U.S. senator from Maine (1940–73).

Smith |smiTH|, Richard (1735–1803) colonial American lawyer. A signer of the Declaration of Independence, he wrote a detailed diary of the Continental Congress.

Smith |smiTH|, Robert Weston (1938–95) U.S. radio, television, and movie entertainer. Known as **Wolfman Jack**. He was a rock and roll radio disk jockey based in San Diego (1987–95); his movies include *American Graffiti* (1973).

Smith |smiTH|, Samuel (1752–1839) U.S. politician. He was a Revolutionary War leader, a member of the U.S. House of Representatives from Maryland (1793–1803, 1816–22), and a U.S. senator (1803–15, 1835–38).

Smith |smiTH|, Samuel Francis (1808–95) U.S. clergyman. He wrote the hymn "America" (1831).

Smith |smiTH|, Seba (1792–1868) U.S. journalist. Pseudonym **Major Jack Downing**. He founded Maine's *Portland Courier* (1829); his letters were an inspiration to homespun political philosophers.

Smith |smiTH|, (Robert) Sidney (1877–1935) U.S. cartoonist. He drew the cartoon "The Gumps" from 1917–1935.

Smith |smiTH|, Stevie (1902–71) English poet and novelist; pseudonym of *Florence Margaret Smith*. She is mainly remembered for her witty, caustic, and enigmatic verse; collections include *A Good Time Was Had by All* (1937) and *Not Waving But Drowning* (1957).

Smith |smiTH|, Sydney (1771–1845) English Anglican churchman, essayist, and wit. He is notable for his *Letters of Peter Plymley* (1807), which defended Catholic Emancipation.

Smith |smiTH|, Theobald (1859–1934) U.S. microbiologist. Known for his work on the causes and nature of infectious and parasitic diseases, he developed the theory of immunization (1884–86).

Smith |smiTH|, William (1769–1839) English geologist. An English land surveyor and geologist, he pioneered the study of stratigraphical geology.

Smith |smiTH|, Willie (1897–1973) U.S. jazz pianist. Born *William Henry Joseph Bonaparte Bertholoff*; known as **The Lion**. His is known for his stride style solo recordings in 1939.

Smith·son |'smiTHsən|, James (1765–1829) English chemist. Known as **James Louis Macie** until 1801. He bequeathed money for the establishment of the Smithsonian Institution.

Smol·lett |'smälət|, Tobias (George) (1721–71) Scottish novelist. His humorous and fast-moving picaresque novels include *The Adventures of Roderick Random* (1748) and *The Adventures of Peregrine Pickle* (1751).

Smuck·er |'sməkər|, Jerome (1858–1948) U.S. businessman. He founded the J. M. Smucker Co., a manufacturer of apple butter; his sons expanded the company to include jellies and preserves.

Smuts |smyts; sməts|, Jan (Christiaan) (1870–1950) South African statesman, soldier, and prime minister (1919–24 and 1939–48). He led Boer forces during the Second Boer War, but afterwards supported the policy of Anglo-Boer cooperation. He commanded Allied troops against German East Africa (1916) and later helped to found the League of Nations.

Snead |snēd|, Sam (1912–) U.S. golfer. Full name *Samuel Jackson Snead*. He holds the PGA Tour career victory record (81).

Snod·grass |'snäd,græs|, W. D. (1926–) U.S. poet and educator. Full name *William DeWitt Snodgrass*. Notable works: *Heart's Needle* (1959, Pulitzer Prize).

Snor·ri Stur·lu·son |'snawrē 'stərləsən| (1178–1241) Icelandic historian and poet. A leading figure of medieval Icelandic literature, he wrote the *Younger Edda* or *Prose Edda* and the *Heimskringla*, a history of the kings of Norway from mythical times to the year 1177.

Snow |snō|, C. P., 1st Baron Snow of Leicester (1905–80) English novelist and scientist; full name *Charles Percy Snow*. He is best known for his sequence of eleven novels *Strangers and Brothers*, which deals with moral dilemmas in the academic world, and for his lecture "The Two Cultures" (1959).

Sny·der |'snīdər|, John P. (1926–97) U.S. chemical engineer and cartographer. He determined the method for converting a spherical globe to a flat map.

Soane |sōn|, Sir John (1753–1837) English architect. His later work avoided unnecessary ornament and adopted structural necessity as the basis of design. His designs included the Bank of England (1788–1833, since rebuilt) and his house in London, now a museum.

So·bies·ki |sō'byeskē|, John see JOHN III.

So·bre·ro |sō'brerō|, Ascanio (1812–88) Italian chemist. He discovered nitroglycerin (1847).

Soc·ra·tes |'säkrə,tēz| (c. 470–399 BC) ancient Athenian philosopher. As represented in the writings of his disciple Plato, he engaged in dialogue with others in an attempt to reach understanding and ethical concepts by exposing and dispelling error (the *Socratic method*). Charged with introducing strange gods and corrupting the young, he committed suicide as required.

Sol·o·mon |'säləmən| (c. 970–c. 930 BC) son of David, king of ancient Israel (c. 970–c. 930 BC). In the Bible, Solomon is traditionally considered the writer of the Song of Solomon, Ecclesiastes, and Proverbs, and he is proverbial for his wisdom. Discontent with his rule, however, led to the secession of the northern tribes in the reign of his son Rehoboam.

So·lon |'sōlən; 'sō,län| (c. 630–c. 560 BC) Athenian statesman and lawgiver. One of the Seven Sages, he revised the code of laws established by Draco, making it less severe. His division of the citizens into four classes based on wealth rather than birth laid the foundations of Athenian democracy.

Sol·ti |'sнōltē|, Sir Georg (1912–97) Hungarian-born British conductor. He revivified Covent Garden as musical director (1961–71) and was conductor of the Chicago Symphony Orchestra (1969–91) and the London Philharmonic Orchestra (1979–83).

Sol·zhe·ni·tsyn |ˌsōlzHə'nētsən|, Alexander (1918–) Russian novelist; Russian name *Aleksandr Isayevich Solzhenitsyn*. He spent eight years in a labor camp for criticizing Stalin and began writing on his release. From 1963 his books were banned in the Soviet Union, and he was exiled in 1974, eventually returning to Russia in 1994. Notable works: *One Day in the Life of Ivan Denisovich* (1962), *The First Circle* (1968), *August 1914* (1971), and *The Gulag Archipelago* (1974). Nobel Prize for Literature (1970).

So·mo·za |sə'mōsə| the name of a family of Nicaraguan statesmen: **Anastasio** (1896–1956), president 1937–47 and 1951–56; full name *Anastasio Somoza García*. He took presidential office following a military coup in 1936. Somoza ruled Nicaragua as a virtual dictator and was assassinated. **Luis** (1922–67), president 1957–63, son of Anastasio; full name *Luis Somoza Debayle*. **Anastasio** (1925–80), President 1967–79, younger brother of Luis; full name *Anastasio Somoza Debayle*. His dictatorial regime was overthrown by the Sandinistas, and he was assassinated while in exile in Paraguay.

Sond·heim |'sänd,hīm|, Stephen (Joshua) (1930–) U.S. composer and lyricist. He became famous with his lyrics for Leonard Bernstein's *West Side Story* (1957). He has since written a number of musicals, including *A Little Night Music* (1973), *Sweeney Todd* (1979), and *Sunday in the Park with George* (1984).

Son·tag |'sän,tæg|, Susan (1933–) U.S. writer and critic. She established her reputation as a radical intellectual with *Against Interpretation* (essays, 1966). Other notable works: *On Photography* (1976) and *Illness as Metaphor* (1979).

Sont·hei·mer |'sänt,hīmər|, Carl G. (*c.* 1915–98) U.S. electronics engineer and entrepreneur. He brought the Cuisinart food processor to the U.S.

Soph·o·cles |'säfə,klēz| (*c.* 496–406 BC) Greek dramatist. His seven surviving plays are notable for their complexity of plot and depth of characterization, and for their examination of the relationship between mortals and the divine order. Notable plays: *Antigone, Electra,* and *Oedipus Rex* (also called *Oedipus Tyrannus*).

Sop·with |'säpwiTH|, Sir Thomas (Octave Murdoch) (1888–1989) English aircraft designer. During the First World War he designed the fighter biplane the Sopwith Camel, while in World War II, as chairman of the Hawker Siddeley company, he was responsible for the production of aircraft such as the Hurricane fighter.

Sor·en |'sawrən|, Tabitha L. (1967–) U.S. television newscaster and writer.

Sou·sa |'sōōzə|, John Philip (1854–1932) U.S. composer and band conductor, known as the "March King." He wrote more than a hundred marches, including *The Stars and Stripes Forever, Semper Fidelis,* and *The Washington Post March*. The sousaphone, invented in 1898, was named in his honor.

Sou·ter |'sōōtər|, David Hackett (1939–) U.S. Supreme Court justice (1990–).

Sou·they |'sowTHē; 'səTHē|, Robert (1774–1843) English poet. Associated with the Lake Poets, he is best known for his shorter poems, such as the "Battle of Blenheim" (1798). He was made Poet Laureate in 1813.

Sou·tine |sōō'tēn|, Chaim (1893–1943) French painter, born in Lithuania. A major exponent of expressionism, he produced pictures of grotesque figures during the 1920s, while from 1925 he increasingly painted still lifes.

So·yin·ka |swoi'iNGkə|, Wole (1934–) Nigerian dramatist, novelist, and critic. Born *Akinwande Oluwole Soyinka*. In 1986 he became the first African to receive the Nobel Prize for Literature. Notable works: *The Lion and the Jewel* (play, 1959) and *The Interpreters* (novel, 1965).

Spaak |späk|, Paul-Henri Charles (1899–1972) Belgian statesman. As prime minister of Belgium (1938–39, 1946, 1947–50), he helped draft the charters of the UN, NATO, and the Common Market.

Spaatz |späts|, Carl (1891–1974) U.S. air force officer. Born *Carl Spatz*; known as **Tooey**. He led the U.S. bombing force in Germany (1944) and Japan (1945) and was the first chief of staff of the independent U.S. air force (1947).

Spahn |spän|, Warren (Edward) (1921–) U.S. baseball player. He holds the pitching record for most career wins by a left-hander (363).

Spal·lan·za·ni |ˌspälänt'sänē|, Lazzaro (1729–99) Italian physiologist and biologist. He is known today for his experiments in subjects such as the circulation of the blood and the digestive system of animals. He also disproved the theory of spontaneous generation.

Span·ier |'spænyər|, Muggsy (1906–67) U.S. jazz cornetist and bandleader. Full name *Francis Joseph Spanier*. He organized his Ragtime Band (1939) and made 16 recordings that helped revive interest in New Orleans jazz in 1940s.

Spark |spärk|, Dame Muriel (1918–) Scottish novelist. Notable works: *The Prime of Miss Jean Brodie* (1961) and *The Mandelbaum Gate* (1965).

Spark·man |'spärkmən|, John Jackson (1899–1985) U.S. politician. He served as an Alabama member of the U.S. House of Representatives (1937–46) and of the U.S. Senate (1946–79); he also was a Democratic vice presidential candidate (1952).

Spar·ta·cus |'spärtəkəs| (died *c.* 71 BC) Thracian slave and gladiator. He led a revolt against Rome in 73, but was eventually defeated by Crassus in 71 and crucified.

Spas·sky |'spæskē|, Boris (Vasilyevich) (1937–) Russian chess player, world champion (1969–72).

Spea·ker |'spēkər|, Tris (1888–1958) U.S. baseball player. Full name *Tristram E. Speaker*. He is the all-time leader in outfield assists (449) and doubles (793).

Speare |spir|, Elizabeth George (1908–94) U.S. author. She wrote historical fiction for children, including *The Witch of Blackbird Pond* (Newbery Award, 1958), *The Bronze Bow* (Newbery Award,

1961), and *Life in Colonial America* (1963).

Spec·tor |'spektər|, Phil (1940–) U.S. record producer and songwriter. Full name *Phillip Harvey Spector*. He pioneered a "wall of sound" style, using echo and tape loops, and had a succession of hit recordings in the 1960s with groups such as the Ronettes and the Crystals.

Speer |spir; SHpär|, Albert (1905–81) German architect and Nazi government official, designer of the Nuremberg stadium for the 1934 Nazi Party congress. He was also minister for armaments and munitions. Following the Nuremberg trials, he served twenty years in Spandau prison.

Speke |spēk|, John Hanning (1827–64) English explorer. With Sir Richard Burton, he became the first European to discover Lake Tanganyika (1858). He also discovered Lake Victoria, naming it in honor of the queen.

Spel·ling |'speliNG|, Aaron (*c.* 1928–) U.S. television producer and writer. He produced numerous television programs, including "Dynasty."

Spence |spens|, Sir Basil (Urwin) (1907–76) British architect, born in India.

Spen·cer |'spensər|, Herbert (1820–1903) English philosopher and sociologist. He sought to apply the theory of natural selection to human societies, developing social Darwinism and coining the phrase the "survival of the fittest" (1864).

Spen·cer |'spensər|, Sir Stanley (1891–1959) English painter. He is best known for his religious and visionary works in the modern setting of his native village of Cookham in Berkshire, such as *Resurrection: Cookham* (1926).

Spen·der |'spendər|, Sir Stephen Harold (1909–) British poet and critic. Notable works: *Poems of Dedication* (1946) and *World within World* (1951).

Speng·ler |SHpeNGglər; 'speNGglər|, Oswald (1880–1936) German philosopher. In his book *The Decline of the West* (1918–22) he argues that civilizations undergo a seasonal cycle of a thousand years and are subject to growth and decay analogous to biological species.

Spen·ser |'spensər|, Edmund (c. 1552–99) English poet. He is best known for his allegorical romance the *Faerie Queene* (1590; 1596), celebrating Queen Elizabeth I and written in the Spenserian stanza.

Sper·ry |'sperē|, Elmer Ambrose (1860–1930) U.S. electrical engineer, industrialist, and inventor. He founded eight manufacturing companies and held over 400 patents, including the Sperry Gyroscopic Compass (1910).

Spie·gel·man |'spēgəlmən|, Art (1948–) U.S. artist and author, born in Sweden. Notable works: *Maus* (1986, Pulitzer Prize), *Raw* (1989), and *Open Me—I'm a Dog* (1997).

Spiel·berg |'spēl,bərg|, Steven (1947–) U.S. filmmaker. Notable films: *Jaws* (1975), *Close Encounters of the Third Kind* (1977), *E.T. the Extra-Terrestrial* (1982), *Jurassic Park* (1993), *Schindler's List* (1993), and *Saving Private Ryan* (1998).

Spil·lane |spə'lān|, Mickey (1918–) U.S. writer; pseudonym of *Frank Morrison Spillane*. His popular detective novels include *I, the Jury* (1947), *My Gun Is Quick* (1950), and *The Big Kill* (1951).

Spin·garn |'spin,gärn|, Joel Elias (1875–1939) U.S. author. The founder of the National Association for the Advancement of Colored People (1909), he was also a founder of Harcourt, Brace & Co. (1919–32).

Spi·no·za |spi'nōzə|, Baruch (or Benedict) de (1632–77) Dutch philosopher, of Portuguese-Jewish descent. He espoused a pantheistic system, seeing "God or nature" as a single infinite substance, with mind and matter being two incommensurable ways of conceiving the one reality.

Spitz |spits|, Mark (Andrew) (1950–) U.S. swimmer. He won seven gold medals in the 1972 Olympic Games at Munich and set twenty-seven world records for freestyle and butterfly (1967–72).

Spock |späk|, Benjamin McLane (1903–98) U.S. pediatrician and writer; known as **Dr. Spock**. His influential manual *The Common Sense Book of Baby and Child Care* (1946) challenged traditional ideas in child-rearing in favor of a psychological approach.

Spotts·wood |'späts,wŏod|, Stephen Gill (1897–1974) He was chairman of the NAACP (1961–74).

Spring·field |'spriNG,fēld|, Dusty (1939–99) British pop-rock vocalist. Born *Mary O'Brien*. Her hits include "You Don't Have to Say You Love Me" (1966) and "What Have I Done to Deserve This" (1987).

Spring·steen |'spriNG,stēn|, Bruce (Frederick Joseph) (1949–) U.S. rock singer, songwriter, and guitarist, noted for his songs about working-class life in the U.S. Notable albums: *Born to Run* (1975) and *Born in the USA* (1984).

Spru·ance |'sprōōəns|, Raymond Ames (1886–1969) U.S. admiral. He was commander in chief of the U.S. Pacific fleet (1945–46).

Spy·ri |'SHpērē|, Johanna (1827–1901) Swiss author. Her children's story *Heidi's Years of Wandering and Learning* (1880) was published in the U.S. as *Heidi* (1884).

Squan·to |'skwäntō| (died 1622) Pawtuxet Indian. He befriended the Pilgrims in Plymouth Colony (1621), acting as an interpreter and giving them advice on planting and fishing, assistance that proved vital to their survival.

Squibb |skwib|, Edward Robinson (1819–1900) U.S. navy physician and businessman. He founded a pharmaceutical company to provide a source of reliable drugs and vitamins to the armed forces (1859).

Staël |stäl|, Mme de see DE STAËL.

Stagg |stæg|, Amos Alonzo (1862–1965) U.S. athlete, football coach, and inventor. A coach at the University of Chicago and College of the Pacific, he invented the tackling dummy; he was elected to both the college football and basketball halls of fame.

St. Agnes, St. Barnabas, etc. see AGNES, ST., BARNABAS, ST.

Stahl |stäl|, Lesley Rene (1941–) U.S. journalist. She is a correspondent for CBS News, appearing on the television program "60 Minutes."

Stai·ner |'stānər|, Sir John (1840–1901) English composer. He is remembered for his church music, including hymns, cantatas, and the oratorio *Crucifixion* (1887).

Sta·lin |'stälən|, Joseph (1879–1953) Soviet statesman, general secretary of the Communist Party of the USSR 1922–53; born *Iosif Vissarionovich Dzhugashvili*. His adoptive name Stalin means "man of steel." Having isolated his political rival Trotsky, by 1927 Stalin was the uncontested leader of the Communist Party. In 1928 he launched a succession of five-year plans for rapid industrialization and the enforced collectivization of agriculture; as a result of this process some 10 million peasants are thought to have died. His large-scale purges of the intelligentsia in the 1930s were equally ruthless. After the World War II victory over Hitler in 1945 he maintained a firm grip on neighboring Communist states.

Stal·lone |stə'lōn|, Sylvester Enzio (1946–　) U.S. actor, director, and producer. He is best known for his *Rocky* and *Rambo* movies.

Stan·dish |'stændɪsʜ|, Myles (*c.* 1584–1656) American colonist, from England. First name also **Miles**. He accompanied the Pilgrims to America (1620) and became the military leader of Plymouth Colony. He was a cofounder of Duxbury, Massachusetts (1631). He is romanticized as the lovelorn suitor in Longfellow's fictional poem "The Courtship of Miles Standish."

Stan·ford |'stænfərd|, A. Leland (1824–93) U.S. railroad official and philanthropist. Full name *Amasa Leland Stanford*. He was governor of California (1861–63); a member of the U.S. Senate (1885–93); promoter, financier, and director of two railroads, the Central Pacific and the Southern Pacific; and founder of Stanford University (1885).

Stan·ford |'stænfərd|, Sir Charles (Villiers) (1852–1924) British composer, born in Ireland. He is noted especially for his Anglican church music and numerous choral works.

Stan·ier |'stænir|, Sir William (Arthur) (1876–1965) English railroad engineer. He is chiefly remembered for his standard locomotive designs for the London Midland and Scottish Railway.

Stan·i·slaus |'stænə,slaws|, St. (1030–

79) patron saint of Poland; Polish name *Stanislaw*; known as **St. Stanislaus of Cracow**. As bishop of Cracow (1072–79) he excommunicated King Boleslaus II. According to tradition Stanislaus was murdered by Boleslaus while taking Mass. Feast day, April 11 (formerly May 7).

Stan·i·slav·sky |,stænə'släfskē|, Konstantin (Sergeyevich) (1863–1938) Russian theater director and actor; born *Konstantin Sergeyevich Alekseyev*. Stanislavsky trained his actors to take a psychological approach and use latent powers of self-expression when taking on roles; his theory and technique were later developed into method acting.

Stan·ley |'stænlē| U.S. inventors. **Francis Edgar Stanley** (1849–1918) and his twin brother **Freelan Oscar Stanley** (1849–1940) designed and built steam cars (1902–17).

Stan·ley |'stænlē|, Sir Henry Morton (1841–1904) Welsh explorer; born *John Rowlands*. As a newspaper correspondent he was sent in 1869 to central Africa to find David Livingstone; two years later he found him at Lake Tanganyika. After Livingstone's death in 1873, Stanley continued his explorations in Africa, charting Lake Victoria, tracing the course of the Congo, and mapping Lake Albert.

Stan·ley |'stænlē|, William, Jr. (1858–1916) U.S. electrical engineer and inventor. He installed the first alternating current distribution system (1886, Great Barrington, Massachusetts).

Stan·ton |'stæntən|, Edwin McMasters (1814–69) U.S. lawyer and public official. He was secretary of war under Abraham Lincoln and played a pivotal role in the impeachment proceedings against President Andrew Johnson; in 1869 he was appointed to the U.S. Supreme Court but died before taking office.

Stan·ton |'stæntən|, Elizabeth (Cady) (1815–1902) U.S. social reformer. With Lucretia Mott, she organized the first U.S. women's rights convention, in Seneca Falls, New York (1848). From 1852, she led the women's rights movement with Susan B. Anthony. She was president of the National Woman Suffrage Association (1869–90) and editor of the radical feminist magazine *Revolution* (1868–70).

Sta·ple·ton |'stāpəltən|, Maureen (1925–) U.S. actress. Notable movies: *Reds* (1981, Academy Award).

Star·ling |'stärliNG|, Ernest Henry (1866–1927) English physiologist and founder of the science of endocrinology. He demonstrated the existence of peristalsis, and coined the term *hormone* for the substance secreted by the pancreas which stimulates the secretion of digestive juices.

Starr |stär|, Bart (1934–) U.S. football player. Full name *Bryan B. Starr*. Elected to the Football Hall of Fame (1977).

Starr |stär|, Kenneth Winston (1946–) U.S. attorney. He was appointed independent counsel (1994) to investigate the Clinton Whitewater real estate venture and other scandals, including the president's affair with Monica Lewinsky.

Starr |stär|, Ringo (1940–) English rock and pop drummer; born *Richard Starkey*. He became the drummer for the Beatles in 1962. After the band split up (1970), he pursued a solo career.

Sta·ti·us |'stāsHəs|, Publius Papinius (*c.* 45–96 AD) Roman poet. He is best known for the *Silvae*, a miscellany of poems addressed to friends, and the *Thebais*, an epic concerning the bloody quarrel between the sons of Oedipus.

Stau·bach |'staw,bäk; 'stawbæk|, Roger (Thomas) (1942–) U.S. football player. He was a five-time passing leader in the National Football Conference.

Stau·ding·er |'sHtowdiNGər|, Hermann (1881–1965) German chemist. His studies of polymers won him the Nobel Prize for Chemistry in 1953.

Ste·ber, Eleanor (1916–90) U.S. operatic soprano. She sang with the Metropolitan Opera for 22 seasons, beginning with her debut in 1940 as Sophie.

Steel |stēl|, Danielle (Fernande) (1947–) U.S. author. Notable works: *Full Circle* (1984), *Five Days in Paris* (1995), and *Long Road Home* (1998).

Steele |stēl|, Sir Richard (1672–1729) Irish essayist and dramatist. He founded and wrote for the periodicals the

Tatler (1709–11) and the *Spectator* (1711–12), the latter in collaboration with Joseph Addison.

Stef·fens |'stefənz|, (Joseph) Lincoln (1866–1936) U.S. journalist. The leader of the muckraking movement, he was editor of *McClure's* (1902–06).

Steg·ner |'stegnər|, Wallace (Earle) (1909–93) U.S. author and professor. Notable works: *Angle of Repose* (1971, Pulitzer Prize) and *The Spectator Bird* (1976, National Book Award).

Stei·chen |'stīkən|, Edward Jean (1879–1973) U.S. photographer, born in Luxembourg. First name originally *Edouard*. He is credited with transforming photography to an art form.

Steig |stīg|, William (1907–) U.S. cartoonist and artist. He created the "Small Fry" drawings appearing in *The New Yorker* magazine.

Stei·ger |'stīgər|, Rod (1925–) U.S. actor. Notable movies: *In the Heat of the Night* (1967, Academy Award).

Stein |stīn|, Gertrude (1874–1946) U.S. writer. Stein developed an esoteric stream-of-consciousness style, notably in *The Autobiography of Alice B. Toklas* (1933). Her home in Paris became a focus for the avant-garde during the 1920s and 1930s.

Stein·beck |'stīn,bek|, John (Ernst) (1902–68) U.S. novelist. His work, for example *Of Mice and Men* (1937) and *The Grapes of Wrath* (1939), is noted for its sympathetic and realistic portrayal of the migrant agricultural workers of California. His later novels include *Cannery Row* (1945) and *East of Eden* (1952). Nobel Prize for Literature (1962).

Stein·bren·ner |'stīn,brenər|, George Michael III (1930–) U.S. businessman. The principal owner of the New York Yankees (1973–), he is also chairman of the board of the American Ship Building Co. (1978–).

Stei·nem |'stīnəm|, Gloria (1934–) U.S. social refromer and journalist. A women's rights activist, she cofounded and edited *Ms.* magazine (1971–87).

Stei·ner |'stīnər|, Rudolf (1861–1925) Austrian philosopher, founder of anthroposophy. He founded the Anthroposophical Society in 1912, aiming to integrate the practical and psychological in education. The society has contributed to child-centered education, especially with its Steiner schools.

Stein·metz |'stīn,mets|, Charles Proteus (1865–1923) German inventor. Born *Karl August Rudolf Steinmetz*. His theories for alternating current enabled the expansion of the electric power industry in U.S.

Stein·way |'stīn,wā|, Henry (Engelhard) (1797–1871) German pianobuilder, resident in the U.S. from 1849; born *Heinrich Engelhard Steinweg*. He founded his famous piano-making firm in New York in 1853.

Stel·la |'stelə|, Frank (Philip) (1936–) U.S. painter, an important figure in minimalism known for his series of all-black paintings.

Stel·ler |'sHtelər; 'stelər|, Georg Wilhelm (1709–46) Last name originally *Stoeller*. German naturalist and geographer. Steller was a research member of Vitus Bering's second expedition to Kamchatka and Alaska and described many new birds and mammals, several of which now bear his name.

Sten·dhal |steN'däl; sten'däl| (1783–1842) French novelist; pseudonym of *Marie Henri Beyle*. His two best-known novels are *Le Rouge et le noir* (1830), relating the rise and fall of a young man from the provinces, and *La Chartreuse de Parme* (1839).

Sten·gel |'steNGgəl|, Casey (c. 1890–1975) U.S. baseball player and manager. Full name *Charles Dillon Stengel*. He guided the New York Yankees to ten American League pennants and seven World Series (1949–60).

Sten·nis |'stenəs|, John Cornelius (1901–95) U.S. politician. He was a U.S. senator from Mississippi for more than 41 years (1947–89).

Ste·pha·no·pou·los |,stefə'näpələs|, George (1961–) U.S. political official. He was a senior adviser during the Clinton administration.

Ste·phen |'stēvən| (c. 1097–1154) grandson of William the Conqueror, king of England 1135–54. Stephen seized the throne from Matilda a few months after the death of Henry I. Civil war followed until Matilda was defeated and forced to leave England in 1148.

Ste·phen |'stēvən|, St. (died c. 35 AD) Christian martyr. One of the original seven deacons in Jerusalem appointed by the Apostles, he was charged with blasphemy and stoned, thus becoming the first Christian martyr. Feast day (in the Western Church) December 26; (in the Eastern Church) December 27.

Ste·phen |'stēvən|, St. (c. 977–1038) king and patron saint of Hungary (reigned 1000–38). The first king of Hungary, he took steps to Christianize the country. Feast day, September 2 or (in Hungary) August 20.

Stern |stərn|, Howard (Allan) (1954–) U.S. disk jockey and talk-show host. He has been labeled a "shock jock" for his trademark broadcasting of crass and explicit material.

Stern |stərn|, Isaac (1920–) U.S. violinist, born in Russia. He made his New York debut in 1937 in Carnegie Hall; he was the first American to perform in Russia after World War II (1956), and he was invited to China in 1979.

Stern |stərn|, Otto (1888–1969) U.S. physicist, born in Germany. He used molecular beams to establish the existence of atomic magnetic moments. Nobel Prize for Physics, 1943.

Stern |stərn|, Richard (Gustave) (1928–) U.S. author. Notable works: *Other Men's Daughters* (1973) and *A Father's Words: A Novel* (1986).

Sterne |stərn|, Laurence (1713–68) Irish novelist. He is best known for his nine-volume work *The Life and Opinions of Tristram Shandy* (1759–67), which parodied the developing conventions of the novel form. Other notable works: *A Sentimental Journey through France and Italy* (1768).

Stet·son |'stetsən|, John Batterson (1830–1906) U.S. entrepreneur. He created the Stetson hat and gave financial support to Stetson University in Florida.

Steu·ben |'sHtoibən; 'sto͞obən|, Friedrich von (1730–94) American army officer, born in Prussia. Full name *Friedrich Wilhelm Ludolf Gerhard Augustin von Steuben*. Arriving in America in December 1777, he joined Washington at Valley Forge, where he introduced European methods of training and discipline. Appointed inspector general of the Continental Army (1778), he turned raw troops into a legitimate military force.

Ste·vens |'stēvənz|, George (*c.* 1904–75) U.S. director. Notable movies: *A Place in the Sun* (1951 Academy Award).

Ste·vens |'stēvənz|, John Paul (1920–) U.S. Supreme Court justice (1975–)

Ste·vens |'stēvənz|, Wallace (1879–1955) U.S. poet. He wrote poetry privately and mostly in isolation from the literary community, developing an original and colorful style. His *Collected Poems* (1954) won a Pulitzer Prize.

Ste·ven·son |'stēvənsən|, Adlai Ewing (1900–65) U.S. statesman and politician. A popular supporter of social reform and internationalism, he was governor of Illinois (1949–53) and was twice the unsuccessful Democratic candidate for the presidency (1952, 1956).

Ste·ven·son |'stēvənsən|, James (*c.* 1929–) U.S. cartoonist, author, and illustrator. His books for children include *Are We Almost There?* (1985) and *The Supreme Souvenir Factory* (1988).

Ste·ven·son |'stēvənsən|, Robert Louis (Balfour) (1850–94) Scottish novelist, poet, and travel writer. Stevenson made his name with the adventure story *Treasure Island* (1883). He is also known for *A Child's Garden of Verses*, a collection of poetry. Other notable works: *The Strange Case of Dr. Jekyll and Mr. Hyde* and *Kidnapped* (both 1886).

Stew·art |'stōōərt|, Jackie (1939–) Scottish racecar driver and television commentator; born *John Young Stewart*. He was three times world champion (1969; 1971; 1973).

Stew·art |'stōōərt|, James (Maitland) (1908–97) U.S. actor, famous for roles in which he was seen as embodying the all-American hero. His movies include *The Philadelphia Story* (1940), which earned him an Oscar, Frank Capra's *It's a Wonderful Life* (1946), Alfred Hitchcock's *Vertigo* (1958), and westerns such as *The Man from Laramie* (1955).

Stew·art |'stōōərt|, Martha (1941–) U.S. businesswoman. She turned her home decorating and cooking ideas into an industry, including an "Ask Martha" radio talk show, a television program, a magazine, and a signature line of housewares.

Stew·art |'stōōərt|, Mary (1916–) English author. Notable works: *The Hollow Hills* (1973).

Stew·art |'stōōərt|, Potter (1915–85) U.S. Supreme Court justice (1958–81). He upheld the First Amendment claim in the Pentagon Papers case, and he was noted for his 1964 opinion on pornography, "I know it when I see it."

Stew·art |'stōōərt|, Rod (1945–) English pop singer and songwriter; full name *Roderick David Stewart*.

Stibitz |'stibəts|, George Robert (1904–95) U.S. inventor. Considered the father of the modern digital computer, he helped design the Model I complex number calculator.

Stick·ley |'stiklē|, Gustave (1858–1942) U.S. furniture designer and manufacturer. His style came to be known as Craftsman.

Stieg·litz |'stēglitz|, Alfred (1864–1946) U.S. photographer, husband of Georgia O'Keefe. He was important for his pioneering work to establish photography as a fine art in the U.S.

Stif·fel |'stifəl|, Theodopholous A. (1899–1971) U.S. businessman. The designer of Stiffel Lamps, he began marketing moderately priced creations and then changed to more elegant productions.

Stiles |stīlz|, Ezra (1727–95) U.S. scholar, teacher, lawyer, and minister. A Congregational minister, he was a president of Yale College (1778–95) and a founder of Brown University.

Stil·ler |'stilər|, Jerry (1926–) U.S. actor. He and his wife Anne Meara form the comedy duo Stiller and Meara.

Stills |stilz|, Stephen (1945–) U.S. rock musician. He was a rock guitarist and keyboardist, as well as a singer with the group Crosby, Stills, Nash (and Young).

Stil·well |'stil,wel|, Joseph Warren (1883–1946) U.S. army officer. Known as **Uncle Joe** or **Vinegar Joe**. He commanded U.S. troops in the China-Burma-India theater (1942–44), U.S. army ground forces under Douglas

MacArthur (1945), and the U.S. 10th Army in the Pacific (1945–46).

Stim·son |'stimsən|, Henry Lewis (1867–1950) U.S. lawyer and statesman. He was the first American to serve in the cabinets of four presidents; among these posts, he served as secretary of state (1929–33) and twice as secretary of war (1911–13 and 1940–45). He authored the Stimson Doctrine against Japan.

Stine |stīn|, R. L. (1943–) U.S. author. He wrote the "Goosebumps" series for children.

Sting |stiNG| (1951–) British pop musician. Born *Gordon Matthew Sumner*. Formerly the lead singer with The Police, as a solo artist he has recorded "If Ever I Lose My Faith in You" (1993, Grammy Award) and "Fields of Gold" (1993).

Stir·ling |'stərliNG|, Sir James Frazer (1926–92) Scottish architect. Working at first in a brutalist style, he became known for his use of geometric shapes and colored decoration in public buildings such as the Neuestaatsgalerie in Stuttgart (1977).

Stitt |stit|, Sonny (1924–82) U.S. jazz saxophonist. Full name *Edward Stitt*. He was a disciple of Charlie Parker.

Stock·hau·sen |'sHtäk,howzən|, Karlheinz (1928–) German composer. An important avant-garde composer and exponent of serialism, he cofounded an electronic music studio for West German radio and in 1980 embarked on his *Licht* cycle of musical ceremonies.

Sto·ker |'stōkər|, Bram (1847–1912) Irish novelist and theater manager; full name *Abraham Stoker*. He is chiefly remembered as the author of the vampire story *Dracula* (1897).

Stokes |stōks|, Carl (1927–1996) U.S. politician. He was the first African-American mayor of a major U.S. city (Cleveland, 1967–72).

Sto·kow·ski |stə'kowskē|, Leopold (1882–1977) British-born U.S. conductor, of Polish descent. Full name *Leopold Antoni Stanislaw Boleslawowicz Stokowski*. He is best known for arranging and conducting the music for Walt Disney's movie *Fantasia* (1940), which

sought to bring classical music to cinema audiences by means of cartoons.

Stone |stōn|, Edward Durell (1902–78) U.S. architect. Notable designs include the U.S. Embassy in India and the Museum of Modern Art (New York, 1938–39).

Stone |stōn|, Harlan Fiske (1872–1946) Chief Justice of the U.S. (1941–46) and U.S. Supreme Court justice (1925–41).

Stone |stōn|, Lucy (1818–93) U.S. feminist and abolitionist. The first woman in Massachusetts to earn a college degree, she traveled widely during the 1850s lecturing on women's rights, and she founded the American Woman Suffrage Association (1869)

Stone |stōn|, Oliver (1946–) U.S. movie director, screenwriter, and producer. He won Oscars for his adaptation of the novel *Midnight Express* (1978) and his direction of *Platoon* (1986) and *Born on the Fourth of July* (1989), both of which indict U.S. involvement in the Vietnam War. Other notable films: *JFK* (1991) and *Natural Born Killers* (1994).

Stone |stōn|, Robert (1937–) U.S. author. Notable works: *Images of War* (1986) and *Outerbridge Reach* (1992).

Stone |stōn|, Sharon (1958–) U.S. actress.

Sto·ner |'stōnər|, Eugene (1922–97) U.S. gun designer. He built the prototype for the M-16, a standard-issue weapon of the American soldier.

Stookey |'stŏŏkē|, (Noel) Paul (1937–) U.S. guitarist and singer. He was part of the singing trio Peter, Paul and Mary (see TRAVERS).

Stop·pard |'stäpərd|, Sir Tom (1937–) British dramatist, born in Czechoslovakia; born *Thomas Straussler*. His best-known plays are comedies, often dealing with metaphysical and ethical questions, for example *Rosencrantz and Guildenstern are Dead* (1966), which is based on the characters in *Hamlet*. Other notable works: *Jumpers* (1972), *The Real Thing* (1982), and *Arcadia* (1993).

Sto·ry |'stawrē|, Joseph (1779–1845) U.S. Supreme Court justice (1811–45). He was a pioneer in organizing and directing teaching at Havard Law School.

Stouf·fer |'stōfər|, Vernon (1901–74) U.S. businessman. He founded the restaurant chain and frozen food business that bear his name.

Stout |stowt|, Rex (Todhunter) (1886–1975) U.S. author. He created the *Nero Wolfe* detective novels.

Stowe |stō|, Harriet (Elizabeth) Beecher (1811–96) U.S. novelist. She won fame with her antislavery novel *Uncle Tom's Cabin* (1852), which strengthened the contemporary abolitionist cause with its descriptions of the sufferings caused by slavery.

Stra·bo |'strābō| (c. 63 BC–c. 23 AD) historian and geographer of Greek descent. His only extant work, *Geographica*, in seventeen volumes, provides a detailed physical and historical geography of the ancient world during the reign of Augustus.

Stra·chey |'strāCHē|, (Giles) Lytton (1880–1932) British biographer. Notable works: *Eminent Victorians* (1969).

Stra·di·va·ri |,strädə'värē; ,strædə 'verē|, Antonio (c. 1644–1737) Italian violin-maker. He devised the proportions of the modern violin, giving a more powerful and rounded sound than earlier instruments possessed. About 650 of his celebrated violins, violas, and violoncellos are still in existence.

Strand |strænd|, Mark (1934–) U.S. poet and author, born in Canada. He was Poet Laureate of the U.S. (1990–91). Notable works: *Selected Poems* (1980) and *Mr. And Mrs. Baby and Other Stories* (1985).

Strand |strænd|, Paul (1890–1976) U.S. photographer and documentary cameraman. He is known for his landscapes.

Stras·berg |'stræs,bərg|, Lee (1901–82) U.S. actor, director, and drama teacher, born in Austria; born *Israel Strassberg*. As artistic director of the Actors' Studio in New York City (1948–82), he was the leading figure in the development of method acting in the U.S.

Strat·e·mey·er |'strætə,mīər|, Edward (1863–1930) U.S. author. Pseudonyms **Arthur M. Winfield** and **Laura Lee Hope**. He authored the *Bobbsey Twins* and *Nancy Drew* series. Father of Harriet Stratemeyer Adams.

Strauss |SHtrows| the name of two Austrian composers: **Johann** (1804–49), a leading composer of waltzes; known as **Strauss the Elder**. His best-known work is the *Radetzky March* (1838). **Johann** (1825–99), son of Strauss the Elder; known as **Strauss the Younger**. He became known as "the waltz king," composing many famous waltzes, such as *The Blue Danube* (1867). He is also noted for the operetta *Die Fledermaus* (1874).

Strauss |strows|, Levi (c. 1829–1902) U.S. manufacturer, born in Germany. He established Levi Strauss & Co. (1850) to sell pants made of tent canvas to gold miners.

Strauss |SHtrows|, Richard (Georg) (1864–1949) German composer. With the librettist Hugo von Hofmannsthal he produced operas such as *Der Rosenkavalier* (1911). Often regarded as the last of the 19th-century romantic composers, Strauss is also well known for the symphonic poem *Also Sprach Zarathustra* (1896).

Stra·vin·sky |strə'vinskē|, Igor (Fyodorovich) (1882–1971) Russian-born composer, resident in the U.S. from 1939. He made his name with the ballets *The Firebird* (1910) and *The Rite of Spring* (1913); both shocked Paris audiences with their irregular rhythms and frequent dissonances. Stravinsky later developed a neoclassical style typified by *The Rake's Progress* (opera, 1948–51) and experimented with serialism in *Threni*.

Stray·horn |'strā,hawrn|, Billy (1915–67) U.S. jazz composer and pianist. Full name *William Thomas Strayhorn*; known as **Swee' Pea**. He was in close collaboration with Duke Ellington for 30 years; his ballads include "Lush Life," "Chelsea Bridge," and "Lotus Blossom."

Streep |strēp|, Meryl (1949–) U.S. actress; born *Mary Louise Streep*. She won Oscars for her parts in *Kramer vs. Kramer* (1980) and *Sophie's Choice* (1982). Other notable movies: *The French Lieutenant's Woman* (1981), *Out of Africa* (1986), and *One True Thing* (1998).

Stree·ter |'strētər|, Edward (1891–

1976) U.S. author. Notable works: *Father of the Bride* (1949).

Strei·sand |'strī,sænd; 'strī,zænd|, Barbra (Joan) (1942–) U.S. singer, actress, and movie director. She won an Oscar for her performance in *Funny Girl* (1968). She later played the lead in *A Star is Born* (1976); the movie's song "Evergreen", composed by Streisand, won an Oscar. Streisand also starred in, produced, and directed *Yentl* (1983).

Strind·berg |'strin(d),bərg|, (Johan) August (1849–1912) Swedish dramatist and novelist. His satire *The Red Room* (1879) is regarded as Sweden's first modern novel. His later plays are typically tense, psychic dramas, such as *A Dream Play* (1902).

Stro·heim |'strō,hīm; 'SHtrō,hīm|, Eric (1885–1957) U.S. movie actor and director, born in Austria. Born *Erich Oswald Stroheim*. He acted in *La Grande Illusion* (1937) and was director of *The Merry Widow* (1925).

Strong |strawNG|, William (1808–95) U.S. Supreme Court justice (1870–80). He wrote the majority opinion in the Supreme Court's reversal of its decision declaring the Legal Tender Act of 1862 unconstitutional (1871).

Stu·art |'stōōərt|, Charles Edward (1720–88) son of James Stuart, pretender to the British throne; known as **the Young Pretender** or **Bonnie Prince Charlie**. He led the Jacobite uprising of 1745–46. However, he was driven back to Scotland and defeated at the Battle of Culloden (1746).

Stu·art |'stōōərt|, Gilbert Charles (1755–1828) U.S. artist. He is best known for his portraits of the early presidents, especially his five life-size portrayals of George Washington.

Stu·art |'stōōərt|, James (Francis Edward) (1688–1766) son of James II (James VII of Scotland), pretender to the British throne; known as **the Old Pretender**. He arrived in Scotland too late to alter the outcome of the 1715 Jacobite uprising and left the leadership of the 1745–46 uprising to his son Charles Edward Stuart.

Stu·art |'stōōərt|, Jeb (1833–64) Confederate cavalry officer. Full name *James Ewell Brown Stuart*. He was known for

his brazen missions of reconnaissance during the Civil War. His stunning raid that surrounded McClellan's army (1862) is praised as a superb military action. He was mortally wounded at Yellow Tavern.

Stu·art |'stōōərt|, Mary see MARY, QUEEN OF SCOTS.

Stubbs |stəbz|, George (1724–1806) English painter and engraver. He is particularly noted for his sporting scenes and paintings of horses and lions, such as the *Mares and Foals in a Landscape* series (*c*.1760–70).

Stubbs |stəbz|, William (1825–1901) English historian and ecclesiastic. He wrote the influential *Constitutional History of England* (three volumes 1874–78).

Stu·de·ba·ker |'stōōdə,bākər|, Clement (1831–1901) U.S. wagon and carriage manufacturer. With his brother Henry (1826–95), he founded H & C Studebaker (1852), which became Studebaker Brothers (1868); the company experimented with automobiles and manufactured Studebaker automobiles after 1901.

Stur·geon |'stərjən|, Theodore (Hamilton) (1918–85) U.S. author. His works of fantasy and science fiction include *More Than Human* (1953).

Sturt |stərt|, Charles (1795–1869) English explorer. He led three expeditions into the Australian interior, becoming the first European to discover the Darling River (1828) and the source of the Murray (1830).

Stuy·ve·sant |'stīvəsənt|, Peter (*c*. 1610–72) Dutch administrator in North America. First name originally *Petrus*. Appointed colonial governor of New Netherland in 1647, he served until the colony was captured by English forces (1664).

Sty·ron |'stīrən|, William (1925–) U.S. author. Notable works: *Sophie's Choice* (1979) and *A Tidewater Morning: Three Tales from Youth* (1993).

Suck·ling |'səkliNG|, Sir John (1609–42) English poet, dramatist, and Royalist leader, one of the Cavalier poets in the court of Charles I.

Suckow, Ruth (1892–1960) U.S. author. Her birthplace, rural Iowa, is the setting for most of her fiction.

Su·cre |'so͞o,krä|, Antonio José de (1795–1830) Venezuelan revolutionary and statesman, president of Bolivia (1826–28). He served as Simón Bolívar's chief of staff, liberating Ecuador, Peru, and Bolivia from the Spanish, and was the first president of Bolivia.

Sue·to·ni·us |swē'tōnēəs| (c. 69–c. 140 AD) Roman biographer and historian; full name *Gaius Suetonius Tranquillus*. His surviving works include *Lives of the Caesars*.

Su·har·to |so͞o'härtō|, Raden (1921–) Indonesian president (1967–98).

Sui, Anna (1955–) U.S. fashion designer. She founded Anna Sui Inc. (1992).

Su·kar·no |so͞o'kärnō|, Achmed (1901–70) Indonesian statesman, president (1945–67). He led the struggle for independence, which was formally granted in 1949, but lost power in the 1960s after having been implicated in the abortive communist coup of 1965.

Su·lei·man I |,so͞ola'män| (c. 1494–1566) sultan of the Ottoman Empire (1520–66). Also **Soliman** or **Solyman**; also known as **Suleiman the Magnificent** or **Suleiman the Lawgiver**. The Ottoman Empire reached its fullest extent under his rule.

Sul·la |'so͞olə| (138–78 BC) Roman general and politician; full name *Lucius Cornelius Sulla Felix*. After a victorious campaign against Mithridates VI, Sulla invaded Italy in 83. He was elected dictator in 82 and implemented constitutional reforms in favor of the Senate.

Sul·li·van |'mäsē|, Anne (1866–1936) U.S. teacher. Married name *Anne Sullivan Macy*. She was the constant companion of Helen Keller.

Sul·li·van |'sələvən|, Sir Arthur (Seymour) (1842–1900) English composer. His fame rests on the fourteen light operas which he wrote in collaboration with the librettist W. S. Gilbert.

Sul·li·van |'sələvən|, Ed (1902–74) U.S. actor. Full name *Edward Vincent Sullivan*. He was host of television's "Ed Sullivan Show" (1948–71) where he gave national exposure to many performers, including Elvis Presley and the Beatles.

Sul·li·van |'sələvən|, Harry Stack (1892–1949) U.S. psychiatrist. He developed techniques for the treatment of schizophrenia.

Sul·li·van |'sələvən|, John Lawrence (1858–1918) U.S. boxer. The world heavyweight champion (1882–92), he was the last of the bare-knuckle champions.

Sul·li·van |'sələvən|, Louis Henry (1856–1924) U.S. architect. He developed modern functionalism in architecture by designing skyscrapers. Notable works: the Auditorium Building (Chicago, 1886–90).

Sul·ly |'sələ|, Thomas (1783–1872) U.S. painter. He painted portraits of the Marquis de Lafayette, Thomas Jefferson, James Madison, and Andrew Jackson.

Sulz·ber·ger |'səlts,bərgər|, Arthur Ochs (1926–) U.S. publisher. He worked for *The New York Times* from 1951, serving as its president fron 1963 to 1979.

Sum·ner |'səmnər|, Charles (1811–74) U.S. politician. He served as a member of the U.S. Senate from Massachusetts (1851–74), where he was a leader in the anti-slavery movement. One of his orations attacked Andrew Butler, and in response, Butler's nephew, Preston S. Brooks, brutally caned Sumner in the Senate chamber.

Sun King the nickname of Louis XIV of France (see LOUIS).

Sun Yat-sen |'so͞on 'yät 'sen| (1866–1925) Chinese statesman. Also **Sun Yixian**. He was provisional president of the Republic of China (1911–12) and president of the Southern Chinese Republic (1923–25). He organized the Kuomintang force and played a vital part in the revolution of 1911 that overthrew the Manchu dynasty. Following opposition, however, he resigned as president to establish a secessionist government at Guangzhou.

Sur·tees |'sər,tēz|, Robert Smith (1803–64) English journalist and novelist. He is best remembered for his comic sketches of Mr. Jorrocks, the sporting Cockney grocer, collected in *Jorrocks's Jaunts and Jollities* (1838).

Su·sann |so͞o'zæn|, Jacqueline (c.

1926–74) U.S. author. Notable works include *Valley of the Dolls* (1968).

Suth·er·land |'sǝTHǝrlǝnd|, George (1862–1942) U.S. Supreme Court justice (1922–38). He wrote many opinions opposing Franklin Roosevelt's programs.

Suth·er·land |'sǝTHǝrlǝnd|, Graham (Vivian) (1903–80) English painter. During World War II he was an official war artist. His postwar work included the tapestry *Christ in Majesty* (1962) in Coventry cathedral.

Suth·er·land |'sǝTHǝrlǝnd|, Dame Joan (1926–) Australian operatic soprano, noted for her dramatic coloratura roles, particularly the title role in Donizetti's *Lucia di Lammermoor*.

Sut·ton |'sǝtn|, Walter Stanborough (1877–1916) U.S. geneticist. He made the first clear formulation of the theory that chromosomes carry physical units determining inheritance.

Su·zu·ki |sǝ'zo͞okē|, Shinichi (1898–1998) Japanese musician. He developed the Suzuki method of teaching young children to play the violin.

Swan |swän|, Sir Joseph Wilson (1828–1914) English physicist and chemist. He devised an electric light bulb in 1860 and in 1883 he formed a partnership with Thomas Edison to manufacture it.

Swan·son |'swänsǝn|, Gloria (1899–1983) U.S. actress; born *Gloria May Josephine Svensson*. She was a major star of silent movies such as *Sadie Thompson* (1928) but is chiefly known for her performance as the fading movie star in *Sunset Boulevard* (1950).

Swayne |swän|, Noah Haynes (1804–84) U.S. Supreme Court justice (1862–81).

Swe·den·borg |'swēdn,bawrg|, Emanuel (1688–1772) Swedish scientist, philosopher, and mystic. The spiritual beliefs that he expounded after a series of mystical experiences blended Christianity with pantheism and theosophy.

Swen·son |'swensǝn|, May (1919–89) U.S. poet. Notable works: *The Complete Poems to Solve* (1993).

Sweyn I |svän| (died 1014) king of Denmark (*c.*985–1014). Also **Sven**; known as **Sweyn Forkbeard**. From 1003 he launched a series of attacks on England, finally driving Ethelred the Unready to flee to Normandy at the end of 1013. Sweyn then became king of England but died five weeks later. He was the father of Canute.

Swift |swift|, Gustavus Franklin (1839–1903) U.S. meat packer. He commissioned the development of the refrigerated railroad car (1877) and incorporated his business as Swift and Co. (1885).

Swift |swift|, Jonathan (1667–1745) Irish satirist, poet, and Anglican cleric; known as **Dean Swift**. He is best known for *Gulliver's Travels* (1726), a satire on human society in the form of a fantastic tale of travels in imaginary lands. He also wrote *A Modest Proposal* (1729), ironically urging that the children of the poor should be fattened to feed the rich.

Swin·burne |'swin,bǝrn|, Algernon Charles (1837–1909) English poet and critic. Associated as a poet with the Pre-Raphaelites, he also contributed to the revival of interest in Elizabethan and Jacobean drama and produced influential studies of William Blake and the Brontës.

Swin·ner·ton |'swinǝrt(ǝ)n|, James Guilford (1875–1974) U.S. cartoonist. He is best known for the comic strip "Little Jimmy."

Swith·in |'swiTHǝn|, St. (died 862) English ecclesiastic. Also **Swithun**. He was bishop of Winchester from 852. The tradition that if it rains on St. Swithin's Day it will do so for the next forty days may have its origin in the heavy rain said to have occurred when his relics were to be transferred to a shrine in Winchester cathedral. Feast day, July 15.

Swit·zer |'switsǝr|, Robert (1904–97) U.S. inventor. With his brother Joseph, he invented fluorescent paint and founded the Day-Glo Co..

Synge |siNG|, J. M. (1871–1909) Irish dramatist; full name *Edmund John Millington Synge*. His play *The Playboy of the Western World* (1907) caused riots at the Abbey Theatre, Dublin, because of its explicit language and its implication that Irish peasants would condone a brutal murder.

Szell |sel|, George (1897–1970) U.S. pianist and conductor, born in Hungary.

First name originally *Georg*. He was conductor of the Cleveland Orchestra (1946–70).

Szent-Györgyi |ˌsänt ˈjawrj|, Albert von Nagyrapolt (1893–1986) American biochemist, born in Hungary. He discovered ascorbic acid, later identified with vitamin C.

Szi·lard |ˈzilˌärd; zəˈlärd|, Leo (1898–1964) U.S. physicist, born in Hungary. He fled from Nazi Germany to the U.S., where he became a central figure in the Manhattan Project to develop the atom bomb.

Tt

Tac·i·tus |ˈtæsətəs| (c. 56–c. 120 AD) Roman historian; full name *Publius*, or *Gaius, Cornelius Tacitus*. His *Annals* (covering the years 14–68) and *Histories* (69–96) are major works on the history of the Roman Empire.

Taft |tæft|, U.S. political family, including: **William Howard Taft** (1857–1930) see box. **Helen Herron Taft** (1861–1943), wife of William Howard Taft and U.S. first lady (1909–13). **Robert Alphonso Taft** (1889–1953), their son, known as **Mr. Republican**. A prominent Ohio conservative, he was a U.S. senator (1938–53) who opposed President Franklin D. Roosevelt's New Deal and Fair Deal programs. He coauthored the Taft-Hartley Act (1947), which imposed new restrictions on labor. In the 1950s, he defended the antisubversive activities of Senator Joseph McCarthy.

Tag·li·a·bue |ˈtæɡlēə,b(y)o͞o|, Paul (1940–) U.S. journalist. He is the commissioner of the National Football League (1989–).

Ta·gore |təˈɡawr|, Rabindranath (1861–1941) Indian writer and philosopher. His poetry pioneered the use of colloquial Bengali, and his own translations established his reputation in the West. Nobel Prize for Literature (1913).

Tail·le·ferre |ˌtīəˈfer|, Germaine (1892–1983) French composer and pianist. A member of Les Six, she composed concertos for unusual combinations of instruments.

Tal·bert |ˈtælbərt|, Mary Burnett (1866–1923) U.S. educator and civil rights advocate. She served as president of the National Association of Colored Women (1916–21) and was a crusader for the Dyer anti-lynching bill (1921). She was the first African-American woman to win the Spingarn Medal (1922).

Tal·bot |ˈtawlbət|, (William Henry) Fox (1800–77) English pioneer of photography. He produced the first photograph on paper in 1835. Five years later he discovered a process for producing a neg-

---

Taft, William Howard
27th U.S. president

Life dates: 1857–1930
Place of birth: Cincinnati, Ohio
Mother: Louise Maria Torrey Taft
Father: Alphonso Taft
Wife: Helen Herron Taft
Children: Robert, Helen, Charles
College/University: Yale; Cincinnati Law School
Career: Lawyer; judge; law professor
Political career: U.S. Solicitor General; U.S. Federal Circuit Court judge; civil governor-general of the Philippine Islands; U.S. secretary of war; president; U.S. Supreme Court chief justice
Party: Republican
Home state: Ohio
Opponents in presidential races: William Jennings Bryan; Woodrow Wilson; Theodore Roosevelt
Term of office: March 4, 1909–March 3, 1913
Vice president: James Schoolcraft Sherman
Notable events of presidency: Tariff Board established; parcel post service authorized; New Mexico admitted as 47th state; Arizona admitted as 48th state; Alaska granted full territorial government
Other achievements: admitted to the Ohio bar; Superior Court judge, Cincinnati; dean, University of Cincinnati Law School; professor of law, Yale
Place of burial: Arlington National Cemetery, Arlington, Va.

---

ative from which multiple positive prints could be made, though the independently developed daguerreotype proved to be superior.

Tal·ley·rand |ˈtælē,rænd|, Charles Maurice de (1754–1838) French statesman; full surname *Talleyrand-Périgord*. Involved in the coup that brought Napoleon to power, he became head of the new government after the fall of Napoleon (1814) and was later instrumental in the overthrow of Charles X and the accession of Louis Philippe (1830).

Tal·lis |'tæləs|, Thomas (*c.* 1505–85) English composer. Organist of the Chapel Royal jointly with William Byrd, he served under Henry VIII, Edward VI, Mary, and Elizabeth I. His works include the 40-part motet *Spem in Alium*.

Tam·bo |'tämbō|, Oliver (1917–93) South African politician. He joined the African National Congress in 1944, became its acting president in 1967, and was president from 1977 until 1991, when he resigned in favor of Nelson Mandela, recently released from prison.

Tam·er·lane |'tæmər,län| (1336–1405) Mongol ruler of Samarkand (1369–1405). Also **Tamburlaine**; Tartar name *Timur Lenk* ("lame Timur"). Leading a force of Mongols and Turks, he conquered Persia, northern India, and Syria and established his capital at Samarkand. He was the ancestor of the Mogul dynasty in India.

Tames |tämz|, George (1919–94) U.S. photographer. He chronicled presidents and political leaders.

Tan |tæn|, Amy (1952–   ) U.S. author. Notable works: *The Joy Luck Club* (1989) and *The Kitchen God's Wife* (1991).

Ta·na·ka |tə'näkə|, Tomoyuki (1909–97) Japanese movie producer.

Tan·dy |'tændē|, Jessica (1909–94) U.S. actress, born in England. She made many stage appearances, some with her husband Hume Cronyn, including *The Gin Game*; her films include *Driving Miss Daisy* (1989, Academy Award)

Ta·ney |'tawnē|, Roger Brooke (1777–1864) Chief Justice of the U.S. (1836–64). He upheld the principle of federal supremacy over states' rights.

Tange |'täNGgä|, Kenzo (1913–   ) Japanese architect. His work, which includes the Peace Center at Hiroshima (1955), is characterized by the use of modern materials while retaining a feeling for traditional Japanese architecture.

Ta·ni·za·ki |,tänē'zäkē|, Jun'ichiro (1886–1965) Japanese novelist and playwright. Notable works: *Some Prefer Nettles* (1955) and *Diary of an Old Man* (1965).

Tann·häu·ser |'tän,hoizər| (*c.* 1200–*c.* 1270) German poet. In reality a Minnesinger whose works included lyrics

and love poetry, he became a legendary figure as a knight who visited Venus's grotto and spent seven years in debauchery, then repented and sought absolution from the Pope.

Tan·sen |'tæn,sen| (*c.* 1500–89) Indian musician and singer. A leading exponent of northern Indian classical music, he became an honored member of the court of Akbar the Great.

Ta·ran·ti·no |,tærən'tēnō|, Quentin (Jerome) (1963–   ) U.S. movie director, screenwriter, and actor. He came to sudden prominence with *Reservoir Dogs* (1992), followed in 1994 by *Pulp Fiction*. Both aroused controversy for their amorality and violence but also won admiration for their wit and style.

Tar·bell |'tärbəl|, Ida M. (1857–1944) U.S. author. She was a leader of the muckraking movement and a writer for *McClure's* magazine. Notable works: *The History of the Standard Oil Co.* (1904).

Tar·ken·ton |'tärkəntən|, Fran (1940–   ) U.S. football player. He passed for 47,003 yards and 342 touchdowns, both NFL records.

Tar·king·ton |'tärkiNGtən|, Booth (1869–1946) U.S. author. Full name *Newton Booth Tarkington*. Notable novels: *The Magnificent Ambersons* (1918) and *Alice Adams* (1921).

Tar·kov·sky |tär'kawfskē|, Andrei (Arsenevich) (1932–86) Russian movie director. Featuring a poetic and impressionistic style, his movies include *Ivan's Childhood* (1962), *Solaris* (1972), and *The Sacrifice* (1986), which won the special grand prize at the Cannes Film Festival.

Tar·quin·i·us |tär'kwinēəs| the name of two semi-legendary Etruscan kings of ancient Rome; anglicized name *Tarquin*: **Tarquinius Priscus**, died 578 BC; reigned *c.*616–*c.*578 BC; full name *Lucius Tarquinius Priscus*. According to tradition he was murdered by the sons of the previous king. **Tarquinius Superbus**, reigned *c.*534–*c.*510 BC; full name *Lucius Tarquinius Superbus*; known as **Tarquin the Proud**. According to tradition he was the son or grandson of Tarquinius Priscus. Noted for his cruelty, he was expelled from the city and the Republic was founded. He repeatedly but unsuccessfully attacked Rome, assisted by Lars Porsenna.

Tar·ti·koff |'tärti,kawf|, Brandon (1949–97) U.S. television network executive. He began as a director of comedy programs and later became president of NBC (1980–   ).

Tas·man |'tăsmän|, Abel (Janszoon) (1603–c. 1659) Dutch navigator. Sent in 1642 by the Governor General of the Dutch East Indies, Anthony van Diemen (1593–1645), to explore Australian waters, he reached Tasmania (which he named Van Diemen's Land) and New Zealand, and in 1643 arrived at Tonga and Fiji.

Tas·so |'tăsō|, Torquato (1544–95) Italian poet, known for his epic poem *Gerusalemme liberata* (1581).

Tate |tät|, James (Vincent) (1943–   ) U.S. poet and educator. Notable works: *Selected Poems* (1992, Pulitzer Prize) and *Worshipful Company of Fletchers* (1994, National Book Award).

Tate |tät|, (John Orley) Allen (1899–1979) U.S. author and educator. He was a leader of the "New Criticism" and the author of poetry, biography, literary criticism, and anthologies.

Tate |tät|, Nahum (1652–1715) Irish dramatist and poet, resident in London from the 1670s. He was appointed Poet Laureate in 1692.

Ta·ti |tä'tē|, Jacques (1908–82) French movie director and actor; born *Jacques Tatischeff*. He introduced the comically inept character Monsieur Hulot in *Monsieur Hulot's Holiday* (1953), seen again in movies including the Oscar-winning *Mon oncle* (1958).

Ta·tum |'tātəm|, Art (1910–56) U.S. jazz pianist; full name *Arthur Tatum*. Born with cataracts in both eyes, he was almost completely blind. He became famous in the 1930s for his solo and trio work.

Ta·tum |'tātəm|, Edward Lawrie (1909–75) U.S. biochemist. He shared the 1958 Nobel Prize for Physiology or Medicine with George Wells Beadle (1903–89) for his work showing that one gene codes for one enzyme.

Tave·ner |'tævənər|, John (Kenneth) (1944–   ) English composer. His music is primarily religious and has been influenced by his conversion to the Russian Orthodox Church.

Tav·er·ner |'tævə(r)nər|, John (c. 1490–1545) English composer, an influential writer of early polyphonic church music.

Tay·lor |'tālər|, Art (1929–95) U.S. jazz drummer. Full name *Arthur S. Taylor, Jr.* He performed and recorded with many different groups and was host of a radio interview program.

Tay·lor |'tālər|, Edward Thompson (1793–1871) U.S. Methodist minister. Known as **Father Taylor**. Herman Melville based Father Mapple's sermon in *Moby Dick* on Taylor's style.

Tay·lor |'tālər|, Elizabeth (1932–   ) U.S. actress, born in England. Notable movies include *National Velvet* (made when she was still a child in 1944), *Cleopatra* (1963), and *Who's Afraid of Virginia Woolf?* (1966), for which she won an Oscar. She has been married numerous times, including twice to the actor Richard Burton.

Tay·lor |'tālər|, Frederick Winslow

Taylor, Zachary
12th U.S. president

Life dates: 1784–1850
Place of birth: near Barboursville, Va.
Mother: Sarah Dabney Strother Taylor
Father: Richard Taylor
Wife: Margaret Mackall Smith Taylor
Children: Anne, Sarah, Octavia, Margaret, Mary Elizabeth, Richard
Nickname: "Old Rough and Ready"
College/University: none (privately tutored)
Military service: served during the War of 1812; defeated the Seminoles in Florida in 1837; won several battles during the Mexican War
Career: Farmer; soldier
Political career: none prior to the presidency
Party: Whig
Home state: Kentucky
Opponents in presidential race: Lewis Cass
Term of office: March 4, 1849–Jul. 9, 1850 (died in office)
Vice president: Millard Fillmore
Notable events of presidency: Clayton-Bulwer Treaty with Great Britain
Place of burial: Louisville, KY

(1856–1915) U.S. industrial engineer. His time and motion studies became known as the "Taylorization" of mass labor production.

Tay·lor |'tālər|, Henry (Splawn) (1942–) U.S. author and educator. Notable works: *The Flying Change* (1985, Pulitzer Prize).

Tay·lor |'tālər|, James (1948–) U.S. pop musician. His hit songs include "You've Got a Friend" and "Fire and Rain."

Tay·lor |'tālər|, Jeremy (1613–67) English Anglican churchman and writer. Chaplain to Charles I during the English Civil War, he is now remembered chiefly for his devotional writings.

Tay·lor |'tālər|, John (1753–1824) U.S. politician and agriculturist. Known as **John Taylor of Caroline**. He was a member of the U.S. Senate from Virginia (1792–94, 1803, and 1822–24) and a strong advocate of states' rights.

Tay·lor |'tālər|, Lawrence (1959–) U.S. football player. He played in a record ten professional bowl games.

Tay·lor |'tālər|, Paul (1930–) U.S. choreographer. He performed with Martha Graham and the New York City Ballet, before forming his own Paul Taylor Dance Co. (1955).

Tay·lor |'tālər| Zachary, see box. **Margaret Mackall Smith Taylor** (1788–1852), wife of Zachary Taylor and U.S. first lady (1849–50).

Tchai·kov·sky |CHī'kawfskē|, Pyotr (Ilich) (1840–93) Russian composer. Notable works include the ballets *Swan Lake* (1877) and *The Nutcracker* (1892), the First Piano Concerto (1875), the opera *Eugene Onegin* (1879), the *1812 Overture* (1880), and his sixth symphony, the "Pathétique" (1893).

Te Ka·na·wa |tä 'känəwə|, Dame Kiri (Janette) (1944–) New Zealand operatic soprano, resident in Britain since 1966. She made her debut in London in 1970 and since then has sung in the world's leading opera houses.

Tea·gar·den |'tē,gärdn|, Jack (1905–64) U.S. jazz trombonist and singer.

Teale |tēl|, Edwin Way (1899–1980) U.S. author. Notable works: *Wandering Through Winter* (1965, Pulitzer Prize).

Teas·dale |'tēz,dāl|, Sara (1884–1933) U.S. poet. Notable works: *Love Songs* (1917, special Pulitzer award).

Te·cum·seh |tə'kəmsə| (1768–1813) Shawnee chief. Also **Tecumtha**. His plans to organize a military confederacy of tribes to resist U.S. encroachment was thwarted by the defeat of his brother, Tenskatawa ("the Prophet"), at Tippecanoe (1811). An ally of the British in the War of 1812, he fought and died in the Battle of the Thames.

Teil·hard de Char·din |tā'yär də SHär-'deN|, Pierre (1881–1955) French Jesuit philosopher and palaeontologist. He is best known for his theory, blending science and Christianity, that man is evolving mentally and socially towards a perfect spiritual state. The Roman Catholic Church declared his views unorthodox, and his major works (e.g. *The Phenomenon of Man*, 1955) were published posthumously.

Tel·e·mann |'telə,män|, Georg Philipp (1681–1767) German composer and organist. His prolific output includes 600 cantatas, 44 Passions, and 40 operas.

Tel·ford |'telfərd|, Thomas (1757–1834) Scottish civil engineer.

Tel·ler |'telər|, Edward (1908–) Hungarian-born U.S. physicist. After moving to the U.S. he worked on the first atomic reactor and the first atom bombs. Work under his guidance led to the detonation of the first hydrogen bomb in 1952.

Tem·pest |'tempəst|, Dame Marie (1864–1942) English actress; born *Mary Susan Etherington*. She was noted for her playing of elegant middle-aged women; the role of Judith Bliss in *Hay Fever* (1925) was created for her by Noel Coward.

Tem·ple |'tempəl|, Shirley (1928–) U.S. child star and political figure; married name *Shirley Temple Black*. In the 1930s she appeared in a succession of movies, such as *Rebecca of Sunnybrook Farm* (1938). She later became active in Republican politics and represented the U.S. at the United Nations and as an ambassador.

Te·niers |tə'nirs; 'tenyərz|, David (1610–90) Flemish painter; known as **David Teniers the Younger**. From

1651 he was court painter to successive regents of the Netherlands.

Ten·niel |'tenēəl|, Sir John (1820–1914) English illustrator and cartoonist. He illustrated Lewis Carroll's *Alice's Adventures in Wonderland* (1865) and *Through the Looking Glass* (1871).

Ten·ny·son |'tenəsən|, Alfred, 1st Baron Tennyson of Aldworth and Freshwater (1809–92) known as *Alfred, Lord Tennyson.* English poet, Poet Laureate from 1850. His reputation was established by *In Memoriam* (1850), a long poem concerned with immortality, change, and evolution. Other notable works: "The Charge of the Light Brigade" (1854).

Ten·zing Nor·gay |'tenziNG 'nawr,gä| (1914–86) Sherpa mountaineer. In 1953, as members of the British expedition, he and Sir Edmund Hillary were the first to reach the summit of Mount Everest.

Ter·ence |'terəns| (*c.* 190–159 BC) Roman comic dramatist; Latin name *Publius Terentius Afer.* His six surviving comedies are based on the Greek New Comedy; they are marked by more realism and a greater consistency of plot than the works of Plautus.

Te·re·sa |tə'rēsə; tə'rāsə|, Mother (1910–97) Roman Catholic nun and missionary. Also **Theresa**; born *Agnes Gonxha Bojaxhiu* in what is now Macedonia, of Albanian parentage. She became an Indian citizen in 1948. She founded the Order of Missionaries of Charity, which became noted for its work among the poor in Calcutta and now operates in many parts of the world. Nobel Peace Prize (1979).

Te·re·sa of Ávi·la |'ävēlə|, St. (1515–82) Spanish Carmelite nun and mystic. She instituted the "discalced" reform movement with St. John of the Cross. Her writings include *The Way of Perfection* (1583) and *The Interior Castle* (1588). Feast day, October 15.

Te·re·sa of Li·sieux |lēz'yOE|, St. (1873–97) French Carmelite nun. Also **Thérèse**; born *Marie-Françoise Thérèse Martin.* In her autobiography, *L'Histoire d'une âme* (1898), she taught that sanctity can be attained through continual renunciation in small matters, and not

only through extreme self-mortification. Feast day, October 3.

Te·resh·ko·va |,terəSH'kawvə|, Valentina (Vladimirovna) (1937–) Russian cosmonaut. In June 1963 she became the first woman in space.

Ter·hune |tər'hyOOn|, Albert Payson (1872–1942) U.S. author. His fiction about collies includes *Lad: A Dog* (1919).

Ter·kel |'tərkəl|, Studs Louis (1912–) U.S. author and radio and television journalist. Notable works: *The Good War* (1984, Pulitzer Prize).

Ter·man |'tərmən|, Lewis Madison (1877–1956) U.S. psychologist and educator. He revised the Binet-Simon Intelligence Tests and introduced the term "intelligence quotient."

Ter·ry |'terē|, Dame (Alice) Ellen (1847–1928) English actress. She played in many of Henry Irving's Shakespearean productions, and George Bernard Shaw created a number of roles for her.

Ter·ry |'terē|, Eli (1772–1852) U.S. manufacturer and inventor. He invented the mantel clock and was the first to mass-produce clocks.

Ter·ry |'terē|, Paul (1887–1971) U.S. cartoonist. He was the animator of Mighty Mouse.

Ter·tul·lian |tər'təlyən| (*c.* 160–*c.* 220) early Christian theologian; Latin name *Quintus Septimius Florens Tertullianus.* His writings include Christian apologetics and attacks on pagan idolatry and Gnosticism.

Tes·la |'teslə|, Nikola (1856–1943) American electrical engineer and inventor, born in what is now Croatia of Serbian descent. He developed the first alternating-current induction motor, as well as several forms of oscillators, the tesla coil, and a wireless guidance system for ships.

Te·traz·zi·ni |,täträ'tsēnē|, Luisa (1871–1940) Italian operatic soprano. She made her debut in Florence in 1890 as Inès and toured extensively worldwide.

Thack·er·ay |'THækərē; 'THækə,rā|, William Makepeace (1811–63) British novelist. He established his reputation with *Vanity Fair* (1847–8), a satire of the upper middle class of early 19th-century society.

Thad·dae·us |ˈTHædēəs| (1st century AD) an Apostle named in St. Matthew's Gospel, traditionally identified with St. Jude.

Tha·les |ˈTHāˌlēz| (c. 624–c. 545 BC) Greek philosopher, mathematician, and astronomer, living at Miletus. Judged by Aristotle to be the founder of physical science, he is also credited with founding geometry. He proposed that water was the primary substance from which all things were derived.

Thant |THänt; THænt|, U (1909–74) Burmese statesman. He served as secretary general of the UN (1961–71).

Tharp |THärp|, Twyla (1941–) U.S. dancer and choreographer. She performed with the Paul Taylor Dance Co., the Joffrey Ballet, and the American Ballet Theater and later formed her own modern dance troupe (1965).

Thatch·er |ˈTHæCHər|, Margaret (Hilda), Baroness Thatcher of Kesteven (1925–) British Conservative stateswoman, prime minister (1979–90). She was Britain's first woman prime minister, and became the longest-serving British prime minister of the 20th century. Her period in office was marked by an emphasis on monetarist policies, privatization of nationalized industries, and labor union legislation. She became known for her determination and her emphasis on individual responsibility and enterprise.

Thaves, Bob (1924–) U.S. cartoonist. He created the "Frank and Ernest" comic strip.

Thax·ter |ˈTHækstər|, Celia Laighton (1835–94) U.S. author. Notable works: *An Island Garden* (1894).

Thay·er |ˈTHāər|, Abbott Handerson (1849–1921) U.S. artist. His study of protective coloration led to the development of camouflage.

The·mis·to·cles |THəˈmistəˌklēz| (c. 528–460 BC) Athenian statesman. He helped build up the Athenian fleet, and defeated the Persian fleet at Salamis in 480.

The·oc·ri·tus |THēˈäkrətəs| (c. 310–c. 250 BC) Greek poet, born in Sicily. He is chiefly known for his *Idylls*, hexame-

ter poems presenting the lives of imaginary shepherds which were the model for Virgil's *Eclogues*.

The·o·do·ra |THēəˈdawrə| (c. 500–48) Byzantine empress, wife of Justinian. As Justinian's closest adviser, she exercised a considerable influence on political affairs and the theological questions of the time.

The·o·do·ra·kis |ˌTHēədəˈräkis|, Mikis (1925–) Greek composer and politician. He was imprisoned by the military government for his left-wing political activities (1967–70). His compositions include the ballet *Antigone* (1958), and the score for the movie *Zorba the Greek* (1965).

The·od·o·ric |ˌTHēˈädərik| (c. 454–526) king of the Ostrogoths 471–526; known as **Theodoric the Great**. At its greatest extent his empire included Italy, Sicily, Dalmatia, and parts of Germany.

The·o·do·sius I |ˌTHēəˈdōsHəs| (c. 346–95) Roman emperor 379–95; full name *Flavius Theodosius*; known as **Theodosius the Great**. Proclaimed co-emperor by the Emperor Gratian in 379, he took control of the Eastern Empire and ended the war with the Visigoths. A pious Christian, he banned all forms of pagan worship in 391.

The·o·phras·tus |ˌTHēəˈfræstəs| (c. 370–c. 287 .) Greek philosopher and scientist, the pupil and successor of Aristotle. The most influential of his works was *Characters*, a collection of sketches of psychological types.

The·re·sa, Mother |təˈrēsə; təˈräsə| see TERESA, MOTHER.

The·roux |THəˈrōō|, Paul (1941–) U.S. author. He has written fiction and nonfiction, including *The Mosquito Coast* (1982) and *Kowloon Tong* (1997).

Thes·i·ger |ˈTHesəjər|, Wilfred (Patrick) (1910–) English explorer. He explored many countries, notably Saudi Arabia and Oman. Notable works: *Arabian Sands* (1959) and *The Marsh Arabs* (1964).

Thes·pis |ˈTHespəs| (6th century BC) Greek dramatic poet, regarded as the founder of Greek tragedy.

Thom |täm|, Alexander (1894–1985) Scottish expert on prehistoric stone circles. An engineer, he began a detailed survey of the stone circles of Britain and Brittany in the 1930s.

Tho·mas |'täməs|, Clarence (1948–) U.S. Supreme Court justice (1991–). His appointment to the Court was approved only after a lengthy and controversial Senate hearing in which he had to respond to charges of sexual harassment.

Tho·mas |'täməs|, Danny (1914–91) U.S. television producer and actor. Born *Amos Jacobs*; father of actress Marlo Thomas. He starred in the television series "Make Room for Daddy" (1953–64).

Tho·mas |'täməs|, Dylan (Marlais) (1914–53) Welsh poet. In 1953 he narrated on radio *Under Milk Wood*, a portrait of a small Welsh town, interspersing poetic alliterative prose with songs and ballads. Other notable works: *Portrait of the Artist as a Young Dog* (prose, 1940).

Tho·mas |'täməs|, (Philip) Edward (1878–1917) English poet. His work offers a sympathetic but unidealized depiction of rural English life, adapting colloquial speech rhythms to poetic meter.

Tho·mas |'täməs|, George Henry (1816–70) U.S. army officer. A Virginia loyalist, he commanded volunteers and won several key battles in the Civil War.

Tho·mas |'täməs|, Isaiah (1749–1831) U.S. printer and publisher. He founded the American Antiquarian Society (1812) and authored *The History of Printing in America* (1810).

Tho·mas |'täməs|, Norman (1884–1968) U.S. social reformer and politician. He helped found the American Civil Liberties Union (1920) and was a Socialist Party presidential candidate six times (1928–48).

Tho·mas |'täməs |, St. (1st century AD) Apostle; known as **Doubting Thomas**. He earned his nickname by saying that he would not believe that Christ had risen again until he had seen and touched his wounds (John 20:24–9). Feast day, December 21.

Tho·mas à Kem·pis |'täməs ə 'kempəs| (*c.* 1380–1471) German theologian; born *Thomas Hemerken*. He is the probable author of *On the Imitation of Christ* (*c.*1415–24), a manual of spiritual devotion.

Tho·mas Aqui·nas |'täməs ə'kwīnəs|, St. see AQUINAS, ST. THOMAS.

Tho·mas More |'täməs mawr|, St. see MORE.

Thomp·son |'täm(p)sən|, Benjamin, Count Rumford. (1753–1814) U.S. scientist and inventor. He established the kinetic theory of heat and invented the drip coffeepot and the Rumford stove. He was a loyalist during the American Revolution.

Thomp·son |'täm(p)sən|, Daley (1958–) English decathlon athlete.

Thomp·son |'täm(p)sən|, Emma (1959–) English actress and screenwriter. Her movies include *Howard's End* (1992), for which she won an Oscar for best actress; *Sense and Sensibility* (1996), for which she also wrote the Oscar-winning screenplay; and *Primary Colors* (1998).

Thomp·son |'täm(p)sən|, Flora (Jane) (1876–1947) English writer. She is remembered for her semi-autobiographical trilogy *Lark Rise to Candleford* (1945).

Thomp·son |'täm(p)sən|, Francis (1859–1907) English poet. His best-known work, such as *The Hound of Heaven* (1893), uses powerful imagery to convey intense religious experience.

Thomp·son |'täm(p)sən|, J. Walter (1847–1928) U.S. businessman. Full name *James Walter Thompson*. He established an advertising firm in New York City (1878) and developed it into one of the most successful in U.S.

Thomp·son |'täm(p)sən|, Smith (1768–1843) U.S. Supreme Court justice (1823–43).

Thom·son |'tämsən|, Elihu (1853–1937) U.S. electrical engineer and inventor, born in England. He was the inventor of electric welding and of the standard three-phase, alternating-current generator (1890); his company merged with Thomas Edison's to form the General Electric Co. (1892).

Thom·son |'tämsən|, British family of scientists, including: **Sir Joseph John** (1856–1940), English atomic physicist. He discovered the electron, deducing its existence as a particle smaller than the atom from his experiments. Thomson received the 1906 Nobel Prize for Physics for his research into the electrical conductivity of gases. His son, **Sir George Paget Thomson** (1892–1975), shared the 1937 Nobel Prize for Physics for his discovery of electron diffraction by crystals.

Thom·son |'tämsən|, Roy Herbert, 1st Baron (1894–1976) British newspaper publisher and businessman, born in Canada. He owned television stations and a chain of newspapers in Canada, England, and Scotland.

Thom·son |'tämsən|, Tom (1877–1917) Canadian painter; full name *Thomas John Thomson.* Notable works: *Northern Lake* (1913), *The West Wind* (1917), and *The Jack Pine* (1917).

Thom·son |'tämsən|, Virgil Garnett (1896–1989) U.S. composer, music critic, and conductor. He was music critic of the *New York Herald Tribune* (1940–54). His movie score for *Louisiana Story* won the 1949 Pulitzer Prize.

Tho·reau |THə'rō|, Henry David (1817–62) U.S. essayist and poet. A key figure of Transcendentalism, he is best known for his book *Walden, or Life in the Woods* (1854), an account of a two-year experiment in self-sufficiency at Walden Pond in Concord, Massachusetts. His essay "On the Duty of Civil Disobedience" (1849) influenced Mahatma Gandhi's policy of passive resistance.

Thorn·dike |'THawrn,dĭk|, Dame (Agnes) Sybil (1882–1976) English actress. She played the title part in the first London production of George Bernard Shaw's *St. Joan* (1924).

Thorn·ton |'THawrnt(ə)n|, William (1759–1828) U.S. architect, born in the British West Indies. He designed the Capitol building in Washington, D.C. (1792).

Thorpe |'THawrp|, Jim (1888–1953) U.S. athlete. After winning Olympic gold medals in the pentathlon and decathlon (1912), he played both baseball and football professionally.

Thor·vald·sen |'tŏor,välsən|, Bertel (*c.* 1770–1844) Danish sculptor. Also **Thorwaldsen**. Major works include a statue of Jason in Rome (1803) and the tomb of Pius VII (1824–31).

Thrale |THräl|, Hester Lynch (1741–1821) English writer; second married name *Hester Lynch Piozzi* She was a close friend of Dr. Samuel Johnson, who lived with her and her husband for several years.

Thu·cyd·i·des |THŌŌ'sidə,dēz| (*c.* 455–*c.* 400 BC) Greek historian. He is remembered for his *History of the Peloponnesian War,* which analyzes the origins and course of the war; he fought in the conflict on the Athenian side.

Thumb |THəm|, General Tom (1838–83) U.S. circus entertainer. Born *Charles S. Stratton.* A 40-inch-tall dwarf, he worked as a sideshow attraction in the shows of P. T. Barnum.

Thur·ber |'THərbər|, James (Grover) (1894–1961) U.S. humorist and cartoonist. He published many of his essays, stories, and sketches in *The New Yorker* magazine. His collections of essays, stories, and sketches include *My World—And Welcome to It* (1942), which contains the story "The Secret Life of Walter Mitty."

Thur·mond |'THərmənd|, (James) Strom (1902–　) U.S. politician. He was governor of South Carolina (1947–51) and a member of the U.S. Senate from South Carolina (1955–　); he was a States' Rights Party presidential candidate (1948).

Tib·bett |'tibət|, Lawrence (1896–1960) U.S. operatic baritone. He sang for 27 seasons with the Metropolitan Opera, beginning with his debut in 1923 as Lovitsky.

Ti·be·ri·us |tī'birēəs| (42 BC–AD 37) Roman emperor (AD 14–37); full name *Tiberius Julius Caesar Augustus.* The adopted successor of his stepfather and father-in-law Augustus, he became increasingly tyrannical, and his reign was marked by a growing number of treason trials and executions.

Ti·bul·lus |tə'bələs|, Albius (*c.* 50–19 BC) Roman poet. He is known for his elegiac love poetry and for his celebration of peaceful rural life.

Tick·nor |'tiknər|, William Davis (1810–64) U.S. publisher. He founded a publishing company (1832), which became Ticknor and Fields (1854), publishers of the *Atlantic Monthly*

(1859), as well as works by Emerson, Thoreau, Hawthorne, and Longfellow.

Tie·po·lo |tē'epə,lō|, Giovanni Battista (1696–1770) Italian painter. He painted numerous rococo frescoes and altarpieces including the *Antony and Cleopatra* frescoes in the Palazzo Labia, Venice (*c.*1750), and the decoration of the residence of the Prince-Bishop at Würzburg (1751–3).

Tif·fa·ny |'tifənē|, Louis Comfort (1848–1933) U.S. glass-maker and interior decorator. A leading exponent of American art nouveau, he established a decorating firm in New York that produced stained glass, vases, lamps, and mosaic.

Tiglath-pileser |'tig,læTH-pī'lēzər| the name of three kings of Assyria, notably: **Tiglath-pileser I**, reigned *c.*1115–*c.*1077 BC. He extended Assyrian territory, taking Cappadocia, reaching Syria, and defeating the king of Babylonia. **Tiglath-pileser III**, reigned *c.*745–727 BC. He brought the Assyrian empire to the height of its power, subduing large parts of Syria and Palestine, and conquered Babylonia.

Til·den |'tildən|, Bill (1893–1953) U.S. tennis player. He led the U.S. to seven straight Davis Cup victories (1920–26).

Til·den |'tildən|, Samuel Jones (1814–86) U.S. politician. He was a Democratic candidate in the 1876 presidential election, which he won by popular vote but lost by settlement of electoral commission. He contributed to the endowment of the New York Public Library.

Til·lich |'tilik|, Paul (Johannes) (1886–1965) German-born U.S. theologian and philosopher. He proposed a form of Christian existentialism. Notable works: *Systematic Theology* (1951–63).

Ti·mo·shen·ko |,timə'sHeNGkō|, Semyon Konstantinovich (1895–1970) Soviet army commander. He directed the defense of Stalingrad (1941–42).

Tim·o·thy |'timəTHē|, St. (1st century AD) convert and disciple of St. Paul. Traditionally he was the first bishop of Ephesus and was martyred in the reign of the Roman emperor Nerva. Feast day, January 22 or 26.

Tin·ber·gen |'tin,berg(ə)n| Dutch family including: **Niko Tinbergen** (1907–88); full name *Nikolaas Tinbergen*, a zoologist. He studied social patterns among animals and applied many findings on animal aggression to humans. He shared the 1973 Nobel Prize for Physiology or Medicine with Konrad Lorenz and Karl von Frisch. His brother **Jan Tinbergen** (1903–94), an economist, shared the first Nobel Prize for Economics (1969) with Ragnar Frisch for his pioneering work on econometrics.

Tin·to·ret·to |,tintə'retō| (1518–94) Italian painter; born *Jacopo Robusti*. His work was typified by a mannerist style, including unusual perspectives and chiaroscuro effects.

Tip·pett |'tipət|, Sir Michael (Kemp) (1905–98) English composer. He established his reputation with the oratorio *A Child of Our Time* (1941), which drew on jazz, madrigals, and spirituals in addition to classical sources. Other works include five operas, four symphonies, and several song cycles.

Tir·pitz |'tirpəts|, Alfred von (1849–1930) German naval commander. As secretary of state in the Imperial Navy department (1897–1916), he created the German high seas fleet.

Ti·tian |'tisHən| (*c.* 1488–1576) Italian painter; Italian name *Tiziano Vecellio*. The most important painter of the Venetian school, he experimented with vivid colors and often broke conventions of composition. He painted many sensual mythological works, including *Bacchus and Ariadne* (*c.*1518–23).

Ti·to |'tētō| (1892–1980) Yugoslav Marshal and statesman, prime minister (1945–53) and president (1953–80); born *Josip Broz*. He organized a communist resistance movement against the German invasion of Yugoslavia (1941). He became head of the new government at the end of the war, establishing Yugoslavia as a non-aligned Communist state with a federal constitution.

Tit·tle |'titl|, Y. A. (1926–) U.S. football player. Full name *Yelberton Abraham Tittle*. Elected to the Football Hall of Fame (1971).

Ti·tus |'tītəs| (AD 39–81) Roman emperor 79–81, son of Vespasian; born

Titus Flavius Vespasianus. In 70 he ended a revolt in Judaea with the conquest of Jerusalem.

Ti·tus |'tītəs|, St. (1st century AD) Greek churchman. A convert and helper of St. Paul, he was traditionally the first bishop of Crete. Feast day (in the Eastern Church) August 23; (in the Western Church) February 6.

To·bi·as |tə'bīəs|, Channing Heggie (1882–1961) U.S. religious and civic leader. He was secretary of the National Council of the YMCA (1911–23) and chairman of the board of the NAACP (1953–59). Spingarn Medal, 1948.

To·bit |'tōbət| a pious Israelite living during the Babylonian Captivity (597–538 BC), described in the Apocrypha.

Tocque·ville |'tōk,vil|, Alexis de (1805–59) French politician and historian. Full name *Alexis Charles Henri Maurice Clérel de Tocqueville.* He is best known for his classic work of political analysis, *Democracy in America* (1835).

Todd |täd|, Baron Alexander Robertus (1907–) British biochemist. He won a 1957 Nobel Prize for Chemistry for his work in determining the chemical structure of nucleotides.

Todd |täd|, Mabel Loomis (1856–1932) U.S. author. She edited Emily Dickinson's *Poems* (1890–91, 1896) and *Letters of Emily Dickinson* (1894).

Todd |täd|, Thomas (1765–1826) U.S. Supreme Court justice (1807–26).

Tof·fler |'tawflər|, Alvin (1928–) U.S. author. Known for his futurist nonfiction, he first gained popularity with the publication of *Future Shock* (1971).

To·jo |'tō,jō|, Hideki (1884–1948) Japanese military leader and statesman, prime minister (1941–44). He initiated the Japanese attack on Pearl Harbor, and by 1944 he had assumed virtual control of all political and military decision-making. After Japan's surrender, he was tried and hanged as a war criminal.

To·klas |'tōkləs|, Alice Babette (1877–1967) U.S. author. She was a companion and secretary of Gertrude Stein.

Tol·kien |'tōl,kēn; 'täl,kēn|, J. R. R. (1892–1973) British novelist and literary scholar, born in South Africa; full name *John Ronald Reuel Tolkien.* He is famous for the fantasy adventures *The Hobbit* (1937) and *The Lord of the Rings* (1954–5), set in Middle Earth.

Tol·son |'tawlsən|, Melvin Beaunorus (1898–1966) U.S. author. Notable works: *Black Boy* (1963).

Tol·stoy |'tawl,stoi; 'tōl,stoi|, Count Leo (1828–1910) Russian writer; Russian name *Lev Nikolaevich Tolstoi.* He is best known for the novels *War and Peace* (1863–9), an epic tale of the Napoleonic invasion, and *Anna Karenina* (1873–77).

Tom·baugh |'täm,baw|, Clyde William (1906–97) American astronomer. His chief discovery was that of the planet Pluto on March 13, 1930, which he made from the Lowell Observatory in Arizona. Tombaugh subsequently discovered numerous asteroids.

To·mei |tō'mā|, Marisa (1964–) U.S. actress. Notable movies: *My Cousin Vinny* (1992, Academy Award).

Tom·lin |'tämlən|, Lily (1939–) U.S. comedian and actress. Born *Mary Jean Tomlon.* She has starred in the television series "Rowan & Martin's Laugh-In" (1969–73) and a one-woman Broadway show *The Search for Signs of Intelligent Life in the Universe* (Tony Award, 1985). Notable movies: *Nine to Five* (1980).

Tomp·kins |'täm(p)kənz|, Daniel D. (1774–1825) vice president of the U.S. (1817–25).

Tone |tōn|, (Theobald) Wolfe (1763–98) Irish nationalist. In 1794 he promoted a French invasion of Ireland that failed to overthrow English rule. Tone was captured by the British during the Irish insurrection in 1798 and committed suicide in prison.

Toole |tool|, John Kennedy (1937–69) U.S. author. Notable works: *A Confederacy of Dunces* (1980, Pulitzer Prize), published posthumously.

Too·mer |'toomər|, Jean (1894–1967) U.S. author. Notable works: *Cane* (1923).

Tor·que·ma·da |,tawrkə'mädə|, Tomás de (*c.* 1420–98) Spanish cleric and Grand Inquisitor. A Dominican monk, he became confessor to Ferdinand and Isabella, whom he persuaded to institute the Inquisition in 1478. He was also the prime mover behind the expulsion of the Jews from Spain in and after 1492.

Tor·rence |'tawrəns|, (Frederic) Ridgely (1875–1950) U.S. author. Notable works: *Poems* (1941, 1952).

Tor·rey |'tawrē|, John (1796–1873) U.S. chemist, botanist, and author. With Asa Gray, he published *A Flora of North America* (two vols., 1838–43).

Tor·ri·cel·li |,tawrə'cHelē|, Evangelista (1608–47) Italian mathematician and physicist. He invented the mercury barometer, with which he demonstrated that the atmosphere exerts a pressure sufficient to support a column of mercury in an inverted closed tube.

Tor·te·lier |,tawrtl'yä|, Paul (1914–90) French cellist. He was noted for his interpretations of Bach and Elgar and was appointed professor at the Paris Conservatoire in 1957.

Tos·ca·ni·ni |,täskə'nēnē|, Arturo (1867–1957) Italian conductor. He was musical director at La Scala in Milan (1898–1903; 1906–8) before becoming conductor of the Metropolitan Opera, New York (1908–21) and the New York Philharmonic Orchestra (1928–36). He founded the NBC Symphony Orchestra (1937).

Tough |təf|, Dave (1908–48) U.S. jazz drummer. Full name *David Jaffray Tough*. He played with Tommy Dorsey's Band and with the Benny Goodman Orchestra.

Toulouse-Lautrec |tə,lo͞oz- lō'trek|, Henri (Marie Raymond) de (1864–1901) French painter and lithographer. His reputation is based on his color lithographs from the 1890s, depicting actors, music-hall singers, prostitutes, and waitresses in Paris; particularly well known is the *Moulin Rouge* series (1894).

Tous·saint L'Ou·ver·ture |to͞o'seN ,lo͞over'tYr|, Pierre Dominique (*c.* 1743–1803) Haitian revolutionary leader. One of the leaders of a rebellion (1791) that emancipated the island's slaves, he was appointed governor general by the revolutionary government of France in 1797. In 1802 Napoleon (wishing to restore slavery) took over the island, and Toussaint died in prison in France.

Townes |townz|, Charles Hard (1915–) U.S. physicist. His development of microwave oscillators and am-

plifiers led to his invention of the maser in 1954. Townes later showed that an optical maser (a laser) was possible, though the first working laser was constructed by others. Nobel Prize for Physics (1964).

Town·send |'townzənd|, Willard (1895–1957) U.S. labor organizer. He organized the United Transport Service Employees, or "redcaps" (1935).

Town·shend |'townzənd|, Peter Dennis Blandford (1945–) British rock musician. He performed with The Who and composed the rock opera *Tommy* (Tony Award, 1993).

Toyn·bee |'toinbē|, Arnold (1852–83) English economist and social reformer. He taught both undergraduates and adult education classes in Oxford and worked with the poor in London's East End. He is best known for his pioneering work *The Industrial Revolution* (1884).

Toyn·bee |'toinbē|, Arnold (Joseph) (1889–1975) English historian. He is best known for his twelve-volume *Study of History* (1934–61), in which he traced the pattern of growth, maturity, and decay of different civilizations.

Tra·cy |'trāsē|, Spencer (1900–67) U.S. actor, particularly known for his screen partnership with Katharine Hepburn, with whom he costarred in movies such as *Guess Who's Coming to Dinner?* (1967). Other notable movies: *Captains Courageous* (1937, for which he won an Oscar); *Boys Town* (1938, for which he won an Oscar); *Adam's Rib* (1949); *Inherit the Wind* (1960); and *Judgment at Nuremberg* (1961).

Tra·herne |trə'hərn|, Thomas (1637–74) English religious writer and metaphysical poet. His major prose work *Centuries* (1699) was rediscovered in 1896 and republished as *Centuries of Meditation* (1908).

Tra·jan |'trājən| (*c.* 53–117 AD) Roman emperor 98–117; Latin name *Marcus Ulpius Traianus*. His reign is noted for the many public works undertaken and for the Dacian wars (101–6), which ended in the annexation of Dacia as a province.

Trav·ers |'trævərz|, Mary (1937–) U.S. folk singer. She was part of trio Peter, Paul, and Mary from the early

1960s through 1990s; their songs, reflecting the social concerns of the 1960s, include "Blowin' in the Wind" and "If I Had a Hammer."

Trav·is |'trævəs|, Merle (1917–83) U.S. country singer, guitarist, and songwriter.

Tre·vi·no |trə'vēnō|, Lee (Buck) (1939–) U.S. golfer. In 1971 he became the first man to win all three Open championships (Canadian, U.S., and British) in the same year.

Trev·or |'trevər|, William (1928–) Irish novelist and short-story writer; pseudonym of *William Trevor Cox*. His works deal insightfully with the elderly, the lonely, and the unsuccessful. They include the novels *The Old Boys* (1964) and *Fools of Fortune* (1983).

Tril·lin |'trilən|, Calvin (1935–) U.S. journalist and author. Notable works: *Remembering Denny* (1993).

Tril·ling |'trilɪNG| U.S. family of writers, including: **Lionel Trilling** (1905–75), a literary critic. Notable works: *The Liberal Imagination* (1950). **Diana Trilling** (1905–), his wife and an author. Notable works: *Mrs. Harris* (1981).

Trim·ble |'trimbəl|, Robert (1777–1828) U.S. Supreme Court justice (1826–28).

Tris·ta·no |trə'tänō|, Lennie (1919–78) U.S. jazz pianist and teacher. Full name *Leonard Joseph Tristano*. He founded a school of jazz in New York, where he excelled as a teacher.

Trol·lope |'träləp| English family of writers, including: **Anthony Trollope** (1815–82), a novelist. He is best known for the six Barsetshire novels, including *The Warden* (1855) and *Barchester Towers* (1857), and for the six political Palliser novels. **Frances Trollope** (1780–1863), his mother, and the author of *Domestic Manners of the Americans* (1832).

Trot·sky |'trätskē|, Leon (1879–1940) Russian revolutionary; born *Lev Davidovich Bronstein*. He helped to organize the October Revolution with Lenin and built up the Red Army. He was expelled from the party by Stalin in 1927 and exiled in 1929. He settled in Mexico in 1937, where he was later murdered by a Stalinist assassin.

Troyes |trwä|, Chrétien de see CHRÉTIEN DE TROYES.

Tru·deau |trōo'dō|, Garry B. (1948–) U.S. cartoonist. He was the creator of "Doonesbury." Pulitzer Prize, 1975.

Tru·deau |trōo'dō|, Pierre (Elliott) (1919–) Canadian Liberal statesman, prime minister of Canada (1968–79 and 1980–84). Noted for his commitment to federalism, Trudeau held a provincial referendum in Quebec in 1980, which rejected independence, and saw the transfer of residual constitutional powers from Britain to Canada in 1982.

Truf·faut |trōo'fō|, François (1932–84) French movie director. His first feature movie, *The 400 Blows* (1959), established him as a leading director of the *nouvelle vague*. Other movies include *Jules et Jim* (1961) and *The Last Metro* (1980).

Tru·ji·llo |trōo'hēyō|, Rafael (1891–1961) Dominican statesman, president of the Dominican Republic (1930–38 and 1942–52); born *Rafael Leónidas Trujillo Molina*; known as **Generalissimo**. Although he was formally president for only two periods, he wielded dictatorial powers from 1930 until his death.

Tru·man |'trōomən| U.S. family, including: **Harry S Truman** see box. **Bess Truman** (1885–1982), wife of Harry S Truman and U.S. first lady (1945–53); born *Elizabeth Virginia Wallace*. **Margaret Truman** (1924–), their daughter, a novelist; married name *Margaret Truman Daniel*. Notable novels: *Murder in the White House* (1980) and *Murder in the Pentagon* (1991).

Trum·bo |'trəmbō|, Dalton (1905–76) U.S. author and screenwriter. Notable works: *Johnny Got His Gun* (1939), *Exodus*, and *Spartacus* (1960).

Trum·bull |'trəmbəl|, John (1756–1843) U.S. artist. He created paintings for the rotunda of the Capitol building in Washington, D.C., and painted several portraits of George Washington.

Trump |trəmp|, Donald John (1946–) U.S. real estate developer.

Truth |trōoTH|, Sojourner (*c.* 1797–1883) U.S. evangelist and reformer; previously *Isabella Van Wagener*. Born into slavery, she was sold to Isaac Van Wagener, who released her in 1827. She

---

Truman, Harry S
33rd U.S. president

Life dates: 1884–1972
Place of birth: Lamar, Missouri
Mother: Martha Ellen Young Truman
Father: John Anderson Truman
Wife: Bess (Elizabeth Virginia) Wallace Truman
Children: (Mary) Margaret
College/University: none
Military service: Missouri National Guard; during World War I served in combat in France
Career: Farmer; owner, men's clothing store
Political career: U.S. Senate; vice president (under Franklin D. Roosevelt); president
Party: Democratic
Home state: Missouri
Opponents in presidential race: Thomas E. Dewey, Henry A. Wallace, James Strom Thurmond
Term of office: Apr. 12, 1945–Jan. 20, 1953 (succeeded to the presidency on the death of Franklin D. Roosevelt)
Vice president: Alben W. Barkley
Notable events of presidency: Germany surrenders to Allied forces; Potsdam Conference; atomic bombing of Hiroshima and Nagasaki, Japan; Japan surrenders, ending World War II; Truman Doctrine; Labor-Management Relations Act (Taft-Hartley Act); Economic Cooperation Administration created (European Recovery Program or Marshall Plan); North Atlantic Treaty Organization (NATO) established; Korean War begins
Other achievements: chairman, Special Senate Committee to Investigate the National Defense Program (Truman Committee)
Place of burial: Independence, Missouri

---

became a zealous evangelist, preaching in favor of black rights and women's suffrage.

Tshom·be |'cʜawmbā|, Moise (1919–69) Prime minister of Belgian Congo (1964–65).

Tsiol·kov·sky |ˌcʜēəl'kawfskē|, Konstantin (Eduardovich) (1857–1935) Russian aeronautical engineer. Tsiolkovsky carried out pioneering theoretical work on multistage rockets, jet engines, and space flight, and his pro-

posal for the use of liquid fuel pre-dated the work of R. H. Goddard by nearly forty years.

Tsu·bo·u·chi |ˌtso͞obə'oͦocʜē|, Shōyō (1859–1935) Japanese writer, scholar, translator. He began the *shingeki* (New Theater) movement, translated Shakespeare into Japanese, and wrote the first major work of modern Japanese literary criticism.

Tubb |təb|, Ernest (1914–84) U.S. country singer, songwriter, guitarist. Notable songs: "The Yellow Rose of Texas."

Tub·man |'təbmən|, Harriet (c. 1820–1913) U.S. aboloitionist. Known as **the Moses of Her People.** She was born a slave in Maryland, but escaped via the Underground Railroad (1849). Following what she called direct messages from God, she returned to Maryland numerous times, leading some 300 slaves to safety. During the Civil War, she went on many spying missions for the Union.

Tub·man |'təbmən|, William Vacanarat Shadrach (1895–1971) president of Liberia (1944–71).

Tuch·man |'təkmən|, Barbara (1912–89) U.S. historian and author. Notable works: *The Guns of August* (1962, Pulitzer Prize) and *Stilwell and the American Experience in China, 1911–45* (1971, Pulitzer Prize).

Tuck·er |təkər|, Richard (1913–75) U.S. operatic tenor. Born *Rubin Ticker.* He sang with the Metropolitan Opera for 30 seasons, beginning with his debut in 1945.

Tuck·er |təkər|, Sophie (1884–1966) U.S. burlesque and vaudeville entertainer, born in Russia. Born *Sophie Abuza.* She joined the Ziegfeld Follies (1909) and later starred in the Schubert Gaieties and the Earl Carroll Vanities; she was known as the "last of the red hot mamas."

Tuck·er |təkər|, Tanya (1958–) U.S. country and pop musician. Notable album: *Can't Run From Yourself* (1992).

Tu·dor |'toͦodər|, Henry. Henry VII of England (see HENRY).

Tu·dor |'toͦodər|, Mary. Mary I of England (see MARY).

Tu Fu |'doͦo 'foͦo| (AD 712–70) Chinese poet. Also **Du Fu.** He is noted for his bitter satiric poems attacking social injustice and corruption at court.

Tull |təl|, Jethro (1674–1741) English agriculturalist. In 1701 he invented the seed drill, a machine that could sow seeds in accurately spaced rows at a controlled rate, reducing the need for farm laborers.

Tul·ley |'təlē|, John (c. 1639–1701) U.S. author, born in England. He wrote the first continuous series of humorous almanacs in the U.S., beginning in 1687.

Tul·ly |'təlē|, Alice (1902–93) U.S. singer, philanthropist, and arts patron.

Tul·si·das |'tŏolsē,däs| (c. 1543–1623) Indian poet. A leading Hindu devotional poet, he is chiefly remembered for the *Ramcaritmanas* (c. 1574–7), a work consisting of seven cantos based on the Sanskrit epic, the *Ramayana*.

Tune |tŏon|, Tommy (1939–) U.S. dancer and choreographer. Notable musicals: *The Best Little Whorehouse in Texas* (1978).

Tu·nick |'tŏonək|, Jonathan (1938–) U.S. musician. He orchestrated Broadway shows, including *Promises, Promises* (1968), *A Little Night Music* (1973), and *A Chorus Line* (1975).

Tun·ney |'tənē|, Gene (James Joseph) (1898–1978) U.S. heavyweight boxer. He was a world heavyweight champion with a career record of 76 wins and one loss.

Tu·po·lev |'tŏopəlyif|, Andrei Nikolaievich (1888–1972) Soviet aeronautical engineer. He designed over 100 military and passenger aircraft and created the first supersonic airliner (1969).

Tup·per |'təpər|, Earl (1907–83) U.S. inventor. He invented the plastic food storage containers known as Tupperware (1946).

Tur·ge·nev |tŏor'gänyəf|, Ivan (Sergeevich) (1818–83) Russian novelist, dramatist, and short-story writer. His novels, such as *Fathers and Sons* (1862), examine individual lives to illuminate the social, political, and philosophical issues of the day.

Tu·ring |'tŏoriNG|, Alan Mathison (1912–54) British mathematician. He developed the concept of a theoretical computing machine, a key step in the development of the first computer, and

carried out important code-breaking work in World War II. He also investigated artificial intelligence.

Tur·ner |'tərnər|, Frederick Jackson (1861–1932) U.S. historian, educator and author. He revolutionized the study of the American frontier with his book *The Significance of Sections in American History* (1932, Pulitzer Prize).

Tur·ner |'tərnər|, J. M.W. (1775–1851) English painter; full name *Joseph Mallord William Turner*. He made his name with landscapes and stormy seascapes, becoming increasingly concerned with depicting the power of light by the use of primary colors, often arranged in a swirling vortex. Notable works: *Rain, Steam, Speed* (1844); *The Fighting Téméraire* (1838).

Tur·ner |'tərnər|, Joe (1911–85) U.S. rock and blues singer. He was a blues shouter of hits such as "Shake, Rattle, and Roll" and "Chains of Love."

Tur·ner |'tərnər|, Nat (1800–31) U.S. slave leader. Hanged on charges of murder and insurrection, he had organized a slave uprising in Southampton, Virginia, in which at least 50 whites were killed (August 1831).

Tur·ner |'tərnər|, Ted (1938–) U.S. broadcasting executive. Full name *Robert Edward Turner III*. His Turner Broadcasting System includes the television networks TBS ("the SuperStation"), Cable News Network (CNN), Turner Classic Movies (TCM), and the Cartoon Network. He owns the Atlanta Braves baseball team and the Atlanta Hawks basketball team. An accomplished yachtsman, he won the America's Cup (1977).

Tur·ner |'tərnər|, Tina (1939–) U.S. rock musician. Born *Anna Mae Bullock*. With her husband she was part of the duo Ike and Tina Turner; her hits include "What's Love Got to Do with It" and "We Don't Need Another Hero."

Tu·row |'tŏorō|, Scott F. (1949–) U.S. author. Notable works: *Laws of Our Fathers* (1996) and *Presumed Innocent* (1996).

Tur·pin |'tərpən|, Dick (1706–39) English highwayman. He was a cattle and deer thief in Essex before entering into partnership with Tom King, a notorious highwayman. Turpin was hanged at York for horse-stealing.

Tus·saud |'to͞osō; tə'sawd|, Madame (1761–1850) French founder of Madame Tussaud's waxworks museum, resident in Britain from 1802; née *Marie Grosholtz*. She took death masks in wax of prominent victims of the French Revolution and later toured Britain with her wax models. In 1835 she founded a permanent waxworks exhibition in London.

Tut·ankh·a·men |ˌto͞oˌtäNG'kämən| (died *c.* 1352 BC) Egyptian pharaoh of the 18th dynasty, reigned *c.*1361–*c.*1352 BC. Also **Tutankhamun**. His tomb, with its rich and varied contents, was discovered virtually intact by the English archaeologist Howard Carter in 1922.

Tuth·mo·sis III |to͝ot'mōsəs| (died *c.* 1450 BC) son of Tuthmosis II, Egyptian pharaoh of the 18th dynasty *c.*1504–*c.*1450 BC. His reign was marked by extensive building; the monuments he erected included Cleopatra's Needles (*c.*1475 BC).

Tu·tu |'to͞oˌto͞o|, Desmond (Mpilo) (1931–) South African clergyman. As General Secretary of the South African Council of Churches (1979–84), he became a leading voice in the struggle against apartheid. He was archbishop of Cape Town 1986–96. Nobel Peace Prize (1984).

Twain |twān|, Mark (1835–1910) U.S. novelist and humorist; pseudonym of *Samuel Langhorne Clemens*. After gaining a reputation as a humorist with early work, he wrote his best-known novels, *The Adventures of Tom Sawyer* (1876) and *The Adventures of Huckleberry Finn* (1885), which give a vivid evocation of Mississippi frontier life.

Tweed |twēd|, William Marcy (1823–78) U.S. politician. Known as **Boss Tweed**. A New York Democrat, he served in the U.S. House of Representatives (1853–55) and as New York City commissioner of schools (1856–57). By the time he was elected to the state senate (1867–71), he had become the leader of a ring of political corruption, which, until exposed in 1870, swindled the state treasury out of as much as $200

million. He was convicted (1873) but fled to Cuba and Spain (1875–76). He was extradited (1876) and returned to a New York jail, where he died.

Twich·ell |'twiCHəl|, Joseph Hopkins (1838–1918) U.S. Congregational clergyman. He was a member of the Nook Farm community in Hartford, Connecticut, where Mark Twain lived.

Twit·ty |'twitē|, Conway (1933–93) U.S. country singer, songwriter, and guitarist. Born *Harold Lloyd Jenkins*. Notable songs: "Hello, Darlin'" and "After the Fire is Gone."

Ty·cho Bra·he |'tīkō 'brähē| see BRAHE.

Ty·ler |'tīlər|, Anne (1941–) U.S. author. Notable works: *A Patchwork Planet* (1998) and *The Accidental Tourist* (1986).

Ty·ler |'tīlər| John, see box. **Letitia**

Tyler, John
10th U.S. president

Life dates: 1790–1862
Place of birth: Charles City County, Va.
Mother: Mary Marot Armistead Tyler
Father: John Tyler
Wife: Letitia Christian Tyler (died 1842); Julia Gardiner (married 1844)
Children: (by first wife) Mary, Robert, John, Letitia, Elizabeth, Anne, Alice, Tazewell; David, John, Julia, Lachlan, Lyon, Robert, Pearl
College/University: College of William and Mary
Career: Farmer; lawyer
Political career: Virginia House of Delegates; U.S. House of Representatives; governor of Virginia; U.S. Senate; vice president (under Harrison); president; elected to Confederate House of Representatives
Party: Democratic; Whig
Home state: Virginia
Opponents in presidential race: none
Term of office: Apr. 6, 1841–March 3, 1845 (succeeded to the presidency on the death of William Henry Harrison)
Vice president: none
Notable events of presidency: Pre-Emption Act; treaty with China; annexation of Texas; Florida admitted as the 27th state
Other achievements: admitted to the Virginia bar
Place of burial: Richmond, Va.

Christian Tyler (1790–1842), wife of John Tyler and U.S. first lady (1841–42).

Julia Gardener Tyler (1820–89), wife of John Tyler and U.S. first lady (1844–45).

Ty·ler |'tɪlər|, Moses Coit (1835–1900) U.S. historian and educator. He helped organize the American Historical Association (1884). Notable works: *A History of American Literature, 1607–1765* (1878) and *The Literary History of the American Revolution, 1763–83* (1897).

Ty·ler |'tɪlər|, Wat (died 1381) English leader of the Peasants' Revolt of 1381. He captured Canterbury and went on to take London and secure Richard II's concession to the rebels' demands, which included the lifting of the newly imposed poll tax. He was killed by royal supporters.

Tyn·dale |'tɪndəl|, William (*c.* 1494–1536) English translator and Protestant martyr. Faced with ecclesiastical opposition to his project for translating the Bible into English, Tyndale left England in 1524. His translations of the Bible later formed the basis of the authorized version. He was burnt at the stake as a heretic in Antwerp.

Ty·son |'tɪsən|, Mike (1966–) U.S. heavyweight boxing champion; full name *Michael Gerald Tyson*.

Ty·us |'tɪəs|, Wyomia (1945–) U.S. track and field athlete. She was the first woman to win consecutive Olympic gold medals (1964, 1968) in the 100-meter dash.

Tza·ra |'tsärə|, Tristan (1896–1963) Romanian-born French poet; born *Samuel Rosenstock*. He was one of the founders of the Dada movement and wrote its manifestos. His poetry, with its continuous flow of unconnected images, helped form the basis for surrealism.

Uu

Uc·cel·lo |o͞o'cHelō|, Paolo (*c.* 1397–1475) Italian painter; born *Paolo di Dono*. His paintings are associated with the early use of perspective and include *The Rout of San Romano* (*c.*1454–57) and *A Hunt in a Forest* (after 1460), one of the earliest known paintings on canvas.

Udall |'yo͞o,dawl|, Morris King (1922–98) U.S. politician. He was a member of the U.S. House of Representatives from Arizona (1961–91).

Uhry |'yo͞orē|, Alfred (1937–) U.S. playwright. Notable works: *Driving Miss Daisy* (1987, Pulitzer Prize).

Ula·no·va |yo͞o'länəvə|, Galina (Sergeyevna) (1910–98) Russian ballet dancer. She gave notable interpretations of *Swan Lake* and *Giselle*, and also danced the leading roles, composed especially for her, in all three of Prokofiev's ballets.

Ul·fi·las |'əlfə,læs| (*c.* 311–*c.* 381) Christian bishop and translator. Also **Wulfila**. Believed to be of Cappadocian descent, he became bishop of the Visigoths in 341. His translation of the Bible from Greek into Gothic (of which fragments survive) is the earliest known translation of the Bible into a Germanic language. Ulfilas is traditionally held to have invented the Gothic alphabet, based on Latin and Greek characters.

Ull·man |'əlmən|, Tracey (1959–) English actress.

Ul·pi·an |'əlpēən| (died *c.* 228) Roman jurist, born in Phoenicia; Latin name *Domitius Ulpianus*. His numerous legal writings provided one of the chief sources for Justinian's *Digest* of 533.

Ul·ya·nov |'o͞olyə,nawf|, Vladimir Ilich see LENIN.

Un·cas |'əNGkəs| (*c.* 1600–1683) chief of the Mohegan Indians. He sided with the British in the Pequot War (1637).

Un·der·wood |'əndər,wo͝od|, William (1787–1864) U.S. businessman. He founded a cannery (1821), whose "red devil" is thought to be the oldest registered food trademark.

Un·ga·ro, Emanuel Matteotti (1933–) French fashion designer.

Uni·tas |yo͞o'nītəs|, Johnny (1933–) U.S. football player. Full name *John Constantine Unitas*. He led the Baltimore Colts to 2 NFL titles and a Super Bowl win.

Un·ser |'ənsər|,Al (1939–) U.S. racecar driver. He retired in 1994, ranked third on the all-time Indy car list with 39 wins.

Un·ter·mey·er |'əntər,mīər|, Louis (1885–1977) U.S. author. He published critical anthologies, including *Modern American Poetry* (1919, with many revisions), as well as his own poetry.

Up·dike |'əp,dīk|, John (Hoyer) (1932–) U.S. novelist, poet, and short-story writer. He is noted for his quartet of novels *Rabbit, Run* (1960), *Rabbit Redux* (1971), *Rabbit is Rich* (1981, Pulitzer Prize), and *Rabbit at Rest* (1990, Pulitzer Prize). Other novels include *The Witches of Eastwick* (1984), and *S* (1998).

Up·john |'əp,jän|, Richard (1802–78) U.S. architect. Notable designs: Trinity Church (New York).

Urann, Marcus Libby (1873–1963) U.S. lawyer and businessman. He founded Ocean Spray Preserving Co. in order to mass-market cranberry sauce.

Ur·bahn |'o͝or,bän|, Max O. (1912–95) U.S. architect. Notable works: Vehicle Assembly Building (Cape Canaveral, Florida).

Urey |'yo͝orē|, Harold Clayton (1893–1981) U.S. chemist He discovered deuterium in 1932, pioneered the use of isotope labeling, and became director of the Manhattan Project at Columbia University. Nobel Prize for Chemistry (1934).

Uris |'yo͝orəs|, Leon Marcus (1924–) U.S. author. Notable works: *QB VII* (1970) and *Trinity* (1976).

Usti·nov |'yo͞ostə,nawf|, Sir Peter (Alexander) (1921–) British actor, director, and dramatist, of Russian descent. He has written and acted in a number of plays, including *Romanoff* *and Juliet* (1956). Notable movies: *Spartacus* (1960) and *Death on the Nile* (1978).

Uta·ma·ro |ˌo͞otəˈmärō|, Kitagawa (1753–1806) Japanese painter and printmaker; born *Kitagawa Nebsuyoshi*. A leading exponent of the ukiyo-e school, he was noted for his sensual depictions of women.

Utril·lo |o͞oˈtrēō|, Maurice (1883–1955) French painter, chiefly known for his depictions of Paris street scenes, especially the Montmartre district.

Vv

Va·ga·no·va |vəˈgänəvə|, Agrippina Yakovlevna (1879–1951) Russian ballet teacher. He codified a Soviet ballet technique that developed acrobatic virtuousity.

Vail |vāl|, Theodore Newton (1845–1920) U.S. businessman. He began as a telegraph operator for Western Union in New York City (1864–66) and general manager of Bell Telephone (1878–87). In 1885 he incorporated the American Telephone & Telegraph company (AT&T) to unify the industry and provide long-distance service; he served as the company's president (1885–89, 1907–19).

Va·len·ti |vəˈlentē|, Jack Joseph (1921–) U.S. movie executive. He is the CEO of the Motion Picture Association of America, Inc. (1966–) and chairman of the Alliance of Motion Picture and television Producers, Inc. (1966–).

Val·en·ti·no |ˌvælənˈtēnō|, Mario (1933–) Italian fashion designer.

Val·en·ti·no |ˌvælənˈtēnō|, Rudolph (1895–1926) Italian-born U.S. actor; born *Rodolfo Alfonzo Raffaelo Pierre Filibert Guglielmi di Valentina d'Antonguolla.* He played the romantic hero in silent movies such as *The Sheikh* (1921).

Va·le·ra |vəˈlerə|, Eamon de see DE VALERA.

Va·le·rian |vəˈlirēən| (died 260) Roman emperor 253–60; Latin name *Publius Licinius Valerianus.* He renewed the persecution of the Christians initiated by Decius.

Va·lé·ry |ˌväləˈrē|, Paul (1871–1945) Full name *Ambroise Paul Toussaint Jules Valéry.* French poet, essayist, and critic. His poetry includes *La Jeune parque* (1917) and "Le Cimetière marin" (1922).

Val·ois |välˈwä|, Dame Ninette de see DE VALOIS.

Van Al·len |væn ˈælən|, James Alfred (1914–) U.S. physicist who discovered Van Allen belts. He used balloons and rockets to study cosmic radiation in the upper atmosphere, showing that specific zones of high radiation were the result of charged particles from the solar wind being trapped in two belts around the earth.

Van Brock·lin |væn ˈbräklən|, Norm (1926–83) U.S. football player. Full name *Norman Mack Van Brocklin.* He led the NFL in passing three times and punting twice.

Van·brugh |ˈvænbrə|, Sir John (1664–1726) English architect and dramatist. His comedies include *The Relapse* (1696) and *The Provok'd Wife* (1697); among his architectural works are Castle Howard (1702) and Blenheim Palace (1705), both produced in collaboration with Nicholas Hawksmoor.

Van Bu·ren |væn ˈbyŏŏrən|, Martin (1782–1862) see box. Hannah Hoes Van Buren (1783–1819), wife of Martin Van Buren.

Van·cou·ver |vænˈkŏŏvər|, George (1757–98) English navigator. He led an

---

Van Buren, Martin
8th U.S. president

Life dates: 1782–1862
Place of birth: Kinderhook, New York
Mother: Maria Hoes Van Buren
Father: Abraham Van Buren
Wife: Hannah Hoes Van Buren
Children: Abraham, John, Martin, Smith
College/University: none
Career: Lawyer
Political career: New York Senate; U.S. Senate; governor of New York; U.S. secretary of state; vice president; president
Party: Democratic-Republican; Democratic
Home state: New York
Opponents in presidential races: William Henry Harrison
Term of office: March 4, 1837–March 3, 1841
Vice president: Richard M. Johnson
Notable events of presidency: Financial panic of 1837; Iowa territorial government authorized; Aroostook War; independent federal treasury system created
Place of burial: Kinderhook, New York

exploration of the coasts of Australia, New Zealand, and Hawaii (1791–92), and later charted much of the west coast of North America between southern Alaska and California. Vancouver Island and the city of Vancouver, Canada, are named after him.

Van de Graaf |'væn də ,græf|, Robert Jemison (1901–67) U.S. physicist. He invented the high-voltage *Van de Graaf generator* in about 1929, which was later adapted for use as a particle accelerator and as a high-energy X-ray generator for medical treatment and industrial use.

Van·den·berg |'vændənbərg|, Arthur Hendrick (1884–1951) U.S. journalist and politician. He was editor of the *Grand Rapids Herald* (1906–28); as a member of the U.S. Senate from Michigan (1928–51), he led the Republican opposition to President Franklin Roosevelt's foreign policy but later became a chief Republican architect of bipartisan foreign policy.

Van·der·bilt |'vændər,bilt|, Cornelius (1794–1877) U.S. businessman and philanthropist. He amassed a fortune from shipping and railroads and made an endowment to found Vanderbilt University in Nashville, Tennessee (1873).

Van·der·lyn |'vændərlən|, John (1775–1852) U.S. artist. A neoclassicist, he painted *The Landing of Columbus* (1842–44) for the U.S. Capitol rotunda.

Van der Post |'væn dər ,pōst|, Sir Laurens (Jan) (1906–96) South African explorer and writer. His books, including *Venture to the Interior* (1952) and *The Lost World of the Kalahari* (1958), combine travel writing and descriptions of fauna with philosophical speculation.

Van De·van·ter |'væn də'væntər|, Willis (1859–1941) U.S. Supreme Court justice (1910–37).

van de Vel·de |,væn də 'veldə|, family of Dutch painters, including: **Willem** (1611–93); known as **Willem van de Velde the Elder**. He painted marine subjects and was official artist to the Dutch fleet. He also worked for Charles II. **Willem** (1633–1707), son of Willem the Elder; known as **Willem van de Velde the Younger**. He was also a notable marine artist who painted for Charles II. **Adriaen** (1636–72); son of

Willem the Elder. He painted landscapes, portraits, and biblical and genre scenes.

van de Vel·de |,væn də 'veldə|, Henri (Clemens) (1863–1957) Belgian architect, designer, and teacher, who pioneered the development of art nouveau design and architecture in Europe. His buildings include the Werkbund Theatre in Cologne (1914).

Van Do·ren |væn 'dawrən| U.S. writers. **Carl (Clinton) Van Doren** (1885–1950), a historian and literary critic, is noted as the author of *Benjamin Franklin* (1938, Pulitzer Prize). His brother, **Mark (Albert) Van Doren** (1894–1972), was a poet and educator. Notable works: *Collected Poems* (1939, Pulitzer Prize).

Van Dru·ten |væn 'drōotn|, John (William) (1901–57) U.S. playwright and author, born in England. Notable works: *I Remember Mama* (1944).

van Duyn |væn 'dīn|, Mona (1921–) U.S. poet. Poet Laureate of the U.S., 1992–93.

Van Dyck |væn 'dīk|, Sir Anthony (1599–1641) Flemish painter. Also **Vandyke**. He is famous for his portraits of members of the English court, which determined the course of portraiture in England for more than 200 years.

Van Dyke |væn 'dīk|, Dick (1925–) U.S. actor. He starred in the television series "The Dick Van Dyke Show" (1961–66) and the movie *Mary Poppins* (1965).

Van Eyck |væn 'āk; væn 'īk|, Jan (*c.* 1370–1441) Flemish painter. He made innovative use of oils, bringing greater flexibility, richer and denser color, and a wider range from light to dark. Notable works: *The Adoration of the Lamb* (known as the Ghent Altarpiece, 1432) in the church of St. Bavon in Ghent and *The Arnolfini Marriage* (1434).

Van Gogh |væn 'gō|, Vincent (Willem) (1853–90) Dutch painter. He is best known for his post-Impressionist work, influenced by contact with Impressionist painting and Japanese woodcuts after he moved to Paris in 1886. His most famous pictures include several studies of sunflowers and *A Starry Night* (1889). Suffering from severe depression, he cut off part of his own ear and eventually committed suicide.

Van Ha·len |væn 'hälən|, Eddie (1957–) U. S. rock musician, born in the Netherlands. Grammy Award, 1991.

van Ley·den |v&aen. 'lidən|, Lucas see LUCAS VAN LEYDEN.

Van Rens·se·laer |,væn ,rensə'lir; ,væn 'rensələr|, Stephen (1764–1839) U.S. army officer and politician. He was a member of the U.S. House of Representatives from New York (1822–29) and founded the technical school (1824) that became Rensselaer Polytechnic Institute.

Van Vech·ten |væn 'vektən|, Carl (1880–1964) U.S. art and music critic. Notable works: *Nigger Heaven* (1926).

Van·zet·ti |væn'zetē|, Bartolomeo (1888–1927) U.S. political radical, born in Italy. Along with Nicola Sacco, he was accused of murder in a sensational trial.

Va·rèse |və'rez|, Edgard (1883–1965) U.S. composer and conductor, born in France. Born *EdgarVictorAchille Charles Varèse*. He was a pioneer in electronic music. Notable works: *Nocturnal* (1961).

Var·gas |'värgəs|, Getúlio Dornelles (1883–1954) Brazilian statesman, president (1930–45 and 1951–54). After seizing power he ruled as a virtual dictator until overthrown by a coup. Returned to power after elections in 1951, he later committed suicide after widespread calls for his resignation.

Var·gas Llo·sa |'värgəs 'yösə|, Mario (1936–) Full name *Jorge Mario Pedro Vargas Llosa*. Peruvian novelist, dramatist, and essayist. Novels include *Aunt Julia and the Scriptwriter* (1977), *TheWar of the End of theWorld* (1982), and *A Fish in theWater* (1994).

Var·ro |'värō|, Marcus Terentius (116–27 BC) Roman scholar and satirist. His works covered many subjects, including philosophy, agriculture, the Latin language, and education.

Va·sa·rely |,väsə'relē|, Viktor (1908–97) Hungarian-born French painter. A pioneer of op art, he was best known for a style of geometric abstraction that used repeated geometric forms and interacting colors to create visual disorientation.

Va·sa·ri |vä'zärē|, Giorgio (1511–74)

Italian painter, architect, and biographer. His *Lives of the Most Excellent Painters, Sculptors, and Architects* (1550, enlarged 1568) laid the basis for later study of art history in the West.

Vas·co da Ga·ma see DA GAMA.

Vaughan |vawn|, Henry (c. 1621–95) Welsh religious writer and metaphysical poet.

Vaughan |vawn|, Sarah Lois (1924–90) U.S. jazz singer. Known as **The Divine One**. She made her first recording with Billy Eckstine's Orchestra (1944).

Vaughan |vawn|, Stevie Ray (1955–90) U.S. blues-rock guitarist. Notable songs: "Pride and Joy."

Vaughn Wil·liams |,vawn 'wilyəmz|, Ralph (1872–1958) English composer. His strongly melodic music frequently reflects his interest in Tudor composers and English folk songs. Notable works: *Fantasia on a Theme by Thomas Tallis* (1910), *A London Symphony* (1914), and the Mass in G minor (1922).

Vaux |vöz; vawks; vöks|, Calvert (1824–95) U.S. architect and landscape gardener. He is known for his work in New York City, including, with Frederick Law Olmsted, the design of Central Park.

Veb·len |'veblən|, Thorstein (Bunde) (1857–1929) U.S. economist and social scientist. His works include the critique of capitalism *The Theory of the Leisure Class* (1899) and *The Theory of Business Enterprise* (1904).

Ve·ga |'vägə|, Lope de (1562–1635) Spanish dramatist and poet; full name *Lope Felix de Vega Carpio*. He is regarded as the founder of Spanish drama.

Ve·láz·quez |və'läs,käs|, Diego Rodríguez de Silva y (1599–1660) Spanish painter, court painter to Philip IV. His portraits humanized the formal Spanish tradition of idealized figures. Notable works: *Pope Innocent X* (1650), *The Toilet ofVenus* (known as The Rokeby Venus, c. 1651), and *Las Meninas* (c. 1656).

Ve·láz·quez de Cuél·lar |və'läs,käs dä 'kwä,är|, Diego (c. 1465–1524) Spanish conquistador. After sailing with Columbus to the New World in 1493, he began the conquest of Cuba in 1511; he later initiated expeditions to conquer Mexico.

Vel·de, van de |'veldə |,Willem and sons see VAN DE VELDE.

Vel·de, van de |'veldə|, Henri see VAN DE VELDE.

Vel·le·ius Pa·ter·cu·lus |və'lēəs pə 'tərkyələs| (c. 19 BC–c. 30 AD) Roman historian and soldier. His *Roman History*, covering the period from the early history of Rome to AD 30, is notable for its eulogistic depiction of Tiberius.

Ven·ing Mei·nesz |'veniNG 'mānəs|, Felix Andries (1887–1966) Dutch geophysicist. He devised a technique for making accurate gravity measurements with the aid of a pendulum and pioneered the use of submarines for marine gravity surveys. He located negative gravity anomalies in the deep trenches near island arcs in the Pacific, correctly interpreting them as being due to the downward buckling of the oceanic crust.

Ven·tu·ra |ven'tŏŏrə; ven'CHŏŏrə|, Jesse (1951–) U.S. politician. Born *James George Janos*. A former professional wrestler (known as **The Body**), he is the governor of Minnesota (1998–).

Ven·tu·ri |ven'tyŏŏrē; ven'CHŏŏrē|, Robert (Charles) (1925–) U.S. architect, pioneer of postmodernist architecture. Among his buildings are the Humanities Classroom Building of the State University of New York (1973) and the Sainsbury Wing of the National Gallery in London (1991).

Ve·nu·ti |ve'nŏŏtē|, Joe (1903–78) U.S. jazz violinist. Born *Guiseppe Venuti*. The first great jazz violinist, he led a big band (1935–43) before returning to small groups.

Ve·ra Cruz |,verə 'krŏŏz|, Phillip (1905–94) U.S. social reformer, born in the Philipines. He helped found the United Farm Workers Union.

Ver·di |'verdē|, Giuseppe (Fortunino Francesco) (1813–1901) Italian composer. His many operas, such as *La Traviata* (1853), *Aida* (1871), and *Otello* (1887), emphasize the dramatic element, treating personal stories on a heroic scale and often against backgrounds that reflect his political interests. He is also famous for his *Requiem* (1874).

Ver·gil variant spelling of VIRGIL.

Ver·laine |ver'len|, Paul Marie (1844–96) French symbolist poet. Notable collections of poetry include *Poèmes saturniens* (1867), *Fêtes galantes* (1869), and *Romances sans paroles* (1874).

Ver·meer |vər'mir|, Jan (1632–75) Dutch painter. He generally painted domestic genre scenes, for example *The Kitchen Maid* (c. 1658). His work is distinguished by its clear design and simple form.

Verne |vərn|, Jules (1828–1905) French novelist. One of the first writers of science fiction, he often anticipated later scientific and technological developments, as in *Twenty Thousand Leagues under the Sea* (1870). Other novels include *Journey to the Center of the Earth* (1864) and *Around the World in Eighty Days* (1873).

Ve·ro·ne·se |,verə'nāzē|, Paolo (c. 1528–88) Italian painter; born *Paolo Caliari*. He gained many commissions in Venice, including the painting of frescoes in the Doges' Palace. He is particularly known for his richly colored feast scenes (for example *The Marriage at Cana*, 1562).

Ver·ra·za·no |,verät'sänō|, Giovanni da (c. 1480–1528) Italian navigator in the service of France. He was the first European to enter New York Bay (1524).

Ver·sa·ce |vər'säCHē|, Gianni (1946–97) Italian fashion designer.

Ver·woerd |fər'vŏŏrt|, Hendrik (Frensch) (1901–66) South African statesman, prime minister (1958–66). As minister of Bantu Affairs (1950–58) he developed the segregation policy of apartheid. As premier he banned the African National Congress and the Pan-Africanist Congress in 1960, following the Sharpeville massacre. He withdrew South Africa from the Commonwealth and declared it a republic in 1961.

Ve·ry |'verē|, Jones (1813–80) U.S. poet and religious thinker. He was incarcerated in an asylum for the insane; his mystical poetry and essays were published under the patronage of Ralph Waldo Emerson (1839).

Ve·sa·li·us |və'sälēəs|, Andreas (1514–64) Flemish anatomist, the founder of modern anatomy. His major work, *De Humani Corporis Fabrica* (1543), contained accurate descriptions of human anatomy, but owed much of its great historical impact to the woodcuts of his dissections.

Ves·pa·sian |vəs'pāzнən| (AD 9–79) Roman emperor (69–79) and founder of the Flavian dynasty; Latin name *Titus Flavius Sabinus Vespasianus.* He was acclaimed emperor by the legions in Egypt during the civil wars following the death of Nero and gained control of Italy after the defeat of Vitellius. His reign saw the restoration of financial and military order and the initiation of a public building program.

Ves·puc·ci |vəs'pōoснē|, Amerigo (1451–1512) Italian merchant and explorer. He traveled to the New World, reaching the coast of Venezuela on his first voyage (1499–1500) and exploring the Brazilian coastline in 1501–02. The Latin form of his first name is believed to have given rise to the name of America.

Viar·dot |vyär'dō|, Pauline (1821–1910) French operatic mezzo-soprano. She made her debut in London in 1839 as Desdemona in *Otello* and sang at Covent Garden (1849–55) and with the Paris Opera until 1860.

Vi·cen·te |vē'säntä|, Gil (*c.* 1465–*c.* 1536) Portuguese dramatist and poet. He is regarded as Portugal's most important dramatist; many of his works were written to commemorate national or court events and include religious dramas, farces, pastoral plays, and satirical comedies.

Vi·co |'vēkō|, Giambattista (1668–1744) Italian philosopher. In *Scienza Nuova* (1725) he asserted that civilizations are subject to recurring cycles of barbarism, heroism, and reason, accompanied by corresponding cultural, linguistic, and political modes. His historicist approach influenced later philosophers such as Marx.

Vic·tor Em·man·u·el II |'viktər i 'mænyəwəl| (1820–78) ruler of the kingdom of Sardinia 1849–61 and first king of united Italy 1861–78. He hastened the drive toward Italian unification by appointing Cavour as premier of Piedmont in 1852. After being crowned king of Italy he added Venetia to the kingdom in 1866 and Rome in 1870.

Vic·tor Em·man·u·el III |'viktər i 'mænyəwəl| (1869–1947) last king of Italy 1900–46. He invited Mussolini to form a government in 1922 and lost all political power. After the loss of Sicily to the Allies (1943), he acted to dismiss Mussolini and conclude an armistice. He abdicated in 1946.

Vic·to·ria |vik'tawrēə|, Tomás Luis de (1548–1611) Spanish composer. His music, all of it religious, resembles that of Palestrina in its contrapuntal nature; it includes motets, masses, and hymns.

Vic·to·ria |vik'tawrēə| (1819–1901) queen of Great Britain and Ireland 1837–1901 and empress of India 1876–1901. Full name *Alexandrina Victoria.* She took an active interest in the policies of her ministers, but largely retired from public life after the death of her husband, Prince Albert, in 1861. Her reign was the longest in British history.

Vi·dal |vi'däl|, Gore (1925–) U.S. novelist, dramatist, and essayist; born *Eugene Luther Vidal.* His novels, many of them satirical comedies, include *Williwaw* (1946) and *Myra Breckenridge* (1968) and *Creation* (1981), as well as historical fiction such as *Lincoln* (1984).

Vigée-Lebrun |vē'zнɑ lə'brŒN|, (Marie Louise) Élisabeth (1755–1842) French painter. She is known for her portraits of women and children, especially Marie Antoinette and Lady Hamilton.

Vi·gno·la |vēn'yōlə|, Giacomo Barozzi da (1507–73) Italian architect. His designs were mannerist in style and include the Palazzo Farnese near Viterbo (1559–73) and the church of Il Gesù in Rome (begun 1568).

Vi·gny |vēn'yē|, Alfred Victor, Comte de (1797–1863) French poet, novelist, and dramatist. His poetry reveals his faith in "man's unconquerable mind." Other works include the play *Chatterton* (1835).

Vi·go |'vēgō|, Jean (1905–34) French movie director. His experimental movies, which combine lyrical, surrealist, and realist elements, include *Zéro de conduite* (1933) and *L'Atalante* (1934).

Vil·la |'vē(y)ə|, Pancho (1878–1923) Mexican revolutionary. Full name *Francisco Villa;* born *Doroteo Arango.* After playing a prominent role in the revolution of 1910–11 he overthrew the dictatorial regime of General Victoriano Huerta in 1914 together with Venustiano Carranza, but then rebelled against Carranza's regime with Emiliano Zapata.

Villa-Lobos |ˌvēlə-'lōbōs|, Heitor (1887–1959) Brazilian composer. He used folk music in many of his instrumental compositions, notably the nine *Bachianas brasileiras* (1930–45).

Vil·lard |vē'lär(d)|, Henry U.S. journalists and businessmen, born in Germany. **Henry Villard** (1835–1900), born *Ferdinand Heinrich Gustav Hilgard*, served as president (1881–84) and later chairman (1889–93) of the Northern Pacific Railroad. He also was president of the Edison General Electric Co. (1890–92) and purchased the *New York Evening Post* (1881). **Oswald Garrison Villard** (1872–1949), his son, was president of the *New York Evening Post* (1900–18) and editor (1918–32) and owner (1918–35) of *The Nation.*

Vil·lon |vē'yawN|, François (1431–63) French poet; born *François de Montcorbier* or *François des Loges*. He is best known for *Le Lais* or *Le Petit testament* (1456) and the longer, more serious *Le Grand testament* (1461).

Vin·cent de Paul |'vinsənt də 'pawl|, St. (1581–1660) French priest. He devoted his life to work among the poor and the sick and established institutions to continue his work, including the Daughters of Charity (Sister of Charity of St. Vincent de Paul) (1633). Feast day, July 19.

Vin·ci |'vinCHē|, Leonardo da see LEONARDO DA VINCI.

Vine |vīn|, Frederick John (1939–) English geologist. Vine and his colleague **Drummond H. Matthews** (1931–97) contributed to the theory of plate tectonics, showing that magnetic data from the earth's crust under the Atlantic Ocean provided evidence for sea-floor spreading.

Vin·son |'vinsən|, Frederick Moore (1890–1953) U.S. Supreme Court justice (1946–53).

Vir·chow |'firkō|, Rudolf Karl (1821–1902) German physician and pathologist, founder of cellular pathology. He argued that the cell was the basis of life and that diseases were reflected in specific cellular abnormalities. Virchow also stressed the importance of environmental factors in disease.

Vir·gil |'vərjəl| (70–19 BC) Roman poet. Also **Vergil**; Latin name *Publius Vergilius Maro*. He wrote three major works: the *Eclogues*, ten pastoral poems, blending traditional themes of Greek bucolic poetry with contemporary political and literary themes; the *Georgics*, a didactic poem on farming; and the *Aeneid* (see AENEID), an epic poem about the Trojan Aeneas.

Virgin Mary mother of Jesus (see MARY).

Vis·con·ti |vis'käntē|, Luchino (1906–76) Italian movie and theater director; full name *Don Luchino Visconti, Conte di Modrone*. His movies include *The Leopard* (1963) and *Death in Venice* (1971). His first movie, *Obsession* (1942), was regarded as the forerunner of neorealism.

Vi·tel·li·us |və'telēəs|, Aulus (15–69) Roman emperor. He was acclaimed emperor in January 69 by the legions in Germany during the civil wars that followed the death of Nero. He defeated Otho but was killed by the supporters of Vespasian.

Vi·tru·vi·us |və'trōōvēəs| (1st century BC) Roman architect and military engineer; full name *Marcus Vitruvius Pollio*. He wrote a comprehensive ten-volume treatise on architecture that includes matters such as acoustics and water supply as well as the more obvious aspects of architectural design, decoration, and building.

Vi·tus |'vītəs|, St. (died *c.* 300) Christian martyr. He was the patron of those who suffered from epilepsy and certain nervous disorders, including St. Vitus's dance (Sydenham's chorea). Feast day, June 15.

Vi·val·di |vi'väldē|, Antonio (Lucio) (1678–1741) Italian composer and violinist, one of the most important baroque composers. His feeling for texture and melody is evident in his numerous compositions such as *The Four Seasons* (concerto, 1725).

Vi·ve·ka·nan·da |ˌvivəkə'nändə|,

Swami (1863–1902) Indian spiritual leader and reformer; born *Narendranath Datta*. He spread the teachings of the Indian mystic Ramakrishna and introduced Vedantic philosophy to the U.S. and Europe.

Viz·e·tel·ly |‚vizə'telē|, Frank Horace (1864–1938) U.S. lexicographer and editor, born in England. He edited Funk and Wagnall's *New Standard Dictionary*.

Vla·di·mir I |'vlædə‚mir| (956–1015) grand prince of Kiev (980–1015); known as **Vladimir the Great**; canonized as **St. Vladimir**. His marriage to a sister of the Byzantine emperor Basil II resulted in his conversion to Christianity and in Christianity in Russia developing close association with the Orthodox Church. Feast day, July 15.

Vla·minck |vlə'meNk|, Maurice de (1876–1958) French painter and writer. With Derain and Matisse he became a leading exponent of Fauvism, though later his color became more subdued.

Vol·ta |'vōltə|, Alessandro Giuseppe Antonio Anastasio (1745–1827) Italian physicist. He discovered methane gas (1778) and developed the first electric battery (1800). The volt, a unit of electrical potential, is named after him.

Vol·taire |vōl'ter| (1694–1778) French writer, dramatist, and poet; pseudonym of *François-Marie Arouet*. He was a leading figure of the Enlightenment, and frequently came into conflict with the establishment as a result of his radical views and satirical writings. Notable works: *Lettres philosophiques* (1734) and the satire *Candide* (1759).

Vol·wi·ler |'vawl‚wilər|, Ernest H. (1893–1992) U.S. inventor. With Donalee Tabern he invented Pentothal while looking for an anesthetic for direct injection into the bloodstream.

von Braun |vän 'brown|, Wernher Magnus Maximilian see BRAUN.

Von Für·sten·berg |vän 'fərstən‚bərg|, Diane Halfin (1946–) U.S. fashion designer, born in Belgium.

von Kar·man |vän 'kärmən|, Theodore

(1881–1963) U.S. physicist and aeronautical engineer, born in Hungary. He was instrumental in the development of rocket technology and was a cofounder of the Jet Propulsion Laboratory (1944).

von Laue |vän 'lowə|, Max Theodor Felix (1879–1960) German physicist. He won a 1914 Nobel Prize for Physics for his discovery of diffraction of X-rays by atoms or ions in crystals.

Von·ne·gut |'vänəgət|, Kurt, Jr. (1922–) U.S. novelist and short-story writer. His works blend elements of realism, science fiction, fantasy, and satire, and include *Cat's Cradle* (1963), *Slaughterhouse Five* (1969), and *Hocus Pocus* (1991).

von Neu·mann |vän 'nōōmən|, John (1903–57) U.S. mathematician, born in Hungary. He contributed to the development of high-speed computers and of the hydrogen bomb; he coined the term "cybernetics."

von Stern·berg |vän 'stərn‚bərg|, Josef (1894–1969) Austrian-born U.S. movie director. His best-known movie *Der Blaue Engel* (1930; *The Blue Angel*) made Marlene Dietrich an international star.

Vo·ro·shi·lov |vərə'sHēləf|, Kliment Yefremovich (1881–1969) Soviet statesman and marshal. He was president after Stalin's death (1953–60).

Vree·land |'vrēlənd|, Diane (c. 1903–89) U.S. editor, born in France. She edited *Harper's Bazaar* (1939–62) and *Vogue* (1962–71) and was a fashion consultant to the Metropolitan Museum of Art in New York.

Vuil·lard |‚vwē'yär(d)|, (Jean) Édouard (1868–1940) French painter and graphic artist. Full name *Jean-Édouard Vuillard*. A member of the Nabi Group, he produced decorative panels, murals, paintings, and lithographs, particularly of domestic interiors and portraits.

Vy·shin·sky |və'sHinskē|, Andrei Yanuaryevich (1883–1954) Soviet lawyer and statesman. He was foreign minister (1949–53) and served as chief prosecuter in Stalin's "purge trials."

Ww

Wade |wād|, (Sarah)Virginia (1945–   ) English tennis player.

Wag·ner |'wægnər|, Honus (1874–1955) U.S. baseball player and coach. Full name *John Peter Wagner*; known as **the Flying Dutchman**. Elected to Baseball Hall of Fame (1936).

Wag·ner |'vägnər|, (Wilhelm) Richard (1813–83) German composer. He developed an operatic genre which he called music drama, synthesizing music, drama, verse, legend, and spectacle. Notable works: *The Flying Dutchman* (opera, 1841), *Der Ring des Nibelungen* (a cycle of four operas, 1847–74), *Tristan and Isolde* (music drama, 1859), and the *Siegfried Idyll* (1870).

Wain |wān|, John (Barrington) (1925–94) English writer and critic. One of the "Angry Young Men" of the early 1950s, he was later professor of poetry at Oxford (1973–8).

Wain·wright |'wān,rīt|, Jonathan Mayhew (1883–1953) U.S. army officer. He was forced to surrender at Corregidor (1942) and was held as a prisoner of war until 1945.

Waite |wāt|, Morrison Remick (1816–88) Chief Justice of the U.S. (1874–88). He wrote over 100 opinions, including the Granger cases (1877), which upheld the power of state governments to regulate business.

Waits |wāts|, Tom (1949–   ) U.S. singer and songwriter. His *Bone Machine* album won a 1992 Grammy Award.

Wajda |'widə|, Andrzej (1926–   ) Polish movie director. Notable movies: *Ashes and Diamonds* (1958), *Man of Iron* (1981), and *Danton* (1983).

Waks·man |'wæksmən|, Selman Abraham (1888–1973) U.S. biochemist, born in Russia. Russian-born American microbiologist. He discovered the antibiotic streptomycin, used especially against tuberculosis. Nobel Prize for Physiology or Medicine, 1952.

Wal·cott |'wawlkət|, Charles Doolittle (1850–1927) U.S. geologist and paleontologist. He was director of the U.S. Geological Survey (1894–1907) and

Secretary of the Smithsonian Institution (1907–   ).

Wald |wawld|, Lillian D. (1867–1940) U.S. nurse and social worker. She organized the Visiting Nurse Service known as the Henry Street Settlement in New York City (1893).

Wald·heim |'väld,hīm|, Kurt (1918–   ) Austrian diplomat and statesman, president (1986–92). He was Secretary General of the United Nations (1972–81). His later career was blemished by revelations about his service as a German officer in World War II.

Walesa |və'lensə; və'wensə|, Lech (1943–   ) Polish labor leader and statesman, president (1990–95). As shipyard worker in Gdańsk, he founded the labor union called Solidarity (1980), and was imprisoned 1981–82 after the movement was banned. After Solidarity's landslide victory in the 1989 elections he became president. Nobel Peace Prize (1983).

Wales, Prince of |wālz| see PRINCE OF WALES; CHARLES, PRINCE.

Wal·green |'wawl,grēn|, Charles Rudolph (1873–1939) U.S. businessman. He founded the drugstore chain that bears his name (1902).

Walk·er |'wawkər|, Alice (Malsenior) (1944–   ) U.S. writer and critic. Notable novels: *The Color Purple* (Pulitzer Prize, 1982), *In Search of Our Mothers' Gardens: Womanist Prose* (1983), and *Possessing the Secret of Joy* (1992).

Walk·er |'wawkər|, Jimmy (1881–1946) U.S. politician. Full name *James John Walker*. He was mayor of New York City (1926–32) but resigned when his involvement in fraud was exposed.

Walk·er |'wawkər|, John (1952–   ) New Zealand track athlete. He was the first athlete to run a mile in less than 3 minutes 50 seconds (1975).

Walk·er |'wawkər|, Margaret Abigail (1915–   ) U.S. poet. Notable works: *For My People* (1942) and *Jubilee* (1965).

Walk·er |'wawkər|, Mort (1923–   ) U.S. cartoonist. Full name *Addison*

Morton Walker. He was the creator of the comic strip "Beetle Baily" and the co-creator of the strip "Hi and Lois."

Walk·er |'wawkər|, Ralph Thomas (1889–1973) U.S. architect. Notable designs: the New York Telephone building and the IBM Research Lab (New York).

Walk·er |'wawkər|, Robert (1801–69) U.S. politician. He was a member of the U.S. Senate from Mississippi (1835–45); he also served as U.S. secretary of the treasury (1845–49) and was largely responsible for creation of the Department of the Interior (1849).

Walk·er |'wawkər|, Sarah Breedlove (1867–1919) U.S. businesswoman. Known as **Madame C. J.** She invented and marketed a preparation to straighten kinky hair (1905) and built her business into the largest African-American–owned firm in the U.S, the Madame C. J. Walker Manufacturing Co. She bequeathed her fortune to educational institutions and charities.

Walk·er |'wawkər|, T-Bone (1910–75) U.S. guitarist. Full name *Aaron Thibeaux Walker*; known as **Daddy of the Blues.** He pioneered the electric blues guitar sound. Notable songs: "Viola Lee Blues" and "Stormy Monday Blues."

Wal·lace |'wawləs; 'wäləs|, Alfred Russel (1823–1913) English naturalist and a founder of zoogeography. He independently formulated a theory of the origin of species that was very similar to that of Charles Darwin.

Wal·lace |'wawləs; 'wäləs|, (Richard Horatio) Edgar (1875–1932) English novelist, screenwriter, and dramatist, noted for his crime novels.

Wal·lace |'wawləs; 'wäləs|, Henry Agard (1888–1965) U.S. politician and editor. He was editor of *Wallaces' Farmer* and its successor (1910–33). He served as vice president of the U.S. (1941–45) and was a Progressive party candidate for president (1948).

Wal·lace |'wawləs; 'wäləs|, George Corley (1919–98) U.S. politician. A four-term governor of Alabama (1963–67, 1971–79, 1983–87), he gained national attention in the early 1960s when he defied the civil rights legislation that out-lawed segregation in public schools. After losing the 1968 presidential race as a third-party candidate, he sought the presidential nomination as a Democrat (1972). While campaigning, he was shot and paralyzed by would-be assassin Arthur Bremner.

Wal·lace |'wawləs; 'wäləs|, Lewis (1827–1905) U.S. soldier and author. He served as major general in the Mexican War and the Civil War. Notable works: Ben Hur (1880).

Wal·lace |'wawləs; 'wäləs|, Mike (1918–) U.S. journalist. Born *Myron Leon Wallace.* A radio and television news commentator, he appears on the television program "60 Minutes."

Wal·lace |'wawləs; 'wäləs|, Sir William (c. 1270–1305) Scottish national hero. He was a leader of Scottish resistance to Edward I, defeating the English army at Stirling in 1297. After Edward's second invasion of Scotland in 1298, Wallace was defeated and subsequently executed.

Wal·lace |'wawləs; 'wäləs|, William Roy DeWitt (1889–1981) U.S. editor and publisher. With his wife Lila, he founded and edited the *Reader's Digest* magazine; they donated much of their fortune to charity.

Wal·len·berg |'wawlən,bərg; 'wälən-,bərg|, Raoul Gustav (1912–47) Swedish diplomat. In 1944 in Budapest he helped many thousands of Jews to escape death by issuing them Swedish passports. In 1945 he was arrested by Soviet forces and imprisoned in Moscow. Although the Soviet authorities stated that Wallenberg had died in prison in 1947, his fate remains uncertain.

Wal·ler |'wawlər; 'wälər|, Fats (1904–43) U.S. jazz pianist, composer, bandleader, and singer. Full name *Thomas Waller.* He was a stride style pianist and a composer of hits such as "Ain't Misbehavin'" (1928) and "Honeysuckle Rose" (1929).

Wal·ler |'wawlər; 'wälər|, Robert James (1939–) U.S. author. Notable works: *The Bridges of Madison County* (1992).

Wal·lis |'wawləs; 'wäləs|, Sir Barnes Neville (1887–1979) English inventor. His designs include the bouncing bomb used against the Ruhr dams in Germany in the Second World War.

Wal·pole |'wawl,pōl|, Horace, 4th Earl of Orford (1717–97) English writer and Whig politician, son of Sir Robert Walpole. He wrote *The Castle of Otranto* (1764), one of the first Gothic novels.

Wal·pole |'wawl,pōl|, Sir Hugh (Seymour) (1884–1941) British novelist, born in New Zealand. He is best known for *The Herries Chronicle* (1930–33), a historical sequence set in England's Lake District.

Wal·pole |'wawl,pōl|, Sir Robert, 1st Earl of Orford (1676–1745) British Whig statesman, First Lord of the Treasury and chancellor of the Exchequer (1715–17 and 1721–42), father of Horace Walpole. Walpole is generally regarded as the first British prime minister, having presided over the cabinet for George I and George II.

Wal·sing·ham |'wawlziNGəm|, Sir Francis (c. 1530–90) English politician. As secretary of state to Queen Elizabeth I he developed a spy network that gathered information about Catholic plots against the queen.

Wal·ter |'wawltər|, Bruno (1876–1962) U.S. conductor, born in Germany. Born *Bruno Walter Schlesinger.* He is noted as the standard interpreter of Mozart and as a supreme conductor of Brahms, Mahler, and Bruckner.

Wal·ters |'wawltərz|, Barbara (1931–) U.S. television journalist. She appears on the television program "20/20" (1979–).

Wal·ton |'wawltn|, Ernest Thomas Sinton (1903–95) Irish physicist. In 1932 he succeeded, with Sir John Cockcroft, in splitting the atom. Nobel Prize for Physics (1951, shared with Cockcroft).

Wal·ton |'wawltn|, Izaak (1593–1683) English writer. He is chiefly known for *The Compleat Angler* (1653; largely rewritten, 1655), which combines practical information on fishing with folklore, interspersed with pastoral songs and ballads.

Wal·ton |'wawltn|, Sam (1918–92) U.S. businessman. He was the founder of Wal-Mart discount stores.

Wal·ton |'wawltn|, Sir William (Turner) (1902–83) English composer. Notable

works: *Façade* (1921–3, a setting of poems by Edith Sitwell for recitation), the oratorio *Belshazzar's Feast* (1930–1), and movie scores for three Shakespeare plays and the movie *The Battle of Britain* (1969).

Wam·baugh |'wäm,bow|, Joseph Aloysius, Jr. (1937–) U.S. author. Notable works: *Floaters* (1996).

Wan·a·ma·ker |'wänə,mākər|, John (1838–1922) U.S. businessman. He was a pioneering department store merchant; in 1861 he founded a men's clothing store in Philadelphia, which he expanded into a department store (1877). He served as U.S. postmaster general (1889–93).

Wang |wäNG|, An (1920–90) U.S. computer engineer, born in China. The founder of Wang Laboratories (1951), he held 40 patents.

Wan·kel |'wæNGkəl; 'väNGkəl|, Felix Heinrich (1902–88) German engineer. He was the inventor and developer of the practical rotary combustion engine.

War·beck |'wawr,bek|, Perkin (1474–99) Flemish claimant to the English throne. In an attempt to overthrow Henry VII, he claimed to be one of the Princes in the Tower. After attempting to begin a revolt, he was captured and imprisoned in the Tower of London in 1497 and later executed.

War·burg |'wawr,bərg|, Aby (Moritz) (1866–1929) German art historian. From 1905 he built up a library in Hamburg, dedicated to preserving the classical heritage of Western culture. In 1933 it was transferred to England and housed in the Warburg Institute (part of the University of London).

War·burg |'wawr,bərg|, Otto Heinrich (1883–1970) German biochemist. He pioneered the use of the techniques of chemistry for biochemical investigations, especially for his work on intracellular respiration. Nobel Prize for Physiology or Medicine (1931); he was prevented by the Nazi regime from accepting a second one in 1944 because of his Jewish ancestry.

Ward |wawrd|, Aaron Montgomery (1843–1913) U.S. businessman. In 1872 he founded founded a dry-goods business, which became the first mail-order firm in the U.S., Montgomery Ward & Co..

Ward |wawrd|, Artemas (1727–1800) American politician and soldier. He served as a Revolutionary War commander, second in command to George Washington; later he was a member of the Continental Congress (1780–82) and of the U.S. House of Representatives (1791–95).

Ward |wawrd|, Mrs. Humphry (1851–1920) English writer and anti-suffrage campaigner, niece of Matthew Arnold; née *Mary Augusta Arnold*. She is best known for several novels dealing with social and religious themes, especially *Robert Elsmere* (1888). An active opponent of the women's suffrage movement, she became the first president of the Anti-Suffrage League in 1908.

Ware |wer|, Henry (1764–1845) U.S. clergyman and educator. He was responsible for the separation of the Unitarians from the Congregationalists, and he developed a curriculum for Harvard Divinity School (1816).

War·hol |'wawr,hawl|, Andy (*c.* 1928–87) U.S. painter, graphic artist, and movie-maker; born *Andrew Warhola*. A major exponent of pop art, he achieved fame for a series of silk-screen prints and acrylic paintings of familiar objects (such as Campbell's soup cans) and famous people (such as Marilyn Monroe), treated with objectivity and precision.

War·ner |'wawrnər|, Charles Dudley (1829–1900) U.S. author. Notable works: *The Gilded Age* (1873), with Samuel Clemens.

War·ner |'wawrnər|, Harry (1881–1958) U.S. movie executive, born in Poland. Born *Harry Morris Eichelbaum*. With brothers Albert (1884–1967), Samuel Louis (1887–1927), and Jack Leonard (1892–1978, born in Canada), he founded Warner Brothers Pictures (1923). The company produced *The Jazz Singer* (1927), the first talking movie.

War·ner |'wawrnər|, Pop (1871–1954) U.S. football coach. Full name *Glenn Scobey Warner*. He coached Olympic gold medalist and football player Jim Thorpe, as well as the football teams at

Pittsburgh (1915–23) and at Stanford University (1924–32).

War·ren |'wawrən; 'wärən| U.S. family of physicians. **Joseph Warren** (1741–75), a Revolutionary War patriot, was killed at the Battle of Bunker Hill. His brother, **John Warren** (1753–1815), was a leading medical practitioner in New England, a surgeon in the Revolutionary War, and the founder of Harvard Medical School (1783). **John Collins Warren** (1778–1856), son of John Warren, founded Massachusetts General Hospital (1811).

War·ren |'wawrən; 'wärən|, Charles (1868–1954) U.S. attorney and constitutional law scholar. Notable works: *A History of the American Bar...to 1860* (1911), *The Supreme Court in U.S. History* (two vols., revised 1937) and *Congress, the Constitution, and the Supreme Court* (1935).

War·ren |'wawrən; 'wärən|, Earl (1891–1974) Chief Justice of the U.S. (1953–69). He did much to extend civil liberties, including prohibiting segregation in schools. He is also remembered for heading the Warren Commission (1964) into the assassination of President Kennedy.

War·ren |'wawrən; 'wärən|, Leonard (1911–60) U.S. operatic baritone. Born *Leonard Warrenoff*. He sang for 22 seasons with the Metropolitan Opera, beginning with his debut in 1939. He collapsed and died onstage during a battle scene in *La Forza del Destino*.

War·ren |'wawrən; 'wärən|, Mercy Otis (1728–1814) U.S. author and political satirist. Notable works: *The Adulateur* (1773).

War·ren |'wawrən; 'wärən|, Robert Penn (1905–89) U.S. poet, novelist, and critic. An advocate of New Criticism, he was the first person to win Pulitzer Prizes in both fiction and poetry, and in 1986 he was made the first American Poet Laureate.

War·wick |'wawrwik|, Dionne (1941–) U.S. singer. Notable songs: "Do You Know the Way to San Jose" and "I'll Never Fall in Love Again."

War·wick |'wawr(w)ik|, Richard Neville, Earl of (1428–71) English statesman; known as **Warwick the**

Kingmaker. During the Wars of the Roses he fought first on the Yorkist side, helping Edward IV to gain the throne (1461), and then on the Lancastrian side, briefly restoring Henry VI to the throne (1470). Warwick was killed at the Battle of Barnet.

Wash·a·kie |'wäsHəkē| (c. 1804–1900) chief of the Shoshone Indians. He was an ally of the U.S. against the Blackfoot, Cheyenne and Sioux tribes and was given a military funeral.

Wash·ing·ton |'wawsHiNGtən; 'wäsH-iNGtən| George, see box. **Martha Dandridge Custis Washington** (1731–

Washington, George
1st U.S. president

Life dates: 1732–1799

Place of birth: Westmoreland County, Va.

Mother: Mary Ball Washington

Father: Augustine Washington

Wife: Martha Dandridge Custis Washington

Children: none

Nickname: "Father of His Country"

College/University: none

Military service: aide-de-camp, French and Indian War; general and commander-in-chief, Army of the United Colonies during the Revolutionary War

Career: Farmer; surveyor; soldier

Political career: Virginia House of Burgesses; First Continental Congress; Second Continental Congress; president

Party: Federalist

Home state: Virginia

Term of office: Apr. 30, 1789–March 3, 1797

Vice president: John Adams

Notable events of presidency: Post Office Department created; first U.S. census; Bank of the United States chartered; District of Columbia established; Vermont admitted as the 14th state; Bill of Rights; Kentucky admitted as 15th state; Tennessee admitted as the 16th state; cornerstone of White House and Capitol laid

Other achievements: commander-in-chief, Virginia armed forces; appointed Lieutenant-General and Commander-in-Chief of all the armies of the United States by President John Adams

Place of burial: Mount Vernon, Va.

1802), wife of George Washington and U.S. first lady (1789–97).

Wash·ing·ton |'wawsHiNGtən; 'wäsH-iNGtən|, Booker T. (1856–1915) U.S. educationist; full name *Booker Taliaferro Washington*. A leading commentator for black Americans, Washington established the Tuskegee Institute in Alabama (1881) and published his influential autobiography *Up from Slavery* in 1901. His support for segregation and his emphasis on black people's vocational skills attracted criticism from other black leaders.

Wash·ing·ton |'wawsHiNGtən; 'wäsH-iNGtən|, Bushrod (1762–1829) U.S. Supreme Court justice (1798–1829).

Wash·ing·ton |'wawsHiNGtən; 'wäsH-iNGtən|, Denzel (1954–) U.S. actor. Notable movies: *Glory* (1989, Academy Award).

Wash·ing·ton |'wawsHiNGtən; 'wäsH-iNGtən|, Dinah (1924–63) U.S. jazz singer. Born *Ruth Lee Jones*; known as **the Queen of the Blues**. Notable songs: "What a Difference a Day Makes" (1959).

Wash·ing·ton |'wawsHiNGtən; 'wäsH-iNGtən|, Harold (1922–87) U.S. politician. He was the first African-American mayor of Chicago (1983–87).

Was·ser·man |'wäsərmən|, Lew R. (1913–) U.S. corporate executive. Full name *Lewis Robert Wasserman*. He is an executive with Music Corp. of America, Inc.

Was·ser·stein |'wäsər,stīn; 'wäsər,stēn|, Wendy (1950–) U.S. playwright. Notable works: *The Heidi Chronicles* (1989).

Wa·ter·house |'wawtər,hows; 'wätər,hows|, Alfred (1830–1905) English architect.

Wa·ter·house |'wawtər,hows; 'wätər,hows|, Benjamin (1754–1846) U.S. physician. He established a safe vaccination method as a general practice in America.

Wa·ters |'wawtərz; 'wätərz|, Ethel (1896–1977) U.S. jazz and blues singer. He began as "cake-walking baby" and moved to mainstream popular music.

Wa·ters |'wawtərz; 'wätərz|, Muddy (1915–83) U.S. blues singer and guitarist; born *McKinley Morganfield*. He became famous with his song "Rollin' Stone" (1950). Waters impressed new rhythm-and-blues bands such as the Rolling Stones, who took their name from his 1950 song.

Wat·son |'wätsən|, James Dewey (1928–) American biologist. Together with Francis Crick he proposed a model for the structure of the DNA molecule. He shared the Nobel Prize for Physiology or Medicine with Crick and Maurice Wilkins in 1962.

Wat·son |'wätsən|, John Broadus (1878–1958) U.S. psychologist. Founder of the school of behaviorism. He held that the role of the psychologist was to discern, through observation and experimentation, the innate and acquired behavior in an individual.

Wat·son |'wätsən|, Johnny (1935–96) U.S. rhythm and blues guitarist.

Wat·son |'wätsən|, Thomas John (1874–1956) U.S. businessman. He worked for Computing-Tabulating-Recording Co., which became known in 1924 as International Business Machines; he served as the company's president (1914–49) and chairman (1949–56).

Wat·son |'wätsən|, Tom (1949–) U.S. golfer. He is a six-time PGA Player of the Year.

Watson-Watt |,wätsən'wät|, Sir Robert Alexander (1892–1973) Scottish physicist. He led a team that developed radar into a practical system for locating aircraft; this played a vital role in the Second World War.

Wat·teau |wä'tō|, Jean Antoine (1684–1721) French painter, of Flemish descent. An initiator of the rococo style, he is also known for his invention of the *fête galante*, the depiction of elegantly dressed people at play in a rural setting.

Wat·ter·son |'wawtərsən; 'wätərsən|, Bill (1958–) U.S. cartoonist and author. He created the comic strip "Calvin and Hobbes."

Wat·ter·son |'wawtərsən; 'wätərsən|, Henry (1840–1921) U.S. journalist. He was editor of the Louisville (Kentucky) *Courier-Journal*, which he controlled for 51 years.

Watts |wäts|, George Frederick (1817–1904) English painter and sculptor. He

is best known for his portraits of public figures, including Gladstone, Tennyson, and J. S. Mill. He was married to the actress Ellen Terry from 1864 to 1877.

Watts |wäts|, Isaac (1674–1748) English hymn writer and poet, remembered for hymns such as "O God, Our Help in Ages Past" (1719).

Waugh |waw|, Evelyn (Arthur St. John) (1903–66) English novelist. His work was profoundly influenced by his conversion to Roman Catholicism in 1930. Notable works: *Decline and Fall* (1928); and *Brideshead Revisited* (1945).

Wa·vell |'wävəl|, Archibald Percival, 1st Earl (1883–1950) British army officer. The commander in chief of British forces in the Middle East (1938–41), he was defeated by Rommel; he later became viceroy of India (1943–47).

Wayne |wän|, Anthony (1745–96) American revolutionary officer. Known as **Mad Anthony**. Noted for his courage and military brilliance, he participated in several critical Revolutionary War battles and is credited with saving West Point from British occupation following Benedict Arnold's betrayal. He retired in 1783, but returned to active duty in the 1790s, defeating the Indians at the Battle at Fallen Timbers (1794).

Wayne |wän|, James Moore (1790–1867) U.S. Supreme Court justice (1835–67).

Wayne |wän|, John (1907–79) U.S. actor; born *Marion Michael Morrison*. Associated with the movie director John Ford from 1930, Wayne became a Hollywood star with *Stagecoach* (1939) and appeared in classic westerns such as *Red River* (1948), *The Searchers* (1956) and *True Grit* (1969), for which he won an Oscar.

Webb |web| English socialists, economists, and historians. (Martha) Beatrice Potter Webb (1858–1943) and her husband Sidney (James) Webb, Baron Passfield (1859–1947), were prominent members of the Fabian Society and helped to establish the London School of Economics (1895). They wrote *The History of Trade Unionism* (1894) and *Industrial Democracy* (1897), as well as founding the *New Statesman* (1913).

Webb |web|, Chick (1902–39) U.S. jazz

band leader and drummer. Full name *William Henry Webb*. His band at the Savoy Ballroom in New York, became an outstanding band of the swing period.

Webb |web|, Jack (1920–82) U.S. actor and producer. He starred in the television series "Dragnet" (1952–59, 1967–70).

Webb |web|, Mary (Gladys Meredith) (1881–1927) English novelist. Her novels, such as *Gone to Earth* (1917) and *Precious Bane* (1924), are representative of regional English fiction popular at the beginning of the century.

We·ber |'vābər|, Carl Maria (Friedrich Ernst) von (1786–1826) German composer. He is regarded as the founder of the German romantic school of opera. Notable operas: *Der Freishütz* (1817–21), *Euryanthe* (1822–3).

We·ber |'vābər|, Max (1864–1920) German economist and sociologist, regarded as one of the founders of modern sociology. Notable works: *The Protestant Ethic and the Spirit of Capitalism* (1904) and *Economy and Society* (1922).

We·ber |'vābər|, Wilhelm Eduard (1804–91) German physicist. He proposed a unified system for electrical units and determined the ratio between the units of electrostatic and electromagnetic charge.

We·bern |'vābərn|, Anton (Friedrich Ernst) von (1883–1945) Austrian composer, a leading exponent of atonality and 12-tone composition. His music is marked by its brevity: *Five Pieces for Orchestra* (1911–13) lasts under a minute.

Web·ster |'webstər|, Ben (1909–73) U.S. jazz tenor saxophonist. Full name *Benjamin Francis Webster*. He played with Duke Ellington's band (1940–43).

Web·ster |'webstər|, Daniel (1782–1852) U.S. statesman and lawyer. A famed orator, he represented New Hampshire in the U.S. House of Representatives (1813–17) and Massachusetts in the U.S. House (1823–27) and Senate (1827–41, 1845–50). As secretary of state (1841–43) under President W. H. Harrison, he negotiated the Webster-Ashburton Treaty, which settled boundary disputes with Canada. He was again secretary of state (1850–52) under President Fillmore.

Web·ster |'webstər|, John (*c.* 1580–*c.* 1625) English dramatist. Notable works: *The White Devil* (1612) and *The Duchess of Malfi* (1623), both revenge tragedies.

Web·ster |'webstər|, Noah (1758–1843) U.S. lexicographer. His *American Dictionary of the English Language* (1828) in two volumes and containing 70,000 words was the first dictionary to give comprehensive coverage of American usage.

We·de·kind |'vādə,kint|, Frank (1864–1918) German dramatist. A key figure of expressionist drama, he scandalized contemporary German society with the explicit and sardonic portrayal of sexual awakening in *The Awakening of Spring* (1891).

Wedg·wood |'wej,wŏod|, Josiah (1730–95) English inventor and potter. He founded Wedgwood China and created many patterns for monarchs and aristocrats.

We·ge·ner |'vāgənər|, Alfred Lothar (1880–1930) German meteorologist and geologist. He was the first serious proponent of the theory of continental drift.

Weid·man |'wīdmən|, Jerome (1913–) U.S. author. Notable works: *I Can Get It For You Wholesale* (1937) and, with George Abbott, *Fiorello!* (1960, Pulitzer Prize).

Weil |vil|, Simone (1909–43) French essayist, philosopher, and mystic. During World War II she joined the resistance movement in England and died of tuberculosis while weakened by voluntary starvation with her French compatriots.

Weill |vīl|, Kurt (Julian) (1900–50) German composer, resident in the U.S. from 1935. He is best known for the operas he wrote with Bertolt Brecht, political satires including *The Threepenny Opera* (1928).

Wein·berg |'wīn,bərg|, Steven (1933–) American theoretical physicist. He devised a theory to unify electromagnetic interactions and the weak forces within the nucleus of an atom, for which he shared the Nobel Prize for Physics in 1979.

Weis·mann |'vīs,män|, August Fried-rich Leopold (1834–1914) German bi-ologist and one of the founders of mod-ern genetics. He expounded the theory of germ plasm, which ruled out the transmission of acquired characteristics and suggested that variability in indi-viduals came from the recombination of chromosomes during reproduction.

Weiss·mul·ler |'wis,mələr|, Johnny (1904–84) U.S. swimmer and actor; full name *Peter John Weissmuller*. He won three Olympic gold medals in 1924 and two in 1928. In the 1930s and 1940s he was the star of the Tarzan movies and later starred on television.

Weiz·mann |'vītsmən|, Chaim (Azriel) (1874–1952) Russian-born Israeli statesman, president (1949–52). He played an important role in persuading the U.S. government to recognize the new state of Israel (1948) and became its first president.

Welch |welcH; welsH|, John Francis, Jr. (1935–) U.S. businessman. He is the CEO of General Electric (1981–).

Welch |welcH; welsH|, Thomas B. (1825–1903) U.S. inventor and busi-nessman. A dentist who invented non-alcoholic grape juice to replace wine used in his church's communion ser-vices, he founded Welch's Grape Juice (1869).

Welch |welcH; welsH|, William Henry (1850–1934) U.S. physician. He helped organize the Johns Hopkins Medical School (1893) and Hospital (1889) and made notable contributions to bacteri-ology and immunology.

Welles |welz|, (George) Orson (1915–85) U.S. movie director and actor. His realistic radio dramatization in 1938 of H. G. Wells's *The War of the Worlds* per-suaded many listeners that a Martian in-vasion was really happening. Notable movies: *Citizen Kane* (1941), *The Lady from Shanghai* (1948), and *The Third Man* (1949).

Wel·ling·ton |'weliNGtən|, Arthur Wellesley, 1st Duke of (1769–1852) British soldier and Tory statesman, prime minister (1828–30 and 1834); known as **the Iron Duke**. He served as commander of the British forces in the Peninsular War (1808–14) and in 1815

defeated Napoleon at the Battle of Wa-terloo, so ending the Napoleonic Wars.

Wells |welz|, Henry (1805–78) U.S. pi-oneer in express shipping. He founded the American Express Co. (1850) and (with William G. Fargo) Wells, Fargo & Co. (1852).

Wells |welz|, H. G. (1866–1946) Eng-lish novelist; full name *Herbert George Wells*. He wrote some of the earliest sci-ence-fiction novels, such as *The War of the Worlds* (1898), which combined po-litical satire with warnings about the powers of science.

Wells |welz|, Horace (1815–48) U.S. physician. He discovered anesthesia in the U.S., but his demonstration in 1845 before a Harvard medical class failed.

Wells |welz|, Ida Bell (1862–1931) U.S. journalist. Last name also **Wells-Bar-nett**. The editor of *Memphis Free Speech* (1891–92), she founded the Negro Fel-lowship League (1910).

Wells |welz|, Mary (1943–92) U.S. pop singer. She was associated with the Mo-town sound. Notable songs: "My Guy" (1964).

Wel·ty |'weltē|, Eudora (1909–) U.S. novelist, short-story writer, and critic. Welty's novels chiefly focus on life in the South and contain Gothic elements; they include *The Optimist's Daughter* (1972), which won the Pulitzer Prize. Other works: *Collected Stories of Eudora Welty* (1980).

Wen·ce·slas |'wensəs,läs| (1361–1419) king of Bohemia (as Wenceslas IV, 1378–1419). Also **Wenceslaus**. He be-came king of Germany, Holy Roman emperor, and king of Bohemia in the same year, but was deposed by the Ger-man Electors in 1400.

Wen·ce·slas |'wensəs,läs|, St. (*c.* 907–929) Duke of Bohemia and patron saint of the Czech Republic. Also **Wences-laus**; also known as **Good King Wenceslas**. He worked to Christianize the people of Bohemia but was mur-dered by his brother; he later became venerated as a martyr. Feast day, Sep-tember 28.

Wer·ner |'vernər|, Abraham Gottlob (1749–1817) German geologist. He was the chief exponent of the theory of Nep-tunism, eventually shown to be incorrect, and attempted to establish a universal stratigraphic sequence.

Wes·ley |'weslē; 'wezlē|, John (1703–91) English preacher and cofounder of Methodism. Wesley was a committed Christian evangelist who won many working-class converts, often through open-air preaching. The opposition they encountered from the Church establishment led to the Methodists forming a separate denomination in 1791. His brother **Charles** (1707–88) was also a founding Methodist, and both wrote many hymns.

Wes·son |'wesən|, Daniel Baird (1825–1906) U.S. inventor and manufacturer. With Horace Smith he patented and manufactured revolvers (1854, 1857).

West |west|, Benjamin (1738–1820) U.S. painter, resident in Britain from 1763. He became historical painter to George III in 1769 and the second president of the Royal Academy in 1792. Notable works: *The Death of General Wolfe* (1771).

West |west|, Dorothy (1907–98) U.S. author. A writer of the Harlem Renaissance, she became a best-selling novelist at age 88 with *The Wedding* (1995).

West |west|, Dottie (1932–91) U.S. country singer and songwriter. Her Grand Ole Opry songs include "Here Comes My Baby."

West |west|, Jerry (1938–) U.S. basketball player and team executive. His silhouette serves as the NBA's logo. Elected to the Basketball Hall of Fame (1979).

West |west|, Mae (c. 1892–1980) U.S. actress and author. She made her name on Broadway in her own comedies *Sex* (1926) and *Diamond Lil* (1928), memorable for their spirited approach to sexual matters, before embarking on her successful Hollywood career in the 1930s.

West |west|, Nathanael (1903–40) U.S. novelist. Pseudonym of *Nathan Wallenstein Weinstein*. He wrote mainly during the Great Depression of the 1930s. Notable works: *Miss Lonelyhearts* (1933) and *The Day of the Locust* (1959).

West |west|, Dame Rebecca (1892–1983) Irish-born British writer and feminist; born *Cicily Isabel Fairfield*. She is best remembered for her study of the Nuremberg trials, *The Meaning of Treason* (1949). Other notable works: *The Fountain Overflows* (novel, 1957).

West·hei·mer |'west,hīmər|, (Karola) Ruth Siegel (1929–) U.S. psychologist, born in Germany. Known as **Dr. Ruth**. In her radio and television talk shows she dispenses advice on sexual matters.

West·ing·house |'westiNG,hows|, George (1846–1914) U.S. inventor and manufacturer. His achievements covered several fields, but he is best known for developing vacuum-operated safety brakes and electrically controlled signals for railways. He built up a huge company, Westinghouse Electric, to manufacture his products.

Wes·ton |'westən|, Edward (1886–1958) U.S. photographer. A pioneer of modern photography with an emphasis on sharp realism, he is known for his landscapes of the American West.

West·o·ver |'wes,tōvər|, Russ (1887–1966) U.S. cartoonist. Full name *Russell Channing Westover*. He created the popular flapper comic strip "Tillie the Toiler."

Wex·ler |'wekslər|, Jerry (1917–) U.S. record producer. He is credited with coining the term "rhythm and blues," a label he used to describe black popular music in his *Billboard* column (1948–51). As co-owner of Atlantic Records (1953–78), he produced the works of such recording artists as Ray Charles, Otis Redding, Aretha Franklin, and Wilson Pickett.

Wey·den |'vīdn|, Rogier van der (c. 1400–64) Flemish painter; French name *Rogier de la Pasture*. He was particularly influential in the development of Dutch portrait painting. Notable works: *The Last Judgment* and *The Deposition in the Tomb* (both c.1450).

Whar·ton |'(h)wawrtn|, Edith (Newbold) (1862–1937) U.S. novelist and short-story writer, resident in France from 1907. Her novels are concerned with the conflict between social and individual fulfillment. They include *The Age of Innocence* (1920), which won a Pulitzer Prize.

Wheat·ley |'(h)wētlē|, Phillis (c. 1752–

84) U.S. poet. She was born in Africa and sold as a slave at age eight to the John Wheatley family of Boston. She was educated by them and then sent to London, where she published her first volume of poems, *Poems on Various Subjects, Religious and Moral* (1773). Her *Memoirs and Poems* were published in 1834.

Whea·ton |'(h)wētn|, Henry (1785–1848) U.S. jurist and diplomat. Notable works: *Elements of International Law* (1836) and *History of the Law of Nations* (1845).

Wheat·stone |'(h)wēt,stōn|, Sir Charles (1802–75) English physicist and inventor. He is best known for his electrical inventions, which included an electric clock, the Wheatstone bridge, the rheostat, and, with Sir W. F. Cooke, the electric telegraph.

Whee·ler |'(h)wēlər|, John Archibald (1911–) U.S. theoretical physicist. He worked with Niels Bohr on nuclear fission, and collaborated with Richard Feynman on problems concerning the retarded effects of action at a distance. He coined the term "black hole" in 1968.

Whee·ler |'(h)wēlər|, William Almon (1819–87) vice president of the U.S. (1877–81).

Whee·lock |'(h)wē,läk|, Eleazar (1711–79) U.S. clergyman and educator. He founded Dartmouth College (1769) and served as its first president (1770–79).

Whip·ple |'(h)wipəl|, Fred Lawrence (1906–) U.S. astronomer. He discovered six new comets.

Whis·tler |'(h)wislər|, James (Abbott) McNeill (1834–1903) U.S. painter and etcher. Notable works: *Arrangement in Gray and Black: The Artist's Mother* (portrait, 1872).

White |(h)wīt| U.S. family, including: **Richard Grant White** (1821–85), author and literary critic. His edition of Shakespeare was republished as the Riverside text. **Stanford White** (1853–1906), his son, an architect. Notable designs: the Washington Arch in Washington Square Park (New York) and Madison Square Garden (New York).

White |(h)wīt|, Andrew Dickson (1832–1918) U.S. educator and diplomat. With Ezra Cornell, he cofounded Cornell University and served as its first president (1867–85); he was also first president of the American Historical Association and chairman of the U.S. delegation to the Hague Peace Conference (1899).

White |(h)wīt|, Byron R. (1917–) U.S. Supreme Court justice (1962–93).

White |(h)wīt|, E. B. (1899–85) U.S. author. Full name *Elwyn Brooks White*. He was a chief contributor to *The New Yorker* and the author of the children's classics *Stuart Little* (1945) and *Charlotte's Web* (1952). Special Pulitzer Prize, 1978.

White |(h)wīt|, Edward Douglas (1845–1921) Chief Justice of the U.S. (1910–21) and U.S. Supreme Court justice (1894–1910).

White |(h)wīt|, Edward Higgins, II (1930–67) U.S. astronaut. The first U.S. astronaut to maneuver in space outside a spacecraft (1965), he was killed in a flash fire in the Apollo 1 capsule.

White |(h)wīt|, John (c. 1577–c. 1593) English artist. He was a Virginia colonist on Roanoke Island (1585); his watercolors were the first authentic pictorial records of life in the New World.

White |(h)wīt|, Patrick (Victor Martindale) (1912–90) Australian novelist, born in Britain. White's reputation is chiefly based on his two novels *The Tree of Man* (1955) and *Voss* (1957). Nobel Prize for Literature (1973).

White |(h)wīt|, Paul Dudley (1886–) U.S. physician. A heart specialist and the author of *Heart Disease* (1931), he was Eisenhower's specialist at the time of the president's heart attack (1955).

White |(h)wīt|, Pearl Fay (1889–1938) U.S. actress. Her movie credits include *The Perils of Pauline* (1914).

White |(h)wīt|, T. H. (1906–64) British novelist, born in India; full name *Terence Hanbury White*. He is best known for the tetralogy *The Once and Future King*, his reworking of the Arthurian legend that began with *The Sword in the Stone* (1937).

White |(h)wīt|, Walter Francis (1893–1955) U.S. civil rights leader and author. He served as executive secretary of the NAACP (1931–55).

White |(h)wīt|, William Allen (1868–

1944) U.S. journalist. Known as the **Sage of Emporia**. He edited Kansas's *Emporia Gazette* from 1895; he won a Pulitzer Prize for his editorials (1923) and another for his autobiography (1946).

White·head |'(h)wīt,hed|, Alfred North (1861–1947) English philosopher and mathematician. He is remembered chiefly for *Principia Mathematica* (1910–13), on which he collaborated with his pupil Bertrand Russell.

White·man |'(h)wītmən|, Paul (1891–1967) U.S. symphony conductor. Known as **Pops**. He conducted the premiere of George Gershwin's *Rhapsody in Blue* (1924), which introduced symphonic jazz.

Whit·lam |'(h)witləm|, (Edward) Gough (1916–) Australian Labour statesman and prime minister (1972–75). Whitlam ended compulsory military service and relaxed the immigration laws. In 1975 he refused to call a general election and became the first elected prime minister to be dismissed by the British Crown.

Whit·man |'(h)witmən|, Marcus (1802–47) U.S. missionary physician and pioneer. He was murdered in Oregon by Cayuse Indians.

Whit·man |'(h)witmən|, Charles Otis (1842–1910) U.S. zoologist. He was the founder and first director of the Marine Biological Laboratory at Woods Hole, Massachusetts (1893–1908).

Whit·man |'(h)witmən|, Christine Todd (1946–) U.S. politician and governor of New Jersey (1994–).

Whit·man |'(h)witmən|, Walt (1819–92) U.S. poet; full name *Walter Whitman*. In 1855 he published the free verse collection *Leaves of Grass*, incorporating "I Sing the Body Electric" and "Song of Myself"; eight further editions followed in Whitman's lifetime. Other notable works: *Drum-Taps* (1865) and *Sequel to Drum-Taps* (1865).

Whit·ney |'(h)witnē| U.S. family, including: **Josiah Dwight Whitney** (1819–96). He was the state geologist of California (1860–74) and the person for whom Mount Whitney was named. **William Dwight Whitney** (1827–94), his brother, a philologist and educator.

He edited the *Century Dictionary* (1889–91).

Whit·ney |'(h)witnē|, Eli (1765–1825) U.S. inventor. He is best known for his invention of the cotton gin (patented 1794), a machine for automating the removal of seeds from raw cotton. He also is known to have developed the idea of mass-producing interchangeable parts. This he applied in his fulfillment of a contract (1797) to supply muskets for the U.S. government.

Whit·ney |'(h)witnē|, Gertrude Vanderbilt (1876–1942) U.S. sculptor and philanthropist. She sculpted the *Titanic Memorial* in Washington, D.C., and founded the Whitney Museum of American Art, the first museum in the U.S. devoted exclusively to native art (1931). Daughter of Cornelius Vanderbilt.

Whit·ney |'(h)witnē|, William Collins (1841–1904) U.S. financier and politician. As U.S. secretary of the navy (1885–89), he laid the basis for the modern "steel navy."

Whit·ta·ker |'(h)witikər|, Charles Evans (1901–73) U.S. Supreme Court justice (1957–62).

Whit·ti·er |'(h)witēər|, John Greenleaf (1807–92) U.S. poet and abolitionist. He is best known for his poems on rural themes, especially "Snow-Bound" (1866).

Whit·ting·ton |'(h)witiNGtən|, Dick (*c.* 1358–1423) English merchant and Lord Mayor of London; full name *Sir Richard Whittington*. He was a dry goods merchant who became Lord Mayor three times (1397–98; 1406–07; 1419–20). The legend of his early life as a poor orphan was first recorded in 1605.

Whit·tle |'(h)witl|, Sir Frank (1907–96) English aeronautical engineer, test pilot, and inventor of the jet aircraft engine. He took out the first patent for a turbojet engine in 1930, and in 1941 the first flight using Whittle's jet engine was made.

Whit·worth |'(h)wit,wərTH|, Kathy (1939–) U.S. golfer. She is a seven-time LPGA Player of the Year.

Whorf |wawrf|, Benjamin Lee (1897–1941) U.S. linguist and insurance executive, known for his contribution to the Sapir-Whorf hypothesis, which states that the structure of a language influences the culture in which it is spoken.

Whym·per |'(h)wimpər|, Edward (1840–1911) English mountaineer. After seven attempts he finally succeeded in climbing the Matterhorn in 1865, but on the way down, four of his fellow climbers fell to their deaths.

Wide·man |'wīdmən|, John Edgar (1941–) U.S. author. Notable works: *Fatheralong: A Meditation on Father and Sons, Race and Society* (1994).

Wie·ner |'wēnər|, Norbert (1894–1964) American mathematician. He is best known for establishing the science of cybernetics in the late 1940s. Wiener made major contributions to the study of stochastic processes, integral equations, harmonic analysis, and related fields.

Wie·sel |vē'zel|, Elie (1928–) Romanian-born U.S. human rights campaigner, novelist, and academic; full name *Eliezer Wiesel*. A survivor of Auschwitz and Buchenwald concentration camps, Wiesel became an authority on the Holocaust, documenting and publicizing Nazi war crimes. Nobel Peace Prize (1986).

Wie·sen·thal |'vēzən,täl; 'wēzən,THäl|, Simon (1908–) Austrian Jewish investigator of Nazi war crimes. After spending three years in concentration camps, he began a campaign to bring Nazi war criminals to justice, tracing some 1,000 unprosecuted criminals, including Adolf Eichmann.

Wig·gin |'wigən|, Kate Douglas (1856–1923) U.S. author. Notable works: *Rebecca of Sunnybrook Farm* (1903).

Wig·gles·worth |'wigəlz,wərTH|, Michael (1631–1705) U.S. clergyman and poet, born in England. Notable works include the theological poem *The Day of Doom* (1662).

Wig·more |'wig,mawr|, John Henry (1863–1943) U.S. legal scholar. The dean of the law faculty at Northwestern University (1901–29), he wrote the *Treatise on the Anglo-American System of Evidence* (1904–5).

Wig·ner |'wignər|, Eugene Paul (1902–) U.S. mathematical physicist, born in Hungary. He formulated the laws governing the mechanics of nuclear

particles and shared a Nobel Prize with Maria Mayer and J. H. D. Jensen (1963).

Wil·ber·force |'wilbər,fawrs|, William (1759–1833) English politician and social reformer. He was a prominent campaigner for the abolition of the slave trade, his efforts resulting in its outlawing in the British West Indies (1807) and in the 1833 Slavery Abolition Act.

Wil·bur |'wilbər|, Richard (Purdy) (1921–) U.S. poet and professor. Poet Laureate of the U.S., 1987–88. Notable works: *Things of This World* (1956, Pulitzer Prize), *New and Collected Poems* (1988), and *Runaway Opposites* (1995).

Wil·cox |'wil,käks|, Ella Wheeler (1850–1919) U.S. poet, novelist, and short-story writer. She wrote many volumes of romantic verse, the most successful one being *Poems of Passion* (1883).

Wilde |wīld|, Oscar (Fingal O'Flahertie Wills) (1854–1900) Irish dramatist, novelist, poet, and wit. His advocacy of "art for art's sake" is evident in his only novel, *The Picture of Dorian Gray* (1890). As a dramatist he achieved success with the comedies *Lady Windermere's Fan* (1892) and *The Importance of Being Earnest* (1895). Wilde was imprisoned (1895–97) for homosexual offenses and died in exile.

Wil·der |'wildər|, Billy (1906–) Austrian-born U.S. movie director and screenwriter; born *Samuel Wilder*. He earned recognition as a writer-director with the *film noir* classic *Double Indemnity* (1944). Other movies include *Sunset Boulevard* (1950), *Some Like It Hot* (1959), and *The Apartment* (1960), which won three Oscars.

Wil·der |'wildər|, Gene (1935–) U.S. actor. Born *Jerome Silberman*. He cowrote and starred in *Young Frankenstein* (1974) and *Blazing Saddles* (1973).

Wil·der |'wildər|, Laura Ingalls (1867–1957) U.S. author. Notable works: *Little House on the Prairie* (1935).

Wil·der |'wildər|, Thornton (Niven) (1897–1975) U.S. novelist and dramatist. He won several Pulitzer Prizes. Notable works: *The Bridge of San Luis Rey* (novel, 1927), *Our Town* (play, 1938), and *Skin of Our Teeth* (play, 1942).

Wil·helm I |'vil,helm| (1797–1888) king of Prussia (1861–88) and emperor of

Germany (1871–88). His reign saw the unification of Germany. He became the first emperor of Germany after Prussia's victory against France in 1871. The latter part of his reign was marked by the rise of German socialism, to which he responded with harsh, repressive measures.

Wil·helm II |'vil,helm| (1859–1941) emperor of Germany 1888–1918, grandson of Wilhelm I and also of Queen Victoria; known as **Kaiser Wilhelm**. After forcing Bismarck to resign in 1890, he proved unable to exercise a strong or consistent influence over German policies. He was vilified by Allied propaganda as the instigator of the First World War. In 1918 he abdicated and went into exile.

Wil·hel·mi·na |,vilhel'mēnə| (1880–1962) queen of the Netherlands 1890–1948. During World War II she maintained a government in exile in London and through frequent radio broadcasts became a symbol of resistance among the Dutch people. She returned to the Netherlands in 1945.

Wil·kens |'wilkənz|, Lenny (1937–) U.S. basketball player and coach. He was inducted into the Basketball Hall of Fame in 1988.

Wilkes |wilks|, Charles (1798–1877) U.S. naval officer. He was the surveyor who determined that Antarctica is a continent (1838–42); Wilkes Land was named in his honor.

Wil·kie |'wilkē|, Sir David (1785–1841) Scottish painter. He made his name with the painting *Village Politicians* (1806). His style contributed to the growing prestige of genre painting.

Wil·kins |'wilkənz|, Maurice Hugh Frederick (1916–) New Zealand-born British biochemist and molecular biologist. From X-ray diffraction analysis of DNA, he and his colleague Rosalind Franklin confirmed the double helix structure proposed by Francis Crick and James Watson in 1953. Nobel Prize for Physiology or Medicine (1962, shared with Crick and Watson).

Wil·kins |'wilkənz|, Roy (1901–81) U.S. civil rights leader. He served as executive secretary of the NAACP (1955–77). Presidential Medal of Freedom, 1969.

Will |wil|, George F. (1941–) U.S. journalist. A columnist and television commentator, he won a Pulitzer Prize for commentary (1977).

Wil·lard |'wilərd|, Archibald MacNeal (1836–1918) U.S. painter. His *Yankee Doodle, or the Spirit of '76* was exhibited at the Centennial exposition in Philadelphia (1876).

Wil·lard |'wilərd|, Emma (1787–1870) U.S. educational reformer. She founded a boarding school in Vermont (1814) to teach subjects not then available to women, such as mathematics and philosophy. The school moved to New York (1821) as the Troy Female Seminary; it served as a model for subsequent women's colleges in the U.S. and Europe.

Wil·lard |'wilərd|, Frances Elizabeth Caroline (1839–98) U.S. women's rights and temperance activist. She was president of the Women's Christian Temperance Union (1879) and an organizer of the Prohibition party.

Wil·lard |'wilərd|, Frank (1893–1958) U.S. cartoonist. He created the comic strip "Moon Mullins" in the early 1920s.

Wil·liam |'wilyəm| (*c.* 1027–87) the name of two kings of England and two of Great Britain and Ireland: **William I** (*c.* 1027–87), reigned 1066–87, the first Norman king of England; known as **William the Conqueror**. He invaded England and defeated Harold II at the Battle of Hastings (1066). He introduced Norman institutions and customs (including feudalism) and instigated the Domesday Book. **William II** (*c.* 1060–1100), son of William I, reigned 1087–1100; known as **William Rufus**. William crushed rebellions in 1088 and 1095 and also campaigned against his brother Robert, Duke of Normandy (1089–96), ultimately acquiring the duchy. He was killed by an arrow while out hunting. **William III** (1650–1702), grandson of Charles I, husband of Mary II, reigned 1689–1702; known as **William of Orange**. In 1688 he deposed James II at the invitation of disaffected politicians and, having accepted the Declaration of Rights, was crowned along with his wife Mary.

William IV (1765–1837), son of George III, reigned 1830–37; known as **the Sailor King**. Having served in the Royal Navy, he came to the throne after the death of his brother George IV. In 1834 he intervened in political affairs by imposing the Conservative Robert Peel as Prime Minister, despite a Whig majority in Parliament.

Wil·liam I |'wilyəm| (1143–1214) grandson of David I, king of Scotland (1165–1214); known as **William the Lion**. He attempted to reassert Scottish independence but was forced to pay homage to Henry II of England after being captured by him in 1174.

Wil·liam I |'wilyəm| (1533–84) prince of the House of Orange, chief magistrate of the United Provinces of the Netherlands (1572–84); known as **William the Silent**. He led a revolt against Spain from 1568 and was assassinated by a Spanish agent.

Wil·liam of Oc·cam |'wilyəm əv 'äkəm| (c. 1285–1349) English philosopher and Franciscan friar. Also **Ockham**. He is known for the maxim called "Occam's razor," which states that in explaining a thing, no more assumptions should be made than are necessary.

Wil·liam of Orange |'wilyəm| William III of Great Britain and Ireland (see WILLIAM).

Wil·liam Rufus |'wilyəm 'rōōfəs| William II of of England (see WILLIAM).

Wil·liams |'wilyəmz| U.S. country singers and songwriters: **Hank Williams** (1923–53); born *Hiram King Williams*. He had the first of many country hits, "Lovesick Blues," in 1949; "Your Cheatin' Heart" (recorded 1952) was released after his sudden death. **Hank Williams, Jr.**, his son. Notable songs: "Texas Women" (1981).

Wil·liams |'wilyəmz|, Cootie (1911–85) U.S. jazz trumpeter and band leader. Full name *Charles Melvin Williams*. He performed with Duke Ellington (1929–40), who was inpired by his playing to write "Concerto for Cootie" (1940) and "New Concerto for Cootie" (1963).

Wil·liams |'wilyəmz|, Daniel Hale (1858–1931) U.S. physician. He performed one of the first two open-heart operations (1893) and was the first African American elected as a fellow of the American College of Surgeons.

Wil·liams |'wilyəmz|, Ephraim (1714–55) U.S. army officer. He served as captain of the Massachusetts militia patrolling the northern Massachusetts border. He bequeathed funds for the school that became Williams College.

Wil·liams |'wilyəmz|, Jody (1950–) U.S. political activst. She won a Nobel Peace Prize in 1997 for her work to ban landmines.

Wil·liams |'wilyəmz|, John (1664–1729) U.S. clergyman and author. He was taken captive by Indians and ransomed (1706); after his release he wrote *The Redeemed Captive Returning to Zion* (1707).

Wil·liams |'wilyəmz|, John Towner (1932–) U.S. composer and conductor. He conducted the Boston Pops Orchestra (1980–98) and wrote the movie scores to *Jaws*, the *Star Wars* trilogy, *Raiders of the Lost Ark*, and *Close Encounters of the Third Kind*.

Wil·liams |'wilyəmz|, J. R. (1888–1957) U.S. cartoonist, born in Canada. Full name *James Robert Williams*. He created the panel "Out Our Way" in 1922.

Wil·liams |'wilyəmz|, Mary Lou (1914–81) U.S. jazz pianist and composer. She composed "Trumpet No End" (1946) for Duke Ellington; her sacred works include *Christ of the Andes* (1963) and three masses.

Wil·liams |'wilyəmz|, Robert R., Jr. (1886–1965) Indian inventor. He synthesized Vitamin B₁.

Wil·liams |'wilyəmz|, Robin (1952–) U.S. actor. His stage, television, and film credits include *Dead Poets Society* (1989) and *Mrs. Doubtfire* (1993).

Wil·liams |'wilyəmz|, Roger (c. 1603–83) American clergyman and founder of Rhode Island (1644).

Wil·liams |'wilyəmz|, Ted (1918–) U.S. baseball player. Full name *Theodore Samuel Williams*. He was the last player to bat over .400 for a season (1941). Elected to the Baseball Hall of Fame (1966).

Wil·liams |'wilyəmz|, Tennessee (1911–83) U.S. dramatist; born *Thomas Lanier Williams*. He achieved success with *The*

Glass Menagerie (1944) and *A Streetcar Named Desire* (1947), which deal with the tragedy of vulnerable heroines living in fragile fantasy worlds shattered by brutal reality. Other notable works: *Cat on a Hot Tin Roof* (1955) and *The Night of the Iguana* (1962).

Wil·liams |'wilyəmz|, William Carlos (1883–1963) U.S. physician and writer. His poetry is characterized by avoidance of emotional content and the use of American vernacular. Collections include *Spring and All* (1923).

Wil·liam-son |'wilyəmsən|, Henry (1895–1977) English novelist. His works include *Tarka the Otter* (1927) and the fifteen-volume semi-autobiographical sequence *A Chronicle of Ancient Sunlight* (1951–69).

Wi·liam the Conqueror |'wilyəm| William I of England (see WILLIAM).

Will·kie |'wilkē|, Wendell Lewis (1882–1944) U.S. politician and lawyer. He was a Republican presidential candidate (1940).

Wills |wilz|, Bob (1905–75) U.S. country singer, bandleader, and songwriter. Full name *Robert James Wills*. His group, the Texas Playboys, popularized western swing.

Wil·son |'wilsən|, Sir Angus (Frank Johnstone) (1913–91) English novelist and short-story writer. His works display his satiric wit, acute social observation, and a love of the macabre and the farcical. Notable novels: *The Old Men at the Zoo* (1961).

Wil·son |'wilsən|, August (1945–) U.S. author and playwright. Notable works: *Fences* (1986, Pulitzer Prize), *The Piano Lesson* (1990, Pulitzer Prize), and *Seven Guitars* (1996).

Wil·son |'wilsən|, Brian (1942–) U.S. rock musician. He popularized the California surfing sound of the Beach Boys, which he formed in 1961 with his brothers Dennis Wilson (1944–83) and Carl Wilson (1946–).

Wil·son |'wilsən|, Charles Thomson Rees (1869–1959) Scottish physicist. He is chiefly remembered for inventing the cloud chamber, which became a major tool of particle physicists. Nobel Prize for Physics (1927).

Wil·son |'wilsən|, Edmund (1895–1972) U.S. critic, essayist, and short-story writer. He is remembered chiefly for works of literary and social criticism, including *Axel's Castle* (1931), *To the Finland Station* (1940), and *Patriotic Gore: Studies in the Literature of the American Civil War* (1962).

Wil·son |'wilsən|, Edward Osborne (1929–) American social biologist. He has worked principally on social insects, extrapolating his findings to the social behavior of other animals including humans. Notable works: *Sociobiology: the New Synthesis* (1975).

Wil·son |'wilsən|, Gahan (1930–) U.S. cartoonist and author. His macabre cartoons were mainly published in *Playboy* magazine.

Wil·son |'wilsən|, (James) Harold, Baron Wilson of Rievaulx (1916–95) British Labour statesman, prime minister (1964–70 and 1974–76). In both terms of office he faced severe economic problems. His government introduced a number of social reforms and renegotiated Britain's terms of entry into the European Economic Community, which was confirmed after a referendum in 1975.

Wil·son |'wilsən|, Harriet (1808–c. 1870) U.S. author. She wrote *Our Nig: Sketches from the Life of a Free Black, in a Two-Story White House, North, Showing That Slavery's Shadows Fall Even There* (1859), the first novel by an African American published in the U.S.

Wil·son |'wilsən|, Harry Leon (1867–1939) U.S. author. Notable works: *Merton of the Movies* (1922).

Wil·son |'wilsən|, Henry (1812–75) U.S. politician. Born *Jeremiah Jones Colbath*. He was a founder of the Republican party, a member of the U.S. Senate from Massachusetts (1855–73), and vice president of the U.S. (1873–75).

Wil·son |'wilsən|, James (1742–98) U.S. Supreme Court justice (1789–98).

Wil·son |'wilsən|, John Tuzo (1908–93) Canadian geophysicist. Wilson was a pioneer in the study of plate tectonics, introducing the term *plate* in this context and identifying transform faults.

Wil·son |'wilsən|, Lanford (1937–) U.S. playwright. Notable works: *Talley's Folly* (1979, Pulitzer Prize).

Wilson, Woodrow
28th U.S. president

Life dates: 1856–1924
Place of birth: Staunton, Virginia
Mother: Janet (Jessie) Woodrow Wilson
Father: Joseph Ruggles Wilson
Wives: Ellen Louise Axson Wilson (died 1914); Edith Bolling Galt Wilson (married 1915)
Children: Margaret, Jessie Woodrow, Eleanor
College/University: Princeton University; University of Virginia Law School; Johns Hopkins University
Career: Lawyer; professor
Political career: governor of New Jersey
Party: Democratic
Home state: New Jersey
Opponents in presidential races: William Howard Taft, Theodore Roosevelt; Charles Evans Hughes
Term of office: March 4, 1913–March 3, 1921
Vice president: Thomas R. Marshall
Notable events of presidency: Federal Reserve Act; Federal Trade Commission established; Clayton Anti-Trust Act; World War I; sinking of the *Lusitania*; Fourteen Points speech to Congress; 18th Amendment to the Constitution ratified (Prohibition)
Other achievements: Ph.D. in political science from Johns Hopkins University; president, Princeton University; awarded 1919 Nobel Peace Prize
Place of burial: Washington, D.C.

Wil·son |'wilsən|, Nancy Sue (1937–) U.S. jazz and pop singer.

Wil·son |'wilsən|, Teddy (1912–86) U.S. jazz pianist. Full name *Theodore Shaw Wilson*. He performed with Benny Goodman (1935–39).

Wil·son |'wilsən|, Tom (1931–) U.S. cartoonist. He created the cartoon character Ziggy.

Wil·son |'wilsən| (Thomas) Woodrow, see box. **Ellen Louise Axson Wilson** (1860–1914), wife of Woodrow Wilson and U.S. first lady (1913–14). **Edith Bolling Galt Wilson** (1872–1961), wife of Woodrow Wilson and U.S. first lady (1915–21).

Winck·el·mann |'viNGkəl,män|, Johann (Joachim) (1717–68) German archaeologist and art historian, born in Prussia. He took part in the excavations at Pompeii and Herculaneum and his best-known work, *History of the Art of Antiquity* (1764), was particularly influential in popularizing the art and culture of ancient Greece.

Wind·ing, Kai (1922–83) U.S. jazz trombonist, born in Denmark.

Wind·sor, Duke of |'winzər|, the title conferred on Edward VIII on his abdication in 1936.

Wines |winz|, Enoch Cobb (1806–79) U.S. reformer. He tried to make prisons into places of reform and correction instead of punishment.

Win·frey |'winfrē|, Oprah (1954–) U.S. actress and television talk show host. She began her confessional-style "Oprah Winfrey Show" in 1986.

Win·ston |'winstən|, Harry (1896–1978) U.S. businessman. He founded a famous jewelry store in New York City.

Win·ter·hal·ter |'vintər,hältər|, Franz Xaver (1806–73) German painter. He painted many portraits of European royalty and aristocracy.

Win·ter·son |'wintərsən|, Jeanette (1959–) English writer. She has received several honors for her fiction, including a Whitbread Award (1985).

Win·throp |'winTHrəp|, American colonists and politicians, born in England: **John Winthrop** (1588–1649) was the first governor of the Massachusetts Bay Colony (from 1629). **John Winthrop, Jr.**, his eldest son (1606–76), was an early astronomer and the governor of Connecticut (1657, 1659–76).

Win·throp |'winTHrəp|, John (1714–79) U.S. astronomer and physicist. He was the first American to practice rigorous experimental science, predicting the return of Halley's Comet in 1759 and giving laboratory demonstrations of electricity (1746). He was descended from Governor John Winthrop.

Win·tour |'wintər|, Anna (1949–) U.S. journalist, born in England. She was creative director of *Vogue* (1983–86) and editor of *House and Garden* (1987–88).

Win·wood |'win,wŏŏd|, Steve (1948–) British pop musician. Notable songs: "Higher Love" (1986, Grammy Award).

Wise |wīz|, Isaac Mayer (1819–1900) U.S. rabbi and scholar, born in Germany. Born *Isaac Mayer Weis*. He founded Reformed Judaism in the U.S. and established Hebrew Union College (1875).

Wise |wīz|, John (1652–1725) American clergyman. He was a Congregational pastor in Ipswich, Massachusetts, who opposed the Mathers' attempts to regulate churches. Notable works: *A Vindication of the Government of New England Churches* (1717).

Wis·sler |'wislər|, Clark (1870–1947) U.S. anthropologist and author. He was the curator of the American Museum of Natural History (1906–41).

Wis·tar |'wistər|, Caspar (1761–1818) U.S. educator and author. He was a professor of anatomy at the University of Pennsylvania and a leader in the intellectual life of Philadelphia; the genus *Wisteria* was named for him.

With·er·spoon |'wiTHər,spōōn|, John (1723–94) colonial American clergyman and educator, born in Scotland. As president of the College of New Jersey (now Princeton University) (1768–94), he was a signer of the Declaration of Independence and a member of the Continental Congress (1776–79, 1780–81).

Witt |vit|, Katarina (1965–) German figure skater. A four-time world champion, she won Olympic gold medals for East Germany in 1984 and 1988.

Witt·gen·stein |'vitgən,SHtīn|, Ludwig (Josef Johann) (1889–1951) British philosopher, born in Austria. His two major works, *Tractatus Logico-Philosophicus* (1921) and *Philosophical Investigations* (1953), examine language and its relationship to the world.

Władysław II see LADISLAUS II.

Wode·house |'wŏŏd,hows|, Sir P. G. (1881–1975) English writer; full name *Pelham Grenville Wodehouse*. His best-known works are humorous stories of the upper-class world of Bertie Wooster and his valet, Jeeves.

Wolf |wŏŏlf|, Hugo (Philipp Jakob) (1860–1903) Austrian composer. He is chiefly known as a composer of lieder, some of which are settings of Goethe and Heinrich Heine.

Wolfe |wŏŏlf|, James (1727–59) British general. One of the leaders of the expedition sent to seize French Canada, he commanded the attack on the French capital, Quebec (1759). He was fatally wounded while leading his troops to victory on the Plains of Abraham, the scene of the battle that led to British control of Canada.

Wolfe |wŏŏlf|, Thomas (Clayton) (1900–38) U.S. novelist. His intense, romantic works, including his first, autobiographical novel, *Look Homeward Angel* (1929), dwell idealistically on America. Other notable works: *Of Time and the River* (1935), *The Web and the Rock* (1938), and *You Can't Go Home Again* (1940).

Wolfe |wŏŏlf|, Tom (1931–) U.S. writer; born *Thomas Kennerley Wolfe, Jr.* Having been a news reporter for the *Washington Post* and the *Herald Tribune*, he examined contemporary American culture in *The Electric Kool-Aid Acid Test* (1968), the novel *The Bonfire of the Vanities* (1988), and *A Man in Full* (1998).

Wolff |wŏŏlf|, Tobias (1945–) U.S. author. Notable works: *This Boy's Life: A Memoir* (1989).

Wolf·man Jack see SMITH, ROBERT WESTON.

Wol·las·ton |'wŏŏləstən|, William Hyde (1766–1828) English chemist and physicist. He discovered palladium and rhodium, and pioneered techniques in powder metallurgy. Wollaston also demonstrated that static and current electricity were the same, invented a kind of slide rule for use in chemistry, and was the first to observe the dark lines in the solar spectrum.

Woll·stone·craft |'wŏŏlstən,kræft|, Mary (1759–97) English writer and feminist, of Irish descent. Her best-known work, *A Vindication of the Rights of Woman* (1792), defied assumptions about male supremacy and championed educational equality for women. In 1797 she married William Godwin and died shortly after giving birth to their daughter, Mary Shelley.

Wol·per |'wŏlpər|, David Lloyd (1928–) U.S. movie and television executive. He is the president of Wolper Pictures, Ltd. (1958–) and an executive producer at Warner Bros., Inc. (1976–).

Wol·sey |'wŏŏlzē|, Thomas (*c.* 1474–1530) English prelate and statesman; known as **Cardinal Wolsey**. Wolsey dominated foreign and domestic policy in the early part of Henry VIII's reign, but incurred royal displeasure through his failure to secure the papal dispensation necessary for Henry's divorce from Catherine of Aragon. He was arrested on a charge of treason and died on his way to trial.

Won·der |'wəndər|, Stevie (1950–) U.S. singer, songwriter, and musician; born *Steveland Judkins Morris*. His repertoire has included soul, rock, funk, and romantic ballads, as heard on albums such as *Innervisions* (1973). He has been blind since birth.

Wood |wŏŏd|, Mrs. Henry (1814–87) English novelist; born *Ellen Price*. Her ingenious and sensational plots about murders, thefts, and forgeries make her one of the forerunners of the modern detective novelist. Notable works: *East Lynne* (1861).

Wood |wŏŏd|, Sir Henry (Joseph) (1869–1944) English conductor. In 1895 he instituted the first of the Promenade Concerts, which he conducted every year until he died. He arranged the *Fantasia on British Sea Songs* (including "Rule, Britannia").

Wood |wŏŏd|, Grant De Volsen (1892–1942) U.S. artist. Notable paintings: *American Gothic* (1930) and *Daughters of Revolution* (1932).

Wood |wŏŏd|, Natalie (1938–81) U.S. actress. She played the vulnerable adolescent heroine of *Rebel Without A Cause* (1955) and similar roles in *Cry in the Night* (1956), *West Side Story* (1961), and *Inside Daisy Clover* (1966).

Wood·bu·ry |'wŏŏd,berē; 'wŏŏdbərē|, Levi (1789–1851) U.S. Supreme Court justice (1845–51).

Wood·en |'wŏŏdn|, John (1910–) U.S. college basketball player and coach. He coached UCLA to ten national titles.

Woods |wŏŏdz|, Granville T. (1856–1910) U.S. inventor. He invented the air brake and the third-rail system now used in subways.

Woods |wŏŏdz|, Rose Mary (1917–) U.S. government employee. She was Richard Nixon's personal secretary (1951–75) and is best known for her role in the Watergate coverup.

Woods |wŏŏdz|, Tiger (1975–) U.S. golfer; born *Eldrick Woods*.

Woods |wŏŏdz|, William Burnham (1824–87) U.S. Supreme Court justice (1880–87).

Wood·son |'wŏŏdsən|, Carter Godwin (1875–1950) U.S. historian. He founded the Association for the Study of Negro Life and History (1916).

Wood·ward |'wŏŏdwərd|, C. Vann (1908–) U.S. historian of the American South. Full name *Comer Vann Woodward*. Notable works: *Oxford History of the U.S.* (11 vols., 1982–) and *Mary Chesnut's Civil War* (1981, Pulitzer Prize).

Wood·ward |'wŏŏdwərd|, Joanne (1930–) U.S. actress. Notable movies: *The Three Faces of Eve* (1957, Academy Award)

Wood·ward |'wŏŏdwərd|, Robert Burns (1917–79) American organic chemist. He was the first to synthesize quinine, cholesterol, chlorophyll, and vitamin B_{12}, and with the Polish-born American chemist **Roald Hoffmann**, (1937–) discovered symmetry-based rules governing the course of rearrangement reactions involving cyclic intermediates. Nobel Prize for Chemistry (1965).

Wood·ward |'wŏŏdwərd|, Robert Upshur (1943–) U.S. journalist. He was assistant managing editor of *The Washington Post* (1981–) and co-author with Carl Bernstein of *All the President's Men* (1974).

Woolf |wŏŏlf|, Virginia (1882–1941) English novelist, essayist, and critic; born *Adeline Virginia Stephen*. A member of the Bloomsbury Group, she gained recognition with *Jacob's Room* (1922). Subsequent novels, such as *Mrs. Dalloway* (1925) and *To the Lighthouse* (1927), characterized by their poetic Impressionism, established her as an exponent of modernism.

Wooll·cott |'wŏŏlkət|, Alexander (Humphreys) (1887–1943) U.S. critic and actor. *The Man Who Came to Din-*

ner, a play by Moss Hart and George S. Kaufman, is based on the character of Woollcott, who appeared in the leading role (1939).

Wool·ley |'woŏlē|, Sir (Charles) Leonard (1880–1960) British archaeologist. He directed a British-American excavation of the Sumerian city of Ur (1922–34), which uncovered rich royal tombs and thousands of clay tablets.

Wool·worth |'woŏl,wərTH|, Frank Winfield (1852–1919) U.S. businessman. He pioneered the concept of low-priced retailing in 1878 and from this built a large international chain of stores.

Worces·ter |'woŏstər|, Joseph Emerson (1784–1865) U.S. lexicographer. He published gazetteers and school texts (mainly dictionaries); his dictionary rivaled that of Noah Webster.

Words·worth |'wərdz,wərTH|, William (1770–1850) English poet. Much of his work was inspired by the geography of England's Lake District. His *Lyrical Ballads* (1798), which was composed with Samuel Taylor Coleridge and included "Tintern Abbey," was a landmark in Romanticism. Other notable poems: "I Wandered Lonely as a Cloud" (sonnet, 1815), and *The Prelude* (1850). He was appointed Poet Laureate in 1843.

Worth |wərTH|, Charles Frederick (1825–95) English couturier, resident in France from 1845. Regarded as the founder of Parisian *haute couture*, he is noted for designing gowns with crinolines and for introducing the bustle.

Wouk |wōk; woŏk|, Herman (1915–) U.S. author. Notable novels: *The Caine Mutiny: A Novel of World War II* (1951), *Marjorie Morningstar* (1955), and *The Winds of War* (1971).

Woz·ni·ak |'wäznē,æk|, Steve (1950–) U.S. inventor. With Steve Jobs he created the first successful personal computer.

Wren |ren|, Sir Christopher (1632–1723) English architect. Following the Fire of London (1666), Wren was responsible for the design of the new St. Paul's Cathedral (1675–1711) and many of the city's churches. Other works include the Greenwich Observatory (1675) and a partial rebuilding of Hampton Court (1689–94).

Wren |ren|, P. C. (1885–1941) English novelist; full name *Percival Christopher Wren*. He is best known for his romantic adventure stories dealing with life in the French Foreign Legion, the first of which was *Beau Geste* (1924).

Wright |rīt|, Elizur (1804–85) U.S. reformer and actuary. As the Massachusetts commissioner of insurance (1858–66), he lobbied the state legislature for reform of life insurance practices.

Wright |rīt|, Fanny (1795–1852) U.S. reformer, born in Scotland. Born *Frances Wright*. With Robert Dale Owen she published the *Free Enquirer* from 1829, and she was active in the U.S. women's rights movement.

Wright |rīt|, Frank Lloyd (1869–1959) U.S. architect. His "prairie-style" houses revolutionized American domestic architecture. He advocated an "organic" architecture, characterized by a close relationship among building, landscape, and the materials used. Notable buildings include the Kaufmann House, which incorporated a waterfall, in Pennsylvania (1935–39) and the Guggenheim Museum of Art in New York (1956–59).

Wright |rīt|, Mickey (1935–) U.S. golfer.

Wright |rīt|, Orville (1871–1948) U.S. aviation pioneer. In 1903 he and his brother **Wilbur Wright** (1867–1912) were the first to make brief, powered, sustained and controlled flights in an airplane, which they had designed and built themselves. They were also the first to make and fly a fully practical powered airplane (1905) and a passenger-carrying airplane (1908).

Wright |rīt|, Richard Nathaniel (1908–60) U.S. author. Notable novels: *Native Son* (1940) and *The Long Dream* (1958). Notable nonfiction: *Black Power* (1954) and *White Man, Listen!* (1957).

Wright |rīt|, Sewall (1889–1988) U.S. geneticist and mathematician. He developed the concept of genetic drift known as the Sewall Wright effect.

Wright |rīt|, Willard Huntington (1888–1939) U.S. author. Pseudonym **S. S. Van Dine**. He created the master sleuth

Philo Vance, who appeared in various novels, including *The Benson Murder Case* (1926).

Wrig·ley |'riglē|, William, Jr. (1861–1932) U.S. businessman. He began as a manufacturer's sales representative for his father's soap company, giving free gum as an incentive; in 1891 he went into business for himself manufacturing chewing gum.

Wurde·mann |'wərdmən|, Audrey (1911–60) U.S. poet and novelist. Notable works: *Splendor in the Grass* (1936) and *Bright Ambush* (1934, Pulitzer Prize). She was wife of Joseph Auslander.

Wur·lit·zer |'wərlitsər|, Rudolph (1831–1914) U.S. businessman, born in Germany. He introduced the jukebox in 1934 and founded Wurlitzer Instruments.

Wurst·er |'wərstər|, William (1895–1973) U.S. architect. Notable designs: Ghirardelli Square (San Francisco).

Wy·att |'wīət|, James (1746–1813) English architect. He was both a neoclassicist and a leading figure in the Gothic revival, the latter seen most notably in his design for Fonthill Abbey in Wiltshire (1796–1807).

Wy·att |'wīət|, Sir Thomas (1503–42) English poet. He went to Italy (1527) as a diplomat in the service of Henry VIII; this visit probably stimulated his translation of Petrarch. His work also includes sonnets, rondeaux, songs for the lute, and satires.

Wych·er·ley |'wiCHərlē|, William (*c.* 1640–1716) English dramatist. His Restoration comedies are characterized by their acute examination of sexual morality and marriage conventions. Notable works: *The Country Wife* (1675).

Wyc·liffe |'wiklif; 'wīklif|, John (*c.* 1330–84) English religious reformer. Also **Wycliffe**. He criticized the wealth and power of the Church and upheld the Bible as the sole guide for doctrine; his teachings were disseminated by itinerant preachers and are regarded as precursors of the Reformation. Wyclif instituted the first English translation of the complete Bible. His followers were known as Lollards.

Wy·eth |'wīəTH|, U.S. family of artists: **N. C. Wyeth** (1882–1945); full name *Newell Convers Wyeth*. He created thousands of oil-paint illustrations, which appeared in countless publications, including such classic novels as Daniel Defoe's *Robinson Crusoe*, Robert Louis Stevenson's *Treasure Island*, and James Fenimore Cooper's *The Deerslayer*. **Andrew Newell Wyeth** (1917–), his son. Notable paintings: *Christina's World* (1948) and The Helga Pictures (a series, 1971–85). **Jamie Wyeth** (1946–), son of Andrew Newell Wyeth; full name *James Browning Wyeth*. Notable paintings: *Portrait of J.F.K.* (1965) and *Wolfbane* (1984).

Wy·ler |'wīlər|, William (1902–81) U.S. director. Notable movies: *Mrs. Miniver* (1942, Academy Award).

Wy·lie |'wīlē|, Eleanor (Hoyt) (1885–1928) U.S. poet and novelist. Notable works: *Nets To Catch the Wind* (1921).

Wynd·ham |'windəm|, John (1903–69) English writer of science fiction; pseudonym of *John Wyndham Parkes Lucas Beynon Harris*. His fiction often examines the psychological impact of catastrophe. Notable novels: *The Day of the Triffids* (1951), *The Chrysalids* (1955), and *The Midwich Cuckoos* (1957).

Wy·nette |wī'net|, Tammy (1942–98) U.S. country singer; born *Tammy Wynette Pugh*. Her unique lamenting voice brought her success with songs such as "Apartment No. 9" (1966) and "Stand by Your Man" (1968).

Wythe |wiTH|, George (1726–1806) colonial American jurist and statesman. He was a signer of the Declaration of Independence and a judge in the Virginia high court of chancery (1778–1806).

Xx

Xan·thip·pe |zæn'tipē| (5th century BC) wife of the philosopher Socrates. Also **Xantippe**. Her allegedly bad-tempered behavior toward her husband has made her proverbial as a shrew.

Xa·vi·er |'zāveər|, St. Francis (1506–52) Spanish Catholic missionary; known as **the Apostle of the Indies**. One of the original seven Jesuits, from 1540 he traveled to southern India, Sri Lanka, Malacca, the Moluccas, and Japan, makng thousands of converts. Feast day, December 3.

Xe·na·kis |zə'näkis|, Iannis (1922–) French composer and architect, of Greek descent. He is noted for his use of electronic and aleatory techniques in music.

Xe·noph·a·nes |zə'näfə,nēz| (c. 570–c. 480 BC) Greek philosopher. A member of the Eleatic school, he argued for a form of pantheism, criticizing belief in anthropomorphic gods.

Xen·o·phon |'zenəfən| (c. 435–c. 354 BC) Greek historian, writer, and military leader. From 401 he fought with Cyrus the Younger against Artaxerxes II, and led an army of 10,000 Greek mercenaries in their retreat of about 900 miles (1,500 km) after Cyrus was killed; the campaign and retreat are recorded in the *Anabasis*. Other notable writings include the *Hellenica*, a history of Greece.

Xer·xes I |'zərk,sēz| (c. 519–465 BC) son of Darius I, king of Persia 486–465. His invasion of Greece achieved victories in 480 at Artemisium and Thermopylae, but defeats at Salamis (480) and Plataea (479) forced him to withdraw.

Yy

Yale |yāl|, Elihu (1649–1721) English colonial administrator. Because of his gift of books and goods to the Collegiate School in Saybrook, Connecticut, the school changed its name to Yale College (1718).

Yale |yāl|, Linus (1821–68) U.S. inventor and manufacturer. He invented the pin tumbler cylinder lock and the combination lock, and he founded the Yale Lock Manufacturing Co. (1868).

Ya·ma·gu·chi |ˌyäməˈgo͞ocHē|, Kristi (1971–) U.S. figure skater. In 1992 she won national, world, and Olympic titles.

Ya·ma·mo·to |ˌyäməˈmōtō|, Isoroku (1884–1943) Japanese admiral. As commander in chief of the Combined Fleet (air and naval forces) from 1939, he was responsible for planning the Japanese attack on Pearl Harbor (1941).

Ya·ma·sa·ki |ˌyäməˈsäkē|, Minoru (1912–86) U.S. architect. He designed the influential barrel-vaulted St. Louis Municipal Airport Terminal (1956) and the World Trade Center in New York (1972).

Yan·cey |ˈyænsē|, Jimmy (1894–1951) U.S. jazz pianist. Full name *James Edward Yancey*. He appeared with his wife, Mama Yancey, at Carnegie Hall in 1948.

Yang |yäNG|, Chen Ning (1922–) U.S. physicist, born in China. He shared the 1957 Nobel Prize for Physics with Tsun-Dao Lee for his discovery that parity is not conserved in the weak interaction.

Yard |yärd|, Molly (c. 1910–) U.S. journalist. She was president of the National Organization for Women (1986–91).

Yard·ley |ˈyärdlē|, Jonathan (1939–) U.S. journalist and author. A book critic for the *Washington Post* (1981–), he won a Pulitzer Prize for criticism (1981).

Yar·row |ˈyærō|, Peter (1938–) U.S. guitarist and singer. He was part of the trio Peter, Paul, and Mary.

Yas·trzem·ski |yəˈstremskē|, Carl Michael (1939–) U.S. baseball player. Known as **Yaz**. He led the American

League in batting three times. Elected to the Baseball Hall of Fame (1989).

Yea·ger |ˈyāgər|, Chuck (1923–) U.S. pilot; full name *Charles Elwood Yeager*. He became the first person to break the sound barrier when he piloted the Bell X-1 rocket research aircraft at high altitude to a level-flight speed of 670 mph in 1947.

Yeats |yāts|, W. B. (1865–1939) Irish poet and dramatist; full name *William Butler Yeats*. His play *The Countess Cathleen* (1892) and his collection of stories *The Celtic Twilight* (1893) stimulated Ireland's theatrical, cultural, and literary revival. Notable poetry: *The Tower* (1928), containing "Sailing to Byzantium" and "Leda and the Swan", and *The Winding Stair* (1929). Nobel Prize for Literature (1923).

Yelt·sin |ˈyeltsən|, Boris (Nikolayevich) (1931–) Russian statesman, president of the Russian Federation since 1991. Impatient with the slow pace of Gorbachev's reforms, Yeltsin resigned from the Communist Party after becoming president of the Russian Soviet Federative Socialist Republic in 1990. As president of the independent Russian Federation he faced opposition to his reforms and in 1993 survived an attempted coup, but he was re-elected in 1996.

Yer·by |ˈyərbē|, Frank (Garvin) (1916–91) U.S. author. After the success of *The Foxes of Harrow* (1946), he turned from stories about racial injustice to historical adventure novels.

Yer·kes |ˈyərkēz|, Charles Tyson (1837–1905) U.S. financier. He established his own banking house (1862) but was jailed for embezzlement (1871); he made a second fortune in street railroad operations in Philadelphia and Chicago.

Yer·kes |ˈyərkēz|, Robert Mearns (1876–1956) U.S. psychologist and educator. A pioneer in the study of animal behavior, he was a leading authority on comparative psychology and psychobiology. Notable works: *The Mental Life of Monkeys and Apes* (1916).

Yev·tu·shen·ko |ˌyevtəˈsHeNGkō|, Yevgeni (Aleksandrovich) (1933–) Russian poet. *Third Snow* (1955) and *Zima Junction* (1956) were regarded as encapsulating the feelings and aspirations of the post-Stalin generation, and he incurred official hostility because of the outspoken nature of some of his poetry, notably *Babi Yar* (1961).

Ye·zier·ska |yəzˈyirskə|, Anzia (1885–1970) U.S. author, born in Russia. She wrote novels and short story collections including *Bread Givers* (1925), as well as an autobiography, *Red Ribbon on a White Horse* (1950), with an introduction by W. H. Auden.

Yo·len |ˈyōlən|, Jane H. (1939–) U.S. children's author and editor. Notable works: *The Girl Who Cried Flowers and Other Tales* (1974).

Yo·shi·mo·to |ˌyōsHēˈmōtō|, Banana (1964–) Japanese author.

Young |yəNG|, Andrew Jackson, Jr. (1932–) U.S. clergyman, politician, and civil rights leader. He served as U.S. ambassador to the United Nations (1977–79) and as mayor of Atlanta, Georgia (1982–). Spingarn Medal, 1978.

Young |yəNG|, Art (1866–1943) U.S. cartoonist. Full name *Arthur Henry Young*. He was a political radical and satirist who published in *The Masses* (1911–17).

Young |yəNG|, Brigham (1801–77) U.S. Mormon leader. He succeeded Joseph Smith as the leader of the Mormons in 1844, led them westward, and established their headquarters at Salt Lake City, Utah. He served as governor of the territory of Utah from 1850 until 1857.

Young |yəNG|, Chic (1901–73) U.S. cartoonist. Full name *Murat Bernard Young*. He created the comic strip "Blondie."

Young |yəNG|, Coleman Alexander (1918–) U.S. politician. He was the longest-serving mayor of Detroit (1974–94).

Young |yəNG|, Denton True (1867–

1955) U.S. baseball player. Known as **Cy Young**. He was the all-time pitching leader in wins (511), complete games (750), and innings pitched (7,355).

Young |yəNG|, Loretta (Gretchen) (1913–) U.S. actress. Notable movies: *The Farmer's Daughter* (1947, Academy Award).

Young |yəNG|, Mahonri (Mackintosh) (1877–1957) U.S. sculptor. He is known for his bronzes *Stevedore* and *Man with Pick*; he is a grandson of Brigham Young.

Young |yəNG|, Neil (Percival) (1945–) Canadian singer, songwriter, and guitarist. He performs both solo and with his group Crazy Horse, combining plaintive acoustic material with distinctively distorted electric-guitar playing. Notable albums: *Harvest* (1972).

Young |yəNG|, Owen D. (1874–1962) U.S. lawyer and corporate executive. He formulated the Young Plan for German reparations at the end of World War I and was president of General Electric (1922–39).

Young |yəNG|, Pres (1909–59) U.S. jazz tenor saxophonist and composer. Full name *Lester Willis Young*. He often accompanied Billie Holiday on records. Notable songs: "Lady Be Good" and "Lester Leaps In."

Young |yəNG|, Steve (1961–) U.S. football player. He was the only quarterback to lead the NFL in passer rating for four straight years.

Young Pretender see STUART.

Your·ce·nar |ˌyo͞orsəˈnär|, Marguerite (1903–87) French writer. Born *Marguerite de Crayencour*. Many of her novels are meticulous historical reconstructions, including *Mémoires d'Hadrian* (1951). Her interest in male homosexuality is reflected in the novel *Alexis ou le Traité du vain combat* (1929).

Yu·ka·wa |yo͞oˈkäwə|, Hideki (1907–81) Japanese physicist. He won the 1949 Nobel Prize for Physics for his prediction of the existence of the particle pi-meson (pion) in 1935.

Zz

Za·har·i·as |zəˈhærēəs|, Babe (1914–56) U.S. track and field athlete and golfer. Full name *Mildred Ella Didrikson Zaharias*. After winning two gold medals in the 1932 Olympics, she became a professional golfer and won 12 major titles; she helped found the LPGA (1949).

Zam·bo·ni |zæmˈbōnē|, Frank J. (1901–) U.S. inventor. He invented the Zamboni ice-resurfacing machine.

Za·mo·ra |zəˈmawrə|, Pedro (1972–94) U.S. AIDS activist, born in Cuba.

Zan·uck |ˈzænək|, Darryl Francis (1902–79) U.S. movie producer; full name *Darryl Francis Zanuck*. He was the controlling executive of Twentieth Century Fox, and its president from 1965 until his retirement in 1971.

Za·pa·ta |zəˈpätə|, Emiliano (1879–1919) Mexican revolutionary. He attempted to implement his program of agrarian reform by means of guerrilla warfare. From 1914 he and Pancho Villa fought against the regimes of General Huerta and Venustiano Carranza.

Zap·pa |ˈzæpə|, Frank (1940–93) U.S. rock singer, musician, and songwriter. Full name *Francis Vincent Zappa, Jr.*. In 1965 he formed the Mothers of Invention, who combined psychedelic rock with elements of jazz and satire. In Zappa's later career he often mixed flowing guitar improvisations with scatological humor.

Za·to·pek |ˈzätō,pek|, Emil (1922–) Czech long-distance runner. In the 1952 Olympic Games he won gold medals in the 5,000 meters, 10,000 meters, and marathon.

Zee·man |ˈzā,män|, Pieter (1865–1943) Dutch physicist. His work on the interaction of light and magnets yielded what is now known as the Zeeman effect. Nobel Prize for Physics, 1902.

Zef·fi·rel·li |,zefəˈrelē|, Franco (1923–) Italian movie and theater director; born *Gianfranco Corsi*. His operatic productions are noted for the opulence of their sets and costumes. Notable movies: *Romeo and Juliet* (1968), *Brother Sun, Sister Moon* (1973),

and the television movie *Jesus of Nazareth* (1977).

Ze·no[1] |ˈzēnō| (*c.*495–*c.*430 BC) Greek philosopher; known as **Zeno of Elea**. A member of the Eleatic school, he defended Parmenides' theories by formulating paradoxes that appeared to demonstrate the impossibility of motion, one of which shows that once Achilles has given a tortoise a start he can never overtake it, since each time he arrives where it was, it has already moved on.

Ze·no[2] |ˈzēnō| (*c.*355–263 BC) Greek philosopher; known as **Zeno of Citium**. He founded the school of Stoic philosophy (*c.* 300), but all that remains of his treatises are fragments of quotations.

Ze·no·bia |zəˈnōbēə| (3rd century AD) queen of Palmyra *c.*267–272. Full name *Septimia Zenobia*. She conquered Egypt and much of Asia Minor. When she proclaimed her son emperor, the Roman emperor Aurelian attacked, defeated, and captured her.

Zep·pe·lin |ˈzep(ə)lin|, Ferdinand (Adolf August Heinrich), Count von (1838–1917) German aviation pioneer. An army officer until his retirement in 1890, he devoted the rest of his life to the development of the dirigible named after him.

Zeux·is |ˈzoōksəs| (*fl.* late 5th century BC) Greek painter, born at Heraclea in southern Italy. His works are known only through the reports of ancient writers, who make reference to monochrome techniques and his use of shading to create an illusion of depth, while his verisimilitude is the subject of many anecdotes.

Zhou En·lai |ˈjō ˈenˈli| (1898–1976) Chinese Communist statesman and prime minister of China (1949–76). Also **Chou En-lai**. A founder of the Chinese Communist Party, he organized a Communist workers' revolt in 1927 in Shanghai in support of the Kuomintang forces surrounding the city. As premier, he was a moderating influence during the Cultural Revolution and presided over the moves towards détente with the U.S. in 1972–73.

Zhu De |ˈjo͞o ˈdä| (1886–1976) Chinese military and political leader. He was founder and commander in chief of the Chinese People's Liberation Army and was closely associated with Mao Ze-dong.

Zhu·kov |ˈzHo͞o͝,kawf| Georgi (Konstantinovich) (1896–1974) Soviet military leader, born in Russia. In the course of World War II he defeated the Germans at Stalingrad (1943), lifted the siege of Leningrad (1944), and led the final assault on Germany and the capture of Berlin (1945). After the war he commanded the Soviet zone in occupied Germany.

Zia-ul-Haq |ˈzēə əl ˈhäk| Muhammad (1924–88) Pakistani general, statesman, and president (1978–88). As chief of staff he led the coup that deposed President Zulfikar Bhutto in 1977. He banned all political parties and began to introduce strict Islamic laws.

Zi·aur |zēˈowr| Rahman (1935–81) Bengali nationalist and president of Bangladesh (1977–81).

Zieg·feld |ˈzēg,feld| Florenz (1869–1932) U.S. theater manager. In 1907 he produced the first of a series of revues in New York, based on those of the Folies-Bergère, entitled the *Ziegfeld Follies*. Among the many famous performers he promoted were W. C. Fields and Fred Astaire.

Zin·del |ˈzindəl| Paul (1936–) U.S. playwright. Notable works: *The Effect of Gamma Rays on Man-in-the-Moon Marigolds* (1964, Pulitzer Prize).

Zinne·mann |ˈzinmən| Fred (1907–97) Austrian-born U.S. movie director. He joined MGM in 1937 and won Oscars for the short *That Mothers Might Live* (1938) and the feature movies *From Here to Eternity* (1953) and *A Man For All Seasons* (1966).

Zof·fany |ˈzäfənē| Johann (c. 1733–1810) German-born painter, resident in England from 1758. Many of his earlier paintings depict scenes from the contemporary theater and feature the actor David Garrick (e.g. *The Farmer's Return*, 1762).

Zog I |zôg| (1895–1961) Albanian prime minister (1922–24), president (1925–28), and king (1928–39); full name *Ahmed Bey Zogu*. He initially headed a republican government, proclaiming himself king in 1928. His autocratic rule resulted in relative political stability, but when the country was invaded by Italy in 1939 he went into exile. He abdicated in 1946 after Albania became a Communist state.

Zo·la |zōˈlä| Émile (Édouard Charles Antoine) (1840–1902) French novelist and critic. His series of twenty novels collectively entitled *Les Rougon-Macquart* (1871–93), including *Nana* (1880), *Germinal* (1885), and *La Terre* (1887), attempts to show how human behavior is determined by environment and heredity. In 1898 he published *J'accuse*, a noted pamphlet in support of Alfred Dreyfus.

Zo·rach |ˈzawr,äk| William (1887–1966) U.S. sculptor. Notable works include *Mother and Child* (1930) and *Spirit of Dance* (1932).

Zo·ro·as·ter |ˈzawrō,æstər| (c. 628–c. 551 BC) Persian prophet and founder of Zoroastrianism; Avestan name *Zarathustra*. Little is known of his life, but traditionally he was born in Persia and began to preach the tenets of what was later called Zoroastrianism after receiving a vision from Ahura Mazda.

Zsig·mon·dy |ˈzHig,mawndē| Richard Adolf (1865–1929) Austrian-born German chemist. He investigated the properties of various colloidal solutions and invented the ultramicroscope for counting colloidal particles. Nobel Prize for Chemistry (1925).

Zu·kor |ˈzo͞okər| Adolph (1873–1976) U.S. movie producer and corporate executive. He founded Famous Players Film Co. (1912), which merged with another company to become Paramount Pictures, Inc.

Zur·ba·rán |,zo͞orbəˈrän| Francisco de (1598–1664) Spanish painter. He carried out commissions for many churches and for Philip IV, for whom he painted *The Defence of Cadiz* (1634) and the series *The Labors of Hercules* (1634). Much of his subject matter is religious.

Zwing·li |ˈzwiNGlē; ˈtsfiNGglē| Ulrich (or *Huldreich*) (1484–1531) Swiss

Protestant reformer, the principal figure of the Swiss Reformation. He rejected papal authority and many orthodox doctrines, and although he had strong local support in Zurich, his ideas met with fierce resistance in some regions. Zwingli was killed in the civil war that resulted from his reforms.

Zwor·y·kin |'zwawrəkin|, Vladimir Kosma (1889–1982) Russian-born U.S. physicist and television pioneer. He invented a precursor of the television camera, the first to scan the image electronically.

Appendixes

PRESIDENTS OF THE UNITED STATES OF AMERICA

Name and life dates	Party (term in office)
1. George Washington 1732-99	Federalist (1789-97)
2. John Adams 1735-1826	Federalist (1797-1801)
3. Thomas Jefferson 1743-1826	Democratic-Republican (1801-09)
4. James Madison 1751-1836	Democratic-Republican (1809-17)
5. James Monroe 1758-1831	Democratic-Republican (1817-25)
6. John Quincy Adams 1767-1848	Independent (1825-29)
7 Andrew Jackson 1767-1845	Democrat (1829-37)
8. Martin Van Buren 1782-1862	Democrat (1837-41)
9. William H. Harrison 1773-1841	Whig (1841)
10. John Tyler 1790-1862	Whig, then Democrat (1841-45)
11. James K. Polk 1795-1849	Democrat (1845-49)
12. Zachary Taylor 1784-1850	Whig (1849-50)
13. Millard Fillmore 1800-74	Whig (1850-53)
14. Franklin Pierce 1804-69	Democrat (1853-57)
15. James Buchanan 1791-1868	Democrat (1857-61)
16. Abraham Lincoln 1809-65	Republican (1861-65)
17. Andrew Johnson 1808-75	Democrat (1865-69)
18. Ulysses S. Grant 1822-85	Republican (1869-77)
19. Rutherford B. Hayes 1822-93	Republican (1877-81)
20. James A. Garfield 1831-81	Republican (1881)
21. Chester A. Arthur 1830-86	Republican (1881-85)
22. Grover Cleveland 1837-1908	Democrat (1885-89)
23. Benjamin Harrison 1833-1901	Republican (1889-93)
24. Grover Cleveland (see above)	Democrat (1893-97)
25. William McKinley 1843-1901	Republican (1897-1901)
26. Theodore Roosevelt 1858-1919	Republican (1901-09)
27. William H. Taft 1857-1930	Republican (1909-13)
28. Woodrow Wilson 1856-1924	Democrat (1913-21)
29. Warren G. Harding 1865-1923	Republican (1921-23)
30. Calvin Coolidge 1872-1933	Republican (1923-29)
31. Herbert Hoover 1874-1964	Republican (1929-33)
32. Franklin D. Roosevelt 1882-1945	Democrat (1933-45)
33. Harry S Truman 1884-1972	Democrat (1945-53)
34. Dwight D. Eisenhower 1890-1969	Republican (1953-61)
35. John F. Kennedy 1917-63	Democrat (1961-63)
36. Lyndon B. Johnson 1908-73	Democrat (1963-69)
37. Richard M. Nixon 1913-94	Republican (1969-74)
38. Gerald R. Ford 1913-	Republican (1974-77)
39. James Earl Carter 1924-	Democrat (1977-81)
40. Ronald W. Reagan 1911-	Republican (1981-89)
41. George H.W. Bush 1924-	Republican (1989-93)
42. William J. Clinton 1946-	Democrat (1993-)

MONARCHS OF ENGLAND AND BRITAIN

House	Monarch	Reign
Wessex (West Saxon)	Egbert	802-839
	Ethelwulf	839-856
	Ethelbald	856-860
	Ethelbert	860-866
	Ethelred I	866-871
	Alfred the Great	871-899
	Edward the Elder	899-924
	Athelstan	925-939
	Edmund I	939-946
	Edred	946-955
	Edwy	955-957
	Edgar	959-975
	Edward the Martyr	975-978
	Ethelred II (the Unready)	978-1016
	Edmund II (Ironside)	1016
Danish		
	Canute (Cnut)	1016-1035
	Harold I	1035-1040
	Hardecanute	1040-1042
West Saxon (restored)	Edward II (the Confessor)	1042-1066
	Harold II	1066
Normandy	William I (the Conqueror)	1066-1087
	William II	1087-1100
	Henry I	1100-1135
	Stephen	1135-1154
Plantagenet (Anjou)	Henry II	1154-1189
	Richard I (the Lion-heart)	1189-1199
	John	1199-1216
	Henry III	1216-1272
	Edward I	1272-1307
	Edward II	1307-1327
	Edward III	1327-1377
	Richard II	1377-1399
Lancaster	Henry IV	1399-1413
	Henry V	1413-1422
	Henry VI	1422-1461
York	Edward IV	1461-1483
	Edward V	1483
	Richard III	1483-1485
Tudor	Henry VII	1485-1509
	Henry VIII	1509-1547
	Edward VI	1547-1553
	Jane (Lady Jane Grey)	1553

House	Monarch	Reign
	Mary I (Bloody Mary)	1553-1558
	Elizabeth I	1558-1603
(monarchs of Britain)		
Stuart	James I	1603-1625
	Charles I	1625-1649
Commonwealth	Long Parliament	1649-1660
Protectorate	Oliver Cromwell	1653-1658
	Richard Cromwell	1658-1660
Stuart	Charles II	1660-1685
	James II	1685-1688
interregnum		1688-1689
	William III and Mary II	1689-1694
	Anne	1702-1714
Hanover	George I	1714-1727
	George II	1727-1760
	George III	1760-1820
	George IV	1820-1830
	William IV	1830-1837
Saxe-Coburg-Gotha	Victoria	1837-1901
	Edward VII	1901-1910
Windsor	George V	1910-1936
	Edward VIII	1936
	George VI	1936-1952
	Elizabeth II	1952-

PRIME MINISTERS OF GREAT BRITAIN AND THE UNITED KINGDOM

Name	Party	Dates in Power
Sir Robert Walpole	Whig	1721-1742
Earl of Wilmington	Whig	1742-1743
Henry Pelham	Whig	1743-1754
Duke of Newcastle	Whig	1754-1756
Earl of Bute	Tory	1762-1763
George Grenville	Whig	1763-1765
Marquis of Rockingham	Whig	1765-1766
Earl of Chatham	Whig	1766-1768
Duke of Grafton	Whig	1768-1770
Lord North	Tory	1770-1782
Marquis of Rockingham	Whig	1782
Earl of Shelburne	Whig	1782-1783
Duke of Portland	coalition	1783
William Pitt	Tory	1783-1801
Henry Addington	Tory	1801-1804
William Pitt	Tory	1804-1806

Name	Party	Dates in Power
Lord William Grenville	Whig	1806-1807
Duke of Portland	Tory	1807-1808
Spencer Perceval	Tory	1809-1812
Earl of Liverpool	Tory	1812-1827
George Canning	Tory	1827
Viscount Goderich	Tory	1827-1828
Duke of Wellington	Tory	1828-1830
Earl Grey	Whig	1830-1834
Viscount Melbourne	Whig	1834
Duke of Wellington	Tory	1834
Sir Robert Peel	Conservative	1834-1835
Viscount Melbourne	Whig	1835-1841
Sir Robert Peel	Conservative	1841-1846
Lord John Russell	Whig	1846-1852
Earl of Derby	Conservative	1852
Earl of Aberdeen	coalition	1852-1855
Viscount Palmerston	Liberal	1855-1858
Earl of Derby	Conservative	1858-1859
Viscount Palmerston	Liberal	1859-1865
Earl Russell	Liberal	1865-1866
Earl of Derby	Conservative	1866-1868
Benjamin Disraeli	Conservative	1868
William Ewart Gladstone	Liberal	1868-1874
Benjamin Disraeli	Conservative	1874-1880
William Ewart Gladstone	Liberal	1880-1885
Marquis of Salisbury	Conservative	1885-1886
William Ewart Gladstone	Liberal	1892-1894
Earl of Rosebery	Liberal	1894-1895
Marquis of Salisbury	Conservative	1895-1902
Arthur James Balfour	Conservative	1902-1905
Sir Henry Campbell-Bannerman	Liberal	1905-1908
Herbert Henry Asquith	Liberal	1908-1916
David Lloyd George	coalition	1916-1922
Andrew Bonar Law	Conservative	1922-1923
Stanley Baldwin	Conservative	1923-1924
James Ramsay MacDonald	Labour	1924
Stanley Baldwin	Conservative	1924-1929
James Ramsay MacDonald	coalition	1929-1935
Stanley Baldwin	coalition	1935-1937
Neville Chamberlain	coalition	1937-1940
Sir Winston Spencer Churchill	coalition	1940-1945
Clement Attlee	Labour	1945-1951
Sir Winston Spencer Churchill	Conservative	1951-1955
Sir Anthony Eden	Conservative	1955-1957
Harold Macmillan	Conservative	1957-1963
Sir Alec Douglas-Home	Conservative	1963-1964
Harold Wilson	Labour	1964-1970
Edward Heath	Conservative	1970-1974
Harold Wilson	Labour	1974-1976
James Callaghan	Labour	1976-1979
Margaret Thatcher	Conservative	1979-1990
John Major	Conservative	1990-1997
Anthony Blair	Labour	1997-

ACADEMY AWARD WINNERS

Note: The movie for which the award was given follows the individual's name, in parentheses.

1928
Best actor: Charles Chaplin (*The Circus*)
Best actress: Janet Gaynor (*Seventh Heaven*)
Best director (drama): Frank Borzage (*Seventh Heaven*)
Best director (comedy): Lewis Milestone (*Two Arabian Knights*)

1929
Best actor: Warner Baxter (*In Old Arizona*)
Best actress: Mary Pickford (*Coquette*)
Best director: Frank Lloyd (*The Divine Lady*)

1930
Best actor: George Arliss (*Disraeli*)
Best actress: Norma Shearer (*The Divorceé*)
Best director: Lewis Milestone (*All Quiet on the Western Front*)

1931
Best actor: Lionel Barrymore (*A Free Soul*)
Best actress: Marie Dressler (*Min and Bill*)
Best director: Norman Taurog (*Skippy*)

1932
Best actors: Wallace Berry (*The Champ*), Frederic March (*Dr. Jekyll and Mr. Hyde*)
Best actress: Helen Hayes (*The Sin of Madelon Claudet*)
Best director: Frank Borzage (*Bad Girl*)

1933
Best actor: Charles Laughton (*The Private Life of Henry VIII*)
Best actress: Katharine Hepburn (*Morning Glory*)
Best director: Frank Lloyd (*Cavalcade*

1934
Best actor: Clark Gable (*It Happened One Night*)
Best actress: Claudette Colbert (*It Happened One Night*)
Best director: Frank Capra (*It Happened One Night*)

1935
Best actor: Victor McLaglen (*The Informer*)
Best actress: Bette Davis (*Dangerous*)
Best director: John Ford (*The Informer*)

1936
Best actor: Paul Muni (*The Story of Louis Pasteur*)
Best actress: Luise Rainer (*The Great Ziegfeld*)
Best director: Frank Capra (*Mr. Deeds Goes to Town*)

1937
Best actor: Spencer Tracy (*Captains Courageous*)
Best actress: Luise Rainer (*The Good Earth*)
Best director: Leo McCarey (*The Awful Truth*)

1938
Best actor: Spencer Tracy (*Boys Town*)
Best actress: Bette Davis (*Jezebel*)
Best director: Frank Capra (*You Can't Take It With You*)

1939
Best actor: Robert Donat (*Goodbye Mr. Chips*)
Best actress: Vivien Leigh (*Gone with the Wind*)
Best director: Victor Fleming (*Gone with the Wind*)

1940
Best actor: James Stewart (*The Philadelphia Story*)
Best actress: Ginger Rogers (*Kitty Foyle*)
Best director: John Ford (*The Grapes of Wrath*)

1941
Best actor: Gary Cooper (*Sergeant York*)
Best actress: Joan Fontaine (*Suspicion*)
Best director: John Ford (*How Green Was My Valley*)

1942
Best actor: James Cagney (*Yankee Doodle Dandy*)
Best actress: Greer Garson (*Mrs. Miniver*)
Best director: William Wyler (*Mrs. Miniver*)

1943
Best actor: Paul Lukas (*Watch on the Rhine*)
Best actress: Jennifer Jones (*The Song of Bernadette*)
Best director: Michael Curtiz (*Casablanca*)

1944
Best actor: Bing Crosby (*Going My Way*)
Best actress: Ingrid Bergman (*Gaslight*)
Best director: Leo McCarey (*Going My Way*)

1945
Best actor: Ray Milland (*The Lost Weekend*)
Best actress: Joan Crawford (*Love Letters*)
Best director: Billy Wilder (*The Lost Weekend*)

1946
Best actor: Frederic March (*The Best Years of Our Lives*)
Best actress: Olivia De Havilland (*To Each His Own*)
Best director: William Wyler (*The Best Years of Our Lives*)

1947
Best actor: Ronald Colman (*A Double Life*)
Best actress: Loretta Young (*The Farmer's Daughter*)
Best director: Elia Kazan (*Gentleman's Agreement*)

1948
Best actor: Laurence Olivier (*Hamlet*)
Best actress: Jane Wyman (*Johnny Belinda*)
Best director: John Huston (*The Treasure of the Sierra Madre*)

1949
Best actor: Broderick Crawford (*All the King's Men*)
Best actress: Olivia De Havilland (*The Heiress*)
Best director: Joseph L. Mankiewicz (*A Letter to Three Wives*)

1950
Best actor: Jose Ferrer (*Cyrano De Bergerac*)
Best actress: Judy Holliday (*Born Yesterday*)
Best director: Joseph L. Mankiewicz (*All About Eve*)

1951
Best actor: Humphrey Bogart (*The African Queen*)
Best actress: Vivien Leigh (*A Streetcar Named Desire*)
Best director: George Stevens (*A Place in the Sun*)

1952
Best actor: Gary Cooper (*High Noon*)
Best actress: Shirley Booth (*Come Back, Little Sheba*)
Best director: John Ford (*The Quiet Man*)

1953
Best actor: William Holden (*Stalag 17*)
Best actress: Audrey Hepburn (*Roman Holiday*)
Best director: Fred Zinnemann (*From Here to Eternity*)

1954
Best actor: Marlon Brando (*On the Waterfront*)
Best actress: Grace Kelly (*The Country Girl*)
Best director: Elia Kazan (*On the Waterfront*)

1955
Best actor: Ernest Borgnine (*Marty*)
Best actress: Anna Magnani (*The Rose Tattoo*)
Best director: Delbert Mann (*Marty*)

1956
Best actor: Yul Brynner (*The King and I*)
Best actress: Ingrid Bergman (*Anastasia*)
Best director: George Stevens (*Giant*)

1957
Best actor: Alec Guinness (*The Bridge on the River Kwai*)
Best actress: Joanne Woodward (*The Three Faces of Eve*)
Best director: David Lean (*The Bride on the River Kwai*)

1958
Best actor: David Niven (*Separate Tables*)
Best actress: Susan Hayward (*I Want to Live!*)
Best director: Vincente Minnelli (*The Defiant Ones*)

1959
Best actor: Charlton Heston (*Ben-Hur*)
Best actress: Simone Signoret (*Room at the Top*)
Best director: William Wyler (*Ben-Hur*)

1960
Best actor: Burt Lancaster (*Elmer Gantry*)
Best actress: Elizabeth Taylor (*Butterfield 8*)
Best director: Billy Wilder (*The Apartment*)

1961
Best actor: Maximilian Schell (*Judgment at Nuremberg*)
Best actress: Sophia Loren (*Two Women*)
Best director: Jerome Robbins, Robert Wise (*West Side Story*)

1962
Best actor: Gregory Peck (*To Kill a Mockingbird*)
Best actress: Anne Bancroft (*The Miracle Worker*)
Best director: David Lean (*Lawrence of Arabia*)

1963
Best actor: Sydney Poitier (*Lilies of the Field*)
Best actress: Patricia Neal (*Hud*)
Best director: Tony Richardson (*Tom Jones*)

1964
Best actor: Rex Harrison (*My Fair Lady*)
Best actress: Julie Andrews (*Mary Poppins*)
Best director: George Cukor (*Mary Poppins*)

1965
Best actor: Lee Marvin (*Cat Ballou*)
Best actress: Julie Christie (*Darling*)
Best director: Robert Wise (*The Sound of Music*)

1966
Best actor: Paul Scofield (*A Man for All Seasons*)
Best actress: Elizabeth Taylor (*Who's Afraid of Virginia Wolf?*)
Best director: Fred Zinnemann (*A Man for All Seasons*)

1967
Best actor: Rod Steiger (*In the Heat of the Night*)
Best actress: Katharine Hepburn (*Guess Who's Coming to Dinner*)
Best director: Mike Nichols (*The Graduate*)

1968
Best actor: Cliff Robertson (*Charly*)
Best actress: Barbra Streisand (*Funny Girl*)
Best director: Carol Reed (*Oliver!*)

1969
Best actor: John Wayne (*True Grit*)
Best actress: Maggie Smith (*The Prime of Miss Jean Brodie*)
Best director: John Schlesinger (*Midnight Cowboy*)

1970
Best actor: George C. Scott (*Patton*)
Best actress: Glenda Jackson (*Women in Love*)
Best director: Franklin J. Schaffner (*Patton*)

1971
Best actor: Gene Hackman (*The French Connection*)
Best actress: Jane Fonda (*Klute*)
Best director: William Friedkin (*The French Connection*)

1972
Best actor: Marlon Brando (*The Godfather*)
Best actress: Liza Minnelli (*Cabaret*)
Best director: Bob Fosse (*Cabaret*)

1973
Best actor: Jack Lemmon (*Save the Tiger*)
Best actress: Glenda Jackson (*A Touch of Class*)
Best director: George Roy Hill (*The Sting*)

1974
Best actor: Art Carney (*Harry and Tonto*)
Best actress: Ellen Burstyn (*Alice Doesn't Live Here Anymore*)
Best director: Francis Ford Coppola (*The Godfather, Part II*)

1975
Best actor: Jack Nicholson (*One Flew Over the Cuckoo's Nest*)
Best actress: Louise Fletcher (*One Flew Over the Cuckoo's Nest*)
Best director: Milos Forman (*One Flew Over the Cuckoo's Nest*)

1976
Best actor: Peter Finch (*Network*)
Best actress: Faye Dunaway (*Network*)
Best director: John G. Avildsen (*Rocky*)

1977
Best actor: Richard Dreyfuss (*The Goodbye Girl*)
Best actress: Diane Keaton (*Annie Hall*)
Best director: Woody Allen (*Annie Hall*)

1978
Best actor: Jon Voight (*Coming Home*)
Best actress: Jane Fonda (*Coming Home*)
Best director: Michael Cimino (*The Deer Hunter*)

1979
Best actor: Dustin Hoffman (*Kramer vs. Kramer*)
Best actress: Sally Field (*Norma Rae*)
Best director: Robert Benton (*Kramer vs. Kramer*)

1980
Best actor: Robert De Niro (*Raging Bull*)
Best actress: Sissy Spacek (*Coal Miner's Daughter*)
Best director: Robert Redford (*Ordinary People*)

1981
Best actor: Henry Fonda (*On Golden Pond*)
Best actress: Katharine Hepburn (*On Golden Pond*)
Best director: Warren Beatty (*Reds*)

1982
Best actor: Ben Kingsley (*Gandhi*)
Best actress: Meryl Streep (*Sophie's Choice*)
Best director: Richard Attenborough (*Gandhi*)

1983
Best actor: Robert Duvall (*Tender Mercies*)
Best actress: Shirley MacLaine (*Terms of Endearment*)
Best director: James L. Brooks (*Terms of Endearment*)

1984
Best actor: F. Murray Abraham (*Amadeus*)
Best actress: Sally Field (*Places in the Heart*)
Best director: Milos Forman (*Amadeus*)

1985
Best actor: William Hurt (*Kiss of the Spider Woman*)
Best actress: Geraldine Page (*The Trip to Bountiful*)
Best director: Sydney Pollack (*Out of Africa*)

1986
Best actor: Paul Newman (*The Color of Money*)
Best actress: Marlee Matlin (*Children of a Lesser God*)
Best director: Oliver Stone (*Platoon*)

1987
Best actor: Michael Douglas (*Wall Street*)
Best actress: Cher (*Moonstruck*)
Best director: Bernardo Bertolucci (*The Last Emperor*)

1988
Best actor: Dustin Hoffman (*Rain Man*)
Best actress: Jodie Foster (*The Accused*)
Best director: Barry Levinson (*Rain Man*)

1989
Best actor: Daniel Day-Lewis (*My Left Foot*)
Best actress: Jessica Tandy (*Driving Miss Daisy*)
Best director: Oliver Stone (*Born on the Fourth of July*)

1990
Best actor: Jeremy Irons (*Reversal of Fortune*)
Best actress: Kathy Bates (*Misery*)
Best director: Kevin Costner (*Dances with Wolves*)

1991
Best actor: Anthony Hopkins (*The Silence of the Lambs*)
Best actress: Jodie Foster (*The Silence of the Lambs*)
Best director: Jonathan Demme (*The Silence of the Lambs*)

1992
Best actor: Al Pacino (*Scent of a Woman*)
Best actress: Emma Thompson (*Howards End*)
Best director: Clint Eastwood (*Unforgiven*)

1993
Best actor: Tom Hanks (*Philadelphia*)
Best actress: Holly Hunter (*The Piano*)
Best director: Steven Spielberg (*Schindler's List*)

1994
Best actor: Tom Hanks (*Forrest Gump*)
Best actress: Jessica Lange (*Blue Sky*)
Best director: Robert Zemeckis (*Forrest Gump*)

1995
Best actor: Nicolas Cage (*Leaving Las Vegas*)
Best actress: Susan Sarandon (*Dead Man Walking*)
Best director: Mel Gibson (*Braveheart*)

1996
Best actor: Geoffrey Rush (*Shine*)
Best actress: Frances McDormand (*Fargo*)
Best director: Anthony Minghella (*The English Patient*)

1997
Best actor: Jack Nicholson (*As Good As It Gets*)
Best actress: Helen Hunt (*As Good As It Gets*)
Best director: James Cameron (*Titanic*)

1998
Best actor: Robert Benigni (*Life is Beautiful* [*La Vita è Bella*])
Best actress: Gwyneth Paltrow (*Shakespeare in Love*)
Best director: Steven Spielberg (*Saving Private Ryan*)

BASEBALL HALL OF FAME INDUCTEES

(elected by the Baseball Writers Association of America)

Year of Induction	Player
1999	George Brett
	Nolan Ryan
	Robin Yount
1998	Don Sutton
1997	Phil Niekro
1995	Mike Schmidt
1994	Steve Carlton
1993	Reggie Jackson
1992	Rollie Fingers
	Tom Seaver
1991	Rod Carew
	Ferguson Jenkins
	Gaylord Perry
1990	Jim Palmer
	Joe Morgan
1989	Johnny Bench
	Carl Yastrzemski
1988	Willie Stargell
1987	Billy Williams
	Catfish Hunter
1986	Willie McCovey
1985	Lou Brock
	Hoyt Wilhelm
1983	Juan Marichal
	Brooks Robinson
1982	Hank Aaron
	Frank Robinson
1981	Bob Gibson
1980	Al Kaline
	Duke Snider
1979	Willie Mays
1978	Eddie Mathews
1977	Ernie Banks
1976	Bob Lemon
	Robin Roberts
1975	Ralph Kiner
1974	Whitey Ford
	Mickey Mantle
1973	Warren Spahn
	Roberto Clemente
1972	Yogi Berra
	Sandy Koufax
	Early Wynn
1970	Lou Boudreau
1969	Roy Campanella
	Stan Musial
1968	Joe Medwick
1967	Red Ruffing
	Ted Williams
1964	Luke Appling
1962	Bob Feller
	Jackie Robinson
1956	Joe Cronin
	Hank Greenberg
1955	Joe DiMaggio
	Gabby Hartnett
	Ted Lyons
	Dazzy Vance
1954	Bill Dickey
	Rabbit Maranville
	Bill Terry
1953	Dizzy Dean
	Al Simmons
1952	Harry Heilmann
	Paul Waner
1951	Jimmie Foxx
	Mel Ott
1949	Charlie Gehringer
1948	Herb Pennock
	Pie Traynor
1947	Michey Cochrane
	Frank Frisch
	Lefty Grove
	Carl Hubbell
1942	Rogers Hornsby
1939	Eddie Collins
	Lou Gehrig
	Willic Keeler
	George Sisler
1938	Grover Alexander
1937	Nap Lajoie
	Tris Speaker
	Cy Young
1936	Ty Cobb
	Walter Johnson
	Christy Mathewson
	Babe Ruth
	Honus Wagner

(elected by the Veterans Committee)

Year of Induction	Player
1998	George Davis
	Larry Doby
	Lee MacPhail
	Wilbur Rogan

Year of Induction	Player
1997	Tommy Lasorda
	Nellie Fox
	Willie J. Wells, Sr.
1996	Jim Bunning
	Earl Weaver
	Ned Hanlon
	Bill Foster
1995	Richie Ashburn
	Leon Day
	William Hulbert
	Vic Willis
1994	Leo Durocher
	Phil Rizzuto
1992	Hal Newhouser
	Bill McGowen
1991	Bill Veeck
	Tony Lazzeri
1989	Al Barlick
	Red Schoendienst
1987	Ray Dandridge
1986	Bobby Doerr
	Ernie Lombardi
1985	Enos Slaughter
	Arky Vaughan
1984	Rick Ferrell
	Pee Wee Reese
1983	Walter Alston
	George Kell
1982	Happy Chandler
	Travis Jackson
1981	Johnny Mize
	Rube Foster
1980	Chuck Klein
	Tom Yawkey
1979	Hack Wilson
	Warren Giles
1978	Larry MacPhail
	Addie Joss
1977	Al Lopez
	Amos Rusie
	Joe Sewell
1976	Roger Connor
	Cal Hubbard
	Fred Lindstrom
1975	Earl Averill
	Bucky Harris
	Billy Herman
1974	Jim Bottomley
	Jocko Conlan
	Sam Thompson
1973	Billy Evans
	George Kelly
	Mickey Welch

Year	Player
1972	Lefty Gomez
	William Harridge
	Ross Youngs
1971	Dave Bancroft
	Jake Beckley
	Chick Hafey
	Harry Hopper
	Joe Kelley
	Rube Marquard
	George Weiss
1970	Earle Combs
	Ford Frick
	Jesse Haines
1969	Stan Coveleski
	Waite Hoyt
1968	Kiki Cuyler
	Goose Goslin
1967	Branch Rickey
	Lloyd Waner
1966	Casey Stengel
1965	Pud Galvin
1964	Red Faber
	Burleigh Grimes
	Miller Huggins
	Tim Keefe
	Heine Manush
	John Ward
1963	John Clarkson
	Elmer Flick
	Sam Rice
	Eppa Rixey
1962	Bill McKechnie
	Edd Roush
1961	Max Carey
	Billy Hamilton
1959	Zack Wheat
1957	Sam Crawford
	Joe McCarthy
1955	Frank Baker
	Ray Schalk
1953	Ed Barrow
	Chief Bender
	Thomas Connolly
	Bill Klem
	Bobby Wallace
	Harry Wright
1949	Mordecai Brown
	Kid Nichols
1946	Jesse Burkett
	Frank Chance
	Jack Chesbro
	Johnny Evers
	Clark Griffith
	Tommy McCarthy
	Joe McGinnity

		1938	Alexander Cartwright, Jr.
	Eddie Plank		Henry Chadwick
	Joe Tinker	1936	Morgan Bulkeley
	Rube Waddell		Ban Johnson
	Ed Walsh		John McGraw
1945	Roger Bresnahan		Connie Mack
	Dan Brouthers		George Wright
	Fred Clarke		
	Jimmy Collins		
	Ed Delahanty	(elected by the Negro League
	Hugh Duffy	Committee)
	Hugh Jennings		
	Michael Kelly	**Year of**	
	Jim O'Rourke	**Induction**	**Player**
	Wilbert Robinson	1977	Pop Lloyd
1944	Kenesaw Mountain		Martin Dihigo
	Landis	1976	Oscar Charleston
1939	Cap Anson	1975	Judy Johnson
	Charles Comiskey	1974	Cool Papa Bell
	Candy Cummings	1973	Monte Irvin
	Buck Ewing	1972	Josh Gibson
	Hoss Radbourn		Buck Leonard
	Al Spalding	1971	Satchel Paige

PRO FOOTBALL HALL
OF FAME INDUCTEES

1999
Eric Dickerson
Tom Mack
Ozzie Newsome
Billy Shaw
Lawrence Taylor

1998
Paul Krause
Tommy McDonald
Anthony Munoz
Mike Singletary
Dwight Stephenson

1997
Mike Haynes
Wellington Mara
Don Shula
Mike Webster

1996
Lou Creekmur
Dan Dierdorf
Joe Gibbs
Charlie Joiner
Mel Renfro

1995
Jim Finks
Henry Jordan
Steve Largent
Lee Roy Selmon
Kellen Winslow

1994
Tony Dorsett
Harry (Bud) Grant
Jimmy Johnson
Leroy Kelly
Jackie Smith
Randy White

1993
Dan Fouts
Larry Little
Chuck Noll
Walter Payton
Bill Walsh

1992
Lem Barney
Al Davis
John Mackey
John Riggins

1991
Earl Campbell
John Hannah
Stan Jones
Tex Schramm
Jan Stenerud

1990
Junious (Buck) Buchanan
Bob Griese
Franco Harris
Ted Hendricks
Jack Lambert
Tom Landry
Bob St. Clair

1989
Mel Blount
Terry Bradshaw
Art Shell
Willie Wood

1988
Fred Bilentnikoff
Mike Ditka
Jack Ham
Alan Page

1987
Larry Csonka
Len Dawson
Joe Greene
John Henry Johnson
Jim Langer
Don Maynard
Gene Upshaw

1986
Paul Hornung
Ken Houston
Willie Lanier
Frank Tarkenton
Doak Walter

1985
Frank Gatski
Joe Namath
Pete Rozelle
O.J. Simpson
Roger Staubach

1984
Willie Brown
Mike McCormack
Charley Taylor
Arnie Weinmeister

1983
Bobby Bell
Sid Gillman
Sonny Jurgensen
Bobby Mitchell
Paul Warfield

1982
Doug Atkins
Sam Huff
George Musso
Merlin Olsen

1981
Morris (Red) Badgro
George Blanda
Willie Davis
Jim Ringo

1980
Herb Adderley
David (Deacon) Jones
Bob Lilly
Jim Otto

1979
Dick Butkus
Yale Lary
Ron Mix
Johnny Unitas

1978
Lance Alworth
Weeb Ewbank
Alphonse (Tuffy)
  Leemans
Ray Nitschke
Larry Wilson

1977
Frank Gifford
Forrest Gregg
Gale Sayers
Bart Starr
Bill Willis

1976
Ray Flaherty
Len Ford
Jim Taylor

1975
Roosevelt Brown
George Connor
Dante Lavelli
Lenny Moore

1974
Tony Canadeo
Bill George
Lou Groza
Dick (Night Train) Lane

1973
Raymond Berry
Jim Parker
Joe Schmidt

1972
Lamar Hunt
Gino Marchetti
Ollie Matson
Clarence (Ace) Parker

1971
Jim Brown
Bill Hewitt
Frank (Bruiser) Kinard
Vince Lombardi
Andy Robustelli

Y.A. Tittle
Norm Van Brocklin

1970
Jack Christiansen
Tom Fears
Hugh McElhenny
Pete Pihos

1969
Glen (Turk) Edwards
Earle (Greasy) Neale
Leo Nomellini
Joe Perry
Ernie Stautner

1968
Cliff Battles
Art Donovan
Elroy (Crazylegs) Hirsch
Wayne Millner
Marion Motley
Charley Trippi
Alex Wojciechowicz

1967
Chuck Bednarik
Charles Bidwill
Paul Brown
Bobby Layne
Dan Reeves
Ken Strong
Joe Stydahar
Emlen Tunnell

1966
Bill Dudley
Joy Guyon
Arnie Herber
Walt Kiesling
George McAfee
Steve Owen
Hugh (Shorty) Ray
Clyde (Bulldog) Turner

1965
Guy Chamberlin
John (Paddy) Driscoll
Dan Fortmann
Otto Graham
Sid Luckman
Steve Van Buren
Bob Waterfield

1964	1963	
Jimmy Conzelman	Sammy Baugh	Cal Hubbard
Ed Healey	Bert Bell	Don Hutson
Clark Hinkle	Joe Carr	Earl (Curly) Lambeau
Roy (Link) Lyman	Earl (Dutch) Clark	Tim Mara
August (Mike)	Red Grange	George Preston Marshall
Michaelske	George Halas	Johnny Blood (McNally)
Art Rooney	Mel Hein	Bronko Nagurski
George Trafton	Wilbur (Pete) Henry	Ernie Nevers
		Jim Thorpe

BASKETBALL HALL OF FAME INDUCTEES

Players	Year inducted		
1998	Larry Bird	1983	John Havlicek
	Arnie Risen		Sam Jones
1996	Alex English	1982	Bill Bradley
	Bailey Howell		Dave DeBusschere
1995	George Gervin		Jack Twyman
	Gail Goodrich	1981	Hal Greer
	David Thompson		Slater Martin
	George Yardley		Frank Ramsey
1994	Kareem Abdul-Jabbar		Willis Reed
	Vern Mikkelsen	1979	Jerry Lucas
1993	Harold E. "Buddy" Jeanette		Oscar Robertson
1992	Walt Bellamy		Jerry West
	Julius "Dr. J" Erving	1978	Wilt Chamberlain
	Dan Issel	1977	Paul Arizin
	Dick McGuire		Joe Fulks
	Calvin Murphy		Cliff Hagan
	Bill Walton		Jim Pollard
1991	Connie Hawkins	1976	Elgin Baylor
	Bob Lanier	1975	Tom Gola
1990	Nate "Tiny" Archibald		Bill Sharman
	Dave Cowens	1974	Bill Russell
	Harry "The Horse" Gallatin	1972	Dolph Schayes
1989	Dave Bing	1970	Bob Cousy
	Elvin "The Big E" Hayes		Bob Pettit
	Neil Johnston	1969	Bob Davies
	Earl "The Pearl" Monroe	1966	Joe Lapchick
1988	William "Pop" Gates	1964	John "Honey" Russell
	K.C. Jones	1961	Andy Phillip
	Lenny Wilkens	1960	Edward "Easy Ed" Macauley
1987	Clyde Lovellette	1959	George Mikan
	Wes Unseld		
1986	Rick Barry	**Coaches**	**Year inducted**
	Walt "Clyde" Frazier	1998	Alex Hannum
	Robert Houbregs		Lenny Wilkens
	Pete Maravich	1996	Pete Carril
	Bobby Wanzer	1993	Charles J. "Chuck" Daly
1985	Billy Cunningham	1991	Al McGuire
	Tom Heinsohn		Jack Ramsay
1984	Al Cervi	1985	William "Red" Holzman
	Nate Thurmond	1976	Frank McGuire
		1975	Harry Litwack

1968	Arnold "Red" Auerbach	1965	Walter Brown
1967	Alvin "Doggie" Julian		Bill Mokray
1964	Ken Loeffler	1964	Edward "Ned" Irish
		1959	Harold Olsen

Contributors	Year inducted		
1990	Larry Fleisher		
	Larry O'Brien	Referees	Year inducted
1980	J. Walter Kennedy	1994	Earl Strom
1979	Lester Harrison	1979	J. Dallas Shirley
1978	Pete Newell	1978	Jim Enright
1973	Maurice Podoloff	1977	John Nucatola
1971	Eddie Gottlieb	1959	Matthew "Pat" Kennedy

ROCK AND ROLL HALL OF FAME INDUCTEES

1999
Billy Joel
Curtis Mayfield
Paul McCartney
Del Shannon
Dusty Springfield
Bruce Springsteen
Staple Singers

Non-Performer
George Martin

Early Influences
Charles Brown
Bob Wills and His Texas Playboys

1998
Eagles
Fleetwood Mac
Mamas and Papas
Lloyd Price
Santana
Gene Vincent

Non-Performer
Allen Toussaint

Early Influence
Jelly Roll Morton

1997
Bee Gees
Buffalo Springfield
Crosby, Stills and Nash
Jackson Five
Joni Mitchell

Parliament-Funkadelic
(Young) Rascals

Non-Performer
Syd Nathan

Early Influences
Mahalia Jackson
Bill Monroe

1996
David Bowie
Jefferson Airplane
Little Willie John
Gladys Knight and the Pips
Pink Floyd
Shirelles
Velvet Underground

Non-Performer
Tom Donahue

Early Influence
Pete Seeger

1995
The Allman Brothers Band
Al Green
Janis Joplin
Led Zeppelin
Martha and the Vandellas
Neil Young
Frank Zappa

Non-Performer
Paul Ackerman